COLLINS

POCKET
SPANISH
DICTIONARY

COLLINS
POCKET
SPANISH
DICTIONARY

SPANISH ▶ ENGLISH   ENGLISH ▶ SPANISH

Collins

An Imprint of HarperCollinsPublishers

third edition/tercera edición 1995

© HarperCollins Publishers 1995, 1999
© William Collins Sons & Co. Ltd. 1990

HarperCollins Publishers
P.O. Box, Glasgow G4 0NB, Great Britain
The HarperCollins website address is
www.fireandwater.com
ISBN 0 00 470773 7

Mike Gonzalez • Alicia de Benito de Harland
Soledad Pérez-López • José Ramón Parrondo

contributors/colaboradores
Bob Grossmith • Teresa Álvarez García
Sharon Hunter • Claire Evans

editorial staff/redacción
Joyce Littlejohn • Val McNulty

series editor/colección dirigida por
Lorna Sinclair Knight

Typeset by Morton Word Processing Ltd, Scarborough

*Printed and bound in Great Britain by Caledonian International
Book Manufacturing Ltd, Glasgow, G64*

INTRODUCTION

We are delighted that you have decided to buy the Collins Pocket Spanish Dictionary, and hope you will enjoy and benefit from using it at home, at school, on holiday or at work.

The innovative use of colour guides you quickly and efficiently to the word you want, and the comprehensive wordlist provides a wealth of modern and idiomatic phrases not normally found in a dictionary this size.

In addition, the supplement provides you with guidance on using the dictionary, along with entertaining ways of improving your dictionary skills.

We hope that you will enjoy using it and that it will significantly enhance your language studies.

Note on trademarks

ABREVIATURAS

ABBREVIATIONS

adjetivo, locución adjetiva	**adj**	adjective, adjectival phrase
abreviatura	**ab(b)r**	abbreviation
adverbio, locución adverbial	**adv**	adverb, adverbial phrase
administración, lengua administrativa	**ADMIN**	administration
agricultura	**AGR**	agriculture
América Latina	**AM**	Latin America
anatomía	**ANAT**	anatomy
arquitectura	**ARQ, ARCH**	architecture
artículo	**art**	article
el automóvil	**AUT(O)**	the motor car and motoring
aviación, viajes aéreos	**AVIAT**	flying, air travel
biología	**BIO(L)**	biology
botánica, flores	**BOT**	botany
inglés británico	**BRIT**	British English
química	**CHEM**	chemistry
comercio, finanzas, banca	**COM(M)**	commerce, finance, banking
comparativo	**compar**	comparative
informática	**COMPUT**	computers
conjunción	**conj**	conjunction
construcción	**CONSTR**	building
compuesto	**cpd**	compound element
cocina	**CULIN**	cookery
definido	**def**	definite
demostrativo	**demos**	demonstrative
economía	**ECON**	economics
electricidad, electrónica	**ELEC**	electricity, electronics
enseñanza, sistema escolar y universitario	**ESCOL**	schooling, schools and universities
España	**ESP**	Spain
especialmente	**esp**	especially
exclamación, interjección	**excl**	exclamation, interjection
femenino	**f**	feminine
lengua familiar (! vulgar)	**fam(!)**	informal usage (! particularly offensive)
ferrocarril	**FERRO**	railways
uso figurado	**fig**	figurative use
fotografía	**FOTO**	photography
(verbo inglés) del cual la partícula es inseparable	**fus**	(phrasal verb) where the particle is inseparable
generalmente	**gen**	generally
geografía, geología	**GEO**	geography, geology
geometría	**GEOM**	geometry
indefinido	**indef**	indefinite
lengua familiar (! vulgar)	**inf(!)**	informal usage
infinitivo	**infin**	infinitive
informática	**INFORM**	computers
interrogativo	**interr**	interrogative
invariable	**inv**	invariable
irregular	**irreg**	irregular
lo jurídico	**JUR**	law

ABREVIATURAS

ABBREVIATIONS

América Latina	LAM	Latin America
gramática, lingüística	LING	grammar, linguistics
masculino	m	masculine
matemáticas	MAT(H)	mathematics
medicina	MED	medical term, medicine
masculino/femenino	m/f	masculine/feminine
lo militar, ejército	MIL	military matters
música	MUS	music
sustantivo, nombre	n	noun
navegación, náutica	NAUT	sailing, navigation
sustantivo numérico	num	numeral noun
complemento	obj	(grammatical) object
	o.s.	oneself
peyorativo	pey, pej	derogatory, pejorative
fotografía	PHOT	photography
fisiología	PHYSIOL	physiology
plural	pl	plural
política	POL	politics
participio de pasado	pp	past participle
preposición	prep	preposition
pronombre	pron	pronoun
psicología, psiquiatría	PSICO, PSYCH	psychology, psychiatry
tiempo pasado	pt	past tense
química	QUIM	chemistry
ferrocarril	RAIL	railways
religión, lo eclesiástico	REL	religion, church service
	sb	somebody
enseñanza, sistema escolar y universitario	SCH	schooling, schools and universities
singular	sg	singular
España	SP	Spain
	sth	something
sujeto	su(b)j	(grammatical) subject
subjuntivo	subjun	subjunctive
superlativo	superl	superlative
tauromaquia	TAUR	bullfighting
también	tb	also
técnica, tecnología	TEC(H)	technical term, technology
telecomunicaciones	TELEC, TEL	telecommunications
televisión	TV	television
imprenta, tipografía	TIP, TYP	typography, printing
inglés norteamericano	US	American English
verbo	vb	verb
verbo intransitivo	vi	intransitive verb
verbo pronominal	vr	reflexive verb
verbo transitivo	vt	transitive verb
zoología, animales	ZOOL	zoology
marca registrada	®	registered trademark
indica un equivalente cultural	≈	introduces a cultural equivalent

SPANISH PRONUNCIATION

Consonants

b	[b, ß]	**b**oda **b**om**b**a la**b**or	see notes on **v** below
c	[k]	**c**aja	**c** before **a, o** or **u** is pronounced as in **c**at
ce, ci	[θe, θi]	**ce**ro **ci**elo	**c** before **e** or **i** is pronounced as in **th**in
ch	[tʃ]	**ch**iste	**ch** is pronounced as **ch** in **ch**air
d	[d, ð]	**d**anés ciu**dad**	at the beginning of a phrase or after **l** or **n**, **d** is pronounced as in English. In any other position it is pronounced like **th** in **the**
g	[g, ɣ]	**g**afas pa**g**a	**g** before **a, o** or **u** is pronounced as in **g**ap, if at the beginning of a phrase or after **n**. In other positions the sound is softened
ge, gi	[xe, xi]	**ge**nte **gi**rar	**g** before **e** or **i** is pronounced similar to **ch** in Scottish lo**ch**
h		**h**aber	**h** is always silent in Spanish
j	[x]	**j**ugar	**j** is pronounced similar to **ch** in Scottish lo**ch**
ll	[ʎ]	ta**ll**e	**ll** is pronounced like the **lli** in mi**lli**on
ñ	[ɲ]	ni**ñ**o	**ñ** is pronounced like the **ni** in o**ni**on
q	[k]	**q**ue	**q** is pronounced as **k** in **k**ing
r, rr	[r, rr]	quita**r** ga**rr**a	**r** is always pronounced in Spanish, unlike the silent **r** in dance**r**. **rr** is trilled, like a Scottish **r**
s	[s]	quizá**s** i**s**la	**s** is usually pronounced as in pa**s**s, but before **b, d, g, l, m** or **n** it is pronounced as in ro**s**e
v	[b, ß]	**v**ía di**v**idir	**v** is pronounced something like **b**. At the beginning of a phrase or after **m** or **n** it is pronounced as **b** in **b**oy. In any other position the sound is softened
z	[θ]	tena**z**	**z** is pronounced as **th** in **th**in

f, k, l, m, n, p, t and **x** are pronounced as in English.

Vowels

a	[a]	p**a**ta	not as long as **a** in f**a**r. When followed by a consonant in the same syllable (i.e. in a closed syllable), as in am**a**nte, the **a** is short, as in b**a**t
e	[e]	m**e**	like **e** in th**ey**. In a closed syllable, as in g**e**nte, the **e** is short as in p**e**t
i	[i]	p**i**no	as in m**ea**n or mach**i**ne
o	[o]	l**o**	as in l**o**cal. In a closed syllable, as in c**o**ntrol, the **o** is short as in c**o**t
u	[u]	l**u**nes	as in r**u**le. It is silent after **q**, and in **gue, gui**, unless marked **güe, güi** e.g. antig**üe**dad, when it is pronounced like **w** in **w**olf

Semivowels

i, y	[j]	b**i**en h**i**elo **y**unta	pronounced like **y** in **y**es
u	[w]	h**u**evo f**u**ento antig**ü**edad	unstressed **u** between consonant and vowel is pronounced like **w** in **w**ell. See also notes on **u** above

Diphthongs

ai, ay	[ai]	b**ai**le	as **i** in r**i**de
au	[au]	**au**to	as **ou** in sh**out**
ei, ey	[ei]	bu**ey**	as **ey** in gr**ey**
eu	[eu]	d**eu**da	both elements pronounced independently [e] + [u]
oi, oy	[oi]	h**oy**	as **oy** in t**oy**

Stress

The rules of stress in Spanish are as follows:

(a) when a word ends in a vowel or in **n** or **s**, the second last syllable is stressed: pa**ta**ta, pa**ta**tas, **co**me, **co**men

(b) when a word ends in a consonant other than **n** or **s**, the stress falls on the last syllable: pa**red**, ha**blar**

(c) when the rules set out in (a) and (b) are not applied, an acute accent appears over the stressed vowel: co**mún**, geogra**fía**, in**glés**

In the phonetic transcription, the symbol ['] precedes the syllable on which the stress falls.

PRONUNCIACIÓN INGLESA

Vocales y diptongos

	Ejemplo inglés	*Ejemplo español/explicación*
ɑː	f**a**ther	Entre **a** de p**a**dre y **o** de n**o**che
ʌ	b**u**t, c**o**me	**a** muy breve
æ	m**a**n, c**a**t	Con los labios en la posición de **e** en p**e**na se pronuncia el sonido **a** parecido a la **a** de c**a**rro
ə	fath**er**, **a**go	Vocal neutra parecida a una **e** u **o** casi mudas
əː	b**ir**d, h**ear**d	Entre **e** abierta, y **o** cerrada, sonido alargado
ɛ	g**e**t, b**e**d	Como en p**e**rro
ɪ	**i**t, b**i**g	Más breve que en s**i**
iː	t**e**a, s**ee**	Como en f**i**no
ɔ	h**o**t, w**a**sh	Como en t**o**rre
ɔː	s**aw**, **a**ll	Como en p**o**r
u	p**u**t, b**oo**k	Sonido breve, más cerrado que b**u**rro
uː	t**oo**, y**ou**	Sonido largo, como en **u**no
aɪ	fl**y**, h**igh**	Como en fr**ai**le
au	h**ow**, h**ou**se	Como en p**au**sa
ɛə	th**ere**, b**ear**	Casi como en v**ea**, pero el segundo elemento es la vocal neutra [ə]
eɪ	d**ay**, ob**ey**	**e** cerrada seguida por una **i** débil
ɪə	h**ere**, h**ear**	Como en man**ía**, mezclándose el sonido **a** con la vocal neutra [ə]
əu	g**o**, n**o**te	[ə] seguido por una breve **u**
ɔɪ	b**oy**, **oi**l	Como en v**oy**
uə	p**oor**, s**ure**	**u** bastante larga más la vocal neutra [ə]

Consonantes

	Ejemplo inglés	*Ejemplo español/explicación*
b	**b**ig, lo**bb**y	Como en tum**b**a
d	men**d**e**d**	Como en con**d**e, an**d**ar
g	**g**o, **g**et, bi**g**	Como en **g**rande, **g**ol
dʒ	**g**in, ju**dg**e	Como en la **ll** andaluza y en **G**eneralitat (catalán)
ŋ	si**ng**	Como en ví**n**culo
h	**h**ouse, **h**e	Como la jota hispanoamericana
j	**y**oung, **y**es	Como en **y**a
k	**c**ome, mo**ck**	Como en **c**aña, Es**c**ocia
r	**r**ed, t**r**ead	Se pronuncia con la punta de la lengua hacia atrás y sin hacerla vibrar
s	**s**and, ye**s**	Como en ca**s**a, **s**esión
z	ro**s**e, **z**ebra	Como en de**s**de, mi**s**mo
ʃ	**sh**e, ma**ch**ine	Como en **ch**ambre (francés), ro**x**o (portugués)
tʃ	**ch**in, ri**ch**	Como en **ch**ocolate
v	**v**alley	Como en f, pero se retiran los dientes superiores vibrándolos contra el labio inferior
w	**w**ater, **wh**ich	Como en la **u** de h**u**evo, p**u**ede
ʒ	vi**s**ion	Como en **j**ournal (francés)
θ	**th**ink, my**th**	Como en re**c**eta, **z**apato
ð	**th**is, **th**e	Como en la **d** de habla**d**o, verda**d**

p, f, m, n, l, t iguales que en español
El signo * indica que la r final escrita apenas se pronuncia en inglés británico cuando la palabra siguiente empieza con vocal. El signo [ˈ] indica la sílaba acentuada.

SPANISH VERB TABLES

1 Gerund *2* Imperative *3* Present *4* Preterite *5* Future *6* Present subjunctive *7* Imperfect subjunctive *8* Past participle *9* Imperfect. *Etc* indicates that the irregular root is used for all persons of the tense, e.g. **oir**: *6* oiga *etc* = oigas, oigamos, oigáis, oigan. Forms which consist of the unmodified verb root + verb ending are not shown, e.g. acertamos, acertáis.

acertar *2* acierta *3* acierto, aciertas, acierta, aciertan *6* acierte, aciertes, acierte, acierten

acordar *2* acuerda *3* acuerdo, acuerdas, acuerda, acuerdan *6* acuerde, acuerdes, acuerde, acuerden

advertir *1* advirtiendo *2* advierte *3* advierto, adviertes, advierte, advierten *4* advirtió, advirtieron *6* advierta, adviertas, advierta, advirtamos, advirtáis, adviertan *7* advirtiera *etc*

agradecer *3* agradezco *6* agradezca *etc*

aparecer *3* aparezco *6* aparezca *etc*

aprobar *2* aprueba *3* apruebo, apruebas, aprueba, aprueban *6* apruebe, apruebes, apruebe, aprueben

atravesar *2* atraviesa *3* atravieso, atraviesas, atraviesa, atraviesan *6* atraviese, atravieses, atraviese, atraviesen

caber *3* quepo *4* cupe, cupiste, cupo, cupimos, cupisteis, cupieron *5* cabré *etc* *6* quepa *etc* *7* cupiera *etc*

caer *1* cayendo *3* caigo *4* cayó, cayeron *6* caiga *etc* *7* cayera *etc*

calentar *2* calienta *3* caliento, calientas, calienta, calientan *6* caliente, calientes, caliente, calienten

cerrar *2* cierra *3* cierro, cierras, cierra, cierran *6* cierre, cierres, cierre, cierren

COMER *1* comiendo *2* come, comed *3* como, comes, come, comemos, coméis, comen *4* comí, comiste, comió, comimos, comisteis, comieron *5* comeré, comerás, comerá, comeremos, comeréis, comerán *6* coma, comas, coma, comamos, comáis, coman *7* comiera, comieras, comiera, comiéramos, comierais, comieran *8* comido *9* comía, comías, comía *etc*

conocer *3* conozco *6* conozca *etc*

contar *2* cuenta *3* cuento, cuentas, cuenta, cuentan *6* cuente, cuentes, cuente, cuenten

costar *2* cuesta *3* cuesto, cuestas, cuesta, cuestan *6* cueste, cuestes, cueste, cuesten

dar *3* doy *4* di, diste, dio, dimos, disteis, dieron *7* diera *etc*

decir *2* di *3* digo *4* dije, dijiste, dijo, dijimos, dijisteis, dijeron *5* diré *etc* *6* diga *etc* *7* dijera

etc *8* dicho

despertar *2* despierta *3* despierto, despiertas, despierta, despiertan *6* despierte, despiertes, despierte, despierten

divertir *1* divirtiendo *2* divierte *3* divierto, diviertes, divierte, divierten *4* divirtió, divirtieron *6* divierta, diviertas, divierta, divirtamos, divirtáis, diviertan *7* divirtiera *etc*

dormir *1* durmiendo *2* duerme *3* duermo, duermes, duerme, duermen *4* durmió, durmieron *6* duerma, duermas, duerma, durmamos, durmáis, duerman *7* durmiera *etc*

empezar *2* empieza *3* empiezo, empiezas, empieza, empiezan *4* empecé *6* empiece, empieces, empiece, empecemos, empecéis, empiecen

entender *2* entiende *3* entiendo, entiendes, entiende, entienden *6* entienda, entiendas, entienda, entiendan

ESTAR *2* está *3* estoy, estás, está, están *4* estuve, estuviste, estuvo, estuvimos, estuvisteis, estuvieron *6* esté, estés, esté, estén *7* estuviera *etc*

HABER *3* he, has, ha, hemos, han *4* hube, hubiste, hubo, hubimos, hubisteis, hubieron *5* habré *etc* *6* haya *etc* *7* hubiera *etc*

HABLAR *1* hablando *2* habla, hablad *3* hablo, hablas, habla, hablamos, habláis, hablan *4* hablé, hablaste, habló, hablamos, hablasteis, hablaron *5* hablaré, hablarás, hablará, hablaremos, hablaréis, hablarán *6* hable, hables, hable, hablemos, habléis, hablen *7* hablara, hablaras, hablara, habláramos, hablarais, hablaran *8* hablado *9* hablaba, hablabas, hablaba, hablábamos, hablabais, hablaban

hacer *2* haz *3* hago *4* hice, hiciste, hizo, hicimos, hicisteis, hicieron *5* haré *etc* *6* haga *etc* *7* hiciera *etc* *8* hecho

instruir *1* instruyendo *2* instruye *3* instruyo, instruyes, instruye, instruyen *4* instruyó, instruyeron *6* instruya *etc* *7* instruyera *etc*

ir *1* yendo *2* ve *3* voy, vas, va, vamos, vais, van *4* fui, fuiste, fue, fuimos, fuisteis, fueron *6* vaya, vayas, vaya, vayamos, vayáis, vayan

7 fuera *etc* 9 iba, ibas, iba, íbamos, ibais, iban

jugar *2* juega *3* juego, juegas, juega, juegan *4* jugué *6* juegue *etc*

leer *1* leyendo *4* leyó, leyeron *7* leyera *etc*

morir *1* muriendo *2* muere *3* muero, mueres, muere, mueren *4* murió, murieron *6* muera, mueras, mueras, muramos, muráis, mueran *7* muriera *etc* *8* muerto

mostrar *2* muestra *3* muestro, muestras, muestra, muestran *6* muestre, muestres, muestre, muestren

mover *2* mueve *3* muevo, mueves, mueve, mueven *6* mueva, muevas, mueva, muevan

negar *2* niega *3* niego, niegas, niega, niegan *4* negué *6* niegue, niegues, niegue, neguemos, neguéis, nieguen

ofrecer *3* ofrezco *6* ofrezca *etc*

oír *1* oyendo *2* oye *3* oigo, oyes, oye, oyen *4* oyó, oyeron *6* oiga *etc* *7* oyera *etc*

oler *2* huele *3* huelo, hueles, huele, huelen *6* huela, huelas, huela, huelan

parecer *3* parezco *6* parezca *etc*

pedir *1* pidiendo *2* pide *3* pido, pides, pide, piden *4* pidió, pidieron *6* pida *etc* *7* pidiera *etc*

pensar *2* piensa *3* pienso, piensas, piensa, piensan *6* piense, pienses, piense, piensen

perder *2* pierde *3* pierdo, pierdes, pierde, pierden *6* pierda, pierdas, pierda, pierdan

poder *1* pudiendo *2* puede *3* puedo, puedes, puede, pueden *4* pude, pudiste, pudo, pudimos, pudisteis, pudieron *5* podré *etc* *6* pueda, puedas, pueda, puedan *7* pudiera *etc*

poner *2* pon *3* pongo *4* puse, pusiste, puso, pusimos, pusisteis, pusieron *5* pondré *etc* *6* ponga *etc* *7* pusiera *etc* *8* puesto

preferir *1* prefiriendo *2* prefiere *3* prefiero, prefieres, prefiere, prefieren *4* prefirió, prefirieron *6* prefiera, prefieras, prefiera, prefiramos, prefiráis, prefieran *7* prefiriera *etc*

querer *2* quiere *3* quiero, quieres, quiere, quieren *4* quise, quisiste, quiso, quisimos, quisisteis, quisieron *5* querré *etc* *6* quiera, quieras, quiera, quieran *7* quisiera *etc*

reír *2* ríe *3* río, ríes, ríe, ríen *4* rio, rieron *6* ría, rías, riamos, riáis, rían *7* riera *etc*

repetir *1* repitiendo *2* repite *3* repito, repites, repite, repiten *4* repitió, repitieron *6* repita *etc* *7* repitiera *etc*

rogar *2* ruega *3* ruego, ruegas, ruega, ruegan *4* rogué *6* ruegue, ruegues, ruegue, roguemos, roguéis, rueguen

saber *3* sé *4* supe, supiste, supo, supimos, supisteis, supieron *5* sabré *etc* *6* sepa *etc* supiera *etc*

salir *2* sal *3* salgo *5* saldré *etc* *6* salga *etc*

seguir *1* siguiendo *2* sigue *3* sigo, sigues, sigue, siguen *4* siguió, siguieron *6* siga *etc* *7* siguiera *etc*

sentar *2* sienta *3* siento, sientas, sienta, sientan *6* siente, sientes, siente, sienten

sentir *1* sintiendo *2* siente *3* siento, sientes, siente, sienten *4* sintió, sintieron *6* sienta, sientas, sienta, sintamos, sintáis, sientan *7* sintiera *etc*

SER *2* sé *3* soy, eres, es, somos, sois, son *4* fui, fuiste, fue, fuimos, fuisteis, fueron *6* sea *etc* fuera *etc* *9* era, eras, era, éramos, erais, eran

servir *1* sirviendo *2* sirve *3* sirvo, sirves, sirve, sirven *4* sirvió, sirvieron *6* sirva *etc* *7* sirviera *etc*

soñar *2* sueña *3* sueño, sueñas, sueña, sueñan *6* sueñe, sueñes, sueñe, sueñen

tener *2* ten *3* tengo, tienes, tiene, tienen *4* tuve, tuviste, tuvo, tuvimos, tuvisteis, tuvieron *5* tendré *etc* *6* tenga *etc* *7* tuviera *etc*

traer *1* trayendo *3* traigo *4* traje, trajiste, trajo, trajimos, trajisteis, trajeron *6* traiga *etc* *7* trajera *etc*

valer *2* val *3* valgo *5* valdré *etc* *6* valga *etc*

venir *2* ven *3* vengo, vienes, viene, vienen *4* vine, viniste, vino, vinimos, vinisteis, vinieron *5* vendré *etc* *6* venga *etc* *7* viniera *etc*

ver *3* veo *6* vea *etc* *8* visto *9* veía *etc*

vestir *1* vistiendo *2* viste *3* visto, vistes, viste, visten *4* vistió, vistieron *6* vista *etc* *7* vistiera *etc*

VIVIR *1* viviendo *2* vive, vivid *3* vivo, vives, vive, vivimos, vivís, viven *4* viví, viviste, vivió, vivimos, vivisteis, vivieron *5* viviré, vivirás, vivirá, viviremos, viviréis, vivirán *6* viva, vivas, viva, vivamos, viváis, vivan *7* viviera, vivieras, viviera, viviéramos, vivierais, vivieran *8* vivido *9* vivía, vivías, vivía, vivíamos, vivíais, vivían

volver *2* vuelve *3* vuelvo, vuelves, vuelve, vuelven *6* vuelva, vuelvas, vuelva, vuelvan *8* vuelto

VERBOS IRREGULARES EN INGLÉS

present	pt	pp	present	pt	pp
arise	arose	arisen	feed	fed	fed
awake	awoke	awoken	feel	felt	felt
be (am, is, are; being)	was, were	been	fight	fought	fought
			find	found	found
bear	bore	born(e)	flee	fled	fled
beat	beat	beaten	fling	flung	flung
become	became	become	fly (flies)	flew	flown
begin	began	begun	forbid	forbade	forbidden
behold	beheld	beheld	forecast	forecast	forecast
bend	bent	bent	forego	forewent	foregone
beseech	besought	besought	foresee	foresaw	foreseen
beset	beset	beset	foretell	foretold	foretold
bet	bet, betted	bet, betted	forget	forgot	forgotten
bid	bid, bade	bid, bidden	forgive	forgave	forgiven
bind	bound	bound	forsake	forsook	forsaken
bite	bit	bitten	freeze	froze	frozen
bleed	bled	bled	get	got	got, (US) gotten
blow	blew	blown			
break	broke	broken	give	gave	given
breed	bred	bred	go (goes)	went	gone
bring	brought	brought	grind	ground	ground
build	built	built	grow	grew	grown
burn	burnt, burned	burnt, burned	hang	hung, hanged	hung, hanged
burst	burst	burst	have (has; having)	had	had
buy	bought	bought			
can	could	(been able)	hear	heard	heard
cast	cast	cast	hide	hid	hidden
catch	caught	caught	hit	hit	hit
choose	chose	chosen	hold	held	held
cling	clung	clung	hurt	hurt	hurt
come	came	come	keep	kept	kept
cost	cost	cost	kneel	knelt, kneeled	knelt, kneeled
creep	crept	crept			
cut	cut	cut	know	knew	known
deal	dealt	dealt	lay	laid	laid
dig	dug	dug	lead	led	led
do (3rd person: he/she/it does)	did	done	lean	leant, leaned	leant, leaned
			leap	leapt, leaped	leapt, leaped
draw	drew	drawn			
dream	dreamed, dreamt	dreamed, dreamt	learn	learnt, learned	learnt, learned
drink	drank	drunk	leave	left	left
drive	drove	driven	lend	lent	lent
dwell	dwelt	dwelt	let	let	let
eat	ate	eaten	lie (lying)	lay	lain
fall	fell	fallen	light	lit, lighted	lit, lighted

LOS NÚMEROS

NUMBERS

primer, primero(a), 1º, 1er (1ª, 1era)   first, 1st
segundo(a), 2º (2ª)
tercer, tercero(a), 3º (3ª)
cuarto(a), 4º (4ª)
quinto(a), 5º (5...
sexto(a)...
sépti-
oc...

...son

...edianoche, las doce (de la noche)   one o'...
...una (de la madrugada)   five past one
...una y cinco   ten past one
...una y diez   a quarter past one, one fifteen
...una y cuarto or quince   twenty-five past one, one twenty-five
...una y veinticinco   half-past one, one thirty
...una y media or treinta   twenty-five to two, one thirty-five
...s dos menos veinticinco, la una
...einta y cinco
...s dos menos veinte, la una cuarenta   twenty to two, one forty
...s dos menos cuarto, la una cuarenta   a quarter to two, one forty-five
...cinco
...s dos menos diez, la una cincuenta   ten to two, one fifty
...diodía, las doce (de la tarde)   twelve o'clock, midday, noon
...una (de la tarde)   one o'clock (in the afternoon), one
                                              (p.m.)
...siete (de la tarde)   seven o'clock (in the evening), seven
                                              (p.m.)

...qué hora?   *(at) what time?*

...edianoche   at midnight
...s siete   at seven o'clock

...veinte minutos   in twenty minutes
...e quince minutos   fifteen minutes ago

present	pt	pp	present	pt	pp
lose	lost	lost	spell	spelt, spelled	spelt, spelled
make	made	made			
may	might	—	spend	spent	spent
mean	meant	meant	spill	spilt, spilled	spilt, spilled
meet	met	met			
mistake	mistook	mistaken	spin	spun	spun
mow	mowed	mown, mowed	spit	spat	spat
must	(had to)	(had to)	split	split	split
pay	paid	paid	spoil	spoiled, spoilt	spoiled, spoilt
put	put	put			
quit	quit, quitted	quit, quitted	spread	spread	spread
			spring	sprang	sprung
read	read	read	stand	stood	stood
rid	rid	rid	steal	stole	stolen
ride	rode	ridden	stick	stuck	stuck
ring	rang	rung	sting	stung	stung
rise	rose	risen	stink	stank	stunk
run	ran	run	stride	strode	stridden
saw	sawed	sawn	strike	struck	struck, stricken
say	said	said			
see	saw	seen	strive	strove	striven
seek	sought	sought	swear	swore	sworn
sell	sold	sold	sweep	swept	swept
send	sent	sent	swell	swelled	swollen, swelled
set	set	set			
shake	shook	shaken	swim	swam	swum
shall	should	—	swing	swung	swung
shear	sheared	shorn, sheared	take	took	taken
shed	shed	shed	teach	taught	taught
shine	shone	shone	tear	tore	torn
shoot	shot	shot	tell	told	told
show	showed	shown	think	thought	thought
shrink	shrank	shrunk	throw	threw	thrown
shut	shut	shut	thrust	thrust	thrust
sing	sang	sung	tread	trod	trodden
sink	sank	sunk	wake	woke	woken
sit	sat	sat	waylay	waylaid	waylaid
slay	slew	slain	wear	wore	worn
sleep	slept	slept	weave	wove, weaved	woven, weaved
slide	slid	slid			
sling	slung	slung	wed	wedded, wed	wedded, wed
slit	slit	slit			
smell	smelt, smelled	smelt, smelled	weep	wept	wept
			win	won	won
sow	sowed	sown, sowed	wind	wound	wound
speak	spoke	spoken	wring	wrung	wrung
speed	sped, speeded	sped, speeded	write	wrote	written

LOS NÚMEROS

NUMBERS

Spanish	Number	English
un, uno(a)	1	one
dos	2	two
tres	3	three
cuatro	4	four
cinco	5	five
seis	6	six
siete	7	seven
ocho	8	eight
nueve	9	nine
diez	10	ten
once	11	eleven
doce	12	twelve
trece	13	thirteen
catorce	14	fourteen
quince	15	fifteen
dieciséis	16	sixteen
diecisiete	17	seventeen
dieciocho	18	eighteen
diecinueve	19	nineteen
veinte	20	twenty
veintiuno	21	twenty-one
veintidós	22	twenty-two
treinta	30	thirty
treinta y uno(a)	31	thirty-one
treinta y dos	32	thirty-two
cuarenta	40	forty
cuarenta y uno(a)	41	forty-one
cincuenta	50	fifty
sesenta	60	sixty
setenta	70	seventy
ochenta	80	eighty
noventa	90	ninety
cien, ciento	100	a hundred, one hundred
ciento uno(a)	101	a hundred and one
doscientos(as)	200	two hundred
doscientos(as) uno(a)	201	two hundred and one
trescientos(as)	300	three hundred
trescientos(as) uno(a)	301	three hundred and one
cuatrocientos(as)	400	four hundred
quiniento(as)	500	five hundred
seiscientos(as)	600	six hundred
setecientos(as)	700	seven hundred
ochocientos(as)	800	eight hundred
novecientos(as)	900	nine hundred
mil	1000	a thousand
mil dos	1002	a thousand and two
cinco mil	5000	five thousand
un millón	1000000	a million

	second, 2nd
	third, 3rd
...no(a)	fourth, 4th
	fifth, 5th
...ctavo(a)	sixth, 6th
noveno(a)	seventh
décimo(a)	eighth
	ninth
	tenth
undécimo(a)	eleventh
duodécimo(a)	twelfth
decimotercio(a)	thirteenth
decimocuarto(a)	fourteenth
decimoquinto(a)	fifteenth
decimosexto(a)	sixteenth
decimoséptimo(a)	seventeenth
decimoctavo(a)	eighteenth
decimonoveno(a)	nineteenth
vigésimo(a)	twentieth
vigésimo(a) primero(a)	twenty-first
vigésimo(a) segundo(a)	twenty-second
trigésimo(a)	thirtieth
centésimo(a)	hundredth
centésimo(a) primero(a)	hundred-and-first
milésimo(a)	thousandth

Números Quebrados etc | Fractions etc

un medio	a half
un tercio	a third
dos tercios	two thirds
un cuarto	a quarter
un quinto	a fifth
cero coma cinco, 0,5	(nought) point five, 0.5
tres coma cuatro, 3,4	three point four, 3.4
diez por cien(to)	ten per cent
cien por cien	a hundred per cent

Ejemplos | Examples

va a llegar el 7 (de mayo)	he's arriving on the 7th (of ...
vive en el número 7	he lives at number 7
el capítulo/la página 7	chapter/page 7
llegó séptimo	he came in 7th

N.B. In Spanish the ordinal numbers from 1 to 10 are commonly used; 20 rather less; above 21 they are rarely written and almost never heard The custom is to replace the forms for 21 and above by the cardinal num...

LA HORA

THE TIME

¿qué hora es? *what time is it?*

es... *it's* o *it is*

midnight, twelve p.m.
...o'clock (in the morning), one (a.m.)

ESPAÑOL – INGLÉS
SPANISH – ENGLISH

A, a

a [a] (a+el = al) prep **1** (dirección) to; **fueron ~ Madrid/Grecia** they went to Madrid/Greece; **me voy ~ casa** I'm going home

2 (distancia): **está ~ 15 km de aquí** it's 15 kms from here

3 (posición): **estar ~ la mesa** to be at table; **al lado de** next to, beside; ver tb **puerta**

4 (tiempo): **~ las 10/~ medianoche** at 10/midnight; **~ la mañana siguiente** the following morning; **~ los pocos días** after a few days; **estamos ~ 9 de julio** it's the ninth of July; **~ los 24 años** at the age of 24; **al año/~ la semana** (AM) a year/week later

5 (manera): **~ la francesa** the French way; **~ caballo** on horseback; **~ oscuras** in the dark

6 (medio, instrumento): **~ lápiz** in pencil; **~ mano** by hand; **cocina ~ gas** gas stove

7 (razón): **~ 30 ptas el kilo** at 30 pesetas a kilo; **~ más de 50 km/h** at more than 50 kms per hour

8 (dativo): **se lo di ~ él** I gave it to him; **vi al policía** I saw the policeman; **se lo compré ~ él** I bought it from him

9 (tras ciertos verbos): **voy ~ verle** I'm going to see him; **empezó ~ trabajar** he started working o to work

10 (+infin): **al verle, le reconocí inmediatamente** when I saw him I recognized him at once; **el camino ~ recorrer** the distance we (etc) have to travel; **¡~ callar!** keep quiet!; **¡~ comer!** let's eat!

abad, esa [a'ßað, 'ðesa] nm/f abbot/abbess; **~ía** nf abbey

abajo [a'ßaxo] adv (situación) (down) below, underneath; (en edificio) downstairs; (dirección) down, downwards; **el piso de ~** the downstairs flat; **la parte de ~** the lower part; **¡~ el gobierno!** down with the government!; **cuesta/río ~** downhill/downstream; **de arriba ~** from top to bottom; **el ~ firmante** the undersigned; **más ~** lower o further down

abalanzarse [aßalan'θarse] vr: **~ sobre** o **contra** to throw o.s. at

abandonado, a [aßando'naðo, a] adj derelict; (desatendido) abandoned; (desierto) deserted; (descuidado) neglected

abandonar [aßando'nar] vt to leave; (persona) to abandon, desert; (cosa) to abandon, leave behind; (descuidar) to neglect; (renunciar a) to give up; (INFORM) to quit; **~se** vr: **~se a** to abandon o.s. to; **abandono** nm (acto) desertion, abandonment; (estado) abandon, neglect; (renuncia) withdrawal, retirement; **ganar por abandono** to win by default

abanicar [aßani'kar] vt to fan; **abanico** nm fan; (NAUT) derrick

abaratar [aßara'tar] vt to lower the price of; **~se** vr to go o come down in price

abarcar [aßar'kar] vt to include, embrace; (AM) to monopolize

abarrotado, a [aßarro'taðo, a] adj packed

abarrotar [aßarro'tar] vt (local, estadio, teatro) to fill, pack

abarrotero, a [aßarro'tero, a] (AM) nm/f grocer; **abarrotes** nmpl (AM) groceries, provisions

abastecer [aßaste'θer] vt: **~ (de)** to supply (with); **abastecimiento** nm supply

abasto [a'ßasto] nm supply; **no dar ~ a** to be unable to cope with

abatido, a [aβa'tiðo, a] *adj* dejected, downcast

abatimiento [aβati'mjento] *nm* (*depresión*) dejection, depression

abatir [aβa'tir] *vt* (*muro*) to demolish; (*pájaro*) to shoot *o* bring down; (*fig*) to depress; **~se** *vr* to get depressed; **~se sobre** to swoop *o* pounce on

abdicación [aβðika'θjon] *nf* abdication

abdicar [aβði'kar] *vi* to abdicate

abdomen [aβ'ðomen] *nm* abdomen; **abdominales** *nmpl* (*tb: ejercicios abdominales*) sit-ups

abecedario [aβeθe'ðarjo] *nm* alphabet

abedul [aβe'ðul] *nm* birch

abeja [a'βexa] *nf* bee

abejorro [aβe'xorro] *nm* bumblebee

abertura [aβer'tura] *nf* = **apertura**

abeto [a'βeto] *nm* fir

abierto, a [a'βjerto, a] *pp de* **abrir** ♦ *adj* open; (*AM*) generous

abigarrado, a [aβiɣa'rraðo, a] *adj* multi-coloured

abismal [aβis'mal] *adj* (*fig*) vast, enormous

abismar [aβis'mar] *vt* to humble, cast down; **~se** *vr* to sink; **~se en** (*fig*) to be plunged into

abismo [a'βismo] *nm* abyss

abjurar [aβxu'rar] *vi*: **~ de** to abjure, forswear

ablandar [aβlan'dar] *vt* to soften; **~se** *vr* to get softer

abnegación [aβneɣa'θjon] *nf* self-denial

abnegado, a [aβne'ɣaðo, a] *adj* self-sacrificing

abocado, a [aβo'kaðo, a] *adj*: **verse ~ al desastre** to be heading for disaster

abochornar [aβotʃor'nar] *vt* to embarrass

abofetear [aβofete'ar] *vt* to slap (in the face)

abogado, a [aβo'ɣaðo, a] *nm/f* lawyer; (*notario*) solicitor; (*en tribunal*) barrister (*BRIT*), attorney (*US*); **~ defensor** defence lawyer *o* attorney (*US*)

abogar [aβo'ɣar] *vi*: **~ por** to plead for; (*fig*) to advocate

abolengo [aβo'lengo] *nm* ancestry, lineage

abolición [aβoli'θjon] *nf* abolition

abolir [aβo'lir] *vt* to abolish; (*cancelar*) to cancel

abolladura [aβoʎa'ðura] *nf* dent

abollar [aβo'ʎar] *vt* to dent

abominable [aβomi'naβle] *adj* abominable

abonado, a [aβo'naðo, a] *adj* (*deuda*) paid(-up) ♦ *nm/f* subscriber

abonar [aβo'nar] *vt* (*deuda*) to settle; (*terreno*) to fertilize; (*idea*) to endorse; **~se** *vr* to subscribe; **abono** *nm* payment; fertilizer; subscription

abordar [aβor'ðar] *vt* (*barco*) to board; (*asunto*) to broach

aborigen [aβo'rixen] *nm/f* aborigine

aborrecer [aβorre'θer] *vt* to hate, loathe

abortar [aβor'tar] *vi* (*malparir*) to have a miscarriage; (*deliberadamente*) to have an abortion; **aborto** *nm* miscarriage; abortion

abotonar [aβoto'nar] *vt* to button (up), do up

abovedado, a [aβoβe'ðaðo, a] *adj* vaulted, domed

abrasar [aβra'sar] *vt* to burn (up); (*AGR*) to dry up, parch

abrazar [aβra'θar] *vt* to embrace, hug

abrazo [a'βraθo] *nm* embrace, hug; **un ~** (*en carta*) with best wishes

abrebotellas [aβreβo'teʎas] *nm inv* bottle opener

abrecartas [aβre'kartas] *nm inv* letter opener

abrelatas [aβre'latas] *nm inv* tin (*BRIT*) *o* can opener

abreviar [aβre'βjar] *vt* to abbreviate; (*texto*) to abridge; (*plazo*) to reduce; **abreviatura** *nf* abbreviation

abridor [aβri'ðor] *nm* bottle opener; (*de latas*) tin (*BRIT*) *o* can opener

abrigar [aβri'ɣar] *vt* (*proteger*) to shelter; (*suj: ropa*) to keep warm; (*fig*) to cherish

abrigo [a'βriɣo] *nm* (*prenda*) coat, overcoat; (*lugar protegido*) shelter

abril [a'βril] *nm* April

abrillantar [aßriʎan'tar] *vt* to polish
abrir [a'ßrir] *vt* to open (up) ♦ *vi* to open;
~**se** *vr* to open (up); (*extenderse*) to open
out; (*cielo*) to clear; ~**se paso** to find *o*
force a way through
abrochar [aßro'tʃar] *vt* (*con botones*) to
button (up); (*zapato, con broche*) to do
up
abrumar [aßru'mar] *vt* to overwhelm;
(*sobrecargar*) to weigh down
abrupto, a [a'ßrupto, a] *adj* abrupt;
(*empinado*) steep
absceso [aßs'θeso] *nm* abscess
absentismo [aßsen'tismo] *nm*
absenteeism
absolución [aßsolu'θjon] *nf* (*REL*)
absolution; (*JUR*) acquittal
absoluto, a [aßso'luto, a] *adj* absolute; **en**
~ *adv* not at all
absolver [aßsol'ßer] *vt* to absolve; (*JUR*) to
pardon; (: *acusado*) to acquit
absorbente [aßsor'ßente] *adj* absorbent;
(*interesante*) absorbing
absorber [aßsor'ßer] *vt* to absorb;
(*embeber*) to soak up
absorción [aßsor'θjon] *nf* absorption;
(*COM*) takeover
absorto, a [aß'sorto, a] *pp de* **absorber**
♦ *adj* absorbed, engrossed
abstemio, a [aßs'temjo, a] *adj* teetotal
abstención [aßsten'θjon] *nf* abstention
abstenerse [aßste'nerse] *vr*: ~ **(de)** to
abstain *o* refrain (from)
abstinencia [aßsti'nenθja] *nf* abstinence;
(*ayuno*) fasting
abstracción [aßstrak'θjon] *nf* abstraction
abstracto, a [aß'strakto, a] *adj* abstract
abstraer [aßstra'er] *vt* to abstract; ~**se** *vr*
to be *o* become absorbed
abstraído, a [aßstra'iðo, a] *adj* absent-
minded
absuelto [aß'swelto] *pp de* **absolver**
absurdo, a [aß'surðo, a] *adj* absurd
abuchear [aßutʃe'ar] *vt* to boo
abuelo, a [a'ßwelo, a] *nm/f* grandfather/
mother; ~**s** *nmpl* grandparents
abulia [a'ßulja] *nf* apathy

abultado, a [aßul'taðo, a] *adj* bulky
abultar [aßul'tar] *vi* to be bulky
abundancia [aßun'danθja] *nf*: **una** ~ **de**
plenty of; **abundante** *adj* abundant,
plentiful
abundar [aßun'dar] *vi* to abound, be
plentiful
aburguesarse [aßurɣe'sarse] *vr* to
become middle-class
aburrido, a [aßu'rriðo, a] *adj* (*hastiado*)
bored; (*que aburre*) boring;
aburrimiento *nm* boredom, tedium
aburrir [aßu'rrir] *vt* to bore; ~**se** *vr* to be
bored, get bored
abusar [aßu'sar] *vi* to go too far; ~ **de** to
abuse
abusivo, a [aßu'sißo, a] *adj* (*precio*)
exorbitant
abuso [a'ßuso] *nm* abuse
abyecto, a [aß'jekto, a] *adj* wretched,
abject
acá [a'ka] *adv* (*lugar*) here; **¿de cuándo** ~**?**
since when?
acabado, a [aka'ßaðo, a] *adj* finished,
complete; (*perfecto*) perfect; (*agotado*)
worn out; (*fig*) masterly ♦ *nm* finish
acabar [aka'ßar] *vt* (*llevar a su fin*) to
finish, complete; (*consumir*) to use up;
(*rematar*) to finish off ♦ *vi* to finish, end;
~**se** *vr* to finish, stop; (*terminarse*) to be
over; (*agotarse*) to run out; ~ **con** to put
an end to; ~ **de llegar** to have just
arrived; ~ **por hacer** to end (up) by
doing; **¡se acabó!** it's all over!; (*¡basta!*)
that's enough!
acábose [aka'ßose] *nm*: **esto es el** ~ this
is the last straw
academia [aka'ðemja] *nf* academy;
académico, a *adj* academic
acaecer [akae'θer] *vi* to happen, occur
acallar [aka'ʎar] *vt* (*persona*) to silence;
(*protestas, rumores*) to suppress
acalorado, a [akalo'raðo, a] *adj*
(*discusión*) heated
acalorarse [akalo'rarse] *vr* (*fig*) to get
heated
acampar [akam'par] *vi* to camp

acantilado [akanti'laðo] *nm* cliff
acaparar [akapa'rar] *vt* to monopolize; (*acumular*) to hoard
acariciar [akari'θjar] *vt* to caress; (*esperanza*) to cherish
acarrear [akarre'ar] *vt* to transport; (*fig*) to cause, result in
acaso [a'kaso] *adv* perhaps, maybe; **(por) si ~** (just) in case
acatamiento [akata'mjento] *nm* respect; (*ley*) observance
acatar [aka'tar] *vt* to respect; (*ley*) obey
acatarrarse [akata'rrarse] *vr* to catch a cold
acaudalado, a [akauða'laðo, a] *adj* well-off
acaudillar [akauði'ʎar] *vt* to lead, command
acceder [akθe'ðer] *vi*: **~ a** (*petición etc*) to agree to; (*tener acceso a*) to have access to; (*INFORM*) to access
accesible [akθe'siβle] *adj* accessible
acceso [ak'θeso] *nm* access, entry; (*camino*) access, approach; (*MED*) attack, fit
accesorio, a [akθe'sorjo, a] *adj, nm* accessory
accidentado, a [akθiðen'taðo, a] *adj* uneven; (*montañoso*) hilly; (*azaroso*) eventful ♦ *nm/f* accident victim
accidental [akθiðen'tal] *adj* accidental; **accidentarse** *vr* to have an accident
accidente [akθi'ðente] *nm* accident; **~s** *nmpl* (*de terreno*) unevenness *sg*
acción [ak'θjon] *nf* action; (*acto*) action, act; (*COM*) share; (*JUR*) action, lawsuit; **accionar** *vt* to work, operate; (*INFORM*) to drive
accionista [akθjo'nista] *nm/f* shareholder, stockholder
acebo [a'θeβo] *nm* holly; (*árbol*) holly tree
acechar [aθe'tʃar] *vt* to spy on; (*aguardar*) to lie in wait for; **acecho** *nm*: **estar al acecho (de)** to lie in wait (for)
aceitar [aθei'tar] *vt* to oil, lubricate
aceite [a'θeite] *nm* oil; (*de oliva*) olive oil; **~ra** *nf* oilcan; **aceitoso, a** *adj* oily

aceituna [aθei'tuna] *nf* olive
acelerador [aθelera'ðor] *nm* accelerator
acelerar [aθele'rar] *vt* to accelerate
acelga [a'θelva] *nf* chard, beet
acento [a'θento] *nm* accent; (*acentuación*) stress
acentuar [aθen'twar] *vt* to accent; to stress; (*fig*) to accentuate
acepción [aθep'θjon] *nf* meaning
aceptable [aθep'taβle] *adj* acceptable
aceptación [aθepta'θjon] *nf* acceptance; (*aprobación*) approval
aceptar [aθep'tar] *vt* to accept; (*aprobar*) to approve
acequia [a'θekja] *nf* irrigation ditch
acera [a'θera] *nf* pavement (*BRIT*), sidewalk (*US*)
acerca [a'θerka]: **~ de** *prep* about, concerning
acercar [aθer'kar] *vt* to bring *o* move nearer; **~se** *vr* to approach, come near
acerico [aθe'riko] *nm* pincushion
acero [a'θero] *nm* steel
acérrimo, a [a'θerrimo, a] *adj* (*partidario*) staunch; (*enemigo*) bitter
acertado, a [aθer'taðo, a] *adj* correct; (*apropiado*) apt; (*sensato*) sensible
acertar [aθer'tar] *vt* (*blanco*) to hit; (*solución*) to get right; (*adivinar*) to guess ♦ *vi* to get it right, be right; **~ a** to manage to; **~ con** to happen *o* hit on
acertijo [aθer'tixo] *nm* riddle, puzzle
achacar [atʃa'kar] *vt* to attribute
achacoso, a [atʃa'koso, a] *adj* sickly
achantar [atʃan'tar] *vt* (*fam*) to scare, frighten; **~se** *vr* to back down
achaque *etc* [a'tʃake] *vb ver* **achacar** ♦ *nm* ailment
achicar [atʃi'kar] *vt* to reduce; (*NAUT*) to bale out
achicharrar [atʃitʃa'rrar] *vt* to scorch, burn
achicoria [atʃi'korja] *nf* chicory
aciago, a [a'θjaɣo, a] *adj* ill-fated, fateful
acicalar [aθika'lar] *vt* to polish; (*persona*) to dress up; **~se** *vr* to get dressed up
acicate [aθi'kate] *nm* spur

acidez [aθiˈðeθ] *nf* acidity

ácido, a [ˈaθiðo, a] *adj* sour, acid ♦ *nm* acid

acierto *etc* [aˈθjerto] *vb ver* **acertar** ♦ *nm* success; (*buen paso*) wise move; (*solución*) solution; (*habilidad*) skill, ability

aclamación [aklamaˈθjon] *nf* acclamation; (*aplausos*) applause

aclamar [aklaˈmar] *vt* to acclaim; (*aplaudir*) to applaud

aclaración [aklaraˈθjon] *nf* clarification, explanation

aclarar [aklaˈrar] *vt* to clarify, explain; (*ropa*) to rinse ♦ *vi* to clear up; **~se** *vr* (*explicarse*) to understand; **~se la garganta** to clear one's throat

aclaratorio, a [aklaraˈtorjo, a] *adj* explanatory

aclimatación [aklimataˈθjon] *nf* acclimatization

aclimatar [aklimaˈtar] *vt* to acclimatize; **~se** *vr* to become acclimatized

acné [akˈne] *nm* acne

acobardar [akoβarˈðar] *vt* to intimidate

acodarse [akoˈðarse] *vr*: **~ en** to lean on

acogedor, a [akoxeˈðor, a] *adj* welcoming; (*hospitalario*) hospitable

acoger [akoˈxer] *vt* to welcome; (*abrigar*) to shelter; **~se** *vr* to take refuge

acogida [akoˈxiða] *nf* reception; refuge

acometer [akomeˈter] *vt* to attack; (*emprender*) to undertake; **acometida** *nf* attack, assault

acomodado, a [akomoˈðaðo, a] *adj* (*persona*) well-to-do

acomodador, a [akomoðaˈðor, a] *nm/f* usher(ette)

acomodar [akomoˈðar] *vt* to adjust; (*alojar*) to accommodate; **~se** *vr* to conform; (*instalarse*) to install o.s.; (*adaptarse*): **~se (a)** to adapt (to)

acompañar [akompaˈɲar] *vt* to accompany; (*documentos*) to enclose

acondicionar [akondiθjoˈnar] *vt* to arrange, prepare; (*pelo*) to condition

acongojar [akoŋɡoˈxar] *vt* to distress, grieve

aconsejar [akonseˈxar] *vt* to advise, counsel; **~se** *vr*: **~se con** to consult

acontecer [akonteˈθer] *vi* to happen, occur; **acontecimiento** *nm* event

acopio [aˈkopjo] *nm* store, stock

acoplamiento [akoplaˈmjento] *nm* coupling; joint; **acoplar** *vt* to fit; (*ELEC*) to connect; (*vagones*) to couple

acorazado, a [akoraˈθaðo, a] *adj* armour-plated, armoured ♦ *nm* battleship

acordar [akorˈðar] *vt* (*resolver*) to agree, resolve; (*recordar*) to remind; **~se** *vr* to agree; **~se (de algo)** to remember (sth); **acorde** *adj* (*MUS*) harmonious ♦ *nm* chord; **acorde con** (*medidas etc*) in keeping with

acordeón [akorðeˈon] *nm* accordion

acordonado, a [akorðoˈnaðo, a] *adj* (*calle*) cordoned-off

acorralar [akorraˈlar] *vt* to round up, corral

acortar [akorˈtar] *vt* to shorten; (*duración*) to cut short; (*cantidad*) to reduce; **~se** *vr* to become shorter

acosar [akoˈsar] *vt* to pursue relentlessly; (*fig*) to hound, pester; **acoso** *nm* harassment; **acoso sexual** sexual harassment

acostar [akosˈtar] *vt* (*en cama*) to put to bed; (*en suelo*) to lay down; **~se** *vr* to go to bed; to lie down; **~se con uno** to sleep with sb

acostumbrado, a [akostumˈbraðo, a] *adj* usual; **~ a** used to

acostumbrar [akostumˈbrar] *vt*: **~ a uno a algo** to get sb used to sth ♦ *vi*: **~ (a) hacer** to be in the habit of doing; **~se** *vr*: **~se a** to get used to

acotación [akotaˈθjon] *nf* marginal note; (*GEO*) elevation mark; (*de límite*) boundary mark; (*TEATRO*) stage direction

ácrata [ˈakrata] *adj, nm/f* anarchist

acre [ˈakre] *adj* (*olor*) acrid; (*fig*) biting ♦ *nm* acre

acrecentar [akreθenˈtar] *vt* to increase, augment

acreditar [akreðiˈtar] *vt* (*garantizar*) to

vouch for, guarantee; (*autorizar*) to
authorize; (*dar prueba de*) to prove; (*COM:
abonar*) to credit; (*embajador*) to accredit;
~se *vr* to become famous

acreedor, a [akree'ðor, a] *adj:* ~ **de**
worthy of ♦ *nm/f* creditor

acribillar [akriβi'ʎar] *vt:* ~ **a balazos** to
riddle with bullets

acróbata [a'kroβata] *nm/f* acrobat

acta ['akta] *nf* certificate; (*de comisión*)
minutes *pl*, record; ~ **de nacimiento/de
matrimonio** birth/marriage certificate; ~
notarial affidavit

actitud [akti'tuð] *nf* attitude; (*postura*)
posture

activar [akti'βar] *vt* to activate; (*acelerar*)
to speed up

actividad [aktiβi'ðað] *nf* activity

activo, a [ak'tiβo, a] *adj* active; (*vivo*)
lively ♦ *nm* (*COM*) assets *pl*

acto ['akto] *nm* act, action; (*ceremonia*)
ceremony; (*TEATRO*) act; **en el** ~
immediately

actor [ak'tor] *nm* actor; (*JUR*) plaintiff
♦ *adj:* **parte ~a** prosecution

actriz [ak'triθ] *nf* actress

actuación [aktwa'θjon] *nf* action;
(*comportamiento*) conduct, behaviour;
(*JUR*) proceedings *pl*; (*desempeño*)
performance

actual [ak'twal] *adj* present(-day), current;
~idad *nf* present; **~idades** *nfpl* (*noticias*)
news *sg*; **en la ~idad** at present; (*hoy día*)
nowadays

actualizar [aktwali'θar] *vt* to update,
modernize

actualmente [aktwal'mente] *adv* at
present; (*hoy día*) nowadays

actuar [ak'twar] *vi* (*obrar*) to work,
operate; (*actor*) to act, perform ♦ *vt* to
work, operate; ~ **de** to act as

acuarela [akwa'rela] *nf* watercolour

acuario [a'kwarjo] *nm* aquarium;
(*ASTROLOGÍA*): **A~** Aquarius

acuartelar [akwarte'lar] *vt* (*MIL*) to confine
to barracks

acuático, a [a'kwatiko, a] *adj* aquatic

acuchillar [akutʃi'ʎar] *vt* (*TEC*) to plane
(down), smooth

acuciante [aku'θjante] *adj* urgent

acuciar [aku'θjar] *vt* to urge on

acudir [aku'ðir] *vi* (*asistir*) to attend; (*ir*)
to go; ~ **a** (*fig*) to turn to; ~ **en ayuda de** to
go to the aid of

acuerdo *etc* [a'kwerðo] *vb ver* **acordar**
♦ *nm* agreement; **¡de ~!** agreed!; **de ~
con** (*persona*) in agreement with; (*acción,
documento*) in accordance with; **estar de
~** to be agreed, agree

acumular [akumu'lar] *vt* to accumulate,
collect

acuñar [aku'ɲar] *vt* (*moneda*) to mint;
(*frase*) to coin

acupuntura [akupun'tura] *nf* acupuncture

acurrucarse [akurru'karse] *vr* to crouch;
(*ovillarse*) to curl up

acusación [akusa'θjon] *nf* accusation

acusar [aku'sar] *vt* to accuse; (*revelar*) to
reveal; (*denunciar*) to denounce

acuse [a'kuse] *nm:* ~ **de recibo**
acknowledgement of receipt

acústica [a'kustika] *nf* acoustics *pl*

acústico, a [a'kustiko, a] *adj* acoustic

adaptación [aðapta'θjon] *nf* adaptation

adaptador [aðapta'ðor] *nm* (*ELEC*) adapter

adaptar [aðap'tar] *vt* to adapt; (*acomodar*)
to fit

adecuado, a [aðe'kwaðo, a] *adj* (*apto*)
suitable; (*oportuno*) appropriate

adecuar [aðe'kwar] *vt* to adapt; to make
suitable

a. de J.C. *abr* (= *antes de Jesucristo*) B.C.

adelantado, a [aðelan'taðo, a] *adj*
advanced; (*reloj*) fast; **pagar por ~** to pay
in advance

adelantamiento [aðelanta'mjento] *nm*
(*AUTO*) overtaking

adelantar [aðelan'tar] *vt* to move forward;
(*avanzar*) to advance; (*acelerar*) to speed
up; (*AUTO*) to overtake ♦ *vi* to go
forward, advance; **~se** *vr* to go forward,
advance

adelante [aðe'lante] *adv* forward(s), ahead
♦ *excl* come in!; **de hoy en ~** from now

afiliarse [afiˈljarse] *vr* to affiliate

afín [aˈfin] *adj* (*parecido*) similar; (*conexo*) related

afinar [afiˈnar] *vt* (*TEC*) to refine; (*MUS*) to tune ♦ *vi* (*tocar*) to play in tune; (*cantar*) to sing in tune

afincarse [afinˈkarse] *vr* to settle

afinidad [afiniˈðað] *nf* affinity; (*parentesco*) relationship; **por ~** by marriage

afirmación [afirmaˈθjon] *nf* affirmation

afirmar [afirˈmar] *vt* to affirm, state; **afirmativo, a** *adj* affirmative

aflicción [aflikˈθjon] *nf* affliction; (*dolor*) grief

afligir [afliˈxir] *vt* to afflict; (*apenar*) to distress; **~se** *vr* to grieve

aflojar [afloˈxar] *vt* to slacken; (*desatar*) to loosen, undo; (*relajar*) to relax ♦ *vi* to drop; (*bajar*) to go down; **~se** *vr* to relax

aflorar [afloˈrar] *vi* to come to the surface, emerge

afluente [afluˈente] *adj* flowing ♦ *nm* tributary

afluir [afluˈir] *vi* to flow

afmo, a *abr* (= *afectísimo(a) suyo(a)*) Yours

afónico, a [aˈfoniko, a] *adj*: **estar ~** to have a sore throat; to have lost one's voice

aforo [aˈforo] *nm* (*de teatro etc*) capacity

afortunado, a [afortuˈnaðo, a] *adj* fortunate, lucky

afrancesado, a [afranθeˈsaðo, a] *adj* francophile; (*pey*) Frenchified

afrenta [aˈfrenta] *nf* affront, insult; (*deshonra*) dishonour, shame

África [ˈafrika] *nf* Africa; **africano, a** *adj, nm/f* African

afrontar [afronˈtar] *vt* to confront; (*poner cara a cara*) to bring face to face

afuera [aˈfwera] *adv* out, outside; **~s** *nfpl* outskirts

agachar [aɣaˈtʃar] *vt* to bend, bow; **~se** *vr* to stoop, bend

agalla [aˈɣaʎa] *nf* (*ZOOL*) gill; **tener ~s** (*fam*) to have guts

agarradera [aɣarraˈðera] (*esp AM*) *nf* handle

agarrado, a [aɣaˈrraðo, a] *adj* mean, stingy

agarrar [aɣaˈrrar] *vt* to grasp, grab; (*AM*) to take, catch; (*recoger*) to pick up ♦ *vi* (*planta*) to take root; **~se** *vr* to hold on (tightly)

agarrotar [aɣarroˈtar] *vt* (*persona*) to squeeze tightly; (*reo*) to garrotte; **~se** *vr* (*motor*) to seize up; (*MED*) to stiffen

agasajar [aɣasaˈxar] *vt* to treat well, fête

agazaparse [aɣaθaˈparse] *vr* to crouch down

agencia [aˈxenθja] *nf* agency; **~ inmobiliaria** estate (*BRIT*) *o* real estate (*US*) agent's (office); **~ de viajes** travel agency

agenciarse [axenˈθjarse] *vr* to obtain, procure

agenda [aˈxenda] *nf* diary

agente [aˈxente] *nm/f* agent; (*de policía*) policeman/policewoman; **~ inmobiliario** estate agent (*BRIT*), realtor (*US*); **~ de seguros** insurance agent

ágil [ˈaxil] *adj* agile, nimble; **agilidad** *nf* agility, nimbleness

agilizar [axiliˈθar] *vt* (*trámites*) to speed up

agitación [axitaˈθjon] *nf* (*de mano etc*) shaking, waving; (*de líquido etc*) stirring; (*fig*) agitation

agitado, a [axiˈaðo, a] *adj* hectic; (*viaje*) bumpy

agitar [axiˈtar] *vt* to wave, shake; (*líquido*) to stir; (*fig*) to stir up, excite; **~se** *vr* to get excited; (*inquietarse*) to get worried *o* upset

aglomeración [aɣlomeraˈθjon] *nf*: **~ de tráfico / gente** traffic jam/mass of people

aglomerar [aɣlomeˈrar] *vt* to crowd together; **~se** *vr* to crowd together

agnóstico, a [aɣˈnostiko, a] *adj, nm/f* agnostic

agobiar [aɣoˈβjar] *vt* to weigh down; (*oprimir*) to oppress; (*cargar*) to burden

agolparse [aɣolˈparse] *vr* to crowd together

agonía [aɣoˈnia] *nf* death throes *pl*; (*fig*)

agony, anguish

agonizante [aɣoniˈθante] *adj* dying

agonizar [aɣoniˈθar] *vi* to be dying

agosto [aˈɣosto] *nm* August

agotado, a [aɣoˈtaðo, a] *adj* (*persona*) exhausted; (*libros*) out of print; (*acabado*) finished; (*COM*) sold out

agotador, a [aɣotaˈðor, a] *adj* exhausting

agotamiento [aɣotaˈmjento] *nm* exhaustion

agotar [aɣoˈtar] *vt* to exhaust; (*consumir*) to drain; (*recursos*) to use up, deplete; **~se** *vr* to be exhausted; (*acabarse*) to run out; (*libro*) to go out of print

agraciado, a [aɣraˈθjaðo, a] *adj* (*atractivo*) attractive; (*en sorteo etc*) lucky

agradable [aɣraˈðaßle] *adj* pleasant, nice

agradar [aɣraˈðar] *vt*: **él me agrada** I like him

agradecer [aɣraðeˈθer] *vt* to thank; (*favor etc*) to be grateful for; **agradecido, a** *adj* grateful; **¡muy agradecido!** thanks a lot!; **agradecimiento** *nm* thanks *pl*; gratitude

agradezco *etc vb ver* **agradecer**

agrado [aˈɣraðo] *nm*: **ser de tu** *etc* **~** to be to your *etc* liking

agrandar [aɣranˈdar] *vt* to enlarge; (*fig*) to exaggerate; **~se** *vr* to get bigger

agrario, a [aˈɣrarjo, a] *adj* agrarian, land *cpd*; (*política*) agricultural, farming

agravante [aɣraˈßante] *adj* aggravating ♦ *nm*: **con el ~ de que ...** with the further difficulty that ....

agravar [aɣraˈßar] *vt* (*pesar sobre*) to make heavier; (*irritar*) to aggravate; **~se** *vr* to worsen, get worse

agraviar [aɣraˈßjar] *vt* to offend; (*ser injusto con*) to wrong; **~se** *vr* to take offence; **agravio** *nm* offence; wrong; (*JUR*) grievance

agredir [aɣreˈðir] *vt* to attack

agregado, a [aɣreˈɣaðo, a] *nm/f*: **A~** ≈ teacher (*who is not head of department*) ♦ *nm* aggregate; (*persona*) attaché

agregar [aɣreˈɣar] *vt* to gather; (*añadir*) to add; (*persona*) to appoint

agresión [aɣreˈsjon] *nf* aggression

agresivo, a [aɣreˈsißo, a] *adj* aggressive

agriar [aˈɣrjar] *vt* to (turn) sour; **~se** *vr* to turn sour

agrícola [aˈɣrikola] *adj* farming *cpd*, agricultural

agricultor, a [aɣrikulˈtor, a] *nm/f* farmer

agricultura [aɣrikulˈtura] *nf* agriculture, farming

agridulce [aɣriˈðulθe] *adj* bittersweet; (*CULIN*) sweet and sour

agrietarse [aɣrjeˈtarse] *vr* to crack; (*piel*) to chap

agrimensor, a [aɣrimenˈsor, a] *nm/f* surveyor

agrio, a [ˈaɣrjo, a] *adj* bitter

agrupación [aɣrupaˈθjon] *nf* group; (*acto*) grouping

agrupar [aɣruˈpar] *vt* to group

agua [ˈaɣwa] *nf* water; (*NAUT*) wake; (*ARQ*) slope of a roof; **~s** *nfpl* (*de piedra*) water *sg*, sparkle *sg*; (*MED*) water *sg*, urine *sg*; (*NAUT*) waters; **~s abajo/arriba** downstream/upstream; **~ bendita/ destilada/potable** holy/distilled/drinking water; **~ caliente** hot water; **~ corriente** running water; **~ de colonia** eau de cologne; **~ mineral (con/sin gas)** (carbonated/uncarbonated) mineral water; **~ oxigenada** hydrogen peroxide; **~s jurisdiccionales** territorial waters

aguacate [aɣwaˈkate] *nm* avocado (pear)

aguacero [aɣwaˈθero] *nm* (heavy) shower, downpour

aguado, a [aˈɣwaðo, a] *adj* watery, watered down

aguafiestas [aɣwaˈfjestas] *nm/f inv* spoilsport, killjoy

aguanieve [aɣwaˈnjeße] *nf* sleet

aguantar [aɣwanˈtar] *vt* to bear, put up with; (*sostener*) to hold up ♦ *vi* to last; **~se** *vr* to restrain o.s.; **aguante** *nm* (*paciencia*) patience; (*resistencia*) endurance

aguar [aˈɣwar] *vt* to water down

aguardar [aɣwarˈðar] *vt* to wait for

aguardiente [aɣwarˈðjente] *nm* brandy,

liquor

aguarrás [axwa'rras] *nm* turpentine

agudeza [aɣu'ðeθa] *nf* sharpness; (*ingenio*) wit

agudizar [aɣuði'θar] *vt* (*crisis*) to make worse; **~se** *vr* to get worse

agudo, a [a'ɣuðo, a] *adj* sharp; (*voz*) high-pitched, piercing; (*dolor, enfermedad*) acute

agüero [a'ɣwero] *nm*: **buen/mal ~** good/ bad omen

aguijón [aɣi'xon] *nm* sting; (*fig*) spur

águila ['aɣila] *nf* eagle; (*fig*) genius

aguileño, a [aɣi'leɲo, a] *adj* (*nariz*) aquiline; (*rostro*) sharp-featured

aguinaldo [aɣi'naldo] *nm* Christmas box

aguja [a'ɣuxa] *nf* needle; (*de reloj*) hand; (*ARQ*) spire; (*TEC*) firing-pin; **~s** *nfpl* (*ZOOL*) ribs; (*FERRO*) points

agujerear [aɣuxere'ar] *vt* to make holes in

agujero [aɣu'xero] *nm* hole

agujetas [aɣu'xetas] *nfpl* stitch *sg*; (*rigidez*) stiffness *sg*

aguzar [aɣu'θar] *vt* to sharpen; (*fig*) to incite

ahí [a'i] *adv* there; **de ~ que** so that, with the result that; **~ llega** here he comes; **por ~** that way; (*allá*) over there; **200 o por ~** 200 or so

ahijado, a [ai'xaðo, a] *nm/f* godson/ daughter

ahínco [a'inko] *nm* earnestness

ahogar [ao'ɣar] *vt* to drown; (*asfixiar*) to suffocate, smother; (*fuego*) to put out; **~se** *vr* (*en el agua*) to drown; (*por asfixia*) to suffocate

ahogo [a'oɣo] *nm* breathlessness; (*fig*) financial difficulty

ahondar [aon'dar] *vt* to deepen, make deeper; (*fig*) to study thoroughly ♦ *vi:* **~ en** to study thoroughly

ahora [a'ora] *adv* now; (*hace poco*) a moment ago, just now; (*dentro de poco*) in a moment; **~ voy** I'm coming; **~ mismo** right now; **~ bien** now then; **por ~** for the present

ahorcar [aor'kar] *vt* to hang

ahorita [ao'rita] (*fam: esp AM*) *adv* right now

ahorrar [ao'rrar] *vt* (*dinero*) to save; (*esfuerzos*) to save, avoid; **ahorro** *nm* (*acto*) saving; **ahorros** *nmpl* (*dinero*) savings

ahuecar [awe'kar] *vt* to hollow (out); (*voz*) to deepen; **~se** *vr* to give o.s. airs

ahumar [au'mar] *vt* to smoke, cure; (*llenar de humo*) to fill with smoke ♦ *vi* to smoke; **~se** *vr* to fill with smoke

ahuyentar [aujen'tar] *vt* to drive off, frighten off; (*fig*) to dispel

airado, a [ai'raðo, a] *adj* angry

airar [ai'rar] *vt* to anger; **~se** *vr* to get angry

aire ['aire] *nm* air; (*viento*) wind; (*corriente*) draught; (*MUS*) tune; **~s** *nmpl*: **darse ~s** to give o.s. airs; **al ~ libre** in the open air; **~ acondicionado** air conditioning; **airearse** *vr* (*persona*) to go out for a breath of fresh air; **airoso, a** *adj* windy; draughty; (*fig*) graceful

aislado, a [ais'laðo, a] *adj* isolated; (*incomunicado*) cut-off; (*ELEC*) insulated

aislar [ais'lar] *vt* to isolate; (*ELEC*) to insulate

ajardinado, a [axarði'naðo, a] *adj* landscaped

ajedrez [axe'ðreθ] *nm* chess

ajeno, a [a'xeno, a] *adj* (*que pertenece a otro*) somebody else's; **~ a** foreign to

ajetreado, a [axetre'aðo, a] *adj* busy

ajetreo [axe'treo] *nm* bustle

ají [a'xi] (*AM*) *nm* chil(l)i, red pepper; (*salsa*) chil(l)i sauce

ajillo [a'xiʎo] *nm*: **gambas al ~** garlic prawns

ajo ['axo] *nm* garlic

ajuar [a'xwar] *nm* household furnishings *pl*; (*de novia*) trousseau; (*de niño*) layette

ajustado, a [axus'taðo, a] *adj* (*tornillo*) tight; (*cálculo*) right; (*ropa*) tight(-fitting); (*resultado*) close

ajustar [axus'tar] *vt* (*adaptar*) to adjust; (*encajar*) to fit; (*TEC*) to engage; (*IMPRENTA*) to make up; (*apretar*) to tighten; (*concertar*) to agree (on); (*reconciliar*) to reconcile; (*cuentas, deudas*) to settle ♦ *vi* to fit; **~se** *vr*: **~se a** (*precio etc*) to be in keeping with, fit in with; **~ las cuentas a uno** to get even with sb

ajuste [aˈxuste] *nm* adjustment; (*COSTURA*) fitting; (*acuerdo*) compromise; (*de cuenta*) settlement

al [al] (= **a +el**) *ver* **a**

ala [ˈala] *nf* wing; (*de sombrero*) brim; (*futbolista*) winger; **~ delta** *nf* hangglider

alabanza [alaˈβanθa] *nf* praise

alabar [alaˈβar] *vt* to praise

alacena [alaˈθena] *nf* kitchen cupboard (*BRIT*), kitchen closet (*US*)

alacrán [alaˈkran] *nm* scorpion

alambique [alamˈbike] *nm* still

alambrada [alamˈbraða] *nf* wire fence; (*red*) wire netting

alambrado [alamˈbraðo] *nm* = **alambrada**

alambre [aˈlambre] *nm* wire; **~ de púas** barbed wire

alameda [alaˈmeða] *nf* (*plantío*) poplar grove; (*lugar de paseo*) avenue, boulevard

álamo [ˈalamo] *nm* poplar; **~ temblón** aspen

alarde [aˈlarðe] *nm* show, display; **hacer ~ de** to boast of

alargador [alarɣaˈðor] *nm* (*ELEC*) extension lead

alargar [alarˈɣar] *vt* to lengthen, extend; (*paso*) to hasten; (*brazo*) to stretch out; (*cuerda*) to pay out; (*conversación*) to spin out; **~se** *vr* to get longer

alarido [alaˈriðo] *nm* shriek

alarma [aˈlarma] *nf* alarm

alarmar *vt* to alarm; **~se** to get alarmed; **alarmante** [alarˈmante] *adj* alarming

alba [ˈalβa] *nf* dawn

albacea [alβaˈθea] *nm/f* executor/executrix

albahaca [alˈβaka] *nf* basil

Albania [alˈβanja] *nf* Albania

albañil [alβaˈɲil] *nm* bricklayer; (*cantero*) mason

albarán [alβaˈran] *nm* (*COM*) delivery note, invoice

albaricoque [alβariˈkoke] *nm* apricot

albedrío [alβeˈðrio] *nm*: **libre ~** free will

alberca [alˈβerka] *nf* reservoir; (*AM*) swimming pool

albergar [alβerˈxar] *vt* to shelter

albergue *etc* [alˈβerxe] *vb ver* **albergar** ♦ *nm* shelter, refuge; **~ juvenil** youth hostel

albóndiga [alˈβondiɣa] *nf* meatball

albornoz [alβorˈnoθ] *nm* (*de los árabes*) burnous; (*para el baño*) bathrobe

alborotar [alβoroˈtar] *vi* to make a row ♦ *vt* to agitate, stir up; **~se** *vr* to get excited; (*mar*) to get rough; **alboroto** *nm* row, uproar

alborozar [alβoroˈθar] *vt* to gladden; **~se** *vr* to rejoice

alborozo [alβoˈroθo] *nm* joy

álbum [ˈalβum] (*pl* **~s**, **~es**) *nm* album; **~ de recortes** scrapbook

alcachofa [alkaˈtʃofa] *nf* artichoke

alcalde, esa [alˈkalde, esa] *nm/f* mayor(ess)

alcaldía [alkalˈdia] *nf* mayoralty; (*lugar*) mayor's office

alcance *etc* [alˈkanθe] *vb ver* **alcanzar** ♦ *nm* reach; (*COM*) adverse balance

alcantarilla [alkantaˈriʎa] *nf* (*de aguas cloacales*) sewer; (*en la calle*) gutter

alcanzar [alkanˈθar] *vt* (*algo: con la mano, el pie*) to reach; (*alguien: en el camino etc*) to catch up (with); (*autobús etc*) to catch; (*suj: bala*) to hit, strike ♦ *vi* (*ser suficiente*) to be enough; **~ a hacer** to manage to do

alcaparra [alkaˈparra] *nf* caper

alcayata [alkaˈjata] *nf* hook

alcázar [alˈkaθar] *nm* fortress; (*NAUT*) quarter-deck

alcoba [alˈkoβa] *nf* bedroom

alcohol [alˈkol] *nm* alcohol; **~ metílico** methylated spirits *pl* (*BRIT*), wood alcohol (*US*); **alcohólico, a** *adj*, *nm/f* alcoholic

alcoholímetro [alkoˈlimetro] *nm* Breathalyser ® (*BRIT*), drunkometer (*US*)

alcoholismo [alkoˈlismo] *nm* alcoholism

alcornoque [alkor'noke] *nm* cork tree; (*fam*) idiot

alcurnia [al'kurnja] *nf* lineage

aldaba [al'daβa] *nf* (door) knocker

aldea [al'dea] *nf* village; **~no, a** *adj* village *cpd* ♦ *nm/f* villager

aleación [alea'θjon] *nf* alloy

aleatorio, a [alea'torjo, a] *adj* random

aleccionar [alekθjo'nar] *vt* to instruct; (*adiestrar*) to train

alegación [aleɣa'θjon] *nf* allegation

alegar [ale'ɣar] *vt* to claim; (*JUR*) to plead ♦ *vi* (*AM*) to argue

alegato [ale'ɣato] *nm* (*JUR*) allegation; (*AM*) argument

alegoría [aleɣo'ria] *nf* allegory

alegrar [ale'ɣrar] *vt* (*causar alegría*) to cheer (up); (*fuego*) to poke; (*fiesta*) to liven up; **~se** *vr* (*fam*) to get merry *o* tight; **~se de** to be glad about

alegre [a'leɣre] *adj* happy, cheerful; (*fam*) merry, tight; (*chiste*) risqué, blue; **alegría** *nf* happiness; merriment

alejamiento [alexa'mjento] *nm* removal; (*distancia*) remoteness

alejar [ale'xar] *vt* to remove; (*fig*) to estrange; **~se** *vr* to move away

alemán, ana [ale'man, ana] *adj, nm/f* German ♦ *nm* (*LING*) German

Alemania [ale'manja] *nf*: **~ Occidental / Oriental** West/East Germany

alentador, a [alenta'ðor, a] *adj* encouraging

alentar [alen'tar] *vt* to encourage

alergia [a'lerxja] *nf* allergy

alero [a'lero] *nm* (*de tejado*) eaves *pl*; (*de carruaje*) mudguard

alerta [a'lerta] *adj, nm* alert

aleta [a'leta] *nf* (*de pez*) fin; (*de ave*) wing; (*de foca, DEPORTE*) flipper; (*AUTO*) mudguard

aletargar [aletar'xar] *vt* to make drowsy; (*entumecer*) to make numb; **~se** *vr* to grow drowsy; to become numb

aletear [alete'ar] *vi* to flutter

alevín [ale'ßin] *nm* fry, young fish

alevosía [aleßo'sia] *nf* treachery

alfabeto [alfa'ßeto] *nm* alphabet

alfalfa [al'falfa] *nf* alfalfa, lucerne

alfarería [alfare'ria] *nf* pottery; (*tienda*) pottery shop; **alfarero, a** *nm/f* potter

alféizar [al'feiθar] *nm* window-sill

alférez [al'fereθ] *nm* (*MIL*) second lieutenant; (*NAUT*) ensign

alfil [al'fil] *nm* (*AJEDREZ*) bishop

alfiler [alfi'ler] *nm* pin; (*broche*) clip

alfiletero [alfile'tero] *nm* needlecase

alfombra [al'fombra] *nf* carpet; (*más pequeña*) rug; **alfombrar** *vt* to carpet; **alfombrilla** *nf* rug, mat

alforja [al'forxa] *nf* saddlebag

algarabía [alɣara'ßia] (*fam*) *nf* gibberish; (*griterío*) hullabaloo

algas ['alɣas] *nfpl* seaweed

álgebra ['alxeßra] *nf* algebra

álgido, a ['alxiðo, a] *adj* (*momento etc*) crucial, decisive

algo ['alɣo] *pron* something; anything ♦ *adv* somewhat, rather; **¿~ más?** anything else?; (*en tienda*) is that all?; **por ~ será** there must be some reason for it

algodón [alɣo'ðon] *nm* cotton; (*planta*) cotton plant; **~ de azúcar** candy floss (*BRIT*), cotton candy (*US*); **~ hidrófilo** cotton wool (*BRIT*), absorbent cotton (*US*)

algodonero, a [alɣoðo'nero, a] *adj* cotton *cpd* ♦ *nm/f* cotton grower ♦ *nm* cotton plant

alguacil [alɣwa'θil] *nm* bailiff; (*TAUR*) mounted official

alguien ['alxjen] *pron* someone, somebody; (*en frases interrogativas*) anyone, anybody

alguno, a [al'ɣuno, a] *adj* (*delante de nm*: **algún**) some; (*después de n*): **no tiene talento ~** he has no talent, he doesn't have any talent ♦ *pron* (*alguien*) someone, somebody; **algún que otro libro** some book or other; **algún día iré** I'll go one *o* some day; **sin interés ~** without the slightest interest; **~ que otro** an occasional one; **~s piensan** some (people) think

alhaja [a'laxa] *nf* jewel; (*tesoro*) precious

object, treasure
alhelí [ale'li] *nm* wallflower, stock
aliado, a [a'ljaðo, a] *adj* allied
alianza [a'ljanθa] *nf* alliance; (*anillo*) wedding ring
aliar [a'ljar] *vt* to ally; **~se** *vr* to form an alliance
alias ['aljas] *adv* alias
alicates [ali'kates] *nmpl* pliers; **~ de uñas** nail clippers
aliciente [ali'θjente] *nm* incentive; (*atracción*) attraction
alienación [aljena'θjon] *nf* alienation
aliento [a'ljento] *nm* breath; (*respiración*) breathing; **sin ~** breathless
aligerar [alixe'rar] *vt* to lighten; (*reducir*) to shorten; (*aliviar*) to alleviate; (*mitigar*) to ease; (*paso*) to quicken
alijo [a'lixo] *nm* consignment
alimaña [ali'maɲa] *nf* pest
alimentación [alimenta'θjon] *nf* (*comida*) food; (*acción*) feeding; (*tienda*) grocer's (shop); **alimentador** *nm*: **alimentador de papel** sheet-feeder
alimentar [alimen'tar] *vt* to feed; (*nutrir*) to nourish; **~se** *vr* to feed
alimenticio, a [alimen'tiθjo, a] *adj* food *cpd*; (*nutritivo*) nourishing, nutritious
alimento [ali'mento] *nm* food; (*nutrición*) nourishment
alineación [alinea'θjon] *nf* alignment; (*DEPORTE*) line-up
alinear [aline'ar] *vt* to align; **~se** *vr* (*DEPORTE*) to line up; **~se en** to fall in with
aliñar [ali'ɲar] *vt* (*CULIN*) to season; **aliño** *nm* (*CULIN*) dressing
alioli [ali'oli] *nm* garlic mayonnaise
alisar [ali'sar] *vt* to smooth
aliso [a'liso] *nm* alder
alistarse [alis'tarse] *vr* to enlist; (*inscribirse*) to enrol
aliviar [ali'βjar] *vt* (*carga*) to lighten; (*persona*) to relieve; (*dolor*) to relieve, alleviate
alivio [a'liβjo] *nm* alleviation, relief
aljibe [al'xiβe] *nm* cistern

allá [a'ʎa] *adv* (*lugar*) there; (*por ahí*) over there; (*tiempo*) then; **~ abajo** down there; **más ~** further on; **más ~ de** beyond; **¡~ tú!** that's your problem!
allanamiento [aʎana'mjento] *nm*: **~ de morada** burglary
allanar [aʎa'nar] *vt* to flatten, level (out); (*igualar*) to smooth (out); (*fig*) to subdue; (*JUR*) to burgle, break into
allegado, a [aʎe'xaðo, a] *adj* near, close ♦ *nm/f* relation
allí [a'ʎi] *adv* there; **~ mismo** right there; **por ~** over there; (*por ese camino*) that way
alma ['alma] *nf* soul; (*persona*) person
almacén [alma'θen] *nm* (*depósito*) warehouse, store; (*MIL*) magazine; (*AM*) shop; **(grandes) almacenes** *nmpl* department store *sg*; **almacenaje** *nm* storage
almacenar [almaθe'nar] *vt* to store, put in storage; (*proveerse*) to stock up with; **almacenero** (*AM*) shopkeeper
almanaque [alma'nake] *nm* almanac
almeja [al'mexa] *nf* clam
almendra [al'mendra] *nf* almond; **almendro** *nm* almond tree
almíbar [al'miβar] *nm* syrup
almidón [almi'ðon] *nm* starch; **almidonar** *vt* to starch
almirante [almi'rante] *nm* admiral
almirez [almi'reθ] *nm* mortar
almizcle [al'miθkle] *nm* musk
almohada [almo'aða] *nf* pillow; (*funda*) pillowcase; **almohadilla** *nf* cushion; (*TEC*) pad; (*AM*) pincushion
almohadón [almoa'ðon] *nm* large pillow; bolster
almorranas [almo'rranas] *nfpl* piles, haemorrhoids
almorzar [almor'θar] *vt*: **~ una tortilla** to have an omelette for lunch ♦ *vi* to (have) lunch
almuerzo *etc* [al'mwerθo] *vb ver* **almorzar** ♦ *nm* lunch
alocado, a [alo'kaðo, a] *adj* crazy
alojamiento [aloxa'mjento] *nm* lodging(s)

(*pl*); (*viviendas*) housing

alojar [alo'xar] *vt* to lodge; **~se** *vr* to lodge, stay

alondra [a'londra] *nf* lark, skylark

alpargata [alpar'vata] *nf* rope-soled sandal, espadrille

Alpes ['alpes] *nmpl:* **los ~** the Alps

alpinismo [alpi'nismo] *nm* mountaineering, climbing; **alpinista** *nm/f* mountaineer, climber

alpiste [al'piste] *nm* birdseed

alquilar [alki'lar] *vt* (*suj: propietario: inmuebles*) to let, rent (out); (: *coche*) to hire out; (: *TV*) to rent (out); (*suj: alquilador: inmuebles, TV*) to rent; (: *coche*) to hire; **"se alquila casa"** "house to let (*BRIT*) o for rent (*US*)"

alquiler [alki'ler] *nm* renting; letting; hiring; (*arriendo*) rent; hire charge; **~ de automóviles** car hire; **de ~** for hire

alquimia [al'kimja] *nf* alchemy

alquitrán [alki'tran] *nm* tar

alrededor [alreðe'ðor] *adv* around, about; **~ de** around, about; **mirar a su ~** to look (round) about one; **~es** *nmpl* surroundings

alta ['alta] *nf* (certificate of) discharge; **dar de ~** to discharge

altanería [altane'ria] *nf* haughtiness, arrogance; **altanero, a** *adj* arrogant, haughty

altar [al'tar] *nm* altar

altavoz [alta'ßoθ] *nm* loudspeaker; (*amplificador*) amplifier

alteración [altera'θjon] *nf* alteration; (*alboroto*) disturbance

alterar [alte'rar] *vt* to alter; to disturb; **~se** *vr* (*persona*) to get upset

altercado [alter'kaðo] *nm* argument

alternar [alter'nar] *vt* to alternate ♦ *vi* to alternate; (*turnar*) to take turns; **~se** *vr* to alternate; to take turns; **~ con** to mix with; **alternativa** *nf* alternative; (*elección*) choice; **alternativo, a** *adj* alternative; (*alterno*) alternating; **alterno, a** *adj* alternate; (*ELEC*) alternating

Alteza [al'teθa] *nf* (*tratamiento*) Highness

altibajos [alti'ßaxos] *nmpl* ups and downs

altiplanicie [altipla'niθje] *nf* high plateau

altiplano [alti'plano] *nm* = **altiplanicie**

altisonante [altiso'nante] *adj* high-flown, high-sounding

altitud [alti'tuð] *nf* height; (*AVIAT, GEO*) altitude

altivez [alti'ßeθ] *nf* haughtiness, arrogance; **altivo, a** *adj* haughty, arrogant

alto, a ['alto, a] *adj* high; (*persona*) tall; (*sonido*) high, sharp; (*noble*) high, lofty ♦ *nm* halt; (*MUS*) alto; (*GEO*) hill; (*AM*) pile ♦ *adv* (*de sitio*) high; (*de sonido*) loud, loudly ♦ *excl* halt!; **la pared tiene 2 metros de ~** the wall is 2 metres high; **en alta mar** on the high seas; **en voz alta** in a loud voice; **las altas horas de la noche** the small o wee hours; **en lo ~ de** at the top of; **pasar por ~** to overlook

altoparlante [altopar'lante] (*AM*) *nm* loudspeaker

altruismo [altru'ismo] *nm* altruism

altura [al'tura] *nf* height; (*NAUT*) depth; (*GEO*) latitude; **la pared tiene 1.80 de ~** the wall is 1 metre 80cm high; **a estas ~s** at this stage; **a estas ~s del año** at this time of the year

alubia [a'lußja] *nf* bean

alucinación [aluθina'θjon] *nf* hallucination

alucinar [aluθi'nar] *vi* to hallucinate ♦ *vt* to deceive; (*fascinar*) to fascinate

alud [a'luð] *nm* avalanche; (*fig*) flood

aludir [alu'ðir] *vi:* **~ a** to allude to; **darse por aludido** to take the hint

alumbrado [alum'braðo] *nm* lighting; **alumbramiento** *nm* lighting; (*MED*) childbirth, delivery

alumbrar [alum'brar] *vt* to light (up) ♦ *vi* (*MED*) to give birth

aluminio [alu'minjo] *nm* aluminium (*BRIT*), aluminum (*US*)

alumno, a [a'lumno, a] *nm/f* pupil, student

alunizar [aluni'θar] *vi* to land on the moon

alusión [alu'sjon] *nf* allusion

alusivo, a [alu'sißo, a] *adj* allusive

aluvión [alu'ßjon] *nm* alluvium; (*fig*) flood

alverja [al'ßerxa] (*AM*) *nf* pea

alza ['alθa] *nf* rise; (*MIL*) sight

alzada [al'θaða] *nf* (*de caballos*) height; (*JUR*) appeal

alzamiento [alθa'mjento] *nm* (*rebelión*) rising

alzar [al'θar] *vt* to lift (up); (*precio, muro*) to raise; (*cuello de abrigo*) to turn up; (*AGR*) to gather in; (*IMPRENTA*) to gather; **~se** *vr* to get up, rise; (*rebelarse*) to revolt; (*COM*) to go fraudulently bankrupt; (*JUR*) to appeal

ama ['ama] *nf* lady of the house; (*dueña*) owner; (*institutriz*) governess; (*madre adoptiva*) foster mother; **~ de casa** housewife; **~ de llaves** housekeeper

amabilidad [amaßili'ðað] *nf* kindness; (*simpatía*) niceness; **amable** *adj* kind; nice; **es usted muy amable** that's very kind of you

amaestrado, a [amaes'traðo, a] *adj* (*animal: en circo etc*) performing

amaestrar [amaes'trar] *vt* to train

amago [a'maxo] *nm* threat; (*gesto*) threatening gesture; (*MED*) symptom

amainar [amai'nar] *vi* (*viento*) to die down

amalgama [amal'xama] *nf* amalgam; **amalgamar** *vt* to amalgamate; (*combinar*) to combine, mix

amamantar [amaman'tar] *vt* to suckle, nurse

amanecer [amane'θer] *vi* to dawn ♦ *nm* dawn; **~ afiebrado** to wake up with a fever

amanerado, a [amane'raðo, a] *adj* affected

amansar [aman'sar] *vt* to tame; (*persona*) to subdue; **~se** *vr* (*persona*) to calm down

amante [a'mante] *adj*: **~ de** fond of ♦ *nm/f* lover

amapola [ama'pola] *nf* poppy

amar [a'mar] *vt* to love

amargado, a [amar'xaðo, a] *adj* bitter

amargar [amar'xar] *vt* to make bitter; (*fig*) to embitter; **~se** *vr* to become embittered

amargo, a [a'marxo, a] *adj* bitter; **amargura** *nf* bitterness

amarillento, a [amari'ʎento, a] *adj* yellowish; (*tez*) sallow; **amarillo, a** *adj, nm* yellow

amarrar [ama'rrar] *vt* to moor; (*sujetar*) to tie up

amarras [a'marras] *nfpl*: **soltar ~** to set sail

amasar [ama'sar] *vt* (*masa*) to knead; (*mezclar*) to mix, prepare; (*confeccionar*) to concoct; **amasijo** *nm* kneading; mixing; (*fig*) hotchpotch

amateur ['amatur] *nm/f* amateur

amazona [ama'θona] *nf* horsewoman; **A~s** *nm*: **el A~s** the Amazon

ambages [am'baxes] *nmpl*: **sin ~** in plain language

ámbar ['ambar] *nm* amber

ambición [ambi'θjon] *nf* ambition; **ambicionar** *vt* to aspire to; **ambicioso, a** *adj* ambitious

ambidextro, a [ambi'ðekstro, a] *adj* ambidextrous

ambientación [ambjenta'θjon] *nf* (*CINE, TEATRO etc*) setting; (*RADIO*) sound effects

ambiente [am'bjente] *nm* (*tb fig*) atmosphere; (*medio*) environment

ambigüedad [ambixwe'ðað] *nf* ambiguity; **ambiguo, a** *adj* ambiguous

ámbito ['ambito] *nm* (*campo*) field; (*fig*) scope

ambos, as ['ambos, as] *adj pl, pron pl* both

ambulancia [ambu'lanθja] *nf* ambulance

ambulante [ambu'lante] *adj* travelling *cpd*, itinerant

ambulatorio [ambula'torio] *nm* state health-service clinic

amedrentar [ameðren'tar] *vt* to scare

amén [a'men] *excl* amen; **~ de** besides

amenaza [ame'naθa] *nf* threat

amenazar [amena'θar] *vt* to threaten ♦ *vi*: **~ con hacer** to threaten to do

amenidad [ameni'ðað] *nf* pleasantness

ameno, a [a'meno, a] *adj* pleasant

América [a'merika] *nf* America; **~ del Norte/del Sur** North/South America; **~ Central/Latina** Central/Latin America; **americana** *nf* coat, jacket; *ver tb* **americano; americano, a** *adj, nm/f* American

amerizar [ameri'θar] *vi* (*avión*) to land (on the sea)

ametralladora [ametraʎa'ðora] *nf* machine gun

amianto [a'mjanto] *nm* asbestos

amigable [ami'ɣaßle] *adj* friendly

amígdala [a'miɣðala] *nf* tonsil; **amigdalitis** *nf* tonsillitis

amigo, a [a'miɣo, a] *adj* friendly ♦ *nm/f* friend; (*amante*) lover; **ser ~ de algo** to be fond of sth; **ser muy ~s** to be close friends

amilanar [amila'nar] *vt* to scare; **~se** *vr* to get scared

aminorar [amino'rar] *vt* to diminish; (*reducir*) to reduce; **~ la marcha** to slow down

amistad [amis'tað] *nf* friendship; **~es** *nfpl* (*amigos*) friends; **amistoso, a** *adj* friendly

amnesia [am'nesja] *nf* amnesia

amnistía [amnis'tia] *nf* amnesty

amo ['amo] *nm* owner; (*jefe*) boss

amodorrarse [amoðo'rrarse] *vr* to get sleepy

amoldar [amol'dar] *vt* to mould; (*adaptar*) to adapt

amonestación [amonesta'θjon] *nf* warning; **amonestaciones** *nfpl* (*REL*) marriage banns

amonestar [amones'tar] *vt* to warn; (*REL*) to publish the banns of

amontonar [amonto'nar] *vt* to collect, pile up; **~se** *vr* to crowd together; (*acumularse*) to pile up

amor [a'mor] *nm* love; (*amante*) lover; **hacer el ~** to make love; **~ propio** self-respect

amoratado, a [amora'taðo, a] *adj* purple

amordazar [amorða'θar] *vt* to muzzle; (*fig*) to gag

amorfo, a [a'morfo, a] *adj* amorphous, shapeless

amoroso, a [amo'roso, a] *adj* affectionate, loving

amortajar [amorta'xar] *vt* to shroud

amortiguador [amortiɣwa'ðor] *nm* shock absorber; (*parachoques*) bumper; **~es** *nmpl* (*AUTO*) suspension *sg*

amortiguar [amorti'ɣwar] *vt* to deaden; (*ruido*) to muffle; (*color*) to soften

amortización [amortiθa'θjon] *nf* (*de deuda*) repayment; (*de bono*) redemption

amotinar [amoti'nar] *vt* to stir up, incite (to riot); **~se** *vr* to mutiny

amparar [ampa'rar] *vt* to protect; **~se** *vr* to seek protection; (*de la lluvia etc*) to shelter; **amparo** *nm* help, protection; **al amparo de** under the protection of

amperio [am'perjo] *nm* ampère, amp

ampliación [amplja'θjon] *nf* enlargement; (*extensión*) extension

ampliar [am'pljar] *vt* to enlarge; to extend

amplificación [amplifika'θjon] *nf* enlargement; **amplificador** *nm* amplifier

amplificar [amplifi'kar] *vt* to amplify

amplio, a ['ampljo, a] *adj* spacious; (*de falda etc*) full; (*extenso*) extensive; (*ancho*) wide; **amplitud** *nf* spaciousness; extent; (*fig*) amplitude

ampolla [am'poʎa] *nf* blister; (*MED*) ampoule

ampuloso, a [ampu'loso, a] *adj* bombastic, pompous

amputar [ampu'tar] *vt* to cut off, amputate

amueblar [amwe'ßlar] *vt* to furnish

amurallar [amura'ʎar] *vt* to wall up *o* in

anacronismo [anakro'nismo] *nm* anachronism

anales [a'nales] *nmpl* annals

analfabetismo [analfaße'tismo] *nm* illiteracy; **analfabeto, a** *adj, nm/f* illiterate

analgésico [anal'xesiko] *nm* painkiller, analgesic

análisis [a'nalisis] *nm inv* analysis

analista [ana'lista] *nm/f* (*gen*) analyst

analizar [anali'θar] *vt* to analyse

analogía [analo'xia] *nf* analogy

analógico, a [ana'loxiko, a] *adj* (*INFORM*) analog; (*reloj*) analogue (*BRIT*), analog (*US*)

análogo, a [a'naloxo, a] *adj* analogous, similar

ananá(s) [ana'na(s)] (*AM*) *nm* pineapple

anaquel [ana'kel] *nm* shelf

anarquía [anar'kia] *nf* anarchy; **anarquismo** *nm* anarchism; **anarquista** *nm/f* anarchist

anatomía [anato'mia] *nf* anatomy

anca ['anka] *nf* rump, haunch; **~s** *nfpl* (*fam*) behind *sg*

ancho, a ['antʃo, a] *adj* wide; (*falda*) full; (*fig*) liberal ♦ *nm* width; (*FERRO*) gauge; **ponerse ~** to get conceited; **estar a sus anchas** to be at one's ease

anchoa [an'tʃoa] *nf* anchovy

anchura [an'tʃura] *nf* width; (*extensión*) wideness

anciano, a [an'θjano, a] *adj* old, aged ♦ *nm/f* old man/woman; elder

ancla ['ankla] *nf* anchor; **~dero** *nm* anchorage; **anclar** *vi* to (drop) anchor

andadura [anda'ðura] *nf* gait; (*de caballo*) pace

Andalucía [andalu'θia] *nf* Andalusia; **andaluz, a** *adj, nm/f* Andalusian

andamiaje [anda'mjaxe] *nm* = **andamio**

andamio [an'damjo] *nm* scaffold(ing)

andar [an'dar] *vt* to go, cover, travel ♦ *vi* to go, walk, travel; (*funcionar*) to go, work; (*estar*) to be ♦ *nm* walk, gait, pace; **~se** *vr* to go away; **~ a pie/a caballo/en bicicleta** to go on foot/on horseback/by bicycle; **~ haciendo algo** to be doing sth; **¡anda!** (*sorpresa*) go on!; **anda por** *o* **en los 40** he's about 40

andén [an'den] *nm* (*FERRO*) platform; (*NAUT*) quayside; (*AM: de la calle*) pavement (*BRIT*), sidewalk (*US*)

Andes ['andes] *nmpl*: **los ~** the Andes

Andorra [an'dorra] *nf* Andorra

andrajo [an'draxo] *nm* rag; **~so, a** *adj*
ragged

anduve *etc* [an'duβe] *vb ver* **andar**

anécdota [a'nekðota] *nf* anecdote, story

anegar [ane'ɣar] *vt* to flood; (*ahogar*) to drown; **~se** *vr* to drown; (*hundirse*) to sink

anejo, a [a'nexo, a] *adj, nm* = **anexo**

anemia [a'nemja] *nf* anaemia

anestesia [anes'tesja] *nf* (*sustancia*) anaesthetic; (*proceso*) anaesthesia

anexar [anek'sar] *vt* to annex; (*documento*) to attach; **anexión** *nf* annexation; **anexionamiento** *nm* annexation; **anexo, a** *adj* attached ♦ *nm* annexe

anfibio, a [an'fiβjo, a] *adj* amphibious ♦ *nm* amphibian

anfiteatro [anfite'atro] *nm* amphitheatre; (*TEATRO*) dress circle

anfitrión, ona [anfi'trjon, ona] *nm/f* host(ess)

ángel ['anxel] *nm* angel; **~ de la guarda** guardian angel; **tener ~** to be charming; **angelical** *adj*, **angélico, a** *adj* angelic(al)

angina [an'xina] *nf* (*MED*) inflammation of the throat; **~ de pecho** angina; **tener ~s** to have tonsillitis

anglicano, a [angli'kano, a] *adj, nm/f* Anglican

anglosajón, ona [anglosa'xon, ona] *adj* Anglo-Saxon

angosto, a [an'gosto, a] *adj* narrow

anguila [an'gila] *nf* eel

angula [an'gula] *nf* elver, baby eel

ángulo ['angulo] *nm* angle; (*esquina*) corner; (*curva*) bend

angustia [an'gustja] *nf* anguish; **angustiar** *vt* to distress, grieve

anhelar [ane'lar] *vt* to be eager for; (*desear*) to long for, desire ♦ *vi* to pant, gasp; **anhelo** *nm* eagerness; desire

anidar [ani'ðar] *vi* to nest

anillo [a'niʎo] *nm* ring; **~ de boda** wedding ring

animación [anima'θjon] *nf* liveliness; (*vitalidad*) life; (*actividad*) activity; bustle

animado, a [ani'maðo, a] *adj* lively;

(vivaz) animated; **animador, a** *nm/f*
(TV) host(ess), compère; *(DEPORTE)*
cheerleader

animadversión [animaðßer'sjon] *nf* ill-
will, antagonism

animal [ani'mal] *adj* animal; *(fig)* stupid
♦ *nm* animal; *(fig)* fool; *(bestia)* brute

animar [ani'mar] *vt (BIO)* to animate, give
life to; *(fig)* to liven up, brighten up,
cheer up; *(estimular)* to stimulate; **~se** *vr*
to cheer up; to feel encouraged;
(decidirse) to make up one's mind

ánimo ['animo] *nm (alma)* soul; *(mente)*
mind; *(valentía)* courage ♦ *excl* cheer up!

animoso, a [ani'moso, a] *adj* brave; *(vivo)*
lively

aniquilar [aniki'lar] *vt* to annihilate,
destroy

anís [a'nis] *nm* aniseed; *(licor)* anisette

aniversario [anißer'sarjo] *nm* anniversary

anoche [a'notʃe] *adv* last night; **antes de**
~ the night before last

anochecer [anotʃe'θer] *vi* to get dark
♦ *nm* nightfall, dark; **al ~** at nightfall

anodino, a [ano'ðino, a] *adj* dull,
anodyne

anomalía [anoma'lia] *nf* anomaly

anonadado, a [anona'ðaðo, a] *adj*:
estar/quedar/sentirse ~ to be
overwhelmed *o* amazed

anonimato [anoni'mato] *nm* anonymity

anónimo, a [a'nonimo, a] *adj*
anonymous; *(COM)* limited ♦ *nm (carta)*
anonymous letter; (: *maliciosa)* poison-
pen letter

anormal [anor'mal] *adj* abnormal

anotación [anota'θjon] *nf* note;
annotation

anotar [ano'tar] *vt* to note down;
(comentar) to annotate

anquilosamiento [ankilosa'mjento] *nm*
(fig) paralysis; stagnation

anquilosarse [ankilo'sarse] *vr (fig:*
persona) to get out of touch; *(método,*
costumbres) to go out of date

ansia ['ansja] *nf* anxiety; *(añoranza)*
yearning; **ansiar** *vt* to long for

ansiedad [ansje'ðað] *nf* anxiety

ansioso, a [an'sjoso, a] *adj* anxious;
(anhelante) eager; **~ de** *o* **por algo**
greedy for sth

antagónico, a [anta'ɣoniko, a] *adj*
antagonistic; *(opuesto)* contrasting;
antagonista *nm/f* antagonist

antaño [an'taɲo] *adv* long ago, formerly

Antártico [an'tartiko] *nm*: **el ~** the
Antarctic

ante ['ante] *prep* before, in the presence
of; *(problema etc)* faced with ♦ *nm (piel)*
suede; **~ todo** above all

anteanoche [antea'notʃe] *adv* the night
before last

anteayer [antea'jer] *adv* the day before
yesterday

antebrazo [ante'ßraθo] *nm* forearm

antecedente [anteθe'ðente] *adj* previous
♦ *nm* antecedent; **~s** *nmpl (JUR)*: **~s**
penales criminal record; *(procedencia)*
background

anteceder [anteθe'ðer] *vt* to precede, go
before

antecesor, a [anteθe'sor, a] *nm/f*
predecessor

antedicho, a [ante'ðitʃo, a] *adj*
aforementioned

antelación [antela'θjon] *nf*: **con ~** in
advance

antemano [ante'mano] *adv*: **de ~** *adv*
beforehand, in advance

antena [an'tena] *nf* antenna; *(de televisión*
etc) aerial; **~ parabólica** satellite dish

anteojo [ante'oxo] *nm* eyeglass; **~s** *nmpl*
(AM) glasses, spectacles

antepasados [antepa'saðos] *nmpl*
ancestors

anteponer [antepo'ner] *vt* to place in
front; *(fig)* to prefer

anteproyecto [antepro'jekto] *nm*
preliminary sketch; *(fig)* blueprint

anterior [ante'rjor] *adj* preceding,
previous; **~idad** *nf*: **con ~idad a** prior to,
before

antes ['antes] *adv (con prioridad)* before
♦ *prep*: **~ de** before ♦ *conj*: **~ de ir/de**

que te vayas before going/before you go; **~ bien** (but) rather; **dos días ~** two days before *o* previously; **no quiso venir ~** she didn't want to come any earlier; **tomo el avión ~ que el barco** I take the plane rather than the boat; **~ que yo** before me; **lo ~ posible** as soon as possible; **cuanto ~ mejor** the sooner the better

antiaéreo, a [antia'ereo, a] *adj* anti-aircraft

antibalas [anti'ßalas] *adj inv*: **chaleco ~** bullet-proof jacket

antibiótico [anti'ßjotiko] *nm* antibiotic

anticiclón [antiθi'klon] *nm* anticyclone

anticipación [antiθipa'θjon] *nf* anticipation; **con 10 minutos de ~** 10 minutes early

anticipado, a [antiθi'paðo, a] *adj* (*pago*) advance; **por ~** in advance

anticipar [antiθi'par] *vt* to anticipate; (*adelantar*) to bring forward; (*COM*) to advance; **~se** *vr*: **~se a su época** to be ahead of one's time

anticipo [anti'θipo] *nm* (*COM*) advance

anticonceptivo, a [antikonθep'tißo, a] *adj, nm* contraceptive

anticongelante [antikonxe'lante] *nm* antifreeze

anticuado, a [anti'kwaðo, a] *adj* out-of-date, old-fashioned; (*desusado*) obsolete

anticuario [anti'kwarjo] *nm* antique dealer

anticuerpo [anti'kwerpo] *nm* (*MED*) antibody

antídoto [an'tiðoto] *nm* antidote

antiestético, a [anties'tetiko, a] *adj* unsightly

antifaz [anti'faθ] *nm* mask; (*velo*) veil

antigualla [anti'ɣwaʎa] *nf* antique; (*reliquia*) relic

antiguamente [antixwa'mente] *adv* formerly; (*hace mucho tiempo*) long ago

antigüedad [antixwe'ðað] *nf* antiquity; (*artículo*) antique; (*rango*) seniority

antiguo, a [an'tixwo, a] *adj* old, ancient; (*que fue*) former

Antillas [an'tiʎas] *nfpl*: **las ~** the West

Indies

antílope [an'tilope] *nm* antelope

antinatural [antinatu'ral] *adj* unnatural

antipatía [antipa'tia] *nf* antipathy, dislike; **antipático, a** *adj* disagreeable, unpleasant

antirrobo [anti'rroßo] *adj inv* (*alarma etc*) anti-theft

antisemita [antise'mita] *adj* anti-Semitic
♦ *nm/f* anti-Semite

antiséptico, a [anti'septiko, a] *adj* antiseptic ♦ *nm* antiseptic

antítesis [an'titesis] *nf inv* antithesis

antojadizo, a [antoxa'ðiθo, a] *adj* capricious

antojarse [anto'xarse] *vr* (*desear*): **se me antoja comprarlo** I have a mind to buy it; (*pensar*): **se me antoja que** I have a feeling that

antojo [an'toxo] *nm* caprice, whim; (*rosa*) birthmark; (*lunar*) mole

antología [antolo'xia] *nf* anthology

antorcha [an'tortʃa] *nf* torch

antro ['antro] *nm* cavern

antropófago, a [antro'pofaxo, a] *adj, nm/f* cannibal

antropología [antropolo'xia] *nf* anthropology

anual [a'nwal] *adj* annual

anuario [a'nwarjo] *nm* yearbook

anudar [anu'ðar] *vt* to knot, tie; (*unir*) to join; **~se** *vr* to get tied up

anulación [anula'θjon] *nf* annulment; (*cancelación*) cancellation

anular [anu'lar] *vt* (*contrato*) to annul, cancel; (*ley*) to revoke, repeal; (*suscripción*) to cancel ♦ *nm* ring finger

Anunciación [anunθja'θjon] *nf* (*REL*) Annunciation

anunciante [anun'θjante] *nm/f* (*COM*) advertiser

anunciar [anun'θjar] *vt* to announce; (*proclamar*) to proclaim; (*COM*) to advertise

anuncio [a'nunθjo] *nm* announcement; (*señal*) sign; (*COM*) advertisement; (*cartel*) poster

anzuelo [an'θwelo] *nm* hook; (*para pescar*) fish hook

añadidura [aɲaði'ðura] *nf* addition, extra; **por ~** besides, in addition

añadir [aɲa'ðir] *vt* to add

añejo, a [a'ɲexo, a] *adj* old; (*vino*) mellow

añicos [a'ɲikos] *nmpl:* **hacer ~** to smash, shatter

añil [a'ɲil] *nm* (*BOT, color*) indigo

año ['aɲo] *nm* year; **¡Feliz A~ Nuevo!** Happy New Year!; **tener 15 ~s** to be 15 (years old); **los ~s 90** the nineties; **~ bisiesto/escolar** leap/school year; **el ~ que viene** next year

añoranza [aɲo'ranθa] *nf* nostalgia; (*anhelo*) longing

apabullar [apaßu'ʎar] *vt* (*tb fig*) to crush, squash

apacentar [apaθen'tar] *vt* to pasture, graze

apacible [apa'θißle] *adj* gentle, mild

apaciguar [apaθi'ɣwar] *vt* to pacify, calm (down)

apadrinar [apaðri'nar] *vt* to sponsor, support; (*REL*) to be godfather to

apagado, a [apa'ɣaðo, a] *adj* (*volcán*) extinct; (*color*) dull; (*voz*) quiet; (*sonido*) muted, muffled; (*persona: apático*) listless; **estar ~** (*fuego, luz*) to be out; (*RADIO, TV etc*) to be off

apagar [apa'ɣar] *vt* to put out; (*ELEC, RADIO, TV*) to turn off; (*sonido*) to silence, muffle; (*sed*) to quench

apagón [apa'ɣon] *nm* blackout; power cut

apalabrar [apala'ßrar] *vt* to agree to; (*contratar*) to engage

apalear [apale'ar] *vt* to beat, thrash

apañar [apa'ɲar] *vt* to pick up; (*asir*) to take hold of, grasp; (*reparar*) to mend, patch up; **~se** *vr* to manage, get along

aparador [apara'ðor] *nm* sideboard; (*AM: escaparate*) shop window

aparato [apa'rato] *nm* apparatus; (*máquina*) machine; (*doméstico*) appliance; (*boato*) ostentation; **~ de facsímil** facsimile (machine), fax; **~ digestivo** (*ANAT*) digestive system; **~so,**

a *adj* showy, ostentatious

aparcamiento [aparka'mjento] *nm* car park (*BRIT*), parking lot (*US*)

aparcar [apar'kar] *vt, vi* to park

aparear [apare'ar] *vt* (*objetos*) to pair, match; (*animales*) to mate; **~se** *vr* to make a pair; to mate

aparecer [apare'θer] *vi* to appear; **~se** *vr* to appear

aparejado, a [apare'xaðo, a] *adj* fit, suitable; **llevar** *o* **traer ~** to involve;

aparejador, a *nm/f* (*ARQ*) master builder

aparejo [apa'rexo] *nm* harness; rigging; (*de poleas*) block and tackle

aparentar [aparen'tar] *vt* (*edad*) to look; (*fingir*): **~ tristeza** to pretend to be sad

aparente [apa'rente] *adj* apparent; (*adecuado*) suitable

aparezco *etc vb ver* **aparecer**

aparición [apari'θjon] *nf* appearance; (*de libro*) publication; (*espectro*) apparition

apariencia [apa'rjenθja] *nf* (*outward*) appearance; **en ~** outwardly, seemingly

apartado, a [apar'taðo, a] *adj* separate; (*lejano*) remote ♦ *nm* (*tipográfico*) paragraph; **~ (de correos)** post office box

apartamento [aparta'mento] *nm* apartment, flat (*BRIT*)

apartamiento [aparta'mjento] *nm* separation; (*aislamiento*) remoteness, isolation; (*AM*) apartment, flat (*BRIT*)

apartar [apar'tar] *vt* to separate; (*quitar*) to remove; **~se** *vr* to separate, part; (*irse*) to move away; to keep away

aparte [a'parte] *adv* (*separadamente*) separately; (*además*) besides ♦ *nm* aside; (*tipográfico*) new paragraph

aparthotel [aparto'tel] *nm* serviced apartments

apasionado, a [apasjo'naðo, a] *adj* passionate

apasionar [apasjo'nar] *vt* to excite; **le apasiona el fútbol** she's crazy about football; **~se** *vr* to get excited

apatía [apa'tia] *nf* apathy

apático, a [a'patiko, a] *adj* apathetic

Apdo *abr* (= *Apartado (de Correos)*) PO Box

apeadero [apea'ðero] *nm* halt, stop, stopping place

apearse [ape'arse] *vr* (*jinete*) to dismount; (*bajarse*) to get down *o* out; (*AUTO, FERRO*) to get off *o* out

apechugar [apetʃu'xar] *vr*: ~ **con algo** to face up to sth

apedrear [apeðre'ar] *vt* to stone

apegarse [ape'xarse] *vr*: ~ **a** to become attached to; **apego** *nm* attachment, devotion

apelación [apela'θjon] *nf* appeal

apelar [ape'lar] *vi* to appeal; ~ **a** (*fig*) to resort to

apellidar [apeʎi'ðar] *vt* to call, name; ~**se** *vr*: **se apellida Pérez** her (sur)name's Pérez

apellido [ape'ʎiðo] *nm* surname

apelmazarse [apelma'θarse] *vr* (*masa, arroz*) to go hard; (*prenda de tana*) to shrink

apenar [ape'nar] *vt* to grieve, trouble; (*AM: avergonzar*) to embarrass; ~**se** *vr* to grieve; (*AM*) to be embarrassed

apenas [a'penas] *adv* scarcely, hardly ♦ *conj* as soon as, no sooner

apéndice [a'pendiθe] *nm* appendix; **apendicitis** *nf* appendicitis

aperitivo [aperi'tiβo] *nm* (*bebida*) aperitif; (*comida*) appetizer

apero [a'pero] *nm* (*AGR*) implement; ~**s** *nmpl* farm equipment *sg*

apertura [aper'tura] *nf* opening; (*POL*) liberalization

apesadumbrar [apesaðum'brar] *vt* to grieve, sadden; ~**se** *vr* to distress o.s.

apestar [apes'tar] *vt* to infect ♦ *vi*: ~ **(a)** to stink (of)

apetecer [apete'θer] *vt*: **¿te apetece un café?** do you fancy a (cup of) coffee?; **apetecible** *adj* desirable; (*comida*) appetizing

apetito [ape'tito] *nm* appetite; ~**so, a** *adj* appetizing; (*fig*) tempting

apiadarse [apja'ðarse] *vr*: ~ **de** to take pity on

ápice ['apiθe] *nm* whit, iota

apilar [api'lar] *vt* to pile *o* heap up; ~**se** *vr* to pile up

apiñarse [api'narse] *vr* to crowd *o* press together

apio ['apjo] *nm* celery

apisonadora [apisona'ðora] *nf* steamroller

aplacar [apla'kar] *vt* to placate; ~**se** *vr* to calm down

aplanar [apla'nar] *vt* to smooth, level; (*allanar*) to roll flat, flatten

aplastante [aplas'tante] *adj* overwhelming; (*lógica*) compelling

aplastar [aplas'tar] *vt* to squash (flat); (*fig*) to crush

aplatanarse [aplata'narse] *vr* to get lethargic

aplaudir [aplau'ðir] *vt* to applaud

aplauso [a'plauso] *nm* applause; (*fig*) approval, acclaim

aplazamiento [aplaθa'mjento] *nm* postponement

aplazar [apla'θar] *vt* to postpone, defer

aplicación [aplika'θjon] *nf* application; (*esfuerzo*) effort

aplicado, a [apli'kaðo, a] *adj* diligent, hard-working

aplicar [apli'kar] *vt* (*ejecutar*) to apply; ~**se** *vr* to apply o.s.

aplique *etc* [a'plike] *vb ver* **aplicar** ♦ *nm* wall light

aplomo [a'plomo] *nm* aplomb, self-assurance

apocado, a [apo'kaðo, a] *adj* timid

apodar [apo'ðar] *vt* to nickname

apoderado [apoðe'raðo] *nm* agent, representative

apoderarse [apoðe'rarse] *vr*: ~ **de** to take possession of

apodo [a'poðo] *nm* nickname

apogeo [apo'xeo] *nm* peak, summit

apolillarse [apoli'ʎarse] *vr* to get moth-eaten

apología [apolo'xia] *nf* eulogy; (*defensa*) defence

apoltronarse [apoltro'narse] *vr* to get

lazy
apoplejía [apople'xia] *nf* apoplexy, stroke
apoquinar [apoki'nar] (*fam*) *vt* to fork
out, cough up
aporrear [aporre'ar] *vt* to beat (up)
aportar [apor'tar] *vt* to contribute ♦ *vi* to
reach port; **~se** *vr* (*AM: llegar*) to arrive,
come
aposento [apo'sento] *nm* lodging;
(*habitación*) room
aposta [a'posta] *adv* deliberately, on
purpose
apostar [apos'tar] *vt* to bet, stake; (*tropas
etc*) to station, post ♦ *vi* to bet
apóstol [a'postol] *nm* apostle
apóstrofo [a'postrofo] *nm* apostrophe
apoyar [apo'jar] *vt* to lean, rest; (*fig*) to
support, back; **~se** *vr*: **~se en** to lean on;
apoyo *nm* (*gen*) support; backing, help
apreciable [apre'θjaβle] *adj* considerable;
(*fig*) esteemed
apreciar [apre'θjar] *vt* to evaluate, assess;
(*COM*) to appreciate, value; (*persona*) to
respect; (*tamaño*) to gauge, assess;
(*detalles*) to notice
aprecio [a'preθjo] *nm* valuation, estimate;
(*fig*) appreciation
aprehender [apreen'der] *vt* to apprehend,
detain
apremiante [apre'mjante] *adj* urgent,
pressing
apremiar [apre'mjar] *vt* to compel, force
♦ *vi* to be urgent, press; **apremio** *nm*
urgency
aprender [apren'der] *vt, vi* to learn
aprendiz, a [apren'diθ, a] *nm/f*
apprentice; (*principiante*) learner; **~ de
conductor** learner driver; **~aje** *nm*
apprenticeship
aprensión [apren'sjon] *nm* apprehension,
fear; **aprensivo, a** *adj* apprehensive
apresar [apre'sar] *vt* to seize; (*capturar*) to
capture
aprestar [apres'tar] *vt* to prepare, get
ready; (*TEC*) to prime, size; **~se** *vr* to get
ready
apresurado, a [apresu'raðo, a] *adj*

hurried, hasty; **apresuramiento** *nm*
hurry, haste
apresurar [apresu'rar] *vt* to hurry,
accelerate; **~se** *vr* to hurry, make haste
apretado, a [apre'taðo, a] *adj* tight;
(*escritura*) cramped
apretar [apre'tar] *vt* to squeeze; (*TEC*) to
tighten; (*presionar*) to press together,
pack ♦ *vi* to be too tight
apretón [apre'ton] *nm* squeeze; **~ de
manos** handshake
aprieto [a'prjeto] *nm* squeeze; (*dificultad*)
difficulty; **estar en un ~** to be in a fix
aprisa [a'prisa] *adv* quickly, hurriedly
aprisionar [aprisjo'nar] *vt* to imprison
aprobación [aproβa'θjon] *nf* approval
aprobar [apro'βar] *vt* to approve (of);
(*examen, materia*) to pass ♦ *vi* to pass
apropiación [apropja'θjon] *nf*
appropriation
apropiado, a [apro'pjaðo, a] *adj*
appropriate
apropiarse [apro'pjarse] *vr*: **~ de** to
appropriate
aprovechado, a [aproβe'tʃaðo, a] *adj*
industrious, hard-working; (*económico*)
thrifty; (*pey*) unscrupulous;
aprovechamiento *nm* use; exploitation
aprovechar [aproβe'tʃar] *vt* to use;
(*explotar*) to exploit; (*experiencia*) to profit
from; (*oferta, oportunidad*) to take
advantage of ♦ *vi* to progress, improve;
~se *vr*: **~se de** to make use of; **¡que aproveche!** enjoy
your meal!
aproximación [aproksima'θjon] *nf*
approximation; (*de lotería*) consolation
prize; **aproximado, a** *adj* approximate
aproximar [aproksi'mar] *vt* to bring
nearer; **~se** *vr* to come near, approach
apruebo *etc vb ver* **aprobar**
aptitud [apti'tuð] *nf* aptitude
apto, a ['apto, a] *adj* suitable
apuesta [a'pwesta] *nf* bet, wager
apuesto [a'pwesto, a] *adj* neat, elegant
apuntador [apunta'ðor] *nm* prompter
apuntalar [apunta'lar] *vt* to prop up

apuntar [apun'tar] *vt* (*con arma*) to aim at; (*con dedo*) to point at *o* to; (*anotar*) to note (down); (*TEATRO*) to prompt; **~se** *vr* (*DEPORTE: tanto, victoria*) to score; (*ESCOL*) to enrol

apunte [a'punte] *nm* note

apuñalar [apuɲa'lar] *vt* to stab

apurado, a [apu'raðo, a] *adj* needy; (*difícil*) difficult; (*peligroso*) dangerous; (*AM*) hurried, rushed

apurar [apu'rar] *vt* (*agotar*) to drain; (*recursos*) to use up; (*molestar*) to annoy; **~se** *vr* (*preocuparse*) to worry; (*darse prisa*) to hurry

apuro [a'puro] *nm* (*aprieto*) fix, jam; (*escasez*) want, hardship; (*vergüenza*) embarrassment; (*AM*) haste, urgency

aquejado, a [ake'xaðo, a] *adj*: **~ de** (*MED*) afflicted by

aquél, aquélla [a'kel, a'keʎa] (*pl* **aquéllos, as**) *pron* that (one); (*pl*) those (ones)

aquel, aquella [a'kel, a'keʎa] (*pl* **aquellos, as**) *adj* that; (*pl*) those

aquello [a'keʎo] *pron* that, that business

aquí [a'ki] *adv* (*lugar*) here; (*tiempo*) now; **~ arriba** up here; **~ mismo** right here; **~ yace** here lies; **de ~ a siete días** a week from now

aquietar [akje'tar] *vt* to quieten (down), calm (down)

ara ['ara] *nf*: **en ~s de** for the sake of

árabe ['araβe] *adj, nm/f* Arab ♦ *nm* (*LING*) Arabic

Arabia [a'raβja] *nf*: **~ Saudí** *o* **Saudita** Saudi Arabia

arado [a'raðo] *nm* plough

Aragón [ara'xon] *nm* Aragon; **aragonés, esa** *adj, nm/f* Aragonese

arancel [aran'θel] *nm* tariff, duty; **~ de aduanas** customs (duty)

arandela [aran'dela] *nf* (*TEC*) washer

araña [a'raɲa] *nf* (*ZOOL*) spider; (*lámpara*) chandelier

arañar [ara'ɲar] *vt* to scratch

arañazo [ara'ɲaθo] *nm* scratch

arar [a'rar] *vt* to plough, till

arbitraje [arβi'traxe] *nm* arbitration

arbitrar [arβi'trar] *vt* to arbitrate in; (*DEPORTE*) to referee ♦ *vi* to arbitrate

arbitrariedad [arβitrarje'ðað] *nf* arbitrariness; (*acto*) arbitrary act; **arbitrario, a** *adj* arbitrary

arbitrio [ar'βitrjo] *nm* free will; (*JUR*) adjudication, decision

árbitro ['arβitro] *nm* arbitrator; (*DEPORTE*) referee; (*TENIS*) umpire

árbol ['arβol] *nm* (*BOT*) tree; (*NAUT*) mast; (*TEC*) axle, shaft; **arbolado, a** *adj* wooded; (*camino etc*) tree-lined ♦ *nm* woodland

arboleda [arβo'leða] *nf* grove, plantation

arbusto [ar'βusto] *nm* bush, shrub

arca ['arka] *nf* chest, box

arcada [ar'kaða] *nf* arcade; (*de puente*) arch, span; **~s** *nfpl* (*náuseas*) retching *sg*

arcaico, a [ar'kaiko, a] *adj* archaic

arce ['arθe] *nm* maple tree

arcén [ar'θen] *nm* (*de autopista*) hard shoulder; (*de carretera*) verge

archipiélago [artʃi'pjelaxo] *nm* archipelago

archivador [artʃiβa'ðor] *nm* filing cabinet

archivar [artʃi'βar] *vt* to file (away); **archivo** *nm* file, archive(s) (*pl*)

arcilla [ar'θiʎa] *nf* clay

arco ['arko] *nm* arch; (*MAT*) arc; (*MIL, MUS*) bow; **~ iris** rainbow

arder [ar'ðer] *vi* to burn; **estar que arde** (*persona*) to fume

ardid [ar'ðið] *nm* ploy, trick

ardiente [ar'ðjente] *adj* burning, ardent

ardilla [ar'ðiʎa] *nf* squirrel

ardor [ar'ðor] *nm* (*calor*) heat; (*fig*) ardour; **~ de estómago** heartburn

arduo, a ['arðwo, a] *adj* arduous

área ['area] *nf* area; (*DEPORTE*) penalty area

arena [a'rena] *nf* sand; (*de una lucha*) arena; **~s movedizas** quicksand *sg*

arenal [are'nal] *nm* (*arena movediza*) quicksand

arengar [aren'gar] *vt* to harangue

arenisca [are'niska] *nf* sandstone; (*cascajo*) grit

arenoso, a [are'noso, a] *adj* sandy

arenque [a'renke] *nm* herring

argamasa [arɣa'masa] *nf* mortar, plaster

Argel [ar'xel] *n* Algiers; **Argelia** *nf* Algeria; **argelino, a** *adj, nm/f* Algerian

Argentina [arxen'tina] *nf:* **(la) ~** Argentina

argentino, a [arxen'tino, a] *adj* Argentinian; *(de plata)* silvery ♦ *nm/f* Argentinian

argolla [ar'ɣoʎa] *nf* (large) ring

argot [ar'ɣo] *(pl* **~s)** *nm* slang

argucia [ar'ɣuθja] *nf* subtlety, sophistry

argüir [ar'ɣwir] *vt* to deduce; *(discutir)* to argue; *(indicar)* to indicate, imply; *(censurar)* to reproach ♦ *vi* to argue

argumentación [arɣumenta'θjon] *nf* (line of) argument

argumentar [arɣumen'tar] *vt, vi* to argue

argumento [arɣu'mento] *nm* argument; *(razonamiento)* reasoning; *(de novela etc)* plot; *(CINE, TV)* storyline

aria ['arja] *nf* aria

aridez [ari'ðeθ] *nf* aridity, dryness

árido, a ['ariðo, a] *adj* arid, dry; **~s** *nmpl* *(COM)* dry goods

Aries ['arjes] *nm* Aries

ario, a ['arjo, a] *adj* Aryan

arisco, a [a'risko, a] *adj* surly; *(insociable)* unsociable

aristócrata [aris'tokrata] *nm/f* aristocrat

aritmética [arit'metika] *nf* arithmetic

arma ['arma] *nf* arm; **~s** *nfpl* arms; **~ blanca** blade, knife; *(espada)* sword; **~ de fuego** firearm; **~s cortas** small arms

armada [ar'maða] *nf* armada; *(flota)* fleet

armadillo [arma'ðiʎo] *nm* armadillo

armado, a [ar'maðo, a] *adj* armed; *(TEC)* reinforced

armador [arma'ðor] *nm* *(NAUT)* shipowner

armadura [arma'ðura] *nf* *(MIL)* armour; *(TEC)* framework; *(ZOOL)* skeleton; *(FÍSICA)* armature

armamento [arma'mento] *nm* armament; *(NAUT)* fitting-out

armar [ar'mar] *vt (soldado)* to arm; *(máquina)* to assemble; *(navío)* to fit out; **~la, ~ un lío** to start a row, kick up a fuss

armario [ar'marjo] *nm* wardrobe; *(de cocina, baño)* cupboard

armatoste [arma'toste] *nm (mueble)* monstrosity; *(máquina)* contraption

armazón [arma'θon] *nf o m* body, chassis; *(de mueble etc)* frame; *(ARQ)* skeleton

armería [arme'ria] *nf* gunsmith's

armiño [ar'miɲo] *nm* stoat; *(piel)* ermine

armisticio [armis'tiθjo] *nm* armistice

armonía [armo'nia] *nf* harmony

armónica [ar'monika] *nf* harmonica

armonioso, a [armo'njoso, a] *adj* harmonious

armonizar [armoni'θar] *vt* to harmonize; *(diferencias)* to reconcile ♦ *vi:* **~ con** *(fig)* to be in keeping with; *(colores)* to tone in with, blend

arnés [ar'nes] *nm* armour; **arneses** *nmpl* *(de caballo etc)* harness *sg*

aro ['aro] *nm* ring; *(tejo)* quoit; *(AM: pendiente)* earring

aroma [a'roma] *nm* aroma, scent

aromático, a [aro'matiko, a] *adj* aromatic

arpa ['arpa] *nf* harp

arpía [ar'pia] *nf* shrew

arpillera [arpi'ʎera] *nf* sacking, sackcloth

arpón [ar'pon] *nm* harpoon

arquear [arke'ar] *vt* to arch, bend; **~se** *vr* to arch, bend

arqueología [arkeolo'xia] *nf* archaeology; **arqueólogo, a** *nm/f* archaeologist

arquero [ar'kero] *nm* archer, bowman

arquetipo [arke'tipo] *nm* archetype

arquitecto [arki'tekto] *nm* architect; **arquitectura** *nf* architecture

arrabal [arra'ßal] *nm* suburb; *(AM)* slum; **~es** *nmpl (afueras)* outskirts

arraigado, a [arrai'ɣaðo, a] *adj* deep-rooted; *(fig)* established

arraigar [arrai'ɣar] *vt* to establish ♦ *vi* to take root; **~se** *vr* to take root; *(persona)* to settle

arrancar [arran'kar] *vt (sacar)* to extract, pull out; *(arrebatar)* to snatch (away); *(INFORM)* to boot; *(fig)* to extract ♦ *vi* *(AUTO, máquina)* to start; *(ponerse en marcha)* to get going; **~ de** to stem from

arranque *etc* [aˈrranke] *vb ver* **arrancar**
♦ *nm* sudden start; (*AUTO*) start; (*fig*) fit,
outburst

arrasar [arraˈsar] *vt* (*aplanar*) to level,
flatten; (*destruir*) to demolish

arrastrado, a [arrasˈtraðo, a] *adj* poor,
wretched; (*AM*) servile

arrastrar [arrasˈtrar] *vt* to drag (along);
(*fig*) to drag down, degrade; (*suj: agua,
viento*) to carry away ♦ *vi* to drag, trail on
the ground; **~se** *vr* to crawl; (*fig*) to
grovel; **llevar algo arrastrado** to drag sth
along

arrastre [aˈrrastre] *nm* drag, dragging

arre [ˈarre] *excl* gee up!

arrear [arreˈar] *vt* to drive on, urge on ♦ *vi*
to hurry along

arrebatado, a [arreβaˈtaðo, a] *adj* rash,
impetuous; (*repentino*) sudden, hasty

arrebatar [arreβaˈtar] *vt* to snatch (away),
seize; (*fig*) to captivate; **~se** *vr* to get
carried away, get excited

arrebato [arreˈβato] *nm* fit of rage, fury;
(*éxtasis*) rapture

arrecife [arreˈθife] *nm* (*tb: ~ de coral*) reef

arredrarse [arreˈðrarse] *vr*: **~ (ante algo)**
to be intimidated (by sth)

arreglado, a [arreˈɣlaðo, a] *adj* (*ordenado*)
neat, orderly; (*moderado*) moderate,
reasonable

arreglar [arreˈɣlar] *vt* (*poner orden*) to tidy
up; (*algo roto*) to fix, repair; (*problema*) to
solve; **~se** *vr* to reach an understanding;
arreglárselas (*fam*) to get by, manage

arreglo [aˈrreɣlo] *nm* settlement; (*orden*)
order; (*acuerdo*) agreement; (*MUS*)
arrangement, setting

arrellanarse [arreʎaˈnarse] *vr*: **~ en** to sit
back in/on

arremangar [arremanˈɡar] *vt* to roll up,
turn up; **~se** *vr* to roll up one's sleeves

arremeter [arremeˈter] *vi*: **~ contra** to
attack, rush at

arrendamiento [arrendaˈmjento] *nm*
letting; (*alquilar*) hiring; (*contrato*) lease;
(*alquiler*) rent; **arrendar** *vt* to let, lease;
to rent; **arrendatario, a** *nm/f* tenant

arreos [aˈrreos] *nmpl* (*de caballo*) harness
sg, trappings

arrepentimiento [arrepentiˈmjento] *nm*
regret, repentance

arrepentirse [arrepenˈtirse] *vr* to repent;
~ de to regret

arrestar [arresˈtar] *vt* to arrest; (*encarcelar*)
to imprison; **arresto** *nm* arrest; (*MIL*)
detention; (*audacia*) boldness, daring;
arresto domiciliario house arrest

arriar [aˈrrjar] *vt* (*velas*) to haul down;
(*bandera*) to lower, strike; (*cable*) to pay
out

┌─────────────────────┐
│ *PALABRA CLAVE* │
└─────────────────────┘

arriba [aˈrriβa] *adv* **1** (*posición*) above;
desde ~ from above; **~ de todo** at the
very top, right on top; **Juan está ~** Juan
is upstairs; **lo ~ mencionado** the
aforementioned

2 (*dirección*): **calle ~** up the street

3: **de ~ abajo** from top to bottom; **mirar
a uno de ~ abajo** to look sb up and
down

4: **para ~**: **de 5000 pesetas para ~** from
5000 pesetas up(wards)

♦ *adj*: **de ~**: **el piso de ~** the upstairs flat
(*BRIT*) *o* apartment; **la parte de ~** the top
o upper part

♦ *prep*: **~ de** (*AM*) above; **~ de 200
dólares** more than 200 dollars

♦ *excl*: **¡~!** up!; **¡manos ~!** hands up!; **¡~
España!** long live Spain!

arribar [arriˈβar] *vi* to put into port;
(*llegar*) to arrive

arribista [arriˈβista] *nm/f* parvenu(e),
upstart

arriendo *etc* [aˈrrjendo] *vb ver* **arrendar**
♦ *nm* = **arrendamiento**

arriero [aˈrrjero] *nm* muleteer

arriesgado, a [arrjesˈɣaðo, a] *adj*
(*peligroso*) risky; (*audaz*) bold, daring

arriesgar [arrjesˈɣar] *vt* to risk; (*poner en
peligro*) to endanger; **~se** *vr* to take a risk

arrimar [arriˈmar] *vt* (*acercar*) to bring
close; (*poner de lado*) to set aside; **~se** *vr*

to come close *o* closer; **~se a** to lean on

arrinconar [arrinko'nar] *vt* (*colocar*) to put in a corner; (*enemigo*) to corner; (*fig*) to put on one side; (*abandonar*) to push aside

arrodillarse [arroði'ʎarse] *vr* to kneel (down)

arrogancia [arro'ɣanθja] *nf* arrogance; **arrogante** *adj* arrogant

arrojar [arro'xar] *vt* to throw, hurl; (*humo*) to emit, give out; (*COM*) to yield, produce; **~se** *vr* to throw *o* hurl o.s.

arrojo [a'rroxo] *nm* daring

arrollador, a [arroʎa'ðor, a] *adj* overwhelming

arrollar [arro'ʎar] *vt* (*AUTO etc*) to run over, knock down; (*DEPORTE*) to crush

arropar [arro'par] *vt* to cover, wrap up; **~se** *vr* to wrap o.s. up

arroyo [a'rrojo] *nm* stream; (*de la calle*) gutter

arroz [a'rroθ] *nm* rice; **~ con leche** rice pudding

arruga [a'rruɣa] *nf* (*de cara*) wrinkle; (*de vestido*) crease

arrugar [arru'ɣar] *vt* to wrinkle; to crease; **~se** *vr* to get creased

arruinar [arrwi'nar] *vt* to ruin, wreck; **~se** *vr* to be ruined, go bankrupt

arrullar [arru'ʎar] *vi* to coo ♦ *vt* to lull to sleep

arsenal [arse'nal] *nm* naval dockyard; (*MIL*) arsenal

arsénico [ar'seniko] *nm* arsenic

arte ['arte] (*gen m en sg y siempre f en pl*) *nm* art; (*maña*) skill, guile; **~s** *nfpl* (*bellas ~s*) arts

artefacto [arte'fakto] *nm* appliance

arteria [ar'terja] *nf* artery

artesanía [artesa'nia] *nf* craftsmanship; (*artículos*) handicrafts *pl*; **artesano, a** *nm/f* artisan, craftsman/woman

ártico, a ['artiko, a] *adj* Arctic ♦ *nm*: **el Á~** the Arctic

articulación [artikula'θjon] *nf* articulation; (*MED, TEC*) joint; **articulado, a** *adj* articulated; jointed

articular [artiku'lar] *vt* to articulate; to join together

artículo [ar'tikulo] *nm* article; (*cosa*) thing, article; **~s** *nmpl* (*COM*) goods

artífice [ar'tifiθe] *nm/f* (*fig*) architect

artificial [artifi'θjal] *adj* artificial

artificio [arti'fiθjo] *nm* art, skill; (*astucia*) cunning

artillería [artiʎe'ria] *nf* artillery

artillero [arti'ʎero] *nm* artilleryman, gunner

artilugio [arti'luxjo] *nm* gadget

artimaña [arti'maɲa] *nf* trap, snare; (*astucia*) cunning

artista [ar'tista] *nm/f* (*pintor*) artist, painter; (*TEATRO*) artist, artiste; **~ de cine** film actor/actress; **artístico, a** *adj* artistic

artritis [ar'tritis] *nf* arthritis

arveja [ar'βexa] (*AM*) *nf* pea

arzobispo [arθo'βispo] *nm* archbishop

as [as] *nm* ace

asa ['asa] *nf* handle; (*fig*) lever

asado [a'saðo] *nm* roast (meat); (*AM: barbacoa*) barbecue

asador [asa'ðor] *nm* spit

asadura [asa'ðura] *nf* entrails *pl*, offal

asalariado, a [asala'rjaðo, a] *adj* paid, salaried ♦ *nm/f* wage earner

asaltante [asal'tante] *nm/f* attacker

asaltar [asal'tar] *vt* to attack, assault; (*fig*) to assail; **asalto** *nm* attack, assault; (*DEPORTE*) round

asamblea [asam'blea] *nf* assembly; (*reunión*) meeting

asar [a'sar] *vt* to roast

asbesto [as'ßesto] *nm* asbestos

ascendencia [asθen'denθja] *nf* ancestry; (*AM*) ascendancy; **de ~ francesa** of French origin

ascender [asθen'der] *vi* (*subir*) to ascend, rise; (*ser promovido*) to gain promotion ♦ *vt* to promote; **~ a** to amount to; **ascendiente** *nm* influence ♦ *nm/f* ancestor

ascensión [asθen'sjon] *nf* ascent; (*REL*): **la A~** the Ascension

ascenso [as'θenso] *nm* ascent; (*promoción*) promotion

ascensor [asθen'sor] *nm* lift (*BRIT*), elevator (*US*)

ascético, a [as'θetiko, a] *adj* ascetic

asco ['asko] *nm*: **¡qué ~!** how revolting *o* disgusting; **el ajo me da ~** I hate *o* loathe garlic; **estar hecho un ~** to be filthy

ascua ['askwa] *nf* ember; **estar en ~s** to be on tenterhooks

aseado, a [ase'aðo, a] *adj* clean; (*arreglado*) tidy; (*pulcro*) smart

asear [ase'ar] *vt* to clean, wash; to tidy (up)

asediar [ase'ðjar] *vt* (*MIL*) to besiege, lay siege to; (*fig*) to chase, pester; **asedio** *nm* siege; (*COM*) run

asegurado, a [aseɣu'raðo, a] *adj* insured

asegurador, a *nm/f* insurer

asegurar [aseɣu'rar] *vt* (*consolidar*) to secure, fasten; (*dar garantía de*) to guarantee; (*preservar*) to safeguard; (*afirmar, dar por cierto*) to assure, affirm; (*tranquilizar*) to reassure; (*tomar un seguro*) to insure; **~se** *vr* to assure o.s., make sure

asemejarse [aseme'xarse] *vr* to be alike; **~ a** to be like, resemble

asentado, a [asen'taðo, a] *adj* established, settled

asentar [asen'tar] *vt* (*sentar*) to seat, sit down; (*poner*) to place, establish; (*alisar*) to level, smooth down *o* out; (*anotar*) to note down ♦ *vi* to be suitable, suit

asentir [asen'tir] *vi* to assent, agree; **~ con la cabeza** to nod (one's head)

aseo [a'seo] *nm* cleanliness; **~s** *nmpl* (*servicios*) toilet *sg* (*BRIT*), cloakroom *sg* (*BRIT*), restroom *sg* (*US*)

aséptico, a [a'septiko, a] *adj* germ-free, free from infection

asequible [ase'kiβle] *adj* (*precio*) reasonable; (*meta*) attainable; (*persona*) approachable

aserradero [aserra'ðero] *nm* sawmill; **aserrar** *vt* to saw

asesinar [asesi'nar] *vt* to murder; (*POL*) to assassinate; **asesinato** *nm* murder; assassination

asesino, a [ase'sino, a] *nm/f* murderer, killer; (*POL*) assassin

asesor, a [ase'sor, a] *nm/f* adviser, consultant

asesorar [aseso'rar] *vt* (*JUR*) to advise, give legal advice to; (*COM*) to act as consultant to; **~se** *vr*: **~se con** *o* **de** to take advice from, consult; **asesoría** *nf* (*cargo*) consultancy; (*oficina*) consultant's office

asestar [ases'tar] *vt* (*golpe*) to deal, strike

asfalto [as'falto] *nm* asphalt

asfixia [as'fiksja] *nf* asphyxia, suffocation

asfixiar [asfik'sjar] *vt* to asphyxiate, suffocate; **~se** *vr* to be asphyxiated, suffocate

asgo *etc vb ver* **asir**

así [a'si] *adv* (*de esta manera*) in this way, like this, thus; (*aunque*) although; (*tan pronto como*) as soon as; **~ que** so; **~ como** as well as; **~ y todo** even so; **¿no es ~?** isn't it?, didn't you? *etc*; **~ de grande** this big

Asia ['asja] *nf* Asia; **asiático, a** *adj, nm/f* Asian, Asiatic

asidero [asi'ðero] *nm* handle

asiduidad [asiðwi'ðað] *nf* assiduousness; **asiduo, a** *adj* assiduous; (*frecuente*) frequent ♦ *nm/f* regular (customer)

asiento [a'sjento] *nm* (*mueble*) seat, chair; (*de coche, en tribunal etc*) seat; (*localidad*) seat, place; (*fundamento*) site; **~ delantero/trasero** front/back seat

asignación [asiɣna'θjon] *nf* (*atribución*) assignment; (*reparto*) allocation; (*sueldo*) salary; **~ (semanal)** pocket money

asignar [asiɣ'nar] *vt* to assign, allocate

asignatura [asiɣna'tura] *nf* subject; course

asilado, a [asi'laðo, a] *nm/f* inmate; (*POL*) refugee

asilo [a'silo] *nm* (*refugio*) asylum, refuge; (*establecimiento*) home, institution; **~ político** political asylum

asimilación [asimila'θjon] *nf* assimilation

asimilar [asimi'lar] *vt* to assimilate

asimismo [asi'mismo] *adv* in the same

way, likewise

asir [a'sir] *vt* to seize, grasp

asistencia [asis'tenθja] *nf* audience; (*MED*) attendance; (*ayuda*) assistance; **asistente** *nm/f* assistant; **los asistentes** those present; **asistente social** social worker

asistido, a [asis'tiðo, a] *adj*: ~ **por ordenador** computer-assisted

asistir [asis'tir] *vt* to assist, help ♦ *vi*: ~ **a** to attend, be present at

asma ['asma] *nf* asthma

asno ['asno] *nm* donkey; (*fig*) ass

asociación [asoθja'θjon] *nf* association; (*COM*) partnership; **asociado, a** *adj* associate ♦ *nm/f* associate; (*COM*) partner

asociar [aso'θjar] *vt* to associate

asolar [aso'lar] *vt* to destroy

asomar [aso'mar] *vt* to show, stick out ♦ *vi* to appear; ~**se** *vr* to appear, show up; ~ **la cabeza por la ventana** to put one's head out of the window

asombrar [asom'brar] *vt* to amaze, astonish; ~**se** *vr* (*sorprenderse*) to be amazed; (*asustarse*) to get a fright; **asombro** *nm* amazement, astonishment; (*susto*) fright; **asombroso, a** *adj* astonishing, amazing

asomo [a'somo] *nm* hint, sign

aspa ['aspa] *nf* (*cruz*) cross; (*de molino*) sail; **en** ~ X-shaped

aspaviento [aspa'ßjento] *nm* exaggerated display of feeling; (*fam*) fuss

aspecto [as'pekto] *nm* (*apariencia*) look, appearance; (*fig*) aspect

aspereza [aspe'reθa] *nf* roughness; (*agrura*) sourness; (*de carácter*) surliness; **áspero, a** *adj* rough; bitter, sour; harsh

aspersión [asper'sjon] *nf* sprinkling

aspiración [aspira'θjon] *nf* breath, inhalation; (*MUS*) short pause; **aspiraciones** *nfpl* (*ambiciones*) aspirations

aspirador [aspira'ðor] *nm* = **aspiradora**

aspiradora [aspira'ðora] *nf* vacuum cleaner, Hoover ®

aspirante [aspi'rante] *nm/f* (*candidato*) candidate; (*DEPORTE*) contender

aspirar [aspi'rar] *vt* to breathe in ♦ *vi*: ~ **a** to aspire to

aspirina [aspi'rina] *nf* aspirin

asquear [aske'ar] *vt* to sicken ♦ *vi* to be sickening; ~**se** *vr* to feel disgusted; **asqueroso, a** *adj* disgusting, sickening

asta ['asta] *nf* lance; (*arpón*) spear; (*mango*) shaft, handle; (*ZOOL*) horn; **a media** ~ at half mast

asterisco [aste'risko] *nm* asterisk

astilla [as'tiʎa] *nf* splinter; (*pedacito*) chip; ~**s** *nfpl* (*leña*) firewood *sg*

astillero [asti'ʎero] *nm* shipyard

astringente [astrin'xente] *adj, nm* astringent

astro ['astro] *nm* star

astrología [astrolo'xia] *nf* astrology; **astrólogo, a** *nm/f* astrologer

astronauta [astro'nauta] *nm/f* astronaut

astronave [astro'naße] *nm* spaceship

astronomía [astrono'mia] *nf* astronomy; **astrónomo, a** *nm/f* astronomer

astucia [as'tuθja] *nf* astuteness; (*ardid*) clever trick

asturiano, a [astu'rjano, a] *adj, nm/f* Asturian

astuto, a [as'tuto, a] *adj* astute; (*taimado*) cunning

asumir [asu'mir] *vt* to assume

asunción [asun'θjon] *nf* assumption; (*REL*): **A~** Assumption

asunto [a'sunto] *nm* (*tema*) matter, subject; (*negocio*) business

asustar [asus'tar] *vt* to frighten; ~**se** *vr* to be (*o* become) frightened

atacar [ata'kar] *vt* to attack

atadura [ata'ðura] *nf* bond, tie

atajar [ata'xar] *vt* (*enfermedad, mal*) to stop ♦ *vi* (*persona*) to take a short cut

atajo [a'taxo] *nm* short cut

atañer [ata'ɲer] *vi*: ~ **a** to concern

ataque *etc* [a'take] *vb ver* **atacar** ♦ *nm* attack; ~ **cardíaco** heart attack

atar [a'tar] *vt* to tie, tie up

atardecer [atarðe'θer] *vi* to get dark ♦ *nm* evening; (*crepúsculo*) dusk

atareado, a [atare'aðo, a] *adj* busy

atascar [atas'kar] *vt* to clog up; (*obstruir*) to jam; (*fig*) to hinder; **~se** *vr* to stall; (*cañería*) to get blocked up; **atasco** *nm* obstruction; (*AUTO*) traffic jam

ataúd [ata'uð] *nm* coffin

ataviar [ata'ßjar] *vt* to deck, array; **~se** *vr* to dress up

atavío [ata'ßio] *nm* attire, dress; **~s** *nmpl* finery *sg*

atemorizar [atemori'θar] *vt* to frighten, scare; **~se** *vr* to get scared

Atenas [a'tenas] *n* Athens

atención [aten'θjon] *nf* attention; (*bondad*) kindness ♦ *excl* (be) careful!, look out!

atender [aten'der] *vt* to attend to, look after ♦ *vi* to pay attention

atenerse [ate'nerse] *vr*: **~ a** to abide by, adhere to

atentado [aten'taðo] *nm* crime, illegal act; (*asalto*) assault; **~ contra la vida de uno** attempt on sb's life

atentamente [atenta'mente] *adv*: **Le saluda ~** Yours faithfully

atentar [aten'tar] *vi*: **~ a** *o* **contra** to commit an outrage against

atento, a [a'tento, a] *adj* attentive, observant; (*cortés*) polite, thoughtful

atenuante [ate'nwante] *adj* extenuating

atenuar [ate'nwar] *vt* (*disminuir*) to lessen, minimize

ateo, a [a'teo, a] *adj* atheistic ♦ *nm/f* atheist

aterciopelado, a [aterθjope'laðo, a] *adj* velvety

aterido, a [ate'riðo, a] *adj*: **~ de frío** frozen stiff

aterrador, a [aterra'ðor, a] *adj* frightening

aterrar [ate'rrar] *vt* to frighten; to terrify

aterrizaje [aterri'θaxe] *nm* landing

aterrizar [aterri'θar] *vi* to land

aterrorizar [aterrori'θar] *vt* to terrify

atesorar [ateso'rar] *vt* to hoard

atestado, a [ates'taðo, a] *adj* packed ♦ *nm* (*JUR*) affidavit

atestar [ates'tar] *vt* to pack, stuff; (*JUR*) to attest, testify to

atestiguar [atesti'ɣwar] *vt* to testify to, bear witness to

atiborrar [atißo'rrar] *vt* to fill, stuff; **~se** *vr* to stuff o.s.

ático ['atiko] *nm* attic; **~ de lujo** penthouse (flat (*BRIT*) *o* apartment)

atinado, a [ati'naðo, a] *adj* (*sensato*) wise; (*correcto*) right, correct

atinar [ati'nar] *vi* (*al disparar*): **~ al blanco** to hit the target; (*fig*) to be right

atisbar [atis'ßar] *vt* to spy on; (*echar una ojeada*) to peep at

atizar [ati'θar] *vt* to poke; (*horno etc*) to stoke; (*fig*) to stir up, rouse

atlántico, a [at'lantiko, a] *adj* Atlantic ♦ *nm*: **el (océano) A~** the Atlantic (Ocean)

atlas ['atlas] *nm* atlas

atleta [at'leta] *nm* athlete; **atlético, a** *adj* athletic; **atletismo** *nm* athletics *sg*

atmósfera [at'mosfera] *nf* atmosphere

atolladero [atoʎa'ðero] *nm* (*fig*) jam, fix

atolondramiento [atolondra'mjento] *nm* bewilderment; (*insensatez*) silliness

atómico, a [a'tomiko, a] *adj* atomic

atomizador [atomiθa'ðor] *nm* atomizer; (*de perfume*) spray

átomo ['atomo] *nm* atom

atónito, a [a'tonito, a] *adj* astonished, amazed

atontado, a [aton'taðo, a] *adj* stunned; (*bobo*) silly, daft

atontar [aton'tar] *vt* to stun; **~se** *vr* to become confused

atormentar [atormen'tar] *vt* to torture; (*molestar*) to torment; (*acosar*) to plague, harass

atornillar [atorni'ʎar] *vt* to screw on *o* down

atosigar [atosi'ɣar] *vt* to harass, pester

atracador, a [atraka'ðor, a] *nm/f* robber

atracar [atra'kar] *vt* (*NAUT*) to moor; (*robar*) to hold up, rob ♦ *vi* to moor; **~se** *vr*: **~se (de)** to stuff o.s. (with)

atracción [atrak'θjon] *nf* attraction

atraco [a'trako] *nm* holdup, robbery

atracón [atra'kon] *nm*: **darse** *o* **pegarse**

un ~ **(de)** (fam) to stuff o.s. (with)

atractivo, a [atrak'tiβo, a] adj attractive
♦ nm appeal

atraer [atra'er] vt to attract

atragantarse [atraɣan'tarse] vr: ~ **(con)** to choke (on); **se me ha atragantado el chico** I can't stand the boy

atrancar [atraŋ'kar] vt (puerta) to bar, bolt

atrapar [atra'par] vt to trap; (resfriado etc) to catch

atrás [a'tras] adv (movimiento) back (-wards); (lugar) behind; (tiempo) previously; **ir hacia** ~ to go back(wards); to go to the rear; **estar** ~ to be behind o at the back

atrasado, a [atra'saðo, a] adj slow; (pago) overdue, late; (país) backward

atrasar [atra'sar] vi to be slow; **~se** vr to remain behind; (tren) to be o run late; **atraso** nm slowness; lateness, delay; (de país) backwardness; **atrasos** nmpl (COM) arrears

atravesar [atraβe'sar] vt (cruzar) to cross (over); (traspasar) to pierce; to go through; (poner al través) to lay o put across; **~se** vr to come in between; (intervenir) to interfere

atravieso etc vb ver **atravesar**

atrayente [atra'jente] adj attractive

atreverse [atre'βerse] vr to dare; (insolentarse) to be insolent; **atrevido, a** adj daring; insolent; **atrevimiento** nm daring; insolence

atribución [atriβu'θjon] nf: **atribuciones** (POL) powers; (ADMIN) responsibilities

atribuir [atriβu'ir] vt to attribute; (funciones) to confer

atribular [atriβu'lar] vt to afflict, distress

atributo [atri'βuto] nm attribute

atril [a'tril] nm (para libro) lectern; (MUS) music stand

atrocidad [atroθi'ðað] nf atrocity, outrage

atropellar [atrope'ʎar] vt (derribar) to knock over o down; (empujar) to push (aside); (AUTO) to run over, run down; (agraviar) to insult; **~se** vr to act hastily; **atropello** nm (AUTO) accident; (empujón)

push; (agravio) wrong; (atrocidad) outrage

atroz [a'troθ] adj atrocious, awful

ATS nm/f abr (= Ayudante Técnico Sanitario) nurse

atto, a abr = **atento**

atuendo [a'twendo] nm attire

atún [a'tun] nm tuna

aturdir [atur'ðir] vt to stun; (de ruido) to deafen; (fig) to dumbfound, bewilder

atusar [atu'sar] vt to smooth (down)

audacia [au'ðaθja] nf boldness, audacity; **audaz** adj bold, audacious

audible [au'ðiβle] adj audible

audición [auði'θjon] nf hearing; (TEATRO) audition

audiencia [au'ðjenθja] nf audience; **A~** (JUR) High Court

audífono [au'ðifono] nm (para sordos) hearing aid

auditor [auði'tor] nm (JUR) judge advocate; (COM) auditor

auditorio [auði'torjo] nm audience; (sala) auditorium

auge ['auxe] nm boom; (clímax) climax

augurar [auɣu'rar] vt to predict; (presagiar) to portend

augurio [au'ɣurjo] nm omen

aula ['aula] nf classroom; (en universidad etc) lecture room

aullar [au'ʎar] vi to howl, yell

aullido [au'ʎiðo] nm howl, yell

aumentar [aumen'tar] vt to increase; (precios) to put up; (producción) to step up; (con microscopio, anteojos) to magnify ♦ vi to increase, be on the increase; **~se** vr to increase, be on the increase; **aumento** nm increase; rise

aun [a'un] adv even; ~ **así** even so; ~ **más** even o yet more

aún [a'un] adv: ~ **está aquí** he's still here; ~ **no lo sabemos** we don't know yet; **¿no ha venido ~?** hasn't she come yet?

aunque [a'unke] conj though, although, even though

aúpa [a'upa] excl come on!

aureola [aure'ola] nf halo

auricular [auriku'lar] nm (TEL) earpiece,

receiver; **~es** *nmpl* (*para escuchar música etc*) headphones

aurora [auˈrora] *nf* dawn

auscultar [auskulˈtar] *vt* (*MED: pecho*) to listen to, sound

ausencia [auˈsenθja] *nf* absence

ausentarse [ausenˈtarse] *vr* to go away; (*por poco tiempo*) to go out

ausente [auˈsente] *adj* absent

auspicios [ausˈpiθjos] *nmpl* auspices

austeridad [austeriˈðað] *nf* austerity; **austero, a** *adj* austere

austral [ausˈtral] *adj* southern ♦ *nm* monetary unit of Argentina

Australia [ausˈtralja] *nf* Australia; **australiano, a** *adj, nm/f* Australian

Austria [ˈaustrja] *nf* Austria; **austríaco, a** *adj, nm/f* Austrian

auténtico, a [auˈtentiko, a] *adj* authentic

auto [ˈauto] *nm* (*JUR*) edict, decree; (: *orden*) writ; (*AUTO*) car; **~s** *nmpl* (*JUR*) proceedings; (: *acta*) court record *sg*

autoadhesivo [autoaðeˈsiβo] *adj* self-adhesive; (*sobre*) self-sealing

autobiografía [autoβjoɣraˈfia] *nf* autobiography

autobús [autoˈβus] *nm* bus

autocar [autoˈkar] *nm* coach (*BRIT*), (passenger) bus (*US*)

autóctono, a [auˈtoktono, a] *adj* native, indigenous

autodefensa [autoðeˈfensa] *nf* self-defence

autodeterminación [autoðetermina'θjon] *nf* self-determination

autodidacta [autoðiˈðakta] *adj* self-taught

autoescuela [autoesˈkwela] *nf* driving school

autógrafo [auˈtoɣrafo] *nm* autograph

autómata [auˈtomata] *nm* automaton

automático, a [autoˈmatiko, a] *adj* automatic ♦ *nm* press stud

automotor, triz [automoˈtor, ˈtriθ] *adj* self-propelled ♦ *nm* diesel train

automóvil [autoˈmoβil] *nm* (motor) car (*BRIT*), automobile (*US*); **automovilismo** *nm* (*actividad*) motoring; (*DEPORTE*) motor

racing; **automovilista** *nm/f* motorist, driver; **automovilístico, a** *adj* (*industria*) motor *cpd*

autonomía [autonoˈmia] *nf* autonomy; **autónomo, a** (*ESP*), **autonómico, a** (*ESP*) *adj* (*POL*) autonomous

autopista [autoˈpista] *nf* motorway (*BRIT*), freeway (*US*); **~ de peaje** toll road (*BRIT*), turnpike road (*US*)

autopsia [auˈtopsja] *nf* autopsy, postmortem

autor, a [auˈtor, a] *nm/f* author

autoridad [autoriˈðað] *nf* authority; **autoritario, a** *adj* authoritarian

autorización [autoriθaˈθjon] *nf* authorization; **autorizado, a** *adj* authorized; (*aprobado*) approved

autorizar [autoriˈθar] *vt* to authorize; (*aprobar*) to approve

autorretrato [autorreˈtrato] *nm* self-portrait

autoservicio [autoserˈβiθjo] *nm* (*tienda*) self-service shop (*BRIT*) o store (*US*); (*restaurante*) self-service restaurant

autostop [autoˈstop] *nm* hitch-hiking; **hacer ~** to hitch-hike; **~ista** *nm/f* hitch-hiker

autosuficiencia [autosufiˈθjenθja] *nf* self-sufficiency

autovía [autoˈβia] *nf* ≈ A-road (*BRIT*), dual carriageway (*BRIT*), ≈ state highway (*US*)

auxiliar [auksiˈljar] *vt* to help ♦ *nm/f* assistant; **auxilio** *nm* assistance, help; **primeros auxilios** first aid *sg*

Av *abr* (= *Avenida*) Av(e).

aval [aˈβal] *nm* guarantee; (*persona*) guarantor

avalancha [aβaˈlantʃa] *nf* avalanche

avance [aˈβanθe] *nm* advance; (*pago*) advance payment; (*CINE*) trailer

avanzar [aβanˈθar] *vt, vi* to advance

avaricia [aβaˈriθja] *nf* avarice, greed; **avaricioso, a** *adj* avaricious, greedy

avaro, a [aˈβaro, a] *adj* miserly, mean ♦ *nm/f* miser

avasallar [aβasaˈʎar] *vt* to subdue, subjugate

Avda abr (= Avenida) Av(e).

AVE ['aβe] nm abr (= Alta Velocidad Española) ≈ bullet train

ave ['aβe] nf bird; **~ de rapiña** bird of prey

avecinarse [aβeθi'narse] vr (tormenta, fig) to be on the way

avellana [aβe'ʎana] nf hazelnut; **avellano** nm hazel tree

avemaría [aβema'ria] nm Hail Mary, Ave Maria

avena [a'βena] nf oats pl

avenida [aβe'niða] nf (calle) avenue

avenir [aβe'nir] vt to reconcile; **~se** vr to come to an agreement, reach a compromise

aventajado, a [aβenta'xaðo, a] adj outstanding

aventajar [aβenta'xar] vt (sobrepasar) to surpass, outstrip

aventura [aβen'tura] nf adventure; **aventurado, a** adj risky; **aventurero, a** adj adventurous

avergonzar [aβerɣon'θar] vt to shame; (desconcertar) to embarrass; **~se** vr to be ashamed; to be embarrassed

avería [aβe'ria] nf (TEC) breakdown, fault

averiado, a [aβe'rjaðo, a] adj broken down; **"~"** "out of order"

averiguación [aβeriɣwa'θjon] nf investigation; (descubrimiento) ascertainment

averiguar [aβeri'ɣwar] vt to investigate; (descubrir) to find out, ascertain

aversión [aβer'sjon] nf aversion, dislike

avestruz [aβes'truθ] nm ostrich

aviación [aβja'θjon] nf aviation; (fuerzas aéreas) air force

aviador, a [aβja'ðor, a] nm/f aviator, airman/woman

avicultura [aβikul'tura] nf poultry farming

avidez [aβi'ðeθ] nf avidity, eagerness; **ávido, a** adj avid, eager

avinagrado, a [aβina'ɣraðo, a] adj sour, acid

avión [a'βjon] nm aeroplane; (ave) martin; **~ de reacción** jet (plane)

avioneta [aβjo'neta] nf light aircraft

avisar [aβi'sar] vt (advertir) to warn, notify; (informar) to tell; (aconsejar) to advise, counsel; **aviso** nm warning; (noticia) notice

avispa [a'βispa] nf wasp

avispado, a [aβis'paðo, a] adj sharp, clever

avispero [aβis'pero] nm wasp's nest

avispón [aβis'pon] nm hornet

avistar [aβis'tar] vt to sight, spot

avituallar [aβitwa'ʎar] vt to supply with food

avivar [aβi'βar] vt to strengthen, intensify; **~se** vr to revive, acquire new life

axila [ak'sila] nf armpit

axioma [ak'sjoma] nm axiom

ay [ai] excl (dolor) ow!, ouch!; (aflicción) oh!, oh dear!; **¡~ de mí!** poor me!

aya ['aja] nf governess; (niñera) nanny

ayer [a'jer] adv, nm yesterday; **antes de ~** the day before yesterday

ayote [a'jote] (AM) nm pumpkin

ayuda [a'juða] nf help, assistance ♦ nm page; **ayudante, a** nm/f assistant, helper; (ESCOL) assistant; (MIL) adjutant

ayudar [aju'ðar] vt to help, assist

ayunar [aju'nar] vi to fast; **ayunas** nfpl: **estar en ayunas** to be fasting; **ayuno** nm fast; fasting

ayuntamiento [ajunta'mjento] nm (consejo) town (o city) council; (edificio) town (o city) hall

azabache [aθa'βatʃe] nm jet

azada [a'θaða] nf hoe

azafata [aθa'fata] nf air stewardess

azafrán [aθa'fran] nm saffron

azahar [aθa'ar] nm orange/lemon blossom

azar [a'θar] nm (casualidad) chance, fate; (desgracia) misfortune, accident; **por ~** by chance; **al ~** at random

azoramiento [aθora'mjento] nm alarm; (confusión) confusion

azorar [aθo'rar] vt to alarm; **~se** vr to get alarmed

Azores [a'θores] nfpl: **las ~** the Azores

azotar [aθo'tar] vt to whip, beat; (pegar) to spank; **azote** nm (látigo) whip;

(*latigazo*) lash, stroke; (*en las nalgas*) spank; (*calamidad*) calamity

azotea [aθo'tea] *nf* (flat) roof

azteca [aθ'teka] *adj, nm/f* Aztec

azúcar [a'θukar] *nm* sugar; **azucarado, a** *adj* sugary, sweet

azucarero, a [aθuka'rero, a] *adj* sugar *cpd* ♦ *nm* sugar bowl

azucena [aθu'θena] *nf* white lily

azufre [a'θufre] *nm* sulphur

azul [a'θul] *adj, nm* blue; **~ marino** navy blue

azulejo [aθu'lexo] *nm* tile

azuzar [aθu'θar] *vt* to incite, egg on

B, b

B.A. *abr* (= *Buenos Aires*) B.A.

baba ['baßa] *nf* spittle, saliva; **babear** *vi* to drool, slaver

babero [ba'ßero] *nm* bib

babor [ba'ßor] *nm* port (side)

baboso, a [ba'ßoso, a] (*AM: fam*) *adj* silly

baca ['baka] *nf* (*AUTO*) luggage *o* roof rack

bacalao [baka'lao] *nm* cod(fish)

bache ['batʃe] *nm* pothole, rut; (*fig*) bad patch

bachillerato [batʃiʎe'rato] *nm higher secondary school course*

bacteria [bak'terja] *nf* bacterium, germ

báculo ['bakulo] *nm* stick, staff

bagaje [ba'yaxe] *nm* baggage, luggage

Bahama [ba'ama]: **las (Islas) ~** *nfpl* the Bahamas

bahía [ba'ia] *nf* bay

bailar [bai'lar] *vt, vi* to dance; **~ín, ina** *nm/f* (ballet) dancer; **baile** *nm* dance; (*formal*) ball

baja ['baxa] *nf* drop, fall; (*MIL*) casualty; **dar de ~** (*soldado*) to discharge; (*empleado*) to dismiss

bajada [ba'xaða] *nf* descent; (*camino*) slope; (*de aguas*) ebb

bajar [ba'xar] *vi* to go down, come down; (*temperatura, precios*) to drop, fall ♦ *vt* (*cabeza*) to bow; (*escalera*) to go down, come down; (*precio, voz*) to lower; (*llevar abajo*) to take down; **~se** *vr* (*de coche*) to get out; (*de autobús, tren*) to get off; **~ de** (*coche*) to get out of; (*autobús, tren*) to get off

bajeza [ba'xeθa] *nf* baseness *no pl*; (*una ~*) vile deed

bajío [ba'xio] *nm* (*AM*) lowlands *pl*

bajo, a ['baxo, a] *adj* (*mueble, número, precio*) low; (*piso*) ground; (*de estatura*) small, short; (*color*) pale; (*sonido*) faint, soft, low; (*voz: en tono*) deep; (*metal*) base; (*humilde*) low, humble ♦ *adv* (*hablar*) softly, quietly; (*volar*) low ♦ *prep* under, below, underneath ♦ *nm* (*MUS*) bass; **~ la lluvia** in the rain

bajón [ba'xon] *nm* fall, drop

bakalao [baka'lao] (*fam*) *nm* rave (music)

bala ['bala] *nf* bullet

balance [ba'lanθe] *nm* (*COM*) balance; (: *libro*) balance sheet; (: *cuenta general*) stocktaking

balancear [balanθe'ar] *vt* to balance ♦ *vi* to swing (to and fro); (*vacilar*) to hesitate; **~se** *vr* to swing (to and fro); to hesitate; **balanceo** *nm* swinging

balanza [ba'lanθa] *nf* scales *pl*, balance; (*ASTROLOGÍA*): **B~** Libra; **~ comercial** balance of trade; **~ de pagos** balance of payments

balar [ba'lar] *vi* to bleat

balaustrada [balaus'traða] *nf* balustrade; (*pasamanos*) banisters *pl*

balazo [ba'laθo] *nm* (*golpe*) shot; (*herida*) bullet wound

balbucear [balßuθe'ar] *vi, vt* to stammer, stutter; **balbuceo** *nm* stammering, stuttering

balbucir [balßu'θir] *vi, vt* to stammer, stutter

balcón [bal'kon] *nm* balcony

balde ['balde] *nm* bucket, pail; **de ~** (for) free, for nothing; **en ~** in vain

baldío, a [bal'dio, a] *adj* uncultivated; (*terreno*) waste ♦ *nm* waste land

baldosa [bal'dosa] *nf* (*azulejo*) floor tile; (*grande*) flagstone; **baldosín** *nm* (small) tile

Baleares [bale'ares] *nfpl*: **las (Islas) ~** the Balearic Islands

balido [ba'liðo] *nm* bleat, bleating

baliza [ba'liθa] *nf* (*AVIAT*) beacon; (*NAUT*) buoy

ballena [ba'ʎena] *nf* whale

ballesta [ba'ʎesta] *nf* crossbow; (*AUTO*) spring

ballet [ba'le] (*pl* **~s**) *nm* ballet

balneario, a [balne'arjo, a] *adj*: **estación balnearia** (*AM*) (bathing) resort ♦ *nm* spa, health resort

balón [ba'lon] *nm* ball

baloncesto [balon'θesto] *nm* basketball

balonmano [balon'mano] *nm* handball

balonvolea [balombo'lea] *nm* volleyball

balsa ['balsa] *nf* raft; (*BOT*) balsa wood

bálsamo ['balsamo] *nm* balsam, balm

baluarte [ba'lwarte] *nm* bastion, bulwark

bambolear [bambole'ar] *vi* to swing, sway; (*silla*) to wobble; **~se** *vr* to swing, sway; to wobble; **bamboleo** *nm* swinging, swaying; wobbling

bambú [bam'bu] *nm* bamboo

banana [ba'nana] (*AM*) *nf* banana; **banano** (*AM*) *nm* banana tree

banca ['banka] *nf* (*COM*) banking

bancario, a [ban'karjo, a] *adj* banking *cpd*, bank *cpd*

bancarrota [banka'rrota] *nf* bankruptcy; **hacer ~** to go bankrupt

banco ['banko] *nm* bench; (*ESCOL*) desk; (*COM*) bank; (*GEO*) stratum; **~ de crédito/de ahorros** credit/savings bank; **~ de arena** sandbank; **~ de datos** databank

banda ['banda] *nf* band; (*pandilla*) gang; (*NAUT*) side, edge; **la B~ Oriental** Uruguay; **~ sonora** soundtrack

bandada [ban'daða] *nf* (*de pájaros*) flock; (*de peces*) shoal

bandazo [ban'daθo] *nm*: **dar ~s** to sway from side to side

bandeja [ban'dexa] *nf* tray

bandera [ban'dera] *nf* flag

banderilla [bande'riʎa] *nf* banderilla

banderín [bande'rin] *nm* pennant, small flag

bandido [ban'diðo] *nm* bandit

bando ['bando] *nm* (*edicto*) edict, proclamation; (*facción*) faction; **los ~s** (*REL*) the banns

bandolera [bando'lera] *nf*: **llevar en ~** to wear across one's chest

bandolero [bando'lero] *nm* bandit, brigand

banquero [ban'kero] *nm* banker

banqueta [ban'keta] *nf* stool; (*AM*: *en la calle*) pavement (*BRIT*), sidewalk (*US*)

banquete [ban'kete] *nm* banquet; (*para convidados*) formal dinner

banquillo [ban'kiʎo] *nm* (*JUR*) dock, prisoner's bench; (*banco*) bench; (*para los pies*) footstool

bañador [baɲa'ðor] *nm* swimming costume (*BRIT*), bathing suit (*US*)

bañar [ba'ɲar] *vt* to bath, bathe; (*objeto*) to dip; (*de barniz*) to coat; **~se** *vr* (*en el mar*) to bathe, swim; (*en la bañera*) to have a bath

bañera [ba'ɲera] *nf* bath(tub)

bañero, a [ba'ɲero, a] (*AM*) *nm/f* lifeguard

bañista [ba'ɲista] *nm/f* bather

baño ['baɲo] *nm* (*en bañera*) bath; (*en río*) dip, swim; (*cuarto*) bathroom; (*bañera*) bath(tub); (*capa*) coating

baqueta [ba'keta] *nf* (*MUS*) drumstick

bar [bar] *nm* bar

barahúnda [bara'unda] *nf* uproar, hubbub

baraja [ba'raxa] *nf* pack (of cards); **barajar** *vt* (*naipes*) to shuffle; (*fig*) to jumble up

baranda [ba'randa] *nf* = **barandilla**

barandilla [baran'diʎa] *nf* rail, railing

baratija [bara'tixa] *nf* trinket

baratillo [bara'tiʎo] *nm* (*tienda*) junkshop; (*subasta*) bargain sale; (*conjunto de cosas*) secondhand goods *pl*

barato, a [ba'rato, a] *adj* cheap ♦ *adv* cheap, cheaply

baraúnda [bara'unda] *nf* = **barahúnda**

barba ['barβa] *nf* (*mentón*) chin; (*pelo*) beard

barbacoa [barˈβaˈkoa] *nf* (*parrilla*)
barbecue; (*carne*) barbecued meat
barbaridad [barβariˈðað] *nf* barbarity;
(*acto*) barbarism; (*atrocidad*) outrage; **una
~** (*fam*) loads; **¡qué ~!** (*fam*) how awful!
barbarie [barˈβarje] *nf* barbarism,
savagery; (*crueldad*) barbarity
barbarismo [barβaˈrismo] *nm* = **barbarie**
bárbaro, a [ˈbarβaro, a] *adj* barbarous,
cruel; (*grosero*) rough, uncouth ♦ *nm/f*
barbarian ♦ *adv*: **lo pasamos ~** (*fam*) we
had a great time; **¡qué ~!** (*fam*) how
marvellous!; **un éxito ~** (*fam*) a terrific
success; **es un tipo ~** (*fam*) he's a great
bloke
barbecho [barˈβetʃo] *nm* fallow land
barbero [barˈβero] *nm* barber, hairdresser
barbilla [barˈβiʎa] *nf* chin, tip of the chin
barbo [ˈbarβo] *nm* barbel; **~ de mar** red
mullet
barbotear [barβoteˈar] *vt, vi* to mutter,
mumble
barbudo, a [barˈβuðo, a] *adj* bearded
barca [ˈbarka] *nf* (small) boat; **~ pesquera**
fishing boat; **~ de pasaje** ferry; **~za** *nf*
barge; **~za de desembarco** landing craft
Barcelona [barθeˈlona] *n* Barcelona
barcelonés, esa [barθeloˈnes, esa] *adj* of
o from Barcelona
barco [ˈbarko] *nm* boat; (*grande*) ship; **~
de carga** cargo boat; **~ de vela** sailing
ship
baremo [baˈremo] *nm* (*MAT, fig*) scale
barítono [baˈritono] *nm* baritone
barman [ˈbarman] *nm* barman
Barna *n* = **Barcelona**
barniz [barˈniθ] *nm* varnish; (*en la loza*)
glaze; (*fig*) veneer; **~ar** *vt* to varnish;
(*loza*) to glaze
barómetro [baˈrometro] *nm* barometer
barquero [barˈkero] *nm* boatman
barquillo [barˈkiʎo] *nm* cone, cornet
barra [ˈbarra] *nf* bar, rod; (*de un bar, café*)
bar; (*de pan*) French stick; (*palanca*) lever;
~ de carmín *o* **de labios** lipstick; **~ libre**
free bar
barraca [baˈrraka] *nf* hut, cabin

barranco [baˈrranko] *nm* ravine; (*fig*)
difficulty
barrena [baˈrrena] *nf* drill; **barrenar** *vt* to
drill (through), bore; **barreno** *nm* large
drill
barrer [baˈrrer] *vt* to sweep; (*quitar*) to
sweep away
barrera [baˈrrera] *nf* barrier
barriada [baˈrrjaða] *nf* quarter, district
barricada [barriˈkaða] *nf* barricade
barrida [baˈrriða] *nf* sweep, sweeping
barrido [baˈrriðo] *nm* = **barrida**
barriga [baˈrriɣa] *nf* belly; (*panza*) paunch;
barrigón, ona *adj* potbellied;
barrigudo, a *adj* potbellied
barril [baˈrril] *nm* barrel, cask
barrio [ˈbarrjo] *nm* (*vecindad*) area,
neighborhood (*US*); (*en las afueras*)
suburb; **~ chino** red-light district
barro [ˈbarro] *nm* (*lodo*) mud; (*objetos*)
earthenware; (*MED*) pimple
barroco, a [baˈrroko, a] *adj, nm* baroque
barrote [baˈrrote] *nm* (*de ventana*) bar
barruntar [barrunˈtar] *vt* (*conjeturar*) to
guess; (*presentir*) to suspect; **barrunto**
nm guess; suspicion
bartola [barˈtola]: **a la ~** *adv*: **tirarse a la
~** to take it easy, be lazy
bártulos [ˈbartulos] *nmpl* things,
belongings
barullo [baˈruʎo] *nm* row, uproar
basar [baˈsar] *vt* to base; **~se** *vr*: **~se en**
to be based on
báscula [ˈbaskula] *nf* (platform) scales
base [ˈbase] *nf* base; **a ~ de** on the basis
of; (*mediante*) by means of; **~ de datos**
(*INFORM*) database
básico, a [ˈbasiko, a] *adj* basic
basílica [baˈsilika] *nf* basilica

┌─────────────────┐
│ *PALABRA CLAVE* │
└─────────────────┘

bastante [basˈtante] *adj* **1** (*suficiente*)
enough; **~ dinero** enough *o* sufficient
money; **~s libros** enough books
2 (*valor intensivo*): **~ gente** quite a lot of
people; **tener ~ calor** to be rather hot
♦ *adv*: **~ bueno/malo** quite good/rather

bad; **~ rico** pretty rich; **(lo) ~ inteligente (como) para hacer algo** clever enough *o* sufficiently clever to do sth

bastar [bas'tar] *vi* to be enough *o* sufficient; **~se** *vr* to be self-sufficient; **~ para** to be enough to; **¡basta!** (that's) enough!

bastardilla [bastar'ðiʎa] *nf* italics

bastardo, a [bas'tarðo, a] *adj, nm/f* bastard

bastidor [basti'ðor] *nm* frame; *(de coche)* chassis; *(TEATRO)* wing; **entre ~es** *(fig)* behind the scenes

basto, a ['basto, a] *adj* coarse, rough; **~s** *nmpl (NAIPES)* ≈ clubs

bastón [bas'ton] *nm* stick, staff; *(para pasear)* walking stick

bastoncillo [baston'θiʎo] *nm* cotton bud

basura [ba'sura] *nf* rubbish *(BRIT)*, garbage *(US)*

basurero [basu'rero] *nm (hombre)* dustman *(BRIT)*, garbage man *(US)*; *(lugar)* dump; *(cubo)* (rubbish) bin *(BRIT)*, trash can *(US)*

bata ['bata] *nf (gen)* dressing gown; *(cubretodo)* smock, overall; *(MED, TEC etc)* lab(oratory) coat

batalla [ba'taʎa] *nf* battle; **de ~** *(fig)* for everyday use

batallar [bata'ʎar] *vi* to fight

batallón [bata'ʎon] *nm* battalion

batata [ba'tata] *nf* sweet potato

batería [bate'ria] *nf* battery; *(MUS)* drums; **~ de cocina** kitchen utensils

batido, a [ba'tiðo, a] *adj (camino)* beaten, well-trodden ♦ *nm (CULIN)*: **~ (de leche)** milk shake

batidora [bati'ðora] *nf* beater, mixer; **~ eléctrica** food mixer, blender

batir [ba'tir] *vt* to beat, strike; *(vencer)* to beat, defeat; *(revolver)* to beat, mix; **~se** *vr* to fight; **~ palmas** to clap, applaud

batuta [ba'tuta] *nf* baton; **llevar la ~** *(fig)* to be the boss, be in charge

baúl [ba'ul] *nm* trunk; *(AUTO)* boot *(BRIT)*, trunk *(US)*

bautismo [bau'tismo] *nm* baptism, christening

bautizar [bauti'θar] *vt* to baptize, christen; *(fam: diluir)* to water down; **bautizo** *nm* baptism, christening

baya ['baja] *nf* berry

bayeta [ba'jeta] *nf* floorcloth

bayoneta [bajo'neta] *nf* bayonet

baza ['baθa] *nf* trick; **meter ~** to butt in

bazar [ba'θar] *nm* bazaar

bazofia [ba'θofja] *nf* trash

beato, a [be'ato, a] *adj* blessed; *(piadoso)* pious

bebé [be'ße] *(pl* **~s)** *nm* baby

bebedor, a [beße'ðor, a] *adj* hard-drinking

beber [be'ßer] *vt, vi* to drink

bebida [be'ßiða] *nf* drink; **bebido, a** *adj* drunk

beca ['beka] *nf* grant, scholarship

becario, a [be'karjo, a] *nm/f* scholarship holder, grant holder

bedel [be'ðel] *nm (ESCOL)* janitor; *(UNIV)* porter

béisbol ['beisßol] *nm (DEPORTE)* baseball

belén [be'len] *nm (de navidad)* nativity scene, crib; **B~** Bethlehem

belga ['belxa] *adj, nm/f* Belgian

Bélgica ['belxika] *nf* Belgium

bélico, a ['beliko, a] *adj (actitud)* warlike; **belicoso, a** *adj (guerrero)* warlike; *(agresivo)* aggressive, bellicose

beligerante [belixe'rante] *adj* belligerent

belleza [be'ʎeθa] *nf* beauty

bello, a ['beʎo, a] *adj* beautiful, lovely; **Bellas Artes** Fine Art

bellota [be'ʎota] *nf* acorn

bemol [be'mol] *nm (MUS)* flat; **esto tiene ~es** *(fam)* this is a tough one

bencina [ben'θina] *(AM) nf (gasolina)* petrol *(BRIT)*, gasoline *(US)*

bendecir [bende'θir] *vt* to bless

bendición [bendi'θjon] *nf* blessing

bendito, a [ben'dito, a] *pp de* **bendecir** ♦ *adj* holy; *(afortunado)* lucky; *(feliz)* happy; *(sencillo)* simple ♦ *nm/f* simple soul

beneficencia [benefi'θenθja] *nf* charity
beneficiar [benefi'θjar] *vt* to benefit, be
  of benefit to; **~se** *vr* to benefit, profit;
  ~io, *a nm/f* beneficiary
beneficio [bene'fiθjo] *nm* (*bien*) benefit,
  advantage; (*ganancia*) profit, gain; **~so,**
  a *adj* beneficial
benéfico, a [be'nefiko, a] *adj*
  charitable
beneplácito [bene'plaθito] *nm* approval,
  consent
benevolencia [beneβo'lenθja] *nf*
  benevolence, kindness; **benévolo, a** *adj*
  benevolent, kind
benigno, a [be'niɣno, a] *adj* kind; (*suave*)
  mild; (*MED: tumor*) benign, non-malignant
berberecho [berβe'retʃo] *nm* (*ZOOL,*
  CULIN) cockle
berenjena [beren'xena] *nf* aubergine
  (*BRIT*), eggplant (*US*)
Berlín [ber'lin] *n* Berlin; **berlinés, esa**
  adj of o from Berlin ♦ *nm/f* Berliner
bermudas [ber'muðas] *nfpl* Bermuda
  shorts
berrear [berre'ar] *vi* to bellow, low
berrido [be'rriðo] *nm* bellow(ing)
berrinche [be'rrintʃe] (*fam*) *nm* temper,
  tantrum
berro ['berro] *nm* watercress
berza ['berθa] *nf* cabbage
besamel [besa'mel] *nf* (*CULIN*) white
  sauce, bechamel sauce
besar [be'sar] *vt* to kiss; (*fig: tocar*) to
  graze; **~se** *vr* to kiss (one another); **beso**
  nm kiss
bestia ['bestja] *nf* beast, animal; (*fig*) idiot;
  ~ de carga beast of burden
bestial [bes'tjal] *adj* bestial; (*fam*) terrific;
  ~idad *nf* bestiality; (*fam*) stupidity
besugo [be'suɣo] *nm* sea bream; (*fam*)
  idiot
besuquear [besuke'ar] *vt* to cover with
  kisses; **~se** *vr* to kiss and cuddle
betún [be'tun] *nm* shoe polish; (*QUÍM*)
  bitumen
biberón [biβe'ron] *nm* feeding bottle
Biblia ['biβlja] *nf* Bible

bibliografía [biβljoɣra'fia] *nf* bibliography
biblioteca [biβljo'teka] *nf* library; (*mueble*)
  bookshelves; **~ de consulta** reference
  library; **~rio, a** *nm/f* librarian
bicarbonato [bikarβo'nato] *nm*
  bicarbonate
bicho ['bitʃo] *nm* (*animal*) small animal;
  (*sabandija*) bug, insect; (*TAUR*) bull
bici ['biθi] (*fam*) *nf* bike
bicicleta [biθi'kleta] *nf* bicycle, cycle; **ir en**
  ~ to cycle
bidé [bi'ðe] (*pl* **~s**) *nm* bidet
bidón [bi'ðon] *nm* (*de aceite*) drum; (*de*
  gasolina) can

┌─────────────────┐
│ *PALABRA CLAVE* │
└─────────────────┘

bien [bjen] *nm* 1 (*bienestar*) good; **te lo**
  digo por tu ~ I'm telling you for your
  own good; **el ~ y el mal** good and evil
  2 (*posesión*): **~es** goods; **~es de**
  consumo consumer goods; **~es**
  inmuebles o **raíces/~es muebles** real
  estate *sg*/personal property *sg*
  ♦ *adv* 1 (*de manera satisfactoria, correcta*
  etc) well; **trabaja/come ~** she works/eats
  well; **contestó ~** he answered correctly;
  me siento ~ I feel fine; **no me siento ~** I
  don't feel very well; **se está ~ aquí** it's
  nice here
  2 (*frases*): **hiciste ~ en llamarme** you
  were right to call me
  3 (*valor intensivo*) very; **un cuarto ~**
  caliente a nice warm room; **~ se ve que**
  ... it's quite clear that ...
  4: **estar ~: estoy muy ~ aquí** I feel very
  happy here; **está ~ que vengan** it's all
  right for them to come; **¡está ~! lo haré**
  oh all right, I'll do it
  5 (*de buena gana*): **yo ~ que iría pero ...**
  I'd gladly go but ...
  ♦ *excl*: **¡~!** (*aprobación*) O.K.!; **¡muy ~!**
  well done!
  ♦ *adj inv* (*matiz despectivo*): **niño ~** rich
  kid; **gente ~** posh people
  ♦ *conj* 1: **~ ... ~: ~ en coche ~ en tren**
  either by car or by train
  2: **no ~** 1: (*esp AM*): **no ~ llegue te llamaré**

as soon as I arrive I'll call you
3: si ~ even though; *ver tb* **más**

---

bienal [bje'nal] *adj* biennial

bienaventurado, a [bjenaßentu'raðo, a] *adj* (*feliz*) happy, fortunate

bienestar [bjenes'tar] *nm* well-being, welfare

bienhechor, a [bjene'tʃor, a] *adj* beneficent ♦ *nm/f* benefactor/benefactress

bienvenida [bjembe'niða] *nf* welcome; **dar la ~ a uno** to welcome sb

bienvenido [bjembe'niðo] *excl* welcome!

bife ['bife] (*AM*) *nm* steak

bifurcación [bifurka'θjon] *nf* fork

bifurcarse [bifur'karse] *vr* (*camino, carretera, río*) to fork

bigamia [bi'xamja] *nf* bigamy; **bígamo, a** *adj* bigamous ♦ *nm/f* bigamist

bigote [bi'xote] *nm* moustache; **bigotudo, a** *adj* with a big moustache

bikini [bi'kini] *nm* bikini; (*CULIN*) toasted ham and cheese sandwich

bilbaíno, a [bilßa'ino, a] *adj* from *o* of Bilbao

bilingüe [bi'lingwe] *adj* bilingual

billar [bi'ʎar] *nm* billiards *sg*; (*lugar*) billiard hall; (*mini-casino*) amusement arcade; **~ americano** pool

billete [bi'ʎete] *nm* ticket; (*de banco*) (bank)note (*BRIT*), bill (*US*); (*carta*) note; **~ sencillo, ~ de ida solamente** single (*BRIT*) *o* one-way (*US*) ticket; **~ de ida y vuelta** return (*BRIT*) *o* round-trip (*US*) ticket; **~ de 20 libras** £20 note

billetera [biʎe'tera] *nf* wallet

billetero [biʎe'tero] *nm* = **billetera**

billón [bi'ʎon] *nm* billion

bimensual [bimen'swal] *adj* twice monthly

bimotor [bimo'tor] *adj* twin-engined ♦ *nm* twin-engined plane

biodegradable [bioðevra'ðaßle] *adj* biodegradable

biografía [bjoxra'fia] *nf* biography; **biógrafo, a** *nm/f* biographer

biología [bjolo'xia] *nf* biology; **biológico, a** *adj* biological; **biólogo, a** *nm/f* biologist

biombo ['bjombo] *nm* (folding) screen

biopsia [bi'opsja] *nf* biopsy

biquini [bi'kini] *nm* bikini

birlar [bir'lar] (*fam*) *vt* to pinch

Birmania [bir'manja] *nf* Burma

birria ['birrja] *nf*: **ser una ~** (*película, libro*) to be rubbish

bis [bis] *excl* encore! ♦ *adv*: **viven en el 27 ~** they live at 27a

bisabuelo, a [bisa'ßwelo, a] *nm/f* great-grandfather/mother

bisagra [bi'saxra] *nf* hinge

bisiesto [bi'sjesto] *adj*: **año ~** leap year

bisnieto, a [bis'njeto, a] *nm/f* great-grandson/daughter

bisonte [bi'sonte] *nm* bison

bisté [bis'te] *nm* = **bistec**

bistec [bis'tek] *nm* steak

bisturí [bistu'ri] *nm* scalpel

bisutería [bisute'ria] *nf* imitation *o* costume jewellery

bit [bit] (*INFORM*) bit

bizco, a ['biθko, a] *adj* cross-eyed

bizcocho [biθ'kotʃo] *nm* (*CULIN*) sponge cake

bizquear [biθke'ar] *vi* to squint

blanca ['blanka] *nf* (*MUS*) minim; **estar sin ~** to be broke; *ver tb* **blanco**

blanco, a ['blanko, a] *adj* white ♦ *nm/f* white man/woman, white ♦ *nm* (*color*) white; (*en texto*) blank; (*MIL, fig*) target; **en ~** blank; **noche en ~** sleepless night

blancura [blan'kura] *nf* whiteness

blandir [blan'dir] *vt* to brandish

blando, a ['blando, a] *adj* soft; (*tierno*) tender, gentle; (*carácter*) mild; (*fam*) cowardly; **blandura** *nf* softness, tenderness; mildness

blanquear [blanke'ar] *vt* to whiten; (*fachada*) to whitewash; (*paño*) to bleach ♦ *vi* to turn white; **blanquecino, a** *adj* whitish

blasfemar [blasfe'mar] *vi* to blaspheme, curse; **blasfemia** *nf* blasphemy

blasón [bla'son] *nm* coat of arms

bledo ['bleðo] *nm*: **me importa un ~** I couldn't care less

blindado, a [blin'daðo, a] *adj* (*MIL*) armour-plated; (*antibala*) bullet-proof; **coche** (*ESP*) *o* **carro** (*AM*) **~** armoured car

blindaje [blin'daxe] *nm* armour, armour-plating

bloc [blok] (*pl* **~s**) *nm* writing pad

bloque ['bloke] *nm* block; (*POL*) bloc; **~ de cilindros** cylinder block

bloquear [bloke'ar] *vt* to blockade; **bloqueo** *nm* blockade; (*COM*) freezing, blocking

blusa ['blusa] *nf* blouse

boato [bo'ato] *nm* show, ostentation

bobada [bo'ßaða] *nf* foolish action; foolish statement; **decir ~s** to talk nonsense

bobería [boße'ria] *nf* = **bobada**

bobina [bo'ßina] *nf* (*TEC*) bobbin; (*FOTO*) spool; (*ELEC*) coil

bobo, a ['boßo, a] *adj* (*tonto*) daft, silly; (*cándido*) naïve ♦ *nm/f* fool, idiot ♦ *nm* (*TEATRO*) clown, funny man

boca ['boka] *nf* mouth; (*de crustáceo*) pincer; (*de cañón*) muzzle; (*entrada*) mouth, entrance; **~s** *nfpl* (*de río*) mouth *sg*; **~ abajo/arriba** face down/up; **se me hace agua la ~** my mouth is watering

bocacalle [boka'kaʎe] *nf* (entrance to a) street; **la primera ~** the first turning *o* street

bocadillo [boka'ðiʎo] *nm* sandwich

bocado [bo'kaðo] *nm* mouthful, bite; (*de caballo*) bridle; **~ de Adán** Adam's apple

bocajarro [boka'xarro]: **a ~** *adv* (*disparar, preguntar*) point-blank

bocanada [boka'naða] *nf* (*de vino*) mouthful, swallow; (*de aire*) gust, puff

bocata [bo'kata] (*fam*) *nm* sandwich

bocazas [bo'kaθas] (*fam*) *nm inv* bigmouth

boceto [bo'θeto] *nm* sketch, outline

bochorno [bo'tʃorno] *nm* (*vergüenza*) embarrassment; (*calor*): **hace ~** it's very muggy; **~so, a** *adj* muggy; embarrassing

bocina [bo'θina] *nf* (*MUS*) trumpet; (*AUTO*)

horn; (*para hablar*) megaphone

boda ['boða] *nf* (*tb*: **~s**) wedding, marriage; (*fiesta*) wedding reception; **~s de plata/de oro** silver/golden wedding

bodega [bo'ðexa] *nf* (*de vino*) (wine) cellar; (*depósito*) storeroom; (*de barco*) hold

bodegón [boðe'xon] *nm* (*ARTE*) still life

bofe ['bofe] *nm* (*tb*: **~s**: *de res*) lights

bofetada [bofe'taða] *nf* slap (in the face)

bofetón [bofe'ton] *nm* = **bofetada**

boga ['boxa] *nf*: **en ~** (*fig*) in vogue

bogar [bo'xar] *vi* (*remar*) to row; (*navegar*) to sail

bogavante [boxa'ßante] *nm* lobster

Bogotá [boxo'ta] *n* Bogotá

bohemio, a [bo'emjo, a] *adj, nm/f* Bohemian

boicot [boi'kot] (*pl* **~s**) *nm* boycott; **~ear** *vt* to boycott; **~eo** *nm* boycott

boina ['boina] *nf* beret

bola ['bola] *nf* ball; (*canica*) marble; (*NAIPES*) (grand) slam; (*betún*) shoe polish; (*mentira*) tale, story; **~s** (*AM*) *nfpl* bolas *sg*; **~ de billar** billiard ball; **~ de nieve** snowball

bolchevique [boltʃe'ßike] *adj, nm/f* Bolshevik

boleadoras [bolea'ðoras] (*AM*) *nfpl* bolas *sg*

bolera [bo'lera] *nf* skittle *o* bowling alley

boleta [bo'leta] (*AM*) *nf* (*billete*) ticket; (*permiso*) pass, permit

boletería [bolete'ria] (*AM*) *nf* ticket office

boletín [bole'tin] *nm* bulletin; (*periódico*) journal, review; **~ de noticias** news bulletin

boleto [bo'leto] *nm* ticket

boli ['boli] (*fam*) *nm* Biro ®, pen

bolígrafo [bo'lixrafo] *nm* ball-point pen, Biro ®

bolívar [bo'lißar] *nm* monetary unit of Venezuela

Bolivia [bo'lißja] *nf* Bolivia; **boliviano, a** *adj, nm/f* Bolivian

bollería [boʎe'ria] *nf* cakes *pl* and pastries *pl*

bollo [ˈboʎo] *nm* (*pan*) roll; (*bulto*) bump, lump; (*abolladura*) dent

bolo [ˈbolo] *nm* skittle; (*píldora*) (large) pill; **(juego de) ~s** *nmpl* skittles *sg*

bolsa [ˈbolsa] *nf* bag; (*AM*) pocket; (*ANAT*) cavity, sac; (*COM*) stock exchange; (*MINERÍA*) pocket; **de ~** pocket *cpd*; **~ de agua caliente** hot water bottle; **~ de aire** air pocket; **~ de papel** paper bag; **~ de plástico** plastic bag

bolsillo [bolˈsiʎo] *nm* pocket; (*cartera*) purse; **de ~** pocket(-size)

bolsista [bolˈsista] *nm/f* stockbroker

bolso [ˈbolso] *nm* (*bolsa*) bag; (*de mujer*) handbag

bomba [ˈbomba] *nf* (*MIL*) bomb; (*TEC*) pump ♦ (*fam*) *adj*: **noticia ~** bombshell ♦ (*fam*) *adv*: **pasarlo ~** to have a great time; **~ atómica / de humo / de efecto retardado** atomic/smoke/time bomb

bombardear [bombarðeˈar] *vt* to bombard; (*MIL*) to bomb; **bombardeo** *nm* bombardment; bombing

bombardero [bombarˈðero] *nm* bomber

bombear [bombeˈar] *vt* (*agua*) to pump (out *o* up); **~se** *vr* to warp

bombero [bomˈbero] *nm* fireman

bombilla [bomˈbiʎa] (*ESP*) *nf* (light) bulb

bombín [bomˈbin] *nm* bowler hat

bombo [ˈbombo] *nm* (*MUS*) bass drum; (*TEC*) drum

bombón [bomˈbon] *nm* chocolate

bombona [bomˈbona] *nf* (*de butano, oxígeno*) cylinder

bonachón, ona [bonaˈtʃon, ona] *adj* good-natured, easy-going

bonanza [boˈnanθa] *nf* (*NAUT*) fair weather; (*fig*) bonanza; (*MINERÍA*) rich pocket *o* vein

bondad [bonˈdað] *nf* goodness, kindness; **tenga la ~ de** (please) be good enough to; **~oso, a** *adj* good, kind

bonificación [bonifikaˈθjon] *nf* bonus

bonito, a [boˈnito, a] *adj* pretty; (*agradable*) nice ♦ *nm* (*atún*) tuna (fish)

bono [ˈbono] *nm* voucher; (*FIN*) bond

bonobús [bonoˈßus] (*ESP*) *nm* bus pass

bonoloto [bonoˈloto] *nf* state-run weekly lottery

boquerón [bokeˈron] *nm* (*pez*) (kind of) anchovy; (*agujero*) large hole

boquete [boˈkete] *nm* gap, hole

boquiabierto, a [bokiaˈßjerto, a] *adj*: **quedar ~** to be amazed *o* flabbergasted

boquilla [boˈkiʎa] *nf* (*para riego*) nozzle; (*para cigarro*) cigarette holder; (*MUS*) mouthpiece

borbotón [borßoˈton] *nm*: **salir a borbotones** to gush out

borda [ˈborða] *nf* (*NAUT*) (ship's) rail; **tirar algo / caerse por la ~** to throw sth/fall overboard

bordado [borˈðaðo] *nm* embroidery

bordar [borˈðar] *vt* to embroider

borde [ˈborðe] *nm* edge, border; (*de camino etc*) side; (*en la costura*) hem; **al ~ de** (*fig*) on the verge *o* brink of; **ser ~** (*ESP: fam*) to be rude; **~ar** *vt* to border

bordillo [borˈðiʎo] *nm* kerb (*BRIT*), curb (*US*)

bordo [ˈborðo] *nm* (*NAUT*) side; **a ~** on board

borinqueño, a [borinˈkenjo, a] *adj*, *nm/f* Puerto Rican

borla [ˈborla] *nf* (*adorno*) tassel

borrachera [borraˈtʃera] *nf* (*ebriedad*) drunkenness; (*orgía*) spree, binge

borracho, a [boˈrratʃo, a] *adj* drunk ♦ *nm/f* (*habitual*) drunkard, drunk; (*temporal*) drunk, drunk man/woman

borrador [borraˈðor] *nm* (*escritura*) first draft, rough sketch; (*goma*) rubber (*BRIT*), eraser

borrar [boˈrrar] *vt* to erase, rub out

borrasca [boˈrraska] *nf* storm

borrico, a [boˈrriko, a] *nm/f* donkey/she-donkey; (*fig*) stupid man/woman

borrón [boˈrron] *nm* (*mancha*) stain

borroso, a [boˈrroso, a] *adj* vague, unclear; (*escritura*) illegible

bosque [ˈboske] *nm* wood; (*grande*) forest

bosquejar [boskeˈxar] *vt* to sketch; **bosquejo** *nm* sketch

bostezar [bosteˈθar] *vi* to yawn; **bostezo**

nm yawn

bota ['bota] *nf* (*calzado*) boot; (*para vino*) leather wine bottle; **~s de agua, ~s de goma** Wellingtons

botánica [bo'tanika] *nf* (*ciencia*) botany; *ver tb* **botánico**

botánico, a [bo'taniko, a] *adj* botanical ♦ *nm/f* botanist

botar [bo'tar] *vt* to throw, hurl; (*NAUT*) to launch; (*AM*) to throw out ♦ *vi* to bounce

bote ['bote] *nm* (*salto*) bounce; (*golpe*) thrust; (*vasija*) tin, can; (*embarcación*) boat; **de ~ en ~** packed, jammed full; **~ de la basura** (*AM*) dustbin (*BRIT*), trashcan (*US*); **~ salvavidas** lifeboat

botella [bo'teʎa] *nf* bottle; **botellín** *nm* small bottle

botica [bo'tika] *nf* chemist's (shop) (*BRIT*), pharmacy; **~rio, a** *nm/f* chemist (*BRIT*), pharmacist

botijo [bo'tixo] *nm* (earthenware) jug

botín [bo'tin] *nm* (*calzado*) half boot; (*polaina*) spat; (*MIL*) booty

botiquín [boti'kin] *nm* (*armario*) medicine cabinet; (*portátil*) first-aid kit

botón [bo'ton] *nm* button; (*BOT*) bud; **~ de oro** buttercup

botones [bo'tones] *nm inv* bellboy (*BRIT*), bellhop (*US*)

bóveda ['boβeða] *nf* (*ARQ*) vault

boxeador [boksea'ðor] *nm* boxer

boxear [bokse'ar] *vi* to box

boxeo [bok'seo] *nm* boxing

boya ['boja] *nf* (*NAUT*) buoy; (*de caña*) float

boyante [bo'jante] *adj* prosperous

bozal [bo'θal] *nm* (*de caballo*) halter; (*de perro*) muzzle

bracear [braθe'ar] *vi* (*agitar los brazos*) to wave one's arms

bracero [bra'θero] *nm* labourer; (*en el campo*) farmhand

bragas ['braɣas] *nfpl* (*de mujer*) panties, knickers (*BRIT*)

bragueta [bra'ɣeta] *nf* fly, flies *pl*

braille [breil] *nm* braille

bramar [bra'mar] *vi* to bellow, roar;

bramido [bra'miðo] *nm* bellow, roar

brasa ['brasa] *nf* live *o* hot coal

brasero [bra'sero] *nm* brazier

Brasil [bra'sil] *nm*: **(el) ~** Brazil; **brasileño, a** *adj, nm/f* Brazilian

bravata [bra'βata] *nf* boast

braveza [bra'βeθa] *nf* (*valor*) bravery; (*ferocidad*) ferocity

bravío, a [bra'βio, a] *adj* wild; (*feroz*) fierce

bravo, a ['braβo, a] *adj* (*valiente*) brave; (*feroz*) ferocious; (*salvaje*) wild; (*mar etc*) rough, stormy ♦ *excl* bravo!; **bravura** *nf* bravery; ferocity

braza ['braθa] *nf* fathom; **nadar a la ~** to swim (the) breast-stroke

brazada [bra'θaða] *nf* stroke

brazado [bra'θaðo] *nm* armful

brazalete [braθa'lete] *nm* (*pulsera*) bracelet; (*banda*) armband

brazo ['braθo] *nm* arm; (*ZOOL*) foreleg; (*BOT*) limb, branch; **luchar a ~ partido** to fight hand-to-hand; **ir cogidos del ~** to walk arm in arm

brea ['brea] *nf* pitch, tar

brebaje [bre'βaxe] *nm* potion

brecha ['bretʃa] *nf* (*hoyo, vacío*) gap, opening; (*MIL, fig*) breach

brega ['breɣa] *nf* (*lucha*) struggle; (*trabajo*) hard work

breva ['breβa] *nf* early fig

breve ['breβe] *adj* short, brief ♦ *nf* (*MUS*) breve; **~dad** *nf* brevity, shortness

brezo ['breθo] *nm* heather

bribón, ona [bri'βon, ona] *adj* idle, lazy ♦ *nm/f* (*pícaro*) rascal, rogue

bricolaje [briko'laxe] *nm* do-it-yourself, DIY

brida ['briða] *nf* bridle, rein; (*TEC*) clamp; **a toda ~** at top speed

bridge [britʃ] *nm* bridge

brigada [bri'ɣaða] *nf* (*unidad*) brigade; (*trabajadores*) squad, gang ♦ *nm* ≈ staff-sergeant, sergeant-major

brillante [bri'ʎante] *adj* brilliant ♦ *nm* diamond

brillar [bri'ʎar] *vi* (*tb fig*) to shine; (*joyas*)

to sparkle

brillo ['briʎo] *nm* shine; (*brillantez*) brilliance; (*fig*) splendour; **sacar ~ a** to polish

brincar [briŋ'kar] *vi* to skip about, hop about, jump about; **está que brinca** he's hopping mad

brinco ['briŋko] *nm* jump, leap

brindar [brin'dar] *vi*: **~ a** *o* **por** to drink (a toast) to ♦ *vt* to offer, present

brindis ['brindis] *nm inv* toast

brío ['brio] *nm* spirit, dash; **brioso, a** *adj* spirited, dashing

brisa ['brisa] *nf* breeze

británico, a [bri'taniko, a] *adj* British ♦ *nm/f* Briton, British person

brizna ['briθna] *nf* (*de hierba, paja*) blade; (*de tabaco*) leaf

broca ['broka] *nf* (*TEC*) drill, bit

brocal [bro'kal] *nm* rim

brocha ['brotʃa] *nf* (large) paintbrush; **~ de afeitar** shaving brush

broche ['brotʃe] *nm* brooch

broma ['broma] *nf* joke; **en ~** in fun, as a joke; **~ pesada** practical joke; **bromear** *vi* to joke

bromista [bro'mista] *adj* fond of joking ♦ *nm/f* joker, wag

bronca ['broŋka] *nf* row; **echar una ~ a uno** to tick sb off

bronce ['bronθe] *nm* bronze; **~ado, a** *adj* bronze; (*por el sol*) tanned ♦ *nm* (sun)tan; (*TEC*) bronzing

bronceador [bronθea'ðor] *nm* suntan lotion

broncearse [bronθe'arse] *vr* to get a suntan

bronco, a ['broŋko, a] *adj* (*manera*) rude, surly; (*voz*) harsh

bronquio ['broŋkjo] *nm* (*ANAT*) bronchial tube

bronquitis [broŋ'kitis] *nf inv* bronchitis

brotar [bro'tar] *vi* (*BOT*) to sprout; (*aguas*) to gush (forth); (*MED*) to break out

brote ['brote] *nm* (*BOT*) shoot; (*MED, fig*) outbreak

bruces ['bruθes]: **de ~** *adv*: **caer** *o* **dar de**

~ to fall headlong, fall flat

bruja ['bruxa] *nf* witch; **brujería** *nf* witchcraft

brujo ['bruxo] *nm* wizard, magician

brújula ['bruxula] *nf* compass

bruma ['bruma] *nf* mist; **brumoso, a** *adj* misty

bruñir [bru'ɲir] *vt* to polish

brusco, a ['brusko, a] *adj* (*súbito*) sudden; (*áspero*) brusque

Bruselas [bru'selas] *n* Brussels

brutal [bru'tal] *adj* brutal

brutalidad [brutali'ðað] *nf* brutality

bruto, a ['bruto, a] *adj* (*idiota*) stupid; (*bestial*) brutish; (*peso*) gross; **en ~** raw, unworked

Bs.As. *abr* (= *Buenos Aires*) B.A.

bucal [bu'kal] *adj* oral; **por vía ~** orally

bucear [buθe'ar] *vi* to dive ♦ *vt* to explore; **buceo** *nm* diving

bucle ['bukle] *nm* curl

budismo [bu'ðismo] *nm* Buddhism

buen [bwen] *adj m ver* **bueno**

buenamente [bwena'mente] *adv* (*fácilmente*) easily; (*voluntariamente*) willingly

buenaventura [bwenaßen'tura] *nf* (*suerte*) good luck; (*adivinación*) fortune

---
PALABRA CLAVE
---

bueno, a ['bweno, a] *adj* (*antes de nmsg*: **buen**) **1** (*excelente etc*) good; **es un libro ~, es un buen libro** it's a good book; **hace ~, hace buen tiempo** the weather is fine, it is fine; **el ~ de Paco** good old Paco; **fue muy ~ conmigo** he was very nice *o* kind to me

2 (*apropiado*): **ser ~ para** to be good for; **creo que vamos por buen camino** I think we're on the right track

3 (*irónico*): **!e di un buen rapapolvo** I gave him a good *o* real ticking off; **¡buen conductor estás hecho!** some *o* a fine driver you are!; **¡estaría ~ que ...!** a fine thing it would be if ...!

4 (*atractivo, sabroso*): **está ~ este bizcocho** this sponge is delicious;

Carmen está muy buena Carmen is gorgeous
5 (*saludos*): **¡buen día!, ¡~s días!** (good) morning!; **¡buenas (tardes)!** (good) afternoon!; (*más tarde*) (good) evening!; **¡buenas noches!** good night!
6 (*otras locuciones*): **estar de buenas** to be in a good mood; **por las buenas o por las malas** by hook or by crook; **de buenas a primeras** all of a sudden
♦ *excl*: **¡~!** all right!; **~, ¿y qué?** well, so what?

Buenos Aires *nm* Buenos Aires
buey [bwei] *nm* ox
búfalo ['bufalo] *nm* buffalo
bufanda [bu'fanda] *nf* scarf
bufar [bu'far] *vi* to snort
bufete [bu'fete] *nm* (*despacho de abogado*) lawyer's office
buffer ['bufer] *nm* (*INFORM*) buffer
bufón [bu'fon] *nm* clown
buhardilla [buar'ðiʎa] *nf* attic
búho ['buo] *nm* owl; (*fig*) hermit, recluse
buhonero [buo'nero] *nm* pedlar
buitre ['bwitre] *nm* vulture
bujía [bu'xia] *nf* (*vela*) candle; (*ELEC*) candle (power); (*AUTO*) spark plug
bula ['bula] *nf* (*papal*) bull
bulbo ['bulßo] *nm* bulb
bulevar [bule'ßar] *nm* boulevard
Bulgaria [bul'ɣarja] *nf* Bulgaria; **búlgaro, a** *adj, nm/f* Bulgarian
bulla ['buʎa] *nf* (*ruido*) uproar; (*de gente*) crowd
bullicio [bu'ʎiθjo] *nm* (*ruido*) uproar; (*movimiento*) bustle
bullir [bu'ʎir] *vi* (*hervir*) to boil; (*burbujear*) to bubble
bulto ['bulto] *nm* (*paquete*) package; (*fardo*) bundle; (*tamaño*) size, bulkiness; (*MED*) swelling, lump; (*silueta*) vague shape
buñuelo [bu'ɲwelo] *nm* ≈ doughnut (*BRIT*), ≈ donut (*US*); (*fruta de sartén*) fritter
BUP [bup] *nm abr* (*ESP*: = *Bachillerato*

Unificado Polivalente) *secondary education and leaving certificate for 14–17 age group*
buque ['buke] *nm* ship, vessel
burbuja [bur'ßuxa] *nf* bubble; **burbujear** *vi* to bubble
burdel [bur'ðel] *nm* brothel
burdo, a ['burðo, a] *adj* coarse, rough
burgués, esa [bur'ɣes, esa] *adj* middle-class, bourgeois; **burguesía** *nf* middle class, bourgeoisie
burla ['burla] *nf* (*mofa*) gibe; (*broma*) joke; (*engaño*) trick
burladero [burla'ðero] *nm* (bullfighter's) refuge
burlar [bur'lar] *vt* (*engañar*) to deceive ♦ *vi* to joke; **~se** *vr* to joke; **~se de** to make fun of
burlesco, a [bur'lesko, a] *adj* burlesque
burlón, ona [bur'lon, ona] *adj* mocking
burocracia [buro'kraθja] *nf* civil service
burócrata [bu'rokrata] *nm/f* civil servant
burrada [bu'rraða] *nf*: **decir/soltar ~s** to talk nonsense; **hacer ~s** to act stupid; **una ~** (*mucho*) a (hell of a) lot
burro, a ['burro, a] *nm/f* donkey/she-donkey; (*fig*) ass, idiot
bursátil [bur'satil] *adj* stock-exchange *cpd*
bus [bus] *nm* bus
busca ['buska] *nf* search, hunt ♦ *nm* (*TEL*) bleeper; **en ~ de** in search of
buscar [bus'kar] *vt* to look for, search for, seek ♦ *vi* to look, search, seek; **se busca secretaria** secretary wanted
busque *etc vb ver* **buscar**
búsqueda ['buskeða] *nf* = **busca** *nf*
busto ['busto] *nm* (*ANAT*, *ARTE*) bust
butaca [bu'taka] *nf* armchair; (*de cine, teatro*) stall, seat
butano [bu'tano] *nm* butane (gas)
buzo ['buθo] *nm* diver
buzón [bu'θon] *nm* (*en puerta*) letter box; (*en la calle*) pillar box

C, c

C. abr (= centígrado) C; (= compañía) Co.

c. abr (= capítulo) ch.

C/ abr (= calle) St

c.a. abr (= corriente alterna) AC

cabal [ka'βal] adj (exacto) exact; (correcto) right, proper; (acabado) finished, complete; **~es** nmpl: **estar en sus ~es** to be in one's right mind

cábalas ['kaβalas] nfpl: **hacer ~** to guess

cabalgar [kaβal'ɣar] vt, vi to ride

cabalgata [kaβal'ɣata] nf procession

caballa [ka'βaʎa] nf mackerel

caballeresco, a [kaβaʎe'resko, a] adj noble, chivalrous

caballería [kaβaʎe'ria] nf mount; (MIL) cavalry

caballeriza [kaβaʎe'riθa] nf stable; **caballerizo** nm groom, stableman

caballero [kaβa'ʎero] nm gentleman; (de la orden de caballería) knight; (trato directo) sir

caballerosidad [kaβaʎerosi'ðað] nf chivalry

caballete [kaβa'ʎete] nm (ARTE) easel; (TEC) trestle

caballito [kaβa'ʎito] nm (caballo pequeño) small horse, pony; **~s** nmpl (en verbena) roundabout, merry-go-round

caballo [ka'βaʎo] nm horse; (AJEDREZ) knight; (NAIPES) queen; **ir en ~** to ride; **~ de vapor** o **de fuerza** horsepower; **~ de carreras** racehorse

cabaña [ka'βaɲa] nf (casita) hut, cabin

cabaré [kaβa're] (pl **~s**) nm cabaret

cabaret [kaβa're] (pl **~s**) nm cabaret

cabecear [kaβeθe'ar] vt, vi to nod

cabecera [kaβe'θera] nf head; (IMPRENTA) headline

cabecilla [kaβe'θiʎa] nm ringleader

cabellera [kaβe'ʎera] nf (head of) hair; (de cometa) tail

cabello [ka'βeʎo] nm (tb: **~s**) hair

caber [ka'βer] vi (entrar) to fit, go; **caben**

3 más there's room for 3 more

cabestrillo [kaβes'triʎo] nm sling

cabestro [ka'βestro] nm halter

cabeza [ka'βeθa] nf head; (POL) chief, leader; **~ rapada** skinhead; **~da** nf (golpe) butt; **dar ~das** to nod off; **cabezón, ona** adj (vino) heady; (fam: persona) pig-headed

cabida [ka'βiða] nf space

cabildo [ka'βildo] nm (de iglesia) chapter; (POL) town council

cabina [ka'βina] nf cabin; (de camión) cab; **~ telefónica** telephone box (BRIT) o booth

cabizbajo, a [kaβiθ'βaxo, a] adj crestfallen, dejected

cable ['kaβle] nm cable

cabo ['kaβo] nm (de objeto) end, extremity; (MIL) corporal; (NAUT) rope, cable; (GEO) cape; **al ~ de 3 días** after 3 days

cabra ['kaβra] nf goat

cabré etc vb ver **caber**

cabrear [kaβre'ar] (fam) vt to bug; **~se** vr (enfadarse) to fly off the handle

cabrío, a [ka'βrio, a] adj goatish; **macho ~** (he-)goat, billy goat

cabriola [ka'βrjola] nf caper

cabritilla [kaβri'tiʎa] nf kid, kidskin

cabrito [ka'βrito] nm kid

cabrón [ka'βron] nm cuckold; (fam!) bastard (!)

caca ['kaka] (fam) nf pooh

cacahuete [kaka'wete] (ESP) nm peanut

cacao [ka'kao] nm cocoa; (BOT) cacao

cacarear [kakare'ar] vi (persona) to boast; (gallina) to crow

cacería [kaθe'ria] nf hunt

cacerola [kaθe'rola] nf pan, saucepan

cachalote [katʃa'lote] nm (ZOOL) sperm whale

cacharro [ka'tʃarro] nm earthenware pot; **~s** nmpl pots and pans

cachear [katʃe'ar] vt to search, frisk

cachemir [katʃe'mir] nm cashmere

cacheo [ka'tʃeo] nm searching, frisking

cachete [ka'tʃete] nm (ANAT) cheek; (bofetada) slap (in the face)

cachiporra [katʃiˈporra] nf truncheon
cachivache [katʃiˈβatʃe] nm (trasto) piece of junk; **~s** nmpl junk sg
cacho [ˈkatʃo] nm (small) bit; (AM: cuerno) horn
cachondeo [katʃonˈdeo] (fam) nm farce, joke
cachondo, a [kaˈtʃondo, a] adj (ZOOL) on heat; (fam: sexualmente) randy; (: gracioso) funny
cachorro, a [kaˈtʃorro, a] nm/f (perro) pup, puppy; (león) cub
cacique [kaˈθike] nm chief, local ruler; (POL) local party boss; **caciquismo** nm system of control by the local boss
caco [ˈkako] nm pickpocket
cacto [ˈkakto] nm cactus
cactus [ˈkaktus] nm inv cactus
cada [ˈkaða] adj inv each; (antes de número) every; **~ día** each day, every day; **~ dos días** every other day; **~ uno/a** each one, every one; **~ vez más/menos** more and more/less and less; **uno de ~ diez** one out of every ten
cadalso [kaˈðalso] nm scaffold
cadáver [kaˈðaβer] nm (dead) body, corpse
cadena [kaˈðena] nf chain; (TV) channel; **trabajo en ~** assembly line work; **~ perpetua** (JUR) life imprisonment
cadencia [kaˈðenθja] nf rhythm
cadera [kaˈðera] nf hip
cadete [kaˈðete] nm cadet
caducar [kaðuˈkar] vi to expire; **caduco, a** adj expired; (persona) very old
caer [kaˈer] vi to fall (down); **~se** vr to fall (down); **me cae bien/mal** I get on well with him/I can't stand him; **~ en la cuenta** to realize; **su cumpleaños cae en viernes** her birthday falls on a Friday
café [kaˈfe] (pl **~s**) nm (bebida, planta) coffee; (lugar) café ♦ adj (color) brown; **~ con leche** white coffee; **~ solo** black coffee
cafetera [kafeˈtera] nf coffee pot
cafetería [kafeteˈria] nf (gen) café
cafetero, a [kafeˈtero, a] adj coffee cpd;

ser muy ~ to be a coffee addict
cagar [kaˈvar] (fam!) vt to bungle, mess up ♦ vi to have a shit (!)
caída [kaˈiða] nf fall; (declive) slope; (disminución) fall, drop
caído, a [kaˈiðo, a] adj drooping
caiga etc vb ver **caer**
caimán [kaiˈman] nm alligator
caja [ˈkaxa] nf box; (para reloj) case; (de ascensor) shaft; (COM) cashbox; (donde se hacen los pagos) cashdesk; (: en supermercado) checkout, till; **~ de ahorros** savings bank; **~ de cambios** gearbox; **~ fuerte, ~ de caudales** safe, strongbox
cajero, a [kaˈxero, a] nm/f cashier; **~ automático** cash dispenser
cajetilla [kaxeˈtiʎa] nf (de cigarrillos) packet
cajón [kaˈxon] nm big box; (de mueble) drawer
cal [kal] nf lime
cala [ˈkala] nf (GEO) cove, inlet; (de barco) hold
calabacín [kalaβaˈθin] nm (BOT) baby marrow; (: más pequeño) courgette (BRIT), zucchini (US)
calabaza [kalaˈβaθa] nf (BOT) pumpkin
calabozo [kalaˈβoθo] nm (cárcel) prison; (celda) cell
calada [kaˈlaða] nf (de cigarrillo) puff
calado, a [kaˈlaðo, a] adj (prenda) lace cpd ♦ nm (NAUT) draught
calamar [kalaˈmar] nm squid no pl
calambre [kaˈlambre] nm (tb: **~s**) cramp
calamidad [kalamiˈðað] nf calamity, disaster
calar [kaˈlar] vt to soak, drench; (penetrar) to pierce, penetrate; (comprender) to see through; (vela) to lower; **~se** vr (AUTO) to stall; **~se las gafas** to stick one's glasses on
calavera [kalaˈβera] nf skull
calcar [kalˈkar] vt (reproducir) to trace; (imitar) to copy
calcetín [kalθeˈtin] nm sock
calcinar [kalθiˈnar] vt to burn, blacken

calcio ['kalθjo] *nm* calcium
calcomanía [kalkoma'nia] *nf* transfer
calculador, a [kalkula'ðor, a] *adj* (*persona*) calculating
calculadora [kalkula'ðora] *nf* calculator
calcular [kalku'lar] *vt* (*MAT*) to calculate, compute; ~ **que** ... to reckon that ...; **cálculo** *nm* calculation
caldear [kalde'ar] *vt* to warm (up), heat (up)
caldera [kal'dera] *nf* boiler
calderilla [kalde'riʎa] *nf* (*moneda*) small change
caldero [kal'dero] *nm* small boiler
caldo ['kaldo] *nm* stock; (*consomé*) consommé
calefacción [kalefak'θjon] *nf* heating; ~ **central** central heating
calendario [kalen'darjo] *nm* calendar
calentador [kalenta'ðor] *nm* heater
calentamiento [kalenta'mjento] *nm* (*DEPORTE*) warm-up
calentar [kalen'tar] *vt* to heat (up); **~se** *vr* to heat up, warm up; (*fig: discusión etc*) to get heated
calentura [kalen'tura] *nf* (*MED*) fever, (high) temperature
calibrar [kali'βrar] *vt* to gauge, measure; **calibre** *nm* (*de cañón*) calibre, bore; (*diámetro*) diameter; (*fig*) calibre
calidad [kali'ðað] *nf* quality; **de ~** quality *cpd*; **en ~ de** in the capacity of, as
cálido, a ['kaliðo, a] *adj* hot; (*fig*) warm
caliente *etc* [ka'ljente] *vb ver* **calentar**
♦ *adj* hot; (*fig*) fiery; (*disputa*) heated; (*fam: cachondo*) randy
calificación [kalifika'θjon] *nf* qualification; (*de alumno*) grade, mark
calificar [kalifi'kar] *vt* to qualify; (*alumno*) to grade, mark; **~ de** to describe as
calima [ka'lima] *nf* (*cerca del mar*) mist
cáliz ['kaliθ] *nm* chalice
caliza [ka'liθa] *nf* limestone
calizo, a [ka'liθo, a] *adj* lime *cpd*
callado, a [ka'ʎaðo, a] *adj* quiet
callar [ka'ʎar] *vt* (*asunto delicado*) to keep quiet about, say nothing about; (*persona*,

opinión) to silence ♦ *vi* to keep quiet, be silent; **~se** *vr* to keep quiet, be silent; **¡cállate!** be quiet!, shut up!
calle ['kaʎe] *nf* street; (*DEPORTE*) lane; ~ **arriba/abajo** up/down the street; ~ **de un solo sentido** one-way street
calleja [ka'ʎexa] *nf* alley, narrow street; **callejear** *vi* to wander (about) the streets; **callejero, a** *adj* street *cpd* ♦ *nm* street map; **callejón** *nm* alley, passage; **callejón sin salida** cul-de-sac; **callejuela** *nf* side-street, alley
callista [ka'ʎista] *nm/f* chiropodist
callo ['kaʎo] *nm* callus; (*en el pie*) corn; **~s** *nmpl* (*CULIN*) tripe *sg*
calma ['kalma] *nf* calm
calmante [kal'mante] *nm* sedative, tranquillizer
calmar [kal'mar] *vt* to calm, calm down ♦ *vi* (*tempestad*) to abate; (*mente etc*) to become calm
calmoso, a [kal'moso, a] *adj* calm, quiet
calor [ka'lor] *nm* heat; (*agradable*) warmth; **hace ~** it's hot; **tener ~** to be hot
caloría [kalo'ria] *nf* calorie
calumnia [ka'lumnja] *nf* calumny, slander; **calumnioso, a** *adj* slanderous
caluroso, a [kalu'roso, a] *adj* hot; (*sin exceso*) warm; (*fig*) enthusiastic
calva ['kalβa] *nf* bald patch; (*en bosque*) clearing
calvario [kal'βarjo] *nm* stations *pl* of the cross
calvicie [kal'βiθje] *nf* baldness
calvo, a ['kalβo, a] *adj* bald; (*terreno*) bare, barren; (*tejido*) threadbare
calza ['kalθa] *nf* wedge, chock
calzada [kal'θaða] *nf* roadway, highway
calzado, a [kal'θaðo, a] *adj* shod ♦ *nm* footwear
calzador [kalθa'ðor] *nm* shoehorn
calzar [kal'θar] *vt* (*zapatos etc*) to wear; (*un mueble*) to put a wedge under; **~se** *vr*: **~se los zapatos** to put on one's shoes; **¿qué (número) calza?** what size do you take?
calzón [kal'θon] *nm* (*tb*: **calzones** *nmpl*)

shorts; (*AM: de hombre*) (under)pants; (: *de mujer*) panties

calzoncillos [kalθonˈθiʎos] *nmpl* underpants

cama [ˈkama] *nf* bed; **~ individual/de matrimonio** single/double bed

camafeo [kamaˈfeo] *nm* cameo

camaleón [kamaleˈon] *nm* chameleon

cámara [ˈkamara] *nf* chamber; (*habitación*) room; (*sala*) hall; (*CINE*) camera; (*fotográfica*) camera; **~ de aire** inner tube; **~ de comercio** chamber of commerce; **~ frigorífica** cold-storage room

camarada [kamaˈraða] *nm* comrade, companion

camarera [kamaˈrera] *nf* (*en restaurante*) waitress; (*en casa, hotel*) maid

camarero [kamaˈrero] *nm* waiter

camarilla [kamaˈriʎa] *nf* clique

camarón [kamaˈron] *nm* shrimp

camarote [kamaˈrote] *nm* cabin

cambiable [kamˈbjaßle] *adj* (*variable*) changeable, variable; (*intercambiable*) interchangeable

cambiante [kamˈbjante] *adj* variable

cambiar [kamˈbjar] *vt* to change; (*dinero*) to exchange ♦ *vi* to change; **~se** *vr* (*mudarse*) to move; (*de ropa*) to change; **~ de idea** to change one's mind; **~ de ropa** to change (one's clothes)

cambio [ˈkambjo] *nm* change; (*trueque*) exchange; (*COM*) rate of exchange; (*oficina*) bureau de change; (*dinero menudo*) small change; **en ~** on the other hand; (*en lugar de*) instead; **~ de divisas** foreign exchange; **~ de velocidades** gear lever

camelar [kameˈlar] *vt* to sweet-talk

camello [kaˈmeʎo] *nm* camel; (*fam: traficante*) pusher

camerino [kameˈrino] *nm* dressing room

camilla [kaˈmiʎa] *nf* (*MED*) stretcher

caminante [kamiˈnante] *nm/f* traveller

caminar [kamiˈnar] *vi* (*marchar*) to walk, go ♦ *vt* (*recorrer*) to cover, travel

caminata [kamiˈnata] *nf* long walk; (*por el campo*) hike

camino [kaˈmino] *nm* way, road; (*sendero*) track; **a medio ~** halfway (there); **en el ~** on the way, en route; **~ de** on the way to; **~ particular** private road

---

Camino de Santiago

🛈 *The* **Camino de Santiago** *is a medieval pilgrim route stretching from the Pyrenees to Santiago de Compostela in north-west Spain, where tradition has it the body of the Apostle James is buried. Nowadays it is a popular tourist route as well as a religious one.*

---

camión [kaˈmjon] *nm* lorry (*BRIT*), truck (*US*); **~ cisterna** tanker; **camionero, a** *nm/f* lorry *o* truck driver

camioneta [kamjoˈneta] *nf* van, light truck

camisa [kaˈmisa] *nf* shirt; (*BOT*) skin; **~ de fuerza** straitjacket; **camisería** *nf* outfitter's (shop)

camiseta [kamiˈseta] *nf* (*prenda*) tee-shirt; (: *ropa interior*) vest; (*de deportista*) top

camisón [kamiˈson] *nm* nightdress, nightgown

camorra [kaˈmorra] *nf*: **buscar ~** to look for trouble

campamento [kampaˈmento] *nm* camp

campana [kamˈpana] *nf* bell; **~ de cristal** bell jar; **~da** *nf* peal; **~rio** *nm* belfry

campanilla [kampaˈniʎa] *nf* small bell

campaña [kamˈpaɲa] *nf* (*MIL, POL*) campaign

campechano, a [kampeˈtʃano, a] *adj* (*franco*) open

campeón, ona [kampeˈon, ona] *nm/f* champion; **campeonato** *nm* championship

campesino, a [kampeˈsino, a] *adj* country *cpd*, rural; (*gente*) peasant *cpd* ♦ *nm/f* countryman/woman; (*agricultor*) farmer

campestre [kamˈpestre] *adj* country *cpd*, rural

camping [ˈkampin] (*pl* **~s**) *nm* camping; (*lugar*) campsite; **ir de** *o* **hacer ~** to go

camping
campo ['kampo] *nm* (*fuera de la ciudad*)
country, countryside; (*AGR, ELEC*) field; (*de
fútbol*) pitch; (*de golf*) course; (*MIL*) camp;
~ **de batalla** battlefield; ~ **de deportes**
sports ground, playing field
camposanto [kampo'santo] *nm* cemetery
camuflaje [kamu'flaxe] *nm* camouflage
cana ['kana] *nf* white *o* grey hair; **tener ~s**
to be going grey
Canadá [kana'ða] *nm* Canada;
canadiense *adj, nm/f* Canadian ♦ *nf*
fur-lined jacket
canal [ka'nal] *nm* canal; (*GEO*) channel,
strait; (*de televisión*) channel; (*de tejado*)
gutter; ~ **de Panamá** Panama Canal;
~izar *vt* to channel
canalla [ka'naʎa] *nf* rabble, mob ♦ *nm*
swine
canalón [kana'lon] *nm* (*conducto vertical*)
drainpipe; (*del tejado*) gutter
canapé [kana'pe] (*pl* **~s**) *nm* sofa, settee;
(*CULIN*) canapé
Canarias [ka'narjas] *nfpl*: (**las Islas**) ~ the
Canary Islands, the Canaries
canario, a [ka'narjo, a] *adj, nm/f* (native)
of the Canary Isles ♦ *nm* (*ZOOL*) canary
canasta [ka'nasta] *nf* (round) basket;
canastilla *nf* small basket; (*de niño*)
layette
canasto [ka'nasto] *nm* large basket
cancela [kan'θela] *nf* gate
cancelación [kanθela'θjon] *nf*
cancellation
cancelar [kanθe'lar] *vt* to cancel; (*una
deuda*) to write off
cáncer ['kanθer] *nm* (*MED*) cancer;
(*ASTROLOGÍA*): **C~** Cancer
cancha ['kantʃa] *nf* (*de baloncesto, tenis
etc*) court; (*AM: de fútbol*) pitch
canciller [kanθi'ʎer] *nm* chancellor
canción [kan'θjon] *nf* song; ~ **de cuna**
lullaby; **cancionero** *nm* song book
candado [kan'daðo] *nm* padlock
candente [kan'dente] *adj* red-hot; (*fig:
tema*) burning
candidato, a [kandi'ðato, a] *nm/f*

candidate
candidez [kandi'ðeθ] *nf* (*sencillez*)
simplicity; (*simpleza*) naiveté; **cándido, a**
adj simple; naive
candil [kan'dil] *nm* oil lamp; **~ejas** *nfpl*
(*TEATRO*) footlights
candor [kan'dor] *nm* (*sinceridad*) frankness;
(*inocencia*) innocence
canela [ka'nela] *nf* cinnamon
canelones [kane'lones] *nmpl* cannelloni
cangrejo [kan'grexo] *nm* crab
canguro [kan'guro] *nm* kangaroo; **hacer
de ~** to babysit
caníbal [ka'nißal] *adj, nm/f* cannibal
canica [ka'nika] *nf* marble
canijo, a [ka'nixo, a] *adj* frail, sickly
canino, a [ka'nino, a] *adj* canine ♦ *nm*
canine (tooth)
canjear [kanxe'ar] *vt* to exchange
cano, a ['kano, a] *adj* grey-haired, white-
haired
canoa [ka'noa] *nf* canoe
canon ['kanon] *nm* canon; (*pensión*) rent;
(*COM*) tax
canónigo [ka'noniʝo] *nm* canon
canonizar [kanoni'θar] *vt* to canonize
canoso, a [ka'noso, a] *adj* grey-haired
cansado, a [kan'saðo, a] *adj* tired, weary;
(*tedioso*) tedious, boring
cansancio [kan'sanθjo] *nm* tiredness,
fatigue
cansar [kan'sar] *vt* (*fatigar*) to tire, tire
out; (*aburrir*) to bore; (*fastidiar*) to bother;
~se *vr* to tire, get tired; (*aburrirse*) to get
bored
cantábrico, a [kan'taßriko, a] *adj*
Cantabrian; **mar C~** Bay of Biscay
cantante [kan'tante] *adj* singing ♦ *nm/f*
singer
cantar [kan'tar] *vt* to sing ♦ *vi* to sing;
(*insecto*) to chirp ♦ *nm* (*acción*) singing;
(*canción*) song; (*poema*) poem
cántara ['kantara] *nf* large pitcher
cántaro ['kantaro] *nm* pitcher, jug; **llover
a ~s** to rain cats and dogs
cante ['kante] *nm*: ~ **jondo** flamenco
singing

cantera [kan'tera] *nf* quarry
cantidad [kanti'ðað] *nf* quantity, amount
cantimplora [kantim'plora] *nf* (*frasco*) water bottle, canteen
cantina [kan'tina] *nf* canteen; (*de estación*) buffet
canto ['kanto] *nm* singing; (*canción*) song; (*borde*) edge, rim; (*de un cuchillo*) back; ~ **rodado** boulder
cantor, a [kan'tor, a] *nm/f* singer
canturrear [kanturre'ar] *vi* to sing softly
canuto [ka'nuto] *nm* (*tubo*) small tube; (*fam: droga*) joint
caña ['kaɲa] *nf* (*BOT: tallo*) stem, stalk; (*carrizo*) reed; (*vaso*) tumbler; (*de cerveza*) glass of beer; (*ANAT*) shinbone; ~ **de azúcar** sugar cane; ~ **de pescar** fishing rod
cañada [ka'ɲaða] *nf* (*entre dos montañas*) gully, ravine; (*camino*) cattle track
cáñamo ['kaɲamo] *nm* hemp
cañería [kaɲe'ria] *nf* (*tubo*) pipe
caño ['kaɲo] *nm* (*tubo*) tube, pipe; (*de albañal*) sewer; (*MUS*) pipe; (*de fuente*) jet
cañón [ka'ɲon] *nm* (*MIL*) cannon; (*de fusil*) barrel; (*GEO*) canyon, gorge
caoba [ka'oβa] *nf* mahogany
caos ['kaos] *nm* chaos
cap. *abr* (= *capítulo*) ch.
capa ['kapa] *nf* cloak, cape; (*GEO*) layer, stratum; **so ~ de** under the pretext of; ~ **de ozono** ozone layer
capacidad [kapaθi'ðað] *nf* (*medida*) capacity; (*aptitud*) capacity, ability
capacitar [kapaθi'tar] *vt*: ~ **a algn para (hacer)** to enable sb to (do)
capar [ka'par] *vt* to castrate, geld
caparazón [kapara'θon] *nm* shell
capataz [kapa'taθ] *nm* foreman
capaz [ka'paθ] *adj* able, capable; (*amplio*) capacious, roomy
capcioso, a [kap'θjoso, a] *adj* wily, deceitful
capellán [kape'ʎan] *nm* chaplain; (*sacerdote*) priest
caperuza [kape'ruθa] *nf* hood
capicúa [kapi'kua] *adj inv* (*número, fecha*) reversible

capilla [ka'piʎa] *nf* chapel
capital [kapi'tal] *adj* capital ♦ *nm* (*COM*) capital ♦ *nf* (*ciudad*) capital; ~ **social** share *o* authorized capital
capitalismo [kapita'lismo] *nm* capitalism; **capitalista** *adj, nm/f* capitalist
capitán [kapi'tan] *nm* captain
capitanear [kapitane'ar] *vt* to captain
capitulación [kapitula'θjon] *nf* (*rendición*) capitulation, surrender; (*acuerdo*) agreement, pact; **capitulaciones (matrimoniales)** *nfpl* marriage contract *sg*
capitular [kapitu'lar] *vi* to make an agreement
capítulo [ka'pitulo] *nm* chapter
capó [ka'po] *nm* (*AUTO*) bonnet
capón [ka'pon] *nm* (*gallo*) capon
capota [ka'pota] *nf* (*de mujer*) bonnet; (*AUTO*) hood (*BRIT*), top (*US*)
capote [ka'pote] *nm* (*abrigo: de militar*) greatcoat; (: *de torero*) cloak
capricho [ka'pritʃo] *nm* whim, caprice; ~**so, a** *adj* capricious
Capricornio [kapri'kornjo] *nm* Capricorn
cápsula ['kapsula] *nf* capsule
captar [kap'tar] *vt* (*comprender*) to understand; (*RADIO*) to pick up; (*atención, apoyo*) to attract
captura [kap'tura] *nf* capture; (*JUR*) arrest; **capturar** *vt* to capture; to arrest
capucha [ka'putʃa] *nf* hood, cowl
capullo [ka'puʎo] *nm* (*BOT*) bud; (*ZOOL*) cocoon; (*fam*) idiot
caqui ['kaki] *nm* khaki
cara ['kara] *nf* (*ANAT, de moneda*) face; (*de disco*) side; (*descaro*) boldness; ~ **a** facing; **de** ~ opposite, facing; **dar la** ~ to face the consequences; **¿~ o cruz?** heads or tails?; **¡qué ~ (más dura)!** what a nerve!
carabina [kara'βina] *nf* carbine, rifle; (*persona*) chaperone
Caracas [ka'rakas] *n* Caracas
caracol [kara'kol] *nm* (*ZOOL*) snail; (*concha*) (sea) shell
carácter [ka'rakter] (*pl* **caracteres**) *nm*

character; **tener buen/mal ~** to be good natured/bad tempered
característica [karakte'ristika] *nf* characteristic
característico, a [karakte'ristiko, a] *adj* characteristic
caracterizar [karakteri'θar] *vt* to characterize, typify
caradura [kara'ðura] *nm/f*: **es un ~** he's got a nerve
carajillo [kara'xiʎo] *nm* coffee with a dash of brandy
carajo [ka'raxo] (*fam!*) *nm*: **¡~!** shit! (*!*)
caramba [ka'ramba] *excl* good gracious!
carámbano [ka'rambano] *nm* icicle
caramelo [kara'melo] *nm* (*dulce*) sweet; (*azúcar fundida*) caramel
caravana [kara'ßana] *nf* caravan; (*fig*) group; (*AUTO*) tailback
carbón [kar'ßon] *nm* coal; **papel ~** carbon paper; **carboncillo** *nm* (*ARTE*) charcoal; **carbonero, a** *nm/f* coal merchant; **carbonilla** [-'niʎa] *nf* coal dust
carbonizar [karßoni'θar] *vt* to carbonize; (*quemar*) to char
carbono [kar'ßono] *nm* carbon
carburador [karßura'ðor] *nm* carburettor
carburante [karßu'rante] *nm* (*para motor*) fuel
carcajada [karka'xaða] *nf* (loud) laugh, guffaw
cárcel ['karθel] *nf* prison, jail; (*TEC*) clamp; **carcelero, a** *adj* prison *cpd* ♦ *nm/f* warder
carcoma [kar'koma] *nf* woodworm
carcomer [karko'mer] *vt* to bore into, eat into; (*fig*) to undermine; **~se** *vr* to become worm-eaten; (*fig*) to decay
cardar [kar'ðar] *vt* (*pelo*) to backcomb
cardenal [karðe'nal] *nm* (*REL*) cardinal; (*MED*) bruise
cardíaco, a [kar'ðiako, a] *adj* cardiac, heart *cpd*
cardinal [karði'nal] *adj* cardinal
cardo ['karðo] *nm* thistle
carearse [kare'arse] *vr* to come face to face

carecer [kare'θer] *vi*: **~ de** to lack, be in need of
carencia [ka'renθja] *nf* lack; (*escasez*) shortage; (*MED*) deficiency
carente [ka'rente] *adj*: **~ de** lacking in, devoid of
carestía [kares'tia] *nf* (*escasez*) scarcity, shortage; (*COM*) high cost
careta [ka'reta] *nf* mask
carga ['karya] *nf* (*peso, ELEC*) load; (*de barco*) freight; (*MIL*) charge; (*responsabilidad*) duty, obligation
cargado, a [kar'yaðo, a] *adj* loaded; (*ELEC*) live; (*café, té*) strong; (*cielo*) overcast
cargamento [karya'mento] *nm* (*acción*) loading; (*mercancías*) load, cargo
cargar [kar'yar] *vt* (*barco, arma*) to load; (*ELEC*) to charge; (*COM: algo en cuenta*) to charge; (*INFORM*) to load ♦ *vi* (*MIL*) to charge; (*AUTO*) to load (up); **~ con** to pick up, carry away; (*peso, fig*) to shoulder, bear; **~se** (*fam*) *vr* (*estropear*) to break; (*matar*) to bump off
cargo ['karyo] *nm* (*puesto*) post, office; (*responsabilidad*) duty, obligation; (*JUR*) charge; **hacerse ~ de** to take charge of *o* responsibility for
carguero [kar'yero] *nm* freighter, cargo boat; (*avión*) freight plane
Caribe [ka'rißE] *nm*: **el ~** the Caribbean; **del ~** Caribbean
caribeño, a [kari'ßeɲo, a] *adj* Caribbean
caricatura [karika'tura] *nf* caricature
caricia [ka'riθja] *nf* caress
caridad [kari'ðað] *nf* charity
caries ['karjes] *nf inv* tooth decay
cariño [ka'riɲo] *nm* affection, love; (*caricia*) caress; (*en carta*) love ...; **tener ~ a** to be fond of; **~so, a** *adj* affectionate
carisma [ka'risma] *nm* charisma
caritativo, a [karita'tißo, a] *adj* charitable
cariz [ka'riθ] *nm*: **tener *o* tomar buen/mal ~** to look good/bad
carmesí [karme'si] *adj, nm* crimson
carmín [kar'min] *nm* lipstick
carnal [kar'nal] *adj* carnal; **primo ~** first cousin

carnaval [karna'βal] *nm* carnival

carnaval

ℹ️ **Carnaval** *is the traditional period of fun, feasting and partying which takes place in the three days before the start of Lent ("Cuaresma"). Although in decline during the Franco years the carnival has grown in popularity recently in Spain. Cádiz and Tenerife are particularly well-known for their flamboyant celebrations with fancy-dress parties, parades and firework displays being the order of the day.*

carne ['karne] *nf* flesh; (*CULIN*) meat; ~ **de cerdo/cordero/ternera/vaca** pork/lamb/veal/beef; ~ **de gallina** (*fig*): **se me pone la ~ de gallina sólo verlo** I get the creeps just seeing it

carné [kar'ne] (*pl* ~s) *nm*: ~ **de conducir** driving licence (*BRIT*), driver's license (*US*); ~ **de identidad** identity card

carnero [kar'nero] *nm* sheep, ram; (*carne*) mutton

carnet [kar'ne] (*pl* ~s) *nm* = **carné**

carnicería [karniθe'ria] *nf* butcher's (shop); (*fig: matanza*) carnage, slaughter

carnicero, a [karni'θero, a] *adj* carnivorous ♦ *nm/f* (*tb fig*) butcher; (*carnívoro*) carnivore

carnívoro, a [kar'niβoro, a] *adj* carnivorous

carnoso, a [kar'noso, a] *adj* beefy, fat

caro, a ['karo, a] *adj* dear; (*COM*) dear, expensive ♦ *adv* dear, dearly

carpa ['karpa] *nf* (*pez*) carp; (*de circo*) big top; (*AM: de camping*) tent

carpeta [kar'peta] *nf* folder, file

carpintería [karpinte'ria] *nf* carpentry, joinery; **carpintero** *nm* carpenter

carraspear [karraspe'ar] *vi* to clear one's throat

carraspera [karras'pera] *nf* hoarseness

carrera [ka'rrera] *nf* (*acción*) run(ning); (*espacio recorrido*) run; (*competición*) race; (*trayecto*) course; (*profesión*) career; (*ESCOL*) course

carreta [ka'rreta] *nf* wagon, cart

carrete [ka'rrete] *nm* reel, spool; (*TEC*) coil

carretera [karre'tera] *nf* (main) road, highway; ~ **de circunvalación** ring road; ~ **nacional** ≈ A road (*BRIT*), ≈ state highway (*US*)

carretilla [karre'tiʎa] *nf* trolley; (*AGR*) (wheel)barrow

carril [ka'rril] *nm* furrow; (*de autopista*) lane; (*FERRO*) rail

carrillo [ka'rriʎo] *nm* (*ANAT*) cheek; (*TEC*) pulley

carrito [ka'rrito] *nm* trolley

carro ['karro] *nm* cart, wagon; (*MIL*) tank; (*AM: coche*) car

carrocería [karroθe'ria] *nf* bodywork, coachwork

carroña [ka'rroɲa] *nf* carrion *no pl*

carroza [ka'rroθa] *nf* (*carruaje*) coach

carrusel [karru'sel] *nm* merry-go-round, roundabout

carta ['karta] *nf* letter; (*CULIN*) menu; (*naipe*) card; (*mapa*) map; (*JUR*) document; ~ **de ajuste** (*TV*) test card; ~ **de crédito** credit card; ~ **certificada** registered letter; ~ **marítima** chart; ~ **verde** (*AUTO*) green card

cartabón [karta'βon] *nm* set square

cartel [kar'tel] *nm* (*anuncio*) poster, placard; (*ESCOL*) wall chart; (*COM*) cartel; ~**era** *nf* hoarding, billboard; (*en periódico etc*) entertainments guide; **"en ~era"** "showing"

cartera [kar'tera] *nf* (*de bolsillo*) wallet; (*de colegial, cobrador*) satchel; (*de señora*) handbag; (*para documentos*) briefcase; (*COM*) portfolio; **ocupa la ~ de Agricultura** she is Minister of Agriculture

carterista [karte'rista] *nm/f* pickpocket

cartero [kar'tero] *nm* postman

cartilla [kar'tiʎa] *nf* primer, first reading book; ~ **de ahorros** savings book

cartón [kar'ton] *nm* cardboard; ~ **piedra** papier-mâché

cartucho [kar'tutʃo] *nm* (*MIL*) cartridge

cartulina [kartu'lina] *nf* card

casa ['kasa] *nf* house; (*hogar*) home; (*COM*) firm, company; **en ~** at home; **~ consistorial** town hall; **~ de huéspedes** boarding house; **~ de socorro** first aid post

casado, a [ka'saðo, a] *adj* married ♦ *nm/f* married man/woman

casamiento [kasa'mjento] *nm* marriage, wedding

casar [ka'sar] *vt* to marry; (*JUR*) to quash, annul; **~se** *vr* to marry, get married

cascabel [kaska'ßel] *nm* (small) bell

cascada [kas'kaða] *nf* waterfall

cascanueces [kaska'nweθes] *nm inv* nutcrackers *pl*

cascar [kas'kar] *vt* to crack, split, break (open); **~se** *vr* to crack, split, break (open)

cáscara ['kaskara] *nf* (*de huevo, fruta seca*) shell; (*de fruta*) skin; (*de limón*) peel

casco ['kasko] *nm* (*de bombero, soldado*) helmet; (*NAUT: de barco*) hull; (*ZOOL: de caballo*) hoof; (*botella*) empty bottle; (*de ciudad*): **el ~ antiguo** the old part; **el ~ urbano** the town centre; **los ~s azules** the UN peace-keeping force, the blue berets

cascote [kas'kote] *nm* rubble

caserío [kase'rio] *nm* hamlet; (*casa*) country house

casero, a [ka'sero, a] *adj* (*pan etc*) home-made ♦ *nm/f* (*propietario*) landlord/lady; **ser muy ~** to be home-loving; **"comida casera"** "home cooking"

caseta [ka'seta] *nf* hut; (*para bañista*) cubicle; (*de feria*) stall

casete [ka'sete] *nm o f* cassette

casi ['kasi] *adv* almost, nearly; **~ nada** hardly anything; **~ nunca** hardly ever, almost never; **~ te caes** you almost fell

casilla [ka'siʎa] *nf* (*casita*) hut, cabin; (*AJEDREZ*) square; (*para cartas*) pigeonhole; **casillero** *nm* (*para cartas*) pigeonholes *pl*

casino [ka'sino] *nm* club; (*de juego*) casino

caso ['kaso] *nm* case; **en ~ de ...** in case of ...; **en ~ de que ...** in case ...; **el ~ es**

que the fact is that; **en ese ~** in that case; **hacer ~ a** to pay attention to; **hacer** *o* **venir al ~** to be relevant

caspa ['kaspa] *nf* dandruff

cassette [ka'sete] *nm o f* = **casete**

casta ['kasta] *nf* caste; (*raza*) breed; (*linaje*) lineage

castaña [kas'taɲa] *nf* chestnut

castañetear [kastaɲete'ar] *vi* (*dientes*) to chatter

castaño, a [kas'taɲo, a] *adj* chestnut (-coloured), brown ♦ *nm* chestnut tree

castañuelas [kasta'ɲwelas] *nfpl* castanets

castellano, a [kaste'ʎano, a] *adj, nm/f* Castilian ♦ *nm* (*LING*) Castilian, Spanish

castidad [kasti'ðað] *nf* chastity, purity

castigar [kasti'var] *vt* to punish; (*DEPORTE*) to penalize; **castigo** *nm* punishment; (*DEPORTE*) penalty

Castilla [kas'tiʎa] *nf* Castille

castillo [kas'tiʎo] *nm* castle

castizo, a [kas'tiθo, a] *adj* (*LING*) pure

casto, a ['kasto, a] *adj* chaste, pure

castor [kas'tor] *nm* beaver

castrar [kas'trar] *vt* to castrate

castrense [kas'trense] *adj* (*disciplina, vida*) military

casual [ka'swal] *adj* chance, accidental; **~idad** *nf* chance, accident; (*combinación de circunstancias*) coincidence; **¡qué ~idad!** what a coincidence!

cataclismo [kata'klismo] *nm* cataclysm

catador, a [kata'ðor, a] *nm* wine taster

catalán, ana [kata'lan, ana] *adj, nm/f* Catalan ♦ *nm* (*LING*) Catalan

catalizador [kataliθa'ðor] *nm* catalyst; (*AUT*) catalytic convertor

catalogar [katalo'var] *vt* to catalogue; **~ a algn (de)** (*fig*) to categorize sb (as)

catálogo [ka'talovo] *nm* catalogue

Cataluña [kata'luɲa] *nf* Catalonia

catar [ka'tar] *vt* to taste, sample

catarata [kata'rata] *nf* (*GEO*) waterfall; (*MED*) cataract

catarro [ka'tarro] *nm* catarrh; (*constipado*) cold

catástrofe [ka'tastrofe] *nf* catastrophe

catear [kate'ar] (*fam*) *vt* (*examen, alumno*) to fail

cátedra ['kateðra] *nf* (*UNIV*) chair, professorship

catedral [kate'ðral] *nf* cathedral

catedrático, a [kate'ðratiko, a] *nm/f* professor

categoría [katexo'ria] *nf* category; (*rango*) rank, standing; (*calidad*) quality; **de ~** (*hotel*) top-class

categórico, a [kate'xoriko, a] *adj* categorical

cateto, a ['kateto, a] (*pey*) *nm/f* peasant

catolicismo [katoli'θismo] *nm* Catholicism

católico, a [ka'toliko, a] *adj, nm/f* Catholic

catorce [ka'torθe] *num* fourteen

cauce ['kauθe] *nm* (*de río*) riverbed; (*fig*) channel

caucho ['kautʃo] *nm* rubber; (*AM: llanta*) tyre

caución [kau'θjon] *nf* bail; **caucionar** *vt* (*JUR*) to bail, go bail for

caudal [kau'ðal] *nm* (*de río*) volume, flow; (*fortuna*) wealth; (*abundancia*) abundance; **~oso, a** *adj* (*río*) large

caudillo [kau'ðiʎo] *nm* leader, chief

causa ['kausa] *nf* cause; (*razón*) reason; (*JUR*) lawsuit, case; **a ~ de** because of

causar [kau'sar] *vt* to cause

cautela [kau'tela] *nf* caution, cautiousness; **cauteloso, a** *adj* cautious, wary

cautivar [kauti'βar] *vt* to capture; (*atraer*) to captivate

cautiverio [kauti'βerjo] *nm* captivity

cautividad [kautiβi'ðað] *nf* = **cautiverio**

cautivo, a [kau'tiβo, a] *adj, nm/f* captive

cauto, a ['kauto, a] *adj* cautious, careful

cava ['kaβa] *nm* champagne-type wine

cavar [ka'βar] *vt* to dig

caverna [ka'βerna] *nf* cave, cavern

cavidad [kaβi'ðað] *nf* cavity

cavilar [kaβi'lar] *vt* to ponder

cayado [ka'jaðo] *nm* (*de pastor*) crook; (*de obispo*) crozier

cayendo *etc vb ver* **caer**

caza ['kaθa] *nf* (*acción: gen*) hunting;

(: *con fusil*) shooting; (*una ~*) hunt, chase; (*animales*) game ♦ *nm* (*AVIAT*) fighter

cazador, a [kaθa'ðor, a] *nm/f* hunter; **cazadora** *nf* jacket

cazar [ka'θar] *vt* to hunt; (*perseguir*) to chase; (*prender*) to catch

cazo ['kaθo] *nm* saucepan

cazuela [ka'θwela] *nf* (*vasija*) pan; (*guisado*) casserole

CD *abbr* (= *compact disc*) CD

CD-ROM *abbr m* CD-ROM

CE *nf abr* (= *Comunidad Europea*) EC

cebada [θe'βaða] *nf* barley

cebar [θe'βar] *vt* (*animal*) to fatten (up); (*anzuelo*) to bait; (*MIL, TEC*) to prime

cebo ['θeβo] *nm* (*para animales*) feed, food; (*para peces, fig*) bait; (*de arma*) charge

cebolla [θe'βoʎa] *nf* onion; **cebolleta** *nf* spring onion; **cebollín** *nm* spring onion

cebra ['θeβra] *nf* zebra

cecear [θeθe'ar] *vi* to lisp; **ceceo** *nm* lisp

ceder [θe'ðer] *vt* to hand over, give up, part with ♦ *vi* (*renunciar*) to give in, yield; (*disminuir*) to diminish, decline; (*romperse*) to give way

cedro ['θeðro] *nm* cedar

cédula ['θeðula] *nf* certificate, document

cegar [θe'xar] *vt* to blind; (*tubería etc*) to block up, stop up ♦ *vi* to go blind; **~se** *vr*: **~se (de)** to be blinded (by)

ceguera [θe'xera] *nf* blindness

CEI *abbr* (= *Confederación de Estados Independientes*) CIS

ceja ['θexa] *nf* eyebrow

cejar [θe'xar] *vi* (*fig*) to back down

celador, a [θela'ðor, a] *nm/f* (*de edificio*) watchman; (*de museo etc*) attendant

celda ['θelda] *nf* cell

celebración [θeleβra'θjon] *nf* celebration

celebrar [θele'βrar] *vt* to celebrate; (*alabar*) to praise ♦ *vi* to be glad; **~se** *vr* to occur, take place

célebre ['θeleβre] *adj* famous

celebridad [θeleβri'ðað] *nf* fame; (*persona*) celebrity

celeste [θe'leste] *adj* (*azul*) sky-blue

celestial [θeles'tjal] *adj* celestial, heavenly
celibato [θeli'ßato] *nm* celibacy
célibe ['θeliße] *adj, nm/f* celibate
celo¹ ['θelo] *nm* zeal; (*REL*) fervour; (*ZOOL*): **en ~** on heat; **~s** *nmpl* jealousy *sg*; **tener ~s** to be jealous
celo² ℝ ['θelo] *nm* Sellotape ℝ
celofán [θelo'fan] *nm* cellophane
celoso, a [θe'loso, a] *adj* jealous; (*trabajador*) zealous
celta ['θelta] *adj* Celtic ♦ *nm/f* Celt
célula ['θelula] *nf* cell; **~ solar** solar cell
celulitis [θelu'litis] *nf* cellulite
celuloide [θelu'loiðe] *nm* celluloid
cementerio [θemen'terjo] *nm* cemetery, graveyard
cemento [θe'mento] *nm* cement; (*hormigón*) concrete; (*AM*: *cola*) glue
cena ['θena] *nf* evening meal, dinner
cenagal [θena'xal] *nm* bog, quagmire
cenar [θe'nar] *vt* to have for dinner ♦ *vi* to have dinner
cenicero [θeni'θero] *nm* ashtray
cenit [θe'nit] *nm* zenith
ceniza [θe'niθa] *nf* ash, ashes *pl*
censo ['θenso] *nm* census; **~ electoral** electoral roll
censura [θen'sura] *nf* (*POL*) censorship
censurar [θensu'rar] *vt* (*idea*) to censure; (*cortar: película*) to censor
centella [θen'teʎa] *nf* spark
centellear [θenteʎe'ar] *vi* (*metal*) to gleam; (*estrella*) to twinkle; (*fig*) to sparkle
centenar [θente'nar] *nm* hundred
centenario, a [θente'narjo, a] *adj* centenary; hundred-year-old ♦ *nm* centenary
centeno [θen'teno] *nm* (*BOT*) rye
centésimo, a [θen'tesimo, a] *adj* hundredth
centígrado [θen'tixraðo] *adj* centigrade
centímetro [θen'timetro] *nm* centimetre (*BRIT*), centimeter (*US*)
céntimo ['θentimo] *nm* cent
centinela [θenti'nela] *nm* sentry, guard
centollo [θen'toʎo] *nm* spider crab
central [θen'tral] *adj* central ♦ *nf* head

office; (*TEC*) plant; (*TEL*) exchange; **~ eléctrica** power station; **~ nuclear** nuclear power station; **~ telefónica** telephone exchange
centralita [θentra'lita] *nf* switchboard
centralizar [θentrali'θar] *vt* to centralize
centrar [θen'trar] *vt* to centre
céntrico, a ['θentriko, a] *adj* central
centrifugar [θentrifu'xar] *vt* to spin-dry
centrista [θen'trista] *adj* centre *cpd*
centro ['θentro] *nm* centre; **~ comercial** shopping centre; **~ juvenil** youth club
centroamericano, a [θentroameri'kano, a] *adj, nm/f* Central American
ceñido, a [θe'niðo, a] *adj* (*chaqueta, pantalón*) tight(-fitting)
ceñir [θe'nir] *vt* (*rodear*) to encircle, surround; (*ajustar*) to fit (tightly)
ceño ['θeno] *nm* frown, scowl; **fruncir el ~** to frown, knit one's brow
CEOE *nf abr* (*ESP*: = *Confederación Española de Organizaciones Empresariales*) ≈ CBI (*BRIT*), employers' organization
cepillar [θepi'ʎar] *vt* to brush; (*madera*) to plane (down)
cepillo [θe'piʎo] *nm* brush; (*para madera*) plane; **~ de dientes** toothbrush
cera ['θera] *nf* wax
cerámica [θe'ramika] *nf* pottery; (*arte*) ceramics
cerca ['θerka] *nf* fence ♦ *adv* near, nearby, close; **~ de** near, close to
cercanías [θerka'nias] *nfpl* (*afueras*) outskirts, suburbs
cercano, a [θer'kano, a] *adj* close, near
cercar [θer'kar] *vt* to fence in; (*rodear*) to surround
cerciorar [θerθjo'rar] *vt* (*asegurar*) to assure; **~se** *vr* (*asegurarse*) to make sure
cerco ['θerko] *nm* (*AGR*) enclosure; (*AM*) fence; (*MIL*) siege
cerdo, a ['θerðo, a] *nm/f* pig/sow
cereal [θere'al] *nm* cereal; **~es** *nmpl* cereals, grain *sg*
cerebro [θe'reßro] *nm* brain; (*fig*) brains *pl*
ceremonia [θere'monja] *nf* ceremony; **ceremonial** *adj, nm* ceremonial;

ceremonioso, a *adj* ceremonious

cereza [θeˈreθa] *nf* cherry

cerilla [θeˈriʎa] *nf* (*fósforo*) match

cernerse [θerˈnerse] *vr* to hover

cero [ˈθero] *nm* nothing, zero

cerrado, a [θeˈrraðo, a] *adj* closed, shut; (*con llave*) locked; (*tiempo*) cloudy, overcast; (*curva*) sharp; (*acento*) thick, broad

cerradura [θerraˈðura] *nf* (*acción*) closing; (*mecanismo*) lock

cerrajero [θerraˈxero] *nm* locksmith

cerrar [θeˈrrar] *vt* to close, shut; (*paso, carretera*) to close; (*grifo*) to turn off; (*cuenta, negocio*) to close ♦ *vi* to close, shut; (*la noche*) to come down; **~se** *vr* to close, shut; **~ con llave** to lock; **~ un trato** to strike a bargain

cerro [ˈθerro] *nm* hill

cerrojo [θeˈrroxo] *nm* (*herramienta*) bolt; (*de puerta*) latch

certamen [θerˈtamen] *nm* competition, contest

certero, a [θerˈtero, a] *adj* (*gen*) accurate

certeza [θerˈteθa] *nf* certainty

certidumbre [θertiˈðumßre] *nf* = **certeza**

certificado [θertifiˈkaðo] *nm* certificate

certificar [θertifiˈkar] *vt* (*asegurar, atestar*) to certify

cervatillo [θerßaˈtiʎo] *nm* fawn

cervecería [θerßeθeˈria] *nf* (*fábrica*) brewery; (*bar*) public house, pub

cerveza [θerˈßeθa] *nf* beer

cesante [θeˈsante] *adj* redundant

cesar [θeˈsar] *vi* to cease, stop ♦ *vt* (*funcionario*) to remove from office

cesárea [θeˈsarea] *nf* (*MED*) Caesarean operation *o* section

cese [ˈθese] *nm* (*de trabajo*) dismissal; (*de pago*) suspension

césped [ˈθespeð] *nm* grass, lawn

cesta [ˈθesta] *nf* basket

cesto [ˈθesto] *nm* (large) basket, hamper

cetro [ˈθetro] *nm* sceptre

cfr *abr* (= *confróntese*) cf.

chabacano, a [tʃaßaˈkano, a] *adj* vulgar, coarse

chabola [tʃaˈßola] *nf* shack; **barrio de ~s** shanty town *sg*

chacal [tʃaˈkal] *nm* jackal

chacha [ˈtʃatʃa] (*fam*) *nf* maid

cháchara [ˈtʃatʃara] *nf* chatter; **estar de ~** to chatter away

chacra [ˈtʃakra] (*AM*) *nf* smallholding

chafar [tʃaˈfar] *vt* (*aplastar*) to crush; (*plan etc*) to ruin

chal [tʃal] *nm* shawl

chalado, a [tʃaˈlado, a] (*fam*) *adj* crazy

chalé [tʃaˈle] (*pl* **~s**) *nm* villa; ≈ detached house

chaleco [tʃaˈleko] *nm* waistcoat, vest (*US*); **~ salvavidas** life jacket

chalet [tʃaˈle] (*pl* **~s**) *nm* = **chalé**

champán [tʃamˈpan] *nm* champagne

champaña [tʃamˈpaɲa] *nm* = **champán**

champiñón [tʃampiˈɲon] *nm* mushroom

champú [tʃamˈpu] (*pl* **champúes, champús**) *nm* shampoo

chamuscar [tʃamusˈkar] *vt* to scorch, sear, singe

chance [ˈtʃanθe] (*AM*) *nm* chance

chancho, a [ˈtʃantʃo, a] (*AM*) *nm/f* pig

chanchullo [tʃanˈtʃuʎo] (*fam*) *nm* fiddle

chandal [tʃanˈdal] *nm* tracksuit

chantaje [tʃanˈtaxe] *nm* blackmail

chapa [ˈtʃapa] *nf* (*de metal*) plate, sheet; (*de madera*) board, panel; (*AM: AUTO*) number (*BRIT*) *o* license (*US*) plate; **~do, a** *adj*: **~do en oro** gold-plated

chaparrón [tʃapaˈrron] *nm* downpour, cloudburst

chapotear [tʃapoteˈar] *vi* to splash about

chapurrear [tʃapurreˈar] *vt* (*idioma*) to speak badly

chapuza [tʃaˈpuθa] *nf* botched job

chapuzón [tʃapuˈθon] *nm*: **darse un ~** to go for a dip

chaqueta [tʃaˈketa] *nf* jacket

chaquetón [tʃakeˈton] *nm* long jacket

charca [ˈtʃarka] *nf* pond, pool

charco [ˈtʃarko] *nm* pool, puddle

charcutería [tʃarkuteˈria] *nf* (*tienda*) *shop selling chiefly pork meat products*; (*productos*) cooked pork meats *pl*

charla ['tʃarla] nf talk, chat; (conferencia) lecture

charlar [tʃar'lar] vi to talk, chat

charlatán, ana [tʃarla'tan, ana] nm/f (hablador) chatterbox; (estafador) trickster

charol [tʃa'rol] nm varnish; (cuero) patent leather

chascarrillo [tʃaska'rriʎo] (fam) nm funny story

chasco ['tʃasko] nm (desengaño) disappointment

chasis ['tʃasis] nm inv chassis

chasquear [tʃaske'ar] vt (látigo) to crack; (lengua) to click; **chasquido** nm crack; click

chatarra [tʃa'tarra] nf scrap (metal)

chato, a ['tʃato, a] adj flat; (nariz) snub

chaval, a [tʃa'ßal, a] nm/f kid, lad/lass

checo, a ['tʃeko, a] adj, nm/f Czech ♦ nm (LING) Czech

checo(e)slovaco, a [tʃeko(e)slo'ßako, a] adj, nm/f Czech, Czechoslovak

Checo(e)slovaquia [tʃeko(e)slo'ßakja] nf Czechoslovakia

cheque ['tʃeke] nm cheque (BRIT), check (US); **~ de viajero** traveller's cheque (BRIT), traveler's check (US)

chequeo [tʃe'keo] nm (MED) check-up; (AUTO) service

chequera [tʃe'kera] (AM) nf chequebook (BRIT), checkbook (US)

chicano, a [tʃi'kano, a] adj, nm/f chicano

chícharo ['tʃitʃaro] (AM) nm pea

chichón [tʃi'tʃon] nm bump, lump

chicle ['tʃikle] nm chewing gum

chico, a ['tʃiko, a] adj small, little ♦ nm/f (niño) child; (muchacho) boy/girl

chiflado, a [tʃi'flaðo, a] adj crazy

chiflar [tʃi'flar] vt to hiss, boo

Chile ['tʃile] nm Chile; **chileno, a** adj, nm/f Chilean

chile ['tʃile] nm chilli pepper

chillar [tʃi'ʎar] vi (persona) to yell, scream; (animal salvaje) to howl; (cerdo) to squeal

chillido [tʃi'ʎiðo] nm (de persona) yell, scream; (de animal) howl

chillón, ona [tʃi'ʎon, ona] adj (niño) noisy; (color) loud, gaudy

chimenea [tʃime'nea] nf chimney; (hogar) fireplace

China ['tʃina] nf: (la) ~ China

chinche ['tʃintʃe] nf (insecto) (bed)bug; (TEC) drawing pin (BRIT), thumbtack (US) ♦ nm/f nuisance, pest

chincheta [tʃin'tʃeta] nf drawing pin (BRIT), thumbtack (US)

chino, a ['tʃino, a] adj, nm/f Chinese ♦ nm (LING) Chinese

chipirón [tʃipi'ron] nm (ZOOL, CULIN) squid

Chipre ['tʃipre] nf Cyprus; **chipriota** adj, nm/f Cypriot

chiquillo, a [tʃi'kiʎo, a] nm/f (fam) kid

chirimoya [tʃiri'moja] nf custard apple

chiringuito [tʃirin'ʋito] nm small open-air bar

chiripa [tʃi'ripa] nf fluke

chirriar [tʃi'rrjar] vi to creak, squeak

chirrido [tʃi'rriðo] nm creak(ing), squeak(ing)

chis [tʃis] excl sh!

chisme ['tʃisme] nm (habladurías) piece of gossip; (fam: objeto) thingummyjig

chismoso, a [tʃis'moso, a] adj gossiping ♦ nm/f gossip

chispa ['tʃispa] nf spark; (fig) sparkle; (ingenio) wit; (fam) drunkenness

chispear [tʃispe'ar] vi (lloviznar) to drizzle

chisporrotear [tʃisporrote'ar] vi (fuego) to throw out sparks; (leña) to crackle; (aceite) to hiss, splutter

chiste ['tʃiste] nm joke, funny story

chistoso, a [tʃis'toso, a] adj funny, amusing

chivo, a ['tʃißo, a] nm/f (billy-/nanny-) goat; **~ expiatorio** scapegoat

chocante [tʃo'kante] adj startling; (extraño) odd; (ofensivo) shocking

chocar [tʃo'kar] vi (coches etc) to collide, crash ♦ vt to shock; (sorprender) to startle; **~ con** to collide with; (fig) to run into, run up against; **¡chócala!** (fam) put it there!

chochear [tʃotʃe'ar] vi to dodder, be senile

chocho, a ['tʃotʃo, a] *adj* doddering, senile; (*fig*) soft, doting

chocolate [tʃoko'late] *adj, nm* chocolate; **chocolatina** *nf* chocolate

chofer [tʃo'fer] *nm* = **chófer**

chófer ['tʃofer] *nm* driver

chollo ['tʃoʎo] (*fam*) *nm* bargain, snip

choque *etc* ['tʃoke] *vb ver* **chocar** ♦ *nm* (*impacto*) impact; (*golpe*) jolt; (*AUTO*) crash; (*fig*) conflict; ~ **frontal** head-on collision

chorizo [tʃo'riθo] *nm* hard pork sausage, (type of) salami

chorrada [tʃo'rraða] (*fam*) *nf*: **¡es una ~!** that's crap! (*!*); **decir ~s** to talk crap (*!*)

chorrear [tʃorre'ar] *vi* to gush (out), spout (out); (*gotear*) to drip, trickle

chorro ['tʃorro] *nm* jet; (*fig*) stream

choza ['tʃoθa] *nf* hut, shack

chubasco [tʃu'βasko] *nm* squall

chubasquero [tʃuβas'kero] *nm* lightweight raincoat

chuchería [tʃutʃe'ria] *nf* trinket

chuleta [tʃu'leta] *nf* chop, cutlet

chulo ['tʃulo] *nm* (*de prostituta*) pimp

chupar [tʃu'par] *vt* to suck; (*absorber*) to absorb; **~se** *vr* to grow thin

chupete [tʃu'pete] *nm* dummy (*BRIT*), pacifier (*US*)

chupito [tʃu'pito] (*fam*) *nm* shot

churro ['tʃurro] *nm* (type of) fritter

chusma ['tʃusma] *nf* rabble, mob

chutar [tʃu'tar] *vi* to shoot (at goal)

Cía *abr* (= *compañía*) Co.

cianuro [θja'nuro] *nm* cyanide

cicatriz [θika'triθ] *nf* scar; **~arse** *vr* to heal (up), form a scar

ciclismo [θi'klismo] *nm* cycling

ciclista [θi'klista] *adj* cycle *cpd* ♦ *nm/f* cyclist

ciclo ['θiklo] *nm* cycle

ciclón [θi'klon] *nm* cyclone

cicloturismo [θiklotu'rismo] *nm*: **hacer ~** to go on a cycling holiday

ciego, a ['θjeɣo, a] *adj* blind ♦ *nm/f* blind man/woman

cielo ['θjelo] *nm* sky; (*REL*) heaven; **¡~s!** good heavens!

ciempiés [θjem'pjes] *nm inv* centipede

cien [θjen] *num ver* **ciento**

ciénaga ['θjenaɣa] *nf* marsh, swamp

ciencia ['θjenθja] *nf* science; **~s** *nfpl* (*ESCOL*) science *sg*; **~-ficción** *nf* science fiction

cieno ['θjeno] *nm* mud, mire

científico, a [θjen'tifiko, a] *adj* scientific ♦ *nm/f* scientist

ciento ['θjento] (*tb:* **cien**) *num* hundred; **pagar al 10 por ~** to pay at 10 per cent

cierre *etc* ['θjerre] *vb ver* **cerrar** ♦ *nm* closing, shutting; (*con llave*) locking; ~ **de cremallera** zip (fastener)

cierro *etc vb ver* **cerrar**

cierto, a ['θjerto, a] *adj* sure, certain; (*un tal*) a certain; (*correcto*) right, correct; ~ **hombre** a certain man; **ciertas personas** certain *o* some people; **sí, es ~** yes, that's correct

ciervo ['θjerβo] *nm* deer; (*macho*) stag

cierzo ['θjerθo] *nm* north wind

cifra ['θifra] *nf* number; (*secreta*) code

cifrar [θi'frar] *vt* to code, write in code

cigala [θi'ɣala] *nf* Norway lobster

cigarra [θi'ɣarra] *nf* cicada

cigarrillo [θiɣa'rriʎo] *nm* cigarette

cigarro [θi'ɣarro] *nm* cigarette; (*puro*) cigar

cigüeña [θi'ɣweɲa] *nf* stork

cilíndrico, a [θi'lindriko, a] *adj* cylindrical

cilindro [θi'lindro] *nm* cylinder

cima ['θima] *nf* (*de montaña*) top, peak; (*de árbol*) top; (*fig*) height

cimbrearse [θimbre'arse] *vr* to sway

cimentar [θimen'tar] *vt* to lay the foundations of; (*fig: fundar*) to found

cimiento [θi'mjento] *nm* foundation

cinc [θink] *nm* zinc

cincel [θin'θel] *nm* chisel; **~ar** *vt* to chisel

cinco ['θinko] *num* five

cincuenta [θin'kwenta] *num* fifty

cine ['θine] *nm* cinema

cineasta [θine'asta] *nm/f* film director

cinematográfico, a [θinemato'ɣrafiko, a] *adj* cine-, film *cpd*

cínico, a ['θiniko, a] *adj* cynical ♦ *nm/f* cynic

cinismo [θi'nismo] *nm* cynicism

cinta ['θinta] *nf* band, strip; (*de tela*) ribbon; (*película*) reel; (*de máquina de escribir*) ribbon; **~ adhesiva** sticky tape; **~ de vídeo** videotape; **~ magnetofónica** tape; **~ métrica** tape measure

cintura [θin'tura] *nf* waist

cinturón [θintu'ron] *nm* belt; **~ de seguridad** safety belt

ciprés [θi'pres] *nm* cypress (tree)

circo ['θirko] *nm* circus

circuito [θir'kwito] *nm* circuit

circulación [θirkula'θjon] *nf* circulation; (*AUTO*) traffic

circular [θirku'lar] *adj, nf* circular ♦ *vi, vt* to circulate ♦ *vi* (*AUTO*) to drive; **"circule por la derecha"** "keep (to the) right"

círculo ['θirkulo] *nm* circle; **~ vicioso** vicious circle

circuncidar [θirkunθi'dar] *vt* to circumcise

circundar [θirkun'dar] *vt* to surround

circunferencia [θirkunfe'renθja] *nf* circumference

circunscribir [θirkunskri'ßir] *vt* to circumscribe; **~se** *vr* to be limited

circunscripción [θirkunskrip'θjon] *nf* (*POL*) constituency

circunspecto, a [θirkuns'pekto, a] *adj* circumspect, cautious

circunstancia [θirkuns'tanθja] *nf* circumstance

cirio ['θirjo] *nm* (wax) candle

ciruela [θi'rwela] *nf* plum; **~ pasa** prune

cirugía [θiru'xia] *nf* surgery; **~ estética** *o* **plástica** plastic surgery

cirujano [θiru'xano] *nm* surgeon

cisne ['θisne] *nm* swan

cisterna [θis'terna] *nf* cistern, tank

cita ['θita] *nf* appointment, meeting; (*de novios*) date; (*referencia*) quotation

citación [θita'θjon] *nf* (*JUR*) summons *sg*

citar [θi'tar] *vt* (*gen*) to make an appointment with; (*JUR*) to summons; (*un autor, texto*) to quote; **~se** *vr*: **se citaron en el cine** they arranged to meet at the cinema

cítricos ['θitrikos] *nmpl* citrus fruit(s)

ciudad [θju'ðað] *nf* town; (*más grande*) city; **~anía** *nf* citizenship; **~ano, a** *nm/f* citizen

cívico, a ['θißiko, a] *adj* civic

civil [θi'ßil] *adj* civil ♦ *nm* (*guardia*) policeman

civilización [θißiliθa'θjon] *nf* civilization

civilizar [θißili'θar] *vt* to civilize

civismo [θi'ßismo] *nm* public spirit

cizaña [θi'θaɲa] *nf* (*fig*) discord

cl. *abr* (= *centilitro*) cl.

clamar [kla'mar] *vt* to clamour for, cry out for ♦ *vi* to cry out, clamour

clamor [kla'mor] *nm* clamour, protest

clandestino, a [klandes'tino, a] *adj* clandestine; (*POL*) underground

clara ['klara] *nf* (*de huevo*) egg white

claraboya [klara'ßoja] *nf* skylight

clarear [klare'ar] *vi* (*el día*) to dawn; (*el cielo*) to clear up, brighten up; **~se** *vr* to be transparent

clarete [kla'rete] *nm* rosé (wine)

claridad [klari'ðað] *nf* (*del día*) brightness; (*de estilo*) clarity

clarificar [klarifi'kar] *vt* to clarify

clarinete [klari'nete] *nm* clarinet

clarividencia [klarißi'ðenθja] *nf* clairvoyance; (*fig*) far-sightedness

claro, a ['klaro, a] *adj* clear; (*luminoso*) bright; (*color*) light; (*evidente*) clear, evident; (*poco espeso*) thin ♦ *nm* (*en bosque*) clearing ♦ *adv* clearly ♦ *excl* (*tb*: **~ que sí**) of course!

clase ['klase] *nf* class; **~ alta/media/obrera** upper/middle/working class; **~s particulares** private lessons, private tuition *sg*

clásico, a ['klasiko, a] *adj* classical

clasificación [klasifika'θjon] *nf* classification; (*DEPORTE*) league (table)

clasificar [klasifi'kar] *vt* to classify

claudicar [klauði'kar] *vi* to give in

claustro ['klaustro] *nm* cloister

cláusula ['klausula] *nf* clause

clausura [klau'sura] *nf* closing, closure;

clausurar *vt (congreso etc)* to bring to a close

clavar [klaˈβar] *vt (clavo)* to hammer in; *(cuchillo)* to stick, thrust

clave [ˈklaβe] *nf* key; *(MUS)* clef

clavel [klaˈβel] *nm* carnation

clavícula [klaˈβikula] *nf* collar bone

clavija [klaˈβixa] *nf* peg, dowel, pin; *(ELEC)* plug

clavo [ˈklaβo] *nm (de metal)* nail; *(BOT)* clove

claxon [ˈklakson] *(pl* **~s**) *nm* horn

clemencia [kleˈmenθja] *nf* mercy, clemency

cleptómano, a [klepˈtomano, a] *nm/f* kleptomaniac

clérigo [ˈkleriɣo] *nm* priest

clero [ˈklero] *nm* clergy

cliché [kliˈtʃe] *nm* cliché; *(FOTO)* negative

cliente, a [ˈkljente, a] *nm/f* client, customer

clientela [kljenˈtela] *nf* clientele, customers *pl*

clima [ˈklima] *nm* climate

climatizado, a [klimatiˈθaðo, a] *adj* air-conditioned

clímax [ˈklimaks] *nm inv* climax

clínica [ˈklinika] *nf* clinic; *(particular)* private hospital

clip [klip] *(pl* **~s**) *nm* paper clip

clítoris [ˈklitoris] *nm inv (ANAT)* clitoris

cloaca [kloˈaka] *nf* sewer

cloro [ˈkloro] *nm* chlorine

club [klub] *(pl* **~s** *o* **~es**) *nm* club; **~ de jóvenes** youth club

cm *abr (= centímetro, centímetros)* cm

C.N.T. *(ESP) abr = Confederación Nacional de Trabajo*

coacción [koakˈθjon] *nf* coercion, compulsion; **coaccionar** *vt* to coerce

coagular [koaɣuˈlar] *vt (leche, sangre)* to clot; **~se** *vr* to clot; **coágulo** *nm* clot

coalición [koaliˈθjon] *nf* coalition

coartada [koarˈtaða] *nf* alibi

coartar [koarˈtar] *vt* to limit, restrict

coba [ˈkoβa] *nf*: **dar ~ a uno** to soft-soap sb

cobarde [koˈβarðe] *adj* cowardly ♦ *nm* coward; **cobardía** *nf* cowardice

cobaya [koˈβaja] *nf* guinea pig

cobertizo [koβerˈtiθo] *nm* shelter

cobertura [koβerˈtura] *nf* cover

cobija [koˈβixa] *(AM) nf* blanket

cobijar [koβiˈxar] *vt (cubrir)* to cover; *(proteger)* to shelter; **cobijo** *nm* shelter

cobra [ˈkoβra] *nf* cobra

cobrador, a [koβraˈðor, a] *nm/f (de autobús)* conductor/conductress; *(de impuestos, gas)* collector

cobrar [koˈβrar] *vt (cheque)* to cash; *(sueldo)* to collect, draw; *(objeto)* to recover; *(precio)* to charge; *(deuda)* to collect ♦ *vi* to be paid; **cóbrese al entregar** cash on delivery

cobre [ˈkoβre] *nm* copper; **~s** *nmpl (MUS)* brass instruments

cobro [ˈkoβro] *nm (de cheque)* cashing; **presentar al ~** to cash

cocaína [kokaˈina] *nf* cocaine

cocción [kokˈθjon] *nf (CULIN)* cooking; *(en agua)* boiling

cocear [koθeˈar] *vi* to kick

cocer [koˈθer] *vt, vi* to cook; *(en agua)* to boil; *(en horno)* to bake

coche [ˈkotʃe] *nm (AUTO)* car *(BRIT)*, automobile *(US)*; *(de tren, de caballos)* coach, carriage; *(para niños)* pram *(BRIT)*, baby carriage *(US)*; **ir en ~** to drive; **~ celular** Black Maria, prison van; **~ de bomberos** fire engine; **~ fúnebre** hearse; **coche-cama** *(pl* **coches-cama**) *nm (FERRO)* sleeping car, sleeper

cochera [koˈtʃera] *nf* garage; *(de autobuses, trenes)* depot

coche restaurante *(pl* **coches restaurante**) *nm (FERRO)* dining car, diner

cochinillo [kotʃiˈniʎo] *nm (CULIN)* suckling pig, sucking pig

cochino, a [koˈtʃino, a] *adj* filthy, dirty ♦ *nm/f* pig

cocido [koˈθiðo] *nm* stew

cocina [koˈθina] *nf* kitchen; *(aparato)* cooker, stove; *(acto)* cookery; **~ eléctrica/de gas** electric/gas cooker; **~**

francesa French cuisine; **cocinar** *vt, vi* to cook

cocinero, a [koθi'nero, a] *nm/f* cook

coco ['koko] *nm* coconut

cocodrilo [koko'ðrilo] *nm* crocodile

cocotero [koko'tero] *nm* coconut palm

cóctel ['koktel] *nm* cocktail

codazo [ko'ðaθo] *nm*: **dar un ~ a uno** to nudge sb

codicia [ko'ðiθja] *nf* greed; **codiciar** *vt* to covet; **codicioso, a** *adj* covetous

código ['koðiɣo] *nm* code; **~ de barras** bar code; **~ civil** common law; **~ de (la) circulación** highway code; **~ postal** postcode

codillo [ko'ðiʎo] *nm* (ZOOL) knee; (TEC) elbow (joint)

codo ['koðo] *nm* (ANAT, de tubo) elbow; (ZOOL) knee

codorniz [koðor'niθ] *nf* quail

coerción [koer'θjon] *nf* coercion

coetáneo, a [koe'taneo, a] *adj, nm/f* contemporary

coexistir [koe(k)sis'tir] *vi* to coexist

cofradía [kofra'ðia] *nf* brotherhood, fraternity

cofre ['kofre] *nm* (de joyas) case; (de dinero) chest

coger [ko'xer] (ESP) *vt* to take (hold of); (objeto caído) to pick up; (frutas) to pick, harvest; (resfriado, ladrón, pelota) to catch ♦ *vi*: **~ por el buen camino** to take the right road; **~se** *vr* (el dedo) to catch; **~se a algo** to get hold of sth

cogollo [ko'ɣoʎo] *nm* (de lechuga) heart

cogote [ko'ɣote] *nm* back o nape of the neck

cohabitar [koaβi'tar] *vi* to live together, cohabit

cohecho [ko'etʃo] *nm* (acción) bribery; (soborno) bribe

coherente [koe'rente] *adj* coherent

cohesión [koe'sjon] *nm* cohesion

cohete [ko'ete] *nm* rocket

cohibido, a [koi'βiðo, a] *adj* (PSICO) inhibited; (tímido) shy

cohibir [koi'βir] *vt* to restrain, restrict

coincidencia [koinθi'ðenθja] *nf* coincidence

coincidir [koinθi'ðir] *vi* (en idea) to coincide, agree; (en lugar) to coincide

coito ['koito] *nm* intercourse, coitus

coja *etc vb ver* **coger**

cojear [koxe'ar] *vi* (persona) to limp, hobble; (mueble) to wobble, rock

cojera [ko'xera] *nf* limp

cojín [ko'xin] *nm* cushion; **cojinete** *nm* (TEC) ball bearing

cojo, a *etc* ['koxo, a] *vb ver* **coger** ♦ *adj* (que no puede andar) lame, crippled; (mueble) wobbly ♦ *nm/f* lame person, cripple

cojón [ko'xon] (fam) *nm*: **¡cojones!** shit! (!); **cojonudo, a** (fam) *adj* great, fantastic

col [kol] *nf* cabbage; **~es de Bruselas** Brussels sprouts

cola ['kola] *nf* tail; (de gente) queue; (lugar) end, last place; (para pegar) glue, gum; **hacer ~** to queue (up)

colaborador, a [kolaβora'ðor, a] *nm/f* collaborator

colaborar [kolaβo'rar] *vi* to collaborate

colada [ko'laða] *nf*: **hacer la ~** to do the washing

colador [kola'ðor] *nm* (de líquidos) strainer; (para verduras etc) colander

colapso [ko'lapso] *nm* collapse; **~ nervioso** nervous breakdown

colar [ko'lar] *vt* (líquido) to strain off; (metal) to cast ♦ *vi* to ooze, seep (through); **~se** *vr* to jump the queue; **~se en** to get into without paying; (fiesta) to gatecrash

colcha ['koltʃa] *nf* bedspread

colchón [kol'tʃon] *nm* mattress; **~ inflable** o **neumático** air bed, air mattress

colchoneta [koltʃo'neta] *nf* (en gimnasio) mat; (de playa) air bed

colección [kolek'θjon] *nf* collection; **coleccionar** *vt* to collect; **coleccionista** *nm/f* collector

colecta [ko'lekta] *nf* collection

colectivo, a [kolek'tiβo, a] *adj* collective,

joint ♦ *nm* (*AM*) (small) bus

colega [ko'leɣa] *nm/f* colleague

colegial, a [kole'xjal, a] *nm/f* schoolboy/ girl

colegio [ko'lexjo] *nm* college; (*escuela*) school; (*de abogados etc*) association; ~ **electoral** polling station; ~ **mayor** hall of residence

---
colegio

ⓘ A **colegio** *is normally a private primary or secondary school. In the state system it means a primary school although these are also called* **escuelas**. *State secondary schools are called* **institutos**.

---

colegir [kole'xir] *vt* to infer, conclude

cólera ['kolera] *nf* (*ira*) anger ♦ *nm* (*MED*) cholera; **colérico, a** [ko'leriko, a] *adj* irascible, bad-tempered

colesterol [koleste'rol] *nm* cholesterol

coleta [ko'leta] *nf* pigtail

colgante [kol'ɣante] *adj* hanging ♦ *nm* (*joya*) pendant

colgar [kol'ɣar] *vt* to hang (up); (*ropa*) to hang out ♦ *vi* to hang; (*TELEC*) to hang up

cólico ['koliko] *nm* colic

coliflor [koli'flor] *nf* cauliflower

colilla [ko'liʎa] *nf* cigarette end, butt

colina [ko'lina] *nf* hill

colisión [koli'sjon] *nf* collision; ~ **de frente** head-on crash

collar [ko'ʎar] *nm* necklace; (*de perro*) collar

colmar [kol'mar] *vt* to fill to the brim; (*fig*) to fulfil, realize

colmena [kol'mena] *nf* beehive

colmillo [kol'miʎo] *nm* (*diente*) eye tooth; (*de elefante*) tusk; (*de perro*) fang

colmo ['kolmo] *nm*: **¡es el ~!** it's the limit!

colocación [koloka'θjon] *nf* (*acto*) placing; (*empleo*) job, position

colocar [kolo'kar] *vt* to place, put, position; (*dinero*) to invest; (*poner en empleo*) to find a job for; ~**se** *vr* to get a job

Colombia [ko'lombja] *nf* Colombia; **colombiano, a** *adj, nm/f* Colombian

colonia [ko'lonja] *nf* colony; (*de casas*) housing estate; (*agua de* ~) cologne

colonización [koloniθa'θjon] *nf* colonization; **colonizador, a** [koloniθa'ðor, a] *adj* colonizing ♦ *nm/f* colonist, settler

colonizar [koloni'θar] *vt* to colonize

coloquio [ko'lokjo] *nm* conversation; (*congreso*) conference

color [ko'lor] *nm* colour

colorado, a [kolo'raðo, a] *adj* (*rojo*) red; (*LAM: chiste*) rude

colorante [kolo'rante] *nm* colouring

colorear [kolore'ar] *vt* to colour

colorete [kolo'rete] *nm* blusher

colorido [kolo'riðo] *nm* colouring

columna [ko'lumna] *nf* column; (*pilar*) pillar; (*apoyo*) support

columpiar [kolum'pjar] *vt* to swing; ~**se** *vr* to swing; **columpio** *nm* swing

coma ['koma] *nf* comma ♦ *nm* (*MED*) coma

comadre [ko'maðre] *nf* (*madrina*) godmother; (*chismosa*) gossip; **comadrona** *nf* midwife

comandancia [koman'danθja] *nf* command

comandante [koman'dante] *nm* commandant

comarca [ko'marka] *nf* region

comba ['komba] *nf* (*curva*) curve; (*cuerda*) skipping rope; **saltar a la** ~ to skip

combar [kom'bar] *vt* to bend, curve

combate [kom'bate] *nm* fight; **combatiente** *nm* combatant

combatir [komba'tir] *vt* to fight, combat

combinación [kombina'θjon] *nf* combination; (*QUÍM*) compound; (*prenda*) slip

combinar [kombi'nar] *vt* to combine

combustible [kombus'tiβle] *nm* fuel

combustión [kombus'tjon] *nf* combustion

comedia [ko'meðja] *nf* comedy; (*TEATRO*) play, drama

comediante [kome'ðjante] *nm/f* (comic) actor/actress

comedido, a [kome'ðiðo, a] *adj* moderate

comedor, a [kome'ðor, a] *nm* (*habitación*) dining room; (*cantina*) canteen

comensal [komen'sal] *nm/f* fellow guest (o diner)

comentar [komen'tar] *vt* to comment on

comentario [komen'tarjo] *nm* comment, remark; (*literario*) commentary; (*fig*) gossip *sg*; **~s** *nmpl* (*chismes*) gossip *sg*

comentarista [komenta'rista] *nm/f* commentator

comenzar [komen'θar] *vt, vi* to begin, start; **~ a hacer algo** to begin *o* start doing sth

comer [ko'mer] *vt* to eat; (*DAMAS, AJEDREZ*) to take, capture ♦ *vi* to eat; (*almorzar*) to have lunch; **~se** *vr* to eat up

comercial [komer'θjal] *adj* commercial; (*relativo al negocio*) business *cpd*; **comercializar** *vt* (*producto*) to market; (*pey*) to commercialize

comerciante [komer'θjante] *nm/f* trader, merchant

comerciar [komer'θjar] *vi* to trade, do business

comercio [ko'merθjo] *nm* commerce, trade; (*negocio*) business; (*fig*) dealings *pl*

comestible [komes'tißle] *adj* eatable, edible; **~s** *nmpl* food *sg*, foodstuffs

cometa [ko'meta] *nm* comet ♦ *nf* kite

cometer [kome'ter] *vt* to commit

cometido [kome'tiðo] *nm* task, assignment

comezón [kome'θon] *nf* itch, itching

cómic ['komik] *nm* comic

comicios [ko'miθjos] *nmpl* elections

cómico, a ['komiko, a] *adj* comic(al) ♦ *nm/f* comedian

comida [ko'miða] *nf* (*alimento*) food; (*almuerzo, cena*) meal; (*de mediodía*) lunch

comidilla [komi'ðiʎa] *nf*: **ser la ~ de la ciudad** to be the talk of the town

comienzo *etc* [ko'mjenθo] *vb ver* **comenzar** ♦ *nm* beginning, start

comillas [ko'miʎas] *nfpl* quotation marks

comilona [komi'lona] (*fam*) *nf* blow-out

comino [ko'mino] *nm*: **(no) me importa un ~** I don't give a damn

comisaría [komisa'ria] *nf* (*de policía*) police station; (*MIL*) commissariat

comisario [komi'sarjo] *nm* (*MIL etc*) commissary; (*POL*) commissar

comisión [komi'sjon] *nf* commission

comité [komi'te] (*pl* **~s**) *nm* committee

comitiva [komi'tißa] *nf* retinue

como ['komo] *adv* as; (*tal ~*) like; (*aproximadamente*) about, approximately ♦ *conj* (*ya que, puesto que*) as, since; **¡~ no!** of course!; **~ no lo haga hoy** unless he does it today; **~ si** as if; **es tan alto ~ ancho** it is as high as it is wide

cómo ['komo] *adv* how?, why? ♦ *excl* what?, I beg your pardon? ♦ *nm*: **el ~ y el porqué** the whys and wherefores

cómoda ['komoða] *nf* chest of drawers

comodidad [komoði'ðað] *nf* comfort; **venga a su ~** come at your convenience

comodín [komo'ðin] *nm* joker

cómodo, a ['komoðo, a] *adj* comfortable; (*práctico, de fácil uso*) convenient

compact disc *nm* compact disk player

compacto, a [kom'pakto, a] *adj* compact

compadecer [kompaðe'θer] *vt* to pity, be sorry for; **~se** *vr*: **~se de** to pity, be *o* feel sorry for

compadre [kom'paðre] *nm* (*padrino*) godfather; (*amigo*) friend, pal

compañero, a [kompa'ɲero, a] *nm/f* companion; (*novio*) boy/girlfriend; **~ de clase** classmate

compañía [kompa'ɲia] *nf* company

comparación [kompara'θjon] *nf* comparison; **en ~ con** in comparison with

comparar [kompa'rar] *vt* to compare

comparecer [kompare'θer] *vi* to appear (in court)

comparsa [kom'parsa] *nm/f* (*TEATRO*) extra

compartimiento [komparti'mjento] *nm* (*FERRO*) compartment

compartir [kompar'tir] *vt* to share; (*dinero,*

comida etc) to divide (up), share (out)

compás [kom'pas] *nm* (*MUS*) beat, rhythm; (*MAT*) compasses *pl*; (*NAUT etc*) compass

compasión [kompa'sjon] *nf* compassion, pity

compasivo, a [kompa'siβo, a] *adj* compassionate

compatibilidad [kompatiβili'ðað] *nf* compatibility

compatible [kompa'tiβle] *adj* compatible

compatriota [kompa'trjota] *nm/f* compatriot, fellow countryman/woman

compendiar [kompen'djar] *vt* to summarize; **compendio** *nm* summary

compenetrarse [kompene'trarse] *vr* to be in tune

compensación [kompensa'θjon] *nf* compensation

compensar [kompen'sar] *vt* to compensate

competencia [kompe'tenθja] *nf* (*incumbencia*) domain, field; (*JUR, habilidad*) competence; (*rivalidad*) competition

competente [kompe'tente] *adj* competent

competición [kompeti'θjon] *nf* competition

competir [kompe'tir] *vi* to compete

compilar [kompi'lar] *vt* to compile

complacencia [kompla'θenθja] *nf* (*placer*) pleasure; (*tolerancia excesiva*) complacency

complacer [kompla'θer] *vt* to please; **~se** *vr* to be pleased

complaciente [kompla'θjente] *adj* kind, obliging, helpful

complejo, a [kom'plexo, a] *adj, nm* complex

complementario, a [komplemen'tarjo, a] *adj* complementary

completar [komple'tar] *vt* to complete

completo, a [kom'pleto, a] *adj* complete; (*perfecto*) perfect; (*lleno*) full ♦ *nm* complement

complicado, a [kompli'kaðo, a] *adj* complicated; **estar ~ en** to be mixed up

in

cómplice ['kompliθe] *nm/f* accomplice

complot [kom'plo(t)] (*pl* **~s**) *nm* plot

componer [kompo'ner] *vt* (*MUS, LITERATURA, IMPRENTA*) to compose; (*algo roto*) to mend, repair; (*arreglar*) to arrange; **~se** *vr*: **~se de** to consist of; **componérselas para hacer algo** to manage to do sth

comportamiento [komporta'mjento] *nm* behaviour, conduct

comportarse [kompor'tarse] *vr* to behave

composición [komposi'θjon] *nf* composition

compositor, a [komposi'tor, a] *nm/f* composer

compostura [kompos'tura] *nf* (*actitud*) composure

compra ['kompra] *nf* purchase; **ir de ~s** to go shopping; **comprador, a** *nm/f* buyer, purchaser

comprar [kom'prar] *vt* to buy, purchase

comprender [kompren'der] *vt* to understand; (*incluir*) to comprise, include

comprensión [kompren'sjon] *nf* understanding; **comprensivo, a** *adj* (*actitud*) understanding

compresa [kom'presa] *nf*: **~ higiénica** sanitary towel (*BRIT*) o napkin (*US*)

comprimido, a [kompri'miðo, a] *adj* compressed ♦ *nm* (*MED*) pill, tablet

comprimir [kompri'mir] *vt* to compress

comprobante [kompro'βante] *nm* proof; (*COM*) voucher; **~ de recibo** receipt

comprobar [kompro'βar] *vt* to check; (*probar*) to prove; (*TEC*) to check, test

comprometer [komprome'ter] *vt* to compromise; (*poner en peligro*) to endanger; **~se** *vr* (*involucrarse*) to get involved

compromiso [kompro'miso] *nm* (*obligación*) obligation; (*cometido*) commitment; (*convenio*) agreement; (*apuro*) awkward situation

compuesto, a [kom'pwesto, a] *adj*: **~ de** composed of, made up of ♦ *nm* compound

computador [komputa'ðor] *nm*
computer; ~ **central** mainframe
computer; ~ **personal** personal computer
computadora [komputa'ðora] *nf* =
computador
cómputo ['komputo] *nm* calculation
comulgar [komul'var] *vi* to receive
communion
común [ko'mun] *adj* common ♦ *nm*: **el ~**
the community
comunicación [komunika'θjon] *nf*
communication; (*informe*) report
comunicado [komuni'kaðo] *nm*
announcement; ~ **de prensa** press release
comunicar [komuni'kar] *vt, vi* to
communicate; **~se** *vr* to communicate;
está comunicando (*TEL*) the line's
engaged (*BRIT*) *o* busy (*US*);
comunicativo, a *adj* communicative
comunidad [komuni'ðað] *nf* community;
~ **autónoma** (*POL*) autonomous region;
C~ Económica Europea European
Economic Community
comunión [komu'njon] *nf* communion
comunismo [komu'nismo] *nm*
communism; **comunista** *adj, nm/f*
communist

PALABRA CLAVE
---

con [kon] *prep* **1** (*medio, compañía*) with;
comer ~ cuchara to eat with a spoon;
pasear ~ uno to go for a walk with sb
2 (*a pesar de*): ~ **todo, merece nuestros
respetos** all the same, he deserves our
respect
3 (*para ~*): **es muy bueno para ~ los
niños** he's very good with (the) children
4 (*+infin*): ~ **llegar tan tarde se quedó
sin comer** by arriving so late he missed
out on eating
♦ *conj*: ~ **que: será suficiente ~ que le
escribas** it will be sufficient if you write
to her

---

conato [ko'nato] *nm* attempt; ~ **de robo**
attempted robbery
concebir [konθe'ßir] *vt, vi* to conceive

conceder [konθe'ðer] *vt* to concede
concejal, a [konθe'xal, a] *nm/f* town
councillor
concentración [konθentra'θjon] *nf*
concentration
concentrar [konθen'trar] *vt* to
concentrate; **~se** *vr* to concentrate
concepción [konθep'θjon] *nf* conception
concepto [kon'θepto] *nm* concept
concernir [konθer'nir] *vi* to concern; **en
lo que concierne a …** as far as … is
concerned; **en lo que a mí concierne** as
far as I'm concerned
concertar [konθer'tar] *vt* (*MUS*) to
harmonize; (*acordar: precio*) to agree;
(*: tratado*) to conclude; (*trato*) to arrange,
fix up; (*combinar: esfuerzos*) to coordinate
♦ *vi* to harmonize, be in tune
concesión [konθe'sjon] *nf* concession
concesionario [konθesjo'narjo] *nm*
(licensed) dealer, agent
concha ['kontʃa] *nf* shell
conciencia [kon'θjenθja] *nf* conscience;
tener/tomar ~ de to be/become aware
of; **tener la ~ limpia/tranquila** to have a
clear conscience
concienciar [konθjen'θjar] *vt* to make
aware; **~se** *vr* to become aware
concienzudo, a [konθjen'θuðo, a] *adj*
conscientious
concierto *etc* [kon'θjerto] *vb ver*
concertar ♦ *nm* concert; (*obra*) concerto
conciliar [konθi'ljar] *vt* to reconcile
concilio [kon'θiljo] *nm* council
conciso, a [kon'θiso, a] *adj* concise
concluir [konklu'ir] *vt, vi* to conclude;
~se *vr* to conclude
conclusión [konklu'sjon] *nf* conclusion
concluyente [konklu'jente] *adj* (*prueba,
información*) conclusive
concordar [konkor'ðar] *vt* to reconcile
♦ *vi* to agree, tally
concordia [kon'korðja] *nf* harmony
concretar [konkre'tar] *vt* to make
concrete, make more specific; **~se** *vr* to
become more definite
concreto, a [kon'kreto, a] *adj, nm* (*AM*)

concrete; **en ~** (*en resumen*) to sum up; (*especificamente*) specifically; **no hay nada en ~** there's nothing definite

concurrencia [konku'rrenθja] *nf* turnout

concurrido, a [konku'rriðo, a] *adj* (*calle*) busy; (*local, reunión*) crowded

concurrir [konku'rrir] *vi* (*juntarse: ríos*) to meet, come together; (: *personas*) to gather, meet

concursante [konkur'sante] *nm/f* competitor

concurso [kon'kurso] *nm* (*de público*) crowd; (*ESCOL, DEPORTE, competencia*) competition; (*ayuda*) help, cooperation

condal [kon'dal] *adj*: **la Ciudad C~** Barcelona

conde ['konde] *nm* count

condecoración [kondekora'θjon] *nf* (*MIL*) medal

condecorar [kondeko'rar] *vt* (*MIL*) to decorate

condena [kon'dena] *nf* sentence

condenación [kondena'θjon] *nf* condemnation; (*REL*) damnation

condenar [konde'nar] *vt* to condemn; (*JUR*) to convict; **~se** *vr* (*REL*) to be damned

condensar [konden'sar] *vt* to condense

condesa [kon'desa] *nf* countess

condición [kondi'θjon] *nf* condition; **condicional** *adj* conditional

condicionar [kondiθjo'nar] *vt* (*acondicionar*) to condition; **~ algo a** to make sth conditional on

condimento [kondi'mento] *nm* seasoning

condolerse [kondo'lerse] *vr* to sympathize

condón [kon'don] *nm* condom

conducir [kondu'θir] *vt* to take, convey; (*AUTO*) to drive ♦ *vi* to drive; (*fig*) to lead; **~se** *vr* to behave

conducta [kon'dukta] *nf* conduct, behaviour

conducto [kon'dukto] *nm* pipe, tube; (*fig*) channel

conductor, a [konduk'tor, a] *adj* leading, guiding ♦ *nm* (*FÍSICA*) conductor; (*de*

vehículo) driver

conduje *etc vb ver* **conducir**

conduzco *etc vb ver* **conducir**

conectado, a [konek'taðo, a] *adj* (*INFORM*) on-line

conectar [konek'tar] *vt* to connect (up); (*enchufar*) plug in

conejillo [kone'xiʎo] *nm*: **~ de Indias** (*ZOOL*) guinea pig

conejo [ko'nexo] *nm* rabbit

conexión [konek'sjon] *nf* connection

confección [konfe(k)'θjon] *nf* preparation; (*industria*) clothing industry

confeccionar [konfekθjo'nar] *vt* to make (up)

confederación [konfeðera'θjon] *nf* confederation

conferencia [konfe'renθja] *nf* conference; (*lección*) lecture; (*TEL*) call

conferir [konfe'rir] *vt* to award

confesar [konfe'sar] *vt* to confess, admit

confesión [konfe'sjon] *nf* confession

confesionario [konfesjo'narjo] *nm* confessional

confeti [kon'feti] *nm* confetti

confiado, a [kon'fjaðo, a] *adj* (*crédulo*) trusting; (*seguro*) confident

confianza [kon'fjanθa] *nf* trust; (*seguridad*) confidence; (*familiaridad*) intimacy, familiarity

confiar [kon'fjar] *vt* to entrust ♦ *vi* to trust

confidencia [konfi'ðenθja] *nf* confidence

confidencial [konfiðen'θjal] *adj* confidential

confidente [konfi'ðente] *nm/f* confidant/e; (*policial*) informer

configurar [konfiɣu'rar] *vt* to shape, form

confín [kon'fin] *nm* limit; **confines** *nmpl* confines, limits

confinar [konfi'nar] *vi* to confine; (*desterrar*) to banish

confirmar [konfir'mar] *vt* to confirm

confiscar [konfis'kar] *vt* to confiscate

confite [kon'fite] *nm* sweet (*BRIT*), candy (*US*)

confitería [konfite'ria] *nf* (*tienda*) confectioner's (shop)

confitura [konfi'tura] *nf* jam
conflictivo, a [konflik'tiβo, a] *adj* (*asunto, propuesta*) controversial; (*país, situación*) troubled
conflicto [kon'flikto] *nm* conflict; (*fig*) clash
confluir [kon'flwir] *vi* (*ríos*) to meet; (*gente*) to gather
conformar [konfor'mar] *vt* to shape, fashion ♦ *vi* to agree; **~se** *vr* to conform; (*resignarse*) to resign o.s.
conforme [kon'forme] *adj* (*correspondiente*): **~ con** in line with; (*de acuerdo*): **estar ~s (con algo)** to be in agreement (with sth) ♦ *adv* as ♦ *excl* agreed! ♦ *prep*: **~ a** in accordance with; **quedarse ~ (con algo)** to be satisfied (with sth)
conformidad [konformi'ðað] *nf* (*semejanza*) similarity; (*acuerdo*) agreement; **conformista** *adj, nm/f* conformist
confortable [konfor'taβle] *adj* comfortable
confortar [konfor'tar] *vt* to comfort
confrontar [konfron'tar] *vt* to confront; (*dos personas*) to bring face to face; (*cotejar*) to compare
confundir [konfun'dir] *vt* (*equivocar*) to mistake, confuse; (*turbar*) to confuse; **~se** *vr* (*turbarse*) to get confused; (*equivocarse*) to make a mistake; (*mezclarse*) to mix
confusión [konfu'sjon] *nf* confusion
confuso, a [kon'fuso, a] *adj* confused
congelado, a [konxe'laðo, a] *adj* frozen; **~s** *nmpl* frozen food(s); **congelador** *nm* (*aparato*) freezer, deep freeze
congelar [konxe'lar] *vt* to freeze; **~se** *vr* (*sangre, grasa*) to congeal
congeniar [konxe'njar] *vi* to get on (*BRIT*) *o* along (*US*) well
congestión [konxes'tjon] *nf* congestion
congestionar [konxestjo'nar] *vt* to congest
congoja [kon'goxa] *nf* distress, grief
congraciarse [kongra'θjarse] *vr* to ingratiate o.s.
congratular [kongratu'lar] *vt* to congratulate
congregación [kongreβa'θjon] *nf* congregation
congregar [kongre'βar] *vt* to gather together; **~se** *vr* to gather together
congresista [kongre'sista] *nm/f* delegate, congressman/woman
congreso [kon'greso] *nm* congress
congrio ['kongrjo] *nm* conger eel
conjetura [konxe'tura] *nf* guess; **conjeturar** *vt* to guess
conjugar [konxu'xar] *vt* to combine, fit together; (*LING*) to conjugate
conjunción [konxun'θjon] *nf* conjunction
conjunto, a [kon'xunto, a] *adj* joint, united ♦ *nm* whole; (*MUS*) band; **en ~** as a whole
conjurar [konxu'rar] *vt* (*REL*) to exorcise; (*fig*) to ward off ♦ *vi* to plot
conmemoración [konmemora'θjon] *nf* commemoration
conmemorar [konmemo'rar] *vt* to commemorate
conmigo [kon'mixo] *pron* with me
conmoción [konmo'θjon] *nf* shock; (*fig*) upheaval; **~ cerebral** (*MED*) concussion
conmovedor, a [konmoβe'ðor, a] *adj* touching, moving; (*emocionante*) exciting
conmover [konmo'βer] *vt* to shake, disturb; (*fig*) to move
conmutador [konmuta'ðor] *nm* switch; (*AM: TEL: centralita*) switchboard; (: *central*) telephone exchange
cono ['kono] *nm* cone
conocedor, a [konoθe'ðor, a] *adj* expert, knowledgeable ♦ *nm/f* expert
conocer [kono'θer] *vt* to know; (*por primera vez*) to meet, get to know; (*entender*) to know about; (*reconocer*) to recognize; **~se** *vr* (*una persona*) to know o.s.; (*dos personas*) to (get to) know each other
conocido, a [kono'θiðo, a] *adj* (well-) known ♦ *nm/f* acquaintance
conocimiento [konoθi'mjento] *nm*

knowledge; (MED) consciousness; **~s** nmpl (saber) knowledge sg

conozco etc vb ver **conocer**

conque ['konke] conj and so, so then

conquista [kon'kista] nf conquest; **conquistador, a** adj conquering ♦ nm conqueror

conquistar [konkis'tar] vt to conquer

consagrar [konsa'xrar] vt (REL) to consecrate; (fig) to devote

consciente [kons'θjente] adj conscious

consecución [konseku'θjon] nf acquisition; (de fin) attainment

consecuencia [konse'kwenθja] nf consequence, outcome; (coherencia) consistency

consecuente [konse'kwente] adj consistent

consecutivo, a [konseku'tiβo, a] adj consecutive

conseguir [konse'xir] vt to get, obtain; (objetivo) to attain

consejero, a [konse'xero, a] nm/f adviser, consultant; (POL) councillor

consejo [kon'sexo] nm advice; (POL) council; **~ de administración** (COM) board of directors; **~ de guerra** court martial; **~ de ministros** cabinet meeting

consenso [kon'senso] nm consensus

consentimiento [konsenti'mjento] nm consent

consentir [konsen'tir] vt (permitir, tolerar) to consent to; (mimar) to pamper, spoil; (aguantar) to put up with ♦ vi to agree, consent; **~ que uno haga algo** to allow sb to do sth

conserje [kon'serxe] nm caretaker; (portero) porter

conservación [konserßa'θjon] nf conservation; (de alimentos, vida) preservation

conservador, a [konserßa'ðor, a] adj (POL) conservative ♦ nm/f conservative

conservante [konser'ßante] nm preservative

conservar [konser'ßar] vt to conserve, keep; (alimentos, vida) to preserve; **~se** vr

to survive

conservas [kon'serßas] nfpl canned food(s) (pl)

conservatorio [konserßa'torjo] nm (MUS) conservatoire, conservatory

considerable [konsiðe'raßle] adj considerable

consideración [konsiðera'θjon] nf consideration; (estimación) respect

considerado, a [konsiðe'raðo, a] adj (atento) considerate; (respetado) respected

considerar [konsiðe'rar] vt to consider

consigna [kon'sixna] nf (orden) order, instruction; (para equipajes) left-luggage office

consigo etc [kon'sixo] vb ver **conseguir** ♦ pron (m) with him; (f) with her; (Vd) with you; (reflexivo) with o.s.

consiguiendo etc vb ver **conseguir**

consiguiente [konsi'xjente] adj consequent; **por ~** and so, therefore, consequently

consistente [konsis'tente] adj consistent; (sólido) solid, firm; (válido) sound

consistir [konsis'tir] vi: **~ en** (componerse de) to consist of

consola [kon'sola] nf (mueble) console table; (de videojuegos) console

consolación [konsola'θjon] nf consolation

consolar [konso'lar] vt to console

consolidar [konsoli'ðar] vt to consolidate

consomé [konso'me] (pl **~s**) nm consommé, clear soup

consonante [konso'nante] adj consonant, harmonious ♦ nf consonant

consorcio [kon'sorθjo] nm consortium

conspiración [konspira'θjon] nf conspiracy

conspirador, a [konspira'ðor, a] nm/f conspirator

conspirar [konspi'rar] vi to conspire

constancia [kon'stanθja] nf constancy; **dejar ~ de** to put on record

constante [kons'tante] adj, nf constant

constar [kons'tar] vi (evidenciarse) to be clear o evident; **~ de** to consist of

constatar [konsta'tar] vt to verify

consternación [konsterna'θjon] *nf* consternation

constipado, a [konsti'paðo, a] *adj*: **estar ~** to have a cold ♦ *nm* cold

constitución [konstitu'θjon] *nf* constitution; **constitucional** *adj* constitutional

constituir [konstitu'ir] *vt* (*formar, componer*) to constitute, make up; (*fundar, erigir, ordenar*) to constitute, establish

constituyente [konstitu'jente] *adj* constituent

constreñir [konstre'ɲir] *vt* (*restringir*) to restrict

construcción [konstruk'θjon] *nf* construction, building

constructor, a [konstruk'tor, a] *nm/f* builder

construir [konstru'ir] *vt* to build, construct

construyendo *etc vb ver* **construir**

consuelo [kon'swelo] *nm* consolation, solace

cónsul ['konsul] *nm* consul; **consulado** *nm* consulate

consulta [kon'sulta] *nf* consultation; (*MED*): **horas de ~** surgery hours

consultar [konsul'tar] *vt* to consult

consultorio [konsul'torjo] *nm* (*MED*) surgery

consumar [konsu'mar] *vt* to complete, carry out; (*crimen*) to commit; (*sentencia*) to carry out

consumición [konsumi'θjon] *nf* consumption; (*bebida*) drink; (*comida*) food; **~ mínima** cover charge

consumidor, a [konsumi'ðor, a] *nm/f* consumer

consumir [konsu'mir] *vt* to consume; **~se** *vr* to be consumed; (*persona*) to waste away

consumismo [konsu'mismo] *nm* consumerism

consumo [kon'sumo] *nm* consumption

contabilidad [kontaβili'ðað] *nf* accounting, book-keeping; (*profesión*) accountancy; **contable** *nm/f* accountant

contacto [kon'takto] *nm* contact; (*AUTO*) ignition

contado, a [kon'taðo, a] *adj*: **~s** (*escasos*) numbered, scarce, few ♦ *nm*: **pagar al ~** to pay (in) cash

contador [konta'ðor] *nm* (*aparato*) meter; (*AM: contante*) accountant

contagiar [konta'xjar] *vt* (*enfermedad*) to pass on, transmit; (*persona*) to infect; **~se** *vr* to become infected

contagio [kon'taxjo] *nm* infection; **contagioso, a** *adj* infectious; (*fig*) catching

contaminación [kontamina'θjon] *nf* contamination; (*polución*) pollution

contaminar [kontami'nar] *vt* to contaminate; (*aire, agua*) to pollute

contante [kon'tante] *adj*: **dinero ~ (y sonante)** cash

contar [kon'tar] *vt* (*páginas, dinero*) to count; (*anécdota, chiste etc*) to tell ♦ *vi* to count; **~ con** to rely on, count on

contemplación [kontempla'θjon] *nf* contemplation

contemplar [kontem'plar] *vt* to contemplate; (*mirar*) to look at

contemporáneo, a [kontempo'raneo, a] *adj, nm/f* contemporary

contendiente [konten'djente] *nm/f* contestant

contenedor [kontene'ðor] *nm* container

contener [konte'ner] *vt* to contain, hold; (*retener*) to hold back, contain; **~se** *vr* to control *o* restrain o.s.

contenido, a [konte'niðo, a] *adj* (*moderado*) restrained; (*risa etc*) suppressed ♦ *nm* contents *pl*, content

contentar [konten'tar] *vt* (*satisfacer*) to satisfy; (*complacer*) to please; **~se** *vr* to be satisfied

contento, a [kon'tento, a] *adj* (*alegre*) pleased; (*feliz*) happy

contestación [kontesta'θjon] *nf* answer, reply

contestador [kontesta'ðor] *nm*: **~ automático** answering machine

contestar [kontes'tar] *vt* to answer, reply;

(*JUR*) to corroborate, confirm

contexto [kon'te(k)sto] *nm* context

contienda [kon'tjenda] *nf* contest

contigo [kon'tiɣo] *pron* with you

contiguo, a [kon'tiɣwo, a] *adj* adjacent, adjoining

continente [konti'nente] *adj, nm* continent

contingencia [kontin'xenθja] *nf* contingency; (*riesgo*) risk; **contingente** *adj, nm* contingent

continuación [kontinwa'θjon] *nf* continuation; **a ~** then, next

continuar [konti'nwar] *vt* to continue, go on with ♦ *vi* to continue, go on; **~ hablando** to continue talking *o* to talk

continuidad [kontinwi'ðað] *nf* continuity

continuo, a [kon'tinwo, a] *adj* (*sin interrupción*) continuous; (*acción perseverante*) continual

contorno [kon'torno] *nm* outline; (*GEO*) contour; **~s** *nmpl* neighbourhood *sg*, surrounding area *sg*

contorsión [kontor'sjon] *nf* contortion

contra ['kontra] *prep, adv* against ♦ *nm inv* con ♦ *nf*: **la C~** (*de Nicaragua*) the Contras *pl*

contraataque [kontraa'take] *nm* counter-attack

contrabajo [kontra'ßaxo] *nm* double bass

contrabandista [kontraßan'dista] *nm/f* smuggler

contrabando [kontra'ßando] *nm* (*acción*) smuggling; (*mercancías*) contraband

contracción [kontrak'θjon] *nf* contraction

contracorriente [kontrako'rrjente]: **(a) ~** *adv* against the current

contradecir [kontraðe'θir] *vt* to contradict

contradicción [kontraðik'θjon] *nf* contradiction

contradictorio, a [kontraðik'torjo, a] *adj* contradictory

contraer [kontra'er] *vt* to contract; (*limitar*) to restrict; **~se** *vr* to contract; (*limitarse*) to limit o.s.

contraluz [kontra'luθ] *nf*: **a ~** against the light

contrapartida [kontrapar'tiða] *nf*: **como ~ (de)** in return (for)

contrapelo [kontra'pelo]: **a ~** *adv* the wrong way

contrapesar [kontrape'sar] *vt* to counterbalance; (*fig*) to offset; **contrapeso** *nm* counterweight

contraportada [kontrapor'taða] *nf* (*de revista*) back cover

contraproducente [kontraproðu'θente] *adj* counterproductive

contrariar [kontra'rjar] *vt* (*oponerse*) to oppose; (*poner obstáculo*) to impede; (*enfadar*) to vex

contrariedad [kontrarje'ðað] *nf* (*obstáculo*) obstacle, setback; (*disgusto*) vexation, annoyance

contrario, a [kon'trarjo, a] *adj* contrary; (*persona*) opposed; (*sentido, lado*) opposite ♦ *nm/f* enemy, adversary; (*DEPORTE*) opponent; **al/por el ~** on the contrary; **de lo ~** otherwise

contrarreloj [kontrarre'lo] *nf* (*tb*: **prueba ~**) time trial

contrarrestar [kontrarres'tar] *vt* to counteract

contrasentido [kontrasen'tiðo] *nm*: **es un ~ que él ...** it doesn't make sense for him to ...

contraseña [kontra'seɲa] *nf* (*INFORM*) password

contrastar [kontras'tar] *vt, vi* to contrast

contraste [kon'traste] *nm* contrast

contratar [kontra'tar] *vt* (*firmar un acuerdo para*) to contract for; (*empleados, obreros*) to hire, engage; **~se** *vr* to sign on

contratiempo [kontra'tjempo] *nm* setback

contratista [kontra'tista] *nm/f* contractor

contrato [kon'trato] *nm* contract

contravenir [kontraße'nir] *vi*: **~ a** to contravene, violate

contraventana [kontraßen'tana] *nf* shutter

contribución [kontrißu'θjon] *nf* (*municipal etc*) tax; (*ayuda*) contribution

contribuir [kontrißu'ir] *vt, vi* to

contribute; (COM) to pay (in taxes)

contribuyente [kontriβu'jente] *nm/f*
(COM) taxpayer; (*que ayuda*) contributor

contrincante [kontrin'kante] *nm*
opponent

control [kon'trol] *nm* control; (*inspección*)
inspection, check; **~ador, a** *nm/f*
controller; **~ador aéreo** air-traffic
controller

controlar [kontro'lar] *vt* to control;
(*inspeccionar*) to inspect, check

controversia [kontro'βersja] *nf*
controversy

contundente [kontun'dente] *adj*
(*instrumento*) blunt; (*argumento, derrota*)
overwhelming

contusión [kontu'sjon] *nf* bruise

convalecencia [kombale'θenθja] *nf*
convalescence

convalecer [kombale'θer] *vi* to
convalesce, get better

convaleciente [kombale'θjente] *adj, nm/f*
convalescent

convalidar [kombali'ðar] *vt* (*título*) to
recognize

convencer [komben'θer] *vt* to convince

convencimiento [kombenθi'mjento] *nm*
(*certidumbre*) conviction

convención [komben'θjon] *nf* convention

conveniencia [kombe'njenθja] *nf*
suitability; (*conformidad*) agreement;
(*utilidad, provecho*) usefulness; **~s** *nfpl*
(*convenciones*) conventions; (COM)
property *sg*

conveniente [kombe'njente] *adj* suitable;
(*útil*) useful

convenio [kom'benjo] *nm* agreement,
treaty

convenir [kombe'nir] *vi* (*estar de acuerdo*)
to agree; (*venir bien*) to suit, be suitable

convento [kom'bento] *nm* convent

convenza *etc vb ver* **convencer**

converger [komber'xer] *vi* to converge

convergir [komber'xir] *vi* = **converger**

conversación [kombersa'θjon] *nf*
conversation

conversar [komber'sar] *vi* to talk,
converse

conversión [komber'sjon] *nf* conversion

convertir [komber'tir] *vt* to convert

convicción [kombik'θjon] *nf* conviction

convicto, a [kom'bikto, a] *adj* convicted

convidado, a [kombi'ðaðo, a] *nm/f* guest

convidar [kombi'ðar] *vt* to invite

convincente [kombin'θente] *adj*
convincing

convite [kom'bite] *nm* invitation;
(*banquete*) banquet

convivencia [kombi'βenθja] *nf*
coexistence, living together

convivir [kombi'βir] *vi* to live together

convocar [kombo'kar] *vt* to summon, call
(together)

convocatoria [komboka'torja] *nf* (*de
oposiciones, elecciones*) notice; (*de huelga*)
call

convulsión [kombul'sjon] *nf* convulsion

conyugal [konju'βal] *adj* conjugal;
cónyuge ['konjuxe] *nm/f* spouse

coñac [ko'ɲa(k)] (*pl* **~s**) *nm* cognac,
brandy

coño ['koɲo] (*fam!*) *excl* (*enfado*) shit! (!);
(*sorpresa*) bloody hell! (!)

cooperación [koopera'θjon] *nf*
cooperation

cooperar [koope'rar] *vi* to cooperate

cooperativa [koopera'tiβa] *nf* cooperative

coordinadora [koorðina'ðora] *nf* (*comité*)
coordinating committee

coordinar [koorði'nar] *vt* to coordinate

copa ['kopa] *nf* cup; (*vaso*) glass; (*bebida*):
(**tomar una) ~** (to have a) drink; (*de
árbol*) top; (*de sombrero*) crown; **~s** *nfpl*
(NAIPES) ≈ hearts

copia ['kopja] *nf* copy; **~ de respaldo** *o*
seguridad (INFORM) back-up copy;
copiar *vt* to copy

copioso, a [ko'pjoso, a] *adj* copious,
plentiful

copla ['kopla] *nf* verse; (*canción*) (popular)
song

copo ['kopo] *nm*: **~ de nieve** snowflake;
~s de maíz cornflakes

coqueta [ko'keta] *adj* flirtatious,

coquettish; **coquetear** *vi* to flirt

coraje [ko'raxe] *nm* courage; (*ánimo*) spirit; (*ira*) anger

coral [ko'ral] *adj* choral ♦ *nf* (*MUS*) choir ♦ *nm* (*ZOOL*) coral

coraza [ko'raθa] *nf* (*armadura*) armour; (*blindaje*) armour-plating

corazón [kora'θon] *nm* heart

corazonada [koraθo'naða] *nf* impulse; (*presentimiento*) hunch

corbata [kor'βata] *nf* tie

corchete [kor'tʃete] *nm* catch, clasp

corcho ['kortʃo] *nm* cork; (*PESCA*) float

cordel [kor'ðel] *nm* cord, line

cordero [kor'ðero] *nm* lamb

cordial [kor'ðjal] *adj* cordial; **~idad** *nf* warmth, cordiality

cordillera [korði'ʎera] *nf* range (of mountains)

Córdoba ['korðoβa] *n* Cordova

cordón [kor'ðon] *nm* (*cuerda*) cord, string; (*de zapatos*) lace; (*MIL etc*) cordon

cordura [kor'ðura] *nf*: **con ~** (*obrar, hablar*) sensibly

corneta [kor'neta] *nf* bugle

cornisa [kor'nisa] *nf* (*ARQ*) cornice

coro ['koro] *nm* chorus; (*conjunto de cantores*) choir

corona [ko'rona] *nf* crown; (*de flores*) garland; **coronación** *nf* coronation; **coronar** *vt* to crown

coronel [koro'nel] *nm* colonel

coronilla [koro'niʎa] *nf* (*ANAT*) crown (of the head)

corporación [korpora'θjon] *nf* corporation

corporal [korpo'ral] *adj* corporal, bodily

corpulento, a [korpu'lento a] *adj* (*persona*) heavily-built

corral [ko'rral] *nm* farmyard

correa [ko'rrea] *nf* strap; (*cinturón*) belt; (*de perro*) lead, leash

corrección [korrek'θjon] *nf* correction; (*reprensión*) rebuke; **correccional** *nm* reformatory

correcto, a [ko'rrekto a] *adj* correct; (*persona*) well-mannered

corredizo, a [korre'ðiθo, a] *adj* (*puerta etc*) sliding

corredor, a [korre'ðor, a] *nm* (*pasillo*) corridor; (*balcón corrido*) gallery; (*COM*) agent, broker ♦ *nm/f* (*DEPORTE*) runner

corregir [korre'xir] *vt* (*error*) to correct; **~se** *vr* to reform

correo [ko'rreo] *nm* post, mail; (*persona*) courier; **C~s** *nmpl* Post Office *sg*; **~ aéreo** airmail; **~ electrónico** electronic mail, e-mail

correr [ko'rrer] *vt* to run; (*cortinas*) to draw; (*cerrojo*) to shoot ♦ *vi* to run; (*líquido*) to run, flow; **~se** *vr* to slide, move; (*colores*) to run

correspondencia [korrespon'denθja] *nf* correspondence; (*FERRO*) connection

corresponder [korrespon'der] *vi* to correspond; (*convenir*) to be suitable; (*pertenecer*) to belong; (*concernir*) to concern; **~se** *vr* (*por escrito*) to correspond; (*amarse*) to love one another

correspondiente [korrespon'djente] *adj* corresponding

corresponsal [korrespon'sal] *nm/f* correspondent

corrida [ko'rriða] *nf* (*de toros*) bullfight

corrido, a [ko'rriðo, a] *adj* (*avergonzado*) abashed; **3 noches corridas** 3 nights running; **un kilo ~** a good kilo

corriente [ko'rrjente] *adj* (*agua*) running; (*dinero etc*) current; (*común*) ordinary, normal ♦ *nf* current ♦ *nm* current month; **~ eléctrica** electric current

corrija *etc vb ver* **corregir**

corrillo [ko'rriʎo] *nm* ring, circle (of people); (*fig*) clique

corro ['korro] *nm* ring, circle (of people)

corroborar [korroβo'rar] *vt* to corroborate

corroer [korro'er] *vt* to corrode; (*GEO*) to erode

corromper [korrom'per] *vt* (*madera*) to rot; (*fig*) to corrupt

corrosivo, a [korro'siβo, a] *adj* corrosive

corrupción [korrup'θjon] *nf* rot, decay; (*fig*) corruption

corsé [kor'se] *nm* corset

cortacésped [korta'θespeð] *nm* lawn mower

cortado, a [kor'taðo, a] *adj* (*gen*) cut; (*leche*) sour; (*tímido*) shy; (*avergonzado*) embarrassed ♦ *nm* coffee (with a little milk)

cortar [kor'tar] *vt* to cut; (*suministro*) to cut off; (*un pasaje*) to cut out ♦ *vi* to cut; **~se** *vr* (*avergonzarse*) to become embarrassed; (*leche*) to turn, curdle; **~se el pelo** to have one's hair cut

cortauñas [korta'uɲas] *nm inv* nail clippers *pl*

corte ['korte] *nm* cut, cutting; (*de tela*) piece, length ♦ *nf*: **las C~s** the Spanish Parliament; **~ y confección** dressmaking; **~ de luz** power cut

cortejar [korte'xar] *vt* to court

cortejo [kor'texo] *nm* entourage; **~ fúnebre** funeral procession

cortés [kor'tes] *adj* courteous, polite

cortesía [korte'sia] *nf* courtesy

corteza [kor'teθa] *nf* (*de árbol*) bark; (*de pan*) crust

cortijo [kor'tixo] *nm* farm, farmhouse

cortina [kor'tina] *nf* curtain

corto, a ['korto, a] *adj* (*breve*) short; (*tímido*) bashful; **~ de luces** not very bright; **~ de vista** short-sighted; **estar ~ de fondos** to be short of funds; **~circuito** *nm* short circuit; **~metraje** *nm* (*CINE*) short

cosa ['kosa] *nf* thing; **~ de** about; **eso es ~ mía** that's my business

coscorrón [kosko'rron] *nm* bump on the head

cosecha [ko'setʃa] *nf* (*AGR*) harvest; (*de vino*) vintage

cosechar [kose'tʃar] *vt* to harvest, gather (in)

coser [ko'ser] *vt* to sew

cosmético, a [kos'metiko, a] *adj, nm* cosmetic

cosquillas [kos'kiʎas] *nfpl*: **hacer ~** to tickle; **tener ~** to be ticklish

costa ['kosta] *nf* (*GEO*) coast; **C~ Brava** Costa Brava; **C~ Cantábrica** Cantabrian Coast; **C~ del Sol** Costa del Sol; **a toda ~** at all costs

costado [kos'taðo] *nm* side

costar [kos'tar] *vt* (*valer*) to cost; **me cuesta hablarle** I find it hard to talk to him

Costa Rica *nf* Costa Rica; **costarricense** *adj, nm/f* Costa Rican; **costarriqueño, a** *adj, nm/f* Costa Rican

coste ['koste] *nm* = **costo**

costear [koste'ar] *vt* to pay for

costero, a [kos'tero, a] *adj* (*pueblecito, camino*) coastal

costilla [kos'tiʎa] *nf* rib; (*CULIN*) cutlet

costo ['kosto] *nm* cost, price; **~ de la vida** cost of living; **~so, a** *adj* costly, expensive

costra ['kostra] *nf* (*corteza*) crust; (*MED*) scab

costumbre [kos'tumbre] *nf* custom, habit

costura [kos'tura] *nf* sewing, needlework; (*zurcido*) seam

costurera [kostu'rera] *nf* dressmaker

costurero [kostu'rero] *nm* sewing box *o* case

cotejar [kote'xar] *vt* to compare

cotidiano, a [koti'ðjano, a] *adj* daily, day to day

cotilla [ko'tiʎa] *nm/f* (*fam*) gossip; **cotillear** *vi* to gossip; **cotilleo** *nm* gossip(ing)

cotización [kotiθa'θjon] *nf* (*COM*) quotation, price; (*de club*) dues *pl*

cotizar [koti'θar] *vt* (*COM*) to quote, price; **~se** *vr*: **~se a** to sell at, fetch; (*BOLSA*) to stand at, be quoted at

coto ['koto] *nm* (*terreno cercado*) enclosure; (*de caza*) reserve

cotorra [ko'torra] *nf* parrot

COU [kou] (*ESP*) *nm abr* (= *Curso de Orientación Universitaria*) *1 year course leading to final school-leaving certificate and university entrance examinations*

coyote [ko'jote] *nm* coyote, prairie wolf

coyuntura [kojun'tura] *nf* juncture, occasion

coz [koθ] *nf* kick
crack [krak] *nm* (*droga*) crack
cráneo ['kraneo] *nm* skull, cranium
cráter ['krater] *nm* crater
creación [krea'θjon] *nf* creation
creador, a [krea'ðor, a] *adj* creative
♦ *nm/f* creator
crear [kre'ar] *vt* to create, make
crecer [kre'θer] *vi* to grow; (*precio*) to rise
creces ['kreθes]: **con ~** *adv* amply, fully
crecido, a [kre'θiðo, a] *adj* (*persona, planta*) full-grown; (*cantidad*) large
creciente [kre'θjente] *adj* growing; (*cantidad*) increasing; (*luna*) crescent
♦ *nm* crescent
crecimiento [kreθi'mjento] *nm* growth; (*aumento*) increase
credenciales [kreðen'θjales] *nfpl* credentials
crédito ['kreðito] *nm* credit
credo ['kreðo] *nm* creed
crédulo, a ['kreðulo, a] *adj* credulous
creencia [kre'enθja] *nf* belief
creer [kre'er] *vt, vi* to think, believe; **~se** *vr* to believe o.s. (to be); **~ en** to believe in; ¡ya lo creo! I should think so!
creíble [kre'iβle] *adj* credible, believable
creído, a [kre'iðo, a] *adj* (*engreído*) conceited
crema ['krema] *nf* cream; **~ pastelera** (confectioner's) custard
cremallera [krema'ʎera] *nf* zip (fastener)
crematorio [krema'torjo] *nm* (*tb*: **horno ~**) crematorium
crepitar [krepi'tar] *vi* to crackle
crepúsculo [kre'puskulo] *nm* twilight, dusk
cresta ['kresta] *nf* (GEO, ZOOL) crest
creyendo *vb ver* **creer**
creyente [kre'jente] *nm/f* believer
creyó *etc vb ver* **creer**
crezco *etc vb ver* **crecer**
cría *etc* ['kria] *vb ver* **criar** ♦ *nf* (*de animales*) rearing, breeding; (*animal*) young; *ver tb* **crío**
criadero [kria'ðero] *nm* (ZOOL) breeding place

criado, a [kri'aðo, a] *nm* servant ♦ *nf* servant, maid
criador [kria'ðor] *nm* breeder
crianza [kri'anθa] *nf* rearing, breeding; (*fig*) breeding
criar [kri'ar] *vt* (*educar*) to bring up; (*producir*) to grow, produce; (*animales*) to breed
criatura [kria'tura] *nf* creature; (*niño*) baby, (small) child
criba ['kriβa] *nf* sieve; **cribar** *vt* to sieve
crimen ['krimen] *nm* crime
criminal [krimi'nal] *adj, nm/f* criminal
crin [krin] *nf* (*tb*: **~es** *nfpl*) mane
crío, a ['krio, a] (*fam*) *nm/f* (*niño*) kid
crisis ['krisis] *nf inv* crisis; **~ nerviosa** nervous breakdown
crispar [kris'par] *vt* (*nervios*) to set on edge
cristal [kris'tal] *nm* crystal; (*de ventana*) glass, pane; (*lente*) lens; **~ino, a** *adj* crystalline; (*fig*) clear ♦ *nm* lens (of the eye); **~izar** *vt, vi* to crystallize
cristiandad [kristjan'daθ] *nf* Christendom
cristianismo [kristja'nismo] *nm* Christianity
cristiano, a [kris'tjano, a] *adj, nm/f* Christian
Cristo ['kristo] *nm* Christ; (*crucifijo*) crucifix
criterio [kri'terjo] *nm* criterion; (*juicio*) judgement
crítica ['kritika] *nf* criticism; *ver tb* **crítico**
criticar [kriti'kar] *vt* to criticize
crítico, a ['kritiko, a] *adj* critical ♦ *nm/f* critic
Croacia [kro'aθja] *nf* Croatia
croar [kro'ar] *vi* to croak
cromo ['kromo] *nm* chrome
crónica ['kronika] *nf* chronicle, account
crónico, a ['kroniko, a] *adj* chronic
cronómetro [kro'nometro] *nm* stopwatch
croqueta [kro'keta] *nf* croquette
cruce *etc* ['kruθe] *vb ver* **cruzar** ♦ *nm* crossing; (*de carreteras*) crossroads
crucificar [kruθifi'kar] *vt* to crucify
crucifijo [kruθi'fixo] *nm* crucifix
crucigrama [kruθi'ɣrama] *nm* crossword

(puzzle)

crudo, a ['kruðo, a] *adj* raw; (*no maduro*) unripe; (*petróleo*) crude; (*rudo, cruel*) cruel ♦ *nm* crude (oil)

cruel [krwel] *adj* cruel; **~dad** *nf* cruelty

crujido [kru'xiðo] *nm* (*de madera etc*) creak

crujiente [kru'xjente] *adj* (*galleta etc*) crunchy

crujir [kru'xir] *vi* (*madera etc*) to creak; (*dedos*) to crack; (*dientes*) to grind; (*nieve, arena*) to crunch

cruz [kruθ] *nf* cross; (*de moneda*) tails *sg*; **~ gamada** swastika

cruzada [kru'θaða] *nf* crusade

cruzado, a [kru'θaðo, a] *adj* crossed ♦ *nm* crusader

cruzar [kru'θar] *vt* to cross; **~se** *vr* (*líneas etc*) to cross; (*personas*) to pass each other

Cruz Roja *nf* Red Cross

cuaderno [kwa'ðerno] *nm* notebook; (*de escuela*) exercise book; (*NAUT*) logbook

cuadra ['kwaðra] *nf* (*caballeriza*) stable; (*AM*) block

cuadrado, a [kwa'ðraðo, a] *adj* square ♦ *nm* (*MAT*) square

cuadrar [kwa'ðrar] *vt* to square ♦ *vi*: **~ con** to square with, tally with; **~se** *vr* (*soldado*) to stand to attention

cuadrilátero [kwaðri'latero] *nm* (*DEPORTE*) boxing ring; (*GEOM*) quadrilateral

cuadrilla [kwa'ðriʎa] *nf* party, group

cuadro ['kwaðro] *nm* square; (*ARTE*) painting; (*TEATRO*) scene; (*diagrama*) chart; (*DEPORTE, MED*) team; **tela a ~s** checked (*BRIT*) *o* chequered (*US*) material

cuádruple ['kwaðruple] *adj* quadruple

cuajar [kwa'xar] *vt* (*leche*) to curdle; (*sangre*) to congeal; (*CULIN*) to set; **~se** *vr* to curdle; to congeal; to set; (*llenarse*) to fill up

cuajo ['kwaxo] *nm*: **de ~** (*arrancar*) by the roots; (*cortar*) completely

cual [kwal] *adv* like, as ♦ *pron*: **el ~** *etc* which; (*persona: sujeto*) who; (: *objeto*) whom ♦ *adj* such as; **cada ~** each one;

déjalo tal ~ leave it just as it is

cuál [kwal] *pron interr* which (one)

cualesquier(a) [kwales'kjer(a)] *pl de* **cualquier(a)**

cualidad [kwali'ðað] *nf* quality

cualquier [kwal'kjer] *adj ver* **cualquiera**

cualquiera [kwal'kjera] (*pl* **cualesquiera**) *adj* (*delante de nm y f*: **cualquier**) any ♦ *pron* anybody; **un coche ~ servirá** any car will do; **no es un hombre ~** he isn't just anybody; **cualquier día/libro** any day/book; **eso ~ lo sabe hacer** anybody can do that; **es un ~** he's a nobody

cuando ['kwando] *adv* when; (*aún si*) if, even if ♦ *conj* (*puesto que*) since ♦ *prep*: **yo, ~ niño ...** when I was a child ...; **~ no sea así** even if it is not so; **~ más** at (the) most; **~ menos** at least; **~ no** if not, otherwise; **de ~ en ~** from time to time

cuándo ['kwando] *adv* when; **¿desde ~?, ¿de ~ acá?** since when?

cuantía [kwan'tia] *nf* (*importe: de pérdidas, deuda, daños*) extent

cuantioso, a [kwan'tjoso, a] *adj* substantial

PALABRA CLAVE

---

cuanto, a ['kwanto, a] *adj* **1** (*todo*): **tiene todo ~ desea** he's got everything he wants; **le daremos ~s ejemplares necesite** we'll give him as many copies as *o* all the copies he needs; **~s hombres la ven** all the men who see her

2: **unos ~s**: **había unos ~s periodistas** there were a few journalists

3 (+*más*): **~ más vino bebes peor te sentirás** the more wine you drink the worse you'll feel

♦ *pron*: **tiene ~ desea** he has everything he wants; **tome ~/~s quiera** take as much/many as you want

♦ *adv*: **en ~**: **en ~ profesor** as a teacher; **en ~ a mí** as for me; *ver tb* **antes**

♦ *conj* **1**: **~ más gana menos gasta** the more he earns the less he spends; **~ más joven más confiado** the younger you are the more trusting you are

2: **en ~**: **en ~ llegue/llegué** as soon as I arrive/arrived

cuánto, a ['kwanto, a] *adj* (*exclamación*) what a lot of; (*interr: sg*) how much?; (: *pl*) how many? ♦ *pron, adv* how; (*interr: sg*) how much?; (: *pl*) how many?; **¡cuánta gente!** what a lot of people!; **¿~ cuesta?** how much does it cost?; **¿a ~s estamos?** what's the date?; **Señor no sé ~s** Mr. So-and-So

cuarenta [kwa'renta] *num* forty

cuarentena [kwaren'tena] *nf* quarantine

cuaresma [kwa'resma] *nf* Lent

cuarta ['kwarta] *nf* (*MAT*) quarter, fourth; (*palmo*) span

cuartel [kwar'tel] *nm* (*MIL*) barracks *pl*; **~ general** headquarters *pl*

cuarteto [kwar'teto] *nm* quartet

cuarto, a ['kwarto, a] *adj* fourth ♦ *nm* (*MAT*) quarter, fourth; (*habitación*) room; **~ de baño** bathroom; **~ de estar** living room; **~ de hora** quarter (of an) hour; **~ de kilo** quarter kilo

cuatro ['kwatro] *num* four

Cuba ['kuβa] *nf* Cuba; **cubano, a** *adj*, *nm/f* Cuban

cuba ['kuβa] *nf* cask, barrel

cubata [ku'βata] *nm* (*fam*) large drink (*of rum and coke etc*)

cúbico, a ['kuβiko, a] *adj* cubic

cubierta [ku'βjerta] *nf* cover, covering; (*neumático*) tyre; (*NAUT*) deck

cubierto, a [ku'βjerto, a] *pp de* **cubrir** ♦ *adj* covered ♦ *nm* cover; (*lugar en la mesa*) place; **~s** *nmpl* cutlery *sg*; **a ~** under cover

cubil [ku'βil] *nm* den; **~ete** *nm* (*en juegos*) cup

cubito [ku'βito] *nm*: **~ de hielo** ice-cube

cubo ['kuβo] *nm* (*MATH*) cube; (*balde*) bucket, tub; (*TEC*) drum

cubrecama [kuβre'kama] *nm* bedspread

cubrir [ku'βrir] *vt* to cover; **~se** *vr* (*cielo*) to become overcast

cucaracha [kuka'ratʃa] *nf* cockroach

cuchara [ku'tʃara] *nf* spoon; (*TEC*) scoop;

~da *nf* spoonful; **~dita** *nf* teaspoonful

cucharilla [kutʃa'riʎa] *nf* teaspoon

cucharón [kutʃa'ron] *nm* ladle

cuchichear [kutʃitʃe'ar] *vi* to whisper

cuchilla [ku'tʃiʎa] *nf* (*large*) knife; (*de arma blanca*) blade; **~ de afeitar** razor blade

cuchillo [ku'tʃiʎo] *nm* knife

cuchitril [kutʃi'tril] *nm* hovel

cuclillas [ku'kliʎas] *nfpl*: **en ~** squatting

cuco, a ['kuko, a] *adj* pretty; (*astuto*) sharp ♦ *nm* cuckoo

cucurucho [kuku'rutʃo] *nm* cornet

cuello ['kweʎo] *nm* (*ANAT*) neck; (*de vestido, camisa*) collar

cuenca ['kwenka] *nf* (*ANAT*) eye socket; (*GEO*) bowl, deep valley

cuenco ['kwenko] *nm* bowl

cuenta *etc* ['kwenta] *vb ver* **contar** ♦ *nf* (*cálculo*) count, counting; (*en café, restaurante*) bill (*BRIT*), check (*US*); (*COM*) account; (*de collar*) bead; **a fin de ~s** in the end; **caer en la ~** to catch on; **darse ~ de** to realize; **tener en ~** to bear in mind; **echar ~s** to take stock; **~ corriente/de ahorros** current/savings account; **~ atrás** countdown; **~kilómetros** *nm inv* ≈ milometer; (*de velocidad*) speedometer

cuento *etc* ['kwento] *vb ver* **contar** ♦ *nm* story

cuerda ['kwerða] *nf* rope; (*fina*) string; (*de reloj*) spring; **dar ~ a un reloj** to wind up a clock; **~ floja** tightrope

cuerdo, a ['kwerðo, a] *adj* sane; (*prudente*) wise, sensible

cuerno ['kwerno] *nm* horn

cuero ['kwero] *nm* leather; **en ~s** stark naked; **~ cabelludo** scalp

cuerpo ['kwerpo] *nm* body

cuervo ['kwerβo] *nm* crow

cuesta *etc* ['kwesta] *vb ver* **costar** ♦ *nf* slope; (*en camino etc*) hill; **~ arriba/abajo** uphill/downhill; **a ~s** on one's back

cueste *etc vb ver* **costar**

cuestión [kwes'tjon] *nf* matter, question, issue

cueva ['kweßa] nf cave
cuidado [kwi'ðaðo] nm care, carefulness; (*preocupación*) care, worry ♦ *excl* careful!, look out!
cuidadoso, a [kwiða'ðoso, a] adj careful; (*preocupado*) anxious
cuidar [kwi'ðar] vt (MED) to care for; (*ocuparse de*) to take care of, look after ♦ vi: ~ **de** to take care of, look after; ~**se** vr to look after o.s.; ~**se de hacer algo** to take care to do sth
culata [ku'lata] nf (*de fusil*) butt
culebra [ku'leßra] nf snake
culebrón [kule'ßron] (*fam*) nm (*TV*) soap(-opera)
culinario, a [kuli'narjo, a] adj culinary, cooking *cpd*
culminación [kulmina'θjon] nf culmination
culo ['kulo] nm bottom, backside; (*de vaso, botella*) bottom
culpa ['kulpa] nf fault; (*JUR*) guilt; **por ~ de** because of; **tener la ~ (de)** to be to blame (for); ~**bilidad** nf guilt; ~**ble** adj guilty ♦ nm/f culprit
culpar [kul'par] vt to blame; (*acusar*) to accuse
cultivar [kulti'ßar] vt to cultivate
cultivo [kul'tißo] nm (*acto*) cultivation; (*plantas*) crop
culto, a ['kulto, a] adj (*que tiene cultura*) cultured, educated ♦ nm (*homenaje*) worship; (*religión*) cult
cultura [kul'tura] nf culture
culturismo [kultu'rismo] nm body-building
cumbre ['kumbre] nf summit, top
cumpleaños [kumple'aɲos] nm inv birthday
cumplido, a [kum'pliðo, a] adj (*abundante*) plentiful; (*cortés*) courteous ♦ nm compliment; **visita de ~** courtesy call
cumplidor, a [kumpli'ðor, a] adj reliable
cumplimentar [kumplimen'tar] vt to congratulate
cumplimiento [kumpli'mjento] nm (*de un*

deber) fulfilment; (*acabamiento*) completion
cumplir [kum'plir] vt (*orden*) to carry out, obey; (*promesa*) to carry out, fulfil; (*condena*) to serve ♦ vi: ~ **con** (*deberes*) to carry out, fulfil; ~**se** vr (*plazo*) to expire; **hoy cumple dieciocho años** he is eighteen today
cúmulo ['kumulo] nm heap
cuna ['kuna] nf cradle, cot
cundir [kun'dir] vi (*noticia, rumor, pánico*) to spread; (*rendir*) to go a long way
cuneta [ku'neta] nf ditch
cuña ['kuɲa] nf wedge
cuñado, a [ku'ɲaðo, a] nm/f brother-/sister-in-law
cuota ['kwota] nf (*parte proporcional*) share; (*cotización*) fee, dues pl
cupe etc vb ver **caber**
cupiera etc vb ver **caber**
cupo ['kupo] vb ver **caber** ♦ nm quota
cupón [ku'pon] nm coupon
cúpula ['kupula] nf dome
cura ['kura] nf (*curación*) cure; (*método curativo*) treatment ♦ nm priest
curación [kura'θjon] nf cure; (*acción*) curing
curandero, a [kuran'dero, a] nm/f quack
curar [ku'rar] vt (MED: *herida*) to treat, dress; (: *enfermo*) to cure; (CULIN) to cure, salt; (*cuero*) to tan; ~**se** vr to get well, recover
curiosear [kurjose'ar] vt to glance at, look over ♦ vi to look round, wander round; (*explorar*) to poke about
curiosidad [kurjosi'ðað] nf curiosity
curioso, a [ku'rjoso, a] adj curious ♦ nm/f bystander, onlooker
currante [ku'rrante] (*fam*) nm/f worker
currar [ku'rrar] (*fam*) vi to work
currículo [ku'rrikulo] = **curriculum**
curriculum [ku'rrikulum] nm curriculum vitae
cursi ['kursi] (*fam*) adj affected
cursillo [kur'siλo] nm short course
cursiva [kur'sißa] nf italics pl
curso ['kurso] nm course; **en ~** (*año*)

current; (*proceso*) going on, under
way

cursor [kur'sor] *nm* (*INFORM*) cursor

curtido, a [kur'tiðo, a] *adj* (*cara etc*)
weather-beaten; (*fig: persona*)
experienced

curtir [kur'tir] *vt* (*cuero etc*) to tan

curva ['kurßa] *nf* curve, bend

cúspide ['kuspiðe] *nf* (*GEO*) peak; (*fig*) top

custodia [kus'toðja] *nf* safekeeping;
custody; **custodiar** *vt* (*conservar*) to take
care of; (*vigilar*) to guard

cutis ['kutis] *nm inv* skin, complexion

cutre ['kutre] (*fam*) *adj* (*lugar*) grotty

cuyo, a ['kujo, a] *pron* (*de quien*) whose;
(*de que*) whose, of which; **en ~ caso** in
which case

C.V. *abr* (= *caballos de vapor*) H.P.

D, d

D. *abr* (= *Don*) Esq.

Da. *abr* = **Doña**

dádiva ['daðißa] *nf* (*donación*) donation;
(*regalo*) gift; **dadivoso, a** *adj*
generous

dado, a ['daðo, a] *pp de* **dar** ♦ *nm* die; **~s**
nmpl dice; **~ que** given that

daltónico, a [dal'toniko, a] *adj* colour-
blind

dama ['dama] *nf* (*gen*) lady; (*AJEDREZ*)
queen; **~s** *nfpl* (*juego*) draughts *sg*

damnificar [damnifi'kar] *vt* to harm;
(*persona*) to injure

danés, esa [da'nes, esa] *adj* Danish
♦ *nm/f* Dane

danzar [dan'θar] *vt, vi* to dance

dañar [da'ɲar] *vt* (*objeto*) to damage;
(*persona*) to hurt; **~se** *vr* (*objeto*) to get
damaged

dañino, a [da'ɲino, a] *adj* harmful

daño ['daɲo] *nm* (*a un objeto*) damage; (*a
una persona*) harm, injury; **~s y
perjuicios** (*JUR*) damages; **hacer ~ a** to
damage; (*persona*) to hurt, injure;
hacerse ~ to hurt o.s.

PALABRA CLAVE

dar [dar] *vt* **1** (*gen*) to give; (*obra de
teatro*) to put on; (*film*) to show; (*fiesta*)
to hold; **~ algo a uno** to give sb sth *o* sth
to sb; **~ de beber a uno** to give sb a
drink

2 (*producir: intereses*) to yield; (*fruta*) to
produce

3 (*locuciones +n*): **da gusto escucharle**
it's a pleasure to listen to him; *ver tb*
paseo *y otros sustantivos*

4 (+*n.* = *perifrasis de verbo*): **me da asco**
it sickens me

5 (*considerar*): **~ algo por descontado/
entendido** to take sth for granted/as
read; **~ algo por concluido** to consider
sth finished

6 (*hora*): **el reloj dio las 6** the clock
struck 6 (o'clock)

7: **me da lo mismo** it's all the same to
me; *ver tb* **igual**; ...

♦ *vi* **1**: **~ con: dimos con él dos horas
más tarde** we came across him two
hours later; **al final di con la solución** I
eventually came up with the answer

2: **~ en** (*blanco, suelo*) to hit; **el sol me
da en la cara** the sun is shining (right)
on my face

3: **~ de sí** (*zapatos etc*) to stretch, give

♦ **~se** *vr* **1**: **~se por vencido** to give up

2 (*ocurrir*): **se han dado muchos casos**
there have been a lot of cases

3: **~se a**: **se ha dado a la bebida** he's
taken to drinking

4: **se me dan bien/mal las ciencias** I'm
good/bad at science

5: **dárselas de**: **se las da de experto** he
fancies himself *o* poses as an expert

---

dardo ['darðo] *nm* dart

datar [da'tar] *vi*: **~ de** to date from

dátil ['datil] *nm* date

dato ['dato] *nm* fact, piece of information;
~s personales personal details

DC *abbr m* (= *disco compacto*) CD

d. de J.C. *abr* (= *después de Jesucristo*) A.D.

PALABRA CLAVE

de [de] *prep* (*de+el* = *del*) **1** (*posesión*) of; **la casa ~ Isabel/mis padres** Isabel's/my parents' house; **es ~ ellos** it's theirs **2** (*origen, distancia, con números*) from; **soy ~ Gijón** I'm from Gijón; **~ 8 a 20** from 8 to 20; **salir del cine** to go out of *o* leave the cinema; **~ 2 en 2** 2 by 2, at a time **3** (*valor descriptivo*): **una copa ~ vino** a glass of wine; **la mesa ~ la cocina** the kitchen table; **un billete ~ 1000 pesetas** a 1000 peseta note; **un niño ~ tres años** a three-year-old (child); **una máquina ~ coser** a sewing machine; **ir vestido ~ gris** to be dressed in grey; **la niña del vestido azul** the girl in the blue dress; **trabaja ~ profesora** she works as a teacher; **~ lado** sideways; **~ atrás/delante** rear/front **4** (*hora, tiempo*): **a las 8 ~ la mañana** at 8 o'clock in the morning; **~ día/noche** by day/night; **~ hoy en ocho días** a week from now; **~ niño era gordo** as a child he was fat **5** (*comparaciones*): **más/menos ~ cien personas** more/less than a hundred people; **el más caro ~ la tienda** the most expensive in the shop; **menos/más ~ lo pensado** less/more than expected **6** (*causa*): **del calor** from the heat; **~ puro tonto** out of sheer stupidity **7** (*tema*) about; **clases ~ inglés** English classes; **¿sabes algo ~ él?** do you know anything about him?; **un libro ~ física** a physics book **8** (*adj +de +infin*): **fácil ~ entender** easy to understand **9** (*oraciones pasivas*): **fue respetado ~ todos** he was loved by all **10** (*condicional +infin*) if; **~ ser posible** if possible; **~ no terminarlo hoy** if I *etc* don't finish it today

dé *vb ver* **dar**
deambular [deambu'lar] *vi* to wander
debajo [de'ßaxo] *adv* underneath; **~ de** below, under; **por ~ de** beneath
debate [de'ßate] *nm* debate; **debatir** *vt* to debate
deber [de'ßer] *nm* duty ♦ *vt* to owe ♦ *vi*: **debe (de)** it must, it should; **~es** *nmpl* (*ESCOL*) homework; **debo hacerlo** I must do it; **debe de ir** he should go; **~se** *vr*: **~se a** to be owing *o* due to
debido, a [de'ßiðo, a] *adj* proper, just; **~ a** due to, because of
débil ['deßil] *adj* (*persona, carácter*) weak; (*luz*) dim; **debilidad** *nf* weakness; dimness
debilitar [deßili'tar] *vt* to weaken; **~se** *vr* to grow weak
debutar [deßu'tar] *vi* to make one's debut
década ['dekaða] *nf* decade
decadencia [deka'ðenθja] *nf* (*estado*) decadence; (*proceso*) decline, decay
decaer [deka'er] *vi* (*declinar*) to decline; (*debilitarse*) to weaken
decaído, a [deka'iðo, a] *adj*: **estar ~** (*abatido*) to be down
decaimiento [dekai'mjento] *nm* (*declinación*) decline; (*desaliento*) discouragement; (*MED: estado débil*) weakness
decano, a [de'kano, a] *nm/f* (*de universidad etc*) dean
decapitar [dekapi'tar] *vt* to behead
decena [de'θena] *nf*: **una ~** ten (or so)
decencia [de'θenθja] *nf* decency
decente [de'θente] *adj* decent
decepción [deθep'θjon] *nf* disappointment
decepcionar [deθepθjo'nar] *vt* to disappoint
decidir [deθi'ðir] *vt, vi* to decide; **~se** *vr*: **~se a** to make up one's mind to
décimo, a ['deθimo, a] *adj* tenth ♦ *nm* tenth
decir [de'θir] *vt* to say; (*contar*) to tell; (*hablar*) to speak ♦ *nm* saying; **~se** *vr*: **se dice que** it is said that; **~ para** *o* **entre sí**

to say to o.s.; **querer ~** to mean;
¡dígame! (*TEL*) hello!; (*en tienda*) can I
help you?

decisión [deθi'sjon] *nf* (*resolución*)
decision; (*firmeza*) decisiveness

decisivo, a [deθi'siβo, a] *adj* decisive

declaración [deklara'θjon] *nf*
(*manifestación*) statement; (*de amor*)
declaration; **~ de ingresos** *o* **de la renta**
o **fiscal** income-tax return

declarar [dekla'rar] *vt* to declare ♦ *vi* to
declare; (*JUR*) to testify; **~se** *vr* to propose

declinar [dekli'nar] *vt* (*gen*) to decline;
(*JUR*) to reject ♦ *vi* (*el día*) to draw to a
close

declive [de'kliβe] *nm* (*cuesta*) slope; (*fig*)
decline

decodificador [dekoδifika'δor] *nm*
decoder

decolorarse [dekolo'rarse] *vr* to become
discoloured

decoración [dekora'θjon] *nf* decoration

decorado [deko'raδo] *nm* (*CINE, TEATRO*)
scenery, set

decorar [deko'rar] *vt* to decorate;
decorativo, a *adj* ornamental,
decorative

decoro [de'koro] *nm* (*respeto*) respect;
(*dignidad*) decency; (*recato*) propriety;
~so, a *adj* (*decente*) decent; (*modesto*)
modest; (*digno*) proper

decrecer [dekre'θer] *vi* to decrease,
diminish

decrépito, a [de'krepito, a] *adj* decrepit

decretar [dekre'tar] *vt* to decree; **decreto**
nm decree

dedal [de'δal] *nm* thimble

dedicación [deδika'θjon] *nf* dedication

dedicar [deδi'kar] *vt* (*libro*) to dedicate;
(*tiempo, dinero*) to devote; (*palabras:
decir, consagrar*) to dedicate, devote;
dedicatoria *nf* (*de libro*) dedication

dedo ['deδo] *nm* finger; **~ (del pie)** toe; **~**
pulgar thumb; **~ índice** index finger; **~**
corazón middle finger; **~ anular** ring
finger; **~ meñique** little finger; **hacer ~**
(*fam*) to hitch (a lift)

deducción [deδuk'θjon] *nf* deduction

deducir [deδu'θir] *vt* (*concluir*) to deduce,
infer; (*COM*) to deduct

defecto [de'fekto] *nm* defect, flaw;
defectuoso, a *adj* defective, faulty

defender [defen'der] *vt* to defend

defensa [de'fensa] *nf* defence ♦ *nm*
(*DEPORTE*) defender, back; **defensivo, a**
adj defensive; **a la defensiva** on the
defensive

defensor, a [defen'sor, a] *adj* defending
♦ *nm/f* (*abogado ~*) defending counsel;
(*protector*) protector

deficiencia [defi'θjenθja] *nf* deficiency

deficiente [defi'θjente] *adj* (*defectuoso*)
defective; **~ en** lacking *o* deficient in; **ser**
un ~ mental to be mentally handicapped

déficit ['defiθit] (*pl* **~s**) *nm* deficit

definición [defini'θjon] *nf* definition

definir [defi'nir] *vt* (*determinar*) to
determine, establish; (*decidir*) to define;
(*aclarar*) to clarify; **definitivo, a** *adj*
definitive; **en definitiva** definitively; (*en
resumen*) in short

deformación [deforma'θjon] *nf*
(*alteración*) deformation; (*RADIO etc*)
distortion

deformar [defor'mar] *vt* (*gen*) to deform;
~se *vr* to become deformed; **deforme**
adj (*informe*) deformed; (*feo*) ugly;
(*malhecho*) misshapen

defraudar [defrau'δar] *vt* (*decepcionar*) to
disappoint; (*estafar*) to defraud

defunción [defun'θjon] *nf* death, demise

degeneración [dexenera'θjon] *nf* (*de las
células*) degeneration; (*moral*) degeneracy

degenerar [dexene'rar] *vi* to degenerate

degollar [deɣo'ʎar] *vt* to behead; (*fig*) to
slaughter

degradar [deɣra'δar] *vt* to debase,
degrade; **~se** *vr* to demean o.s.

degustación [deɣusta'θjon] *nf* sampling,
tasting

deificar [deifi'kar] *vt* to deify

dejadez [dexa'δeθ] *nf* (*negligencia*)
neglect; (*descuido*) untidiness, carelessness

dejar [de'xar] *vt* to leave; (*permitir*) to

allow, let; (*abandonar*) to abandon, forsake; (*beneficios*) to produce, yield ♦ *vi*: ~ **de** (*parar*) to stop; (*no hacer*) to fail to; **no dejes de comprar un billete** make sure you buy a ticket; ~ **a un lado** to leave *o* set aside

dejo ['dexo] *nm* (LING) accent

del [del] (= **de**+**el**) *ver* **de**

delantal [delan'tal] *nm* apron

delante [de'lante] *adv* in front, (*enfrente*) opposite; (*adelante*) ahead; ~ **de** in front of, before

delantera [delan'tera] *nf* (*de vestido, casa etc*) front part; (DEPORTE) forward line; **llevar la** ~ **(a uno)** to be ahead (of sb)

delantero, a [delan'tero, a] *adj* front ♦ *nm* (DEPORTE) forward, striker

delatar [dela'tar] *vt* to inform on *o* against, betray; **delator, a** *nm/f* informer

delegación [delexa'θjon] *nf* (*acción, delegados*) delegation; (COM: *oficina*) office, branch; ~ **de policía** police station

delegado, a [dele'xaðo, a] *nm/f* delegate; (COM) agent

delegar [dele'xar] *vt* to delegate

deletrear [deletre'ar] *vt* to spell (out)

deleznable [deleθ'naßle] *adj* brittle; (*excusa, idea*) feeble

delfín [del'fin] *nm* dolphin

delgadez [delxa'ðeθ] *nf* thinness, slimness

delgado, a [del'xaðo, a] *adj* thin; (*persona*) slim, thin; (*tela etc*) light, delicate

deliberación [delißera'θjon] *nf* deliberation

deliberar [deliße'rar] *vt* to debate, discuss

delicadeza [delika'ðeθa] *nf* (*gen*) delicacy; (*refinamiento, sutileza*) refinement

delicado, a [deli'kaðo, a] *adj* (*gen*) delicate; (*sensible*) sensitive; (*quisquilloso*) touchy

delicia [de'liθja] *nf* delight

delicioso, a [deli'θjoso, a] *adj* (*gracioso*) delightful; (*exquisito*) delicious

delimitar [delimi'tar] *vt* (*funciones, responsabilidades*) to define

delincuencia [delin'kwenθja] *nf* delinquency; **delincuente** *nm/f* delinquent; (*criminal*) criminal

delineante [deline'ante] *nm/f* draughtsman/woman

delinear [deline'ar] *vt* (*dibujo*) to draw; (*fig, contornos*) to outline

delinquir [delin'kir] *vi* to commit an offence

delirante [deli'rante] *adj* delirious

delirar [deli'rar] *vi* to be delirious, rave

delirio [de'lirjo] *nm* (MED) delirium; (*palabras insensatas*) ravings *pl*

delito [de'lito] *nm* (*gen*) crime; (*infracción*) offence

delta ['delta] *nm* delta

demacrado, a [dema'kraðo, a] *adj*: **estar** ~ to look pale and drawn, be wasted away

demagogo, a [dema'xoxo, a] *nm/f* demagogue

demanda [de'manda] *nf* (*pedido, COM*) demand; (*petición*) request; (JUR) action, lawsuit

demandante [deman'dante] *nm/f* claimant

demandar [deman'dar] *vt* (*gen*) to demand; (JUR) to sue, file a lawsuit against

demarcación [demarka'θjon] *nf* (*de terreno*) demarcation

demás [de'mas] *adj*: **los** ~ **niños** the other children, the remaining children ♦ *pron*: **los/las** ~ the others, the rest (of them); **lo** ~ the rest (of it)

demasía [dema'sia] *nf* (*exceso*) excess, surplus; **comer en** ~ to eat to excess

demasiado, a [dema'sjaðo, a] *adj*: ~ **vino** too much wine ♦ *adv* (*antes de adj, adv*) too; ~**s libros** too many books; **¡esto es** ~**!** that's the limit!; **hace** ~ **calor** it's too hot; ~ **despacio** too slowly; ~**s** too many

demencia [de'menθja] *nf* (*locura*) madness; **demente** *nm/f* lunatic ♦ *adj* mad, insane

democracia [demo'kraθja] *nf* democracy

demócrata [de'mokrata] *nm/f* democrat;

democrático, a *adj* democratic
demoler [demo'ler] *vt* to demolish;
  demolición *nf* demolition
demonio [de'monjo] *nm* devil, demon;
  ¡~s! hell!, damn!; **¿cómo ~s?** how the
  hell?
demora [de'mora] *nf* delay; **demorar** *vt*
  (*retardar*) to delay, hold back; (*detener*) to
  hold up ♦ *vi* to linger, stay on; **~se** *vr* to
  be delayed
demos *vb ver* **dar**
demostración [demostra'θjon] *nf* (*MAT*)
  proof; (*de afecto*) show, display
demostrar [demos'trar] *vt* (*probar*) to
  prove; (*mostrar*) to show; (*manifestar*) to
  demonstrate
demudado, a [demu'ðaðo, a] *adj* (*rostro*)
  pale
den *vb ver* **dar**
denegar [dene'xar] *vt* (*rechazar*) to refuse;
  (*JUR*) to reject
denigrar [deni'xrar] *vt* (*desacreditar,
  infamar*) to denigrate; (*injuriar*) to insult

Denominación de Origen
---

*❶ The **Denominación de Origen**,
abbreviated to **D.O.**, is a prestigious
classification awarded to food products
such as wines, cheeses, sausages and hams
which meet the stringent quality and
production standards of the designated
region. D.O. labels serve as a guarantee of
quality.*

---

denotar [deno'tar] *vt* to denote
densidad [densi'ðað] *nf* density; (*fig*)
  thickness
denso, a ['denso, a] *adj* dense; (*espeso,
  pastoso*) thick; (*fig*) heavy
dentadura [denta'ðura] *nf* (set of) teeth
  pl; **~ postiza** false teeth *pl*
dentera [den'tera] *nf* (*sensación
  desagradable*) the shivers *pl*
dentífrico, a [den'tifriko, a] *adj* dental
  ♦ *nm* toothpaste
dentista [den'tista] *nm/f* dentist
dentro ['dentro] *adv* inside ♦ *prep*: **~ de**

in, inside; within; **por ~** (on the) inside;
  mirar por ~ to look inside; **~ de tres
  meses** within three months
denuncia [de'nunθja] *nf* (*delación*)
  denunciation; (*acusación*) accusation; (*de
  accidente*) report; **denunciar** *vt* to
  report; (*delatar*) to inform on *o* against
departamento [departa'mento] *nm*
  (*sección administrativa*) department,
  section; (*AM: apartamento*) flat (*BRIT*),
  apartment
dependencia [depen'denθja] *nf*
  dependence; (*POL*) dependency; (*COM*)
  office, section
depender [depen'der] *vi*: **~ de** to depend
  on
dependienta [depen'djenta] *nf*
  saleswoman, shop assistant
dependiente [depen'djente] *adj*
  dependent ♦ *nm* salesman, shop assistant
depilar [depi'lar] *vt* (*con cera*) to wax;
  (*cejas*) to pluck; **depilatorio** *nm* hair
  remover
deplorable [deplo'raβle] *adj* deplorable
deplorar [deplo'rar] *vt* to deplore
deponer [depo'ner] *vt* to lay down ♦ *vi*
  (*JUR*) to give evidence; (*declarar*) to make
  a statement
deportar [depor'tar] *vt* to deport
deporte [de'porte] *nm* sport; **hacer ~** to
  play sports; **deportista** *adj* sports *cpd*
  ♦ *nm/f* sportsman/woman; **deportivo, a**
  adj (*club, periódico*) sports *cpd* ♦ *nm*
  sports car
depositar [deposi'tar] *vt* (*dinero*) to
  deposit; (*mercancías*) to put away, store;
  ~se *vr* to settle; **~io, a** *nm/f* trustee
depósito [de'posito] *nm* (*gen*) deposit;
  (*almacén*) warehouse, store; (*de agua,
  gasolina etc*) tank; **~ de cadáveres**
  mortuary
depreciar [depre'θjar] *vt* to depreciate,
  reduce the value of; **~se** *vr* to depreciate,
  lose value
depredador, a [depreða'ðor, a] *adj*
  predatory ♦ *nm* predator
depresión [depre'sjon] *nf* depression

deprimido, a [depriˈmiðo, a] *adj* depressed

deprimir [depriˈmir] *vt* to depress; **~se** *vr* (*persona*) to become depressed

deprisa [deˈprisa] *adv* quickly, hurriedly

depuración [depuraˈθjon] *nf* purification; (*POL*) purge

depurar [depuˈrar] *vt* to purify; (*purgar*) to purge

derecha [deˈretʃa] *nf* right(-hand) side; (*POL*) right; **a la ~** (*estar*) on the right; (*torcer etc*) (to the) right

derecho, a [deˈretʃo, a] *adj* right, right-hand ♦ *nm* (*privilegio*) right; (*lado*) right(-hand) side; (*leyes*) law ♦ *adv* straight, directly; **~s** *nmpl* (*de aduana*) duty *sg*; (*de autor*) royalties; **tener ~ a** to have a right to

deriva [deˈriβa] *nf*: **ir** *o* **estar a la ~** to drift, be adrift

derivado [deriˈβaðo] *nm* (*COM*) by-product

derivar [deriˈβar] *vt* to derive; (*desviar*) to direct ♦ *vi* to derive, be derived; (*NAUT*) to drift; **~se** *vr* to derive, be derived; to drift

derramamiento [derramaˈmjento] *nm* (*dispersión*) spilling; **~ de sangre** bloodshed

derramar [derraˈmar] *vt* to spill; (*verter*) to pour out; (*esparcir*) to scatter; **~se** *vr* to pour out; **~ lágrimas** to weep

derrame [deˈrrame] *nm* (*de líquido*) spilling; (*de sangre*) shedding; (*de tubo etc*) overflow; (*pérdida*) leakage; (*MED*) discharge

derredor [derreˈðor] *adv*: **al** *o* **en ~ de** around, about

derretido, a [derreˈtiðo, a] *adj* melted; (*metal*) molten

derretir [derreˈtir] *vt* (*gen*) to melt; (*nieve*) to thaw; **~se** *vr* to melt

derribar [derriˈβar] *vt* to knock down; (*construcción*) to demolish; (*persona, gobierno, político*) to bring down

derrocar [derroˈkar] *vt* (*gobierno*) to bring down, overthrow

derrochar [derroˈtʃar] *vt* to squander; **derroche** *nm* (*despilfarro*) waste, squandering

derrota [deˈrrota] *nf* (*NAUT*) course; (*MIL, DEPORTE etc*) defeat, rout; **derrotar** *vt* (*gen*) to defeat; **derrotero** *nm* (*rumbo*) course

derruir [derruˈir] *vt* (*edificio*) to demolish

derrumbar [derrumˈbar] *vt* (*edificio*) to knock down; **~se** *vr* to collapse

derruyendo *etc vb ver* **derruir**

des *vb ver* **dar**

desabotonar [desaβotoˈnar] *vt* to unbutton, undo; **~se** *vr* to come undone

desabrido, a [desaˈβriðo, a] *adj* (*comida*) insipid, tasteless; (*persona*) rude, surly; (*respuesta*) sharp; (*tiempo*) unpleasant

desabrochar [desaβroˈtʃar] *vt* (*botones, broches*) to undo, unfasten; **~se** *vr* (*ropa etc*) to come undone

desacato [desaˈkato] *nm* (*falta de respeto*) disrespect; (*JUR*) contempt

desacertado, a [desaθerˈtaðo, a] *adj* (*equivocado*) mistaken; (*inoportuno*) unwise

desacierto [desaˈθjerto] *nm* mistake, error

desaconsejado, a [desakonseˈxaðo, a] *adj* ill-advised

desaconsejar [desakonseˈxar] *vt* to advise against

desacreditar [desakreðiˈtar] *vt* (*desprestigiar*) to discredit, bring into disrepute; (*denigrar*) to run down

desacuerdo [desaˈkwerðo] *nm* disagreement, discord

desafiar [desaˈfjar] *vt* (*retar*) to challenge; (*enfrentarse a*) to defy

desafilado, a [desafiˈlaðo, a] *adj* blunt

desafinado, a [desafiˈnaðo, a] *adj*: **estar ~** to be out of tune

desafinar [desafiˈnar] *vi* (*al cantar*) to be *o* go out of tune

desafío *etc* [desaˈfio] *vb ver* **desafiar** ♦ *nm* (*reto*) challenge; (*combate*) duel; (*resistencia*) defiance

desaforado, a [desafoˈraðo, a] *adj* (*grito*) ear-splitting; (*comportamiento*) outrageous

desafortunadamente
[desafortunaða'mente] *adv* unfortunately

desafortunado, a [desafortu'naðo, a] *adj*
(*desgraciado*) unfortunate, unlucky

desagradable [desaɣra'ðaßle] *adj*
(*fastidioso, enojoso*) unpleasant; (*irritante*)
disagreeable

desagradar [desaɣra'ðar] *vi* (*disgustar*) to
displease; (*molestar*) to bother

desagradecido, a [desaɣraðe'θiðo, a] *adj*
ungrateful

desagrado [desa'ɣraðo] *nm* (*disgusto*)
displeasure; (*contrariedad*) dissatisfaction

desagraviar [desaɣra'ßjar] *vt* to make
amends to

desagüe [des'aɣwe] *nm* (*de un líquido*)
drainage; (*cañería*) drainpipe; (*salida*)
outlet, drain

desaguisado [desaɣi'saðo] *nm* outrage

desahogado, a [desao'ɣaðo, a] *adj*
(*holgado*) comfortable; (*espacioso*) roomy,
large

desahogar [desao'ɣar] *vt* (*aliviar*) to ease,
relieve; (*ira*) to vent; **~se** *vr* (*relajarse*) to
relax; (*desfogarse*) to let off steam

desahogo [desa'oxo] *nm* (*alivio*) relief;
(*comodidad*) comfort, ease

desahuciar [desau'θjar] *vt* (*enfermo*) to
give up hope for; (*inquilino*) to evict;
desahucio *nm* eviction

desairar [desai'rar] *vt* (*menospreciar*) to
slight, snub

desaire [des'aire] *nm* (*menosprecio*) slight;
(*falta de garbo*) unattractiveness

desajustar [desaxus'tar] *vt* (*desarreglar*) to
disarrange; (*desconcertar*) to throw off
balance; **~se** *vr* to get out of order;
(*aflojarse*) to loosen

desajuste [desa'xuste] *nm* (*de máquina*)
disorder; (*situación*) imbalance

desalentador, a [desalenta'ðor, a] *adj*
discouraging

desalentar [desalen'tar] *vt* (*desanimar*) to
discourage

desaliento *etc* [desa'ljento] *vb ver*
desalentar ♦ *nm* discouragement

desaliño [desa'liɲo] *nm* slovenliness

desalmado, a [desal'maðo, a] *adj* (*cruel*)
cruel, heartless

desalojar [desalo'xar] *vt* (*expulsar, echar*)
to eject; (*abandonar*) to move out of ♦ *vi*
to move out

desamor [desa'mor] *nm* (*frialdad*)
indifference; (*odio*) dislike

desamparado, a [desampa'raðo, a] *adj*
(*persona*) helpless; (*lugar: expuesto*)
exposed; (*desierto*) deserted

desamparar [desampa'rar] *vt* (*abandonar*)
to desert, abandon; (*JUR*) to leave
defenceless; (*barco*) to abandon

desandar [desan'dar] *vt*: **~ lo andado** *o* **el
camino** to retrace one's steps

desangrar [desan'grar] *vt* to bleed; (*fig:
persona*) to bleed dry; **~se** *vr* to lose a lot
of blood

desanimado, a [desani'maðo, a] *adj*
(*persona*) downhearted; (*espectáculo,
fiesta*) dull

desanimar [desani'mar] *vt* (*desalentar*) to
discourage; (*deprimir*) to depress; **~se** *vr*
to lose heart

desapacible [desapa'θißle] *adj* (*gen*)
unpleasant

desaparecer [desapare'θer] *vi* (*gen*) to
disappear; (*el sol, la luz*) to vanish;
desaparecido, a *adj* missing;
desaparición *nf* disappearance

desapasionado, a [desapasjo'naðo, a]
adj dispassionate, impartial

desapego [desa'peɣo] *nm* (*frialdad*)
coolness; (*distancia*) detachment

desapercibido, a [desaperθi'ßiðo, a] *adj*
(*desprevenido*) unprepared; **pasar ~** to go
unnoticed

desaprensivo, a [desapren'sißo, a] *adj*
unscrupulous

desaprobar [desapro'ßar] *vt* (*reprobar*) to
disapprove of; (*condenar*) to condemn;
(*no consentir*) to reject

desaprovechado, a [desaproße'tʃaðo, a]
adj (*oportunidad, tiempo*) wasted;
(*estudiante*) slack

desaprovechar [desaproße'tʃar] *vt* to
waste

desarmar [desar'mar] vt (MIL, fig) to disarm; (TEC) to take apart, dismantle; **desarme** nm disarmament

desarraigar [desarrai'var] vt to uproot; **desarraigo** nm uprooting

desarreglar [desarre'vlar] vt (desordenar) to disarrange; (trastocar) to upset, disturb

desarreglo [desa'rrevlo] nm (de casa, persona) untidiness; (desorden) disorder

desarrollar [desarro'ʎar] vt (gen) to develop; **~se** vr to develop; (ocurrir) to take place; (FOTO) to develop; **desarrollo** nm development

desarticular [desartiku'lar] vt (hueso) to dislocate; (objeto) to take apart; (fig) to break up

desasir [desa'sir] vt to loosen

desasosegar [desasose'var] vt (inquietar) to disturb, make uneasy; **~se** vr to become uneasy

desasosiego etc [desaso'sjevo] vb ver **desasosegar** ♦ nm (intranquilidad) uneasiness, restlessness; (ansiedad) anxiety

desastrado, a [desas'traðo, a] adj (desaliñado) shabby; (sucio) dirty

desastre [de'sastre] nm disaster; **desastroso, a** adj disastrous

desatado, a [desa'taðo, a] adj (desligado) untied; (violento) violent, wild

desatar [desa'tar] vt (nudo) to untie; (paquete) to undo; (separar) to detach; **~se** vr (zapatos) to come untied; (tormenta) to break

desatascar [desatas'kar] vt (cañería) to unblock, clear

desatender [desaten'der] vt (no prestar atención a) to disregard; (abandonar) to neglect

desatento, a [desa'tento, a] adj (distraído) inattentive; (descortés) discourteous

desatinado, a [desati'naðo, a] adj foolish, silly; **desatino** nm (idiotez) foolishness, folly; (error) blunder

desatornillar [desatorni'ʎar] vt to unscrew

desatrancar [desatran'kar] vt (puerta) to unbolt; (cañería) to clear, unblock

desautorizado, a [desautori'θaðo, a] adj unauthorized

desautorizar [desautori'θar] vt (oficial) to deprive of authority; (informe) to deny

desavenencia [desaβe'nenθja] nf (desacuerdo) disagreement; (discrepancia) quarrel

desayunar [desaju'nar] vi to have breakfast ♦ vt to have for breakfast; **desayuno** nm breakfast

desazón [desa'θon] nf anxiety

desazonarse [desaθo'narse] vr to worry, be anxious

desbandarse [desβan'darse] vr (MIL) to disband; (fig) to flee in disorder

desbarajuste [desβara'xuste] nm confusion, disorder

desbaratar [desβara'tar] vt (deshacer, destruir) to ruin

desbloquear [desβloke'ar] vt (negociaciones, tráfico) to get going again; (COM: cuenta) to unfreeze

desbocado, a [desβo'kaðo, a] adj (caballo) runaway

desbordar [desβor'ðar] vt (sobrepasar) to go beyond; (exceder) to exceed; **~se** vr (río) to overflow; (entusiasmo) to erupt

descabalgar [deskaβal'var] vi to dismount

descabellado, a [deskaβe'ʎaðo, a] adj (disparatado) wild, crazy

descafeinado, a [deskafei'naðo, a] adj decaffeinated ♦ nm decaffeinated coffee

descalabro [deska'laβro] nm blow; (desgracia) misfortune

descalificar [deskalifi'kar] vt to disqualify; (desacreditar) to discredit

descalzar [deskal'θar] vt (zapato) to take off; **descalzo, a** adj barefoot(ed)

descambiar [deskam'bjar] vt to exchange

descaminado, a [deskami'naðo, a] adj (equivocado) on the wrong road; (fig) misguided

descampado [deskam'paðo] nm open space

descansado, a [deskan'saðo, a] adj (gen) rested; (que tranquiliza) restful

descansar [deskan'sar] *vt* (*gen*) to rest
♦ *vi* to rest, have a rest; (*echarse*) to lie down

descansillo [deskan'siʎo] *nm* (*de escalera*) landing

descanso [des'kanso] *nm* (*reposo*) rest; (*alivio*) relief; (*pausa*) break; (*DEPORTE*) interval, half time

descapotable [deskapo'taβle] *nm* (*tb:* **coche ~**) convertible

descarado, a [deska'raðo, a] *adj* shameless; (*insolente*) cheeky

descarga [des'karɣa] *nf* (*ARQ , ELEC, MIL*) discharge; (*NAUT*) unloading

descargar [deskar'ɣar] *vt* to unload; (*golpe*) to let fly; **~se** *vr* to unburden o.s.; **descargo** *nm* (*COM*) receipt; (*JUR*) evidence

descaro [des'karo] *nm* nerve

descarriar [deska'rrjar] *vt* (*descaminar*) to misdirect; (*fig*) to lead astray; **~se** *vr* (*perderse*) to lose one's way; (*separarse*) to stray; (*pervertirse*) to err, go astray

descarrilamiento [deskarrila'mjento] *nm* (*de tren*) derailment

descarrilar [deskarri'lar] *vi* to be derailed

descartar [deskar'tar] *vt* (*rechazar*) to reject; (*eliminar*) to rule out; **~se** *vr* (*NAIPES*) to discard; **~se de** to shirk

descascarillado, a [deskaskari'ʎaðo, a] *adj* (*paredes*) peeling

descendencia [desθen'denθja] *nf* (*origen*) origin, descent; (*hijos*) descendants

descender [desθen'der] *vt* (*bajar: escalera*) to go down ♦ *vi* to descend; (*temperatura, nivel*) to fall, drop; **~ de** to be descended from

descendiente [desθen'djente] *nm/f* descendant

descenso [des'θenso] *nm* descent; (*de temperatura*) drop

descifrar [desθi'frar] *vt* to decipher; (*mensaje*) to decode

descolgar [deskol'ɣar] *vt* (*bajar*) to take down; (*teléfono*) to pick up; **~se** *vr* to let o.s. down

descolorido, a [deskolo'riðo, a] *adj* faded; (*pálido*) pale

descompasado, a [deskompa'saðo, a] *adj* (*sin proporción*) out of all proportion; (*excesivo*) excessive

descomponer [deskompo'ner] *vt* (*desordenar*) to disarrange, disturb; (*TEC*) to put out of order; (*dividir*) to break down (into parts); (*fig*) to provoke; **~se** *vr* (*corromperse*) to rot, decompose; (*TEC*) to break down

descomposición [deskomposi'θjon] *nf* (*de un objeto*) breakdown; (*de fruta etc*) decomposition; **~ de vientre** stomach upset, diarrhoea

descompuesto, a [deskom'pwesto, a] *adj* (*corrompido*) decomposed; (*roto*) broken

descomunal [deskomu'nal] *adj* (*enorme*) huge

desconcertado, a [deskonθer'taðo, a] *adj* disconcerted, bewildered

desconcertar [deskonθer'tar] *vt* (*confundir*) to baffle; (*incomodar*) to upset, put out; **~se** *vr* (*turbarse*) to be upset

desconchado, a [deskon'tʃaðo, a] *adj* (*pintura*) peeling

desconcierto *etc* [deskon'θjerto] *vb ver* **desconcertar** ♦ *nm* (*gen*) disorder; (*desorientación*) uncertainty; (*inquietud*) uneasiness

desconectar [deskonek'tar] *vt* to disconnect

desconfianza [deskon'fjanθa] *nf* distrust

desconfiar [deskon'fjar] *vi* to be distrustful; **~ de** to distrust, suspect

descongelar [deskonxe'lar] *vt* to defrost; (*COM, POL*) to unfreeze

descongestionar [deskonxestjo'nar] *vt* (*cabeza, tráfico*) to clear

desconocer [deskono'θer] *vt* (*ignorar*) not to know, be ignorant of

desconocido, a [deskono'θiðo, a] *adj* unknown ♦ *nm/f* stranger

desconocimiento [deskonoθi'mjento] *nm* (*falta de conocimientos*) ignorance

desconsiderado, a [deskonsiðe'raðo, a] *adj* inconsiderate; (*insensible*) thoughtless

desconsolar [deskonso'lar] *vt* to distress; **~se** *vr* to despair

desconsuelo *etc* [deskon'swelo] *vb ver* **desconsolar** ♦ *nm* (*tristeza*) distress; (*desesperación*) despair

descontado, a [deskon'taðo, a] *adj:* **dar por ~ (que)** to take (it) for granted (that)

descontar [deskon'tar] *vt* (*deducir*) to take away, deduct; (*rebajar*) to discount

descontento, a [deskon'tento, a] *adj* dissatisfied ♦ *nm* dissatisfaction, discontent

descorazonar [deskoraθo'nar] *vt* to discourage, dishearten

descorchar [deskor'tʃar] *vt* to uncork

descorrer [desko'rrer] *vt* (*cortinas, cerrojo*) to draw back

descortés [deskor'tes] *adj* (*mal educado*) discourteous; (*grosero*) rude

descoser [desko'ser] *vt* to unstitch; **~se** *vr* to come apart (at the seams)

descosido, a [desko'siðo, a] *adj* (*COSTURA*) unstitched

descrédito [des'kreðito] *nm* discredit

descreído, a [deskre'iðo, a] *adj* (*incrédulo*) incredulous; (*falto de fe*) unbelieving

descremado, a [deskre'maðo, a] *adj* skimmed

describir [deskri'βir] *vt* to describe; **descripción** [deskrip'θjon] *nf* description

descrito [des'krito] *pp de* **describir**

descuartizar [deskwarti'θar] *vt* (*animal*) to cut up

descubierto, a [desku'βjerto, a] *pp de* **descubrir** ♦ *adj* uncovered, bare; (*persona*) bareheaded ♦ *nm* (*bancario*) overdraft; **al ~** in the open

descubrimiento [deskuβri'mjento] *nm* (*hallazgo*) discovery; (*revelación*) revelation

descubrir [desku'βrir] *vt* to discover, find; (*inaugurar*) to unveil; (*vislumbrar*) to detect; (*revelar*) to reveal, show; (*destapar*) to uncover; **~se** *vr* to reveal o.s.; (*quitarse sombrero*) to take off one's hat; (*confesar*) to confess

descuento *etc* [des'kwento] *vb ver*

descontar ♦ *nm* discount

descuidado, a [deskwi'ðaðo, a] *adj* (*sin cuidado*) careless; (*desordenado*) untidy; (*olvidadizo*) forgetful; (*dejado*) neglected; (*desprevenido*) unprepared

descuidar [deskwi'ðar] *vt* (*dejar*) to neglect; (*olvidar*) to overlook; **~se** *vr* (*distraerse*) to be careless; (*abandonarse*) to let o.s. go; (*desprevenirse*) to drop one's guard; **¡descuida!** don't worry!; **descuido** *nm* (*dejadez*) carelessness; (*olvido*) negligence

---
PALABRA CLAVE
---

desde ['desðe] *prep* **1** (*lugar*) from; **~ Burgos hasta mi casa hay 30 km** it's 30 kms from Burgos to my house
2 (*posición*): **hablaba ~ el balcón** she was speaking from the balcony
3 (*tiempo: +adv, n*): **~ ahora** from now on; **~ la boda** since the wedding; **~ niño** since I *etc* was a child; **~ 3 años atrás** since 3 years ago
4 (*tiempo: +vb, fecha*) since; for; **nos conocemos ~ 1992/ ~ hace 20 años** we've known each other since 1992/for 20 years; **no le veo ~ 1997/~ hace 5 años** I haven't seen him since 1997/for 5 years
5 (*gama*): **~ los más lujosos hasta los más económicos** from the most luxurious to the most reasonably priced
6: ~ luego (que no) of course (not)
♦ *conj:* **~ que:** **~ que recuerdo** for as long as I can remember; **~ que llegó no ha salido** he hasn't been out since he arrived

---

desdecirse [desðe'θirse] *vr* to retract; **~ de** to go back on

desdén [des'ðen] *nm* scorn

desdeñar [desðe'ɲar] *vt* (*despreciar*) to scorn

desdicha [des'ðitʃa] *nf* (*desgracia*) misfortune; (*infelicidad*) unhappiness; **desdichado, a** *adj* (*sin suerte*) unlucky; (*infeliz*) unhappy

desdoblar [desðo'ßlar] *vt* (*extender*) to spread out; (*desplegar*) to unfold

desear [dese'ar] *vt* to want, desire, wish for

desecar [dese'kar] *vt* to dry up; **~se** *vr* to dry up

desechar [dese'tʃar] *vt* (*basura*) to throw out *o* away; (*ideas*) to reject, discard; **desechos** *nmpl* rubbish *sg*, waste *sg*

desembalar [desemba'lar] *vt* to unpack

desembarazar [desembara'θar] *vt* (*desocupar*) to clear; (*desenredar*) to free; **~se** *vr*: **~se de** to free o.s. of, get rid of

desembarcar [desembar'kar] *vt* (*mercancías etc*) to unload ♦ *vi* to disembark; **~se** *vr* to disembark

desembocadura [desemboka'ðura] *nf* (*de río*) mouth; (*de calle*) opening

desembocar [desembo'kar] *vi* (*río*) to flow into; (*fig*) to result in

desembolso [desem'bolso] *nm* payment

desembragar [desembra'var] *vi* to declutch

desembrollar [desembro'ʎar] *vt* (*madeja*) to unravel; (*asunto, malentendido*) to sort out

desemejanza [deseme'xanθa] *nf* dissimilarity

desempaquetar [desempake'tar] *vt* (*regalo*) to unwrap; (*mercancía*) to unpack

desempatar [desempa'tar] *vi* to replay, hold a play-off; **desempate** *nm* (*FÚTBOL*) replay, play-off; (*TENIS*) tie-break(er)

desempeñar [desempe'ɲar] *vt* (*cargo*) to hold; (*papel*) to perform; (*lo empeñado*) to redeem; **~ un papel** (*fig*) to play (a role)

desempeño [desem'peɲo] *nm* redeeming; (*de cargo*) occupation

desempleado, a [desemple'aðo, a] *nm/f* unemployed person; **desempleo** *nm* unemployment

desempolvar [desempol'ßar] *vt* (*muebles etc*) to dust; (*lo olvidado*) to revive

desencadenar [desenkaðe'nar] *vt* to unchain; (*ira*) to unleash; **~se** *vr* to break loose; (*tormenta*) to burst; (*guerra*) to break out

desencajar [desenka'xar] *vt* (*hueso*) to dislocate; (*mecanismo, pieza*) to disconnect, disengage

desencanto [desen'kanto] *nm* disillusionment

desenchufar [desentʃu'far] *vt* to unplug

desenfadado, a [desenfa'ðaðo, a] *adj* (*desenvuelto*) uninhibited; (*descarado*) forward; **desenfado** *nm* (*libertad*) freedom; (*comportamiento*) free and easy manner; (*descaro*) forwardness

desenfocado, a [desenfo'kaðo, a] *adj* (*FOTO*) out of focus

desenfrenado, a [desenfre'naðo, a] *adj* (*descontrolado*) uncontrolled; (*inmoderado*) unbridled; **desenfreno** *nm* wildness; (*de las pasiones*) lack of self-control

desenganchar [desengan'tʃar] *vt* (*gen*) to unhook; (*FERRO*) to uncouple

desengañar [desenga'ɲar] *vt* to disillusion; **~se** *vr* to become disillusioned; **desengaño** *nm* disillusionment; (*decepción*) disappointment

desenlace [desen'laθe] *nm* outcome

desenmarañar [desenmara'ɲar] *vt* (*fig*) to unravel

desenmascarar [desenmaska'rar] *vt* to unmask

desenredar [desenre'ðar] *vt* (*pelo*) to untangle; (*problema*) to sort out

desenroscar [desenros'kar] *vt* to unscrew

desentenderse [desenten'derse] *vr*: **~ de** to pretend not to know about; (*apartarse*) to have nothing to do with

desenterrar [desente'rrar] *vt* to exhume; (*tesoro, fig*) to unearth, dig up

desentonar [desento'nar] *vi* (*MUS*) to sing (*o* play) out of tune; (*color*) to clash

desentrañar [desentra'ɲar] *vt* (*misterio*) to unravel

desentumecer [desentume'θer] *vt* (*pierna etc*) to stretch

desenvoltura [desenßol'tura] *nf* ease

desenvolver [desenßol'ßer] *vt* (*paquete*) to unwrap; (*fig*) to develop; **~se** *vr* (*desarrollarse*) to unfold, develop;

(arreglárselas) to cope

deseo [de'seo] *nm* desire, wish; **~so, a**
adj: **estar ~so de** to be anxious to

desequilibrado, a [desekili'ßraðo, a] *adj*
unbalanced

desertar [deser'tar] *vi* to desert

desértico, a [de'sertiko, a] *adj* desert *cpd*

desesperación [desespera'θjon] *nf*
(impaciencia) desperation, despair;
(irritación) fury

desesperar [desespe'rar] *vt* to drive to
despair; *(exasperar)* to drive to distraction
♦ *vi*: **~ de** to despair of; **~se** *vr* to
despair, lose hope

desestabilizar [desestaßili'θar] *vt* to
destabilize

desestimar [desesti'mar] *vt (menospreciar)*
to have a low opinion of; *(rechazar)* to
reject

desfachatez [desfatʃa'teθ] *nf (insolencia)*
impudence; *(descaro)* rudeness

desfalco [des'falko] *nm* embezzlement

desfallecer [desfaʎe'θer] *vi (perder las
fuerzas)* to become weak; *(desvanecerse)*
to faint

desfasado, a [desfa'saðo, a] *adj*
(anticuado) old-fashioned; **desfase** *nm*
(diferencia) gap

desfavorable [desfaßo'raßle] *adj*
unfavourable

desfigurar [desfixu'rar] *vt (cara)* to
disfigure; *(cuerpo)* to deform

desfiladero [desfila'ðero] *nm* gorge

desfilar [desfi'lar] *vi* to parade; **desfile**
nm procession

desfogarse [desfo'xarse] *vr (fig)* to let off
steam

desgajar [desxa'xar] *vt (arrancar)* to tear
off; *(romper)* to break off; **~se** *vr* to come
off

desgana [des'xana] *nf (falta de apetito)*
loss of appetite; *(apatía)* unwillingness;
~do, a *adj*: **estar ~do** *(sin apetito)* to
have no appetite; *(sin entusiasmo)* to have
lost interest

desgarrador, a [desxarra'ðor, a] *adj (fig)*
heartrending

desgarrar [desxa'rrar] *vt* to tear (up); *(fig)*
to shatter; **desgarro** *nm (en tela)* tear;
(aflicción) grief

desgastar [desxas'tar] *vt (deteriorar)* to
wear away *o* down; *(estropear)* to spoil;
~se *vr* to get worn out; **desgaste** *nm*
wear (and tear)

desglosar [desxlo'sar] *vt (factura)* to break
down

desgracia [des'xraθja] *nf* misfortune;
(accidente) accident; *(vergüenza)* disgrace;
(contratiempo) setback; **por ~**
unfortunately

desgraciado, a [desxra'θjaðo, a] *adj (sin
suerte)* unlucky, unfortunate; *(miserable)*
wretched; *(infeliz)* miserable

desgravación [desxraßa'θjon] *nf (COM):* **~**
fiscal tax relief

desgravar [desxra'ßar] *vt (impuestos)* to
reduce the tax *o* duty on

deshabitado, a [desaßi'taðo, a] *adj*
uninhabited

deshacer [desa'θer] *vt (casa)* to break up;
(TEC) to take apart; *(enemigo)* to defeat;
(diluir) to melt; *(contrato)* to break;
(intriga) to solve; **~se** *vr (disolverse)* to
melt; *(despedazarse)* to come apart *o*
undone; **~se de** to get rid of; **~se en**
lágrimas to burst into tears

desharrapado, a [desarra'paðo, a] *adj*
(persona) shabby

deshecho, a [des'etʃo, a] *adj* undone;
(roto) smashed; *(persona)*: **estar ~** to be
shattered

desheredar [desere'ðar] *vt* to disinherit

deshidratar [desiðra'tar] *vt* to dehydrate

deshielo [des'jelo] *nm* thaw

deshonesto, a [deso'nesto, a] *adj*
indecent

deshonra [des'onra] *nf (deshonor)*
dishonour; *(vergüenza)* shame

deshora [des'ora]: **a ~** *adv* at the wrong
time

deshuesar [deswe'sar] *vt (carne)* to bone;
(fruta) to stone

desierto, a [de'sjerto, a] *adj (casa, calle,
negocio)* deserted ♦ *nm* desert

designar [desiɣ'nar] *vt* (*nombrar*) to
designate; (*indicar*) to fix

designio [de'siɣnjo] *nm* plan

desigual [desi'ɣwal] *adj* (*terreno*) uneven;
(*lucha etc*) unequal

desilusión [desilu'sjon] *nf* disillusionment;
(*decepción*) disappointment;
desilusionar *vt* to disillusion; to
disappoint; **desilusionarse** *vr* to become
disillusioned

desinfectar [desinfek'tar] *vt* to disinfect

desinflar [desin'flar] *vt* to deflate

desintegración [desinteɣra'θjon] *nf*
disintegration

desinterés [desinte'res] *nm* (*desgana*)
lack of interest; (*altruismo*) unselfishness

desintoxicarse [desintoksi'karse] *vr*
(*drogadicto*) to undergo detoxification

desistir [desis'tir] *vi* (*renunciar*) to stop,
desist

desleal [desle'al] *adj* (*infiel*) disloyal; (*COM:
competencia*) unfair; **~tad** *nf* disloyalty

desleír [desle'ir] *vt* (*líquido*) to dilute;
(*sólido*) to dissolve

deslenguado, a [deslen'gwaðo, a] *adj*
(*grosero*) foul-mouthed

desligar [desli'ɣar] *vt* (*desatar*) to untie,
undo; (*separar*) to separate; **~se** *vr* (*de un
compromiso*) to extricate o.s.

desliz [des'liθ] *nm* (*fig*) lapse; **~ar** *vt* to
slip, slide

deslucido, a [deslu'θiðo, a] *adj* dull;
(*torpe*) awkward, graceless; (*deslustrado*)
tarnished

deslumbrar [deslum'brar] *vt* to dazzle

desmadrarse [desma'ðrarse] (*fam*) *vr*
(*descontrolarse*) to run wild; (*divertirse*) to
let one's hair down; **desmadre** (*fam*)
nm (*desorganización*) chaos; (*jaleo*)
commotion

desmán [des'man] *nm* (*exceso*) outrage;
(*abuso de poder*) abuse

desmandarse [desman'darse] *vr* (*portarse
mal*) to behave badly; (*excederse*) to get
out of hand; (*caballo*) to bolt

desmantelar [desmante'lar] *vt* (*deshacer*)
to dismantle; (*casa*) to strip

desmaquillador [desmakiʎa'ðor] *nm*
make-up remover

desmayar [desma'jar] *vi* to lose heart;
~se *vr* (*MED*) to faint; **desmayo** *nm*
(*MED: acto*) faint; (: *estado*)
unconsciousness

desmedido, a [desme'ðiðo, a] *adj*
excessive

desmejorar [desmexo'rar] *vt* (*dañar*) to
impair, spoil; (*MED*) to weaken

desmembrar [desmem'brar] *vt* (*MED*) to
dismember; (*fig*) to separate

desmemoriado, a [desmemo'rjaðo, a]
adj forgetful

desmentir [desmen'tir] *vt* (*contradecir*) to
contradict; (*refutar*) to deny

desmenuzar [desmenu'θar] *vt* (*deshacer*)
to crumble; (*carne*) to chop; (*examinar*) to
examine closely

desmerecer [desmere'θer] *vt* to be
unworthy of ♦ *vi* (*deteriorarse*) to
deteriorate

desmesurado, a [desmesu'raðo, a] *adj*
disproportionate

desmontable [desmon'taßle] *adj* (*que se
quita: pieza*) detachable; (*que se puede
plegar etc*) collapsible; folding

desmontar [desmon'tar] *vt* (*deshacer*) to
dismantle; (*tierra*) to level ♦ *vi* to
dismount

desmoralizar [desmorali'θar] *vt* to
demoralize

desmoronar [desmoro'nar] *vt* to wear
away, erode; **~se** *vr* (*edificio, dique*) to
collapse; (*economía*) to decline

desnatado, a [desna'taðo, a] *adj*
skimmed

desnivel [desni'ßel] *nm* (*de terreno*)
unevenness

desnudar [desnu'ðar] *vt* (*desvestir*) to
undress; (*despojar*) to strip; **~se** *vr*
(*desvestirse*) to get undressed; **desnudo,
a** *adj* naked ♦ *nm/f* nude; **desnudo de**
devoid *o* bereft of

desnutrición [desnutri'θjon] *nf*
malnutrition; **desnutrido, a** *adj*
undernourished

desobedecer [desoβeðe'θer] *vt, vi* to disobey; **desobediencia** *nf* disobedience

desocupado, a [desoku'paðo, a] *adj* at leisure; (*desempleado*) unemployed; (*deshabitado*) empty, vacant

desocupar [desoku'par] *vt* to vacate

desodorante [desoðo'rante] *nm* deodorant

desolación [desola'θjon] *nf* (*de lugar*) desolation; (*fig*) grief

desolar [deso'lar] *vt* to ruin, lay waste

desorbitado, a [desorβi'taðo, a] *adj* (*excesivo: ambición*) boundless; (*deseos*) excessive; (: *precio*) exorbitant

desorden [des'orðen] *nm* confusion; (*político*) disorder, unrest

desorganizar [desorvani'θar] *vt* (*desordenar*) to disorganize; **desorganización** *nf* (*de persona*) disorganization; (*en empresa, oficina*) disorder, chaos

desorientar [desorjen'tar] *vt* (*extraviar*) to mislead; (*confundir, desconcertar*) to confuse; **~se** *vr* (*perderse*) to lose one's way

despabilado, a [despaβi'laðo, a] *adj* (*despierto*) wide-awake; (*fig*) alert, sharp

despabilar [despaβi'lar] *vt* (*el ingenio*) to sharpen ♦ *vi* to wake up; (*fig*) to get a move on; **~se** *vr* to wake up; to get a move on

despachar [despa'tʃar] *vt* (*negocio*) to do, complete; (*enviar*) to send, dispatch; (*vender*) to sell, deal in; (*billete*) to issue; (*mandar ir*) to send away

despacho [des'patʃo] *nm* (*oficina*) office; (*de paquetes*) dispatch; (*venta*) sale; (*comunicación*) message

despacio [des'paθjo] *adv* slowly

desparpajo [despar'paxo] *nm* self-confidence; (*pey*) nerve

desparramar [desparra'mar] *vt* (*esparcir*) to scatter; (*líquido*) to spill

despavorido, a [despaβo'riðo, a] *adj* terrified

despecho [des'petʃo] *nm* spite; **a ~ de** in spite of

despectivo, a [despek'tiβo, a] *adj* (*despreciativo*) derogatory; (*LING*) pejorative

despedazar [despeða'θar] *vt* to tear to pieces

despedida [despe'ðiða] *nf* (*adiós*) farewell; (*de obrero*) sacking

despedir [despe'ðir] *vt* (*visita*) to see off, show out; (*empleado*) to dismiss; (*inquilino*) to evict; (*objeto*) to hurl; (*olor etc*) to give out *o* off; **~se** *vr*: **~se de** to say goodbye to

despegar [despe'xar] *vt* to unstick ♦ *vi* (*avión*) to take off; **~se** *vr* to come loose, come unstuck; **despego** *nm* detachment

despegue *etc* [des'pexe] *vb ver* **despegar** ♦ *nm* takeoff

despeinado, a [despei'naðo, a] *adj* dishevelled, unkempt

despejado, a [despe'xaðo, a] *adj* (*lugar*) clear, free; (*cielo*) clear; (*persona*) wide-awake, bright

despejar [despe'xar] *vt* (*gen*) to clear; (*misterio*) to clear up ♦ *vi* (*el tiempo*) to clear; **~se** *vr* (*tiempo, cielo*) to clear (up); (*misterio*) to become clearer; (*cabeza*) to clear

despellejar [despeʎe'xar] *vt* (*animal*) to skin

despensa [des'pensa] *nf* larder

despeñadero [despeɲa'ðero] *nm* (*GEO*) cliff, precipice

despeñarse [despe'ɲarse] *vr* to hurl o.s. down; (*coche*) to tumble over

desperdicio [desper'ðiθjo] *nm* (*despilfarro*) squandering; **~s** *nmpl* (*basura*) rubbish *sg* (*BRIT*), garbage *sg* (*US*); (*residuos*) waste *sg*

desperdigarse [desperði'varse] *vr* (*rebaño, familia*) to scatter, spread out; (*granos de arroz, semillas*) to scatter

desperezarse [despere'θarse] *vr* to stretch

desperfecto [desper'fekto] *nm* (*deterioro*) slight damage; (*defecto*) flaw, imperfection

despertador [desperta'ðor] *nm* alarm clock

despertar [desper'tar] *nm* awakening ♦ *vt* (*persona*) to wake up; (*recuerdos*) to revive; (*sentimiento*) to arouse ♦ *vi* to awaken, wake up; **~se** *vr* to awaken, wake up

despiadado, a [despja'ðaðo, a] *adj* (*ataque*) merciless; (*persona*) heartless

despido *etc* [des'piðo] *vb ver* **despedir** ♦ *nm* dismissal, sacking

despierto, a *etc* [des'pjerto, a] *vb ver* **despertar** ♦ *adj* awake; (*fig*) sharp, alert

despilfarro [despil'farro] *nm* (*derroche*) squandering; (*lujo desmedido*) extravagance

despistar [despis'tar] *vt* to throw off the track *o* scent; (*confundir*) to mislead, confuse; **~se** *vr* to take the wrong road; (*confundirse*) to become confused

despiste [des'piste] *nm* absent-mindedness; **un ~** a mistake, slip

desplazamiento [desplaθa'mjento] *nm* displacement

desplazar [despla'θar] *vt* to move; (*NAUT*) to displace; (*INFORM*) to scroll; (*fig*) to oust; **~se** *vr* (*persona*) to travel

desplegar [desple'ɣar] *vt* (*tela, papel*) to unfold, open out; (*bandera*) to unfurl; **despliegue** *etc* [des'pleɣe] *vb ver* **desplegar** ♦ *nm* display

desplomarse [desplo'marse] *vr* (*edificio, gobierno, persona*) to collapse

desplumar [desplu'mar] *vt* (*ave*) to pluck; (*fam: estafar*) to fleece

despoblado, a [despo'ßlaðo, a] *adj* (*sin habitantes*) uninhabited

despojar [despo'xar] *vt* (*alguien: de sus bienes*) to divest of, deprive of; (*casa*) to strip, leave bare; (*alguien: de su cargo*) to strip of

despojo [des'poxo] *nm* (*acto*) plundering; (*objetos*) plunder, loot; **~s** *nmpl* (*de ave, res*) offal *sg*

desposado, a [despo'saðo, a] *adj, nm/f* newly-wed

desposar [despo'sar] *vt* to marry; **~se** *vr* to get married

desposeer [despose'er] *vt*: **~ a uno de** (*puesto, autoridad*) to strip sb of

déspota ['despota] *nm/f* despot

despreciar [despre'θjar] *vt* (*desdeñar*) to despise, scorn; (*afrentar*) to slight; **desprecio** *nm* scorn, contempt; slight

desprender [despren'der] *vt* (*broche*) to unfasten; (*olor*) to give off; **~se** *vr* (*botón: caerse*) to fall off; (*broche*) to come unfastened; (*olor, perfume*) to be given off; **~se de algo que ...** to draw from sth that ...

desprendimiento [desprendi'mjento] *nm* (*gen*) loosening; (*generosidad*) disinterestedness; (*de tierra, rocas*) landslide

despreocupado, a [despreoku'paðo, a] *adj* (*sin preocupación*) unworried, nonchalant; (*negligente*) careless

despreocuparse [despreoku'parse] *vr* not to worry; **~ de** to have no interest in

desprestigiar [despresti'xjar] *vt* (*criticar*) to run down; (*desacreditar*) to discredit

desprevenido, a [despreße'niðo, a] *adj* (*no preparado*) unprepared, unready

desproporcionado, a [desproporθjo'naðo, a] *adj* disproportionate, out of proportion

desprovisto, a [despro'ßisto, a] *adj*: **~ de** devoid of

después [des'pwes] *adv* afterwards, later; (*próximo paso*) next; **~ de comer** after lunch; **un año ~** a year later; **~ se debatió el tema** next the matter was discussed; **~ de corregido el texto** after the text had been corrected; **~ de todo** after all

desquiciado, a [deski'θjaðo, a] *adj* deranged

desquite [des'kite] *nm* (*satisfacción*) satisfaction; (*venganza*) revenge

destacar [desta'kar] *vt* to emphasize, point up; (*MIL*) to detach, detail ♦ *vi* (*resaltarse*) to stand out; (*persona*) to be outstanding *o* exceptional; **~se** *vr* to stand out; to be outstanding *o* exceptional

destajo [des'taxo] *nm*: **trabajar a ~** to do piecework

destapar [desta'par] *vt* (*botella*) to open; (*cacerola*) to take the lid off; (*descubrir*) to uncover; **~se** *vr* (*revelarse*) to reveal one's true character

destartalado, a [destarta'laðo, a] *adj* (*desordenado*) untidy; (*ruinoso*) tumbledown

destello [des'teλo] *nm* (*de estrella*) twinkle; (*de faro*) signal light

destemplado, a [destem'plaðo, a] *adj* (*MUS*) out of tune; (*voz*) harsh; (*MED*) out of sorts; (*tiempo*) unpleasant, nasty

desteñir [deste'ɲir] *vt* to fade ♦ *vi* to fade; **~se** *vr* to fade; **esta tela no destiñe** this fabric will not run

desternillarse [desterni'λarse] *vr*: **~ de risa** to split one's sides laughing

desterrar [deste'rrar] *vt* (*exilar*) to exile; (*fig*) to banish, dismiss

destiempo [des'tjempo] *nm*: **a ~** *adv* out of turn

destierro *etc* [des'tjerro] *vb ver* **desterrar** ♦ *nm* exile

destilar [desti'lar] *vt* to distil; **destilería** *nf* distillery

destinar [desti'nar] *vt* (*funcionario*) to appoint, assign; (*fondos*): **~ (a)** to set aside (for)

destinatario, a [destina'tarjo, a] *nm/f* addressee

destino [des'tino] *nm* (*suerte*) destiny; (*de avión, viajero*) destination

destituir [destitu'ir] *vt* to dismiss

destornillador [destorniλa'ðor] *nm* screwdriver

destornillar [destorni'λar] *vt* (*tornillo*) to unscrew; **~se** *vr* to unscrew

destreza [des'treθa] *nf* (*habilidad*) skill; (*maña*) dexterity

destrozar [destro'θar] *vt* (*romper*) to smash, break (up); (*estropear*) to ruin; (*nervios*) to shatter

destrozo [des'troθo] *nm* (*acción*)

destruction; (*desastre*) smashing; **~s** *nmpl* (*pedazos*) pieces; (*daños*) havoc *sg*

destrucción [destruk'θjon] *nf* destruction

destruir [destru'ir] *vt* to destroy

desuso [des'uso] *nm* disuse; **caer en ~** to become obsolete

desvalido, a [desßa'liðo, a] *adj* (*desprotegido*) destitute; (*sin fuerzas*) helpless

desvalijar [desßali'xar] *vt* (*persona*) to rob; (*casa, tienda*) to burgle; (*coche*) to break into

desván [des'ßan] *nm* attic

desvanecer [desßane'θer] *vt* (*disipar*) to dispel; (*borrar*) to blur; **~se** *vr* (*humo etc*) to vanish, disappear; (*color*) to fade; (*recuerdo, sonido*) to fade away; (*MED*) to pass out; (*duda*) to be dispelled

desvanecimiento [desßaneθi'mjento] *nm* (*desaparición*) disappearance; (*de colores*) fading; (*evaporación*) evaporation; (*MED*) fainting fit

desvariar [desßa'rjar] *vi* (*enfermo*) to be delirious; **desvarío** *nm* delirium

desvelar [desße'lar] *vt* to keep awake; **~se** *vr* (*no poder dormir*) to stay awake; (*preocuparse*) to be vigilant *o* watchful

desvelos [des'ßelos] *nmpl* worrying *sg*

desvencijado, a [desßenθi'xaðo, a] *adj* (*silla*) rickety; (*máquina*) broken-down

desventaja [desßen'taxa] *nf* disadvantage

desventura [desßen'tura] *nf* misfortune

desvergonzado, a [desßerxon'θaðo, a] *adj* shameless

desvergüenza [desßer'ɣwenθa] *nf* (*descaro*) shamelessness; (*insolencia*) impudence; (*mala conducta*) effrontery

desvestir [desßes'tir] *vt* to undress; **~se** *vr* to undress

desviación [desßja'θjon] *nf* deviation; (*AUTO*) diversion, detour

desviar [des'ßjar] *vt* to turn aside; (*río*) to alter the course of; (*navío*) to divert, re-route; (*conversación*) to sidetrack; **~se** *vr* (*apartarse del camino*) to turn aside; (: *barco*) to go off course

desvío *etc* [des'ßio] *vb ver* **desviar** ♦ *nm*

(*desviación*) detour, diversion; (*fig*) indifference

desvirtuar [desβir'twar] *vt* to distort

desvivirse [desβi'βirse] *vr*: **~ por** (*anhelar*) to long for, crave for; (*hacer lo posible por*) to do one's utmost for

detallar [deta'ʎar] *vt* to detail

detalle [de'taʎe] *nm* detail; (*gesto*) gesture, token; **al ~** in detail; (*COM*) retail

detallista [deta'ʎista] *nm/f* (*COM*) retailer

detective [detek'tiβe] *nm/f* detective

detener [dete'ner] *vt* (*gen*) to stop; (*JUR*) to arrest; (*objeto*) to keep; **~se** *vr* to stop; (*demorarse*): **~se en** to delay over, linger over

detenidamente [deteniða'mente] *adv* (*minuciosamente*) carefully; (*extensamente*) at great length

detenido, a [dete'niðo, a] *adj* (*arrestado*) under arrest ♦ *nm/f* person under arrest, prisoner

detenimiento [deteni'mjento] *nm*: **con ~** thoroughly; (*observar, considerar*) carefully

detergente [deter'xente] *nm* detergent

deteriorar [deterjo'rar] *vt* to spoil, damage; **~se** *vr* to deteriorate; **deterioro** *nm* deterioration

determinación [determina'θjon] *nf* (*empeño*) determination; (*decisión*) decision; **determinado, a** *adj* specific

determinar [determi'nar] *vt* (*plazo*) to fix; (*precio*) to settle; **~se** *vr* to decide

detestar [detes'tar] *vt* to detest

detractor, a [detrak'tor, a] *nm/f* slanderer, libeller

detrás [de'tras] *adv* behind; (*atrás*) at the back; **~ de** behind

detrimento [detri'mento] *nm*: **en ~ de** to the detriment of

deuda ['deuða] *nf* debt

devaluación [deβalwa'θjon] *nf* devaluation

devastar [deβas'tar] *vt* (*destruir*) to devastate

devoción [deβo'θjon] *nf* devotion

devolución [deβolu'θjon] *nf* (*reenvío*) return, sending back; (*reembolso*)

repayment; (*JUR*) devolution

devolver [deβol'βer] *vt* to return; (*lo extraviado, lo prestado*) to give back; (*carta al correo*) to send back; (*COM*) to repay, refund ♦ *vi* (*vomitar*) to be sick

devorar [deβo'rar] *vt* to devour

devoto, a [de'βoto, a] *adj* devout ♦ *nm/f* admirer

devuelto *pp de* **devolver**

devuelva *etc vb ver* **devolver**

di *vb ver* **dar; decir**

día ['dia] *nm* day; **¿qué ~ es?** what's the date?; **estar/poner al ~** to be/keep up to date; **el ~ de hoy/de mañana** today/ tomorrow; **al ~ siguiente** (on) the following day; **vivir al ~** to live from hand to mouth; **de ~** by day, in daylight; **en pleno ~** in full daylight; **D~ de Reyes** Epiphany; **~ festivo** (*ESP*) o **feriado** (*AM*) holiday; **~ libre** day off

diabetes [dja'βetes] *nf* diabetes

diablo ['djaβlo] *nm* devil; **diablura** *nf* prank

diadema [dja'ðema] *nf* tiara

diafragma [dja'fraɣma] *nm* diaphragm

diagnosis [djaɣ'nosis] *nf inv* diagnosis

diagnóstico [djaɣ'nostiko] *nm* = **diagnosis**

diagonal [djaɣo'nal] *adj* diagonal

diagrama [dja'ɣrama] *nm* diagram; **~ de flujo** flowchart

dial [djal] *nm* dial

dialecto [dja'lekto] *nm* dialect

dialogar [djalo'ɣar] *vi*: **~ con** (*POL*) to hold talks with

diálogo ['djaloɣo] *nm* dialogue

diamante [dja'mante] *nm* diamond

diana ['djana] *nf* (*MIL*) reveille; (*de blanco*) centre, bull's-eye

diapositiva [djaposi'tiβa] *nf* (*FOTO*) slide, transparency

diario, a ['djarjo, a] *adj* daily ♦ *nm* newspaper; **a ~** daily; **de ~** everyday

diarrea [dja'rrea] *nf* diarrhoea

dibujar [diβu'xar] *vt* to draw, sketch; **dibujo** *nm* drawing; **dibujos animados** cartoons

diccionario [dikθjo'narjo] *nm* dictionary
dice *etc vb ver* **decir**
dicho, a ['ditʃo, a] *pp de* **decir** ♦ *adj*: **en ~s países** in the aforementioned countries ♦ *nm* saying
dichoso, a [di'tʃoso, a] *adj* happy
diciembre [di'θjembre] *nm* December
dictado [dik'taðo] *nm* dictation
dictador [dikta'ðor] *nm* dictator; **dictadura** *nf* dictatorship
dictamen [dik'tamen] *nm* (*opinión*) opinion; (*juicio*) judgment; (*informe*) report
dictar [dik'tar] *vt* (*carta*) to dictate; (*JUR: sentencia*) to pronounce; (*decreto*) to issue; (*AM: clase*) to give
didáctico, a [di'ðaktiko, a] *adj* educational
diecinueve [djeθi'nweβe] *num* nineteen
dieciocho [djeθi'otʃo] *num* eighteen
dieciséis [djeθi'seis] *num* sixteen
diecisiete [djeθi'sjete] *num* seventeen
diente ['djente] *nm* (*ANAT, TEC*) tooth; (*ZOOL*) fang; (: *de elefante*) tusk; (*de ajo*) clove; **hablar entre ~s** to mutter, mumble
diera *etc vb ver* **dar**
diesel ['disel] *adj*: **motor ~** diesel engine
diestro, a ['djestro, a] *adj* (*derecho*) right; (*hábil*) skilful
dieta ['djeta] *nf* diet; **dietética** *nf*: **tienda de dietética** health food shop; **dietético, a** *adj* diet (*atr*), dietary
diez [djeθ] *num* ten
diezmar [djeθ'mar] *vt* (*población*) to decimate
difamar [difa'mar] *vt* (*JUR: hablando*) to slander; (: *por escrito*) to libel
diferencia [dife'renθja] *nf* difference; **diferenciar** *vt* to differentiate between ♦ *vi* to differ; **diferenciarse** *vr* to differ, be different; (*distinguirse*) to distinguish o.s.
diferente [dife'rente] *adj* different
diferido [dife'riðo] *nm*: **en ~** (*TV etc*) recorded
difícil [di'fiθil] *adj* difficult

dificultad [difikul'tað] *nf* difficulty; (*problema*) trouble
dificultar [difikul'tar] *vt* (*complicar*) to complicate, make difficult; (*estorbar*) to obstruct
difteria [dif'terja] *nf* diphtheria
difundir [difun'dir] *vt* (*calor, luz*) to diffuse; (*RADIO, TV*) to broadcast; **~ una noticia** to spread a piece of news; **~se** *vr* to spread (out)
difunto, a [di'funto, a] *adj* dead, deceased ♦ *nm/f* deceased (person)
difusión [difu'sjon] *nf* (*RADIO, TV*) broadcasting
diga *etc vb ver* **decir**
digerir [dixe'rir] *vt* to digest; (*fig*) to absorb; **digestión** *nf* digestion; **digestivo, a** *adj* digestive
digital [dixi'tal] *adj* digital
dignarse [dix'narse] *vr* to deign to
dignatario, a [dixna'tarjo, a] *nm/f* dignitary
dignidad [dixni'ðað] *nf* dignity
digno, a ['dixno, a] *adj* worthy
digo *etc vb ver* **decir**
dije *etc vb ver* **decir**
dilapidar [dilapi'ðar] *vt* (*dinero, herencia*) to squander, waste
dilatar [dila'tar] *vt* (*cuerpo*) to dilate; (*prolongar*) to prolong
dilema [di'lema] *nm* dilemma
diligencia [dili'xenθja] *nf* diligence; (*ocupación*) errand, job; **~s** *nfpl* (*JUR*) formalities; **diligente** *adj* diligent
diluir [dilu'ir] *vt* to dilute
diluvio [di'luβjo] *nm* deluge, flood
dimensión [dimen'sjon] *nf* dimension
diminuto, a [dimi'nuto, a] *adj* tiny, diminutive
dimitir [dimi'tir] *vi* to resign
dimos *vb ver* **dar**
Dinamarca [dina'marka] *nf* Denmark
dinámico, a [di'namiko, a] *adj* dynamic
dinamita [dina'mita] *nf* dynamite
dínamo ['dinamo] *nf* dynamo
dineral [dine'ral] *nm* large sum of money, fortune

dinero [di'nero] *nm* money; ~ **contante,** ~ **efectivo** (ready) cash; ~ **suelto** (loose) change

dio *vb ver* **dar**

dios [djos] *nm* god; ¡**D~ mío!** (oh,) my God!

diosa ['djosa] *nf* goddess

diploma [di'ploma] *nm* diploma

diplomacia [diplo'maθja] *nf* diplomacy; (*fig*) tact

diplomado, a [diplo'maðo, a] *adj* qualified

diplomático, a [diplo'matiko, a] *adj* diplomatic ♦ *nm/f* diplomat

diputación [diputa'θjon] *nf* (*tb:* ~ **provincial**) ≈ county council

diputado, a [dipu'taðo, a] *nm/f* delegate; (*POL*) ≈ member of parliament (*BRIT*), ≈ representative (*US*)

dique ['dike] *nm* dyke

diré *etc vb ver* **decir**

dirección [direk'θjon] *nf* direction; (*señas*) address; (*AUTO*) steering; (*gerencia*) management; (*POL*) leadership; ~ **única/ prohibida** one-way street/no entry

directa [di'rekta] *nf* (*AUT*) top gear

directiva [direk'tißa] *nf* (*DEP, tb:* **junta** ~) board of directors

directo, a [di'rekto, a] *adj* direct; (*RADIO, TV*) live; **transmitir en** ~ to broadcast live

director, a [direk'tor, a] *adj* leading ♦ *nm/f* director; (*ESCOL*) head(teacher) (*BRIT*), principal (*US*); (*gerente*) manager(ess); (*PRENSA*) editor; ~ **de cine** film director; ~ **general** managing director

dirigente [diri'xente] *nm/f* (*POL*) leader

dirigir [diri'xir] *vt* to direct; (*carta*) to address; (*obra de teatro, film*) to direct; (*MUS*) to conduct; (*negocio*) to manage; ~**se** *vr:* ~**se a** to go towards, make one's way towards; (*hablar con*) to speak to

dirija *etc vb ver* **dirigir**

discernir [disθer'nir] *vt* to discern

disciplina [disθi'plina] *nf* discipline

discípulo, a [dis'θipulo, a] *nm/f* disciple

disco ['disko] *nm* disc; (*DEPORTE*) discus;

(*TEL*) dial; (*AUTO: semáforo*) light; (*MUS*) record; (*INFORM*): ~ **flexible/rígido** floppy/hard disk; ~ **compacto/de larga duración** compact disc/long-playing record; ~ **de freno** brake disc

disconforme [diskon'forme] *adj* differing; **estar** ~ **(con)** to be in disagreement (with)

discordia [dis'korðja] *nf* discord

discoteca [disko'teka] *nf* disco(theque)

discreción [diskre'θjon] *nf* discretion; (*reserva*) prudence; **comer a** ~ to eat as much as one wishes; **discrecional** *adj* (*facultativo*) discretionary

discrepancia [diskre'panθja] *nf* (*diferencia*) discrepancy; (*desacuerdo*) disagreement

discreto, a [dis'kreto, a] *adj* discreet

discriminación [diskrimina'θjon] *nf* discrimination

disculpa [dis'kulpa] *nf* excuse; (*pedir perdón*) apology; **pedir** ~**s a/por** to apologize to/for; **disculpar** *vt* to excuse, pardon; **disculparse** *vr* to excuse o.s.; to apologize

discurrir [disku'rrir] *vi* (*pensar, reflexionar*) to think, meditate; (*el tiempo*) to pass, go by

discurso [dis'kurso] *nm* speech

discusión [disku'sjon] *nf* (*diálogo*) discussion; (*riña*) argument

discutir [disku'tir] *vt* (*debatir*) to discuss; (*pelear*) to argue about; (*contradecir*) to argue against ♦ *vi* (*debatir*) to discuss; (*pelearse*) to argue

disecar [dise'kar] *vt* (*conservar: animal*) to stuff; (*: planta*) to dry

diseminar [disemi'nar] *vt* to disseminate, spread

diseñar [dise'nar] *vt, vi* to design

diseño [di'seno] *nm* design

disfraz [dis'fraθ] *nm* (*máscara*) disguise; (*excusa*) pretext; ~**ar** *vt* to disguise; ~**arse** *vr:* ~**arse de** to disguise o.s. as

disfrutar [disfru'tar] *vt* to enjoy ♦ *vi* to enjoy o.s.; ~ **de** to enjoy, possess

disgregarse [disɣre'ɣarse] *vr*

(*muchedumbre*) to disperse
disgustar [disxus'tar] *vt* (*no gustar*) to displease; (*contrariar, enojar*) to annoy, upset; **~se** *vr* (*enfadarse*) to get upset; (*dos personas*) to fall out
disgusto [dis'xusto] *nm* (*contrariedad*) annoyance; (*tristeza*) grief; (*riña*) quarrel
disidente [disi'ðente] *nm* dissident
disimular [disimu'lar] *vt* (*ocultar*) to hide, conceal ♦ *vi* to dissemble
disipar [disi'par] *vt* to dispel; (*fortuna*) to squander; **~se** *vr* (*nubes*) to vanish; (*indisciplinarse*) to dissipate
dislocarse [dislo'karse] *vr* (*articulación*) to sprain, dislocate
disminución [disminu'θjon] *nf* decrease, reduction
disminuido, a [disminu'iðo, a] *nm/f*: **~ mental/físico** mentally/physically handicapped person
disminuir [disminu'ir] *vt* to decrease, diminish
disociarse [diso'θjarse] *vr*: **~ (de)** to dissociate o.s. (from)
disolver [disol'ßer] *vt* (*gen*) to dissolve; **~se** *vr* to dissolve; (*COM*) to go into liquidation
dispar [dis'par] *adj* different
disparar [dispa'rar] *vt, vi* to shoot, fire
disparate [dispa'rate] *nm* (*tontería*) foolish remark; (*error*) blunder; **decir ~s** to talk nonsense
disparo [dis'paro] *nm* shot
dispensar [dispen'sar] *vt* to dispense; (*disculpar*) to excuse
dispersar [disper'sar] *vt* to disperse; **~se** *vr* to scatter
disponer [dispo'ner] *vt* (*arreglar*) to arrange; (*ordenar*) to put in order; (*preparar*) to prepare, get ready ♦ *vi*: **~ de** to have, own; **~se** *vr*: **~se a** *o* **para hacer** to prepare to do
disponible [dispo'nißle] *adj* available
disposición [disposi'θjon] *nf* arrangement, disposition; (*INFORM*) layout; **a la ~ de** at the disposal of; **~ de ánimo** state of mind

dispositivo [disposi'tißo] *nm* device, mechanism
dispuesto, a [dis'pwesto, a] *pp de* **disponer** ♦ *adj* (*arreglado*) arranged; (*preparado*) disposed
disputar [dispu'tar] *vt* (*carrera*) to compete in
disquete [dis'kete] *nm* floppy disk, diskette
distancia [dis'tanθja] *nf* distance
distanciar [distan'θjar] *vt* to space out; **~se** *vr* to become estranged
distante [dis'tante] *adj* distant
distar [dis'tar] *vi*: **dista 5km de aquí** it is 5km from here
diste *vb ver* **dar**
disteis ['disteis] *vb ver* **dar**
distension [disten'sjon] *nf* (*en las relaciones*) relaxation; (*POL*) détente; (*muscular*) strain
distinción [distin'θjon] *nf* distinction; (*elegancia*) elegance; (*honor*) honour
distinguido, a [distin'giðo, a] *adj* distinguished
distinguir [distin'gir] *vt* to distinguish; (*escoger*) to single out; **~se** *vr* to be distinguished
distintivo [distin'tißo] *nm* badge; (*fig*) characteristic
distinto, a [dis'tinto, a] *adj* different; (*claro*) clear
distracción [distrak'θjon] *nf* distraction; (*pasatiempo*) hobby, pastime; (*olvido*) absent-mindedness, distraction
distraer [distra'er] *vt* (*atención*) to distract; (*divertir*) to amuse; (*fondos*) to embezzle; **~se** *vr* (*entretenerse*) to amuse o.s.; (*perder la concentración*) to allow one's attention to wander
distraído, a [distra'iðo, a] *adj* (*gen*) absent-minded; (*entretenido*) amusing
distribuidor, a [distribui'ðor, a] *nm/f* distributor; **distribuidora** *nf* (*COM*) dealer, agent; (*CINE*) distributor
distribuir [distribu'ir] *vt* to distribute
distrito [dis'trito] *nm* (*sector, territorio*) region; (*barrio*) district

disturbio [dis'turβjo] *nm* disturbance; (*desorden*) riot
disuadir [diswa'ðir] *vt* to dissuade
disuelto [di'swelto] *pp de* **disolver**
disyuntiva [disjun'tiβa] *nf* dilemma
DIU *nm abr* (= *dispositivo intrauterino*) IUD
diurno, a ['djurno, a] *adj* day *cpd*
divagar [diβa'ɣar] *vi* (*desviarse*) to digress
diván [di'βan] *nm* divan
divergencia [diβer'xenθja] *nf* divergence
diversidad [diβersi'ðað] *nf* diversity, variety
diversificar [diβersifi'kar] *vt* to diversify
diversión [diβer'sjon] *nf* (*gen*) entertainment; (*actividad*) hobby, pastime
diverso, a [di'βerso, a] *adj* diverse; **~s libros** several books; **~s** *nmpl* sundries
divertido, a [diβer'tiðo, a] *adj* (*chiste*) amusing; (*fiesta etc*) enjoyable
divertir [diβer'tir] *vt* (*entretener, recrear*) to amuse; **~se** *vr* (*pasarlo bien*) to have a good time; (*distraerse*) to amuse o.s.
dividendos [diβi'ðendos] *nmpl* (*COM*) dividends
dividir [diβi'ðir] *vt* (*gen*) to divide; (*distribuir*) to distribute, share out
divierta *etc vb ver* **divertir**
divino, a [di'βino, a] *adj* divine
divirtiendo *etc vb ver* **divertir**
divisa [di'βisa] *nf* (*emblema*) emblem, badge; **~s** *nfpl* foreign exchange *sg*
divisar [diβi'sar] *vt* to make out, distinguish
división [diβi'sjon] *nf* (*gen*) division; (*de partido*) split; (*de país*) partition
divorciar [diβor'θjar] *vt* to divorce; **~se** *vr* to get divorced; **divorcio** *nm* divorce
divulgar [diβul'ɣar] *vt* (*ideas*) to spread; (*secreto*) to divulge
DNI (*ESP*) *nm abr* (= *Documento Nacional de Identidad*) national identity card

   DNI

ⓘ The **Documento Nacional de Identidad** *is a Spanish ID card which must be carried at all times and produced on request for the police. It contains the holder's photo, fingerprints and personal details. It is also known as the* DNI *or* "carnet de identidad".

Dña. *abr* (= *doña*) Mrs
do [do] *nm* (*MUS*) do, C
dobladillo [doβla'ðiʎo] *nm* (*de vestido*) hem; (*de pantalón: vuelta*) turn-up (*BRIT*), cuff (*US*)
doblar [do'βlar] *vt* to double; (*papel*) to fold; (*caño*) to bend; (*la esquina*) to turn, go round; (*film*) to dub ♦ *vi* to turn; (*campana*) to toll; **~se** *vr* (*plegarse*) to fold (up), crease; (*encorvarse*) to bend
doble ['doβle] *adj* double; (*de dos aspectos*) dual; (*fig*) two-faced ♦ *nm* double ♦ *nm/f* (*TEATRO*) double, stand-in; **~s** *nmpl* (*DEPORTE*) doubles *sg*; **con sentido ~** with a double meaning
doblegar [doβle'ɣar] *vt* to fold, crease; **~se** *vr* to yield
doblez [do'βleθ] *nm* fold, hem ♦ *nf* insincerity, duplicity
doce ['doθe] *num* twelve; **~na** *nf* dozen
docente [do'θente] *adj*: **centro/personal ~** teaching establishment/staff
dócil ['doθil] *adj* (*pasivo*) docile; (*obediente*) obedient
docto, a ['dokto, a] *adj*: **~ en** instructed in
doctor, a [dok'tor, a] *nm/f* doctor
doctorado [dokto'raðo] *nm* doctorate
doctrina [dok'trina] *nf* doctrine, teaching
documentación [dokumenta'θjon] *nf* documentation, papers *pl*
documental [dokumen'tal] *adj, nm* documentary
documento [doku'mento] *nm* (*certificado*) document; **~ national de identidad** identity card
dólar ['dolar] *nm* dollar
doler [do'ler] *vt, vi* to hurt; (*fig*) to grieve; **~se** *vr* (*de su situación*) to grieve, feel sorry; (*de las desgracias ajenas*) to sympathize; **me duele el brazo** my arm hurts
dolor [do'lor] *nm* pain; (*fig*) grief, sorrow; **~ de cabeza** headache; **~ de estómago**

stomachache

domar [doˈmar] *vt* to tame

domesticar [domestiˈkar] *vt* = **domar**

doméstico, a [doˈmestiko, a] *adj* (*vida, servicio*) home; (*tareas*) household; (*animal*) tame, pet

domiciliación [domiθiliaˈθjon] *nf*: ~ **de pagos** (COM) standing order

domicilio [domiˈθiljo] *nm* home; ~ **particular** private residence; ~ **social** (COM) head office; **sin ~ fijo** of no fixed abode

dominante [domiˈnante] *adj* dominant; (*persona*) domineering

dominar [domiˈnar] *vt* (*gen*) to dominate; (*idiomas*) to be fluent in ♦ *vi* to dominate, prevail; ~**se** *vr* to control o.s.

domingo [doˈmingo] *nm* Sunday

dominio [doˈminjo] *nm* (*tierras*) domain; (*autoridad*) power, authority; (*de las pasiones*) grip, hold; (*de idiomas*) command

don [don] *nm* (*talento*) gift; ~ **Juan Gómez** Mr Juan Gómez, Juan Gómez Esq (BRIT)

┌─────────────────────────┐
│ **Don/Doña** │
└─────────────────────────┘

> *The term **don/doña** often abbreviated to **D./Dña** is placed before the first name as a mark of respect to an older or more senior person - eg Don Diego, Doña Inés. Although becoming rarer in Spain it is still used with names and surnames on official documents and formal correspondence - eg "Sr. D. Pedro Rodríguez Hernández", "Sra. Dña. Inés Rodríguez Hernández".*

donaire [doˈnaire] *nm* charm

donar [doˈnar] *vt* to donate

donativo [donaˈtiβo] *nm* donation

doncella [donˈθeʎa] *nf* (*criada*) maid

donde [ˈdonde] *adv* where ♦ *prep*: **el coche está allí ~ el farol** the car is over there by the lamppost *o* where the lamppost is; **en ~** where, in which

dónde [ˈdonde] *adv interrogativo* where?; **¿a ~ vas?** where are you going (to)?;

¿de ~ vienes? where have you been?; **¿por ~?** where?, whereabouts?

dondequiera [dondeˈkjera] *adv* anywhere; **por ~** everywhere, all over the place ♦ *conj*: ~ **que** wherever

doña [ˈdoɲa] *nf*: ~ **Alicia** Alicia; ~ **Victoria Benito** Mrs Victoria Benito

dorado, a [doˈraðo, a] *adj* (*color*) golden; (TEC) gilt

dormir [dorˈmir] *vt*: ~ **la siesta** to have an afternoon nap ♦ *vi* to sleep; ~**se** *vr* to fall asleep

dormitar [dormiˈtar] *vi* to doze

dormitorio [dormiˈtorjo] *nm* bedroom; ~ **común** dormitory

dorsal [dorˈsal] *nm* (DEPORTE) number

dorso [ˈdorso] *nm* (*de mano*) back; (*de hoja*) other side

dos [dos] *num* two

dosis [ˈdosis] *nf inv* dose, dosage

dotado, a [doˈtaðo, a] *adj* gifted; ~ **de** endowed with

dotar [doˈtar] *vt* to endow; **dote** *nf* dowry; **dotes** *nfpl* (*talentos*) gifts

doy *vb ver* **dar**

dragar [draˈxar] *vt* (*río*) to dredge; (*minas*) to sweep

drama [ˈdrama] *nm* drama

dramaturgo [dramaˈturvo] *nm* dramatist, playwright

drástico, a [ˈdrastiko, a] *adj* drastic

drenaje [dreˈnaxe] *nm* drainage

droga [ˈdroxa] *nf* drug

drogadicto, a [droxaˈðikto, a] *nm/f* drug addict

droguería [droxeˈria] *nf* hardware shop (BRIT) *o* store (US)

ducha [ˈdutʃa] *nf* (*baño*) shower; (MED) douche; **ducharse** *vr* to take a shower

duda [ˈduða] *nf* doubt; **dudar** *vt, vi* to doubt; **dudoso, a** [duˈðoso, a] *adj* (*incierto*) hesitant; (*sospechoso*) doubtful

duela *etc vb ver* **doler**

duelo [ˈdwelo] *vb ver* **doler** ♦ *nm* (*combate*) duel; (*luto*) mourning

duende [ˈdwende] *nm* imp, goblin

dueño, a [ˈdweɲo, a] *nm/f* (*propietario*)

owner; (*de pensión, taberna*) landlord/
lady; (*empresario*) employer
duermo *etc vb ver* **dormir**
dulce ['dulθe] *adj* sweet ♦ *adv* gently,
softly ♦ *nm* sweet
dulzura [dul'θura] *nf* sweetness; (*ternura*)
gentleness
duna ['duna] *nf* (*GEO*) dune
dúo ['duo] *nm* duet
duplicar [dupli'kar] *vt* (*hacer el doble de*)
to duplicate; **~se** *vr* to double
duque ['duke] *nm* duke; **~sa** *nf* duchess
duración [dura'θjon] *nf* (*de película, disco
etc*) length; (*de pila etc*) life; (*curso: de
acontecimientos etc*) duration
duradero, a [dura'ðero, a] *adj* (*tela etc*)
hard-wearing; (*fe, paz*) lasting
durante [du'rante] *prep* during
durar [du'rar] *vi* to last; (*recuerdo*) to
remain
durazno [du'raθno] (*AM*) *nm* (*fruta*) peach;
(*árbol*) peach tree
durex ['dureks] (*AM*) *nm* (*tira adhesiva*)
Sellotape ® (*BRIT*), Scotch tape ® (*US*)
dureza [du'reθa] *nf* (*calidad*) hardness
duro, a ['duro, a] *adj* hard; (*carácter*)
tough ♦ *adv* hard ♦ *nm* (*moneda*) five
peseta coin *o* piece

E, e

E *abr* (= *este*) E
e [e] *conj* and
ebanista [eβa'nista] *nm/f* cabinetmaker
ébano ['eβano] *nm* ebony
ebrio, a ['eβrjo, a] *adj* drunk
ebullición [eβuʎi'θjon] *nf* boiling
eccema [ek'θema] *nf* (*MED*) eczema
echar [e'tʃar] *vt* to throw; (*agua, vino*) to
pour (out); (*empleado: despedir*) to fire,
sack; (*hojas*) to sprout; (*cartas*) to post;
(*humo*) to emit, give out ♦ *vi*: **~ a
correr/llorar** to run off/burst into tears;
~se *vr* to lie down; **~ llave a** to lock (up);
~ abajo (*gobierno*) to overthrow; (*edificio*)
to demolish; **~ mano a** to lay hands on;

~ una mano a uno (*ayudar*) to give sb a
hand; **~ de menos** to miss
eclesiástico, a [ekle'sjastiko, a] *adj*
ecclesiastical
eclipse [e'klipse] *nm* eclipse
eco ['eko] *nm* echo; **tener ~** to catch on
ecología [ekolo'xia] *nf* ecology;
ecológico, a *adj* (*producto, método*)
environmentally-friendly; (*agricultura*)
organic; **ecologista** *adj* ecological,
environmental ♦ *nm/f* environmentalist
economato [ekono'mato] *nm* cooperative
store
economía [ekono'mia] *nf* (*sistema*)
economy; (*carrera*) economics
económico, a [eko'nomiko, a] *adj*
(*barato*) cheap, economical; (*ahorrativo*)
thrifty; (*COM: año etc*) financial;
(*: situación*) economic
economista [ekono'mista] *nm/f*
economist
ECU [eku] *nm* ECU
ecuador [ekwa'ðor] *nm* equator; **(el) E~**
Ecuador
ecuánime [e'kwanime] *adj* (*carácter*)
level-headed; (*estado*) calm
ecuatoriano, a [ekwato'rjano, a] *adj*,
nm/f Ecuadorian
ecuestre [e'kwestre] *adj* equestrian
eczema [ek'θema] *nm* = **eccema**
edad [e'ðað] *nf* age; **¿qué ~ tienes?** how
old are you?; **tiene ocho años de ~** he is
eight (years old); **de ~ mediana/
avanzada** middle-aged/advanced in
years; **la E~ Media** the Middle Ages
edición [eði'θjon] *nf* (*acto*) publication;
(*ejemplar*) edition
edificar [edifi'kar] *vt, vi* to build
edificio [eði'fiθjo] *nm* building; (*fig*)
edifice, structure
Edimburgo [eðim'burxo] *nm* Edinburgh
editar [eði'tar] *vt* (*publicar*) to publish;
(*preparar textos*) to edit
editor, a [eði'tor, a] *nm/f* (*que publica*)
publisher; (*redactor*) editor ♦ *adj*: **casa ~a**
publishing house, publisher; **~ial** *adj*
editorial ♦ *nm* leading article, editorial;

casa ~ial publishing house, publisher

edredon [eðreˈðon] *nm* duvet

educación [eðukaˈθjon] *nf* education; (*crianza*) upbringing; (*modales*) (good) manners *pl*

educado, a [eðuˈkaðo, a] *adj*: **bien/mal ~** well/badly behaved

educar [eðuˈkar] *vt* to educate; (*criar*) to bring up; (*voz*) to train

EE. UU. *nmpl abr* (= *Estados Unidos*) US(A)

efectista [efekˈtista] *adj* sensationalist

efectivamente [efectiβaˈmente] *adv* (*como respuesta*) exactly, precisely; (*verdaderamente*) really; (*de hecho*) in fact

efectivo, a [efekˈtiβo, a] *adj* effective; (*real*) actual, real ♦ *nm*: **pagar en ~** to pay (in) cash; **hacer ~ un cheque** to cash a cheque

efecto [eˈfekto] *nm* effect, result; **~s** *nmpl* (*~s personales*) effects; (*bienes*) goods; (*COM*) assets; **en ~** in fact; (*respuesta*) exactly, indeed; **~ invernadero** greenhouse effect

efectuar [efekˈtwar] *vt* to carry out; (*viaje*) to make

eficacia [efiˈkaθja] *nf* (*de persona*) efficiency; (*de medicamento etc*) effectiveness

eficaz [efiˈkaθ] *adj* (*persona*) efficient; (*acción*) effective

eficiente [efiˈθjente] *adj* efficient

efusivo, a [efuˈsiβo, a] *adj* effusive; **mis más efusivas gracias** my warmest thanks

EGB (*ESP*) *nf abr* (*ESCOL*) = *Educación General Básica*

egipcio, a [eˈxipθjo, a] *adj, nm/f* Egyptian

Egipto [eˈxipto] *nm* Egypt

egoísmo [eɣoˈismo] *nm* egoism

egoísta [eɣoˈista] *adj* egoistical, selfish ♦ *nm/f* egoist

egregio, a [eˈɣrexjo, a] *adj* eminent, distinguished

Eire [ˈeire] *nm* Eire

ej. *abr* (= *ejemplo*) eg

eje [ˈexe] *nm* (*GEO, MAT*) axis; (*de rueda*)

axle; (*de máquina*) shaft, spindle

ejecución [exekuˈθjon] *nf* execution; (*cumplimiento*) fulfilment; (*MUS*) performance; (*JUR*: *embargo de deudor*) attachment

ejecutar [exekuˈtar] *vt* to execute, carry out; (*matar*) to execute; (*cumplir*) to fulfil; (*MUS*) to perform; (*JUR*: *embargar*) to attach, distrain (on)

ejecutivo, a [exekuˈtiβo, a] *adj* executive; **el (poder) ~** the executive (power)

ejemplar [exemˈplar] *adj* exemplary ♦ *nm* example; (*ZOOL*) specimen; (*de libro*) copy; (*de periódico*) number, issue

ejemplo [eˈxemplo] *nm* example; **por ~** for example

ejercer [exerˈθer] *vt* to exercise; (*influencia*) to exert; (*un oficio*) to practise ♦ *vi* (*practicar*): **~ (de)** to practise (as)

ejercicio [exerˈθiθjo] *nm* exercise; (*período*) tenure; **~ comercial** financial year

ejército [eˈxerθito] *nm* army; **entrar en el ~** to join the army, join up

ejote [eˈxote] (*AM*) *nm* green bean

PALABRA CLAVE

---

el [el] (*f* **la**, *pl* **los, las**, *neutro* **lo**) *art def* **1** the; **el libro/la mesa/los estudiantes** the book/table/students

2 (*con n abstracto: no se traduce*): **el amor/la juventud** love/youth

3 (*posesión: se traduce a menudo por adj posesivo*): **romperse el brazo** to break one's arm; **levantó la mano** he put his hand up; **se puso el sombrero** she put her hat on

4 (*valor descriptivo*): **tener la boca grande/los ojos azules** to have a big mouth/blue eyes

5 (*con días*) on; **me iré el viernes** I'll leave on Friday; **los domingos suelo ir a nadar** on Sundays I generally go swimming

6 (*lo +adj*): **lo difícil/caro** what is difficult/expensive; (= *cuán*): **no se da cuenta de lo pesado que es** he doesn't realise how boring he is

♦ *pron demos* 1: **mi libro y el de usted** my book and yours; **las de Pepe son mejores** Pepe's are better; **no la(s) blanca(s) sino la(s) gris(es)** not the white one(s) but the grey one(s)

2: **lo de**: **lo de ayer** what happened yesterday; **lo de las facturas** that business about the invoices

♦ *pron relativo*: **el que** *etc* 1 (*indef*): **el (los) que quiera(n) que se vaya(n)** anyone who wants to can leave; **llévese el que más le guste** take the one you like best

2 (*def*): **el que compré ayer** the one I bought yesterday; **los que se van** those who leave

3: **lo que**: **lo que pienso yo/más me gusta** what I think/like most

♦ *conj*: **el que**: **el que lo diga** the fact that he says so; **el que sea tan vago me molesta** his being so lazy bothers me

♦ *excl*: **¡el susto que me diste!** what a fright you gave me!

♦ *pron personal* 1 (*persona: m*) him; (: *f*) her; (: *pl*) them; **lo/las veo** I can see him/them

2 (*animal, cosa: sg*) it; (: *pl*) them; **lo** (*o* **la**) **veo** I can see it; **los** (*o* **las**) **veo** I can see them

3: **lo** (*como sustituto de frase*): **no lo sabía** I didn't know; **ya lo entiendo** I understand now

él [el] *pron* (*persona*) he; (*cosa*) it; (*después de prep: persona*) him; (: *cosa*) it; **de ~** his

elaborar [elaβo'rar] *vt* (*producto*) to make, manufacture; (*preparar*) to prepare; (*madera, metal etc*) to work; (*proyecto etc*) to work on *o* out

elasticidad [elastiθi'ðað] *nf* elasticity

elástico, a [e'lastiko, a] *adj* elastic; (*flexible*) flexible ♦ *nm* elastic; (*un ~*) elastic band

elección [elek'θjon] *nf* election; (*selección*) choice, selection

electorado [elekto'raðo] *nm* electorate,

voters *pl*

electricidad [elektriθi'ðað] *nf* electricity

electricista [elektri'θista] *nm/f* electrician

eléctrico, a [e'lektriko, a] *adj* electric

electro... [elektro] *prefijo* electro...; **~cardiograma** *nm* electrocardiogram; **~cutar** *vt* to electrocute; **~do** *nm* electrode; **~domésticos** *nmpl* (electrical) household appliances; **~magnético, a** *adj* electromagnetic

electrónica [elek'tronika] *nf* electronics *sg*

electrónico, a [elek'troniko, a] *adj* electronic

elefante [ele'fante] *nm* elephant

elegancia [ele'vanθja] *nf* elegance, grace; (*estilo*) stylishness

elegante [ele'vante] *adj* elegant, graceful; (*estiloso*) stylish, fashionable

elegir [ele'xir] *vt* (*escoger*) to choose, select; (*optar*) to opt for; (*presidente*) to elect

elemental [elemen'tal] *adj* (*claro, obvio*) elementary; (*fundamental*) elemental, fundamental

elemento [ele'mento] *nm* element; (*fig*) ingredient; **~s** *nmpl* elements, rudiments

elepé [ele'pe] (*pl* **~s**) *nm* L.P.

elevación [eleβa'θjon] *nf* elevation; (*acto*) raising, lifting; (*de precios*) rise; (*GEO etc*) height, altitude

elevar [ele'βar] *vt* to raise, lift (up); (*precio*) to put up; **~se** *vr* (*edificio*) to rise; (*precios*) to go up

eligiendo *etc vb ver* **elegir**

elija *etc vb ver* **elegir**

eliminar [elimi'nar] *vt* to eliminate, remove

eliminatoria [elimina'torja] *nf* heat, preliminary (round)

elite [e'lite] *nf* elite

ella [e'ʎa] *pron* (*persona*) she; (*cosa*) it; (*después de prep: persona*) her; (: *cosa*) it; **de ~** hers

ellas ['eʎas] *pron* (*personas y cosas*) they; (*después de prep*) them; **de ~** theirs

ello ['eʎo] *pron* it

ellos ['eʎos] *pron* they; (*después de prep*)

them; **de ~** theirs

elocuencia [elo'kwenθja] *nf* eloquence

elogiar [elo'xjar] *vt* to praise; **elogio** *nm* praise

elote [e'lote] (*AM*) *nm* corn on the cob

eludir [elu'ðir] *vt* to avoid

emanar [ema'nar] *vi*: **~ de** to emanate from, come from; (*derivar de*) to originate in

emancipar [emanθi'par] *vt* to emancipate; **~se** *vr* to become emancipated, free o.s.

embadurnar [embaður'nar] *vt* to smear

embajada [emba'xaða] *nf* embassy

embajador, a [embaxa'ðor, a] *nm/f* ambassador/ambassadress

embalaje [emba'laxe] *nm* packing

embalar [emba'lar] *vt* to parcel, wrap (up); **~se** *vr* to go fast

embalsamar [embalsa'mar] *vt* to embalm

embalse [em'balse] *nm* (*presa*) dam; (*lago*) reservoir

embarazada [embara'θaða] *adj* pregnant ♦ *nf* pregnant woman

embarazo [emba'raθo] *nm* (*de mujer*) pregnancy; (*impedimento*) obstacle, obstruction; (*timidez*) embarrassment; **embarazoso, a** *adj* awkward, embarrassing

embarcación [embarka'θjon] *nf* (*barco*) boat, craft; (*acto*) embarkation, boarding

embarcadero [embarka'ðero] *nm* pier, landing stage

embarcar [embar'kar] *vt* (*cargamento*) to ship, stow; (*persona*) to embark, put on board; **~se** *vr* to embark, go on board

embargar [embar'ɣar] *vt* (*JUR*) to seize, impound

embargo [em'barɣo] *nm* (*JUR*) seizure; (*COM, POL*) embargo

embargue [em'barɣe] *etc vb ver* **embargar**

embarque *etc* [em'barke] *vb ver* **embarcar** ♦ *nm* shipment, loading

embaucar [embau'kar] *vt* to trick, fool

embeber [embe'ßer] *vt* (*absorber*) to absorb, soak up; (*empapar*) to saturate ♦ *vi* to shrink; **~se** *vr*: **~se en un libro** to be engrossed *o* absorbed in a book

embellecer [embeʎe'θer] *vt* to embellish, beautify

embestida [embes'tiða] *nf* attack, onslaught; (*carga*) charge

embestir [embes'tir] *vt* to attack, assault; to charge, attack ♦ *vi* to attack

emblema [em'blema] *nm* emblem

embobado, a [embo'ßaðo, a] *adj* (*atontado*) stunned, bewildered

embolia [em'bolja] *nf* (*MED*) clot

émbolo ['embolo] *nm* (*AUTO*) piston

embolsar [embol'sar] *vt* to pocket, put in one's pocket

emborrachar [emborra'tʃar] *vt* to make drunk, intoxicate; **~se** *vr* to get drunk

emboscada [embos'kaða] *nf* ambush

embotar [embo'tar] *vt* to blunt, dull; **~se** *vr* (*adormecerse*) to go numb

embotellamiento [emboteʎa'mjento] *nm* (*AUTO*) traffic jam

embotellar [embote'ʎar] *vt* to bottle

embrague [em'braɣe] *nm* (*tb*: **pedal de ~**) clutch

embriagar [embrja'ɣar] *vt* (*emborrachar*) to make drunk; **~se** *vr* (*emborracharse*) to get drunk

embrión [em'brjon] *nm* embryo

embrollar [embro'ʎar] *vt* (*el asunto*) to confuse, complicate; (*implicar*) to involve, embroil; **~se** *vr* (*confundirse*) to get into a muddle *o* mess

embrollo [em'broʎo] *nm* (*enredo*) muddle, confusion; (*aprieto*) fix, jam

embrujado, a [embru'xaðo, a] *adj* bewitched; **casa embrujada** haunted house

embrutecer [embrute'θer] *vt* (*atontar*) to stupefy; **~se** *vr* to be stupefied

embudo [em'buðo] *nm* funnel

embuste [em'buste] *nm* (*mentira*) lie; **~ro, a** *adj* lying, deceitful ♦ *nm/f* (*mentiroso*) liar

embutido [embu'tiðo] *nm* (*CULIN*) sausage; (*TEC*) inlay

emergencia [emer'xenθja] *nf* emergency;

(*surgimiento*) emergence

emerger [emer'xer] *vi* to emerge, appear

emigración [emiɣra'θjon] *nf* emigration; (*de pájaros*) migration

emigrar [emi'ɣrar] *vi* (*personas*) to emigrate; (*pájaros*) to migrate

eminencia [emi'nenθja] *nf* eminence; **eminente** *adj* eminent, distinguished; (*elevado*) high

emisario [emi'sarjo] *nm* emissary

emisión [emi'sjon] *nf* (*acto*) emission; (*COM etc*) issue; (*RADIO, TV: acto*) broadcasting; (: *programa*) broadcast, programme (*BRIT*), program (*US*)

emisora [emi'sora] *nf* radio *o* broadcasting station

emitir [emi'tir] *vt* (*olor etc*) to emit, give off; (*moneda etc*) to issue; (*opinión*) to express; (*RADIO*) to broadcast

emoción [emo'θjon] *nf* emotion; (*excitación*) excitement; (*sentimiento*) feeling

emocionante [emoθjo'nante] *adj* (*excitante*) exciting, thrilling

emocionar [emoθjo'nar] *vt* (*excitar*) to excite, thrill; (*conmover*) to move, touch; (*impresionar*) to impress

emotivo, a [emo'tiβo, a] *adj* emotional

empacar [empa'kar] *vt* (*gen*) to pack; (*en caja*) to bale, crate

empacho [em'patʃo] *nm* (*MED*) indigestion; (*fig*) embarrassment

empadronarse [empaðro'narse] *vr* (*POL: como elector*) to register

empalagoso, a [empala'ɣoso, a] *adj* cloying; (*fig*) tiresome

empalmar [empal'mar] *vt* to join, connect ♦ *vi* (*dos caminos*) to meet, join; **empalme** *nm* joint, connection; junction; (*de trenes*) connection

empanada [empa'naða] *nf* pie, pasty

empantanarse [empanta'narse] *vr* to get swamped; (*fig*) to get bogged down

empañarse [empa'ɲarse] *vr* (*cristales etc*) to steam up

empapar [empa'par] *vt* (*mojar*) to soak, saturate; (*absorber*) to soak up, absorb;

~se *vr*: **~se de** to soak up

empapelar [empape'lar] *vt* (*paredes*) to paper

empaquetar [empake'tar] *vt* to pack, parcel up

empastar [empas'tar] *vt* (*embadurnar*) to paste; (*diente*) to fill

empaste [em'paste] *nm* (*de diente*) filling

empatar [empa'tar] *vi* to draw, tie; **empate** *nm* draw, tie

empecé [empe'θe] *etc vb ver* **empezar**

empedernido, a [empeðer'niðo, a] *adj* hard, heartless; (*fumador*) inveterate

empedrado, a [empe'ðraðo, a] *adj* paved ♦ *nm* paving

empeine [em'peine] *nm* (*de pie, zapato*) instep

empellón [empe'ʎon] *nm* push, shove

empeñado, a [empe'ɲaðo, a] *adj* (*persona*) determined; (*objeto*) pawned

empeñar [empe'ɲar] *vt* (*objeto*) to pawn, pledge; (*persona*) to compel; **~se** *vr* (*endeudarse*) to get into debt; **~se en** to be set on, be determined to

empeño [em'peɲo] *nm* (*determinación, insistencia*) determination, insistence; **casa de ~s** pawnshop

empeorar [empeo'rar] *vt* to make worse, worsen ♦ *vi* to get worse, deteriorate

empequeñecer [empekeɲe'θer] *vt* to dwarf; (*minusvalorar*) to belittle

emperador [empera'ðor] *nm* emperor; **emperatriz** *nf* empress

empezar [empe'θar] *vt, vi* to begin, start

empiece *etc vb ver* **empezar**

empiezo *etc vb ver* **empezar**

empinar [empi'nar] *vt* to raise; **~se** *vr* (*persona*) to stand on tiptoe; (*animal*) to rear up; (*camino*) to climb steeply

empírico, a [em'piriko, a] *adj* empirical

emplasto [em'plasto] *nm* (*MED*) plaster

emplazamiento [emplaθa'mjento] *nm* site, location; (*JUR*) summons *sg*

emplazar [empla'θar] *vt* (*ubicar*) to site, place, locate; (*JUR*) to summons; (*convocar*) to summon

empleado, a [emple'aðo, a] *nm/f* (*gen*)

employee; (*de banco etc*) clerk
emplear [emple'ar] *vt* (*usar*) to use,
employ; (*dar trabajo a*) to employ; **~se** *vr*
(*conseguir trabajo*) to be employed;
(*ocuparse*) to occupy o.s.
empleo [em'pleo] *nm* (*puesto*) job;
(*puestos: colectivamente*) employment;
(*uso*) use, employment
empobrecer [empoβre'θer] *vt* to
impoverish; **~se** *vr* to become poor *o*
impoverished
empollar [empo'ʎar] (*fam*) *vt, vi* to swot
(up); **empollón, ona** (*fam*) *nm/f* swot
emporio [em'porjo] *nm* (*AM: gran
almacén*) department store
empotrado, a [empo'traðo, a] *adj*
(*armario etc*) built-in
emprender [empren'der] *vt* (*empezar*) to
begin, embark on; (*acometer*) to tackle,
take on
empresa [em'presa] *nf* (*de espíritu etc*)
enterprise; (*COM*) company, firm; **~rio, a**
nm/f (*COM*) businessman/woman
empréstito [em'prestito] *nm* (public) loan
empujar [empu'xar] *vt* to push, shove
empujón [empu'xon] *nm* push, shove
empuñar [empu'ɲar] *vt* (*asir*) to grasp,
take (firm) hold of
emular [emu'lar] *vt* to emulate; (*rivalizar*)
to rival

PALABRA CLAVE

en [en] *prep* **1** (*posición*) in; (: *sobre*) on;
está ~ el cajón it's in the drawer; **~
Argentina/La Paz** in Argentina/La Paz; **~
la oficina/el colegio** at the office/school;
está ~ el suelo/quinto piso it's on the
floor/the fifth floor
2 (*dirección*) into; **entró ~ el aula** she
went into the classroom; **meter algo ~ el
bolso** to put sth into one's bag
3 (*tiempo*) in; on; **~ 1605/3 semanas/
invierno** in 1605/3 weeks/winter; **~ (el
mes de) enero** in (the month of)
January; **~ aquella ocasión/época** on
that occasion/at that time
4 (*precio*) for; **lo vendió ~ 20 dólares** he

sold it for 20 dollars
5 (*diferencia*) by; **reducir/aumentar ~
una tercera parte/un 20 por ciento** to
reduce/increase by a third/20 per cent
6 (*manera*): **~ avión/autobús** by plane/
bus; **escrito ~ inglés** written in English
7 (*después de vb que indica gastar etc*) on;
han cobrado demasiado ~ dietas
they've charged too much to expenses;
se le va la mitad del sueldo ~ comida
he spends half his salary on food
8 (*tema, ocupación*): **experto ~ la
materia** expert on the subject; **trabaja ~
la construcción** he works in the building
industry
9 (*adj + ~ + infin*): **lento ~ reaccionar**
slow to react

---

enaguas [e'naɣwas] *nfpl* petticoat *sg*,
underskirt *sg*
enajenación [enaxena'θjon] *nf*: **~ mental**
mental derangement
enajenar [enaxe'nar] *vt* (*volver loco*) to
drive mad
enamorado, a [enamo'raðo, a] *adj* in
love ♦ *nm/f* lover
enamorar [enamo'rar] *vt* to win the love
of; **~se** *vr*: **~se de alguien** to fall in love
with sb
enano, a [e'nano, a] *adj* tiny ♦ *nm/f*
dwarf
enardecer [enarðe'θer] *vt* (*pasiones*) to
fire, inflame; (*persona*) to fill with
enthusiasm; **~se** *vr*: **~se por** to get
excited about; (*entusiasmarse*) to get
enthusiastic about
encabezamiento [enkaβeθa'mjento] *nm*
(*de carta*) heading; (*de periódico*) headline
encabezar [enkaβe'θar] *vt* (*movimiento,
revolución*) to lead, head; (*lista*) to head,
be at the top of; (*carta*) to put a heading
to
encadenar [enkaðe'nar] *vt* to chain
(together); (*poner grilletes a*) to shackle
encajar [enka'xar] *vt* (*ajustar*): **~ (en)** to fit
(into); (*fam: golpe*) to take ♦ *vi* to fit
(well); (*fig: corresponder a*) to match; **~se**

vr: **~se en un sillón** to squeeze into a chair

encaje [en'kaxe] *nm* (*labor*) lace

encalar [enka'lar] *vt* (*pared*) to whitewash

encallar [enka'ʎar] *vi* (NAUT) to run aground

encaminar [enkami'nar] *vt* to direct, send; **~se** *vr*: **~se a** to set out for

encantado, a [enkan'taðo, a] *adj* (*hechizado*) bewitched; (*muy contento*) delighted; **¡~!** how do you do, pleased to meet you

encantador, a [enkanta'ðor, a] *adj* charming, lovely ♦ *nm/f* magician, enchanter/enchantress

encantar [enkan'tar] *vt* (*agradar*) to charm, delight; (*hechizar*) to bewitch, cast a spell on; **me encanta eso** I love that; **encanto** *nm* (*hechizo*) spell, charm; (*fig*) charm, delight

encarcelar [enkarθe'lar] *vt* to imprison, jail

encarecer [enkare'θer] *vt* to put up the price of; **~se** *vr* to get dearer

encarecimiento [enkareθi'mjento] *nm* price increase

encargado, a [enkar'ɣaðo, a] *adj* in charge ♦ *nm/f* agent, representative; (*responsable*) person in charge

encargar [enkar'ɣar] *vt* to entrust; (*recomendar*) to urge, recommend; **~se** *vr*: **~se de** to look after, take charge of

encargo [en'karɣo] *nm* (*tarea*) assignment, job; (*responsabilidad*) responsibility; (COM) order

encariñarse [enkari'narse] *vr*: **~ con** to grow fond of, get attached to

encarnación [enkarna'θjon] *nf* incarnation, embodiment

encarnizado, a [enkarni'θaðo, a] *adj* (*lucha*) bloody, fierce

encarrilar [enkarri'lar] *vt* (*tren*) to put back on the rails; (*fig*) to correct, put on the right track

encasillar [enkasi'ʎar] *vt* (*tb fig*) to pigeonhole; (*actor*) to typecast

encauzar [enkau'θar] *vt* to channel

encendedor [enθende'ðor] *nm* lighter

encender [enθen'der] *vt* (*con fuego*) to light; (*luz, radio*) to put on, switch on; (*avivar: pasiones*) to inflame; **~se** *vr* to catch fire; (*excitarse*) to get excited; (*de cólera*) to flare up; (*el rostro*) to blush

encendido [enθen'diðo] *nm* (AUTO) ignition

encerado [enθe'raðo] *nm* (ESCOL) blackboard

encerar [enθe'rar] *vt* (*suelo*) to wax, polish

encerrar [enθe'rrar] *vt* (*confinar*) to shut in, shut up; (*comprender, incluir*) to include, contain

encharcado, a [entʃar'kaðo, a] *adj* (*terreno*) flooded

encharcarse [entʃar'karse] *vr* to get flooded

enchufado, a [entʃu'faðo, a] (*fam*) *nm/f* well-connected person

enchufar [entʃu'far] *vt* (ELEC) to plug in; (TEC) to connect, fit together; **enchufe** *nm* (ELEC: *clavija*) plug; (: *toma*) socket; (*de dos tubos*) joint, connection; (*fam: influencia*) contact, connection; (: *puesto*) cushy job

encía [en'θia] *nf* gum

encienda *etc vb ver* **encender**

encierro *etc* [en'θjerro] *vb ver* **encerrar** ♦ *nm* shutting in, shutting up; (*calabozo*) prison

encima [en'θima] *adv* (*sobre*) above, over; (*además*) besides; **~ de** (*en*) on, on top of; (*sobre*) above, over; (*además de*) besides, on top of; **por ~ de** over; **¿llevas dinero ~?** have you (got) any money on you?; **se me vino ~** it took me by surprise

encina [en'θina] *nf* holm oak

encinta [en'θinta] *adj* pregnant

enclenque [en'klenke] *adj* weak, sickly

encoger [enko'xer] *vt* to shrink, contract; **~se** *vr* to shrink, contract; (*fig*) to cringe; **~se de hombros** to shrug one's shoulders

encolar [enko'lar] *vt* (*engomar*) to glue, paste; (*pegar*) to stick down

encolerizar [enkoleri'θar] *vt* to anger, provoke; **~se** *vr* to get angry

encomendar [enkomen'dar] *vt* to entrust, commend; **~se** *vr*: **~se a** to put one's trust in

encomiar [enko'mjar] *vt* to praise, pay tribute to

encomienda *etc* [enko'mjenda] *vb ver* **encomendar ♦** *nf* (*encargo*) charge, commission; (*elogio*) tribute; **~ postal** (*AM*) parcel post

encontrado, a [enkon'traðo, a] *adj* (*contrario*) contrary, conflicting

encontrar [enkon'trar] *vt* (*hallar*) to find; (*inesperadamente*) to meet, run into; **~se** *vr* to meet (each other); (*situarse*) to be (situated); **~se con** to meet; **~se bien (de salud)** to feel well

encrespar [enkres'par] *vt* (*cabellos*) to curl; (*fig*) to anger, irritate; **~se** *vr* (*el mar*) to get rough; (*fig*) to get cross, get irritated

encrucijada [enkruθi'xaða] *nf* crossroads *sg*

encuadernación [enkwaðerna'θjon] *nf* binding

encuadernador, a [enkwaðerna'ðor, a] *nm/f* bookbinder

encuadrar [enkwa'ðrar] *vt* (*retrato*) to frame; (*ajustar*) to fit, insert; (*contener*) to contain

encubrir [enku'ßrir] *vt* (*ocultar*) to hide, conceal; (*criminal*) to harbour, shelter

encuentro *etc* [en'kwentro] *vb ver* **encontrar ♦** *nm* (*de personas*) meeting; (*AUTO etc*) collision, crash; (*DEPORTE*) match, game; (*MIL*) encounter

encuesta [en'kwesta] *nf* inquiry, investigation; (*sondeo*) (public) opinion poll; **~ judicial** post mortem

encumbrar [enkum'brar] *vt* (*persona*) to exalt

endeble [en'deßle] *adj* (*argumento, excusa, persona*) weak

endémico, a [en'demiko, a] *adj* (*MED*) endemic; (*fig*) rife, chronic

endemoniado, a [endemo'njaðo, a] *adj* possessed (of the devil); (*travieso*) devilish

enderezar [endere'θar] *vt* (*poner derecho*) to straighten (out); (: *verticalmente*) to set upright; (*situación*) to straighten *o* sort out; (*dirigir*) to direct; **~se** *vr* (*persona sentada*) to straighten up

endeudarse [endeu'ðarse] *vr* to get into debt

endiablado, a [endja'ßlaðo, a] *adj* devilish, diabolical; (*travieso*) mischievous

endilgar [endil'var] (*fam*) *vt*: **~le algo a uno** to lumber sb with sth; **~le un sermón a uno** to lecture sb

endiñar [endi'ɲar] (*fam*) *vt* (*bofetón*) to land, belt

endosar [endo'sar] *vt* (*cheque etc*) to endorse

endulzar [endul'θar] *vt* to sweeten; (*suavizar*) to soften

endurecer [endure'θer] *vt* to harden; **~se** *vr* to harden, grow hard

enema [e'nema] *nm* (*MED*) enema

enemigo, a [ene'mixo, a] *adj* enemy, hostile **♦** *nm/f* enemy

enemistad [enemis'taθ] *nf* enmity

enemistar [enemis'tar] *vt* to make enemies of, cause a rift between; **~se** *vr* to become enemies; (*amigos*) to fall out

energía [ener'xia] *nf* (*vigor*) energy, drive; (*empuje*) push; (*TEC, ELEC*) energy, power; **~ eolica** wind power; **~ solar** solar energy/power

enérgico, a [e'nerxiko, a] *adj* (*gen*) energetic; (*voz, modales*) forceful

energúmeno, a [ener'xumeno, a] (*fam*) *nm/f* (*fig*) madman/woman

enero [e'nero] *nm* January

enfadado, a [enfa'ðaðo, a] *adj* angry, annoyed

enfadar [enfa'ðar] *vt* to anger, annoy; **~se** *vr* to get angry *o* annoyed

enfado [en'faðo] *nm* (*enojo*) anger, annoyance; (*disgusto*) trouble, bother

énfasis ['enfasis] *nm* emphasis, stress

enfático, a [en'fatiko, a] *adj* emphatic

enfermar [enfer'mar] *vt* to make ill **♦** *vi* to fall ill, be taken ill

enfermedad [enferme'ðað] *nf* illness; ~ **venérea** venereal disease

enfermera [enfer'mera] *nf* nurse

enfermería [enferme'ria] *nf* infirmary; (*de colegio etc*) sick bay

enfermero [enfer'mero] *nm* (male) nurse

enfermizo, a [enfer'miθo, a] *adj* (*persona*) sickly, unhealthy; (*fig*) unhealthy

enfermo, a [en'fermo, a] *adj* ill, sick ♦ *nm/f* invalid, sick person; (*en hospital*) patient

enflaquecer [enflake'θer] *vt* (*adelgazar*) to make thin; (*debilitar*) to weaken

enfocar [enfo'kar] *vt* (*foto etc*) to focus; (*problema etc*) to approach

enfoque *etc* [en'foke] *vb ver* **enfocar** ♦ *nm* focus.

enfrascarse [enfras'karse] *vr*: ~ **en algo** to bury o.s. in sth

enfrentar [enfren'tar] *vt* (*peligro*) to face (up to), confront; (*oponer*) to bring face to face; ~**se** *vr* (*dos personas o* confront each other; (*DEPORTE: dos equipos*) to meet; ~**se a** *o* **con** to face up to, confront

enfrente [en'frente] *adv* opposite; **la casa de** ~ the house opposite, the house across the street; ~ **de** opposite, facing

enfriamiento [enfria'mjento] *nm* chilling, refrigeration; (*MED*) cold, chill

enfriar [enfri'ar] *vt* (*alimentos*) to cool, chill; (*algo caliente*) to cool down; ~**se** *vr* to cool down; (*MED*) to catch a chill; (*amistad*) to cool

enfurecer [enfure'θer] *vt* to enrage, madden; ~**se** *vr* to become furious, fly into a rage; (*mar*) to get rough

engalanar [engala'nar] *vt* (*adornar*) to adorn; (*ciudad*) to decorate; ~**se** *vr* to get dressed up

enganchar [engan'tʃar] *vt* to hook; (*dos vagones*) to hitch up; (*TEC*) to couple, connect; (*MIL*) to recruit; ~**se** *vr* (*MIL*) to enlist, join up

enganche [en'gantʃe] *nm* hook; (*TEC*) coupling, connection; (*acto*) hooking (up); (*MIL*) recruitment, enlistment; (*AM*: *depósito*) deposit

engañar [enga'nar] *vt* to deceive; (*estafar*) to cheat, swindle; ~**se** *vr* (*equivocarse*) to be wrong; (*disimular la verdad*) to deceive o.s.

engaño [en'gaɲo] *nm* deceit; (*estafa*) trick, swindle; (*error*) mistake, misunderstanding; (*ilusión*) delusion; ~**so, a** *adj* (*tramposo*) crooked; (*mentiroso*) dishonest, deceitful; (*aspecto*) deceptive; (*consejo*) misleading

engarzar [engar'θar] *vt* (*joya*) to set, mount; (*fig*) to link, connect

engatusar [engatu'sar] *vt* (*fam*) to coax

engendrar [enxen'drar] *vt* to breed; (*procrear*) to beget; (*causar*) to cause, produce; **engendro** *nm* (*BIO*) foetus; (*fig*) monstrosity

englobar [englo'ßar] *vt* to include, comprise

engordar [engor'ðar] *vt* to fatten ♦ *vi* to get fat, put on weight

engorroso, a [engo'rroso, a] *adj* bothersome, trying

engranaje [engra'naxe] *nm* (*AUTO*) gear

engrandecer [engrande'θer] *vt* to enlarge, magnify; (*alabar*) to praise, speak highly of; (*exagerar*) to exaggerate

engrasar [engra'sar] *vt* (*TEC*: *poner grasa*) to grease; (: *lubricar*) to lubricate, oil; (*manchar*) to make greasy

engreído, a [engre'iðo, a] *adj* vain, conceited

engrosar [engro'sar] *vt* (*ensanchar*) to enlarge; (*aumentar*) to increase; (*hinchar*) to swell

enhebrar [ene'ßrar] *vt* to thread

enhorabuena [enora'ßwena] *excl*: ¡~! congratulations! ♦ *nf*: **dar la** ~ **a** to congratulate

enigma [e'nixma] *nm* enigma; (*problema*) puzzle; (*misterio*) mystery

enjabonar [enxaßo'nar] *vt* to soap; (*fam*: *adular*) to soft-soap

enjambre [en'xambre] *nm* swarm

enjaular [enxau'lar] *vt* to (put in a) cage; (*fam*) to jail, lock up

enjuagar [enxwa'ɣar] vt (ropa) to rinse (out)

enjuague etc [en'xwaxe] vb ver **enjuagar** ♦ nm (MED) mouthwash; (de ropa) rinse, rinsing

enjugar [enxu'ɣar] vt to wipe (off); (lágrimas) to dry; (déficit) to wipe out

enjuiciar [enxwi'θjar] vt (JUR: procesar) to prosecute, try; (fig) to judge

enjuto, a [en'xuto, a] adj (flaco) lean, skinny

enlace [en'laθe] nm link, connection; (relación) relationship; (tb: ~ **matrimonial**) marriage; (de carretera, trenes) connection; ~ **sindical** shop steward

enlatado, a [enla'taðo, a] adj (comida, productos) tinned, canned

enlazar [enla'θar] vt (unir con lazos) to bind together; (atar) to tie; (conectar) to link, connect; (AM) to lasso

enlodar [enlo'ðar] vt to cover in mud; (fig: manchar) to stain; (: rebajar) to debase

enloquecer [enloke'θer] vt to drive mad ♦ vi to go mad; ~**se** vr to go mad

enlutado, a [enlu'taðo, a] adj (persona) in mourning

enmarañar [enmara'ɲar] vt (enredar) to tangle (up), entangle; (complicar) to complicate; (confundir) to confuse; ~**se** vr (enredarse) to become entangled; (confundirse) to get confused

enmarcar [enmar'kar] vt (cuadro) to frame

enmascarar [enmaska'rar] vt to mask; ~**se** vr to put on a mask

enmendar [enmen'dar] vt to emend, correct; (constitución etc) to amend; (comportamiento) to reform; ~**se** vr to reform, mend one's ways; **enmienda** nf correction; amendment; reform

enmohecerse [enmoe'θerse] vr (metal) to rust, go rusty; (muro, plantas) to get mouldy

enmudecer [enmuðe'θer] vi (perder el habla) to fall silent; (guardar silencio) to remain silent

ennegrecer [ennexre'θer] vt (poner negro) to blacken; (oscurecer) to darken; ~**se** vr

to turn black; (oscurecerse) to get dark, darken

ennoblecer [ennoßle'θer] vt to ennoble

enojar [eno'xar] vt (encolerizar) to anger; (disgustar) to annoy, upset; ~**se** vr to get angry; to get annoyed

enojo [e'noxo] nm (cólera) anger; (irritación) annoyance; ~**so, a** adj annoying

enorgullecerse [enorɣuʎe'θerse] vr to be proud; ~ **de** to pride o.s. on, be proud of

enorme [e'norme] adj enormous, huge; (fig) monstrous; **enormidad** nf hugeness, immensity

enrarecido, a [enrare'θiðo, a] adj (atmósfera, aire) rarefied

enredadera [enreða'ðera] nf (BOT) creeper, climbing plant

enredar [enre'ðar] vt (cables, hilos etc) to tangle (up), entangle; (situación) to complicate, confuse; (meter cizaña) to sow discord among o between; (implicar) to embroil, implicate; ~**se** vr to get entangled, get tangled (up); (situación) to get complicated; (persona) to get embroiled; (AM: fam) to meddle

enredo [en'reðo] nm (maraña) tangle; (confusión) mix-up, confusion; (intriga) intrigue

enrejado [enre'xaðo] nm fence, railings pl

enrevesado, a [enreße'saðo, a] adj (asunto) complicated, involved

enriquecer [enrike'θer] vt to make rich, enrich; ~**se** vr to get rich

enrojecer [enroxe'θer] vt to redden ♦ vi (persona) to blush; ~**se** vr to blush

enrolar [enro'lar] vt (MIL) to enlist; (reclutar) to recruit; ~**se** vr (MIL) to join up; (afiliarse) to enrol

enrollar [enro'ʎar] vt to roll (up), wind (up)

enroscar [enros'kar] vt (torcer, doblar) to coil (round), wind; (tornillo, rosca) to screw in; ~**se** vr to coil, wind

ensalada [ensa'laða] nf salad; **ensaladilla (rusa)** nf Russian salad

ensalzar [ensal'θar] vt (alabar) to praise,

extol; (*exaltar*) to exalt

ensamblaje [ensamˈblaxe] *nm* assembly; (*TEC*) joint

ensanchar [ensanˈtʃar] *vt* (*hacer más ancho*) to widen; (*agrandar*) to enlarge, expand; (*COSTURA*) to let out; **~se** *vr* to get wider, expand; **ensanche** *nm* (*de calle*) widening

ensangrentar [ensangrenˈtar] *vt* to stain with blood

ensañar [ensaˈɲar] *vt* to enrage; **~se** *vr*: **~se con** to treat brutally

ensartar [ensarˈtar] *vt* (*cuentas, perlas etc*) to string (together)

ensayar [ensaˈjar] *vt* to test, try (out); (*TEATRO*) to rehearse

ensayo [enˈsajo] *nm* test, trial; (*QUÍM*) experiment; (*TEATRO*) rehearsal; (*DEPORTE*) try; (*ESCOL, LITERATURA*) essay

enseguida [enseˈɣiða] *adv* at once, right away

ensenada [enseˈnaða] *nf* inlet, cove

enseñanza [enseˈɲanθa] *nf* (*educación*) education; (*acción*) teaching; (*doctrina*) teaching, doctrine

enseñar [enseˈɲar] *vt* (*educar*) to teach; (*mostrar, señalar*) to show

enseres [enˈseres] *nmpl* belongings

ensillar [ensiˈʎar] *vt* to saddle (up)

ensimismarse [ensimisˈmarse] *vr* (*abstraerse*) to become lost in thought; (*AM*) to become conceited

ensombrecer [ensombreˈθer] *vt* to darken, cast a shadow over; (*fig*) to overshadow, put in the shade

ensordecer [ensorðeˈθer] *vt* to deafen
♦ *vi* to go deaf

ensortijado, a [ensortiˈxaðo, a] *adj* (*pelo*) curly

ensuciar [ensuˈθjar] *vt* (*manchar*) to dirty, soil; (*fig*) to defile; **~se** *vr* to get dirty; (*niño*) to wet o.s.

ensueño [enˈsweɲo] *nm* (*sueño*) dream, fantasy; (*ilusión*) illusion; (*soñando despierto*) daydream

entablar [entaˈβlar] *vt* (*recubrir*) to board (up); (*AJEDREZ, DAMAS*) to set up;

(*conversación*) to strike up; (*JUR*) to file
♦ *vi* to draw

entablillar [entaβliˈʎar] *vt* (*MED*) to (put in a) splint

entallar [entaˈʎar] *vt* (*traje*) to tailor ♦ *vi*: **el traje entalla bien** the suit fits well

ente [ˈente] *nm* (*organización*) body, organization; (*fam: persona*) odd character

entender [entenˈder] *vt* (*comprender*) to understand; (*darse cuenta*) to realize ♦ *vi* to understand; (*creer*) to think, believe; **~se** *vr* (*comprenderse*) to be understood; (*2 personas*) to get on together; (*ponerse de acuerdo*) to agree, reach an agreement; **~ de** to know all about; **~ algo de** to know a little about; **~ en** to deal with, have to do with; **~se mal** (*2 personas*) to get on badly

entendido, a [entenˈdiðo, a] *adj* (*comprendido*) understood; (*hábil*) skilled; (*inteligente*) knowledgeable ♦ *nm/f* (*experto*) expert ♦ *excl* agreed!; **entendimiento** *nm* (*comprensión*) understanding; (*inteligencia*) mind, intellect; (*juicio*) judgement

enterado, a [enteˈraðo, a] *adj* well-informed; **estar ~ de** to know about, be aware of

enteramente [enteraˈmente] *adv* entirely, completely

enterar [enteˈrar] *vt* (*informar*) to inform, tell; **~se** *vr* to find out, get to know

entereza [enteˈreθa] *nf* (*totalidad*) entirety; (*fig: carácter*) strength of mind; (: *honradez*) integrity

enternecer [enterneˈθer] *vt* (*ablandar*) to soften; (*apiadar*) to touch, move; **~se** *vr* to be touched, be moved

entero, a [enˈtero, a] *adj* (*total*) whole, entire; (*fig: honesto*) honest; (: *firme*) firm, resolute ♦ *nm* (*COM: punto*) point; (*AM: pago*) payment

enterrador [enterraˈðor] *nm* gravedigger

enterrar [enteˈrrar] *vt* to bury

entibiar [entiˈβjar] *vt* (*enfriar*) to cool; (*calentar*) to warm; **~se** *vr* (*fig*) to cool

entidad [enti'ðað] *nf* (*empresa*) firm, company; (*organismo*) body; (*sociedad*) society; (*FILOSOFÍA*) entity

entiendo *etc vb ver* **entender**

entierro [en'tjerro] *nm* (*acción*) burial; (*funeral*) funeral

entonación [entona'θjon] *nf* (*LING*) intonation

entonar [ento'nar] *vt* (*canción*) to intone; (*colores*) to tone; (*MED*) to tone up ♦ *vi* to be in tune

entonces [en'tonθes] *adv* then, at that time; **desde ~** since then; **en aquel ~** at that time; (**pues**) **~** and so

entornar [entor'nar] *vt* (*puerta, ventana*) to half close, leave ajar; (*los ojos*) to screw up

entorpecer [entorpe'θer] *vt* (*entendimiento*) to dull; (*impedir*) to obstruct, hinder; (: *tránsito*) to slow down, delay

entrada [en'traða] *nf* (*acción*) entry, access; (*sitio*) entrance, way in; (*INFORM*) input; (*COM*) receipts *pl*, takings *pl*; (*CULIN*) starter; (*DEPORTE*) innings *sg*; (*TEATRO*) house, audience; (*billete*) ticket; (*COM*): **~s y salidas** income and expenditure; (*TEC*): **~ de aire** air intake *o* inlet; **de ~** from the outset

entrado, a [en'traðo, a] *adj*: **~ en años** elderly; **una vez ~ el verano** in the summer(time), when summer comes

entramparse [entram'parse] *vr* to get into debt

entrante [en'trante] *adj* next, coming; **mes/año ~** next month/year; **~s** *nmpl* starters

entraña [en'traɲa] *nf* (*fig: centro*) heart, core; (*raíz*) root; **~s** *nfpl* (*ANAT*) entrails; (*fig*) heart *sg*; **sin ~s** (*fig*) heartless; **entrañable** *adj* close, intimate; **entrañar** *vt* to entail

entrar [en'trar] *vt* (*introducir*) to bring in; (*INFORM*) to input ♦ *vi* (*meterse*) to go in, come in, enter; (*comenzar*): **~ diciendo** to begin by saying; **hacer ~** to show in; **no me entra** I can't get the hang of it

entre ['entre] *prep* (*dos*) between; (*más de dos*) among(st)

entreabrir [entrea'ßrir] *vt* to half-open, open halfway

entrecejo [entre'θexo] *nm*: **fruncir el ~** to frown

entrecortado, a [entrekor'taðo, a] *adj* (*respiración*) difficult; (*habla*) faltering

entredicho [entre'ðitʃo] *nm* (*JUR*) injunction; **poner en ~** to cast doubt on; **estar en ~** to be in doubt

entrega [en'treȝa] *nf* (*de mercancías*) delivery; (*de novela etc*) instalment

entregar [entre'ȝar] *vt* (*dar*) to hand (over), deliver; **~se** *vr* (*rendirse*) to surrender, give in, submit; (*dedicarse*) to devote o.s.

entrelazar [entrela'θar] *vt* to entwine

entremeses [entre'meses] *nmpl* hors d'œuvres

entremeter [entreme'ter] *vt* to insert, put in; **~se** *vr* to meddle, interfere; **entremetido, a** *adj* meddling, interfering

entremezclar [entremeθ'klar] *vt* to intermingle; **~se** *vr* to intermingle

entrenador, a [entrena'ðor, a] *nm/f* trainer, coach

entrenarse [entre'narse] *vr* to train

entrepierna [entre'pjerna] *nf* crotch

entresacar [entresa'kar] *vt* to pick out, select

entresuelo [entre'swelo] *nm* mezzanine

entretanto [entre'tanto] *adv* meanwhile, meantime

entretejer [entrete'xer] *vt* to interweave

entretener [entrete'ner] *vt* (*divertir*) to entertain, amuse; (*detener*) to hold up, delay; **~se** *vr* (*divertirse*) to amuse o.s.; (*retrasarse*) to delay, linger; **entretenido, a** *adj* entertaining, amusing; **entretenimiento** *nm* entertainment, amusement

entrever [entre'ßer] *vt* to glimpse, catch a glimpse of

entrevista [entre'ßista] *nf* interview; **entrevistar** *vt* to interview;

entrevistarse *vr* to have an interview

entristecer [entriste'θer] *vt* to sadden, grieve; **~se** *vr* to grow sad

entrometerse [entrome'terse] *vr*: **~ (en)** to interfere (in *o* with)

entroncar [entron'kar] *vi* to be connected *o* related

entumecer [entume'θer] *vt* to numb, benumb; **~se** *vr* (*por el frío*) to go *o* become numb; **entumecido, a** *adj* numb, stiff

enturbiar [entur'βjar] *vt* (*el agua*) to make cloudy; (*fig*) to confuse; **~se** *vr* (*oscurecerse*) to become cloudy; (*fig*) to get confused, become obscure

entusiasmar [entusjas'mar] *vt* to excite, fill with enthusiasm; (*gustar mucho*) to delight; **~se** *vr*: **~se con** *o* **por** to get enthusiastic *o* excited about

entusiasmo [entu'sjasmo] *nm* enthusiasm; (*excitación*) excitement

entusiasta [entu'sjasta] *adj* enthusiastic ♦ *nm/f* enthusiast

enumerar [enume'rar] *vt* to enumerate

enunciación [enunθja'θjon] *nf* enunciation

enunciado [enun'θjaðo] *nm* enunciation

envainar [embai'nar] *vt* to sheathe

envalentonar [embalento'nar] *vt* to give courage to; **~se** *vr* (*pey: jactarse*) to boast, brag

envanecer [embane'θer] *vt* to make conceited; **~se** *vr* to grow conceited

envasar [emba'sar] *vt* (*empaquetar*) to pack, wrap; (*enfrascar*) to bottle; (*enlatar*) to can; (*embolsar*) to pocket

envase [em'base] *nm* (*en paquete*) packing, wrapping; (*en botella*) bottling; (*en lata*) canning; (*recipiente*) container; (*paquete*) package; (*botella*) bottle; (*lata*) tin (*BRIT*), can

envejecer [embexe'θer] *vt* to make old, age ♦ *vi* (*volverse viejo*) to grow old; (*parecer viejo*) to age; **~se** *vr* to grow old; to age

envenenar [embene'nar] *vt* to poison; (*fig*) to embitter

envergadura [emberɣa'ðura] *nf* (*fig*) scope, compass

envés [em'bes] *nm* (*de tela*) back, wrong side

enviar [em'bjar] *vt* to send

enviciarse [embi'θjarse] *vr*: **~ (con)** to get addicted (to)

envidia [em'biðja] *nf* envy; **tener ~ a** to envy, be jealous of; **envidiar** *vt* to envy

envío [em'bio] *nm* (*acción*) sending; (*de mercancías*) consignment; (*de dinero*) remittance

enviudar [embju'ðar] *vi* to be widowed

envoltura [embol'tura] *nf* (*cobertura*) cover; (*embalaje*) wrapper, wrapping; **envoltorio** *nm* package

envolver [embol'βer] *vt* to wrap (up); (*cubrir*) to cover; (*enemigo*) to surround; (*implicar*) to involve, implicate

envuelto [em'bwelto] *pp de* **envolver**

enyesar [enje'sar] *vt* (*pared*) to plaster; (*MED*) to put in plaster

enzarzarse [enθar'θarse] *vr*: **~ en** (*pelea*) to get mixed up in; (*disputa*) to get involved in

épica ['epika] *nf* epic

épico, a ['epiko, a] *adj* epic

epidemia [epi'ðemja] *nf* epidemic

epilepsia [epi'lepsja] *nf* epilepsy

epílogo [e'pilovo] *nm* epilogue

episodio [epi'soðjo] *nm* episode

epístola [e'pistola] *nf* epistle

época ['epoka] *nf* period, time; (*HISTORIA*) age, epoch; **hacer ~** to be epoch-making

equilibrar [ekili'βrar] *vt* to balance; **equilibrio** *nm* balance, equilibrium; **equilibrista** *nm/f* (*funámbulo*) tightrope walker; (*acróbata*) acrobat

equipaje [eki'paxe] *nm* luggage; (*avíos*): **~ de mano** hand luggage

equipar [eki'par] *vt* (*proveer*) to equip

equipararse [ekipa'rarse] *vr*: **~ con** to be on a level with

equipo [e'kipo] *nm* (*conjunto de cosas*) equipment; (*DEPORTE*) team; (*de obreros*) shift

equis ['ekis] *nf inv* (the letter) X

equitación [ekita'θjon] *nf* horse riding

equitativo, a [ekita'tiβo, a] *adj* equitable, fair

equivalente [ekiβa'lente] *adj, nm* equivalent

equivaler [ekiβa'ler] *vi* to be equivalent *o* equal

equivocación [ekiβoka'θjon] *nf* mistake, error

equivocado, a [ekiβo'kaðo, a] *adj* wrong, mistaken

equivocarse [ekiβo'karse] *vr* to be wrong, make a mistake; ~ **de camino** to take the wrong road

equívoco, a [e'kiβoko, a] *adj* (*dudoso*) suspect; (*ambiguo*) ambiguous ♦ *nm* ambiguity; (*malentendido*) misunderstanding

era ['era] *vb ver* **ser** ♦ *nf* era, age

erais *vb ver* **ser**

éramos *vb ver* **ser**

eran *vb ver* **ser**

erario [e'rarjo] *nm* exchequer (*BRIT*), treasury

eras *vb ver* **ser**

erección [erek'θjon] *nf* erection

eres *vb ver* **ser**

erguir [er'ɣir] *vt* to raise, lift; (*poner derecho*) to straighten; ~**se** *vr* to straighten up

erigir [eri'xir] *vt* to erect, build; ~**se** *vr*: ~**se en** to set o.s. up as

erizarse [eri'θarse] *vr* (*pelo: de perro*) to bristle; (: *de persona*) to stand on end

erizo [e'riθo] *nm* (*ZOOL*) hedgehog; ~ **de mar** sea-urchin

ermita [er'mita] *nf* hermitage

ermitaño, a [ermi'taɲo, a] *nm/f* hermit

erosión [ero'sjon] *nf* erosion

erosionar [erosjo'nar] *vt* to erode

erótico, a [e'rotiko, a] *adj* erotic; **erotismo** *nm* eroticism

erradicar [erraði'kar] *vt* to eradicate

errante [e'rrante] *adj* wandering, errant

errar [e'rrar] *vi* (*vagar*) to wander, roam; (*equivocarse*) to be mistaken ♦ *vt*: ~ **el camino** to take the wrong road; ~ **el tiro** to miss

erróneo, a [e'rroneo, a] *adj* (*equivocado*) wrong, mistaken

error [e'rror] *nm* error, mistake; (*INFORM*) bug; ~ **de imprenta** misprint

eructar [eruk'tar] *vt* to belch, burp

erudito, a [eru'ðito, a] *adj* erudite, learned

erupción [erup'θjon] *nf* eruption; (*MED*) rash

es *vb ver* **ser**

esa ['esa] (*pl* **esas**) *adj demos ver* **ese**

ésa ['esa] (*pl* **ésas**) *pron ver* **ése**

esbelto, a [es'βelto, a] *adj* slim, slender

esbozo [es'βoθo] *nm* sketch, outline

escabeche [eska'βetʃe] *nm* brine; (*de aceitunas etc*) pickle; **en** ~ pickled

escabroso, a [eska'βroso, a] *adj* (*accidentado*) rough, uneven; (*fig*) tough, difficult; (: *atrevido*) risqué

escabullirse [eskaβu'ʎirse] *vr* to slip away, to clear out

escafandra [eska'fandra] *nf* (*buzo*) diving suit; (~ *espacial*) space suit

escala [es'kala] *nf* (*proporción, MUS*) scale; (*de mano*) ladder; (*AVIAT*) stopover; **hacer** ~ **en** to stop *o* call in at

escalafón [eskala'fon] *nm* (*escala de salarios*) salary scale, wage scale

escalar [eska'lar] *vt* to climb, scale

escalera [eska'lera] *nf* stairs *pl*, staircase; (*escala*) ladder; (*NAIPES*) run; ~ **mecánica** escalator; ~ **de caracol** spiral staircase

escalfar [eskal'far] *vt* (*huevos*) to poach

escalinata [eskali'nata] *nf* staircase

escalofriante [eskalo'frjante] *adj* chilling

escalofrío [eskalo'frio] *nm* (*MED*) chill; ~**s** *nmpl* (*fig*) shivers

escalón [eska'lon] *nm* step, stair; (*de escalera*) rung

escalope [eska'lope] *nm* (*CULIN*) escalope

escama [es'kama] *nf* (*de pez, serpiente*) scale; (*de jabón*) flake; (*fig*) resentment

escamar [eska'mar] *vt* (*fig*) to make wary *o* suspicious

escamotear [eskamote'ar] *vt* (*robar*) to lift, swipe; (*hacer desaparecer*) to make disappear

escampar [eskam'par] *vb impers* to stop raining

escandalizar [eskandali'θar] *vt* to scandalize, shock; **~se** *vr* to be shocked; (*ofenderse*) to be offended

escándalo [es'kandalo] *nm* scandal; (*alboroto, tumulto*) row, uproar; **escandaloso, a** *adj* scandalous, shocking

escandinavo, a [eskandi'naβo, a] *adj, nm/f* Scandinavian

escaño [es'kaɲo] *nm* bench; (*POL*) seat

escapar [eska'par] *vi* (*gen*) to escape, run away; (*DEPORTE*) to break away; **~se** *vr* to escape, get away; (*agua, gas*) to leak (out)

escaparate [eskapa'rate] *nm* shop window

escape [es'kape] *nm* (*de agua, gas*) leak; (*de motor*) exhaust

escarabajo [eskara'βaxo] *nm* beetle

escaramuza [eskara'muθa] *nf* skirmish

escarbar [eskar'βar] *vt* (*tierra*) to scratch

escarceos [eskar'θeos] *nmpl* (*fig*): **en mis ~ con la política ...** in my dealings with politics ...; **~ amorosos** love affairs

escarcha [es'kartʃa] *nf* frost

escarchado, a [eskar'tʃaðo, a] *adj* (*CULIN*: *fruta*) crystallized

escarlata [eskar'lata] *adj inv* scarlet; **escarlatina** *nf* scarlet fever

escarmentar [eskarmen'tar] *vt* to punish severely ♦ *vi* to learn one's lesson

escarmiento *etc* [eskar'mjento] *vb ver* **escarmentar** ♦ *nm* (*ejemplo*) lesson; (*castigo*) punishment

escarnio [es'karnjo] *nm* mockery; (*injuria*) insult

escarola [eska'rola] *nf* endive

escarpado, a [eskar'paðo, a] *adj* (*pendiente*) sheer, steep; (*rocas*) craggy

escasear [eskase'ar] *vi* to be scarce

escasez [eska'seθ] *nf* (*falta*) shortage, scarcity; (*pobreza*) poverty

escaso, a [es'kaso, a] *adj* (*poco*) scarce; (*raro*) rare; (*ralo*) thin, sparse; (*limitado*) limited

escatimar [eskati'mar] *vt* to skimp (on), be sparing with

escayola [eska'jola] *nf* plaster

escena [es'θena] *nf* scene

escenario [esθe'narjo] *nm* (*TEATRO*) stage; (*CINE*) set; (*fig*) scene; **escenografía** *nf* set design

escepticismo [esθepti'θismo] *nm* scepticism; **escéptico, a** *adj* sceptical ♦ *nm/f* sceptic

escisión [esθi'sjon] *nf* (*de partido, secta*) split

esclarecer [esklare'θer] *vt* (*misterio, problema*) to shed light on

esclavitud [esklaβi'tuð] *nf* slavery

esclavizar [esklaβi'θar] *vt* to enslave

esclavo, a [es'klaβo, a] *nm/f* slave

esclusa [es'klusa] *nf* (*de canal*) lock; (*compuerta*) floodgate

escoba [es'koβa] *nf* broom; **escobilla** *nf* brush

escocer [esko'θer] *vi* to burn, sting; **~se** *vr* to chafe, get chafed

escocés, esa [esko'θes, esa] *adj* Scottish ♦ *nm/f* Scotsman/woman, Scot

Escocia [es'koθja] *nf* Scotland

escoger [esko'xer] *vt* to choose, pick, select; **escogido, a** *adj* chosen, selected

escolar [esko'lar] *adj* school *cpd* ♦ *nm/f* schoolboy/girl, pupil

escollo [es'koʎo] *nm* (*obstáculo*) pitfall

escolta [es'kolta] *nf* escort; **escoltar** *vt* to escort

escombros [es'kombros] *nmpl* (*basura*) rubbish *sg*; (*restos*) debris *sg*

esconder [eskon'der] *vt* to hide, conceal; **~se** *vr* to hide; **escondidas** (*AM*) *nfpl*: **a escondidas** secretly; **escondite** *nm* hiding place; (*juego*) hide-and-seek; **escondrijo** *nm* hiding place, hideout

escopeta [esko'peta] *nf* shotgun

escoria [es'korja] *nf* (*de alto horno*) slag; (*fig*) scum, dregs *pl*

Escorpio [es'korpjo] *nm* Scorpio

escorpión [eskor'pjon] *nm* scorpion

escotado, a [esko'taðo, a] *adj* low-cut

escote [es'kote] *nm* (*de vestido*) low neck

pagar a ~ to share the expenses

escotilla [esko'tiʎa] *nf* (*NAUT*) hatch(way)

escozor [esko'θor] *nm* (*dolor*) sting(ing)

escribir [eskri'ßir] *vt*, *vi* to write; **~ a máquina** to type; **¿cómo se escribe?** how do you spell it?

escrito, a [es'krito, a] *pp de* **escribir** ♦ *nm* (*documento*) document; (*manuscrito*) text, manuscript; **por ~** in writing

escritor, a [eskri'tor, a] *nm/f* writer

escritorio [eskri'torjo] *nm* desk

escritura [eskri'tura] *nf* (*acción*) writing; (*caligrafía*) (hand)writing; (*JUR: documento*) deed

escrúpulo [es'krupulo] *nm* scruple; (*minuciosidad*) scrupulousness; **escrupuloso, a** *adj* scrupulous

escrutar [eskru'tar] *vt* to scrutinize, examine; (*votos*) to count

escrutinio [eskru'tinjo] *nm* (*examen atento*) scrutiny; (*POL: recuento de votos*) count(ing)

escuadra [es'kwaðra] *nf* (*MIL etc*) squad; (*NAUT*) squadron; (*de coches etc*) fleet; **escuadrilla** *nf* (*de aviones*) squadron; (*AM: de obreros*) gang

escuadrón [eskwa'ðron] *nm* squadron

escuálido, a [es'kwaliðo, a] *adj* skinny, scraggy; (*sucio*) squalid

escuchar [esku'tʃar] *vt* to listen to ♦ *vi* to listen

escudilla [esku'ðiʎa] *nf* bowl, basin

escudo [es'kuðo] *nm* shield

escudriñar [eskuðri'nar] *vt* (*examinar*) to investigate, scrutinize; (*mirar de lejos*) to scan

escuela [es'kwela] *nf* school; **~ de artes y oficios** (*ESP*) ≈ technical college; **~ normal** teacher training college

escueto, a [es'kweto, a] *adj* plain; (*estilo*) simple

escuincle [es'kwinkle] (*AM: fam*) *nm/f* kid

esculpir [eskul'pir] *vt* to sculpt; (*grabar*) to engrave; (*tallar*) to carve; **escultor, a** *nm/f* sculptor/tress; **escultura** *nf* sculpture

escupidera [eskupi'ðera] *nf* spittoon

escupir [esku'pir] *vt*, *vi* to spit (out)

escurreplatos [eskurre'platos] *nm inv* plate rack

escurridizo, a [eskurri'ðiθo, a] *adj* slippery

escurridor [eskurri'ðor] *nm* colander

escurrir [esku'rrir] *vt* (*ropa*) to wring out; (*verduras, platos*) to drain ♦ *vi* (*líquidos*) to drip; **~se** *vr* (*secarse*) to drain; (*resbalarse*) to slip, slide; (*escaparse*) to slip away

ese ['ese] (*f* **esa**, *pl* **esos, esas**) *adj demos* (*sg*) that; (*pl*) those

ése ['ese] (*f* **ésa**, *pl* **ésos, ésas**) *pron* (*sg*) that (one); (*pl*) those (ones); **~ ... éste ...** the former ... the latter ...; **no me vengas con ésas** don't give me any more of that nonsense

esencia [e'senθja] *nf* essence; **esencial** *adj* essential

esfera [es'fera] *nf* sphere; (*de reloj*) face; **esférico, a** *adj* spherical

esforzarse [esfor'θarse] *vr* to exert o.s., make an effort

esfuerzo *etc* [es'fwerθo] *vb ver* **esforzar** ♦ *nm* effort

esfumarse [esfu'marse] *vr* (*apoyo, esperanzas*) to fade away

esgrima [es'xrima] *nf* fencing

esgrimir [esxri'mir] *vt* (*arma*) to brandish; (*argumento*) to use

esguince [es'xinθe] *nm* (*MED*) sprain

eslabón [esla'ßon] *nm* link

eslip [es'lip] *nm* pants *pl* (*BRIT*), briefs *pl*

eslovaco, a [eslo'ßako, a] *adj*, *nm/f* Slovak, Slovakian ♦ *nm* (*LING*) Slovak, Slovakian

Eslovaquia [eslo'ßakja] *nf* Slovakia

esmaltar [esmal'tar] *vt* to enamel; **esmalte** *nm* enamel; **esmalte de uñas** nail varnish *o* polish

esmerado, a [esme'raðo, a] *adj* careful, neat

esmeralda [esme'ralda] *nf* emerald

esmerarse [esme'rarse] *vr* (*aplicarse*) to take great pains, exercise great care; (*afanarse*) to work hard

esmero [es'mero] *nm* (great) care

esnob [es'nob] (*pl* **~s**) *adj* (*persona*) snobbish ♦ *nm/f* snob; **~ismo** *nm* snobbery

eso ['eso] *pron* that, that thing *o* matter; **~ de su coche** that business about his car; **~ de ir al cine** all that about going to the cinema; **a ~ de las cinco** at about five o'clock; **en ~** thereupon, at that point; **~ es** that's it; **¡~ sí que es vida!** now that is really living!; **por ~ te lo dije** that's why I told you; **y ~ que llovía** in spite of the fact it was raining

esos ['esos] *adj demos ver* **ese**

ésos ['esos] *pron ver* **ése**

espabilar *etc* [espaβi'lar] = **despabilar** *etc*

espacial [espa'θjal] *adj* (*del espacio*) space *cpd*

espaciar [espa'θjar] *vt* to space (out)

espacio [es'paθjo] *nm* space; (*MUS*) interval; (*RADIO, TV*) programme (*BRIT*), program (*US*); **el ~** space; **~so, a** *adj* spacious, roomy

espada [es'paða] *nf* sword; **~s** *nfpl* (*NAIPES*) spades

espaguetis [espa'ɣetis] *nmpl* spaghetti *sg*

espalda [es'palda] *nf* (*gen*) back; **~s** *nfpl* (*hombros*) shoulders; **a ~s de uno** behind sb's back; **tenderse de ~s** to lie (down) on one's back; **volver la ~ a alguien** to cold-shoulder sb

espantajo [espan'taxo] *nm* = **espanta-pájaros**

espantapájaros [espanta'paxaros] *nm inv* scarecrow

espantar [espan'tar] *vt* (*asustar*) to frighten, scare; (*ahuyentar*) to frighten off; (*asombrar*) to horrify, appal; **~se** *vr* to get frightened *o* scared; to be appalled

espanto [es'panto] *nm* (*susto*) fright; (*terror*) terror; (*asombro*) astonishment; **~so, a** *adj* frightening; terrifying; astonishing

España [es'paɲa] *nf* Spain; **español, a** *adj* Spanish ♦ *nm/f* Spaniard ♦ *nm* (*LING*) Spanish

esparadrapo [espara'ðrapo] *nm* (sticking) plaster (*BRIT*), adhesive tape (*US*)

esparcimiento [esparθi'mjento] *nm* (*dispersión*) spreading; (*diseminación*) scattering; (*fig*) cheerfulness

esparcir [espar'θir] *vt* to spread; (*diseminar*) to scatter; **~se** *vr* to spread (out); to scatter; (*divertirse*) to enjoy o.s.

espárrago [es'parraɣo] *nm* asparagus

esparto [es'parto] *nm* esparto (grass)

espasmo [es'pasmo] *nm* spasm

espátula [es'patula] *nf* spatula

especia [es'peθja] *nf* spice

especial [espe'θjal] *adj* special; **~idad** *nf* speciality (*BRIT*), specialty (*US*)

especie [es'peθje] *nf* (*BIO*) species; (*clase*) kind, sort; **en ~** in kind

especificar [espeθifi'kar] *vt* to specify; **específico, a** *adj* specific

espécimen [es'peθimen] (*pl* **especímenes**) *nm* specimen

espectáculo [espek'takulo] *nm* (*gen*) spectacle; (*TEATRO etc*) show

espectador, a [espekta'ðor, a] *nm/f* spectator

espectro [es'pektro] *nm* ghost; (*fig*) spectre

especular [espeku'lar] *vt, vi* to speculate

espejismo [espe'xismo] *nm* mirage

espejo [es'pexo] *nm* mirror; **~ retrovisor** rear-view mirror

espeluznante [espeluθ'nante] *adj* horrifying, hair-raising

espera [es'pera] *nf* (*pausa, intervalo*) wait; (*JUR: plazo*) respite; **en ~ de** waiting for; (*con expectativa*) expecting

esperanza [espe'ranθa] *nf* (*confianza*) hope; (*expectativa*) expectation; **hay pocas ~s de que venga** there is little prospect of his coming

esperar [espe'rar] *vt* (*aguardar*) to wait for; (*tener expectativa de*) to expect; (*desear*) to hope for ♦ *vi* to wait; to expect; to hope

esperma [es'perma] *nf* sperm

espesar [espe'sar] *vt* to thicken; **~se** *vr* to thicken, get thicker

espeso, a [es'peso, a] *adj* thick; **espesor**

nm thickness

espía [es'pia] *nm/f* spy; **espiar** *vt*
(*observar*) to spy on

espiga [es'piɣa] *nf* (*BOT: de trigo etc*) ear

espigón [espi'ɣon] *nm* (*BOT*) ear; (*NAUT*)
breakwater

espina [es'pina] *nf* thorn; (*de pez*) bone; **~
dorsal** (*ANAT*) spine

espinaca [espi'naka] *nf* spinach

espinazo [espi'naθo] *nm* spine, backbone

espinilla [espi'niʎa] *nf* (*ANAT: tibia*)
shin(bone); (*grano*) blackhead

espinoso, a [espi'noso, a] *adj* (*planta*)
thorny, prickly; (*asunto*) difficult

espionaje [espjo'naxe] *nm* spying,
espionage

espiral [espi'ral] *adj, nf* spiral

espirar [espi'rar] *vt* to breathe out, exhale

espiritista [espiri'tista] *adj, nm/f*
spiritualist

espíritu [es'piritu] *nm* spirit; **espiritual**
adj spiritual

espita [es'pita] *nf* tap

espléndido, a [es'plendiðo, a] *adj*
(*magnífico*) magnificent, splendid;
(*generoso*) generous

esplendor [esplen'dor] *nm* splendour

espolear [espole'ar] *vt* to spur on

espoleta [espo'leta] *nf* (*de bomba*) fuse

espolón [espo'lon] *nm* sea wall

espolvorear [espolβore'ar] *vt* to dust,
sprinkle

esponja [es'ponxa] *nf* sponge; (*fig*)
sponger; **esponjoso, a** *adj* spongy

espontaneidad [espontanei'ðað] *nf*
spontaneity; **espontáneo, a** *adj*
spontaneous

esposa [es'posa] *nf* wife; **~s** *nfpl*
handcuffs; **esposar** *vt* to handcuff

esposo [es'poso] *nm* husband

espray [es'prai] *nm* spray

espuela [es'pwela] *nf* spur

espuma [es'puma] *nf* foam; (*de cerveza*)
froth, head; (*de jabón*) lather;
espumadera *nf* (*utensilio*) skimmer;
espumoso, a *adj* frothy, foamy; (*vino*)
sparkling

esqueleto [eske'leto] *nm* skeleton

esquema [es'kema] *nm* (*diagrama*)
diagram; (*dibujo*) plan; (*FILOSOFÍA*) schema

esquí [es'ki] (*pl* **~s**) *nm* (*objeto*) ski;
(*DEPORTE*) skiing; **~ acuático** water-skiing;
esquiar *vi* to ski

esquilar [eski'lar] *vt* to shear

esquimal [eski'mal] *adj, nm/f* Eskimo

esquina [es'kina] *nf* corner

esquinazo [eski'naθo] *nm*: **dar ~ a algn**
to give sb the slip

esquirol [eski'rol] *nm* blackleg

esquivar [eski'βar] *vt* to avoid

esquivo, a [es'kiβo, a] *adj* evasive;
(*tímido*) reserved; (*huraño*) unsociable

esta ['esta] *adj demos ver* **este²**

está *vb ver* **estar**

ésta ['esta] *pron ver* **éste**

estabilidad [estaβili'ðað] *nf* stability;
estable *adj* stable

establecer [estaβle'θer] *vt* to establish;
~se *vr* to establish o.s.; (*echar raíces*) to
settle (down); **establecimiento** *nm*
establishment

establo [es'taβlo] *nm* (*AGR*) stable

estaca [es'taka] *nf* stake, post; (*de tienda
de campaña*) peg

estacada [esta'kaða] *nf* (*cerca*) fence,
fencing; (*palenque*) stockade

estación [esta'θjon] *nf* station; (*del año*)
season; **~ de autobuses** bus station; **~
balnearia** seaside resort; **~ de servicio**
service station

estacionamiento [estaθjona'mjento] *nm*
(*AUTO*) parking; (*MIL*) stationing

estacionar [estaθjo'nar] *vt* (*AUTO*) to park;
(*MIL*) to station; **~io, a** *adj* stationary;
(*COM: mercado*) slack

estadio [es'taðjo] *nm* (*fase*) stage, phase;
(*DEPORTE*) stadium

estadista [esta'ðista] *nm* (*POL*) statesman;
(*ESTADÍSTICA*) statistician

estadística [esta'ðistika] *nf* figure,
statistic; (*ciencia*) statistics *sg*

estado [es'taðo] *nm* (*POL: condición*) state;
~ de ánimo state of mind; **~ de cuenta**
bank statement; **~ de sitio** state of siege;

~ civil marital status; **~ mayor** staff; **estar en ~** to be pregnant; **(los) E~s Unidos** *nmpl* the United States (of America) *sg*

estadounidense [estaðouniˈðense] *adj* United States *cpd*, American ♦ *nm/f* American

estafa [esˈtafa] *nf* swindle, trick; **estafar** *vt* to swindle, defraud

estafeta [estaˈfeta] *nf* (*oficina de correos*) post office; **~ diplomática** diplomatic bag

estáis *vb ver* **estar**

estallar [estaˈʎar] *vi* to burst; (*bomba*) to explode, go off; (*epidemia, guerra, rebelión*) to break out; **~ en llanto** to burst into tears; **estallido** *nm* explosion; (*fig*) outbreak

estampa [esˈtampa] *nf* print, engraving

estampado, a [estamˈpaðo, a] *adj* printed ♦ *nm* (*impresión: acción*) printing; (*: efecto*) print; (*marca*) stamping

estampar [estamˈpar] *vt* (*imprimir*) to print; (*marcar*) to stamp; (*metal*) to engrave; (*poner sello en*) to stamp; (*fig*) to stamp, imprint

estampida [estamˈpiða] *nf* stampede

estampido [estamˈpiðo] *nm* bang, report

están *vb ver* **estar**

estancado, a [estanˈkaðo, a] *adj* stagnant

estancar [estanˈkar] *vt* (*aguas*) to hold up, hold back; (*COM*) to monopolize; (*fig*) to block, hold up; **~se** *vr* to stagnate

estancia [esˈtanθja] *nf* (*permanencia*) stay; (*sala*) room; (*AM*) farm, ranch; **estanciero** (*AM*) *nm* farmer, rancher

estanco, a [esˈtanko, a] *adj* watertight ♦ *nm* tobacconist's (shop), cigar store (*US*)

Estanco

i Cigarettes, tobacco, postage stamps and official forms are all sold under state monopoly in shops called an **estanco**. Although tobacco products can also be bought in bars and **quioscos** they are generally more expensive.

---

estándar [esˈtandar] *adj, nm* standard;

estandarizar *vt* to standardize

estandarte [estanˈdarte] *nm* banner, standard

estanque [esˈtanke] *nm* (*lago*) pool, pond; (*AGR*) reservoir

estanquero, a [estanˈkero, a] *nm/f* tobacconist

estante [esˈtante] *nm* (*armario*) rack, stand; (*biblioteca*) bookcase; (*anaquel*) shelf; (*AM*) prop; **estantería** *nf* shelving, shelves *pl*

estaño [esˈtaɲo] *nm* tin

PALABRA CLAVE

---

estar [esˈtar] *vi* **1** (*posición*) to be; **está en la plaza** it's in the square; **¿está Juan?** is Juan in?; **estamos a 30 km de Junín** we're 30 kms from Junín

2 (*+adj: estado*) to be; **~ enfermo** to be ill; **está muy elegante** he's looking very smart; **¿cómo estás?** how are you keeping?

3 (*+gerundio*) to be; **estoy leyendo** I'm reading

4 (*uso pasivo*): **está condenado a muerte** he's been condemned to death; **está envasado en ...** it's packed in ...

5 (*con fechas*): **¿a cuántos estamos?** what's the date today?; **estamos a 5 de mayo** it's the 5th of May

6 (*locuciones*): **¿estamos?** (*¿de acuerdo?*) okay?; (*¿listo?*) ready?; **¡ya está bien!** that's enough!

7: ~ de: **~ de vacaciones/viaje** to be on holiday/away *o* on a trip; **está de camarero** he's working as a waiter

8: ~ para: **está para salir** he's about to leave; **no estoy para bromas** I'm not in the mood for jokes

9: ~ por (*propuesta etc*) to be in favour of; (*persona etc*) to support, side with; **está por limpiar** it still has to be cleaned

10: ~ sin: **~ sin +infin** to have no money; **está sin terminar** it isn't finished yet

♦ **~se** *vr*: **se estuvo en la cama toda la tarde** he stayed in bed all afternoon

estas ['estas] *adj demos ver* **este²**

éstas ['estas] *pron ver* **éste**

estatal [esta'tal] *adj* state *cpd*

estático, a [es'tatiko, a] *adj* static

estatua [es'tatwa] *nf* statue

estatura [esta'tura] *nf* stature, height

estatuto [esta'tuto] *nm* (JUR) statute; (*de ciudad*) bye-law; (*de comité*) rule

este¹ ['este] *nm* east

este² ['este] (*f* **esta**, *pl* **estos**, **estas**) *adj demos* (*sg*) this; (*pl*) these

esté *etc vb ver* **estar**

éste ['este] (*f* **ésta**, *pl* **éstos**, **éstas**) *pron* (*sg*) this (one); (*pl*) these (ones); **ése ... ~ ...** the former ... the latter ....

estelar [este'lar] *adj* (ASTRO) stellar; (*actuación, reparto*) star (*atr*)

estén *etc vb ver* **estar**

estepa [es'tepa] *nf* (GEO) steppe

estera [es'tera] *nf* mat(ting)

estéreo [es'tereo] *adj inv*, *nm* stereo; **estereotipo** *nm* stereotype

estéril [es'teril] *adj* sterile, barren; (*fig*) vain, futile; **esterilizar** *vt* to sterilize

esterlina [ester'lina] *adj*: **libra ~** pound sterling

estés *etc vb ver* **estar**

estética [es'tetika] *nf* aesthetics *sg*

estético, a [es'tetiko, a] *adj* aesthetic

estibador [estiβa'ðor] *nm* stevedore, docker

estiércol [es'tjerkol] *nm* dung, manure

estigma [es'tiɣma] *nm* stigma

estilarse [esti'larse] *vr* to be in fashion

estilo [es'tilo] *nm* style; (TEC) stylus; (NATACIÓN) stroke; **algo por el ~** something along those lines

estima [es'tima] *nf* esteem, respect

estimación [estima'θjon] *nf* (*evaluación*) estimation; (*aprecio, afecto*) esteem, regard

estimar [esti'mar] *vt* (*evaluar*) to estimate; (*valorar*) to value; (*apreciar*) to esteem, respect; (*pensar, considerar*) to think, reckon

estimulante [estimu'lante] *adj* stimulating ♦ *nm* stimulant

estimular [estimu'lar] *vt* to stimulate; (*excitar*) to excite

estímulo [es'timulo] *nm* stimulus; (*ánimo*) encouragement

estipulación [estipula'θjon] *nf* stipulation, condition

estipular [estipu'lar] *vt* to stipulate

estirado, a [esti'raðo, a] *adj* (*tenso*) (stretched *o* drawn) tight; (*fig: persona*) stiff, pompous

estirar [esti'rar] *vt* to stretch; (*dinero, suma etc*) to stretch out; **~se** *vr* to stretch

estirón [esti'ron] *nm* pull, tug; (*crecimiento*) spurt, sudden growth; **dar un ~** (*niño*) to shoot up

estirpe [es'tirpe] *nf* stock, lineage

estival [esti'βal] *adj* summer *cpd*

esto ['esto] *pron* this, this thing *o* matter; **~ de la boda** this business about the wedding

Estocolmo [esto'kolmo] *nm* Stockholm

estofado [esto'faðo] *nm* stew

estofar [esto'far] *vt* to stew

estómago [es'tomaxo] *nm* stomach; **tener ~** to be thick-skinned

estorbar [estor'βar] *vt* to hinder, obstruct; (*molestar*) to bother, disturb ♦ *vi* to be in the way; **estorbo** *nm* (*molestia*) bother, nuisance; (*obstáculo*) hindrance, obstacle

estornudar [estornu'ðar] *vi* to sneeze

estos ['estos] *adj demos ver* **este²**

éstos ['estos] *pron ver* **éste**

estoy *vb ver* **estar**

estrado [es'traðo] *nm* platform

estrafalario, a [estrafa'larjo, a] *adj* odd, eccentric

estrago [es'traxo] *nm* ruin, destruction; **hacer ~s en** to wreak havoc among

estragón [estra'xon] *nm* tarragon

estrambótico, a [estram'botiko, a] *adj* (*persona*) eccentric; (*peinado, ropa*) outlandish

estrangulador, a [estrangula'ðor, a] *nm/f* strangler ♦ *nm* (TEC) throttle; (AUTO) choke

estrangular [estrangu'lar] *vt* (*persona*) to

strangle; (*MED*) to strangulate
estratagema [estrata'xema] *nf* (*MIL*)
stratagem; (*astucia*) cunning
estrategia [estra'texja] *nf* strategy;
estratégico, a *adj* strategic
estrato [es'trato] *nm* stratum, layer
estrechamente [es'tretʃamente] *adv*
(*íntimamente*) closely, intimately;
(*pobremente: vivir*) poorly
estrechar [estre'tʃar] *vt* (*reducir*) to
narrow; (*COSTURA*) to take in; (*abrazar*) to
hug, embrace; **~se** *vr* (*reducirse*) to
narrow, grow narrow; (*abrazarse*) to
embrace; **~ la mano** to shake hands
estrechez [estre'tʃeθ] *nf* narrowness; (*de
ropa*) tightness; **estrecheces** *nfpl*
(*dificultades económicas*) financial
difficulties
estrecho, a [es'tretʃo, a] *adj* narrow;
(*apretado*) tight; (*íntimo*) close, intimate;
(*miserable*) mean ♦ *nm* strait; **~ de miras**
narrow-minded
estrella [es'treʎa] *nf* star; **~ de mar** (*ZOOL*)
starfish; **~ fugaz** shooting star;
estrellado, a *adj* (*forma*) star-shaped;
(*cielo*) starry
estrellar [estre'ʎar] *vt* (*hacer añicos*) to
smash (to pieces); (*huevos*) to fry; **~se** *vr*
to smash; (*chocarse*) to crash; (*fracasar*) to
fail
estremecer [estreme'θer] *vt* to shake; **~se**
vr to shake, tremble; **estremecimiento**
nm (*temblor*) trembling, shaking
estrenar [estre'nar] *vt* (*vestido*) to wear for
the first time; (*casa*) to move into;
(*película, obra de teatro*) to première; **~se**
vr (*persona*) to make one's début;
estreno *nm* (*CINE etc*) première
estreñido, a [estre'ɲiðo, a] *adj*
constipated
estreñimiento [estreɲi'mjento] *nm*
constipation
estrépito [es'trepito] *nm* noise, racket;
(*fig*) fuss; **estrepitoso, a** *adj* noisy;
(*fiesta*) rowdy
estría [es'tria] *nf* groove
estribación [estriβa'θjon] *nf* (*GEO*) spur,

foothill
estribar [estri'βar] *vi*: **~ en** to lie on
estribillo [estri'βiʎo] *nm* (*LITERATURA*)
refrain; (*MUS*) chorus
estribo [es'triβo] *nm* (*de jinete*) stirrup; (*de
coche, tren*) step; (*de puente*) support;
(*GEO*) spur; **perder los ~s** to fly off the
handle
estribor [estri'βor] *nm* (*NAUT*) starboard
estricto, a [es'trikto, a] *adj* (*riguroso*)
strict; (*severo*) severe
estridente [estri'ðente] *adj* (*color*) loud;
(*voz*) raucous
estropajo [estro'paxo] *nm* scourer
estropear [estrope'ar] *vt* to spoil; (*dañar*)
to damage; **~se** *vr* (*objeto*) to get
damaged; (*persona: la piel etc*) to be
ruined
estructura [estruk'tura] *nf* structure
estruendo [es'trwendo] *nm* (*ruido*) racket,
din; (*fig: alboroto*) uproar, turmoil
estrujar [estru'xar] *vt* (*apretar*) to squeeze;
(*aplastar*) to crush; (*fig*) to drain, bleed
estuario [es'twarjo] *nm* estuary
estuche [es'tutʃe] *nm* box, case
estudiante [estu'ðjante] *nm/f* student;
estudiantil *adj* student *cpd*
estudiar [estu'ðjar] *vt* to study
estudio [es'tuðjo] *nm* study; (*CINE, ARTE,
RADIO*) studio; **~s** *nmpl* studies; (*erudición*)
learning *sg*; **~so, a** *adj* studious
estufa [es'tufa] *nf* heater, fire
estupefaciente [estupefa'θjente] *nm*
drug, narcotic
estupefacto, a [estupe'fakto, a] *adj*
speechless, thunderstruck
estupendo, a [estu'pendo, a] *adj*
wonderful, terrific; (*fam*) great; **¡~!** that's
great!, fantastic!
estupidez [estupi'ðeθ] *nf* (*torpeza*)
stupidity; (*acto*) stupid thing (to do)
estúpido, a [es'tupiðo, a] *adj* stupid, silly
estupor [estu'por] *nm* stupor; (*fig*)
astonishment, amazement
estuve *etc vb ver* **estar**
esvástica [es'βastika] *nf* swastika
ETA ['eta] (*ESP*) *nf abr* (= Euskadi ta

Askatasuna) ETA

etapa [e'tapa] *nf* (*de viaje*) stage; (*DEPORTE*) leg; (*parada*) stopping place; (*fase*) stage, phase

etarra [e'tarra] *nm/f* member of ETA

etc. *abr* (= *etcétera*) etc

etcétera [et'θetera] *adv* etcetera

eternidad [eterni'ðað] *nf* eternity; **eterno, a** *adj* eternal, everlasting

ética ['etika] *nf* ethics *pl*

ético, a ['etiko, a] *adj* ethical

etiqueta [eti'keta] *nf* (*modales*) etiquette; (*rótulo*) label, tag

Eucaristía [eukaris'tia] *nf* Eucharist

eufemismo [eufe'mismo] *nm* euphemism

euforia [eu'forja] *nf* euphoria

eurodiputado, a [eurodipu'taðo, a] *nm/f* Euro MP, MEP

Europa [eu'ropa] *nf* Europe; **europeo, a** *adj, nm/f* European

Euskadi [eus'kaði] *nm* the Basque Country *o* Provinces *pl*

euskera [eus'kera] *nm* (*LING*) Basque

evacuación [eßakwa'θjon] *nf* evacuation

evacuar [eßa'kwar] *vt* to evacuate

evadir [eßa'ðir] *vt* to evade, avoid; **~se** *vr* to escape

evaluar [eßa'lwar] *vt* to evaluate

evangelio [eßan'xeljo] *nm* gospel

evaporar [eßapo'rar] *vt* to evaporate; **~se** *vr* to vanish

evasión [eßa'sjon] *nf* escape, flight; (*fig*) evasion; **~ de capitales** flight of capital

evasiva [eßa'sißa] *nf* (*pretexto*) excuse

evasivo, a [eßa'sißo, a] *adj* evasive, non-committal

evento [e'ßento] *nm* event

eventual [eßen'twal] *adj* possible, conditional (upon circumstances); (*trabajador*) casual, temporary

evidencia [eßi'ðenθja] *nf* evidence, proof; **evidenciar** *vt* (*hacer patente*) to make evident; (*probar*) to prove, show; **evidenciarse** *vr* to be evident

evidente [eßi'ðente] *adj* obvious, clear, evident

evitar [eßi'tar] *vt* (*evadir*) to avoid; (*impedir*) to prevent

evocar [eßo'kar] *vt* to evoke, call forth

evolución [eßolu'θjon] *nf* (*desarrollo*) evolution, development; (*cambio*) change; (*MIL*) manoeuvre; **evolucionar** *vi* to evolve; to manoeuvre

ex [eks] *adj* ex-; **el ~ ministro** the former minister, the ex-minister

exacerbar [eksaθer'ßar] *vt* to irritate, annoy

exactamente [eksakta'mente] *adv* exactly

exactitud [eksakti'tuð] *nf* exactness; (*precisión*) accuracy; (*puntualidad*) punctuality; **exacto, a** *adj* exact; accurate; punctual; **¡exacto!** exactly!

exageración [eksaxera'θjon] *nf* exaggeration

exagerar [eksaxe'rar] *vt, vi* to exaggerate

exaltado, a [eksal'taðo, a] *adj* (*apasionado*) over-excited, worked-up; (*POL*) extreme

exaltar [eksal'tar] *vt* to exalt, glorify; **~se** *vr* (*excitarse*) to get excited *o* worked-up

examen [ek'samen] *nm* examination

examinar [eksami'nar] *vt* to examine; **~se** *vr* to be examined, take an examination

exasperar [eksaspe'rar] *vt* to exasperate; **~se** *vr* to get exasperated, lose patience

Exca. *abr* = **Excelencia**

excavadora [ekskaßa'ðora] *nf* excavator

excavar [ekska'ßar] *vt* to excavate

excedencia [eksθe'ðenθja] *nf*: **estar en ~** to be on leave; **pedir** *o* **solicitar la ~** to ask for leave

excedente [eksθe'ðente] *adj, nm* excess, surplus

exceder [eksθe'ðer] *vt* to exceed, surpass; **~se** *vr* (*extralimitarse*) to go too far

excelencia [eksθe'lenθja] *nf* excellence; **E~** Excellency; **excelente** *adj* excellent

excentricidad [eksθentriθi'ðað] *nf* eccentricity; **excéntrico, a** *adj, nm/f* eccentric

excepción [eksθep'θjon] *nf* exception; **excepcional** *adj* exceptional

excepto [eks'θepto] *adv* excepting, except (for)

exceptuar [eksθep'twar] *vt* to except, exclude

excesivo, a [eksθe'siβo, a] *adj* excessive

exceso [eks'θeso] *nm* (*gen*) excess; (*COM*) surplus; **~ de equipaje/peso** excess luggage/weight

excitación [eksθita'θjon] *nf* (*sensación*) excitement; (*acción*) excitation

excitado, a [eksθi'taðo, a] *adj* excited; (*emociones*) aroused

excitar [eksθi'tar] *vt* to excite; (*incitar*) to urge; **~se** *vr* to get excited

exclamación [eksklama'θjon] *nf* exclamation

exclamar [ekskla'mar] *vi* to exclaim

excluir [eksklu'ir] *vt* to exclude; (*dejar fuera*) to shut out; (*descartar*) to reject; **exclusión** *nf* exclusion

exclusiva [eksklu'siβa] *nf* (*PRENSA*) exclusive, scoop; (*COM*) sole right

exclusivo, a [eksklu'siβo, a] *adj* exclusive; **derecho ~** sole *o* exclusive right

Excmo. *abr* = **excelentísimo**

excomulgar [ekskomul'var] *vt* (*REL*) to excommunicate

excomunión [ekskomu'njon] *nf* excommunication

excursión [ekskur'sjon] *nf* excursion, outing; **excursionista** *nm/f* (*turista*) sightseer

excusa [eks'kusa] *nf* excuse; (*disculpa*) apology

excusar [eksku'sar] *vt* to excuse; **~se** *vr* (*disculparse*) to apologize

exhalar [eksa'lar] *vt* to exhale, breathe out; (*olor etc*) to give off; (*suspiro*) to breathe, heave

exhaustivo, a [eksaus'tiβo, a] *adj* (*análisis*) thorough; (*estudio*) exhaustive

exhausto, a [ek'sausto, a] *adj* exhausted

exhibición [eksiβi'θjon] *nf* exhibition, display, show

exhibir [eksi'βir] *vt* to exhibit, display, show

exhortar [eksor'tar] *vt*: **~ a** to exhort to

exigencia [eksi'xenθja] *nf* demand, requirement; **exigente** *adj* demanding

exigir [eksi'xir] *vt* (*gen*) to demand, require; **~ el pago** to demand payment

exiliado, a [eksi'ljaðo, a] *adj* exiled ♦ *nm/f* exile

exilio [ek'siljo] *nm* exile

eximir [eksi'mir] *vt* to exempt

existencia [eksis'tenθja] *nf* existence; **~s** *nfpl* stock(s) (*pl*)

existir [eksis'tir] *vi* to exist, be

éxito ['eksito] *nm* (*triunfo*) success; (*MUS etc*) hit; **tener ~** to be successful

exonerar [eksone'rar] *vt* to exonerate; **~ de una obligación** to free from an obligation

exorbitante [eksorβi'tante] *adj* (*precio*) exorbitant; (*cantidad*) excessive

exorcizar [eksorθi'θar] *vt* to exorcize

exótico, a [ek'sotiko, a] *adj* exotic

expandir [ekspan'dir] *vt* to expand

expansión [ekspan'sjon] *nf* expansion

expansivo, a [ekspan'siβo, a] *adj*: **onda ~a** shock wave

expatriarse [ekspa'trjarse] *vr* to emigrate; (*POL*) to go into exile

expectativa [ekspekta'tiβa] *nf* (*espera*) expectation; (*perspectiva*) prospect

expedición [ekspeði'θjon] *nf* (*excursión*) expedition

expediente [ekspe'ðjente] *nm* expedient; (*JUR: procedimento*) action, proceedings *pl*; (: *papeles*) dossier, file, record

expedir [ekspe'ðir] *vt* (*despachar*) to send, forward; (*pasaporte*) to issue

expendedor, a [ekspende'ðor, a] *nm/f* (*vendedor*) dealer

expensas [eks'pensas] *nfpl*: **a ~ de** at the expense of

experiencia [ekspe'rjenθja] *nf* experience

experimentado, a [eksperimen'taðo, a] *adj* experienced

experimentar [eksperimen'tar] *vt* (*en laboratorio*) to experiment with; (*probar*) to test, try out; (*notar, observar*) to experience; (*deterioro, pérdida*) to suffer; **experimento** *nm* experiment

experto, a [eks'perto, a] *adj* expert, skilled ♦ *nm/f* expert

expiar [ekspi'ar] *vt* to atone for

expirar [ekspi'rar] *vi* to expire

explanada [ekspla'naða] *nf* (*llano*) plain

explayarse [ekspla'jarse] *vr* (*en discurso*) to speak at length; **~ con uno** to confide in sb

explicación [eksplika'θjon] *nf* explanation

explicar [ekspli'kar] *vt* to explain; **~se** *vr* to explain (o.s.)

explícito, a [eks'pliθito, a] *adj* explicit

explique *etc vb ver* **explicar**

explorador, a [eksplora'ðor, a] *nm/f* (*pionero*) explorer; (*MIL*) scout ♦ *nm* (*MED*) probe; (*TEC*) (*radar*) scanner

explorar [eksplo'rar] *vt* to explore; (*MED*) to probe; (*radar*) to scan

explosión [eksplo'sjon] *nf* explosion; **explosivo, a** *adj* explosive

explotación [eksplota'θjon] *nf* exploitation; (*de planta etc*) running

explotar [eksplo'tar] *vt* to exploit; to run, operate ♦ *vi* to explode

exponer [ekspo'ner] *vt* to expose; (*cuadro*) to display; (*vida*) to risk; (*idea*) to explain; **~se** *vr*: **~se a (hacer) algo** to run the risk of (doing) sth

exportación [eksporta'θjon] *nf* (*acción*) export; (*mercancías*) exports *pl*

exportar [ekspor'tar] *vt* to export

exposición [eksposi'θjon] *nf* (*gen*) exposure; (*de arte*) show, exhibition; (*explicación*) explanation; (*declaración*) account, statement

expresamente [ekspresa'mente] *adv* (*decir*) clearly; (*a propósito*) expressly

expresar [ekspre'sar] *vt* to express; **expresión** *nf* expression

expresivo, a [ekspre'sißo, a] *adj* (*persona, gesto, palabras*) expressive; (*cariñoso*) affectionate

expreso, a [eks'preso, a] *pp de* **expresar** ♦ *adj* (*explícito*) express; (*claro*) specific, clear; (*tren*) fast ♦ *adv*: **mandar ~** to send by express (delivery)

express [eks'pres] (*AM*) *adv*: **enviar algo ~** to send sth special delivery

exprimidor [eksprimi'ðor] *nm* squeezer

exprimir [ekspri'mir] *vt* (*fruta*) to squeeze; (*zumo*) to squeeze out

expropiar [ekspro'pjar] *vt* to expropriate

expuesto, a [eks'pwesto, a] *pp de* **exponer** ♦ *adj* exposed; (*cuadro etc*) on show, on display

expulsar [ekspul'sar] *vt* (*echar*) to eject, throw out; (*alumno*) to expel; (*despedir*) to sack, fire; (*DEPORTE*) to send off; **expulsión** *nf* expulsion; sending-off

exquisito, a [ekski'sito, a] *adj* exquisite; (*comida*) delicious

éxtasis ['ekstasis] *nm* ecstasy

extender [eksten'der] *vt* to extend; (*los brazos*) to stretch out, hold out; (*mapa, tela*) to spread (out), open (out); (*mantequilla*) to spread; (*certificado*) to issue; (*cheque, recibo*) to make out; (*documento*) to draw up; **~se** *vr* (*gen*) to extend; (*persona: en el suelo*) to stretch out; (*epidemia*) to spread; **extendido, a** *adj* (*abierto*) spread out, open; (*brazos*) outstretched; (*costumbre*) widespread

extensión [eksten'sjon] *nf* (*de terreno, mar*) expanse, stretch; (*de tiempo*) length, duration; (*TEL*) extension; **en toda la ~ de la palabra** in every sense of the word

extenso, a [eks'tenso, a] *adj* extensive

extenuar [ekste'nwar] *vt* (*debilitar*) to weaken

exterior [ekste'rjor] *adj* (*de fuera*) external; (*afuera*) outside, exterior; (*apariencia*) outward; (*deuda, relaciones*) foreign ♦ *nm* (*gen*) exterior, outside; (*aspecto*) outward appearance; (*DEPORTE*) wing(er); (*países extranjeros*) abroad; **en el ~** abroad; **al ~** outwardly, on the surface

exterminar [ekstermi'nar] *vt* to exterminate; **exterminio** *nm* extermination

externo, a [eks'terno, a] *adj* (*exterior*) external, outside; (*superficial*) outward ♦ *nm/f* day pupil

extinguir [ekstin'gir] *vt* (*fuego*) to extinguish, put out; (*raza, población*) to wipe out; **~se** *vr* (*fuego*) to go out; (*BIO*) to die out, become extinct

extinto, a [eks'tinto, a] *adj* extinct
extintor [ekstin'tor] *nm* (fire) extinguisher
extirpar [ekstir'par] *vt* (MED) to remove (surgically)
extorsión [ekstor'sjon] *nf* extortion
extra ['ekstra] *adj inv* (*tiempo*) extra; (*chocolate, vino*) good-quality ♦ *nm/f* extra ♦ *nm* extra; (*bono*) bonus
extracción [ekstrak'θjon] *nf* extraction; (*en lotería*) draw
extracto [eks'trakto] *nm* extract
extradición [ekstraði'θjon] *nf* extradition
extraer [ekstra'er] *vt* to extract, take out
extraescolar [ekstraesko'lar] *adj*: **actividad ~** extracurricular activity
extralimitarse [ekstralimi'tarse] *vr* to go too far
extranjero, a [ekstran'xero, a] *adj* foreign ♦ *nm/f* foreigner ♦ *nm* foreign countries *pl*; **en el ~** abroad
extrañar [ekstra'ɲar] *vt* (*sorprender*) to find strange *o* odd; (*echar de menos*) to miss; **~se** *vr* (*sorprenderse*) to be amazed, be surprised
extrañeza [ekstra'ɲeθa] *nf* (*rareza*) strangeness, oddness; (*asombro*) amazement, surprise
extraño, a [eks'traɲo, a] *adj* (*extranjero*) foreign; (*raro, sorprendente*) strange, odd
extraordinario, a [ekstraorði'narjo, a] *adj* extraordinary; (*edición, número*) special ♦ *nm* (*de periódico*) special edition; **horas extraordinarias** overtime *sg*
extrarradio [ekstra'rraðjo] *nm* suburbs
extravagancia [ekstraßa'vanθja] *nf* oddness; outlandishness; **extravagante** *adj* (*excéntrico*) eccentric; (*estrafalario*) outlandish
extraviado, a [ekstra'ßjaðo, a] *adj* lost, missing
extraviar [ekstra'ßjar] *vt* (*persona: desorientar*) to mislead, misdirect; (*perder*) to lose, misplace; **~se** *vr* to lose one's way, get lost; **extravío** *nm* loss; (*fig*) deviation
extremar [ekstre'mar] *vt* to carry to extremes; **~se** *vr* to do one's utmost,

make every effort
extremaunción [ekstremaun'θjon] *nf* extreme unction
extremidad [ekstremi'ðað] *nf* (*punta*) extremity; **~es** *nfpl* (ANAT) extremities
extremo, a [eks'tremo, a] *adj* extreme; (*último*) last ♦ *nm* end; (*límite, grado sumo*) extreme; **en último ~** as a last resort
extrovertido, a [ekstroßer'tiðo, a] *adj, nm/f* extrovert
exuberancia [eksuße'ranθja] *nf* exuberance; **exuberante** *adj* exuberant; (*fig*) luxuriant, lush
eyacular [ejaku'lar] *vt, vi* to ejaculate

F, f

f.a.b. *abr* (= *franco a bordo*) f.o.b.
fabada [fa'ßaða] *nf* bean and sausage stew
fábrica ['faßrika] *nf* factory; **marca de ~** trademark; **precio de ~** factory price
fabricación [faßrika'θjon] *nf* (*manufactura*) manufacture; (*producción*) production; **de ~ casera** home-made; **~ en serie** mass production
fabricante [faßri'kante] *nm/f* manufacturer
fabricar [faßri'kar] *vt* (*manufacturar*) to manufacture, make; (*construir*) to build; (*cuento*) to fabricate, devise
fábula ['faßula] *nf* (*cuento*) fable; (*chisme*) rumour; (*mentira*) fib
fabuloso, a [faßu'loso, a] *adj* (*oportunidad, tiempo*) fabulous, great
facción [fak'θjon] *nf* (POL) faction; **facciones** (*del rostro*) features
faceta [fa'θeta] *nf* facet
facha ['fatʃa] (*fam*) *nf* (*aspecto*) look; (*cara*) face
fachada [fa'tʃaða] *nf* (ARQ) façade, front
fácil ['faθil] *adj* (*simple*) easy; (*probable*) likely
facilidad [faθili'ðað] *nf* (*capacidad*) ease; (*sencillez*) simplicity; (*de palabra*) fluency; **~es** *nfpl* facilities

facilitar [faθili'tar] *vt* (*hacer fácil*) to make easy; (*proporcionar*) to provide

fácilmente ['faθilmente] *adv* easily

facsímil [fak'simil] *nm* facsimile, fax

factible [fak'tiβle] *adj* feasible

factor [fak'tor] *nm* factor

factura [fak'tura] *nf* (*cuenta*) bill; **facturación** *nf* (*de equipaje*) check-in; **facturar** *vt* (*COM*) to invoice, charge for; (*equipaje*) to check in

facultad [fakul'taθ] *nf* (*aptitud, ESCOL etc*) faculty; (*poder*) power

faena [fa'ena] *nf* (*trabajo*) work; (*quehacer*) task, job

faisán [fai'san] *nm* pheasant

faja ['faxa] *nf* (*para la cintura*) sash; (*de mujer*) corset; (*de tierra*) strip

fajo ['faxo] *nm* (*de papeles*) bundle; (*de billetes*) wad

falacia [fa'laθja] *nf* fallacy

falda ['falda] *nf* (*prenda de vestir*) skirt

falla ['faʎa] *nf* (*defecto*) fault, flaw

fallar [fa'ʎar] *vt* (*JUR*) to pronounce sentence on ♦ *vi* (*memoria*) to fail; (*motor*) to miss

---
Fallas

ⓘ *In the week of 19 March (the feast of San José), Valencia honours its patron saint with a spectacular fiesta called* **Las Fallas**. *The* **Fallas** *are huge papier-mâché, cardboard and wooden sculptures which are built by competing teams throughout the year. They depict politicians and well-known public figures and are thrown onto bonfires and set alight once a jury has judged them - only the best sculpture escapes the flames.*

---

fallecer [faʎe'θer] *vi* to pass away, die; **fallecimiento** *nm* decease, demise

fallido, a [fa'ʎiðo, a] *adj* (*gen*) frustrated, unsuccessful

fallo ['faʎo] *nm* (*JUR*) verdict, ruling; (*fracaso*) failure; **~ cardíaco** heart failure

falsedad [false'ðaθ] *nf* falseness; (*hipocresía*) hypocrisy; (*mentira*) falsehood

falsificar [falsifi'kar] *vt* (*firma etc*) to forge; (*moneda*) to counterfeit

falso, a ['falso, a] *adj* false; (*documento, moneda etc*) fake; **en ~** falsely

falta ['falta] *nf* (*defecto*) fault, flaw; (*privación*) lack, want; (*ausencia*) absence; (*carencia*) shortage; (*equivocación*) mistake; (*DEPORTE*) foul; **echar en ~** to miss; **hacer ~ hacer algo** to be necessary to do sth; **me hace ~ una pluma** I need a pen; **~ de educación** bad manners *pl*

faltar [fal'tar] *vi* (*escasear*) to be lacking, be wanting; (*ausentarse*) to be absent, be missing; **faltan 2 horas para llegar** there are 2 hours to go till arrival; **~ al respeto a uno** to be disrespectful to sb; **¡no faltaba más!** (*no hay de qué*) don't mention it

fama ['fama] *nf* (*renombre*) fame; (*reputación*) reputation

famélico, a [fa'meliko, a] *adj* starving

familia [fa'milja] *nf* family; **~ política** in-laws *pl*

familiar [fami'ljar] *adj* (*relativo a la familia*) family *cpd*; (*conocido, informal*) familiar ♦ *nm* relative, relation; **~idad** *nf* (*gen*) familiarity; (*informalidad*) homeliness; **~izarse** *vr*: **~izarse con** to familiarize o.s. with

famoso, a [fa'moso, a] *adj* (*renombrado*) famous

fanático, a [fa'natiko, a] *adj* fanatical ♦ *nm/f* fanatic; (*CINE, DEPORTE*) fan; **fanatismo** *nm* fanaticism

fanfarrón, ona [fanfa'rron, ona] *adj* boastful

fango ['fango] *nm* mud; **~so, a** *adj* muddy

fantasía [fanta'sia] *nf* fantasy, imagination; **joyas de ~** imitation jewellery *sg*

fantasma [fan'tasma] *nm* (*espectro*) ghost, apparition; (*fanfarrón*) show-off

fantástico, a [fan'tastiko, a] *adj* fantastic

farmacéutico, a [farma'θeutiko, a] *adj* pharmaceutical ♦ *nm/f* chemist (*BRIT*), pharmacist

farmacia [far'maθja] *nf* chemist's (shop)

(*BRIT*), pharmacy; **~ de turno** duty chemist; **~ de guardia** all-night chemist

fármaco ['farmako] *nm* drug

faro ['faro] *nm* (*NAUT: torre*) lighthouse; (*AUTO*) headlamp; **~s antiniebla** fog lamps; **~s delanteros/traseros** headlights/rear lights

farol [fa'rol] *nm* lantern, lamp

farola [fa'rola] *nf* street lamp (*BRIT*) *o* light (*US*)

farsa ['farsa] *nf* (*gen*) farce

farsante [far'sante] *nm/f* fraud, fake

fascículo [fas'θikulo] *nm* (*de revista*) part, instalment

fascinar [fasθi'nar] *vt* (*gen*) to fascinate

fascismo [fas'θismo] *nm* fascism; **fascista** *adj, nm/f* fascist

fase ['fase] *nf* phase

fastidiar [fasti'ðjar] *vt* (*molestar*) to annoy, bother; (*estropear*) to spoil; **~se** *vr*: **¡que se fastidie!** (*fam*) he'll just have to put up with it!

fastidio [fas'tiðjo] *nm* (*molestia*) annoyance; **~so, a** *adj* (*molesto*) annoying

fastuoso, a [fas'twoso, a] *adj* (*banquete, boda*) lavish; (*acto*) pompous

fatal [fa'tal] *adj* (*gen*) fatal; (*desgraciado*) ill-fated; (*fam: malo, pésimo*) awful; **~idad** *nf* (*destino*) fate; (*mala suerte*) misfortune

fatiga [fa'tiɣa] *nf* (*cansancio*) fatigue, weariness

fatigar [fati'ɣar] *vt* to tire, weary; **~se** *vr* to get tired

fatigoso, a [fati'ɣoso, a] *adj* (*cansador*) tiring

fatuo, a ['fatwo, a] *adj* (*vano*) fatuous; (*presuntuoso*) conceited

favor [fa'βor] *nm* favour; **estar a ~ de** to be in favour of; **haga el ~ de...** would you be so good as to..., kindly...; **por ~** please; **~able** *adj* favourable

favorecer [faβore'θer] *vt* to favour; (*vestido etc*) to become, flatter; **este peinado le favorece** this hairstyle suits him

favorito, a [faβo'rito, a] *adj, nm/f* favourite

fax [faks] *nm inv* fax; **mandar por ~** to fax

faz [faθ] *nf* face; **la ~ de la tierra** the face of the earth

fe [fe] *nf* (*REL*) faith; (*documento*) certificate; **prestar ~ a** to believe, credit; **actuar con buena/mala ~** to act in good/bad faith; **dar ~ de** to bear witness to

fealdad [feal'daθ] *nf* ugliness

febrero [fe'βrero] *nm* February

febril [fe'βril] *adj* (*fig: actividad*) hectic; (*mente, mirada*) feverish

fecha ['fetʃa] *nf* date; **~ de caducidad** (*de producto alimenticio*) sell-by date; (*de contrato etc*) expiry date; **con ~ adelantada** postdated; **en ~ próxima** soon; **hasta la ~** to date, so far; **poner ~** to date; **fechar** *vt* to date

fecundar [fekun'dar] *vt* (*generar*) to fertilize, make fertile; **fecundo, a** *adj* (*fértil*) fertile; (*fig*) prolific; (*productivo*) productive

federación [feðera'θjon] *nf* federation

felicidad [feliθi'ðaθ] *nf* happiness; **~es** *nfpl* (*felicitaciones*) best wishes, congratulations

felicitación [feliθita'θjon] *nf*: **¡felicitaciones!** congratulations!

felicitar [feliθi'tar] *vt* to congratulate

feligrés, esa [feli'ɣres, esa] *nm/f* parishioner

feliz [fe'liθ] *adj* happy

felpudo [fel'puðo] *nm* doormat

femenino, a [feme'nino, a] *adj, nm* feminine

feminista [femi'nista] *adj, nm/f* feminist

fenómeno [fe'nomeno] *nm* phenomenon; (*fig*) freak, accident ♦ *adj* great ♦ *excl* great!, marvellous!; **fenomenal** *adj* = **fenómeno**

feo, a ['feo, a] *adj* (*gen*) ugly; (*desagradable*) bad, nasty

féretro ['feretro] *nm* (*ataúd*) coffin; (*sarcófago*) bier

feria ['ferja] *nf* (*gen*) fair; (*descanso*) holiday, rest day; (*AM: mercado*) village market; (: *cambio*) loose *o* small change

fermentar [fermen'tar] *vi* to ferment

ferocidad [feroθi'ðað] *nf* fierceness, ferocity

feroz [fe'roθ] *adj* (*cruel*) cruel; (*salvaje*) fierce

férreo, a ['ferreo, a] *adj* iron

ferretería [ferrete'ria] *nf* (*tienda*) ironmonger's (shop) (*BRIT*), hardware store

ferrocarril [ferroka'rril] *nm* railway

ferroviario, a [ferro'βjarjo, a] *adj* rail *cpd*

fértil ['fertil] *adj* (*productivo*) fertile; (*rico*) rich; **fertilidad** *nf* (*gen*) fertility; (*productividad*) fruitfulness

ferviente [fer'βjente] *adj* fervent

fervor [fer'βor] *nm* fervour; **~oso, a** *adj* fervent

festejar [feste'xar] *vt* (*celebrar*) to celebrate

festejo [fes'texo] *nm* celebration; **festejos** *nmpl* (*fiestas*) festivals

festín [fes'tin] *nm* feast, banquet

festival [festi'βal] *nm* festival

festividad [festiβi'ðað] *nf* festivity

festivo, a [fes'tiβo, a] *adj* (*de fiesta*) festive; (*CINE, LITERATURA*) humorous; **día ~** holiday

fétido, a ['fetiðo, a] *adj* foul-smelling

feto ['feto] *nm* foetus

fiable ['fjaβle] *adj* (*persona*) trustworthy; (*máquina*) reliable

fiador, a [fia'ðor, a] *nm/f* (*JUR*) surety, guarantor; (*COM*) backer; **salir ~ por uno** to stand bail for sb

fiambre ['fjambre] *nm* cold meat

fianza ['fjanθa] *nf* surety; (*JUR*): **libertad bajo ~** release on bail

fiar [fi'ar] *vt* (*salir garante de*) to guarantee; (*vender a crédito*) to sell on credit; (*secreto*): **~ a** to confide (to) ♦ *vi* to trust; **~se** *vr* to trust (in), rely on; **~se de uno** to rely on sb

fibra ['fiβra] *nf* fibre; **~ óptica** optical fibre

ficción [fik'θjon] *nf* fiction

ficha ['fitʃa] *nf* (*TEL*) token; (*en juegos*) counter, marker; (*tarjeta*) (index) card; **fichar** *vt* (*archivar*) to file, index; (*DEPORTE*) to sign; **estar fichado** to have

a record; **fichero** *nm* box file; (*INFORM*) file

ficticio, a [fik'tiθjo, a] *adj* (*imaginario*) fictitious; (*falso*) fabricated

fidelidad [fiðeli'ðað] *nf* (*lealtad*) fidelity, loyalty; **alta ~** high fidelity, hi-fi

fideos [fi'ðeos] *nmpl* noodles

fiebre ['fjeβre] *nf* (*MED*) fever; (*fig*) fever, excitement; **~ amarilla/del heno** yellow/hay fever; **~ palúdica** malaria; **tener ~** to have a temperature

fiel [fjel] *adj* (*leal*) faithful, loyal; (*fiable*) reliable; (*exacto*) accurate, faithful ♦ *nm*: **los ~es** the faithful

fieltro ['fjeltro] *nm* felt

fiera ['fjera] *nf* (*animal feroz*) wild animal *o* beast; (*fig*) dragon; *ver tb* **fiero**

fiero, a ['fjero, a] *adj* (*cruel*) cruel; (*feroz*) fierce; (*duro*) harsh

fiesta ['fjesta] *nf* party; (*de pueblo*) festival; (*vacaciones, tb*: **~s**) holiday *sg*; (*REL*): **~ de guardar** day of obligation

---

Fiestas

i **Fiestas** *can be official public holidays or holidays set by each autonomous region, many of which coincide with religious festivals. There are also many* **fiestas** *all over Spain for a local patron saint or the Virgin Mary. These often last several days and can include religious processions, carnival parades, bullfights and dancing.*

---

figura [fi'γura] *nf* (*gen*) figure; (*forma, imagen*) shape, form; (*NAIPES*) face card

figurar [fixu'rar] *vt* (*representar*) to represent; (*fingir*) to figure ♦ *vi* to figure; **~se** *vr* (*imaginarse*) to imagine; (*suponer*) to suppose

fijador [fixa'ðor] *nm* (*FOTO etc*) fixative; (*de pelo*) gel

fijar [fi'xar] *vt* (*gen*) to fix; (*estampilla*) to affix, stick (on); **~se** *vr*: **~se en** to notice

fijo, a ['fixo, a] *adj* (*gen*) fixed; (*firme*) firm; (*permanente*) permanent ♦ *adv*: **mirar ~** to stare

fila ['fila] *nf* row; (*MIL*) rank; **ponerse en ~** to line up, get into line

filántropo, a [fi'lantropo, a] *nm/f* philanthropist

filatelia [fila'telja] *nf* philately, stamp collecting

filete [fi'lete] *nm* (*carne*) fillet steak; (*pescado*) fillet

filiación [filja'θjon] *nf* (*POL*) affiliation

filial [fi'ljal] *adj* filial ♦ *nf* subsidiary

Filipinas [fili'pinas] *nfpl*: **las ~** the Philippines; **filipino, a** *adj, nm/f* Philippine

filmar [fil'mar] *vt* to film, shoot

filo ['filo] *nm* (*gen*) edge; **sacar ~ a** to sharpen; **al ~ del mediodía** at about midday; **de doble ~** double-edged

filón [fi'lon] *nm* (*MINERÍA*) vein, lode; (*fig*) goldmine

filosofía [filoso'fia] *nf* philosophy; **filósofo, a** *nm/f* philosopher

filtrar [fil'trar] *vt, vi* to filter, strain; **~se** *vr* to filter; **filtro** [*TEC, utensilio*] filter

fin [fin] *nm* end; (*objetivo*) aim, purpose; **al ~ y al cabo** when all's said and done; **a ~ de** in order to; **por ~** finally; **en ~** in short; **~ de semana** weekend

final [fi'nal] *adj* final ♦ *nm* end, conclusion ♦ *nf* final; **~idad** *nf* (*propósito*) purpose, intention; **~ista** *nm/f* finalist; **~izar** *vt* to end, finish; (*INFORM*) to log out *o* off ♦ *vi* to end, come to an end

financiar [finan'θjar] *vt* to finance; **financiero, a** *adj* financial ♦ *nm/f* financier

finca ['finka] *nf* (*bien inmueble*) property, land; (*casa de campo*) country house; (*AM*) farm

fingir [fin'xir] *vt* (*simular*) to simulate, feign ♦ *vi* (*aparentar*) to pretend

finlandés, esa [finlan'des, esa] *adj* Finnish ♦ *nm/f* Finn ♦ *nm* (*LING*) Finnish

Finlandia [fin'landja] *nf* Finland

fino, a ['fino, a] *adj* fine; (*delgado*) slender; (*de buenas maneras*) polite, refined; (*jerez*) fino, dry

firma ['firma] *nf* signature; (*COM*) firm, company

firmamento [firma'mento] *nm* firmament

firmar [fir'mar] *vt* to sign

firme ['firme] *adj* firm; (*estable*) stable; (*sólido*) solid; (*constante*) steady; (*decidido*) resolute ♦ *nm* road (surface); **~mente** *adv* firmly; **~za** *nf* firmness; (*constancia*) steadiness; (*solidez*) solidity

fiscal [fis'kal] *adj* fiscal ♦ *nm/f* public prosecutor; **año ~** tax *o* fiscal year

fisco ['fisko] *nm* (*hacienda*) treasury, exchequer (*BRIT*)

fisgar [fis'var] *vt* to pry into

fisgonear [fisvone'ar] *vt* to poke one's nose into ♦ *vi* to pry, spy

física ['fisika] *nf* physics *sg*; *ver tb* **físico**

físico, a ['fisiko, a] *adj* physical ♦ *nm* physique ♦ *nm/f* physicist

fisura [fi'sura] *nf* crack; (*MED*) fracture

flác(c)ido, a ['fla(k)θiðo, a] *adj* flabby

flaco, a ['flako, a] *adj* (*muy delgado*) skinny, thin; (*débil*) weak, feeble

flagrante [fla'xrante] *adj* flagrant

flamante [fla'mante] (*fam*) *adj* brilliant; (*nuevo*) brand-new

flamenco, a [fla'menko, a] *adj* (*de Flandes*) Flemish; (*baile, música*) flamenco ♦ *nm* (*baile, música*) flamenco

flan [flan] *nm* creme caramel

flaqueza [fla'keθa] *nf* (*delgadez*) thinness, leanness; (*fig*) weakness

flash [flaʃ] (*pl* **~s** *o* **~es**) *nm* (*FOTO*) flash

flauta ['flauta] *nf* (*MUS*) flute

flecha ['fletʃa] *nf* arrow

flechazo [fle'tʃaθo] *nm* love at first sight

fleco ['fleko] *nm* fringe

flema ['flema] *nm* phlegm

flequillo [fle'kiʎo] *nm* (*pelo*) fringe

flexible [flek'siβle] *adj* flexible

flexión [flek'sjon] *nf* press-up

flexo ['flekso] *nm* adjustable table-lamp

flojera [flo'xera] (*AM: fam*) *nf*: **me da ~** I can't be bothered

flojo, a ['floxo, a] *adj* (*gen*) loose; (*sin fuerzas*) limp; (*débil*) weak

flor [flor] *nf* flower; **a ~ de** on the surface of; **~ecer** *vi* (*BOT*) to flower, bloom; (*fig*) to flourish; **~eciente** *adj* (*BOT*) in flower, flowering; (*fig*) thriving; **~ero** *nm* vase; **~istería** *nf* florist's (shop)

flota ['flota] *nf* fleet

flotador [flota'ðor] *nm* (*gen*) float; (*para nadar*) rubber ring

flotar [flo'tar] *vi* (*gen*) to float; **flote** *nm*: **a flote** afloat; **salir a flote** (*fig*) to get back on one's feet

fluctuar [fluk'twar] *vi* (*oscilar*) to fluctuate

fluidez [flui'ðeθ] *nf* fluidity; (*fig*) fluency

flúido, a ['fluiðo, a] *adj, nm* fluid

fluir [flu'ir] *vi* to flow

flujo ['fluxo] *nm* flow; **~ y reflujo** ebb and flow

flúor ['fluor] *nm* fluoride

fluvial [flu'ßial] *adj* (*navegación, cuenca*) fluvial, river *cpd*

foca ['foka] *nf* seal

foco ['foko] *nm* focus; (*ELEC*) floodlight; (*AM*) (light) bulb

fofo, a ['fofo, a] *adj* soft, spongy; (*carnes*) flabby

fogata [fo'ɣata] *nf* bonfire

fogón [fo'ɣon] *nm* (*de cocina*) ring, burner

fogoso, a [fo'ɣoso, a] *adj* spirited

folio ['foljo] *nm* folio, page

follaje [fo'ʎaxe] *nm* foliage

folletín [foʎe'tin] *nm* newspaper serial

folleto [fo'ʎeto] *nm* (*POL*) pamphlet

follón [fo'ʎon] (*fam*) *nm* (*lío*) mess; (*conmoción*) fuss; **armar un ~** to kick up a row

fomentar [fomen'tar] *vt* (*MED*) to foment; **fomento** *nm* (*promoción*) promotion

fonda ['fonda] *nf* inn

fondo ['fondo] *nm* (*de mar*) bottom; (*de coche, sala*) back; (*ARTE etc*) background; (*reserva*) fund; **~s** *nmpl* (*COM*) funds, resources; **una investigación a ~** a thorough investigation; **en el ~** at bottom, deep down

fontanería [fontane'ria] *nf* plumbing; **fontanero, a** *nm/f* plumber

footing ['futin] *nm* jogging; **hacer ~** to jog, go jogging

forastero, a [foras'tero, a] *nm/f* stranger

forcejear [forθexe'ar] *vi* (*luchar*) to struggle

forense [fo'rense] *nm/f* pathologist

forjar [for'xar] *vt* to forge

forma ['forma] *nf* (*figura*) form, shape; (*MED*) fitness; (*método*) way, means; **las ~s** the conventions; **estar en ~** to be fit

formación [forma'θjon] *nf* (*gen*) formation; (*educación*) education; **~ profesional** vocational training

formal [for'mal] *adj* (*gen*) formal; (*fig: serio*) serious; (*: de fiar*) reliable; **~idad** *nf* formality; seriousness; **~izar** *vt* (*JUR*) to formalize; (*situación*) to put in order, regularize; **~izarse** *vr* (*situación*) to be put in order, be regularized

formar [for'mar] *vt* (*componer*) to form, shape; (*constituir*) to make up, constitute; (*ESCOL*) to train, educate; **~se** *vr* (*ESCOL*) to be trained, educated; (*cobrar forma*) to form, take form; (*desarrollarse*) to develop

formatear [formate'ar] *vt* to format

formativo, a [forma'tißo, a] *adj* (*lecturas, años*) formative

formato [for'mato] *nm* format

formidable [formi'ðaßle] *adj* (*temible*) formidable; (*estupendo*) tremendous

fórmula ['formula] *nf* formula

formular [formu'lar] *vt* (*queja*) to make, lodge; (*petición*) to draw up; (*pregunta*) to pose

formulario [formu'larjo] *nm* form

fornido, a [for'niðo, a] *adj* well-built

forrar [fo'rrar] *vt* (*abrigo*) to line; (*libro*) to cover; **forro** *nm* (*de cuaderno*) cover; (*COSTURA*) lining; (*de sillón*) upholstery

fortalecer [fortale'θer] *vt* to strengthen

fortaleza [forta'leθa] *nf* (*MIL*) fortress, stronghold; (*fuerza*) strength; (*determinación*) resolution

fortuito, a [for'twito, a] *adj* accidental

fortuna [for'tuna] *nf* (*suerte*) fortune, (good) luck; (*riqueza*) fortune, wealth

forzar [for'θar] *vt* (*puerta*) to force (open); (*compeler*) to compel

forzoso, a [for'θoso, a] *adj* necessary

fosa ['fosa] *nf* (*sepultura*) grave; (*en tierra*)

pit; **~s nasales** nostrils
fósforo ['fosforo] *nm* (*QUÍM*) phosphorus;
(*cerilla*) match
foso ['foso] *nm* ditch; (*TEATRO*) pit; (*AUTO*):
~ de reconocimiento inspection pit
foto ['foto] *nf* photo, snap(shot); **sacar
una ~** to take a photo *o* picture
fotocopia [foto'kopja] *nf* photocopy;
fotocopiadora *nf* photocopier;
fotocopiar *vt* to photocopy
fotografía [fotoɣra'fia] *nf* (*ARTE*)
photography; (*una ~*) photograph;
fotografiar *vt* to photograph
fotógrafo, a [fo'toɣrafo, a] *nm/f*
photographer
fracasar [fraka'sar] *vi* (*gen*) to fail
fracaso [fra'kaso] *nm* failure
fracción [frak'θjon] *nf* fraction;
fraccionamiento (*AM*) *nm* housing
estate
fractura [frak'tura] *nf* fracture, break
fragancia [fra'ɣanθja] *nf* (*olor*) fragrance,
perfume
frágil ['fraxil] *adj* (*débil*) fragile; (*COM*)
breakable
fragmento [fraɣ'mento] *nm* (*pedazo*)
fragment
fragua ['fraɣwa] *nf* forge; **fraguar** *vt* to
forge; (*fig*) to concoct ♦ *vi* to harden
fraile ['fraile] *nm* (*REL*) friar; (*: monje*)
monk
frambuesa [fram'bwesa] *nf* raspberry
francamente [franka'mente] *adv* (*hablar,
decir*) frankly; (*realmente*) really
francés, esa [fran'θes, esa] *adj* French
♦ *nm/f* Frenchman/woman ♦ *nm* (*LING*)
French
Francia ['franθja] *nf* France
franco, a ['franko, a] *adj* (*cándido*) frank,
open; (*COM: exento*) free ♦ *nm* (*moneda*)
franc
francotirador, a [frankotira'ðor, a] *nm/f*
sniper
franela [fra'nela] *nf* flannel
franja ['franxa] *nf* fringe
franquear [franke'ar] *vt* (*camino*) to clear;
(*carta, paquete postal*) to frank, stamp;

(*obstáculo*) to overcome
franqueo [fran'keo] *nm* postage
franqueza [fran'keθa] *nf* (*candor*)
frankness
frasco ['frasko] *nm* bottle, flask; **~ al vacío**
(vacuum) flask
frase ['frase] *nf* sentence; **~ hecha** set
phrase; (*pey*) stock phrase
fraterno, a [fra'terno, a] *adj* brotherly,
fraternal
fraude ['frauðe] *nm* (*cualidad*) dishonesty;
(*acto*) fraud; **fraudulento, a** *adj*
fraudulent
frazada [fra'saða] (*AM*) *nf* blanket
frecuencia [fre'kwenθja] *nf* frequency;
con ~ frequently, often
frecuentar [frekwen'tar] *vt* to frequent
fregadero [freɣa'ðero] *nm* (kitchen) sink
fregar [fre'ɣar] *vt* (*frotar*) to scrub; (*platos*)
to wash (up); (*AM*) to annoy
fregona [fre'ɣona] *nf* mop
freír [fre'ir] *vt* to fry
frenar [fre'nar] *vt* to brake; (*fig*) to check
frenazo [fre'naθo] *nm*: **dar un ~** to brake
sharply
frenesí [frene'si] *nm* frenzy; **frenético, a**
adj frantic
freno ['freno] *nm* (*TEC, AUTO*) brake; (*de
cabalgadura*) bit; (*fig*) check
frente ['frente] *nm* (*ARQ, POL*) front; (*de
objeto*) front part ♦ *nf* forehead, brow; **~
a** in front of; (*en situación opuesta de*)
opposite; **al ~ de** (*fig*) at the head of;
chocar de ~ to crash head-on; **hacer ~ a**
to face up to
fresa ['fresa] (*ESP*) *nf* strawberry
fresco, a ['fresko, a] *adj* (*nuevo*) fresh;
(*frío*) cool; (*descarado*) cheeky ♦ *nm* (*aire*)
fresh air; (*ARTE*) fresco; (*AM: jugo*) fruit
drink ♦ *nm/f* (*fam*): **ser un ~** to have a
nerve; **tomar el ~** to get some fresh air;
frescura *nf* freshness; (*descaro*) cheek,
nerve
frialdad [frial'dað] *nf* (*gen*) coldness;
(*indiferencia*) indifference
fricción [frik'θjon] *nf* (*gen*) friction; (*acto*)
rub(bing); (*MED*) massage

frigidez [frixi'ðeθ] *nf* frigidity

frigorífico [frivo'rifiko] *nm* refrigerator

frijol [fri'xol] *nm* kidney bean

frío, a *etc* ['frio, a] *vb ver* freír ♦ *adj* cold; (*indiferente*) indifferent ♦ *nm* cold; indifference; **hace ~** it's cold; **tener ~** to be cold

frito, a ['frito, a] *adj* fried; **me trae ~ ese hombre** I'm sick and tired of that man; **fritos** *nmpl* fried food

frívolo, a ['friβolo, a] *adj* frivolous

frontal [fron'tal] *adj* frontal; **choque ~** head-on collision

frontera [fron'tera] *nf* frontier; **fronterizo, a** *adj* frontier *cpd*; (*contiguo*) bordering

frontón [fron'ton] *nm* (*DEPORTE: cancha*) pelota court; (*: juego*) pelota

frotar [fro'tar] *vt* to rub; **~se** *vr*: **~se las manos** to rub one's hands

fructífero, a [fruk'tifero, a] *adj* fruitful

fruncir [frun'θir] *vt* to pucker; (*COSTURA*) to pleat; **~ el ceño** to knit one's brow

frustrar [frus'trar] *vt* to frustrate

fruta ['fruta] *nf* fruit; **frutería** *nf* fruit shop; **frutero, a** *adj* fruit *cpd* ♦ *nm/f* fruiterer ♦ *nm* fruit bowl

frutilla [fru'tiʎa] (*AM*) *nf* strawberry

fruto ['fruto] *nm* fruit; (*fig: resultado*) result; (*: beneficio*) benefit; **~s secos** nuts; (*pasas etc*) dried fruit *sg*

fue *vb ver* ser, ir

fuego ['fwevo] *nm* (*gen*) fire; **a ~ lento** on a low heat; **¿tienes ~?** have you (got) a light?; **~s artificiales** *o* **de artificio** fireworks

fuente ['fwente] *nf* fountain; (*manantial, fig*) spring; (*origen*) source; (*plato*) large dish

fuera *etc* ['fwera] *vb ver* ser, ir ♦ *adv* out(side); (*en otra parte*) away; (*excepto, salvo*) except, save ♦ *prep*: **~ de** outside; (*fig*) besides; **~ de sí** beside o.s.; **por ~** (on the) outside

fuera-borda [fwera'ßorða] *nm* speedboat

fuerte ['fwerte] *adj* strong; (*golpe*) hard; (*ruido*) loud; (*comida*) rich; (*lluvia*) heavy; (*dolor*) intense ♦ *adv* strongly; hard; loud(ly)

fuerza *etc* ['fwerθa] *vb ver* forzar ♦ *nf* (*fortaleza*) strength; (*TEC, ELEC*) power; (*coacción*) force; (*MIL: tb:* **~s**) forces *pl*; **a ~ de** by dint of; **cobrar ~s** to recover one's strength; **tener ~s para** to have the strength to; **a la ~** forcibly, by force; **por ~** of necessity; **~ de voluntad** willpower

fuga ['fuva] *nf* (*huida*) flight, escape; (*de gas etc*) leak

fugarse [fu'varse] *vr* to flee, escape

fugaz [fu'vaθ] *adj* fleeting

fugitivo, a [fuxi'tiβo, a] *adj, nm/f* fugitive

fui *vb ver* ser; ir

fulano, a [fu'lano, a] *nm/f* so-and-so, what's-his-name/what's-her-name

fulminante [fulmi'nante] *adj* (*fig: mirada*) fierce; (*MED: enfermedad, ataque*) sudden; (*fam: éxito, golpe*) sudden

fumador, a [fuma'ðor, a] *nm/f* smoker

fumar [fu'mar] *vt, vi* to smoke; **~ en pipa** to smoke a pipe

función [fun'θjon] *nf* function; (*en trabajo*) duties *pl*; (*espectáculo*) show; **entrar en funciones** to take up one's duties

funcionar [funθjo'nar] *vi* (*gen*) to function; (*máquina*) to work; **"no funciona"** "out of order"

funcionario, a [funθjo'narjo, a] *nm/f* civil servant

funda ['funda] *nf* (*gen*) cover; (*de almohada*) pillowcase

fundación [funda'θjon] *nf* foundation

fundamental [fundamen'tal] *adj* fundamental, basic

fundamentar [fundamen'tar] *vt* (*poner base*) to lay the foundations of; (*establecer*) to found; (*fig*) to base; **fundamento** *nm* (*base*) foundation

fundar [fun'dar] *vt* to found; **~se** *vr*: **~se en** to be founded on

fundición [fundi'θjon] *nf* fusing; (*fábrica*) foundry

fundir [fun'dir] *vt* (*gen*) to fuse; (*metal*) to smelt, melt down; (*nieve etc*) to melt; (*COM*) to merge; (*estatua*) to cast; **~se** *vr* (*colores etc*) to merge, blend; (*unirse*) to fuse together; (*ELEC: fusible, lámpara etc*) to fuse, blow; (*nieve etc*) to melt

fúnebre ['funeßre] *adj* funeral *cpd*, funereal

funeral [fune'ral] *nm* funeral; **funeraria** *nf* undertaker's

funesto, a [fu'nesto, a] *adj* (*día*) ill-fated; (*decisión*) fatal

furgón [fur'xon] *nm* wagon; **furgoneta** *nf* (*AUTO, COM*) (transit) van (*BRIT*), pick-up (truck) (*US*)

furia ['furja] *nf* (*ira*) fury; (*violencia*) violence; **furibundo, a** *adj* furious; **furioso, a** *adj* (*iracundo*) furious; (*violento*) violent; **furor** *nm* (*cólera*) rage

furtivo, a [fur'tißo, a] *adj* furtive ♦ *nm* poacher

fusible [fu'sißle] *nm* fuse

fusil [fu'sil] *nm* rifle; **~ar** *vt* to shoot

fusión [fu'sjon] *nf* (*gen*) melting; (*unión*) fusion; (*COM*) merger

fútbol ['futßol] *nm* football; **futbolín** *nm* table football; **futbolista** *nm* footballer

futuro, a [fu'turo, a] *adj, nm* future

G, g

gabardina [gaßar'ðina] *nf* raincoat, gabardine

gabinete [gaßi'nete] *nm* (*POL*) cabinet; (*estudio*) study; (*de abogados etc*) office

gaceta [ga'θeta] *nf* gazette

gachas ['gatʃas] *nfpl* porridge *sg*

gafas ['gafas] *nfpl* glasses; **~ de sol** sunglasses

gafe ['gafe] *nm* jinx

gaita ['gaita] *nf* bagpipes *pl*

gajes ['gaxes] *nmpl*: **los ~ del oficio** occupational hazards

gajo ['gaxo] *nm* (*de naranja*) segment

gala ['gala] *nf* (*traje de etiqueta*) full dress; **~s** *nfpl* (*ropa*) finery *sg*; **estar de ~** to be in one's best clothes; **hacer ~ de** to display

galante [ga'lante] *adj* gallant; **galantería**

nf (*caballerosidad*) gallantry; (*cumplido*) politeness; (*comentario*) compliment

galápago [ga'lapaxo] *nm* (*ZOOL*) turtle

galardón [galar'ðon] *nm* award, prize

galaxia [ga'laksja] *nf* galaxy

galera [ga'lera] *nf* (*nave*) galley; (*carro*) wagon; (*IMPRENTA*) galley

galería [gale'ria] *nf* (*gen*) gallery; (*balcón*) veranda(h); (*pasillo*) corridor

Gales ['gales] *nm* (*tb*: **País de ~**) Wales; **galés, esa** *adj* Welsh ♦ *nm/f* Welshman/woman ♦ *nm* (*LING*) Welsh

galgo, a ['galɣo, a] *nm/f* greyhound

galimatías [galima'tias] *nmpl* (*lenguaje*) gibberish *sg*, nonsense *sg*

gallardía [gaʎar'ðia] *nf* (*valor*) bravery

gallego, a [ga'ʎeɣo, a] *adj, nm/f* Galician

galleta [ga'ʎeta] *nf* biscuit (*BRIT*), cookie (*US*)

gallina [ga'ʎina] *nf* hen ♦ *nm/f* (*fam: cobarde*) chicken; **gallinero** *nm* henhouse; (*TEATRO*) top gallery

gallo ['gaʎo] *nm* cock, rooster

galón [ga'lon] *nm* (*MIL*) stripe; (*COSTURA*) braid; (*medida*) gallon

galopar [galo'par] *vi* to gallop

gama ['gama] *nf* (*fig*) range

gamba ['gamba] *nf* prawn (*BRIT*), shrimp (*US*)

gamberro, a [gam'berro, a] *nm/f* hooligan, lout

gamuza [ga'muθa] *nf* chamois

gana ['gana] *nf* (*deseo*) desire, wish; (*apetito*) appetite; (*voluntad*) will; (*añoranza*) longing; **de buena ~** willingly; **de mala ~** reluctantly; **me da ~s de** I feel like, I want to; **no me da la ~** I don't feel like it; **tener ~s de** to feel like

ganadería [ganaðe'ria] *nf* (*ganado*) livestock; (*ganado vacuno*) cattle *pl*; (*cría, comercio*) cattle raising

ganado [ga'naðo] *nm* livestock; **~ lanar** sheep *pl*; **~ mayor** cattle *pl*; **~ porcino** pigs *pl*

ganador, a [gana'ðor, a] *adj* winning ♦ *nm/f* winner

ganancia [ga'nanθja] *nf* (*lo ganado*) gain;

(*aumento*) increase; (*beneficio*) profit; **~s**
nfpl (*ingresos*) earnings; (*beneficios*) profit
sg, winnings

ganar [ga'nar] *vt* (*obtener*) to get, obtain;
(*sacar ventaja*) to gain; (*salario etc*) to
earn; (*DEPORTE, premio*) to win; (*derrotar
a*) to beat; (*alcanzar*) to reach ♦ *vi*
(*DEPORTE*) to win; **~se** *vr*: **~se la vida** to
earn one's living

ganchillo [gan'tʃiʎo] *nm* crochet

gancho ['gantʃo] *nm* (*gen*) hook;
(*colgador*) hanger

gandul, a [gan'dul, a] *adj, nm/f* good-
for-nothing, layabout

ganga ['ganga] *nf* bargain

gangrena [gan'grena] *nf* gangrene

ganso, a ['ganso, a] *nm/f* (*ZOOL*) goose;
(*fam*) idiot

ganzúa [gan'θua] *nf* skeleton key

garabatear [garaβate'ar] *vi, vt* (*al escribir*)
to scribble, scrawl

garabato [gara'βato] *nm* (*escritura*) scrawl,
scribble

garaje [ga'raxe] *nm* garage

garante [ga'rante] *adj* responsible ♦ *nm/f*
guarantor

garantía [garan'tia] *nf* guarantee

garantizar [garanti'θar] *vt* to guarantee

garbanzo [gar'βanθo] *nm* chickpea (*BRIT*),
garbanzo (*US*)

garbo ['garβo] *nm* grace, elegance

garfio ['garfjo] *nm* grappling iron

garganta [gar'ɣanta] *nf* (*ANAT*) throat; (*de
botella*) neck; **gargantilla** *nf* necklace

gárgaras ['garɣaras] *nfpl*: **hacer ~** to
gargle

garita [ga'rita] *nf* cabin, hut; (*MIL*) sentry
box

garra ['garra] *nf* (*de gato, TEC*) claw; (*de
ave*) talon; (*fam: mano*) hand, paw

garrafa [ga'rrafa] *nf* carafe, decanter

garrapata [garra'pata] *nf* tick

garrote [ga'rrote] *nm* (*palo*) stick; (*porra*)
cudgel; (*suplicio*) garrotte

garza ['garθa] *nf* heron

gas [gas] *nm* gas

gasa ['gasa] *nf* gauze

gaseosa [gase'osa] *nf* lemonade

gaseoso, a [gase'oso, a] *adj* gassy, fizzy

gasoil [ga'soil] *nm* diesel (oil)

gasóleo [ga'soleo] *nm* = **gasoil**

gasolina [gaso'lina] *nf* petrol, gas(oline)
(*US*); **gasolinera** *nf* petrol (*BRIT*) o gas
(*US*) station

gastado, a [gas'taðo, a] *adj* (*dinero*) spent;
(*ropa*) worn out; (*usado: frase etc*) trite

gastar [gas'tar] *vt* (*dinero, tiempo*) to
spend; (*fuerzas*) to use up; (*desperdiciar*)
to waste; (*llevar*) to wear; **~se** *vr* to wear
out; (*estropearse*) to waste; **~ en** to spend
on; **~ bromas** to crack jokes; **¿qué
número gastas?** what size (shoe) do you
take?

gasto ['gasto] *nm* (*desembolso*)
expenditure, spending; (*consumo, uso*)
use; **~s** *nmpl* (*desembolsos*) expenses;
(*cargos*) charges, costs

gastronomía [gastrono'mia] *nf*
gastronomy

gatear [gate'ar] *vi* (*andar a gatas*) to go
on all fours

gatillo [ga'tiʎo] *nm* (*de arma de fuego*)
trigger; (*de dentista*) forceps

gato, a ['gato, a] *nm/f* cat ♦ *nm* (*TEC*) jack;
andar a gatas to go on all fours

gaviota [ga'βjota] *nf* seagull

gay [ɡei] *adj inv, nm* gay, homosexual

gazpacho [gaθ'patʃo] *nm* gazpacho

gel [xel] *nm* (*tb*: **~ de baño/ducha**) gel

gelatina [xela'tina] *nf* jelly; (*polvos etc*)
gelatine

gema ['xema] *nf* gem

gemelo, a [xe'melo, a] *adj, nm/f* twin; **~s**
nmpl (*de camisa*) cufflinks; (*prismáticos*)
field glasses, binoculars

gemido [xe'miðo] *nm* (*quejido*) moan,
groan; (*aullido*) howl

Géminis ['xeminis] *nm* Gemini

gemir [xe'mir] *vi* (*quejarse*) to moan,
groan; (*aullar*) to howl

generación [xenera'θjon] *nf* generation

general [xene'ral] *adj* general ♦ *nm*
general; **por lo** o **en ~** in general; **G~itat**
nf Catalan parliament; **~izar** *vt* to

generalize; **~izarse** *vr* to become generalized, spread; **~mente** *adv* generally

generar [xene'rar] *vt* to generate

género ['xenero] *nm* (*clase*) kind, sort; (*tipo*) type; (*BIO*) genus; (*LING*) gender; (*COM*) material; **~ humano** human race

generosidad [xenerosi'ðað] *nf* generosity; **generoso, a** *adj* generous

genial [xe'njal] *adj* inspired; (*idea*) brilliant; (*afable*) genial

genio ['xenjo] *nm* (*carácter*) nature, disposition; (*humor*) temper; (*facultad creadora*) genius; **de mal ~** bad-tempered

genital [xeni'tal] *adj* genital; **genitales** *nmpl* genitals

gente ['xente] *nf* (*personas*) people *pl*; (*parientes*) relatives *pl*

gentil [xen'til] *adj* (*elegante*) graceful; (*encantador*) charming; **~eza** *nf* grace; charm; (*cortesía*) courtesy

gentío [xen'tio] *nm* crowd, throng

genuino, a [xe'nwino, a] *adj* genuine

geografía [xeoɣra'fia] *nf* geography

geología [xeolo'xia] *nf* geology

geometría [xeome'tria] *nf* geometry

gerencia [xe'renθja] *nf* management; **gerente** *nm/f* (*supervisor*) manager; (*jefe*) director

geriatría [xeria'tria] *nf* (*MED*) geriatrics *sg*

germen ['xermen] *nm* germ

germinar [xermi'nar] *vi* to germinate

gesticular [xestiku'lar] *vi* to gesticulate; (*hacer muecas*) to grimace; **gesticulación** *nf* gesticulation; (*mueca*) grimace

gestión [xes'tjon] *nf* management; (*diligencia, acción*) negotiation; **gestionar** *vt* (*lograr*) to try to arrange; (*dirigir*) to manage

gesto ['xesto] *nm* (*mueca*) grimace; (*ademán*) gesture

Gibraltar [xiβral'tar] *nm* Gibraltar; **gibraltareño, a** *adj, nm/f* Gibraltarian

gigante [xi'ɣante] *adj, nm/f* giant; **gigantesco, a** *adj* gigantic

gilipollas [xili'poʎas] (*fam*) *adj inv* daft

♦ *nm/f inv* wally

gimnasia [xim'nasja] *nf* gymnastics *pl*; **gimnasio** *nm* gymnasium; **gimnasta** *nm/f* gymnast

gimotear [ximote'ar] *vi* to whine, whimper

ginebra [xi'neβra] *nf* gin

ginecólogo, a [xine'koloɣo, a] *nm/f* gynaecologist

gira ['xira] *nf* tour, trip

girar [xi'rar] *vt* (*dar la vuelta*) to turn (around); (: *rápidamente*) to spin; (*COM*: *giro postal*) to draw; (: *letra de cambio*) to issue ♦ *vi* to turn (round); (*rápido*) to spin

girasol [xira'sol] *nm* sunflower

giratorio, a [xira'torjo, a] *adj* revolving

giro ['xiro] *nm* (*movimiento*) turn, revolution; (*LING*) expression; (*COM*) draft; **~ bancario/postal** bank giro/postal order

gis [xis] (*AM*) *nm* chalk

gitano, a [xi'tano, a] *adj, nm/f* gypsy

glacial [gla'θjal] *adj* icy, freezing

glaciar [gla'θjar] *nm* glacier

glándula ['glandula] *nf* gland

global [glo'βal] *adj* global

globo ['gloβo] *nm* (*esfera*) globe, sphere; (*aerostato, juguete*) balloon

glóbulo ['gloβulo] *nm* globule; (*ANAT*) corpuscle

gloria ['glorja] *nf* glory

glorieta [glo'rjeta] *nf* (*de jardín*) bower, arbour; (*plazoleta*) roundabout (*BRIT*), traffic circle (*US*)

glorificar [glorifi'kar] *vt* (*enaltecer*) to glorify, praise

glorioso, a [glo'rjoso, a] *adj* glorious

glotón, ona [glo'ton, ona] *adj* gluttonous, greedy ♦ *nm/f* glutton

glucosa [glu'kosa] *nf* glucose

gobernador, a [goβerna'ðor, a] *adj* governing ♦ *nm/f* governor; **gobernante** *adj* governing

gobernar [goβer'nar] *vt* (*dirigir*) to guide, direct; (*POL*) to rule, govern ♦ *vi* to govern; (*NAUT*) to steer

gobierno *etc* [go'βjerno] *vb ver* **gobernar** ♦ *nm* (*POL*) government; (*dirección*) guidance, direction; (*NAUT*) steering

goce *etc* ['goθe] *vb ver* **gozar** ♦ *nm* enjoyment

gol [gol] *nm* goal

golf [golf] *nm* golf

golfa ['golfa] (*fam!*) *nf* (*mujer*) slut, whore

golfo, a ['golfo, a] *nm* (*GEO*) gulf ♦ *nm/f* (*fam: niño*) urchin; (*gamberro*) lout

golondrina [golon'drina] *nf* swallow

golosina [golo'sina] *nf* (*dulce*) sweet; **goloso, a** *adj* sweet-toothed

golpe ['golpe] *nm* blow; (*de puño*) punch; (*de mano*) smack; (*de remo*) stroke; (*fig: choque*) clash; **no dar ~** to be bone idle; **de un ~** with one blow; **de ~** suddenly; **~ (de estado)** coup (d'état); **golpear** *vt, vi* to strike, knock; (*asestar*) to beat; (*de puño*) to punch; (*golpetear*) to tap

goma ['goma] *nf* (*caucho*) rubber; (*elástico*) elastic; (*una ~*) elastic band; **~ espuma** foam rubber; **~ de pegar** gum, glue; **~ de borrar** eraser, rubber (*BRIT*)

gomina [go'mina] *nf* hair gel

gordo, a ['gorðo, a] *adj* (*gen*) fat; (*fam*) enormous; **el (premio) ~** (*en lotería*) first prize; **gordura** *nf* fat; (*corpulencia*) fatness, stoutness

gorila [go'rila] *nm* gorilla

gorjear [gorxe'ar] *vi* to twitter, chirp

gorra ['gorra] *nf* cap; (*de niño*) bonnet; (*militar*) bearskin; **entrar de ~** (*fam*) to gatecrash; **ir de ~** to sponge

gorrión [go'rrjon] *nm* sparrow

gorro ['gorro] *nm* (*gen*) cap; (*de niño, mujer*) bonnet

gorrón, ona [go'rron, ona] *nm/f* scrounger; **gorronear** (*fam*) *vi* to scrounge

gota ['gota] *nf* (*gen*) drop; (*de sudor*) bead; (*MED*) gout; **gotear** *vi* to drip; (*lloviznar*) to drizzle; **gotera** *nf* leak

gozar [go'θar] *vi* to enjoy o.s.; **~ de** (*disfrutar*) to enjoy; (*poseer*) to possess

gozne ['goθne] *nm* hinge

gozo ['goθo] *nm* (*alegría*) joy; (*placer*) pleasure

gr. *abr* (= *gramo, gramos*) g

grabación [graβa'θjon] *nf* recording

grabado [gra'βaðo] *nm* print, engraving

grabadora [graβa'ðora] *nf* tape-recorder

grabar [gra'βar] *vt* to engrave; (*discos, cintas*) to record

gracia [gra'θja] *nf* (*encanto*) grace, gracefulness; (*humor*) humour, wit; **¡(muchas) ~s!** thanks (very much)!; **~s a** thanks to; **tener ~** (*chiste etc*) to be funny; **no me hace ~** I am not keen; **gracioso, a** *adj* (*divertido*) funny, amusing; (*cómico*) comical ♦ *nm/f* (*TEATRO*) comic character

grada ['graða] *nf* (*de escalera*) step; (*de anfiteatro*) tier, row; **~s** *nfpl* (*DEPORTE: de estadio*) terraces

gradería [graðe'ria] *nf* (*gradas*) (flight of) steps *pl*; (*de anfiteatro*) tiers *pl*, rows *pl*; (*DEPORTE: de estadio*) terraces *pl*; **~ cubierta** covered stand

grado ['graðo] *nm* degree; (*de aceite, vino*) grade; (*grada*) step; (*MIL*) rank; **de buen ~** willingly

graduación [graðwa'θjon] *nf* (*del alcohol*) proof, strength; (*ESCOL*) graduation; (*MIL*) rank

gradual [gra'ðwal] *adj* gradual

graduar [gra'ðwar] *vt* (*gen*) to graduate; (*MIL*) to commission; **~se** *vr* to graduate; **~se la vista** to have one's eyes tested

gráfica ['grafika] *nf* graph

gráfico, a ['grafiko, a] *adj* graphic ♦ *nm* diagram; **~s** *nmpl* (*INFORM*) graphics

grajo ['graxo] *nm* rook

Gral *abr* (= *General*) Gen.

gramática [gra'matika] *nf* grammar

gramo ['gramo] *nm* gramme (*BRIT*), gram (*US*)

gran [gran] *adj ver* **grande**

grana ['grana] *nf* (*color, tela*) scarlet

granada [gra'naða] *nf* pomegranate; (*MIL*) grenade

granate [gra'nate] *adj* deep red

Gran Bretaña [-bre'taɲa] *nf* Great Britain

grande ['grande] (*antes de nmsg*: **gran**) *adj* (*de tamaño*) big, large; (*alto*) tall; (*distinguido*) great; (*impresionante*) grand

♦ *nm* grandee; **grandeza** *nf* greatness
grandioso, a [gran'djoso, a] *adj*
magnificent, grand
granel [gra'nel]: **a ~** *adv* (COM) in bulk
granero [gra'nero] *nm* granary, barn
granito [gra'nito] *nm* (AGR) small grain;
(*roca*) granite
granizado [grani'θaðo] *nm* iced drink
granizar [grani'θar] *vi* to hail; **granizo**
nm hail
granja ['granxa] *nf* (*gen*) farm; **granjear**
vt to win, gain; **granjearse** *vr* to win,
gain; **granjero, a** *nm/f* farmer
grano ['grano] *nm* grain; (*semilla*) seed; (*de
café*) bean; (MED) pimple, spot
granuja [gra'nuxa] *nm/f* rogue; (*golfillo*)
urchin
grapa ['grapa] *nf* staple; (TEC) clamp;
grapadora *nf* stapler
grasa ['grasa] *nf* (*gen*) grease; (*de cocinar*)
fat, lard; (*sebo*) suet; (*mugre*) filth;
grasiento, a *adj* greasy; (*de aceite*) oily;
graso, a *adj* (*leche, queso, carne*) fatty;
(*pelo, piel*) greasy
gratificación [gratifika'θjon] *nf* (*bono*)
bonus; (*recompensa*) reward
gratificar [gratifi'kar] *vt* to reward
gratinar [grati'nar] *vt* to cook au gratin
gratis ['gratis] *adv* free
gratitud [grati'tuð] *nf* gratitude
grato, a ['grato, a] *adj* (*agradable*)
pleasant, agreeable
gratuito, a [gra'twito, a] *adj* (*gratis*) free;
(*sin razón*) gratuitous
gravamen [gra'ßamen] *nm* (*impuesto*) tax
gravar [gra'ßar] *vt* to tax
grave ['graße] *adj* heavy; (*serio*) grave,
serious; **~dad** *nf* gravity
gravilla [gra'ßiʎa] *nf* gravel
gravitar [graßi'tar] *vi* to gravitate; **~ sobre**
to rest on
graznar [graθ'nar] *vi* (*cuervo*) to squawk;
(*pato*) to quack; (*hablar ronco*) to croak
Grecia ['greθja] *nf* Greece
gremio ['gremjo] *nm* trade, industry
greña ['greɲa] *nf* (*cabellos*) shock of hair
gresca ['greska] *nf* uproar

griego, a ['grjexo, a] *adj, nm/f* Greek
grieta ['grjeta] *nf* crack
grifo ['grifo] *nm* tap; (AM: AUTO) petrol
(BRIT) o gas (US) station
grilletes [gri'ʎetes] *nmpl* fetters
grillo ['griʎo] *nm* (ZOOL) cricket
gripe ['gripe] *nf* flu, influenza
gris [gris] *adj* (*color*) grey
gritar [gri'tar] *vt, vi* to shout, yell; **grito**
nm shout, yell; (*de horror*) scream
grosella [gro'seʎa] *nf* (red)currant; **~
negra** blackcurrant
grosería [grose'ria] *nf* (*actitud*) rudeness;
(*comentario*) vulgar comment; **grosero,
a** *adj* (*poco cortés*) rude, bad-mannered;
(*ordinario*) vulgar, crude
grosor [gro'sor] *nm* thickness
grotesco, a [gro'tesko, a] *adj* grotesque
grúa ['grua] *nf* (TEC) crane; (*de petróleo*)
derrick
grueso, a ['grweso, a] *adj* thick; (*persona*)
stout ♦ *nm* bulk; **el ~ de** the bulk of
grulla ['gruʎa] *nf* crane
grumo ['grumo] *nm* clot, lump
gruñido [gru'ɲiðo] *nm* grunt; (*de persona*)
grumble
gruñir [gru'ɲir] *vi* (*animal*) to growl;
(*persona*) to grumble
grupa ['grupa] *nf* (ZOOL) rump
grupo ['grupo] *nm* group; (TEC) unit, set
gruta ['gruta] *nf* grotto
guadaña [gwa'ðaɲa] *nf* scythe
guagua ['gwa'vwa] (AM) *nf* (*niño*) baby;
(*bus*) bus
guante ['gwante] *nm* glove; **~ra** *nf* glove
compartment
guapo, a ['gwapo, a] *adj* good-looking,
attractive; (*elegante*) smart
guarda ['gwarða] *nm/f* (*persona*) guard,
keeper ♦ *nf* (*acto*) guarding; (*custodia*)
custody; **~bosques** *nm inv*
gamekeeper; **~costas** *nm inv*
coastguard vessel ♦ *nm/f* guardian,
protector; **~espaldas** *nm/f inv*
bodyguard; **~meta** *nm/f* goalkeeper;
guardar *vt* (*gen*) to keep; (*vigilar*) to
guard, watch over; (*dinero: ahorrar*) to

save; **guardarse** vr (*preservarse*) to protect o.s.; (*evitar*) to avoid; **guardar cama** to stay in bed; **~rropa** nm (*armario*) wardrobe; (*en establecimiento público*) cloakroom

guardería [gwarðe'ria] nf nursery

guardia ['gwarðja] nf (MIL) guard; (*cuidado*) care, custody ♦ nm/f guard; (*policía*) policeman/woman; **estar de ~** to be on guard; **montar ~** to mount guard; **G~ Civil** Civil Guard; **G~ Nacional** National Guard

guardián, ana [gwar'ðjan, ana] nm/f (*gen*) guardian, keeper

guarecer [gware'θer] vt (*proteger*) to protect; (*abrigar*) to shelter; **~se** vr to take refuge

guarida [gwa'riða] nf (*de animal*) den, lair; (*refugio*) refuge

guarnecer [gwarne'θer] vt (*equipar*) to provide; (*adornar*) to adorn; (TEC) to reinforce; **guarnición** nf (*de vestimenta*) trimming; (*de piedra*) mount; (CULIN) garnish; (*arneses*) harness; (MIL) garrison

guarro, a ['gwarro, a] nm/f pig

guasa ['gwasa] nf joke; **guasón, ona** adj (*bromista*) joking ♦ nm/f wit; joker

Guatemala [gwate'mala] nf Guatemala

guay [gwai] (fam) adj super, great

gubernativo, a [gußerna'tißo, a] adj governmental

guerra ['gerra] nf war; **~ civil** civil war; **~ fría** cold war; **dar ~** to annoy; **guerrear** vi to wage war; **guerrero, a** adj fighting; (*carácter*) warlike ♦ nm/f warrior

guerrilla [ge'rriʎa] nf guerrilla warfare; (*tropas*) guerrilla band o group

guía etc ['gia] vb ver **guiar** ♦ nm/f (*persona*) guide ♦ nf (*libro*) guidebook; **~ de ferrocarriles** railway timetable; **~ telefónica** telephone directory

guiar [gi'ar] vt to guide, direct; (AUTO) to steer; **~se** vr: **~se por** to be guided by

guijarro [gi'xarro] nm pebble

guillotina [giʎo'tina] nf guillotine

guinda ['ginda] nf morello cherry

guindilla [gin'diʎa] nf chilli pepper

guiñapo [gi'ɲapo] nm (*harapo*) rag; (*persona*) reprobate, rogue

guiñar [gi'ɲar] vt to wink

guión [gi'on] nm (LING) hyphen, dash; (CINE) script; **guionista** nm/f scriptwriter

guiri ['giri] (fam: pey) nm/f foreigner

guirnalda [gir'nalda] nf garland

guisado [gi'saðo] nm stew

guisante [gi'sante] nm pea

guisar [gi'sar] vt, vi to cook; **guiso** nm cooked dish

guitarra [gi'tarra] nf guitar

gula ['gula] nf gluttony, greed

gusano [gu'sano] nm worm; (*lombriz*) earthworm

gustar [gus'tar] vt to taste, sample ♦ vi to please, be pleasing; **~ de algo** to like o enjoy sth; **me gustan las uvas** I like grapes; **le gusta nadar** she likes o enjoys swimming

gusto ['gusto] nm (*sentido, sabor*) taste; (*placer*) pleasure; **tiene ~ a menta** it tastes of mint; **tener buen ~** to have good taste; **sentirse a ~** to feel at ease; **mucho ~ (en conocerle)** pleased to meet you; **el ~ es mío** the pleasure is mine; **con ~** willingly, gladly; **~so, a** adj (*sabroso*) tasty; (*agradable*) pleasant

H, h

ha vb ver **haber**

haba ['aßa] nf bean

Habana [a'ßana] nf: **la ~** Havana

habano [a'ßano] nm Havana cigar

habéis vb ver **haber**

PALABRA CLAVE

---

haber [a'ßer] vb aux **1** (*tiempos compuestos*) to have; **había comido** I had eaten; **antes/después de ~lo visto** before seeing/after seeing o having seen it

2: **¡~lo dicho antes!** you should have said so before!

3: **~ de**: **he de hacerlo** I have to do it;

ha de llegar mañana it should arrive tomorrow

♦ *vb impers* **1** (*existencia: sg*) there is; (*: pl*) there are; **hay un hermano / dos hermanos** there is one brother/there are two brothers; **¿cuánto hay de aquí a Sucre?** how far is it from here to Sucre? **2** (*obligación*): **hay que hacer algo** something must be done; **hay que apuntarlo para acordarse** you have to write it down to remember **3**: **¡hay que ver!** well I never! **4**: **¡no hay de** *o* (*AM*) **qué!** don't mention it!, not at all! **5**: **¿qué hay?** (*¿qué pasa?*) what's up?, what's the matter?; (*¿qué tal?*) how's it going?

♦ **~se** *vr*: **habérselas con uno** to have it out with sb

♦ *vt*: **he aquí unas sugerencias** here are some suggestions; **no hay cintas blancas pero sí las hay rojas** there aren't any white ribbons but there are some red ones

♦ *nm* (*en cuenta*) credit side; **~es** *nmpl* assets; **¿cuánto tengo en el ~?** how much do I have in my account?; **tiene varias novelas en su ~** he has several novels to his credit

habichuela [aßi'tʃwela] *nf* kidney bean
hábil ['aßil] *adj* (*listo*) clever, smart; (*capaz*) fit, capable; (*experto*) expert; **día ~** working day; **habilidad** *nf* skill, ability
habilitar [aßili'tar] *vt* (*capacitar*) to enable; (*dar instrumentos*) to equip; (*financiar*) to finance
hábilmente [aßil'mente] *adv* skilfully, expertly
habitación [aßita'θjon] *nf* (*cuarto*) room; (*BIO: morada*) habitat; **~ sencilla** *o* **individual** single room; **~ doble** *o* **de matrimonio** double room
habitante [aßi'tante] *nm/f* inhabitant
habitar [aßi'tar] *vt* (*residir en*) to inhabit; (*ocupar*) to occupy ♦ *vi* to live
hábito ['aßito] *nm* habit

habitual [aßi'twal] *adj* usual
habituar [aßi'twar] *vt* to accustom; **~se** *vr*: **~se a** to get used to
habla ['aßla] *nf* (*capacidad de hablar*) speech; (*idioma*) language; (*dialecto*) dialect; **perder el ~** to become speechless; **de ~ francesa** French-speaking; **estar al ~** to be in contact; (*TEL*) to be on the line; **¡González al ~!** (*TEL*) González speaking!
hablador, a [aßla'ðor, a] *adj* talkative ♦ *nm/f* chatterbox
habladuría [aßlaðu'ria] *nf* rumour; **~s** *nfpl* gossip *sg*
hablante [a'ßlante] *adj* speaking ♦ *nm/f* speaker
hablar [a'ßlar] *vt* to speak, talk ♦ *vi* to speak; **~se** *vr* to speak to each other; **~ con** to speak to; **~ de** to speak of *o* about; **"se habla inglés"** "English spoken here"; **¡ni ~!** it's out of the question!
habré *etc vb ver* **haber**
hacendoso, a [aθen'doso, a] *adj* industrious

| PALABRA CLAVE |

hacer [a'θer] *vt* **1** (*fabricar, producir*) to make; (*construir*) to build; **~ una película / un ruido** to make a film/noise; **el guisado lo hice yo** I made *o* cooked the stew **2** (*ejecutar: trabajo etc*) to do; **~ la colada** to do the washing; **~ la comida** to do the cooking; **¿qué haces?** what are you doing?; **~ el malo** *o* **el papel del malo** (*TEATRO*) to play the villain **3** (*estudios, algunos deportes*) to do; **~ español / económicas** to do *o* study Spanish/economics; **~ yoga / gimnasia** to do yoga/go to gym **4** (*transformar, incidir en*): **esto lo hará más difícil** this will make it more difficult; **salir te hará sentir mejor** going out will make you feel better **5** (*cálculo*): **2 y 2 hacen 4** 2 and 2 make 4; **éste hace 100** this one makes 100

6 (+*subjun*): **esto hará que ganemos** this will make us win; **harás que no quiera venir** you'll stop him wanting to come
7 (*como sustituto de vb*) to do; **él bebió y yo hice lo mismo** he drank and I did likewise
8: no hace más que criticar all he does is criticize
♦ *vb semi-aux*: **hacer +infin 1** (*directo*): **les hice venir** I made *o* had them come; **~ trabajar a los demás** to get others to work
2 (*por intermedio de otros*): **~ reparar algo** to get sth repaired
♦ *vi* **1: haz como que no lo sabes** act as if you don't know
2 (*ser apropiado*): **si os hace** if it's alright with you
3: ~ de: ~ de madre para uno to be like a mother to sb; (*TEATRO*): **~ de Otelo** to play Othello
♦ *vb impers* **1: hace calor/frío** it's hot/cold; *ver tb* **bueno; sol; tiempo**
2 (*tiempo*): **hace 3 años** 3 years ago; **hace un mes que voy/no voy** I've been going/I haven't been for a month
3: ¿cómo has hecho para llegar tan rápido? how did you manage to get here so quickly?
♦ **~se** *vr* **1** (*volverse*) to become; **se hicieron amigos** they became friends
2 (*acostumbrarse*): **~se a** to get used to
3: se hace con huevos y leche it's made out of eggs and milk; **eso no se hace** that's not done
4 (*obtener*): **~se de** *o* **con algo** to get hold of sth
5 (*fingirse*): **~se el sueco** to turn a deaf ear

hacha ['atʃa] *nf* axe; (*antorcha*) torch
hachís [a'tʃis] *nm* hashish
hacia ['aθja] *prep* (*en dirección de*) towards; (*cerca de*) near; (*actitud*) towards; **~ arriba/abajo** up(wards)/down(wards); **~ mediodía** about noon
hacienda [a'θjenda] *nf* (*propiedad*) property; (*finca*) farm; (*AM*) ranch; **~ pública** public finance; **(Ministerio de) H~** Exchequer (*BRIT*), Treasury Department (*US*)
hada ['aða] *nf* fairy
hago *etc vb ver* **hacer**
Haití [ai'ti] *nm* Haiti
halagar [ala'xar] *vt* to flatter
halago [a'laxo] *nm* flattery; **halagüeño, a** *adj* flattering
halcón [al'kon] *nm* falcon, hawk
hallar [a'ʎar] *vt* (*gen*) to find; (*descubrir*) to discover; (*toparse con*) to run into; **~se** to be (situated); **hallazgo** *nm* discovery; (*cosa*) find
halterofilia [altero'filja] *nf* weightlifting
hamaca [a'maka] *nf* hammock
hambre ['ambre] *nf* hunger; (*plaga*) famine; (*deseo*) longing; **tener ~** to be hungry; **hambriento, a** *adj* hungry, starving
hamburguesa [ambur'xesa] *nf* hamburger; **hamburguesería** *nf* burger bar
han *vb ver* **haber**
harapiento, a [ara'pjento, a] *adj* tattered, in rags
harapos [a'rapos] *nmpl* rags
haré *etc vb ver* **hacer**
harina [a'rina] *nf* flour
hartar [ar'tar] *vt* to satiate, glut; (*fig*) to tire, sicken; **~se** *vr* (*de comida*) to fill o.s., gorge o.s.; (*cansarse*) to get fed up (*de* with); **hartazgo** *nm* surfeit, glut; **harto, a** *adj* (*lleno*) full; (*cansado*) fed up ♦ *adv* (*bastante*) enough; (*muy*) very; **estar harto de** to be fed up with
has *vb ver* **haber**
hasta ['asta] *adv* even ♦ *prep* (*alcanzando a*) as far as; up to; down to; (*de tiempo: a tal hora*) till, until; (*antes de*) before ♦ *conj*: **~ que** until; **~ luego/el sábado** see you soon/on Saturday
hastiar [as'tjar] *vt* (*gen*) to weary; (*aburrir*) to bore; **~se** *vr*: **~se de** to get fed up with; **hastío** *nm* weariness; boredom
hatillo [a'tiʎo] *nm* belongings *pl*, kit;

(*montón*) bundle, heap

hay *vb ver* **haber**

Haya ['aja] *nf:* **la ~** The Hague

haya *etc* ['aja] *vb ver* **haber** ♦ *nf* beech tree

haz [aθ] *vb ver* **hacer** ♦ *nm* (*de luz*) beam

hazaña [a'θaɲa] *nf* feat, exploit

hazmerreír [aθmerre'ir] *nm inv* laughing stock

he *vb ver* **haber**

hebilla [e'βiʎa] *nf* buckle, clasp

hebra ['eβra] *nf* thread; (*BOT: fibra*) fibre, grain

hebreo, a [e'βreo, a] *adj, nm/f* Hebrew ♦ *nm* (*LING*) Hebrew

hechizar [etʃi'θar] *vt* to cast a spell on, bewitch

hechizo [e'tʃiθo] *nm* witchcraft, magic; (*acto de magía*) spell, charm

hecho, a ['etʃo, a] *pp de* **hacer** ♦ *adj* (*carne*) done; (*COSTURA*) ready-to-wear ♦ *nm* deed, act; (*dato*) fact; (*cuestión*) matter; (*suceso*) event ♦ *excl* agreed!, done!; **¡bien ~!** well done!; **de ~** in fact, as a matter of fact

hechura [e'tʃura] *nf* (*forma*) form, shape; (*de persona*) build

hectárea [ek'tarea] *nf* hectare

heder [e'ðer] *vi* to stink, smell

hediondo, a [e'ðjondo, a] *adj* stinking

hedor [e'ðor] *nm* stench

helada [e'laða] *nf* frost

heladera [ela'ðera] (*AM*) *nf* (*refrigerador*) refrigerator

helado, a [e'laðo, a] *adj* frozen; (*glacial*) icy; (*fig*) chilly, cold ♦ *nm* ice cream

helar [e'lar] *vt* to freeze, ice (up); (*dejar atónito*) to amaze; (*desalentar*) to discourage ♦ *vi* to freeze; **~se** *vr* to freeze

helecho [e'letʃo] *nm* fern

hélice ['eliθe] *nf* (*TEC*) propeller

helicóptero [eli'koptero] *nm* helicopter

hembra ['embra] *nf* (*BOT, ZOOL*) female; (*mujer*) woman; (*TEC*) nut

hemorragia [emo'rraxja] *nf* haemorrhage

hemorroides [emo'rroiðes] *nfpl* haemorrhoids, piles

hemos *vb ver* **haber**

hendidura [endi'ðura] *nf* crack, split

heno ['eno] *nm* hay

herbicida [erβi'θiða] *nm* weedkiller

heredad [ere'ðað] *nf* landed property; (*granja*) farm

heredar [ere'ðar] *vt* to inherit; **heredero, a** *nm/f* heir(ess)

hereje [e'rexe] *nm/f* heretic

herencia [e'renθja] *nf* inheritance

herida [e'riða] *nf* wound, injury; *ver tb* **herido**

herido, a [e'riðo, a] *adj* injured, wounded ♦ *nm/f* casualty

herir [e'rir] *vt* to wound, injure; (*fig*) to offend

hermanastro, a [erma'nastro, a] *nm/f* stepbrother/sister

hermandad [erman'dað] *nf* brotherhood

hermano, a [er'mano, a] *nm/f* brother/sister; **~ gemelo** twin brother; **hermana gemela** twin sister; **~ político** brother-in-law; **hermana política** sister-in-law

hermético, a [er'metiko, a] *adj* hermetic; (*fig*) watertight

hermoso, a [er'moso, a] *adj* beautiful, lovely; (*estupendo*) splendid; (*guapo*) handsome; **hermosura** *nf* beauty

hernia ['ernja] *nf* hernia

héroe ['eroe] *nm* hero

heroína [ero'ina] *nf* (*mujer*) heroine; (*droga*) heroin

heroísmo [ero'ismo] *nm* heroism

herradura [erra'ðura] *nf* horseshoe

herramienta [erra'mjenta] *nf* tool

herrero [e'rrero] *nm* blacksmith

herrumbre [e'rrumbre] *nf* rust

hervidero [erβi'ðero] *nm* (*fig*) swarm; (*POL etc*) hotbed

hervir [er'βir] *vi* to boil; (*burbujear*) to bubble; (*fig*): **~ de** to teem with; **~ a fuego lento** to simmer; **hervor** *nm* boiling; (*fig*) ardour, fervour

heterosexual [eterosek'swal] *adj* heterosexual

hice *etc vb ver* **hacer**

hidratante [iðra'tante] *adj:* **crema ~**

moisturizing cream, moisturizer; **hidratar**
vt (*piel*) to moisturize; **hidrato** *nm*:
hidratos de carbono carbohydrates

hidráulica [i'ðraulika] *nf* hydraulics *sg*

hidráulico, a [i'ðrauliko, a] *adj* hydraulic

hidro... [iðro] *prefijo* hydro..., water-...;
~eléctrico, a *adj* hydroelectric; **~fobia**
nf hydrophobia, rabies; **hidrógeno** *nm*
hydrogen

hiedra ['jeðra] *nf* ivy

hiel [jel] *nf* gall, bile; (*fig*) bitterness

hiela *etc vb ver* **helar**

hielo ['jelo] *nm* (*gen*) ice; (*escarcha*) frost;
(*fig*) coldness, reserve

hiena ['jena] *nf* hyena

hierba ['jerβa] *nf* (*pasto*) grass; (*CULIN,
MED: planta*) herb; **mala ~** weed; (*fig*) evil
influence; **~buena** *nf* mint

hierro ['jerro] *nm* (*metal*) iron; (*objeto*)
iron object

hígado ['ixaðo] *nm* liver

higiene [i'xjene] *nf* hygiene; **higiénico,
a** *adj* hygienic

higo ['ixo] *nm* fig; **higuera** *nf* fig tree

hijastro, a [i'xastro, a] *nm/f* stepson/
daughter

hijo, a ['ixo, a] *nm/f* son/daughter, child;
~s *nmpl* children, sons and daughters; **~
de papá/mamá** daddy's/mummy's boy;
~ de puta (*fam!*) bastard (*!*), son of a
bitch (*!*)

hilar [i'lar] *vt* to spin; **~ fino** to split hairs

hilera [i'lera] *nf* row, file

hilo ['ilo] *nm* thread; (*BOT*) fibre; (*metal*)
wire; (*de agua*) trickle, thin stream

hilvanar [ilβa'nar] *vt* (*COSTURA*) to tack
(*BRIT*), baste (*US*); (*fig*) to do hurriedly

himno ['imno] *nm* hymn; **~ nacional**
national anthem

hincapié [inka'pje] *nm*: **hacer ~ en** to
emphasize

hincar [in'kar] *vt* to drive (in), thrust (in);
~se *vr*: **~se de rodillas** to kneel down

hincha ['intʃa] (*fam*) *nm/f* fan

hinchado, a [in'tʃaðo, a] *adj* (*gen*)
swollen; (*persona*) pompous

hinchar [in'tʃar] *vt* (*gen*) to swell; (*inflar*)

to blow up, inflate; (*fig*) to exaggerate;
~se *vr* (*inflarse*) to swell up; (*fam: de
comer*) to stuff o.s.; **hinchazón** *nf* (*MED*)
swelling; (*altivez*) arrogance

hinojo [i'noxo] *nm* fennel

hipermercado [ipermer'kaðo] *nm*
hypermarket, superstore

hípico, a ['ipiko, a] *adj* horse *cpd*

hipnotismo [ipno'tismo] *nm* hypnotism;
hipnotizar *vt* to hypnotize

hipo ['ipo] *nm* hiccups *pl*

hipocresía [ipokre'sia] *nf* hypocrisy;
hipócrita *adj* hypocritical ♦ *nm/f*
hypocrite

hipódromo [i'poðromo] *nm* racetrack

hipopótamo [ipo'potamo] *nm*
hippopotamus

hipoteca [ipo'teka] *nf* mortgage

hipótesis [i'potesis] *nf inv* hypothesis

hiriente [i'rjente] *adj* offensive, wounding

hispánico, a [is'paniko, a] *adj* Hispanic

hispano, a [is'pano, a] *adj* Hispanic,
Spanish, Hispano- ♦ *nm/f* Spaniard;
H~américa *nf* Latin America;
~americano, a *adj, nm/f* Latin
American

histeria [is'terja] *nf* hysteria

historia [is'torja] *nf* history; (*cuento*) story,
tale; **~s** *nfpl* (*chismes*) gossip *sg*; **dejarse
de ~s** to come to the point; **pasar a la ~**
to go down in history; **~dor, a** *nm/f*
historian; **historial** *nm* (*profesional*)
curriculum vitae, C.V.; (*MED*) case history;
histórico, a *adj* historical; (*memorable*)
historic

historieta [isto'rjeta] *nf* tale, anecdote;
(*dibujos*) comic strip

hito ['ito] *nm* (*fig*) landmark

hizo *vb ver* **hacer**

Hnos *abr* (= *Hermanos*) Bros.

hocico [o'θiko] *nm* snout

hockey ['xoki] *nm* hockey; **~ sobre hielo**
ice hockey

hogar [o'xar] *nm* fireplace, hearth; (*casa*)
home; (*vida familiar*) home life; **~eño, a**
adj home *cpd*; (*persona*) home-loving

hoguera [o'xera] *nf* (*gen*) bonfire

hoja ['oxa] *nf* (*gen*) leaf; (*de flor*) petal; (*de papel*) sheet; (*página*) page; **~ de afeitar** razor blade

hojalata [oxa'lata] *nf* tin(plate)

hojaldre [o'xaldre] *nm* (*CULIN*) puff pastry

hojear [oxe'ar] *vt* to leaf through, turn the pages of

hola ['ola] *excl* hello!

Holanda [o'landa] *nf* Holland; **holandés, esa** *adj* Dutch ♦ *nm/f* Dutchman/ woman ♦ *nm* (*LING*) Dutch

holgado, a [ol'xaðo, a] *adj* (*ropa*) loose, baggy; (*rico*) comfortable

holgar [ol'xar] *vi* (*descansar*) to rest; (*sobrar*) to be superfluous; **huelga decir que** it goes without saying that

holgazán, ana [olxa'θan, ana] *adj* idle, lazy ♦ *nm/f* loafer

holgura [ol'xura] *nf* looseness, bagginess; (*TEC*) play, free movement; (*vida*) comfortable living

hollín [o'ʎin] *nm* soot

hombre ['ombre] *nm* (*gen*) man; (*raza humana*): **el ~** man(kind) ♦ *excl* **¡sí ~!** (*claro*) of course!; (*para énfasis*) man, old boy; **~ de negocios** businessman; **~ de pro** honest man; **~-rana** frogman

hombrera [om'brera] *nf* shoulder strap

hombro ['ombro] *nm* shoulder

hombruno, a [om'bruno, a] *adj* mannish

homenaje [ome'naxe] *nm* (*gen*) homage; (*tributo*) tribute

homicida [omi'θiða] *adj* homicidal ♦ *nm/f* murderer; **homicidio** *nm* murder, homicide

homologar [omolo'ðar] *vt* (*COM*: *productos, tamaños*) to standardize; **homólogo, a** *nm/f*: **su** *etc* **homólogo** his *etc* counterpart *o* opposite number

homosexual [omosek'swal] *adj, nm/f* homosexual

hondo, a ['ondo, a] *adj* deep; **lo ~** the depth(s) (*pl*), the bottom; **~nada** *nf* hollow, depression; (*cañón*) ravine

Honduras [on'duras] *nf* Honduras

hondureño, a [ondu'reɲo, a] *adj, nm/f* Honduran

honestidad [onesti'ðað] *nf* purity, chastity; (*decencia*) decency; **honesto, a** *adj* chaste; decent, honest; (*justo*) just

hongo ['ongo] *nm* (*BOT*: *gen*) fungus; (: *comestible*) mushroom; (: *venenoso*) toadstool

honor [o'nor] *nm* (*gen*) honour; **en ~ a la verdad** to be fair; **~able** *adj* honourable

honorario, a [ono'rarjo, a] *adj* honorary; **~s** *nmpl* fees

honra ['onra] *nf* (*gen*) honour; (*renombre*) good name; **~dez** *nf* honesty; (*de persona*) integrity; **~do, a** *adj* honest, upright

honrar [on'rar] *vt* to honour; **~se** *vr*: **~se con algo/de hacer algo** to be honoured by sth/to do sth

honroso, a [on'roso, a] *adj* (*honrado*) honourable; (*respetado*) respectable

hora ['ora] *nf* (*una ~*) hour; (*tiempo*) time; **¿qué ~ es?** what time is it?; **¿a qué ~?** at what time?; **media ~** half an hour; **a la ~ de recreo** at playtime; **a primera ~** first thing (in the morning); **a última ~** at the last moment; **a altas ~s** in the small hours; **¡a buena ~!** about time, too!; **dar la ~** to strike the hour; **~s de oficina/de trabajo** office/working hours; **~s de visita** visiting times; **~s extras** *o* **extraordinarias** overtime *sg*; **~s punta** rush hours

horadar [ora'ðar] *vt* to drill, bore

horario, a [o'rarjo, a] *adj* hourly, hour *cpd* ♦ *nm* timetable; **~ comercial** business hours *pl*

horca ['orka] *nf* gallows *sg*

horcajadas [orka'xaðas]: **a ~** *adv* astride

horchata [or'tʃata] *nf* cold drink made *from tiger nuts and water*, tiger nut milk

horizontal [oriθon'tal] *adj* horizontal

horizonte [ori'θonte] *nm* horizon

horma ['orma] *nf* mould

hormiga [or'mixa] *nf* ant; **~s** *nfpl* (*MED*) pins and needles

hormigón [ormi'xon] *nm* concrete; **~ armado/pretensado** reinforced/ prestressed concrete

hormigueo [ormi'ɣeo] *nm* (*comezón*) itch

hormona [or'mona] *nf* hormone

hornada [or'naða] *nf* batch (of loaves *etc*)

hornillo [or'niʎo] *nm* (*cocina*) portable stove

horno ['orno] *nm* (CULIN) oven; (TEC) furnace; **alto ~** blast furnace

horóscopo [o'roskopo] *nm* horoscope

horquilla [or'kiʎa] *nf* hairpin; (AGR) pitchfork

horrendo, a [o'rrendo, a] *adj* horrendous, frightful

horrible [o'rriβle] *adj* horrible, dreadful

horripilante [orripi'lante] *adj* hair-raising, horrifying

horror [o'rror] *nm* horror, dread; (*atrocidad*) atrocity; **¡qué ~!** (*fam*) how awful!; **~izar** *vt* to horrify, frighten; **~izarse** *vr* to be horrified; **~oso, a** *adj* horrifying, ghastly

hortaliza [orta'liθa] *nf* vegetable

hortelano, a [orte'lano, a] *nm/f* (market) gardener

hortera [or'tera] (*fam*) *adj* tacky

hosco, a ['osko, a] *adj* sullen, gloomy

hospedar [ospe'ðar] *vt* to put up; **~se** *vr* to stay, lodge

hospital [ospi'tal] *nm* hospital

hospitalario, a [ospita'larjo, a] *adj* (*acogedor*) hospitable; **hospitalidad** *nf* hospitality

hostal [os'tal] *nm* small hotel

hostelería [ostele'ria] *nf* hotel business *o* trade

hostia ['ostja] *nf* (REL) host, consecrated wafer; (*fam!: golpe*) whack, punch ♦ *excl* (*fam!*): **¡~(s)!** damn!

hostigar [osti'ɣar] *vt* to whip; (*fig*) to harass, pester

hostil [os'til] *adj* hostile; **~idad** *nf* hostility

hotel [o'tel] *nm* hotel; **~ero, a** *adj* hotel *cpd* ♦ *nm/f* hotelier

---
hotel

ⓘ *In Spain you can choose from the following categories of accommodation, in descending order of quality and price:*

hotel *(from 5 stars to 1),* **hostal, pensión, casa de huéspedes, fonda.** *The State also runs luxury hotels called* **paradores,** *which are usually sited in places of particular historical interest and are often historic buildings themselves.*

---

hoy [oi] *adv* (*este día*) today; (*la actualidad*) now(adays) ♦ *nm* present time; **~ (en) día** now(adays)

hoyo ['ojo] *nm* hole, pit; **hoyuelo** *nm* dimple

hoz [oθ] *nf* sickle

hube *etc vb ver* **haber**

hucha ['utʃa] *nf* money box

hueco, a ['weko, a] *adj* (*vacío*) hollow, empty; (*resonante*) booming ♦ *nm* hollow, cavity

huelga *etc vb ver* **holgar** ♦ *nf* strike; **declararse en ~** to go on strike, come out on strike; **~ de hambre** hunger strike

huelguista [wel'ɣista] *nm/f* striker

huella ['weʎa] *nf* (*pisada*) tread; (*marca del paso*) footprint, footstep; (: *de animal, máquina*) track; **~ digital** fingerprint

huelo *etc vb ver* **oler**

huérfano, a ['werfano, a] *adj* orphan(ed) ♦ *nm/f* orphan

huerta ['werta] *nf* market garden; (*en Murcia y Valencia*) irrigated region

huerto ['werto] *nm* kitchen garden; (*de árboles frutales*) orchard

hueso ['weso] *nm* (ANAT) bone; (*de fruta*) stone

huésped, a ['wespeð, a] *nm/f* guest

huesudo, a [we'suðo, a] *adj* bony, big-boned

hueva ['weβa] *nf* roe

huevera [we'βera] *nf* eggcup

huevo ['weβo] *nm* egg; **~ duro/ escalfado/frito** (ESP) *o* **estrellado** (AM)/ **pasado por agua** hard-boiled/poached/ fried/soft-boiled egg; **~s revueltos** scrambled eggs

huida [u'iða] *nf* escape, flight

huidizo, a [ui'ðiθo, a] *adj* shy

huir [u'ir] *vi (escapar)* to flee, escape; *(evitar)* to avoid; **~se** *vr (escaparse)* to escape
hule ['ule] *nm* oilskin
humanidad [umani'ðað] *nf (género humano)* man(kind); *(cualidad)* humanity
humanitario, a [umani'tarjo, a] *adj* humanitarian
humano, a [u'mano, a] *adj (gen)* human; *(humanitario)* humane ♦ *nm* human; **ser ~** human being
humareda [uma'reða] *nf* cloud of smoke
humedad [ume'ðað] *nf (del clima)* humidity; *(de pared etc)* dampness; **a prueba de ~** damp-proof; **humedecer** *vt* to moisten, wet; **humedecerse** *vr* to get wet
húmedo, a ['umeðo, a] *adj (mojado)* damp, wet; *(tiempo etc)* humid
humildad [umil'dað] *nf* humility, humbleness; **humilde** *adj* humble, modest
humillación [umiʎa'θjon] *nf* humiliation; **humillante** *adj* humiliating
humillar [umi'ʎar] *vt* to humiliate; **~se** *vr* to humble o.s., grovel
humo ['umo] *nm (de fuego)* smoke; *(gas nocivo)* fumes *pl*; *(vapor)* steam, vapour; **~s** *nmpl (fig)* conceit *sg*
humor [u'mor] *nm (disposición)* mood, temper; *(lo que divierte)* humour; **de buen/mal ~** in a good/bad mood; **~ista** *nm/f* comic; **~ístico, a** *adj* funny, humorous
hundimiento [undi'mjento] *nm (gen)* sinking; *(colapso)* collapse
hundir [un'dir] *vt* to sink; *(edificio, plan)* to ruin, destroy; **~se** *vr* to sink, collapse
húngaro, a ['ungaro, a] *adj, nm/f* Hungarian
Hungría [un'gria] *nf* Hungary
huracán [ura'kan] *nm* hurricane
huraño, a [u'raɲo, a] *adj (antisocial)* unsociable
hurgar [ur'xar] *vt* to poke, jab; *(remover)* to stir (up); **~se** *vr*: **~se (las narices)** to pick one's nose

hurón, ona [u'ron, ona] *nm (ZOOL)* ferret
hurtadillas [urta'ðiʎas]: **a ~** *adv* stealthily, on the sly
hurtar [ur'tar] *vt* to steal; **hurto** *nm* theft, stealing
husmear [usme'ar] *vt (oler)* to sniff out, scent; *(fam)* to pry into
huyo *etc vb ver* **huir**

I, i

iba *etc vb ver* **ir**
ibérico, a [i'ßeriko, a] *adj* Iberian
iberoamericano, a [ißeroameri'kano, a] *adj, nm/f* Latin American
Ibiza [i'ßiθa] *nf* Ibiza
iceberg [iðe'ßer] *nm* iceberg
icono [i'kono] *nm* ikon, icon
iconoclasta [ikono'klasta] *adj* iconoclastic ♦ *nm/f* iconoclast
ictericia [ikte'riθja] *nf* jaundice
I + D *abr* (= *Investigación y Desarrollo*) R & D
ida ['iða] *nf* going, departure; **~ y vuelta** round trip, return
idea [i'ðea] *nf* idea; **no tengo la menor ~** I haven't a clue
ideal [iðe'al] *adj, nm* ideal; **~ista** *nm/f* idealist; **~izar** *vt* to idealize
idear [iðe'ar] *vt* to think up; *(aparato)* to invent; *(viaje)* to plan
ídem ['iðem] *pron* ditto
idéntico, a [i'ðentiko, a] *adj* identical
identidad [iðenti'ðað] *nf* identity
identificación [iðentifika'θjon] *nf* identification
identificar [iðentifi'kar] *vt* to identify; **~se** *vr*: **~se con** to identify with
ideología [iðeolo'xia] *nf* ideology
idilio [i'ðiljo] *nm* love-affair
idioma [i'ðjoma] *nm (gen)* language
idiota [i'ðjota] *adj* idiotic ♦ *nm/f* idiot; **idiotez** *nf* idiocy
ídolo ['iðolo] *nm (tb fig)* idol
idóneo, a [i'ðoneo, a] *adj* suitable
iglesia [i'xlesja] *nf* church

ignorancia [ixno'ranθja] *nf* ignorance;
  ignorante *adj* ignorant, uninformed
  ♦ *nm/f* ignoramus
ignorar [ixno'rar] *vt* not to know, be
  ignorant of; (*no hacer caso a*) to ignore
igual [i'ɣwal] *adj* (*gen*) equal; (*similar*) like,
  similar; (*mismo*) (the) same; (*constante*)
  constant; (*temperatura*) even ♦ *nm/f*
  equal; **~ que** like, the same as; **me da** *o*
  es ~ I don't care; **son ~es** they're the
  same; **al ~ que** *prep, conj* like, just like
igualada [iɣwa'laða] *nf* equaliser
igualar [iɣwa'lar] *vt* (*gen*) to equalize,
  make equal; (*allanar, nivelar*) to level (off),
  even (out); **~se** *vr* (*platos de balanza*) to
  balance out
igualdad [iɣwal'daθ] *nf* equality;
  (*similaridad*) sameness; (*uniformidad*)
  uniformity
igualmente [iɣwal'mente] *adv* equally;
  (*también*) also, likewise ♦ *excl* the same
  to you!
ikurriña [iku'rriɲa] *nf* Basque flag
ilegal [ile'ɣal] *adj* illegal
ilegítimo, a [ile'xitimo, a] *adj* illegitimate
ileso, a [i'leso, a] *adj* unhurt
ilícito, a [i'liθito] *adj* illicit
ilimitado, a [ilimi'taðo, a] *adj* unlimited
ilógico, a [i'loxiko, a] *adj* illogical
iluminación [ilumina'θjon] *nf*
  illumination; (*alumbrado*) lighting
iluminar [ilumi'nar] *vt* to illuminate, light
  (up); (*fig*) to enlighten
ilusión [ilu'sjon] *nf* illusion; (*quimera*)
  delusion; (*esperanza*) hope; **hacerse**
  ilusiones to build up one's hopes;
  ilusionado, a *adj* excited; **ilusionar**
  vi: **le ilusiona ir de vacaciones** he's
  looking forward to going on holiday;
  ilusionarse *vr*: **ilusionarse (con)** to get
  excited (about)
ilusionista [ilusjo'nista] *nm/f* conjurer
iluso, a [i'luso, a] *adj* easily deceived
  ♦ *nm/f* dreamer
ilusorio, a [ilu'sorjo, a] *adj* (*de ilusión*)
  illusory, deceptive; (*esperanza*) vain
ilustración [ilustra'θjon] *nf* illustration;

(*saber*) learning, erudition; **la l~** the
  Enlightenment; **ilustrado, a** *adj*
  illustrated; learned
ilustrar [ilus'trar] *vt* to illustrate; (*instruir*)
  to instruct; (*explicar*) to explain, make
  clear; **~se** *vr* to acquire knowledge
ilustre [i'lustre] *adj* famous, illustrious
imagen [i'maxen] *nf* (*gen*) image; (*dibujo*)
  picture
imaginación [imaxina'θjon] *nf*
  imagination
imaginar [imaxi'nar] *vt* (*gen*) to imagine;
  (*idear*) to think up; (*suponer*) to suppose;
  ~se *vr* to imagine; **~io, a** *adj* imaginary;
  imaginativo, a *adj* imaginative
imán [i'man] *nm* magnet
imbécil [im'beθil] *nm/f* imbecile, idiot
imitación [imita'θjon] *nf* imitation
imitar [imi'tar] *vt* to imitate; (*parodiar,*
  remedar) to mimic, ape
impaciencia [impa'θjenθja] *nf*
  impatience; **impaciente** *adj* impatient;
  (*nervioso*) anxious
impacto [im'pakto] *nm* impact
impar [im'par] *adj* odd
imparcial [impar'θjal] *adj* impartial, fair
impartir [impar'tir] *vt* to impart, give
impasible [impa'siβle] *adj* impassive
impecable [impe'kaβle] *adj* impeccable
impedimento [impeði'mento] *nm*
  impediment, obstacle
impedir [impe'ðir] *vt* (*obstruir*) to impede,
  obstruct; (*estorbar*) to prevent
impenetrable [impene'traβle] *adj*
  impenetrable; (*fig*) incomprehensible
imperar [impe'rar] *vi* (*reinar*) to rule,
  reign; (*fig*) to prevail, reign; (*precio*) to be
  current
imperativo, a [impera'tiβo, a] *adj*
  (*urgente, LING*) imperative
imperceptible [imperθep'tiβle] *adj*
  imperceptible
imperdible [imper'ðiβle] *nm* safety pin
imperdonable [imperðo'naβle] *adj*
  unforgivable, inexcusable
imperfección [imperfek'θjon] *nf*
  imperfection

imperfecto, a [imper'fekto, a] *adj*
imperfect

imperial [impe'rjal] *adj* imperial; **~ismo**
nm imperialism

imperio [im'perjo] *nm* empire; (*autoridad*)
rule, authority; (*fig*) pride, haughtiness;
~so, a *adj* imperious; (*urgente*) urgent;
(*imperativo*) imperative

impermeable [imperme'aßle] *adj*
waterproof ♦ *nm* raincoat, mac (*BRIT*)

impersonal [imperso'nal] *adj* impersonal

impertinencia [imperti'nenθja] *nf*
impertinence; **impertinente** *adj*
impertinent

imperturbable [impertur'ßaßle] *adj*
imperturbable

ímpetu ['impetu] *nm* (*impulso*) impetus,
impulse; (*impetuosidad*) impetuosity;
(*violencia*) violence

impetuoso, a [impe'twoso, a] *adj*
impetuous; (*río*) rushing; (*acto*) hasty

impío, a [im'pio, a] *adj* impious, ungodly

implacable [impla'kaßle] *adj* implacable

implantar [implan'tar] *vt* to introduce

implicar [impli'kar] *vt* to involve;
(*entrañar*) to imply

implícito, a [im'pliθito, a] *adj* (*tácito*)
implicit; (*sobreentendido*) implied

implorar [implo'rar] *vt* to beg, implore

imponente [impo'nente] *adj*
(*impresionante*) impressive, imposing;
(*solemne*) grand

imponer [impo'ner] *vt* (*gen*) to impose;
(*exigir*) to exact; **~se** *vr* to assert o.s.;
(*prevalecer*) to prevail; **imponible** *adj*
(*COM*) taxable

impopular [impopu'lar] *adj* unpopular

importación [importa'θjon] *nf* (*acto*)
importing; (*mercancías*) imports *pl*

importancia [impor'tanθja] *nf*
importance; (*valor*) value, significance;
(*extensión*) size, magnitude; **importante**
adj important; valuable, significant

importar [impor'tar] *vt* (*del extranjero*) to
import; (*costar*) to amount to ♦ *vi* to be
important, matter; **me importa un
rábano** I couldn't care less; **no importa** it

doesn't matter; **¿le importa que fume?**
do you mind if I smoke?

importe [im'porte] *nm* (*total*) amount;
(*valor*) value

importunar [importu'nar] *vt* to bother,
pester

imposibilidad [imposißili'ðað] *nf*
impossibility; **imposibilitar** *vt* to make
impossible, prevent

imposible [impo'sißle] *adj* (*gen*)
impossible; (*insoportable*) unbearable,
intolerable

imposición [imposi'θjon] *nf* imposition;
(*COM: impuesto*) tax; (*: inversión*) deposit

impostor, a [impos'tor, a] *nm/f* impostor

impotencia [impo'tenθja] *nf* impotence;
impotente *adj* impotent

impracticable [imprakti'kaßle] *adj*
(*irrealizable*) impracticable; (*intransitable*)
impassable

impreciso, a [impre'θiso, a] *adj*
imprecise, vague

impregnar [impreɣ'nar] *vt* to impregnate;
~se *vr* to become impregnated

imprenta [im'prenta] *nf* (*acto*) printing;
(*aparato*) press; (*casa*) printer's; (*letra*)
print

imprescindible [impresθin'dißle] *adj*
essential, vital

impresión [impre'sjon] *nf* (*gen*)
impression; (*IMPRENTA*) printing; (*edición*)
edition; (*FOTO*) print; (*marca*) imprint; **~
digital** fingerprint

impresionable [impresjo'naßle] *adj*
(*sensible*) impressionable

impresionante [impresjo'nante] *adj*
impressive; (*tremendo*) tremendous;
(*maravilloso*) great, marvellous

impresionar [impresjo'nar] *vt* (*conmover*)
to move; (*afectar*) to impress, strike;
(*película fotográfica*) to expose; **~se** *vr* to
be impressed; (*conmoverse*) to be moved

impreso, a [im'preso, a] *pp de* **imprimir**
♦ *adj* printed; **~s** *nmpl* printed matter;
impresora *nf* printer

imprevisto, a [impre'ßisto, a] *adj* (*gen*)
unforeseen; (*inesperado*) unexpected

imprimir [impri'mir] *vt* to imprint, impress, stamp; *(textos)* to print; *(INFORM)* to output, print out

improbable [impro'ßaßle] *adj* improbable; *(inverosímil)* unlikely

improcedente [improθe'ðente] *adj* inappropriate

improductivo, a [improðuk'tißo, a] *adj* unproductive

improperio [impro'perjo] *nm* insult

impropio, a [im'propjo, a] *adj* improper

improvisado, a [improßi'saðo, a] *adj* improvised

improvisar [improßi'sar] *vt* to improvise

improviso, a [impro'ßiso, a] *adj*: **de ~** unexpectedly, suddenly

imprudencia [impru'ðenθja] *nf* imprudence; *(indiscreción)* indiscretion; *(descuido)* carelessness; **imprudente** *adj* unwise, imprudent; *(indiscreto)* indiscreet

impúdico, a [im'puðiko, a] *adj* shameless; *(lujurioso)* lecherous

impuesto, a [im'pwesto, a] *adj* imposed ♦ *nm* tax; **~ sobre el valor añadido** value added tax

impugnar [impuɣ'nar] *vt* to oppose, contest; *(refutar)* to refute, impugn

impulsar [impul'sar] *vt* to drive; *(promover)* to promote, stimulate

impulsivo, a [impul'sißo, a] *adj* impulsive; **impulso** *nm* impulse; *(fuerza, empuje)* thrust, drive; *(fig: sentimiento)* urge, impulse

impune [im'pune] *adj* unpunished

impureza [impu'reθa] *nf* impurity; **impuro, a** *adj* impure

imputar [impu'tar] *vt* to attribute

inacabable [inaka'ßaßle] *adj* *(infinito)* endless; *(interminable)* interminable

inaccesible [inakθe'sißle] *adj* inaccessible

inacción [inak'θjon] *nf* inactivity

inaceptable [inaθep'taßle] *adj* unacceptable

inactividad [inaktißi'ðað] *nf* inactivity; *(COM)* dullness; **inactivo, a** *adj* inactive

inadecuado, a [inaðe'kwaðo, a] *adj* *(insuficiente)* inadequate; *(inapto)* unsuitable

inadmisible [inaðmi'sißle] *adj* inadmissible

inadvertido, a [inaðßer'tiðo, a] *adj* *(no visto)* unnoticed

inagotable [inaɣo'taßle] *adj* inexhaustible

inaguantable [inaɣwan'taßle] *adj* unbearable

inalterable [inalte'raßle] *adj* immutable, unchangeable

inanición [inani'θjon] *nf* starvation

inanimado, a [inani'maðo, a] *adj* inanimate

inapreciable [inapre'θjaßle] *adj* *(cantidad, diferencia)* imperceptible; *(ayuda, servicio)* invaluable

inaudito, a [inau'ðito, a] *adj* unheard-of

inauguración [inauɣura'θjon] *nf* inauguration; opening

inaugurar [inauɣu'rar] *vt* to inaugurate; *(exposición)* to open

inca ['inka] *nm/f* Inca

incalculable [inkalku'laßle] *adj* incalculable

incandescente [inkandes'θente] *adj* incandescent

incansable [inkan'saßle] *adj* tireless, untiring

incapacidad [inkapaθi'ðað] *nf* incapacity; *(incompetencia)* incompetence; **~ física/mental** physical/mental disability

incapacitar [inkapaθi'tar] *vt* *(inhabilitar)* to incapacitate, render unfit; *(descalificar)* to disqualify

incapaz [inka'paθ] *adj* incapable

incautación [inkauta'θjon] *nf* confiscation

incautarse [inkau'tarse] *vr*: **~ de** to seize, confiscate

incauto, a [in'kauto, a] *adj* *(imprudente)* incautious, unwary

incendiar [inθen'djar] *vt* to set fire to; *(fig)* to inflame; **~se** *vr* to catch fire; **~io, a** *adj* incendiary

incendio [in'θendjo] *nm* fire

incentivo [inθen'tißo] *nm* incentive

incertidumbre [inθerti'ðumbre] *nf* *(inseguridad)* uncertainty; *(duda)* doubt

incesante [inθe'sante] *adj* incessant

incesto [in'θesto] *nm* incest

incidencia [inθi'ðenθja] *nf* (*MAT*) incidence

incidente [inθi'ðente] *nm* incident

incidir [inθi'ðir] *vi* (*influir*) to influence; (*afectar*) to affect; **~ en un error** to fall into error

incienso [in'θjenso] *nm* incense

incierto, a [in'θjerto, a] *adj* uncertain

incineración [inθinera'θjon] *nf* incineration; (*de cadáveres*) cremation

incinerar [inθine'rar] *vt* to burn; (*cadáveres*) to cremate

incipiente [inθi'pjente] *adj* incipient

incisión [inθi'sjon] *nf* incision

incisivo, a [inθi'siβo, a] *adj* sharp, cutting; (*fig*) incisive

incitar [inθi'tar] *vt* to incite, rouse

inclemencia [inkle'menθja] *nf* (*severidad*) harshness, severity; (*del tiempo*) inclemency

inclinación [inklina'θjon] *nf* (*gen*) inclination; (*de tierras*) slope, incline; (*de cabeza*) nod, bow; (*fig*) leaning, bent

inclinar [inkli'nar] *vt* to incline; (*cabeza*) to nod, bow ♦ *vi* to lean, slope; **~se** *vr* to bow; (*encorvarse*) to stoop; **~se a** (*parecerse a*) to take after, resemble; **~se ante** to bow down to; **me inclino a pensar que** I'm inclined to think that

incluir [inklu'ir] *vt* to include; (*incorporar*) to incorporate; (*meter*) to enclose

inclusive [inklu'siβe] *adv* inclusive ♦ *prep* including

incluso [in'kluso] *adv* even

incógnita [in'koɣnita] *nf* (*MAT*) unknown quantity

incógnito [in'koɣnito] *nm*: **de ~** incognito

incoherente [inkoe'rente] *adj* incoherent

incoloro, a [inko'loro, a] *adj* colourless

incólume [in'kolume] *adj* unhurt, unharmed

incomodar [inkomo'ðar] *vt* to inconvenience; (*molestar*) to bother, trouble; (*fastidiar*) to annoy; **~se** *vr* to put o.s. out; (*fastidiarse*) to get annoyed

incomodidad [inkomoði'ðað] *nf* inconvenience; (*fastidio, enojo*) annoyance; (*de vivienda*) discomfort

incómodo, a [in'komoðo, a] *adj* (*inconfortable*) uncomfortable; (*molesto*) annoying; (*inconveniente*) inconvenient

incomparable [inkompa'raβle] *adj* incomparable

incompatible [inkompa'tiβle] *adj* incompatible

incompetencia [inkompe'tenθja] *nf* incompetence; **incompetente** *adj* incompetent

incompleto, a [inkom'pleto, a] *adj* incomplete, unfinished

incomprensible [inkompren'siβle] *adj* incomprehensible

incomunicado, a [inkomuni'kaðo, a] *adj* (*aislado*) cut off, isolated; (*confinado*) in solitary confinement

inconcebible [inkonθe'βiβle] *adj* inconceivable

incondicional [inkondiθjo'nal] *adj* unconditional; (*apoyo*) wholehearted; (*partidario*) staunch

inconexo, a [inko'nekso, a] *adj* (*gen*) unconnected; (*desunido*) disconnected

inconfundible [inkonfun'diβle] *adj* unmistakable

incongruente [inkon'ɣrwente] *adj* incongruous

inconsciencia [inkons'θjenθja] *nf* unconsciousness; (*fig*) thoughtlessness; **inconsciente** *adj* unconscious; thoughtless

inconsecuente [inkonse'kwente] *adj* inconsistent

inconsiderado, a [inkonsiðe'raðo, a] *adj* inconsiderate

inconsistente [inkonsis'tente] *adj* weak; (*tela*) flimsy

inconstancia [inkon'stanθja] *nf* inconstancy; (*inestabilidad*) unsteadiness; **inconstante** *adj* inconstant

incontable [inkon'taβle] *adj* countless, innumerable

incontestable [inkontes'taβle] *adj*

unanswerable; (*innegable*) undeniable

incontinencia [inkonti'nenθja] *nf*
incontinence

inconveniencia [inkombe'njenθja] *nf*
unsuitability, inappropriateness;
(*descortesía*) impoliteness;
inconveniente *adj* unsuitable; impolite
♦ *nm* obstacle; (*desventaja*) disadvantage;
el inconveniente es que ... the trouble
is that ...

incordiar [inkor'ðjar] (*fam*) *vt* to bug,
annoy

incorporación [inkorpora'θjon] *nf*
incorporation

incorporar [inkorpo'rar] *vt* to incorporate;
~se *vr* to sit up

incorrección [inkorrek'θjon] *nf* (*gen*)
incorrectness, inaccuracy; (*descortesía*)
bad-mannered behaviour; **incorrecto, a**
adj (*gen*) incorrect, wrong;
(*comportamiento*) bad-mannered

incorregible [inkorre'xiβle] *adj*
incorrigible

incredulidad [inkreðuli'ðað] *nf*
incredulity; (*escepticismo*) scepticism;
incrédulo, a *adj* incredulous,
unbelieving, sceptical

increíble [inkre'iβle] *adj* incredible

incremento [inkre'mento] *nm* increment;
(*aumento*) rise, increase

increpar [inkre'par] *vt* to reprimand

incruento, a [in'krwento, a] *adj* bloodless

incrustar [inkrus'tar] *vt* to incrust;
(*piedras: en joya*) to inlay

incubar [inku'βar] *vt* to incubate

inculcar [inkul'kar] *vt* to inculcate

inculpar [inkul'par] *vt* (*acusar*) to accuse;
(*achacar, atribuir*) to charge, blame

inculto, a [in'kulto, a] *adj* (*persona*)
uneducated; (*grosero*) uncouth ♦ *nm/f*
ignoramus

incumplimiento [inkumpli'mjento] *nm*
non-fulfilment; **~ de contrato** breach of
contract

incurrir [inku'rrir] *vi*: **~ en** to incur;
(*crimen*) to commit; **~ en un error** to
make a mistake

indagación [indaɣa'θjon] *nf* investigation;
(*búsqueda*) search; (*JUR*) inquest

indagar [inda'ɣar] *vt* to investigate; to
search; (*averiguar*) to ascertain

indecente [inde'θente] *adj* indecent,
improper; (*lascivo*) obscene

indecible [inde'θiβle] *adj* unspeakable;
(*indescriptible*) indescribable

indeciso, a [inde'θiso, a] *adj* (*por decidir*)
undecided; (*vacilante*) hesitant

indefenso, a [inde'fenso, a] *adj*
defenceless

indefinido, a [indefi'niðo, a] *adj*
indefinite; (*vago*) vague, undefined

indeleble [inde'leβle] *adj* indelible

indemne [in'demne] *adj* (*objeto*)
undamaged; (*persona*) unharmed, unhurt

indemnizar [indemni'θar] *vt* to indemnify;
(*compensar*) to compensate

independencia [indepen'denθja] *nf*
independence

independiente [indepen'djente] *adj*
(*libre*) independent; (*autónomo*) self-
sufficient

indeterminado, a [indetermi'naðo, a] *adj*
indefinite; (*desconocido*) indeterminate

India ['indja] *nf*: **la ~** India

indicación [indika'θjon] *nf* indication;
(*señal*) sign; (*sugerencia*) suggestion, hint

indicado, a [indi'kaðo, a] *adj* (*momento,
método*) right; (*tratamiento*) appropriate;
(*solución*) likely

indicador [indika'ðor] *nm* indicator; (*TEC*)
gauge, meter

indicar [indi'kar] *vt* (*mostrar*) to indicate,
show; (*termómetro etc*) to read, register;
(*señalar*) to point to

índice ['indiθe] *nm* index; (*catálogo*)
catalogue; (*ANAT*) index finger, forefinger

indicio [in'diθjo] *nm* indication, sign; (*en
pesquisa etc*) clue

indiferencia [indife'renθja] *nf*
indifference; (*apatía*) apathy;
indiferente *adj* indifferent

indígena [in'dixena] *adj* indigenous,
native ♦ *nm/f* native

indigencia [indi'xenθja] *nf* poverty, need

indigestión [indixes'tjon] *nf* indigestion

indigesto, a [indi'xesto, a] *adj (alimento)* indigestible; *(fig)* turgid

indignación [indiɣna'θjon] *nf* indignation

indignar [indiɣ'nar] *vt* to anger, make indignant; **~se** *vr*: **~se por** to get indignant about

indigno, a [in'diɣno, a] *adj (despreciable)* low, contemptible; *(inmerecido)* unworthy

indio, a ['indjo, a] *adj, nm/f* Indian

indirecta [indi'rekta] *nf* insinuation, innuendo; *(sugerencia)* hint

indirecto, a [indi'rekto, a] *adj* indirect

indiscreción [indiskre'θjon] *nf (imprudencia)* indiscretion; *(irreflexión)* tactlessness; *(acto)* gaffe, faux pas

indiscreto, a [indis'kreto, a] *adj* indiscreet

indiscriminado, a [indiskrimi'naðo, a] *adj* indiscriminate

indiscutible [indisku'tiβle] *adj* indisputable, unquestionable

indispensable [indispen'saβle] *adj* indispensable, essential

indisponer [indispo'ner] *vt* to spoil, upset; *(salud)* to make ill; **~se** *vr* to fall ill; **~se con uno** to fall out with sb

indisposición [indisposi'θjon] *nf* indisposition

indispuesto, a [indis'pwesto, a] *adj (enfermo)* unwell, indisposed

indistinto, a [indis'tinto, a] *adj* indistinct; *(vago)* vague

individual [indiβi'ðwal] *adj* individual; *(habitación)* single ♦ *nm (DEPORTE)* singles *sg*

individuo, a [indi'βiðwo, a] *adj, nm* individual

índole ['indole] *nf (naturaleza)* nature; *(clase)* sort, kind

indómito, a [in'domito, a] *adj* indomitable

inducir [indu'θir] *vt* to induce; *(inferir)* to infer; *(persuadir)* to persuade

indudable [indu'ðaβle] *adj* undoubted; *(incuestionable)* unquestionable

indulgencia [indul'xenθja] *nf* indulgence

indultar [indul'tar] *vt (perdonar)* to

pardon, reprieve; *(librar de pago)* to exempt; **indulto** *nm* pardon; exemption

industria [in'dustrja] *nf* industry; *(habilidad)* skill; **industrial** *adj* industrial ♦ *nm* industrialist

inédito, a [in'eðito, a] *adj (texto)* unpublished; *(nuevo)* new

inefable [ine'faβle] *adj* ineffable, indescribable

ineficaz [inefi'kaθ] *adj (inútil)* ineffective; *(ineficiente)* inefficient

ineludible [inelu'ðiβle] *adj* inescapable, unavoidable

ineptitud [inepti'tuð] *nf* ineptitude, incompetence; **inepto, a** *adj* inept, incompetent

inequívoco, a [ine'kiβoko, a] *adj* unequivocal; *(inconfundible)* unmistakable

inercia [in'erθja] *nf* inertia; *(pasividad)* passivity

inerme [in'erme] *adj (sin armas)* unarmed; *(indefenso)* defenceless

inerte [in'erte] *adj* inert; *(inmóvil)* motionless

inesperado, a [inespe'raðo, a] *adj* unexpected, unforeseen

inestable [ines'taβle] *adj* unstable

inevitable [ineβi'taβle] *adj* inevitable

inexactitud [ineksakti'tuð] *nf* inaccuracy; **inexacto, a** *adj* inaccurate; *(falso)* untrue

inexperto, a [inek'sperto, a] *adj (novato)* inexperienced

infalible [infa'liβle] *adj* infallible; *(plan)* foolproof

infame [in'fame] *adj* infamous; *(horrible)* dreadful; **infamia** *nf* infamy; *(deshonra)* disgrace

infancia [in'fanθja] *nf* infancy, childhood

infantería [infante'ria] *nf* infantry

infantil [infan'til] *adj (pueril, aniñado)* infantile; *(cándido)* childlike; *(literatura, ropa etc)* children's

infarto [in'farto] *nm (tb: ~ de miocardio)* heart attack

infatigable [infati'βaβle] *adj* tireless, untiring

infección [infek'θjon] *nf* infection;
  infeccioso, a *adj* infectious
infectar [infek'tar] *vt* to infect; **~se** *vr* to
  become infected
infeliz [infe'liθ] *adj* unhappy, wretched
  ♦ *nm/f* wretch
inferior [infe'rjor] *adj* inferior; (*situación*)
  lower ♦ *nm/f* inferior, subordinate
inferir [infe'rir] *vt* (*deducir*) to infer,
  deduce; (*causar*) to cause
infestar [infes'tar] *vt* to infest
infidelidad [infiðeli'ðað] *nf* (*gen*)
  infidelity, unfaithfulness
infiel [in'fjel] *adj* unfaithful, disloyal;
  (*erróneo*) inaccurate ♦ *nm/f* infidel,
  unbeliever
infierno [in'fjerno] *nm* hell
infiltrarse [infil'trarse] *vr*: **~ en** to infiltrate
  in(to); (*persona*) to work one's way in(to)
ínfimo, a ['infimo, a] *adj* (*más bajo*)
  lowest; (*despreciable*) vile, mean
infinidad [infini'ðað] *nf* infinity;
  (*abundancia*) great quantity
infinito, a [infi'nito, a] *adj, nm* infinite
inflación [infla'θjon] *nf* (*hinchazón*)
  swelling; (*monetaria*) inflation; (*fig*)
  conceit; **inflacionario, a** *adj* inflationary
inflamar [infla'mar] *vt* (*MED, fig*) to
  inflame; **~se** *vr* to catch fire; to become
  inflamed
inflar [in'flar] *vt* (*hinchar*) to inflate, blow
  up; (*fig*) to exaggerate; **~se** *vr* to swell
  (up); (*fig*) to get conceited
inflexible [inflek'siβle] *adj* inflexible; (*fig*)
  unbending
infligir [infli'xir] *vt* to inflict
influencia [influ'enθja] *nf* influence;
  influenciar *vt* to influence
influir [influ'ir] *vt* to influence
influjo [in'fluxo] *nm* influence
influya *etc vb ver* **influir**
influyente [influ'jente] *adj* influential
información [informa'θjon] *nf*
  information; (*noticias*) news *sg*; (*JUR*)
  inquiry; **I~** (*oficina*) Information Office;
  (*mostrador*) Information Desk; (*TEL*)
  Directory Enquiries

informal [infor'mal] *adj* (*gen*) informal
informar [infor'mar] *vt* (*gen*) to inform;
  (*revelar*) to reveal, make known ♦ *vi* (*JUR*)
  to plead; (*denunciar*) to inform; (*dar
  cuenta de*) to report on; **~se** *vr* to find
  out; **~se de** to inquire into
informática [infor'matika] *nf* computer
  science, information technology
informe [in'forme] *adj* shapeless ♦ *nm*
  report
infortunio [infor'tunjo] *nm* misfortune
infracción [infrak'θjon] *nf* infraction,
  infringement
infranqueable [infranke'aβle] *adj*
  impassable; (*fig*) insurmountable
infravalorar [infrabalo'rar] *vt* to
  undervalue, underestimate
infringir [infrin'xir] *vt* to infringe,
  contravene
infructuoso, a [infruk'twoso, a] *adj*
  fruitless, unsuccessful
infundado, a [infun'daðo, a] *adj*
  groundless, unfounded
infundir [infun'dir] *vt* to infuse, instil
infusión [infu'sjon] *nf* infusion; **~ de
  manzanilla** camomile tea
ingeniar [inxe'njar] *vt* to think up, devise;
  ~se *vr*: **~se para** to manage to
ingeniería [inxenje'ria] *nf* engineering; **~
  genética** genetic engineering;
  ingeniero, a *nm/f* engineer; **ingeniero
  de caminos/de sonido** civil engineer/
  sound engineer
ingenio [in'xenjo] *nm* (*talento*) talent;
  (*agudeza*) wit; (*habilidad*) ingenuity,
  inventiveness; **~ azucarero** (*AM*) sugar
  refinery
ingenioso, a [inxe'njoso, a] *adj*
  ingenious, clever; (*divertido*) witty
ingenuidad [inxenwi'ðað] *nf*
  ingenuousness; (*sencillez*) simplicity;
  ingenuo, a *adj* ingenuous
ingerir [inxe'rir] *vt* to ingest; (*tragar*) to
  swallow; (*consumir*) to consume
Inglaterra [ingla'terra] *nf* England
ingle ['ingle] *nf* groin
inglés, esa [in'gles, esa] *adj* English

♦ *nm/f* Englishman/woman ♦ *nm* (*LING*) English

ingratitud [ingrati'tuð] *nf* ingratitude; **ingrato, a** *adj* (*gen*) ungrateful

ingrediente [ingre'ðjente] *nm* ingredient

ingresar [ingre'sar] *vt* (*dinero*) to deposit ♦ *vi* to come in; ~ **en un club** to join a club; ~ **en el hospital** to go into hospital

ingreso [in'greso] *nm* (*entrada*) entry; (: *en hospital etc*) admission; ~**s** *nmpl* (*dinero*) income *sg*; (: *COM*) takings *pl*

inhabitable [inaβi'taβle] *adj* uninhabitable

inhalar [ina'lar] *vt* to inhale

inherente [ine'rente] *adj* inherent

inhibir [ini'βir] *vt* to inhibit

inhóspito, a [i'nospito, a] *adj* (*región, paisaje*) inhospitable

inhumano, a [inu'mano, a] *adj* inhuman

inicial [ini'θjal] *adj, nf* initial

iniciar [ini'θjar] *vt* (*persona*) to initiate; (*empezar*) to begin, commence; (*conversación*) to start up

iniciativa [iniθja'tiβa] *nf* initiative; **la ~ privada** private enterprise

ininterrumpido, a [ininterrum'piðo, a] *adj* uninterrupted

injerencia [inxe'renθja] *nf* interference

injertar [inxer'tar] *vt* to graft; **injerto** *nm* graft

injuria [in'xurja] *nf* (*agravio, ofensa*) offence; (*insulto*) insult; **injuriar** *vt* to insult; **injurioso, a** *adj* offensive; insulting

injusticia [inxus'tiθja] *nf* injustice

injusto, a [in'xusto, a] *adj* unjust, unfair

inmadurez [inmaðu'reθ] *nf* immaturity

inmediaciones [inmeðja'θjones] *nfpl* neighbourhood *sg*, environs

inmediato, a [inme'ðjato, a] *adj* immediate; (*contiguo*) adjoining; (*rápido*) prompt; (*próximo*) neighbouring, next; **de ~** immediately

inmejorable [inmexo'raβle] *adj* unsurpassable; (*precio*) unbeatable

inmenso, a [in'menso, a] *adj* immense, huge

inmerecido, a [inmere'θiðo, a] *adj* undeserved

inmigración [inmiɣra'θjon] *nf* immigration

inmiscuirse [inmisku'irse] *vr* to interfere, meddle

inmobiliaria [inmoβi'ljarja] *nf* estate agency

inmobiliario, a [inmoβi'ljarjo, a] *adj* real-estate *cpd*, property *cpd*

inmolar [inmo'lar] *vt* to immolate, sacrifice

inmoral [inmo'ral] *adj* immoral

inmortal [inmor'tal] *adj* immortal; ~**izar** *vt* to immortalize

inmóvil [in'moβil] *adj* immobile

inmueble [in'mweβle] *adj*: **bienes ~s** real estate, landed property ♦ *nm* property

inmundicia [inmun'diθja] *nf* filth; **inmundo, a** *adj* filthy

inmune [in'mune] *adj*: ~ **(a)** (*MED*) immune (to)

inmunidad [inmuni'ðað] *nf* immunity

inmutarse [inmu'tarse] *vr* to turn pale; **no se inmutó** he didn't turn a hair

innato, a [in'nato, a] *adj* innate

innecesario, a [inneθe'sarjo, a] *adj* unnecessary

innoble [in'noβle] *adj* ignoble

innovación [innoβa'θjon] *nf* innovation

innovar [inno'βar] *vt* to introduce

inocencia [ino'θenθja] *nf* innocence

inocentada [inoθen'taða] *nf* practical joke

inocente [ino'θente] *adj* (*ingenuo*) naive, innocent; (*inculpable*) innocent; (*sin malicia*) harmless ♦ *nm/f* simpleton

---

Día de los Santos Inocentes

i The 28th December, **el día de los (Santos) Inocentes**, *is when the Church commemorates the story of Herod's slaughter of the innocent children of Judaea. On this day Spaniards play* **inocentadas** *(practical jokes) on each other, much like our April Fool's Day pranks.*

---

inodoro [ino'ðoro] *nm* toilet, lavatory

(*BRIT*)

inofensivo, a [inofen'siβo, a] *adj* inoffensive, harmless

inolvidable [inolβi'ðaβle] *adj* unforgettable

inopinado, a [inopi'naðo, a] *adj* unexpected

inoportuno, a [inopor'tuno, a] *adj* untimely; (*molesto*) inconvenient

inoxidable [inoksi'ðaβle] *adj*: **acero ~** stainless steel

inquebrantable [inkeβran'taβle] *adj* unbreakable

inquietar [inkje'tar] *vt* to worry, trouble; **~se** *vr* to worry, get upset; **inquieto, a** *adj* anxious, worried; **inquietud** *nf* anxiety, worry

inquilino, a [inki'lino, a] *nm/f* tenant

inquirir [inki'rir] *vt* to enquire into, investigate

insaciable [insa'θjaβle] *adj* insatiable

insalubre [insa'luβre] *adj* unhealthy

inscribir [inskri'βir] *vt* to inscribe; **~ a uno en** (*lista*) to put sb on; (*censo*) to register sb on

inscripción [inskrip'θjon] *nf* inscription; (*ESCOL etc*) enrolment; (*censo*) registration

insecticida [insekti'θiða] *nm* insecticide

insecto [in'sekto] *nm* insect

inseguridad [inseɣuri'ðað] *nf* insecurity

inseguro, a [inse'ɣuro, a] *adj* insecure; (*inconstante*) unsteady; (*incierto*) uncertain

insensato, a [insen'sato, a] *adj* foolish, stupid

insensibilidad [insensiβili'ðað] *nf* (*gen*) insensitivity; (*dureza de corazón*) callousness

insensible [insen'siβle] *adj* (*gen*) insensitive; (*movimiento*) imperceptible; (*sin sentido*) numb

insertar [inser'tar] *vt* to insert

inservible [inser'βiβle] *adj* useless

insidioso, a [insi'ðjoso, a] *adj* insidious

insignia [in'siɣnja] *nf* (*señal distintiva*) badge; (*estandarte*) flag

insignificante [insiɣnifi'kante] *adj* insignificant

insinuar [insi'nwar] *vt* to insinuate, imply

insípido, a [in'sipiðo, a] *adj* insipid

insistencia [insis'tenθja] *nf* insistence

insistir [insis'tir] *vi* to insist; **~ en algo** to insist on sth; (*enfatizar*) to stress sth

insolación [insola'θjon] *nf* (*MED*) sunstroke

insolencia [inso'lenθja] *nf* insolence; **insolente** *adj* insolent

insólito, a [in'solito, a] *adj* unusual

insoluble [inso'luβle] *adj* insoluble

insolvencia [insol'βenθja] *nf* insolvency

insomnio [in'somnjo] *nm* insomnia

insondable [inson'daβle] *adj* bottomless; (*fig*) impenetrable

insonorizado, a [insonori'θaðo, a] *adj* (*cuarto etc*) soundproof

insoportable [insopor'taβle] *adj* unbearable

insospechado, a [insospe'tʃaðo, a] *adj* (*inesperado*) unexpected

inspección [inspek'θjon] *nf* inspection, check; **inspeccionar** (*examinar*) to inspect, examine; (*controlar*) to check

inspector, a [inspek'tor, a] *nm/f* inspector

inspiración [inspira'θjon] *nf* inspiration

inspirar [inspi'rar] *vt* to inspire; (*MED*) to inhale; **~se** *vr*: **~se en** to be inspired by

instalación [instala'θjon] *nf* (*equipo*) fittings *pl*, equipment; **~ eléctrica** wiring

instalar [insta'lar] *vt* (*establecer*) to instal; (*erguir*) to set up, erect; **~se** *vr* to establish o.s.; (*en una vivienda*) to move into

instancia [ins'tanθja] *nf* (*JUR*) petition; (*ruego*) request; **en última ~** as a last resort

instantánea [instan'tanea] *nf* snap(shot)

instantáneo, a [instan'taneo, a] *adj* instantaneous; **café ~** instant coffee

instante [ins'tante] *nm* instant, moment

instar [ins'tar] *vt* to press, urge

instaurar [instau'rar] *vt* (*costumbre*) to establish; (*normas, sistema*) to bring in, introduce; (*gobierno*) to instal

instigar [insti'ɣar] *vt* to instigate

instinto [ins'tinto] *nm* instinct; **por ~**

instinctively

institución [institu'θjon] *nf* institution, establishment

instituir [institu'ir] *vt* to establish; (*fundar*) to found; **instituto** *nm* (*gen*) institute; (*ESP: ESCOL*) ≈ comprehensive (*BRIT*) o high (*US*) school

institutriz [institu'triθ] *nf* governess

instrucción [instruk'θjon] *nf* instruction

instructivo, a [instruk'tiβo, a] *adj* instructive

instruir [instru'ir] *vt* (*gen*) to instruct; (*enseñar*) to teach, educate

instrumento [instru'mento] *nm* (*gen*) instrument; (*herramienta*) tool, implement

insubordinarse [insuβorði'narse] *vr* to rebel

insuficiencia [insufi'θjenθja] *nf* (*carencia*) lack; (*inadecuación*) inadequacy; **insuficiente** *adj* (*gen*) insufficient; (*ESCOL: calificación*) unsatisfactory

insufrible [insu'friβle] *adj* insufferable

insular [insu'lar] *adj* insular

insultar [insul'tar] *vt* to insult; **insulto** *nm* insult

insumiso, a [insu'miso, a] *nm/f* (*POL*) *person who refuses to do military service or its substitute, community service*

insuperable [insupe'raβle] *adj* (*excelente*) unsurpassable; (*problema etc*) insurmountable

insurgente [insur'xente] *adj, nm/f* insurgent

insurrección [insurrek'θjon] *nf* insurrection, rebellion

intachable [inta'tʃaβle] *adj* irreproachable

intacto, a [in'takto, a] *adj* intact

integral [inte'ɣral] *adj* integral; (*completo*) complete; **pan ~** wholemeal (*BRIT*) o wholewheat (*US*) bread

integrar [inte'ɣrar] *vt* to make up, compose; (*MAT, fig*) to integrate

integridad [inteɣri'ðað] *nf* wholeness; (*carácter*) integrity; **íntegro, a** *adj* whole, entire; (*honrado*) honest

intelectual [intelek'twal] *adj, nm/f* intellectual

inteligencia [inteli'xenθja] *nf* intelligence; (*ingenio*) ability; **inteligente** *adj* intelligent

inteligible [inteli'xiβle] *adj* intelligible

intemperie [intem'perje] *nf*: **a la ~** out in the open, exposed to the elements

intempestivo, a [intempes'tiβo, a] *adj* untimely

intención [inten'θjon] *nf* (*gen*) intention, purpose; **con segundas intenciones** maliciously; **con ~** deliberately

intencionado, a [intenθjo'naðo, a] *adj* deliberate; **bien ~** well-meaning; **mal ~** ill-disposed, hostile

intensidad [intensi'ðað] *nf* (*gen*) intensity; (*ELEC, TEC*) strength; **llover con ~** to rain hard

intenso, a [in'tenso, a] *adj* intense; (*sentimiento*) profound, deep

intentar [inten'tar] *vt* (*tratar*) to try, attempt; **intento** *nm* attempt

interactivo, a [interak'tiβo, a] *adj* (*INFORM*) interactive

intercalar [interka'lar] *vt* to insert

intercambio [inter'kambjo] *nm* exchange, swap

interceder [interθe'ðer] *vi* to intercede

interceptar [interθep'tar] *vt* to intercept

intercesión [interθe'sjon] *nf* intercession

interés [inte'res] *nm* (*gen*) interest; (*parte*) share, part; (*pey*) self-interest; **intereses creados** vested interests

interesado, a [intere'saðo, a] *adj* interested; (*prejuiciado*) prejudiced; (*pey*) mercenary, self-seeking

interesante [intere'sante] *adj* interesting

interesar [intere'sar] *vt, vi* to interest, be of interest to; **~se** *vr*: **~se en** o **por** to take an interest in

interferir [interfe'rir] *vt* to interfere with; (*TEL*) to jam ♦ *vi* to interfere

interfono [inter'fono] *nm* intercom

interino, a [inte'rino, a] *adj* temporary ♦ *nm/f* temporary holder of a post; (*MED*) locum; (*ESCOL*) supply teacher

interior [inte'rjor] *adj* inner, inside; (*COM*) domestic, internal ♦ *nm* interior, inside;

(*fig*) soul, mind; **Ministerio del I~**
≈ Home Office (*BRIT*), ≈ Department of
the Interior (*US*)
interjección [interxek'θjon] *nf* interjection
interlocutor, a [interloku'tor, a] *nm/f*
speaker
intermediario, a [interme'ðjarjo, a] *nm/f*
intermediary
intermedio, a [inter'meðjo, a] *adj*
intermediate ♦ *nm* interval
interminable [intermi'naßle] *adj* endless
intermitente [intermi'tente] *adj*
intermittent ♦ *nm* (*AUTO*) indicator
internacional [internaθjo'nal] *adj*
international
internado [inter'naðo] *nm* boarding
school
internar [inter'nar] *vt* to intern; (*en un
manicomio*) to commit; **~se** *vr* (*penetrar*)
to penetrate
interno, a [in'terno, a] *adj* internal,
interior; (*POL etc*) domestic ♦ *nm/f*
(*alumno*) boarder
interponer [interpo'ner] *vt* to interpose,
put in; **~se** *vr* to intervene
interpretación [interpreta'θjon] *nf*
interpretation
interpretar [interpre'tar] *vt* to interpret;
(*TEATRO, MUS*) to perform, play;
intérprete *nm/f* (*LING*) interpreter,
translator; (*MUS, TEATRO*) performer,
artist(e)
interrogación [interroxa'θjon] *nf*
interrogation; (*LING: tb:* **signo de ~**)
question mark
interrogar [interro'var] *vt* to interrogate,
question
interrumpir [interrum'pir] *vt* to interrupt
interrupción [interrup'θjon] *nf*
interruption
interruptor [interrup'tor] *nm* (*ELEC*) switch
intersección [intersek'θjon] *nf*
intersection
interurbano, a [interur'ßano, a] *adj*:
llamada interurbana long-distance call
intervalo [inter'ßalo] *nm* interval;
(*descanso*) break; **a ~s** at intervals, every

now and then
intervenir [interße'nir] *vt* (*controlar*) to
control, supervise; (*MED*) to operate on
♦ *vi* (*participar*) to take part, participate;
(*mediar*) to intervene
interventor, a [interßen'tor, a] *nm/f*
inspector; (*COM*) auditor
intestino [intes'tino] *nm* intestine
intimar [inti'mar] *vi* to become friendly
intimidad [intimi'ðað] *nf* intimacy;
(*familiaridad*) familiarity; (*vida privada*)
private life; (*JUR*) privacy
íntimo, a ['intimo, a] *adj* intimate
intolerable [intole'raßle] *adj* intolerable,
unbearable
intoxicación [intoksika'θjon] *nf* poisoning
intranquilizarse [intrankili'θarse] *vr* to
get worried *o* anxious; **intranquilo, a**
adj worried
intransigente [intransi'xente] *adj*
intransigent
intransitable [intransi'taßle] *adj*
impassable
intrépido, a [in'trepiðo, a] *adj* intrepid
intriga [in'triva] *nf* intrigue; (*plan*) plot;
intrigar *vt, vi* to intrigue
intrincado, a [intrin'kaðo, a] *adj* intricate
intrínseco, a [in'trinseko, a] *adj* intrinsic
introducción [introðuk'θjon] *nf*
introduction
introducir [introðu'θir] *vt* (*gen*) to
introduce; (*moneda etc*) to insert;
(*INFORM*) to input, enter
intromisión [intromi'sjon] *nf* interference,
meddling
introvertido, a [introßer'tiðo, a] *adj, nm/f*
introvert
intruso, a [in'truso, a] *adj* intrusive
♦ *nm/f* intruder
intuición [intwi'θjon] *nf* intuition
inundación [inunda'θjon] *nf* flood(ing);
inundar *vt* to flood; (*fig*) to swamp,
inundate
inusitado, a [inusi'taðo, a] *adj* unusual,
rare
inútil [in'util] *adj* useless; (*esfuerzo*) vain,
fruitless; **inutilidad** *nf* uselessness

inutilizar [inutili'θar] *vt* to make *o* render useless; **~se** *vr* to become useless

invadir [imba'ðir] *vt* to invade

inválido, a [im'baliðo, a] *adj* invalid
♦ *nm/f* invalid

invariable [imba'rjaβle] *adj* invariable

invasión [imba'sjon] *nf* invasion

invasor, a [imba'sor, a] *adj* invading
♦ *nm/f* invader

invención [imben'θjon] *nf* invention

inventar [imben'tar] *vt* to invent

inventario [imben'tarjo] *nm* inventory

inventiva [imben'tiβa] *nf* inventiveness

invento [im'bento] *nm* invention

inventor, a [imben'tor, a] *nm/f* inventor

invernadero [imberna'ðero] *nm* greenhouse

inverosímil [imbero'simil] *adj* implausible

inversión [imber'sjon] *nf* (COM) investment

inverso, a [im'berso, a] *adj* inverse, opposite; **en el orden ~** in reverse order; **a la inversa** inversely, the other way round

inversor, a [imber'sor, a] *nm/f* (COM) investor

invertir [imber'tir] *vt* (COM) to invest; (*volcar*) to turn upside down; (*tiempo etc*) to spend

investigación [imbestiβa'θjon] *nf* investigation; (ESCOL) research; **~ de mercado** market research

investigar [imbesti'βar] *vt* to investigate; (ESCOL) to do research into

invierno [im'bjerno] *nm* winter

invisible [imbi'siβle] *adj* invisible

invitado, a [imbi'taðo, a] *nm/f* guest

invitar [imbi'tar] *vt* to invite; (*incitar*) to entice; (*pagar*) to buy, pay for

invocar [imbo'kar] *vt* to invoke, call on

involucrar [imbolu'krar] *vt*: **~ en** to involve in; **~se** *vr* (*persona*): **~ en** to get mixed up in

involuntario, a [imbolun'tarjo, a] *adj* (*movimiento, gesto*) involuntary; (*error*) unintentional

inyección [injek'θjon] *nf* injection

inyectar [injek'tar] *vt* to inject

PALABRA CLAVE
---

ir [ir] *vi* **1** to go; (*a pie*) to walk; (*viajar*) to travel; **~ caminando** to walk; **fui en tren** I went *o* travelled by train; **¡(ahora) voy!** (I'm just) coming!

2: **~ (a) por**: **~ (a) por el médico** to fetch the doctor

3 (*progresar: persona, cosa*) to go; **el trabajo va muy bien** work is going very well; **¿cómo te va?** how are things going?; **me va muy bien** I'm getting on very well; **le fue fatal** it went awfully badly for him

4 (*funcionar*): **el coche no va muy bien** the car isn't running very well

5: **te va estupendamente ese color** that colour suits you fantastically well

6 (*locuciones*): **¿vino? – ¡qué va!** did he come? – of course not!; **vamos, no llores** come on, don't cry; **¡vaya coche!** what a car!, that's some car!

7: **no vaya a ser: tienes que correr, no vaya a ser que pierdas el tren** you'll have to run so as not to miss the train

8 (+*pp*): **iba vestido muy bien** he was very well dressed

9: **no me** *etc* **va ni me viene** I *etc* don't care

♦ *vb aux* **1**: **~ a**: **voy/iba a hacerlo hoy** I am/was going to do it today

2 (+*gerundio*): **iba anocheciendo** it was getting dark; **todo se me iba aclarando** everything was gradually becoming clearer to me

3 (+*pp = pasivo*): **van vendidos 300 ejemplares** 300 copies have been sold so far

♦ **~se** *vr* **1**: **¿por dónde se va al zoológico?** which is the way to the zoo?

2 (*marcharse*) to leave; **ya se habrán ido** they must already have left *o* gone

---

ira ['ira] *nf* anger, rage

Irak [i'rak] *nm* = **Iraq**

Irán [i'ran] *nm* Iran; **iraní** *adj, nm/f*

Iranian

Iraq [i'rak] *nm* Iraq; **iraquí** *adj, nm/f* Iraqui

iris ['iris] *nm inv* (*tb:* **arco ~**) rainbow; (*ANAT*) iris

Irlanda [ir'landa] *nf* Ireland; **irlandés, esa** *adj* Irish ♦ *nm/f* Irishman/woman; **los irlandeses** the Irish

ironía [iro'nia] *nf* irony; **irónico, a** *adj* ironic(al)

IRPF [i 'erre 'pe 'efe] *nm abr* (= *Impuesto sobre la Renta de las Personas Físicas*) (personal) income tax

irreal [irre'al] *adj* unreal

irrecuperable [irrekupe'raßle] *adj* irrecoverable, irretrievable

irreflexión [irreflek'sjon] *nf* thoughtlessness

irregular [irreɣu'lar] *adj* (*gen*) irregular; (*situación*) abnormal

irremediable [irreme'ðjaßle] *adj* irremediable; (*vicio*) incurable

irreparable [irrepa'raßle] *adj* (*daños*) irreparable; (*pérdida*) irrecoverable

irresoluto, a [irreso'luto, a] *adj* irresolute, hesitant

irrespetuoso, a [irrespe'twoso, a] *adj* disrespectful

irresponsable [irrespon'saßle] *adj* irresponsible

irreversible [irreßer'sible] *adj* irreversible

irrigar [irri'ɣar] *vt* to irrigate

irrisorio, a [irri'sorjo, a] *adj* derisory, ridiculous

irritar [irri'tar] *vt* to irritate, annoy

irrupción [irrup'θjon] *nf* irruption; (*invasión*) invasion

isla ['isla] *nf* island

islandés, esa [islan'des, esa] *adj* Icelandic ♦ *nm/f* Icelander

Islandia [is'landja] *nf* Iceland

isleño, a [is'leɲo, a] *adj* island *cpd* ♦ *nm/f* islander

Israel [isra'el] *nm* Israel; **israelí** *adj, nm/f* Israeli

istmo ['istmo] *nm* isthmus

Italia [i'talja] *nf* Italy; **italiano, a** *adj,* *nm/f* Italian

itinerario [itine'rarjo] *nm* itinerary, route

IVA ['ißa] *nm abr* (= *impuesto sobre el valor añadido*) VAT

izar [i'θar] *vt* to hoist

izdo, a *abr* (= *izquierdo, a*) l.

izquierda [iθ'kjerda] *nf* left; (*POL*) left (wing); **a la ~** (*estar*) on the left; (*torcer etc*) (to the) left

izquierdista [iθkjer'ðista] *nm/f* left-winger, leftist

izquierdo, a [iθ'kjerðo, a] *adj* left

J, j

jabalí [xaßa'li] *nm* wild boar

jabalina [xaßa'lina] *nf* javelin

jabón [xa'ßon] *nm* soap; **jabonar** *vt* to soap

jaca ['xaka] *nf* pony

jacinto [xa'θinto] *nm* hyacinth

jactarse [xak'tarse] *vr* to boast, brag

jadear [xaðe'ar] *vi* to pant, gasp for breath; **jadeo** *nm* panting, gasping

jaguar [xa'ɣwar] *nm* jaguar

jalea [xa'lea] *nf* jelly

jaleo [xa'leo] *nm* racket, uproar; **armar un ~** to kick up a racket

jalón [xa'lon] (*AM*) *nm* tug

jamás [xa'mas] *adv* never

jamón [xa'mon] *nm* ham; **~ dulce, ~ de York** cooked ham; **~ serrano** cured ham

Japón [xa'pon] *nm*: **el ~** Japan; **japonés, esa** *adj, nm/f* Japanese ♦ *nm* (*LING*) Japanese

jaque ['xake] *nm*: **~ mate** checkmate

jaqueca [xa'keka] *nf* (very bad) headache, migraine

jarabe [xa'raße] *nm* syrup

jarcia ['xarθja] *nf* (*NAUT*) ropes *pl*, rigging

jardín [xar'ðin] *nm* garden; **~ de infancia** (*ESP*) *o* **de niños** (*AM*) nursery (school); **jardinería** *nf* gardening; **jardinero, a** *nm/f* gardener

jarra ['xarra] *nf* jar; (*jarro*) jug

jarro ['xarro] *nm* jug

jarrón [xa'rron] *nm* vase
jaula ['xaula] *nf* cage
jauría [xau'ria] *nf* pack of hounds
jazmín [xaθ'min] *nm* jasmine
J. C. *abr* (= *Jesucristo*) J.C.
jefa ['xefa] *nf ver* **jefe**
jefatura [xefa'tura] *nf*: ~ **de policía** police headquarters *sg*
jefe, a ['xefe, a] *nm/f* (*gen*) chief, head; (*patrón*) boss; ~ **de cocina** chef; ~ **de estación** stationmaster; ~ **de estado** head of state
jengibre [xen'xiβre] *nm* ginger
jeque ['xeke] *nm* sheik
jerarquía [xerar'kia] *nf* (*orden*) hierarchy; (*rango*) rank; **jerárquico, a** *adj* hierarchic(al)
jerez [xe'reθ] *nm* sherry
jerga ['xerɣa] *nf* jargon
jeringa [xe'ringa] *nf* syringe; (*AM*) annoyance, bother; ~ **de engrase** grease gun; **jeringar** *vt* (*fam*) to annoy, bother; **jeringuilla** *nf* syringe
jeroglífico [xero'ɣlifiko] *nm* hieroglyphic
jersey [xer'sei] (*pl* ~**s**) *nm* jersey, pullover, jumper
Jerusalén [xerusa'len] *n* Jerusalem
Jesucristo [xesu'kristo] *nm* Jesus Christ
jesuita [xe'swita] *adj, nm* Jesuit
Jesús [xe'sus] *nm* Jesus; ¡~! good heavens!; (*al estornudar*) bless you!
jinete, a [xi'nete, a] *nm/f* horseman/woman, rider
jipijapa [xipi'xapa] (*AM*) *nm* straw hat
jirafa [xi'rafa] *nf* giraffe
jirón [xi'ron] *nm* rag, shred
jocoso, a [xo'koso, a] *adj* humorous, jocular
joder [xo'ðer] (*fam!*) *vt, vi* to fuck(!)
jofaina [xo'faina] *nf* washbasin
jornada [xor'naða] *nf* (*viaje de un día*) day's journey; (*camino o viaje entero*) journey; (*día de trabajo*) working day
jornal [xor'nal] *nm* (day's) wage; ~**ero** *nm* (day) labourer
joroba [xo'roβa] *nf* hump, hunched back; ~**do, a** *adj* hunchbacked ♦ *nm/f*

hunchback
jota ['xota] *nf* (the letter) J; (*danza*) Aragonese dance; **no saber ni** ~ to have no idea
joven ['xoβen] (*pl* **jóvenes**) *adj* young ♦ *nm* young man, youth ♦ *nf* young woman, girl
jovial [xo'βjal] *adj* cheerful, jolly
joya ['xoja] *nf* jewel, gem; (*fig: persona*) gem; **joyería** *nf* (*joyas*) jewellery; (*tienda*) jeweller's (shop); **joyero** *nm* (*persona*) jeweller; (*caja*) jewel case
juanete [xwa'nete] *nm* (*del pie*) bunion
jubilación [xuβila'θjon] *nf* (*retiro*) retirement
jubilado, a [xuβi'laðo, a] *adj* retired ♦ *nm/f* pensioner (*BRIT*), senior citizen
jubilar [xuβi'lar] *vt* to pension off, retire; (*fam*) to discard; ~**se** *vr* to retire
júbilo ['xuβilo] *nm* joy, rejoicing; **jubiloso, a** *adj* jubilant
judía [xu'ðia] *nf* (*CULIN*) bean; ~ **verde** French bean; *ver tb* **judío**
judicial [xuði'θjal] *adj* judicial
judío, a [xu'ðio, a] *adj* Jewish ♦ *nm/f* Jew(ess)
judo ['juðo] *nm* judo
juego *etc* ['xweɣo] *vb ver* **jugar** ♦ *nm* (*gen*) play; (*pasatiempo, partido*) game; (*en casino*) gambling; (*conjunto*) set; **fuera de** ~ (*DEPORTE: persona*) offside; (: *pelota*) out of play; **J~s Olímpicos** Olympic Games
juerga ['xwerɣa] *nf* binge; (*fiesta*) party; **ir de** ~ to go out on a binge
jueves ['xweβes] *nm inv* Thursday
juez [xweθ] *nm/f* judge; ~ **de línea** linesman; ~ **de salida** starter
jugada [xu'ɣaða] *nf* play; **buena** ~ good move/shot/stroke *etc*
jugador, a [xuɣa'ðor, a] *nm/f* player; (*en casino*) gambler
jugar [xu'ɣar] *vt, vi* to play; (*en casino*) to gamble; (*apostar*) to bet; ~ **al fútbol** to play football
juglar [xu'ɣlar] *nm* minstrel
jugo ['xuɣo] *nm* (*BOT*) juice; (*fig*) essence, substance; ~ **de fruta** (*AM*) fruit juice;

~so, a *adj* juicy; *(fig)* substantial, important

juguete [xu'ɣete] *nm* toy; **~ar** *vi* to play; **~ría** *nf* toyshop

juguetón, ona [xuɣe'ton, ona] *adj* playful

juicio ['xwiθjo] *nm* judgement; *(razón)* sanity, reason; *(opinión)* opinion; **~so, a** *adj* wise, sensible

julio ['xuljo] *nm* July

junco ['xunko] *nm* rush, reed

jungla ['xungla] *nf* jungle

junio ['xunjo] *nm* June

junta ['xunta] *nf (asamblea)* meeting, assembly; *(comité, consejo)* board, council, committee; *(TEC)* joint

juntar [xun'tar] *vt* to join, unite; *(maquinaria)* to assemble, put together; *(dinero)* to collect; **~se** *vr* to join, meet; *(reunirse: personas)* to meet, assemble; *(arrimarse)* to approach, draw closer; **~se con uno** to join sb

junto, a ['xunto, a] *adj* joined; *(unido)* united; *(anexo)* near, close; *(contiguo, próximo)* next, adjacent ♦ *adv*: **todo ~** all at once; **~s** together; **~ a** near (to), next to

jurado [xu'raðo] *nm (JUR: individuo)* juror; *(: grupo)* jury; *(de concurso: grupo)* panel (of judges); *(: individuo)* member of a panel

juramento [xura'mento] *nm* oath; *(maldición)* oath, curse; **prestar ~** to take the oath; **tomar ~ a** to swear in, administer the oath to

jurar [xu'rar] *vt, vi* to swear; **~ en falso** to commit perjury; **jurárselas a uno** to have it in for sb

jurídico, a [xu'riðiko, a] *adj* legal

jurisdicción [xurisðik'θjon] *nf (poder, autoridad)* jurisdiction; *(territorio)* district

jurisprudencia [xurispru'ðenθja] *nf* jurisprudence

jurista [xu'rista] *nm/f* jurist

justamente [xusta'mente] *adv* justly, fairly; *(precisamente)* just, exactly

justicia [xus'tiθja] *nf* justice; *(equidad)* fairness, justice; **justiciero, a** *adj* just, righteous

justificación [xustifika'θjon] *nf* justification; **justificar** *vt* to justify

justo, a ['xusto, a] *adj (equitativo)* just, fair, right; *(preciso)* exact, correct; *(ajustado)* tight ♦ *adv (precisamente)* exactly, precisely; *(AM: apenas a tiempo)* just in time

juvenil [xuβe'nil] *adj* youthful

juventud [xuβen'tuð] *nf (adolescencia)* youth; *(jóvenes)* young people *pl*

juzgado [xuθ'ɣaðo] *nm* tribunal; *(JUR)* court

juzgar [xuθ'ɣar] *vt* to judge; **a ~ por ...** to judge by ..., judging by ...

K, k

kg *abr* (= *kilogramo*) kg

kilo ['kilo] *nm* kilo ♦ *pref*: **~gramo** *nm* kilogramme; **~metraje** *nm* distance in kilometres, ≈ mileage; **kilómetro** *nm* kilometre; **~vatio** *nm* kilowatt

kiosco ['kjosko] *nm* = **quiosco**

km *abr* (= *kilómetro*) km

kv *abr* (= *kilovatio*) kw

L, l

l *abr* (= *litro*) l

la [la] *art def* the ♦ *pron* her; *(Ud.)* you; *(cosa)* it ♦ *nm* (MUS) la; **~ del sombrero rojo** the girl in the red hat; *tb ver* **el**

laberinto [laβe'rinto] *nm* labyrinth

labia ['laβja] *nf* fluency; *(pey)* glib tongue

labio ['laβjo] *nm* lip

labor [la'βor] *nf* labour; *(AGR)* farm work; *(tarea)* job, task; *(COSTURA)* needlework; **~able** *adj* (AGR) workable; **día ~able** working day; **~al** *adj (accidente)* at work; *(jornada)* working

laboratorio [laβora'torjo] *nm* laboratory

laborioso, a [laβo'rjoso, a] *adj (persona)* hard-working; *(trabajo)* tough

laborista [laβo'rista] *adj*: **Partido L~**

Labour Party

labrado, a [la'ßraðo, a] *adj* worked; (*madera*) carved; (*metal*) wrought

labrador, a [laßra'ðor, a] *adj* farming *cpd* ♦ *nm/f* farmer

labranza [la'ßranθa] *nf* (*AGR*) cultivation

labrar [la'ßrar] *vt* (*gen*) to work; (*madera etc*) to carve; (*fig*) to cause, bring about

labriego, a [la'ßrjeɣo, a] *nm/f* peasant

laca ['laka] *nf* lacquer

lacayo [la'kajo] *nm* lackey

lacio, a ['laθjo, a] *adj* (*pelo*) lank, straight

lacón [la'kon] *nm* shoulder of pork

lacónico, a [la'koniko, a] *adj* laconic

lacra ['lakra] *nf* (*fig*) blot; **lacrar** *vt* (*cerrar*) to seal (with sealing wax); **lacre** *nm* sealing wax

lactancia [lak'tanθja] *nf* lactation

lactar [lak'tar] *vt, vi* to suckle

lácteo, a ['lakteo, a] *adj*: **productos ~s** dairy products

ladear [laðe'ar] *vt* to tip, tilt ♦ *vi* to tilt; **~se** *vr* to lean

ladera [la'ðera] *nf* slope

lado ['laðo] *nm* (*gen*) side; (*fig*) protection; (*MIL*) flank; **al ~ de** beside; **poner de ~** to put on its side; **poner a un ~** to put aside; **por todos ~s** on all sides, all round (*BRIT*)

ladrar [la'ðrar] *vi* to bark; **ladrido** *nm* bark, barking

ladrillo [la'ðriʎo] *nm* (*gen*) brick; (*azulejo*) tile

ladrón, ona [la'ðron, ona] *nm/f* thief

lagartija [laɣar'tixa] *nf* (*ZOOL*) (small) lizard

lagarto [la'ɣarto] *nm* (*ZOOL*) lizard

lago ['laɣo] *nm* lake

lágrima ['laɣrima] *nf* tear

laguna [la'ɣuna] *nf* (*lago*) lagoon; (*hueco*) gap

laico, a ['laiko, a] *adj* lay

lamentable [lamen'taßle] *adj* lamentable, regrettable; (*miserable*) pitiful

lamentar [lamen'tar] *vt* (*sentir*) to regret; (*deplorar*) to lament; **lo lamento mucho** I'm very sorry; **~se** *vr* to lament;

lamento *nm* lament

lamer [la'mer] *vt* to lick

lámina ['lamina] *nf* (*plancha delgada*) sheet; (*para estampar, estampa*) plate

lámpara ['lampara] *nf* lamp; **~ de alcohol/gas** spirit/gas lamp; **~ de pie** standard lamp

lamparón [lampa'ron] *nm* grease spot

lana ['lana] *nf* wool

lancha ['lantʃa] *nf* launch; **~ de pesca** fishing boat; **~ salvavidas/torpedera** lifeboat/torpedo boat

langosta [lan'gosta] *nf* (*crustáceo*) lobster; (: *de río*) crayfish; **langostino** *nm* Dublin Bay prawn

languidecer [langiðe'θer] *vi* to languish; **languidez** *nf* languor; **lánguido, a** *adj* (*gen*) languid; (*sin energía*) listless

lanilla [la'niʎa] *nf* nap

lanza ['lanθa] *nf* (*arma*) lance, spear

lanzamiento [lanθa'mjento] *nm* (*gen*) throwing; (*NAUT, COM*) launch, launching; **~ de peso** putting the shot

lanzar [lan'θar] *vt* (*gen*) to throw; (*DEPORTE: pelota*) to bowl; (*NAUT, COM*) to launch; (*JUR*) to evict; **~se** *vr* to throw o.s.

lapa ['lapa] *nf* limpet

lapicero [lapi'θero] *nm* pencil; (*AM: bolígrafo*) Biro ®

lápida ['lapiða] *nf* stone; **~ mortuoria** headstone; **~ conmemorativa** memorial stone; **lapidario, a** *adj, nm* lapidary

lápiz ['lapiθ] *nm* pencil; **~ de color** coloured pencil; **~ de labios** lipstick

lapón, ona [la'pon, ona] *nm/f* Laplander, Lapp

lapso ['lapso] *nm* (*de tiempo*) interval; (*error*) error

lapsus ['lapsus] *nm inv* error, mistake

largar [lar'ɣar] *vt* (*soltar*) to release; (*aflojar*) to loosen; (*lanzar*) to launch; (*fam*) to let fly; (*velas*) to unfurl; (*AM*) to throw; **~se** *vr* (*fam*) to beat it; **~se a** (*AM*) to start to

largo, a ['larɣo, a] *adj* (*longitud*) long; (*tiempo*) lengthy; (*fig*) generous ♦ *nm* length; (*MUS*) largo; **dos años ~s** two

long years; **tiene 9 metros de ~** it is 9
metres long; **a lo ~ de** along; (*tiempo*) all
through, throughout; **~metraje** *nm*
feature film

laringe [la'rinxe] *nf* larynx; **laringitis** *nf*
laryngitis

larva ['larßa] *nf* larva

las [las] *art def* the ♦ *pron* them; **~ que
cantan** the ones/women/girls who sing;
tb ver **el**

lascivo, a [las'θißo, a] *adj* lewd

láser ['laser] *nm* laser

lástima ['lastima] *nf* (*pena*) pity; **dar ~** to
be pitiful; **es una ~ que** it's a pity that;
¡qué ~! what a pity!; **ella está hecha
una ~** she looks pitiful

lastimar [lasti'mar] *vt* (*herir*) to wound;
(*ofender*) to offend; **~se** *vr* to hurt o.s.;
lastimero, a *adj* pitiful, pathetic

lastre ['lastre] *nm* (*TEC, NAUT*) ballast; (*fig*)
dead weight

lata ['lata] *nf* (*metal*) tin; (*caja*) tin (*BRIT*),
can; (*fam*) nuisance; **en ~** tinned (*BRIT*),
canned; **dar (la) ~** to be a nuisance

latente [la'tente] *adj* latent

lateral [late'ral] *adj* side *cpd*, lateral ♦ *nm*
(*TEATRO*) wings

latido [la'tiðo] *nm* (*del corazón*) beat

latifundio [lati'fundjo] *nm* large estate;
latifundista *nm/f* owner of a large
estate

latigazo [lati'vaθo] *nm* (*golpe*) lash;
(*sonido*) crack

látigo ['lativo] *nm* whip

latín [la'tin] *nm* Latin

latino, a [la'tino, a] *adj* Latin;
~americano, a *adj, nm/f* Latin-
American

latir [la'tir] *vi* (*corazón, pulso*) to beat

latitud [lati'tuð] *nf* (*GEO*) latitude

latón [la'ton] *nm* brass

latoso, a [la'toso, a] *adj* (*molesto*)
annoying; (*aburrido*) boring

laúd [la'uð] *nm* lute

laurel [lau'rel] *nm* (*BOT*) laurel; (*CULIN*) bay

lava ['laßa] *nf* lava

lavabo [la'ßaßo] *nm* (*pila*) washbasin; (*tb*:

~s) toilet

lavado [la'ßaðo] *nm* washing; (*de ropa*)
laundry; (*ARTE*) wash; **~ de cerebro**
brainwashing; **~ en seco** dry-cleaning

lavadora [laßa'ðora] *nf* washing machine

lavanda [la'ßanda] *nf* lavender

lavandería [laßande'ria] *nf* laundry;
(*automática*) launderette

lavaplatos [laßa'platos] *nm inv*
dishwasher

lavar [la'ßar] *vt* to wash; (*borrar*) to wipe
away; **~se** *vr* to wash o.s.; **~se las
manos** to wash one's hands; **~se los
dientes** to brush one's teeth; **~ y marcar**
(*pelo*) to shampoo and set; **~ en seco** to
dry-clean; **~ los platos** to wash the dishes

lavavajillas [laßaßa'xiλas] *nm inv*
dishwasher

laxante [lak'sante] *nm* laxative

lazada [la'θaða] *nf* bow

lazarillo [laθa'riλo] *nm*: **perro ~** guide dog

lazo ['laθo] *nm* knot; (*lazada*) bow; (*para
animales*) lasso; (*trampa*) snare; (*vínculo*)
tie

le [le] *pron* (*directo*) him (o her); (: *usted*)
you; (*indirecto*) to him (o her o it);
(: *usted*) to you

leal [le'al] *adj* loyal; **~tad** *nf* loyalty

lección [lek'θjon] *nf* lesson

leche ['letʃe] *nf* milk; **tiene mala ~** (*fam!*)
he's a swine (!); **~ condensada/en polvo**
condensed/powdered milk; **~ desnatada**
skimmed milk; **~ra** *nf* (*vendedora*)
milkmaid; (*recipiente*) (milk) churn; (*AM*)
cow; **~ro, a** *adj* dairy

lecho ['letʃo] *nm* (*cama, de río*) bed; (*GEO*)
layer

lechón [le'tʃon] *nm* sucking (*BRIT*) o
suckling (*US*) pig

lechoso, a [le'tʃoso, a] *adj* milky

lechuga [le'tʃuxa] *nf* lettuce

lechuza [le'tʃuθa] *nf* owl

lector, a [lek'tor, a] *nm/f* reader ♦ *nm*: **~
de discos compactos** CD player

lectura [lek'tura] *nf* reading

leer [le'er] *vt* to read

legado [le'xaðo] *nm* (*don*) bequest;

(*herencia*) legacy; (*enviado*) legate
legajo [le'xaxo] *nm* file
legal [le'yal] *adj* (*gen*) legal; (*persona*)
trustworthy; **~idad** *nf* legality
legalizar [leyali'θar] *vt* to legalize;
(*documento*) to authenticate
legaña [le'xaɲa] *nf* sleep (*in eyes*)
legar [le'yar] *vt* to bequeath, leave
legendario, a [lexen'darjo, a] *adj*
legendary
legión [le'xjon] *nf* legion; **legionario, a**
adj legionary ♦ *nm* legionnaire
legislación [lexisla'θjon] *nf* legislation
legislar [lexis'lar] *vi* to legislate
legislatura [lexisla'tura] *nf* (*POL*) period of
office
legitimar [lexiti'mar] *vt* to legitimize;
legítimo, a *adj* (*genuino*) authentic;
(*legal*) legitimate
lego, a ['leyo, a] *adj* (*REL*) secular;
(*ignorante*) ignorant ♦ *nm* layman
legua ['leywa] *nf* league
legumbres [le'yumbres] *nfpl* pulses
leído, a [le'iðo, a] *adj* well-read
lejanía [lexa'nia] *nf* distance; **lejano, a**
adj far-off; (*en el tiempo*) distant; (*fig*)
remote
lejía [le'xia] *nf* bleach
lejos ['lexos] *adv* far, far away; **a lo ~** in
the distance; **de** *o* **desde ~** from afar; **~**
de far from
lelo, a ['lelo, a] *adj* silly ♦ *nm/f* idiot
lema ['lema] *nm* motto; (*POL*) slogan
lencería [lenθe'ria] *nf* linen, drapery
lengua ['lengwa] *nf* tongue; (*LING*)
language; **morderse la ~** to hold one's
tongue
lenguado [len'gwaðo] *nm* sole
lenguaje [len'gwaxe] *nm* language
lengüeta [len'gweta] *nf* (*ANAT*) epiglottis;
(*zapatos*) tongue; (*MUS*) reed
lente ['lente] *nf* lens; (*lupa*) magnifying
glass; **~s** *nfpl* (*gafas*) glasses; **~s de**
contacto contact lenses
lenteja [len'texa] *nf* lentil; **lentejuela** *nf*
sequin
lentilla [len'tiʎa] *nf* contact lens

lentitud [lenti'tuð] *nf* slowness; **con ~**
slowly
lento, a ['lento, a] *adj* slow
leña ['leɲa] *nf* firewood; **~dor, a** *nm/f*
woodcutter
leño ['leɲo] *nm* (*trozo de árbol*) log;
(*madera*) timber; (*fig*) blockhead
Leo ['leo] *nm* Leo
león [le'on] *nm* lion; **~ marino** sea lion
leopardo [leo'parðo] *nm* leopard
leotardos [leo'tarðos] *nmpl* tights
lepra ['lepra] *nf* leprosy; **leproso, a** *nm/f*
leper
lerdo, a ['lerðo, a] *adj* (*lento*) slow;
(*patoso*) clumsy
les [les] *pron* (*directo*) them; (: *ustedes*)
you; (*indirecto*) to them; (: *ustedes*) to you
lesbiana [les'ßjana] *adj, nf* lesbian
lesión [le'sjon] *nf* wound, lesion; (*DEPORTE*)
injury; **lesionado, a** *adj* injured ♦ *nm/f*
injured person
letal [le'tal] *adj* lethal
letanía [leta'nia] *nf* litany
letargo [le'tarxo] *nm* lethargy
letra ['letra] *nf* letter; (*escritura*)
handwriting; (*MUS*) lyrics *pl*; **~ de cambio**
bill of exchange; **~ de imprenta** print;
~do, a *adj* learned ♦ *nm/f* lawyer;
letrero *nm* (*cartel*) sign; (*etiqueta*) label
letrina [le'trina] *nf* latrine
leucemia [leu'θemja] *nf* leukaemia
levadizo [leßa'ðiθo] *adj*: **puente ~**
drawbridge
levadura [leßa'ðura] *nf* (*para el pan*) yeast;
(*de la cerveza*) brewer's yeast
levantamiento [leßanta'mjento] *nm*
raising, lifting; (*rebelión*) revolt, uprising; **~**
de pesos weight-lifting
levantar [leßan'tar] *vt* (*gen*) to raise; (*del*
suelo) to pick up; (*hacia arriba*) to lift
(up); (*plan*) to make, draw up; (*mesa*) to
clear; (*campamento*) to strike; (*fig*) to
cheer up, hearten; **~se** *vr* to get up;
(*enderezarse*) to straighten up; (*rebelarse*)
to rebel; **~ el ánimo** to cheer up
levante [le'ßante] *nm* east coast; **el L~**
region of Spain extending from Castellón

to Murcia

levar [leˈßar] *vt* to weigh

leve [ˈleße] *adj* light; (*fig*) trivial; **~dad** *nf* lightness

levita [leˈßita] *nf* frock coat

léxico [ˈleksiko] *nm* (*vocabulario*) vocabulary

ley [lei] *nf* (*gen*) law; (*metal*) standard

leyenda [leˈjenda] *nf* legend

leyó *etc vb ver* **leer**

liar [liˈar] *vt* to tie (up); (*unir*) to bind; (*envolver*) to wrap (up); (*enredar*) to confuse; (*cigarrillo*) to roll; **~se** *vr* (*fam*) to get involved; **~se a palos** to get involved in a fight

Líbano [ˈlißano] *nm*: **el ~** (the) Lebanon

libelo [liˈßelo] *nm* satire, lampoon

libélula [liˈßelula] *nf* dragonfly

liberación [lißeraˈθjon] *nf* liberation; (*de la cárcel*) release

liberal [lißeˈral] *adj, nm/f* liberal; **~idad** *nf* liberality, generosity

liberar [lißeˈrar] *vt* to liberate

libertad [lißerˈtað] *nf* liberty, freedom; **~ de culto/de prensa/de comercio** freedom of worship/of the press/of trade; **~ condicional** probation; **~ bajo palabra** parole; **~ bajo fianza** bail

libertar [lißerˈtar] *vt* (*preso*) to set free; (*de una obligación*) to release; (*eximir*) to exempt

libertino, a [lißerˈtino, a] *adj* permissive ♦ *nm/f* permissive person

libra [ˈlißra] *nf* pound; (*ASTROLOGÍA*): **L~** Libra; **~ esterlina** pound sterling

librar [liˈßrar] *vt* (*de peligro*) to save; (*batalla*) to wage, fight; (*de impuestos*) to exempt; (*cheque*) to make out; (*JUR*) to exempt; **~se** *vr*: **~se de** to escape from, free o.s. from

libre [ˈlißre] *adj* free; (*lugar*) unoccupied; (*asiento*) vacant; (*de deudas*) free of debts; **~ de impuestos** free of tax; **tiro ~** free kick; **los 100 metros ~** the 100 metres free-style (race); **al aire ~** in the open air

librería [lißreˈria] *nf* (*tienda*) bookshop; **librero, a** *nm/f* bookseller

libreta [liˈßreta] *nf* notebook; **~ de ahorros** savings book

libro [ˈlißro] *nm* book; **~ de bolsillo** paperback; **~ de caja** cashbook; **~ de cheques** chequebook (*BRIT*), checkbook (*US*); **~ de texto** textbook

Lic. *abr* = **licenciado, a**

licencia [liˈθenθja] *nf* (*gen*) licence; (*permiso*) permission; **~ por enfermedad** sick leave; **~ de caza** game licence; **~do, a** *adj* licensed ♦ *nm/f* graduate;

licenciar *vt* (*empleado*) to dismiss; (*permitir*) to permit, allow; (*soldado*) to discharge; (*estudiante*) to confer a degree upon; **licenciarse** *vr*: **licenciarse en letras** to graduate in arts

licencioso, a [liθenˈθjoso, a] *adj* licentious

licitar [liθiˈtar] *vt* to bid for; (*AM*) to sell by auction

lícito, a [ˈliθito, a] *adj* (*legal*) lawful; (*justo*) fair, just; (*permisible*) permissible

licor [liˈkor] *nm* spirits *pl* (*BRIT*), liquor (*US*); (*de frutas etc*) liqueur

licuadora [likwaˈðora] *nf* blender

licuar [liˈkwar] *vt* to liquidize

líder [ˈliðer] *nm/f* leader; **liderato** *nm* leadership; **liderazgo** *nm* leadership

lidia [ˈliðja] *nf* bullfighting; (*una ~*) bullfight; **toros de ~** fighting bulls; **lidiar** *vt, vi* to fight

liebre [ˈljeßre] *nf* hare

lienzo [ˈljenθo] *nm* linen; (*ARTE*) canvas; (*ARQ*) wall

liga [ˈliɣa] *nf* (*de medias*) garter, suspender; (*AM: gomita*) rubber band; (*confederación*) league

ligadura [liɣaˈðura] *nf* bond, tie; (*MED, MUS*) ligature

ligamento [liɣaˈmento] *nm* ligament

ligar [liˈɣar] *vt* (*atar*) to tie; (*unir*) to join; (*MED*) to bind up; (*MUS*) to slur ♦ *vi* to mix, blend; (*fam*): (**él) liga mucho** he pulls a lot of women; **~se** *vr* to commit o.s.

ligereza [lixeˈreθa] *nf* lightness; (*rapidez*) swiftness; (*agilidad*) agility; (*superficialidad*) flippancy

ligero, a [liˈxero, a] *adj* (*de peso*) light; (*tela*) thin; (*rápido*) swift, quick; (*ágil*) agile, nimble; (*de importancia*) slight; (*de carácter*) flippant, superficial ♦ *adv*: **a la ligera** superficially

liguero [liˈɣero] *nm* suspender (*BRIT*) *o* garter (*US*) belt

lija [ˈlixa] *nf* (*ZOOL*) dogfish; (*tb*: **papel de** ~) sandpaper

lila [ˈlila] *nf* lilac

lima [ˈlima] *nf* file; (*BOT*) lime; ~ **de uñas** nailfile; **limar** *vt* to file

limitación [limitaˈθjon] *nf* limitation, limit; ~ **de velocidad** speed limit

limitar [limiˈtar] *vt* to limit; (*reducir*) to reduce, cut down ♦ *vi*: ~ **con** to border on; ~**se** *vr*: ~**se a** to limit o.s. to

límite [ˈlimite] *nm* (*gen*) limit; (*fin*) end; (*frontera*) border; ~ **de velocidad** speed limit

limítrofe [liˈmitrofe] *adj* neighbouring

limón [liˈmon] *nm* lemon ♦ *adj*: **amarillo** ~ lemon-yellow; **limonada** *nf* lemonade

limosna [liˈmosna] *nf* alms *pl*; **vivir de** ~ to live on charity

limpiaparabrisas [limpjaparaˈβrisas] *nm inv* windscreen (*BRIT*) *o* windshield (*US*) wiper

limpiar [limˈpjar] *vt* to clean; (*con trapo*) to wipe; (*quitar*) to wipe away; (*zapatos*) to shine, polish; (*fig*) to clean up

limpieza [limˈpjeθa] *nf* (*estado*) cleanliness; (*acto*) cleaning; (: *de las calles*) cleansing; (: *de zapatos*) polishing; (*habilidad*) skill; (*fig: POLICÍA*) clean-up; (*pureza*) purity; (*MIL*): **operación de** ~ mopping-up operation; ~ **en seco** dry cleaning

limpio, a [ˈlimpjo, a] *adj* clean; (*moralmente*) pure; (*COM*) clear, net; (*fam*) honest ♦ *adv*: **jugar** ~ to play fair; **pasar a** (*ESP*) *o* **en** (*AM*) ~ to make a clean copy

linaje [liˈnaxe] *nm* lineage, family

lince [ˈlinθe] *nm* lynx

linchar [linˈtʃar] *vt* to lynch

lindar [linˈdar] *vi* to adjoin; ~ **con** to

border on; **linde** *nm o f* boundary; **lindero, a** *adj* adjoining ♦ *nm* boundary

lindo, a [ˈlindo, a] *adj* pretty, lovely ♦ *adv*: **nos divertimos de lo** ~ we had a marvellous time; **canta muy** ~ (*AM*) he sings beautifully

línea [ˈlinea] *nf* (*gen*) line; **en** ~ (*INFORM*) on line; ~ **aérea** airline; ~ **de meta** goal line; (*de carrera*) finishing line; ~ **recta** straight line

lingote [linˈɡote] *nm* ingot

lingüista [linˈɡwista] *nm/f* linguist; **lingüística** *nf* linguistics *sg*

lino [ˈlino] *nm* linen; (*BOT*) flax

linóleo [liˈnoleo] *nm* lino, linoleum

linterna [linˈterna] *nf* torch (*BRIT*), flashlight (*US*)

lío [ˈlio] *nm* bundle; (*fam*) fuss; (*desorden*) muddle, mess; **armar un** ~ to make a fuss

liquen [ˈliken] *nm* lichen

liquidación [likiðaˈθjon] *nf* liquidation; **venta de** ~ clearance sale

liquidar [likiˈðar] *vt* (*mercancías*) to liquidate; (*deudas*) to pay off; (*empresa*) to wind up

líquido, a [ˈlikiðo, a] *adj* liquid; (*ganancia*) net ♦ *nm* liquid; ~ **imponible** net taxable income

lira [ˈlira] *nf* (*MUS*) lyre; (*moneda*) lira

lírico, a [ˈliriko, a] *adj* lyrical

lirio [ˈlirjo] *nm* (*BOT*) iris

lirón [liˈron] *nm* (*ZOOL*) dormouse; (*fig*) sleepyhead

Lisboa [lisˈβoa] *n* Lisbon

lisiado, a [liˈsjaðo, a] *adj* injured ♦ *nm/f* cripple

lisiar [liˈsjar] *vt* to maim; ~**se** *vr* to injure o.s.

liso, a [ˈliso, a] *adj* (*terreno*) flat; (*cabello*) straight; (*superficie*) even; (*tela*) plain

lisonja [liˈsonxa] *nf* flattery

lista [ˈlista] *nf* list; (*de alumnos*) school register; (*de libros*) catalogue; (*de platos*) menu; (*de precios*) price list; **pasar** ~ to call the roll; ~ **de correos** poste restante; ~ **de espera** waiting list; **tela de** ~**s** striped material; **listín** *nm*: ~ (**telefónico**) telephone directory

listo, a ['listo, a] *adj* (*perspicaz*) smart, clever; (*preparado*) ready

listón [lis'ton] *nm* (*de madera, metal*) strip

litera [li'tera] *nf* (*en barco, tren*) berth; (*en dormitorio*) bunk, bunk bed

literal [lite'ral] *adj* literal

literario, a [lite'rarjo, a] *adj* literary

literato, a [lite'rato, a] *adj* literary ♦ *nm/f* writer

literatura [litera'tura] *nf* literature

litigar [liti'ɣar] *vt* to fight ♦ *vi* (*JUR*) to go to law; (*fig*) to dispute, argue

litigio [li'tixjo] *nm* (*JUR*) lawsuit; (*fig*): **en ~ con** in dispute with

litografía [litoɣra'fia] *nf* lithography; (*una* ~) lithograph

litoral [lito'ral] *adj* coastal ♦ *nm* coast, seaboard

litro ['litro] *nm* litre

liviano, a [li'βjano, a] *adj* (*cosa, objeto*) trivial

lívido, a ['lißiðo, a] *adj* livid

llaga ['ʎaɣa] *nf* wound

llama ['ʎama] *nf* flame; (*ZOOL*) llama

llamada [ʎa'maða] *nf* call; ~ **al orden** call to order; ~ **a pie de página** reference note

llamamiento [ʎama'mjento] *nm* call

llamar [ʎa'mar] *vt* to call; (*atención*) to attract ♦ *vi* (*por teléfono*) to telephone; (*a la puerta*) to knock (*o* ring); (*por señas*) to beckon; (*MIL*) to call up; **~se** *vr* to be called, be named; **¿cómo se llama usted?** what's your name?

llamarada [ʎama'raða] *nf* (*llamas*) blaze; (*rubor*) flush

llamativo, a [ʎama'tißo, a] *adj* showy; (*color*) loud

llano, a ['ʎano, a] *adj* (*superficie*) flat; (*persona*) straightforward; (*estilo*) clear ♦ *nm* plain, flat ground

llanta ['ʎanta] *nf* (*wheel*) rim; (*AM*): ~ (**de goma**) tyre; (: *cámara*) inner (tube)

llanto ['ʎanto] *nm* weeping

llanura [ʎa'nura] *nf* plain

llave ['ʎaße] *nf* key; (*del agua*) tap; (*MECÁNICA*) spanner; (*de la luz*) switch; (*MUS*) key; ~ **inglesa** monkey wrench; ~ **maestra** master key; ~ **de contacto** (*AUTO*) ignition key; ~ **de paso** stopcock; **echar la ~ a** to lock up; ~**ro** *nm* keyring

llegada [ʎe'ɣaða] *nf* arrival

llegar [ʎe'ɣar] *vi* to arrive; (*alcanzar*) to reach; (*bastar*) to be enough; **~se** *vr*: **~se a** to approach; ~ **a** to manage to, succeed in; ~ **a saber** to find out; ~ **a ser** to become; ~ **a las manos de** to come into the hands of

llenar [ʎe'nar] *vt* to fill; (*espacio*) to cover; (*formulario*) to fill in *o* up; (*fig*) to heap

lleno, a ['ʎeno, a] *adj* full, filled; (*repleto*) full up ♦ *nm* (*TEATRO*) full house; **dar de ~ contra un muro** to hit a wall head-on

llevadero, a [ʎeßa'ðero, a] *adj* bearable, tolerable

llevar [ʎe'ßar] *vt* to take; (*ropa*) to wear; (*cargar*) to carry; (*quitar*) to take away; (*en coche*) to drive; (*transportar*) to transport; (*traer: dinero*) to carry; (*conducir*) to lead; (*MAT*) to carry ♦ *vi* (*suj: camino etc*): ~ **a** to lead to; **~se** *vr* to carry off, take away; **llevamos dos días aquí** we have been here for two days; **él me lleva 2 años** he's 2 years older than me; (*COM*): ~ **los libros** to keep the books; **~se bien** to get on well (together)

llorar [ʎo'rar] *vt, vi* to cry, weep; ~ **de risa** to cry with laughter

lloriquear [ʎorike'ar] *vi* to snivel, whimper

lloro ['ʎoro] *nm* crying, weeping; **llorón, ona** *adj* tearful ♦ *nm/f* cry-baby; **~so, a** *adj* (*gen*) weeping, tearful; (*triste*) sad, sorrowful

llover [ʎo'ßer] *vi* to rain

llovizna [ʎo'ßiθna] *nf* drizzle; **lloviznar** *vi* to drizzle

llueve *etc vb ver* **llover**

lluvia ['ʎußja] *nf* rain; ~ **radioactiva** (radioactive) fallout; **lluvioso, a** *adj* rainy

lo [lo] *art def*: ~ **bello** the beautiful, what is beautiful, that which is beautiful ♦ *pron* (*persona*) him; (*cosa*) it; *tb ver* **el**

loable [lo'aβle] *adj* praiseworthy; **loar** *vt* to praise

lobo ['loβo] *nm* wolf; **~ de mar** (*fig*) sea dog; **~ marino** seal

lóbrego, a ['loβreɣo, a] *adj* dark; (*fig*) gloomy

lóbulo ['loβulo] *nm* lobe

local [lo'kal] *adj* local ♦ *nm* place, site; (*oficinas*) premises *pl*; **~idad** *nf* (*barrio*) locality; (*lugar*) location; (*TEATRO*) seat, ticket; **~izar** *vt* (*ubicar*) to locate, find; (*restringir*) to localize; (*situar*) to place

loción [lo'θjon] *nf* lotion

loco, a ['loko, a] *adj* mad ♦ *nm/f* lunatic, mad person

locomotora [lokomo'tora] *nf* engine, locomotive

locuaz [lo'kwaθ] *adj* loquacious

locución [loku'θjon] *nf* expression

locura [lo'kura] *nf* madness; (*acto*) crazy act

locutor, a [loku'tor, a] *nm/f* (*RADIO*) announcer; (*comentarista*) commentator; (*TV*) newsreader

locutorio [loku'torjo] *nm* (*en telefónica*) telephone booth

lodo ['loðo] *nm* mud

lógica ['loxika] *nf* logic

lógico, a ['loxiko, a] *adj* logical

logística [lo'xistika] *nf* logistics *sg*

logotipo [loɣo'tipo] *nm* logo

logrado, a [lo'ðraðo, a] *adj* (*interpretación, reproducción*) polished, excellent

lograr [lo'ɣrar] *vt* to achieve; (*obtener*) to get, obtain; **~ hacer** to manage to do; **~ que uno venga** to manage to get sb to come

logro ['loɣro] *nm* achievement, success

loma ['loma] *nf* hillock (*BRIT*), small hill

lombriz [lom'briθ] *nf* worm

lomo ['lomo] *nm* (*de animal*) back; (*CULIN: de cerdo*) pork loin; (: *de vaca*) rib steak; (*de libro*) spine

lona ['lona] *nf* canvas

loncha ['lontʃa] *nf* = **lonja**

lonche ['lontʃe] (*AM*) *nm* lunch; **~ría** (*AM*) *nf* snack bar, diner (*US*)

Londres ['londres] *n* London

longaniza [longa'niθa] *nf* pork sausage

longitud [lonxi'tuð] *nf* length; (*GEO*) longitude; **tener 3 metros de ~** to be 3 metres long; **~ de onda** wavelength

lonja ['lonxa] *nf* slice; (*de tocino*) rasher; **~ de pescado** fish market

loro ['loro] *nm* parrot

los [los] *art def* the ♦ *pron* them; (*ustedes*) you; **mis libros y ~ tuyos** my books and yours; *tb ver* **el**

losa ['losa] *nf* stone; **~ sepulcral** gravestone

lote ['lote] *nm* portion; (*COM*) lot

lotería [lote'ria] *nf* lottery; (*juego*) lotto

Lotería

i *Millions of pounds are spent on lotteries each year in Spain, two of which are state-run: the **Lotería Primitiva** and the **Lotería Nacional**, with money raised going directly to the government. One of the most famous lotteries is run by the wealthy and influential society for the blind, "la ONCE".*

---

loza ['loθa] *nf* crockery

lubina [lu'βina] *nf* sea bass

lubricante [luβri'kante] *nm* lubricant

lubricar [luβri'kar] *vt* to lubricate

lucha ['lutʃa] *nf* fight, struggle; **~ de clases** class struggle; **~ libre** wrestling; **luchar** *vi* to fight

lucidez [luθi'ðeθ] *nf* lucidity

lúcido, a ['luθiðo, a] *adj* (*persona*) lucid; (*mente*) logical; (*idea*) crystal-clear

luciérnaga [lu'θjernaɣa] *nf* glow-worm

lucir [lu'θir] *vt* to illuminate, light (up); (*ostentar*) to show off ♦ *vi* (*brillar*) to shine; **~se** *vr* (*irónico*) to make a fool of o.s.

lucro ['lukro] *nm* profit, gain

lúdico, a ['luðiko, a] *adj* (*aspecto, actividad*) play *cpd*

luego ['lweɣo] *adv* (*después*) next; (*más tarde*) later, afterwards

lugar [lu'ɣar] *nm* place; (*sitio*) spot; **en ~ de** instead of; **hacer ~** to make room; **fuera de ~** out of place; **tener ~** to take place; **~ común** commonplace

lugareño, a [luɣa'reɲo, a] *adj* village *cpd* ♦ *nm/f* villager

lugarteniente [luɣarte'njente] *nm* deputy

lúgubre ['luɣuβre] *adj* mournful

lujo ['luxo] *nm* luxury; (*fig*) profusion, abundance; **~so, a** *adj* luxurious

lujuria [lu'xurja] *nf* lust

lumbre ['lumbre] *nf* fire; (*para cigarrillo*) light

lumbrera [lum'brera] *nf* luminary

luminoso, a [lumi'noso, a] *adj* luminous, shining

luna ['luna] *nf* moon; (*de un espejo*) glass; (*de gafas*) lens; (*fig*) crescent; **~ llena/ nueva** full/new moon; **estar en la ~** to have one's head in the clouds; **~ de miel** honeymoon

lunar [lu'nar] *adj* lunar ♦ *nm* (*ANAT*) mole; **tela de ~es** spotted material

lunes ['lunes] *nm inv* Monday

lupa ['lupa] *nf* magnifying glass

lustrar [lus'trar] *vt* (*mueble*) to polish; (*zapatos*) to shine; **lustre** *nm* polish; (*fig*) lustre; **dar lustre a** to polish; **lustroso, a** *adj* shining

luto ['luto] *nm* mourning; **llevar el** *o* **vestirse de ~** to be in mourning

Luxemburgo [luksem'burxo] *nm* Luxembourg

luz [luθ] (*pl* **luces**) *nf* light; **dar a ~ un niño** to give birth to a child; **sacar a la ~** to bring to light; **dar** *o* **encender** (*ESP*) *o* **prender** (*AM*)/**apagar la ~** to switch the light on/off; **a todas luces** by any reckoning; **tener pocas luces** to be dim *o* stupid; **~ roja/verde** red/green light; **~ de freno** brake light; **luces de tráfico** traffic lights; **traje de luces** bullfighter's costume

M, m

m *abr* (= *metro*) m; (= *minuto*) m

macarrones [maka'rrones] *nmpl* macaroni *sg*

macedonia [maθe'ðonja] *nf*: **~ de frutas** fruit salad

macerar [maθe'rar] *vt* to macerate

maceta [ma'θeta] *nf* (*de flores*) pot of flowers; (*para plantas*) flowerpot

machacar [matʃa'kar] *vt* to crush, pound ♦ *vi* (*insistir*) to go on, keep on

machete [ma'tʃete] (*AM*) *nm* machete, (large) knife

machismo [ma'tʃismo] *nm* male chauvinism; **machista** *adj, nm* sexist

macho ['matʃo] *adj* male; (*fig*) virile ♦ *nm* male; (*fig*) he-man

macizo, a [ma'θiθo, a] *adj* (*grande*) massive; (*fuerte, sólido*) solid ♦ *nm* mass, chunk

madeja [ma'ðexa] *nf* (*de lana*) skein, hank; (*de pelo*) mass, mop

madera [ma'ðera] *nf* wood; (*fig*) nature, character; **una ~** a piece of wood

madero [ma'ðero] *nm* beam

madrastra [ma'ðrastra] *nf* stepmother

madre ['maðre] *adj* mother *cpd*; (*AM*) tremendous ♦ *nf* mother; (*de vino etc*) dregs *pl*; **~ política/soltera** mother-in-law/unmarried mother

Madrid [ma'ðrið] *n* Madrid

madriguera [maðri'ɣera] *nf* burrow

madrileño, a [maðri'leɲo, a] *adj* of *o* from Madrid ♦ *nm/f* native of Madrid

madrina [ma'ðrina] *nf* godmother; (*ARQ*) prop, shore; (*TEC*) brace; (*de boda*) bridesmaid

madrugada [maðru'ɣaða] *nf* early morning; (*alba*) dawn, daybreak

madrugador, a [maðruɣa'ðor, a] *adj* early-rising

madrugar [maðru'ɣar] *vi* to get up early; (*fig*) to get ahead

madurar [maðu'rar] *vt, vi* (*fruta*) to ripen;

(fig) to mature; **madurez** *nf* ripeness; maturity; **maduro, a** *adj* ripe; mature
maestra [ma'estra] *nf ver* **maestro**
maestría [maes'tria] *nf* mastery; *(habilidad)* skill, expertise
maestro, a [ma'estro, a] *adj* masterly; *(principal)* main ♦ *nm/f* master/mistress; *(profesor)* teacher ♦ *nm (autoridad)* authority; *(MUS)* maestro; *(AM)* skilled workman; **~ albañil** master mason
magdalena [max'ða'lena] *nf* fairy cake
magia ['maxja] *nf* magic; **mágico, a** *adj* magic(al) ♦ *nm/f* magician
magisterio [maxis'terjo] *nm (enseñanza)* teaching; *(profesión)* teaching profession; *(maestros)* teachers *pl*
magistrado [maxis'traðo] *nm* magistrate
magistral [maxis'tral] *adj* magisterial; *(fig)* masterly
magnánimo, a [max'nanimo, a] *adj* magnanimous
magnate [max'nate] *nm* magnate, tycoon
magnético, a [max'netiko, a] *adj* magnetic; **magnetizar** *vt* to magnetize
magnetofón [maxneto'fon] *nm* tape recorder; **magnetofónico, a** *adj*: **cinta magnetofónica** recording tape
magnetófono [maxne'tofono] *nm* = **magnetofón**
magnífico, a [max'nifiko, a] *adj* splendid, magnificent
magnitud [maxni'tuð] *nf* magnitude
mago, a ['maxo, a] *nm/f* magician; **los Reyes M~s** the Magi, the Three Wise Men
magro, a ['maxro, a] *adj (carne)* lean
maguey [ma'vei] *nm* agave
magullar [maxu'λar] *vt (amoratar)* to bruise; *(dañar)* to damage
mahometano, a [maome'tano, a] *adj* Mohammedan
mahonesa [mao'nesa] *nf* mayonnaise
maíz [ma'iθ] *nm* maize *(BRIT)*, corn *(US)*; sweet corn
majadero, a [maxa'ðero, a] *adj* silly, stupid
majestad [maxes'taθ] *nf* majesty;

majestuoso, a *adj* majestic
majo, a ['maxo, a] *adj* nice; *(guapo)* attractive, good-looking; *(elegante)* smart
mal [mal] *adv* badly; *(equivocadamente)* wrongly ♦ *adj* = **malo** ♦ *nm* evil; *(desgracia)* misfortune; *(daño)* harm, damage; *(MED)* illness; **~ que bien** rightly or wrongly; **ir de ~ en peor** to get worse and worse
malabarismo [malaβa'rismo] *nm* juggling; **malabarista** *nm/f* juggler
malaria [ma'larja] *nf* malaria
malcriado, a [mal'krjaðo, a] *adj* spoiled
maldad [mal'daθ] *nf* evil, wickedness
maldecir [malde'θir] *vt* to curse ♦ *vi*: **~ de** to speak ill of
maldición [maldi'θjon] *nf* curse
maldito, a [mal'dito, a] *adj (condenado)* damned; *(perverso)* wicked; **¡~ sea!** damn it!
maleante [male'ante] *nm/f* criminal, crook
maledicencia [maleði'θenθja] *nf* slander, scandal
maleducado, a [maleðu'kaðo, a] *adj* bad-mannered, rude
malentendido [malenten'diðo] *nm* misunderstanding
malestar [males'tar] *nm (gen)* discomfort; *(fig: inquietud)* uneasiness; *(POL)* unrest
maleta [ma'leta] *nf* case, suitcase; *(AUTO)* boot *(BRIT)*, trunk *(US)*; **hacer las ~s** to pack; **maletera** *(AM) nf*, **maletero** *nm (AUTO)* boot *(BRIT)*, trunk *(US)*; **maletín** *nm* small case, bag
malévolo, a [ma'leβolo, a] *adj* malicious, spiteful
maleza [ma'leθa] *nf (hierbas malas)* weeds *pl*; *(arbustos)* thicket
malgastar [malvas'tar] *vt (tiempo, dinero)* to waste; *(salud)* to ruin
malhechor, a [male'tʃor, a] *nm/f* delinquent
malhumorado, a [malumo'raðo, a] *adj* bad-tempered
malicia [ma'liθja] *nf (maldad)* wickedness; *(astucia)* slyness, guile; *(mala intención)* malice, spite; *(carácter travieso)*

mischievousness; **malicioso, a** *adj* wicked, evil; sly, crafty; malicious, spiteful; mischievous

maligno, a [maˈliɣno, a] *adj* evil; (*malévolo*) malicious; (*MED*) malignant

malla [ˈmaʎa] *nf* mesh; (*de baño*) swimsuit; (*de ballet, gimnasia*) leotard; **~s** *nfpl* tights; **~ de alambre** wire mesh

Mallorca [maˈʎorka] *nf* Majorca

malo, a [ˈmalo, a] *adj* bad; (*falso*) false ♦ *nm/f* villain; **estar ~** to be ill

malograr [maloˈɣrar] *vt* to spoil; (*plan*) to upset; (*ocasión*) to waste; **~se** *vr* (*plan etc*) to fail, come to grief; (*persona*) to die before one's time

malparado, a [malpaˈraðo, a] *adj*: **salir ~** to come off badly

malpensado, a [malpenˈsaðo, a] *adj* nasty

malsano, a [malˈsano, a] *adj* unhealthy

malteada [malteˈaða] (*AM*) *nf* milk shake

maltratar [maltraˈtar] *vt* to ill-treat, mistreat

maltrecho, a [malˈtretʃo, a] *adj* battered, damaged

malvado, a [malˈβaðo, a] *adj* evil, villainous

malversar [malβerˈsar] *vt* to embezzle, misappropriate

Malvinas [malˈβinas]: **Islas ~** *nfpl* Falkland Islands

malvivir [malβiˈβir] *vi* to live poorly

mama [ˈmama] *nf* (*de animal*) teat; (*de mujer*) breast

mamá [maˈma] (*pl* **~s**) (*fam*) *nf* mum, mummy

mamar [maˈmar] *vt, vi* to suck

mamarracho [mamaˈrratʃo] *nm* sight, mess

mamífero [maˈmifero] *nm* mammal

mampara [mamˈpara] *nf* (*entre habitaciones*) partition; (*biombo*) screen

mampostería [mamposteˈria] *nf* masonry

manada [maˈnaða] *nf* (*ZOOL*) herd; (: *de leones*) pride; (: *de lobos*) pack

manantial [mananˈtjal] *nm* spring

manar [maˈnar] *vi* to run, flow

mancha [ˈmantʃa] *nf* stain, mark; (*ZOOL*) patch; **manchar** *vt* (*gen*) to stain, mark; (*ensuciar*) to soil, dirty

manchego, a [manˈtʃeɣo, a] *adj* of o from La Mancha

manco, a [ˈmanko, a] *adj* (*de un brazo*) one-armed; (*de una mano*) one-handed; (*fig*) defective, faulty

mancomunar [mankomuˈnar] *vt* to unite, bring together; (*recursos*) to pool; (*JUR*) to make jointly responsible; **mancomunidad** *nf* union, association; (*comunidad*) community; (*JUR*) joint responsibility

mandamiento [mandaˈmjento] *nm* (*orden*) order, command; (*REL*) commandment; **~ judicial** warrant

mandar [manˈdar] *vt* (*ordenar*) to order; (*dirigir*) to lead, command; (*enviar*) to send; (*pedir*) to order, ask for ♦ *vi* to be in charge; (*pey*) to be bossy; **¿mande?** pardon?, excuse me?; **~ hacer un traje** to have a suit made

mandarina [mandaˈrina] *nf* tangerine, mandarin (orange)

mandato [manˈdato] *nm* (*orden*) order; (*POL: período*) term of office; (: *territorio*) mandate; **~ judicial** (search) warrant

mandíbula [manˈdiβula] *nf* jaw

mandil [manˈdil] *nm* apron

mando [ˈmando] *nm* (*MIL*) command; (*de país*) rule; (*el primer lugar*) lead; (*POL*) term of office; (*TEC*) control; **~ a la izquierda** left-hand drive

mandón, ona [manˈdon, ona] *adj* bossy, domineering

manejable [maneˈxaβle] *adj* manageable

manejar [maneˈxar] *vt* to manage; (*máquina*) to work, operate; (*caballo etc*) to handle; (*casa*) to run, manage; (*AM: AUTO*) to drive; **~se** *vr* (*comportarse*) to act, behave; (*arreglárselas*) to manage; **manejo** *nm* management; handling; running; driving; (*facilidad de trato*) ease, confidence; **manejos** *nmpl* (*intrigas*) intrigues

manera [maˈnera] *nf* way, manner,

fashion; **~s** *nfpl* (*modales*) manners; **su ~
de ser** the way he is; (*aire*) his manner;
de ninguna ~ no way, by no means; **de
otra ~** otherwise; **de todas ~s** at any
rate; **no hay ~ de persuadirle** there's no
way of convincing him
manga ['maŋga] *nf* (*de camisa*) sleeve; (*de
riego*) hose
mangar [maŋ'gar] (*fam*) *vt* to pinch, nick
mango ['maŋgo] *nm* handle; (*BOT*) mango
mangonear [maŋgone'ar] *vi* (*meterse*) to
meddle, interfere; (*ser mandón*) to boss
people about
manguera [maŋ'gera] *nf* hose
manía [ma'nia] *nf* (*MED*) mania; (*fig:
moda*) rage, craze; (*disgusto*) dislike;
(*malicia*) spite; **maníaco, a** *adj*
maniac(al) ♦ *nm/f* maniac
maniatar [manja'tar] *vt* to tie the hands of
maniático, a [ma'njatiko, a] *adj*
maniac(al) ♦ *nm/f* maniac
manicomio [mani'komjo] *nm* mental
hospital (*BRIT*), insane asylum (*US*)
manifestación [manifesta'θjon] *nf*
(*declaración*) statement, declaration; (*de
emoción*) show, display; (*POL: desfile*)
demonstration; (: *concentración*) mass
meeting
manifestar [manifes'tar] *vt* to show,
manifest; (*declarar*) to state, declare;
manifiesto, a *adj* clear, manifest ♦ *nm*
manifesto
manillar [mani'ʎar] *nm* handlebars *pl*
maniobra [ma'njoßra] *nf* manœuvre; **~s**
nfpl (*MIL*) manœuvres; **maniobrar** *vt* to
manœuvre
manipulación [manipula'θjon] *nf*
manipulation
manipular [manipu'lar] *vt* to manipulate;
(*manejar*) to handle
maniquí [mani'ki] *nm* dummy ♦ *nm/f*
model
manirroto, a [mani'rroto, a] *adj* lavish,
extravagant ♦ *nm/f* spendthrift
manivela [mani'ßela] *nf* crank
manjar [man'xar] *nm* (tasty) dish
mano ['mano] *nf* hand; (*ZOOL*) foot, paw;

(*de pintura*) coat; (*serie*) lot, series; **a ~** by
hand; **a ~ derecha/izquierda** on the
right(-hand side)/left(-hand side); **de
primera ~** (at) first hand; **de segunda ~**
(at) second hand; **robo a ~ armada**
armed robbery; **~ de obra** labour,
manpower; **estrechar la ~ a uno** to
shake sb's hand
manojo [ma'noxo] *nm* handful, bunch; **~
de llaves** bunch of keys
manopla [ma'nopla] *nf* mitten
manoseado, a [manose'aðo, a] *adj* well-
worn
manosear [manose'ar] *vt* (*tocar*) to
handle, touch; (*desordenar*) to mess up,
rumple; (*insistir en*) to overwork; (*AM*) to
caress, fondle
manotazo [mano'taθo] *nm* slap, smack
mansalva [man'salßa]: **a ~** *adv*
indiscriminately
mansedumbre [manse'ðumbre] *nf*
gentleness, meekness
mansión [man'sjon] *nf* mansion
manso, a ['manso, a] *adj* gentle, mild;
(*animal*) tame
manta ['manta] *nf* blanket; (*AM: poncho*)
poncho
manteca [man'teka] *nf* fat; (*AM*) butter; **~
de cacahuete/cacao** peanut/cocoa
butter; **~ de cerdo** lard
mantecado [mante'kaðo] (*AM*) *nm* ice
cream
mantel [man'tel] *nm* tablecloth
mantendré *etc vb ver* **mantener**
mantener [mante'ner] *vt* to support,
maintain; (*alimentar*) to sustain;
(*conservar*) to keep; (*TEC*) to maintain,
service; **~se** *vr* (*seguir de pie*) to be still
standing; (*no ceder*) to hold one's
ground; (*subsistir*) to sustain o.s., keep
going; **mantenimiento** *nm*
maintenance; sustenance; (*sustento*)
support
mantequilla [mante'kiʎa] *nf* butter
mantilla [man'tiʎa] *nf* mantilla; **~s** *nfpl*
(*de bebé*) baby clothes
manto ['manto] *nm* (*capa*) cloak; (*de*

ceremonia) robe, gown

mantuve *etc vb ver* **mantener**

manual [ma'nwal] *adj* manual ♦ *nm* manual, handbook

manufactura [manufak'tura] *nf* manufacture; *(fábrica)* factory; **manufacturado, a** *adj (producto)* manufactured

manuscrito, a [manus'krito, a] *adj* handwritten ♦ *nm* manuscript

manutención [manuten'θjon] *nf* maintenance; *(sustento)* support

manzana [man'θana] *nf* apple; *(ARQ)* block (of houses)

manzanilla [manθa'niʎa] *nf (planta)* camomile; *(infusión)* camomile tea

manzano [man'θano] *nm* apple tree

maña ['maɲa] *nf (gen)* skill, dexterity; *(pey)* guile; *(destreza)* trick, knack

mañana [ma'ɲana] *adv* tomorrow ♦ *nm* future ♦ *nf* morning; **de** *o* **por la ~** in the morning; **¡hasta ~!** see you tomorrow!; **~ por la ~** tomorrow morning

mañoso, a [ma'ɲoso, a] *adj (hábil)* skilful; *(astuto)* smart, clever

mapa ['mapa] *nm* map

maqueta [ma'keta] *nf* (scale) model

maquillaje [maki'ʎaxe] *nm* make-up; *(acto)* making up

maquillar [maki'ʎar] *vt* to make up; **~se** *vr* to put on (some) make-up

máquina ['makina] *nf* machine; *(de tren)* locomotive, engine; *(FOTO)* camera; *(AM: coche)* car; *(fig)* machinery; **escrito a ~** typewritten; **~ de escribir** typewriter; **~ de coser/lavar** sewing/washing machine

maquinación [makina'θjon] *nf* machination, plot

maquinal [maki'nal] *adj (fig)* mechanical, automatic

maquinaria [maki'narja] *nf (máquinas)* machinery; *(mecanismo)* mechanism, works *pl*

maquinilla [maki'niʎa] *nf*: **~ de afeitar** razor

maquinista [maki'nista] *nm/f (de tren)* engine driver; *(TEC)* operator; *(NAUT)*

engineer

mar [mar] *nm o f* sea; **~ adentro** *o* **afuera** out at sea; **en alta ~** on the high seas; **la ~ de** *(fam)* lots of; **el M~ Negro/Báltico** the Black/Baltic Sea

maraña [ma'raɲa] *nf (maleza)* thicket; *(confusión)* tangle

maravilla [mara'ßiʎa] *nf* marvel, wonder; *(BOT)* marigold; **maravillar** *vt* to astonish, amaze; **maravillarse** *vr* to be astonished, be amazed; **maravilloso, a** *adj* wonderful, marvellous

marca ['marka] *nf (gen)* mark; *(sello)* stamp; *(COM)* make, brand; **de ~** excellent, outstanding; **~ de fábrica** trademark; **~ registrada** registered trademark

marcado, a [mar'kaðo, a] *adj* marked, strong

marcador [marka'ðor] *nm (DEPORTE)* scoreboard; *(: persona)* scorer

marcapasos [marka'pasos] *nm inv* pacemaker

marcar [mar'kar] *vt (gen)* to mark; *(número de teléfono)* to dial; *(gol)* to score; *(números)* to record, keep a tally of; *(pelo)* to set ♦ *vi (DEPORTE)* to score; *(TEL)* to dial

marcha ['martʃa] *nf* march; *(TEC)* running, working; *(AUTO)* gear; *(velocidad)* speed; *(fig)* progress; *(dirección)* course; **poner en ~** to put into gear; *(fig)* to set in motion, get going; **dar ~ atrás** to reverse, put into reverse; **estar en ~** to be under way, be in motion

marchar [mar'tʃar] *vi (ir)* to go; *(funcionar)* to work, go; **~se** *vr* to go (away), leave

marchitar [martʃi'tar] *vt* to wither, dry up; **~se** *vr (BOT)* to wither; *(fig)* to fade away; **marchito, a** *adj* withered, faded; *(fig)* in decline

marcial [mar'θjal] *adj* martial, military

marciano, a [mar'θjano, a] *adj, nm/f* Martian

marco ['marko] *nm* frame; *(moneda)* mark; *(fig)* framework

marea [ma'rea] *nf* tide

marear [mare'ar] *vt* (*fig*) to annoy, upset; (*MED*): ~ **a uno** to make sb feel sick; ~**se** *vr* (*tener náuseas*) to feel sick; (*desvanecerse*) to feel faint; (*aturdirse*) to feel dizzy; (*fam: emborracharse*) to get tipsy

maremoto [mare'moto] *nm* tidal wave

mareo [ma'reo] *nm* (*náusea*) sick feeling; (*en viaje*) travel sickness; (*aturdimiento*) dizziness; (*fam: lata*) nuisance

marfil [mar'fil] *nm* ivory

margarina [marva'rina] *nf* margarine

margarita [marva'rita] *nf* (*BOT*) daisy; (**rueda**) ~ daisywheel

margen ['marxen] *nm* (*borde*) edge, border; (*fig*) margin, space ♦ *nf* (*de río etc*) bank; **dar ~ para** to give an opportunity for; **mantenerse al ~** to keep out (of things)

marginar [marxi'nar] *vt* (*socialmente*) to marginalize, ostracize

marica [ma'rika] (*fam*) *nm* sissy

maricón [mari'kon] (*fam*) *nm* queer

marido [ma'riðo] *nm* husband

marihuana [mari'wana] *nf* marijuana, cannabis

marina [ma'rina] *nf* navy; ~ **mercante** merchant navy

marinero, a [mari'nero, a] *adj* sea *cpd* ♦ *nm* sailor, seaman

marino, a [ma'rino, a] *adj* sea *cpd*, marine ♦ *nm* sailor

marioneta [marjo'neta] *nf* puppet

mariposa [mari'posa] *nf* butterfly

mariquita [mari'kita] *nf* ladybird (*BRIT*), ladybug (*US*)

mariscos [ma'riskos] *nmpl* shellfish *inv*, seafood(s)

marítimo, a [ma'ritimo, a] *adj* sea *cpd*, maritime

mármol ['marmol] *nm* marble

marqués, esa [mar'kes, esa] *nm/f* marquis/marchioness

marrón [ma'rron] *adj* brown

marroquí [marro'ki] *adj, nm/f* Moroccan ♦ *nm* Morocco (leather)

Marruecos [ma'rrwekos] *nm* Morocco

martes ['martes] *nm inv* Tuesday

Martes y Trece

According to Spanish superstition Tuesday is an unlucky day, even more so if it falls on the 13th of the month.

---

martillo [mar'tiʎo] *nm* hammer; ~ **neumático** pneumatic drill (*BRIT*), jackhammer

mártir ['martir] *nm/f* martyr; **martirio** *nm* martyrdom; (*fig*) torture, torment

marxismo [mark'sismo] *nm* Marxism; **marxista** *adj, nm/f* Marxist

marzo ['marθo] *nm* March

PALABRA CLAVE

más [mas] *adj, adv* **1**: ~ **(que/de)** (*compar*) more (than), ...+er (than); ~ **grande/inteligente** bigger/more intelligent; **trabaja ~ (que yo)** he works more (than me); *ver tb* **cada**

2 (*superl*): **el ~** the most, ...+est; **el ~ grande/inteligente (de)** the biggest/ most intelligent (in)

3 (*negativo*): **no tengo ~ dinero** I haven't got any more money; **no viene ~ por aquí** he doesn't come round here any more

4 (*adicional*): **no le veo ~ solución que ...** I see no other solution than to ...; **¿quién ~?** anybody else?

5 (+*adj: valor intensivo*): **¡qué perro ~ sucio!** what a filthy dog!; **¡es ~ tonto!** he's so stupid!

6 (*locuciones*): ~ **o menos** more or less; **los ~** most people; **es ~** furthermore; ~ **bien** rather; **¡qué ~ da!** what does it matter!; *ver tb* **no**

7: **por ~**: **por ~ que te esfuerces** no matter how hard you try; **por ~ que quisiera ...** much as I should like to ...

8: **de ~**: **veo que aquí estoy de ~** I can see I'm not needed here; **tenemos uno de ~** we've got one extra

♦ *prep*: **2 ~ 2 son 4** 2 and *o* plus 2 are 4

♦ *nm inv*: **este trabajo tiene sus ~ y**

sus menos this job's got its good points and its bad points

---

mas [mas] *conj* but

masa ['masa] *nf* (*mezcla*) dough; (*volumen*) volume, mass; (*FÍSICA*) mass; **en ~** en masse; **las ~s** (*POL*) the masses

masacre [ma'sakre] *nf* massacre

masaje [ma'saxe] *nm* massage

máscara ['maskara] *nf* mask; **mascarilla** *nf* (*de belleza, MED*) mask

masculino, a [masku'lino, a] *adj* masculine; (*BIO*) male

masía [ma'sia] *nf* farmhouse

masificación [masifika'θjon] *nf* overcrowding

masivo, a [ma'siβo, a] *adj* mass *cpd*

masón [ma'son] *nm* (free)mason

masoquista [maso'kista] *nm/f* masochist

masticar [masti'kar] *vt* to chew

mástil ['mastil] *nm* (*de navío*) mast; (*de guitarra*) neck

mastín [mas'tin] *nm* mastiff

masturbación [masturβa'θjon] *nf* masturbation

masturbarse [mastur'βarse] *vr* to masturbate

mata ['mata] *nf* (*arbusto*) bush, shrub; (*de hierba*) tuft

matadero [mata'ðero] *nm* slaughterhouse, abattoir

matador, a [mata'ðor, a] *adj* killing ♦ *nm/f* killer ♦ *nm* (*TAUR*) matador, bullfighter

matamoscas [mata'moskas] *nm inv* (*palo*) fly swat

matanza [ma'tanθa] *nf* slaughter

matar [ma'tar] *vt, vi* to kill; **~se** *vr* (*suicidarse*) to kill o.s., commit suicide; (*morir*) to be o get killed; **~ el hambre** to stave off hunger

matasellos [mata'seʎos] *nm inv* postmark

mate ['mate] *adj* matt ♦ *nm* (*en ajedrez*) (check)mate; (*AM: hierba*) maté; (*: vasija*) gourd

matemáticas [mate'matikas] *nfpl* mathematics; **matemático, a** *adj*

mathematical ♦ *nm/f* mathematician

materia [ma'terja] *nf* (*gen*) matter; (*TEC*) material; (*ESCOL*) subject; **en ~ de** on the subject of; **~ prima** raw material;

material *adj* material ♦ *nm* material; (*TEC*) equipment; **materialismo** *nm* materialism; **materialista** *adj* materialist(ic); **materialmente** *adv* materially; (*fig*) absolutely

maternal [mater'nal] *adj* motherly, maternal

maternidad [materni'ðað] *nf* motherhood, maternity; **materno, a** *adj* maternal; (*lengua*) mother *cpd*

matinal [mati'nal] *adj* morning *cpd*

matiz [ma'tiθ] *nm* shade; **~ar** *vt* (*variar*) to vary; (*ARTE*) to blend; **~ar de** to tinge with

matón [ma'ton] *nm* bully

matorral [mato'rral] *nm* thicket

matraca [ma'traka] *nf* rattle

matrícula [ma'trikula] *nf* (*registro*) register; (*AUTO*) registration number; (*: placa*) number plate; **matricular** *vt* to register, enrol

matrimonial [matrimo'njal] *adj* matrimonial

matrimonio [matri'monjo] *nm* (*pareja*) (married) couple; (*unión*) marriage

matriz [ma'triθ] *nf* (*ANAT*) womb; (*TEC*) mould; **casa ~** (*COM*) head office

matrona [ma'trona] *nf* (*persona de edad*) matron; (*comadrona*) midwife

maullar [mau'ʎar] *vi* to mew, miaow

maxilar [maksi'lar] *nm* jaw(bone)

máxima ['maksima] *nf* maxim

máxime ['maksime] *adv* especially

máximo, a ['maksimo, a] *adj* maximum; (*más alto*) highest; (*más grande*) greatest ♦ *nm* maximum

mayo ['majo] *nm* May

mayonesa [majo'nesa] *nf* mayonnaise

mayor [ma'jor] *adj* main, chief; (*adulto*) adult; (*de edad avanzada*) elderly; (*MUS*) major; (*compar: de tamaño*) bigger; (*: de edad*) older; (*superl: de tamaño*) biggest; (*: de edad*) oldest ♦ *nm* (*adulto*) adult; **al**

por ~ wholesale; **~ de edad** adult; **~es** *nmpl* (*antepasados*) ancestors

mayoral [majo'ral] *nm* foreman

mayordomo [major'ðomo] *nm* butler

mayoría [majo'ria] *nf* majority, greater part

mayorista [majo'rista] *nm/f* wholesaler

mayoritario, a [majori'tarjo, a] *adj* majority *cpd*

mayúscula [ma'juskula] *nf* capital letter

mayúsculo, a [ma'juskulo, a] *adj* (*fig*) big, tremendous

mazapán [maθa'pan] *nm* marzipan

mazo ['maθo] *nm* (*martillo*) mallet; (*de flores*) bunch; (*DEPORTE*) bat

me [me] *pron* (*directo*) me; (*indirecto*) (to) me; (*reflexivo*) (to) myself; **¡dámelo!** give it to me!

mear [me'ar] (*fam*) *vi* to pee, piss (*!*)

mecánica [me'kanika] *nf* (*ESCOL*) mechanics *sg*; (*mecanismo*) mechanism; *ver tb* **mecánico**

mecánico, a [me'kaniko, a] *adj* mechanical ♦ *nm/f* mechanic

mecanismo [meka'nismo] *nm* mechanism; (*marcha*) gear

mecanografía [mekanoɣra'fia] *nf* typewriting; **mecanógrafo, a** *nm/f* typist

mecate [me'kate] (*AM*) *nm* rope

mecedora [meθe'ðora] *nf* rocking chair

mecer [me'θer] *vt* (*cuna*) to rock; **~se** *vr* to rock; (*ramo*) to sway

mecha ['metʃa] *nf* (*de vela*) wick; (*de bomba*) fuse

mechero [me'tʃero] *nm* (*cigarette*) lighter

mechón [me'tʃon] *nm* (*gen*) tuft; (*de pelo*) lock

medalla [me'ðaʎa] *nf* medal

media ['meðja] *nf* (*ESP*) stocking; (*AM*) sock; (*promedio*) average

mediado, a [me'ðjaðo, a] *adj* half-full; (*trabajo*) half-completed; **a ~s de** in the middle of, halfway through

mediano, a [me'ðjano, a] *adj* (*regular*) medium, average; (*mediocre*) mediocre

medianoche [meðja'notʃe] *nf* midnight

mediante [me'ðjante] *adv* by (means of), through

mediar [me'ðjar] *vi* (*interceder*) to mediate, intervene

medicación [meðika'θjon] *nf* medication, treatment

medicamento [meðika'mento] *nm* medicine, drug

medicina [meði'θina] *nf* medicine

medición [meði'θjon] *nf* measurement

médico, a ['meðiko, a] *adj* medical ♦ *nm/f* doctor

medida [me'ðiða] *nf* measure; (*medición*) measurement; (*prudencia*) moderation, prudence; **en cierta / gran ~** up to a point/to a great extent; **un traje a la ~** made-to-measure suit; **~ de cuello** collar size; **a ~ de** in proportion to; (*de acuerdo con*) in keeping with; **a ~ que** (*conforme*) as

medio, a ['meðjo, a] *adj* half (a); (*punto*) mid, middle; (*promedio*) average ♦ *adv* half ♦ *nm* (*centro*) middle, centre; (*promedio*) average; (*método*) means, way; (*ambiente*) environment; **~s** *nmpl* means, resources; **~ litro** half a litre; **las tres y media** half past three; **medio ambiente** environment; **M~ Oriente** Middle East; **a ~ terminar** half finished; **pagar a medias** to share the cost; **~ambiental** *adj* (*política, efectos*) environmental

mediocre [me'ðjokre] *adj* mediocre

mediodía [meðjo'ðia] *nm* midday, noon

medir [me'ðir] *vt, vi* (*gen*) to measure

meditar [meði'tar] *vt* to ponder, think over, meditate on; (*planear*) to think out

mediterráneo, a [meðite'rraneo, a] *adj* Mediterranean ♦ *nm*: **el M~** the Mediterranean (Sea)

médula ['meðula] *nf* (*ANAT*) marrow; **~ espinal** spinal cord

medusa [me'ðusa] (*ESP*) *nf* jellyfish

megafonía [meɣafo'nia] *nf* public address system, PA system; **megáfono** *nm* megaphone

megalómano, a [meɣa'lomano, a] *nm/f* megalomaniac

mejicano, a [mexi'kano, a] *adj, nm/f* Mexican

Méjico ['mexiko] *nm* Mexico

mejilla [me'xiʎa] *nf* cheek

mejillón [mexi'ʎon] *nm* mussel

mejor [me'xor] *adj, adv* (*compar*) better; (*superl*) best; **a lo ~** probably; (*quizá*) maybe; **~ dicho** rather; **tanto ~** so much the better

mejora [me'xora] *nf* improvement; **mejorar** *vt* to improve, make better ♦ *vi* to improve, get better; **mejorarse** *vr* to improve, get better

melancólico, a [melan'koliko, a] *adj* (*triste*) sad, melancholy; (*soñador*) dreamy

melena [me'lena] *nf* (*de persona*) long hair; (*ZOOL*) mane

mellizo, a [me'ʎiθo, a] *adj, nm/f* twin; **~s** *nmpl* (*AM*) cufflinks

melocotón [meloko'ton] (*ESP*) *nm* peach

melodía [melo'ðia] *nf* melody, tune

melodrama [melo'ðrama] *nm* melodrama; **melodramático, a** *adj* melodramatic

melón [me'lon] *nm* melon

membrete [mem'brete] *nm* letterhead

membrillo [mem'briʎo] *nm* quince; **carne de ~** quince jelly

memorable [memo'raβle] *adj* memorable

memoria [me'morja] *nf* (*gen*) memory; **~s** *nfpl* (*de autor*) memoirs; **memorizar** *vt* to memorize

menaje [me'naxe] *nm*: **~ de cocina** kitchenware

mencionar [menθjo'nar] *vt* to mention

mendigar [mendi'ɣar] *vt* to beg (for)

mendigo, a [men'diɣo, a] *nm/f* beggar

mendrugo [men'druɣo] *nm* crust

menear [mene'ar] *vt* to move; **~se** *vr* to shake; (*balancearse*) to sway; (*moverse*) to move; (*fig*) to get a move on

menestra [me'nestra] *nf*: **~ de verduras** vegetable stew

menguante [men'gwante] *adj* decreasing, diminishing

menguar [men'gwar] *vt* to lessen, diminish ♦ *vi* to diminish, decrease

menopausia [meno'pausja] *nf* menopause

menor [me'nor] *adj* (*más pequeño*: *compar*) smaller; (: *superl*) smallest; (*más joven*: *compar*) younger; (: *superl*) youngest; (*MUS*) minor ♦ *nm/f* (*joven*) young person, juvenile; **no tengo la ~ idea** I haven't the faintest idea; **al por ~** retail; **~ de edad** person under age

Menorca [me'norka] *nf* Minorca

PALABRA CLAVE

---

menos [menos] *adj* 1: **~ (que/de)** (*compar*: *cantidad*) less (than); (: *número*) fewer (than); **con ~ entusiasmo** with less enthusiasm; **~ gente** fewer people; *ver tb* **cada**

2 (*superl*): **es el que ~ culpa tiene** he is the least to blame

♦ *adv* 1 (*compar*): **~ (que, de)** less (than); **me gusta ~ que el otro** I like it less than the other one

2 (*superl*): **es el ~ listo (de su clase)** he's the least bright in his class; **de todas ellas es la que ~ me agrada** out of all of them she's the one I like least; **(por) lo ~** at (the very) least

3 (*locuciones*): **no quiero verle y ~ visitarle** I don't want to see him let alone visit him; **tenemos 7 de ~** we're seven short

♦ *prep* except; (*cifras*) minus; **todos ~ él** everyone except (for) him; **5 ~ 2** 5 minus 2

♦ *conj*: **a ~ que: a ~ que venga mañana** unless he comes tomorrow

---

menospreciar [menospre'θjar] *vt* to underrate, undervalue; (*despreciar*) to scorn, despise

mensaje [men'saxe] *nm* message; **~ro, a** *nm/f* messenger

menstruación [menstrua'θjon] *nf* menstruation

menstruar [mens'trwar] *vi* to menstruate

mensual [men'swal] *adj* monthly; **1000 ptas ~es** 1000 ptas a month; **~idad** *nf* (*salario*) monthly salary; (*COM*) monthly payment, monthly instalment

menta ['menta] *nf* mint

mental [men'tal] *adj* mental; **~idad** *nf* mentality; **~izar** *vt* (*sensibilizar*) to make aware; (*convencer*) to convince; (*padres*) to prepare (mentally); **~izarse** *vr* (*concienciarse*) to become aware; **~izarse (de)** to get used to the idea (of); **~izarse de que ...** (*convencerse*) to get it into one's head that ...

mentar [men'tar] *vt* to mention, name

mente ['mente] *nf* mind

mentir [men'tir] *vi* to lie

mentira [men'tira] *nf* (*una* ~) lie; (*acto*) lying; (*invención*) fiction; **parece ~ que ...** it seems incredible that ..., I can't believe that ...

mentiroso, a [menti'roso, a] *adj* lying ♦ *nm/f* liar

menú [me'nu] (*pl* **~s**) *nm* menu; (*AM*) set meal; **~ del día** set menu

menudo, a [me'nuðo, a] *adj* (*pequeño*) small, tiny; (*sin importancia*) petty, insignificant; **¡~ negocio!** (*fam*) some deal!; **a ~** often, frequently

meñique [me'nike] *nm* little finger

meollo [me'oʎo] *nm* (*fig*) core

mercado [mer'kaðo] *nm* market

mercancía [merkan'θia] *nf* commodity; **~s** *nfpl* goods, merchandise *sg*

mercantil [merkan'til] *adj* mercantile, commercial

mercenario, a [merθe'narjo, a] *adj, nm* mercenary

mercería [merθe'ria] *nf* haberdashery (*BRIT*), notions (*US*); (*tienda*) haberdasher's (*BRIT*), notions store (*US*); (*AM*) drapery

mercurio [mer'kurjo] *nm* mercury

merecer [mere'θer] *vt* to deserve, merit ♦ *vi* to be deserving, be worthy; **merece la pena** it's worthwhile; **merecido, a** *adj* (well) deserved; **llevar su merecido** to get one's deserts

merendar [meren'dar] *vt* to have for tea ♦ *vi* to have tea; (*en el campo*) to have a picnic; **merendero** *nm* open-air cafe

merengue [me'renge] *nm* meringue

meridiano [meri'ðjano] *nm* (*GEO*) meridian

merienda [me'rjenda] *nf* (light) tea, afternoon snack; (*de campo*) picnic

mérito ['merito] *nm* merit; (*valor*) worth, value

merluza [mer'luθa] *nf* hake

merma ['merma] *nf* decrease; (*pérdida*) wastage; **mermar** *vt* to reduce, lessen ♦ *vi* to decrease, dwindle

mermelada [merme'laða] *nf* jam

mero, a ['mero, a] *adj* mere; (*AM: fam*) very

merodear [meroðe'ar] *vi*: **~ por** to prowl about

mes [mes] *nm* month

mesa ['mesa] *nf* table; (*de trabajo*) desk; (*GEO*) plateau; **~ directiva** board; **~ redonda** (*reunión*) round table; **poner/ quitar la ~** to lay/clear the table; **mesero, a** (*AM*) *nm/f* waiter/waitress

meseta [me'seta] *nf* (*GEO*) meseta, tableland

mesilla [me'siʎa] *nf*: **~ (de noche)** bedside table

mesón [me'son] *nm* inn

mestizo, a [mes'tiθo, a] *adj* half-caste, of mixed race ♦ *nm/f* half-caste

mesura [me'sura] *nf* moderation, restraint

meta ['meta] *nf* goal; (*de carrera*) finish

metabolismo [metaßo'lismo] *nm* metabolism

metáfora [me'tafora] *nf* metaphor

metal [me'tal] *nm* (*materia*) metal; (*MUS*) brass; **metálico, a** *adj* metallic; (*de metal*) metal ♦ *nm* (*dinero contante*) cash

metalurgia [meta'lurxja] *nf* metallurgy

meteoro [mete'oro] *nm* meteor; **~logía** *nf* meteorology

meter [me'ter] *vt* (*colocar*) to put, place; (*introducir*) to put in, insert; (*involucrar*) to involve; (*causar*) to make, cause; **~se** *vr*: **~se en** to go into, enter; (*fig*) to interfere in, meddle in; **~se a** to start; **~se a escritor** to become a writer; **~se con uno** to provoke sb, pick a quarrel with sb

meticuloso, a [metiku'loso, a] *adj*

meticulous, thorough

metódico, a [me'toðiko, a] *adj* methodical

método ['metoðo] *nm* method

metralleta [metra'ʎeta] *nf* sub-machine-gun

métrico, a ['metriko, a] *adj* metric

metro ['metro] *nm* metre; (*tren*) underground (*BRIT*), subway (*US*)

México ['mexiko] *nm* Mexico; **Ciudad de ~** Mexico City

mezcla ['meθkla] *nf* mixture; **mezclar** *vt* to mix (up); **mezclarse** *vr* to mix, mingle; **mezclarse en** to get mixed up in, get involved in

mezquino, a [meθ'kino, a] *adj* mean

mezquita [meθ'kita] *nf* mosque

mg. *abr* (= *miligramo*) mg

mi [mi] *adj* my ♦ *nm* (*MUS*) E

mí [mi] *pron* me; myself

mía ['mia] *pron ver* **mío**

miaja ['mjaxa] *nf* crumb

michelín [mitʃe'lin] (*fam*) *nm* (*de grasa*) spare tyre

micro ['mikro] (*AM*) *nm* minibus

microbio [mi'kroβjo] *nm* microbe

micrófono [mi'krofono] *nm* microphone

microondas [mikro'ondas] *nm inv* (*tb:* **horno ~**) microwave (oven)

microscopio [mikro'skopjo] *nm* microscope

miedo ['mjeðo] *nm* fear; (*nerviosismo*) apprehension, nervousness; **tener ~** to be afraid; **de ~** wonderful, marvellous; **hace un frío de ~** (*fam*) it's terribly cold; **~so, a** *adj* fearful, timid

miel [mjel] *nf* honey

miembro ['mjembro] *nm* limb; (*socio*) member; **~ viril** penis

mientras ['mjentras] *conj* while; (*duración*) as long as ♦ *adv* meanwhile; **~ tanto** meanwhile; **~ más tiene, más quiere** the more he has, the more he wants

miércoles ['mjerkoles] *nm inv* Wednesday

mierda ['mjerða] (*fam!*) *nf* shit (*!*)

miga ['miɣa] *nf* crumb; (*fig: meollo*) essence; **hacer buenas ~s** (*fam*) to get

on well

migración [miɣra'θjon] *nf* migration

mil [mil] *num* thousand; **dos ~ libras** two thousand pounds

milagro [mi'laɣro] *nm* miracle; **~so, a** *adj* miraculous

milésima [mi'lesima] *nf* (*de segundo*) thousandth

mili ['mili] (*fam*) *nf*: **hacer la ~** to do one's military service

milicia [mi'liθja] *nf* militia; (*servicio militar*) military service

milímetro [mi'limetro] *nm* millimetre

militante [mili'tante] *adj* militant

militar [mili'tar] *adj* military ♦ *nm/f* soldier ♦ *vi* (*MIL*) to serve; (*en un partido*) to be a member

milla ['miʎa] *nf* mile

millar [mi'ʎar] *nm* thousand

millón [mi'ʎon] *num* million; **millonario, a** *nm/f* millionaire

mimar [mi'mar] *vt* to spoil, pamper

mimbre ['mimbre] *nm* wicker

mímica ['mimika] *nf* (*para comunicarse*) sign language; (*imitación*) mimicry

mimo ['mimo] *nm* (*caricia*) caress; (*de niño*) spoiling; (*TEATRO*) mime; (*: actor*) mime artist

mina ['mina] *nf* mine; **minar** *vt* to mine; (*fig*) to undermine

mineral [mine'ral] *adj* mineral ♦ *nm* (*GEO*) mineral; (*mena*) ore

minero, a [mi'nero, a] *adj* mining *cpd* ♦ *nm/f* miner

miniatura [minja'tura] *adj inv, nf* miniature

minifalda [mini'falda] *nf* miniskirt

mínimo, a ['minimo, a] *adj, nm* minimum

minino, a [mi'nino, a] (*fam*) *nm/f* puss, pussy

ministerio [minis'terjo] *nm* Ministry; **M~ de Hacienda / de Asuntos Exteriores** Treasury (*BRIT*), Treasury Department (*US*)/Foreign Office (*BRIT*), State Department (*US*)

ministro, a [mi'nistro, a] *nm/f* minister

minoría [mino'ria] *nf* minority

minucioso, a [minu'θjoso, a] *adj* thorough, meticulous; (*prolijo*) very detailed

minúscula [mi'nuskula] *nf* small letter

minúsculo, a [mi'nuskulo, a] *adj* tiny, minute

minusválido, a [minus'ßaliðo, a] *adj* (physically) handicapped ♦ *nm/f* (physically) handicapped person

minuta [mi'nuta] *nf* (*de comida*) menu

minutero [minu'tero] *nm* minute hand

minuto [mi'nuto] *nm* minute

mío, a ['mio, a] *pron*: **el ~/la mía** mine; **un amigo ~** a friend of mine; **lo ~** what is mine

miope [mi'ope] *adj* short-sighted

mira ['mira] *nf* (*de arma*) sight(s) (*pl*); (*fig*) aim, intention

mirada [mi'raða] *nf* look, glance; (*expresión*) look, expression; **clavar la ~ en** to stare at; **echar una ~ a** to glance at

mirado, a [mi'raðo, a] *adj* (*sensato*) sensible; (*considerado*) considerate; **bien/mal ~** well/not well thought of; **bien ~** all things considered

mirador [mira'ðor] *nm* viewpoint, vantage point

mirar [mi'rar] *vt* to look at; (*observar*) to watch; (*considerar*) to consider, think over; (*vigilar, cuidar*) to watch, look after ♦ *vi* to look; (*ARQ*) to face; **~se** *vr* (*dos personas*) to look at each other; **~ bien/mal** to think highly of/have a poor opinion of; **~se al espejo** to look at o.s. in the mirror

mirilla [mi'riʎa] *nf* spyhole, peephole

mirlo ['mirlo] *nm* blackbird

misa ['misa] *nf* mass

miserable [mise'raßle] *adj* (*avaro*) mean, stingy; (*nimio*) miserable, paltry; (*lugar*) squalid; (*fam*) vile, despicable ♦ *nm/f* (*malvado*) rogue

miseria [mi'serja] *nf* (*pobreza*) poverty; (*tacañería*) meanness, stinginess; (*condiciones*) squalor; **una ~** a pittance

misericordia [miseri'korðja] *nf*

(*compasión*) compassion, pity; (*piedad*) mercy

misil [mi'sil] *nm* missile

misión [mi'sjon] *nf* mission; **misionero, a** *nm/f* missionary

mismo, a ['mismo, a] *adj* (*semejante*) same; (*después de pron*) -self; (*para énfasis*) very ♦ *adv*: **aquí/hoy ~** right here/this very day; **ahora ~** right now ♦ *conj*: **lo ~ que** just like, just as; **el ~ traje** the same suit; **en ese ~ momento** at that very moment; **vino el ~ Ministro** the minister himself came; **yo ~ lo vi** I saw it myself; **lo ~ the same (thing); **da lo ~** it's all the same; **quedamos en las mismas** we're no further forward; **por lo ~** for the same reason

misterio [mis'terjo] *nm* mystery; **~so, a** *adj* mysterious

mitad [mi'tað] *nf* (*medio*) half; (*centro*) middle; **a ~ de precio** (at) half-price; **en** *o* **a ~ del camino** halfway along the road; **cortar por la ~** to cut through the middle

mitigar [miti'var] *vt* to mitigate; (*dolor*) to ease; (*sed*) to quench

mitin ['mitin] (*pl* **mítines**) *nm* meeting

mito ['mito] *nm* myth

mixto, a ['miksto, a] *adj* mixed

ml. *abr* (= *mililitro*) ml

mm. *abr* (= *milímetro*) mm

mobiliario [moßi'ljarjo] *nm* furniture

mochila [mo'tʃila] *nf* rucksack (*BRIT*), back-pack

moción [mo'θjon] *nf* motion

moco ['moko] *nm* mucus; **~s** *nmpl* (*fam*) snot; **limpiarse los ~s de la nariz** (*fam*) to wipe one's nose

moda ['moða] *nf* fashion; (*estilo*) style; **a la** *o* **de ~** in fashion, fashionable; **pasado de ~** out of fashion

modales [mo'ðales] *nmpl* manners

modalidad [moðali'ðað] *nf* kind, variety

modelar [moðe'lar] *vt* to model

modelo [mo'ðelo] *adj inv, nm/f* model

módem ['moðem] *nm* (*INFORM*) modem

moderado, a [moðe'raðo, a] *adj*

moderate
moderar [moðe'rar] *vt* to moderate; (*violencia*) to restrain, control; (*velocidad*) to reduce; **~se** *vr* to restrain o.s., control o.s.

modernizar [moðerni'θar] *vt* to modernize

moderno, a [mo'ðerno, a] *adj* modern; (*actual*) present-day

modestia [mo'ðestja] *nf* modesty; **modesto, a** *adj* modest

módico, a ['moðiko, a] *adj* moderate, reasonable

modificar [moðifi'kar] *vt* to modify

modisto, a [mo'ðisto, a] *nm/f* (*diseñador*) couturier, designer; (*que confecciona*) dressmaker

modo ['moðo] *nm* way, manner; (*MUS*) mode; **~s** *nmpl* manners; **de ningún ~** in no way; **de todos ~s** at any rate; **~ de empleo** directions *pl* (for use)

modorra [mo'ðorra] *nf* drowsiness

mofa ['mofa] *nf*: **hacer ~ de** to mock; **mofarse** *vr*: **mofarse de** to mock, scoff at

mogollón [moɣo'ʎon] (*fam*) *adv* a hell of a lot

moho ['moo] *nm* mould, mildew; (*en metal*) rust; **~so, a** *adj* mouldy; rusty

mojar [mo'xar] *vt* to wet; (*humedecer*) to damp(en), moisten; (*calar*) to soak; **~se** *vr* to get wet

mojón [mo'xon] *nm* boundary stone

molde ['molde] *nm* mould; (*COSTURA*) pattern; (*fig*) model; **~ado** *nm* soft perm; **~ar** *vt* to mould

mole ['mole] *nf* mass, bulk; (*edificio*) pile

moler [mo'ler] *vt* to grind, crush

molestar [moles'tar] *vt* to bother; (*fastidiar*) to annoy; (*incomodar*) to inconvenience, put out ♦ *vi* to be a nuisance; **~se** *vr* to bother; (*incomodarse*) to go to trouble; (*ofenderse*) to take offence; **¿(no) te molesta si ...?** do you mind if ...?

molestia [mo'lestja] *nf* bother, trouble; (*incomodidad*) inconvenience; (*MED*)

discomfort; **es una ~** it's a nuisance; **molesto, a** *adj* (*que fastidia*) annoying; (*incómodo*) inconvenient; (*inquieto*) uncomfortable, ill at ease; (*enfadado*) annoyed

molido, a [mo'liðo, a] *adj*: **estar ~** (*fig*) to be exhausted *o* dead beat

molinillo [moli'niʎo] *nm*: **~ de carne/café** mincer/coffee grinder

molino [mo'lino] *nm* (*edificio*) mill; (*máquina*) grinder

momentáneo, a [momen'taneo, a] *adj* momentary

momento [mo'mento] *nm* moment; **de ~** at the moment, for the moment

momia ['momja] *nf* mummy

monarca [mo'narka] *nm/f* monarch, ruler; **monarquía** *nf* monarchy; **monárquico, a** *nm/f* royalist, monarchist

monasterio [monas'terjo] *nm* monastery

mondar [mon'dar] *vt* to peel; **~se de risa** (*fam*) to split one's sides laughing

moneda [mo'neða] *nf* (*tipo de dinero*) currency, money; (*pieza*) coin; **una ~ de 5 pesetas** a 5 peseta piece; **monedero** *nm* purse; **monetario, a** *adj* monetary, financial

monitor, a [moni'tor, a] *nm/f* instructor, coach ♦ *nm* (*TV*) set; (*INFORM*) monitor

monja ['monxa] *nf* nun

monje ['monxe] *nm* monk

mono, a ['mono, a] *adj* (*bonito*) lovely, pretty; (*gracioso*) nice, charming ♦ *nm/f* monkey, ape ♦ *nm* dungarees *pl*; (*overoles*) overalls *pl*

monopatín [monopa'tin] *nm* skateboard

monopolio [mono'poljo] *nm* monopoly; **monopolizar** *vt* to monopolize

monotonía [monoto'nia] *nf* (*sonido*) monotone; (*fig*) monotony

monótono, a [mo'notono, a] *adj* monotonous

monstruo ['monstrwo] *nm* monster ♦ *adj inv* fantastic; **~so, a** *adj* monstrous

montaje [mon'taxe] *nm* assembly; (*TEATRO*) décor; (*CINE*) montage

montaña [mon'taɲa] *nf* (*monte*)
mountain; (*sierra*) mountains *pl*,
mountainous area; (*AM: selva*) forest; ~
rusa roller coaster; **montañero, a** *nm/f*
mountaineer; **montañés, esa** *nm/f*
highlander; **montañismo** *nm*
mountaineering

montar [mon'tar] *vt* (*subir a*) to mount,
get on; (*TEC*) to assemble, put together;
(*negocio*) to set up; (*arma*) to cock;
(*colocar*) to lift on to; (*CULIN*) to beat ♦ *vi*
to mount, get on; (*sobresalir*) to overlap;
~ **en cólera** to get angry; ~ **a caballo** to
ride, go horseriding

monte ['monte] *nm* (*montaña*) mountain;
(*bosque*) woodland; (*área sin cultivar*) wild
area, wild country; **M~ de Piedad**
pawnshop

montón [mon'ton] *nm* heap, pile; (*fig*): **un**
~ **de** heaps of, lots of

monumento [monu'mento] *nm*
monument

monzón [mon'θon] *nm* monsoon

moño ['moɲo] *nm* bun

moqueta [mo'keta] *nf* fitted carpet

mora ['mora] *nf* blackberry; *ver tb* **moro**

morada [mo'raða] *nf* (*casa*) dwelling,
abode

morado, a [mo'raðo, a] *adj* purple, violet
♦ *nm* bruise

moral [mo'ral] *adj* moral ♦ *nf* (*ética*) ethics
pl; (*moralidad*) morals *pl*, morality;
(*ánimo*) morale

moraleja [mora'lexa] *nf* moral

moralidad [morali'ðað] *nf* morals *pl*,
morality

morboso, a [mor'ßoso, a] *adj* morbid

morcilla [mor'θiʎa] *nf* blood sausage,
≈ black pudding (*BRIT*)

mordaz [mor'ðaθ] *adj* (*crítica*) biting,
scathing

mordaza [mor'ðaθa] *nf* (*para la boca*) gag;
(*TEC*) clamp

morder [mor'ðer] *vt* to bite; (*fig: consumir*)
to eat away, eat into; **mordisco** *nm* bite

moreno, a [mo'reno, a] *adj* (*color*) (dark)
brown; (*de tez*) dark; (*de pelo* ~) dark-

haired; (*negro*) black

morfina [mor'fina] *nf* morphine

moribundo, a [mori'ßundo, a] *adj* dying

morir [mo'rir] *vi* to die; (*fuego*) to die
down; (*luz*) to go out; **~se** *vr* to die; (*fig*)
to be dying; **murió en un accidente** he
was killed in an accident; **~se por algo** to
be dying for sth

moro, a ['moro, a] *adj* Moorish ♦ *nm/f*
Moor

moroso, a [mo'roso, a] *nm/f* bad debtor,
defaulter

morral [mo'rral] *nm* haversack

morro ['morro] *nm* (*ZOOL*) snout, nose;
(*AUTO, AVIAT*) nose

morsa ['morsa] *nf* walrus

mortadela [morta'ðela] *nf* mortadella

mortaja [mor'taxa] *nf* shroud

mortal [mor'tal] *adj* mortal; (*golpe*) deadly;
~idad *nf* mortality

mortero [mor'tero] *nm* mortar

mortífero, a [mor'tifero, a] *adj* deadly,
lethal

mortificar [mortifi'kar] *vt* to mortify

mosca ['moska] *nf* fly

Moscú [mos'ku] *n* Moscow

mosquearse [moske'arse] (*fam*) *vr*
(*enojarse*) to get cross; (*ofenderse*) to take
offence

mosquitero [moski'tero] *nm* mosquito
net

mosquito [mos'kito] *nm* mosquito

mostaza [mos'taθa] *nf* mustard

mosto ['mosto] *nm* (unfermented) grape
juice

mostrador [mostra'ðor] *nm* (*de tienda*)
counter; (*de café*) bar

mostrar [mos'trar] *vt* to show; (*exhibir*) to
display, exhibit; (*explicar*) to explain; **~se**
vr: **~se amable** to be kind; to prove to
be kind; **no se muestra muy inteligente**
he doesn't seem (to be) very intelligent

mota ['mota] *nf* speck, tiny piece; (*en
diseño*) dot

mote ['mote] *nm* nickname

motín [mo'tin] *nm* (*del pueblo*) revolt,
rising; (*del ejército*) mutiny

motivar [moti'ßar] *vt* (*causar*) to cause, motivate; (*explicar*) to explain, justify; **motivo** *nm* motive, reason

moto ['moto] (*fam*) *nf* = **motocicleta**

motocicleta [motoθi'kleta] *nf* motorbike (*BRIT*), motorcycle

motor [mo'tor] *nm* motor, engine; ~ **a chorro** *o* **de reacción/de explosión** jet engine/internal combustion engine

motora [mo'tora] *nf* motorboat

movedizo, a [moße'ðiθo, a] *adj ver* **arena**

mover [mo'ßer] *vt* to move; (*cabeza*) to shake; (*accionar*) to drive; (*fig*) to cause, provoke; **~se** *vr* to move; (*fig*) to get a move on

móvil ['moßil] *adj* mobile; (*pieza de máquina*) moving; (*mueble*) movable ♦ *nm* motive; **movilidad** *nf* mobility; **movilizar** *vt* to mobilize

movimiento [moßi'mjento] *nm* movement; (*TEC*) motion; (*actividad*) activity

mozo, a ['moθo, a] *adj* (*joven*) young ♦ *nm/f* youth, young man/girl

muchacho, a [mu'tʃatʃo, a] *nm/f* (*niño*) boy/girl; (*criado*) servant; (*criada*) maid

muchedumbre [mutʃe'ðumbre] *nf* crowd

⌐ PALABRA CLAVE ⌐

mucho, a ['mutʃo, a] *adj* **1** (*cantidad*) a lot of, much; (*número*) lots of, a lot of, many; ~ **dinero** a lot of money; **hace ~ calor** it's very hot; **muchas amigas** lots *o* a lot of friends

2 (*sg: grande*): **ésta es mucha casa para él** this house is much too big for him

♦ *pron*: **tengo ~ que hacer** I've got a lot to do; **~s dicen que ...** a lot of people say that ...; *ver tb* **tener**

♦ *adv* **1**: **me gusta ~** I like it a lot; **lo siento ~** I'm very sorry; **come ~** he eats a lot; **¿te vas a quedar ~?** are you going to be staying long?

2 (*respuesta*) very; **¿estás cansado? – ¡~!** are you tired? – very!

3 (*locuciones*): **como ~** at (the) most; **con ~: el mejor con ~** by far the best; **ni ~**

---

menos: no es rico ni ~ menos he's far from being rich

4: **por ~ que: por ~ que le creas** no matter how *o* however much you believe her

---

muda ['muða] *nf* change of clothes

mudanza [mu'ðanθa] *nf* (*de casa*) move

mudar [mu'ðar] *vt* to change; (*ZOOL*) to shed ♦ *vi* to change; **~se** *vr* (*la ropa*) to change; **~se de casa** to move house

mudo, a ['muðo, a] *adj* dumb; (*callado*, *CINE*) silent

mueble ['mweßle] *nm* piece of furniture; **~s** *nmpl* furniture *sg*

mueca ['mweka] *nf* face, grimace; **hacer ~s a** to make faces at

muela ['mwela] *nf* (*back*) tooth

muelle ['mweʎe] *nm* spring; (*NAUT*) wharf; (*malecón*) pier

muero *etc vb ver* **morir**

muerte ['mwerte] *nf* death; (*homicidio*) murder; **dar ~ a** to kill

muerto, a ['mwerto, a] *pp de* **morir** ♦ *adj* dead ♦ *nm/f* dead man/woman; (*difunto*) deceased; (*cadáver*) corpse; **estar ~ de cansancio** to be dead tired

muestra ['mwestra] *nf* (*señal*) indication, sign; (*demostración*) demonstration; (*prueba*) proof; (*estadística*) sample; (*modelo*) model, pattern; (*testimonio*) token

muestreo [mwes'treo] *nm* sample, sampling

muestro *etc vb ver* **mostrar**

muevo *etc vb ver* **mover**

mugir [mu'xir] *vi* (*vaca*) to moo

mugre ['muxre] *nf* dirt, filth; **mugriento, a** *adj* dirty, filthy

mujer [mu'xer] *nf* woman; (*esposa*) wife; **~iego** *nm* womanizer

mula ['mula] *nf* mule

muleta [mu'leta] *nf* (*para andar*) crutch; (*TAUR*) stick with red cape attached

mullido, a [mu'ʎiðo, a] *adj* (*cama*) soft; (*hierba*) soft, springy

multa ['multa] *nf* fine; **poner una ~ a** to

fine; **multar** *vt* to fine
multicines [multi'θines] *nmpl* multiscreen cinema
multinacional [multinaθjo'nal] *nf* multinational
múltiple ['multiple] *adj* multiple; (*pl*) many, numerous
multiplicar [multipli'kar] *vt* (*MAT*) to multiply; (*fig*) to increase; **~se** *vr* (*BIO*) to multiply; (*fig*) to be everywhere at once
multitud [multi'tuð] *nf* (*muchedumbre*) crowd; **~ de** lots of
mundano, a [mun'dano, a] *adj* worldly
mundial [mun'djal] *adj* world-wide, universal; (*guerra, récord*) world *cpd*
mundo ['mundo] *nm* world; **todo el ~** everybody; **tener ~** to be experienced, know one's way around
munición [muni'θjon] *nf* ammunition
municipal [muniθi'pal] *adj* municipal, local
municipio [muni'θipjo] *nm* (*ayuntamiento*) town council, corporation; (*territorio administrativo*) town, municipality
muñeca [mu'ɲeka] *nf* (*ANAT*) wrist; (*juguete*) doll
muñeco [mu'ɲeko] *nm* (*figura*) figure; (*marioneta*) puppet; (*fig*) puppet, pawn
mural [mu'ral] *adj* mural, wall *cpd* ♦ *nm* mural
muralla [mu'raʎa] *nf* (city) wall(s) (*pl*)
murciélago [mur'θjelaɣo] *nm* bat
murmullo [mur'muʎo] *nm* murmur(ing); (*cuchicheo*) whispering
murmuración [murmura'θjon] *nf* gossip; **murmurar** *vi* to murmur, whisper; (*cotillear*) to gossip
muro ['muro] *nm* wall
muscular [musku'lar] *adj* muscular
músculo ['muskulo] *nm* muscle
museo [mu'seo] *nm* museum; **~ de arte** art gallery
musgo ['musɣo] *nm* moss
música ['musika] *nf* music; *ver tb* **músico**
músico, a ['musiko, a] *adj* musical ♦ *nm/f* musician
muslo ['muslo] *nm* thigh

mustio, a ['mustjo, a] *adj* (*persona*) depressed, gloomy; (*planta*) faded, withered
musulmán, ana [musul'man, ana] *nm/f* Moslem
mutación [muta'θjon] *nf* (*BIO*) mutation; (*cambio*) (sudden) change
mutilar [muti'lar] *vt* to mutilate; (*a una persona*) to maim
mutismo [mu'tismo] *nm* (*de persona*) uncommunicativeness; (*de autoridades*) silence
mutuamente [mutwa'mente] *adv* mutually
mutuo, a ['mutwo, a] *adj* mutual
muy [mwi] *adv* very; (*demasiado*) too; **M~ Señor mío** Dear Sir; **~ de noche** very late at night; **eso es ~ de él** that's just like him

N, n

N *abr* (= *norte*) N
nabo ['naβo] *nm* turnip
nácar ['nakar] *nm* mother-of-pearl
nacer [na'θer] *vi* to be born; (*de huevo*) to hatch; (*vegetal*) to sprout; (*río*) to rise; **nací en Barcelona** I was born in Barcelona; **nació una sospecha en su mente** a suspicion formed in her mind; **nacido, a** *adj* born; **recién nacido** newborn; **naciente** *adj* new, emerging; (*sol*) rising; **nacimiento** *nm* birth; (*de Navidad*) Nativity; (*de río*) source
nación [na'θjon] *nf* nation; **nacional** *adj* national; **nacionalismo** *nm* nationalism; **nacionalista** *nm/f* nationalist; **nacionalizar** *vt* to nationalize; **nacionalizarse** *vr* (*persona*) to become naturalized
nada ['naða] *pron* nothing ♦ *adv* not at all, in no way; **no decir ~** to say nothing, not to say anything; **~ más** nothing else; **de ~** don't mention it
nadador, a [naða'ðor, a] *nm/f* swimmer
nadar [na'ðar] *vi* to swim

nadie ['naðje] *pron* nobody, no-one; **~ habló** nobody spoke; **no había ~** there was nobody there, there wasn't anybody there

nado ['naðo]: **a ~** *adv*: **pasar a ~** to swim across

nafta ['nafta] (*AM*) *nf* petrol (*BRIT*), gas (*US*)

naipe ['naipe] *nm* (playing) card; **~s** *nmpl* cards

nalgas ['nalɣas] *nfpl* buttocks

nana ['nana] *nf* lullaby

naranja [na'ranxa] *adj inv*, *nf* orange; **media ~** (*fam*) better half; **naranjada** *nf* orangeade; **naranjo** *nm* orange tree

narciso [nar'θiso] *nm* narcissus

narcótico, a [nar'kotiko, a] *adj*, *nm* narcotic; **narcotizar** *vt* to drug; **narcotráfico** *nm* drug trafficking *o* running

nardo ['narðo] *nm* lily

narigudo, a [nari'ɣuðo, a] *adj* big-nosed

nariz [na'riθ] *nf* nose

narración [narra'θjon] *nf* narration; **narrador, a** *nm/f* narrator

narrar [na'rrar] *vt* to narrate, recount; **narrativa** *nf* narrative

nata ['nata] *nf* cream

natación [nata'θjon] *nf* swimming

natal [na'tal] *adj*: **ciudad ~** home town; **~idad** *nf* birth rate

natillas [na'tiʎas] *nfpl* custard *sg*

nativo, a [na'tiβo, a] *adj*, *nm/f* native

nato, a ['nato, a] *adj* born; **un músico ~** a born musician

natural [natu'ral] *adj* natural; (*fruta etc*) fresh ♦ *nm/f* native ♦ *nm* (*disposición*) nature

naturaleza [natura'leθa] *nf* nature; (*género*) nature, kind; **~ muerta** still life

naturalidad [naturali'ðað] *nf* naturalness

naturalmente [natural'mente] *adv* (*de modo natural*) in a natural way; **¡~!** of course!

naufragar [naufra'ɣar] *vi* to sink; **naufragio** *nm* shipwreck; **náufrago, a** *nm/f* castaway, shipwrecked person

nauseabundo, a [nausea'βundo, a] *adj* nauseating, sickening

náuseas ['nauseas] *nfpl* nausea *sg*; **me da ~** it makes me feel sick

náutico, a ['nautiko, a] *adj* nautical

navaja [na'βaxa] *nf* knife; (*de barbero, peluquero*) razor

naval [na'βal] *adj* naval

Navarra [na'βarra] *n* Navarre

nave ['naβe] *nf* (*barco*) ship, vessel; (*ARQ*) nave; **~ espacial** spaceship

navegación [naβeɣa'θjon] *nf* navigation; (*viaje*) sea journey; **~ aérea** air traffic; **~ costera** coastal shipping; **navegante** *nm/f* navigator; **navegar** *vi* (*barco*) to sail; (*avión*) to fly

Navidad [naβi'ðað] *nf* Christmas; **~es** *nfpl* Christmas time; **Feliz N~** Merry Christmas; **navideño, a** *adj* Christmas *cpd*

navío [na'βio] *nm* ship

nazca *etc vb ver* **nacer**

nazi ['naθi] *adj*, *nm/f* Nazi

NE *abr* (= *nor(d)este*) NE

neblina [ne'βlina] *nf* mist

nebulosa [neβu'losa] *nf* nebula

necesario, a [neθe'sarjo, a] *adj* necessary

neceser [neθe'ser] *nm* toilet bag; (*bolsa grande*) holdall

necesidad [neθesi'ðað] *nf* need; (*lo inevitable*) necessity; (*miseria*) poverty, need; **en caso de ~** in case of need *o* emergency; **hacer sus ~es** to relieve o.s.

necesitado, a [neθesi'taðo, a] *adj* needy, poor; **~ de** in need of

necesitar [neθesi'tar] *vt* to need, require

necio, a ['neθjo, a] *adj* foolish

necrópolis [ne'kropolis] *nf inv* cemetery

nectarina [nekta'rina] *nf* nectarine

nefasto, a [ne'fasto, a] *adj* ill-fated, unlucky

negación [neɣa'θjon] *nf* negation; (*rechazo*) refusal, denial

negar [ne'ɣar] *vt* (*renegar, rechazar*) to refuse; (*prohibir*) to refuse, deny; (*desmentir*) to deny; **~se** *vr*: **~se a** to refuse to

negativa [neɣa'tiβa] *nf* negative; (*rechazo*)

refusal, denial

negativo, a [neɣa'tiβo, a] *adj, nm* negative

negligencia [neɣli'xenθja] *nf* negligence; **negligente** *adj* negligent

negociado [neɣo'θjaðo] *nm* department, section

negociante [neɣoθ'jante] *nm/f* businessman/woman

negociar [neɣo'θjar] *vt, vi* to negotiate; ~ **en** to deal in, trade in

negocio [ne'ɣoθjo] *nm* (*COM*) business; (*asunto*) affair, business; (*operación comercial*) deal, transaction; (*AM*) firm; (*lugar*) place of business; **los ~s** business *sg*; **hacer ~** to do business

negra ['neɣra] *nf* (*MUS*) crotchet; *ver tb* **negro**

negro, a ['neɣro, a] *adj* black; (*suerte*) awful ♦ *nm* black ♦ *nm/f* black man/woman

nene, a ['nene, a] *nm/f* baby, small child

nenúfar [ne'nufar] *nm* water lily

neologismo [neolo'xismo] *nm* neologism

neón [ne'on] *nm*: **luces/lámpara de ~** neon lights/lamp

neoyorquino, a [neojor'kino, a] *adj* (of) New York

nervio ['nerβjo] *nm* nerve; **nerviosismo** *nm* nervousness, nerves *pl*; **~so, a** *adj* nervous

neto, a ['neto, a] *adj* net

neumático, a [neu'matiko, a] *adj* pneumatic ♦ *nm* (*ESP*) tyre (*BRIT*), tire (*US*); ~ **de recambio** spare tyre

neurasténico, a [neuras'teniko, a] *adj* (*fig*) hysterical

neurólogo, a [neu'roloɣo, a] *nm/f* neurologist

neurona [neu'rona] *nf* nerve cell

neutral [neu'tral] *adj* neutral; **~izar** *vt* to neutralize; (*contrarrestar*) to counteract

neutro, a ['neutro, a] *adj* (*BIO, LING*) neuter

neutrón [neu'tron] *nm* neutron

nevada [ne'βaða] *nf* snowstorm; (*caída de nieve*) snowfall

nevar [ne'βar] *vi* to snow

nevera [ne'βera] *nf* (*ESP*) refrigerator (*BRIT*), icebox (*US*)

nevería [neβe'ria] *nf* (*AM*) ice-cream parlour

nexo ['nekso] *nm* link, connection

ni [ni] *conj* nor, neither; (*tb*: ~ **siquiera**) not ... even; ~ **aunque que** not even if; ~ **blanco ~ negro** neither white nor black

Nicaragua [nika'raɣwa] *nf* Nicaragua; **nicaragüense** *adj, nm/f* Nicaraguan

nicho ['nitʃo] *nm* niche

nicotina [niko'tina] *nf* nicotine

nido ['niðo] *nm* nest

niebla ['njeβla] *nf* fog; (*neblina*) mist

niego *etc vb ver* **negar**

nieto, a ['njeto, a] *nm/f* grandson/daughter; **~s** *nmpl* grandchildren

nieve *etc* ['njeβe] *vb ver* **nevar** ♦ *nf* snow; (*AM*) icecream

N.I.F. *nm abr* (= *Número de Identificación Fiscal*) *personal identification number used for financial and tax purposes*

nimiedad [nimje'ðað] *nf* triviality

nimio, a ['nimjo, a] *adj* trivial, insignificant

ninfa ['ninfa] *nf* nymph

ningún [nin'ɡun] *adj ver* **ninguno**

ninguno, a [nin'ɡuno, a] (*delante de nm*: **ningún**) *adj no* ♦ *pron* (*nadie*) nobody; (*ni uno*) none, not one; (*ni uno ni otro*) neither; **de ninguna manera** by no means, not at all

niña ['niɲa] *nf* (*ANAT*) pupil; *ver tb* **niño**

niñera [ni'ɲera] *nf* nursemaid, nanny; **niñería** *nf* childish act

niñez [ni'ɲeθ] *nf* childhood; (*infancia*) infancy

niño, a ['niɲo, a] *adj* (*joven*) young; (*inmaduro*) immature ♦ *nm/f* child, boy/girl

nipón, ona [ni'pon, ona] *adj, nm/f* Japanese

níquel ['nikel] *nm* nickel; **niquelar** *vt* (*TEC*) to nickel-plate

níspero ['nispero] *nm* medlar

nitidez [niti'ðeθ] *nf* (*claridad*) clarity; (: *de imagen*) sharpness; **nítido, a** *adj* clear;

sharp

nitrato [ni'trato] *nm* nitrate

nitrógeno [ni'troxeno] *nm* nitrogen

nivel [ni'ßel] *nm* (GEO) level; (*norma*) level, standard; (*altura*) height; **~ de aceite** oil level; **~ de aire** air level; **~ de vida** standard of living; **~ar** *vt* to level out; (*fig*) to even up; (COM) to balance

NN. UU. *nfpl abr* (= *Naciones Unidas*) UN *sg*

no [no] *adv* no; not; (*con verbo*) not ♦ *excl* no!; **~ tengo nada** I don't have anything, I have nothing; **~ es el mío** it's not mine; **ahora ~** not now; **¿~ lo sabes?** don't you know?; **~ mucho** not much; **~ bien termine, lo entregaré** as soon as I finish I'll hand it over; **~ más: ayer ~ más** just yesterday; **¡pase ~ más!** come in!; **¡a que ~ lo sabes!** I bet you don't know!; **¡cómo ~!** of course!; **los países ~ alineados** the non-aligned countries; **la ~ intervención** non-intervention

noble ['noßle] *adj, nm/f* noble; **~za** *nf* nobility

noche ['notʃe] *nf* night, night-time; (*la tarde*) evening; **de ~, por la ~** at night; **es de ~** it's dark

---
Noche de San Juan

ⓘ The **Noche de San Juan** *on the 24th June is a* **fiesta** *coinciding with the summer solstice and which has taken the place of other ancient pagan festivals. Traditionally fire plays a major part in these festivities with celebrations and dancing taking place around bonfires in towns and villages across the country.*

---

nochebuena [notʃe'ßwena] *nf* Christmas Eve

Nochebuena

ⓘ Traditional Christmas celebrations in Spanish-speaking countries mainly take place on the night of **Nochebuena,** *Christmas Eve. Families gather together for a large meal and the more religiously*

inclined attend Midnight Mass. While presents are traditionally given by **los Reyes Magos** *on the 6th January, more and more people are exchanging gifts on Christmas Eve.*

---

nochevieja [notʃe'ßjexa] *nf* New Year's Eve

noción [no'θjon] *nf* notion

nocivo, a [no'θißo, a] *adj* harmful

noctámbulo, a [nok'tambulo, a] *nm/f* sleepwalker

nocturno, a [nok'turno, a] *adj* (*de la noche*) nocturnal, night *cpd*; (*de la tarde*) evening *cpd* ♦ *nm* nocturne

nodriza [no'ðriθa] *nf* wet nurse; **buque** *o* **nave ~** supply ship

nogal [no'val] *nm* walnut tree

nómada ['nomaða] *adj* nomadic ♦ *nm/f* nomad

nombramiento [nombra'mjento] *nm* naming; (*a un empleo*) appointment

nombrar [nom'brar] *vt* (*designar*) to name; (*mencionar*) to mention; (*dar puesto a*) to appoint

nombre ['nombre] *nm* name; (*sustantivo*) noun; **~ y apellidos** name in full; **~ común/propio** common/proper noun; **~ de pila/de soltera** Christian/maiden name; **poner ~ a** to call, name

nómina ['nomina] *nf* (*lista*) payroll; (*hoja*) payslip

nominal [nomi'nal] *adj* nominal

nominar [nomi'nar] *vt* to nominate

nominativo, a [nomina'tißo, a] *adj* (COM): **cheque ~ a X** cheque made out to X

nono, a ['nono, a] *adj* ninth

nordeste [nor'ðeste] *adj* north-east, north-eastern, north-easterly ♦ *nm* north-east

nórdico, a ['norðiko, a] *adj* Nordic

noreste [no'reste] *adj, nm* = **nordeste**

noria ['norja] *nf* (AGR) waterwheel; (*de carnaval*) big (BRIT) *o* Ferris (US) wheel

norma ['norma] *nf* rule (of thumb)

normal [nor'mal] *adj* (*corriente*) normal;

(*habitual*) usual, natural; **~idad** *nf* normality; **restablecer la ~idad** to restore order; **~izar** *vt* (*reglamentar*) to normalize; (*TEC*) to standardize; **~izarse** *vr* to return to normal; **~mente** *adv* normally

normando, a [nor'mando, a] *adj, nm/f* Norman

normativa [norma'tiβa] *nf* (set of) rules *pl*, regulations *pl*

noroeste [noro'este] *adj* north-west, north-western, north-westerly ♦ *nm* north-west

norte ['norte] *adj* north, northern, northerly ♦ *nm* north; (*fig*) guide

norteamericano, a [norteameri'kano, a] *adj, nm/f* (North) American

Noruega [no'rweɣa] *nf* Norway

noruego, a [no'rweɣo, a] *adj, nm/f* Norwegian

nos [nos] *pron* (*directo*) us; (*indirecto*) us; to us; for us; from us; (*reflexivo*) (to) ourselves; (*recíproco*) (to) each other; **~ levantamos a las 7** we get up at 7

nosotros, as [no'sotros, as] *pron* (*sujeto*) we; (*después de prep*) us

nostalgia [nos'talxja] *nf* nostalgia

nota ['nota] *nf* note; (*ESCOL*) mark

notable [no'taβle] *adj* notable; (*ESCOL*) outstanding

notar [no'tar] *vt* to notice, note; **~se** *vr* to be obvious; **se nota que ...** one observes that ...

notarial [nota'rjal] *adj*: **acta ~** affidavit

notario [no'tarjo] *nm* notary

noticia [no'tiθja] *nf* (*información*) piece of news; **las ~s** the news *sg*; **tener ~s de alguien** to hear from sb

noticiero [noti'θjero] (*AM*) *nm* news bulletin

notificación [notifika'θjon] *nf* notification; **notificar** *vt* to notify, inform

notoriedad [notorje'ðað] *nf* fame, renown; **notorio, a** *adj* (*público*) well-known; (*evidente*) obvious

novato, a [no'βato, a] *adj* inexperienced ♦ *nm/f* beginner, novice

novecientos, as [noβe'θjentos, as] *num* nine hundred

novedad [noβe'ðað] *nf* (*calidad de nuevo*) newness; (*noticia*) piece of news; (*cambio*) change, (new) development

novel [no'βel] *adj* new; (*inexperto*) inexperienced ♦ *nm/f* beginner

novela [no'βela] *nf* novel

noveno, a [no'βeno, a] *adj* ninth

noventa [no'βenta] *num* ninety

novia ['noβja] *nf* ver **novio**

noviazgo [no'βjaθɣo] *nm* engagement

novicio, a [no'βiθjo, a] *nm/f* novice

noviembre [no'βjembre] *nm* November

novillada [noβi'ʎaða] *nf* (*TAUR*) bullfight with young bulls; **novillero** *nm* novice bullfighter; **novillo** *nm* young bull, bullock; **hacer novillos** (*fam*) to play truant

novio, a ['noβjo, a] *nm/f* boyfriend/girlfriend; (*prometido*) fiancé/fiancée; (*recién casado*) bridegroom/bride; **los ~s** the newly-weds

nubarrón [nuβa'rron] *nm* storm cloud

nube ['nuβe] *nf* cloud

nublado, a [nu'βlaðo, a] *adj* cloudy; **nublarse** *vr* to grow dark

nubosidad [nuβosi'ðað] *nf* cloudiness; **había mucha ~** it was very cloudy

nuca ['nuka] *nf* nape of the neck

nuclear [nukle'ar] *adj* nuclear

núcleo ['nukleo] *nm* (*centro*) core; (*FÍSICA*) nucleus

nudillo [nu'ðiʎo] *nm* knuckle

nudista [nu'ðista] *adj* nudist

nudo ['nuðo] *nm* knot; **~so, a** *adj* knotty

nuera ['nwera] *nf* daughter-in-law

nuestro, a ['nwestro, a] *adj* our ♦ *pron* ours; **~ padre** our father; **un amigo ~** a friend of ours; **es el ~** it's ours

nueva ['nweβa] *nf* piece of news

nuevamente [nweβa'mente] *adv* (*otra vez*) again; (*de nuevo*) anew

Nueva York [-'jɔrk] *n* New York

Nueva Zelanda [-θe'landa] *nf* New Zealand

nueve ['nweβe] *num* nine

nuevo, a ['nweßo, a] *adj* (*gen*) new; **de ~**
again

nuez [nweθ] *nf* walnut; **~ de Adán** Adam's
apple; **~ moscada** nutmeg

nulidad [nuli'ðað] *nf* (*incapacidad*)
incompetence; (*abolición*) nullity

nulo, a ['nulo, a] *adj* (*inepto, torpe*)
useless; (*inválido*) (null and) void;
(*DEPORTE*) drawn, tied

núm. *abr* (= *número*) no

numeración [numera'θjon] *nf* (*cifras*)
numbers *pl*; (*arábiga, romana etc*)
numerals *pl*

numeral [nume'ral] *nm* numeral

numerar [nume'rar] *vt* to number

número ['numero] *nm* (*gen*) number;
(*tamaño: de zapato*) size; (*ejemplar: de
diario*) number, issue; **sin ~** numberless,
unnumbered; **~ de matrícula/de
teléfono** registration/telephone number;
~ atrasado back number

numeroso, a [nume'roso, a] *adj*
numerous

nunca ['nunka] *adv* (*jamás*) never; **~ lo
pensé** I never thought it; **no viene ~** he
never comes; **~ más** never again; **más
que ~** more than ever

nupcias ['nupθjas] *nfpl* wedding *sg*,
nuptials

nutria ['nutrja] *nf* otter

nutrición [nutri'θjon] *nf* nutrition

nutrido, a [nu'triðo, a] *adj* (*alimentado*)
nourished; (*fig: grande*) large; (*abundante*)
abundant

nutrir [nu'trir] *vt* (*alimentar*) to nourish;
(*dar de comer*) to feed; (*fig*) to strengthen;
nutritivo, a *adj* nourishing, nutritious

nylon [ni'lon] *nm* nylon

Ñ, ñ

ñato, a ['ɲato, a] (*AM*) *adj* snub-nosed

ñoñería [ɲoɲe'ria] *nf* insipidness

ñoño, a ['ɲoɲo, a] *adj* (*AM: tonto*) silly,
stupid; (*soso*) insipid; (*persona*) spineless

O, o

O *abr* (= *oeste*) W

o [o] *conj* or

o/ *abr* (= *orden*) o.

oasis [o'asis] *nm inv* oasis

obcecarse [oßθe'karse] *vr* to get *o*
become stubborn

obedecer [oßeðe'θer] *vt* to obey;
obediencia *nf* obedience; **obediente**
adj obedient

obertura [oßer'tura] *nf* overture

obesidad [oßesi'ðað] *nf* obesity; **obeso,
a** *adj* obese

obispo [o'ßispo] *nm* bishop

objeción [oßxe'θjon] *nf* objection; **poner
objeciones** to raise objections

objetar [oßxe'tar] *vt*, *vi* to object

objetivo, a [oßxe'tißo, a] *adj, nm*
objective

objeto [oß'xeto] *nm* (*cosa*) object; (*fin*)
aim

objetor, a [oßxe'tor, a] *nm/f* objector

oblicuo, a [o'ßlikwo, a] *adj* oblique;
(*mirada*) sidelong

obligación [oßlixa'θjon] *nf* obligation;
(*COM*) bond

obligar [oßli'var] *vt* to force; **~se** *vr* to
bind o.s.; **obligatorio, a** *adj*
compulsory, obligatory

oboe [o'ßoe] *nm* oboe

obra ['oßra] *nf* work; (*ARQ*) construction,
building; (*TEATRO*) play; **~ maestra**
masterpiece; **~s públicas** public works;
por ~ de thanks to (the efforts of); **obrar**
vt to work; (*tener efecto*) to have an effect
on ♦ *vi* to act, behave; (*tener efecto*) to
have an effect; **la carta obra en su
poder** the letter is in his/her possession

obrero, a [o'ßrero, a] *adj* (*clase*) working;
(*movimiento*) labour *cpd* ♦ *nm/f* (*gen*)
worker; (*sin oficio*) labourer

obscenidad [oßsθeni'ðað] *nf* obscenity;
obsceno, a *adj* obscene

obscu... = oscu...

obsequiar [oβse'kjar] *vt* (*ofrecer*) to present with; (*agasajar*) to make a fuss of, lavish attention on; **obsequio** *nm* (*regalo*) gift; (*cortesía*) courtesy, attention

observación [oβserβa'θjon] *nf* observation; (*reflexión*) remark

observador, a [oβserβa'ðor, a] *nm/f* observer

observar [oβser'βar] *vt* to observe; (*anotar*) to notice; **~se** *vr* to keep to, observe

obsesión [oβse'sjon] *nf* obsession; **obsesivo, a** *adj* obsessive

obsoleto, a [oβso'leto, a] *adj* obsolete

obstáculo [oβs'takulo] *nm* obstacle; (*impedimento*) hindrance, drawback

obstante [oβs'tante]: **no ~** *adv* nevertheless

obstinado, a [oβsti'naðo, a] *adj* obstinate, stubborn

obstinarse [oβsti'narse] *vr* to be obstinate; **~ en** to persist in

obstrucción [oβstruk'θjon] *nf* obstruction; **obstruir** *vt* to obstruct

obtener [oβte'ner] *vt* (*gen*) to obtain; (*premio*) to win

obturador [oβtura'ðor] *nm* (*FOTO*) shutter

obvio, a ['oββjo, a] *adj* obvious

oca ['oka] *nf* (*animal*) goose; (*juego*) ≈ snakes and ladders

ocasión [oka'sjon] *nf* (*oportunidad*) opportunity, chance; (*momento*) occasion, time; (*causa*) cause; **de ~** secondhand; **ocasionar** *vt* to cause

ocaso [o'kaso] *nm* (*fig*) decline

occidente [okθi'ðente] *nm* west

OCDE *nf abr* (= *Organización de Cooperación y Desarrollo Económico*) OECD

océano [o'θeano] *nm* ocean; **el ~ Índico** the Indian Ocean

ochenta [o'tʃenta] *num* eighty

ocho ['otʃo] *num* eight; **~ días** a week

ocio ['oθjo] *nm* (*tiempo*) leisure; (*pey*) idleness; **~so, a** *adj* (*inactivo*) idle; (*inútil*) useless

octavilla [okta'viʎa] *nf* leaflet, pamphlet

octavo, a [ok'taβo, a] *adj* eighth

octubre [ok'tuβre] *nm* October

ocular [oku'lar] *adj* ocular, eye *cpd*; **testigo ~** eyewitness

oculista [oku'lista] *nm/f* oculist

ocultar [okul'tar] *vt* (*esconder*) to hide; (*callar*) to conceal; **oculto, a** *adj* hidden; (*fig*) secret

ocupación [okupa'θjon] *nf* occupation

ocupado, a [oku'paðo, a] *adj* (*persona*) busy; (*plaza*) occupied, taken; (*teléfono*) engaged; **ocupar** *vt* (*gen*) to occupy; **ocuparse** *vr*: **ocuparse de** *o* **en** (*gen*) to concern o.s. with; (*cuidar*) to look after

ocurrencia [oku'rrenθja] *nf* (*idea*) bright idea

ocurrir [oku'rrir] *vi* to happen; **~se** *vr*: **se me ocurrió que ...** it occurred to me that ...

odiar [o'ðjar] *vt* to hate; **odio** *nm* hate, hatred; **odioso, a** *adj* (*gen*) hateful; (*malo*) nasty

odontólogo, a [oðon'toloɣo, a] *nm/f* dentist, dental surgeon

OEA *nf abr* (= *Organización de Estados Americanos*) OAS

oeste [o'este] *nm* west; **una película del ~** a western

ofender [ofen'der] *vt* (*agraviar*) to offend; (*insultar*) to insult; **~se** *vr* to take offence; **ofensa** *nf* offence; **ofensiva** *nf* offensive; **ofensivo, a** *adj* offensive

oferta [o'ferta] *nf* offer; (*propuesta*) proposal; **la ~ y la demanda** supply and demand; **artículos en ~** goods on offer

oficial [ofi'θjal] *adj* official ♦ *nm* (*MIL*) officer

oficina [ofi'θina] *nf* office; **~ de correos** post office; **~ de turismo** tourist office; **oficinista** *nm/f* clerk

oficio [o'fiθjo] *nm* (*profesión*) profession; (*puesto*) post; (*REL*) service; **ser del ~** to be an old hand; **tener mucho ~** to have a lot of experience; **~ de difuntos** funeral service

oficioso, a [ofi'θjoso, a] *adj* (*pey*) officious; (*no oficial*) unofficial, informal

ofimática [ofi'matika] *nf* office

automation

ofrecer [ofre'θer] vt (dar) to offer; (proponer) to propose; **~se** vr (persona) to offer o.s., volunteer; (situación) to present itself; **¿qué se le ofrece?, ¿se le ofrece algo?** what can I do for you?, can I get you anything?

ofrecimiento [ofreθi'mjento] nm offer

oftalmólogo, a [oftal'moloɣo, a] nm/f ophthalmologist

ofuscar [ofus'kar] vt (por pasión) to blind; (por luz) to dazzle

oída [o'iða] nf: **de ~s** by hearsay

oído [o'iðo] nm (ANAT) ear; (sentido) hearing

oigo etc vb ver **oír**

oír [o'ir] vt (gen) to hear; (atender a) to listen to; **¡oiga!** listen!; **~ misa** to attend mass

OIT nf abr (= Organización Internacional del Trabajo) ILO

ojal [o'xal] nm buttonhole

ojalá [oxa'la] excl if only (it were so)!, some hope! ♦ conj if only ...!, would that ...!; **~ (que) venga hoy** I hope he comes today

ojeada [oxe'aða] nf glance

ojera [o'xera] nf: **tener ~s** to have bags under one's eyes

ojeriza [oxe'riθa] nf ill-will

ojeroso, a [oxe'roso, a] adj haggard

ojo ['oxo] nm eye; (de puente) span; (de cerradura) keyhole ♦ excl careful!; **tener ~ para** to have an eye for; **~ de buey** porthole

okupa [o'kupa] (fam) nm/f squatter

ola ['ola] nf wave

olé [o'le] excl bravo!, olé!

oleada [ole'aða] nf big wave, swell; (fig) wave

oleaje [ole'axe] nm swell

óleo ['oleo] nm oil; **oleoducto** nm (oil) pipeline

oler [o'ler] vt (gen) to smell; (inquirir) to pry into; (fig: sospechar) to sniff out ♦ vi to smell; **~ a** to smell of

olfatear [olfate'ar] vt to smell; (inquirir) to

pry into; **olfato** nm sense of smell

oligarquía [oliɣar'kia] nf oligarchy

olimpíada [olim'piaða] nf: **las O~s** the Olympics; **olímpico, a** [o'limpiko, a] adj Olympic

oliva [o'liβa] nf (aceituna) olive; **aceite de ~** olive oil; **olivo** nm olive tree

olla ['oʎa] nf pan; (comida) stew; **~ a presión** o **exprés** pressure cooker; **~ podrida** type of Spanish stew

olmo ['olmo] nm elm (tree)

olor [o'lor] nm smell; **~oso, a** adj scented

olvidar [olβi'ðar] vt to forget; (omitir) to omit; **~se** vr (fig) to forget o.s.; **se me olvidó** I forgot

olvido [ol'βiðo] nm oblivion; (despiste) forgetfulness

ombligo [om'bliɣo] nm navel

omisión [omi'sjon] nf (abstención) omission; (descuido) neglect

omiso, a [o'miso, a] adj: **hacer caso ~ de** to ignore, pass over

omitir [omi'tir] vt to omit

omnipotente [omnipo'tente] adj omnipotent

omóplato [o'moplato] nm shoulder blade

OMS nf abr (= Organización Mundial de la Salud) WHO

once ['onθe] num eleven; **~s** (AM) nfpl tea break

onda ['onda] nf wave; **~ corta/larga/ media** short/long/medium wave; **ondear** vt, vi to wave; (tener ondas) to be wavy; (agua) to ripple; **ondearse** vr to swing, sway

ondulación [ondula'θjon] nf undulation; **ondulado, a** adj wavy

ondular [ondu'lar] vt (el pelo) to wave ♦ vi to undulate; **~se** vr to undulate

ONG nf abr (= organización no gubernamental) NGO

ONU ['onu] nf abr (= Organización de las Naciones Unidas) UNO

opaco, a [o'pako, a] adj opaque

opción [op'θjon] nf (gen) option; (derecho) right, option

OPEP ['opep] nf abr (= Organización de

Países Exportadores de Petróleo) OPEC

ópera ['opera] *nf* opera; **~ bufa** *o* **cómica** comic opera

operación [opera'θjon] *nf* (*gen*) operation; (*COM*) transaction, deal

operador, a [opera'ðor, a] *nm/f* operator; (*CINE: proyección*) projectionist; (: *rodaje*) cameraman

operar [ope'rar] *vt* (*producir*) to produce, bring about; (*MED*) to operate on ♦ *vi* (*COM*) to operate, deal; **~se** *vr* to occur; (*MED*) to have an operation

opereta [ope'reta] *nf* operetta

opinar [opi'nar] *vi* to think ♦ *vi* to give one's opinion; **opinión** *nf* (*creencia*) belief; (*criterio*) opinion

opio ['opjo] *nm* opium

oponente [opo'nente] *nm/f* opponent

oponer [opo'ner] *vt* (*resistencia*) to put up, offer; **~se** *vr* (*objetar*) to object; (*estar frente a frente*) to be opposed; (*dos personas*) to oppose each other; **~ A a B** to set A against B; **me opongo a pensar que ...** I refuse to believe *o* think that ...

oportunidad [oportuni'ðað] *nf* (*ocasión*) opportunity; (*posibilidad*) chance

oportuno, a [opor'tuno, a] *adj* (*en su tiempo*) opportune, timely; (*respuesta*) suitable; **en el momento ~** at the right moment

oposición [oposi'θjon] *nf* opposition; **oposiciones** *nfpl* (*ESCOL*) public examinations

opositor, a [oposi'tor, a] *nm/f* (*adversario*) opponent; (*candidato*): **~ (a)** candidate (for)

opresión [opre'sjon] *nf* oppression; **opresivo, a** *adj* oppressive; **opresor, a** *nm/f* oppressor

oprimir [opri'mir] *vt* to squeeze; (*fig*) to oppress

optar [op'tar] *vi* (*elegir*) to choose; **~ por** to opt for; **optativo, a** *adj* optional

óptico, a ['optiko, a] *adj* optic(al) ♦ *nm/f* optician; **óptica** *nf* optician's (shop); **desde esta óptica** from this point of view

optimismo [opti'mismo] *nm* optimism; **optimista** *nm/f* optimist

óptimo, a ['optimo, a] *adj* (*el mejor*) very best

opuesto, a [o'pwesto, a] *adj* (*contrario*) opposite; (*antagónico*) opposing

opulencia [opu'lenθja] *nf* opulence; **opulento, a** *adj* opulent

oración [ora'θjon] *nf* (*REL*) prayer; (*LING*) sentence

orador, a [ora'ðor, a] *nm/f* (*conferenciante*) speaker, orator

oral [o'ral] *adj* oral

orangután [orangu'tan] *nm* orangutan

orar [o'rar] *vi* to pray

oratoria [ora'torja] *nf* oratory

órbita ['orßita] *nf* orbit

orden ['orðen] *nm* (*gen*) order ♦ *nf* (*gen*) order; (*INFORM*) command; **~ del día** agenda; **de primer ~** first-rate; **en ~ de prioridad** in order of priority

ordenado, a [orðe'naðo, a] *adj* (*metódico*) methodical; (*arreglado*) orderly

ordenador [orðena'ðor] *nm* computer; **~ central** mainframe computer

ordenanza [orðe'nanθa] *nf* ordinance

ordenar [orðe'nar] *vt* (*mandar*) to order; (*poner orden*) to put in order, arrange; **~se** *vr* (*REL*) to be ordained

ordeñar [orðe'ɲar] *vt* to milk

ordinario, a [orði'narjo, a] *adj* (*común*) ordinary, usual; (*vulgar*) vulgar, common

orégano [o'reɣano] *nm* oregano

oreja [o'rexa] *nf* ear; (*MECÁNICA*) lug, flange

orfanato [orfa'nato] *nm* orphanage

orfandad [orfan'dað] *nf* orphanhood

orfebrería [orfeße'ria] *nf* gold/silver work

orgánico, a [or'ɣaniko, a] *adj* organic

organigrama [orɣani'ɣrama] *nm* flow chart

organismo [orɣa'nismo] *nm* (*BIO*) organism; (*POL*) organization

organización [orɣaniθa'θjon] *nf* organization; **organizar** *vt* to organize

órgano ['orɣano] *nm* organ

orgasmo [or'ɣasmo] *nm* orgasm

orgía [or'xia] *nf* orgy

orgullo [or'ɣuʎo] *nm* pride; **orgulloso, a** *adj* (*gen*) proud; (*altanero*) haughty

orientación [orjenta'θjon] *nf* (*posición*) position; (*dirección*) direction

oriental [orjen'tal] *adj* eastern; (*del Lejano Oriente*) oriental

orientar [orjen'tar] *vt* (*situar*) to orientate; (*señalar*) to point; (*dirigir*) to direct; (*guiar*) to guide; **~se** *vr* to get one's bearings

oriente [o'rjente] *nm* east; **Cercano/Medio/Lejano O~** Near/Middle/Far East

origen [o'rixen] *nm* origin

original [orixi'nal] *adj* (*nuevo*) original; (*extraño*) odd, strange; **~idad** *nf* originality

originar [orixi'nar] *vt* to start, cause; **~se** *vr* to originate; **~io, a** *adj* original; **~io de** native of

orilla [o'riʎa] *nf* (*borde*) border; (*de río*) bank; (*de bosque, tela*) edge; (*de mar*) shore

orina [o'rina] *nf* urine; **orinal** *nm* (chamber) pot; **orinar** *vi* to urinate; **orinarse** *vr* to wet o.s.; **orines** *nmpl* urine

oriundo, a [o'rjundo, a] *adj*: **~ de** native of

ornitología [ornitolo'xia] *nf* ornithology, bird-watching

oro ['oro] *nm* gold; **~s** *nmpl* (*NAIPES*) hearts

oropel [oro'pel] *nm* tinsel

orquesta [or'kesta] *nf* orchestra; **~ de cámara/sinfónica** chamber/symphony orchestra

orquídea [or'kiðea] *nf* orchid

ortiga [or'tiɣa] *nf* nettle

ortodoxo, a [orto'ðokso, a] *adj* orthodox

ortografía [ortoɣra'fia] *nf* spelling

ortopedia [orto'peðja] *nf* orthopaedics *sg*; **ortopédico, a** *adj* orthopaedic

oruga [o'ruɣa] *nf* caterpillar

orzuelo [or'θwelo] *nm* stye

os [os] *pron* (*gen*) you; (*a vosotros*) to you

osa ['osa] *nf* (she-)bear; **O~ Mayor/Menor** Great/Little Bear

osadía [osa'ðia] *nf* daring

osar [o'sar] *vi* to dare

oscilación [osθila'θjon] *nf* (*movimiento*) oscillation; (*fluctuación*) fluctuation

oscilar [osθi'lar] *vi* to oscillate; to fluctuate

oscurecer [oskure'θer] *vt* to darken ♦ *vi* to grow dark; **~se** *vr* to grow *o* get dark

oscuridad [oskuri'ðað] *nf* obscurity; (*tinieblas*) darkness

oscuro, a [os'kuro, a] *adj* dark; (*fig*) obscure; **a oscuras** in the dark

óseo, a ['oseo, a] *adj* bone *cpd*

oso ['oso] *nm* bear; **~ de peluche** teddy bear; **~ hormiguero** anteater

ostentación [ostenta'θjon] *nf* (*gen*) ostentation; (*acto*) display

ostentar [osten'tar] *vt* (*gen*) to show; (*pey*) to flaunt, show off; (*poseer*) to have, possess

ostra ['ostra] *nf* oyster

OTAN ['otan] *nf abr* (= *Organización del Tratado del Atlántico Norte*) NATO

otear [ote'ar] *vt* to observe; (*fig*) to look into

otitis [o'titis] *nf* earache

otoñal [oto'ɲal] *adj* autumnal

otoño [o'toɲo] *nm* autumn

otorgar [otor'ɣar] *vt* (*conceder*) to concede; (*dar*) to grant

otorrino [oto'rrino, a], **otorrinolaringólogo, a** [otorrinolarin'ɡoloɣo, a] *nm/f* ear, nose and throat specialist

---

PALABRA CLAVE

---

otro, a ['otro, a] *adj* **1** (*distinto: sg*) another; (: *pl*) other; **con ~s amigos** with other *o* different friends

2 (*adicional*): **tráigame ~ café (más), por favor** can I have another coffee please; **~s 10 días más** another ten days

♦ *pron* **1**: **el ~** the other one; **(los) ~s** (the) others; **de ~** somebody else's; **que lo haga ~** let somebody else do it

2 (*recíproco*): **se odian (la) una a (la) otra** they hate one another *o* each other

3: **~ tanto: comer ~ tanto** to eat the

same *o* as much again; **recibió una decena de telegramas y otras tantas llamadas** he got about ten telegrams and as many calls

---

ovación [oβa'θjon] *nf* ovation
oval [o'βal] *adj* oval; **~ado, a** *adj* oval;
  óvalo *nm* oval
ovario [o'βarjo] *nm* ovary
oveja [o'βexa] *nf* sheep
overol [oβe'rol] (*AM*) *nm* overalls *pl*
ovillo [o'βiʎo] *nm* (*de lana*) ball of wool;
  hacerse un ~ to curl up
OVNI ['oβni] *nm abr* (= *objeto volante no identificado*) UFO
ovulación [oβula'θjon] *nf* ovulation;
  óvulo *nm* ovum
oxidación [oksiða'θjon] *nf* rusting
oxidar [oksi'ðar] *vt* to rust; **~se** *vr* to go rusty
óxido ['oksiðo] *nm* oxide
oxigenado, a [oksixe'naðo, a] *adj* (*QUÍM*) oxygenated; (*pelo*) bleached
oxígeno [ok'sixeno] *nm* oxygen
oyente [o'jente] *nm/f* listener, hearer
oyes *etc vb ver* **oír**
ozono [o'θono] *nm* ozone

P, p

P *abr* (= *padre*) Fr.
pabellón [paβe'ʎon] *nm* bell tent; (*ARQ*) pavilion; (*de hospital etc*) block, section; (*bandera*) flag
pacer [pa'θer] *vi* to graze
paciencia [pa'θjenθja] *nf* patience
paciente [pa'θjente] *adj*, *nm/f* patient
pacificación [paθifika'θjon] *nf* pacification
pacificar [paθifi'kar] *vt* to pacify; (*tranquilizar*) to calm
pacífico, a [pa'θifiko, a] *adj* (*persona*) peaceable; (*existencia*) peaceful; **el (océano) P~** the Pacific (Ocean)
pacifismo [paθi'fismo] *nm* pacifism;

pacifista *nm/f* pacifist
pacotilla [pako'tiʎa] *nf*: **de ~** (*actor, escritor*) third-rate; (*mueble etc*) cheap
pactar [pak'tar] *vt* to agree to *o* on ♦ *vi* to come to an agreement
pacto ['pakto] *nm* (*tratado*) pact; (*acuerdo*) agreement
padecer [paðe'θer] *vt* (*sufrir*) to suffer; (*soportar*) to endure, put up with;
  padecimiento *nm* suffering
padrastro [pa'ðrastro] *nm* stepfather
padre ['paðre] *nm* father ♦ *adj* (*fam*): **un éxito ~** a tremendous success; **~s** *nmpl* parents
padrino [pa'ðrino] *nm* (*REL*) godfather; (*tb*: **~ de boda**) best man; (*fig*) sponsor, patron; **~s** *nmpl* godparents
padrón [pa'ðron] *nm* (*censo*) census, roll
paella [pa'eʎa] *nf* paella, *dish of rice with meat, shellfish etc*
paga ['paɣa] *nf* (*pago*) payment; (*sueldo*) pay, wages *pl*
pagano, a [pa'ɣano, a] *adj*, *nm/f* pagan, heathen
pagar [pa'ɣar] *vt* to pay; (*las compras, crimen*) to pay for; (*fig*: *favor*) to repay ♦ *vi* to pay; **~ al contado/a plazos** to pay (in) cash/in instalments
pagaré [paɣa're] *nm* I.O.U.
página ['paxina] *nf* page
pago ['paɣo] *nm* (*dinero*) payment; **~ anticipado/a cuenta/contra reembolso/en especie** advance payment/payment on account/cash on delivery/payment in kind; **en ~ de** in return for
pág(s). *abr* (= *página(s)*) p(p).
pague *etc vb ver* **pagar**
país [pa'is] *nm* (*gen*) country; (*región*) land; **los P~es Bajos** the Low Countries; **el P~ Vasco** the Basque Country
paisaje [pai'saxe] *nm* landscape, scenery
paisano, a [pai'sano, a] *adj* of the same country ♦ *nm/f* (*compatriota*) fellow countryman/woman; **vestir de ~** (*soldado*) to be in civvies; (*guardia*) to be in plain clothes

paja ['paxa] *nf* straw; (*fig*) rubbish (*BRIT*), trash (*US*)

pajarita [paxa'rita] *nf* (*corbata*) bow tie

pájaro ['paxaro] *nm* bird; **~ carpintero** woodpecker

pajita [pa'xita] *nf* (drinking) straw

pala ['pala] *nf* spade, shovel; (*raqueta etc*) bat; (: *de tenis*) racquet; (*CULIN*) slice; **~ matamoscas** fly swat

palabra [pa'laβra] *nf* word; (*facultad*) (power of) speech; (*derecho de hablar*) right to speak; **tomar la ~** (*en mitin*) to take the floor

palabrota [pala'brota] *nf* swearword

palacio [pa'laθjo] *nm* palace; (*mansión*) mansion, large house; **~ de justicia** courthouse; **~ municipal** town/city hall

paladar [pala'ðar] *nm* palate; **paladear** *vt* to taste

palanca [pa'lanka] *nf* lever; (*fig*) pull, influence

palangana [palan'gana] *nf* washbasin

palco ['palko] *nm* box

Palestina [pales'tina] *nf* Palestine; **palestino, a** *nm/f* Palestinian

paleta [pa'leta] *nf* (*de pintor*) palette; (*de albañil*) trowel; (*de ping-pong*) bat; (*AM*) ice lolly

paleto, a [pa'leto, a] (*fam, pey*) *nm/f* yokel

paliar [pa'ljar] *vt* (*mitigar*) to mitigate, alleviate; **paliativo** *nm* palliative

palidecer [paliðe'θer] *vi* to turn pale; **palidez** *nf* paleness; **pálido, a** *adj* pale

palillo [pa'liʎo] *nm* (*mondadientes*) toothpick; (*para comer*) chopstick

paliza [pa'liθa] *nf* beating, thrashing

palma ['palma] *nf* (*ANAT*) palm; (*árbol*) palm tree; **batir** *o* **dar ~s** to clap, applaud; **~da** *nf* slap; **~das** *nfpl* clapping *sg*, applause *sg*

palmar [pal'mar] (*fam*) *vi* (*tb*: **~la**) to die, kick the bucket

palmear [palme'ar] *vi* to clap

palmera [pal'mera] *nf* (*BOT*) palm tree

palmo ['palmo] *nm* (*medida*) span; (*fig*) small amount; **~ a ~** inch by inch

palo ['palo] *nm* stick; (*poste*) post; (*de*

tienda de campaña) pole; (*mango*) handle, shaft; (*golpe*) blow, hit; (*de golf*) club; (*de béisbol*) bat; (*NAUT*) mast; (*NAIPES*) suit

paloma [pa'loma] *nf* dove, pigeon

palomitas [palo'mitas] *nfpl* popcorn *sg*

palpar [pal'par] *vt* to touch, feel

palpitación [palpita'θjon] *nf* palpitation

palpitante [palpi'tante] *adj* palpitating; (*fig*) burning

palpitar [palpi'tar] *vi* to palpitate; (*latir*) to beat

palta ['palta] (*AM*) *nf* avocado (pear)

paludismo [palu'ðismo] *nm* malaria

pamela [pa'mela] *nf* picture hat, sun hat

pampa ['pampa] (*AM*) *nf* pampas, prairie

pan [pan] *nm* bread; (*una barra*) loaf; **~ integral** wholemeal (*BRIT*) *o* wholewheat (*US*) bread; **~ rallado** breadcrumbs *pl*

pana ['pana] *nf* corduroy

panadería [panaðe'ria] *nf* baker's (shop); **panadero, a** *nm/f* baker

Panamá [pana'ma] *nm* Panama; **panameño, a** *adj* Panamanian

pancarta [pan'karta] *nf* placard, banner

panda ['panda] *nm* (*ZOOL*) panda

pandereta [pande'reta] *nf* tambourine

pandilla [pan'diʎa] *nf* set, group; (*de criminales*) gang; (*pey: camarilla*) clique

panecillo [pane'θiʎo] *nm* (bread) roll

panel [pa'nel] *nm* panel; **~ solar** solar panel

panfleto [pan'fleto] *nm* pamphlet

pánico ['paniko] *nm* panic

panorama [pano'rama] *nm* panorama; (*vista*) view

pantalla [pan'taʎa] *nf* (*de cine*) screen; (*de lámpara*) lampshade

pantalón [panta'lon] *nm* trousers; **pantalones** *nmpl* trousers

pantano [pan'tano] *nm* (*ciénaga*) marsh, swamp; (*depósito: de agua*) reservoir; (*fig*) jam, difficulty

panteón [pante'on] *nm*: **~ familiar** family tomb

pantera [pan'tera] *nf* panther

panti(e)s ['pantis] *nmpl* tights

pantomima [panto'mima] *nf* pantomime

pantorrilla [panto'rriʎa] *nf* calf (of the leg)

pantufla [pan'tufla] *nf* slipper

panty(s) ['panti(s)] *nm(pl)* tights

panza ['panθa] *nf* belly, paunch

pañal [pa'ɲal] *nm* nappy (*BRIT*), diaper (*US*); **~es** *nmpl* (*fig*) early stages, infancy *sg*

paño ['paɲo] *nm* (*tela*) cloth; (*pedazo de tela*) (piece of) cloth; (*trapo*) duster, rag; **~ higiénico** sanitary towel; **~s menores** underclothes

pañuelo [pa'ɲwelo] *nm* handkerchief, hanky (*fam*); (*para la cabeza*) (head)scarf

papa ['papa] *nm*: **el P~** the Pope ♦ *nf* (*AM*) potato

papá [pa'pa] (*pl* **~s**) (*fam*) *nm* dad(dy), pa (*US*)

papada [pa'paða] *nf* double chin

papagayo [papa'ɣajo] *nm* parrot

papanatas [papa'natas] (*fam*) *nm inv* simpleton

paparrucha [papa'rrutʃa] *nf* piece of nonsense

papaya [pa'paja] *nf* papaya

papear [pape'ar] (*fam*) *vt, vi* to scoff

papel [pa'pel] *nm* paper; (*hoja de ~*) sheet of paper; (*TEATRO, fig*) role; **~ de calco/ carbón/de cartas** tracing paper/carbon paper/stationery; **~ de envolver/pintado** wrapping paper/wallpaper; **~ de aluminio/higiénico** aluminium (*BRIT*) *o* aluminum (*US*) foil/toilet paper; **~ de estaño** *o* **plata** tinfoil; **~ de lija** sandpaper; **~ moneda** paper money; **~ secante** blotting paper

papeleo [pape'leo] *nm* red tape

papelera [pape'lera] *nf* wastepaper basket; (*en la calle*) litter bin

papelería [papele'ria] *nf* stationer's (shop)

papeleta [pape'leta] *nf* (*POL*) ballot paper; (*ESCOL*) report

paperas [pa'peras] *nfpl* mumps *sg*

papilla [pa'piʎa] *nf* (*para niños*) baby food

paquete [pa'kete] *nm* (*de cigarrillos etc*) packet; (*CORREOS etc*) parcel; (*AM*) package tour; (*: fam*) nuisance

par [par] *adj* (*igual*) like, equal; (*MAT*) even ♦ *nm* equal; (*de guantes*) pair; (*de veces*) couple; (*POL*) peer; (*GOLF, COM*) par; **abrir de ~ en ~** to open wide

para ['para] *prep* for; **no es ~ comer** it's not for eating; **decir ~ sí** to say to o.s.; **¿~ qué lo quieres?** what do you want it for?; **se casaron ~ separarse otra vez** they married only to separate again; **lo tendré ~ mañana** I'll have it (for) tomorrow; **ir ~ casa** to go home, head for home; **~ profesor es muy estúpido** he's very stupid for a teacher; **¿quién es usted ~ gritar así?** who are you to shout like that?; **tengo bastante ~ vivir** I have enough to live on; *ver tb* **con**

parabién [para'βjen] *nm* congratulations *pl*

parábola [pa'raβola] *nf* parable; (*MAT*) parabola; **parabólica** *nf* (*tb*: **antena ~**) satellite dish

parabrisas [para'βrisas] *nm inv* windscreen (*BRIT*), windshield (*US*)

paracaídas [paraka'iðas] *nm inv* parachute; **paracaidista** *nm/f* parachutist; (*MIL*) paratrooper

parachoques [para'tʃokes] *nm inv* (*AUTO*) bumper; (*MECÁNICA etc*) shock absorber

parada [pa'raða] *nf* stop; (*acto*) stopping; (*de industria*) shutdown, stoppage; (*lugar*) stopping place; **~ de autobús** bus stop

paradero [para'ðero] *nm* stopping-place; (*situación*) whereabouts

parado, a [pa'raðo, a] *adj* (*persona*) motionless, standing still; (*fábrica*) closed, at a standstill; (*coche*) stopped; (*AM*) standing (up); (*sin empleo*) unemployed, idle

paradoja [para'ðoxa] *nf* paradox

parador [para'ðor] *nm* parador, state-run hotel

paráfrasis [pa'rafrasis] *nf inv* paraphrase

paraguas [pa'raɣwas] *nm inv* umbrella

Paraguay [para'ɣwai] *nm*: **el ~** Paraguay; **paraguayo, a** *adj, nm/f* Paraguayan

paraíso [para'iso] *nm* paradise, heaven

paraje [pa'raxe] *nm* place, spot

paralelo, a [para'lelo, a] *adj* parallel
parálisis [pa'ralisis] *nf inv* paralysis; **paralítico, a** *adj, nm/f* paralytic
paralizar [parali'θar] *vt* to paralyse; **~se** *vr* to become paralysed; *(fig)* to come to a standstill
paramilitar [paramili'tar] *adj* paramilitary
páramo ['paramo] *nm* bleak plateau
parangón [paraŋ'gon] *nm*: **sin ~** incomparable
paranoico, a [para'noiko, a] *nm/f* paranoiac
parapente [para'pente] *nm* (*deporte*) paragliding; *(aparato)* paraglider
parapléjico, a [para'plexiko, a] *adj, nm/f* paraplegic
parar [pa'rar] *vt* to stop; *(golpe)* to ward off ♦ *vi* to stop; **~se** *vr* to stop; (*AM*) to stand up; **ha parado de llover** it has stopped raining; **van a ir a ~ a comisaría** they're going to end up in the police station; **~se en** to pay attention to
pararrayos [para'rrajos] *nm inv* lightning conductor
parásito, a [pa'rasito, a] *nm/f* parasite
parcela [par'θela] *nf* plot, piece of ground
parche ['partʃe] *nm* (*gen*) patch
parchís [par'tʃis] *nm* ludo
parcial [par'θjal] *adj* (*pago*) part-; *(eclipse)* partial; *(JUR)* prejudiced, biased; *(POL)* partisan; **~idad** *nf* prejudice, bias
pardillo, a [par'ðiʎo, a] (*pey*) *adj* yokel
parecer [pare'θer] *nm* (*opinión*) opinion, view; *(aspecto)* looks *pl* ♦ *vi* (*tener apariencia*) to seem, look; *(asemejarse)* to look *o* seem like; *(aparecer, llegar)* to appear; **~se** *vr* to look alike, resemble each other; **~se a** to look like, resemble; **según parece** evidently, apparently; **me parece que** I think (that), it seems to me that
parecido, a [pare'θiðo, a] *adj* similar ♦ *nm* similarity, likeness, resemblance; **bien ~** good-looking, nice-looking
pared [pa'reð] *nf* wall
pareja [pa'rexa] *nf* (*par*) pair; *(dos personas)* couple; *(otro: de un par)* other

one (of a pair); *(persona)* partner
parentela [paren'tela] *nf* relations *pl*
parentesco [paren'tesko] *nm* relationship
paréntesis [pa'rentesis] *nm inv* parenthesis; *(en escrito)* bracket
parezco *etc vb ver* **parecer**
pariente, a [pa'rjente, a] *nm/f* relative, relation
parir [pa'rir] *vt* to give birth to ♦ *vi* (*mujer*) to give birth, have a baby
París [pa'ris] *n* Paris
parking ['parkin] *nm* car park (*BRIT*), parking lot (*US*)
parlamentar [parlamen'tar] *vi* to parley
parlamentario, a [parlamen'tarjo, a] *adj* parliamentary ♦ *nm/f* member of parliament
parlamento [parla'mento] *nm* parliament
parlanchín, ina [parlan'tʃin, ina] *adj* indiscreet ♦ *nm/f* chatterbox
parlar [par'lar] *vi* to chatter (away)
paro ['paro] *nm* (*huelga*) stoppage (of work), strike; *(desempleo)* unemployment; **subsidio de ~** unemployment benefit
parodia [pa'roðja] *nf* parody; **parodiar** *vt* to parody
parpadear [parpaðe'ar] *vi* (*ojos*) to blink; *(luz)* to flicker
párpado ['parpaðo] *nm* eyelid
parque ['parke] *nm* (*lugar verde*) park; **~ de atracciones/infantil/zoológico** fairground/playground/zoo
parqué [par'ke] *nm* parquet (flooring)
parquímetro [par'kimetro] *nm* parking meter
parra ['parra] *nf* (grape)vine
párrafo ['parrafo] *nm* paragraph; **echar un ~** *(fam)* to have a chat
parranda [pa'rranda] *(fam) nf* spree, binge
parrilla [pa'rriʎa] *nf* (*CULIN*) grill; *(de coche)* grille; **(carne a la) ~** barbecue; **~da** *nf* barbecue
párroco ['parroko] *nm* parish priest
parroquia [pa'rrokja] *nf* parish; *(iglesia)* parish church; *(COM)* clientele, customers *pl*; **~no, a** *nm/f* parishioner; client, customer

parsimonia [parsi'monja] *nf* calmness, level-headedness

parte ['parte] *nm* message; (*informe*) report ♦ *nf* part; (*lado, cara*) side; (*de reparto*) share; (*JUR*) party; **en alguna ~ de Europa** somewhere in Europe; **en/por todas ~s** everywhere; **en gran ~** to a large extent; **la mayor ~ de los españoles** most Spaniards; **de un tiempo a esta ~** for some time past; **de ~ de alguien** on sb's behalf; **¿de ~ de quién?** (*TEL*) who is speaking?; **por ~ de** on the part of; **yo por mi ~** I for my part; **por otra ~** on the other hand; **dar ~ to** inform; **tomar ~** to take part

partición [parti'θjon] *nf* division, sharing-out; (*POL*) partition

participación [partiθipa'θjon] *nf* (*acto*) participation, taking part; (*parte, COM*) share; (*de lotería*) shared prize; (*aviso*) notice, notification

participante [partiθi'pante] *nm/f* participant

participar [partiθi'par] *vt* to notify, inform ♦ *vi* to take part, participate

partícipe [par'tiθipe] *nm/f* participant

particular [partiku'lar] *adj* (*especial*) particular, special; (*individual, personal*) private, personal ♦ *nm* (*punto, asunto*) particular, point; (*individuo*) individual; **tiene coche ~** he has a car of his own

partida [par'tiða] *nf* (*salida*) departure; (*COM*) entry, item; (*juego*) game; (*grupo de personas*) band, group; **mala ~** dirty trick; **~ de nacimiento / matrimonio / defunción** birth/marriage/death certificate

partidario, a [parti'ðarjo, a] *adj* partisan ♦ *nm/f* supporter, follower

partido [par'tiðo] *nm* (*POL*) party; (*DEPORTE*) game, match; **sacar ~ de** to profit *o* benefit from; **tomar ~** to take sides

partir [par'tir] *vt* (*dividir*) to split, divide; (*compartir, distribuir*) to share (out), distribute; (*romper*) to break open, split open; (*rebanada*) to cut (off) ♦ *vi* (*ponerse*

en camino) to set off *o* out; (*comenzar*) to start (off *o* out); **~se** *vr* to crack *o* split *o* break (in two *etc*); **a ~ de** (starting) from

partitura [parti'tura] *nf* (*MUS*) score

parto ['parto] *nm* birth; (*fig*) product, creation; **estar de ~** to be in labour

pasa ['pasa] *nf* raisin; **~ de Corinto/de Esmirna** currant/sultana

pasada [pa'saða] *nf* passing, passage; **de ~** in passing, incidentally; **una mala ~** a dirty trick

pasadizo [pasa'ðiθo] *nm* (*pasillo*) passage, corridor; (*callejuela*) alley

pasado, a [pa'saðo, a] *adj* past; (*malo: comida, fruta*) bad; (*muy cocido*) overdone; (*anticuado*) out of date ♦ *nm* past; **~ mañana** the day after tomorrow; **el mes ~** last month

pasador [pasa'ðor] *nm* (*cerrojo*) bolt; (*de pelo*) hair slide; (*horquilla*) grip

pasaje [pa'saxe] *nm* passage; (*pago de viaje*) fare; (*los pasajeros*) passengers *pl*; (*pasillo*) passageway

pasajero, a [pasa'xero, a] *adj* passing; (*situación, estado*) temporary; (*amor, enfermedad*) brief ♦ *nm/f* passenger

pasamontañas [pasamon'tañas] *nm inv* balaclava helmet

pasaporte [pasa'porte] *nm* passport

pasar [pa'sar] *vt* to pass; (*tiempo*) to spend; (*desgracias*) to suffer, endure; (*noticia*) to give, pass on; (*río*) to cross; (*barrera*) to pass through; (*falta*) to overlook, tolerate; (*contrincante*) to surpass, do better than; (*coche*) to overtake; (*CINE*) to show; (*enfermedad*) to give, infect with ♦ *vi* (*gen*) to pass; (*terminarse*) to be over; (*ocurrir*) to happen; **~se** *vr* (*flores*) to fade; (*comida*) to go bad *o* off; (*fig*) to overdo it, go too far; **~ de** to go beyond, exceed; **~ por** (*AM*) to fetch; **~lo bien/mal** to have a good/bad time; **¡pase!** come in!; **hacer ~** to show in; **~se al enemigo** to go over to the enemy; **se me pasó** I forgot; **no se le pasa nada** he misses nothing; **pase lo que pase** come what may; **¿qué**

pasa? what's going on?, what's up?;
¿qué te pasa? what's wrong?

pasarela [pasa'rela] *nf* footbridge; (*en barco*) gangway

pasatiempo [pasa'tjempo] *nm* pastime, hobby

Pascua ['paskwa] *nf*: ~ **(de Resurrección)** Easter; ~ **de Navidad** Christmas; **~s** *nfpl* Christmas (time); **¡felices ~s!** Merry Christmas!

pase ['pase] *nm* pass; (*CINE*) performance, showing

pasear [pase'ar] *vt* to take for a walk; (*exhibir*) to parade, show off ♦ *vi* to walk, go for a walk; **~se** *vr* to walk, go for a walk; ~ **en coche** to go for a drive;
  paseo *nm* (*avenida*) avenue; (*distancia corta*) walk, stroll; **dar un** *o* **ir de paseo** to go for a walk

pasillo [pa'siʎo] *nm* passage, corridor

pasión [pa'sjon] *nf* passion

pasivo, a [pa'siβo, a] *adj* passive; (*inactivo*) inactive ♦ *nm* (*COM*) liabilities *pl*, debts *pl*

pasmar [pas'mar] *vt* (*asombrar*) to amaze, astonish; **pasmo** *nm* amazement, astonishment; (*resfriado*) chill; (*fig*) wonder, marvel; **pasmoso, a** *adj* amazing, astonishing

paso, a ['paso, a] *adj* dried ♦ *nm* step; (*modo de andar*) walk; (*huella*) footprint; (*rapidez*) speed, pace, rate; (*camino accesible*) way through, passage; (*cruce*) crossing; (*pasaje*) passing, passage; (*GEO*) pass; (*estrecho*) strait; ~ **a nivel** (*FERRO*) level-crossing; ~ **de peatones** pedestrian crossing; **a ese** ~ (*fig*) at that rate; **salir al** ~ **de** *o* **a** to waylay; **estar de** ~ to be passing through; ~ **elevado** flyover; **prohibido el** ~ no entry; **ceda el** ~ give way

pasota [pa'sota] (*fam*) *adj, nm/f* ≈ dropout; **ser un (tipo)** ~ to be a bit of a dropout; (*ser indiferente*) not to care about anything

pasta ['pasta] *nf* paste; (*CULIN: masa*) dough; (: *de bizcochos etc*) pastry; (*fam*)

dough; **~s** *nfpl* (*bizcochos*) pastries, small cakes; (*fideos, espaguetis etc*) pasta; ~ **de dientes** *o* **dentífrica** toothpaste

pastar [pas'tar] *vt, vi* to graze

pastel [pas'tel] *nm* (*dulce*) cake; (*ARTE*) pastel; ~ **de carne** meat pie; **~ería** *nf* cake shop

pasteurizado, a [pasteuri'θaðo, a] *adj* pasteurized

pastilla [pas'tiʎa] *nf* (*de jabón, chocolate*) bar; (*píldora*) tablet, pill

pasto ['pasto] *nm* (*hierba*) grass; (*lugar*) pasture, field

pastor, a [pas'tor, a] *nm/f* shepherd/ess ♦ *nm* (*REL*) clergyman, pastor; ~ **alemán** Alsatian

pata ['pata] *nf* (*pierna*) leg; (*pie*) foot; (*de muebles*) leg; **~s arriba** upside down; **metedura de** ~ (*fam*) gaffe; **meter la** ~ (*fam*) to put one's foot in it; (*TEC*): ~ **de cabra** crowbar; **tener buena/mala** ~ to be lucky/unlucky; **~da** *nf* kick; (*en el suelo*) stamp

patalear [patale'ar] *vi* (*en el suelo*) to stamp one's feet

patata [pa'tata] *nf* potato; **~s fritas** chips, French fries; (*de bolsa*) crisps

paté [pa'te] *nm* pâté

patear [pate'ar] *vt* (*pisar*) to stamp on, trample (on); (*pegar con el pie*) to kick ♦ *vi* to stamp (with rage), stamp one's feet

patentar [paten'tar] *vt* to patent

patente [pa'tente] *adj* obvious, evident; (*COM*) patent ♦ *nf* patent

paternal [pater'nal] *adj* fatherly, paternal; **paterno, a** *adj* paternal

patético, a [pa'tetiko, a] *adj* pathetic, moving

patilla [pa'tiʎa] *nf* (*de gafas*) side(piece); **~s** *nfpl* sideburns

patín [pa'tin] *nm* skate; (*de trineo*) runner; **patinaje** *nm* skating; **patinar** *vi* to skate; (*resbalarse*) to skid, slip; (*fam*) to slip up, blunder

patio ['patjo] *nm* (*de casa*) patio, courtyard; ~ **de recreo** playground

pato ['pato] *nm* duck; **pagar el ~** (*fam*) to take the blame, carry the can

patológico, a [pato'loxiko, a] *adj* pathological

patoso, a [pa'toso, a] (*fam*) *adj* clumsy

patraña [pa'traɲa] *nf* story, fib

patria ['patrja] *nf* native land, mother country

patrimonio [patri'monjo] *nm* inheritance; (*fig*) heritage

patriota [pa'trjota] *nm/f* patriot; **patriotismo** *nm* patriotism

patrocinar [patroθi'nar] *vt* to sponsor; **patrocinio** *nm* sponsorship

patrón, ona [pa'tron, ona] *nm/f* (*jefe*) boss, chief, master/mistress; (*propietario*) landlord/lady; (*REL*) patron saint ♦ *nm* (*TEC, COSTURA*) pattern

patronal [patro'nal] *adj:* **la clase ~** management

patronato [patro'nato] *nm* sponsorship; (*acto*) patronage; (*fundación benéfica*) trust, foundation

patrulla [pa'truʎa] *nf* patrol

pausa ['pausa] *nf* pause, break

pausado, a [pau'saðo, a] *adj* slow, deliberate

pauta ['pauta] *nf* line, guide line

pavimento [paβi'mento] *nm* (*con losas*) pavement, paving

pavo ['paβo] *nm* turkey; **~ real** peacock

pavor [pa'βor] *nm* dread, terror

payaso [pa'jaso, a] *nm/f* clown

payo, a ['pajo, a] *nm/f* non-gipsy

paz [paθ] *nf* peace; (*tranquilidad*) peacefulness, tranquillity; **hacer las paces** to make peace; (*fig*) to make up

pazo ['paθo] *nm* country house

P.D. *abr* (= *posdata*) P.S., p.s.

peaje [pe'axe] *nm* toll

peatón [pea'ton] *nm* pedestrian

peca ['peka] *nf* freckle

pecado [pe'kaðo] *nm* sin; **pecador, a** *adj* sinful ♦ *nm/f* sinner

pecaminoso, a [pekami'noso, a] *adj* sinful

pecar [pe'kar] *vi* (*REL*) to sin; **peca de**

generoso he is generous to a fault

pecera [pe'θera] *nf* fish tank; (*redonda*) goldfish bowl

pecho ['petʃo] *nm* (*ANAT*) chest; (*de mujer*) breast; **dar el ~ a** to breast-feed; **tomar algo a ~** to take sth to heart

pechuga [pe'tʃuxa] *nf* breast

peculiar [peku'ljar] *adj* special, peculiar; (*característico*) typical, characteristic; **~idad** *nf* peculiarity; special feature, characteristic

pedal [pe'ðal] *nm* pedal; **~ear** *vi* to pedal

pedante [pe'ðante] *adj* pedantic ♦ *nm/f* pedant; **~ría** *nf* pedantry

pedazo [pe'ðaθo] *nm* piece, bit; **hacerse ~s** to smash, shatter

pedernal [peðer'nal] *nm* flint

pediatra [pe'ðjatra] *nm/f* paediatrician

pedido [pe'ðiðo] *nm* (*COM*) order; (*petición*) request

pedir [pe'ðir] *vt* to ask for, request; (*comida, COM: mandar*) to order; (*necesitar*) to need, demand, require ♦ *vi* to ask; **me pidió que cerrara la puerta** he asked me to shut the door; **¿cuánto piden por el coche?** how much are they asking for the car?

pedo ['peðo] (*fam!*) *nm* fart

pega ['pexa] *nf* snag; **poner ~s (a)** to complain (about)

pegadizo, a [pexa'ðiθo, a] *adj* (*MUS*) catchy

pegajoso, a [pexa'xoso, a] *adj* sticky, adhesive

pegamento [pexa'mento] *nm* gum, glue

pegar [pe'var] *vt* (*papel, sellos*) to stick (on); (*cartel*) to stick up (on); (*coser*) to sew (on); (*unir: partes*) to join, fix together; (*MED*) to give, infect with; (*dar: golpe*) to give, deal ♦ *vi* (*adherirse*) to stick, adhere; (*ir juntos: colores*) to match, go together; (*golpear*) to hit; (*quemar: el sol*) to strike hot, burn (*fig*); **~se** *vr* (*gen*) to stick; (*dos personas*) to hit each other, fight; (*fam*): **~ un grito** to let out a yell; **~ un salto** to jump (with fright); **~ en** to touch; **~se un tiro** to shoot o.s.

pegatina [peɣaˈtina] *nf* sticker

pegote [peˈɣote] (*fam*) *nm* eyesore, sight

peinado [peiˈnaðo] *nm* hairstyle

peinar [peiˈnar] *vt* to comb; (*hacer estilo*) to style; **~se** *vr* to comb one's hair

peine [ˈpeine] *nm* comb; **~ta** *nf* ornamental comb

p.ej. *abr* (= *por ejemplo*) e.g.

Pekín [peˈkin] *n* Pekin(g)

pelado, a [peˈlaðo, a] *adj* (*fruta, patata etc*) peeled; (*cabeza*) shorn; (*campo, fig*) bare; (*fam: sin dinero*) broke

pelaje [peˈlaxe] *nm* (*ZOOL*) fur, coat; (*fig*) appearance

pelar [peˈlar] *vt* (*fruta, patatas etc*) to peel; (*cortar el pelo a*) to cut the hair of; (*quitar la piel: animal*) to skin; **~se** *vr* (*la piel*) to peel off; **voy a ~me** I'm going to get my hair cut

peldaño [pelˈdaɲo] *nm* step

pelea [peˈlea] *nf* (*lucha*) fight; (*discusión*) quarrel, row

peleado, a [peleˈaðo, a] *adj*: **estar ~ (con uno)** to have fallen out (with sb)

pelear [peleˈar] *vi* to fight; **~se** *vr* to fight; (*reñirse*) to fall out, quarrel

peletería [peleteˈria] *nf* furrier's, fur shop

pelícano [peˈlikano] *nm* pelican

película [peˈlikula] *nf* film; (*cobertura ligera*) thin covering; (*FOTO: rollo*) roll o reel of film

peligro [peˈliɣro] *nm* danger; (*riesgo*) risk; **correr ~ de** to run the risk of; **~so, a** *adj* dangerous, risky

pelirrojo, a [peliˈrroxo, a] *adj* red-haired, red-headed ♦ *nm/f* redhead

pellejo [peˈʎexo] *nm* (*de animal*) skin, hide

pellizcar [peʎiθˈkar] *vt* to pinch, nip

pelma [ˈpelma] (*fam*) *nm/f* pain (in the neck)

pelmazo [pelˈmaθo] (*fam*) *nm* = **pelma**

pelo [ˈpelo] *nm* (*cabellos*) hair; (*de barba, bigote*) whisker; (*de animal: pellejo*) hair, fur, coat; **al ~** just right; **venir al ~** to be exactly what one needs; **un hombre de ~ en pecho** a brave man; **por los ~s** by the skin of one's teeth; **no tener ~s en la lengua** to be outspoken, not mince words; **tomar el ~ a uno** to pull sb's leg

pelota [peˈlota] *nf* ball; **en ~** stark naked; **hacer la ~ (a uno)** (*fam*) to creep (to sb); **~ vasca** pelota

pelotari [peloˈtari] *nm* pelota player

pelotón [peloˈton] *nm* (*MIL*) squad, detachment

peluca [peˈluka] *nf* wig

peluche [peˈlutʃe] *nm*: **oso/muñeco de ~** teddy bear/soft toy

peludo, a [peˈluðo, a] *adj* hairy, shaggy

peluquería [pelukeˈria] *nf* hairdresser's; **peluquero, a** *nm/f* hairdresser

pelusa [peˈlusa] *nf* (*BOT*) down; (*en tela*) fluff

pena [ˈpena] *nf* (*congoja*) grief, sadness; (*remordimiento*) regret; (*dificultad*) trouble; (*dolor*) pain; (*JUR*) sentence; **merecer o valer la ~** to be worthwhile; **a duras ~s** with great difficulty; **~ de muerte** death penalty; **~ pecuniaria** fine; **¡qué ~!** what a shame!

penal [peˈnal] *adj* penal ♦ *nm* (*cárcel*) prison

penalidad [penaliˈðað] *nf* (*problema, dificultad*) trouble, hardship; (*JUR*) penalty, punishment; **~es** *nfpl* trouble, hardship

penalti, penalty [peˈnalti] (*pl* **~s** o **~es**) *nm* penalty (kick)

pendiente [penˈdjente] *adj* pending, unsettled ♦ *nm* earring ♦ *nf* hill, slope

pene [ˈpene] *nm* penis

penetración [penetraˈθjon] *nf* (*acto*) penetration; (*agudeza*) sharpness, insight

penetrante [peneˈtrante] *adj* (*herida*) deep; (*persona, arma*) sharp; (*sonido*) penetrating, piercing; (*mirada*) searching; (*viento, ironía*) biting

penetrar [peneˈtrar] *vt* to penetrate, pierce; (*entender*) to grasp ♦ *vi* to penetrate, go in; (*entrar*) to enter, go in; (*líquido*) to soak in; (*fig*) to pierce

penicilina [peniθiˈlina] *nf* penicillin

península [peˈninsula] *nf* peninsula; **peninsular** *adj* peninsular

penique [peˈnike] *nm* penny

penitencia [peni'tenθja] *nf* penance

penoso, a [pe'noso, a] *adj* (*lamentable*) distressing; (*difícil*) arduous, difficult

pensador, a [pensa'ðor, a] *nm/f* thinker

pensamiento [pensa'mjento] *nm* thought; (*mente*) mind; (*idea*) idea

pensar [pen'sar] *vt* to think; (*considerar*) to think over, think out; (*proponerse*) to intend, plan; (*imaginarse*) to think up, invent ♦ *vi* to think; ~ **en** to aim at, aspire to; **pensativo, a** *adj* thoughtful, pensive

pensión [pen'sjon] *nf* (*casa*) boarding o guest house; (*dinero*) pension; (*cama y comida*) board and lodging; ~ **completa** full board; **media ~** half-board; **pensionista** *nm/f* (*jubilado*) (old-age) pensioner; (*huésped*) lodger

penúltimo, a [pe'nultimo, a] *adj* penultimate, last but one

penumbra [pe'numbra] *nf* half-light

penuria [pe'nurja] *nf* shortage, want

peña ['peɲa] *nf* (*roca*) rock; (*cuesta*) cliff, crag; (*grupo*) group, circle; (*AM: club*) folk club

peñasco [pe'ɲasko] *nm* large rock, boulder

peñón [pe'ɲon] *nm* wall of rock; **el P~** the Rock (of Gibraltar)

peón [pe'on] *nm* labourer; (*AM*) farm labourer, farmhand; (*AJEDREZ*) pawn

peonza [pe'onθa] *nf* spinning top

peor [pe'or] *adj* (*comparativo*) worse; (*superlativo*) worst ♦ *adv* worse; worst; **de mal en ~** from bad to worse

pepinillo [pepi'niʎo] *nm* gherkin

pepino [pe'pino] *nm* cucumber; **(no) me importa un ~** I don't care one bit

pepita [pe'pita] *nf* (*BOT*) pip; (*MINERÍA*) nugget

pepito [pe'pito] *nm*: ~ **(de ternera)** steak sandwich

pequeñez [peke'ɲeθ] *nf* smallness, littleness; (*trivialidad*) trifle, triviality

pequeño, a [pe'keɲo, a] *adj* small, little

pera ['pera] *nf* pear; **peral** *nm* pear tree

percance [per'kanθe] *nm* setback,
misfortune

percatarse [perka'tarse] *vr*: ~ **de** to notice, take note of

percebe [per'θeβe] *nm* barnacle

percepción [perθep'θjon] *nf* (*vista*) perception; (*idea*) notion, idea

percha ['pertʃa] *nf* (*coat*)hanger; (*ganchos*) coat hooks *pl*; (*de ave*) perch

percibir [perθi'βir] *vt* to perceive, notice; (*COM*) to earn, get

percusión [perku'sjon] *nf* percussion

perdedor, a [perðe'ðor, a] *adj* losing ♦ *nm/f* loser

perder [per'ðer] *vt* to lose; (*tiempo, palabras*) to waste; (*oportunidad*) to lose, miss; (*tren*) to miss ♦ *vi* to lose; **~se** *vr* (*extraviarse*) to get lost; (*desaparecer*) to disappear, be lost to view; (*arruinarse*) to be ruined; **echar a ~** (*comida*) to spoil, ruin; (*oportunidad*) to waste

perdición [perði'θjon] *nf* perdition, ruin

pérdida [per'ðiða] *nf* loss; (*de tiempo*) waste; **~s** *nfpl* (*COM*) losses

perdido, a [per'ðiðo, a] *adj* lost

perdiz [per'ðiθ] *nf* partridge

perdón [per'ðon] *nm* (*disculpa*) pardon, forgiveness; (*clemencia*) mercy; **¡~!** sorry!, I beg your pardon!; **perdonar** *vt* to pardon, forgive; (*la vida*) to spare; (*excusar*) to exempt, excuse; **¡perdone (usted)!** sorry!, I beg your pardon!

perdurar [perðu'rar] *vi* (*resistir*) to last, endure; (*seguir existiendo*) to stand, still exist

perecedero, a [pereθe'ðero, a] *adj* perishable

perecer [pere'θer] *vi* to perish, die

peregrinación [pereɣrina'θjon] *nf* (*REL*) pilgrimage

peregrino, a [pere'ɣrino, a] *adj* (*idea*) strange, absurd ♦ *nm/f* pilgrim

perejil [pere'xil] *nm* parsley

perenne [pe'renne] *adj* everlasting, perennial

pereza [pe'reθa] *nf* laziness, idleness; **perezoso, a** *adj* lazy, idle

perfección [perfek'θjon] *nf* perfection;

perfeccionar *vt* to perfect; (*mejorar*) to improve; (*acabar*) to complete, finish
perfectamente [perfekta'mente] *adv* perfectly
perfecto, a [per'fekto, a] *adj* perfect; (*total*) complete
perfil [per'fil] *nm* profile; (*contorno*) silhouette, outline; (*ARQ*) (cross) section; **~es** *nmpl* features; **~ar** *vt* (*trazar*) to outline; (*fig*) to shape, give character to
perforación [perfora'θjon] *nf* perforation; (*con taladro*) drilling; **perforadora** *nf* punch
perforar [perfo'rar] *vt* to perforate; (*agujero*) to drill, bore; (*papel*) to punch a hole in ♦ *vi* to drill, bore
perfume [per'fume] *nm* perfume, scent
pericia [pe'riθja] *nf* skill, expertise
periferia [peri'ferja] *nf* periphery; (*de ciudad*) outskirts *pl*
periférico [peri'feriko] (*AM*) *nm* ring road (*BRIT*), beltway (*US*)
perímetro [pe'rimetro] *nm* perimeter
periódic, a [pe'rjoðiko, a] *adj* periodic(al) ♦ *nm* newspaper
periodismo [perjo'ðismo] *nm* journalism; **periodista** *nm/f* journalist
periodo [pe'rjoðo] *nm* period
período [pe'rioðo] *nm* = **periodo**
periquito [peri'kito] *nm* budgerigar, budgie
perito, a [pe'rito, a] *adj* (*experto*) expert; (*diestro*) skilled, skilful ♦ *nm/f* expert; skilled worker; (*técnico*) technician
perjudicar [perxuði'kar] *vt* (*gen*) to damage, harm; **perjudicial** *adj* damaging, harmful; (*en detrimento*) detrimental; **perjuicio** *nm* damage, harm
perjurar [perxu'rar] *vi* to commit perjury
perla ['perla] *nf* pearl; **me viene de ~s** it suits me fine
permanecer [permane'θer] *vi* (*quedarse*) to stay, remain; (*seguir*) to continue to be
permanencia [perma'nenθja] *nf* permanence; (*estancia*) stay
permanente [perma'nente] *adj*

permanent, constant ♦ *nf* perm
permiso [per'miso] *nm* permission; (*licencia*) permit, licence; **con ~** excuse me; **estar de ~** (*MIL*) to be on leave; **~ de conducir** driving licence (*BRIT*), driver's license (*US*)
permitir [permi'tir] *vt* to permit, allow
pernera [per'nera] *nf* trouser leg
pernicioso, a [perni'θjoso, a] *adj* pernicious
pero ['pero] *conj* but; (*aún*) yet ♦ *nm* (*defecto*) flaw, defect; (*reparo*) objection
perpendicular [perpendiku'lar] *adj* perpendicular
perpetrar [perpe'trar] *vt* to perpetrate
perpetuar [perpe'twar] *vt* to perpetuate; **perpetuo, a** *adj* perpetual
perplejo, a [per'plexo, a] *adj* perplexed, bewildered
perra ['perra] *nf* (*ZOOL*) bitch; **estar sin una ~** to be flat broke
perrera [pe'rrera] *nf* kennel
perrito [pe'rrito] *nm*: **~ caliente** hot dog
perro ['perro] *nm* dog
persa ['persa] *adj, nm/f* Persian
persecución [perseku'θjon] *nf* pursuit, chase; (*REL, POL*) persecution
perseguir [perse'vir] *vt* to pursue, hunt; (*cortejar*) to chase after; (*molestar*) to pester, annoy; (*REL, POL*) to persecute
perseverante [perseβe'rante] *adj* persevering, persistent
perseverar [perseβe'rar] *vi* to persevere, persist
persiana [per'sjana] *nf* (Venetian) blind
persignarse [persiv'narse] *vr* to cross o.s.
persistente [persis'tente] *adj* persistent
persistir [persis'tir] *vi* to persist
persona [per'sona] *nf* person; **~ mayor** elderly person
personaje [perso'naxe] *nm* important person, celebrity; (*TEATRO etc*) character
personal [perso'nal] *adj* (*particular*) personal; (*para una persona*) single, for one person ♦ *nm* personnel, staff; **~idad** *nf* personality
personarse [perso'narse] *vr* to appear in

person

personificar [personifiˈkar] *vt* to personify

perspectiva [perspekˈtiβa] *nf* perspective; (*vista, panorama*) view, panorama; (*posibilidad futura*) outlook, prospect

perspicacia [perspiˈkaθja] *nf* discernment, perspicacity

perspicaz [perspiˈkaθ] *adj* shrewd

persuadir [perswaˈðir] *vt* (*gen*) to persuade; (*convencer*) to convince; **~se** *vr* to become convinced; **persuasión** *nf* persuasion; **persuasivo, a** *adj* persuasive; convincing

pertenecer [perteneˈθer] *vi* to belong; (*fig*) to concern; **perteneciente** *adj*: **perteneciente a** belonging to; **pertenencia** *nf* ownership; **pertenencias** *nfpl* (*bienes*) possessions, property *sg*

pertenezca *etc vb ver* **pertenecer**

pértiga [ˈpertiɣa] *nf*: **salto de ~** pole vault

pertinente [pertiˈnente] *adj* relevant, pertinent; (*apropiado*) appropriate; **~ a** concerning, relevant to

perturbación [perturβaˈθjon] *nf* (*POL*) disturbance; (*MED*) upset, disturbance

perturbado, a [perturˈβaðo, a] *adj* mentally unbalanced

perturbar [perturˈβar] *vt* (*el orden*) to disturb; (*MED*) to upset, disturb; (*mentalmente*) to perturb

Perú [peˈru] *nm*: **el ~** Peru; **peruano, a** *adj, nm/f* Peruvian

perversión [perβerˈsjon] *nf* perversion; **perverso, a** *adj* perverse; (*depravado*) depraved

pervertido, a [perβerˈtiðo, a] *adj* perverted ♦ *nm/f* pervert

pervertir [perβerˈtir] *vt* to pervert, corrupt

pesa [ˈpesa] *nf* weight; (*DEPORTE*) shot

pesadez [pesaˈðeθ] *nf* (*peso*) heaviness; (*lentitud*) slowness; (*aburrimiento*) tediousness

pesadilla [pesaˈðiʎa] *nf* nightmare, bad dream

pesado, a [peˈsaðo, a] *adj* heavy; (*lento*) slow; (*difícil, duro*) tough, hard; (*aburrido*) boring, tedious; (*tiempo*) sultry

pésame [ˈpesame] *nm* expression of condolence, message of sympathy; **dar el ~** to express one's condolences

pesar [peˈsar] *vt* to weigh ♦ *vi* to weigh; (*ser pesado*) to weigh a lot, be heavy; (*fig: opinión*) to carry weight; **no pesa mucho** it is not very heavy ♦ *nm* (*arrepentimiento*) regret; (*pena*) grief, sorrow; **a ~ de** *o* **pese a (que)** in spite of, despite

pesca [ˈpeska] *nf* (*acto*) fishing; (*lo pescado*) catch; **ir de ~** to go fishing

pescadería [peskaðeˈria] *nf* fish shop, fishmonger's (*BRIT*)

pescadilla [peskaˈðiʎa] *nf* whiting

pescado [pesˈkaðo] *nm* fish

pescador, a [peskaˈðor, a] *nm/f* fisherman/woman

pescar [pesˈkar] *vt* (*tomar*) to catch; (*intentar tomar*) to fish for; (*conseguir: trabajo*) to manage to get ♦ *vi* to fish, go fishing

pescuezo [pesˈkweθo] *nm* neck

pesebre [peˈseβre] *nm* manger

peseta [peˈseta] *nf* peseta

pesimista [pesiˈmista] *adj* pessimistic ♦ *nm/f* pessimist

pésimo, a [ˈpesimo, a] *adj* awful, dreadful

peso [ˈpeso] *nm* weight; (*balanza*) scales *pl*; (*moneda*) peso; **~ bruto/neto** gross/net weight; **vender al ~** to sell by weight

pesquero, a [pesˈkero, a] *adj* fishing *cpd*

pesquisa [pesˈkisa] *nf* inquiry, investigation

pestaña [pesˈtaɲa] *nf* (*ANAT*) eyelash; (*borde*) rim; **pestañear** *vi* to blink

peste [ˈpeste] *nf* plague; (*mal olor*) stink, stench

pesticida [pestiˈθiða] *nm* pesticide

pestillo [pesˈtiʎo] *nm* (*cerrojo*) bolt; (*picaporte*) doorhandle

petaca [peˈtaka] *nf* (*de cigarros*) cigarette case; (*de pipa*) tobacco pouch; (*AM: maleta*) suitcase

pétalo [ˈpetalo] *nm* petal

petardo [peˈtardo] *nm* firework, firecracker

petición [peti'θjon] *nf* (*pedido*) request, plea; (*memorial*) petition; (*JUR*) plea

petrificar [petrifi'kar] *vt* to petrify

petróleo [pe'troleo] *nm* oil, petroleum; **petrolero, a** *adj* petroleum *cpd* ♦ *nm* (oil) tanker

peyorativo, a [pejora'tiβo, a] *adj* pejorative

pez [peθ] *nm* fish

pezón [pe'θon] *nm* teat, nipple

pezuña [pe'θuɲa] *nf* hoof

piadoso, a [pja'δoso, a] *adj* (*devoto*) pious, devout; (*misericordioso*) kind, merciful

pianista [pja'nista] *nm/f* pianist

piano ['pjano] *nm* piano

piar [pjar] *vi* to cheep

pibe, a ['piβe, a] (*AM*) *nm/f* boy/girl

picadero [pika'δero] *nm* riding school

picadillo [pika'δiʎo] *nm* mince, minced meat

picado, a [pi'kaδo, a] *adj* pricked, punctured; (*CULIN*) minced, chopped; (*mar*) choppy; (*diente*) bad; (*tabaco*) cut; (*enfadado*) cross

picador [pika'δor] *nm* (*TAUR*) picador; (*minero*) faceworker

picadura [pika'δura] *nf* (*pinchazo*) puncture; (*de abeja*) sting; (*de mosquito*) bite; (*tabaco picado*) cut tobacco

picante [pi'kante] *adj* hot; (*comentario*) racy, spicy

picaporte [pika'porte] *nm* (*manija*) doorhandle; (*pestillo*) latch

picar [pi'kar] *vt* (*agujerear, perforar*) to prick, puncture; (*abeja*) to sting; (*mosquito, serpiente*) to bite; (*CULIN*) to mince, chop; (*incitar*) to incite, goad; (*dañar, irritar*) to annoy, bother; (*quemar: lengua*) to burn, sting ♦ *vi* (*pez*) to bite, take the bait; (*sol*) to burn, scorch; (*abeja, MED*) to sting; (*mosquito*) to bite; **~se** *vr* (*agriarse*) to turn sour, go off; (*ofenderse*) to take offence

picardía [pikar'δia] *nf* villainy; (*astucia*) slyness, craftiness; (*una ~*) dirty trick; (*palabra*) rude/bad word *o* expression

pícaro, a ['pikaro, a] *adj* (*malicioso*) villainous; (*travieso*) mischievous ♦ *nm* (*astuto*) crafty sort; (*sinvergüenza*) rascal, scoundrel

pichón [pi'tʃon] *nm* young pigeon

pico ['piko] *nm* (*de ave*) beak; (*punta*) sharp point; (*TEC*) pick, pickaxe; (*GEO*) peak, summit; **y ~** and a bit

picor [pi'kor] *nm* itch

picotear [pikote'ar] *vt* to peck ♦ *vi* to nibble, pick

picudo, a [pi'kuδo, a] *adj* pointed, with a point

pidió *etc vb ver* **pedir**

pido *etc vb ver* **pedir**

pie [pje] (*pl* ~**s**) *nm* foot; (*fig: motivo*) motive, basis; (*: fundamento*) foothold; **ir a ~** to go on foot, walk; **estar de ~** to be standing (up); **ponerse de ~** to stand up; **de ~s a cabeza** from top to bottom; **al ~ de la letra** (*citar*) literally, verbatim; (*copiar*) exactly, word for word; **en ~ de guerra** on a war footing; **dar ~ a** to give cause for; **hacer ~** (*en el agua*) to touch (the) bottom

piedad [pje'δaδ] *nf* (*lástima*) pity, compassion; (*clemencia*) mercy; (*devoción*) piety, devotion

piedra ['pjeδra] *nf* stone; (*roca*) rock; (*de mechero*) flint; (*METEOROLOGÍA*) hailstone

piel [pjel] *nf* (*ANAT*) skin; (*ZOOL*) skin, hide, fur; (*cuero*) leather; (*BOT*) skin, peel

pienso *etc vb ver* **pensar**

pierdo *etc vb ver* **perder**

pierna ['pjerna] *nf* leg

pieza ['pjeθa] *nf* piece; (*habitación*) room; **~ de recambio** *o* **repuesto** spare (part)

pigmeo, a [piɣ'meo, a] *adj, nm/f* pigmy

pijama [pi'xama] *nm* pyjamas *pl*

pila ['pila] *nf* (*ELEC*) battery; (*montón*) heap, pile; (*lavabo*) sink

píldora ['pilδora] *nf* pill; **la ~ (anticonceptiva)** the (contraceptive) pill

pileta [pi'leta] *nf* basin, bowl; (*AM*) swimming pool

pillaje [pi'ʎaxe] *nm* pillage, plunder

pillar [pi'ʎar] *vt* (*saquear*) to pillage,

plunder; (*fam: coger*) to catch; (*: agarrar*) to grasp, seize; (*: entender*) to grasp, catch on to; **~se** *vr*: **~se un dedo con la puerta** to catch one's finger in the door

pillo, a ['piʎo, a] *adj* villainous; (*astuto*) sly, crafty ♦ *nm/f* rascal, rogue, scoundrel

piloto [pi'loto] *nm* pilot; (*de aparato*) (pilot) light; (*AUTO: luz*) tail *o* rear light; (*: conductor*) driver

pimentón [pimen'ton] *nm* paprika

pimienta [pi'mjenta] *nf* pepper

pimiento [pi'mjento] *nm* pepper, pimiento

pin [pin] (*pl* **pins**) *nm* badge

pinacoteca [pinako'teka] *nf* art gallery

pinar [pi'nar] *nm* pine forest (*BRIT*), pine grove (*US*)

pincel [pin'θel] *nm* paintbrush

pinchadiscos [pintʃa'ðiskos] *nm/f inv* disc-jockey, DJ

pinchar [pin'tʃar] *vt* (*perforar*) to prick, pierce; (*neumático*) to puncture; (*fig*) to prod

pinchazo [pin'tʃaθo] *nm* (*perforación*) prick; (*de neumático*) puncture; (*fig*) prod

pincho ['pintʃo] *nm* savoury (snack); **~ moruno** shish kebab; **~ de tortilla** small slice of omelette

ping-pong ['pin'pon] *nm* table tennis

pingüino [pin'gwino] *nm* penguin

pino ['pino] *nm* pine (tree)

pinta ['pinta] *nf* spot; (*de líquidos*) spot, drop; (*aspecto*) appearance, look(s) (*pl*); **~do, a** *adj* spotted; (*de colores*) colourful; **~das** *nfpl* graffiti *sg*

pintar [pin'tar] *vt* to paint ♦ *vi* to paint; (*fam*) to count, be important; **~se** *vr* to put on make-up

pintor, a [pin'tor, a] *nm/f* painter

pintoresco, a [pinto'resko, a] *adj* picturesque

pintura [pin'tura] *nf* painting; **~ a la acuarela** watercolour; **~ al óleo** oil painting

pinza ['pinθa] *nf* (*ZOOL*) claw; (*para colgar ropa*) clothes peg; (*TEC*) pincers *pl*; **~s** *nfpl* (*para depilar etc*) tweezers *pl*

piña ['piɲa] *nf* (*fruto del pino*) pine cone; (*fruta*) pineapple; (*fig*) group

piñón [pi'ɲon] *nm* (*fruto*) pine nut; (*TEC*) pinion

pío, a ['pio, a] *adj* (*devoto*) pious, devout; (*misericordioso*) merciful

piojo ['pjoxo] *nm* louse

pionero, a [pjo'nero, a] *adj* pioneering ♦ *nm/f* pioneer

pipa ['pipa] *nf* pipe; **~s** *nfpl* (*BOT*) (edible) sunflower seeds

pipí [pi'pi] (*fam*) *nm*: **hacer ~** to have a wee(-wee) (*BRIT*), have to go (wee-wee) (*US*)

pique ['pike] *nm* (*resentimiento*) pique, resentment; (*rivalidad*) rivalry, competition; **irse a ~** to sink; (*esperanza, familia*) to be ruined

piqueta [pi'keta] *nf* pick(axe)

piquete [pi'kete] *nm* (*MIL*) squad, party; (*de obreros*) picket

pirado, a [pi'raðo, a] (*fam*) *adj* round the bend ♦ *nm/f* nutter

piragua [pi'raɣwa] *nf* canoe; **piragüismo** *nm* canoeing

pirámide [pi'ramiðe] *nf* pyramid

pirata [pi'rata] *adj, nm* pirate ♦ *nm/f*: **~ informático/a** hacker

Pirineo(s) [piri'neo(s)] *nm(pl)* Pyrenees *pl*

pirómano, a [pi'romano, a] *nm/f* (*MED, JUR*) arsonist

piropo [pi'ropo] *nm* compliment, (piece of) flattery

pirueta [pi'rweta] *nf* pirouette

pis [pis] (*fam*) *nm* pee, piss; **hacer ~** to have a pee; (*para niños*) to wee-wee

pisada [pi'saða] *nf* (*paso*) footstep; (*huella*) footprint

pisar [pi'sar] *vt* (*caminar sobre*) to walk on, tread on; (*apretar con el pie*) to press; (*fig*) to trample on, walk all over ♦ *vi* to tread, step, walk

piscina [pis'θina] *nf* swimming pool

Piscis ['pisθis] *nm* Pisces

piso ['piso] *nm* (*suelo, planta*) floor; (*apartamento*) flat (*BRIT*), apartment; **primer ~** (*ESP*) first floor; (*AM*) ground floor

pisotear [pisote'ar] *vt* to trample (on *o* underfoot)

pista ['pista] *nf* track, trail; (*indicio*) clue; ~ **de aterrizaje** runway; ~ **de baile** dance floor; ~ **de hielo** ice rink; ~ **de tenis** tennis court

pistola [pis'tola] *nf* pistol; (*TEC*) spray-gun; **pistolero, a** *nm/f* gunman/woman, gangster

pistón [pis'ton] *nm* (*TEC*) piston; (*MUS*) key

pitar [pi'tar] *vt* (*silbato*) to blow; (*rechiflar*) to whistle at, boo ♦ *vi* to whistle; (*AUTO*) to sound *o* toot one's horn; (*AM*) to smoke

pitillo [pi'tiʎo] *nm* cigarette

pito ['pito] *nm* whistle; (*de coche*) horn

pitón [pi'ton] *nm* (*ZOOL*) python

pitonisa [pito'nisa] *nf* fortune-teller

pitorreo [pito'rreo] *nm* joke; **estar de ~** to be joking

pizarra [pi'θarra] *nf* (*piedra*) slate; (*encerado*) blackboard

pizca ['piθka] *nf* pinch, spot; (*fig*) spot, speck; **ni ~** not a bit

placa ['plaka] *nf* plate; (*distintivo*) badge, insignia; ~ **de matrícula** number plate

placentero, a [plaθen'tero, a] *adj* pleasant, agreeable

placer [pla'θer] *nm* pleasure ♦ *vt* to please

plácido, a ['plaθiðo, a] *adj* placid

plaga ['plaɣa] *nf* pest; (*MED*) plague; (*abundancia*) abundance; **plagar** *vt* to infest, plague; (*llenar*) to fill

plagio ['plaxjo] *nm* plagiarism

plan [plan] *nm* (*esquema, proyecto*) plan; (*idea, intento*) idea, intention; **tener ~** (*fam*) to have a date; **tener un ~** (*fam*) to have an affair; **en ~ económico** (*fam*) on the cheap; **vamos en ~ de turismo** we're going as tourists; **si te pones en ese ~ ...** if that's your attitude ...

plana ['plana] *nf* sheet (of paper), page; (*TEC*) trowel; **en primera ~** on the front page; ~ **mayor** staff

plancha ['plantʃa] *nf* (*para planchar*) iron; (*rótulo*) plate, sheet; (*NAUT*) gangway; **a la ~** (*CULIN*) grilled; ~**do** *nm* ironing; **planchar** *vt* to iron ♦ *vi* to do the ironing

planeador [planea'ðor] *nm* glider

planear [plane'ar] *vt* to plan ♦ *vi* to glide

planeta [pla'neta] *nm* planet

planicie [pla'niθje] *nf* plain

planificación [planifika'θjon] *nf* planning; ~ **familiar** family planning

plano, a ['plano, a] *adj* flat, level, even ♦ *nm* (*MAT, TEC*) plane; (*FOTO*) shot; (*ARQ*) plan; (*GEO*) map; (*de ciudad*) map, street plan; **primer ~** close-up; **caer de ~** to fall flat

planta ['planta] *nf* (*BOT, TEC*) plant; (*ANAT*) sole of the foot, foot; (*piso*) floor; (*AM: personal*) staff; ~ **baja** ground floor

plantación [planta'θjon] *nf* (*AGR*) plantation; (*acto*) planting

plantar [plan'tar] *vt* (*BOT*) to plant; (*levantar*) to erect, set up; ~**se** *vr* to stand firm; ~ **a uno en la calle** to throw sb out; **dejar plantado a uno** (*fam*) to stand sb up

plantear [plante'ar] *vt* (*problema*) to pose; (*dificultad*) to raise

plantilla [plan'tiʎa] *nf* (*de zapato*) insole; (*personal*) personnel; **ser de ~** to be on the staff

plantón [plan'ton] *nm* (*MIL*) guard, sentry; (*fam*) long wait; **dar (un) ~ a uno** to stand sb up

plasmar [plas'mar] *vt* (*dar forma*) to mould, shape; (*representar*) to represent; ~**se** *vr*: ~**se en** to take the form of

plasta ['plasta] (*fam*) *adj inv* boring ♦ *nm/f* bore

plástico, a ['plastiko, a] *adj* plastic ♦ *nm* plastic

Plastilina ® [plasti'lina] *nf* Plasticine ®

plata ['plata] *nf* (*metal*) silver; (*cosas hechas de* ~) silverware; (*AM*) cash, dough; **hablar en ~** to speak bluntly *o* frankly

plataforma [plata'forma] *nf* platform; ~ **de lanzamiento/perforación** launch(ing) pad/drilling rig

plátano ['platano] *nm* (*fruta*) banana;

(*árbol*) plane tree; banana tree
platea [pla'tea] *nf* (*TEATRO*) pit
plateado, a [plate'aðo, a] *adj* silver; (*TEC*) silver-plated
plática ['platika] *nf* talk, chat; **platicar** *vi* to talk, chat
platillo [pla'tiʎo] *nm* saucer; **~s** *nmpl* (*MUS*) cymbals; **~ volador** *o* **volante** flying saucer
platino [pla'tino] *nm* platinum; **~s** *nmpl* (*AUTO*) contact points
plato ['plato] *nm* plate, dish; (*parte de comida*) course; (*comida*) dish; **~ combinado** set main course (*served on one plate*); **~ fuerte** main course; **primer ~** first course
playa ['plaja] *nf* beach; (*costa*) seaside; **~ de estacionamiento** (*AM*) car park
playera [pla'jera] *nf* (*AM: camiseta*) T-shirt; **~s** *nfpl* (*zapatos*) canvas shoes
plaza ['plaθa] *nf* square; (*mercado*) market(place); (*sitio*) room, space; (*en vehículo*) seat, place; (*colocación*) post, job; **~ de toros** bullring
plazo ['plaθo] *nm* (*lapso de tiempo*) time, period; (*fecha de vencimiento*) expiry date; (*pago parcial*) instalment; **a corto/largo ~** short-/long-term; **comprar algo a ~s** to buy sth on hire purchase (*BRIT*) *o* on time (*US*)
plazoleta [plaθo'leta] *nf* small square
pleamar [plea'mar] *nf* high tide
plebe ['pleβe] *nf*: **la ~** the common people *pl*, the masses *pl*; (*pey*) the plebs *pl*; **~yo, a** *adj* plebeian; (*pey*) coarse, common
plebiscito [pleβis'θito] *nm* plebiscite
plegable [ple'xaβle] *adj* collapsible; (*silla*) folding
plegar [ple'xar] *vt* (*doblar*) to fold, bend; (*COSTURA*) to pleat; **~se** *vr* to yield, submit
pleito ['pleito] *nm* (*JUR*) lawsuit, case; (*fig*) dispute, feud
plenilunio [pleni'lunjo] *nm* full moon
plenitud [pleni'tuð] *nf* plenitude, fullness; (*abundancia*) abundance
pleno, a ['pleno, a] *adj* full; (*completo*)

complete ♦ *nm* plenum; **en ~ día** in broad daylight; **en ~ verano** at the height of summer; **en plena cara** full in the face
pliego *etc* ['pljexo] *vb ver* **plegar** ♦ *nm* (*hoja*) sheet (of paper); (*carta*) sealed letter/document; **~ de condiciones** details *pl*, specifications *pl*
pliegue *etc* ['pljexe] *vb ver* **plegar** ♦ *nm* fold, crease; (*de vestido*) pleat
plomero [plo'mero] *nm* (*AM*) plumber
plomo ['plomo] *nm* (*metal*) lead; (*ELEC*) fuse; **sin ~** unleaded
pluma ['pluma] *nf* feather; (*para escribir*): **~ (estilográfica)** ink pen; **~ fuente** (*AM*) fountain pen
plumero [plu'mero] *nm* (*para el polvo*) feather duster
plumón [plu'mon] *nm* (*de ave*) down; (*AM: fino*) felt-tip pen; (*: ancho*) marker
plural [plu'ral] *adj* plural; **~idad** *nf* plurality
pluriempleo [pluriem'pleo] *nm* having more than one job
plus [plus] *nm* bonus; **~valía** *nf* (*COM*) appreciation
población [poβla'θjon] *nf* population; (*pueblo, ciudad*) town, city
poblado, a [po'βlaðo, a] *adj* inhabited ♦ *nm* (*aldea*) village; (*pueblo*) (small) town; **densamente ~** densely populated
poblador, a [poβla'ðor, a] *nm/f* settler, colonist
poblar [po'βlar] *vt* (*colonizar*) to colonize; (*fundar*) to found; (*habitar*) to inhabit
pobre ['poβre] *adj* poor ♦ *nm/f* poor person; **~za** *nf* poverty
pocilga [po'θilxa] *nf* pigsty
pócima ['poθima] *nf* potion

┌─────────────────┐
│ *PALABRA CLAVE* │
└─────────────────┘

poco, a ['poko, a] *adj* **1** (*sg*) little, not much; **~ tiempo** little *o* not much time; **de ~ interés** of little interest, not very interesting; **poca cosa** not much
2 (*pl*) few, not many; **unos ~s** a few, some; **~s niños comen lo que les**

conviene few children eat what they should
♦ *adv* **1** little, not much; **cuesta ~** it doesn't cost much
2 (*+adj: = negativo, antónimo*): **~ amable/inteligente** not very nice/intelligent
3: por ~ me caigo I almost fell
4: a ~: a ~ de haberse casado shortly after getting married
5: ~ a ~ little by little
♦ *nm* a little, a bit; **un ~ triste/de dinero** a little sad/money

podar [po'ðar] *vt* to prune

PALABRA CLAVE

poder [po'ðer] *vi* **1** (*capacidad*) can, be able to; **no puedo hacerlo** I can't do it, I'm unable to do it
2 (*permiso*) can, may, be allowed to; **¿se puede?** may I (*o* we)?; **puedes irte ahora** you may go now; **no se puede fumar en este hospital** smoking is not allowed in this hospital
3 (*posibilidad*) may, might, could; **puede llegar mañana** he may *o* might arrive tomorrow; **pudiste haberte hecho daño** you might *o* could have hurt yourself; **¡podías habérmelo dicho antes!** you might have told me before!
4: puede ser: puede ser perhaps; **puede ser que lo sepa Tomás** may *o* might know
5: ¡no puedo más! I've had enough!; **no pude menos que dejarlo** I couldn't help but leave it; **es tonto a más no ~** he's as stupid as they come
6: ~ con: no puedo con este crío this kid's too much for me
♦ *nm* power; **~ adquisitivo** purchasing power; **detentar** *o* **ocupar** *o* **estar en el ~** to be in power

poderoso, a [poðe'roso, a] *adj* (*político, país*) powerful
podio ['poðjo] *nm* (*DEPORTE*) podium

podium ['poðjum] = **podio**
podrido, a [po'ðriðo, a] *adj* rotten, bad; (*fig*) rotten, corrupt
podrir [po'ðrir] = **pudrir**
poema [po'ema] *nm* poem
poesía [poe'sia] *nf* poetry
poeta [po'eta] *nm/f* poet; **poético, a** *adj* poetic(al)
poetisa [poe'tisa] *nf* (woman) poet
póker ['poker] *nm* poker
polaco, a [po'lako, a] *adj* Polish ♦ *nm/f* Pole
polar [po'lar] *adj* polar; **~idad** *nf* polarity; **~izarse** *vr* to polarize
polea [po'lea] *nf* pulley
polémica [po'lemika] *nf* polemics *sg*; (*una ~*) controversy, polemic
polen ['polen] *nm* pollen
policía [poli'θia] *nm/f* policeman/woman ♦ *nf* police; **~co, a** *adj* police *cpd*; **novela policíaca** detective story; **policial** *adj* police *cpd*
polideportivo [poliðepor'tiβo] *nm* sports centre *o* complex
poligamia [poli'γamja] *nf* polygamy
polígono [po'liγono] *nm* (*MAT*) polygon; **~ industrial** industrial estate
polilla [po'liʎa] *nf* moth
polio ['poljo] *nf* polio
política [po'litika] *nf* politics *sg*; (*económica, agraria etc*) policy; *ver tb* **político**
político, a [po'litiko, a] *adj* political; (*discreto*) tactful; (*de familia*) -in-law ♦ *nm/f* politician; **padre ~** father-in-law
póliza ['poliθa] *nf* certificate, voucher; (*impuesto*) tax stamp; **~ de seguros** insurance policy
polizón [poli'θon] *nm* stowaway
pollera [po'ʎera] (*AM*) *nf* skirt
pollería [poʎe'ria] *nf* poulterer's (shop)
pollo ['poʎo] *nm* chicken
polo ['polo] *nm* (*GEO, ELEC*) pole; (*helado*) ice lolly; (*DEPORTE*) polo; (*suéter*) polo-neck; **~ Norte/Sur** North/South Pole
Polonia [po'lonja] *nf* Poland
poltrona [pol'trona] *nf* easy chair

polución [polu'θjon] *nf* pollution
polvera [pol'ßera] *nf* powder compact
polvo [ˈpolßo] *nm* dust; (*QUÍM, CULIN, MED*) powder; **~s** *nmpl* (*maquillaje*) powder *sg*; **quitar el ~** to dust; **~ de talco** talcum powder; **estar hecho ~** (*fam*) to be worn out *o* exhausted
pólvora ['polßora] *nf* gunpowder; (*fuegos artificiales*) fireworks *pl*
polvoriento, a [polßo'rjento, a] *adj* (*superficie*) dusty; (*sustancia*) powdery
pomada [po'maða] *nf* cream, ointment
pomelo [po'melo] *nm* grapefruit
pómez ['pomeθ] *nf*: **piedra ~** pumice stone
pomo ['pomo] *nm* doorknob
pompa ['pompa] *nf* (*burbuja*) bubble; (*bomba*) pump; (*esplendor*) pomp, splendour; **pomposo, a** *adj* splendid, magnificent; (*pey*) pompous
pómulo ['pomulo] *nm* cheekbone
pon [pon] *vb ver* **poner**
ponche ['pontʃe] *nm* punch
poncho ['pontʃo] *nm* poncho
ponderar [ponde'rar] *vt* (*considerar*) to weigh up, consider; (*elogiar*) to praise highly, speak in praise of
pondré *etc vb ver* **poner**

PALABRA CLAVE

poner [po'ner] *vt* **1** (*colocar*) to put; (*telegrama*) to send; (*obra de teatro*) to put on; (*película*) to show; **ponlo más fuerte** turn it up; **¿qué ponen en el Excelsior?** what's on at the Excelsior?
2 (*tienda*) to open; (*instalar: gas etc*) to put in; (*radio, TV*) to switch *o* turn on
3 (*suponer*): **pongamos que ...** let's suppose that ...
4 (*contribuir*): **el gobierno ha puesto otro millón** the government has contributed another million
5 (*TELEC*): **póngame con el Sr. López** can you put me through to Mr. López?
6: **~ de**: **le han puesto de director general** they've appointed him general manager

7 (*+adj*) to make; **me estás poniendo nerviosa** you're making me nervous
8 (*dar nombre*): **al hijo le pusieron Diego** they called their son Diego
♦ *vi* (*gallina*) to lay
♦ **~se** *vr* **1** (*colocarse*): **se puso a mi lado** he came and stood beside me; **tú ponte en esa silla** you go and sit on that chair
2 (*vestido, cosméticos*) to put on; **¿por qué no te pones el vestido nuevo?** why don't you put on *o* wear your new dress?
3 (*+adj*) to turn; to get; become; **se puso muy serio** he got very serious; **después de lavarla la tela se puso azul** after washing it the material turned blue
4: **~se a**: **se puso a llorar** he started to cry; **tienes que ~te a estudiar** you must get down to studying
5: **~se a bien con uno** to make it up with sb; **~se a mal con uno** to get on the wrong side of sb

pongo *etc vb ver* **poner**
poniente [po'njente] *nm* (*occidente*) west; (*viento*) west wind
pontífice [pon'tifiθe] *nm* pope, pontiff
popa ['popa] *nf* stern
popular [popu'lar] *adj* popular; (*cultura*) of the people, folk *cpd*; **~idad** *nf* popularity; **~izarse** *vr* to become popular

PALABRA CLAVE

por [por] *prep* **1** (*objetivo*) for; **luchar ~ la patria** to fight for one's country
2 (*+infin*): **~ no llegar tarde** so as not to arrive late; **~ citar unos ejemplos** to give a few examples
3 (*causa*) out of, because of; **~ escasez de fondos** through *o* for lack of funds
4 (*tiempo*): **~ la mañana/noche** in the morning/at night; **se queda ~ una semana** she's staying (for) a week
5 (*lugar*): **pasar ~ Madrid** to pass through Madrid; **ir a Guayaquil ~ Quito** to go to Guayaquil via Quito; **caminar ~ la calle** to walk along the street; **ver tb**

todo
6 (*cambio, precio*): **te doy uno nuevo ~ el que tienes** I'll give you a new one (in return) for the one you've got
7 (*valor distributivo*): **550 pesetas ~ hora/cabeza** 550 pesetas an *o* per hour/ a *o* per head
8 (*modo, medio*) by; **~ correo/avión** by post/air; **día ~ día** day by day; **entrar ~ la entrada principal** to go in through the main entrance
9: **10 ~ 10 son 100** 10 times 10 is 100
10 (*en lugar de*): **vino él ~ su jefe** he came instead of his boss
11: **~ mí que revienten** as far as I'm concerned they can drop dead
12: **¿~ qué?** why?; **¿~ qué no?** why not?

porcelana [porθe'lana] *nf* porcelain; (*china*) china
porcentaje [porθen'taxe] *nm* percentage
porción [por'θjon] *nf* (*parte*) portion, share; (*cantidad*) quantity, amount
pordiosero, a [pordjo'sero, a] *nm/f* beggar
porfiar [por'fjar] *vi* to persist, insist; (*disputar*) to argue stubbornly
pormenor [porme'nor] *nm* detail, particular
pornografía [pornoɣra'fia] *nf* pornography
poro ['poro] *nm* pore; **~so, a** *adj* porous
porque ['porke] *conj* (*a causa de*) because; (*ya que*) since; (*con el fin de*) so that, in order that
porqué [por'ke] *nm* reason, cause
porquería [porke'ria] *nf* (*suciedad*) filth, dirt; (*acción*) dirty trick; (*objeto*) small thing, trifle; (*fig*) rubbish
porra ['porra] *nf* (*arma*) stick, club
porrazo [po'rraθo] *nm* blow, bump
porro ['porro] (*fam*) *nm* (*droga*) joint (*fam*)
porrón [po'rron] *nm* glass wine jar with a long spout
portaaviones [porta'(a)βjones] *nm inv* aircraft carrier

portada [por'taða] *nf* (*de revista*) cover
portador, a [porta'ðor, a] *nm/f* carrier, bearer; (*COM*) bearer, payee
portaequipajes [portaeki'paxes] *nm inv* (*AUTO: maletero*) boot; (: *baca*) luggage rack
portal [por'tal] *nm* (*entrada*) vestibule, hall; (*portada*) porch, doorway; (*puerta de entrada*) main door
portamaletas [portama'letas] *nm inv* (*AUTO: maletero*) boot; (: *baca*) roof rack
portarse [por'tarse] *vr* to behave, conduct o.s.
portátil [por'tatil] *adj* portable
portavoz [porta'βoθ] *nm/f* spokesman/ woman
portazo [por'taθo] *nm*: **dar un ~** to slam the door
porte ['porte] *nm* (*COM*) transport; (*precio*) transport charges *pl*
portento [por'tento] *nm* marvel, wonder; **~so, a** *adj* marvellous, extraordinary
porteño, a [por'teno, a] *adj* of *o* from Buenos Aires
portería [porte'ria] *nf* (*oficina*) porter's office; (*DEPORTE*) goal
portero, a [por'tero, a] *nm/f* porter; (*conserje*) caretaker; (*ujier*) doorman; (*DEPORTE*) goalkeeper; **~ automático** intercom
pórtico ['portiko] *nm* (*patio*) portico, porch; (*fig*) gateway; (*arcada*) arcade
portorriqueño, a [portorri'keno, a] *adj* Puerto Rican
Portugal [portu'βal] *nm* Portugal; **portugués, esa** *adj, nm/f* Portuguese
♦ *nm* (*LING*) Portuguese
porvenir [porβe'nir] *nm* future
pos [pos] *prep*: **en ~ de** after, in pursuit of
posada [po'saða] *nf* (*refugio*) shelter, lodging; (*mesón*) guest house; **dar ~ a** to give shelter to, take in
posaderas [posa'ðeras] *nfpl* backside *sg*, buttocks
posar [po'sar] *vt* (*en el suelo*) to lay down, put down; (*la mano*) to place, put gently
♦ *vi* (*modelo*) to sit, pose; **~se** *vr* to

settle; (*pájaro*) to perch; (*avión*) to land, come down

posavasos [posa'basos] *nm inv* coaster; (*para cerveza*) beermat

posdata [pos'ðata] *nf* postscript

pose ['pose] *nf* pose

poseedor, a [posee'ðor, a] *nm/f* owner, possessor; (*de récord, puesto*) holder

poseer [pose'er] *vt* to possess, own; (*ventaja*) to enjoy; (*récord, puesto*) to hold

posesión [pose'sjon] *nf* possession; **posesionarse** *vr*: **posesionarse de** to take possession of, take over

posesivo, a [pose'siβo, a] *adj* possessive

posgrado [pos'graðo] *nm*: **curso de ~** postgraduate course

posibilidad [posiβili'ðað] *nf* possibility; (*oportunidad*) chance; **posibilitar** *vt* to make possible; (*hacer realizable*) to make feasible

posible [po'siβle] *adj* possible; (*realizable*) feasible; **de ser ~** if possible; **en lo ~** as far as possible

posición [posi'θjon] *nf* position; (*rango social*) status

positivo, a [posi'tiβo, a] *adj* positive

poso ['poso] *nm* sediment; (*heces*) dregs *pl*

posponer [pospo'ner] *vt* (*relegar*) to put behind/below; (*aplazar*) to postpone

posta ['posta] *nf*: **a ~** deliberately, on purpose

postal [pos'tal] *adj* postal ♦ *nf* postcard

poste ['poste] *nm* (*de telégrafos etc*) post, pole; (*columna*) pillar

póster ['poster] (*pl* **pósteres, pósters**) *nm* poster

postergar [poster'xar] *vt* to postpone, delay

posteridad [posteri'ðað] *nf* posterity

posterior [poste'rjor] *adj* back, rear; (*siguiente*) following, subsequent; (*más tarde*) later; **~idad** *nf*: **con ~idad** later, subsequently

postgrado [post'graðo] *nm* = **posgrado**

postizo, a [pos'tiθo, a] *adj* false, artificial ♦ *nm* hairpiece

postor, a [pos'tor, a] *nm/f* bidder

postre ['postre] *nm* sweet, dessert

postrero, a [pos'trero, a] (*delante de nmsg*: **postrer**) *adj* (*último*) last; (*que viene detrás*) rear

postulado [postu'laðo] *nm* postulate

póstumo, a ['postumo, a] *adj* posthumous

postura [pos'tura] *nf* (*del cuerpo*) posture, position; (*fig*) attitude, position

potable [po'taβle] *adj* drinkable; **agua ~** drinking water

potaje [po'taxe] *nm* thick vegetable soup

pote ['pote] *nm* pot, jar

potencia [po'tenθja] *nf* power; **~l** [poten'θjal] *adj, nm* potential; **~r** *vt* to boost

potente [po'tente] *adj* powerful

potro, a ['potro, a] *nm/f* (*ZOOL*) colt/filly ♦ *nm* (*de gimnasia*) vaulting horse

pozo ['poθo] *nm* well; (*de río*) deep pool; (*de mina*) shaft

P.P. *abr* (= *porte pagado*) CP

práctica ['praktika] *nf* practice; (*método*) method; (*arte, capacidad*) skill; **en la ~** in practice

practicable [prakti'kaβle] *adj* practicable; (*camino*) passable

practicante [prakti'kante] *nm/f* (*MED*: *ayudante de doctor*) medical assistant; (: *enfermero*) nurse; (*quien practica algo*) practitioner ♦ *adj* practising

practicar [prakti'kar] *vt* to practise; (*DEPORTE*) to play; (*realizar*) to carry out, perform

práctico, a ['praktiko, a] *adj* practical; (*instruido: persona*) skilled, expert

practique *etc vb ver* **practicar**

pradera [pra'ðera] *nf* meadow; (*US etc*) prairie

prado ['praðo] *nm* (*campo*) meadow, field; (*pastizal*) pasture

Praga ['praxa] *n* Prague

pragmático, a [praɣ'matiko, a] *adj* pragmatic

preámbulo [pre'ambulo] *nm* preamble, introduction

precario, a [pre'karjo, a] *adj* precarious

precaución [prekau'θjon] *nf (medida preventiva)* preventive measure, precaution; *(prudencia)* caution, wariness

precaver [preka'βer] *vt* to guard against; *(impedir)* to forestall; **~se** *vr*: **~se de** *o* **contra algo** to (be on one's) guard against sth; **precavido, a** *adj* cautious, wary

precedente [preθe'ðente] *adj* preceding; *(anterior)* former ♦ *nm* precedent

preceder [preθe'ðer] *vt, vi* to precede, go before, come before

precepto [pre'θepto] *nm* precept

preciado, a [pre'θjaðo, a] *adj (estimado)* esteemed, valuable

preciarse [pre'θjarse] *vr* to boast; **~se de** to pride o.s. on, boast of being

precinto [pre'θinto] *nm (tb:* **~ de garantía)** seal

precio ['preθjo] *nm* price; *(costo)* cost; *(valor)* value, worth; *(de viaje)* fare; **~ al contado/de coste/de oportunidad** cash/cost/bargain price; **~ al detalle** *o* **al por menor** retail price; **~ tope** top price

preciosidad [preθjosi'ðað] *nf (valor)* (high) value, (great) worth; *(encanto)* charm; *(cosa bonita)* beautiful thing; **es una ~** it's lovely, it's really beautiful

precioso, a [pre'θjoso, a] *adj* precious; *(de mucho valor)* valuable; *(fam)* lovely, beautiful

precipicio [preθi'piθjo] *nm* cliff, precipice; *(fig)* abyss

precipitación [preθipita'θjon] *nf* haste; *(lluvia)* rainfall

precipitado, a [preθipi'taðo, a] *adj (conducta)* hasty, rash; *(salida)* hasty, sudden

precipitar [preθipi'tar] *vt (arrojar)* to hurl down, throw; *(apresurar)* to hasten; *(acelerar)* to speed up, accelerate; **~se** *vr* to throw o.s.; *(apresurarse)* to rush; *(actuar sin pensar)* to act rashly

precisamente [preθisa'mente] *adv* precisely; *(exactamente)* precisely, exactly

precisar [preθi'sar] *vt (necesitar)* to need, require; *(fijar)* to determine exactly, fix;

(especificar) to specify

precisión [preθi'sjon] *nf (exactitud)* precision

preciso, a [pre'θiso, a] *adj (exacto)* precise; *(necesario)* necessary, essential

preconcebido, a [prekonθe'βiðo, a] *adj* preconceived

precoz [pre'koθ] *adj (persona)* precocious; *(calvicie etc)* premature

precursor, a [prekur'sor, a] *nm/f* predecessor, forerunner

predecir [preðe'θir] *vt* to predict, forecast

predestinado, a [preðesti'naðo, a] *adj* predestined

predicar [preði'kar] *vt, vi* to preach

predicción [preðik'θjon] *nf* prediction

predilecto, a [preði'lekto, a] *adj* favourite

predisponer [preðispo'ner] *vt* to predispose; *(pey)* to prejudice; **predisposición** *nf* inclination; prejudice, bias

predominante [preðomi'nante] *adj* predominant

predominar [preðomi'nar] *vt* to dominate ♦ *vi* to predominate; *(prevalecer)* to prevail; **predominio** *nm* predominance; prevalence

preescolar [pre(e)sko'lar] *adj* preschool

prefabricado, a [prefaβri'kaðo, a] *adj* prefabricated

prefacio [pre'faθjo] *nm* preface

preferencia [prefe'renθja] *nf* preference; **de ~** preferably, for preference

preferible [prefe'riβle] *adj* preferable

preferir [prefe'rir] *vt* to prefer

prefiero *etc vb ver* **preferir**

prefijo [pre'fixo] *nm (TELEC)* (dialling) code

pregonar [prevo'nar] *vt* to proclaim, announce

pregunta [pre'vunta] *nf* question; **hacer una ~** to ask a question

preguntar [prevun'tar] *vt* to ask; *(cuestionar)* to question ♦ *vi* to ask; **~se** *vr* to wonder; **~ por alguien** to ask for sb

preguntón, ona [prevun'ton, ona] *adj* inquisitive

prehistórico, a [preis'toriko, a] *adj*

prehistoric

prejuicio [pre'xwiθjo] *nm* (*acto*) prejudgement; (*idea preconcebida*) preconception; (*parcialidad*) prejudice, bias

preliminar [prelimi'nar] *adj* preliminary

preludio [pre'luðjo] *nm* prelude

prematuro, a [prema'turo, a] *adj* premature

premeditación [premeðita'θjon] *nf* premeditation

premeditar [premeði'tar] *vt* to premeditate

premiar [pre'mjar] *vt* to reward; (*en un concurso*) to give a prize to

premio ['premjo] *nm* reward; prize; (*COM*) premium

premonición [premoni'θjon] *nf* premonition

prenatal [prena'tal] *adj* antenatal, prenatal

prenda ['prenda] *nf* (*ropa*) garment, article of clothing; (*garantía*) pledge; ~s *nfpl* (*talentos*) talents, gifts

prendedor [prende'ðor] *nm* brooch

prender [pren'der] *vt* (*captar*) to catch, capture; (*detener*) to arrest; (*COSTURA*) to pin, attach; (*sujetar*) to fasten ♦ *vi* to catch; (*arraigar*) to take root; ~**se** *vr* (*encenderse*) to catch fire

prendido, a [pren'diðo, a] (*AM*) *adj* (*luz etc*) on

prensa ['prensa] *nf* press; **la** ~ the press; **prensar** *vt* to press

preñado, a [pre'ɲaðo, a] *adj* pregnant; ~ **de** pregnant with, full of

preocupación [preokupa'θjon] *nf* worry, concern; (*ansiedad*) anxiety

preocupado, a [preoku'paðo, a] *adj* worried, concerned; (*ansioso*) anxious

preocupar [preoku'par] *vt* to worry; ~**se** *vr* to worry; ~**se de algo** (*hacerse cargo*) to take care of sth

preparación [prepara'θjon] *nf* (*acto*) preparation; (*estado*) readiness; (*entrenamiento*) training

preparado, a [prepa'raðo, a] *adj* (*dispuesto*) prepared; (*CULIN*) ready (to

serve) ♦ *nm* preparation

preparar [prepa'rar] *vt* (*disponer*) to prepare, get ready; (*TEC: tratar*) to prepare, process; (*entrenar*) to teach, train; ~**se** *vr*: ~**se a** *o* **para** to prepare to *o* for, get ready to *o* for; **preparativo, a** *adj* preparatory, preliminary; **preparativos** *nmpl* preparations; **preparatoria** (*AM*) *nf* sixth-form college (*BRIT*), senior high school (*US*)

prerrogativa [prerroɣa'tißa] *nf* prerogative, privilege

presa ['presa] *nf* (*cosa apresada*) catch; (*víctima*) victim; (*de animal*) prey; (*de agua*) dam

presagiar [presa'xjar] *vt* to presage, forebode; **presagio** *nm* omen

prescindir [presθin'dir] *vi*: ~ **de** (*privarse de*) to do without, go without; (*descartar*) to dispense with

prescribir [preskri'ßir] *vt* to prescribe; **prescripción** *nf* prescription

presencia [pre'senθja] *nf* presence; **presencial** *adj*: **testigo presencial** eyewitness; **presenciar** *vt* to be present at; (*asistir a*) to attend; (*ver*) to see, witness

presentación [presenta'θjon] *nf* presentation; (*introducción*) introduction

presentador, a [presenta'ðor, a] *nm/f* presenter, compère

presentar [presen'tar] *vt* to present; (*ofrecer*) to offer; (*mostrar*) to show, display; (*a una persona*) to introduce; ~**se** *vr* (*llegar inesperadamente*) to appear, turn up; (*ofrecerse como candidato*) to run, stand; (*aparecer*) to show, appear; (*solicitar empleo*) to apply

presente [pre'sente] *adj* present ♦ *nm* present; **hacer** ~ to state, declare; **tener** ~ to remember, bear in mind

presentimiento [presenti'mjento] *nm* premonition, presentiment

presentir [presen'tir] *vt* to have a premonition of

preservación [preserßa'θjon] *nf* protection, preservation

preservar [preser'ßar] *vt* to protect, preserve; **preservativo** *nm* sheath, condom

presidencia [presi'ðenθja] *nf* presidency; (*de comité*) chairmanship

presidente [presi'ðente] *nm/f* president; (*de comité*) chairman/woman

presidiario [presi'ðjarjo] *nm* convict

presidio [pre'sidjo] *nm* prison, penitentiary

presidir [presi'ðir] *vt* (*dirigir*) to preside at, preside over; (*: comité*) to take the chair at; (*dominar*) to dominate, rule ♦ *vi* to preside; to take the chair

presión [pre'sjon] *nf* pressure; **presionar** *vt* to press; (*fig*) to press, put pressure on ♦ *vi*: **presionar para** to press for

preso, a ['preso, a] *nm/f* prisoner; **tomar** *o* **llevar ~ a uno** to arrest sb, take sb prisoner

prestación [presta'θjon] *nf* service; (*subsidio*) benefit; **prestaciones** *nfpl* (*TEC, AUT*) performance features

prestado, a [pres'taðo, a] *adj* on loan; **pedir ~** to borrow

prestamista [presta'mista] *nm/f* moneylender

préstamo ['prestamo] *nm* loan; **~ hipotecario** mortgage

prestar [pres'tar] *vt* to lend, loan; (*atención*) to pay; (*ayuda*) to give

presteza [pres'teθa] *nf* speed, promptness

prestigio [pres'tixjo] *nm* prestige; **~so, a** *adj* (*honorable*) prestigious; (*famoso, renombrado*) renowned, famous

presto, a ['presto, a] *adj* (*rápido*) quick, prompt; (*dispuesto*) ready ♦ *adv* at once, right away.

presumido, a [presu'miðo, a] *adj* (*persona*) vain

presumir [presu'mir] *vt* to presume ♦ *vi* (*tener aires*) to be conceited; **según cabe ~** as may be presumed, presumably; **presunción** *nf* presumption; **presunto, a** *adj* (*supuesto*) supposed, presumed; (*así llamado*) so-called; **presuntuoso, a** *adj* conceited, presumptuous

presuponer [presupo'ner] *vt* to presuppose

presupuesto [presu'pwesto] *pp de* **presuponer** ♦ *nm* (*FINANZAS*) budget; (*estimación: de costo*) estimate

pretencioso, a [preten'θjoso, a] *adj* pretentious

pretender [preten'der] *vt* (*intentar*) to try to, seek to; (*reivindicar*) to claim; (*buscar*) to seek, try for; (*cortejar*) to woo, court; **~ que** to expect that; **pretendiente** *nm/f* (*amante*) suitor; (*al trono*) pretender; **pretensión** *nf* (*aspiración*) aspiration; (*reivindicación*) claim; (*orgullo*) pretension

pretexto [pre'teksto] *nm* pretext; (*excusa*) excuse

prevalecer [preßale'θer] *vi* to prevail

prevención [preßen'θjon] *nf* prevention; (*precaución*) precaution

prevenido, a [preße'niðo, a] *adj* prepared, ready; (*cauteloso*) cautious

prevenir [preße'nir] *vt* (*impedir*) to prevent; (*predisponer*) to prejudice, bias; (*avisar*) to warn; (*preparar*) to prepare, get ready; **~se** *vr* to get ready, prepare; **~se contra** to take precautions against; **preventivo, a** *adj* preventive, precautionary

prever [pre'ßer] *vt* to foresee

previo, a ['preßjo, a] *adj* (*anterior*) previous; (*preliminar*) preliminary ♦ *prep*: **~ acuerdo de los otros** subject to the agreement of the others

previsión [preßi'sjon] *nf* (*perspicacia*) foresight; (*predicción*) forecast; **previsto, a** *adj* anticipated, forecast

prima ['prima] *nf* (*COM*) bonus; **~ de seguro** insurance premium; *ver tb* **primo**

primacía [prima'θia] *nf* primacy

primario, a [pri'marjo, a] *adj* primary

primavera [prima'ßera] *nf* spring(-time)

primera [pri'mera] *nf* (*AUTO*) first gear; (*FERRO: tb: ~ clase*) first class; **de ~** (*fam*) first-class, first-rate

primero, a [pri'mero, a] (*delante de nmsg:* **primer**) *adj* first; (*principal*) prime ♦ *adv*

first; (más bien) sooner, rather; **primera
plana** front page

primicia [pri'miθja] nf (tb: ~ **informativa**)
scoop

primitivo, a [primi'tiβo, a] adj primitive;
(original) original

primo, a ['primo, a] adj prime ♦ nm/f
cousin; (fam) fool, idiot; ~ **hermano** first
cousin; **materias primas** raw materials

primogénito, a [primo'xenito, a] adj
first-born

primordial [primor'ðjal] adj basic,
fundamental

primoroso, a [primo'roso, a] adj
exquisite, delicate

princesa [prin'θesa] nf princess

principal [prinθi'pal] adj principal, main
♦ nm (jefe) chief, principal

príncipe ['prinθipe] nm prince

principiante [prinθi'pjante] nm/f
beginner

principio [prin'θipjo] nm (comienzo)
beginning, start; (origen) origin; (primera
etapa) rudiment, basic idea; (moral)
principle; **a ~s de** at the beginning of

pringoso, a [prin'ɣoso, a] adj (grasiento)
greasy; (pegajoso) sticky

pringue ['pringe] nm (grasa) grease, fat,
dripping

prioridad [priori'ðað] nf priority

prisa ['prisa] nf (apresuramiento) hurry,
haste; (rapidez) speed; (urgencia) (sense
of) urgency; **a o de ~** quickly; **correr ~** to
be urgent; **darse ~** to hurry up; **estar de
o tener ~** to be in a hurry

prisión [pri'sjon] nf (cárcel) prison;
(período de cárcel) imprisonment;
prisionero, a nm/f prisoner

prismáticos [pris'matikos] nmpl
binoculars

privación [priβa'θjon] nf deprivation;
(falta) want, privation

privado, a [pri'βaðo, a] adj private

privar [pri'βar] vt to deprive; **privativo, a**
adj exclusive

privilegiado, a [priβile'xjaðo, a] adj
privileged; (memoria) very good

privilegiar [priβile'xjar] vt to grant a
privilege to; (favorecer) to favour

privilegio [priβi'lexjo] nm privilege;
(concesión) concession

pro [pro] nm o f profit, advantage ♦ prep:
asociación ~ ciegos association for the
blind ♦ prefijo: ~ **soviético/americano**
pro-Soviet/American; **en ~ de** on behalf
of, for; **los ~s y los contras** the pros and
cons

proa ['proa] nf bow, prow; **de ~** bow cpd,
fore

probabilidad [proβaβili'ðað] nf
probability, likelihood; (oportunidad,
posibilidad) chance, prospect; **probable**
adj probable, likely

probador [proβa'ðor] nm (en tienda)
fitting room

probar [pro'βar] vt (demostrar) to prove;
(someter a prueba) to test, try out; (ropa)
to try on; (comida) to taste ♦ vi to try;
~se un traje to try on a suit

probeta [pro'βeta] nf test tube

problema [pro'βlema] nm problem

procedente [proθe'ðente] adj (razonable)
reasonable; (conforme a derecho) proper,
fitting; ~ **de** coming from, originating in

proceder [proθe'ðer] vi (avanzar) to
proceed; (actuar) to act; (ser correcto) to
be right and (proper), be fitting ♦ nm
(comportamiento) behaviour, conduct; ~
de to come from, originate in;
procedimiento nm procedure;
(proceso) process; (método) means pl,
method

procesado, a [proθe'saðo, a] nm/f
accused

procesador [proθesa'ðor] nm: ~ **de
textos** word processor

procesar [proθe'sar] vt to try, put on trial

procesión [proθe'sjon] nf procession

proceso [pro'θeso] nm process; (JUR) trial

proclamar [prokla'mar] vt to proclaim

procreación [prokrea'θjon] nf procreation

procrear [prokre'ar] vt, vi to procreate

procurador, a [prokura'ðor, a] nm/f
attorney

procurar [proku'rar] *vt* (*intentar*) to try, endeavour; (*conseguir*) to get, obtain; (*asegurar*) to secure; (*producir*) to produce

prodigio [pro'ðixjo] *nm* prodigy; (*milagro*) wonder, marvel; **~so, a** *adj* prodigious, marvellous

pródigo, a ['proðiɣo, a] *adj*: **hijo ~** prodigal son

producción [proðuk'θjon] *nf* (*gen*) production; (*producto*) output; **~ en serie** mass production

producir [proðu'θir] *vt* to produce; (*causar*) to cause, bring about; **~se** *vr* (*cambio*) to come about; (*accidente*) to take place; (*problema etc*) to arise; (*hacerse*) to be produced, be made; (*estallar*) to break out

productividad [proðuktißi'ðað] *nf* productivity; **productivo, a** *adj* productive; (*provechoso*) profitable

producto [pro'ðukto] *nm* product

productor, a [proðuk'tor, a] *adj* productive, producing ♦ *nm/f* producer

proeza [pro'eθa] *nf* exploit, feat

profanar [profa'nar] *vt* to desecrate, profane; **profano, a** *adj* profane ♦ *nm/f* layman/woman

profecía [profe'θia] *nf* prophecy

proferir [profe'rir] *vt* (*palabra, sonido*) to utter; (*injuria*) to hurl, let fly

profesión [profe'sjon] *nf* profession; **profesional** *adj* professional

profesor, a [profe'sor, a] *nm/f* teacher; **~ado** *nm* teaching profession

profeta [pro'feta] *nm/f* prophet; **profetizar** *vt, vi* to prophesy

prófugo, a ['profuɣo, a] *nm/f* fugitive; (*MIL: desertor*) deserter

profundidad [profundi'ðað] *nf* depth; **profundizar** *vi*: **profundizar en** to go deeply into; **profundo, a** *adj* deep; (*misterio, pensador*) profound

progenitor [proxeni'tor] *nm* ancestor; **~es** *nmpl* (*padres*) parents

programa [pro'ɣrama] *nm* programme (*BRIT*), program (*US*); **~ción** *nf* programming; **~dor, a** *nm/f*

programmer; **programar** *vt* to program

progresar [proɣre'sar] *vi* to progress, make progress; **progresista** *adj, nm/f* progressive; **progresivo, a** *adj* progressive; (*gradual*) gradual; (*continuo*) continuous; **progreso** *nm* progress

prohibición [proißi'θjon] *nf* prohibition, ban

prohibir [proi'ßir] *vt* to prohibit, ban, forbid; **se prohibe fumar, prohibido fumar** no smoking; **"prohibido el paso"** "no entry"

prójimo, a ['proximo, a] *nm/f* fellow man; (*vecino*) neighbour

proletariado [proleta'rjaðo] *nm* proletariat

proletario, a [prole'tarjo, a] *adj, nm/f* proletarian

proliferación [prolifera'θjon] *nf* proliferation

proliferar [prolife'rar] *vi* to proliferate; **prolífico, a** *adj* prolific

prólogo ['proloɣo] *nm* prologue

prolongación [prolonga'θjon] *nf* extension; **prolongado, a** *adj* (*largo*) long; (*alargado*) lengthy

prolongar [prolon'xar] *vt* to extend; (*reunión etc*) to prolong; (*calle, tubo*) to extend

promedio [pro'meðjo] *nm* average; (*de distancia*) middle, mid-point

promesa [pro'mesa] *nf* promise

prometer [prome'ter] *vt* to promise ♦ *vi* to show promise; **~se** *vr* (*novios*) to get engaged; **prometido, a** *adj* promised; engaged ♦ *nm/f* fiancé/fiancée

prominente [promi'nente] *adj* prominent

promiscuo, a [pro'miskwo, a] *adj* promiscuous

promoción [promo'θjon] *nf* promotion

promotor [promo'tor] *nm* promoter; (*instigador*) instigator

promover [promo'ßer] *vt* to promote; (*causar*) to cause; (*instigar*) to instigate, stir up

promulgar [promul'xar] *vt* to promulgate; (*anunciar*) to proclaim

pronombre [pro'nombre] *nm* pronoun

pronosticar [pronosti'kar] *vt* to predict, foretell, forecast; **pronóstico** *nm* prediction, forecast; **pronóstico del tiempo** weather forecast

pronto, a ['pronto, a] *adj (rápido)* prompt, quick; *(preparado)* ready ♦ *adv* quickly, promptly; *(en seguida)* at once, right away; *(dentro de poco)* soon; *(temprano)* early ♦ *nm*: **tener ~s de enojo** to be quick-tempered; **de ~** suddenly; **por lo ~** meanwhile, for the present

pronunciación [pronunθja'θjon] *nf* pronunciation

pronunciar [pronun'θjar] *vt* to pronounce; *(discurso)* to make, deliver; **~se** *vr* to revolt, rebel; *(declararse)* to declare o.s.

propagación [propaɣa'θjon] *nf* propagation

propaganda [propa'ɣanda] *nf (política)* propaganda; *(comercial)* advertising

propagar [propa'ɣar] *vt* to propagate

propensión [propen'sjon] *nf* inclination, propensity; **propenso, a** *adj* inclined to; **ser propenso a** to be inclined to, have a tendency to

propicio, a [pro'piθjo, a] *adj* favourable, propitious

propiedad [propje'ðað] *nf* property; *(posesión)* possession, ownership; **~ particular** private property

propietario, a [propje'tarjo, a] *nm/f* owner, proprietor

propina [pro'pina] *nf* tip

propio, a ['propjo, a] *adj* own, of one's own; *(característico)* characteristic, typical; *(debido)* proper; *(mismo)* selfsame, very; **el ~ ministro** the minister himself; **¿tienes casa propia?** have you a house of your own?

proponer [propo'ner] *vt* to propose, put forward; *(problema)* to pose; **~se** *vr* to propose, intend

proporción [propor'θjon] *nf* proportion; *(MAT)* ratio; **proporciones** *nfpl (dimensiones)* dimensions; *(fig)* size *sg*; **proporcionado, a** *adj* proportionate;

(regular) medium, middling; *(justo)* just right; **proporcionar** *vt (dar)* to give, supply, provide

proposición [proposi'θjon] *nf* proposition; *(propuesta)* proposal

propósito [pro'posito] *nm* purpose; *(intento)* aim, intention ♦ *adv*: **a ~** by the way, incidentally; *(a posta)* on purpose, deliberately; **a ~ de** about, with regard to

propuesta [pro'pwesta] *vb ver* **proponer** ♦ *nf* proposal

propulsar [propul'sar] *vt* to drive, propel; *(fig)* to promote, encourage; **propulsión** *nf* propulsion; **propulsión a chorro** *o* **por reacción** jet propulsion

prórroga ['prorroxa] *nf* extension; *(JUR)* stay; *(COM)* deferment; *(DEPORTE)* extra time; **prorrogar** *vt (período)* to extend; *(decisión)* to defer, postpone

prorrumpir [prorrum'pir] *vi* to burst forth, break out

prosa ['prosa] *nf* prose

proscrito, a [pro'skrito, a] *adj* banned

proseguir [prose'ɣir] *vt* to continue, carry on ♦ *vi* to continue, go on

prospección [prospek'θjon] *nf* exploration; *(del oro)* prospecting

prospecto [pros'pekto] *nm* prospectus

prosperar [prospe'rar] *vi* to prosper, thrive, flourish; **prosperidad** *nf* prosperity; *(éxito)* success; **próspero, a** *adj* prosperous, flourishing; *(que tiene éxito)* successful

prostíbulo [pros'tiβulo] *nm* brothel *(BRIT)*, house of prostitution *(US)*

prostitución [prostitu'θjon] *nf* prostitution

prostituir [prosti'twir] *vt* to prostitute; **~se** *vr* to prostitute o.s., become a prostitute

prostituta [prosti'tuta] *nf* prostitute

protagonista [protaɣo'nista] *nm/f* protagonist

protagonizar [protaɣoni'θar] *vt* to take the chief rôle in

protección [protek'θjon] *nf* protection

protector, a [protek'tor, a] *adj* protective, protecting ♦ *nm/f* protector

proteger [prote'xer] *vt* to protect; **protegido, a** *nm/f* protégé/protégée
proteína [prote'ina] *nf* protein
protesta [pro'testa] *nf* protest; (*declaración*) protestation
protestante [protes'tante] *adj* Protestant
protestar [protes'tar] *vt* to protest, declare ♦ *vi* to protest
protocolo [proto'kolo] *nm* protocol
prototipo [proto'tipo] *nm* prototype
prov. *abr* (= *provincia*) prov
provecho [pro'βetʃo] *nm* advantage, benefit; (*FINANZAS*) profit; ¡**buen ~!** bon appétit!; **en ~ de** to the benefit of; **sacar ~ de** to benefit from, profit by
proveer [proβe'er] *vt* to provide, supply ♦ *vi*: ~ **a** to provide for
provenir [proβe'nir] *vi*: ~ **de** to come from, stem from
proverbio [pro'βerβjo] *nm* proverb
providencia [proβi'ðenθja] *nf* providence
provincia [pro'βinθja] *nf* province; ~**no, a** *adj* provincial; (*del campo*) country *cpd*
provisión [proβi'sjon] *nf* provision; (*abastecimiento*) provision, supply; (*medida*) measure, step
provisional [proβisjo'nal] *adj* provisional
provocación [proβoka'θjon] *nf* provocation
provocar [proβo'kar] *vt* to provoke; (*alentar*) to tempt, invite; (*causar*) to bring about, lead to; (*promover*) to promote; (*estimular*) to rouse, stimulate; ¿**te provoca un café?** (*AM*) would you like a coffee?; **provocativo, a** *adj* provocative
próximamente [proksima'mente] *adv* shortly, soon
proximidad [proksimi'ðað] *nf* closeness, proximity; **próximo, a** *adj* near, close; (*vecino*) neighbouring; (*siguiente*) next
proyectar [projek'tar] *vt* (*objeto*) to hurl, throw; (*luz*) to cast, shed; (*CINE*) to screen, show; (*planear*) to plan
proyectil [projek'til] *nm* projectile, missile
proyecto [pro'jekto] *nm* plan; (*estimación de costo*) detailed estimate

proyector [projek'tor] *nm* (*CINE*) projector
prudencia [pru'ðenθja] *nf* (*sabiduría*) wisdom; (*cuidado*) care; **prudente** *adj* sensible, wise; (*conductor*) careful
prueba *etc* ['prweβa] *vb ver* **probar** ♦ *nf* proof; (*ensayo*) test, trial; (*degustación*) tasting, sampling; (*de ropa*) fitting; **a ~** on trial; **a ~ de** proof against; **a ~ de agua/fuego** waterproof/fireproof; **someter a ~** to put to the test
prurito [pru'rito] *nm* itch; (*de bebé*) nappy (*BRIT*) o diaper (*US*) rash
psico... [siko] *prefijo* psycho...; ~**análisis** *nm inv* psychoanalysis; ~**logía** *nf* psychology; ~**lógico, a** *adj* psychological; **psicólogo, a** *nm/f* psychologist; **psicópata** *nm/f* psychopath; ~**sis** *nf inv* psychosis
psiquiatra [si'kjatra] *nm/f* psychiatrist; **psiquiátrico, a** *adj* psychiatric
psíquico, a ['sikiko, a] *adj* psychic(al)
PSOE [pe'soe] *nm abr* = **Partido Socialista Obrero Español**
pta(s) *abr* = **peseta(s)**
pts *abr* = **pesetas**
púa ['pua] *nf* (*BOT*, *ZOOL*) prickle, spine; (*para guitarra*) plectrum (*BRIT*), pick (*US*); **alambre de ~** barbed wire
pubertad [puβer'tað] *nf* puberty
publicación [puβlika'θjon] *nf* publication
publicar [puβli'kar] *vt* (*editar*) to publish; (*hacer público*) to publicize; (*divulgar*) to make public, divulge
publicidad [puβliθi'ðað] *nf* publicity; (*COM*: *propaganda*) advertising; **publicitario, a** *adj* publicity *cpd*; advertising *cpd*
público, a ['puβliko, a] *adj* public ♦ *nm* public; (*TEATRO etc*) audience
puchero [pu'tʃero] *nm* (*CULIN*: *guiso*) stew; (: *olla*) cooking pot; **hacer ~s** to pout
pude *etc vb ver* **poder**
púdico, a ['puðiko, a] *adj* modest
pudiente [pu'ðjente] *adj* (*rico*) wealthy, well-to-do
pudiera *etc vb ver* **poder**
pudor [pu'ðor] *nm* modesty

pudrir [pu'ðrir] *vt* to rot; **~se** *vr* to rot,
decay
pueblo ['pweßlo] *nm* people; (*nación*)
nation; (*aldea*) village
puedo *etc vb ver* **poder**
puente ['pwente] *nm* bridge; **hacer ~** (*inf*)
*to take extra days off work between 2
public holidays*; *to take a long weekend*;
~ aéreo shuttle service; **~ colgante**
suspension bridge

---
hacer puente
---

i When a public holiday in Spain falls
on a Tuesday or Thursday it is
common practice for employers to make
the Monday or Friday a holiday as well
and to give everyone a four-day weekend.
This is known as **hacer puente**. When a
named public holiday such as the **Día de
la Constitución** falls on a Tuesday or
Thursday, people refer to the whole
holiday period as e.g. the **puente de la
Constitución**.

---

puerco, a ['pwerko, a] *nm/f* pig/sow ♦ *adj*
(*sucio*) dirty, filthy; (*obsceno*) disgusting; **~
de mar** porpoise; **~ marino** dolphin
pueril [pwe'ril] *adj* childish
puerro ['pwerro] *nm* leek
puerta ['pwerta] *nf* door; (*de jardín*) gate;
(*portal*) doorway; (*fig*) gateway; (*portería*)
goal; **a la ~** at the door; **a ~ cerrada**
behind closed doors; **~ giratoria** revolving
door
puerto ['pwerto] *nm* port; (*paso*) pass; (*fig*)
haven, refuge
Puerto Rico [pwerto'riko] *nm* Puerto
Rico; **puertorriqueño, a** *adj, nm/f*
Puerto Rican
pues [pwes] *adv* (*entonces*) then; (*bueno*)
well, well then; (*así que*) so ♦ *conj* (*ya
que*) since; **¡~!** (*sí*) yes!, certainly!
puesta ['pwesta] *nf* (*apuesta*) bet, stake; **~
en marcha** starting; **~ del sol** sunset
puesto, a ['pwesto, a] *pp de* **poner** ♦ *adj*:
tener algo ~ to have sth on, be wearing
sth ♦ *nm* (*lugar, posición*) place; (*trabajo*)

post, job; (*COM*) stall ♦ *conj*: **~ que** since,
as
púgil ['puxil] *nm* boxer
pugna ['puɣna] *nf* battle, conflict; **pugnar**
vi (*luchar*) to struggle, fight; (*pelear*) to
fight
pujar [pu'xar] *vi* (*en subasta*) to bid;
(*esforzarse*) to struggle, strain
pulcro, a ['pulkro, a] *adj* neat, tidy
pulga ['pulɣa] *nf* flea
pulgada [pul'ɣaða] *nf* inch
pulgar [pul'xar] *nm* thumb
pulir [pu'lir] *vt* to polish; (*alisar*) to
smooth; (*fig*) to polish up, touch up
pulla ['puʎa] *nf* cutting remark
pulmón [pul'mon] *nm* lung; **pulmonía** *nf*
pneumonia
pulpa ['pulpa] *nf* pulp; (*de fruta*) flesh, soft
part
pulpería [pulpe'ria] (*AM*) *nf* (*tienda*) small
grocery store
púlpito ['pulpito] *nm* pulpit
pulpo ['pulpo] *nm* octopus
pulsación [pulsa'θjon] *nf* beat;
pulsaciones pulse rate
pulsar [pul'sar] *vt* (*tecla*) to touch, tap;
(*MUS*) to play; (*botón*) to press, push ♦ *vi*
to pulsate; (*latir*) to beat, throb; (*MED*): **~
a uno** to take sb's pulse
pulsera [pul'sera] *nf* bracelet
pulso ['pulso] *nm* (*ANAT*) pulse; (*fuerza*)
strength; (*firmeza*) steadiness, steady
hand
pulverizador [pulßeriθa'ðor] *nm* spray,
spray gun
pulverizar [pulßeri'θar] *vt* to pulverize;
(*líquido*) to spray
puna ['puna] (*AM*) *nf* mountain sickness
punitivo, a [puni'tißo, a] *adj* punitive
punta ['punta] *nf* point, tip; (*extremidad*)
end; (*fig*) touch, trace; **horas ~s** peak
hours, rush hours; **sacar ~ a** to sharpen
puntada [pun'taða] *nf* (*COSTURA*) stitch
puntal [pun'tal] *nm* prop, support
puntapié [punta'pje] *nm* kick
puntear [punte'ar] *vt* to tick, mark
puntería [punte'ria] *nf* (*de arma*) aim,

aiming; (*destreza*) marksmanship
puntero, a [pun'tero, a] *adj* leading ♦ *nm*
(*palo*) pointer
puntiagudo, a [puntja'ɣuðo, a] *adj* sharp,
pointed
puntilla [pun'tiʎa] *nf* (*encaje*) lace edging
o trim; (**andar) de ~s** (to walk) on tiptoe
punto ['punto] *nm* (*gen*) point; (*señal
diminuta*) spot, dot; (*COSTURA, MED*) stitch;
(*lugar*) spot, place; (*momento*) point,
moment; **a ~** ready; **estar a ~ de** to be
on the point of *o* about to; **en ~** on the
dot; **~ muerto** dead centre; (*AUTO*)
neutral (gear); **~ final** full stop (*BRIT*),
period (*US*); **~ y coma** semicolon; **~ de
interrogación** question mark; **~ de vista**
point of view, viewpoint; **hacer ~** (*tejer*)
to knit
puntuación [puntwa'θjon] *nf* punctuation;
(*puntos: en examen*) mark(s) (*pl*);
(*: DEPORTE*) score
puntual [pun'twal] *adj* (*a tiempo*)
punctual; (*exacto*) exact, accurate; **~idad**
nf punctuality; exactness, accuracy; **~izar**
vt to fix, specify
puntuar [pun'twar] *vi* (*DEPORTE*) to score,
count
punzada [pun'θaða] *nf* (*de dolor*) twinge
punzante [pun'θante] *adj* (*dolor*) shooting,
sharp; (*herramienta*) sharp; **punzar** *vt* to
prick, pierce ♦ *vi* to shoot, stab
puñado [pu'ɲaðo] *nm* handful
puñal [pu'ɲal] *nm* dagger; **~ada** *nf* stab
puñetazo [puɲe'taθo] *nm* punch
puño ['puɲo] *nm* (*ANAT*) fist; (*cantidad*)
fistful, handful; (*COSTURA*) cuff; (*de
herramienta*) handle
pupila [pu'pila] *nf* pupil
pupitre [pu'pitre] *nm* desk
puré [pu're] *nm* puree; (*sopa*) (thick) soup;
~ de patatas mashed potatoes
pureza [pu'reθa] *nf* purity
purga ['purɣa] *nf* purge; **purgante** *adj,
nm* purgative; **purgar** *vt* to purge
purgatorio [purɣa'torjo] *nm* purgatory
purificar [purifi'kar] *vt* to purify; (*refinar*)
to refine

puritano, a [puri'tano, a] *adj* (*actitud*)
puritanical; (*iglesia, tradición*) puritan
♦ *nm/f* puritan
puro, a ['puro, a] *adj* pure; (*verdad*)
simple, plain ♦ *adv*: **de ~ cansado** out of
sheer tiredness ♦ *nm* cigar
púrpura ['purpura] *nf* purple; **purpúreo,
a** *adj* purple
pus [pus] *nm* pus
puse *etc vb ver* **poner**
pusiera *etc vb ver* **poner**
pústula ['pustula] *nf* pimple, sore
puta ['puta] (*fam!*) *nf* whore, prostitute
putrefacción [putrefak'θjon] *nf* rotting,
putrefaction
PVP *abr* (*ESP*: = *precio venta al público*)
RRP
pyme, PYME ['pime] *nf abr* (= *Pequeña
y Mediana Empresa*) SME

Q, q

PALABRA CLAVE

que [ke] *conj* **1** (*con oración subordinada:
muchas veces no se traduce*) that; **dijo ~
vendría** he said (that) he would come;
espero ~ lo encuentres I hope (that)
you find it; *ver tb* **el**
2 (*en oración independiente*): **¡~ entre!**
send him in; **¡~ se mejore tu padre!** I
hope your father gets better
3 (*enfático*): **¿me quieres? - ¡~ sí!** do
you love me? – of course!
4 (*consecutivo: muchas veces no se
traduce*) that; **es tan grande ~ no lo
puedo levantar** it's so big (that) I can't
lift it
5 (*comparaciones*) than; **yo ~ tú/él** if I
were you/him; *ver tb* **más; menos;
mismo**
6 (*valor disyuntivo*): **~ le guste o no**
whether he likes it or not; **~ venga o ~
no venga** whether he comes or not
7 (*porque*): **no puedo, ~ tengo ~
quedarme en casa** I can't, I've got to

stay in
♦ *pron* **1** (*cosa*) that, which; (*+prep*) which; **el sombrero ~ te compraste** the hat (that *o* which) you bought; **la cama en ~ dormí** the bed (that *o* which) I slept in
2 (*persona: suj*) that, who; (*: objeto*) that, whom; **el amigo ~ me acompañó al museo** the friend that *o* who went to the museum with me: **la chica ~ invité** the girl (that *o* whom) I invited

qué [ke] *adj* what?, which? ♦ *pron* what?; **¡~ divertido!** how funny!; **¿~ edad tienes?** how old are you?; **¿de ~ me hablas?** what are you saying to me?; **¿~ tal?** how are you?, how are things?; **¿~ hay (de nuevo)?** what's new?

quebradizo, a [keßra'ðiθo, a] *adj* fragile; (*persona*) frail
quebrado, a [ke'ßraðo, a] *adj* (*roto*) broken ♦ *nm/f* bankrupt ♦ *nm* (*MAT*) fraction
quebrantar [keßran'tar] *vt* (*infringir*) to violate, transgress; **~se** *vr* (*persona*) to fail in health
quebranto [ke'ßranto] *nm* damage, harm; (*dolor*) grief, pain
quebrar [ke'ßrar] *vt* to break, smash ♦ *vi* to go bankrupt; **~se** *vr* to break, get broken; (*MED*) to be ruptured
quedar [ke'ðar] *vi* to stay, remain; (*encontrarse: sitio*) to be; (*haber aún*) to remain, be left; **~se** *vr* to remain, stay (behind); **~se (con) algo** to keep sth; **~ en** (*acordar*) to agree on/to; **~ en nada** to come to nothing; **~ por hacer** to be still to be done; **~ ciego/mudo** to be left blind/dumb; **no te queda bien ese vestido** that dress doesn't suit you; **eso queda muy lejos** that's a long way (away); **quedamos a las seis** we agreed to meet at six
quedo, a ['keðo, a] *adj* still ♦ *adv* softly, gently
quehacer [kea'θer] *nm* task, job; **~es (domésticos)** *nmpl* household chores

queja ['kexa] *nf* complaint; **quejarse** *vr* (*enfermo*) to moan, groan; (*protestar*) to complain; **quejarse de que** to complain (about the fact) that; **quejido** *nm* moan
quemado, a [ke'maðo, a] *adj* burnt
quemadura [kema'ðura] *nf* burn, scald
quemar [ke'mar] *vt* to burn; (*fig: malgastar*) to burn up, squander ♦ *vi* to be burning hot; **~se** *vr* (*consumirse*) to burn (up); (*del sol*) to get sunburnt
quemarropa [kema'rropa]: **a ~** *adv* point-blank
quepo *etc vb ver* **caber**
querella [ke'reʎa] *nf* (*JUR*) charge; (*disputa*) dispute; **~rse** *vr* (*JUR*) to file a complaint

---

PALABRA CLAVE

---

querer [ke'rer] *vt* **1** (*desear*) to want; **quiero más dinero** I want more money; **quisiera** *o* **querría un té** I'd like a tea; **sin ~** unintentionally; **quiero ayudar/que vayas** I want to help/you to go
2 (*preguntas: para pedir algo*): **¿quiere abrir la ventana?** could you open the window?; **¿quieres echarme una mano?** can you give me a hand?
3 (*amar*) to love; (*tener cariño a*) to be fond of; **quiere mucho a sus hijos** he's very fond of his children
4 (*requerir*): **esta planta quiere más luz** this plant needs more light
5: le pedí que me dejara ir pero no quiso I asked him to let me go but he refused

---

querido, a [ke'riðo, a] *adj* dear ♦ *nm/f* darling; (*amante*) lover
queso ['keso] *nm* cheese
quicio ['kiθjo] *nm* hinge; **sacar a uno de ~** to get on sb's nerves
quiebra ['kjeßra] *nf* break, split; (*COM*) bankruptcy; (*ECON*) slump
quiebro ['kjeßro] *nm* (*del cuerpo*) swerve
quien [kjen] *pron* who; **hay ~ piensa que** there are those who think that; **no hay ~ lo haga** no-one will do it

quién [kjen] *pron* who, whom; **¿~ es?** who's there?

quienquiera [kjen'kjera] (*pl* **quienesquiera**) *pron* whoever

quiero *etc vb ver* **querer**

quieto, a ['kjeto, a] *adj* still; (*carácter*) placid; **quietud** *nf* stillness

quilate [ki'late] *nm* carat

quilla ['kiʎa] *nf* keel

quimera [ki'mera] *nf* chimera; **quimérico, a** *adj* fantastic

químico, a ['kimiko, a] *adj* chemical ♦ *nm/f* chemist ♦ *nf* chemistry

quincalla [kin'kaʎa] *nf* hardware, ironmongery

quince ['kinθe] *num* fifteen; **~ días** a fortnight; **~añero, a** *nm/f* teenager; **~na** *nf* fortnight; (*pago*) fortnightly pay; **~nal** *adj* fortnightly

quiniela [ki'njela] *nf* football pools *pl*; **~s** *nfpl* (*impreso*) pools coupon *sg*

quinientos, as [ki'njentos, as] *adj, num* five hundred

quinina [ki'nina] *nf* quinine

quinto, a ['kinto, a] *adj* fifth ♦ *nf* country house; (*MIL*) call-up, draft

quiosco ['kjosko] *nm* (*de música*) bandstand; (*de periódicos*) news stand

quirófano [ki'rofano] *nm* operating theatre

quirúrgico, a [ki'rurxiko, a] *adj* surgical

quise *etc vb ver* **querer**

quisiera *etc vb ver* **querer**

quisquilloso, a [kiski'ʎoso, a] *adj* (*susceptible*) touchy; (*meticuloso*) pernickety

quiste ['kiste] *nm* cyst

quitaesmalte [kitaes'malte] *nm* nail-polish remover

quitamanchas [kita'mantʃas] *nm inv* stain remover

quitanieves [kita'njeßes] *nm inv* snowplough (*BRIT*), snowplow (*US*)

quitar [ki'tar] *vt* to remove, take away; (*ropa*) to take off; (*dolor*) to relieve; **¡quita de ahí!** get away!; **~se** *vr* to withdraw; (*ropa*) to take off; **se quitó el sombrero**

he took off his hat

quite ['kite] *nm* (*esgrima*) parry; (*evasión*) dodge

Quito ['kito] *n* Quito

quizá(s) [ki'θa(s)] *adv* perhaps, maybe

R, r

rábano ['raßano] *nm* radish; **me importa un ~** I don't give a damn

rabia ['raßja] *nf* (*MED*) rabies *sg*; (*ira*) fury, rage; **rabiar** *vi* to have rabies; to rage, be furious; **rabiar por algo** to long for sth

rabieta [ra'ßjeta] *nf* tantrum, fit of temper

rabino [ra'ßino] *nm* rabbi

rabioso, a [ra'ßjoso, a] *adj* rabid; (*fig*) furious

rabo ['raßo] *nm* tail

racha ['ratʃa] *nf* gust of wind: **buena/ mala ~** spell of good/bad luck

racial [ra'θjal] *adj* racial, race *cpd*

racimo [ra'θimo] *nm* bunch

raciocinio [raθjo'θinjo] *nm* reason

ración [ra'θjon] *nf* portion; **raciones** *nfpl* rations

racional [raθjo'nal] *adj* (*razonable*) reasonable; (*lógico*) rational; **~izar** *vt* to rationalize

racionar [raθjo'nar] *vt* to ration (out)

racismo [ra'θismo] *nm* racism; **racista** *adj, nm/f* racist

radar [ra'ðar] *nm* radar

radiactivo, a [raðiak'tißo, a] *adj* = **radioactivo**

radiador [raðja'ðor] *nm* radiator

radiante [ra'ðjante] *adj* radiant

radical [raði'kal] *adj, nm/f* radical

radicar [raði'kar] *vi*: **~ en** (*dificultad, problema*) to lie in; (*solución*) to consist in; **~se** *vr* to establish o.s., put down (one's) roots

radio ['raðjo] *nf* radio; (*aparato*) radio (set) ♦ *nm* (*MAT*) radius; (*QUÍM*) radium; **~actividad** *nf* radioactivity; **~activo, a** *adj* radioactive; **~difusión** *nf* broadcasting; **~emisora** *nf* transmitter, radio station; **~escucha** *nm/f* listener; **~grafía** *nf* X-ray; **~grafiar** *vt* to X-ray; **~terapia** *nf* radiotherapy; **~yente** *nm/f* listener

ráfaga [ˈrafaɣa] *nf* gust; (*de luz*) flash; (*de tiros*) burst

raído, a [raˈiðo, a] *adj* (*ropa*) threadbare

raigambre [raiˈɣambre] *nf* (*BOT*) roots *pl*; (*fig*) tradition

raíz [raˈiθ] *nf* root; **~ cuadrada** square root; **a ~ de** as a result of

raja [ˈraxa] *nf* (*de melón etc*) slice; (*grieta*) crack; **rajar** *vt* to split; (*fam*) to slash; **rajarse** *vr* to split, crack; **rajarse de** to back out of

rajatabla [raxaˈtaβla]: **a ~** *adv* (*estrictamente*) strictly, to the letter

rallador [raʎaˈðor] *nm* grater

rallar [raˈʎar] *vt* to grate

rama [ˈrama] *nf* branch; **~je** *nm* branches *pl*, foliage; **ramal** *nm* (*de cuerda*) strand; (*FERRO*) branch line (*BRIT*); (*AUTO*) branch (road) (*BRIT*)

rambla [ˈrambla] *nf* (*avenida*) avenue

ramificación [ramifikaˈθjon] *nf* ramification

ramificarse [ramifiˈkarse] *vr* to branch out

ramillete [ramiˈʎete] *nm* bouquet

ramo [ˈramo] *nm* branch; (*sección*) department, section

rampa [ˈrampa] *nf* ramp

ramplón, ona [ramˈplon, ona] *adj* uncouth, coarse

rana [ˈrana] *nf* frog; **salto de ~** leapfrog

ranchero [ranˈtʃero] *nm* (*AM*) rancher; smallholder

rancho [ˈrantʃo] *nm* (*grande*) ranch; (*pequeño*) small farm

rancio, a [ˈranθjo, a] *adj* (*comestibles*) rancid; (*vino*) aged, mellow; (*fig*) ancient

rango [ˈrango] *nm* rank, standing

ranura [raˈnura] *nf* groove; (*de teléfono etc*) slot

rapar [raˈpar] *vt* to shave; (*los cabellos*) to crop

rapaz [raˈpaθ] (*nf*: **rapaza**) *nm/f* young

boy/girl ♦ *adj* (*ZOOL*) predatory

rape [ˈrape] *nm* (*pez*) monkfish; **al ~** cropped

rapé [raˈpe] *nm* snuff

rapidez [rapiˈðeθ] *nf* speed, rapidity; **rápido, a** *adj* fast, quick ♦ *adv* quickly ♦ *nm* (*FERRO*) express; **rápidos** *nmpl* rapids

rapiña [raˈpiɲa] *nm* robbery; **ave de ~** bird of prey

raptar [rapˈtar] *vt* to kidnap; **rapto** *nm* kidnapping; (*impulso*) sudden impulse; (*éxtasis*) ecstasy, rapture

raqueta [raˈketa] *nf* racquet

raquítico, a [raˈkitiko, a] *adj* stunted; (*fig*) poor, inadequate; **raquitismo** *nm* rickets *sg*

rareza [raˈreθa] *nf* rarity; (*fig*) eccentricity

raro, a [ˈraro, a] *adj* (*poco común*) rare; (*extraño*) odd, strange; (*excepcional*) remarkable

ras [ras] *nm*: **a ~ de** level with; **a ~ de tierra** at ground level

rasar [raˈsar] *vt* (*igualar*) to level

rascacielos [raskaˈθjelos] *nm inv* skyscraper

rascar [rasˈkar] *vt* (*con las uñas etc*) to scratch; (*raspar*) to scrape; **~se** *vr* to scratch (o.s.)

rasgar [rasˈɣar] *vt* to tear, rip (up)

rasgo [ˈrasɣo] *nm* (*con pluma*) stroke; **~s** *nmpl* (*facciones*) features, characteristics; **a grandes ~s** in outline, broadly

rasguñar [rasɣuˈɲar] *vt* to scratch; **rasguño** *nm* scratch

raso, a [ˈraso, a] *adj* (*liso*) flat, level; (*a baja altura*) very low ♦ *nm* satin; **cielo ~** clear sky

raspadura [raspaˈðura] *nf* (*acto*) scrape, scraping; (*marca*) scratch; **~s** *nfpl* (*de papel etc*) scrapings

raspar [rasˈpar] *vt* to scrape; (*arañar*) to scratch; (*limar*) to file

rastra [ˈrastra] *nf* (*AGR*) rake; **a ~s** by dragging; (*fig*) unwillingly

rastreador [rastreaˈðor] *nm* tracker; **~ de minas** minesweeper

rastrear [rastre'ar] *vt* (*seguir*) to track
rastrero, a [ras'trero, a] *adj* (*BOT, ZOOL*) creeping; (*fig*) despicable, mean
rastrillo [ras'triʎo] *nm* rake
rastro ['rastro] *nm* (*AGR*) rake; (*pista*) track, trail; (*vestigio*) trace; **el R~** the Madrid fleamarket
rastrojo [ras'troxo] *nm* stubble
rasurador [rasura'ðor] (*AM*) *nm* electric shaver
rasuradora [rasura'ðora] (*AM*) *nf* = **rasurador**
rasurarse [rasu'rarse] *vr* to shave
rata ['rata] *nf* rat
ratear [rate'ar] *vt* (*robar*) to steal
ratero, a [ra'tero, a] *adj* light-fingered ♦ *nm/f* (*carterista*) pickpocket; (*AM: de casas*) burglar
ratificar [ratifi'kar] *vt* to ratify
rato ['rato] *nm* while, short time; **a ~s** from time to time; **hay para ~** there's still a long way to go; **al poco ~** soon afterwards; **pasar el ~** to kill time; **pasar un buen/mal ~** to have a good/rough time; **en mis ~s libres** in my spare time
ratón [ra'ton] *nm* mouse; **ratonera** *nf* mousetrap
raudal [rau'ðal] *nm* torrent; **a ~es** in abundance
raya ['raja] *nf* line; (*marca*) scratch; (*en tela*) stripe; (*de pelo*) parting; (*límite*) boundary; (*pez*) ray; (*puntuación*) dash; **a ~s** striped; **pasarse de la ~** to go too far: **tener a ~** to keep in check; **rayar** *vt* to line; to scratch; (*subrayar*) to underline ♦ *vi*: **rayar en** *o* **con** to border on
rayo ['rajo] *nm* (*del sol*) ray, beam; (*de luz*) shaft; (*en una tormenta*) (flash of) lightning; **~s X** X-rays
raza ['raθa] *nf* race; **~ humana** human race
razón [ra'θon] *nf* reason; (*justicia*) right, justice; (*razonamiento*) reasoning; (*motivo*) reason, motive; (*MAT*) ratio; **a ~ de 10 cada día** at the rate of 10 a day; **"~: ..."** "inquiries to ..."; with regard to; **dar ~ a uno** to agree that sb is right; **tener ~** to be right; **~ directa/inversa**

direct/inverse proportion; **~ de ser** raison d'être; **razonable** *adj* reasonable; (*justo, moderado*) fair; **razonamiento** *nm* (*juicio*) judg(e)ment; (*argumento*) reasoning; **razonar** *vt, vi* to reason, argue
reacción [reak'θjon] *nf* reaction; **avión a ~** jet plane; **~ en cadena** chain reaction; **reaccionar** *vi* to react; **reaccionario, a** *adj* reactionary
reacio, a [re'aθjo, a] *adj* stubborn
reactivar [reakti'βar] *vt* to revitalize
reactor [reak'tor] *nm* reactor
readaptación [reaðapta'θjon] *nf*: **~ profesional** industrial retraining
reajuste [rea'xuste] *nm* readjustment
real [re'al] *adj* real; (*del rey, fig*) royal
realce [re'alθe] *nm* (*lustre, fig*) splendour; **poner de ~** to emphasize
realidad [reali'ðað] *nf* reality, fact; (*verdad*) truth
realista [rea'lista] *nm/f* realist
realización [realiθa'θjon] *nf* fulfilment
realizador, a [realiθa'ðor, a] *nm/f* film-maker
realizar [reali'θar] *vt* (*objetivo*) to achieve; (*plan*) to carry out; (*viaje*) to make, undertake; **~se** *vr* to come about, come true
realmente [real'mente] *adv* really, actually
realquilar [realki'lar] *vt* to sublet
realzar [real'θar] *vt* to enhance; (*acentuar*) to highlight
reanimar [reani'mar] *vt* to revive; (*alentar*) to encourage; **~se** *vr* to revive
reanudar [reanu'ðar] *vt* (*renovar*) to renew; (*historia, viaje*) to resume
reaparición [reapari'θjon] *nf* reappearance
rearme [re'arme] *nm* rearmament
rebaja [re'βaxa] *nf* (*COM*) reduction; (: *descuento*) discount; **~s** *nfpl* (*COM*) sale; **rebajar** *vt* (*bajar*) to lower; (*reducir*) to reduce; (*disminuir*) to lessen; (*humillar*) to humble
rebanada [reβa'naða] *nf* slice
rebañar [reβa'ɲar] *vt* (*comida*) to scrape

up; (*plato*) to scrape clean

rebaño [re'βaɲo] *nm* herd; (*de ovejas*) flock

rebasar [reβa'sar] *vt* (*tb*: ~ **de**) to exceed

rebatir [reβa'tir] *vt* to refute

rebeca [re'βeka] *nf* cardigan

rebelarse [reβe'larse] *vr* to rebel, revolt

rebelde [re'βelde] *adj* rebellious; (*niño*) unruly ♦ *nm/f* rebel; **rebeldía** *nf* rebelliousness; (*desobediencia*) disobedience

rebelión [reβe'ljon] *nf* rebellion

reblandecer [reβlande'θer] *vt* to soften

rebobinar [reβoβi'nar] *vt* (*cinta, película de video*) to rewind

rebosante [reβo'sante] *adj* overflowing

rebosar [reβo'sar] *vi* (*líquido, recipiente*) to overflow; (*abundar*) to abound, be plentiful

rebotar [reβo'tar] *vt* to bounce; (*rechazar*) to repel ♦ *vi* (*pelota*) to bounce; (*bala*) to ricochet; **rebote** *nm* rebound; **de rebote** on the rebound

rebozado, a [reβo'θaðo, a] *adj* fried in batter *o* breadcrumbs

rebozar [reβo'θar] *vt* to wrap up; (*CULIN*) to fry in batter *o* breadcrumbs

rebuscado, a [reβus'kaðo, a] *adj* (*amanerado*) affected; (*palabra*) recherché; (*idea*) far-fetched

rebuscar [reβus'kar] *vi*: ~ **(en/por)** to search carefully (in/for)

rebuznar [reβuθ'nar] *vi* to bray

recado [re'kaðo] *nm* (*mensaje*) message; (*encargo*) errand; **tomar un** ~ (*TEL*) to take a message

recaer [reka'er] *vi* to relapse; ~ **en** to fall to *o* on; (*criminal etc*) to fall back into, relapse into; **recaída** *nf* relapse

recalcar [rekal'kar] *vt* (*fig*) to stress, emphasize

recalcitrante [rekalθi'trante] *adj* recalcitrant

recalentar [rekalen'tar] *vt* (*volver a calentar*) to reheat; (*calentar demasiado*) to overheat

recámara [re'kamara] (*AM*) *nf* bedroom

recambio [re'kambjo] *nm* spare; (*de pluma*) refill

recapacitar [rekapaθi'tar] *vi* to reflect

recargado, a [rekar'xaðo, a] *adj* overloaded

recargar [rekar'xar] *vt* to overload; (*batería*) to recharge; **recargo** *nm* surcharge; (*aumento*) increase

recatado, a [reka'taðo, a] *adj* (*modesto*) modest, demure; (*prudente*) cautious

recato [re'kato] *nm* (*modestia*) modesty, demureness; (*cautela*) caution

recaudación [rekauða'θjon] *nf* (*acción*) collection; (*cantidad*) takings *pl*; (*en deporte*) gate; **recaudador, a** *nm/f* tax collector

recelar [reθe'lar] *vt*: ~ **que** (*sospechar*) to suspect that; (*temer*) to fear that ♦ *vi*: ~ **de** to distrust; **recelo** *nm* distrust, suspicion; **receloso, a** *adj* distrustful, suspicious

recepción [reθep'θjon] *nf* reception; **recepcionista** *nm/f* receptionist

receptáculo [reθep'takulo] *nm* receptacle

receptivo, a [reθep'tiβo, a] *adj* receptive

receptor, a [reθep'tor, a] *nm/f* recipient ♦ *nm* (*TEL*) receiver

recesión [reθe'sjon] *nf* (*COM*) recession

receta [re'θeta] *nf* (*CULIN*) recipe; (*MED*) prescription

rechazar [retʃa'θar] *vt* to reject; (*oferta*) to turn down; (*ataque*) to repel

rechazo [re'tʃaθo] *nm* rejection

rechifla [re'tʃifla] *nf* hissing, booing; (*fig*) derision

rechinar [retʃi'nar] *vi* to creak; (*dientes*) to grind

rechistar [retʃis'tar] *vi*: **sin** ~ without a murmur

rechoncho, a [re'tʃontʃo, a] (*fam*) *adj* thickset (*BRIT*), heavy-set (*US*)

rechupete [retʃu'pete]: **de** ~ (*comida*) delicious, scrumptious

recibidor, a [reθiβi'ðor, a] *nm* entrance hall

recibimiento [reθiβi'mjento] *nm* reception, welcome

recibir [reθi'ßir] *vt* to receive; (*dar la bienvenida*) to welcome ♦ *vi* to entertain; **~se** *vr*: **~se de** to qualify as; **recibo** *nm* receipt

reciclar [reθi'klar] *vt* to recycle

recién [re'θjen] *adv* recently, newly; **los ~ casados** the newly-weds; **el ~ llegado** the newcomer; **el ~ nacido** the newborn child

reciente [re'θjente] *adj* recent; (*fresco*) fresh; **~mente** *adv* recently

recinto [re'θinto] *nm* enclosure; (*área*) area, place

recio, a ['reθjo, a] *adj* strong, tough; (*voz*) loud ♦ *adv* hard; loud(ly)

recipiente [reθi'pjente] *nm* receptacle

reciprocidad [reθiproθi'ðað] *nf* reciprocity; **recíproco, a** *adj* reciprocal

recital [reθi'tal] *nm* (*MUS*) recital; (*LITERATURA*) reading

recitar [reθi'tar] *vt* to recite

reclamación [reklama'θjon] *nf* claim, demand; (*queja*) complaint

reclamar [rekla'mar] *vt* to claim, demand ♦ *vi*: **~ contra** to complain about; **~ a uno en justicia** to take sb to court; **reclamo** *nm* (*anuncio*) advertisement; (*tentación*) attraction

reclinar [rekli'nar] *vt* to recline, lean; **~se** *vr* to lean back

recluir [reklu'ir] *vt* to intern, confine

reclusión [reklu'sjon] *nf* (*prisión*) prison; (*refugio*) seclusion; **~ perpetua** life imprisonment

recluta [re'kluta] *nm/f* recruit ♦ *nf* recruitment; **reclutar** *vt* (*datos*) to collect; (*dinero*) to collect up; **~miento** [rekluta'mjento] *nm* recruitment

recobrar [reko'ßrar] *vt* (*salud*) to recover; (*rescatar*) to get back; **~se** *vr* to recover

recodo [re'koðo] *nm* (*de río, camino*) bend

recogedor [rekoxe'ðor] *nm* dustpan

recoger [reko'xer] *vt* to collect; (*AGR*) to harvest; (*levantar*) to pick up; (*juntar*) to gather; (*pasar a buscar*) to come for, get; (*dar asilo*) to give shelter to; (*faldas*) to gather up; (*pelo*) to put up; **~se** *vr* (*retirarse*) to retire; **recogido, a** *adj* (*lugar*) quiet, secluded; (*pequeño*) small ♦ *nf* (*CORREOS*) collection; (*AGR*) harvest

recolección [rekolek'θjon] *nf* (*AGR*) harvesting; (*colecta*) collection

recomendación [rekomenda'θjon] *nf* (*sugerencia*) suggestion, recommendation; (*referencia*) reference

recomendar [rekomen'dar] *vt* to suggest, recommend; (*confiar*) to entrust

recompensa [rekom'pensa] *nf* reward, recompense; **recompensar** *vt* to reward, recompense

recomponer [rekompo'ner] *vt* to mend

reconciliación [rekonθilja'θjon] *nf* reconciliation

reconciliar [rekonθi'ljar] *vt* to reconcile; **~se** *vr* to become reconciled

recóndito, a [re'kondito, a] *adj* (*lugar*) hidden, secret

reconfortar [rekonfor'tar] *vt* to comfort

reconocer [rekono'θer] *vt* to recognize; (*registrar*) to search; (*MED*) to examine; **reconocido, a** *adj* recognized; (*agradecido*) grateful; **reconocimiento** *nm* recognition; search; examination; gratitude; (*confesión*) admission

reconquista [rekon'kista] *nf* reconquest; **la R~** the Reconquest (of Spain)

reconstituyente [rekonstitu'jente] *nm* tonic

reconstruir [rekonstru'ir] *vt* to reconstruct

reconversión [rekonßer'sjon] *nf*: **~ industrial** industrial rationalization

recopilación [rekopila'θjon] *nf* (*resumen*) summary; (*compilación*) compilation; **recopilar** *vt* to compile

récord ['rekorð] (*pl* **~s**) *adj inv, nm* record

recordar [rekor'ðar] *vt* (*acordarse de*) to remember; (*acordar a otro*) to remind ♦ *vi* to remember

recorrer [reko'rrer] *vt* (*país*) to cross, travel through; (*distancia*) to cover; (*registrar*) to search; (*repasar*) to look over; **recorrido** *nm* run, journey; **tren de largo recorrido** main-line train

recortado, a [rekor'taðo, a] *adj* uneven,

irregular

recortar [rekor'tar] *vt* to cut out; **recorte** *nm* (*acción, de prensa*) cutting; (*de telas, chapas*) trimming; **recorte presupuestario** budget cut

recostado, a [rekos'taðo, a] *adj* leaning; **estar ~** to be lying down

recostar [rekos'tar] *vt* to lean; **~se** *vr* to lie down

recoveco [reko'ßeko] *nm* (*de camino, río etc*) bend; (*en casa*) cubby hole

recreación [rekrea'θjon] *nf* recreation

recrear [rekre'ar] *vt* (*entretener*) to entertain; (*volver a crear*) to recreate; **recreativo, a** *adj* recreational; **recreo** *nm* recreation; (*ESCOL*) break, playtime

recriminar [rekrimi'nar] *vt* to reproach ♦ *vi* to recriminate; **~se** *vr* to reproach each other

recrudecer [rekruðe'θer] *vt, vi* to worsen; **~se** *vr* to worsen

recrudecimiento [rekruðeθi'mjento] *nm* upsurge

recta ['rekta] *nf* straight line

rectángulo, a [rek'tangulo, a] *adj* rectangular ♦ *nm* rectangle

rectificar [rektifi'kar] *vt* to rectify; (*volverse recto*) to straighten ♦ *vi* to correct o.s.

rectitud [rekti'tuð] *nf* straightness; (*fig*) rectitude

recto, a ['rekto, a] *adj* straight; (*persona*) honest, upright ♦ *nm* rectum

rector, a [rek'tor, a] *adj* governing

recuadro [re'kwaðro] *nm* box; (*TIPOGRAFÍA*) inset

recubrir [reku'ßrir] *vt*: **~ (con)** (*pintura, crema*) to cover (with)

recuento [re'kwento] *nm* inventory; **hacer el ~ de** to count *o* reckon up

recuerdo [re'kwerðo] *nm* souvenir; **~s** *nmpl* (*memorias*) memories; **¡~s a tu madre!** give my regards to your mother!

recular [reku'lar] *vi* to back down

recuperable [rekupe'raßle] *adj* recoverable

recuperación [rekupera'θjon] *nf* recovery

recuperar [rekupe'rar] *vt* to recover;

(*tiempo*) to make up; **~se** *vr* to recuperate

recurrir [reku'rrir] *vi* (*JUR*) to appeal; **~ a** to resort to; (*persona*) to turn to; **recurso** *nm* resort; (*medios*) means *pl*, resources *pl*; (*JUR*) appeal

recusar [reku'sar] *vt* to reject, refuse

red [reð] *nf* net, mesh; (*FERRO etc*) network; (*trampa*) trap

redacción [reðak'θjon] *nf* (*acción*) editing; (*personal*) editorial staff; (*ESCOL*) essay, composition

redactar [reðak'tar] *vt* to draw up, draft; (*periódico*) to edit

redactor, a [reðak'tor, a] *nm/f* editor

redada [re'ðaða] *nf*: **~ policial** police raid, round-up

rededor [reðe'ðor] *nm*: **al** *o* **en ~** around, round about

redención [reðen'θjon] *nf* redemption

redicho, a [re'ðitʃo, a] *adj* affected

redil [re'ðil] *nm* sheepfold

redimir [reði'mir] *vt* to redeem

rédito ['reðito] *nm* interest, yield

redoblar [reðo'ßlar] *vt* to redouble ♦ *vi* (*tambor*) to roll

redomado, a [reðo'maðo, a] *adj* (*astuto*) sly, crafty; (*perfecto*) utter

redonda [re'ðonda] *nf*: **a la ~** around, round about

redondear [reðonde'ar] *vt* to round, round off

redondel [reðon'del] *nm* (*círculo*) circle; (*TAUR*) bullring, arena

redondo, a [re'ðondo, a] *adj* (*circular*) round; (*completo*) complete

reducción [reðuk'θjon] *nf* reduction

reducido, a [reðu'θiðo, a] *adj* reduced; (*limitado*) limited; (*pequeño*) small

reducir [reðu'θir] *vt* to reduce; to limit; **~se** *vr* to diminish

redundancia [reðun'danθja] *nf* redundancy

reembolsar [re(e)mbol'sar] *vt* (*persona*) to reimburse; (*dinero*) to repay, pay back; (*depósito*) to refund; **reembolso** *nm* reimbursement; refund

reemplazar [re(e)mpla'θar] *vt* to replace;

reemplazo *nm* replacement; **de reemplazo** (*MIL*) reserve

reencuentro [re(e)n'kwentro] *nm* reunion

referencia [refe'renθja] *nf* reference; **con ~ a** with reference to

referéndum [refe'rendum] (*pl* **~s**) *nm* referendum

referente [refe'rente] *adj*: **~ a** concerning, relating to

referir [refe'rir] *vt* (*contar*) to tell, recount; (*relacionar*) to refer, relate; **~se** *vr*: **~se a** to refer to

refilón [refi'lon]: **de ~** *adv* obliquely

refinado, a [refi'naðo, a] *adj* refined

refinamiento [refina'mjento] *nm* refinement

refinar [refi'nar] *vt* to refine; **refinería** *nf* refinery

reflejar [refle'xar] *vt* to reflect; **reflejo, a** *adj* reflected; (*movimiento*) reflex ♦ *nm* reflection; (*ANAT*) reflex

reflexión [reflek'sjon] *nf* reflection;

reflexionar *vt* to reflect on ♦ *vi* to reflect; (*detenerse*) to pause (to think)

reflexivo, a [reflek'sißo, a] *adj* thoughtful; (*LING*) reflexive

reflujo [re'fluxo] *nm* ebb

reforma [re'forma] *nf* reform; (*ARQ etc*) repair; **~ agraria** agrarian reform

reformar [refor'mar] *vt* to reform; (*modificar*) to change, alter; (*ARQ*) to repair; **~se** *vr* to mend one's ways

reformatorio [reforma'torjo] *nm* reformatory

reforzar [refor'θar] *vt* to strengthen; (*ARQ*) to reinforce; (*fig*) to encourage

refractario, a [refrak'tarjo, a] *adj* (*TEC*) heat-resistant

refrán [re'fran] *nm* proverb, saying

refregar [refre'xar] *vt* to scrub

refrenar [refre'nar] *vt* to check, restrain

refrendar [refren'dar] *vt* (*firma*) to endorse, countersign; (*ley*) to approve

refrescante [refres'kante] *adj* refreshing, cooling

refrescar [refres'kar] *vt* to refresh ♦ *vi* to cool down; **~se** *vr* to get cooler; (*tomar aire fresco*) to go out for a breath of fresh air; (*beber*) to have a drink

refresco [re'fresko] *nm* soft drink, cool drink; **"~s"** "refreshments"

refriega [re'frjeɣa] *nf* scuffle, brawl

refrigeración [refrixera'θjon] *nf* refrigeration; (*de sala*) air-conditioning

refrigerador [refrixera'ðor] *nm* refrigerator (*BRIT*), icebox (*US*)

refrigerar [refrixe'rar] *vt* to refrigerate; (*sala*) to air-condition

refuerzo [re'fwerθo] *nm* reinforcement; (*TEC*) support

refugiado, a [refu'xjaðo, a] *nm/f* refugee

refugiarse [refu'xjarse] *vr* to take refuge, shelter

refugio [re'fuxjo] *nm* refuge; (*protección*) shelter

refunfuñar [refunfu'ɲar] *vi* to grunt, growl; (*quejarse*) to grumble

refutar [refu'tar] *vt* to refute

regadera [reɣa'ðera] *nf* watering can

regadío [reɣa'ðio] *nm* irrigated land

regalado, a [reɣa'laðo, a] *adj* comfortable, luxurious; (*gratis*) free, for nothing

regalar [reɣa'lar] *vt* (*dar*) to give (as a present); (*entregar*) to give away; (*mimar*) to pamper, make a fuss of

regaliz [reɣa'liθ] *nm* liquorice

regalo [re'ɣalo] *nm* (*obsequio*) gift, present; (*gusto*) pleasure

regañadientes [reɣaɲa'ðjentes]: **a ~** *adv* reluctantly

regañar [reɣa'ɲar] *vt* to scold ♦ *vi* to grumble; **regañón, ona** *adj* nagging

regar [re'ɣar] *vt* to water, irrigate; (*fig*) to scatter, sprinkle

regatear [reɣate'ar] *vt* (*COM*) to bargain over; (*escatimar*) to be mean with ♦ *vi* to bargain, haggle; (*DEPORTE*) to dribble; **regateo** *nm* bargaining; dribbling; (*del cuerpo*) swerve, dodge

regazo [re'ɣaθo] *nm* lap

regeneración [rexenera'θjon] *nf* regeneration

regenerar [rexene'rar] *vt* to regenerate

regentar [rexen'tar] *vt* to direct, manage; **regente** *nm* (COM) manager; (POL) regent

régimen ['reximen] (*pl* **regímenes**) *nm* regime; (MED) diet

regimiento [rexi'mjento] *nm* regiment

regio, a ['rexjo, a] *adj* royal, regal; (*fig: suntuoso*) splendid; (AM: *fam*) great, terrific

región [re'xjon] *nf* region

regir [re'xir] *vt* to govern, rule; (*dirigir*) to manage, run ♦ *vi* to apply, be in force

registrar [rexis'trar] *vt* (*buscar*) to search; (: *en cajón*) to look through; (*inspeccionar*) to inspect; (*anotar*) to register, record; (INFORM) to log; **~se** *vr* to register; (*ocurrir*) to happen

registro [re'xistro] *nm* (*acto*) registration; (MUS, *libro*) register; (*inspección*) inspection, search; **~ civil** registry office

regla ['rexla] *nf* (*ley*) rule, regulation; (*de medir*) ruler, rule; (MED: *período*) period

reglamentación [rexlamenta'θjon] *nf* (*acto*) regulation; (*lista*) rules *pl*

reglamentar [rexlamen'tar] *vt* to regulate; **reglamentario, a** *adj* statutory; **reglamento** *nm* rules *pl*, regulations *pl*

regocijarse [rexoθi'xarse] *vr*: **~ de** to rejoice at, be happy about; **regocijo** *nm* joy, happiness

regodearse [rexoðe'arse] *vr* to be glad, be delighted; **regodeo** *nm* delight

regresar [rexre'sar] *vi* to come back, go back, return; **regresivo, a** *adj* backward; (*fig*) regressive; **regreso** *nm* return

reguero [re'xero] *nm* (*de sangre etc*) trickle; (*de humo*) trail

regulador [rexula'ðor] *nm* regulator; (*de radio etc*) knob, control

regular [rexu'lar] *adj* regular; (*normal*) normal, usual; (*común*) ordinary; (*organizado*) regular, orderly; (*mediano*) average; (*fam*) not bad, so-so ♦ *adv* so-so, alright ♦ *vt* (*controlar*) to control, regulate; (TEC) to adjust; **por lo ~** as a rule; **~idad** *nf* regularity; **~izar** *vt* to regularize

regusto [re'xusto] *nm* aftertaste

rehabilitación [reaβilita'θjon] *nf* rehabilitation; (ARQ) restoration

rehabilitar [reaβili'tar] *vt* to rehabilitate; (ARQ) to restore; (*reintegrar*) to reinstate

rehacer [rea'θer] *vt* (*reparar*) to mend, repair; (*volver a hacer*) to redo, repeat; **~se** *vr* (MED) to recover

rehén [re'en] *nm* hostage

rehuir [reu'ir] *vt* to avoid, shun

rehusar [reu'sar] *vt, vi* to refuse

reina ['reina] *nf* queen; **~do** *nm* reign

reinante [rei'nante] *adj* (*fig*) prevailing

reinar [rei'nar] *vi* to reign

reincidir [reinθi'ðir] *vi* to relapse

reincorporarse [reinkorpo'rarse] *vr*: **~ a** to rejoin

reino ['reino] *nm* kingdom; **el R~ Unido** the United Kingdom

reintegrar [reinte'xrar] *vt* (*reconstituir*) to reconstruct; (*persona*) to reinstate; (*dinero*) to refund, pay back; **~se** *vr*: **~se a** to return to

reír [re'ir] *vi* to laugh; **~se** *vr* to laugh; **~se de** to laugh at

reiterar [reite'rar] *vt* to reiterate

reivindicación [reiβindika'θjon] *nf* (*demanda*) claim, demand; (*justificación*) vindication

reivindicar [reiβindi'kar] *vt* to claim

reja ['rexa] *nf* (*de ventana*) grille, bars *pl*; (*en la calle*) grating

rejilla [re'xiʎa] *nf* grating, grille; (*muebles*) wickerwork; (*de ventilación*) vent; (*de coche etc*) luggage rack

rejoneador [rexonea'ðor] *nm* mounted bullfighter

rejuvenecer [rexuβene'θer] *vt, vi* to rejuvenate

relación [rela'θjon] *nf* relation, relationship; (MAT) ratio; (*narración*) report; **relaciones públicas** public relations; **con ~ a, en ~ con** in relation to; **relacionar** *vt* to relate, connect; **relacionarse** *vr* to be connected, be linked

relajación [relaxa'θjon] *nf* relaxation
relajado, a [rela'xaðo, a] *adj* (*disoluto*)
  loose; (*cómodo*) relaxed; (*MED*) ruptured
relajar [rela'xar] *vt* to relax; **~se** *vr* to relax
relamerse [rela'merse] *vr* to lick one's lips
relamido, a [rela'miðo, a] *adj* (*pulcro*)
  overdressed; (*afectado*) affected
relámpago [re'lampaɣo] *nm* flash of
  lightning; **visita/huelga ~** lightning visit/
  strike; **relampaguear** *vi* to flash
relatar [rela'tar] *vt* to tell, relate
relativo, a [rela'tiβo, a] *adj* relative; **en lo
  ~ a** concerning
relato [re'lato] *nm* (*narración*) story, tale
relegar [rele'ɣar] *vt* to relegate
relevante [rele'βante] *adj* eminent,
  outstanding
relevar [rele'βar] *vt* (*sustituir*) to relieve;
  ~se *vr* to relay; **~ a uno de un cargo** to
  relieve sb of his post
relevo [re'leβo] *nm* relief; **carrera de ~s**
  relay race
relieve [re'ljeβe] *nm* (*ARTE, TEC*) relief; (*fig*)
  prominence, importance; **bajo ~** bas-relief
religión [reli'xjon] *nf* religion; **religioso,
  a** *adj* religious ♦ *nm/f* monk/nun
relinchar [relin'tʃar] *vi* to neigh; **relincho**
  nm neigh; (*acto*) neighing
reliquia [re'likja] *nf* relic; **~ de familia**
  heirloom
rellano [re'ʎano] *nm* (*ARQ*) landing
rellenar [reʎe'nar] *vt* (*llenar*) to fill up;
  (*CULIN*) to stuff; (*COSTURA*) to pad;
  relleno, a *adj* full up; stuffed ♦ *nm*
  stuffing; (*de tapicería*) padding
reloj [re'lo(x)] *nm* clock; **~ (de pulsera)**
  wristwatch; **~ despertador** alarm (clock);
  poner el ~ to set one's watch (*o* the
  clock); **~ero, a** *nm/f* clockmaker;
  watchmaker
reluciente [relu'θjente] *adj* brilliant,
  shining
relucir [relu'θir] *vi* to shine; (*fig*) to excel
relumbrar [relum'brar] *vi* to dazzle, shine
  brilliantly
remachar [rema'tʃar] *vt* to rivet; (*fig*) to
  hammer home, drive home; **remache**

nm rivet
remanente [rema'nente] *nm* remainder;
  (*COM*) balance; (*de producto*) surplus
remangar [reman'gar] *vt* to roll up
remanso [re'manso] *nm* pool
remar [re'mar] *vi* to row
rematado, a [rema'taðo, a] *adj* complete,
  utter
rematar [rema'tar] *vt* to finish off; (*COM*)
  to sell off cheap ♦ *vi* to end, finish off;
  (*DEPORTE*) to shoot
remate [re'mate] *nm* end, finish; (*punta*)
  tip; (*DEPORTE*) shot; (*ARQ*) top; **de *o* para
  ~** to crown it all (*BRIT*), to top it off
remedar [reme'ðar] *vt* to imitate
remediar [reme'ðjar] *vt* to remedy;
  (*subsanar*) to make good, repair; (*evitar*)
  to avoid
remedio [re'meðjo] *nm* remedy; (*alivio*)
  relief, help; (*JUR*) recourse, remedy; **poner
  ~ a** to correct, stop; **no tener más ~** to
  have no alternative; **¡qué ~!** there's no
  choice!; **sin ~** hopeless
remedo [re'meðo] *nm* imitation; (*pey*)
  parody
remendar [remen'dar] *vt* to repair; (*con
  parche*) to patch
remesa [re'mesa] *nf* remittance; (*COM*)
  shipment
remiendo [re'mjendo] *nm* mend; (*con
  parche*) patch; (*cosido*) darn
remilgado, a [remil'xaðo, a] *adj* prim;
  (*afectado*) affected
remilgo [re'milxo] *nm* primness;
  (*afectación*) affectation
reminiscencia [reminis'θenθja] *nf*
  reminiscence
remiso, a [re'miso, a] *adj* slack, slow
remite [re'mite] *nm* (*en sobre*) name and
  address of sender
remitir [remi'tir] *vt* to remit, send ♦ *vi* to
  slacken; (*en carta*): **remite: X** sender: X;
  remitente *nm/f* sender
remo ['remo] *nm* (*de barco*) oar; (*DEPORTE*)
  rowing
remojar [remo'xar] *vt* to steep, soak;
  (*galleta etc*) to dip, dunk

remojo [re'moxo] *nm*: **dejar la ropa en ~** to leave clothes to soak

remolacha [remo'latʃa] *nf* beet, beetroot

remolcador [remolka'ðor] *nm* (*NAUT*) tug; (*AUTO*) breakdown lorry

remolcar [remol'kar] *vt* to tow

remolino [remo'lino] *nm* eddy; (*de agua*) whirlpool; (*de viento*) whirlwind; (*de gente*) crowd

remolque [re'molke] *nm* tow, towing; (*cuerda*) towrope; **llevar a ~** to tow

remontar [remon'tar] *vt* to mend; **~se** *vr* to soar; **~se a** (*COM*) to amount to; **~ el vuelo** to soar

remorder [remor'ðer] *vt* to distress, disturb; **~le la conciencia a uno** to have a guilty conscience; **remordimiento** *nm* remorse

remoto, a [re'moto, a] *adj* remote

remover [remo'ßer] *vt* to stir; (*tierra*) to turn over; (*objetos*) to move round

remozar [remo'θar] *vt* (*ARQ*) to refurbish

remuneración [remunera'θjon] *nf* remuneration

remunerar [remune'rar] *vt* to remunerate; (*premiar*) to reward

renacer [rena'θer] *vi* to be reborn; (*fig*) to revive; **renacimiento** *nm* rebirth; **el Renacimiento** the Renaissance

renacuajo [rena'kwaxo] *nm* (*ZOOL*) tadpole

renal [re'nal] *adj* renal, kidney *cpd*

rencilla [ren'θiʎa] *nf* quarrel

rencor [ren'kor] *nm* rancour, bitterness; **~oso, a** *adj* spiteful

rendición [rendi'θjon] *nf* surrender

rendido, a [ren'diðo, a] *adj* (*sumiso*) submissive; (*cansado*) worn-out, exhausted

rendija [ren'dixa] *nf* (*hendedura*) crack, cleft

rendimiento [rendi'mjento] *nm* (*producción*) output; (*TEC*, *COM*) efficiency

rendir [ren'dir] *vt* (*vencer*) to defeat; (*producir*) to produce; (*dar beneficio*) to yield; (*agotar*) to exhaust ♦ *vi* to pay; **~se** *vr* (*someterse*) to surrender; (*cansarse*) to

wear o.s. out; **~ homenaje** *o* **culto a** to pay homage to

renegar [rene'xar] *vi* (*renunciar*) to renounce; (*blasfemar*) to blaspheme; (*quejarse*) to complain

RENFE ['renfe] *nf abr* (= *Red Nacional de los Ferrocarriles Españoles*) ≈ BR (*BRIT*)

renglón [ren'glon] *nm* (*línea*) line; (*COM*) item, article; **a ~ seguido** immediately after

renombrado, a [renom'braðo, a] *adj* renowned

renombre [re'nombre] *nm* renown

renovación [renoßa'θjon] *nf* (*de contrato*) renewal; (*ARQ*) renovation

renovar [reno'ßar] *vt* to renew; (*ARQ*) to renovate

renta ['renta] *nf* (*ingresos*) income; (*beneficio*) profit; (*alquiler*) rent; **~ vitalicia** annuity; **rentable** *adj* profitable; **rentar** *vt* to produce, yield

renuncia [re'nunθja] *nf* resignation

renunciar [renun'θjar] *vt* to renounce; (*tabaco, alcohol etc*): **~ a** to give up; (*oferta, oportunidad*) to turn down; (*puesto*) to resign ♦ *vi* to resign

reñido, a [re'ɲiðo, a] *adj* (*batalla*) bitter, hard-fought; **estar ~ con uno** to be on bad terms with sb

reñir [re'ɲir] *vt* (*regañar*) to scold ♦ *vi* (*estar peleado*) to quarrel, fall out; (*combatir*) to fight

reo ['reo] *nm/f* culprit, offender; **~ de muerte** prisoner condemned to death

reojo [re'oxo]: **de ~** *adv* out of the corner of one's eye

reparación [repara'θjon] *nf* (*acto*) mending, repairing; (*TEC*) repair; (*fig*) amends, reparation

reparar [repa'rar] *vt* to repair; (*fig*) to make amends for; (*observar*) to observe ♦ *vi*: **~ en** (*darse cuenta de*) to notice; (*prestar atención a*) to pay attention to

reparo [re'paro] *nm* (*advertencia*) observation; (*duda*) doubt; (*dificultad*) difficulty; **poner ~s (a)** to raise objections (to)

repartición [reparti'θjon] *nf* distribution; (*división*) division; **repartidor, a** *nm/f* distributor

repartir [repar'tir] *vt* to distribute, share out; (*CORREOS*) to deliver; **reparto** *nm* distribution; delivery; (*TEATRO, CINÉ*) cast; (*AM: urbanización*) housing estate (*BRIT*), real estate development (*US*)

repasar [repa'sar] *vt* (*ESCOL*) to revise; (*MECÁNICA*) to check, overhaul; (*COSTURA*) to mend; **repaso** *nm* revision; overhaul, checkup; mending

repatriar [repa'trjar] *vt* to repatriate

repecho [re'petʃo] *nm* steep incline

repelente [repe'lente] *adj* repellent, repulsive

repeler [repe'ler] *vt* to repel

repensar [repen'sar] *vt* to reconsider

repente [re'pente] *nm*: **de ~** suddenly; **~ de ira** fit of anger

repentino, a [repen'tino, a] *adj* sudden

repercusión [reperku'sjon] *nf* repercussion

repercutir [reperku'tir] *vi* (*objeto*) to rebound; (*sonido*) to echo; **~ en** (*fig*) to have repercussions on

repertorio [reper'torjo] *nm* list; (*TEATRO*) repertoire

repetición [repeti'θjon] *nf* repetition

repetir [repe'tir] *vt* to repeat; (*plato*) to have a second helping of ♦ *vi* to repeat; (*sabor*) to come back; **~se** *vr* (*volver sobre un tema*) to repeat o.s.

repetitivo, a [repeti'tiβo, a] *adj* repetitive, repetitious

repicar [repi'kar] *vt* (*campanas*) to ring

repique [re'pike] *nm* pealing, ringing; **~teo** *nm* pealing; (*de tambor*) drumming

repisa [re'pisa] *nf* ledge, shelf; (*de ventana*) windowsill; **~ de chimenea** mantelpiece

repito *etc vb ver* **repetir**

replantearse [replante'arse] *vr*: **~ un problema** to reconsider a problem

replegarse [reple'varse] *vr* to fall back, retreat

repleto, a [re'pleto, a] *adj* replete, full up

réplica ['replika] *nf* answer; (*ARTE*) replica

replicar [repli'kar] *vi* to answer; (*objetar*) to argue, answer back

repliegue [re'pljexe] *nm* (*MIL*) withdrawal

repoblación [repoβla'θjon] *nf* repopulation; (*de río*) restocking; **~ forestal** reafforestation

repoblar [repo'βlar] *vt* to repopulate; (*con árboles*) to reafforest

repollo [re'poʎo] *nm* cabbage

reponer [repo'ner] *vt* to replace, put back; (*TEATRO*) to revive; **~se** *vr* to recover; **~ que** to reply that

reportaje [repor'taxe] *nm* report, article

reportero, a [repor'tero, a] *nm/f* reporter

reposacabezas [reposaka'βeθas] *nm inv* headrest

reposado, a [repo'saðo, a] *adj* (*descansado*) restful; (*tranquilo*) calm

reposar [repo'sar] *vi* to rest, repose

reposición [reposi'θjon] *nf* replacement; (*CINÉ*) remake

reposo [re'poso] *nm* rest

repostar [repos'tar] *vt* to replenish; (*AUTO*) to fill up (with petrol (*BRIT*) *o* gasoline (*US*))

repostería [reposte'ria] *nf* confectioner's (shop); **repostero, a** *nm/f* confectioner

reprender [repren'der] *vt* to reprimand

represa [re'presa] *nf* dam; (*lago artificial*) lake, pool

represalia [repre'salja] *nf* reprisal

representación [representa'θjon] *nf* representation; (*TEATRO*) performance; **representante** *nm/f* representative; performer

representar [represen'tar] *vt* to represent; (*TEATRO*) to perform; (*edad*) to look; **~se** *vr* to imagine; **representativo, a** *adj* representative

represión [repre'sjon] *nf* repression

reprimenda [repri'menda] *nf* reprimand, rebuke

reprimir [repri'mir] *vt* to repress

reprobar [repro'βar] *vt* to censure, reprove

reprochar [repro'tʃar] *vt* to reproach; **reproche** *nm* reproach

reproducción [reproðuk'θjon] *nf* reproduction

reproducir [reproðu'θir] *vt* to reproduce; **~se** *vr* to breed; (*situación*) to recur

reproductor, a [reproðuk'tor, a] *adj* reproductive

reptil [rep'til] *nm* reptile

república [re'puβlika] *nf* republic; **R~ Dominicana** Dominican Republic; **republicano, a** *adj, nm/f* republican

repudiar [repu'ðjar] *vt* to repudiate; (*fe*) to renounce

repuesto [re'pwesto] *nm* (*pieza de recambio*) spare (part); (*abastecimiento*) supply; **rueda de ~** spare wheel

repugnancia [repuɣ'nanθja] *nf* repugnance; **repugnante** *adj* repugnant, repulsive

repugnar [repuɣ'nar] *vt* to disgust

repulsa [re'pulsa] *nf* rebuff

repulsión [repul'sjon] *nf* repulsion, aversion; **repulsivo, a** *adj* repulsive

reputación [reputa'θjon] *nf* reputation

requemado, a [reke'maðo, a] *adj* (*quemado*) scorched; (*bronceado*) tanned

requerimiento [rekeri'mjento] *nm* request; (*JUR*) summons

requerir [reke'rir] *vt* (*pedir*) to ask, request; (*exigir*) to require; (*llamar*) to send for, summon

requesón [reke'son] *nm* cottage cheese

requete... [re'kete] *prefijo* extremely

réquiem ['rekjem] (*pl* **~s**) *nm* requiem

requisito [reki'sito] *nm* requirement, requisite

res [res] *nf* beast, animal

resaca [re'saka] *nf* (*en el mar*) undertow, undercurrent; (*fam*) hangover

resaltar [resal'tar] *vi* to project, stick out; (*fig*) to stand out

resarcir [resar'θir] *vt* to compensate; **~se** *vr* to make up for

resbaladizo, a [resβala'ðiθo, a] *adj* slippery

resbalar [resβa'lar] *vi* to slip, slide; (*fig*) to slip (up); **~se** *vr* to slip, slide; to slip (up); **resbalón** *nm* (*acción*) slip

rescatar [reska'tar] *vt* (*salvar*) to save, rescue; (*objeto*) to get back, recover; (*cautivos*) to ransom

rescate [res'kate] *nm* rescue; (*de objeto*) recovery; **pagar un ~** to pay a ransom

rescindir [resθin'dir] *vt* to rescind

rescisión [resθi'sjon] *nf* cancellation

rescoldo [res'koldo] *nm* embers *pl*

resecar [rese'kar] *vt* to dry thoroughly; (*MED*) to cut out, remove; **~se** *vr* to dry up

reseco, a [re'seko, a] *adj* very dry; (*fig*) skinny

resentido, a [resen'tiðo, a] *adj* resentful

resentimiento [resenti'mjento] *nm* resentment, bitterness

resentirse [resen'tirse] *vr* (*debilitarse*: *persona*) to suffer; **~ de** (*consecuencias*) to feel the effects of; **~ de (o por) algo** to resent sth, be bitter about sth

reseña [re'seɲa] *nf* (*cuenta*) account; (*informe*) report; (*LITERATURA*) review

reseñar [rese'ɲar] *vt* to describe; (*LITERATURA*) to review

reserva [re'serβa] *nf* reserve; (*reservación*) reservation; **a ~ de que ...** unless ...; **con toda ~** in strictest confidence

reservado, a [reser'βaðo, a] *adj* reserved; (*retraído*) cold, distant ♦ *nm* private room

reservar [reser'βar] *vt* (*guardar*) to keep; (*habitación, entrada*) to reserve; **~se** *vr* to save o.s.; (*callar*) to keep to o.s.

resfriado [resfri'aðo] *nm* cold; **resfriarse** *vr* to cool; (*MED*) to catch (a) cold

resguardar [resɣwar'ðar] *vt* to protect, shield; **~se** *vr*: **~se de** to guard against; **resguardo** *nm* defence; (*vale*) voucher; (*recibo*) receipt, slip

residencia [resi'ðenθja] *nf* residence; **~l** *nf* (*urbanización*) housing estate

residente [resi'ðente] *adj, nm/f* resident

residir [resi'ðir] *vi* to reside, live; **~ en** to reside in, lie in

residuo [re'siðwo] *nm* residue

resignación [resiɣna'θjon] *nf* resignation; **resignarse** *vr*: **resignarse a** *o* **con** to resign o.s. to, be resigned to

resina [re'sina] *nf* resin

resistencia [resis'tenθja] *nf* (*dureza*) endurance, strength; (*oposición, ELEC*) resistance; **resistente** *adj* strong, hardy; resistant

resistir [resis'tir] *vt* (*soportar*) to bear; (*oponerse a*) to resist, oppose; (*aguantar*) to put up with ♦ *vi* to resist; (*aguantar*) to last, endure; **~se** *vr*: **~se a** to refuse to, resist

resolución [resolu'θjon] *nf* resolution; (*decisión*) decision; **resoluto, a** *adj* resolute

resolver [resol'βer] *vt* to resolve; (*solucionar*) to solve, resolve; (*decidir*) to decide, settle; **~se** *vr* to make up one's mind

resonancia [reso'nanθja] *nf* (*del sonido*) resonance; (*repercusión*) repercussion

resonar [reso'nar] *vi* to ring, echo

resoplar [reso'plar] *vi* to snort; **resoplido** *nm* heavy breathing

resorte [re'sorte] *nm* spring; (*fig*) lever

respaldar [respal'dar] *vt* to back (up), support; **~se** *vr* to lean back; **~se con** *o* **en** (*fig*) to take one's stand on; **respaldo** *nm* (*de sillón*) back; (*fig*) support, backing

respectivo, a [respek'tiβo, a] *adj* respective; **en lo ~ a** with regard to

respecto [res'pekto] *nm*: **al ~** on this matter; **con ~ a, ~ de** with regard to, in relation to

respetable [respe'taβle] *adj* respectable

respetar [respe'tar] *vt* to respect; **respeto** *nm* respect; (*acatamiento*) deference; **respetos** *nmpl* respects; **respetuoso, a** *adj* respectful

respingo [res'pingo] *nm* start, jump

respiración [respira'θjon] *nf* breathing; (*MED*) respiration; (*ventilación*) ventilation

respirar [respi'rar] *vi* to breathe; **respiratorio, a** *adj* respiratory; **respiro** *nm* breathing; (*fig: descanso*) respite

resplandecer [resplande'θer] *vi* to shine; **resplandeciente** *adj* resplendent, shining; **resplandor** *nm* brilliance,

brightness; (*de luz, fuego*) blaze

responder [respon'der] *vt* to answer ♦ *vi* to answer; (*fig*) to respond; (*pey*) to answer back; **~ de** *o* **por** to answer for; **respondón, ona** *adj* cheeky

responsabilidad [responsaβili'ðað] *nf* responsibility

responsabilizarse [responsaβili'θarse] *vr* to make o.s. responsible, take charge

responsable [respon'saβle] *adj* responsible

respuesta [res'pwesta] *nf* answer, reply

resquebrajar [reskeβra'xar] *vt* to crack, split; **~se** *vr* to crack, split

resquemor [reske'mor] *nm* resentment

resquicio [res'kiθjo] *nm* chink; (*hendedura*) crack

resta ['resta] *nf* (*MAT*) remainder

restablecer [restaβle'θer] *vt* to re-establish, restore; **~se** *vr* to recover

restallar [resta'ʎar] *vi* to crack

restante [res'tante] *adj* remaining; **lo ~** the remainder

restar [res'tar] *vt* (*MAT*) to subtract; (*fig*) to take away ♦ *vi* to remain, be left

restauración [restaura'θjon] *nf* restoration

restaurante [restau'rante] *nm* restaurant

restaurar [restau'rar] *vt* to restore

restitución [restitu'θjon] *nf* return, restitution

restituir [restitu'ir] *vt* (*devolver*) to return, give back; (*rehabilitar*) to restore

resto ['resto] *nm* (*residuo*) rest, remainder; (*apuesta*) stake; **~s** *nmpl* remains

restregar [restre'var] *vt* to scrub, rub

restricción [restrik'θjon] *nf* restriction

restrictivo, a [restrik'tiβo, a] *adj* restrictive

restringir [restrin'xir] *vt* to restrict, limit

resucitar [resuθi'tar] *vt, vi* to resuscitate, revive

resuello [re'sweʎo] *nm* (*aliento*) breath; **estar sin ~** to be breathless

resuelto, a [re'swelto, a] *pp de* **resolver** ♦ *adj* resolute, determined

resultado [resul'taðo] *nm* result; (*conclusión*) outcome; **resultante** *adj* resulting, resultant

resultar [resul'tar] *vi* (*ser*) to be; (*llegar a ser*) to turn out to be; (*salir bien*) to turn out well; (*COM*) to amount to; ~ **de** to stem from; **me resulta difícil hacerlo** it's difficult for me to do it

resumen [re'sumen] (*pl* **resúmenes**) *nm* summary, résumé; **en ~** in short

resumir [resu'mir] *vt* to sum up; (*cortar*) to abridge, cut down; (*condensar*) to summarize

resurgir [resur'xir] *vi* (*reaparecer*) to reappear

resurrección [resurre(k)'θjon] *nf* resurrection

retablo [re'taβlo] *nm* altarpiece

retaguardia [reta'ɣwarðja] *nf* rearguard

retahíla [reta'ila] *nf* series, string

retal [re'tal] *nm* remnant

retar [re'tar] *vt* to challenge; (*desafiar*) to defy, dare

retardar [retar'ðar] *vt* (*demorar*) to delay; (*hacer más lento*) to slow down; (*retener*) to hold back

retazo [re'taθo] *nm* snippet (*BRIT*), fragment

retener [rete'ner] *vt* (*intereses*) to withhold

reticente [reti'θente] *adj* (*tono*) insinuating; (*postura*) reluctant; **ser ~ a hacer algo** to be reluctant *o* unwilling to do sth

retina [re'tina] *nf* retina

retintín [retin'tin] *nm* jangle, jingle

retirada [reti'raða] *nf* (*MIL, refugio*) retreat; (*de dinero*) withdrawal; (*de embajador*) recall; **retirado, a** *adj* (*lugar*) remote; (*vida*) quiet; (*jubilado*) retired

retirar [reti'rar] *vt* to withdraw; (*quitar*) to remove; (*jubilar*) to retire, pension off; **~se** *vr* to retreat, withdraw; to retire; (*acostarse*) to retire, go to bed; **retiro** *nm* retreat; retirement; (*pago*) pension

reto ['reto] *nm* dare, challenge

retocar [reto'kar] *vt* (*fotografía*) to touch up, retouch

retoño [re'toɲo] *nm* sprout, shoot; (*fig*) offspring, child

retoque [re'toke] *nm* retouching

retorcer [retor'θer] *vt* to twist; (*manos, lavado*) to wring; **~se** *vr* to become twisted; (*mover el cuerpo*) to writhe

retorcido, a [retor'θiðo, a] *adj* (*persona*) devious

retórica [re'torika] *nf* rhetoric; (*pey*) affectedness; **retórico, a** *adj* rhetorical

retornar [retor'nar] *vt* to return, give back ♦ *vi* to return, go/come back; **retorno** *nm* return

retortijón [retorti'xon] *nm* twist, twisting

retozar [reto'θar] *vi* (*juguetear*) to frolic, romp; (*saltar*) to gambol; **retozón, ona** *adj* playful

retracción [retrak'θjon] *nf* retraction

retractarse [retrak'tarse] *vr* to retract; **me retracto** I take that back

retraerse [retra'erse] *vr* to retreat, withdraw; **retraído, a** *adj* shy, retiring; **retraimiento** *nm* retirement; (*timidez*) shyness

retransmisión [retransmi'sjon] *nf* repeat (broadcast)

retransmitir [retransmi'tir] *vt* (*mensaje*) to relay; (*TV etc*) to repeat, retransmit; (: *en vivo*) to broadcast live

retrasado, a [retra'saðo, a] *adj* late; (*MED*) mentally retarded; (*país etc*) backward, underdeveloped

retrasar [retra'sar] *vt* (*demorar*) to postpone, put off; (*retardar*) to slow down ♦ *vi* (*atrasarse*) to be late; (*reloj*) to be slow; (*producción*) to fall (off); (*quedarse atrás*) to lag behind; **~se** *vr* to be late; to be slow; to fall (off); to lag behind

retraso [re'traso] *nm* (*demora*) delay; (*lentitud*) slowness; (*tardanza*) lateness; (*atraso*) backwardness; **~s** (*FINANZAS*) *nmpl* arrears; **llegar con ~** to arrive late; **~ mental** mental deficiency

retratar [retra'tar] *vt* (*ARTE*) to paint the portrait of; (*fotografiar*) to photograph; (*fig*) to depict, describe; **~se** *vr* to have one's portrait painted; to have one's photograph taken; **retrato** *nm* portrait;

(fig) likeness; **retrato-robot** *nm* Identikit
® picture
retreta [re'treta] *nf* retreat
retrete [re'trete] *nm* toilet
retribución [retriβu'θjon] *nf* (*recompensa*)
reward; (*pago*) pay, payment
retribuir [retri'βwir] *vt* (*recompensar*) to
reward; (*pagar*) to pay
retro... ['retro] *prefijo* retro...
retroactivo, a [retroak'tiβo, a] *adj*
retroactive, retrospective
retroceder [retroθe'ðer] *vi* (*echarse atrás*)
to move back(wards); (*fig*) to back down
retroceso [retro'θeso] *nm* backward
movement; (*MED*) relapse; (*fig*) backing
down
retrógrado, a [re'troxraðo, a] *adj*
retrograde, retrogressive; (*POL*) reactionary
retrospectivo, a [retrospek'tiβo, a] *adj*
retrospective
retrovisor [retroβi'sor] *nm* (*tb*: **espejo ~**)
rear-view mirror
retumbar [retum'bar] *vi* to echo, resound
reúma [re'uma], **reuma** ['reuma] *nm*
rheumatism
reumatismo [reuma'tismo] *nm* = **reúma**
reunificar [reunifi'kar] *vt* to reunify
reunión [reu'njon] *nf* (*asamblea*) meeting;
(*fiesta*) party
reunir [reu'nir] *vt* (*juntar*) to reunite, join
(together); (*recoger*) to gather (together);
(*personas*) to get together; (*cualidades*) to
combine; **~se** *vr* (*personas: en asamblea*)
to meet, gather
revalidar [reβali'ðar] *vt* (*ratificar*) to
confirm, ratify
revalorizar [reβalori'θar] *vt* to revalue,
reassess
revancha [re'βantʃa] *nf* revenge
revelación [reβela'θjon] *nf* revelation
revelado [reβe'laðo] *nm* developing
revelar [reβe'lar] *vt* to reveal; (*FOTO*) to
develop
reventa [re'βenta] *nf* (*de entradas: para
concierto*) touting
reventar [reβen'tar] *vt* to burst, explode
reventón [reβen'ton] *nm* (*AUTO*) blow-out

(*BRIT*), flat (*US*)
reverencia [reβe'renθja] *nf* reverence;
reverenciar *vt* to revere
reverendo, a [reβe'rendo, a] *adj* reverend
reverente [reβe'rente] *adj* reverent
reversible [reβer'siβle] *adj* (*prenda*)
reversible
reverso [re'βerso] *nm* back, other side; (*de
moneda*) reverse
revertir [reβer'tir] *vi* to revert
revés [re'βes] *nm* back, wrong side; (*fig*)
reverse, setback; (*DEPORTE*) backhand; **al ~**
the wrong way round; (*de arriba abajo*)
upside down; (*ropa*) inside out; **volver
algo del ~** to turn sth round; (*ropa*) to
turn sth inside out
revestir [reβes'tir] *vt* (*cubrir*) to cover, coat
revisar [reβi'sar] *vt* (*examinar*) to check;
(*texto etc*) to revise; **revisión** *nf* revision
revisor, a [reβi'sor, a] *nm/f* inspector;
(*FERRO*) ticket collector
revista [re'βista] *nf* magazine, review;
(*TEATRO*) revue; (*inspección*) inspection;
pasar ~ a to review, inspect
revivir [reβi'βir] *vi* to revive
revocación [reβoka'θjon] *nf* repeal
revocar [reβo'kar] *vt* to revoke
revolcarse [reβol'karse] *vr* to roll about
revolotear [reβolote'ar] *vi* to flutter
revoltijo [reβol'tixo] *nm* mess, jumble
revoltoso, a [reβol'toso, a] *adj* (*travieso*)
naughty, unruly
revolución [reβolu'θjon] *nf* revolution;
revolucionar *vt* to revolutionize;
revolucionario, a *adj, nm/f*
revolutionary
revolver [reβol'βer] *vt* (*desordenar*) to
disturb, mess up; (*mover*) to move about
♦ *vi*: **~ en** to go through, rummage
(about) in; **~se** *vr* (*volver contra*) to turn
on *o* against
revólver [re'βolβer] *nm* revolver
revuelo [re'βwelo] *nm* fluttering; (*fig*)
commotion
revuelta [re'βwelta] *nf* (*motín*) revolt;
(*agitación*) commotion
revuelto, a [re'βwelto, a] *pp de* **revolver**

♦ *adj* (*mezclado*) mixed-up, in disorder
rey [rei] *nm* king; **Día de R~es** Twelfth Night

Reyes Magos
---

i On the night before the 6th January (the Epiphany), children go to bed expecting **los Reyes Magos** (the Three Wise Men) to bring them presents. Twelfth Night processions, known as **cabalgatas**, take place that evening when 3 people dressed as **los Reyes Magos** arrive in the town by land or sea to the delight of the children.

---

reyerta [re'jerta] *nf* quarrel, brawl
rezagado, a [reθa'xaðo, a] *nm/f* straggler
rezagar [reθa'xar] *vt* (*dejar atrás*) to leave behind; (*retrasar*) to delay, postpone
rezar [re'θar] *vi* to pray; **~ con** (*fam*) to concern, have to do with; **rezo** *nm* prayer
rezongar [reθoŋ'gar] *vi* to grumble
rezumar [reθu'mar] *vt* to ooze
ría ['ria] *nf* estuary
riada [ri'aða] *nf* flood
ribera [ri'ßera] *nf* (*de río*) bank; (: *área*) riverside
ribete [ri'ßete] *nm* (*de vestido*) border; (*fig*) addition; **~ar** *vt* to edge, border
ricino [ri'θino] *nm*: **aceite de ~** castor oil
rico, a ['riko, a] *adj* rich; (*adinerado*) wealthy, rich; (*lujoso*) luxurious; (*comida*) delicious; (*niño*) lovely, cute ♦ *nm/f* rich person
rictus ['riktus] *nm* (*mueca*) sneer, grin
ridiculez [riðiku'leθ] *nf* absurdity
ridiculizar [riðikuli'θar] *vt* to ridicule
ridículo, a [ri'ðikulo, a] *adj* ridiculous; **hacer el ~** to make a fool of o.s.; **poner a uno en ~** to make a fool of sb
riego ['rjeɣo] *nm* (*aspersión*) watering; (*irrigación*) irrigation
riel [rjel] *nm* rail
rienda ['rjenda] *nf* rein; **dar ~ suelta a** to give free rein to
riesgo ['rjesɣo] *nm* risk; **correr el ~ de** to run the risk of

rifa ['rifa] *nf* (*lotería*) raffle; **rifar** *vt* to raffle
rifle ['rifle] *nm* rifle
rigidez [rixi'ðeθ] *nf* rigidity, stiffness; (*fig*) strictness; **rígido, a** *adj* rigid, stiff; strict, inflexible
rigor [ri'ɣor] *nm* strictness, rigour; (*inclemencia*) harshness; **de ~** de rigueur, essential; **riguroso, a** *adj* rigorous; harsh; (*severo*) severe
rimar [ri'mar] *vi* to rhyme
rimbombante [rimbom'bante] *adj* pompous
rímel ['rimel] *nm* mascara
rímmel ['rimel] *nm* = **rímel**
rincón [rin'kon] *nm* corner (*inside*)
rinoceronte [rinoθe'ronte] *nm* rhinoceros
riña ['riɲa] *nf* (*disputa*) argument; (*pelea*) brawl
riñón [ri'ɲon] *nm* kidney
río *etc* ['rio] *vb ver* **reir** ♦ *nm* river; (*fig*) torrent, stream; **~ abajo/arriba** downstream/upstream; **~ de la Plata** River Plate
rioja [ri'oxa] *nm* (*vino*) rioja (wine)
rioplatense [riopla'tense] *adj* of o from the River Plate region
riqueza [ri'keθa] *nf* wealth, riches *pl*; (*cualidad*) richness
risa ['risa] *nf* laughter; (*una ~*) laugh; **¡qué ~!** what a laugh!
risco ['risko] *nm* crag, cliff
risible [ri'sißle] *adj* ludicrous, laughable
risotada [riso'taða] *nf* guffaw, loud laugh
ristra ['ristra] *nf* string
risueño, a [ri'sweɲo, a] *adj* (*sonriente*) smiling; (*contento*) cheerful
ritmo ['ritmo] *nm* rhythm; **a ~ lento** slowly; **trabajar a ~ lento** to go slow
rito ['rito] *nm* rite
ritual [ri'twal] *adj*, *nm* ritual
rival [ri'ßal] *adj*, *nm/f* rival; **~idad** *nf* rivalry; **~izar** *vi*: **~izar con** to rival, vie with
rizado, a [ri'θaðo, a] *adj* curly ♦ *nm* curls *pl*
rizar [ri'θar] *vt* to curl; **~se** *vr* (*pelo*) to

curl; (*agua*) to ripple; **rizo** *nm* curl; ripple

RNE *nf abr* = **Radio Nacional de España**

robar [ro'βar] *vt* to rob; (*objeto*) to steal; (*casa etc*) to break into; (*NAIPES*) to draw

roble ['roβle] *nm* oak; **~dal** *nm* oakwood

robo ['roβo] *nm* robbery, theft

robot [ro'βot] *nm* robot; **~ (de cocina)** food processor

robustecer [roβuste'θer] *vt* to strengthen

robusto, a [ro'βusto, a] *adj* robust, strong

roca ['roka] *nf* rock

roce ['roθe] *nm* (*caricia*) brush; (*TEC*) friction; (*en la piel*) graze; **tener ~ con** to be in close contact with

rociar [ro'θjar] *vt* to spray

rocín [ro'θin] *nm* nag, hack

rocío [ro'θio] *nm* dew

rocoso, a [ro'koso, a] *adj* rocky

rodaballo [roða'baʎo] *nm* turbot

rodado, a [ro'ðaðo, a] *adj* (*con ruedas*) wheeled

rodaja [ro'ðaxa] *nf* slice

rodaje [ro'ðaxe] *nm* (*CINE*) shooting, filming; (*AUTO*): **en ~** running in

rodar [ro'ðar] *vt* (*vehículo*) to wheel (along); (*escalera*) to roll down; (*viajar por*) to travel (over) ♦ *vi* to roll; (*coche*) to go, run; (*CINE*) to shoot, film

rodear [roðe'ar] *vt* to go round; **~se** *vr*: **~se de amigos** to surround o.s. with friends

rodeo [ro'ðeo] *nm* (*ruta indirecta*) detour; (*evasión*) evasion; (*AM*) rodeo; **hablar sin ~s** to come to the point, speak plainly

rodilla [ro'ðiʎa] *nf* knee; **de ~s** kneeling; **ponerse de ~s** to kneel (down)

rodillo [ro'ðiʎo] *nm* roller; (*CULIN*) rolling-pin

roedor, a [roe'ðor, a] *adj* gnawing ♦ *nm* rodent

roer [ro'er] *vt* (*masticar*) to gnaw; (*corroer, fig*) to corrode

rogar [ro'ɣar] *vt, vi* (*pedir*) to ask for; (*suplicar*) to beg, plead; **se ruega no fumar** please do not smoke

rojizo, a [ro'xiθo, a] *adj* reddish

rojo, a ['roxo, a] *adj, nm* red; **al ~ vivo** red-hot

rol [rol] *nm* list, roll; (*papel*) role

rollito [ro'ʎito] *nm*: **~ de primavera** spring roll

rollizo, a [ro'ʎiθo, a] *adj* (*objeto*) cylindrical; (*persona*) plump

rollo ['roʎo] *nm* roll; (*de cuerda*) coil; (*madera*) log; (*fam*) bore; **¡qué ~!** what a carry-on!

Roma ['roma] *n* Rome

romance [ro'manθe] *nm* (*amoroso*) romance; (*LITERATURA*) ballad

romano, a [ro'mano, a] *adj, nm/f* Roman; **a la romana** in batter

romanticismo [romanti'θismo] *nm* romanticism

romántico, a [ro'mantiko, a] *adj* romantic

rombo ['rombo] *nm* (*GEOM*) rhombus

romería [rome'ria] *nf* (*REL*) pilgrimage; (*excursión*) trip, outing

---
Romería

🛈 *Originally a pilgrimage to a shrine or church to express devotion to the Virgin Mary or a local Saint, the* **romería** *has also become a rural festival which accompanies the pilgrimage. People come from all over to attend, bringing their own food and drink, and spend the day in celebration.*

---

romero, a [ro'mero, a] *nm/f* pilgrim ♦ *nm* rosemary

romo, a ['romo, a] *adj* blunt; (*fig*) dull

rompecabezas [rompeka'βeθas] *nm inv* riddle, puzzle; (*juego*) jigsaw (puzzle)

rompeolas [rompe'olas] *nm inv* breakwater

romper [rom'per] *vt* to break; (*hacer pedazos*) to smash; (*papel, tela etc*) to tear, rip ♦ *vi* (*olas*) to break; (*sol, diente*) to break through; **~ un contrato** to break a contract; **~ a** (*empezar a*) to start (suddenly) to; **~ a llorar** to burst into tears; **~ con uno** to fall out with sb

ron [ron] *nm* rum

roncar [ron'kar] *vi* to snore

ronco, a ['ronko, a] *adj* (*afónico*) hoarse; (*áspero*) raucous

ronda ['ronda] *nf* (*gen*) round; (*patrulla*) patrol; **rondar** *vt* to patrol ♦ *vi* to patrol; (*fig*) to prowl round

ronquido [ron'kiðo] *nm* snore, snoring

ronronear [ronrone'ar] *vi* to purr; **ronroneo** *nm* purr

roña ['roɲa] *nf* (*VETERINARIA*) mange; (*mugre*) dirt, grime; (*óxido*) rust

roñoso, a [ro'ɲoso, a] *adj* (*mugriento*) filthy; (*tacaño*) mean

ropa ['ropa] *nf* clothes *pl*, clothing; **~ blanca** linen; **~ de cama** bed linen; **~ interior** underwear; **~ para lavar** washing; **~je** *nm* gown, robes *pl*

ropero [ro'pero] *nm* linen cupboard; (*guardarropa*) wardrobe

rosa ['rosa] *adj* pink ♦ *nf* rose; **~ de los vientos** the compass

rosado, a [ro'saðo, a] *adj* pink ♦ *nm* rosé

rosal [ro'sal] *nm* rosebush

rosario [ro'sarjo] *nm* (*REL*) rosary; **rezar el ~** to say the rosary

rosca ['roska] *nf* (*de tornillo*) thread; (*de humo*) coil, spiral; (*pan, postre*) ring-shaped roll/pastry

rosetón [rose'ton] *nm* rosette; (*ARQ*) rose window

rosquilla [ros'kiʎa] *nf* doughnut-shaped fritter

rostro ['rostro] *nm* (*cara*) face

rotación [rota'θjon] *nf* rotation; **~ de cultivos** crop rotation

rotativo, a [rota'tiβo, a] *adj* rotary

roto, a ['roto, a] *pp de* **romper** ♦ *adj* broken

rotonda [ro'tonda] *nf* roundabout

rótula ['rotula] *nf* kneecap; (*TEC*) ball-and-socket joint

rotulador [rotula'ðor] *nm* felt-tip pen

rotular [rotu'lar] *vt* (*carta, documento*) to head, entitle; (*objeto*) to label; **rótulo** *nm* heading, title; label; (*letrero*) sign

rotundamente [rotunda'mente] *adv* (*negar*) flatly; (*responder, afirmar*) emphatically; **rotundo, a** *adj* round;

(*enfático*) emphatic

rotura [ro'tura] *nf* (*acto*) breaking; (*MED*) fracture

roturar [rotu'rar] *vt* to plough

rozadura [roθa'ðura] *nf* abrasion, graze

rozar [ro'θar] *vt* (*frotar*) to rub; (*arañar*) to scratch; (*tocar ligeramente*) to shave, touch lightly; **~se** *vr* to rub (together); **~se con** (*fam*) to rub shoulders with

rte. *abr* (= *remite, remitente*) sender

RTVE *nf abr* = **Radiotelevisión Española**

rubí [ru'βi] *nm* ruby; (*de reloj*) jewel

rubio, a ['ruβjo, a] *adj* fair-haired, blond(e) ♦ *nm/f* blond/blonde; **tabaco ~** Virginia tobacco

rubor [ru'βor] *nm* (*sonrojo*) blush; (*timidez*) bashfulness; **~izarse** *vr* to blush

rúbrica [ru'βrika] *nf* (*de la firma*) flourish; **rubricar** *vt* (*firmar*) to sign with a flourish; (*concluir*) to sign and seal

rudimentario, a [ruðimen'tarjo, a] *adj* rudimentary; **rudimento** *nm* rudiment

rudo, a ['ruðo, a] *adj* (*sin pulir*) unpolished; (*grosero*) coarse; (*violento*) violent; (*sencillo*) simple

rueda ['rweða] *nf* wheel; (*círculo*) ring, circle; (*rodaja*) slice, round; **~ delantera/trasera/de repuesto** front/back/spare wheel; **~ de prensa** press conference

ruedo ['rweðo] *nm* (*círculo*) circle; (*TAUR*) arena, bullring

ruego *etc* ['rweɣo] *vb ver* **rogar** ♦ *nm* request

rufián [ru'fjan] *nm* scoundrel

rugby ['ruɣβi] *nm* rugby

rugido [ru'xiðo] *nm* roar

rugir [ru'xir] *vi* to roar

rugoso, a [ru'ɣoso, a] *adj* (*arrugado*) wrinkled; (*áspero*) rough; (*desigual*) ridged

ruido ['rwiðo] *nm* noise; (*sonido*) sound; (*alboroto*) racket, row; (*escándalo*) commotion, rumpus; **~so, a** *adj* noisy, loud; (*fig*) sensational

ruin [rwin] *adj* contemptible, mean

ruina ['rwina] *nf* ruin; (*colapso*) collapse; (*de persona*) ruin, downfall

ruindad [rwin'dað] *nf* lowness, meanness;

(acto) low *o* mean act
ruinoso, a [rwi'noso, a] *adj* ruinous;
(destartalado) dilapidated, tumbledown;
(COM) disastrous
ruiseñor [rwise'ɲor] *nm* nightingale
ruleta [ru'leta] *nf* roulette
rulo ['rulo] *nm (para el pelo)* curler
Rumanía [ruma'nia] *nf* Rumania
rumba ['rumba] *nf* rumba
rumbo ['rumbo] *nm (ruta)* route, direction;
(ángulo de dirección) course, bearing; *(fig)*
course of events; **ir con ~ a** to be
heading for
rumboso, a [rum'boso, a] *adj* generous
rumiante [ru'mjante] *nm* ruminant
rumiar [ru'mjar] *vt* to chew; *(fig)* to chew
over ♦ *vi* to chew the cud
rumor [ru'mor] *nm (ruido sordo)* low
sound; *(murmuración)* murmur, buzz
rumorearse [rumore'arse] *vr:* **se rumorea
que** it is rumoured that
runrún [run'run] *nm (voces)* murmur,
sound of voices; *(fig)* rumour
rupestre [ru'pestre] *adj* rock *cpd*
ruptura [rup'tura] *nf* rupture
rural [ru'ral] *adj* rural
Rusia ['rusja] *nf* Russia; **ruso, a** *adj, nm/f*
Russian
rústica ['rustika] *nf:* **libro en ~** paperback
(book); *ver tb* **rústico**
rústico, a ['rustiko, a] *adj* rustic;
(ordinario) coarse, uncouth ♦ *nm/f* yokel
ruta ['ruta] *nf* route
rutina [ru'tina] *nf* routine; **~rio, a** *adj*
routine

S, s

S *abr (= santo, a)* St; *(= sur)* S
s. *abr (= siglo)* C.; *(= siguiente)* foll
S.A. *abr (= Sociedad Anónima)* Ltd. *(BRIT)*,
Inc. *(US)*
sábado ['saβaðo] *nm* Saturday
sábana ['saβana] *nf* sheet
sabandija [saβan'dixa] *nf* bug, insect
sabañón [saβa'ɲon] *nm* chilblain

saber [sa'ßer] *vt* to know; *(llegar a
conocer)* to find out, learn; *(tener
capacidad de)* to know how to ♦ *vi:* **~ a**
to taste of, taste like ♦ *nm* knowledge,
learning; **a ~** namely; **¿sabes conducir/
nadar?** can you drive/swim?; **¿sabes
francés?** do you speak French?; **~ de
memoria** to know by heart; **hacer ~ algo
a uno** to inform sb of sth, let sb know sth
sabiduría [saßiðu'ria] *nf (conocimientos)*
wisdom; *(instrucción)* learning
sabiendas [sa'ßjendas]: **a ~** *adv*
knowingly
sabio, a ['saßjo,a] *adj (docto)* learned;
(prudente) wise, sensible
sabor [sa'ßor] *nm* taste, flavour; **~ear** *vt*
to taste, savour; *(fig)* to relish
sabotaje [saßo'taxe] *nm* sabotage
saboteador, a [saßotea'ðor, a] *nm/f*
saboteur
sabotear [saßote'ar] *vt* to sabotage
sabré *etc vb ver* **saber**
sabroso, a [sa'ßroso, a] *adj* tasty; *(fig:
fam)* racy, salty
sacacorchos [saka'kortʃos] *nm inv*
corkscrew
sacapuntas [saka'puntas] *nm inv* pencil
sharpener
sacar [sa'kar] *vt* to take out; *(fig: extraer)*
to get (out); *(quitar)* to remove, get out;
(hacer salir) to bring out; *(conclusión)* to
draw; *(novela etc)* to publish, bring out;
(ropa) to take off; *(obra)* to make;
(premio) to receive; *(entradas)* to get;
(TENIS) to serve; **~ adelante** *(niño)* to
bring up; *(negocio)* to carry on, go on
with; **~ a uno a bailar** to get sb up to
dance; **~ una foto** to take a photo; **~ la
lengua** to stick out one's tongue; **~
buenas/malas notas** to get good/bad
marks
sacarina [saka'rina] *nf* saccharin(e)
sacerdote [saθer'ðote] *nm* priest
saciar [sa'θjar] *vt (hambre, sed)* to satisfy;
~se *vr (de comida)* to get full up; **comer
hasta ~se** to eat one's fill
saco ['sako] *nm* bag; *(grande)* sack; *(su*

contenido) bagful; (*AM*) jacket; **~ de dormir** sleeping bag

sacramento [sakra'mento] *nm* sacrament

sacrificar [sakrifi'kar] *vt* to sacrifice; **sacrificio** *nm* sacrifice

sacrilegio [sakri'lexjo] *nm* sacrilege; **sacrílego, a** *adj* sacrilegious

sacristía [sakris'tia] *nf* sacristy

sacro, a ['sakro, a] *adj* sacred

sacudida [saku'ðiða] *nf* (*agitación*) shake, shaking; (*sacudimiento*) jolt, bump; **~ eléctrica** electric shock

sacudir [saku'ðir] *vt* to shake; (*golpear*) to hit

sádico, a ['saðiko, a] *adj* sadistic ♦ *nm/f* sadist; **sadismo** *nm* sadism

saeta [sa'eta] *nf* (*flecha*) arrow

sagacidad [saxaθi'ðað] *nf* shrewdness, cleverness; **sagaz** *adj* shrewd, clever

sagitario [saxi'tarjo] *nm* Sagittarius

sagrado, a [sa'vraðo, a] *adj* sacred, holy

Sáhara ['saara] *nm*: **el ~** the Sahara (desert)

sal [sal] *vb ver* **salir** ♦ *nf* salt

sala ['sala] *nf* room; (*~ de estar*) living room; (*TEATRO*) house, auditorium; (*de hospital*) ward; **~ de apelación** court; **~ de espera** waiting room; **~ de estar** living room; **~ de fiestas** dance hall

salado, a [sa'laðo, a] *adj* salty; (*fig*) witty, amusing; **agua salada** salt water

salar [sa'lar] *vt* to salt, add salt to

salarial [sala'rjal] *adj* (*aumento, revisión*) wage *cpd*, salary *cpd*

salario [sa'larjo] *nm* wage, pay

salchicha [sal'tʃitʃa] *nf* (pork) sausage; **salchichón** *nm* (salami-type) sausage

saldar [sal'dar] *vt* to pay; (*vender*) to sell off; (*fig*) to settle, resolve; **saldo** *nm* (*pago*) settlement; (*de una cuenta*) balance; (*lo restante*) remnant(s) (*pl*), remainder; **saldos** *nmpl* (*en tienda*) sale

saldré *etc vb ver* **salir**

salero [sa'lero] *nm* salt cellar

salgo *etc vb ver* **salir**

salida [sa'liða] *nf* (*puerta etc*) exit, way out; (*acto*) leaving, going out; (*de tren*,

AVIAT) departure; (*TEC*) output, production; (*fig*) way out; (*COM*) opening; (*GEO, válvula*) outlet; (*de gas*) leak; **calle sin ~** cul-de-sac; **~ de incendios** fire escape

saliente [sa'ljente] *adj* (*ARQ*) projecting; (*sol*) rising; (*fig*) outstanding

---

PALABRA CLAVE

---

salir [sa'lir] *vi* 1 (*partir: tb*: **~ de**) to leave; **Juan ha salido** Juan is out; **salió de la cocina** he came out of the kitchen

2 (*aparecer*) to appear; (*disco, libro*) to come out; **anoche salió en la tele** she appeared *o* was on TV last night; **salió en todos los periódicos** it was in all the papers

3 (*resultar*): **la muchacha nos salió muy trabajadora** the girl turned out to be a very hard worker; **la comida te ha salido exquisita** the food was delicious; **sale muy caro** it's very expensive

4: **~le a uno algo: la entrevista que hice me salió bien/mal** the interview I did went *o* turned out well/badly

5: **~ adelante: no sé como haré para ~ adelante** I don't know how I'll get by

♦ **~se** *vr* (*líquido*) to spill; (*animal*) to escape

---

saliva [sa'liβa] *nf* saliva

salmo ['salmo] *nm* psalm

salmón [sal'mon] *nm* salmon

salmonete [salmo'nete] *nm* red mullet

salmuera [sal'mwera] *nf* pickle, brine

salón [sa'lon] *nm* (*de casa*) living room, lounge; (*muebles*) lounge suite; **~ de belleza** beauty parlour; **~ de baile** dance hall

salpicadero [salpika'ðero] *nm* (*AUTO*) dashboard

salpicar [salpi'kar] *vt* (*rociar*) to sprinkle, spatter; (*esparcir*) to scatter

salpicón [salpi'kon] *nm*: **~ de mariscos** seafood salad

salsa ['salsa] *nf* sauce; (*con carne asada*) gravy; (*fig*) spice

saltamontes [salta'montes] *nm inv* grasshopper

saltar [sal'tar] *vt* to jump (over), leap (over); (*dejar de lado*) to skip, miss out ♦ *vi* to jump, leap; (*pelota*) to bounce; (*al aire*) to fly up; (*quebrarse*) to break; (*al agua*) to dive; (*fig*) to explode, blow up

salto ['salto] *nm* jump, leap; (*al agua*) dive; **~ de agua** waterfall; **~ de altura** high jump

saltón, ona [sal'ton, ona] *adj* (*ojos*) bulging, popping; (*dientes*) protruding

salud [sa'luð] *nf* health; **¡(a su) ~!** cheers!, good health!; **~able** *adj* (*de buena ~*) healthy; (*provechoso*) good, beneficial

saludar [salu'ðar] *vt* to greet; (*MIL*) to salute; **saludo** *nm* greeting; **"saludos"** (*en carta*) "best wishes", "regards"

salva ['salßa] *nf*: **~ de aplausos** ovation

salvación [salßa'θjon] *nf* salvation; (*rescate*) rescue

salvado [sal'ßaðo] *nm* bran

salvaguardar [salßaɣwar'ðar] *vt* to safeguard

salvajada [salßa'xaða] *nf* atrocity

salvaje [sal'ßaxe] *adj* wild; (*tribu*) savage; **salvajismo** *nm* savagery

salvamento [salßa'mento] *nm* rescue

salvar [sal'ßar] *vt* (*rescatar*) to save, rescue; (*resolver*) to overcome, resolve; (*cubrir distancias*) to cover, travel; (*hacer excepción*) to except, exclude; (*barco*) to salvage

salvavidas [salßa'ßiðas] *adj inv*: **bote/ chaleco/cinturón ~** lifeboat/life jacket/life belt

salvo, a ['salßo, a] *adj* safe ♦ *adv* except (for), save; **a ~** out of danger; **~ que** unless; **~conducto** *nm* safe-conduct

san [san] *adj* saint; **S~ Juan** St John

sanar [sa'nar] *vt* (*herida*) to heal; (*persona*) to cure ♦ *vi* (*persona*) to get well, recover; (*herida*) to heal

sanatorio [sana'torjo] *nm* sanatorium

sanción [san'θjon] *nf* sanction; **sancionar** *vt* to sanction

sandalia [san'dalja] *nf* sandal

sandez [san'deθ] *nf* foolishness

sandía [san'dia] *nf* watermelon

sandwich ['sandwitʃ] (*pl* **~s, ~es**) *nm* sandwich

saneamiento [sanea'mjento] *nm* sanitation

sanear [sane'ar] *vt* to clean up; (*terreno*) to drain

┌─────────────────┐
│ **Sanfermines** │
└─────────────────┘

The **Sanfermines** *is a week-long festival in Pamplona made famous by Ernest Hemingway. From the 7th July, the feast of "San Fermín", crowds of mainly young people take to the streets drinking, singing and dancing. Early in the morning bulls are released along the narrow streets leading to the bullring, and young men risk serious injury to show their bravery by running out in front of them, a custom which is also typical of many Spanish villages.*

sangrar [san'grar] *vt, vi* to bleed; **sangre** *nf* blood

sangría [san'gria] *nf* sangria, *sweetened drink of red wine with fruit*

sangriento, a [san'grjento, a] *adj* bloody

sanguijuela [sangi'xwela] *nf* (*ZOOL, fig*) leech

sanguinario, a [sangi'narjo, a] *adj* bloodthirsty

sanguíneo, a [san'gineo, a] *adj* blood *cpd*

sanidad [sani'ðað] *nf*: **~ (pública)** public health

┌─────────────────┐
│ **San Isidro** │
└─────────────────┘

San Isidro *is the patron saint of Madrid, and gives his name to the week-long festivities which take place around the 15th May. Originally an 18th-century trade fair, the* **San Isidro** *celebrations now include music, dance, a famous* **romería**, *theatre and bullfighting.*

sanitario, a [sani'tarjo, a] *adj* health *cpd*; **~s** *nmpl* toilets (*BRIT*), washroom (*US*)

sano, a ['sano, a] *adj* healthy; (*sin daños*)
sound; (*comida*) wholesome; (*entero*)
whole, intact; **~ y salvo** safe and sound

Santiago [san'tjaɣo] *nm*: **~ (de Chile)**
Santiago

santiamén [santja'men] *nm*: **en un ~** in
no time at all

santidad [santi'ðað] *nf* holiness, sanctity

santiguarse [santi'ɣwarse] *vr* to make the
sign of the cross

santo, a ['santo, a] *adj* holy; (*fig*)
wonderful, miraculous ♦ *nm/f* saint ♦ *nm*
saint's day; **~ y seña** password

santuario [san'twarjo] *nm* sanctuary,
shrine

saña ['sana] *nf* rage, fury

sapo ['sapo] *nm* toad

saque ['sake] *nm* (*TENIS*) service, serve;
(*FÚTBOL*) throw-in; **~ de esquina** corner
(kick)

saquear [sake'ar] *vt* (*MIL*) to sack; (*robar*)
to loot, plunder; (*fig*) to ransack; **saqueo**
nm sacking; looting, plundering;
ransacking

sarampión [saram'pjon] *nm* measles *sg*

sarcasmo [sar'kasmo] *nm* sarcasm;
sarcástico, a *adj* sarcastic

sardina [sar'ðina] *nf* sardine

sargento [sar'xento] *nm* sergeant

sarmiento [sar'mjento] *nm* (*BOT*) vine
shoot

sarna ['sarna] *nf* itch; (*MED*) scabies

sarpullido [sarpu'ʎiðo] *nm* (*MED*) rash

sarro ['sarro] *nm* (*en dientes*) tartar, plaque

sartén [sar'ten] *nf* frying pan

sastre ['sastre] *nm* tailor; **~ría** *nf* (*arte*)
tailoring; (*tienda*) tailor's (shop)

Satanás [sata'nas] *nm* Satan

satélite [sa'telite] *nm* satellite

sátira ['satira] *nf* satire

satisfacción [satisfak'θjon] *nf* satisfaction

satisfacer [satisfa'θer] *vt* to satisfy;
(*gastos*) to meet; (*pérdida*) to make good;
~se *vr* to satisfy o.s., to be satisfied;
(*vengarse*) to take revenge; **satisfecho,
a** *adj* satisfied; (*contento*) content(ed),
happy; (*tb:* **satisfecho de sí mismo**)

self-satisfied, smug

saturar [satu'rar] *vt* to saturate; **~se** *vr*
(*mercado, aeropuerto*) to reach saturation
point

sauce ['sauθe] *nm* willow; **~ llorón**
weeping willow

sauna ['sauna] *nf* sauna

savia ['saßja] *nf* sap

saxofón [sakso'fon] *nm* saxophone

sazonar [saθo'nar] *vt* to ripen; (*CULIN*) to
flavour, season

SE *abr* (= *sudeste*) SE

PALABRA CLAVE

se [se] *pron* **1** (*reflexivo: sg: m*) himself; (*: f*)
herself; (*: pl*) themselves; (*: cosa*) itself;
(*: de Vd*) yourself; (*: de Vds*) yourselves; **~
está preparando** she's preparing herself;
*para usos léxicos del pron ver el vb en
cuestión, p.ej.* **arrepentirse**

2 (*con complemento indirecto*) to him; to
her; to them; to it; to you; **a usted ~ lo
dije ayer** I told you yesterday; **~ compró
un sombrero** he bought himself a hat; **~
rompió la pierna** he broke his leg

3 (*uso recíproco*) each other, one another;
~ miraron (el uno al otro) they looked at
each other *o* one another

4 (*en oraciones pasivas*): **se han vendido
muchos libros** a lot of books have been
sold

5 (*impers*): **~ dice que** people say that, it
is said that; **allí ~ come muy bien** the
food there is very good, you can eat very
well there

---

sé *vb ver* **saber; ser**

sea *etc vb ver* **ser**

sebo ['seßo] *nm* fat, grease

secador [seka'ðor] *nm*: **~ de pelo** hair-
dryer

secadora [seka'ðora] *nf* tumble dryer

secar [se'kar] *vt* to dry; **~se** *vr* to dry (off);
(*río, planta*) to dry up

sección [sek'θjon] *nf* section

seco, a ['seko, a] *adj* dry; (*carácter*) cold;
(*respuesta*) sharp, curt; **habrá pan a**

secas there will be just bread; **decir algo a secas** to say sth curtly; **parar en ~** to stop dead

secretaría [sekreta'ria] *nf* secretariat

secretario, a [sekre'tarjo, a] *nm/f* secretary

secreto, a [se'kreto, a] *adj* secret; (*persona*) secretive ♦ *nm* secret; (*calidad*) secrecy

secta ['sekta] *nf* sect; **~rio, a** *adj* sectarian

sector [sek'tor] *nm* sector

secuela [se'kwela] *nf* consequence

secuencia [se'kwenθja] *nf* sequence

secuestrar [sekwes'trar] *vt* to kidnap; (*bienes*) to seize, confiscate; **secuestro** *nm* kidnapping; seizure, confiscation

secular [seku'lar] *adj* secular

secundar [sekun'dar] *vt* to second, support

secundario, a [sekun'darjo, a] *adj* secondary

sed [seð] *nf* thirst; **tener ~** to be thirsty

seda ['seða] *nf* silk

sedal [se'ðal] *nm* fishing line

sedante [se'ðante] *nm* sedative

sede ['seðe] *nf* (*de gobierno*) seat; (*de compañía*) headquarters *pl*; **Santa S~** Holy See

sedentario, a [seðen'tarjo, a] *adj* sedentary

sediento, a [se'ðjento, a] *adj* thirsty

sedimento [seði'mento] *nm* sediment

sedoso, a [se'ðoso, a] *adj* silky, silken

seducción [seðuk'θjon] *nf* seduction

seducir [seðu'θir] *vt* to seduce; (*cautivar*) to charm, fascinate; (*atraer*) to attract; **seductor, a** *adj* seductive, charming, fascinating; attractive ♦ *nm/f* seducer

segar [se'var] *vt* (*mies*) to reap, cut; (*hierba*) to mow, cut

seglar [se'vlar] *adj* secular, lay

segregación [sevreva'θjon] *nf* segregation. **~ racial** racial segregation

segregar [sevre'var] *vt* to segregate, separate

seguida [se'viða] *nf*: **en ~** at once, right away

seguido, a [se'viðo, a] *adj* (*continuo*) continuous, unbroken; (*recto*) straight ♦ *adv* (*directo*) straight (on); (*después*) after; (*AM: a menudo*) often; **~s** consecutive, successive; **5 días ~s** 5 days running, 5 days in a row

seguimiento [sevi'mjento] *nm* chase, pursuit; (*continuación*) continuation

seguir [se'vir] *vt* to follow; (*venir después*) to follow on, come after; (*proseguir*) to continue; (*perseguir*) to chase, pursue ♦ *vi* (*gen*) to follow; (*continuar*) to continue, carry *o* go on; **~se** *vr* to follow; **sigo sin comprender** I still don't understand; **sigue lloviendo** it's still raining

según [se'vun] *prep* according to ♦ *adv*: **¿irás? – ~** are you going? — it all depends ♦ *conj* as; **~ caminamos** while we walk

segundo, a [se'vundo, a] *adj* second ♦ *nm* second ♦ *nf* second meaning; **de segunda mano** second-hand; **segunda (clase)** second class; **segunda enseñanza** secondary education; **segunda (marcha)** (*AUT*) second (gear)

seguramente [sevura'mente] *adv* surely; (*con certeza*) for sure, with certainty

seguridad [sevuri'ðað] *nf* safety; (*del estado, de casa etc*) security; (*certidumbre*) certainty; (*confianza*) confidence; (*estabilidad*) stability; **~ social** social security

seguro, a [se'vuro, a] *adj* (*cierto*) sure, certain; (*fiel*) trustworthy; (*libre de peligro*) safe; (*bien defendido, firme*) secure ♦ *adv* for sure, certainly ♦ *nm* (*COM*) insurance; **~ contra terceros/a todo riesgo** third party/comprehensive insurance; **~s sociales** social security *sg*

seis [seis] *num* six

seísmo [se'ismo] *nm* tremor, earthquake

selección [selek'θjon] *nf* selection; **seleccionar** *vt* to pick, choose, select

selectividad [selektiβi'ðað] (*ESP*) *nf* university entrance examination

selecto, a [se'lekto, a] *adj* select, choice; (*escogido*) selected

sellar [se'ʎar] vt (*documento oficial*) to seal; (*pasaporte, visado*) to stamp

sello ['seʎo] nm stamp; (*precinto*) seal

selva ['selβa] nf (*bosque*) forest, woods pl; (*jungla*) jungle

semáforo [se'maforo] nm (*AUTO*) traffic lights pl; (*FERRO*) signal

semana [se'mana] nf week; **entre ~** during the week; **S~ Santa** Holy Week; **semanal** adj weekly; **~rio** nm weekly magazine

---
Semana Santa

ⓘ *In Spain celebrations for* **Semana Santa** *(Holy Week) are often spectacular. "Viernes Santo", "Sábado Santo" and "Domingo de Resurrección" (Good Friday, Holy Saturday, Easter Sunday) are all national public holidays, with additional days being given as local holidays. There are fabulous* **procesiones** *all over the country, with members of "cofradías" (brotherhoods) dressing in hooded robes and parading their "pasos" (religious floats and sculptures) through the streets. Seville has the most famous Holy Week processions.*

---

semblante [sem'blante] nm face; (*fig*) look

sembrar [sem'brar] vt to sow; (*objetos*) to sprinkle, scatter about; (*noticias etc*) to spread

semejante [seme'xante] adj (*parecido*) similar ♦ nm fellow man, fellow creature; **~s** alike, similar; **nunca hizo cosa ~** he never did any such thing; **semejanza** nf similarity, resemblance

semejar [seme'xar] vi to seem like, resemble; **~se** vr to look alike, be similar

semen ['semen] nm semen

semestral [semes'tral] adj half-yearly, bi-annual

semicírculo [semi'θirkulo] nm semicircle

semidesnatado, a [semiðesna'taðo, a] adj semi-skimmed

semifinal [semifi'nal] nf semifinal

semilla [se'miʎa] nf seed

seminario [semi'narjo] nm (*REL*) seminary; (*ESCOL*) seminar

sémola ['semola] nf semolina

Sena ['sena] nm: **el ~** the (river) Seine

senado [se'naðo] nm senate; **senador, a** nm/f senator

sencillez [senθi'ʎeθ] nf simplicity; (*de persona*) naturalness; **sencillo, a** adj simple; natural, unaffected

senda ['senda] nf path, track

senderismo [sende'rismo] nm hiking

sendero [sen'dero] nm path, track

sendos, as ['sendos, as] adj pl: **les dio ~ golpes** he hit both of them

senil [se'nil] adj senile

seno ['seno] nm (*ANAT*) bosom, bust; (*fig*) bosom; **~s** breasts

sensación [sensa'θjon] nf sensation; (*sentido*) sense; (*sentimiento*) feeling; **sensacional** adj sensational

sensato, a [sen'sato, a] adj sensible

sensible [sen'sible] adj sensitive; (*apreciable*) perceptible, appreciable; (*pérdida*) considerable; **~ro, a** adj sentimental

sensitivo, a [sensi'tiβo, a] adj sense cpd

sensorial [senso'rjal] adj sensory

sensual [sen'swal] adj sensual

sentada [sen'taða] nf sitting; (*protesta*) sit-in

sentado, a [sen'taðo, a] adj: **estar ~** to sit, be sitting (down); **dar por ~** to take for granted, assume

sentar [sen'tar] vt to sit, seat; (*fig*) to establish ♦ vi (*vestido*) to suit; (*alimento*): **~ bien/mal a** to agree/disagree with; **~se** vr (*persona*) to sit, sit down; (*los depósitos*) to settle

sentencia [sen'tenθja] nf (*máxima*) maxim, saying; (*JUR*) sentence; **sentenciar** vt to sentence

sentido, a [sen'tiðo, a] adj (*pérdida*) regrettable; (*carácter*) sensitive ♦ nm sense; (*sentimiento*) feeling; (*significado*) sense, meaning; (*dirección*) direction; **mi más ~ pésame** my deepest sympathy; **~**

del humor sense of humour; **~ único** one-way (street); **tener ~** to make sense

sentimental [sentimen'tal] *adj* sentimental; **vida ~** love life

sentimiento [senti'mjento] *nm* feeling

sentir [sen'tir] *vt* to feel; (*percibir*) to perceive, sense; (*lamentar*) to regret, be sorry for ♦ *vi* (*tener la sensación*) to feel; (*lamentarse*) to feel sorry ♦ *nm* opinion, judgement; **~se bien/mal** to feel well/ill; **lo siento** I'm sorry

seña ['sena] *nf* sign; (*MIL*) password; **~s** *nfpl* (*dirección*) address *sg*; **~s personales** personal description *sg*

señal [se'nal] *nf* sign; (*síntoma*) symptom; (*FERRO, TELEC*) signal; (*marca*) mark; (*COM*) deposit; **en ~ de** as a token of, as a sign of; **~ar** *vt* to mark; (*indicar*) to point out, indicate

señor [se'nor] *nm* (*hombre*) man; (*caballero*) gentleman; (*dueño*) owner, master; (*trato: antes de nombre propio*) Mr; (: *hablando directamente*) sir; **muy ~ mío** Dear Sir; **el ~ alcalde/presidente** the mayor/president

señora [se'nora] *nf* (*dama*) lady; (*trato: antes de nombre propio*) Mrs; (: *hablando directamente*) madam; (*esposa*) wife; **Nuestra S~** Our Lady

señorita [seno'rita] *nf* (*con nombre y/o apellido*) Miss; (*mujer joven*) young lady

señorito [seno'rito] *nm* young gentleman; (*pey*) rich kid

señuelo [se'nwelo] *nm* decoy

sepa *etc vb ver* **saber**

separación [separa'θjon] *nf* separation; (*división*) division; (*hueco*) gap

separar [sepa'rar] *vt* to separate; (*dividir*) to divide; **~se** *vr* (*parte*) to come away; (*partes*) to come apart; (*persona*) to leave, go away; (*matrimonio*) to separate; **separatismo** *nm* separatism

sepia ['sepja] *nf* cuttlefish

septentrional [septentrjo'nal] *adj* northern

septiembre [sep'tjembre] *nm* September

séptimo, a ['septimo, a] *adj, nm* seventh

sepulcral [sepul'kral] *adj* (*fig: silencio, atmósfera*) deadly; **sepulcro** *nm* tomb, grave

sepultar [sepul'tar] *vt* to bury; **sepultura** *nf* (*acto*) burial; (*tumba*) grave, tomb

sequedad [seke'ðað] *nf* dryness; (*fig*) brusqueness, curtness

sequía [se'kia] *nf* drought

séquito ['sekito] *nm* (*de rey etc*) retinue; (*seguidores*) followers *pl*

PALABRA CLAVE

ser [ser] *vi* **1** (*descripción*) to be; **es médica/muy alta** she's a doctor/very tall; **la familia es de Cuzco** his (*o her etc*) family is from Cuzco; **soy Ana** (*TELEC*) Ana speaking *o* here

2 (*propiedad*): **es de Joaquín** it's Joaquín's, it belongs to Joaquín

3 (*horas, fechas, números*): **es la una** it's one o'clock; **son las seis y media** it's half-past six; **es el 1 de junio** it's the first of June; **somos/son seis** there are six of us/them

4 (*en oraciones pasivas*): **ha sido descubierto ya** it's already been discovered

5: **es de esperar que ...** it is to be hoped *o* I *etc* hope that ...

6 (*locuciones con sub*): **o sea** that is to say; **sea él sea su hermana** either him or his sister

7: **a no ~ por él ...** but for him ...

8: **a no ~ que: a no ~ que tenga uno ya** unless he's got one already

♦ *nm* being; **~ humano** human being

---

serenarse [sere'narse] *vr* to calm down

sereno, a [se'reno, a] *adj* (*persona*) calm, unruffled; (*el tiempo*) fine, settled; (*ambiente*) calm, peaceful ♦ *nm* night watchman

serial [ser'jal] *nm* serial

serie ['serje] *nf* series; (*cadena*) sequence, succession; **fuera de ~** out of order; (*fig*) special, out of the ordinary; **fabricación en ~** mass production

seriedad [serje'ðað] *nf* seriousness; (*formalidad*) reliability; **serio, a** *adj* serious; reliable, dependable, grave, serious; **en serio** *adv* seriously

serigrafía [seriɣra'fia] *nf* silk-screen printing

sermón [ser'mon] *nm* (REL) sermon

seropositivo, a [seroposi'tiβo, a] *adj* HIV positive

serpentear [serpente'ar] *vi* to wriggle; (*camino, río*) to wind, snake

serpentina [serpen'tina] *nf* streamer

serpiente [ser'pjente] *nf* snake; **~ de cascabel** rattlesnake

serranía [serra'nia] *nf* mountainous area

serrar [se'rrar] *vt* = **aserrar**

serrín [se'rrin] *nm* = **aserrín**

serrucho [se'rrutʃo] *nm* saw

servicio [ser'βiθjo] *nm* service; **~s** *nmpl* toilet(s); **~ incluido** service charge included; **~ militar** military service

servidumbre [serβi'ðumbre] *nf* (*sujeción*) servitude; (*criados*) servants *pl*, staff

servil [ser'βil] *adj* servile

servilleta [serβi'ʎeta] *nf* serviette, napkin

servir [ser'βir] *vt* to serve ♦ *vi* to serve; (*tener utilidad*) to be of use, be useful; **~se** *vr* to serve o help o.s.; **~se de algo** to make use of sth, use sth; **sírvase pasar** please come in

sesenta [se'senta] *num* sixty

sesgo [ˈsesɣo] *nm* slant; (*fig*) slant, twist

sesión [se'sjon] *nf* (POL) session, sitting; (*CINE*) showing

seso [ˈseso] *nm* brain; **sesudo, a** *adj* sensible, wise

seta [ˈseta] *nf* mushroom; **~ venenosa** toadstool

setecientos, as [sete'θjentos, as] *adj, num* seven hundred

setenta [se'tenta] *num* seventy

seto [ˈseto] *nm* hedge

seudónimo [seu'ðonimo] *nm* pseudonym

severidad [seβeri'ðað] *nf* severity; **severo, a** *adj* severe

Sevilla [se'βiʎa] *n* Seville; **sevillano, a** *adj* of o from Seville ♦ *nm/f* native o

inhabitant of Seville

sexo [ˈsekso] *nm* sex

sexto, a [ˈseksto, a] *adj, nm* sixth

sexual [sek'swal] *adj* sexual; **vida ~** sex life

si [si] *conj* if; **me pregunto ~ ...** I wonder if o whether ...

sí [si] *adv* yes ♦ *nm* consent ♦ *pron* (*uso impersonal*) oneself; (*sg: m*) himself; (: *f*) herself; (: *de cosa*) itself; (*de usted*) yourself; (*pl*) themselves; (*de ustedes*) yourselves; (*recíproco*) each other; **él no quiere pero yo ~** he doesn't want to but I do; **ella ~ vendrá** she will certainly come, she is sure to come; **claro que ~** of course; **creo que ~** I think so

siamés, esa [sja'mes, esa] *adj, nm/f* Siamese

SIDA [ˈsiða] *nm abr* (= *Síndrome de Inmunodeficiencia Adquirida*) AIDS

siderúrgico, a [siðe'rurxico, a] *adj* iron and steel *cpd*

sidra [ˈsiðra] *nf* cider

siembra [ˈsjembra] *nf* sowing

siempre [ˈsjempre] *adv* always; (*todo el tiempo*) all the time; **~ que** (*cada vez*) whenever; (*dado que*) provided that; **como ~** as usual; **para ~** for ever

sien [sjen] *nf* temple

siento *etc vb ver* **sentar; sentir**

sierra [ˈsjerra] *nf* (TEC) saw; (*cadena de montañas*) mountain range

siervo, a [ˈsjerβo, a] *nm/f* slave

siesta [ˈsjesta] *nf* siesta, nap; **echar la ~** to have an afternoon nap o a siesta

siete [ˈsjete] *num* seven

sífilis [ˈsifilis] *nf* syphilis

sifón [si'fon] *nm* syphon; **whisky con ~** whisky and soda

sigla [ˈsiɣla] *nf* abbreviation; acronym

siglo [ˈsiɣlo] *nm* century; (*fig*) age

significación [siɣnifika'θjon] *nf* significance

significado [siɣnifi'kaðo] *nm* (*de palabra etc*) meaning

significar [siɣnifi'kar] *vt* to mean, signify; (*notificar*) to make known, express; **significativo, a** *adj* significant

signo ['siɣno] *nm* sign; **~ de admiración** *o* **exclamación** exclamation mark; **~ de interrogación** question mark

sigo *etc vb ver* **seguir**

siguiente [si'ɣjente] *adj* next, following

siguió *etc vb ver* **seguir**

sílaba ['silaβa] *nf* syllable

silbar [sil'βar] *vt, vi* to whistle; **silbato** *nm* whistle; **silbido** *nm* whistle, whistling

silenciador [silenθja'ðor] *nm* silencer

silenciar [silen'θjar] *vt* (*persona*) to silence; (*escándalo*) to hush up; **silencio** *nm* silence, quiet; **silencioso, a** *adj* silent, quiet

silla ['siʎa] *nf* (*asiento*) chair; (*tb:* **~ de montar**) saddle; **~ de ruedas** wheelchair

sillón [si'ʎon] *nm* armchair, easy chair

silueta [si'lweta] *nf* silhouette; (*de edificio*) outline; (*figura*) figure

silvestre [sil'βestre] *adj* wild

simbólico, a [sim'βoliko, a] *adj* symbolic(al)

simbolizar [simboli'θar] *vt* to symbolize

símbolo ['simbolo] *nm* symbol

simetría [sime'tria] *nf* symmetry

simiente [si'mjente] *nf* seed

similar [simi'lar] *adj* similar

simio ['simjo] *nm* ape

simpatía [simpa'tia] *nf* liking; (*afecto*) affection; (*amabilidad*) kindness; **simpático, a** *adj* nice, pleasant; kind

simpatizante [simpati'θante] *nm/f* sympathizer

simpatizar [simpati'θar] *vi*: **~ con** to get on well with

simple ['simple] *adj* simple; (*elemental*) simple, easy; (*mero*) mere; (*puro*) pure, sheer ♦ *nm/f* simpleton; **~za** *nf* simpleness; (*necedad*) silly thing; **simplificar** *vt* to simplify

simposio [sim'posjo] *nm* symposium

simular [simu'lar] *vt* to simulate

simultáneo, a [simul'taneo, a] *adj* simultaneous

sin [sin] *prep* without; **la ropa está ~ lavar** the clothes are unwashed; **~ que** without;

~ embargo however, still

sinagoga [sina'ɣoɣa] *nf* synagogue

sinceridad [sinθeri'ðað] *nf* sincerity; **sincero, a** *adj* sincere

sincronizar [sinkroni'θar] *vt* to synchronize

sindical [sindi'kal] *adj* union *cpd*, trade-union *cpd*; **~ista** *adj*, *nm/f* trade unionist

sindicato [sindi'kato] *nm* (*de trabajadores*) trade(s) union; (*de negociantes*) syndicate

síndrome ['sindrome] *nm* (*MED*) syndrome; **~ de abstinencia** (*MED*) withdrawal symptoms

sinfín [sin'fin] *nm*: **un ~ de** a great many, no end of

sinfonía [sinfo'nia] *nf* symphony

singular [singu'lar] *adj* singular; (*fig*) outstanding, exceptional; (*raro*) peculiar, odd; **~idad** *nf* singularity, peculiarity; **~izarse** *vr* to distinguish o.s., stand out

siniestro, a [si'njestro, a] *adj* sinister ♦ *nm* (*accidente*) accident

sinnúmero [sin'numero] *nm* = **sinfín**

sino ['sino] *nm* fate, destiny ♦ *conj* (*pero*) but; (*salvo*) except, save

sinónimo, a [si'nonimo, a] *adj* synonymous ♦ *nm* synonym

síntesis ['sintesis] *nf* synthesis; **sintético, a** *adj* synthetic

sintetizar [sinteti'θar] *vt* to synthesize

sintió *vb ver* **sentir**

síntoma ['sintoma] *nm* symptom

sintonía [sinto'nia] *nf* (*RADIO, MUS: de programa*) tuning; **sintonizar** *vt* (*RADIO: emisora*) to tune (in)

sinvergüenza [simber'ɣwenθa] *nm/f* rogue, scoundrel; **¡es un ~!** he's got a nerve!

siquiera [si'kjera] *conj* even if, even though ♦ *adv* at least; **ni ~** not even

sirena [si'rena] *nf* siren

Siria ['sirja] *nf* Syria

sirviente, a [sir'βjente, a] *nm/f* servant

sirvo *etc vb ver* **servir**

sisear [sise'ar] *vt, vi* to hiss

sistema [sis'tema] *nm* system; (*método*) method; **sistemático, a** *adj* systematic

---

sistema educativo

i *The reform of the Spanish* **sistema educativo** *(education system) begun in the early 90s has replaced the courses* **EGB**, **BUP** *and* **COU** *with the following: "Primaria" a compulsory 6 years; "Secundaria" a compulsory 4 years and "Bachillerato" an optional 2-year secondary school course, essential for those wishing to go on to higher education.*

---

sitiar [si'tjar] *vt* to besiege, lay siege to
sitio ['sitjo] *nm* (*lugar*) place; (*espacio*) room, space; (MIL) siege
situación [sitwa'θjon] *nf* situation, position; (*estatus*) position, standing
situado, a [situ'aðo] *adj* situated, placed
situar [si'twar] *vt* to place, put; (*edificio*) to locate, situate
slip [slip] *nm* pants *pl*, briefs *pl*
smoking ['smokin, es'mokin] (*pl* ~s) *nm* dinner jacket (BRIT), tuxedo (US)
snob [es'nob] = **esnob**
SO *abr* (= *suroeste*) SW
sobaco [so'βako] *nm* armpit
sobar [so'βar] *vt* (*ropa*) to rumple; (*comida*) to play around with
soberanía [soβera'nia] *nf* sovereignty; **soberano, a** *adj* sovereign; (*fig*) supreme ♦ *nm/f* sovereign
soberbia [so'βerβja] *nf* pride; haughtiness, arrogance; magnificence
soberbio, a [so'βerβjo, a] *adj* (*orgulloso*) proud; (*altivo*) haughty, arrogant; (*estupendo*) magnificent, superb
sobornar [soβor'nar] *vt* to bribe; **soborno** *nm* bribe
sobra ['soβra] *nf* excess, surplus; **~s** *nfpl* left-overs, scraps; **de ~** surplus, extra; **tengo de ~** I've more than enough; **~do, a** *adj* (*más que suficiente*) more than enough; (*superfluo*) excessive; **sobrante** *adj* remaining, extra ♦ *nm* surplus, remainder
sobrar [so'βrar] *vt* to exceed, surpass ♦ *vi* (*tener de más*) to be more than enough;

(*quedar*) to remain, be left (over)
sobrasada [soβra'saða] *nf* pork sausage spread
sobre ['soβre] *prep* (*gen*) on; (*encima*) on (top of); (*por encima de, arriba de*) over, above; (*más que*) more than; (*además*) in addition to, besides; (*alrededor de*) about ♦ *nm* envelope; **~ todo** above all
sobrecama [soβre'kama] *nf* bedspread
sobrecargar [soβrekar'xar] *vt* (*camión*) to overload; (COM) to surcharge
sobredosis [soβre'ðosis] *nf inv* overdose
sobreentender [soβre(e)nten'der] *vt* to deduce, infer; **~se** *vr*: **se sobreentiende que ...** it is implied that ...
sobrehumano, a [soβreu'mano, a] *adj* superhuman
sobrellevar [soβreʎe'βar] *vt* to bear, endure
sobremesa [soβre'mesa] *nf*: **durante la ~** after dinner; **ordenador de ~** desktop computer
sobrenatural [soβrenatu'ral] *adj* supernatural
sobrenombre [soβre'nombre] *nm* nickname
sobrepasar [soβrepa'sar] *vt* to exceed, surpass
sobreponerse [soβrepo'nerse] *vr*: **~ a** to overcome
sobresaliente [soβresa'ljente] *adj* outstanding, excellent
sobresalir [soβresa'lir] *vi* to project, jut out; (*fig*) to stand out, excel
sobresaltar [soβresal'tar] *vt* (*asustar*) to scare, frighten; (*sobrecoger*) to startle; **sobresalto** *nm* (*movimiento*) start; (*susto*) scare; (*turbación*) sudden shock
sobretodo [soβre'toðo] *nm* overcoat
sobrevenir [soβreβe'nir] *vi* (*ocurrir*) to happen (unexpectedly); (*resultar*) to follow, ensue
sobreviviente [soβreβi'βjente] *adj* surviving ♦ *nm/f* survivor
sobrevivir [soβreβi'βir] *vi* to survive
sobrevolar [soβreβo'lar] *vt* to fly over
sobriedad [soβrje'ðað] *nf* sobriety,

soberness; (*moderación*) moderation, restraint

sobrino, a [so'βrino, a] *nm/f* nephew/ niece

sobrio, a ['soβrjo, a] *adj* sober; (*moderado*) moderate, restrained

socarrón, ona [soka'rron, ona] *adj* (*sarcástico*) sarcastic, ironic(al)

socavar [soka'βar] *vt* (*tb fig*) to undermine

socavón [soka'βon] *nm* (*hoyo*) hole

sociable [so'θjaβle] *adj* (*persona*) sociable, friendly; (*animal*) social

social [so'θjal] *adj* social; (*COM*) company *cpd*

socialdemócrata [soθjalde'mokrata] *nm/f* social democrat

socialista [soθja'lista] *adj, nm/f* socialist

socializar [soθjali'θar] *vt* to socialize

sociedad [soθje'ðað] *nf* society; (*COM*) company; ~ **anónima** limited company; ~ **de consumo** consumer society

socio, a ['soθjo, a] *nm/f* (*miembro*) member; (*COM*) partner

sociología [soθjolo'xia] *nf* sociology; **sociólogo, a** *nm/f* sociologist

socorrer [soko'rrer] *vt* to help; **socorrista** *nm/f* first aider; (*en piscina, playa*) lifeguard; **socorro** *nm* (*ayuda*) help, aid; (*MIL*) relief; **¡socorro!** help!

soda ['soða] *nf* (*sosa*) soda; (*bebida*) soda (water)

sofá [so'fa] (*pl* ~**s**) *nm* sofa, settee; ~-**cama** studio couch; sofa bed

sofisticación [sofistika'θjon] *nf* sophistication

sofocar [sofo'kar] *vt* to suffocate; (*apagar*) to smother, put out; ~**se** *vr* to suffocate; (*fig*) to blush, feel embarrassed; **sofoco** *nm* suffocation; embarrassment

sofreír [sofre'ir] *vt* (*CULIN*) to fry lightly

soga ['soxa] *nf* rope

sois *vb ver* **ser**

soja ['soxa] *nf* soya

sol [sol] *nm* sun; (*luz*) sunshine, sunlight; **hace** ~ it is sunny

solamente [sola'mente] *adv* only, just

solapa [so'lapa] *nf* (*de chaqueta*) lapel; (*de*

libro) jacket

solapado, a [sola'paðo, a] *adj* (*intenciones*) underhand; (*gestos, movimiento*) sly

solar [so'lar] *adj* solar, sun *cpd*

solaz [so'laθ] *nm* recreation, relaxation; ~**ar** *vt* (*divertir*) to amuse

soldado [sol'daðo] *nm* soldier; ~ **raso** private

soldador [solda'ðor] *nm* soldering iron; (*persona*) welder

soldar [sol'dar] *vt* to solder, weld

soleado, a [sole'aðo, a] *adj* sunny

soledad [sole'ðað] *nf* solitude; (*estado infeliz*) loneliness

solemne [so'lemne] *adj* solemn; **solemnidad** *nf* solemnity

soler [so'ler] *vi* to be in the habit of, be accustomed to; **suele salir a las ocho** she usually goes out at 8 o'clock

solfeo [sol'feo] *nm* solfa

solicitar [soliθi'tar] *vt* (*permiso*) to ask for, seek; (*puesto*) to apply for; (*votos*) to canvass for; (*atención*) to attract

solícito, a [so'liθito, a] *adj* (*diligente*) diligent; (*cuidadoso*) careful; **solicitud** *nf* (*calidad*) great care; (*petición*) request; (*a un puesto*) application

solidaridad [soliðari'ðað] *nf* solidarity; **solidario, a** *adj* (*participación*) joint, common; (*compromiso*) mutually binding

solidez [soli'ðeθ] *nf* solidity; **sólido, a** *adj* solid

soliloquio [soli'lokjo] *nm* soliloquy

solista [so'lista] *nm/f* soloist

solitario, a [soli'tarjo, a] *adj* (*persona*) lonely, solitary; (*lugar*) lonely, desolate ♦ *nm/f* (*recluso*) recluse; (*en la sociedad*) loner ♦ *nm* solitaire

sollozar [soλo'θar] *vi* to sob; **sollozo** *nm* sob

solo, a ['solo, a] *adj* (*único*) single, sole; (*sin compañía*) alone; (*solitario*) lonely; **hay una sola dificultad** there is just one difficulty; **a solas** alone, by oneself

sólo ['solo] *adv* only, just

solomillo [solo'miλo] *nm* sirloin

soltar [sol'tar] *vt* (*dejar ir*) to let go of; (*desprender*) to unfasten, loosen; (*librar*) to release, set free; (*risa etc*) to let out

soltero, a [sol'tero, a] *adj* single, unmarried ♦ *nm/f* bachelor/single woman; **solterón, ona** *nm/f* old bachelor/spinster

soltura [sol'tura] *nf* looseness, slackness; (*de los miembros*) agility, ease of movement; (*en el hablar*) fluency, ease

soluble [so'luβle] *adj* (*QUÍM*) soluble; (*problema*) solvable; **~ en agua** soluble in water

solución [solu'θjon] *nf* solution; **solucionar** *vt* (*problema*) to solve; (*asunto*) to settle, resolve

solventar [solβen'tar] *vt* (*pagar*) to settle, pay; (*resolver*) to resolve; **solvente** *adj* (*ECON: empresa, persona*) solvent

sombra ['sombra] *nf* shadow; (*como protección*) shade; **~s** *nfpl* (*oscuridad*) darkness *sg*, shadows; **tener buena/mala ~** to be lucky/unlucky

sombrero [som'brero] *nm* hat

sombrilla [som'briʎa] *nf* parasol, sunshade

sombrío, a [som'brio, a] *adj* (*oscuro*) dark; (*triste*) sombre, sad; (*persona*) gloomy

somero, a [so'mero, a] *adj* superficial

someter [some'ter] *vt* (*país*) to conquer; (*persona*) to subject to one's will; (*informe*) to present, submit; **~se** *vr* to give in, yield, submit; **~ a** to subject to

somier [so'mjer] (*pl* **somiers**) *n* spring mattress

somnífero [som'nifero] *nm* sleeping pill

somnolencia [somno'lenθja] *nf* sleepiness, drowsiness

somos *vb ver* **ser**

son [son] *vb ver* **ser** ♦ *nm* sound; **en ~ de broma** as a joke

sonajero [sona'xero] *nm* (baby's) rattle

sonambulismo [sonambu'lismo] *nm* sleepwalking; **sonámbulo, a** *nm/f* sleepwalker

sonar [so'nar] *vt* to ring ♦ *vi* to sound; (*hacer ruido*) to make a noise; (*pronunciarse*) to be sounded, be pronounced; (*ser conocido*) to sound familiar; (*campana*) to ring; (*reloj*) to strike, chime; **~se** *vr*: **~se (las narices)** to blow one's nose; **me suena ese nombre** that name rings a bell

sonda ['sonda] *nf* (*NAUT*) sounding; (*TEC*) bore, drill; (*MED*) probe

sondear [sonde'ar] *vt* to sound; to bore (into), drill; to probe, sound; (*fig*) to sound out; **sondeo** *nm* sounding; boring, drilling; (*fig*) poll, enquiry

sonido [so'niðo] *nm* sound

sonoro, a [so'noro, a] *adj* sonorous; (*resonante*) loud, resonant

sonreír [sonre'ir] *vi* to smile; **~se** *vr* to smile; **sonriente** *adj* smiling; **sonrisa** *nf* smile

sonrojarse [sonro'xarse] *vr* to blush, go red; **sonrojo** *nm* blush

soñador, a [soɲa'ðor, a] *nm/f* dreamer

soñar [so'ɲar] *vt, vi* to dream; **~ con** to dream about *o* of

soñoliento, a [soɲo'ljento, a] *adj* sleepy, drowsy

sopa ['sopa] *nf* soup

sopesar [sope'sar] *vt* to consider, weigh up

soplar [so'plar] *vt* (*polvo*) to blow away, blow off; (*inflar*) to blow up; (*vela*) to blow out ♦ *vi* to blow; **soplo** *nm* blow, puff; (*de viento*) puff, gust

soplón, ona [so'plon, ona] (*fam*), *nm/f* (*niño*) telltale; (*de policía*) grass (*fam*)

sopor [so'por] *nm* drowsiness

soporífero [sopo'rifero] *nm* sleeping pill

soportable [sopor'taβle] *adj* bearable

soportar [sopor'tar] *vt* to bear, carry; (*fig*) to bear, put up with; **soporte** *nm* support; (*fig*) pillar, support

soprano [so'prano] *nf* soprano

sorber [sor'βer] *vt* (*chupar*) to sip; (*absorber*) to soak up, absorb

sorbete [sor'βete] *nm* iced fruit drink

sorbo ['sorβo] *nm* (*trago: grande*) gulp, swallow; (: *pequeño*) sip

sordera [sor'ðera] *nf* deafness

sórdido, a ['sorðiðo, a] *adj* dirty, squalid

sordo, a ['sorðo, a] *adj (persona)* deaf
♦ *nm/f* deaf person; **~mudo, a** *adj* deaf
and dumb

sorna ['sorna] *nf* sarcastic tone

soroche [so'rotʃe] *(AM) nm* mountain
sickness

sorprendente [sorpren'dente] *adj*
surprising

sorprender [sorpren'der] *vt* to surprise;
sorpresa *nf* surprise

sortear [sorte'ar] *vt* to draw lots for; *(rifar)*
to raffle; *(dificultad)* to avoid; **sorteo** *nm*
(en lotería) draw; *(rifa)* raffle

sortija [sor'tixa] *nf* ring; *(rizo)* ringlet, curl

sosegado, a [sose'vaðo, a] *adj* quiet,
calm

sosegar [sose'var] *vt* to quieten, calm; *(el
ánimo)* to reassure ♦ *vi* to rest; **sosiego**
nm quiet(ness), calm(ness)

soslayo [sos'lajo]: **de ~** *adv* obliquely,
sideways

soso, a ['soso, a] *adj (CULIN)* tasteless;
(aburrido) dull, uninteresting

sospecha [sos'petʃa] *nf* suspicion;
sospechar *vt* to suspect;
sospechoso, a *adj* suspicious;
(testimonio, opinión) suspect ♦ *nm/f*
suspect

sostén [sos'ten] *nm (apoyo)* support;
(sujetador) bra; *(alimentación)* sustenance,
food

sostener [soste'ner] *vt* to support;
(mantener) to keep up, maintain;
(alimentar) to sustain, keep going; **~se** *vr*
to support o.s.; *(seguir)* to continue,
remain; **sostenido, a** *adj* continuous,
sustained; *(prolongado)* prolonged

sotana [so'tana] *nf (REL)* cassock

sótano ['sotano] *nm* basement

soviético, a [so'ßjetiko, a] *adj* Soviet; **los
~s** the Soviets

soy *vb ver* **ser**

Sr. *abr (= Señor)* Mr

Sra. *abr (= Señora)* Mrs

S.R.C. *abr (= se ruega contestación)*
R.S.V.P.

Sres. *abr (= Señores)* Messrs

Srta. *abr (= Señorita)* Miss

Sta. *abr (= Santa)* St

status ['status, e'status] *nm inv* status

Sto. *abr (= Santo)* St

su [su] *pron (de él)* his; *(de ella)* her; *(de
una cosa)* its; *(de ellos, ellas)* their; *(de
usted, ustedes)* your

suave ['swaße] *adj* gentle; *(superficie)*
smooth; *(trabajo)* easy; *(música, voz)* soft,
sweet; **suavidad** *nf* gentleness;
smoothness; softness, sweetness;
suavizante *nm (de ropa)* softener; *(del
pelo)* conditioner; **suavizar** *vt* to soften;
(quitar la aspereza) to smooth (out)

subalimentado, a [sußalimen'taðo, a]
adj undernourished

subasta [su'ßasta] *nf* auction; **subastar**
vt to auction (off)

subcampeón, ona [sußkampe'on, ona]
nm/f runner-up

subconsciente [sußkon'sθjente] *adj, nm*
subconscious

subdesarrollado, a [sußðesarro'ʎaðo, a]
adj underdeveloped

subdesarrollo [sußðesa'rroʎo] *nm*
underdevelopment

subdirector, a [sußðirek'tor, a] *nm/f*
assistant director

súbdito, a ['sußðito, a] *nm/f* subject

subestimar [sußesti'mar] *vt* to
underestimate, underrate

subida [su'ßiða] *nf (de montaña etc)*
ascent, climb; *(de precio)* rise, increase;
(pendiente) slope, hill

subir [su'ßir] *vt (objeto)* to raise, lift up;
(cuesta, calle) to go up; *(colina, montaña)*
to climb; *(precio)* to raise, put up ♦ *vi* to
go up, come up; *(a un coche)* to get in;
(a un autobús, tren o avión) to get on,
board; *(precio)* to rise, go up; *(río, marea)*
to rise; **~se** *vr* to get up, climb

súbito, a ['sußito, a] *adj (repentino)*
sudden; *(imprevisto)* unexpected

subjetivo, a [sußxe'tißo, a] *adj* subjective

sublevación [sußleßa'θjon] *nf* revolt,
rising

sublevar [sußle'ßar] *vt* to rouse to revolt;

~**se** *vr* to revolt, rise

sublime [su'ßlime] *adj* sublime

submarinismo [sußmari'nismo] *nm* scuba diving

submarino, a [sußma'rino, a] *adj* underwater ♦ *nm* submarine

subnormal [sußnor'mal] *adj* subnormal ♦ *nm/f* subnormal person

subordinado, a [sußorði'naðo, a] *adj, nm/f* subordinate

subrayar [sußra'jar] *vt* to underline

subsanar [sußsa'nar] *vt* to rectify

subscribir [sußskri'ßir] *vt* = **suscribir**

subsidio [suß'siðjo] *nm* (*ayuda*) aid, financial help; (*subvención*) subsidy, grant; (*de enfermedad, paro etc*) benefit, allowance

subsistencia [sußsis'tenθja] *nf* subsistence

subsistir [sußsis'tir] *vi* to subsist; (*sobrevivir*) to survive, endure

subterráneo, a [sußte'rraneo, a] *adj* underground, subterranean ♦ *nm* underpass, underground passage

subtítulo [suß'titulo] *nm* (*CINE*) subtitle

suburbano, a [sußur'ßano, a] *adj* suburban

suburbio [su'ßurßjo] *nm* (*barrio*) slum quarter

subvención [sußßen'θjon] *nf* (*ECON*) subsidy, grant; **subvencionar** *vt* to subsidize

subversión [sußßer'sjon] *nf* subversion; **subversivo, a** *adj* subversive

subyugar [sußju'var] *vt* (*país*) to subjugate, subdue; (*enemigo*) to overpower; (*voluntad*) to dominate

sucedáneo, a [suθe'ðaneo, a] *adj* substitute ♦ *nm* substitute (food)

suceder [suθe'ðer] *vt, vi* to happen; (*seguir*) to succeed, follow; **lo que sucede es que ...** the fact is that ...; **sucesión** *nf* succession; (*serie*) sequence, series

sucesivamente [suθesißa'mente] *adv*: **y así ~** and so on

sucesivo, a [suθe'sißo, a] *adj* successive, following; **en lo ~** in future, from now on

suceso [su'θeso] *nm* (*hecho*) event, happening; (*incidente*) incident

suciedad [suθje'ðað] *nf* (*estado*) dirtiness; (*mugre*) dirt, filth

sucinto, a [su'θinto, a] *adj* (*conciso*) succinct, concise

sucio, a ['suθjo, a] *adj* dirty

suculento, a [suku'lento, a] *adj* succulent

sucumbir [sukum'bir] *vi* to succumb

sucursal [sukur'sal] *nf* branch (office)

sudadera [suða'ðera] *nf* sweatshirt

Sudáfrica [suð'afrika] *nf* South Africa

Sudamérica [suða'merika] *nf* South America; **sudamericano, a** *adj, nm/f* South American

sudar [su'ðar] *vt, vi* to sweat

sudeste [su'ðeste] *nm* south-east

sudoeste [suðo'este] *nm* south-west

sudor [su'ðor] *nm* sweat; ~**oso, a** *adj* sweaty, sweating

Suecia ['sweθja] *nf* Sweden; **sueco, a** *adj* Swedish ♦ *nm/f* Swede

suegro, a ['swevro, a] *nm/f* father-/ mother-in-law

suela ['swela] *nf* sole

sueldo ['sweldo] *nm* pay, wage(s) (*pl*)

suele *etc vb ver* **soler**

suelo ['swelo] *nm* (*tierra*) ground; (*de casa*) floor

suelto, a ['swelto, a] *adj* loose; (*libre*) free; (*separado*) detached; (*ágil*) quick, agile ♦ *nm* (*loose*) change, small change

sueño *etc* ['sweno] *vb ver* **soñar** ♦ *nm* sleep; (*somnolencia*) sleepiness, drowsiness; (*lo soñado, fig*) dream; **tener ~** to be sleepy

suero ['swero] *nm* (*MED*) serum; (*de leche*) whey

suerte ['swerte] *nf* (*fortuna*) luck; (*azar*) chance; (*destino*) fate, destiny; (*especie*) sort, kind; **tener ~** to be lucky; **de otra ~** otherwise, if not; **de ~ que** so that, in such a way that

suéter ['sweter] *nm* sweater

suficiente [sufi'θjente] *adj* enough, sufficient ♦ *nm* (*ESCOL*) pass

sufragio [su'fraxjo] *nm* (*voto*) vote; (*derecho de voto*) suffrage

sufrido, a [su'friðo, a] *adj* (*persona*) tough; (*paciente*) long-suffering, patient

sufrimiento [sufri'mjento] *nm* (*dolor*) suffering

sufrir [su'frir] *vt* (*padecer*) to suffer; (*soportar*) to bear, put up with; (*apoyar*) to hold up, support ♦ *vi* to suffer

sugerencia [suxe'renθja] *nf* suggestion

sugerir [suxe'rir] *vt* to suggest; (*sutilmente*) to hint

sugestión [suxes'tjon] *nf* suggestion; (*sutil*) hint; **sugestionar** *vt* to influence

sugestivo, a [suxes'tiβo, a] *adj* stimulating; (*fascinante*) fascinating

suicida [sui'θiða] *adj* suicidal ♦ *nm/f* suicidal person; (*muerto*) suicide, person who has committed suicide; **suicidarse** *vr* to commit suicide, kill o.s.; **suicidio** *nm* suicide

Suiza ['swiθa] *nf* Switzerland; **suizo, a** *adj*, *nm/f* Swiss

sujeción [suxe'θjon] *nf* subjection

sujetador [suxeta'ðor] *nm* (*sostén*) bra

sujetar [suxe'tar] *vt* (*fijar*) to fasten; (*detener*) to hold down; **~se** *vr* to subject o.s.; **sujeto, a** *adj* fastened, secure ♦ *nm* subject; (*individuo*) individual; **sujeto a** subject to

suma ['suma] *nf* (*cantidad*) total, sum; (*de dinero*) sum; (*acto*) adding (up), addition; **en ~** in short

sumamente [suma'mente] *adv* extremely, exceedingly

sumar [su'mar] *vt* to add (up) ♦ *vi* to add up

sumario, a [su'marjo, a] *adj* brief, concise ♦ *nm* summary

sumergir [sumer'xir] *vt* to submerge; (*hundir*) to sink

suministrar [sumini'strar] *vt* to supply, provide; **suministro** *nm* supply; (*acto*) supplying, providing

sumir [su'mir] *vt* to sink, submerge; (*fig*) to plunge

sumisión [sumi'sjon] *nf* (*acto*) submission; (*calidad*) submissiveness, docility; **sumiso, a** *adj* submissive, docile

sumo, a ['sumo, a] *adj* great, extreme; (*autoridad*) highest, supreme

suntuoso, a [sun'twoso, a] *adj* sumptuous, magnificent

supe *etc vb ver* **saber**

supeditar [supeði'tar] *vt*: **~ algo a algo** to subordinate sth to sth

super... [super] *prefijo* super..., over...; **~bueno** *adj* great, fantastic

súper ['super] *nf* (*gasolina*) three-star (petrol)

superar [supe'rar] *vt* (*sobreponerse a*) to overcome; (*rebasar*) to surpass, do better than; (*pasar*) to go beyond; **~se** *vr* to excel o.s.

superávit [supe'raβit] *nm inv* surplus

superficial [superfi'θjal] *adj* superficial; (*medida*) surface *cpd*, of the surface

superficie [super'fiθje] *nf* surface; (*área*) area

superfluo, a [su'perflwo, a] *adj* superfluous

superior [supe'rjor] *adj* (*piso, clase*) upper; (*temperatura, número, nivel*) higher; (*mejor: calidad, producto*) superior, better ♦ *nm/f* superior; **~idad** *nf* superiority

supermercado [supermer'kaðo] *nm* supermarket

superponer [superpo'ner] *vt* to superimpose

supersónico, a [super'soniko, a] *adj* supersonic

superstición [supersti'θjon] *nf* superstition; **supersticioso, a** *adj* superstitious

supervisar [superβi'sar] *vt* to supervise

supervivencia [superβi'βenθja] *nf* survival

superviviente [superβi'βjente] *adj* surviving

supiera *etc vb ver* **saber**

suplantar [suplan'tar] *vt* to supplant

suplemento [suple'mento] *nm* supplement

suplente [su'plente] *adj*, *nm/f* substitute

supletorio, a [suple'torjo, a] *adj*

supplementary ♦ *nm* supplement; **teléfono ~** extension

súplica ['suplika] *nf* request; (*JUR*) petition

suplicar [supli'kar] *vt* (*cosa*) to beg (for), plead for; (*persona*) to beg, plead with

suplicio [su'pliθjo] *nm* torture

suplir [su'plir] *vt* (*compensar*) to make good, make up for; (*reemplazar*) to replace, substitute ♦ *vi*: **~ a** to take the place of, substitute for

supo *etc vb ver* **saber**

suponer [supo'ner] *vt* to suppose; **suposición** *nf* supposition

supremacía [suprema'θia] *nf* supremacy

supremo, a [su'premo, a] *adj* supreme

supresión [supre'sjon] *nf* suppression; (*de derecho*) abolition; (*de palabra etc*) deletion; (*de restricción*) cancellation, lifting

suprimir [supri'mir] *vt* to suppress; (*derecho, costumbre*) to abolish; (*palabra etc*) to delete; (*restricción*) to cancel, lift

supuesto, a [su'pwesto, a] *pp de* **suponer** ♦ *adj* (*hipotético*) supposed ♦ *nm* assumption, hypothesis; **~ que** since; **por ~** of course

sur [sur] *nm* south

surcar [sur'kar] *vt* to plough; **surco** *nm* (*en metal, disco*) groove; (*AGR*) furrow

surgir [sur'xir] *vi* to arise, emerge; (*dificultad*) to come up, crop up

suroeste [suro'este] *nm* south-west

surtido, a [sur'tiðo, a] *adj* mixed, assorted ♦ *nm* (*selección*) selection, assortment; (*abastecimiento*) supply, stock; **~r** *nm* (*tb:* **~r de gasolina**) petrol pump (*BRIT*), gas pump (*US*)

surtir [sur'tir] *vt* to supply, provide ♦ *vi* to spout, spurt

susceptible [susθep'tiβle] *adj* susceptible; (*sensible*) sensitive; **~ de** capable of

suscitar [susθi'tar] *vt* to cause, provoke; (*interés, sospechas*) to arouse

suscribir [suskri'βir] *vt* (*firmar*) to sign; (*respaldar*) to subscribe to, endorse; **~se** *vr* to subscribe; **suscripción** *nf* subscription

susodicho, a [suso'ðitʃo, a] *adj* above-mentioned

suspender [suspen'der] *vt* (*objeto*) to hang (up), suspend; (*trabajo*) to stop, suspend; (*ESCOL*) to fail; (*interrumpir*) to adjourn; (*atrasar*) to postpone; **suspensión** *nf* suspension; (*fig*) stoppage, suspension

suspenso, a [sus'penso, a] *adj* hanging, suspended; (*ESCOL*) failed ♦ *nm* (*ESCOL*) fail; **quedar** *o* **estar en ~** to be pending

suspicacia [suspi'kaθja] *nf* suspicion, mistrust; **suspicaz** *adj* suspicious, distrustful

suspirar [suspi'rar] *vi* to sigh; **suspiro** *nm* sigh

sustancia [sus'tanθja] *nf* substance

sustentar [susten'tar] *vt* (*alimentar*) to sustain, nourish; (*objeto*) to hold up, support; (*idea, teoría*) to maintain, uphold; (*fig*) to sustain, keep going; **sustento** *nm* support; (*alimento*) sustenance, food

sustituir [sustitu'ir] *vt* to substitute, replace; **sustituto, a** *nm/f* substitute, replacement

susto ['susto] *nm* fright, scare

sustraer [sustra'er] *vt* to remove, take away; (*MAT*) to subtract

susurrar [susu'rrar] *vi* to whisper; **susurro** *nm* whisper

sutil [su'til] *adj* (*aroma, diferencia*) subtle; (*tenue*) thin; (*inteligencia, persona*) sharp; **~eza** *nf* subtlety; thinness

suyo, a ['sujo, a] (*con artículo o después del verbo* **ser**) *adj* (*de él*) his; (*de ella*) hers; (*de ellos, ellas*) theirs; (*de Ud, Uds*) yours; **un amigo ~** a friend of his (*o* hers *o* theirs *o* yours)

T, t

tabacalera [taßaka'lera] *nf*: **T~** *Spanish state tobacco monopoly*

tabaco [ta'ßako] *nm* tobacco; (*fam*) cigarettes *pl*

taberna [ta'ßerna] *nf* bar, pub (*BRIT*)

tabique [ta'ßike] *nm* partition (wall)

tabla ['taßla] *nf* (*de madera*) plank; (*estante*) shelf; (*de vestido*) pleat; (*ARTE*) panel; **~s** *nfpl*: **estar** *o* **quedar en ~s** to draw; **~do** *nm* (*plataforma*) platform; (*TEATRO*) stage

tablao [ta'ßlao] *nm* (*tb*: **~ flamenco**) flamenco show

tablero [ta'ßlero] *nm* (*de madera*) plank, board; (*de ajedrez, damas*) board; **~ de anuncios** notice (*BRIT*) *o* bulletin (*US*) board

tableta [ta'ßleta] *nf* (*MED*) tablet; (*de chocolate*) bar

tablón [ta'ßlon] *nm* (*de suelo*) plank; (*de techo*) beam; **~ de anuncios** notice board (*BRIT*), bulletin board (*US*)

tabú [ta'ßu] *nm* taboo

tabular [taßu'lar] *vt* to tabulate

taburete [taßu'rete] *nm* stool

tacaño, a [ta'kaɲo, a] *adj* mean

tacha ['tatʃa] *nf* flaw; (*TEC*) stud; **tachar** *vt* (*borrar*) to cross out; **tachar de** to accuse of

tácito, a ['taθito, a] *adj* tacit

taciturno, a [taθi'turno, a] *adj* silent

taco ['tako] *nm* (*BILLAR*) cue; (*libro de billetes*) book; (*AM: de zapato*) heel; (*tarugo*) peg; (*palabrota*) swear word

tacón [ta'kon] *nm* heel; **de ~ alto** high-heeled; **taconeo** *nm* (*heel*) stamping

táctica ['taktika] *nf* tactics *pl*

táctico, a ['taktiko, a] *adj* tactical

tacto ['takto] *nm* touch; (*fig*) tact

taimado, a [tai'maðo, a] *adj* (*astuto*) sly

tajada [ta'xaða] *nf* slice

tajante [ta'xante] *adj* sharp

tajo ['taxo] *nm* (*corte*) cut; (*GEO*) cleft

tal [tal] *adj* such; **~ vez** perhaps ♦ *pron* (*persona*) someone, such a one; (*cosa*) something, such a thing; **~ como** such as; **~ para cual** (*dos iguales*) two of a kind ♦ *adv*: **~ como** (*igual*) just as; **~ cual** (*como es*) just as it is; **¿qué ~?** how are things?; **¿qué ~ te gusta?** how do you like it? ♦ *conj*: **con ~ de que** provided that

taladrar [tala'ðrar] *vt* to drill; **taladro** *nm* drill

talante [ta'lante] *nm* (*humor*) mood; (*voluntad*) will, willingness

talar [ta'lar] *vt* to fell, cut down; (*devastar*) to devastate

talco ['talko] *nm* (*polvos*) talcum powder

talego [ta'leɣo] *nm* sack

talento [ta'lento] *nm* talent; (*capacidad*) ability

TALGO ['talɣo] (*ESP*) *nm abr* (= *tren articulado ligero Goicoechea-Oriol*) ≈ HST (*BRIT*)

talismán [talis'man] *nm* talisman

talla ['taʎa] *nf* (*estatura, fig, MED*) height, stature; (*palo*) measuring rod; (*ARTE*) carving; (*medida*) size

tallado, a [ta'ʎaðo, a] *adj* carved ♦ *nm* carving

tallar [ta'ʎar] *vt* (*madera*) to carve; (*metal etc*) to engrave; (*medir*) to measure

tallarines [taʎa'rines] *nmpl* noodles

talle ['taʎe] *nm* (*ANAT*) waist; (*fig*) appearance

taller [ta'ʎer] *nm* (*TEC*) workshop; (*de artista*) studio

tallo ['taʎo] *nm* (*de planta*) stem; (*de hierba*) blade; (*brote*) shoot

talón [ta'lon] *nm* (*ANAT*) heel; (*COM*) counterfoil; (*cheque*) cheque (*BRIT*), check (*US*)

talonario [talo'narjo] *nm* (*de cheques*) chequebook (*BRIT*), checkbook (*US*); (*de recibos*) receipt book

tamaño, a [ta'maɲo, a] *adj* (*tan grande*) such a big; (*tan pequeño*) such a small ♦ *nm* size; **de ~ natural** full-size

tamarindo [tama'rindo] *nm* tamarind

tambalearse [tambale'arse] *vr* (*persona*) to stagger; (*vehículo*) to sway

también [tam'bjen] *adv* (*igualmente*) also, too, as well; (*además*) besides

tambor [tam'bor] *nm* drum; (*ANAT*) eardrum; **~ del freno** brake drum

tamiz [ta'miθ] *nm* sieve; **~ar** *vt* to sieve

tampoco [tam'poko] *adv* nor, neither; **yo ~ lo compré** I didn't buy it either

tampón [tam'pon] *nm* tampon

tan [tan] *adv* so; **~ es así que ...** so much so that ....

tanda ['tanda] *nf* (*gen*) series; (*turno*) shift

tangente [tan'xente] *nf* tangent

Tánger ['tanxer] *n* Tangier(s)

tangible [tan'xiβle] *adj* tangible

tanque ['tanke] *nm* (*cisterna, MIL*) tank; (*AUTO*) tanker

tantear [tante'ar] *vt* (*calcular*) to reckon (up); (*medir*) to take the measure of; (*probar*) to test, try out; (*tomar la medida: persona*) to take the measurements of; (*situación*) to weigh up; (*persona: opinión*) to sound out ♦ *vi* (*DEPORTE*) to score; **tanteo** *nm* (*cálculo*) (rough) calculation; (*prueba*) test, trial; (*DEPORTE*) scoring

tanto, a ['tanto, a] *adj* (*cantidad*) so much, as much; **~s** so many, as many; **20 y ~s** 20-odd ♦ *adv* (*cantidad*) so much, as much; (*tiempo*) so long, as long ♦ *conj*: **en ~ que** while; **hasta ~ (que)** until such time as ♦ *nm* (*suma*) certain amount; (*proporción*) so much; (*punto*) point; (*gol*) goal; **un ~ perezoso** somewhat lazy ♦ *pron*: **cada uno paga ~** each one pays so much; **~ tú como yo** both you and I; **~ como eso** as much as that; **~ más ... cuanto que** all the more ... because; **~ mejor/peor** so much the better/the worse; **~ si viene como si va** whether he comes or whether he goes; **~ es así que** so much so that; **por ○ por lo ~** therefore; **me he vuelto ronco de ○ con ~ hablar** I have become hoarse with so much talking; **a ~s de agosto** on such and such a day in August

tapa ['tapa] *nf* (*de caja, olla*) lid; (*de botella*) top; (*de libro*) cover; (*comida*) snack

tapadera [tapa'ðera] *nf* lid, cover

tapar [ta'par] *vt* (*cubrir*) to cover; (*envolver*) to wrap ○ cover up; (*la vista*) to obstruct; (*persona, falta*) to conceal; (*AM*) to fill; **~se** *vr* to wrap o.s. up

taparrabo [tapa'rraβo] *nm* loincloth

tapete [ta'pete] *nm* table cover

tapia ['tapja] *nf* (*garden*) wall; **tapiar** *vt* to wall in

tapicería [tapiθe'ria] *nf* tapestry; (*para muebles*) upholstery; (*tienda*) upholsterer's (shop)

tapiz [ta'piθ] *nm* (*alfombra*) carpet; (*tela tejida*) tapestry; **~ar** *vt* (*muebles*) to upholster

tapón [ta'pon] *nm* (*de botella*) top; (*de lavabo*) plug; **~ de rosca** screw-top

taquigrafía [takiɣra'fia] *nf* shorthand; **taquígrafo, a** *nm/f* shorthand writer, stenographer

taquilla [ta'kiʎa] *nf* (*donde se compra*) booking office; (*suma recogida*) takings *pl*; **taquillero, a** *adj*: **función taquillera** box office success ♦ *nm/f* ticket clerk

tara ['tara] *nf* (*defecto*) defect; (*COM*) tare

tarántula [ta'rantula] *nf* tarantula

tararear [tarare'ar] *vi* to hum

tardar [tar'ðar] *vi* (*tomar tiempo*) to take a long time; (*llegar tarde*) to be late; (*demorar*) to delay; **¿tarda mucho el tren?** does the train take (very) long?; **a más ~** at the latest; **no tardes en venir** come soon

tarde ['tarðe] *adv* late ♦ *nf* (*de día*) afternoon; (*al anochecer*) evening; **de ~ en ~** from time to time; **¡buenas ~s!** good afternoon!; **a ○ por la ~** in the afternoon; in the evening

tardío, a [tar'ðio, a] *adj* (*retrasado*) late; (*lento*) slow (to arrive)

tarea [ta'rea] *nf* task; (*faena*) chore; (*ESCOL*) homework

tarifa [ta'rifa] *nf* (*lista de precios*) price list; (*precio*) tariff

tarima [ta'rima] *nf* (*plataforma*) platform

tarjeta [tar'xeta] *nf* card; ~ **postal/de crédito/de Navidad** postcard/credit card/Christmas card

tarro ['tarro] *nm* jar, pot

tarta ['tarta] *nf* (*pastel*) cake; (*de base dura*) tart

tartamudear [tartamuðe'ar] *vi* to stammer; **tartamudo, a** *adj* stammering ♦ *nm/f* stammerer

tártaro, a ['tartaro, a] *adj*: **salsa tártara** tartar(e) sauce

tasa ['tasa] *nf* (*precio*) (fixed) price, rate; (*valoración*) valuation; (*medida, norma*) measure, standard; ~ **de cambio/interés** exchange/interest rate; ~**s universitarias** university fees; ~**s de aeropuerto** airport tax; ~**ción** *nf* valuation; ~**dor, a** *nm/f* valuer

tasar [ta'sar] *vt* (*arreglar el precio*) to fix a price for; (*valorar*) to value, assess

tasca ['taska] (*fam*) *nf* pub

tatarabuelo, a [tatara'ßwelo, a] *nm/f* great-great-grandfather/mother

tatuaje [ta'twaxe] *nm* (*dibujo*) tattoo; (*acto*) tattooing

tatuar [ta'twar] *vt* to tattoo

taurino, a [tau'rino, a] *adj* bullfighting *cpd*

Tauro ['tauro] *nm* Taurus

tauromaquia [tauro'makja] *nf* tauromachy, (art of) bullfighting

taxi ['taksi] *nm* taxi

taxista [tak'sista] *nm/f* taxi driver

taza ['taθa] *nf* cup; (*de retrete*) bowl; ~ **para café** coffee cup; **tazón** *nm* (*taza grande*) mug, large cup; (*de fuente*) basin

te [te] *pron* (*complemento de objeto*) you; (*complemento indirecto*) (to) you; (*reflexivo*) (to) yourself; ¿~ **duele mucho el brazo?** does your arm hurt a lot?; ~ **equivocas** you're wrong; ¡**cálma~!** calm down!

té [te] *nm* tea

tea ['tea] *nf* torch

teatral [tea'tral] *adj* theatre *cpd*; (*fig*) theatrical

teatro [te'atro] *nm* theatre; (*LITERATURA*) plays *pl*, drama

tebeo [te'ßeo] *nm* comic

techo ['tetʃo] *nm* (*externo*) roof; (*interno*) ceiling; ~ **corredizo** sunroof

tecla ['tekla] *nf* key; ~**do** *nm* keyboard; **teclear** *vi* (*MUS*) to strum; (*con los dedos*) to tap ♦ *vt* (*INFORM*) to key in

técnica ['teknika] *nf* technique; (*tecnología*) technology; *ver tb* **técnico**

técnico, a ['tekniko, a] *adj* technical ♦ *nm/f* technician; (*experto*) expert

tecnología [teknolo'xia] *nf* technology; **tecnológico, a** *adj* technological

tedio ['teðjo] *nm* boredom, tedium; ~**so, a** *adj* boring, tedious

teja ['texa] *nf* tile; (*BOT*) lime (tree); ~**do** *nm* (tiled) roof

tejemaneje [texema'nexe] *nm* (*lío*) fuss; (*intriga*) intrigue

tejer [te'xer] *vt* to weave; (*hacer punto*) to knit; (*fig*) to fabricate; **tejido** *nm* (*tela*) material, fabric; (*telaraña*) web; (*ANAT*) tissue

tel [tel] *abr* (= *teléfono*) tel

tela ['tela] *nf* (*tejido*) material; (*telaraña*) web; (*en líquido*) skin; **telar** *nm* (*máquina*) loom

telaraña [tela'raɲa] *nf* cobweb

tele ['tele] (*fam*) *nf* telly (*BRIT*), tube (*US*)

tele... ['tele] *prefijo* tele...; ~**comunicación** *nf* telecommunication; ~**control** *nm* remote control; ~**diario** *nm* television news; ~**difusión** *nf* (television) broadcast; ~**dirigido, a** *adj* remote-controlled

teléf *abr* (= *teléfono*) tel

teleférico [tele'feriko] *nm* (*de esquí*) ski-lift

telefonear [telefone'ar] *vi* to telephone

telefónico, a [tele'foniko, a] *adj* telephone *cpd*

telefonillo [telefo'niʎo] *nm* (*de puerta*) intercom

telefonista [telefo'nista] *nm/f* telephonist

teléfono [te'lefono] *nm* (tele)phone; **estar hablando al** ~ to be on the phone; **llamar a uno por** ~ to ring sb (up) *o* phone sb (up); ~ **móvil** car phone; ~ **portátil** mobile phone

telegrafía [teleɣraˈfia] *nf* telegraphy

telégrafo [teˈleɣrafo] *nm* telegraph

telegrama [teleˈɣrama] *nm* telegram

tele: **~impresor** *nm* teleprinter (*BRIT*), teletype (*US*); **~novela** *nf* soap (opera); **~objetivo** *nm* telephoto lens; **~patía** *nf* telepathy; **~pático, a** *adj* telepathic; **~scópico, a** *adj* telescopic; **~scopio** *nm* telescope; **~silla** *nm* chairlift; **~spectador, a** *nm/f* viewer; **~squí** *nm* ski-lift; **~tarjeta** *nf* phonecard; **~tipo** *nm* teletype

televidente [teleβiˈðente] *nm/f* viewer

televisar [teleβiˈsar] *vt* to televise

televisión [teleβiˈsjon] *nf* television; **~ en colores** colour television

televisor [teleβiˈsor] *nm* television set

télex [ˈteleks] *nm inv* telex

telón [teˈlon] *nm* curtain; **~ de acero** (*POL*) iron curtain; **~ de fondo** backcloth, background

tema [ˈtema] *nm* (*asunto*) subject, topic; (*MUS*) theme; **temática** *nf* (*social, histórica, artística*) range of topics; **temático, a** *adj* thematic

temblar [temˈblar] *vi* to shake, tremble; (*de frío*) to shiver; **temblón, ona** *adj* shaking; **temblor** *nm* trembling; (*de tierra*) earthquake; **tembloroso, a** *adj* trembling

temer [teˈmer] *vt* to fear ♦ *vi* to be afraid; **temo que llegue tarde** I am afraid he may be late

temerario, a [temeˈrarjo, a] *adj* (*descuidado*) reckless; (*irreflexivo*) hasty; **temeridad** *nf* (*imprudencia*) rashness; (*audacia*) boldness

temeroso, a [temeˈroso, a] *adj* (*miedoso*) fearful; (*que inspira temor*) frightful

temible [teˈmiβle] *adj* fearsome

temor [teˈmor] *nm* (*miedo*) fear; (*duda*) suspicion

témpano [ˈtempano] *nm*: **~ de hielo** ice-floe

temperamento [temperaˈmento] *nm* temperament

temperatura [temperaˈtura] *nf* temperature

tempestad [tempesˈtað] *nf* storm; **tempestuoso, a** *adj* stormy

templado, a [temˈplaðo, a] *adj* (*moderado*) moderate; (*frugal*) frugal; (*agua*) lukewarm; (*clima*) mild; (*MUS*) well-tuned; **templanza** *nf* moderation; mildness

templar [temˈplar] *vt* (*moderar*) to moderate; (*furia*) to restrain; (*calor*) to reduce; (*afinar*) to tune (up); (*acero*) to temper; (*tuerca*) to tighten up; **temple** *nm* (*ajuste*) tempering; (*afinación*) tuning; (*pintura*) tempera

templo [ˈtemplo] *nm* (*iglesia*) church; (*pagano etc*) temple

temporada [tempoˈraða] *nf* time, period; (*estación*) season

temporal [tempoˈral] *adj* (*no permanente*) temporary; (*REL*) temporal ♦ *nm* storm

tempranero, a [tempraˈnero, a] *adj* (*BOT*) early; (*persona*) early-rising

temprano, a [temˈprano, a] *adj* early; (*demasiado pronto*) too soon, too early

ten *vb ver* **tener**

tenaces [teˈnaθes] *adj pl ver* **tenaz**

tenacidad [tenaθiˈðað] *nf* tenacity; (*dureza*) toughness; (*terquedad*) stubbornness

tenacillas [tenaˈθiʎas] *nfpl* tongs; (*para el pelo*) curling tongs (*BRIT*) *o* iron *sg* (*US*); (*MED*) forceps

tenaz [teˈnaθ] *adj* (*material*) tough; (*persona*) tenacious; (*creencia, resistencia*) stubborn

tenaza(s) [teˈnaθa(s)] *nf(pl)* (*MED*) forceps; (*TEC*) pliers; (*ZOOL*) pincers

tendedero [tendeˈðero] *nm* (*para ropa*) drying place; (*cuerda*) clothes line

tendencia [tenˈdenθja] *nf* tendency; **tener ~ a** to tend to, have a tendency to; **tendencioso, a** *adj* tendentious

tender [tenˈder] *vt* (*extender*) to spread out; (*colgar*) to hang out; (*vía férrea, cable*) to lay; (*estirar*) to stretch ♦ *vi*: **~ a** to tend to, have a tendency towards; **~se** *vr* to lie down; **~ la cama/la mesa** (*AM*) to make the bed/lay (*BRIT*) *o* set (*US*) the table

tenderete [tende'rete] *nm* (*puesto*) stall; (*exposición*) display of goods

tendero, a [ten'dero, a] *nm/f* shopkeeper

tendido, a [ten'diðo, a] *adj* (*acostado*) lying down, flat; (*colgado*) hanging ♦ *nm* (*TAUR*) front rows of seats; **a galope ~** flat out

tendón [ten'don] *nm* tendon

tendré *etc vb ver* **tener**

tenebroso, a [tene'ßroso, a] *adj* (*oscuro*) dark; (*fig*) gloomy

tenedor [tene'ðor] *nm* (*CULIN*) fork; **~ de libros** book-keeper

tenencia [te'nenθja] *nf* (*de casa*) tenancy; (*de oficio*) tenure; (*de propiedad*) possession

--- PALABRA CLAVE ---

tener [te'ner] *vt* **1** (*poseer, gen*) to have; (*en la mano*) to hold; **¿tienes un boli?** have you got a pen?; **va a ~ un niño** she's going to have a baby; **¡ten (*o* tenga)!, ¡aquí tienes (*o* tiene)!** here you are!

2 (*edad, medidas*) to be; **tiene 7 años** she's 7 (years old); **tiene 15 cm de largo** it's 15 cm long; *ver* **calor**; **hambre** *etc*

3 (*considerar*): **lo tengo por brillante** I consider him to be brilliant; **~ en mucho a uno** to think very highly of sb

4 (+*pp*: = *pretérito*): **tengo terminada ya la mitad del trabajo** I've done half the work already

5: **~ que hacer algo** to have to do sth; **tengo que acabar este trabajo hoy** I have to finish this job today

6: **¿qué tienes, estás enfermo?** what's the matter with you, are you ill?

♦ **~se** *vr* **1**: **~se en pie** to stand up

2: **~se por** to think o.s.; **se tiene por muy listo** he thinks himself very clever

tengo *etc vb ver* **tener**

tenia ['tenja] *nf* tapeworm

teniente [te'njente] *nm* (*rango*) lieutenant;

(*ayudante*) deputy

tenis ['tenis] *nm* tennis; **~ de mesa** table tennis; **~ta** *nm/f* tennis player

tenor [te'nor] *nm* (*sentido*) meaning; (*MUS*) tenor; **a ~ de** on the lines of

tensar [ten'sar] *vt* to tighten; (*arco*) to draw

tensión [ten'sjon] *nf* tension; (*TEC*) stress; (*MED*): **~ arterial** blood pressure; **tener la ~ alta** to have high blood pressure

tenso, a ['tenso, a] *adj* tense

tentación [tenta'θjon] *nf* temptation

tentáculo [ten'takulo] *nm* tentacle

tentador, a [tenta'ðor, a] *adj* tempting

tentar [ten'tar] *vt* (*seducir*) to tempt; (*atraer*) to attract; **tentativa** *nf* attempt; **tentativa de asesinato** attempted murder

tentempié [tentem'pje] *nm* snack

tenue ['tenwe] *adj* (*delgado*) thin, slender; (*neblina*) light; (*lazo, vínculo*) slight

teñir [te'nir] *vt* to dye; (*fig*) to tinge; **~se** *vr* to dye; **~se el pelo** to dye one's hair

teología [teolo'xia] *nf* theology

teoría [teo'ria] *nf* theory; **en ~** in theory; **teóricamente** *adv* theoretically; **teórico, a** *adj* theoretic(al) ♦ *nm/f* theoretician, theorist; **teorizar** *vi* to theorize

terapéutico, a [tera'peutiko, a] *adj* therapeutic

terapia [te'rapja] *nf* therapy

tercer [ter'θer] *adj ver* **tercero**

tercermundista [terθermun'dista] *adj* Third World *cpd*

tercero, a [ter'θero, a] *adj* (*delante de nmsg*: **tercer**) third ♦ *nm* (*JUR*) third party

terceto [ter'θeto] *nm* trio

terciar [ter'θjar] *vi* (*participar*) to take part; (*hacer de árbitro*) to mediate; **~se** *vr* to come up; **~io, a** *adj* tertiary

tercio ['terθjo] *nm* third

terciopelo [terθjo'pelo] *nm* velvet

terco, a ['terko, a] *adj* obstinate

tergal ® [ter'val] *nm* type of polyester

tergiversar [terxißer'sar] *vt* to distort

termal [ter'mal] *adj* thermal

termas ['termas] *nfpl* hot springs
térmico, a ['termiko, a] *adj* thermal
terminación [termina'θjon] *nf* (*final*) end; (*conclusión*) conclusion, ending
terminal [termi'nal] *adj, nm, nf* terminal
terminante [termi'nante] *adj* (*final*) final, definitive; (*tajante*) categorical; **~mente** *adv*: **~mente prohibido** strictly forbidden
terminar [termi'nar] *vt* (*completar*) to complete, finish; (*concluir*) to end ♦ *vi* (*llegar a su fin*) to end; (*parar*) to stop; (*acabar*) to finish; **~se** *vr* to come to an end; **~ por hacer algo** to end up (by) doing sth
término ['termino] *nm* end, conclusion; (*parada*) terminus; (*límite*) boundary; **~ medio** average; (*fig*) middle way; **en último ~** (*a fin de cuentas*) in the last analysis; (*como último recurso*) as a last resort
terminología [terminolo'xia] *nf* terminology
termodinámico, a [termoði'namiko, a] *adj* thermodynamic
termómetro [ter'mometro] *nm* thermometer
termonuclear [termonukle'ar] *adj* thermonuclear
termo(s) ® ['termo(s)] *nm* Thermos ® (flask)
termostato [termo'stato] *nm* thermostat
ternero, a [ter'nero, a] *nm/f* (*animal*) calf ♦ *nf* (*carne*) veal
ternura [ter'nura] *nf* (*trato*) tenderness; (*palabra*) endearment; (*cariño*) fondness
terquedad [terke'ðað] *nf* obstinacy
terrado [te'rraðo] *nm* terrace
terraplén [terra'plen] *nm* embankment
terrateniente [terrate'njente] *nm/f* landowner
terraza [te'rraθa] *nf* (*balcón*) balcony; (*tejado*) (flat) roof; (*AGR*) terrace
terremoto [terre'moto] *nm* earthquake
terrenal [terre'nal] *adj* earthly
terreno [te'rreno] *nm* (*tierra*) land; (*parcela*) plot; (*suelo*) soil; (*fig*) field; **un ~** a piece of land

terrestre [te'rrestre] *adj* terrestrial; (*ruta*) land *cpd*
terrible [te'rriβle] *adj* terrible, awful
territorio [terri'torjo] *nm* territory
terrón [te'rron] *nm* (*de azúcar*) lump; (*de tierra*) clod, lump
terror [te'rror] *nm* terror; **~ífico, a** *adj* terrifying; **~ista** *adj, nm/f* terrorist
terso, a ['terso, a] *adj* (*liso*) smooth; (*pulido*) polished; **tersura** *nf* smoothness
tertulia [ter'tulja] *nf* (*reunión informal*) social gathering; (*grupo*) group, circle
tesis ['tesis] *nf inv* thesis
tesón [te'son] *nm* (*firmeza*) firmness; (*tenacidad*) tenacity
tesorero, a [teso'rero, a] *nm/f* treasurer
tesoro [te'soro] *nm* treasure; (*COM, POL*) treasury
testaferro [testa'ferro] *nm* figurehead
testamentario, a [testamen'tarjo, a] *adj* testamentary ♦ *nm/f* executor/executrix
testamento [testa'mento] *nm* will
testar [tes'tar] *vi* to make a will
testarudo, a [testa'ruðo, a] *adj* stubborn
testículo [tes'tikulo] *nm* testicle
testificar [testifi'kar] *vt* to testify; (*fig*) to attest ♦ *vi* to give evidence
testigo [tes'tiγo] *nm/f* witness; **~ de cargo/descargo** witness for the prosecution/defence; **~ ocular** eye witness
testimoniar [testimo'njar] *vt* to testify to; (*fig*) to show; **testimonio** *nm* testimony
teta ['teta] *nf* (*de biberón*) teat; (*ANAT: fam*) breast
tétanos ['tetanos] *nm* tetanus
tetera [te'tera] *nf* teapot
tétrico, a ['tetriko, a] *adj* gloomy, dismal
textil [teks'til] *adj* textile
texto ['teksto] *nm* text; **textual** *adj* textual
textura [teks'tura] *nf* (*de tejido*) texture
tez [teθ] *nf* (*cutis*) complexion
ti [ti] *pron* you; (*reflexivo*) yourself
tía ['tia] *nf* (*pariente*) aunt; (*fam*) chick, bird
tibieza [ti'βjeθa] *nf* (*temperatura*) tepidness; (*actitud*) coolness; **tibio, a** *adj* lukewarm
tiburón [tiβu'ron] *nm* shark

tic [tik] *nm* (*ruido*) click; (*de reloj*) tick; (*MED*): ~ **nervioso** nervous tic

tictac [tik'tak] *nm* (*de reloj*) tick tock

tiempo ['tjempo] *nm* time; (*época, período*) age, period; (*METEOROLOGÍA*) weather; (*LING*) tense; (*DEPORTE*) half; **a** ~ in time; **a un** *o* **al mismo** ~ at the same time; **al poco** ~ very soon (after); **se quedó poco** ~ he didn't stay very long; **hace poco** ~ not long ago; **mucho** ~ a long time; **de** ~ **en** ~ from time to time; **hace buen/mal** ~ the weather is fine/bad; **estar a** ~ to be in time; **hace** ~ some time ago; **hacer** ~ to while away the time; **motor de 2** ~**s** two-stroke engine; **primer** ~ first half

tienda ['tjenda] *nf* shop, store; ~ (**de campaña**) tent; ~ **de alimentación** *o* **comestibles** grocer's (*BRIT*), grocery store (*US*)

tienes *etc vb ver* **tener**

tienta *etc* ['tjenta] *vb ver* **tentar** ♦ *nf*: **andar a** ~**s** to grope one's way along

tiento ['tjento] *vb ver* **tentar** ♦ *nm* (*tacto*) touch; (*precaución*) wariness

tierno, a ['tjerno, a] *adj* (*blando*) tender; (*fresco*) fresh; (*amable*) sweet

tierra ['tjerra] *nf* earth; (*suelo*) soil; (*mundo*) earth, world; (*país*) country, land; ~ **adentro** inland

tieso, a ['tjeso, a] *adj* (*rígido*) rigid; (*duro*) stiff; (*fam: orgulloso*) conceited

tiesto ['tjesto] *nm* flowerpot

tifoidea [tifoi'ðea] *nf* typhoid

tifón [ti'fon] *nm* typhoon

tifus ['tifus] *nm* typhus

tigre ['tivre] *nm* tiger

tijera [ti'xera] *nf* scissors *pl*; (*ZOOL*) claw; ~**s** *nfpl* scissors; (*para plantas*) shears

tijeretear [tixerete'ar] *vt* to snip

tila ['tila] *nf* lime blossom tea

tildar [til'dar] *vt*: ~ **de** to brand as

tilde ['tilde] *nf* (*TIP*) tilde

tilín [ti'lin] *nm* tinkle

tilo ['tilo] *nm* lime tree

timar [ti'mar] *vt* (*estafar*) to swindle

timbal [tim'bal] *nm* small drum

timbrar [tim'brar] *vt* to stamp

timbre ['timbre] *nm* (*sello*) stamp; (*campanilla*) bell; (*tono*) timbre; (*COM*) stamp duty

timidez [timi'ðeθ] *nf* shyness; **tímido, a** *adj* shy

timo ['timo] *nm* swindle

timón [ti'mon] *nm* helm, rudder; **timonel** *nm* helmsman

tímpano ['timpano] *nm* (*ANAT*) eardrum; (*MUS*) small drum

tina ['tina] *nf* tub; (*baño*) bath(tub); **tinaja** *nf* large jar

tinglado [tin'glaðo] *nm* (*cobertizo*) shed; (*fig: truco*) trick; (*intriga*) intrigue

tinieblas [ti'njeßlas] *nfpl* darkness *sg*; (*sombras*) shadows

tino ['tino] *nm* (*habilidad*) skill; (*juicio*) insight

tinta ['tinta] *nf* ink; (*TEC*) dye; (*ARTE*) colour

tinte ['tinte] *nm* dye

tintero [tin'tero] *nm* inkwell

tintinear [tintine'ar] *vt* to tinkle

tinto ['tinto] *nm* red wine

tintorería [tintore'ria] *nf* dry cleaner's

tintura [tin'tura] *nf* (*QUÍM*) dye; (*farmacéutico*) tincture

tío ['tio] *nm* (*pariente*) uncle; (*fam: individuo*) bloke (*BRIT*), guy

tiovivo [tio'ßißo] *nm* merry-go-round

típico, a ['tipiko, a] *adj* typical

tipo ['tipo] *nm* (*clase*) type, kind; (*hombre*) fellow; (*ANAT: de hombre*) build; (: *de mujer*) figure; (*IMPRENTA*) type; ~ **bancario/de descuento/de interés/de cambio** bank/discount/interest/exchange rate

tipografía [tipovra'fia] *nf* printing *cpd*; **tipográfico, a** *adj* printing *cpd*

tíquet ['tiket] (*pl* ~**s**) *nm* ticket; (*en tienda*) cash slip

tiquismiquis [tikis'mikis] *nm inv* fussy person ♦ *nmpl* (*querellas*) squabbling *sg*; (*escrúpulos*) silly scruples

tira ['tira] *nf* strip; (*fig*) abundance; ~ **y afloja** give and take

tirabuzón [tiraßu'θon] *nm* (*rizo*) curl

tirachinas [tira'tʃinas] *nm inv* catapult

tirada [ti'raða] *nf* (*acto*) cast, throw; (*serie*) series; (*TIP*) printing, edition; **de una ~** at one go

tirado, a [ti'raðo, a] *adj* (*barato*) dirt-cheap; (*fam: fácil*) very easy

tirador [tira'ðor] *nm* (*mango*) handle

tiranía [tira'nia] *nf* tyranny; **tirano, a** *adj* tyrannical ♦ *nm/f* tyrant

tirante [ti'rante] *adj* (*cuerda etc*) tight, taut; (*relaciones*) strained ♦ *nm* (*ARQ*) brace; **~s** *nmpl* (*de pantalón*) braces (*BRIT*), suspenders (*US*); **tirantez** *nf* tightness; (*fig*) tension

tirar [ti'rar] *vt* to throw; (*dejar caer*) to drop; (*volcar*) to upset; (*derribar*) to knock down *o* over; (*desechar*) to throw out *o* away; (*dinero*) to squander; (*imprimir*) to print ♦ *vi* (*disparar*) to shoot; (*de la puerta etc*) to pull; (*fam: andar*) to go; (*tender a, buscar realizar*) to tend to; (*DEPORTE*) to shoot; **~se** *vr* to throw o.s.; **~ abajo** to bring down, destroy; **tira más a su padre** he takes more after his father; **ir tirando** to manage; **a todo ~** at the most

tirita [ti'rita] *nf* (sticking) plaster (*BRIT*), bandaid (*US*)

tiritar [tiri'tar] *vi* to shiver

tiro ['tiro] *nm* (*lanzamiento*) throw; (*disparo*) shot; (*DEPORTE*) shot; (*GOLF, TENIS*) drive; (*alcance*) range; **~ al blanco** target practice; **caballo de ~** cart-horse; **andar de ~s largos** to be all dressed up; **al ~** (*AM*) at once

tirón [ti'ron] *nm* (*sacudida*) pull, tug; **de un ~** in one go, all at once

tiroteo [tiro'teo] *nm* exchange of shots, shooting

tísico, a ['tisiko, a] *adj* consumptive

tisis ['tisis] *nf inv* consumption, tuberculosis

títere ['titere] *nm* puppet

titiritero, a [titiri'tero, a] *nm/f* puppeteer

titubeante [tituße'ante] *adj* (*al andar*) shaky, tottering; (*al hablar*) stammering; (*dudoso*) hesitant

titubear [tituße'ar] *vi* to stagger; to

stammer; (*fig*) to hesitate; **titubeo** *nm* staggering; stammering; hesitation

titulado, a [titu'laðo, a] *adj* (*libro*) entitled; (*persona*) titled

titular [titu'lar] *adj* titular ♦ *nm/f* holder ♦ *nm* headline ♦ *vt* to title; **~se** *vr* to be entitled; **título** *nm* title; (*de diario*) headline; (*certificado*) professional qualification; (*universitario*) (university) degree; **a título de** in the capacity of

tiza ['tiθa] *nf* chalk

tiznar [tiθ'nar] *vt* to blacken

tizón [ti'θon] *nm* brand

toalla [to'aʎa] *nf* towel

tobillo [to'ßiʎo] *nm* ankle

tobogán [toßo'ɣan] *nm* (*montaña rusa*) roller-coaster; (*de niños*) chute, slide

tocadiscos [toka'ðiskos] *nm inv* record player

tocado, a [to'kaðo, a] *adj* (*fam*) touched ♦ *nm* headdress

tocador [toka'ðor] *nm* (*mueble*) dressing table; (*cuarto*) boudoir; (*fam*) ladies' toilet (*BRIT*) *o* room (*US*)

tocante [to'kante]: **~ a** *prep* with regard to

tocar [to'kar] *vt* to touch; (*MUS*) to play; (*referirse a*) to allude to; (*timbre*) to ring ♦ *vi* (*a la puerta*) to knock (on *o* at the door); (*ser de turno*) to fall to, be the turn of; (*ser hora*) to be due; **~se** *vr* (*cubrirse la cabeza*) to cover one's head; (*tener contacto*) to touch (each other); **por lo que a mí me toca** as far as I am concerned; **te toca a tí** it's your turn

tocayo, a [to'kajo, a] *nm/f* namesake

tocino [to'θino] *nm* bacon

todavía [toða'ßia] *adv* (*aun*) even; (*aún*) still, yet; **~ más** yet more; **~ no** not yet

---

PALABRA CLAVE

---

todo, a ['toðo, a] *adj* **1** (*con artículo sg*) all; **toda la carne** all the meat; **toda la noche** all night, the whole night; **~ el libro** the whole book; **toda una botella** a whole bottle; **~ lo contrario** quite the opposite; **está toda sucia** she's all dirty; **por ~ el país** throughout the whole

country
2 (*con artículo pl*) all; every; **~s los libros** all the books; **todas las noches** every night; **~s los que quieran salir** all those who want to leave
♦ *pron* **1** everything, all; **~s** everyone, everybody; **lo sabemos ~** we know everything; **~s querían más tiempo** everybody *o* everyone wanted more time; **nos marchamos ~s** all of us left
2: con ~: con ~ él me sigue gustando even so I still like him
♦ *adv* all; **vaya ~ seguido** keep straight on *o* ahead
♦ *nm:* **como un ~** as a whole; **del ~: no me agrada del ~** I don't entirely like it

todopoderoso, a [toðopoðe'roso, a] *adj* all powerful; (*REL*) almighty
toga ['toxa] *nf* toga; (*ESCOL*) gown
Tokio ['tokjo] *n* Tokyo
toldo ['toldo] *nm* (*para el sol*) sunshade (*BRIT*), parasol; (*tienda*) marquee
tolerancia [tole'ranθja] *nf* tolerance; **tolerante** *adj* (*sociedad*) liberal; (*persona*) open-minded
tolerar [tole'rar] *vt* to tolerate; (*resistir*) to endure
toma ['toma] *nf* (*acto*) taking; (*MED*) dose; **~ (de corriente)** socket
tomar [to'mar] *vt* to take; (*aspecto*) to take on; (*beber*) to drink ♦ *vi* to take; (*AM*) to drink; **~se** *vr* to take; **~se por** to consider o.s. to be; **~ a bien/a mal** to take well/badly; **~ en serio** to take seriously; **~ el pelo a alguien** to pull sb's leg; **~la con uno** to pick a quarrel with sb; **¡tome!** here you are!; **~ el sol** to sunbathe
tomate [to'mate] *nm* tomato
tomillo [to'miʎo] *nm* thyme
tomo ['tomo] *nm* (*libro*) volume
ton [ton] *abr* = **tonelada** ♦ *nm:* **sin ~ ni son** without rhyme or reason
tonada [to'naða] *nf* tune
tonalidad [tonali'ðað] *nf* tone
tonel [to'nel] *nm* barrel
tonelada [tone'laða] *nf* ton; **tonelaje** *nm*

tonnage
tónica ['tonika] *nf* (*MUS*) tonic; (*fig*) keynote
tónico, a ['toniko, a] *adj* tonic ♦ *nm* (*MED*) tonic
tonificar [tonifi'kar] *vt* to tone up
tono ['tono] *nm* tone; **fuera de ~** inappropriate; **darse ~** to put on airs
tontería [tonte'ria] *nf* (*estupidez*) foolishness; (*cosa*) stupid thing; (*acto*) foolish act; **~s** *nfpl* (*disparates*) rubbish *sg*, nonsense *sg*
tonto, a ['tonto, a] *adj* stupid, silly ♦ *nm/f* fool
topar [to'par] *vi:* **~ contra** *o* **en** to run into; **~ con** to run up against
tope ['tope] *adj* maximum ♦ *nm* (*fin*) end; (*límite*) limit; (*FERRO*) buffer; (*AUTO*) bumper; **al ~** end to end
tópico, a ['topiko, a] *adj* topical ♦ *nm* platitude
topo ['topo] *nm* (*ZOOL*) mole; (*fig*) blunderer
topografía [topoxra'fia] *nf* topography; **topógrafo, a** *nm/f* topographer
toque *etc* ['toke] *vb ver* **tocar** ♦ *nm* touch; (*MUS*) beat; (*de campana*) peal; **dar un ~ a** to warn; **~ de queda** curfew
toqué *vb ver* **tocar**
toquetear [tokete'ar] *vt* to finger
toquilla [to'kiʎa] *nf* (*pañuelo*) headscarf; (*chal*) shawl
tórax ['toraks] *nm* thorax
torbellino [torbe'ʎino] *nm* whirlwind; (*fig*) whirl
torcedura [torθe'ðura] *nf* twist; (*MED*) sprain
torcer [tor'θer] *vt* to twist; (*la esquina*) to turn; (*MED*) to sprain ♦ *vi* (*desviar*) to turn off; **~se** *vr* (*ladearse*) to bend; (*desviarse*) to go astray; (*fracasar*) to go wrong; **torcido, a** *adj* twisted; (*fig*) crooked ♦ *nm* curl
tordo, a ['torðo, a] *adj* dappled ♦ *nm* thrush
torear [tore'ar] *vt* (*fig: evadir*) to avoid; (*jugar con*) to tease ♦ *vi* to fight bulls;

toreo *nm* bullfighting; **torero, a** *nm/f* bullfighter

tormenta [tor'menta] *nf* storm; (*fig: confusión*) turmoil

tormento [tor'mento] *nm* torture; (*fig*) anguish

tornar [tor'nar] *vt* (*devolver*) to return, give back; (*transformar*) to transform ♦ *vi* to go back; **~se** *vr* (*ponerse*) to become

tornasolado, a [tornaso'laðo, a] *adj* (*brillante*) iridescent; (*reluciente*) shimmering

torneo [tor'neo] *nm* tournament

tornillo [tor'niʎo] *nm* screw

torniquete [torni'kete] *nm* (*MED*) tourniquet

torno ['torno] *nm* (*TEC*) winch; (*tambor*) drum; **en ~ (a)** round, about

toro ['toro] *nm* bull; (*fam*) he-man; **los ~s** bullfighting

toronja [to'ronxa] *nf* grapefruit

torpe ['torpe] *adj* (*poco hábil*) clumsy, awkward; (*necio*) dim; (*lento*) slow

torpedo [tor'peðo] *nm* torpedo

torpeza [tor'peθa] *nf* (*falta de agilidad*) clumsiness; (*lentitud*) slowness; (*error*) mistake

torre ['torre] *nf* tower; (*de petróleo*) derrick

torrefacto, a [torre'facto, a] *adj* roasted

torrente [to'rrente] *nm* torrent

tórrido, a ['torriðo, a] *adj* torrid

torrija [to'rrixa] *nf* French toast

torsión [tor'sjon] *nf* twisting

torso ['torso] *nm* torso

torta ['torta] *nf* cake; (*fam*) slap

tortícolis [tor'tikolis] *nm inv* stiff neck

tortilla [tor'tiʎa] *nf* omelette; (*AM*) maize pancake; **~ francesa/española** plain/ potato omelette

tórtola ['tortola] *nf* turtledove

tortuga [tor'tuɣa] *nf* tortoise

tortuoso, a [tor'twoso, a] *adj* winding

tortura [tor'tura] *nf* torture; **torturar** *vt* to torture

tos [tos] *nf* cough; **~ ferina** whooping cough

tosco, a ['tosko, a] *adj* coarse

toser [to'ser] *vi* to cough

tostada [tos'taða] *nf* piece of toast; **tostado, a** [tos'taðo, a] *adj* toasted; (*por el sol*) dark brown; (*piel*) tanned

tostador [tosta'ðor] *nm* toaster

tostar [tos'tar] *vt* to toast; (*café*) to roast; (*persona*) to tan; **~se** *vr* to get brown

total [to'tal] *adj* total ♦ *adv* in short; (*al fin y al cabo*) when all is said and done ♦ *nm* total; **~ que** to cut (*BRIT*) o make (*US*) a long story short

totalidad [totali'ðað] *nf* whole

totalitario, a [totali'tarjo, a] *adj* totalitarian

tóxico, a ['toksiko, a] *adj* toxic ♦ *nm* poison; **toxicómano, a** *nm/f* drug addict

toxina [to'ksina] *nf* toxin

tozudo, a [to'θuðo, a] *adj* obstinate

traba ['traßa] *nf* bond, tie; (*cadena*) shackle

trabajador, a [traßaxa'ðor, a] *adj* hard-working ♦ *nm/f* worker

trabajar [traßa'xar] *vt* to work; (*AGR*) to till; (*empeñarse en*) to work at; (*convencer*) to persuade ♦ *vi* to work; (*esforzarse*) to strive; **trabajo** *nm* work; (*tarea*) task; (*POL*) labour; (*fig*) effort; **tomarse el trabajo de** to take the trouble to; **trabajo por turno/a destajo** shift work/ piecework; **trabajoso, a** *adj* hard

trabalenguas [traßa'lengwas] *nm inv* tongue twister

trabar [tra'ßar] *vt* (*juntar*) to join, unite; (*atar*) to tie down, fetter; (*agarrar*) to seize; (*amistad*) to strike up; **~se** *vr* to become entangled; **trabársele a uno la lengua** to be tongue-tied

tracción [trak'θjon] *nf* traction; **~ delantera/trasera** front-wheel/rear-wheel drive

tractor [trak'tor] *nm* tractor

tradición [traði'θjon] *nf* tradition; **tradicional** *adj* traditional

traducción [traðuk'θjon] *nf* translation

traducir [traðu'θir] *vt* to translate; **traductor, a** *nm/f* translator

traer [tra'er] *vt* to bring; (*llevar*) to carry; (*llevar puesto*) to wear; (*incluir*) to carry; (*causar*) to cause; **~se** *vr*: **~se algo** to be up to sth

traficar [trafi'kar] *vi* to trade

tráfico ['trafiko] *nm* (*COM*) trade; (*AUTO*) traffic

tragaluz [traɣa'luθ] *nm* skylight

tragaperras [traɣa'perras] *nm o f inv* slot machine

tragar [tra'ɣar] *vt* to swallow; (*devorar*) to devour, bolt down; **~se** *vr* to swallow

tragedia [tra'xeðja] *nf* tragedy; **trágico, a** *adj* tragic

trago ['traɣo] *nm* (*líquido*) drink; (*bocado*) gulp; (*fam: de bebida*) swig; (*desgracia*) blow

traición [trai'θjon] *nf* treachery; (*JUR*) treason; (*una ~*) act of treachery; **traicionar** *vt* to betray

traicionero, a [traiθjo'nero, a] *adj* treacherous

traidor, a [trai'ðor, a] *adj* treacherous ♦ *nm/f* traitor

traigo *etc vb ver* **traer**

traje ['traxe] *vb ver* **traer** ♦ *nm* (*de hombre*) suit; (*de mujer*) dress; (*vestido típico*) costume; **~ de baño** swimsuit; **~ de luces** bullfighter's costume

trajera *etc vb ver* **traer**

trajín [tra'xin] *nm* (*fam: movimiento*) bustle; **trajinar** *vi* (*moverse*) to bustle about

trama ['trama] *nf* (*intriga*) plot; (*de tejido*) weft (*BRIT*), woof (*US*); **tramar** *vt* to plot; (*TEC*) to weave

tramitar [trami'tar] *vt* (*asunto*) to transact; (*negociar*) to negotiate

trámite ['tramite] *nm* (*paso*) step; (*JUR*) transaction; **~s** *nmpl* (*burocracia*) procedure *sg*; (*JUR*) proceedings

tramo ['tramo] *nm* (*de tierra*) plot; (*de escalera*) flight; (*de vía*) section

tramoya [tra'moja] *nf* (*TEATRO*) piece of stage machinery; **tramoyista** *nm/f* scene shifter; (*fig*) trickster

trampa ['trampa] *nf* trap; (*en el suelo*)

trapdoor; (*truco*) trick; (*engaño*) fiddle; **trampear** *vt*, *vi* to cheat

trampolín [trampo'lin] *nm* (*de piscina etc*) diving board

tramposo, a [tram'poso, a] *adj* crooked, cheating ♦ *nm/f* crook, cheat

tranca ['tranka] *nf* (*palo*) stick; (*de puerta, ventana*) bar; **trancar** *vt* to bar

trance ['tranθe] *nm* (*momento difícil*) difficult moment *o* juncture; (*estado hipnotizado*) trance

tranquilidad [trankili'ðað] *nf* (*calma*) calmness, stillness; (*paz*) peacefulness

tranquilizar [trankili'θar] *vt* (*calmar*) to calm (down); (*asegurar*) to reassure; **~se** *vr* to calm down; **tranquilo, a** *adj* (*calmado*) calm; (*apacible*) peaceful; (*mar*) calm; (*mente*) untroubled

transacción [transak'θjon] *nf* transaction

transbordador [transβorða'ðor] *nm* ferry

transbordar [transβor'ðar] *vt* to transfer; **transbordo** *nm* transfer; **hacer transbordo** to change (trains *etc*)

transcurrir [transku'rrir] *vi* (*tiempo*) to pass; (*hecho*) to take place

transcurso [trans'kurso] *nm*: **~ del tiempo** lapse (of time)

transeúnte [transe'unte] *nm/f* passer-by

transferencia [transfe'renθja] *nf* transference; (*COM*) transfer

transferir [transfe'rir] *vt* to transfer

transformador [transforma'ðor] *nm* (*ELEC*) transformer

transformar [transfor'mar] *vt* to transform; (*convertir*) to convert

tránsfuga ['transfuɣa] *nm/f* (*MIL*) deserter; (*POL*) turncoat

transfusión [transfu'sjon] *nf* transfusion

transición [transi'θjon] *nf* transition

transigir [transi'xir] *vi* to compromise, make concessions

transistor [transis'tor] *nm* transistor

transitar [transi'tar] *vi* to go (from place to place); **tránsito** *nm* transit; (*AUTO*) traffic; **transitorio, a** *adj* transitory

transmisión [transmi'sjon] *nf* (*TEC*) transmission; (*transferencia*) transfer; **~ en**

directo/exterior live/outside broadcast
transmitir [transmi'tir] *vt* to transmit; (*RADIO, TV*) to broadcast
transparencia [transpa'renθja] *nf* transparency; (*claridad*) clearness, clarity; (*foto*) slide
transparentar [transparen'tar] *vt* to reveal ♦ *vi* to be transparent; **transparente** *adj* transparent; (*claro*) clear
transpirar [transpi'rar] *vi* to perspire
transportar [transpor'tar] *vt* to transport; (*llevar*) to carry; **transporte** *nm* transport; (*COM*) haulage
transversal [transβer'sal] *adj* transverse, cross
tranvía [tram'bia] *nm* tram
trapecio [tra'peθjo] *nm* trapeze; **trapecista** *nm/f* trapeze artist
trapero, a [tra'pero, a] *nm/f* ragman
trapicheo [trapi'tʃeo] (*fam*) *nm* scheme, fiddle
trapo ['trapo] *nm* (*tela*) rag; (*de cocina*) cloth
tráquea ['trakea] *nf* windpipe
traqueteo [trake'teo] *nm* rattling
tras [tras] *prep* (*detrás*) behind; (*después*) after
trasatlántico [trasat'lantiko] *nm* (*barco*) (cabin) cruiser
trascendencia [trasθen'denθja] *nf* (*importancia*) importance; (*FILOSOFÍA*) transcendence
trascendental [trasθenden'tal] *adj* important; (*FILOSOFÍA*) transcendental
trascender [trasθen'der] *vi* (*noticias*) to come out; (*suceso*) to have a wide effect
trasero, a [tra'sero, a] *adj* back, rear ♦ *nm* (*ANAT*) bottom
trasfondo [tras'fondo] *nm* background
trasgredir [trasvre'ðir] *vt* to contravene
trashumante [trasu'mante] *adj* (*animales*) migrating
trasladar [trasla'ðar] *vt* to move; (*persona*) to transfer; (*postergar*) to postpone; (*copiar*) to copy; **~se** *vr* (*mudarse*) to move; **traslado** *nm* move; (*mudanza*) move, removal

traslucir [traslu'θir] *vt* to show; **~se** *vr* to be translucent; (*fig*) to be revealed
trasluz [tras'luθ] *nm* reflected light; **al ~** against *o* up to the light
trasnochador, a [trasnotʃa'ðor, a] *nm/f* night owl
trasnochar [trasno'tʃar] *vi* (*acostarse tarde*) to stay up late
traspapelar [traspape'lar] *vt* (*document, carta*) to mislay, misplace
traspasar [traspa'sar] *vt* (*suj: bala etc*) to pierce, go through; (*propiedad*) to sell, transfer; (*calle*) to cross over; (*límites*) to go beyond; (*ley*) to break; **traspaso** *nm* (*venta*) transfer, sale
traspié [tras'pje] *nm* (*tropezón*) trip; (*error*) blunder
trasplantar [trasplan'tar] *vt* to transplant
traste ['traste] *nm* (*MUS*) fret; **dar al ~ con algo** to ruin sth
trastero [tras'tero] *nm* storage room
trastienda [tras'tjenda] *nf* back of shop
trasto ['trasto] (*pey*) *nm* (*cosa*) piece of junk; (*persona*) dead loss
trastornado, a [trastor'naðo, a] *adj* (*loco*) mad, crazy
trastornar [trastor'nar] *vt* (*fig: planes*) to disrupt; (*: nervios*) to shatter; (*: persona*) to drive crazy; **~se** *vr* (*volverse loco*) to go mad *o* crazy; **trastorno** *nm* (*acto*) overturning; (*confusión*) confusion
tratable [tra'taßle] *adj* friendly
tratado [tra'taðo] *nm* (*POL*) treaty; (*COM*) agreement
tratamiento [trata'mjento] *nm* treatment; **~ de textos** (*INFORM*) word processing *cpd*
tratar [tra'tar] *vt* (*ocuparse de*) to treat; (*manejar, TEC*) to handle; (*MED*) to treat; (*dirigirse a: persona*) to address ♦ *vi*: **~ de** (*hablar sobre*) to deal with, be about; (*intentar*) to try to; **~se** *vr* to treat each other; **~ con** (*COM*) to trade in; (*negociar*) to negotiate with; (*tener contactos*) to have dealings with; **¿de qué se trata?** what's it about?; **trato** *nm* dealings *pl*; (*relaciones*) relationship; (*comportamiento*)

manner; (COM) agreement

trauma ['trauma] nm trauma

través [tra'βes] nm (fig) reverse; **al ~** across, crossways; **a ~ de** across; (sobre) over; (por) through

travesaño [traβe'saɲo] nm (ARQ) crossbeam; (DEPORTE) crossbar

travesía [traβe'sia] nf (calle) cross-street; (NAUT) crossing

travesura [traβe'sura] nf (broma) prank; (ingenio) wit

traviesa [tra'βjesa] nf (ARQ) crossbeam

travieso, a [tra'βjeso, a] adj (niño) naughty

trayecto [tra'jekto] nm (ruta) road, way; (viaje) journey; (tramo) stretch; **~ria** nf trajectory; (fig) path

traza ['traθa] nf (aspecto) looks pl; (señal) sign; **~do, a** adj: **bien ~do** shapely, well-formed ♦ nm (ARQ) plan, design; (fig) outline

trazar [tra'θar] vt (ARQ) to plan; (ARTE) to sketch; (fig) to trace; (plan) to draw up; **trazo** nm (línea) line; (bosquejo) sketch

trébol ['treβol] nm (BOT) clover

trece ['treθe] num thirteen

trecho ['tretʃo] nm (distancia) distance; (de tiempo) while; **de ~ en ~** at intervals

tregua ['trexwa] nf (MIL) truce; (fig) respite

treinta ['treinta] num thirty

tremendo, a [tre'mendo, a] adj (terrible) terrible; (imponente: cosa) imposing; (fam: fabuloso) tremendous

trémulo, a ['tremulo, a] adj quivering

tren [tren] nm train; **~ de aterrizaje** undercarriage

trenca ['trenka] nf duffel coat

trenza ['trenθa] nf (de pelo) plait (BRIT), braid (US); **trenzar** vt (pelo) to plait, braid; **trenzarse** vr (AM) to become involved

trepadora [trepa'ðora] nf (BOT) climber

trepar [tre'par] vt, vi to climb

trepidante [trepi'ðante] adj (acción) fast; (ritmo) hectic

tres [tres] num three

tresillo [tre'siʎo] nm three-piece suite;

(MUS) triplet

treta ['treta] nf trick

triángulo ['trjangulo] nm triangle

tribu ['triβu] nf tribe

tribuna [tri'βuna] nf (plataforma) platform; (DEPORTE) (grand)stand

tribunal [triβu'nal] nm (JUR) court; (comisión, fig) tribunal

tributar [triβu'tar] vt (gen) to pay; **tributo** nm (COM) tax

tricotar [triko'tar] vi to knit

trigal [tri'val] nm wheat field

trigo ['trivo] nm wheat

trigueño, a [tri'xeɲo, a] adj (pelo) corn-coloured

trillado, a [tri'ʎaðo, a] adj threshed; (asunto) trite, hackneyed; **trilladora** nf threshing machine

trillar [tri'ʎar] vt (AGR) to thresh

trimestral [trimes'tral] adj quarterly; (ESCOL) termly

trimestre [tri'mestre] nm (ESCOL) term

trinar [tri'nar] vi (pájaros) to sing; (rabiar) to fume, be angry

trinchar [trin'tʃar] vt to carve

trinchera [trin'tʃera] nf (fosa) trench

trineo [tri'neo] nm sledge

trinidad [trini'ðað] nf trio; (REL): **la T~** the Trinity

trino ['trino] nm trill

tripa ['tripa] nf (ANAT) intestine; (fam: tb: **~s**) insides pl

triple ['triple] adj triple

triplicado, a [tripli'kaðo, a] adj: **por ~** in triplicate

tripulación [tripula'θjon] nf crew

tripulante [tripu'lante] nm/f crewman/woman

tripular [tripu'lar] vt (barco) to man; (AUTO) to drive

triquiñuela [triki'ɲwela] nf trick

tris [tris] nm inv crack; **en un ~** in an instant

triste ['triste] adj sad; (lamentable) sorry, miserable; **~za** nf (aflicción) sadness; (melancolía) melancholy

triturar [tritu'rar] vt (moler) to grind;

(*mascar*) to chew

triunfar [trjun'far] *vi* (*tener éxito*) to triumph; (*ganar*) to win; **triunfo** *nm* triumph

trivial [tri'βjal] *adj* trivial; **~izar** *vt* to minimize, play down

triza ['triθa] *nf*: **hacer ~s** to smash to bits; (*papel*) to tear to shreds

trocar [tro'kar] *vt* to exchange

trocear [troθe'ar] *vt* (*carne, manzana*) to cut up, cut into pieces

trocha ['trotʃa] *nf* short cut

troche ['trotʃe]: **a ~ y moche** *adv* helter-skelter, pell-mell

trofeo [tro'feo] *nm* (*premio*) trophy; (*éxito*) success

tromba ['tromba] *nf* downpour

trombón [trom'bon] *nm* trombone

trombosis [trom'bosis] *nf inv* thrombosis

trompa ['trompa] *nf* horn; (*trompo*) humming top; (*hocico*) snout; (*fam*): **cogerse una ~** to get tight

trompazo [trom'paθo] *nm* bump, bang

trompeta [trom'peta] *nf* trumpet; (*clarín*) bugle

trompicón [trompi'kon]: **a ~es** *adv* in fits and starts

trompo ['trompo] *nm* spinning top

trompón [trom'pon] *nm* bump

tronar [tro'nar] *vt* (*AM*) to shoot ♦ *vi* to thunder; (*fig*) to rage

tronchar [tron'tʃar] *vt* (*árbol*) to chop down; (*fig: vida*) to cut short; (: *esperanza*) to shatter; (*persona*) to tire out; **~se** *vr* to fall down

tronco ['tronko] *nm* (*de árbol, ANAT*) trunk

trono ['trono] *nm* throne

tropa ['tropa] *nf* (*MIL*) troop; (*soldados*) soldiers *pl*

tropel [tro'pel] *nm* (*muchedumbre*) crowd

tropezar [trope'θar] *vi* to trip, stumble; (*errar*) to slip up; **~ con** to run into; (*topar con*) to bump into; **tropezón** *nm* trip; (*fig*) blunder

tropical [tropi'kal] *adj* tropical

trópico ['tropiko] *nm* tropic

tropiezo [tro'pjeθo] *vb ver* **tropezar** ♦ *nm*

(*error*) slip, blunder; (*desgracia*) misfortune; (*obstáculo*) snag

trotamundos [trota'mundos] *nm inv* globetrotter

trotar [tro'tar] *vi* to trot; **trote** *nm* trot; (*fam*) travelling; **de mucho trote** hard-wearing

trozo ['troθo] *nm* bit, piece

trucha ['trutʃa] *nf* trout

truco ['truko] *nm* (*habilidad*) knack; (*engaño*) trick

trueno ['trweno] *nm* thunder; (*estampido*) bang

trueque *etc* ['trweke] *vb ver* **trocar** ♦ *nm* exchange; (*COM*) barter

trufa ['trufa] *nf* (*BOT*) truffle

truhán, ana [tru'an, ana] *nm/f* rogue

truncar [trun'kar] *vt* (*cortar*) to truncate; (*fig: la vida etc*) to cut short; (: *el desarrollo*) to stunt

tu [tu] *adj* your

tú [tu] *pron* you

tubérculo [tu'βerkulo] *nm* (*BOT*) tuber

tuberculosis [tußerku'losis] *nf inv* tuberculosis

tubería [tuße'ria] *nf* pipes *pl*; (*conducto*) pipeline

tubo ['tußo] *nm* tube, pipe; **~ de ensayo** test tube; **~ de escape** exhaust (pipe)

tuerca ['twerka] *nf* nut

tuerto, a ['twerto, a] *adj* blind in one eye ♦ *nm/f* one-eyed person

tuerza *etc vb ver* **torcer**

tuétano ['twetano] *nm* marrow; (*BOT*) pith

tufo ['tufo] *nm* (*hedor*) stench

tul [tul] *nm* tulle

tulipán [tuli'pan] *nm* tulip

tullido, a [tu'ʎiðo, a] *adj* crippled

tumba ['tumba] *nf* (*sepultura*) tomb

tumbar [tum'bar] *vt* to knock down; **~se** *vr* (*echarse*) to lie down; (*extenderse*) to stretch out

tumbo ['tumbo] *nm*: **dar ~s** to stagger

tumbona [tum'bona] *nf* (*butaca*) easy chair; (*de playa*) deckchair (*BRIT*), beach chair (*US*)

tumor [tu'mor] *nm* tumour

tumulto [tu'multo] *nm* turmoil
tuna ['tuna] *nf* (MUS) student music group;
ver tb **tuno**

┌─────────────┐
│ **tuna** │
└─────────────┘

> ❶ *A* **tuna** *is a musical group made up of*
> *university students or former students*
> *who dress up in costumes from the "Edad*
> *de Oro", the Spanish Golden Age. These*
> *groups go through the town playing their*
> *guitars, lutes and tambourines and*
> *serenade the young ladies in the halls of*
> *residence or make impromptu appearances*
> *at weddings or parties singing traditional*
> *Spanish songs for a few* **pesetas.**

tunante [tu'nante] *nm/f* rascal
tunda ['tunda] *nf* (*golpeo*) beating
túnel ['tunel] *nm* tunnel
Túnez ['tuneθ] *nm* Tunisia; (*ciudad*) Tunis
tuno, a ['tuno, a] *nm/f* (*fam*) rogue ♦ *nm*
member of student music group
tupido, a [tu'piðo, a] *adj* (*denso*) dense;
(*tela*) close-woven
turba ['turβa] *nf* crowd
turbante [tur'βante] *nm* turban
turbar [tur'βar] *vt* (*molestar*) to disturb;
(*incomodar*) to upset; **~se** *vr* to be
disturbed
turbina [tur'βina] *nf* turbine
turbio, a ['turβjo, a] *adj* cloudy; (*tema etc*)
confused
turbulencia [turβu'lenθja] *nf* turbulence;
(*fig*) restlessness; **turbulento, a** *adj*
turbulent; (*fig: intranquilo*) restless;
(: *ruidoso*) noisy
turco, a ['turko, a] *adj* Turkish ♦ *nm/f*
Turk
turismo [tu'rismo] *nm* tourism; (*coche*)
car; **turista** *nm/f* tourist; **turístico, a**
adj tourist *cpd*
turnar [tur'nar] *vi* to take (it in) turns; **~se**
vr to take (it in) turns; **turno** *nm* (*de
trabajo*) shift; (*juegos etc*) turn
turquesa [tur'kesa] *nf* turquoise
Turquía [tur'kia] *nf* Turkey
turrón [tu'rron] *nm* (*dulce*) nougat

tutear [tute'ar] *vt* to address as familiar
"tú"; **~se** *vr* to be on familiar terms
tutela [tu'tela] *nf* (*legal*) guardianship;
tutelar *adj* tutelary ♦ *vt* to protect
tutor, a [tu'tor, a] *nm/f* (*legal*) guardian;
(ESCOL) tutor
tuve *etc vb ver* **tener**
tuviera *etc vb ver* **tener**
tuyo, a ['tujo, a] *adj* yours, of yours ♦ *pron*
yours; **un amigo ~** a friend of yours; **los
~s** (*fam*) your relations, your family
TV ['te'βe] *nf abr* (= *televisión*) TV
TVE *nf abr* = **Televisión Española**

U, u

u [u] *conj* or
ubicar [uβi'kar] *vt* to place, situate; (AM:
encontrar) to find; **~se** *vr* to lie, be
located
ubre ['uβre] *nf* udder
UCI *nf abr* (= *Unidad de Cuidados
Intensivos*) ICU
Ud(s) *abr* = **usted(es)**
UE *nf abr* (= *Unión Europea*) EU
ufanarse [ufa'narse] *vr* to boast; **~ de**
to pride o.s. on; **ufano, a** *adj* (*arrogante*)
arrogant; (*presumido*) conceited
UGT *nf abr* = **Unión General de
Trabajadores**
ujier [u'xjer] *nm* usher; (*portero*)
doorkeeper
úlcera ['ulθera] *nf* ulcer
ulcerar [ulθe'rar] *vt* to make sore; **~se** *vr*
to ulcerate
ulterior [ulte'rjor] *adj* (*más allá*) farther,
further; (*subsecuente, siguiente*)
subsequent
últimamente ['ultimamente] *adv*
(*recientemente*) lately, recently
ultimar [ulti'mar] *vt* to finish; (*finalizar*) to
finalize; (AM: *rematar*) to finish off
ultimátum [ulti'matum] (*pl* **~s**) ultimatum
último, a ['ultimo, a] *adj* last; (*más
reciente*) latest, most recent; (*más bajo*)
bottom; (*más alto*) top; **en las últimas**

on one's last legs; **por ~** finally
ultra ['ultra] *adj* ultra ♦ *nm/f* extreme
right-winger
ultrajar [ultra'xar] *vt* (*ofender*) to outrage;
(*insultar*) to insult, abuse; **ultraje** *nm*
outrage; insult
ultramar [ultra'mar] *nm*: **de** *o* **en ~**
abroad, overseas
ultramarinos [ultrama'rinos] *nmpl*
groceries; **tienda de ~** grocer's (shop)
ultranza [ul'tranθa]: **a ~** *adv* (*a todo
trance*) at all costs; (*completo*) outright
ultratumba [ultra'tumba] *nf*: **la vida de ~**
the next life
umbral [um'bral] *nm* (*gen*) threshold
umbrío, a [um'brio, a] *adj* shady

PALABRA CLAVE

un, una [un, 'una] *art indef* a; (*antes de
vocal*) an; **una mujer/naranja** a woman/
an orange
♦ *adj*: **unos** (*o* **unas**): **hay unos regalos
para ti** there are some presents for you;
hay unas cervezas en la nevera there
are some beers in the fridge

---

unánime [u'nanime] *adj* unanimous;
unanimidad *nf* unanimity
undécimo, a [un'deθimo, a] *adj* eleventh
ungir [un'xir] *vt* to anoint
ungüento [un'gwento] *nm* ointment
únicamente ['unikamente] *adv* solely,
only
único, a ['uniko, a] *adj* only, sole; (*sin par*)
unique
unidad [uni'ðað] *nf* unity; (*COM, TEC etc*)
unit
unido, a [u'niðo, a] *adj* joined, linked; (*fig*)
united
unificar [unifi'kar] *vt* to unite, unify
uniformar [unifor'mar] *vt* to make
uniform, level up; (*persona*) to put into
uniform
uniforme [uni'forme] *adj* uniform, equal;
(*superficie*) even ♦ *nm* uniform;
uniformidad *nf* uniformity; (*de terreno*)
levelness, evenness

unilateral [unilate'ral] *adj* unilateral
unión [u'njon] *nf* union; (*acto*) uniting,
joining; (*unidad*) unity; (*TEC*) joint; **la U~
Europea** the European Union; **la U~
Soviética** the Soviet Union
unir [u'nir] *vt* (*juntar*) to join, unite; (*atar*)
to tie, fasten; (*combinar*) to combine; **~se**
vr to join together, unite; (*empresas*) to
merge
unísono [u'nisono] *nm*: **al ~** in unison
universal [uniβer'sal] *adj* universal;
(*mundial*) world *cpd*
universidad [uniβersi'ðað] *nf* university
universitario, a [uniβersi'tarjo, a] *adj*
university *cpd* ♦ *nm/f* (*profesor*) lecturer;
(*estudiante*) (university) student;
(*graduado*) graduate
universo [uni'βerso] *nm* universe

PALABRA CLAVE

uno, a ['uno, a] *adj* one; **es todo ~** it's all
one and the same; **~s pocos** a few; **~s
cien** about a hundred
♦ *pron* **1** one; **quiero sólo ~** I only want
one; **~ de ellos** one of them
2 (*alguien*) somebody, someone; **conozco
a ~ que se te parece** I know somebody
o someone who looks like you; **~ mismo**
oneself; **~s querían quedarse** some
(people) wanted to stay
3 (**los**) **~s ... (los) otros ...** some ...
others; **una y otra son muy agradables**
they're both very nice
♦ *nf* one; **es la una** it's one o'clock
♦ *nm* (number) one

---

untar [un'tar] *vt* (*mantequilla*) to spread;
(*engrasar*) to grease, oil
uña ['uɲa] *nf* (*ANAT*) nail; (*garra*) claw;
(*casco*) hoof; (*arrancaclavos*) claw
uranio [u'ranjo] *nm* uranium
urbanidad [urβani'ðað] *nf* courtesy,
politeness
urbanismo [urβa'nismo] *nm* town
planning
urbanización [urβaniθa'θjon] *nf* (*barrio,
colonia*) housing estate

urbanizar [urβaniˈθar] *vt* (*zona*) to develop, urbanize

urbano, a [urˈβano, a] *adj* (*de ciudad*) urban; (*cortés*) courteous, polite

urbe [ˈurβe] *nf* large city

urdimbre [urˈðimbre] *nf* (*de tejido*) warp; (*intriga*) intrigue

urdir [urˈðir] *vt* to warp; (*complot*) to plot, contrive

urgencia [urˈxenθja] *nf* urgency; (*prisa*) haste, rush; (*emergencia*) emergency; **servicios de ~** emergency services; **"Urgencias"** "Casualty"; **urgente** *adj* urgent

urgir [urˈxir] *vi* to be urgent; **me urge** I'm in a hurry for it

urinario, a [uriˈnarjo, a] *adj* urinary ♦ *nm* urinal

urna [ˈurna] *nf* urn; (*POL*) ballot box

urraca [uˈrraka] *nf* magpie

URSS *nf*: **la ~** the USSR

Uruguay [uruˈɣwai] *nm*: **el ~** Uruguay; **uruguayo, a** *adj*, *nm/f* Uruguayan

usado, a [uˈsaðo, a] *adj* used; (*de segunda mano*) secondhand

usar [uˈsar] *vt* to use; (*ropa*) to wear; (*tener costumbre*) to be in the habit of; **~se** *vr* to be used; **uso** *nm* use; wear; (*costumbre*) usage, custom; (*moda*) fashion; **al uso** in keeping with custom; **al uso de** in the style of

usted [usˈteð] *pron* (*sg*) you *sg*; (*pl*): **~es** you *pl*

usual [uˈswal] *adj* usual

usuario, a [usuˈarjo, a] *nm/f* user

usura [uˈsura] *nf* usury; **usurero, a** *nm/f* usurer

usurpar [usurˈpar] *vt* to usurp

utensilio [utenˈsiljo] *nm* tool; (*CULIN*) utensil

útero [ˈutero] *nm* uterus, womb

útil [ˈutil] *adj* useful ♦ *nm* tool; **utilidad** *nf* usefulness; (*COM*) profit; **utilizar** *vt* to use, utilize

utopía [utoˈpia] *nf* Utopia; **utópico, a** *adj* Utopian

uva [ˈuβa] *nf* grape

---

las uvas

i In Spain **las uvas** *play a big part on New Year's Eve* (**Nochevieja**), *when on the stroke of midnight people gather at home, in restaurants or in the* **plaza mayor** *and eat a grape for each stroke of the clock of the* **Puerta del Sol** *in Madrid. It is said to bring luck for the following year.*

V, v

v *abr* (= *voltio*) v

va *vb ver* **ir**

vaca [ˈbaka] *nf* (*animal*) cow; **carne de ~** beef

vacaciones [bakaˈθjones] *nfpl* holidays

vacante [baˈkante] *adj* vacant, empty ♦ *nf* vacancy

vaciar [baˈθjar] *vt* to empty out; (*ahuecar*) to hollow out; (*moldear*) to cast; **~se** *vr* to empty

vacilante [baθiˈlante] *adj* unsteady; (*habla*) faltering; (*dudoso*) hesitant

vacilar [baθiˈlar] *vi* to be unsteady; (*al hablar*) to falter; (*dudar*) to hesitate, waver; (*memoria*) to fail

vacío, a [baˈθio, a] *adj* empty; (*puesto*) vacant; (*desocupado*) idle; (*vano*) vain ♦ *nm* emptiness; (*FÍSICA*) vacuum; (*un ~*) (empty) space

vacuna [baˈkuna] *nf* vaccine; **vacunar** *vt* to vaccinate

vacuno, a [baˈkuno, a] *adj* cow *cpd*; **ganado ~** cattle

vacuo, a [ˈbakwo, a] *adj* empty

vadear [baðeˈar] *vt* (*río*) to ford; **vado** *nm* ford

vagabundo, a [baɣaˈβundo, a] *adj* wandering ♦ *nm* tramp

vagamente [baɣaˈmente] *adv* vaguely

vagancia [baˈɣanθja] *nf* (*pereza*) idleness, laziness

vagar [baˈɣar] *vi* to wander; (*no hacer*

nada) to idle
vagina [ba'xina] *nf* vagina
vago, a ['baɣo, a] *adj* vague; (*perezoso*)
lazy ♦ *nm/f* (*vagabundo*) tramp; (*flojo*)
lazybones *sg*, idler
vagón [ba'ɣon] *nm* (*FERRO: de pasajeros*)
carriage; (: *de mercancías*) wagon
vaguedad [baɣe'ðað] *nf* vagueness
vaho ['bao] *nm* (*vapor*) vapour, steam;
(*respiración*) breath
vaina ['baina] *nf* sheath
vainilla [bai'niʎa] *nf* vanilla
vainita [bai'nita] (*AM*) *nf* green *o* French
bean
vais *vb ver* **ir**
vaivén [bai'ßen] *nm* to-and-fro movement;
(*de tránsito*) coming and going; **vaivenes**
nmpl (*fig*) ups and downs
vajilla [ba'xiʎa] *nf* crockery, dishes *pl*;
lavar la ~ to do the washing-up (*BRIT*),
wash the dishes (*US*)
valdré *etc vb ver* **valer**
vale ['bale] *nm* voucher; (*recibo*) receipt;
(*pagaré*) IOU
valedero, a [bale'ðero, a] *adj* valid
valenciano, a [balen'θjano, a] *adj*
Valencian
valentía [balen'tia] *nf* courage, bravery
valer [ba'ler] *vt* to be worth; (*MAT*) to
equal; (*costar*) to cost ♦ *vi* (*ser útil*) to be
useful; (*ser válido*) to be valid; **~se** *vr* to
take care of oneself; **~se de** to make use
of, take advantage of; **~ la pena** to be
worthwhile; **¿vale?** (*ESP*) OK?
valeroso, a [bale'roso, a] *adj* brave,
valiant
valgo *etc vb ver* **valer**
valía [ba'lia] *nf* worth, value
validar [bali'ðar] *vt* to validate; **validez** *nf*
validity; **válido, a** *adj* valid
valiente [ba'ljente] *adj* brave, valiant ♦ *nm*
hero
valioso, a [ba'ljoso, a] *adj* valuable
valla ['baʎa] *nf* fence; (*DEPORTE*) hurdle; **~
publicitaria** hoarding; **vallar** *vt* to fence
in
valle ['baʎe] *nm* valley

valor [ba'lor] *nm* value, worth; (*precio*)
price; (*valentía*) valour, courage;
(*importancia*) importance; **~es** *nmpl*
(*COM*) securities; **~ar** *vt* to value
vals [bals] *nm inv* waltz
válvula ['balßula] *nf* valve
vamos *vb ver* **ir**
vampiro, resa [bam'piro, 'resa] *nm/f*
vampire
van *vb ver* **ir**
vanagloriarse [banaɣlo'rjarse] *vr* to boast
vandalismo [banda'lismo] *nm* vandalism;
vándalo, a *nm/f* vandal
vanguardia [ban'gwardja] *nf* vanguard;
(*ARTE etc*) avant-garde
vanidad [bani'ðað] *nf* vanity; **vanidoso,
a** *adj* vain, conceited
vano, a ['bano, a] *adj* vain
vapor [ba'por] *nm* vapour; (*vaho*) steam;
al ~ (*CULIN*) steamed; **~izador** *nm*
atomizer; **~izar** *vt* to vaporize; **~oso, a**
adj vaporous
vapulear [bapule'ar] *vt* to beat, thrash
vaquero, a [ba'kero, a] *adj* cattle *cpd*
♦ *nm* cowboy; **~s** *nmpl* (*pantalones*)
jeans
vaquilla [ba'kiʎa] *nf* (*ZOOL*) heifer
vara ['bara] *nf* stick; (*TEC*) rod; **~ mágica**
magic wand
variable [ba'rjaßle] *adj, nf* variable
variación [barja'θjon] *nf* variation
variar [bar'jar] *vt* to vary; (*modificar*) to
modify; (*cambiar de posición*) to switch
around ♦ *vi* to vary
varicela [bari'θela] *nf* chickenpox
varices [ba'riθes] *nfpl* varicose veins
variedad [barje'ðað] *nf* variety
varilla [ba'riʎa] *nf* stick; (*BOT*) twig; (*TEC*)
rod; (*de rueda*) spoke
vario, a ['barjo, a] *adj* varied; **~s** various,
several
varita [ba'rita] *nf:* **~ mágica** magic wand
varón [ba'ron] *nm* male, man; **varonil** *adj*
manly, virile
Varsovia [bar'soßja] *n* Warsaw
vas *vb ver* **ir**
vasco, a ['basko, a] *adj, nm/f* Basque

vascongado, a [baskon'gaðo, a] *adj* Basque; **las Vascongadas** the Basque Country

vascuence [bas'kwenθe] *adj* = **vascongado**

vaselina [base'lina] *nf* Vaseline ®

vasija [ba'sixa] *nf* container, vessel

vaso ['baso] *nm* glass, tumbler; (*ANAT*) vessel

vástago ['bastaxo] *nm* (*BOT*) shoot; (*TEC*) rod; (*fig*) offspring

vasto, a ['basto, a] *adj* vast, huge

Vaticano [bati'kano] *nm*: **el ~** the Vatican

vatio ['batjo] *nm* (*ELEC*) watt

vaya *etc vb ver* **ir**

Vd(s) *abr* = **usted(es)**

ve *vb ver* **ir; ver**

vecindad [beθin'daθ] *nf* neighbourhood; (*habitantes*) residents *pl*

vecindario [beθin'darjo] *nm* neighbourhood; residents *pl*

vecino, a [be'θino, a] *adj* neighbouring ♦ *nm/f* neighbour; (*residente*) resident

veda ['beða] *nf* prohibition

vedar [be'ðar] *vt* (*prohibir*) to ban, prohibit; (*impedir*) to stop, prevent

vegetación [bexeta'θjon] *nf* vegetation

vegetal [bexe'tal] *adj, nm* vegetable

vegetariano, a [bexeta'rjano, a] *adj, nm/f* vegetarian

vehemencia [be(e)'menθja] *nf* vehemence; **vehemente** *adj* vehement

vehículo [be'ikulo] *nm* vehicle; (*MED*) carrier

veía *etc vb ver* **ver**

veinte ['beinte] *num* twenty

vejación [bexa'θjon] *nf* vexation; (*humillación*) humiliation

vejar [be'xar] *vt* (*irritar*) to annoy, vex; (*humillar*) to humiliate

vejez [be'xeθ] *nf* old age

vejiga [be'xixa] *nf* (*ANAT*) bladder

vela ['bela] *nf* (*de cera*) candle; (*NAUT*) sail; (*insomnio*) sleeplessness; (*vigilia*) vigil; (*MIL*) sentry duty; **estar a dos ~s** (*fam: sin dinero*) to be skint

velado, a [be'laðo, a] *adj* veiled; (*sonido*) muffled; (*FOTO*) blurred ♦ *nf* soirée

velar [be'lar] *vt* (*vigilar*) to keep watch over ♦ *vi* to stay awake; **~ por** to watch over, look after

velatorio [bela'torjo] *nm* (*funeral*) wake

veleidad [belei'ðað] *nf* (*ligereza*) fickleness; (*capricho*) whim

velero [be'lero] *nm* (*NAUT*) sailing ship; (*AVIAT*) glider

veleta [be'leta] *nf* weather vane

veliz [be'lis] (*AM*) *nm* suitcase

vello ['beʎo] *nm* down, fuzz

velo ['belo] *nm* veil

velocidad [beloθi'ðað] *nf* speed; (*TEC, AUTO*) gear

velocímetro [belo'θimetro] *nm* speedometer

veloz [be'loθ] *adj* fast

ven *vb ver* **venir**

vena ['bena] *nf* vein

venado [be'naðo] *nm* deer

vencedor, a [benθe'ðor, a] *adj* victorious ♦ *nm/f* victor, winner

vencer [ben'θer] *vt* (*dominar*) to defeat, beat; (*derrotar*) to vanquish; (*superar, controlar*) to overcome, master ♦ *vi* (*triunfar*) to win (through), triumph; (*plazo*) to expire; **vencido, a** *adj* (*derrotado*) defeated, beaten; (*COM*) due ♦ *adv*: **pagar vencido** to pay in arrears; **vencimiento** *nm* (*COM*) maturity

venda ['benda] *nf* bandage; **vendaje** *nm* bandage, dressing; **vendar** *vt* to bandage; **vendar los ojos** to blindfold

vendaval [benda'βal] *nm* (*viento*) gale

vendedor, a [bende'ðor, a] *nm/f* seller

vender [ben'der] *vt* to sell; **~ al contado/al por mayor/al por menor** to sell for cash/wholesale/retail

vendimia [ben'dimja] *nf* grape harvest

vendré *etc vb ver* **venir**

veneno [be'neno] *nm* poison; (*de serpiente*) venom; **~so, a** *adj* poisonous; venomous

venerable [bene'raβle] *adj* venerable; **venerar** *vt* (*respetar*) to revere; (*adorar*) to worship

venéreo, a [be'nereo, a] *adj*: **enfermedad venérea** venereal disease

venezolano, a [beneθo'lano, a] *adj* Venezuelan

Venezuela [bene'θwela] *nf* Venezuela

venganza [ben'ganθa] *nf* vengeance, revenge; **vengar** *vt* to avenge; **vengarse** *vr* to take revenge; **vengativo, a** *adj* (*persona*) vindictive

vengo *etc vb ver* **venir**

venia ['benja] *nf* (*perdón*) pardon; (*permiso*) consent

venial [be'njal] *adj* venial

venida [be'niða] *nf* (*llegada*) arrival; (*regreso*) return

venidero, a [beni'ðero, a] *adj* coming, future

venir [be'nir] *vi* to come; (*llegar*) to arrive; (*ocurrir*) to happen; (*fig*): **~ de** to stem from; **~ bien/mal** to be suitable/ unsuitable; **el año que viene** next year; **~se abajo** to collapse

venta ['benta] *nf* (*COM*) sale; **~ a plazos** hire purchase; **~ al contado/al por mayor/al por menor** *o* **al detalle** cash sale/wholesale/retail; **~ con derecho a retorno** sale or return; **"en ~"** "for sale"

ventaja [ben'taxa] *nf* advantage; **ventajoso, a** *adj* advantageous

ventana [ben'tana] *nf* window; **ventanilla** *nf* (*de taquilla*) window (*of booking office etc*)

ventilación [bentila'θjon] *nf* ventilation; (*corriente*) draught

ventilador [bentila'ðor] *nm* fan

ventilar [benti'lar] *vt* to ventilate; (*para secar*) to put out to dry; (*asunto*) to air, discuss

ventisca [ben'tiska] *nf* blizzard

ventrílocuo, a [ben'trilokwo, a] *nm/f* ventriloquist

ventura [ben'tura] *nf* (*felicidad*) happiness; (*buena suerte*) luck; (*destino*) fortune; **a la (buena) ~** at random; **venturoso, a** *adj* happy; (*afortunado*) lucky, fortunate

veo *etc vb ver* **ver**

ver [ber] *vt* to see; (*mirar*) to look at,

watch; (*entender*) to understand; (*investigar*) to look into; ♦ *vi* to see; to understand; **~se** *vr* (*encontrarse*) to meet; (*dejarse* **~**) to be seen; (*hallarse: en un apuro*) to find o.s., be; **a ~** let's see; **no tener nada que ~ con** to have nothing to do with; **a mi modo de ~** as I see it

vera ['bera] *nf* edge, verge; (*de río*) bank

veracidad [beraθi'ðað] *nf* truthfulness

veranear [berane'ar] *vi* to spend the summer; **veraneo** *nm* summer holiday; **veraniego, a** *adj* summer *cpd*

verano [be'rano] *nm* summer

veras ['beras] *nfpl* truth *sg*; **de ~** really, truly

veraz [be'raθ] *adj* truthful

verbal [ber'ßal] *adj* verbal

verbena [ber'ßena] *nf* (*baile*) open-air dance

verbo ['berßo] *nm* verb; **~so, a** *adj* verbose

verdad [ber'ðað] *nf* truth; (*fiabilidad*) reliability; **de ~** real, proper; **a decir ~** to tell the truth; **~ero, a** *adj* (*veraz*) true, truthful; (*fiable*) reliable; (*fig*) real

verde ['berðe] *adj* green; (*chiste*) blue, dirty ♦ *nm* green; **viejo ~** dirty old man; **~ar** *vi* to turn green; **verdor** *nm* greenness

verdugo [ber'ðuxo] *nm* executioner

verdulero, a [berðu'lero, a] *nm/f* greengrocer

verduras [ber'ðuras] *nfpl* (*CULIN*) greens

vereda [be'reða] *nf* path; (*AM*) pavement (*BRIT*), sidewalk (*US*)

veredicto [bere'ðikto] *nm* verdict

vergonzoso, a [bervon'θoso, a] *adj* shameful; (*tímido*) timid, bashful

vergüenza [ber'xwenθa] *nf* shame, sense of shame; (*timidez*) bashfulness; (*pudor*) modesty; **me da ~** I'm ashamed

verídico, a [be'riðiko, a] *adj* true, truthful

verificar [berifi'kar] *vt* to check; (*corroborar*) to verify; (*llevar a cabo*) to carry out; **~se** *vr* (*predicción*) to prove to be true

verja ['berxa] *nf* (*cancela*) iron gate; (*valla*)

iron railings *pl*; (*de ventana*) grille

vermut [ber'mut] (*pl* ~s) *nm* vermouth

verosímil [bero'simil] *adj* likely, probable; (*relato*) credible

verruga [be'rruxa] *nf* wart

versado, a [ber'saðo, a] *adj*: ~ **en** versed in

versátil [ber'satil] *adj* versatile

versión [ber'sjon] *nf* version

verso ['berso] *nm* verse; **un** ~ a line of poetry

vértebra ['berteβra] *nf* vertebra

verter [ber'ter] *vt* (*líquido: adrede*) to empty, pour (out); (: *sin querer*) to spill; (*basura*) to dump ♦ *vi* to flow

vertical [berti'kal] *adj* vertical

vértice ['bertiθe] *nm* vertex, apex

vertidos [ber'tiðos] *nmpl* waste *sg*

vertiente [ber'tjente] *nf* slope; (*fig*) aspect

vertiginoso, a [bertixi'noso, a] *adj* giddy, dizzy

vértigo ['bertixo] *nm* vertigo; (*mareo*) dizziness

vesícula [be'sikula] *nf* blister

vespino ® [bes'pino] *nm o nf* moped

vestíbulo [bes'tiβulo] *nm* hall; (*de teatro*) foyer

vestido [bes'tiðo] *pp de* **vestir**; ~ **de azul/marinero** dressed in blue/as a sailor ♦ *nm* (*ropa*) clothes *pl*, clothing; (*de mujer*) dress, frock

vestigio [bes'tixjo] *nm* (*huella*) trace; ~**s** *nmpl* (*restos*) remains

vestimenta [besti'menta] *nf* clothing

vestir [bes'tir] *vt* (*poner: ropa*) to put on; (*llevar: ropa*) to wear; (*proveer de ropa a*) to clothe; (*suj: sastre*) to make clothes for ♦ *vi* to dress; (*verse bien*) to look good; ~**se** *vr* to get dressed, dress o.s.

vestuario [bes'twarjo] *nm* clothes *pl*, wardrobe; (*TEATRO: cuarto*) dressing room; (*DEPORTE*) changing room

veta ['beta] *nf* (*vena*) vein, seam; (*en carne*) streak; (*de madera*) grain

vetar [be'tar] *vt* to veto

veterano, a [bete'rano, a] *adj, nm* veteran

veterinaria [beteri'narja] *nf* veterinary

science; *ver tb* **veterinario**

veterinario, a [beteri'narjo, a] *nm/f* vet(erinary surgeon)

veto ['beto] *nm* veto

vez [beθ] *nf* time; (*turno*) turn; **a la** ~ **que** at the same time as; **a su** ~ in its turn; **otra** ~ again; **una** ~ once; **de una** ~ in one go; **de una** ~ **para siempre** once and for all; **en** ~ **de** instead of; **a** *o* **algunas veces** sometimes; **una y otra** ~ repeatedly; **de** ~ **en cuando** from time to time; **7 veces 9** 7 times 9; **hacer las veces de** to stand in for; **tal** ~ perhaps

vía ['bia] *nf* track, route; (*FERRO*) line; (*fig*) way; (*ANAT*) passage, tube ♦ *prep* via, by way of; **por** ~ **judicial** by legal means; **por** ~ **oficial** through official channels; **en** ~**s de** in the process of; ~ **aérea** airway; **V~ Láctea** Milky Way; ~ **pública** public road *o* thoroughfare

viable ['bjaβle] *adj* (*solución, plan, alternativa*) feasible

viaducto [bja'ðukto] *nm* viaduct

viajante [bja'xante] *nm* commercial traveller

viajar [bja'xar] *vi* to travel; **viaje** *nm* journey; (*gira*) tour; (*NAUT*) voyage; **estar de viaje** to be on a trip; **viaje de ida y vuelta** round trip; **viaje de novios** honeymoon; **viajero, a** *adj* travelling; (*ZOOL*) migratory ♦ *nm/f* (*quien viaja*) traveller; (*pasajero*) passenger

vial [bjal] *adj* road *cpd*, traffic *cpd*

víbora ['biβora] *nf* viper; (*AM*) poisonous snake

vibración [biβra'θjon] *nf* vibration

vibrar [bi'βrar] *vt, vi* to vibrate

vicario [bi'karjo] *nm* curate

vicepresidente [biθepresi'ðente] *nm/f* vice-president

viceversa [biθe'βersa] *adv* vice versa

viciado, a [bi'θjaðo, a] *adj* (*corrompido*) corrupt; (*contaminado*) foul, contaminated; **viciar** *vt* (*pervertir*) to pervert; (*JUR*) to nullify; (*estropear*) to spoil; **viciarse** *vr* to become corrupted

vicio [bi'θjo] *nm* vice; (*mala costumbre*)

bad habit; **~so, a** adj (muy malo)
vicious; (corrompido) depraved ♦ nm/f
depraved person

vicisitud [biθisi'tuð] nf vicissitude

víctima ['biktima] nf victim

victoria [bik'torja] nf victory; **victorioso,
a** adj victorious

vid [bið] nf vine

vida ['biða] nf (gen) life; (duración) lifetime;
de por ~ for life; **en la/mi ~** never; **estar
con ~** to be still alive; **ganarse la ~** to
earn one's living

vídeo ['biðeo] nm video ♦ adj inv:
película ~ video film; **videocámara** nf
camcorder; **videocasete** nm video cassette, videotape; **videoclub** nm video
club; **videojuego** nm video game

vidriero, a [bi'ðrjero, a] nm/f glazier ♦ nf
(ventana) stained-glass window; (AM: de
tienda) shop window; (puerta) glass door

vidrio ['biðrjo] nm glass

vieira ['bjeira] nf scallop

viejo, a ['bjexo, a] adj old ♦ nm/f old
man/woman; **hacerse ~** to get old

Viena ['bjena] n Vienna

vienes etc vb ver **venir**

vienés, esa [bje'nes, esa] adj Viennese

viento ['bjento] nm wind; **hacer ~** to be
windy

vientre ['bjentre] nm belly; (matriz) womb

viernes ['bjernes] nm inv Friday; **V~
Santo** Good Friday

Vietnam [bjet'nam] nm: **el ~** Vietnam;
vietnamita adj Vietnamese

viga ['biɣa] nf beam, rafter; (de metal)
girder

vigencia [bi'xenθja] nf validity; **estar en ~**
to be in force; **vigente** adj valid, in
force; (imperante) prevailing

vigésimo, a [bi'xesimo, a] adj twentieth

vigía [bi'xia] nm look-out

vigilancia [bixi'lanθja] nf: **tener a uno
bajo ~** to keep watch on sb

vigilar [bixi'lar] vt to watch over ♦ vi (gen)
to be vigilant; (hacer guardia) to keep
watch; **~ por** to take care of

vigilia [vi'xilja] nf wakefulness, being

awake; (REL) fast

vigor [bi'ɣor] nm vigour, vitality; **en ~** in
force; **entrar/poner en ~** to come/put
into effect; **~oso, a** adj vigorous

VIH nm abr (= virus de la
inmunodeficiencia humana) HIV; **~
positivo/negativo** HIV-positive/-negative

vil [bil] adj vile, low; **~eza** nf vileness;
(acto) base deed

vilipendiar [bilipen'djar] vt to vilify, revile

villa ['biʎa] nf (casa) villa; (pueblo) small
town; (municipalidad) municipality; **~
miseria** (AM) shantytown

villancico [biʎan'θiko] nm (Christmas)
carol

villorrio [bi'ʎorrjo] nm shantytown

vilo ['bilo]: **en ~** adv in the air, suspended;
(fig) on tenterhooks, in suspense

vinagre [bi'naɣre] nm vinegar

vinagreta [bina'ɣreta] nf vinaigrette,
French dressing

vinculación [binkula'θjon] nf (lazo) link,
bond; (acción) linking

vincular [binku'lar] vt to link, bind;
vínculo nm link, bond

vine etc vb ver **venir**

vinicultura [binikul'tura] nf wine growing

viniera etc vb ver **venir**

vino ['bino] vb ver **venir** ♦ nm wine; **~
blanco/tinto** white/red wine

viña ['biɲa] nf vineyard; **viñedo** nm
vineyard

viola ['bjola] nf viola

violación [bjola'θjon] nf violation; **~
(sexual)** rape

violar [bjo'lar] vt to violate; (sexualmente)
to rape

violencia [bjo'lenθja] nf violence, force;
(incomodidad) embarrassment; (acto
injusto) unjust act; **violentar** vt to force;
(casa) to break into; (agredir) to assault;
(violar) to violate; **violento, a** adj
violent; (furioso) furious; (situación)
embarrassing; (acto) forced, unnatural

violeta [bjo'leta] nf violet

violín [bjo'lin] nm violin

violón [bjo'lon] nm double bass

viraje [bi'raxe] *nm* turn; (*de vehículo*) swerve; (*fig*) change of direction; **virar** *vi* to change direction

virgen ['birxen] *adj*, *nf* virgin

Virgo ['birɣo] *nm* Virgo

viril [bi'ril] *adj* virile; **~idad** *nf* virility

virtud [bir'tuð] *nf* virtue; **en ~ de** by virtue of; **virtuoso, a** *adj* virtuous ♦ *nm/f* virtuoso

viruela [bi'rwela] *nf* smallpox

virulento, a [biru'lento, a] *adj* virulent

virus ['birus] *nm inv* virus

visa ['bisa] (*AM*) *nf* = **visado**

visado [bi'saðo] *nm* visa

víscera ['bisθera] *nf* (*ANAT, ZOOL*) gut, bowel; **~s** *nfpl* entrails

visceral [bisθe'ral] *adj* (*odio*) intense; **reacción ~** gut reaction

viscoso, a [bis'koso, a] *adj* viscous

visera [bi'sera] *nf* visor

visibilidad [bisiβili'ðað] *nf* visibility; **visible** *adj* visible; (*fig*) obvious

visillos [bi'siʎos] *nmpl* lace curtains

visión [bi'sjon] *nf* (*ANAT*) vision, (eye)sight; (*fantasía*) vision, fantasy

visita [bi'sita] *nf* call, visit; (*persona*) visitor; **hacer una ~** to pay a visit

visitar [bisi'tar] *vt* to visit, call on

vislumbrar [bislum'brar] *vt* to glimpse, catch a glimpse of

viso ['biso] *nm* (*del metal*) glint, gleam; (*de tela*) sheen; (*aspecto*) appearance

visón [bi'son] *nm* mink

visor [bi'sor] *nm* (*FOTO*) viewfinder

víspera ['bispera] *nf*: **la ~ de ...** the day before ...

vista ['bista] *nf* sight, vision; (*capacidad de ver*) (eye)sight; (*mirada*) look(s) (*pl*); **a primera ~** at first glance; **hacer la ~ gorda** to turn a blind eye; **volver la ~** to look back; **está a la ~ que** it's obvious that; **en ~ de** in view of; **en ~ de que** in view of the fact that; **¡hasta la ~!** so long!, see you!; **con ~s a** with a view to; **~zo** *nm* glance; **dar o echar un ~zo a** to glance at a

visto, a ['bisto, a] *pp de* **ver** ♦ *vb ver tb*

vestir ♦ *adj* seen; (*considerado*) considered ♦ *nm*: **~ bueno** approval; **"~ bueno"** "approved"; **por lo ~** apparently; **está ~ que** it's clear that; **está bien/mal ~** it's acceptable/unacceptable; **~ que** since, considering that

vistoso, a [bis'toso, a] *adj* colourful

visual [bi'swal] *adj* visual

vital [bi'tal] *adj* life *cpd*, living *cpd*; (*fig*) vital; (*persona*) lively, vivacious; **~icio, a** *adj* for life; **~idad** *nf* (*de persona, negocio*) energy; (*de ciudad*) liveliness

vitamina [bita'mina] *nf* vitamin

viticultor, a [bitikul'tor, a] *nm/f* wine grower; **viticultura** *nf* wine growing

vitorear [bitore'ar] *vt* to cheer, acclaim

vitrina [bi'trina] *nf* show case; (*AM*) shop window

viudez *nf* widowhood

viudo, a ['bjuðo, a] *nm/f* widower/widow

viva ['biβa] *excl* hurrah!: **¡~ el rey!** long live the king!

vivacidad [biβaθi'ðað] *nf* (*vigor*) vigour; (*vida*) liveliness

vivaracho, a [biβa'ratʃo, a] *adj* jaunty, lively; (*ojos*) bright, twinkling

vivaz [bi'βaθ] *adj* lively

víveres ['biβeres] *nmpl* provisions

vivero [bi'βero] *nm* (*para plantas*) nursery; (*para peces*) fish farm; (*fig*) hotbed

viveza [bi'βeθa] *nf* liveliness; (*agudeza: mental*) sharpness

vivienda [bi'βjenda] *nf* housing; (*una ~*) house; (*piso*) flat (*BRIT*), apartment (*US*)

viviente [bi'βjente] *adj* living

vivir [bi'βir] *vt*, *vi* to live ♦ *nm* life, living

vivo, a ['biβo, a] *adj* living, alive; (*fig: descripción*) vivid; (*persona: astuto*) smart, clever; **en ~** (*transmisión etc*) live

vocablo [bo'kaβlo] *nm* (*palabra*) word; (*término*) term

vocabulario [bokaβu'larjo] *nm* vocabulary

vocación [boka'θjon] *nf* vocation; **vocacional** (*AM*) *nf* ≈ technical college

vocal [bo'kal] *adj* vocal ♦ *nf* vowel; **~izar** *vt* to vocalize

vocear [boθe'ar] *vt* (*para vender*) to cry;

(aclamar) to acclaim; *(fig)* to proclaim
♦ *vi* to yell; **vocerío** *nm* shouting
vocero [bo'θero] *nm/f* spokesman/woman
voces ['boθes] *pl de* **voz**
vociferar [boθife'rar] *vt* to shout ♦ *vi* to
yell
vodka ['boðka] *nm o f* vodka
vol *abr* = **volumen**
volador, a [bola'ðor, a] *adj* flying
volandas [bo'landas]: **en ~** *adv* in the air
volante [bo'lante] *adj* flying ♦ *nm (de
coche)* steering wheel; *(de reloj)* balance
volar [bo'lar] *vt (edificio)* to blow up ♦ *vi*
to fly
volátil [bo'latil] *adj* volatile
volcán [bol'kan] *nm* volcano; **~ico, a** *adj*
volcanic
volcar [bol'kar] *vt* to upset, overturn;
(tumbar, derribar) to knock over; *(vaciar)*
to empty out ♦ *vi* to overturn; **~se** *vr* to
tip over
voleibol [bolei'ßol] *nm* volleyball
volqué *etc vb ver* **volcar**
voltaje [bol'taxe] *nm* voltage
voltear [bolte'ar] *vt* to turn over; *(volcar)*
to turn upside down
voltereta [bolte'reta] *nf* somersault
voltio ['boltjo] *nm* volt
voluble [bo'lußle] *adj* fickle
volumen [bo'lumen] *(pl* **volúmenes)** *nm*
volume; **voluminoso, a** *adj*
voluminous; *(enorme)* massive
voluntad [bolun'tað] *nf* will; *(resolución)*
willpower; *(deseo)* desire, wish
voluntario, a [bolun'tarjo, a] *adj*
voluntary ♦ *nm/f* volunteer
voluntarioso, a [bolunta'rjoso, a] *adj*
headstrong
voluptuoso, a [bolup'twoso, a] *adj*
voluptuous
volver [bol'ßer] *vt (gen)* to turn; *(dar
vuelta a)* to turn (over); *(voltear)* to turn
round, turn upside down; *(poner al revés)*
to turn inside out; *(devolver)* to return
♦ *vi* to return, go back, come back; **~se**
vr to turn round; **~ la espalda** to turn
one's back; **~ triste** *etc* **a uno** to make sb

sad *etc*; **~ a hacer** to do again; **~ en sí** to
come to; **~se insoportable/muy caro** to
get *o* become unbearable/very expensive;
~se loco to go mad
vomitar [bomi'tar] *vt, vi* to vomit;
vómito *nm* vomit
voraz [bo'raθ] *adj* voracious
vos [bos] *(AM) pron* you
vosotros, as [bo'sotros, as] *pron* you;
(reflexivo): **entre/para ~** among/for
yourselves
votación [bota'θjon] *nf (acto)* voting;
(voto) vote
votar [bo'tar] *vi* to vote; **voto** *nm* vote;
(promesa) vow; **votos** (good) wishes
voy *vb ver* **ir**
voz [boθ] *nf* voice; *(grito)* shout; *(rumor)*
rumour; *(LING)* word; **dar voces** to shout,
yell; **a media ~** in a low voice; **a ~ en
cuello** *o* **en grito** at the top of one's
voice; **de viva ~** verbally; **en ~ alta** aloud;
~ de mando command
vuelco ['bwelko] *vb ver* **volcar** ♦ *nm* spill,
overturning
vuelo ['bwelo] *vb ver* **volar** ♦ *nm* flight;
(encaje) lace, frill; **coger al ~** to catch in
flight; **~ charter/regular** charter/
scheduled flight; **~ libre** *(DEPORTE)* hang-
gliding
vuelque *etc vb ver* **volcar**
vuelta ['bwelta] *nf (gen)* turn; *(curva)*
bend, curve; *(regreso)* return; *(revolución)*
revolution; *(de circuito)* lap; *(de papel,
tela)* reverse; *(cambio)* change; **a la ~** on
one's return; **a ~ de correo** by return of
post; **dar ~s** *(suj: cabeza)* to spin; **dar ~s
a una idea** to turn over an idea (in one's
head); **estar de ~** to be back; **dar una ~**
to go for a walk; *(en coche)* to go for a
drive; **~ ciclista** *(DEPORTE)* (cycle) tour
vuelto *pp de* **volver**
vuelvo *etc vb ver* **volver**
vuestro, a ['bwestro, a] *adj* your; **un
amigo ~** a friend of yours ♦ *pron*: **el ~/la
vuestra,** the vuestra/ yours/ yours; **los ~s/las vuestras** yours
vulgar [bul'xar] *adj (ordinario)* vulgar;
(común) common; **~idad** *nf*

commonness; (*acto*) vulgarity; (*expresión*) coarse expression; **~izar** *vt* to popularize
vulgo ['bulxo] *nm* common people
vulnerable [bulne'raßle] *adj* vulnerable
vulnerar [bulne'rar] *vt* (*ley, acuerdo*) to violate, breach; (*derechos, intimidad*) to violate; (*reputación*) to damage

W, w

Walkman ® [wak'man] *nm* Walkman ®
wáter ['bater] *nm* toilet
whisky ['wiski] *nm* whisky, whiskey

X, x

xenofobia [kseno'foßja] *nf* xenophobia
xilófono [ksi'lofono] *nm* xylophone

Y, y

y [i] *conj* and
ya [ja] *adv* (*gen*) already; (*ahora*) now; (*en seguida*) at once; (*pronto*) soon ♦ *excl* all right! ♦ *conj* (*ahora que*) now that; **~ lo sé** I know; **~ que** since
yacer [ja'θer] *vi* to lie
yacimiento [jaθi'mjento] *nm* (*de mineral*) deposit; (*arqueológico*) site
yanqui ['janki] *adj, nm/f* Yankee
yate ['jate] *nm* yacht
yazco *etc vb ver* **yacer**
yedra ['jeðra] *nf* ivy
yegua ['jexwa] *nf* mare
yema ['jema] *nf* (*del huevo*) yoke; (*BOT*) leaf bud; (*fig*) best part; **~ del dedo** fingertip
yergo *etc vb ver* **erguir**
yermo, a ['jermo, a] *adj* (*estéril, fig*) barren ♦ *nm* wasteland
yerno ['jerno] *nm* son-in-law
yerro *etc vb ver* **errar**
yeso ['jeso] *nm* plaster
yo [jo] *pron* I; **soy ~** it's me, it is I

yodo ['joðo] *nm* iodine
yoga ['joxa] *nm* yoga
yogur(t) [jo'xur(t)] *nm* yoghurt
yugo ['juxo] *nm* yoke
Yugoslavia [juxos'laßja] *nf* Yugoslavia
yugular [juxu'lar] *adj* jugular
yunque ['junke] *nm* anvil
yunta ['junta] *nf* yoke
yuxtaponer [jukstapo'ner] *vt* to juxtapose; **yuxtaposición** *nf* juxtaposition

Z, z

zafar [θa'far] *vt* (*soltar*) to untie; (*superficie*) to clear; **~se** *vr* (*escaparse*) to escape; (*TEC*) to slip off
zafio, a ['θafjo, a] *adj* coarse
zafiro [θa'firo] *nm* sapphire
zaga ['θaxa] *nf*: **a la ~** behind, in the rear
zaguán [θa'ɣwan] *nm* hallway
zaherir [θae'rir] *vt* (*criticar*) to criticize
zaino, a ['θaino, a] *adj* (*caballo*) chestnut
zalamería [θalame'ria] *nf* flattery; **zalamero, a** *adj* flattering; (*cobista*) suave
zamarra [θa'marra] *nf* (*chaqueta*) sheepskin jacket
zambullirse [θambu'ʎirse] *vr* to dive
zampar [θam'par] *vt* to gobble down
zanahoria [θana'orja] *nf* carrot
zancada [θan'kaða] *nf* stride
zancadilla [θanka'ðiʎa] *nf* trip
zanco ['θanko] *nm* stilt
zancudo, a [θan'kuðo, a] *adj* long-legged ♦ *nm* (*AM*) mosquito
zángano ['θangano] *nm* drone
zanja ['θanxa] *nf* ditch; **zanjar** *vt* (*resolver*) to resolve
zapata [θa'pata] *nf* (*MECÁNICA*) shoe
zapatear [θapate'ar] *vi* to tap with one's feet
zapatería [θapate'ria] *nf* (*oficio*) shoemaking; (*tienda*) shoe shop; (*fábrica*) shoe factory; **zapatero, a** *nm/f*

shoemaker
zapatilla [θapa'tiʎa] *nf* slipper; **~ de deporte** training shoe
zapato [θa'pato] *nm* shoe
zapping ['θapin] *nm* channel-hopping; **hacer ~** to flick through the channels
zar [θar] *nm* tsar, czar
zarandear [θarande'ar] *(fam) vt* to shake vigorously
zarpa ['θarpa] *nf (garra)* claw
zarpar [θar'par] *vi* to weigh anchor
zarza ['θarθa] *nf (BOT)* bramble; **zarzal** *nm (matorral)* bramble patch
zarzamora [θarθa'mora] *nf* blackberry
zarzuela [θar'θwela] *nf* Spanish light opera
zigzag [θiɣ'θaɣ] *nm* zigzag; **zigzaguear** *vi* to zigzag
zinc [θink] *nm* zinc
zócalo ['θokalo] *nm (ARQ)* plinth, base
zodíaco [θo'ðiako] *nm (ASTRO)* zodiac
zona ['θona] *nf* zone; **~ fronteriza** border area

zoo ['θoo] *nm* zoo
zoología [θoolo'xia] *nf* zoology; **zoológico, a** *adj* zoological ♦ *nm (tb:* **parque ~)** zoo; **zoólogo, a** *nm/f* zoologist
zoom [θum] *nm* zoom lens
zopilote [θopi'lote] *(AM) nm* buzzard
zoquete [θo'kete] *nm (fam)* blockhead
zorro, a ['θorro, a] *adj* crafty ♦ *nm/f* fox/vixen
zozobra [θo'θoßra] *nf (fig)* anxiety; **zozobrar** *vi (hundirse)* to capsize; *(fig)* to fail
zueco ['θweko] *nm* clog
zumbar [θum'bar] *vt (golpear)* to hit ♦ *vi* to buzz; **zumbido** *nm* buzzing
zumo ['θumo] *nm* juice
zurcir [θur'θir] *vt (coser)* to darn
zurdo, a ['θurðo, a] *adj (persona)* left-handed
zurrar [θu'rrar] *(fam) vt* to wallop

USING YOUR COLLINS POCKET DICTIONARY

Supplement by
Roy Simon
reproduced by kind permission of
Tayside Region Education Department

USING YOUR COLLINS POCKET DICTIONARY

Introduction

We are delighted that you have decided to invest in this Collins Pocket Dictionary! Whether you intend to use it in school, at home, on holiday or at work, we are sure that you will find it very useful.

The purpose of this supplement is to help you become aware of the wealth of vocabulary and grammatical information your dictionary contains, to explain how this information is presented and also to point out some of the traps one can fall into when using a Spanish-English English-Spanish dictionary.

In the pages which follow you will find explanations and wordgames (not too difficult!) designed to give you practice in exploring the dictionary's contents and in retrieving information for a variety of purposes. Answers are provided at the end. If you spend a little time on these pages you should be able to use your dictionary more efficiently and effectively. Have fun!

Contents

HOW INFORMATION IS PRESENTED IN YOUR DICTIONARY

A great deal of information is packed into your Collins Pocket Dictionary using colour, various typefaces, sizes of type, symbols, abbreviations and brackets. The purpose of this section is to acquaint you with the conventions used in presenting information.

Headwords

A headword is the word you look up in a dictionary. Headwords are listed in alphabetical order throughout the dictionary. They are printed in colour so that they stand out clearly from all the other words on the dictionary page.

Note that at the top of each page two headwords appear. These tell you which is the first and last word dealt with on the page in question. They are there to help you scan through the dictionary more quickly.

The Spanish alphabet consists of 27 letters: the same 26 letters as the English alphabet, in the same order, plus 'ñ', which comes after letter 'n'. You will need to remember that words containing this letter will be listed slightly differently from what you would expect according to English alphabetical order: thus 'caña' does not come immediately after 'cana', but follows the last word beginning with 'can-' in the list, namely 'canuto'.

Where two Spanish words are distinguished only by an accent, the accented form follows the unaccented, e.g. 'de', 'dé'.

A dictionary entry

An entry is made up of a headword and all the information about that headword. Entries will be short or long depending on how frequently a word is used in either English or Spanish and how many meanings it has. Inevitably, the fuller the dictionary entry the more care is needed in sifting through it to find the information you require.

Meanings

The translations of a headword are given in ordinary type. Where there is more than one meaning or usage, a semi-colon separates one from the other.

completo, a [kom'pleto, a] *adj* complete;
  (*perfecto*) perfect; (*lleno*) full ♦ *nm* full
  complement
complicado, a [kompli'kaðo, a] *adj*
  complicated; **estar ~ en** to be mixed up
  in
cómplice ['kompliθe] *nm/f* accomplice
complot [kom'plo(t)] (*pl* **~s**) *nm* plot

  aiming; (*destreza*) marksmanship
puntero, a [pun'tero, a] *adj* leading ♦ *nm*
  (*palo*) pointer
puntiagudo, a [puntja'ɣuðo, a] *adj* sharp,
  pointed
puntilla [pun'tiʎa] *nf* (*encaje*) lace edging

puritano, a [puri'tano, a] *adj* (*actitud*)
  puritanical; (*iglesia, tradición*) puritan
  ♦ *nm/f* puritan
puro, a ['puro, a] *adj* pure; (*verdad*)
  simple, plain ♦ *adv*: **de ~ cansado** out of
  sheer tiredness ♦ *nm* cigar

nevar [ne'ßar] *vi* to snow

cuenta *etc* ['kwenta] *vb ver* **contar** ♦ *nf*
  (*cálculo*) count, counting; (*en café,
  restaurante*) bill (*BRIT*), check (*US*); (*COM*)
  account; (*de collar*) bead; **a fin de ~s** in
  the end; **caer en la ~** to catch on; **darse
  ~ de** to realize; **tener en ~** to bear in
  mind; **echar ~s** to take stock; **~
  corriente/de ahorros** current/savings
  account; **~ atrás** countdown;
  ~kilómetros *nm inv* ≈ milometer; (*de
  velocidad*) speedometer

titubear [tituße'ar] *vi* to stagger; to
  stammer; (*fig*) to hesitate; **titubeo** *nm*
  staggering; stammering; hesitation

iii

In addition, you will often find other words appearing in *italics* in brackets before the translations. These either give some notion of the contexts in which the headword might appear (as with 'lane' opposite – 'lane in the country', 'lane in a race', etc.) or else they provide synonyms (as with 'hit' opposite – 'strike', 'reach', etc.).

Phonetic spellings

The phonetic spelling of each headword – i.e. its pronunciation – is given in square brackets immediately after it. The phonetic transcription of Spanish and English vowels and consonants is given on pages viii to xi at the front of your dictionary.

Additional information about headwords

Information about the usage or form of certain headwords is given in brackets between the phonetics and the translation or translations. Have a look at the entries for 'COU', 'cuenca', 'mast', 'R.S.V.P.' and 'burro' opposite.

This information is usually given in abbreviated form. A helpful list of abbreviations is given on pages vi and vii at the front of your dictionary.

You should be particularly careful with colloquial words or phrases. Words labelled (*fam*) would not normally be used in formal speech, while those labelled (*fam!*) would be considered offensive.

Careful consideration of such style labels will help indicate the degree of formality and appropriateness of a word and could help you avoid many an embarrassing situation when using Spanish!

Expressions in which the headword appears

An entry will often feature certain common expressions in which the headword appears. These expressions are in **bold** type, but in black as opposed to colour. A swung dash (~) is used instead of repeating a headword in an entry. 'Tono' and 'mano' opposite illustrate this point.

Related words

In the Pocket Dictionary words related to certain headwords are sometimes given at the end of an entry, as with 'ambición' and 'accept' opposite. These are easily picked out as they are also in colour. To help you find these words, they are placed in alphabetical order after the headword to which they belong: cf. 'accept', 'general' opposite.

lane [leɪn] n (in country) camino; (AUT) carril m; (in race) calle f

embrollar [embroˈʎar] vt (el asunto) to confuse, complicate; (implicar) to involve, embroil; **~se** vr (confundirse) to get into a muddle o mess

COU [kou] (ESP) nm abr (= Curso de Orientación Universitaria) 1 year course leading to final school-leaving certificate and university entrance examinations

cuenca [ˈkwenka] nf (ANAT) eye socket; (GEO) bowl, deep valley

menudo, a [meˈnuðo, a] adj (pequeño) small, tiny; (sin importancia) petty, insignificant; ¡**~ negocio!** (fam) some deal!; **a ~** often, frequently

tono [ˈtono] nm tone; **fuera de ~** inappropriate; **darse ~** to put on airs

ambición [ambiˈθjon] nf ambition; **ambicionar** vt to aspire to; **ambicioso, a** adj ambitious

accept [əkˈsept] vt aceptar; (responsibility, blame) admitir; **~able** adj aceptable; **~ance** n aceptación f

hit [hɪt] (pt, pp **hit**) vt (strike) golpear, pegar; (reach: target) alcanzar; (collide with: car) chocar contra; (fig: affect) afectar ♦ n golpe m; (success) éxito; **to ~ it off with sb** llevarse bien con uno; **~-and-run driver** n conductor(a) que atropella y huye

repoblación [repoβlaˈθjon] nf repopulation; (de río) restocking; **~ forestal** reafforestation

mast [maːst] n (NAUT) mástil m; (RADIO etc) torre f

R.S.V.P. abbr (= répondez s'il vous plaît) SRC

burro, a [ˈburro, a] nm/f donkey/she-donkey; (fig) ass, idiot

bocazas [boˈkaθas] (fam) nm inv bigmouth

cabrón [kaˈβron] nm cuckold; (fam!) bastard (!)

mano [ˈmano] nf hand; (ZOOL) foot, paw; (de pintura) coat; (serie) lot, series; **a ~** by hand; **a ~ derecha/izquierda** on the right(-hand side)/left(-hand side); **de primera ~** (at) first hand; **de segunda ~** (at) second hand; **robo a ~ armada** armed robbery; **~ de obra** labour, manpower; **estrechar la ~ a uno** to shake sb's hand

general [xeneˈral] adj general ♦ nm general; **por lo** o **en ~** in general; **G~itat** nf Catalan parliament; **~izar** vt to generalize; **~izarse** vr to become generalized, spread; **~mente** adv generally

v

'Key' words

Your Collins Pocket Dictionary gives special status to certain Spanish and English words which can be looked on as 'key' words in each language. These are words which have many different usages. 'Poder', 'menos' and 'se' opposite are typical examples in Spanish. You are likely to become familiar with them in your day-to-day language studies.

There will be occasions, however, when you want to check on a particular usage. Your dictionary can be very helpful here. Note how with 'poder', for example, different parts of speech and different usages are clearly indicated by a combination of lozenges - ♦ - and numbers. In addition, further guides to usage are given in the language of the user who needs them. These are bracketed and in italics.

poder [poˈðer] *vi* **1** (*capacidad*) can, be
able to; **no puedo hacerlo** I can't do it,
I'm unable to do it
2 (*permiso*) can, may, be allowed to; **¿se
puede?** may I (o we)?; **puedes irte
ahora** you may go now; **no se puede
fumar en este hospital** smoking is not
allowed in this hospital
3 (*posibilidad*) may, might, could; **puede
llegar mañana** he may *o* might arrive
tomorrow; **pudiste haberte hecho daño**
you might *o* could have hurt yourself;
¡podías habérmelo dicho antes! you
might have told me before!
4: puede ser: puede ser perhaps;
puede ser que lo sepa Tomás Tomás
may *o* might know
5: ¡no puedo más! I've had enough!; **no
pude menos que dejarlo** I couldn't help
but leave it; **es tonto a más no ~** he's as
stupid as they come
6: ~ con: no puedo con este crío this
kid's too much for me
♦ *nm* power; **~ adquisitivo** purchasing
power; **detentar** *o* **ocupar** *o* **estar en el
~** to be in power

se |se| *pron* **1** (*reflexivo: sg: m*) himself; (*: f*)
herself; (*: pl*) themselves; (*: cosa*) itself;
(*: de Vd*) yourself; (*: de Vds*) yourselves; **~
está preparando** she's preparing herself;
*para usos léxicos del pron ver el vb en
cuestión, p.ej.* **arrepentirse**
2 (*con complemento indirecto*) to him; to
her; to them; to it; to you; **a usted ~ lo
dije ayer** I told you yesterday; **~ compró
un sombrero** he bought himself a hat; **~
rompió la pierna** he broke his leg
3 (*uso recíproco*) each other, one another;
~ miraron (el uno al otro) they looked at
each other *o* one another
4 (*en oraciones pasivas*): **se han vendido
muchos libros** a lot of books have been
sold
5 (*impers*): **~ dice que** people say that, it
is said that; **allí ~ come muy bien** the
food there is very good, you can eat very
well there

menos [menos] *adj* **1: ~ (que/de)**
(*compar: cantidad*) less (than); (*: número*)
fewer (than); **con ~ entusiasmo** with less
enthusiasm; **~ gente** fewer people; *ver tb*
cada
2 (*superl*): **es el que ~ culpa tiene** he is
the least to blame
♦ *adv* **1** (*compar*): **~ (que, de)** less (than);
me gusta ~ que el otro I like it less than
the other one
2 (*superl*): **es el ~ listo (de su clase)** he's
the least bright in his class; **de todas
ellas es la que ~ me agrada** out of all of
them she's the one I like least; **(por) lo ~**
at (the very) least
3 (*locuciones*): **no quiero verle y ~
visitarle** I don't want to see him let alone
visit him; **tenemos 7 de ~** we're seven
short
♦ *prep* except; (*cifras*) minus; **todos ~ él**
everyone except (for) him; **5 ~ 2** 5 minus
2
♦ *conj*: **a ~ que: a ~ que venga mañana**
unless he comes tomorrow

WORDGAME 1

HEADWORDS

Study the following sentences. In each sentence a wrong word spelt very similarly to the correct word has deliberately been put in and the sentence doesn't make sense. This word is shaded each time. Write out each sentence again, putting in the <u>correct</u> word which you will find in your dictionary near the wrong word.

Example: Aparcar aquí no es delirio.

['Delirio' (= delirium) is the wrong word and should be replaced by 'delito' (= offence)]

1.   El mecánico se negó a arrebatarme el coche.

2.   El baúl estaba cubierto de pólvora.

3.   Es muy caro reventar las fotos en esa tienda.

4.   Les gusta mucho dar pasillos a caballo.

5.   Para ayunar a su madre pone la mesa todos los días.

6.   La ballesta es el animal más grande del mundo.

7.   Mientras esquiábamos nos cayó una nevera tremenda.

8.   No me gustó el último capota del libro.

9.   Tuvimos un pincho y hubo que parar el coche.

10. Hay que cerrar la puerta con candidato.

WORDGAME 2

DICTIONARY ENTRIES

Complete the crossword below by looking up the English words in the list and finding the correct Spanish translations. There is a slight catch, however! All the English words can be translated several ways into Spanish, but only one translation will fit correctly into each part of the crossword. So look carefully through the entries in the English-Spanish section of your dictionary.

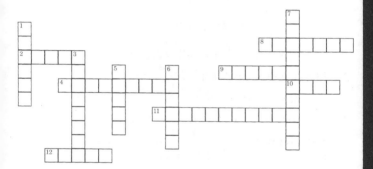

1. HORN	7. AMUSE
2. THROW	8. OLD
3. REMEMBER	9. BELL
4. PERFORMANCE	10. MATERIAL
5. SPEECH	11. ENDING
6. WHOLE	12. PART

WORDGAME 3

FINDING MEANINGS

In this list there are eight pairs of words that have some sort of connection with each other. For example, **'curso'** (= 'course') and **'estudiante'** (= 'student') are linked. Find the other pairs by looking up the words in your dictionary.

1. bata
2. nido
3. cuero
4. zapatillas
5. campanario
6. estudiante
7. libro
8. bolso
9. pasarela
10. aleta
11. curso
12. estante
13. urraca
14. barco
15. veleta
16. tiburón

WORDGAME 4

SYNONYMS

Complete the crossword by supplying SYNONYMS of the words below. You will sometimes find the synonym you are looking for in italics bracketed at the entries for the words listed below. Sometimes you will have to turn to the English-Spanish section for help.

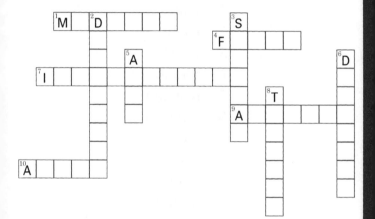

1. maneras
2. desilusión
3. exceder
4. incendio
5. cariño
6. vencer
7. inacabable
8. éxito
9. complacer
10. aeroplano

WORDGAME 5

SPELLING

You will often use your dictionary to check spellings. The person who has compiled this list of ten Spanish words has made <u>three</u> spelling mistakes. Find the three words which have been misspelt and write them out correctly.

1. pájaro
2. acienda
3. oleaje
4. gigante
5. avarrotar
6. peregil
7. ahora
8. velocidad
9. quinientos
10. abridor

WORDGAME 6

ANTONYMS

Complete the crossword by supplying ANTONYMS (i.e. opposites) in Spanish of the words below. Use your dictionary to help.

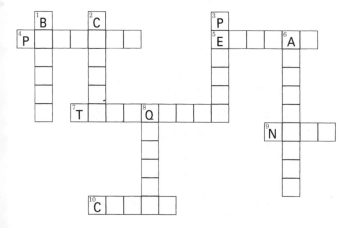

1. feo		6. engordar
2. abrir		7. inquieto
3. ligero		8. poner
4. riqueza		9. todo
5. salir		10. oscuro

WORDGAME 7

PHONETIC SPELLINGS

The phonetic transcriptions of twenty Spanish words are given below.
If you study pages viii and ix at the front of your dictionary you should be
able to work out what the words are.

1. 'aɣwa
2. θju'ðað
3. alreðe'ðor
4. mu'tʃatʃo
5. 'bjento
6. 'niɲo
7. bol'βer
8. 'kaʎe
9. θiɣ'θaɣ
10. 'xenjo
11. 'gwarða
12. 'tʃoke
13. em'bjar
14. ka'βaʎo
15. aβo'ɣaðo
16. korre'xir
17. ko'mjenθo
18. 'eʎos
19. xer'sei
20. i'ɣwal

WORDGAME 8

EXPRESSIONS IN WHICH THE HEADWORD APPEARS

If you look up the headword 'mismo' in the Spanish-English section of your dictionary you will find that the word can have many meanings. Study the entry carefully and translate the following sentences into English.

1. Ahora mismo se lo llevo.

2. A mí me da lo mismo.

3. Lo mismo que tú estudias francés yo estudio español.

4. En ese mismo momento llegó la policía.

5. Acudió el mismo Presidente.

6. Todos los domingos se ponía el mismo traje.

7. Lo hice yo mismo.

8. Era un hipócrita, y por lo mismo despreciado por todos.

9. Tenemos que empezar hoy mismo.

10. Lo vi aquí mismo.

WORDGAME 9

RELATED WORDS

Fill in the blanks in the pairs of sentences below. The missing words are related to the headwords on the left. Choose the correct 'relative' each time. You will find it in your dictionary near the headword provided.

HEADWORD	RELATED WORDS
estudiante	1. Realiza sus _____ en la Universidad. 2. Hay que _____ bien el texto.
pertenecer	3. Estos son los terrenos _____ al Ayuntamiento. 4. Recogió todas sus _____ y se fue.
empleo	5. Es _____ de banco. 6. Voy a _____ todos los medios a mi alcance.
atractivo	7. Esa perspectiva no me _____ nada. 8. Aquella mujer ejercía una gran _____ sobre él.
terminante	9. Al _____ de la reunión todos se fueron a tomar café. 10. No le dejaron _____ lo que estaba diciendo.
falsedad	11. Lo que estás diciendo es completamente _____ 12. Se dedicaban a _____ billetes de banco.

WORDGAME 10

'KEY' WORDS

Study carefully the entry **hacer** in your dictionary and find translations for the following:

1. it's cold

2. I made them come

3. to study Economics

4. this will make it more difficult

5. to do the cooking

6. they became friends

7. I've been going for a month

8. to turn a deaf ear

9. if it's alright with you

10. to get hold of something

THE DICTIONARY AND GRAMMAR

While it is true that a dictionary can never be a substitute for a detailed grammar reference book, it nevertheless provides a great deal of grammatical information. If you know how to extract this information you will be able to use Spanish more accurately both in speech and in writing.

The Collins Pocket Dictionary presents grammatical information as follows.

Parts of speech

Parts of speech are given in italics immediately after the phonetic spellings of headwords. Abbreviated forms are used. Abbreviations can be checked on pages vi and vii.

Changes in parts of speech within an entry – for example, from adjective to adverb to noun, or from noun to intransitive verb to transitive verb – are indicated by means of lozenges - ♦ - as with the Spanish 'derecho' and the English 'act' opposite.

Genders of Spanish nouns

The gender of each noun in the Spanish-English section of the dictionary is indicated in the following way:

> *nm* = nombre masculino
>
> *nf* = nombre femenino

You will occasionally see *nm/f* beside an entry. This indicates that a noun – 'habitante', for example – can be either masculine or feminine.

Feminine forms of nouns are shown, as with 'ministro' opposite: the feminine ending is substituted for the masculine, so that 'ministro' becomes 'ministra' in the feminine.

In the English-Spanish section of the dictionary, genders are not shown for masculine nouns ending in '-o' or feminine nouns ending in '-a'. Otherwise, the gender immediately follows the translation. If a noun can be either masculine or feminine, this is shown by '*m/f*' if the form of the noun does not change, or by the feminine ending if it does change, as with 'graduate' and 'dentist' opposite. Note that when an ending is added on to a word rather than substituted for another ending it appears in brackets.

It is most important that you know the correct gender of a Spanish noun, since it is going to determine the form of both adjectives and past participles. If you are in any doubt as to the gender of a noun, it is always best to check it in your dictionary.

estría [es'tria] *nf* groove

tenue ['tenwe] *adj* (*delgado*) thin, slender; (*neblina*) light; (*lazo, vínculo*) slight

criterio [kri'terjo] *nm* criterion; (*juicio*) judgement

manguera [man'gera] *nf* hose

habitante [aßi'tante] *nm/f* inhabitant

ministro, a [mi'nistro, a] *nm/f* minister

derecho, a [de'retʃo, a] *adj* right, right-hand ♦ *nm* (*privilegio*) right; (*lado*) right(-hand) side; (*leyes*) law ♦ *adv* straight, directly; **~s** *nmpl* (*de aduana*) duty *sg*; (*de autor*) royalties; **tener ~ a** to have a right to

act [ækt] *n* acto, acción *f*; (*of play*) acto; (*in music hall etc*) número; (*LAW*) decreto, ley *f* ♦ *vi* (*behave*) comportarse; (*have effect: drug, chemical*) hacer efecto; (*THEATRE*) actuar; (*pretend*) fingir; (*take action*) obrar ♦ *vt* (*part*) hacer el papel de; **in the ~ of:** **to catch sb in the ~ of ...** pillar a uno en el momento en que ...; **to ~ as** actuar *or* hacer de; **~ing** *adj* suplente ♦ *n* (*activity*) actuación *f*; (*profession*) profesión *f* de actor

graduate [*n* 'grædjuɪt, *vb* 'grædjueɪt] *n* (*US: of high school*) graduado/a; (*of university*) licenciado/a ♦ *vi* graduarse; licenciarse; **graduation** [-'eɪʃən] *n* (*ceremony*) entrega del título

dentist ['dɛntɪst] *n* dentista *m/f*

Adjectives

Adjectives are given in both their masculine and feminine forms, where these are different. The usual rule is to drop the 'o' of the masculine form and add an 'a' to make an adjective feminine, as with 'negro' opposite.

Some adjectives have identical masculine and feminine forms. Where this occurs, there is no 'a' beside the basic masculine form.

Adverbs

The normal 'rule' for forming adverbs in Spanish is to add '-mente' to the feminine form of the adjective. Thus:

seguro > segura > seguramente

The '-mente' ending is often the equivalent of the English '-ly':

seguramente – surely
lentamente – slowly

In your dictionary Spanish adverbs are not generally given, since the English translation can usually be derived from the relevant translation of the adjective headword. Usually the translation can be formed by adding '-ly' to the relevant adjective translation: e.g.

fiel – faithful
fielmente – faithfully

In cases where the basic translation for the adverb cannot be derived from those for the adjective, the adverb is likely to be listed as a headword in alphabetical order. This means it may not be immediately adjacent to the adjective headword: see 'actual' and 'actualmente' opposite.

Information about verbs

A major problem facing language learners is that the form of a verb will change according to the subject and/or the tense being used. A typical Spanish verb can take many different forms – too many to list in a dictionary entry.

negro, a ['neɣro, a] *adj* black; (*suerte*) awful ♦ *nm* black ♦ *nm/f* black man/woman

valiente [ba'ljente] *adj* brave, valiant ♦ *nm* hero

seguramente [seɣura'mente] *adv* surely; (*con certeza*) for sure, with certainty

actual [ak'twal] *adj* present(-day), current; **~idad** *nf* present; **~idades** *nfpl* (*noticias*) news *sg*; **en la ~idad** at present; (*hoy día*) nowadays
actualizar [aktwali'θar] *vt* to update, modernize
actualmente [aktwal'mente] *adv* at present; (*hoy día*) nowadays

Yet, although verbs are listed in your dictionary in their infinitive forms only, this does not mean that the dictionary is of limited value when it comes to handling the verb system of the Spanish language. On the contrary, it contains much valuable information.

First of all, your dictionary will help you with the meanings of unfamiliar verbs. If you came across the word 'decidió' in a text and looked it up in your dictionary you wouldn't find it. What you must do is assume that it is part of a verb and look for the infinitive form. Thus you will deduce that 'decidió' is a form of the verb 'decidir'. You now have the basic meaning of the word you are concerned with – something to do with English verb 'decide' – and this should be enough to help you understand the text you are reading.

It is usually an easy task to make the connection between the form of a verb and the infinitive. For example, 'decidieran', 'decidirá', 'decidimos' and 'decidido' are all recognisable as parts of the infinitive 'decidir'. However, sometimes it is less obvious – for example, 'pueda', 'podrán' and 'pude' are all parts of 'poder'. The only real solution to this problem is to learn the various forms of the main Spanish regular and irregular verbs.

And this is the second source of help offered by your dictionary as far as verbs are concerned. The verb tables on page xii of the Collins Pocket Dictionary provide a summary of some of the main forms of the main tenses of regular and irregular verbs. Consider the verb 'poder' below where the following information is given:

1	pudiendo	– Present Participle
2	puede	– Imperative
3	puedo, puedes, puede, pueden	– Present Tense forms
4	pude, pudiste, pudo, pudimos, pudisteis, pudieron	– Preterite forms
5	podré *etc*	– 1st Person Singular of the Future Tense
6	pueda, puedas, pueda, puedan	– Present Subjunctive forms
7	pudiera *etc*	– 1st Person Singular of the Imperfect Subjunctive

The regular '-ar', '-er', and '-ir' verbs – 'hablar', 'comer' and 'vivir' – are presented in greater detail. The main tenses and the different endings are given in full. This information can be transferred and applied to all verbs in the list. In addition, the main parts of the most common irregular verbs are listed in the body of the dictionary.

HABLAR

1 hablando
2 habla, hablad
3 hablo, hablas, habla, hablamos, habláis, hablan
4 hablé, hablaste, habló, hablamos, hablasteis, hablaron
5 hablaré, hablarás, hablará, hablaremos, hablaréis, hablarán
6 hable, hables, hable, hablemos, habléis, hablen
7 hablara, hablaras, hablara, habláramos, hablarais, hablaran
8 hablado
9 hablaba, hablabas, hablaba, hablábamos, hablabais, hablaban

In order to make maximum use of the information contained in these pages, a good working knowledge of the various rules affecting Spanish verbs is required. You will acquire this in the course of your Spanish studies and your Collins dictionary will serve as a useful reminder. If you happen to forget how to form the second person singular form of the Future Tense of 'poder' (i.e. how to translate 'you will be able to'), there will be no need to panic – your dictionary contains the information!

WORDGAME 11

PARTS OF SPEECH

In each sentence below a word has been shaded. Put a tick in the appropriate box to indicate the <u>part of speech</u> each time.

SENTENCE	Noun	Adj	Adv	Verb
1. Es estudiante de derecho.				
2. No hables tan alto.				
3. No tiene mucho dinero en su haber.				
4. Es un escrito muy largo.				
5. Vaya todo seguido.				
6. Es un dicho muy frecuente.				
7. Llegamos a casa muy tarde.				
8. Le gusta mucho andar por el campo.				
9. Lo hacemos por tu bien.				
10. A mi parecer es una buena película.				

WORDGAME 12

MEANING CHANGING WITH GENDER

Some Spanish nouns change meaning according to their gender, i.e. according to whether they are masculine or feminine. Look at the pairs of sentences below and fill in the blanks with either 'un', 'una', 'el' or 'la'. Use your dictionary to help.

1. No podía comprender_____ cólera de su padre.

   _____ cólera hace estragos en las regiones tropicales.

2. Perdí_____ pendiente en su casa.

   El coche no podía subir por_____ pendiente.

3. Los niños jugaban con _____cometa.

   Dicen que en abril caerá _____cometa.

4. Vimos_____policía dentro de su coche.

   _____ policía ha descubierto una red de traficantes de droga.

5. Hay que cambiar_____ order de los números.

   En cuanto recibió_____orden se puso en camino.

6. ¿Ha llegado_____ parte de la policía?

   _____ parte de atrás de la casa es muy sombría.

7. Pasó dos días en _____coma profundo.

   Tienes que poner_____ coma ahí.

8. Los soldados están todavía en _____frente.

   El pelo le cubría_____ frente.

WORDGAME 13

ADVERBS

Translate the following Spanish adverbs into English (generally by adding **-ly** to the adjective).

1. recientemente
2. lamentablemente
3. constantemente
4. mensualmente
5. pesadamente
6. inconscientemente
7. inmediatamente
8. ampliamente
9. tenazmente
10. brillantemente

WORDGAME 14

VERB TENSES

Use your dictionary to help you fill in the blanks in the table below.
(Remember the important pages at the front of your dictionary.)

INFINITIVE	PRESENT SUBJUNCTIVE	PRETERITE	FUTURE
tener		yo	
hacer			yo
poder			yo
decir		yo	
agradecer	yo		
saber			yo
reír	yo		
querer		yo	
caber	yo		
ir	yo		
salir			yo
ser		yo	

WORDGAME 15

IRREGULAR VERBS

Use your dictionary to find the <u>first person</u> present indicative of these verbs.

INFINITIVE	PRESENT INDICATIVE
conocer	
saber	
estar	
ofrecer	
poder	
ser	
poner	
divertir	
traer	
decir	
preferir	
negar	
dar	
instruir	

WORDGAME 16

IDENTIFYING INFINITIVES

In the sentences below you will see various Spanish verbs shaded. Use your dictionary to help you find the **infinitive** form of each verb.

1. Cuando erá pequeño dormía en la misma habitación que mi hermano.

2. Mis amigos vienen conmigo.

3. No cupieron todos los libros en el estante.

4. ¿Es que no veías lo que pasaba?

5. El sábado saldremos todos juntos.

6. Ya hemos visto la casa.

7. ¿Quieres que lo ponga aquí?

8. Le dije que viniera a las ocho.

9. Nos han escrito tres cartas ya.

10. No sabían qué hacer.

11. Tuvimos que salir temprano.

12. En cuanto supe lo de su padre la llamé por teléfono.

13. ¿Por qué no trajiste el dinero?

14. Prefiero quedarme en casa.

15. Quiero que conozcas a mi padre.

MORE ABOUT MEANING

In this section we will consider some of the problems associated with using a bilingual dictionary.

Overdependence on your dictionary

That the dictionary is an invaluable tool for the language learner is beyond dispute. Nevertheless, it is possible to become overdependent on your dictionary, turning to it in an almost automatic fashion every time you come up against a new word or phrase in a Spanish text. Tackling an unfamiliar text in this way will turn reading in Spanish into an extremely tedious activity. It is possible to argue that if you stop to look up every new word you may actually be *hindering* your ability to read in Spanish – you are so concerned with the individual words that you pay no attention to the text as a whole and to the context which gives them meaning. It is therefore important to develop appropriate reading skills – using clues such as titles, headlines, illustrations, etc., understanding relations within a sentence, etc. to predict or infer what a text is about.

A detailed study of the development of reading skills is not within the scope of this supplement; we are concerned with knowing how to use a dictionary, which is only one of several important skills involved in reading. Nevertheless, it may be instructive to look at one example. You see the following text in a Spanish newspaper and are interested in working out what it is about.

Contextual clues here include the heading in large type, which indicates that this is some sort of announcement, and the names. The verb 'recibir' is very much like the English 'receive' and you will also know 'form' words such as 'una', 'y' and so forth from your general studies in Spanish, as well as essential vocabulary such as 'niña', 'hijos', 'nombre'. Given that this extract appeared in a newspaper,

> **Natalicios**
>
> La señora de García Rodríguez (don Alfonso), de soltera Laura Montes de la Torre, ha dado a luz una niña, cuarta de sus hijos, que recibirá el nombre de Beatriz y tendrá como padrinos a doña Mercedes Sánchez Serrano y don Felipe Gómez Morales.

you will probably have worked out by now that this is an announcement placed in the 'Personal Column'.

So you have used contextual and word-formation clues to get you to the point where you have understood that this notice has been placed in the personal column because something has happened to señora de García Rodríguez and that somebody is going to be given the name of 'Beatriz'. And you have reached this point *without* opening your dictionary once. Common sense and your knowledge of newspaper contents in this country will suggest that this must be an announcement of someone's birth or death. Thus 'dar a luz' ('to give birth') and 'padrinos' ('godparents') become the only words that you need to look up in order to confirm that this is indeed a birth announcement.

When learning Spanish we are helped considerably by the fact that many Spanish and English words look and sound alike and have exactly the same meaning. Such words are called 'COGNATES'. Many words which look similar in Spanish and English come from a common Latin root. Other words are the same or nearly the same in both languages because the Spanish language has borrowed a word from English or vice versa. The dictionary will often not be necessary where cognates are concerned – provided you know the English word that the Spanish word resembles!

Words with more than one meaning

The need to examine with care *all* the information contained in a dictionary entry must be stressed. This is particularly important with the many Spanish words which have more than one meaning. For example, the Spanish 'destino' can mean 'destiny' as well as 'destination'. How you translated the word would depend on the context in which you found it.

Similarly, if you were trying to translate a phrase such as 'sigo sin saber', you would have to look through the whole entry for 'seguir' to get the right translation. If you restricted your search to the first line of the entry and saw that the first meaning given is 'to follow', you might be tempted to assume that the phrase meant 'I follow without knowing'. But if you examined the entry closely you would see that 'seguir sin ...' means 'to still do ...' or 'to still be ...'. So 'sigo sin saber' means 'I still don't know'.

The same need for care applies when you are using the English-Spanish section of your dictionary to translate a word from English into Spanish. Watch out in particular for the lozenges indicating changes in parts of speech.

The noun 'sink' is 'fregadero', while the verb is 'hundir'. If you don't watch what you are doing, you could end up with ridiculous non-Spanish e.g. 'Dejó los platos en el hundir'!

sink [sɪŋk] (*pt* **sank**, *pp* **sunk**) *n* fregadero ♦ *vt* hundir, echar a pique; (*foundations*) excavar ♦ *vi* (*gen*) hundirse; **to ~ sth into** hundir algo en; **~ in** *vi* (*fig*) penetrar, calar

Phrasal verbs

Another potential source of difficulty is English phrasal verbs. These consist of a common verb ('make', 'get', etc.) plus an adverb and/or a preposition to give English expressions such as 'to make out', 'to get on', etc. Entries for such verbs tend to be fairly full, so close examination of the contents is required. Note how these verbs appear in colour within the entry.

make [meɪk] (*pt, pp* **made**) *vt* hacer; (*manufacture*) fabricar; (*mistake*) cometer; (*speech*) pronunciar; (*cause to be*): **to ~ sb sad** poner triste a alguien; (*force*): **to ~ sb do sth** obligar a alguien a hacer algo; (*earn*) ganar; (*equal*): **2 and 2 ~ 4** 2 y 2 son 4 ♦ *n* marca; **to ~ the bed** hacer la cama; **to ~ a fool of sb** poner a alguien en ridículo; **to ~ a profit/loss** obtener ganancias/sufrir pérdidas; **to ~ it?** (*arrive*) llegar; (*achieve sth*) tener éxito; **what time do you ~ it?** ¿qué hora tienes?; **to ~ do with** contentarse con; **~ for** *vt fus* (*place*) dirigirse a; **~ out** *vt* (*decipher*) descifrar; (*understand*) entender; (*see*) distinguir; (*cheque*) extender; **~ up** *vt* (*invent*) inventar; (*prepare*) hacer; (*constitute*) constituir ♦ *vi* reconciliarse;

Falsos amigos

We noted above that many Spanish and English words have similar forms *and* meanings. There are, however, many Spanish words which *look* like English words but have a completely *different* meaning. For example, 'la carpeta' means 'the folder'; 'sensible' means 'sensitive'. This can easily lead to serious mistranslations.

Sometimes the meaning of the Spanish word is quite close to the English. For example, 'la moneda' means 'coin' rather than 'money'; 'simpático' means 'nice' rather than 'sympathetic'. But some Spanish words which look similar to English words have two meanings, one the same as the English, the other completely different! 'El plato' can mean 'course' (in a meal) as well as 'plate'; 'la cámara' can mean 'camera', but also 'chamber'.

Such words are often referred to as FALSOS AMIGOS ('false friends'). You will have to look at the context in which they appear to arrive at the correct meaning. If they seem to fit in with the sense of the passage as a whole, you will probably not need to look them up. If they don't make sense, however, you may well be dealing with 'falsos amigos'.

WORDGAME 17

WORDS IN CONTEXT

Study the sentences below. Translations of the shaded words are given at the bottom. Match the number of the sentence and the letter of the translation correctly each time.

1. Tendremos que atarlo con una cuerda.
2. La cuerda del reloj se ha roto.
3. Iremos al cine para entretener a los niños.
4. No me entretengas, que llegaré tarde.
5. Le dieron una patada en la espinilla.
6. Tenía una espinilla enorme en la nariz.
7. Siempre le da mucho sueño después de comer.
8. Anoche me desperté sobresaltada por un mal sueño.
9. El niño tocaba todo lo que veía.
10. Su padre tocaba muy bien la guitarra.
11. Tuvo un acceso de tos.
12. Todas las vías de acceso estaban cerradas.
13. Me gustaría estudiar la carrera de Derecho.
14. Todos querían participar en la carrera.
15. He quebrado el plato sin darme cuenta.
16. No sabían que esa empresa había quebrado.

a. touched	e. fit	i. rope	m. gone bankrupt
b. shin(bone)	f. course	j. hold up	n. played
c. entertain	g. sleepiness	k. entry	o. dream
d. spring	h. blackhead	l. race	p. broken

WORDGAME 18

WORDS WITH MORE THAN ONE MEANING

Look at the advertisements below. The words which are shaded can have more than one meaning. Use your dictionary to help you work out the correct translation in the context.

1

El Pescador
RESTAURANTE

Mariscos de viveros propios
Teléfono 406 12 80 – MADRID 6

P FÁCIL
APARCAMIENTO

2

Restaurante
LOS CEREZOS

ALTA COCINA REGIONAL
Para amantes de lo tradicional
RESERVAS: 574 34 11/12

3

INTERLANGUE
ANUNCIA CURSO MASTER DE
INGLÉS JURÍDICO PARA
PROFESIONALES DEL DERECHO
Inicio: 20 de octubre

4

¡¡¡BUTACAS PIEL A MEDIDA!!!
APROVECHE GRANDES REBAJAS EN OCTUBRE
¡En fábrica, más calidad y menor precio!
Horario continuado de 9,30 a 20,30 –
incluso sábados

GRANDES ALMACENES "EL CONDOR"
IMPORTANTES REBAJAS DE FIN DE TEMPORADA

5

6

Guía **TELEVISION**
JUEVES, 19

19.00. – Partido adelantado de la
JORNADA DE LIGA de PRIMERA DIVISION:
Atlético de Madrid – Barcelona (TV-2)

7

Bar-restaurante **"La Ballena"**

platos combinados desde 300 ptas.
helados, postres nuestra especialidad

8

ULTIMAS VIVIENDAS
de 2 y 3 dormitorios con
plaza de garaje opcional
Lunes a Viernes mañanas de 11 a 13,30.
Tardes de 16,30 a 19,30.

9

Calle de
ISABEL LA CATOLICA
N.ºs 50 - 56

**PISOS EXTERIORES
DE 80 m^2**

FINANCIACION A 11 AÑOS
13 Y 13,5% CON LA CAJA DE BARCELONA

WORDGAME 19

FALSE FRIENDS

Look at the advertisements below. The words which are shaded resemble English words but have different meanings here. Find a correct translation for each word in the context.

1

LA MAYOR COLECCION DE
ALFOMBRAS
PERSAS Y
ORIENTALES
¡¡¡VENTA DE LIQUIDACION
POR CAMBIO DE DOMICILIO!!!

2

Teatro Nacional:
"El Alcalde de Zalamea"
Localidades en venta a partir de mañana

3

PRODUCTOS BENGOLEA
¡NO RECURRA A
LA COMPETENCIA!
Visite nuestro local en Castellana 500

4

OFERTA ESPECIAL
cubiertos de acero inoxidable de
primerísima calidad en planta baja

5

INTERSEGUR SEGUROS

ASEGURE HOY SU
JUBILACIÓN DE MAÑANA

6

HOSTAL DEL REY

Habitaciones con baño
Muy céntrico

Tel. 315 48 67

7

PENSION "LA GAVIOTA"

camas, comidas, a dos minutos de la
playa, habitaciones muy cómodas a
un precio incomparable.

8

VENDO LOCAL

Ortega y Gasset
piso interior
10.750.000 pesetas

Teléfono 593 87 60

9

SEGUROS "NON PLUS ULTRA"

Desea comunicarle su nueva
dirección a partir del 1º
de enero:

**DIAGONAL 348
BARCELONA 07008**

Tel. 260 7000/1/2

HAVE FUN WITH YOUR DICTIONARY

Here are some word games for you to try. You will find your dictionary helpful as you attempt the activities.

WORDGAME 20

CODED WORDS

In the boxes below the letters of eight Spanish words have been replaced by numbers. A number represents the same letter each time (though an accent may be required sometimes).

Try to crack the code and find the eight words. If you need help, use your dictionary.

Here is a clue: all the words you are looking for have something to do with TRANSPORT.

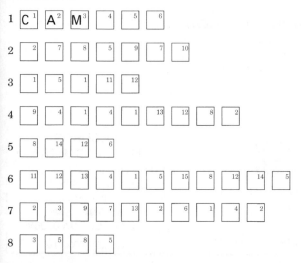

1 C¹ A² M³ ☐⁴ ☐⁵ ☐⁶

2 ☐² ☐⁷ ☐⁸ ☐⁵ ☐⁹ ☐⁷ ☐¹⁰

3 ☐¹ ☐⁵ ☐¹ ☐¹¹ ☐¹²

4 ☐⁹ ☐⁴ ☐¹ ☐⁴ ☐¹ ☐¹³ ☐¹² ☐⁸ ☐²

5 ☐⁸ ☐¹⁴ ☐¹² ☐⁶

6 ☐¹¹ ☐¹² ☐¹³ ☐⁴ ☐¹ ☐⁵ ☐¹⁵ ☐⁸ ☐¹² ☐¹⁴ ☐⁵

7 ☐² ☐³ ☐⁹ ☐⁷ ☐¹³ ☐² ☐⁶ ☐¹ ☐⁴ ☐²

8 ☐³ ☐⁵ ☐⁸ ☐⁵

WORDGAME 21

BEHEADED WORDS

If you 'behead' certain Spanish words, i.e. take away their first letter, you are left with another Spanish word. For example, if you behead **'aplomo'** (= 'self-assurance'), you get **'plomo'** (= 'lead'), and **'bala'** (= 'bullet') gives **'ala'** (= 'wing').

The following words have their heads chopped off, i.e. the first letter has been removed. Use your dictionary to help you form a new Spanish word by adding one letter to the start of each word below. You will find that some of them can have more than one answer. Write down the new Spanish word and its meaning.

1. bajo (= low)
2. oler (= to smell)
3. año (= year)
4. oro (= gold)
5. reparar (= to repair)
6. ama (= owner)
7. rendido (= worn-out)
8. cuerdo (= sane)
9. ave (= bird)
10. batir (= to beat)
11. resto (= rest)
12. precio (= price)
13. cera (= wax)
14. hora (= hour)
15. pinar (= pine forest)

WORDGAME 22

PALABRAS CRUZADAS

Complete this crossword by looking up the words listed below in the English-Spanish section of your dictionary. Remember to read through the entry carefully to find the word that will fit.

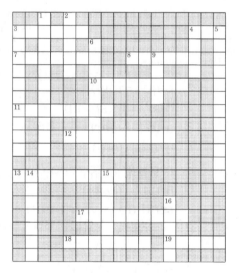

ACROSS

- 3. to bark
- 4. wing
- 7. lie
- 8. above
- 10. to work out
- 11. to lighten
- 12. to need
- 13. usual
- 17. cornet
- 18. to stink
- 19. radius

DOWN

- 1. to identify
- 2. to go out
- 3. regrettable
- 4. to love
- 5. streamlined
- 6. heating
- 9. expensive
- 14. to oblige
- 15. tricks
- 16. now

WORDGAME 23

There are twelve Spanish words hidden in the grid below. Each word is made up of five letters but has been split into two parts.

Find the Spanish words. Each group of letters can only be used once.

Use your dictionary to help you.

bla	lir	bu	ma	que	go
gor	ar	ver	vi	asi	jor
cal	me	ha	jo	lar	so
bo	jía	lo	vol	sa	eno

WORDGAME 24

Here is a list of Spanish words for things you will find in the kitchen. Unfortunately, they have all been jumbled up. Try to work out what each word is and put the word in the boxes on the right. You will see that there are seven shaded boxes below. With the seven letters in the shaded boxes make up <u>another</u> Spanish word for an object you can find in the kitchen.

1. azta   ¿Quieres una ____ de café?   ☐☐☐☐

2. eanevr   ¡Mete la mantequilla en la ____!   ☐☐☐☐☐☐

3. asme   ¡La comida está en la ____!   ☐☐☐☐

4. zoac   Su madre está calentando la leche en el ____   ☐☐☐☐

5. roegcanldo   ¡No saques el helado del ____ todavía!   ☐☐☐☐☐☐☐☐☐☐

6. uclclohi   ¿Dónde has puesto el ____ del queso?   ☐☐☐☐☐☐☐☐

7. rgoif   ¿Puedes cerrar ya el ____ del agua caliente?   ☐☐☐☐☐

The word you are looking for is:

☐☐☐☐☐☐☐

WORDGAME 25

PALABRAS CRUZADAS

Take the four letters given each time and put them in the four empty boxes in the centre of each grid. Arrange them in such a way that you form four six-letter words. Use your dictionary to check the words.

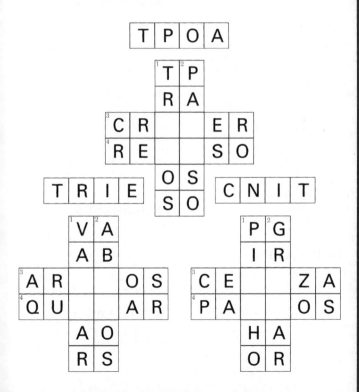

ANSWERS

WORDGAME 1

1 arreglarme	6 ballena
2 polvo	7 nevada
3 revelar	8 capítulo
4 paseos	9 pinchazo
5 ayudar	10 candado

WORDGAME 2

1 cuerno	7 entretener
2 echar	8 antiguo
3 recordar	9 timbre
4 actuación	10 tela
5 habla	11 terminación
6 entero	12 parte

WORDGAME 3

bata + zapatillas
nido + urraca
cuero + bolso
campanario + veleta
estudiante + curso
libro + estante
pasarela + barco
aleta + tiburón

WORDGAME 4

1 modales	6 derrotar
2 decepción	7 interminable
3 superar	8 triunfo
4 fuego	9 agradar
5 amor	10 avión

WORDGAME 5

2 hacienda
5 abalorios
6 perejil

WORDGAME 6

1 bonito	6 adelgazar
2 cerrar	7 tranquilo
3 pesado	8 quitar
4 pobreza	9 nada
5 entrar	10 claro

WORDGAME 7

agua, ciudad, alrededor,
muchacho, viento, niño,
volver, calle, zigzag,
genio, guarda, choque,
enviar, caballo, abogado,
corregir, comienzo, ellos,
jersey, igual

WORDGAME 9

1 estudios	7 atrae
2 estudiar	8 atracción
3 pertenecientes	9 término
4 pertenencias	10 terminar
5 empleado	11 falso
6 emplear	12 falsificar

WORDGAME 11

1 n 2 adv 3 n 4 n 5 adv
6 n 7 adv 8 v 9 n 10 n

WORDGAME 12

1	la; El	5	el; la
2	el; la	6	el; La
3	una; un	7	un; una
4	un; La	8	el; la

WORDGAME 14

tuve	ría
haré	quise
podré	quepa
dije	vaya
agradezca	saldré
sabré	fui

WORDGAME 15

conozco	divierto
sé	traigo
estoy	digo
ofrezco	prefiero
puedo	niego
soy	doy
pongo	instruyo

WORDGAME 16

1	dormir	9	escribir
2	venir	10	saber
3	caber	11	tener
4	ver	12	saber
5	salir	13	traer
6	ver	14	preferir
7	poner	15	conocer
8	venir		

WORDGAME 17

1	i	5	b	9	a	13	f
2	d	6	h	10	n	14	l
3	c	7	g	11	e	15	p
4	j	8	o	12	k	16	m

WORDGAME 18

1 fish farm
2 cuisine
3 law
4 leather
5 significant
6 league
7 set main course
8 space
9 savings bank

WORDGAME 19

1 clearance sale;
  home (Here: address)
2 tickets
3 competition
4 cutlery
5 retirement
6 small hotel; rooms
7 guest house
8 premises
9 address

WORDGAME 20

1	camión	5	tren
2	autobús	6	helicóptero
3	coche	7	ambulancia
4	bicicleta	8	moto

WORDGAME 21

1	abajo	7	prendido
2	doler; moler; soler	8	acuerdo
		9	nave
3	baño; paño; daño; caño	10	abatir
		11	presto
4	coro; loro; moro; poro	12	aprecio
		13	acera
5	preparar	14	ahora
6	cama; dama; fama; gama; mama; rama	15	opinar

WORDGAME 22

ACROSS:
3 ladrar
4 ala
7 mentira
8 encima
10 elaborar
11 aligerar
12 necesitar
13 corriente
17 cucurucho
18 apestar
19 radio

DOWN:
1 identificar
2 salir
3 lamentable
4 amar
5 aerodinámico
6 calefacción
9 caro
14 obligar
15 trucos
16 ahora

WORDGAME 23

enojo	verbo
queso	calma
salir	asilo
volar	largo
vigor	mejor
bujía	habla

WORDGAME 24

1	taza	5	congelador
2	nevera	6	cuchillo
3	mesa	7	grifo
4	cazo		

Missing word – ARMARIO

WORDGAME 25

1)	1 trapos		2	patoso
	3 cráter		4	reposo
2)	1 variar		2	abetos
	3 arreos		4	quitar
3)	1 pincho		2	gritar
	3 ceniza		4	pactos

ENGLISH – SPANISH
INGLÉS – ESPAÑOL

A, a

A [eɪ] *n* (*MUS*) la *m*

a [ə] *indef art* (*before vowel or silent h: an*)
1 un(a); **~ book** un libro; **an apple** una
manzana; **she's ~ doctor** (ella) es médica
2 (*instead of the number "one"*) un(a); **~
year ago** hace un año; **~ hundred/
thousand** *etc* **pounds** cien/mil *etc* libras
3 (*in expressing ratios, prices etc*): **3 ~
day/week** 3 al día/a la semana; **10 km
an hour** 10 km por hora; **£5 ~ person** £5
por persona; **30p ~ kilo** 30p el kilo

A.A. *n abbr* (= *Automobile Association:
BRIT*) ≈ RACE *m* (*SP*); (= *Alcoholics
Anonymous*) Alcohólicos Anónimos
A.A.A. (*US*) *n abbr* (= *American
Automobile Association*) ≈ RACE *m* (*SP*)
aback [ə'bæk] *adv*: **to be taken ~** quedar
desconcertado
abandon [ə'bændən] *vt* abandonar; (*give
up*) renunciar a
abate [ə'beɪt] *vi* (*storm*) amainar; (*anger*)
aplacarse; (*terror*) disminuir
abattoir ['æbətwɑː*] (*BRIT*) *n* matadero
abbey ['æbɪ] *n* abadía
abbot ['æbət] *n* abad *m*
abbreviation [ə'briːvɪ'eɪʃən] *n* abreviatura
abdicate ['æbdɪkeɪt] *vt* renunciar a ♦ *vi*
abdicar
abdomen ['æbdəmən] *n* abdomen *m*
abduct [æb'dʌkt] *vt* raptar, secuestrar
abeyance [ə'beɪəns] *n*: **in ~** (*law*) en
desuso; (*matter*) en suspenso
abide [ə'baɪd] *vt*: **I can't ~ it/him** no lo/le
puedo ver; **~ by** *vt fus* atenerse a
ability [ə'bɪlɪtɪ] *n* habilidad *f*, capacidad *f*;
(*talent*) talento
abject ['æbdʒɛkt] *adj* (*poverty*) miserable;

(*apology*) rastrero
ablaze [ə'bleɪz] *adj* en llamas, ardiendo
able ['eɪbl] *adj* capaz; (*skilled*) hábil; **to be
~ to do sth** poder hacer algo; **~-bodied**
adj sano; **ably** *adv* hábilmente
abnormal [æb'nɔːməl] *adj* anormal
aboard [ə'bɔːd] *adv* a bordo ♦ *prep* a
bordo de
abode [ə'bəud] *n*: **of no fixed ~** sin
domicilio fijo
abolish [ə'bɔlɪʃ] *vt* suprimir, abolir
aborigine [æbə'rɪdʒɪnɪ] *n* aborigen *m/f*
abort [ə'bɔːt] *vt*, *vi* abortar; **~ion** [ə'bɔːʃən]
n aborto; **to have an ~ion** abortar,
hacerse abortar; **~ive** *adj* malogrado

about [ə'baut] *adv* **1** (*approximately*) más o
menos, aproximadamente; **~ a
hundred/thousand** *etc* unos(unas) cien/
mil *etc*; **it takes ~ 10 hours** se tarda unas
or más o menos 10 horas; **at ~ 2 o'clock**
sobre las dos; **I've just ~ finished** casi he
terminado
2 (*referring to place*) por todas partes; **to
leave things lying ~** dejar las cosas
(tiradas) por ahí; **to run ~** correr por
todas partes; **to walk ~** pasearse, ir y
venir
3: **to be ~ to do sth** estar a punto de
hacer algo
♦ *prep* **1** (*relating to*) de, sobre, acerca
de; **a book ~ London** un libro sobre *or*
acerca de Londres; **what is it ~?** ¿de qué
se trata?, ¿qué pasa?; **we talked ~ it**
hablamos de eso *or* ello; **what** *or* **how ~
doing this?** ¿qué tal si hacemos esto?
2 (*referring to place*) por; **to walk ~ the
town** caminar por la ciudad

above [ə'bʌv] *adv* encima, por encima, arriba ♦ *prep* encima de; (*greater than: in number*) más de; (: *in rank*) superior a; **mentioned ~** susodicho; **~ all** sobre todo; **~ board** *adj* legítimo

abrasive [ə'breɪzɪv] *adj* abrasivo; (*manner*) brusco

abreast [ə'brest] *adv* de frente; **to keep ~ of** (*fig*) mantenerse al corriente de

abroad [ə'brɔːd] *adv* (*to be*) en el extranjero; (*to go*) al extranjero

abrupt [ə'brʌpt] *adj* (*sudden*) brusco; (*curt*) áspero

abruptly [ə'brʌptlɪ] *adv* (*leave*) repentinamente; (*speak*) bruscamente

abscess ['æbsɪs] *n* absceso

abscond [əb'skɔnd] *vi* (*thief*): **to ~ with** fugarse con; (*prisoner*): **to ~ (from)** escaparse (de)

absence ['æbsəns] *n* ausencia

absent ['æbsənt] *adj* ausente; **~ee** [-'tiː] *n* ausente *m/f*; **~-minded** *adj* distraído

absolute ['æbsəluːt] *adj* absoluto; **~ly** [-'luːtlɪ] *adv* (*totally*) totalmente; (*certainly!*) ¡por supuesto (que sí)!

absolve [əb'zɔlv] *vt*: **to ~ sb (from)** absolver a alguien (de)

absorb [əb'zɔːb] *vt* absorber; **to be ~ed in a book** estar absorto en un libro; **~ent cotton** (*US*) *n* algodón *m* hidrófilo; **~ing** *adj* absorbente

absorption [əb'zɔːpʃən] *n* absorción *f*

abstain [əb'steɪn] *vi*: **to ~ (from)** abstenerse (de)

abstinence ['æbstɪnəns] *n* abstinencia

abstract ['æbstrækt] *adj* abstracto

absurd [əb'səːd] *adj* absurdo

abundance [ə'bʌndəns] *n* abundancia

abuse [*n* ə'bjuːs, *vb* ə'bjuːz] *n* (*insults*) insultos *mpl*, injurias *fpl*; (*ill-treatment*) malos tratos *mpl*; (*misuse*) abuso ♦ *vt* insultar; maltratar; abusar de; **abusive** *adj* ofensivo

abysmal [ə'bɪzməl] *adj* pésimo; (*failure*) garrafal; (*ignorance*) supino

abyss [ə'bɪs] *n* abismo

AC *abbr* (= *alternating current*) corriente *f* alterna

academic [ækə'demɪk] *adj* académico, universitario; (*pej: issue*) puramente teórico ♦ *n* estudioso/a; profesor(a) *m/f* universitario/a

academy [ə'kædəmɪ] *n* (*learned body*) academia; (*school*) instituto, colegio; **~ of music** conservatorio

accelerate [æk'seləreɪt] *vt, vi* acelerar; **accelerator** (*BRIT*) *n* acelerador *m*

accent ['æksent] *n* acento; (*fig*) énfasis *m*

accept [ək'sept] *vt* aceptar; (*responsibility, blame*) admitir; **~able** *adj* aceptable; **~ance** *n* aceptación *f*

access ['ækses] *n* acceso; **to have ~ to** tener libre acceso a; **~ible** [-'sesəbl] *adj* (*place, person*) accesible; (*knowledge etc*) asequible

accessory [æk'sesərɪ] *n* accesorio; (*LAW*): **~ to** cómplice de

accident ['æksɪdənt] *n* accidente *m*; (*chance event*) casualidad *f*; **by ~** (*unintentionally*) sin querer; (*by chance*) por casualidad; **~al** [-'dentl] *adj* accidental, fortuito; **~ally** [-'dentəlɪ] *adv* sin querer; por casualidad; **~ insurance** *n* seguro contra accidentes; **~-prone** *adj* propenso a los accidentes

acclaim [ə'kleɪm] *vt* aclamar, aplaudir ♦ *n* aclamación *f*, aplausos *mpl*

acclimatize [ə'klaɪmətaɪz] (*US* **acclimate**) *vt*: **to become ~d** aclimatarse

accommodate [ə'kɔmədeɪt] *vt* (*subj: person*) alojar, hospedar; (: *car, hotel etc*) tener cabida para; (*oblige, help*) complacer; **accommodating** *adj* servicial, complaciente

accommodation [əkɔmə'deɪʃən] *n* (*US* **accommodations** *npl*) alojamiento

accompany [ə'kʌmpənɪ] *vt* acompañar

accomplice [ə'kʌmplɪs] *n* cómplice *m/f*

accomplish [ə'kʌmplɪʃ] *vt* (*finish*) concluir; (*achieve*) lograr; **~ed** *adj* experto, hábil; **~ment** *n* (*skill: gen pl*) talento; (*completion*) realización *f*

accord [ə'kɔːd] *n* acuerdo ♦ *vt* conceder;

of his own ~ espontáneamente; **~ance** *n*: **in ~ance with** de acuerdo con; **~ing**: **~ing to** *prep* según; (*in accordance with*) conforme a; **~ingly** *adv* (*appropriately*) de acuerdo con esto; (*as a result*) en consecuencia

accordion [ə'kɔːdɪən] *n* acordeón *m*

accost [ə'kɔst] *vt* abordar, dirigirse a

account [ə'kaunt] *n* (COMM) cuenta; (*report*) informe *m*; **~s** *npl* (COMM) cuentas *fpl*; **of no ~** de ninguna importancia; **on ~** a cuenta; **on no ~** bajo ningún concepto; **on ~ of** a causa de, por motivo de; **to take into ~, take ~ of** tener en cuenta; **~ for** *vt fus* (*explain*) explicar; (*represent*) representar; **~able** *adj*: **~able (to)** responsable (ante); **~ancy** *n* contabilidad *f*; **~ant** *n* contable *m/f*, contador(a) *m/f*; **~ number** *n* (*at bank etc*) número de cuenta

accrued interest [ə'kruːd-] *n* interés *m* acumulado

accumulate [ə'kjuːmjuleɪt] *vt* acumular ♦ *vi* acumularse

accuracy ['ækjurəsɪ] *n* (*of total*) exactitud *f*; (*of description etc*) precisión *f*

accurate ['ækjurɪt] *adj* exacto; (*description*) preciso; (*person*) cuidadoso; (*device*) de precisión; **~ly** *adv* con precisión

accusation [ækjuˈzeɪʃən] *n* acusación *f*

accuse [ə'kjuːz] *vt*: **to ~ sb (of sth)** acusar a uno (de algo); **~d** *n* (LAW) acusado/a

accustom [ə'kʌstəm] *vt* acostumbrar; **~ed** *adj*: **~ed to** acostumbrado a

ace [eɪs] *n* as *m*

ache [eɪk] *n* dolor *m* ♦ *vi* doler; **my head ~s** me duele la cabeza

achieve [ə'tʃiːv] *vt* (*aim, result*) alcanzar; (*success*) lograr, conseguir; **~ment** *n* (*completion*) realización *f*; (*success*) éxito

acid ['æsɪd] *adj* ácido; (*taste*) agrio ♦ *n* (CHEM, *inf*: LSD) ácido; **~ rain** *n* lluvia ácida

acknowledge [ək'nɔlɪdʒ] *vt* (*letter: also*: **~ receipt of**) acusar recibo de; (*fact, situation, person*) reconocer; **~ment** *n*

acuse *m* de recibo

acne ['æknɪ] *n* acné *m*

acorn ['eɪkɔːn] *n* bellota

acoustic [ə'kuːstɪk] *adj* acústico; **~s** *n*, *npl* acústica *sg*

acquaint [ə'kweɪnt] *vt*: **to ~ sb with sth** (*inform*) poner a uno al corriente de algo; **to be ~ed with** conocer; **~ance** *n* (*person*) conocido/a; (*with person, subject*) conocimiento

acquire [ə'kwaɪə*] *vt* adquirir;

acquisition [ækwɪ'zɪʃən] *n* adquisición *f*

acquit [ə'kwɪt] *vt* absolver, exculpar; **to ~ o.s. well** salir con éxito

acre ['eɪkə*] *n* acre *m*

acrid ['ækrɪd] *adj* acre

acrobat ['ækrəbæt] *n* acróbata *m/f*

across [ə'krɔs] *prep* (*on the other side of*) al otro lado de, del otro lado de; (*crosswise*) a través de ♦ *adv* de un lado a otro, de una parte a otra; a través, al través; (*measurement*): **the road is 10m ~** la carretera tiene 10m de ancho; **to run/ swim ~** atravesar corriendo/nadando; **~ from** enfrente de

acrylic [ə'krɪlɪk] *adj* acrílico ♦ *n* acrílica

act [ækt] *n* acto, acción *f*; (*of play*) acto; (*in music hall etc*) número; (LAW) decreto, ley *f* ♦ *vi* (*behave*) comportarse; (*have effect*: *drug, chemical*) hacer efecto; (THEATRE) actuar; (*pretend*) fingir; (*take action*) obrar ♦ *vt* (*part*) hacer el papel de; **in the ~ of**: **to catch sb in the ~ of ...** pillar a uno en el momento en que ...; **to ~ as** actuar *or* hacer de; **~ing** *adj* suplente ♦ *n* (*activity*) actuación *f*; (*profession*) profesión *f* de actor

action ['ækʃən] *n* acción *f*, acto; (MIL) acción *f*, batalla; (LAW) proceso, demanda; **out of ~** (*person*) fuera de combate; (*thing*) estropeado; **to take ~** tomar medidas; **~ replay** *n* (TV) repetición *f*

activate ['æktɪveɪt] *vt* activar

active ['æktɪv] *adj* activo, enérgico; (*volcano*) en actividad; **~ly** *adv* (*participate*) activamente; (*discourage,* dislike) enérgicamente; **activity** [-'tɪvɪtɪ] n actividad f; **activity holiday** n vacaciones fpl con actividades organizadas

actor ['æktə*] n actor m

actress ['æktrɪs] n actriz f

actual ['æktjʊəl] adj verdadero, real; (emphatic use) propiamente dicho; **~ly** adv realmente, en realidad; (even) incluso

acumen ['ækjumən] n perspicacia

acute [ə'kju:t] adj agudo

ad [æd] n abbr = **advertisement**

A.D. adv abbr (= anno Domini) A.C.

adamant ['ædəmənt] adj firme, inflexible

adapt [ə'dæpt] vt adaptar ♦ vi: **to ~ (to)** adaptarse (a), ajustarse (a); **~able** adj adaptable; **~er, ~or** n (ELEC) adaptador m

add [æd] vt añadir, agregar; (figures: also: ~ up) sumar ♦ vi: **to ~ to** (increase) aumentar, acrecentar; **it doesn't ~ up** (fig) no tiene sentido

adder ['ædə*] n víbora

addict ['ædɪkt] n adicto/a; (enthusiast) entusiasta m/f; **~ed** [ə'dɪktɪd] adj: **to be ~ed to** ser adicto a; (football etc) ser fanático de; **~ion** [ə'dɪkʃən] n (to drugs etc) adicción f; **~ive** [ə'dɪktɪv] adj que causa adicción

addition [ə'dɪʃən] n (adding up) adición f; (thing added) añadidura, añadido; **in ~** además, por añadidura; **in ~ to** además de; **~al** adj adicional

additive ['ædɪtɪv] n aditivo

address [ə'drɛs] n dirección f, señas fpl; (speech) discurso ♦ vt (letter) dirigir; (speak to) dirigirse a, dirigir la palabra a; (problem) tratar

adept ['ædɛpt] adj: **~ at** experto or hábil en

adequate ['ædɪkwɪt] adj (satisfactory) adecuado; (enough) suficiente

adhere [əd'hɪə*] vi: **to ~ to** (stick to) pegarse a; (fig: abide by) observar; (: belief etc) ser partidario de

adhesive [əd'hi:zɪv] n adhesivo; **~ tape** n (BRIT) cinta adhesiva; (US: MED)

esparadrapo

ad hoc [æd'hɔk] adj ad hoc

adjacent [ə'dʒeɪsənt] adj: **~ to** contiguo a, inmediato a

adjective ['ædʒɛktɪv] n adjetivo

adjoining [ə'dʒɔɪnɪŋ] adj contiguo, vecino

adjourn [ə'dʒə:n] vt aplazar ♦ vi suspenderse

adjudicate [ə'dʒu:dɪkeɪt] vi sentenciar

adjust [ə'dʒʌst] vt (change) modificar; (clothing) arreglar; (machine) ajustar ♦ vi: **to ~ (to)** adaptarse (a); **~able** adj ajustable; **~ment** n adaptación f; (of machine, prices) ajuste m

ad-lib [æd'lɪb] vt, vi improvisar; **ad lib** adv de forma improvisada

administer [əd'mɪnɪstə*] vt administrar; **administration** [-'treɪʃən] n (management) administración f; (government) gobierno; **administrative** [-trətɪv] adj administrativo

admiral ['ædmərəl] n almirante m; **A~ty** (BRIT) n Ministerio de Marina, Almirantazgo

admiration [ædmə'reɪʃən] n admiración f

admire [əd'maɪə*] vt admirar; **~r** n (fan) admirador(a) m/f

admission [əd'mɪʃən] n (to university, club) ingreso; (entry fee) entrada; (confession) confesión f

admit [əd'mɪt] vt (confess) confesar; (permit to enter) dejar entrar, dar entrada a; (to club, organization) admitir; (accept: defeat) reconocer; **to be ~ted to hospital** ingresar en el hospital; **~ to** vt fus confesarse culpable de; **~tance** n entrada; **~tedly** adv es cierto or verdad que

admonish [əd'mɔnɪʃ] vt amonestar

ad nauseam [æd'nɔ:sɪæm] adv hasta el cansancio

ado [ə'du:] n: **without (any) more ~** sin más (ni más)

adolescent [ædəu'lɛsnt] adj, n adolescente m/f

adopt [ə'dɔpt] vt adoptar; **~ed** adj adoptivo; **~ion** [ə'dɔpʃən] n adopción f

adore [əˈdɔː*] vt adorar
Adriatic [eɪdrɪˈætɪk] n: **the ~ (Sea)** el (Mar) Adriático
adrift [əˈdrɪft] adv a la deriva
adult [ˈædʌlt] n adulto/a ♦ adj (grown-up) adulto; (for adults) para adultos
adultery [əˈdʌltərɪ] n adulterio
advance [ədˈvɑːns] n (progress) adelanto, progreso; (money) anticipo, préstamo; (MIL) avance m ♦ adj: **~ booking** venta anticipada; **~ notice, ~ warning** previo aviso ♦ vt (money) anticipar; (theory, idea) proponer (para la discusión) ♦ vi avanzar, adelantarse; **to make ~s (to sb)** hacer proposiciones (a alguien); **in ~** por adelantado; **~d** adj avanzado; (SCOL: studies) adelantado
advantage [ədˈvɑːntɪdʒ] n (also TENNIS) ventaja; **to take ~ of** (person) aprovecharse de; (opportunity) aprovechar
Advent [ˈædvənt] n (REL) Adviento
adventure [ədˈventʃə*] n aventura; **adventurous** [-tʃərəs] adj atrevido; aventurero
adverb [ˈædvɜːb] n adverbio
adverse [ˈædvɜːs] adj adverso, contrario
adversity [ədˈvɜːsɪtɪ] n infortunio
advert [ˈædvɜːt] (BRIT) n abbr = **advertisement**
advertise [ˈædvətaɪz] vi (in newspaper etc) anunciar, hacer publicidad; **to ~ for** (staff, accommodation etc) buscar por medio de anuncios ♦ vt anunciar; **~ment** [ədˈvɜːtɪsmənt] n (COMM) anuncio; **~r** n anunciante m/f; **advertising** n publicidad f, anuncios mpl; (industry) industria publicitaria
advice [ədˈvaɪs] n consejo, consejos mpl; (notification) aviso; **a piece of ~** un consejo; **to take legal ~** consultar con un abogado
advisable [ədˈvaɪzəbl] adj aconsejable, conveniente
advise [ədˈvaɪz] vt aconsejar; (inform): **to ~ sb of sth** informar a uno de algo; **to ~ sb against sth/doing sth** desaconsejar algo a uno/aconsejar a uno que no haga algo;

~dly [ədˈvaɪzɪdlɪ] adv (deliberately) deliberadamente; **~r** n = **advisor**; **advisor** n consejero/a; (consultant) asesor(a) m/f; **advisory** adj consultivo
advocate [ˈædvəkeɪt] vt abogar por ♦ n [-kɪt] (lawyer) abogado/a; (supporter): **~ of** defensor(a) m/f de
Aegean [iːˈdʒiːən] n: **the ~ (Sea)** el (Mar) Egeo
aerial [ˈɛərɪəl] n antena ♦ adj aéreo
aerobics [ɛəˈrəʊbɪks] n aerobic m
aeroplane [ˈɛərəpleɪn] (BRIT) n avión m
aerosol [ˈɛərəsɔl] n aerosol m
aesthetic [iːsˈθetɪk] adj estético
afar [əˈfɑː*] adv: **from ~** desde lejos
affair [əˈfɛə*] n asunto; (also: **love ~**) aventura (amorosa)
affect [əˈfekt] vt (influence) afectar, influir en; (afflict, concern) afectar; (move) conmover; **~ed** adj afectado
affection [əˈfekʃən] n afecto, cariño; **~ate** adj afectuoso, cariñoso
affinity [əˈfɪnɪtɪ] n (bond, rapport): **to feel an ~ with** sentirse identificado con; (resemblance) afinidad f
afflict [əˈflɪkt] vt afligir
affluence [ˈæfluəns] n opulencia, riqueza
affluent [ˈæfluənt] adj (wealthy) acomodado; **the ~ society** la sociedad opulenta
afford [əˈfɔːd] vt (provide) proporcionar; **can we ~ (to buy) it?** ¿tenemos bastante dinero para comprarlo?
Afghanistan [æfˈgænɪstæn] n Afganistán m
afield [əˈfiːld] adv: **far ~** muy lejos
afloat [əˈfləʊt] adv (floating) a flote
afoot [əˈfʊt] adv: **there is something ~** algo se está tramando
afraid [əˈfreɪd] adj: **to be ~ of** (person) tener miedo a; (thing) tener miedo de; **to be ~ to** tener miedo de, temer; **I am ~ that** me temo que; **I am ~ not/so** lo siento, pero no/es así
afresh [əˈfreʃ] adv de nuevo, otra vez
Africa [ˈæfrɪkə] n África; **~n** adj, n africano/a m/f

after ['ɑ:ftə*] *prep* (*time*) después de; (*place, order*) detrás de, tras ♦ *adv* después ♦ *conj* después (de) que; **what/ who are you ~?** ¿qué/a quién busca usted?; **~ having done/he left** después de haber hecho/después de que se marchó; **to name sb ~ sb** llamar a uno por uno; **it's twenty ~ eight** (*US*) son las ocho y veinte; **to ask ~ sb** preguntar por alguien; **~ all** después de todo, al fin y al cabo; **~ you!** ¡pase usted!; **~-effects** *npl* consecuencias *fpl*, efectos *mpl*; **~math** *n* consecuencias *fpl*, resultados *mpl*; **~noon** *n* tarde *f*; **~s** (*inf*) *n* (*dessert*) postre *m*; **~-sales service** (*BRIT*) *n* servicio de asistencia pos-venta; **~-shave (lotion)** *n* aftershave *m*; **~sun (lotion/cream)** *n* loción *f*/crema para después del sol, aftersun *m*; **~thought** *n* ocurrencia (tardía), **~wards** (*US* **~ward**) *adv* después, más tarde

again [ə'gen] *adv* otra vez, de nuevo; **to do sth ~** volver a hacer algo; **~ and ~** una y otra vez

against [ə'genst] *prep* (*in opposition to*) en contra de; (*leaning on, touching*) contra, junto a

age [eɪdʒ] *n* edad *f*; (*period*) época ♦ *vi* envejecer(se) ♦ *vt* envejecer; **she is 20 years of ~** tiene 20 años; **to come of ~** llegar a la mayoría de edad; **it's been ~s since I saw you** hace siglos que no te veo; **~d 10** de 10 años de edad; **the ~d** ['eɪdʒɪd] *npl* los ancianos; **~ group** *n*: **to be in the same ~ group** tener la misma edad; **~ limit** *n* edad *f* mínima (*or* máxima)

agency ['eɪdʒənsɪ] *n* agencia

agenda [ə'dʒendə] *n* orden *m* del día

agent ['eɪdʒənt] *n* agente *m/f*; (*COMM: holding concession*) representante *m/f*, delegado,a; (*CHEM, fig*) agente *m*

aggravate ['ægrəveɪt] *vt* (*situation*) agravar; (*person*) irritar

aggregate ['ægrɪgeɪt] *n* conjunto

aggressive [ə'gresɪv] *adj* (*belligerent*) agresivo,a; (*assertive*) enérgico

aggrieved [ə'gri:vd] *adj* ofendido, agraviado

aghast [ə'gɑ:st] *adj* horrorizado

agile ['ædʒaɪl] *adj* ágil

agitate ['ædʒɪteɪt] *vt* (*trouble*) inquietar ♦ *vi*: **to ~ for/against** hacer campaña pro *or* en favor de/en contra de

AGM *n abbr* (= *annual general meeting*) asamblea anual

ago [ə'gəu] *adv*: **2 days ~** hace 2 días; **not long ~** hace poco; **how long ~?** ¿hace cuánto tiempo?

agog [ə'gɔg] *adj* (*eager*) ansioso; (*excited*) emocionado

agonizing ['ægənaɪzɪŋ] *adj* (*pain*) atroz; (*decision, wait*) angustioso

agony ['ægənɪ] *n* (*pain*) dolor *m* agudo; (*distress*) angustia; **to be in ~** retorcerse de dolor

agree [ə'gri:] *vt* (*price, date*) acordar, quedar en ♦ *vi* (*have same opinion*): **to ~ (with/that)** estar de acuerdo (con/que); (*correspond*) coincidir, concordar; (*consent*) acceder; **to ~ with** (*subj: person*) estar de acuerdo con, ponerse de acuerdo con; (: *food*) sentar bien a; (*LING*) concordar con; **to ~ to sth/to do sth** consentir en algo/aceptar hacer algo; **to ~ that** (*admit*) estar de acuerdo en que; **~able** *adj* (*sensation*) agradable; (*person*) simpático,a; (*willing*) de acuerdo, conforme; **~d** *adj* (*time, place*) convenido; **~ment** *n* acuerdo; (*contract*) contrato; **in ~ment** de acuerdo, conforme

agricultural [ægrɪ'kʌltʃərəl] *adj* agrícola

agriculture ['ægrɪkʌltʃə*] *n* agricultura

aground [ə'graund] *adv*: **to run ~** (*NAUT*) encallar, embarrancar

ahead [ə'hed] *adv* (*in front*) delante; (*into the future*): **she had no time to think ~** no tenía tiempo de hacer planes para el futuro; **~ of** delante de; (*in advance of*) antes de; **~ of time** antes de la hora; **go right** *or* **straight ~** (*direction*) siga adelante; (*permission*) hazlo or hágalo

aid [eɪd] *n* ayuda, auxilio; (*device*) aparato ♦ *vt* ayudar, auxiliar; **in ~ of** a beneficio

de
aide [eɪd] n (person, also MIL) ayudante m/f
AIDS [eɪdz] n abbr (= acquired immune deficiency syndrome) SIDA m
ailment ['eɪlmənt] n enfermedad f, achaque m
aim [eɪm] vt (gun, camera) apuntar; (missile, remark) dirigir; (blow) asestar ♦ vi (also: **take ~**) apuntar ♦ n (in shooting: skill) puntería; (objective) propósito, meta; **to ~ at** (with weapon) apuntar a; (objective) aspirar a, pretender; **to ~ to do** tener la intención de hacer; **~less** adj sin propósito, sin objeto
ain't [eɪnt] (inf) = **am not; aren't; isn't**
air [ɛə*] n aire m; (appearance) aspecto ♦ vt (room) ventilar; (clothes, ideas) airear ♦ cpd aéreo; **to throw sth into the ~** (ball etc) lanzar algo al aire; **by ~** (travel) en avión; **to be on the ~** (RADIO, TV) estar en antena; **~bed** (BRIT) n colchón m neumático; **~-conditioned** adj climatizado; **~ conditioning** n aire acondicionado; **~craft** n inv avión m; **~craft carrier** n porta(a)viones m inv; **~field** n campo de aviación; **A~ Force** n fuerzas fpl aéreas, aviación f; **~ freshener** n ambientador m; **~gun** n escopeta de aire comprimido; **~ hostess** (BRIT) n azafata; **~ letter** (BRIT) n carta aérea; **~lift** n puente m aéreo; **~line** n línea aérea; **~liner** n avión m de pasajeros; **~mail** n: **by ~mail** por avión; **~plane** (US) n avión m; **~port** n aeropuerto; **~ raid** n ataque m aéreo; **~sick** adj: **to be ~sick** marearse (en avión); **~space** n espacio aéreo; **~tight** adj hermético; **~-traffic controller** n controlador(a) m/f aéreo/a; **~y** adj (room) bien ventilado; (fig: manner) desenfadado
aisle [aɪl] n (of church) nave f; (of theatre, supermarket) pasillo; **~ seat** n (on plane) asiento de pasillo
ajar [ə'dʒɑ:*] adj entreabierto
alarm [ə'lɑ:m] n (in shop, bank) alarma; (anxiety) inquietud f ♦ vt asustar,

inquietar; **~ call** n (in hotel etc) alarma; **~ clock** n despertador m
alas [ə'læs] adv desgraciadamente
albeit [ɔ:l'bi:ɪt] conj aunque
album ['ælbəm] n álbum m; (L.P.) elepé m
alcohol ['ælkəhɔl] n alcohol m; **~ic** [-'hɔlɪk] adj, n alcohólico/a m/f
ale [eɪl] n cerveza
alert [ə'lə:t] adj (attentive) atento; (to danger, opportunity) alerta ♦ n alerta m, alarma ♦ vt poner sobre aviso; **to be on the ~** (also MIL) estar alerta or sobre aviso
algebra ['ældʒɪbrə] n álgebra
Algeria [æl'dʒɪərɪə] n Argelia
alias ['eɪlɪəs] adv alias, conocido por ♦ n (of criminal) apodo; (of writer) seudónimo
alibi ['ælɪbaɪ] n coartada
alien ['eɪlɪən] n (foreigner) extranjero/a; (extraterrestrial) extraterrestre m/f ♦ adj: **~ to** ajeno a; **~ate** vt enajenar, alejar
alight [ə'laɪt] adj ardiendo; (eyes) brillante ♦ vi (person) apearse, bajar; (bird) posarse
align [ə'laɪn] vt alinear
alike [ə'laɪk] adj semejantes, iguales ♦ adv igualmente, del mismo modo; **to look ~** parecerse
alimony ['ælɪmənɪ] n manutención f
alive [ə'laɪv] adj vivo; (lively) alegre

┌──────────────┐
│ KEYWORD │
└──────────────┘

all [ɔ:l] adj (sg) todo/a; (pl) todos/as; **~ day** todo el día; **~ night** toda la noche; **~ men** todos los hombres; **~ five came** vinieron los cinco; **~ the books** todos los libros; **~ his life** toda su vida
♦ pron **1** todo; **I ate it ~, I ate ~ of it** me lo comí todo; **~ of us went** fuimos todos; **~ the boys went** fueron todos los chicos; **is that ~?** ¿eso es todo?, ¿algo más?; (in shop) ¿algo más?, ¿alguna cosa más?
2 (in phrases): **above ~** sobre todo; por encima de todo; **after ~** después de todo; **at ~: not at ~** (in answer to question) en absoluto; (in answer to thanks) ¡de nada!, ¡no hay de qué!; **I'm not at ~ tired** no estoy nada cansado/a; **anything at ~ will do** cualquier cosa viene bien; **~ in ~** a fin

de cuentas
♦ *adv*: ~ **alone** completamente solo/a;
it's not as hard as ~ that no es tan
difícil como lo pintas; ~ **the more/the
better** tanto más/mejor; ~ **but** casi; **the
score is 2** ~ están empatados a 2

all clear *n* (*after attack etc*) fin *m* de la
alerta; (*fig*) luz *f* verde
allege [ə'lɛdʒ] *vt* pretender; ~**dly**
[ə'lɛdʒɪdlɪ] *adv* supuestamente, según se
afirma
allegiance [ə'li:dʒəns] *n* lealtad *f*
allergy ['ælədʒɪ] *n* alergia
alleviate [ə'li:vɪeɪt] *vt* aliviar
alley ['ælɪ] *n* callejuela
alliance [ə'laɪəns] *n* alianza
allied ['ælaɪd] *adj* aliado
alligator ['ælɪgeɪtə*] *n* (*ZOOL*) caimán *m*
all-in (*BRIT*) *adj*, *adv* (*charge*) todo incluido
all-night *adj* (*café, shop*) abierto toda la
noche; (*party*) que dura toda la noche
allocate ['æləkeɪt] *vt* (*money etc*) asignar
allot [ə'lɒt] *vt* asignar; ~**ment** *n* ración *f*;
(*garden*) parcela
all-out *adj* (*effort etc*) supremo; **all out**
adv con todas las fuerzas
allow [ə'lau] *vt* permitir, dejar; (*a claim*)
admitir; (*sum, time etc*) dar, conceder;
(*concede*) **to ~ that** reconocer que; **to ~
sb to do** permitir a alguien hacer; **he is
~ed to ...** se le permite ...; ~ **for** *vt fus*
tener en cuenta; ~**ance** *n* subvención *f*;
(*welfare payment*) subsidio, pensión *f*;
(*pocket money*) dinero de bolsillo; (*tax
~ance*) desgravación *f*; **to make ~ances
for** (*person*) disculpar a; (*thing*) tener en
cuenta
alloy ['ælɔɪ] *n* mezcla
all: ~ **right** *adv* bien; (*as answer*)
¡conforme!, ¡está bien!; ~-**rounder** *n*:
he's a good ~-rounder se le da bien
todo; ~-**time** *adj* (*record*) de todos los
tiempos
alluring [ə'ljuərɪŋ] *adj* atractivo,
tentador(a)
ally ['ælaɪ] *n* aliado/a ♦ *vt*: **to ~ o.s. with**

aliarse con
almighty [ɔːl'maɪtɪ] *adj* todopoderoso;
(*row etc*) imponente
almond ['ɑːmənd] *n* almendra
almost ['ɔːlməust] *adv* casi
alone [ə'ləun] *adj, adv* solo; **to leave sb ~**
dejar a uno en paz; **to leave sth ~** no
tocar algo, dejar algo sin tocar; **let ~ ...** y
mucho menos ...
along [ə'lɒŋ] *prep* a lo largo de, por ♦ *adv*:
is he coming ~ with us? ¿viene con
nosotros?; **he was limping ~** iba
cojeando; ~ **with** junto con; **all ~** (*all the
time*) desde el principio; ~**side** *prep* al
lado de ♦ *adv* al lado
aloof [ə'luːf] *adj* reservado ♦ *adv*: **to stand
~** mantenerse apartado
aloud [ə'laud] *adv* en voz alta
alphabet ['ælfəbet] *n* alfabeto
Alps [ælps] *npl*: **the ~** los Alpes
already [ɔːl'redɪ] *adv* ya
alright ['ɔːl'raɪt] (*BRIT*) *adv* = **all right**
Alsatian [æl'seɪʃən] *n* (*dog*) pastor *m*
alemán
also ['ɔːlsəu] *adv* también, además
altar ['ɔːltə*] *n* altar *m*
alter ['ɔːltə*] *vt* cambiar, modificar ♦ *vi*
cambiar; ~**ation** [ɔːltə'reɪʃən] *n* cambio; (*to
clothes*) arreglo; (*to building*) arreglos *mpl*
alternate [*adj* æl'tɜːnɪt, *vb* 'ɔːltəneɪt] *adj*
(*actions etc*) alternativo; (*events*) alterno;
(*US*) = **alternative** ♦ *vi*: **to ~** (**with**)
alternar (con); **on ~ days** un día sí y otro
no; **alternating current** [-neɪtɪŋ] *n*
corriente *f* alterna
alternative [ɔl'tɜːnətɪv] *adj* alternativo ♦ *n*
alternativa; ~ **medicine** medicina
alternativa; ~**ly** *adv*: ~**ly one could ...**
por otra parte se podría ...
although [ɔːl'ðəu] *conj* aunque
altitude ['æltɪtjuːd] *n* altura
alto ['æltəu] *n* (*female*) contralto *f*; (*male*)
alto
altogether [ɔːltə'geðə*] *adv*
completamente, del todo; (*on the whole*)
en total, en conjunto
aluminium [ælju'mɪnɪəm] (*BRIT*),

aluminum [ə'lu:mɪnəm] (*US*) *n* aluminio

always ['ɔ:lweɪz] *adv* siempre

Alzheimer's (disease) ['æltshaɪməz-] *n* enfermedad *f* de Alzheimer

am [æm] *vb see* **be**

a.m. *adv abbr* (= *ante meridiem*) de la mañana

amalgamate [ə'mælgəmeɪt] *vi* amalgamarse ♦ *vt* amalgamar, unir

amateur ['æmətə*] *n* aficionado/a, amateur *m/f*; **~ish** *adj* inexperto, superficial

amaze [ə'meɪz] *vt* asombrar, pasmar; **to be ~d (at)** quedar pasmado (de); **~ment** *n* asombro, sorpresa; **amazing** *adj* extraordinario; (*fantastic*) increíble

Amazon ['æməzən] *n* (*GEO*) Amazonas *m*

ambassador [æm'bæsədə*] *n* embajador(a) *m/f*

amber ['æmbə*] *n* ámbar *m*; **at ~** (*BRIT: AUT*) en el amarillo

ambiguous [æm'bɪgjuəs] *adj* ambiguo

ambition [æm'bɪʃən] *n* ambición *f*; **ambitious** [-ʃəs] *adj* ambicioso

ambulance ['æmbjuləns] *n* ambulancia

ambush ['æmbuʃ] *n* emboscada ♦ *vt* tender una emboscada a

amenable [ə'mi:nəbl] *adj*: **to be ~ to** dejarse influir por

amend [ə'mend] *vt* enmendar; **to make ~s** dar cumplida satisfacción

amenities [ə'mi:nɪtɪz] *npl* comodidades *fpl*

America [ə'merɪkə] *n* (*USA*) Estados *mpl* Unidos; **~n** *adj, n* norteamericano/a *m/f*; estadounidense *m/f*

amiable ['eɪmɪəbl] *adj* amable, simpático

amicable ['æmɪkəbl] *adj* amistoso, amigable

amid(st) [ə'mɪd(st)] *prep* entre, en medio de

amiss [ə'mɪs] *adv*: **to take sth ~** tomar algo a mal; **there's something ~** pasa algo

ammonia [ə'məunɪə] *n* amoníaco

ammunition [æmju'nɪʃən] *n* municiones *fpl*

amnesty ['æmnɪstɪ] *n* amnistía

amok [ə'mɔk] *adv*: **to run ~** enloquecerse, desbocarse

among(st) [ə'mʌŋ(st)] *prep* entre, en medio de

amorous ['æmərəs] *adj* amoroso

amount [ə'maunt] *n* (*gen*) cantidad *f*; (*of bill etc*) suma, importe *m* ♦ *vi*: **to ~ to** sumar; (*be same as*) equivaler a, significar

amp(ère) ['æmp(εə*)] *n* amperio

ample ['æmpl] *adj* (*large*) grande; (*abundant*) abundante; (*enough*) bastante, suficiente

amplifier ['æmplɪfaɪə*] *n* amplificador *m*

amuse [ə'mju:z] *vt* divertir; (*distract*) distraer, entretener; **~ment** *n* diversión *f*; (*pastime*) pasatiempo; (*laughter*) risa; **~ment arcade** *n* salón *m* de juegos; **~ment park** *n* parque *m* de atracciones

an [æn] *indef art see* **a**

anaemic [ə'ni:mɪk] (*US* **anemic**) *adj* anémico; (*fig*) soso, insípido

anaesthetic [ænɪs'θetɪk] *n* (*US* **anesthetic**) anestesia

analog(ue) ['ænəlɔg] *adj* (*computer, watch*) analógico

analyse ['ænəlaɪz] (*US* **analyze**) *vt* analizar; **analysis** [ə'næləsɪs] (*pl* **analyses**) *n* análisis *m inv*; **analyst** [-lɪst] *n* (*political analyst, psychoanalyst*) analista *m/f*

analyze ['ænəlaɪz] (*US*) *vt* = **analyse**

anarchist ['ænəkɪst] *n* anarquista *m/f*

anatomy [ə'nætəmɪ] *n* anatomía

ancestor ['ænsɪstə*] *n* antepasado

anchor ['æŋkə*] *n* ancla, áncora ♦ *vi* (*also*: **to drop ~**) anclar ♦ *vt* anclar; **to weigh ~** levar anclas

anchovy ['æntʃəvɪ] *n* anchoa

ancient ['eɪnʃənt] *adj* antiguo

ancillary [æn'sɪlərɪ] *adj* auxiliar

and [ænd] *conj* y; (*before i-, hi- +consonant*) e; **men ~ women** hombres y mujeres; **father ~ son** padre e hijo; **trees ~ grass** árboles y hierba; **~ so on** etcétera, y así sucesivamente; **try ~ come** procura venir; **he talked ~ talked** habló sin parar; **better ~ better** cada vez mejor

Andes ['ændiːz] *npl*: **the ~** los Andes
anemic *etc* [ə'niːmɪk] (*US*) = **anaemic** *etc*
anesthetic *etc* [ænɪs'θetɪk] (*US*) = **anaesthetic** *etc*
anew [ə'njuː] *adv* de nuevo, otra vez
angel ['eɪndʒəl] *n* ángel *m*
anger ['æŋgə*] *n* cólera
angina [æn'dʒaɪnə] *n* angina (del pecho)
angle ['æŋgl] *n* ángulo; **from their ~** desde su punto de vista
angler ['æŋglə*] *n* pescador(a) *m/f* (de caña)
Anglican ['æŋglɪkən] *adj, n* anglicano/a *m/f*
angling ['æŋglɪŋ] *n* pesca con caña
Anglo... ['æŋgləu] *prefix* anglo...
angrily ['æŋgrɪlɪ] *adv* coléricamente, airadamente
angry ['æŋgrɪ] *adj* enfadado, airado; (*wound*) inflamado; **to be ~ with sb/at sth** estar enfadado con alguien/por algo; **to get ~** enfadarse, enojarse
anguish ['æŋgwɪʃ] *n* (*physical*) tormentos *mpl*; (*mental*) angustia
animal ['ænɪməl] *n* animal *m*; (*pej: person*) bestia ♦ *adj* animal
animate ['ænɪmɪt] *adj* vivo; **~d** [-meɪtɪd] *adj* animado
aniseed ['ænɪsiːd] *n* anís *m*
ankle ['æŋkl] *n* tobillo *m*; **~ sock** calcetín *m* corto
annex [*n* 'æneks, *vb* æ'neks] *n* (*also: BRIT: annexe*) (*building*) edificio anexo ♦ *vt* (*territory*) anexionar
annihilate [ə'naɪəleɪt] *vt* aniquilar
anniversary [ænɪ'vəːsərɪ] *n* aniversario
announce [ə'nauns] *vt* anunciar; **~ment** *n* anuncio; (*official*) declaración *f*; **~r** *n* (*RADIO*) locutor(a) *m/f*; (*TV*) presentador(a) *m/f*
annoy [ə'nɔɪ] *vt* molestar, fastidiar; **don't get ~ed!** ¡no se enfade!; **~ance** *n* enojo; **~ing** *adj* molesto, fastidioso; (*person*) pesado
annual ['ænjuəl] *adj* anual ♦ *n* (*BOT*) anual *m*; (*book*) anuario; **~ly** *adv* anualmente, cada año

annul [ə'nʌl] *vt* anular
annum ['ænəm] *n see* **per**
anonymous [ə'nɔnɪməs] *adj* anónimo
anorak ['ænəræk] *n* anorak *m*
anorexia [ænə'reksɪə] *n* (*MED: also:* **~ nervosa**) anorexia
another [ə'nʌðə*] *adj* (*one more, a different one*) otro ♦ *pron* otro; *see* **one**
answer ['ɑːnsə*] *n* contestación *f*, respuesta; (*to problem*) solución *f* ♦ *vi* contestar, responder ♦ *vt* (*reply to*) contestar a, responder a; (*problem*) resolver; (*prayer*) escuchar; **in ~ to your letter** contestando en or en contestación a su carta; **to ~ the phone** contestar or coger el teléfono; **to ~ the bell** or **the door** acudir a la puerta; **~ back** *vi* replicar, ser respondón/ona; **~ for** *vt fus* responder de or por; **~ to** *vt fus* (*description*) corresponder a; **~able** *adj*: **~able to sb for sth** responsable ante uno de algo; **~ing machine** *n* contestador *m* automático
ant [ænt] *n* hormiga
antagonism [æn'tægənɪzm] *n* antagonismo, hostilidad *f*
antagonize [æn'tægənaɪz] *vt* provocar la enemistad de
Antarctic [ænt'ɑːktɪk] *n*: **the ~** el Antártico
antelope ['æntɪləup] *n* antílope *m*
antenatal ['æntɪ'neɪtl] *adj* antenatal, prenatal; **~ clinic** *n* clínica prenatal
anthem ['ænθəm] *n*: **national ~** himno nacional
anthropology [ænθrə'pɔlədʒɪ] *n* antropología
anti... [æntɪ] *prefix* anti...; **~aircraft** [-'eəkrɑːft] *adj* antiaéreo; **~biotic** [-baɪ'ɔtɪk] *n* antibiótico; **~body** ['æntɪbɔdɪ] *n* anticuerpo
anticipate [æn'tɪsɪpeɪt] *vt* prever; (*expect*) esperar, contar con; (*look forward to*) esperar con ilusión; (*do first*) anticiparse a, adelantarse a; **anticipation** [-'peɪʃən] *n* (*expectation*) previsión *f*; (*eagerness*) ilusión *f*, expectación *f*
anticlimax [æntɪ'klaɪmæks] *n* decepción *f*

anticlockwise [ˈæntɪˈklɔkwaɪz] (BRIT) adv
en dirección contraria a la de las agujas
del reloj

antics [ˈæntɪks] npl gracias fpl

anticyclone [ˈæntɪˈsaɪkləun] n anticiclón m

antidote [ˈæntɪdəut] n antídoto

antifreeze [ˈæntɪfriːz] n anticongelante m

antihistamine [ˈæntɪˈhɪstəmiːn] n
antihistamínico

antiquated [ˈæntɪkweɪtɪd] adj anticuado

antique [ænˈtiːk] n antigüedad f ♦ adj
antiguo; ~ **dealer** n anticuario/a; ~
shop n tienda de antigüedades

antiquity [ænˈtɪkwɪtɪ] n antigüedad f

anti-Semitism [ˈæntɪˈsemɪtɪzm] n
antisemitismo

antiseptic [ˈæntɪˈseptɪk] adj, n antiséptico

antlers [ˈæntləz] npl cuernas fpl,
cornamenta sg

anus [ˈeɪnəs] n ano

anvil [ˈænvɪl] n yunque m

anxiety [æŋˈzaɪətɪ] n inquietud f; (MED)
ansiedad f; ~ **to do** deseo de hacer

anxious [ˈæŋkʃəs] adj inquieto,
preocupado; (worrying) preocupante;
(keen): **to be ~ to do** tener muchas ganas
de hacer

KEYWORD

any [ˈenɪ] adj 1 (in questions etc) algún/
alguna; **have you ~ butter/children?**
¿tienes mantequilla/hijos?; **if there are ~
tickets left** si quedan billetes, si queda
algún billete

2 (with negative): **I haven't ~ money/
books** no tengo dinero/libros

3 (no matter which) cualquier; ~ **excuse
will do** valdrá or servirá cualquier excusa;
choose ~ book you like escoge el libro
que quieras; ~ **teacher you ask will tell
you** cualquier profesor al que preguntes
te lo dirá

4 (in phrases): **in ~ case** de todas formas,
en cualquier caso; ~ **day now** cualquier
día (de estos); **at ~ moment** en cualquier
momento, de un momento a otro; **at ~
rate** en todo caso; ~ **time: come (at) ~**

time ven cuando quieras; **he might come
(at) ~ time** podría llegar de un momento
a otro

♦ pron 1 (in questions etc): **have you got
~?** ¿tienes alguno(s)/a(s)?; **can ~ of you
sing?** ¿sabe cantar alguno de vosotros/
ustedes?

2 (with negative): **I haven't ~ (of them)**
no tengo ninguno

3 (no matter which one(s)): **take ~ of
those books (you like)** toma el libro que
quieras de ésos

♦ adv 1 (in questions etc): **do you want ~
more soup/sandwiches?** ¿quieres más
sopa/bocadillos?; **are you feeling ~
better?** ¿te sientes algo mejor?

2 (with negative): **I can't hear him ~
more** ya no le oigo; **don't wait ~ longer**
no esperes más

---

anybody [ˈenɪbɔdɪ] pron cualquiera; (in
interrogative sentences) alguien; (in
negative sentences): **I don't see ~** no veo
a nadie; **if ~ should phone ...** si llama
alguien ...

anyhow [ˈenɪhau] adv (at any rate) de
todos modos, de todas formas;
(haphazard): **do it ~ you like** hazlo como
quieras; **she leaves things just ~** deja las
cosas como quiera or de cualquier modo;
I shall go ~ de todos modos iré

anyone [ˈenɪwʌn] pron = **anybody**

anything [ˈenɪθɪŋ] pron (in questions etc)
algo, alguna cosa; (with negative) nada;
can you see ~? ¿ves algo?; **if ~ happens
to me ...** si algo me ocurre ...; (no matter
what): **you can say ~ you like** puedes
decir lo que quieras; ~ **will do** vale todo
or cualquier cosa; **he'll eat ~** come de
todo or lo que sea

anyway [ˈenɪweɪ] adv (at any rate) de
todos modos, de todas formas; **I shall go
~** iré de todos modos; (besides): **~, I
couldn't come even if I wanted to**
además, no podría venir aunque quisiera,
why are you phoning, ~? ¿entonces, por
qué llamas?, ¿por qué llamas, pues?

anywhere [ˈɛnɪweə*] *adv* (*in questions etc*): **can you see him ~?** ¿le ves por algún lado?; **are you going ~?** ¿vas a algún sitio?; (*with negative*): **I can't see him ~** no le veo por ninguna parte; **~ in the world** (*no matter where*) en cualquier parte (del mundo); **put the books down ~** deja los libros donde quieras

apart [əˈpɑːt] *adv* (*aside*) aparte; (*situation*): **~ (from)** separado (de); (*movement*): **to pull ~** separar; **10 miles ~** separados por 10 millas; **to take ~** desmontar; **~ from** *prep* aparte de

apartheid [əˈpɑːteɪt] *n* apartheid *m*

apartment [əˈpɑːtmənt] *n* (*US*) piso (*SP*), departamento (*AM*), apartamento; (*room*) cuarto; **~ building** (*US*) *n* edificio de apartamentos

apathetic [æpəˈθɛtɪk] *adj* apático, indiferente

ape [eɪp] *n* mono ♦ *vt* imitar, remedar

aperitif [əˈpɛrɪtɪf] *n* aperitivo

aperture [ˈæpətʃuə*] *n* rendija, resquicio; (*PHOT*) abertura

APEX [ˈeɪpɛks] *n abbr* (= *Advanced Purchase Excursion Fare*) tarifa APEX *f*

apex *n* ápice *m*; (*fig*) cumbre *f*

apiece [əˈpiːs] *adv* cada uno

aplomb [əˈplɒm] *n* aplomo

apologetic [əpɒləˈdʒɛtɪk] *adj* de disculpa; (*person*) arrepentido

apologize [əˈpɒlədʒaɪz] *vi*: **to ~ (for sth to sb)** disculparse (con alguien de algo)

apology [əˈpɒlədʒɪ] *n* disculpa, excusa

apostrophe [əˈpɒstrəfɪ] *n* apóstrofo *m*

appal [əˈpɔːl] *vt* horrorizar, espantar; **~ling** *adj* espantoso; (*awful*) pésimo

apparatus [æpəˈreɪtəs] *n* (*equipment*) equipo; (*organization*) aparato; (*in gymnasium*) aparatos *mpl*

apparel [əˈpærl] (*US*) *n* ropa

apparent [əˈpærənt] *adj* aparente; (*obvious*) evidente; **~ly** *adv* por lo visto, al parecer

appeal [əˈpiːl] *vi* (*LAW*) apelar ♦ *n* (*LAW*) apelación *f*; (*request*) llamamiento; (*plea*) petición *f*; (*charm*) atractivo; **to ~ for**

reclamar; **to ~ to** (*be attractive to*) atraer; **it doesn't ~ to me** no me atrae, no me llama la atención; **~ing** *adj* (*attractive*) atractivo

appear [əˈpɪə*] *vi* aparecer, presentarse; (*LAW*) comparecer; (*publication*) salir (a luz), publicarse; (*seem*) parecer; **to ~ on TV/in "Hamlet"** salir por la tele/hacer un papel en "Hamlet"; **it would ~ that** parecería que; **~ance** *n* aparición *f*; (*look*) apariencia, aspecto

appease [əˈpiːz] *vt* (*pacify*) apaciguar; (*satisfy*) satisfacer

appendices [əˈpɛndɪsiːz] *npl of* **appendix**

appendicitis [əpɛndɪˈsaɪtɪs] *n* apendicitis *f*

appendix [əˈpɛndɪks] (*pl* **appendices**) *n* apéndice *m*

appetite [ˈæpɪtaɪt] *n* apetito; (*fig*) deseo, anhelo

appetizer [ˈæpɪtaɪzə*] *n* (*drink*) aperitivo; (*food*) tapas *fpl* (*SP*)

applaud [əˈplɔːd] *vt, vi* aplaudir

applause [əˈplɔːz] *n* aplausos *mpl*

apple [ˈæpl] *n* manzana; **~ tree** *n* manzano

appliance [əˈplaɪəns] *n* aparato

applicable [əˈplɪkəbl] *adj* (*relevant*): **to be ~ (to)** referirse (a)

applicant [ˈæplɪkənt] *n* candidato/a; solicitante *m/f*

application [æplɪˈkeɪʃən] *n* aplicación *f*; (*for a job etc*) solicitud *f*, petición *f*; **~ form** *n* solicitud *f*

applied [əˈplaɪd] *adj* aplicado

apply [əˈplaɪ] *vt* (*paint etc*) poner; (*law etc*: *put into practice*) poner en vigor ♦ *vi*: **to ~ to** (*ask*) dirigirse a; (*be applicable*) ser aplicable a; **to ~ for** (*permit, grant, job*) solicitar; **to ~ o.s. to** aplicarse a, dedicarse a

appoint [əˈpɔɪnt] *vt* (*to post*) nombrar; **~ed** *adj*: **at the ~ed time** a la hora señalada; **~ment** *n* (*with client*) cita; (*act*) nombramiento; (*post*) puesto; (*at hairdresser etc*): **to have an ~ment** tener hora; **to make an ~ment (with sb)** citarse (con uno)

appraisal [əˈpreɪzl] *n* valoración *f*

appreciate [əˈpriːʃɪeɪt] *vt* apreciar, tener en mucho; (*be grateful for*) agradecer; (*be aware of*) comprender ♦ *vi* (*COMM*) aumentar(se) en valor; **appreciation** [-ˈeɪʃən] *n* apreciación *f*; (*gratitude*) reconocimiento, agradecimiento; (*COMM*) aumento en valor

appreciative [əˈpriːʃɪətɪv] *adj* apreciativo; (*comment*) agradecido

apprehensive [æprɪˈhensɪv] *adj* aprensivo

apprentice [əˈprentɪs] *n* aprendiz/a *m/f*; **~ship** *n* aprendizaje *m*

approach [əˈprəʊtʃ] *vi* acercarse ♦ *vt* acercarse a; (*ask, apply to*) dirigirse a; (*situation, problem*) abordar ♦ *n* acercamiento; (*access*) acceso; (*to problem, situation*): **~ (to)** actitud *f* (ante); **~able** *adj* (*person*) abordable; (*place*) accesible

appropriate [*adj* əˈprəʊprɪɪt, *vb* əˈprəʊprɪeɪt] *adj* apropiado, conveniente ♦ *vt* (*take*) apropiarse de

approval [əˈpruːvəl] *n* aprobación *f*, visto bueno; (*permission*) consentimiento; **on ~** (*COMM*) a prueba

approve [əˈpruːv] *vt* aprobar; **~ of** *vt fus* (*thing*) aprobar; (*person*): **they don't ~ of her** (ella) no les parece bien

approximate [əˈprɒksɪmɪt] *adj* aproximado; **~ly** *adv* aproximadamente, más o menos

apricot [ˈeɪprɪkɒt] *n* albaricoque *m* (*SP*), damasco (*AM*)

April [ˈeɪprəl] *n* abril *m*; **~ Fools' Day** *n* el primero de abril; ≈ día *m* de los Inocentes (*28 December*)

apron [ˈeɪprən] *n* delantal *m*

apt [æpt] *adj* acertado, apropiado; (*likely*): **~ to do** propenso a hacer

aquarium [əˈkweərɪəm] *n* acuario *m*

Aquarius [əˈkweərɪəs] *n* Acuario

Arab [ˈærəb] *adj, n* árabe *m/f*

Arabian [əˈreɪbɪən] *adj* árabe

Arabic [ˈærəbɪk] *adj* árabe; (*numerals*) arábigo ♦ *n* árabe *m*

arable [ˈærəbl] *adj* cultivable

Aragon [ˈærəgən] *n* Aragón *m*

arbitrary [ˈɑːbɪtrərɪ] *adj* arbitrario

arbitration [ɑːbɪˈtreɪʃən] *n* arbitraje *m*

arcade [ɑːˈkeɪd] *n* (*round a square*) soportales *mpl*; (*shopping mall*) galería comercial

arch [ɑːtʃ] *n* arco; (*of foot*) arco del pie ♦ *vt* arquear

archaeologist [ɑːkɪˈɒlədʒɪst] (*US* **archeologist**) *n* arqueólogo/a

archaeology [ɑːkɪˈɒlədʒɪ] (*US* **archeology**) *n* arqueología

archbishop [ɑːtʃˈbɪʃəp] *n* arzobispo

archeology *etc* [ɑːkɪˈɒlədʒɪ] (*US*) = **archaeology** *etc*

archery [ˈɑːtʃərɪ] *n* tiro al arco

architect [ˈɑːkɪtekt] *n* arquitecto/a; **~ure** *n* arquitectura

archives [ˈɑːkaɪvz] *npl* archivo

Arctic [ˈɑːktɪk] *adj* ártico ♦ *n*: **the ~** el Ártico

ardent [ˈɑːdənt] *adj* ardiente, apasionado

arduous [ˈɑːdjuəs] *adj* (*task*) arduo; (*journey*) agotador(a)

are [ɑː*] *vb see* **be**

area [ˈeərɪə] *n* área, región *f*; (*part of place*) zona; (*MATH etc*) área, superficie *f*; (*in room: e.g. dining ~*) parte *f*; (*of knowledge, experience*) campo

arena [əˈriːnə] *n* estadio; (*of circus*) pista

aren't [ɑːnt] = **are not**

Argentina [ɑːdʒənˈtiːnə] *n* Argentina; **Argentinian** [-ˈtɪnɪən] *adj, n* argentino/a *m/f*

arguably [ˈɑːgjuəblɪ] *adv* posiblemente

argue [ˈɑːgjuː] *vi* (*quarrel*) discutir, pelearse; (*reason*) razonar, argumentar; **to ~ that** sostener que

argument [ˈɑːgjumənt] *n* discusión *f*, pelea; (*reasons*) argumento; **~ative** [-ˈmentətɪv] *adj* discutidor(a)

Aries [ˈeərɪz] *n* Aries *m*

arise [əˈraɪz] (*pt* **arose**, *pp* **arisen**) *vi* surgir, presentarse

arisen [əˈrɪzn] *pp of* **arise**

aristocrat [ˈærɪstəkræt] *n* aristócrata *m/f*

arithmetic [əˈrɪθmətɪk] *n* aritmética

ark [ɑːk] *n*: **Noah's A~** el Arca *f* de Noé

arm [ɑːm] *n* brazo ♦ *vt* armar; **~s** *npl* armas *fpl*; **~ in ~** cogidos del brazo

armaments [ˈɑːməmənts] *npl* armamento

armchair [ˈɑːmtʃɛə*] *n* sillón *m*, butaca

armed [ɑːmd] *adj* armado; **~ robbery** *n* robo a mano armada

armour (*US* **armor**) [ˈɑːmə*] *n* armadura; (*MIL: tanks*) blindaje *m*; **~ed car** *n* coche *m* (*SP*) or carro (*AM*) blindado

armpit [ˈɑːmpɪt] *n* sobaco, axila

armrest [ˈɑːmrest] *n* apoyabrazos *m inv*

army [ˈɑːmɪ] *n* ejército; (*fig*) multitud *f*

aroma [əˈrəumə] *n* aroma *m*, fragancia; **~therapy** *n* aromaterapia

arose [əˈrəuz] *pt of* **arise**

around [əˈraund] *adv* alrededor; (*in the area*): **there is no one else ~** no hay nadie más por aquí ♦ *prep* alrededor de

arouse [əˈrauz] *vt* despertar; (*anger*) provocar

arrange [əˈreɪndʒ] *vt* arreglar, ordenar; (*organize*) organizar; **to ~ to do sth** quedar en hacer algo; **~ment** *n* arreglo; (*agreement*) acuerdo; **~ments** *npl* (*preparations*) preparativos *mpl*

array [əˈreɪ] *n*: **~ of** (*things*) serie *f* de; (*people*) conjunto *m*

arrears [əˈrɪəz] *npl* atrasos *mpl*; **to be in ~ with one's rent** estar retrasado en el pago del alquiler

arrest [əˈrest] *vt* detener; (*sb's attention*) llamar ♦ *n* detención *f*; **under ~** detenido

arrival [əˈraɪvəl] *n* llegada; **new ~** recién llegado/a; (*baby*) recién nacido

arrive [əˈraɪv] *vi* llegar; (*baby*) nacer

arrogant [ˈærəgənt] *adj* arrogante

arrow [ˈærəu] *n* flecha

arse [ɑːs] (*BRIT: inf!*) *n* culo, trasero

arson [ˈɑːsn] *n* incendio premeditado

art [ɑːt] *n* arte *m*; (*skill*) destreza; **A~s** *npl* (*SCOL*) Letras *fpl*

artery [ˈɑːtərɪ] *n* arteria

art gallery *n* pinacoteca; (*saleroom*) galería de arte

arthritis [ɑːˈθraɪtɪs] *n* artritis *f*

artichoke [ˈɑːtɪtʃəuk] *n* alcachofa;

Jerusalem ~ aguaturma

article [ˈɑːtɪkl] *n* artículo; (*BRIT: LAW: training*): **~s** *npl* contrato de aprendizaje; **~ of clothing** prenda de vestir

articulate [*adj* ɑːˈtɪkjulɪt, *vb* ɑːˈtɪkjuleɪt] *adj* claro, bien expresado ♦ *vt* expresar; **~d lorry** (*BRIT*) *n* trailer *m*

artificial [ɑːtɪˈfɪʃəl] *adj* artificial; (*affected*) afectado

artillery [ɑːˈtɪlərɪ] *n* artillería

artisan [ˈɑːtɪzæn] *n* artesano

artist [ˈɑːtɪst] *n* artista *m/f*; (*MUS*) intérprete *m/f*; **~ic** [ɑːˈtɪstɪk] *adj* artístico; **~ry** *n* arte *m*, habilidad *f* (artística)

art school *n* escuela de bellas artes

KEYWORD

as [æz] *conj* **1** (*referring to time*) cuando, mientras; a medida que; **~ the years went by** con el paso de los años; **he came in ~ I was leaving** entró cuando me marchaba; **~ from tomorrow** desde *or* a partir de mañana

2 (*in comparisons*): **~ big ~** tan grande como; **twice ~ big ~** el doble de grande que; **~ much money/many books ~** tanto dinero/tantos libros como; **~ soon ~** en cuanto

3 (*since, because*) como, ya que; **he left early ~ he had to be home by 10** se fue temprano ya que tenía que estar en casa a las 10

4 (*referring to manner, way*): **do ~ you wish** haz lo que quieras; **~ she said** como dijo; **he gave it to me ~ a present** me lo dio de regalo

5 (*in the capacity of*): **he works ~ a barman** trabaja de barman; **~ chairman of the company, he ...** como presidente de la compañía, ...

6 (*concerning*): **~ for** *or* **to that** por *or* en lo que respecta a eso

7: **~ if** *or* **though** como si; **he looked ~ if he was ill** parecía como si estuviera enfermo, tenía aspecto de enfermo; *see also* **long**; **such**; **well**

a.s.a.p. *abbr* (= *as soon as possible*) cuanto antes

asbestos [æz'bestəs] *n* asbesto, amianto

ascend [ə'send] *vt* subir; (*throne*) ascender or subir a

ascent [ə'sent] *n* subida; (*slope*) cuesta, pendiente *f*

ascertain [æsə'teɪn] *vt* averiguar

ash [æʃ] *n* ceniza; (*tree*) fresno

ashamed [ə'ʃeɪmd] *adj* avergonzado, apenado (*AM*); **to be ~ of** avergonzarse de

ashore [ə'ʃɔː*] *adv* en tierra; (*swim etc*) a tierra

ashtray [æʃtreɪ] *n* cenicero

Ash Wednesday *n* miércoles *m* de Ceniza

Asia ['eɪʃə] *n* Asia; **~n** *adj*, *n* asiático/a *m/f*

aside [ə'saɪd] *adv* a un lado ♦ *n* aparte *m*

ask [ɑːsk] *vt* (*question*) preguntar; (*invite*) invitar; **to ~ sth/to do sth** preguntar algo a alguien/pedir a alguien que haga algo; **to ~ sb about sth** preguntar algo a alguien; **to ~ (sb) a question** hacer una pregunta (a alguien); **to ~ sb out to dinner** invitar a cenar a uno; **~ after** *vt fus* preguntar por; **~ for** *vt fus* pedir; (*trouble*) buscar

asking price *n* precio inicial

asleep [ə'sliːp] *adj* dormido; **to fall ~** dormirse, quedarse dormido

asparagus [əs'pærəgəs] *n* (*plant*) espárrago; (*food*) espárragos *mpl*

aspect ['æspekt] *n* aspecto, apariencia; (*direction in which a building etc faces*) orientación *f*

aspersions [əs'pɜːʃənz] *npl*: **to cast ~ on** difamar a, calumniar a

asphyxiation [æsfɪksɪ'eɪʃən] *n* asfixia

aspire [əs'paɪə*] *vi*: **to ~ to** aspirar a, ambicionar

aspirin ['æsprɪn] *n* aspirina

ass [æs] *n* asno, burro; (*inf: idiot*) imbécil *m/f*; (*US: inf!*) culo, trasero

assailant [ə'seɪlənt] *n* asaltador(a) *m/f*, agresor(a) *m/f*

assassinate [ə'sæsɪneɪt] *vt* asesinar;

assassination [əsæsɪ'neɪʃən] *n* asesinato

assault [ə'sɔːlt] *n* asalto; (*LAW*) agresión *f* ♦ *vt* asaltar, atacar; (*sexually*) violar

assemble [ə'sembl] *vt* reunir, juntar; (*TECH*) montar ♦ *vi* reunirse, juntarse

assembly [ə'semblɪ] *n* reunión *f*, asamblea; (*parliament*) parlamento; (*construction*) montaje *m*; **~ line** *n* cadena de montaje

assent [ə'sent] *n* asentimiento, aprobación *f*

assert [ə'sɜːt] *vt* afirmar; (*authority*) hacer valer; **~ion** [-ʃən] *n* afirmación *f*

assess [ə'ses] *vt* valorar, calcular; (*tax, damages*) fijar; (*for tax*) gravar; **~ment** *n* valoración *f*; (*for tax*) gravamen *m*; **~or** *n* asesor(a) *m/f*

asset ['æset] *n* ventaja; **~s** *npl* (*COMM*) activo; (*property, funds*) fondos *mpl*

assign [ə'saɪn] *vt*: **to ~ (to)** (*date*) fijar (para); (*task*) asignar (a); (*resources*) destinar (a); **~ment** *n* tarea

assist [ə'sɪst] *vt* ayudar; **~ance** *n* ayuda, auxilio; **~ant** *n* ayudante *m/f*; (*BRIT: also:* **shop ~ant**) dependiente/a *m/f*

associate [*adj*, *n* ə'səʊʃɪɪt, *vb* ə'səʊʃɪeɪt] *adj* asociado ♦ *n* (*at work*) colega *m/f* ♦ *vt* asociar; (*ideas*) relacionar ♦ *vi*: **to ~ with sb** tratar con alguien

association [əsəʊsɪ'eɪʃən] *n* asociación *f*

assorted [ə'sɔːtɪd] *adj* surtido, variado

assortment [ə'sɔːtmənt] *n* (*of shapes, colours*) surtido; (*of books*) colección *f*; (*of people*) mezcla

assume [ə'sjuːm] *vt* suponer; (*responsibilities*) asumir; (*attitude*) adoptar, tomar

assumption [ə'sʌmpʃən] *n* suposición *f*, presunción *f*; (*of power etc*) toma

assurance [ə'ʃʊərəns] *n* garantía, promesa; (*confidence*) confianza, aplomo; (*insurance*) seguro

assure [ə'ʃʊə*] *vt* asegurar

asthma ['æsmə] *n* asma

astonish [ə'stɒnɪʃ] *vt* asombrar, pasmar; **~ment** *n* asombro, sorpresa

astound [ə'staʊnd] *vt* asombrar, pasmar

astray [ə'streɪ] *adv*: **to go ~** extraviarse; **to lead ~** (*morally*) llevar por mal camino
astride [ə'straɪd] *prep* a caballo *or* horcajadas sobre
astrology [æs'trɒlədʒɪ] *n* astrología
astronaut ['æstrənɔːt] *n* astronauta *m/f*
astronomy [æs'trɒnəmɪ] *n* astronomía
asylum [ə'saɪləm] *n* (*refuge*) asilo; (*mental hospital*) manicomio

---

KEYWORD

at [æt] *prep* **1** (*referring to position*) en; (*direction*) a; **~ the top** en lo alto; **~ home/school** en casa/la escuela; **to look ~ sth/sb** mirar algo/a uno
2 (*referring to time*): **~ 4 o'clock** a las 4; **~ night** por la noche; **~ Christmas** en Navidad; **~ times** a veces
3 (*referring to rates, speed etc*): **~ £1 a kilo** a una libra el kilo; **two ~ a time** de dos en dos; **~ 50 km/h** a 50 km/h
4 (*referring to manner*): **~ a stroke** de un golpe; **~ peace** en paz
5 (*referring to activity*): **to be ~ work** estar trabajando; (*in the office etc*) estar en el trabajo; **to play ~ cowboys** jugar a los vaqueros; **to be good ~ sth** ser bueno en algo
6 (*referring to cause*): **shocked/surprised/annoyed ~ sth** asombrado/sorprendido/fastidiado por algo; **I went ~ his suggestion** fui a instancias suyas

---

ate [eɪt] *pt of* **eat**
atheist ['eɪθɪɪst] *n* ateo/a
Athens ['æθɪnz] *n* Atenas
athlete ['æθliːt] *n* atleta *m/f*
athletic [æθ'letɪk] *adj* atlético; **~s** *n* atletismo
Atlantic [ət'læntɪk] *adj* atlántico ♦ *n*: **the ~ (Ocean)** el (Océano) Atlántico
atlas ['ætləs] *n* atlas *m*
A.T.M. *n abbr* (= *automated telling machine*) cajero automático
atmosphere ['ætməsfɪə*] *n* atmósfera; (*of place*) ambiente *m*
atom ['ætəm] *n* átomo; **~ic** [ə'tɒmɪk] *adj*

atómico; **~(ic) bomb** *n* bomba atómica; **~izer** ['ætəmaɪzə*] *n* atomizador *m*
atone [ə'təun] *vi*: **to ~ for** expiar
atrocious [ə'trəuʃəs] *adj* atroz
attach [ə'tætʃ] *vt* (*fasten*) atar; (*join*) unir, sujetar; (*document, letter*) adjuntar; (*importance etc*) dar, conceder; **to be ~ed to sb/sth** (*to like*) tener cariño a alguien/algo
attaché case [ə'tæʃeɪ-] *n* maletín *m*
attachment [ə'tætʃmənt] *n* (*tool*) accesorio; (*love*): **~ (to)** apego (a)
attack [ə'tæk] *vt* (MIL) atacar; (*subj: criminal*) agredir, asaltar; (*criticize*) criticar; (*task*) emprender ♦ *n* ataque *m*, asalto; (*on sb's life*) atentado; (*fig: criticism*) crítica; (*of illness*) ataque *m*; **heart ~** infarto (de miocardio); **~er** *n* agresor(a) *m/f*, asaltante *m/f*
attain [ə'teɪn] *vt* (*also*: **~ to**) alcanzar; (*achieve*) lograr, conseguir
attempt [ə'tempt] *n* tentativa, intento; (*attack*) atentado ♦ *vt* intentar; **~ed** *adj*: **~ed burglary/murder/suicide** tentativa *or* intento de robo/asesinato/suicidio
attend [ə'tend] *vt* asistir a; (*patient*) atender; **~ to** *vt fus* ocuparse de; (*customer, patient*) atender a; **~ance** *n* asistencia, presencia; (*people present*) concurrencia; **~ant** *n* ayudante *m/f*; (*in garage etc*) encargado/a ♦ *adj* (*dangers*) concomitante
attention [ə'tenʃən] *n* atención *f*; (*care*) atenciones *fpl* ♦ *excl* (MIL) ¡firme(s)!; **for the ~ of ...** (ADMIN) atención ...
attentive [ə'tentɪv] *adj* atento
attic ['ætɪk] *n* desván *m*
attitude ['ætɪtjuːd] *n* actitud *f*; (*disposition*) disposición *f*
attorney [ə'tɜːnɪ] *n* (*lawyer*) abogado/a; **A~ General** *n* (BRIT) ≈ Presidente *m* del Consejo del Poder Judicial (SP); (US) ≈ ministro de justicia
attract [ə'trækt] *vt* atraer; (*sb's attention*) llamar; **~ion** [ə'trækʃən] *n* encanto; (*gen pl: amusements*) diversiones *fpl*; (PHYSICS) atracción *f*; (*fig: towards sb, sth*) atractivo;

~ive *adj* guapo; (*interesting*) atrayente

attribute [*n* 'ætrıbjuːt, *vb* ə'trıbjuːt] *n* atributo ♦ *vt*: **to ~ sth** atribuir algo a

attrition [ə'trıʃən] *n*: **war of ~** guerra de agotamiento

aubergine ['əubəʒiːn] (*BRIT*) *n* berenjena; (*colour*) morado

auburn ['ɔːbən] *adj* color castaño rojizo

auction ['ɔːkʃən] *n* (*also: sale by ~*) subasta ♦ *vt* subastar; **~eer** [-'nɪə*] *n* subastador(a) *m/f*

audible ['ɔːdıbl] *adj* audible, que se puede oír

audience ['ɔːdıəns] *n* público; (*RADIO*) radioescuchas *mpl*; (*TV*) telespectadores *mpl*; (*interview*) audiencia

audio-visual [ɔːdıəu'vızjuəl] *adj* audiovisual; **~ aid** *n* ayuda audiovisual

audit ['ɔːdıt] *vt* revisar, intervenir

audition [ɔː'dıʃən] *n* audición *f*

auditor ['ɔːdıtə*] *n* interventor(a) *m/f*, censor(a) *m/f* de cuentas

augment [ɔːg'ment] *vt* aumentar

augur ['ɔːgə*] *vi*: **it ~s well** es un buen augurio

August ['ɔːgəst] *n* agosto

aunt [ɑːnt] *n* tía; **~ie** *n diminutive of* **aunt**; **~y** *n diminutive of* **aunt**

au pair ['əu'peə*] *n* (*also: ~ girl*) (chica) au pair *f*

auspicious [ɔːs'pıʃəs] *adj* propicio, de buen augurio

Australia [ɒs'treılıə] *n* Australia; **~n** *adj*, *n* australiano/a *m/f*

Austria ['ɒstrıə] *n* Austria; **~n** *adj*, *n* austríaco/a *m/f*

authentic [ɔː'θentık] *adj* auténtico

author ['ɔːθə*] *n* autor(a) *m/f*

authoritarian [ɔːθɒrı'teərıən] *adj* autoritario

authoritative [ɔː'θɒrıtətıv] *adj* autorizado; (*manner*) autoritario

authority [ɔː'θɒrıtı] *n* autoridad *f*; (*official permission*) autorización *f*; **the authorities** *npl* las autoridades

authorize ['ɔːθəraız] *vt* autorizar

auto ['ɔːtəu] (*US*) *n* coche *m* (*SP*), carro *m* (*AM*), automóvil *m*

auto: **~biography** [ɔːtəbaı'ɒgrəfı] *n* autobiografía; **~graph** ['ɔːtəgrɑːf] *n* autógrafo ♦ *vt* (*photo etc*) dedicar; (*programme*) firmar; **~mated** ['ɔːtəmeıtıd] *adj* automatizado; **~matic** [ɔːtə'mætık] *adj* automático ♦ *n* (*gun*) pistola automática; (*car*) coche *m* automático; **~matically** *adv* automáticamente; **~mation** [ɔːtə'meıʃən] *n* reconversión *f*; **~mobile** ['ɔːtəməbiːl] (*US*) *n* coche *m* (*SP*), carro (*AM*), automóvil *m*; **~nomy** [ɔː'tɒnəmı] *n* autonomía

autumn ['ɔːtəm] *n* otoño

auxiliary [ɔːg'zılıərı] *adj*, *n* auxiliar *m/f*

avail [ə'veıl] *vt*: **to ~ o.s. of** aprovechar(se) de ♦ *n*: **to no ~** en vano, sin resultado

available [ə'veıləbl] *adj* disponible; (*unoccupied*) libre; (*person: unattached*) soltero y sin compromiso

avalanche ['ævəlɑːnʃ] *n* alud *m*, avalancha

avant-garde ['ævɑ̃'gɑːd] *adj* de vanguardia

Ave. *abbr* = **avenue**

avenge [ə'vendʒ] *vt* vengar

avenue ['ævənjuː] *n* avenida; (*fig*) camino

average ['ævərıdʒ] *n* promedio, término medio ♦ *adj* medio, de término medio; (*ordinary*) regular, corriente ♦ *vt* sacar un promedio de; **on ~** por regla general; **~ out** *vi*: **to ~ out at** salir en un promedio de

averse [ə'vəːs] *adj*: **to be ~ to sth/doing** sentir aversión *or* antipatía por algo/por hacer

avert [ə'vəːt] *vt* prevenir; (*blow*) desviar; (*one's eyes*) apartar

aviary ['eıvıərı] *n* pajarera, avería

avocado [ævə'kɑːdəu] *n* (*also: BRIT: ~ pear*) aguacate *m* (*SP*), palta (*AM*)

avoid [ə'vɔıd] *vt* evitar, eludir

await [ə'weıt] *vt* esperar, aguardar

awake [ə'weık] (*pt* **awoke**, *pp* **awoken** *or* **awaked**) *adj* despierto ♦ *vt* despertar ♦ *vi* despertarse; **to be ~** estar despierto; **~ning** *n* el despertar

award [ə'wɔːd] *n* premio; (*LAW*: *damages*) indemnización *f* ♦ *vt* otorgar, conceder; (*LAW*: *damages*) adjudicar

aware [ə'wɛə*] *adj*: **~ (of)** consciente (de); **to become ~ of/that** (*realize*) darse cuenta de/de que; (*learn*) enterarse de/de que; **~ness** *n* conciencia; (*knowledge*) conocimiento

away [ə'weɪ] *adv* fuera; (*movement*): **she went ~** se marchó; (*far ~*) lejos; **two kilometres ~** a dos kilómetros de distancia; **two hours ~ by car** a dos horas en coche; **the holiday was two weeks ~** faltaban dos semanas para las vacaciones; **he's ~ for a week** estará ausente una semana; **to take ~ (from)** quitar (a); (*subtract*) substraer (de); **to work/pedal ~** seguir trabajando/pedaleando; **to fade ~** (*colour*) desvanecerse; (*sound*) apagarse; **~ game** *n* (*SPORT*) partido de fuera

awe [ɔ:] *n* admiración *f* respetuosa; **~-inspiring** *adj* imponente

awful ['ɔ:fəl] *adj* horroroso; (*quantity*): **an ~ lot (of)** cantidad de (de); **~ly** *adv* (*very*) terriblemente

awkward ['ɔ:kwəd] *adj* desmañado, torpe; (*shape*) incómodo; (*embarrassing*) delicado, difícil

awning ['ɔ:nɪŋ] *n* (*of tent, caravan, shop*) toldo

awoke [ə'wəuk] *pt of* **awake**

awoken [ə'wəukən] *pp of* **awake**

awry [ə'raɪ] *adv*: **to be ~** estar descolocado *or* mal puesto

axe [æks] (*US* **ax**) *n* hacha ♦ *vt* (*project*) cortar; (*jobs*) reducir

axes ['æksi:z] *npl of* **axis**

axis ['æksɪs] (*pl* **axes**) *n* eje *m*

axle ['æksl] *n* eje *m*, árbol *m*

ay(e) [aɪ] *excl* sí

B, b

B [bi:] *n* (*MUS*) si *m*

B.A. *abbr* = **Bachelor of Arts**

baby ['beɪbɪ] *n* bebé *m/f*; (*US: inf: darling*) mi amor; **~ carriage** (*US*) *n* cochecito; **~-sit** *vi* hacer de canguro; **~-sitter** *n* canguro/a; **~ wipe** *n* toallita húmeda (*para bebés*)

bachelor ['bætʃələ*] *n* soltero; **B~ of Arts/Science** licenciado/a en Filosofía y Letras/Ciencias

back [bæk] *n* (*of person*) espalda; (*of animal*) lomo; (*of hand*) dorso; (*as opposed to front*) parte *f* de atrás; (*of chair*) respaldo; (*of page*) reverso; (*of book*) final *m*; (*FOOTBALL*) defensa *m*; (*of crowd*): **the ones at the ~** los del fondo ♦ *vt* (*candidate: also*: **~ up**) respaldar, apoyar; (*horse: at races*) apostar a; (*car*) dar marcha atrás a *or* con ♦ *vi* (*car etc*) ir (*or* salir *or* entrar) marcha atrás ♦ *adj* (*payment, rent*) atrasado; (*seats, wheels*) de atrás ♦ *adv* (*not forward*) (*hacia*) atrás; (*returned*): **he's ~** está de vuelta, ha vuelto; **he ran ~** volvió corriendo; (*restitution*): **throw the ball ~** devuelve la pelota; **can I have it ~?** ¿me lo devuelve?; (*again*): **he called ~** llamó de nuevo; **~ down** *vi* echarse atrás; **~ out** *vi* (*of promise*) volverse atrás; **~ up** *vt* (*person*) apoyar, respaldar; (*theory*) defender; (*COMPUT*) hacer una copia preventiva *or* de reserva; **~bencher** (*BRIT*) *n* miembro del parlamento sin cargo relevante; **~bone** *n* columna vertebral; **~date** *vt* (*pay rise*) dar efecto retroactivo a; (*letter*) poner fecha atrasada a; **~drop** *n* telón *m* de fondo; **~fire** *vi* (*AUT*) petardear; (*plans*) fallar, salir mal; **~ground** *n* fondo; (*of events*) antecedentes *mpl*; (*basic knowledge*) bases *fpl*; (*experience*) conocimientos *mpl*, educación *f*; **family ~ground** origen *m*, antecedentes *mpl*; **~hand** *n* (*TENNIS*:

also: ~**hand stroke**) revés *m*; ~**hander** (BRIT) *n* (*bribe*) soborno; ~**ing** *n* (*fig*) apoyo, respaldo; ~**lash** *n* reacción *f*; ~**log** *n*: ~**log of work** trabajo atrasado; ~**number** *n* (*of magazine etc*) número atrasado; ~**pack** *n* mochila; ~**packer** *n* mochilero/a; ~ **pay** *n* pago atrasado; ~**side** (*inf*) *n* trasero, culo; ~**stage** *adv* entre bastidores; ~**stroke** *n* espalda; ~**up** *adj* suplementario; (COMPUT) de reserva ♦ *n* (*support*) apoyo; (*also*: ~**up file**) copia preventiva *or* de reserva; ~**ward** *adj* (*person, country*) atrasado; ~**wards** *adv* hacia atrás; (*read a list*) al revés; (*fall*) de espaldas; ~**yard** *n* traspatio

bacon ['beɪkən] *n* tocino, beicon *m*

bad [bæd] *adj* malo; (*mistake, accident*) grave; (*food*) podrido, pasado; **his ~ leg** su pierna lisiada; **to go ~** (*food*) pasarse

badge [bædʒ] *n* insignia; (*policeman's*) chapa, placa

badger ['bædʒə*] *n* tejón *m*

badly ['bædlɪ] *adv* mal; **to reflect ~ on sb** influir negativamente en la reputación de uno; ~ **wounded** gravemente herido; **he needs it** ~ le hace gran falta; **to be ~ off (for money)** andar mal de dinero

badminton ['bædmɪntən] *n* bádminton *m*

bad-tempered *adj* de mal genio *or* carácter; (*temporarily*) de mal humor

bag [bæg] *n* bolsa; (*handbag*) bolso; (*satchel*) mochila; (*case*) maleta; ~**s of** (*inf*) un montón de; ~**gage** *n* equipaje *m*; ~**gage allowance** *n* límite *m* de equipaje; ~**gage reclaim** *n* recogida de equipajes; ~**gy** *adj* amplio; ~**pipes** *npl* gaita

Bahamas [bə'hɑːməz] *npl*: **the ~** las Islas Bahamas

bail [beɪl] *n* fianza ♦ *vt* (*prisoner: gen: grant ~ to*) poner en libertad bajo fianza; (*boat: also*: ~ **out**) achicar; **on ~** (*prisoner*) bajo fianza; **to ~ sb out** obtener la libertad de uno bajo fianza; *see also* **bale**

bailiff ['beɪlɪf] *n* alguacil *m*

bait [beɪt] *n* cebo ♦ *vt* poner cebo en;

(*tease*) tomar el pelo a

bake [beɪk] *vt* cocer (al horno) ♦ *vi* cocerse; ~**d beans** *npl* judías *fpl* en salsa de tomate; ~**d potato** *n* patata al horno; ~**r** *n* panadero; ~**ry** *n* panadería; (*for cakes*) pastelería; **baking** *n* (*act*) amasar *m*; (*batch*) hornada; **baking powder** *n* levadura (en polvo)

balance ['bæləns] *n* equilibrio; (COMM: *sum*) balance *m*; (*remainder*) resto; (*scales*) balanza ♦ *vt* equilibrar; (*budget*) nivelar; (*account*) saldar; (*make equal*) equilibrar; ~ **of trade/payments** balanza de comercio/pagos; ~**d** *adj* (*personality, diet*) equilibrado; (*report*) objetivo; ~ **sheet** *n* balance *m*

balcony ['bælkənɪ] *n* (*open*) balcón *m*; (*closed*) galería; (*in theatre*) anfiteatro

bald [bɔːld] *adj* calvo; (*tyre*) liso

bale [beɪl] *n* (AGR) paca, fardo; (*of papers etc*) fajo; ~ **out** *vi* lanzarse en paracaídas

Balearics [bælɪ'ærɪks] *npl*: **the ~** las Baleares

ball [bɔːl] *n* pelota; (*football*) balón *m*; (*of wool, string*) ovillo; (*dance*) baile *m*; **to play ~** (*fig*) cooperar

ballast ['bæləst] *n* lastre *m*

ball bearings *npl* cojinetes *mpl* de bolas

ballerina [bælə'riːnə] *n* bailarina

ballet ['bæleɪ] *n* ballet *m*; ~ **dancer** *n* bailarín/ina *m/f*

balloon [bə'luːn] *n* globo

ballot ['bælət] *n* votación *f*; ~ **paper** *n* papeleta (para votar)

ballpoint (pen) ['bɔːlpɔɪnt-] *n* bolígrafo

ballroom ['bɔːlrum] *n* salón *m* de baile

Baltic ['bɔːltɪk] *n*: **the ~ (Sea)** el (Mar) Báltico

ban [bæn] *n* prohibición *f*, proscripción *f* ♦ *vt* prohibir, proscribir

banal [bə'nɑːl] *adj* banal, vulgar

banana [bə'nɑːnə] *n* plátano (SP), banana (AM)

band [bænd] *n* grupo; (*strip*) faja, tira; (*stripe*) lista; (MUS: *jazz*) orquesta; (: *rock*) grupo; (: MIL) banda; ~ **together** *vi* juntarse, asociarse

bandage ['bændɪdʒ] *n* venda, vendaje *m*
♦ *vt* vendar
Bandaid ® ['bændeɪd] (*US*) *n* tirita
bandit ['bændɪt] *n* bandido
bandy-legged ['bændɪ'legd] *adj* estevado
bang [bæŋ] *n* (*of gun, exhaust*) estallido,
detonación *f*; (*of door*) portazo; (*blow*)
golpe *m* ♦ *vt* (*door*) cerrar de golpe;
(*one's head*) golpear ♦ *vi* estallar; (*door*)
cerrar de golpe
Bangladesh [bɑːŋglə'deʃ] *n* Bangladesh *m*
bangs [bæŋz] (*US*) *npl* flequillo
banish ['bænɪʃ] *vt* desterrar
banister(s) ['bænɪstə(z)] *n(pl)* barandilla,
pasamanos *m inv*
bank [bæŋk] *n* (*COMM*) banco; (*of river,
lake*) ribera, orilla; (*of earth*) terraplén *m*
♦ *vi* (*AVIAT*) ladearse; ~ **on** *vt fus* contar
con; ~ **account** *n* cuenta de banco; ~
card *n* tarjeta bancaria; ~**er** *n* banquero;
~**er's card** (*BRIT*) *n* = ~ **card**; **B~
holiday** (*BRIT*) *n* día *m* festivo; ~**ing** *n*
banca; ~**note** *n* billete *m* de banco; ~
rate *n* tipo de interés bancario

---

bank holiday

ⓘ *El término* **bank holiday** *se aplica en
el Reino Unido a todo día festivo
oficial en el que cierran bancos y
comercios. Los más importantes son en
Navidad, Semana Santa, finales de mayo
y finales de agosto y, al contrario que en
los países de tradición católica, no
coinciden necesariamente con una
celebración religiosa.*

---

bankrupt ['bæŋkrʌpt] *adj* quebrado,
insolvente; **to go** ~ hacer bancarrota; **to
be** ~ estar en quiebra; ~**cy** *n* quiebra
bank statement *n* balance *m or* detalle
m de cuenta
banner ['bænə*] *n* pancarta
bannister(s) ['bænɪstə(z)] *n(pl)*
= **banister(s)**
baptism ['bæptɪzəm] *n* bautismo; (*act*)
bautizo
bar [bɑː*] *n* (*pub*) bar *m*; (*counter*)

mostrador *m*; (*rod*) barra; (*of window,
cage*) reja; (*of soap*) pastilla; (*of chocolate*)
tableta; (*fig: hindrance*) obstáculo;
(*prohibition*) proscripción *f*; (*MUS*) barra
♦ *vt* (*road*) obstruir; (*person*) excluir;
(*activity*) prohibir; **the B~** (*LAW*) la
abogacía; **behind ~s** entre rejas; ~ **none**
sin excepción
barbaric [bɑː'bærɪk] *adj* bárbaro
barbecue ['bɑːbɪkjuː] *n* barbacoa
barbed wire ['bɑːbd-] *n* alambre *m* de
púas
barber ['bɑːbə*] *n* peluquero, barbero
bar code *n* código de barras
bare [beə*] *adj* desnudo; (*trees*) sin hojas;
(*necessities etc*) básico ♦ *vt* desnudar;
(*teeth*) enseñar; ~**back** *adv* a pelo, sin
silla; ~**faced** *adj* descarado; ~**foot** *adj,
adv* descalzo; ~**ly** *adv* apenas
bargain ['bɑːgɪn] *n* pacto, negocio; (*good
buy*) ganga ♦ *vi* negociar; (*haggle*)
regatear; **into the** ~ además, por
añadidura; ~ **for** *vt fus*: **he got more
than he** ~**ed for** le resultó peor de lo que
esperaba
barge [bɑːdʒ] *n* barcaza; ~ **in** *vi* irrumpir;
(*interrupt: conversation*) interrumpir
bark [bɑːk] *n* (*of tree*) corteza; (*of dog*)
ladrido ♦ *vi* ladrar
barley ['bɑːlɪ] *n* cebada
barmaid ['bɑːmeɪd] *n* camarera
barman ['bɑːmən] *n* camarero, barman *m*
barn [bɑːn] *n* granero
barometer [bə'rɒmɪtə*] *n* barómetro
baron ['bærən] *n* barón *m*; (*press ~ etc*)
magnate *m*; ~**ess** *n* baronesa
barracks ['bærəks] *npl* cuartel *m*
barrage ['bærɑːʒ] *n* (*MIL*) descarga,
bombardeo; (*dam*) presa; (*of criticism*)
lluvia, aluvión *m*
barrel ['bærəl] *n* barril *m*; (*of gun*) cañón
m
barren ['bærən] *adj* estéril
barricade [bærɪ'keɪd] *n* barricada
barrier ['bærɪə*] *n* barrera
barring ['bɑːrɪŋ] *prep* excepto, salvo
barrister ['bærɪstə*] (*BRIT*) *n* abogado/a

barrow [ˈbærəʊ] n (cart) carretilla (de mano)

bartender [ˈbɑːtendə*] (US) n camarero, barman m

barter [ˈbɑːtə*] vt: **to ~ sth for sth** trocar algo por algo

base [beɪs] n base f ♦ vt: **to ~ sth on** basar or fundar algo en ♦ adj bajo, infame

baseball [ˈbeɪsbɔːl] n béisbol m

basement [ˈbeɪsmənt] n sótano m

bases¹ [ˈbeɪsiːz] npl of **basis**

bases² [ˈbeɪsɪz] npl of **base**

bash [bæʃ] (inf) vt golpear

bashful [ˈbæʃful] adj tímido, vergonzoso

basic [ˈbeɪsɪk] adj básico; **~ally** adv fundamentalmente, en el fondo; (simply) sencillamente; **~s** npl: **the ~s** los fundamentos

basil [ˈbæzl] n albahaca

basin [ˈbeɪsn] n cuenco, tazón m; (GEO) cuenca; (also: **wash~**) lavabo

basis [ˈbeɪsɪs] (pl **bases**) n base f; **on a part-time/trial ~** a tiempo parcial/a prueba

bask [bɑːsk] vi: **to ~ in the sun** tomar el sol

basket [ˈbɑːskɪt] n cesta, cesto; canasta; **~ball** n baloncesto

Basque [bæsk] adj, n vasco/a m/f; **~ Country** n Euskadi m, País m Vasco

bass [beɪs] n (MUS: instrument) bajo; (double ~) contrabajo; (singer) bajo

bassoon [bəˈsuːn] n fagot m

bastard [ˈbɑːstəd] n bastardo; (inf!) hijo de puta (!)

bat [bæt] n (ZOOL) murciélago; (for ball games) palo; (BRIT: for table tennis) pala ♦ vt: **he didn't ~ an eyelid** ni pestañeó

batch [bætʃ] n (of bread) hornada; (of letters etc) lote m

bated [ˈbeɪtɪd] adj: **with ~ breath** sin respirar

bath [bɑːθ, pl bɑːðz] n (action) baño; (~tub) baño (SP), bañera (SP), tina (AM) ♦ vt bañar; **to have a ~** bañarse, tomar un baño; see also **baths**

bathe [beɪð] vi bañarse ♦ vt (wound) lavar; **~r** n bañista m/f

bathing [ˈbeɪðɪŋ] n el bañarse; **~ costume** (US ~ **suit**) n traje m de baño

bath: **~robe** n (man's) batín m; (woman's) bata; **~room** n (cuarto de) baño; **~s** npl (also: **swimming ~s**) piscina; **~ towel** n toalla de baño

baton [ˈbætən] n (MUS) batuta; (ATHLETICS) testigo; (weapon) porra

batter [ˈbætə*] vt maltratar; (subj: rain etc) azotar ♦ n masa (para rebozar); **~ed** adj (hat, pan) estropeado

battery [ˈbætərɪ] n (AUT) batería; (of torch) pila

battle [ˈbætl] n batalla; (fig) lucha ♦ vi luchar; **~ship** n acorazado

bawl [bɔːl] vi chillar, gritar; (child) berrear

bay [beɪ] n (GEO) bahía; **B~ of Biscay** ≈ mar Cantábrico; **to hold sb at ~** mantener a alguien a raya; **~ leaf** n hoja de laurel

bay window n ventana salediza

bazaar [bəˈzɑː*] n bazar m; (fete) venta con fines benéficos

B. & B. n abbr (= bed and breakfast) cama y desayuno

BBC n abbr (= British Broadcasting Corporation) cadena de radio y televisión estatal británica

B.C. adv abbr (= before Christ) a. de C.

KEYWORD

be [biː] (pt **was**, **were**, pp **been**) aux vb **1** (with present participle: forming continuous tenses): **what are you doing?** ¿qué estás haciendo?, ¿qué haces?; **they're coming tomorrow** vienen mañana; **I've been waiting for you for hours** llevo horas esperándote

2 (with pp: forming passives): ser (but often replaced by active or reflective constructions); **to ~ murdered** ser asesinado; **the box had been opened** habían abierto la caja; **the thief was nowhere to ~ seen** no se veía al ladrón por ninguna parte

3 (*in tag questions*): **it was fun, wasn't it?** fue divertido, ¿no? *or* ¿verdad?; **he's good-looking, isn't he?** es guapo, ¿no te parece?; **she's back again, is she?** entonces, ¿ha vuelto?
4 (*+to +infin*): **the house is to ~ sold** (*necessity*) hay que vender la casa; (*future*) van a vender la casa; **he's not to open it** no tiene que abrirlo
♦ *vb +complement* **1** (*with n or num complement, but see also* **3, 4, 5** *and impers vb below*) ser; **he's a doctor** es médico; **2 and 2 are 4** 2 y 2 son 4
2 (*with adj complement: expressing permanent or inherent quality*) ser; (*: expressing state seen as temporary or reversible*) estar; **I'm English** soy inglés/ esa; **she's tall/pretty** es alta/bonita; **he's young** es joven; **~ careful/good/quiet** ten cuidado/pórtate bien/cállate; **I'm tired** estoy cansado/a; **it's dirty** está sucio/a
3 (*of health*) estar; **how are you?** ¿cómo estás?; **he's very ill** está muy enfermo; **I'm better now** ya estoy mejor
4 (*of age*) tener; **how old are you?** ¿cuántos años tienes?; **I'm sixteen (years old)** tengo dieciséis años
5 (*cost*) costar; ser; **how much was the meal?** ¿cuánto fue *or* costó la comida?; **that'll ~ £5.75, please** son £5.75, por favor; **this shirt is £17** esta camisa cuesta £17
♦ *vi* **1** (*exist, occur etc*) existir, haber; **the best singer that ever was** el mejor cantante que existió jamás; **is there a God?** ¿hay un Dios?, ¿existe Dios?; **~ that as it may** sea como sea; **so ~ it** así sea
2 (*referring to place*) estar; **I won't ~ here tomorrow** no estaré aquí mañana
3 (*referring to movement*): **where have you been?** ¿dónde has estado?
♦ *impers vb* **1** (*referring to time*): **it's 5 o'clock** son las 5; **it's the 28th of April** estamos a 28 de abril
2 (*referring to distance*): **it's 10 km to the village** el pueblo está a 10 km

3 (*referring to the weather*): **it's too hot/ cold** hace demasiado calor/frío; **it's windy today** hace viento hoy
4 (*emphatic*): **it's me** soy yo; **it was Maria who paid the bill** fue María la que pagó la cuenta

beach [biːtʃ] *n* playa ♦ *vt* varar
beacon ['biːkən] *n* (*lighthouse*) faro; (*marker*) guía
bead [biːd] *n* cuenta; (*of sweat etc*) gota
beak [biːk] *n* pico
beaker ['biːkə*] *n* vaso de plástico
beam [biːm] *n* (ARCH) viga, travesaño; (*of light*) rayo, haz *m* de luz ♦ *vi* brillar; (*smile*) sonreír
bean [biːn] *n* judía; **runner/broad ~** habichuela/haba; **coffee ~** grano de café; **~sprouts** *npl* brotes *mpl* de soja
bear [bɛə*] (*pt* bore, *pp* borne) *n* oso ♦ *vt* (*weight etc*) llevar; (*cost*) pagar; (*responsibility*) tener; (*endure*) soportar, aguantar; (*children*) parir, tener; (*fruit*) dar ♦ *vi*: **to ~ right/left** torcer a la derecha/ izquierda; **~ out** *vt* (*suspicions*) corroborar, confirmar; (*person*) dar la razón a; **~ up** *vi* (*remain cheerful*) mantenerse animado
beard [bɪəd] *n* barba; **~ed** *adj* con barba, barbudo
bearer ['bɛərə*] *n* portador(a) *m/f*
bearing ['bɛərɪŋ] *n* porte *m*, comportamiento; (*connection*) relación *f*; **~s** *npl* (*also*: **ball ~s**) cojinetes *mpl* a bolas; **to take a ~** tomar marcaciones; **to find one's ~s** orientarse
beast [biːst] *n* bestia; (*inf*) bruto, salvaje *m*; **~ly** (*inf*) *adj* horrible
beat [biːt] (*pt* beat, *pp* beaten) *n* (*of heart*) latido; (MUS) ritmo, compás *m*; (*of policeman*) ronda ♦ *vt* pegar, golpear; (*eggs*) batir; (*defeat: opponent*) vencer, derrotar; (*: record*) sobrepasar ♦ *vi* (*heart*) latir; (*drum*) redoblar; (*rain, wind*) azotar; **off the ~en track** aislado; **to ~ it** (*inf*) largarse; **~ off** *vt* rechazar; **~ up** *vt* (*attack*) dar una paliza a; **~ing** *n* paliza

beautiful ['bjuːtɪful] *adj* precioso, hermoso, bello; **~ly** *adv* maravillosamente

beauty ['bjuːtɪ] *n* belleza; **~ salon** *n* salón *m* de belleza; **~ spot** *n* (*TOURISM*) lugar *m* pintoresco

beaver ['biːvə*] *n* castor *m*

became [bɪ'keɪm] *pt of* **become**

because [bɪ'kɒz] *conj* porque; **~ of** debido a, a causa de

beckon ['bekən] *vt* (*also:* **~ to**) llamar con señas

become [bɪ'kʌm] (*irreg: like* **come**) *vt* (*suit*) favorecer, sentar bien a ♦ *vi* (+*n*) hacerse, llegar a ser; (+*adj*) ponerse, volverse; **to ~ fat** engordar

becoming [bɪ'kʌmɪŋ] *adj* (*behaviour*) decoroso; (*clothes*) favorecedor(a)

bed [bed] *n* cama; (*of flowers*) macizo; (*of coal, clay*) capa; (*of river*) lecho; (*of sea*) fondo; **to go to ~** acostarse; **~ and breakfast** *n* (*place*) pensión *f*; (*terms*) cama y desayuno; **~clothes** *npl* ropa de cama; **~ding** *n* ropa de cama

---
bed and breakfast

ⓘ *Se llama* **bed and breakfast** *a una forma de alojamiento, en el campo o la ciudad, que ofrece cama y desayuno a precios inferiores a los de un hotel. El servicio se suele anunciar con carteles en los que a menudo se usa únicamente la abreviatura* B. & B.

---

bedraggled [bɪ'drægld] *adj* (*untidy: person*) desastrado; (*clothes, hair*) desordenado

bed: **~ridden** *adj* postrado (en cama); **~room** *n* dormitorio; **~side** *n*: **at the ~side of** a la cabecera de; **~sit(ter)** (*BRIT*) *n* estudio (*SP*), suite *m* (*AM*); **~spread** *n* cubrecama *m*, colcha; **~time** *n* hora de acostarse

bee [biː] *n* abeja

beech [biːtʃ] *n* haya

beef [biːf] *n* carne *f* de vaca; **roast ~** rosbif *m*; **~burger** *n* hamburguesa; **B~eater** *n* alabardero de la Torre de Londres

beehive ['biːhaɪv] *n* colmena

beeline ['biːlaɪn] *n*: **to make a ~ for** ir derecho a

been [biːn] *pp of* **be**

beer [bɪə*] *n* cerveza

beet [biːt] (*US*) *n* (*also:* **red ~**) remolacha

beetle ['biːtl] *n* escarabajo

beetroot ['biːtruːt] (*BRIT*) *n* remolacha

before [bɪ'fɔː*] *prep* (*of time*) antes de; (*of space*) delante de ♦ *conj* antes (de) que ♦ *adv* antes, anteriormente; delante, adelante; **~ going** antes de marcharse; **~ she goes** antes de que se vaya; **the week ~** la semana anterior; **I've never seen it ~** no lo he visto nunca; **~hand** *adv* de antemano, con anticipación

beg [beg] *vi* pedir limosna ♦ *vt* pedir, rogar; (*entreat*) suplicar; **to ~ sb to do sth** rogar a uno que haga algo; *see also* **pardon**

began [bɪ'gæn] *pt of* **begin**

beggar ['begə*] *n* mendigo/a

begin [bɪ'gɪn] (*pt* **began**, *pp* **begun**) *vt, vi* empezar, comenzar; **to ~ doing** *or* **to do sth** empezar a hacer algo; **~ner** *n* principiante *m/f*; **~ning** *n* principio, comienzo

begun [bɪ'gʌn] *pp of* **begin**

behalf [bɪ'hɑːf] *n*: **on ~ of** en nombre de, por; (*for benefit of*) en beneficio de; **on my/his ~** por mí/él

behave [bɪ'heɪv] *vi* (*person*) portarse, comportarse; (*well: also:* **~ o.s.**) portarse bien; **behaviour** (*US* **behavior**) *n* comportamiento, conducta

behind [bɪ'haɪnd] *prep* detrás de; (*supporting*): **to be ~ sb** apoyar a alguien ♦ *adv* detrás, por detrás, atrás ♦ *n* trasero; **to be ~ (schedule)** ir retrasado; **~ the scenes** (*fig*) entre bastidores

behold [bɪ'həʊld] (*irreg: like* **hold**) *vt* contemplar

beige [beɪʒ] *adj* color beige

Beijing ['beɪ'dʒɪŋ] *n* Pekín *m*

being ['biːɪŋ] *n* ser *m*; (*existence*): **in ~** existente; **to come into ~** aparecer

Beirut [beɪ'ruːt] *n* Beirut *m*

Belarus [bɛləˈrus] *n* Bielorrusia

belated [bɪˈleɪtɪd] *adj* atrasado, tardío

belch [bɛltʃ] *vi* eructar ♦ *vt* (*gen*: ~ **out**: *smoke etc*) arrojar

Belgian [ˈbɛldʒən] *adj, n* belga *m/f*

Belgium [ˈbɛldʒəm] *n* Bélgica

belief [bɪˈliːf] *n* opinión *f*; (*faith*) fe *f*

believe [bɪˈliːv] *vt, vi* creer; **to ~ in** creer en; **~r** *n* partidario/a; (*REL*) creyente *m/f*, fiel *m/f*

belittle [bɪˈlɪtl] *vt* quitar importancia a

bell [bɛl] *n* campana; (*small*) campanilla; (*on door*) timbre *m*

belligerent [bɪˈlɪdʒərənt] *adj* agresivo

bellow [ˈbɛləu] *vi* bramar; (*person*) rugir

belly [ˈbɛlɪ] *n* barriga, panza

belong [bɪˈlɔŋ] *vi*: **to ~ to** pertenecer a; (*club etc*) ser socio de; **this book ~s here** este libro va aquí; **~ings** *npl* pertenencias *fpl*

beloved [bɪˈlʌvɪd] *adj* querido/a

below [bɪˈləu] *prep* bajo, debajo de; (*less than*) inferior a ♦ *adv* abajo, (por) debajo; **see ~** véase más abajo

belt [bɛlt] *n* cinturón *m*; (*TECH*) correa, cinta ♦ *vt* (*thrash*) pegar con correa; **~way** (*US*) *n* (*AUT*) carretera de circunvalación

bench [bɛntʃ] *n* banco; (*BRIT*: *POL*): **the Government/Opposition ~es** (los asientos de) los miembros del Gobierno/ de la Oposición; **the B~** (*LAW*: *judges*) magistratura

bend [bɛnd] (*pt, pp* **bent**) *vt* doblar ♦ *vi* inclinarse ♦ *n* (*BRIT*: *in road, river*) curva; (*in pipe*) codo; **~ down** *vi* inclinarse, doblarse; **~ over** *vi* inclinarse

beneath [bɪˈniːθ] *prep* bajo, debajo de; (*unworthy of*) indigno de ♦ *adv* abajo, (por) debajo

benefactor [ˈbɛnɪfæktə*] *n* bienhechor *m*

beneficial [bɛnɪˈfɪʃəl] *adj* beneficioso

benefit [ˈbɛnɪfɪt] *n* beneficio; (*allowance of money*) subsidio ♦ *vt* beneficiar ♦ *vi*: **he'll ~ from it** le sacará provecho

benevolent [bɪˈnɛvələnt] *adj* (*person*) benévolo

benign [bɪˈnaɪn] *adj* benigno; (*smile*) afable

bent [bɛnt] *pt, pp of* **bend** ♦ *n* inclinación *f* ♦ *adj*: **to be ~ on** estar empeñado en

bequest [bɪˈkwɛst] *n* legado

bereaved [bɪˈriːvd] *npl*: **the ~** los íntimos de una persona afligidos por su muerte

beret [ˈbɛreɪ] *n* boina

Berlin [bəːˈlɪn] *n* Berlín

berm [bəːm] (*US*) *n* (*AUT*) arcén *m*

Bermuda [bəːˈmjuːdə] *n* las Bermudas

berry [ˈbɛrɪ] *n* baya

berserk [bəˈsəːk] *adj*: **to go ~** perder los estribos

berth [bəːθ] *n* (*bed*) litera; (*cabin*) camarote *m*; (*for ship*) amarradero ♦ *vi* atracar, amarrar

beseech [bɪˈsiːtʃ] (*pt, pp* **besought**) *vt* suplicar

beset [bɪˈsɛt] (*pt, pp* **beset**) *vt* (*person*) acosar

beside [bɪˈsaɪd] *prep* junto a, al lado de; **to be ~ o.s. with anger** estar fuera de sí; **that's ~ the point** eso no tiene nada que ver; **~s** *adv* además ♦ *prep* además de

besiege [bɪˈsiːdʒ] *vt* sitiar; (*fig*) asediar

best [bɛst] *adj* (el/la) mejor ♦ *adv* (lo) mejor; **the ~ part of** (*quantity*) la mayor parte de; **at ~** en el mejor de los casos; **to make the ~ of sth** sacar el mejor partido de algo; **to do one's ~** hacer todo lo posible; **to the ~ of my knowledge** que yo sepa; **to the ~ of my ability** como mejor puedo; **~-before date** *n* fecha de consumo preferente; **~ man** *n* padrino de boda

bestow [bɪˈstəu] *vt* (*title*) otorgar

bestseller [ˈbɛstˈsɛlə*] *n* éxito de librería, bestseller *m*

bet [bɛt] (*pt, pp* **bet** or **betted**) *n* apuesta ♦ *vt*: **to ~ money on** apostar dinero por; **to ~ sb sth** apostar algo a uno ♦ *vi* apostar

betray [bɪˈtreɪ] *vt* traicionar; (*trust*) faltar a; **~al** *n* traición *f*

better [ˈbɛtə*] *adj, adv* mejor ♦ *vt* superar ♦ *n*: **to get the ~ of sb** quedar por encima de alguien; **you had ~ do it** más vale que lo hagas; **he thought ~ of it** cambió de parecer; **to get ~** (MED) mejorar(se); **~ off** adj mejor; (wealthier) más acomodado

betting ['betɪŋ] n juego, el apostar; **~ shop** (BRIT) n agencia de apuestas

between [bɪ'twiːn] prep entre ♦ adv (time) mientras tanto; (place) en medio

beverage ['bevərɪdʒ] n bebida

beware [bɪ'weə*] vi: **to ~ (of)** tener cuidado (con); **"~ of the dog"** "perro peligroso"

bewildered [bɪ'wɪldəd] adj aturdido, perplejo

beyond [bɪ'jɔnd] prep más allá de; (past: understanding) fuera de; (after: date) después de, más allá de; (above) superior a ♦ adv (in space) más allá; (in time) posteriormente; **~ doubt** fuera de toda duda; **~ repair** irreparable

bias ['baɪəs] n (prejudice) prejuicio, pasión f; (preference) predisposición f; **~(s)ed** adj parcial

bib [bɪb] n babero

Bible ['baɪbl] n Biblia

bicarbonate of soda [baɪ'kɑːbənɪt-] n bicarbonato sódico

bicker ['bɪkə*] vi pelearse

bicycle ['baɪsɪkl] n bicicleta

bid [bɪd] (pt **bade** or **bid**, pp **bidden** or **bid**) n oferta, postura; (in tender) licitación f; (attempt) tentativa, conato ♦ vi hacer una oferta ♦ vt (offer) ofrecer; **to ~ sb good day** dar a uno los buenos días; **~der** n: **the highest ~der** el mejor postor; **~ding** n (at auction) ofertas fpl

bide [baɪd] vt: **to ~ one's time** esperar el momento adecuado

bifocals [baɪ'fəuklz] npl gafas fpl (SP) or anteojos mpl (AM) bifocales

big [bɪg] adj grande; (brother, sister) mayor

bigheaded ['bɪg'hedɪd] adj engreído

bigot ['bɪgət] n fanático/a, intolerante m/f; **~ed** adj fanático, intolerante; **~ry** n fanatismo, intolerancia

big top n (at circus) carpa

bike [baɪk] n bici f

bikini [bɪ'kiːnɪ] n bikini m

bilingual [baɪ'lɪŋgwəl] adj bilingüe

bill [bɪl] n cuenta; (invoice) factura; (POL) proyecto de ley; (US: banknote) billete m; (of bird) pico; (of show) programa m; **"post no ~s"** "prohibido fijar carteles"; **to fit** or **fill the ~** (fig) cumplir con los requisitos; **~board** (US) n cartelera

billet ['bɪlɪt] n alojamiento

billfold ['bɪlfəuld] (US) n cartera

billiards ['bɪljədz] n billar m

billion ['bɪljən] n (BRIT) billón m (millón de millones); (US) mil millones mpl

bimbo ['bɪmbəu] (inf) n tía buena sin seso

bin [bɪn] n (for rubbish) cubo (SP) or bote m (AM) de la basura; (container) recipiente m

bind [baɪnd] (pt, pp **bound**) vt atar; (book) encuadernar; (oblige) obligar ♦ n (inf: nuisance) lata; **~ing** adj (contract) obligatorio

binge [bɪndʒ] (inf) n: **to go on a ~** ir de juerga

bingo ['bɪŋgəu] n bingo m

binoculars [bɪ'nɔkjuləz] npl prismáticos mpl

bio... [baɪə] prefix: **~chemistry** n bioquímica; **~degradable** [baɪəudr'greɪdəbl] adj biodegradable; **~graphy** [baɪ'ɔgrəfɪ] n biografía; **~logical** adj biológico; **~logy** [baɪ'ɔlədʒɪ] n biología

birch [bəːtʃ] n (tree) abedul m

bird [bəːd] n ave f, pájaro; (BRIT: inf: girl) chica; **~'s eye view** n (aerial view) vista de pájaro; (overview) visión f de conjunto; **~ watcher** n ornitólogo/a

Biro ® ['baɪrəu] n bolígrafo

birth [bəːθ] n nacimiento; **to give ~ to** parir, dar a luz; **~ certificate** n partida de nacimiento; **~ control** n (policy) control m de natalidad; (methods) métodos mpl anticonceptivos; **~day** n cumpleaños m inv ♦ cpd (cake, card etc) de cumpleaños; **~place** n lugar m de nacimiento; **~ rate** n (tasa de) natalidad

f
biscuit ['bɪskɪt] (*BRIT*) *n* galleta, bizcocho (*AM*)
bisect [baɪ'sɛkt] *vt* bisecar
bishop ['bɪʃəp] *n* obispo; (*CHESS*) alfil *m*
bit [bɪt] *pt of* **bite** ♦ *n* trozo, pedazo, pedacito; (*COMPUT*) bit *m*, bitio; (*for horse*) freno, bocado; **a ~ of** un poco de; **a ~ mad** un poco loco; **~ by ~** poco a poco
bitch [bɪtʃ] *n* perra; (*inf!: woman*) zorra (!)
bite [baɪt] (*pt* **bit**, *pp* **bitten**) *vt*, *vi* morder; (*insect etc*) picar ♦ *n* (*insect ~*) picadura; (*mouthful*) bocado; **to ~ one's nails** comerse las uñas; **let's have a ~ (to eat)** (*inf*) vamos a comer algo
bitter ['bɪtə*] *adj* amargo; (*wind*) cortante, penetrante; (*battle*) encarnizado ♦ *n* (*BRIT: beer*) cerveza típica británica a base de lúpulos; **~ness** *n* lo amargo, amargura; (*anger*) rencor *m*
bizarre [bɪ'zɑ:*] *adj* raro, extraño
black [blæk] *adj* negro; (*tea, coffee*) solo ♦ *n* color *m* negro; (*person*): **B~** negro/a ♦ *vt* (*BRIT: INDUSTRY*) boicotear; **to give sb a ~ eye** ponerle a uno el ojo morado; **~ and blue** (*bruised*) amoratado; **to be in the ~** (*bank account*) estar en números negros; **~berry** *n* zarzamora; **~bird** *n* mirlo; **~board** *n* pizarra; **~ coffee** *n* café *m* solo; **~currant** *n* grosella negra; **~en** *vt* (*fig*) desacreditar; **~ ice** *n* hielo invisible en la carretera; **~leg** (*BRIT*) *n* esquirol *m*, rompehuelgas *m inv*; **~list** *n* lista negra; **~mail** *n* chantaje *m* ♦ *vt* chantajear; **~ market** *n* mercado negro; **~out** *n* (*MIL*) oscurecimiento; (*power cut*) apagón *m*; (*TV, RADIO*) interrupción *f* de programas; (*fainting*) desvanecimiento; **B~ Sea** *n*: **the B~ Sea** el Mar Negro; **~ sheep** *n* (*fig*) oveja negra; **~smith** *n* herrero *m*; **~ spot** *n* (*AUT*) lugar *m* peligroso; (*for unemployment etc*) punto negro
bladder ['blædə*] *n* vejiga
blade [bleɪd] *n* hoja; (*of propeller*) paleta; **a ~ of grass** una brizna de hierba

blame [bleɪm] *n* culpa ♦ *vt*: **to ~ sb for sth** echar a uno la culpa de algo; **to be to ~** tener la culpa de
bland [blænd] *adj* (*music, taste*) soso
blank [blæŋk] *adj* en blanco; (*look*) sin expresión ♦ *n* (*of memory*): **my mind is a ~** no puedo recordar nada; (*on form*) blanco, espacio en blanco; (*cartridge*) cartucho sin bala *or* de fogueo; **~ cheque** *n* cheque *m* en blanco
blanket ['blæŋkɪt] *n* manta (*SP*), cobija (*AM*); (*of snow*) capa; (*of fog*) manto
blare [blɛə*] *vi* sonar estrepitosamente
blasé ['blɑːzeɪ] *adj* hastiado
blast [blɑːst] *n* (*of wind*) ráfaga, soplo; (*explosive*) explosión *f* ♦ *vt* (*blow up*) volar; **~-off** *n* (*SPACE*) lanzamiento
blatant ['bleɪtənt] *adj* descarado
blaze [bleɪz] *n* (*fire*) fuego; (*fig: of colour*) despliegue *m*; (: *of glory*) esplendor *m* ♦ *vi* arder en llamas; (*fig*) brillar ♦ *vt*: **to ~ a trail** (*fig*) abrir (un) camino; **in a ~ of publicity** con gran publicidad
blazer ['bleɪzə*] *n* chaqueta de uniforme de colegial *o* de socio de club
bleach [bliːtʃ] *n* (*also:* **household ~**) lejía ♦ *vt* blanquear; **~ed** *adj* (*hair*) teñido (de rubio); **~ers** (*US*) *npl* (*SPORT*) gradas *fpl* al sol
bleak [bliːk] *adj* (*countryside*) desierto; (*prospect*) poco prometedor(a); (*weather*) crudo; (*smile*) triste
bleat [bliːt] *vi* balar
bleed [bliːd] (*pt*, *pp* **bled**) *vt*, *vi* sangrar; **my nose is ~ing** me está sangrando la nariz
bleeper ['bliːpə*] *n* busca *m*
blemish ['blɛmɪʃ] *n* marca, mancha; (*on reputation*) tacha
blend [blɛnd] *n* mezcla ♦ *vt* mezclar; (*colours etc*) combinar, mezclar ♦ *vi* (*colours etc: also:* **~ in**) combinarse, mezclarse
bless [blɛs] (*pt*, *pp* **blessed** *or* **blest**) *vt* bendecir; **~ you!** (*after sneeze*) ¡Jesús!; **~ing** *n* (*approval*) aprobación *f*; (*godsend*) don *m* del cielo, bendición *f*; (*advantage*)

beneficio, ventaja

blew [bluː] *pt of* **blow**

blind [blaɪnd] *adj* ciego; (*fig*): ~ **(to)** ciego (a) ♦ *n* (*for window*) persiana ♦ *vt* cegar; (*dazzle*) deslumbrar; (*deceive*): **to ~ sb to ...** cegar a uno a ...; **the ~** *npl* los ciegos; ~ **alley** *n* callejón *m* sin salida; ~ **corner** (*BRIT*) *n* esquina escondida; ~**fold** *n* venda ♦ *adv* con los ojos vendados ♦ *vt* vendar los ojos a; ~**ly** *adv* a ciegas, ciegamente; ~**ness** *n* ceguera; ~ **spot** *n* (*AUT*) ángulo ciego

blink [blɪŋk] *vi* parpadear, pestañear; (*light*) oscilar; ~**ers** *npl* anteojeras *fpl*

bliss [blɪs] *n* felicidad *f*

blister ['blɪstə*] *n* ampolla ♦ *vi* (*paint*) ampollarse

blizzard ['blɪzəd] *n* ventisca

bloated ['bləʊtɪd] *adj* hinchado; (*person: full*) ahíto

blob [blɔb] *n* (*drop*) gota; (*indistinct object*) bulto

bloc [blɔk] *n* (*POL*) bloque *m*

block [blɔk] *n* bloque *m*; (*in pipes*) obstáculo; (*of buildings*) manzana (*SP*), cuadra (*AM*) ♦ *vt* obstruir, cerrar; (*progress*) estorbar; ~ **of flats** (*BRIT*) bloque *m* de pisos; **mental ~** bloqueo mental; ~**ade** [-'keɪd] *n* bloqueo ♦ *vt* bloquear; ~**age** *n* estorbo, obstrucción *f*; ~**buster** *n* (*book*) bestseller *m*; (*film*) éxito de público; ~ **letters** *npl* letras *fpl* de molde

bloke [bləʊk] (*BRIT: inf*) *n* tipo, tío

blond(e) [blɔnd] *adj, n* rubio/a *m/f*

blood [blʌd] *n* sangre *f*; ~ **donor** *n* donante *m/f* de sangre; ~ **group** *n* grupo sanguíneo; ~**hound** *n* sabueso; ~ **poisoning** *n* envenenamiento de la sangre; ~ **pressure** *n* presión *f* sanguínea; ~**shed** *n* derramamiento de sangre; ~**shot** *adj* inyectado en sangre; ~**stream** *n* corriente *f* sanguínea; ~ **test** *n* análisis *m inv* de sangre; ~**thirsty** *adj* sanguinario; ~ **vessel** *n* vaso sanguíneo; ~**y** *adj* sangriento; (*nose etc*) lleno de sangre; (*BRIT: inf!*): **this ~y...** este

condenado *o* puñetero ... (!) ♦ *adv*: ~**y strong/good** (*BRIT: inf!*) terriblemente fuerte/bueno; ~**y-minded** (*BRIT: inf*) *adj* puñetero (!)

bloom [bluːm] *n* flor *f* ♦ *vi* florecer

blossom ['blɔsəm] *n* flor *f* ♦ *vi* (*also fig*) florecer

blot [blɔt] *n* borrón *m*; (*fig*) mancha ♦ *vt* (*stain*) manchar; ~ **out** *vt* (*view*) tapar

blotchy ['blɔtʃɪ] *adj* (*complexion*) lleno de manchas

blotting paper ['blɔtɪŋ-] *n* papel *m* secante

blouse [blaʊz] *n* blusa

blow [bləʊ] (*pt* **blew**, *pp* **blown**) *n* golpe *m*; (*with sword*) espadazo ♦ *vi* soplar; (*dust, sand etc*) volar; (*fuse*) fundirse ♦ *vt* (*subj: wind*) llevarse; (*fuse*) quemar; (*instrument*) tocar; **to ~ one's nose** sonarse; ~ **away** *vt* llevarse, arrancar; ~ **down** *vt* derribar; ~ **off** *vt* arrebatar; ~ **out** *vi* apagarse; ~ **over** *vi* amainar; ~ **up** *vi* estallar ♦ *vt* volar; (*tyre*) inflar; (*PHOT*) ampliar; ~-**dry** *n* moldeado (con secador); ~**lamp** (*BRIT*) *n* soplete *m*, lámpara de soldar; ~-**out** *n* (*of tyre*) pinchazo; ~**torch** *n* = ~**lamp**

blue [bluː] *adj* azul; (*depressed*) deprimido; ~ **film/joke** película/chiste *m* verde; **out of the** ~ (*fig*) de repente; ~**bell** *n* campanilla, campánula azul; ~**bottle** *n* moscarda, mosca azul; ~**print** *n* (*fig*) anteproyecto

bluff [blʌf] *vi* tirarse un farol, farolear ♦ *n* farol *m*; **to call sb's ~** coger a uno la palabra

blunder ['blʌndə*] *n* patinazo, metedura de pata ♦ *vi* cometer un error, meter la pata

blunt [blʌnt] *adj* (*pencil*) despuntado; (*knife*) desafilado, romo; (*person*) franco, directo

blur [bləː*] *n* (*shape*): **to become a ~** hacerse borroso ♦ *vt* (*vision*) enturbiar; (*distinction*) borrar

blush [blʌʃ] *vi* ruborizarse, ponerse colorado ♦ *n* rubor *m*

blustery ['blʌstəri] *adj* (*weather*)
tempestuoso, tormentoso

boar [bɔː*] *n* verraco, cerdo

board [bɔːd] *n* (*card~*) cartón *m*; (*wooden*)
tabla, tablero; (*on wall*) tablón *m*; (*for
chess etc*) tablero; (*committee*) junta,
consejo; (*in firm*) mesa *or* junta directiva;
(*NAUT, AVIAT*): **on ~** a bordo ♦ *vt* (*ship*)
embarcarse en; (*train*) subir a; **full ~** (*BRIT*)
pensión completa; **half ~** (*BRIT*) media
pensión; **to go by the ~** (*fig*) ser
abandonado *or* olvidado; **~ up** *vt* (*door*)
tapiar; **~ and lodging** *n* casa y comida;
~er *n* (*SCOL*) interno/a; **~ing card** (*BRIT*)
n tarjeta de embarque; **~ing house** *n*
casa de huéspedes; **~ing pass** (*US*) *n* =
~ing card; **~ing school** *n* internado; **~
room** *n* sala de juntas

boast [bəust] *vi*: **to ~ (about *or* of)**
alardear (de)

boat [bəut] *n* barco, buque *m*; (*small*)
barca, bote *m*

bob [bɔb] *vi* (*also*: **~ up and down**)
menearse, balancearse; **~ up** *vi*
(re)aparecer de repente

bobby ['bɔbɪ] (*BRIT*: *inf*) *n* poli *m*

bobsleigh ['bɔbsleɪ] *n* bob *m*

bode [bəud] *vi*: **to ~ well/ill (for)** ser
prometedor/poco prometedor (para)

bodily ['bɔdɪlɪ] *adj* corporal ♦ *adv* (*move:
person*) en peso

body ['bɔdɪ] *n* cuerpo; (*corpse*) cadáver *m*;
(*of car*) caja, carrocería; (*fig: group*) grupo;
(: *organization*) organismo; **~-building** *n*
culturismo; **~guard** *n* guardaespaldas *m
inv*; **~work** *n* carrocería

bog [bɔg] *n* pantano, ciénaga ♦ *vt*: **to get
~ged down** (*fig*) empantanarse, atascarse

bogus ['bəugəs] *adj* falso, fraudulento

boil [bɔɪl] *vt* (*water*) hervir; (*eggs*) pasar por
agua, cocer ♦ *vi* hervir; (*fig: with anger*)
estar furioso; (: *with heat*) asfixiarse ♦ *n*
(*MED*) furúnculo, divieso; **to come to the
~, to come to a ~** (*US*) comenzar a
hervir; **to ~ down to** (*fig*) reducirse a; **~
over** *vi* salirse, rebosar; (*anger etc*) llegar
al colmo; **~ed egg** *n* huevo cocido (*SP*)

or pasado (*AM*); **~ed potatoes** *npl*
patatas *fpl* (*SP*) *or* papas *fpl* (*AM*) hervidas;
~er *n* caldera; **~er suit** (*BRIT*) *n* mono;
~ing point *n* punto de ebullición

boisterous ['bɔɪstərəs] *adj* (*noisy*)
bullicioso; (*excitable*) exuberante; (*crowd*)
tumultuoso

bold [bəuld] *adj* valiente, audaz; (*pej*)
descarado; (*colour*) llamativo

Bolivia [bə'lɪvɪə] *n* Bolivia; **~n** *adj*, *n*
boliviano/a *m/f*

bollard ['bɔləd] (*BRIT*) *n* (*AUT*) poste *m*

bolt [bəult] *n* (*lock*) cerrojo; (*with nut*)
perno, tornillo ♦ *adv*: **~ upright** rígido,
erguido ♦ *vt* (*door*) echar el cerrojo a;
(*also*: **~ together**) sujetar con tornillos;
(*food*) engullir ♦ *vi* fugarse; (*horse*)
desbocarse

bomb [bɔm] *n* bomba ♦ *vt* bombardear; **~
disposal** *n* desmontaje *m* de explosivos;
~er *n* (*AVIAT*) bombardero; **~shell** *n* (*fig*)
bomba

bond [bɔnd] *n* (*promise*) fianza; (*FINANCE*)
bono; (*link*) vínculo, lazo; (*COMM*): **in ~** en
depósito bajo fianza

bondage ['bɔndɪdʒ] *n* esclavitud *f*

bone [bəun] *n* hueso; (*of fish*) espina ♦ *vt*
deshuesar; quitar las espinas a; **~ idle** *adj*
gandul; **~ marrow** *n* médula

bonfire ['bɔnfaɪə*] *n* hoguera, fogata

bonnet ['bɔnɪt] *n* gorra; (*BRIT: of car*) capó
m

bonus ['bəunəs] *n* (*payment*) paga
extraordinaria, plus *m*; (*fig*) bendición *f*

bony ['bəunɪ] *adj* (*arm, face*) huesudo;
(*MED: tissue*) óseo; (*meat*) lleno de huesos;
(*fish*) lleno de espinas

boo [buː] *excl* ¡uh! ♦ *vt* abuchear, rechiflar

booby trap ['buːbɪ-] *n* trampa explosiva

book [buk] *n* libro; (*of tickets*) taco; (*of
stamps etc*) librito ♦ *vt* (*ticket*) sacar; (*seat,
room*) reservar; **~s** *npl* (*COMM*) cuentas
fpl, contabilidad *f*; **~case** *n* librería,
estante *m* para libros; **~ing office** *n*
(*BRIT: RAIL*) despacho de billetes (*SP*) *or*
boletos (*AM*); (*THEATRE*) taquilla (*SP*),
boletería (*AM*); **~-keeping** *n* contabilidad

f; **~let** *n* folleto; **~maker** *n* corredor *m* de apuestas; **~seller** *n* librero; **~shop, ~ store** *n* librería

boom [bu:m] *n* (*noise*) trueno, estampido; (*in prices etc*) alza rápida; (ECON, *in population*) boom *m* ♦ *vi* (*cannon*) hacer gran estruendo, retumbar; (ECON) estar en alza

boon [bu:n] *n* favor *m*, beneficio

boost [bu:st] *n* estímulo, empuje *m* ♦ *vt* estimular, empujar; **~er** *n* (MED) reinyección *f*

boot [bu:t] *n* bota; (BRIT: *of car*) maleta, maletero ♦ *vt* (COMPUT) arrancar; **to ~** (*in addition*) además, por añadidura

booth [bu:ð] *n* (*telephone* ~, *voting* ~) cabina

booze [bu:z] (*inf*) *n* bebida

border ['bɔ:də*] *n* borde *m*, margen *m*; (*of a country*) frontera; (*for flowers*) arriate *m* ♦ *vt* (*road*) bordear; (*another country*: *also*: **~ on**) lindar con; **B~s** *n*: **the B~s** región fronteriza entre Escocia e Inglaterra; **~ on** *vt fus* (*insanity etc*) rayar en; **~line** *n*: **on the ~line** en el límite; **~line case** *n* caso dudoso

bore [bɔ:*] *pt of* **bear** ♦ *vt* (*hole*) hacer un agujero en; (*well*) perforar; (*person*) aburrir ♦ *n* (*person*) pelmazo, pesado; (*of gun*) calibre *m*; **to be ~d** estar aburrido; **~dom** *n* aburrimiento

boring ['bɔ:rɪŋ] *adj* aburrido

born [bɔ:n] *adj*: **to be ~** nacer; **I was ~ in 1960** nací en 1960

borne [bɔ:n] *pp of* **bear**

borough ['bʌrə] *n* municipio

borrow ['bɔrəu] *vt*: **to ~ sth (from sb)** tomar algo prestado (a alguien)

Bosnia(-Herzegovina) ['bɔsnɪə(hɛrzə'gəuvɪ:nə)] *n* Bosnia (-Herzegovina)

bosom ['buzəm] *n* pecho

boss [bɔs] *n* jefe *m* ♦ *vt* (*also*: **~ about** *or* **around**) mangonear; **~y** *adj* mandón/ona

bosun ['bəusn] *n* contramaestre *m*

botany ['bɔtənɪ] *n* botánica

botch [bɔtʃ] *vt* (*also*: **~ up**) arruinar,

estropear

both [bəuθ] *adj, pron* ambos/as, los/las dos; **~ of us went, we ~ went** fuimos los dos, ambos fuimos ♦ *adv*: **~ A and B** tanto A como B

bother ['bɔðə*] *vt* (*worry*) preocupar; (*disturb*) molestar, fastidiar ♦ *vi* (*also*: **~ o.s.**) molestarse ♦ *n* (*trouble*) dificultad *f*; (*nuisance*) molestia, lata; **to ~ doing** tomarse la molestia de hacer

bottle ['bɔtl] *n* botella; (*small*) frasco; (*baby's*) biberón *m* ♦ *vt* embotellar; **~ up** *vt* suprimir; **~ bank** *n* contenedor *m* de vidrio; **~neck** *n* (AUT) embotellamiento; (*in supply*) obstáculo; **~-opener** *n* abrebotellas *m inv*

bottom ['bɔtəm] *n* (*of box, sea*) fondo; (*buttocks*) trasero, culo; (*of page*) pie *m*; (*of list*) final *m*; (*of class*) último/a ♦ *adj* (*lowest*) más bajo; (*last*) último

bough [bau] *n* rama

bought [bɔ:t] *pt, pp of* **buy**

boulder ['bəuldə*] *n* canto rodado

bounce [bauns] *vi* (*ball*) (re)botar; (*cheque*) ser rechazado ♦ *vt* hacer (re)botar ♦ *n* (*rebound*) (re)bote *m*; **~r** (*inf*) *n* gorila *m* (*que echa a los alborotadores de un bar, club etc*)

bound [baund] *pt, pp of* **bind** ♦ *n* (*leap*) salto; (*gen pl*: *limit*) límite *m* ♦ *vi* (*leap*) saltar ♦ *vt* (*border*) rodear ♦ *adj*: **~ by** rodeado de; **to be ~ to do sth** (*obliged*) tener el deber de hacer algo; **he's ~ to come** es seguro que vendrá; **out of ~s** prohibido el paso; **~ for** con destino a

boundary ['baundrɪ] *n* límite *m*

bouquet ['bukeɪ] *n* (*of flowers*) ramo

bourgeois ['buəʒwa:] *adj* burgués/esa *m/f*

bout [baut] *n* (*of malaria etc*) ataque *m*; (*of activity*) período; (BOXING *etc*) combate *m*, encuentro

bow[1] [bəu] *n* (*knot*) lazo; (*weapon, MUS*) arco

bow[2] [bau] *n* (*of the head*) reverencia; (NAUT: *also*: **~s**) proa ♦ *vi* inclinarse, hacer una reverencia; (*yield*): **to ~** *or* **before** ceder ante, someterse a

bowels [baʊəlz] *npl* intestinos *mpl*, vientre *m*; (*fig*) entrañas *fpl*

bowl [bəʊl] *n* tazón *m*, cuenco; (*ball*) bola ♦ *vi* (*CRICKET*) arrojar la pelota; *see also* **bowls**

bow-legged ['bəʊ'lɛgɪd] *adj* estevado

bowler ['bəʊlə*] *n* (*CRICKET*) lanzador *m* (de la pelota); (*BRIT: also:* **~ hat**) hongo, bombín *m*

bowling ['bəʊlɪŋ] *n* (*game*) bochas *fpl*, bolos *mpl*; **~ alley** *n* bolera; **~ green** *n* pista para bochas

bowls [bəʊlz] *n* juego de las bochas, bolos *mpl*

bow tie ['bəʊ-] *n* corbata de lazo, pajarita

box [bɒks] *n* (*also:* **cardboard ~**) caja, cajón *m*; (*THEATRE*) palco ♦ *vt* encajonar ♦ *vi* (*SPORT*) boxear; **~er** ['bɒksə*] *n* (*person*) boxeador *m*; **~ing** ['bɒksɪŋ] *n* (*SPORT*) boxeo; **B~ing Day** (*BRIT*) *n* día en que se dan los aguinaldos, 26 de diciembre; **~ing gloves** *npl* guantes *mpl* de boxeo; **~ing ring** *n* ring *m*, cuadrilátero; **~ office** *n* taquilla (*SP*), boletería (*AM*); **~room** *n* trastero

---
Boxing Day

> ***ⓘ*** *El día 26 de diciembre se conoce como* **Boxing Day** *y es día festivo en todo el Reino Unido. En el siglo XIX era tradición entregar "Christmas boxes" (aguinaldos) a empleados, carteros y otros proveedores en este día, y de ahí el nombre.*
---

boy [bɔɪ] *n* (*young*) niño; (*older*) muchacho, chico; (*son*) hijo

boycott ['bɔɪkɒt] *n* boicot *m* ♦ *vt* boicotear

boyfriend ['bɔɪfrɛnd] *n* novio

boyish ['bɔɪɪʃ] *adj* juvenil; (*girl*) con aspecto de muchacho

B.R. *n* *abbr* (*formerly = British Rail*) ≈ RENFE *f* (*SP*)

bra [brɑː] *n* sostén *m*, sujetador *m*

brace [breɪs] *n* (*BRIT: also:* **~s**: *on teeth*) corrector *m*, aparato; (*tool*) berbiquí *m*

♦ *vt* (*knees, shoulders*) tensionar; **~s** *npl* (*BRIT*) tirantes *mpl*; **to ~ o.s.** (*fig*) prepararse

bracelet ['breɪslɪt] *n* pulsera, brazalete *m*

bracing ['breɪsɪŋ] *adj* vigorizante, tónico

bracket ['brækɪt] *n* (*TECH*) soporte *m*, puntal *m*; (*group*) clase *f*, categoría; (*also:* **brace ~**) soporte *m*, abrazadera; (*also:* **round ~**) paréntesis *m inv*; (*also:* **square ~**) corchete *m* ♦ *vt* (*word etc*) poner entre paréntesis

brag [bræg] *vi* jactarse

braid [breɪd] *n* (*trimming*) galón *m*; (*of hair*) trenza

brain [breɪn] *n* cerebro; **~s** *npl* sesos *mpl*; **she's got ~s** es muy lista; **~wash** *vt* lavar el cerebro; **~wave** *n* idea luminosa; **~y** *adj* muy inteligente

braise [breɪz] *vt* cocer a fuego lento

brake [breɪk] *n* (*on vehicle*) freno ♦ *vi* frenar; **~ light** *n* luz *f* de frenado

bran [bræn] *n* salvado

branch [brɑːntʃ] *n* rama; (*COMM*) sucursal *f*; **~ out** *vi* (*fig*) extenderse

brand [brænd] *n* marca; (*fig: type*) tipo ♦ *vt* (*cattle*) marcar con hierro candente; **~-new** *adj* flamante, completamente nuevo

brandy ['brændɪ] *n* coñac *m*

brash [bræʃ] *adj* (*forward*) descarado

brass [brɑːs] *n* latón *m*; **the ~** (*MUS*) los cobres; **~ band** *n* banda de metal

brat [bræt] (*pej*) *n* mocoso/a

brave [breɪv] *adj* valiente, valeroso ♦ *vt* (*face up to*) desafiar; **~ry** *n* valor *m*, valentía

brawl [brɔːl] *n* pelea, reyerta

brazen ['breɪzn] *adj* descarado, cínico ♦ *vt*: **to ~ it out** echarle cara

Brazil [brə'zɪl] *n* (el) Brasil; **~ian** *adj*, *n* brasileño/a *m/f*

breach [briːtʃ] *vt* abrir brecha en ♦ *n* (*gap*) brecha; (*breaking*): **~ of contract** infracción *f* de contrato; **~ of the peace** perturbación *f* del orden público

bread [brɛd] *n* pan *m*; **~ and butter** *n* pan con mantequilla; (*fig*) pan (de cada

día); **~bin** n panera; **~crumbs** npl
migajas fpl; (CULIN) pan rallado; **~line** n:
on the ~line en la miseria
breadth [brɛdθ] n anchura; (fig) amplitud f
breadwinner ['brɛdwɪnə*] n sustento m
de la familia
break [breɪk] (pt **broke**, pp **broken**) vt
romper; (promise) faltar a; (law) violar,
infringir; (record) batir ♦ vi romperse,
quebrarse; (storm) estallar; (weather)
cambiar; (dawn) despuntar; (news etc)
darse a conocer ♦ n (gap) abertura;
(fracture) fractura; (time) intervalo; (: at
school) (período de) recreo; (chance)
oportunidad f; **to ~ the news to sb**
comunicar la noticia a uno; **~ down** vt
(figures, data) analizar, descomponer ♦ vi
(machine) estropearse; (AUT) averiarse;
(person) romper a llorar; (talks) fracasar; **~
even** vi cubrir los gastos; **~ free** or
loose vi escaparse; **~ in** vt (horse etc)
domar ♦ vi (burglar) forzar una entrada;
(interrupt) interrumpir; **~ into** vt fus
(house) forzar; **~ off** vi (speaker) pararse,
detenerse; (branch) partir; **~ open** vt
(door etc) abrir por la fuerza, forzar; **~
out** vi estallar; (prisoner) escaparse; **to ~
out in spots** salirle a uno granos; **~ up** vi
(ship) hacerse pedazos; (crowd, meeting)
disolverse; (marriage) deshacerse; (SCOL)
terminar (el curso) ♦ vt (rocks etc) partir;
(journey) partir; (fight etc) acabar con;
~age n rotura; **~down** n (AUT) avería;
(in communications) interrupción f; (MED:
also: **nervous ~down**) colapso, crisis f
nerviosa; (of marriage, talks) fracaso; (of
statistics) análisis m inv; **~down van**
(BRIT) n (camión m) grúa; **~er** n (ola)
rompiente f
breakfast ['brɛkfəst] n desayuno
break: **~-in** n robo con allanamiento de
morada; **~ing and entering** n (LAW)
violación f de domicilio, allanamiento de
morada; **~through** n (also fig) avance m;
~water n rompeolas m inv
breast [brɛst] n (of woman) pecho, seno;
(chest) pecho; (of bird) pechuga; **~-feed**

(irreg: like **feed**) vt, vi amamantar, criar a
los pechos; **~-stroke** n braza (de pecho)
breath [brɛθ] n aliento, respiración f; **to
take a deep ~** respirar hondo; **out of ~**
sin aliento, sofocado
Breathalyser ® ['brɛθəlaɪzə*] (BRIT) n
alcoholímetro m
breathe [briːð] vt, vi respirar; **~ in** vt, vi
aspirar; **~ out** vt, vi espirar; **~r** n respiro;
breathing n respiración f
breath: **~less** adj sin aliento, jadeante;
~taking adj imponente, pasmoso
breed [briːd] (pt, pp **bred**) vt criar ♦ vi
reproducirse, procrear ♦ n (ZOOL) raza,
casta; (type) tipo; **~ing** n (of person)
educación f
breeze [briːz] n brisa
breezy ['briːzɪ] adj de mucho viento,
ventoso; (person) despreocupado
brevity ['brɛvɪtɪ] n brevedad f
brew [bruː] vt (tea) hacer; (beer) elaborar
♦ vi (fig: trouble) prepararse; (storm)
amenazar; **~ery** n fábrica de cerveza,
cervecería
bribe [braɪb] n soborno ♦ vt sobornar,
cohechar; **~ry** n soborno, cohecho
bric-a-brac ['brɪkəbræk] n inv baratijas fpl
brick [brɪk] n ladrillo; **~layer** n albañil m
bridal ['braɪdl] adj nupcial
bride [braɪd] n novia; **~groom** n novio;
~smaid n dama de honor
bridge [brɪdʒ] n puente m; (NAUT) puente
m de mando; (of nose) caballete m;
(CARDS) bridge m ♦ vt (fig): **to ~ a gap**
llenar un vacío
bridle ['braɪdl] n brida, freno; **~ path** n
camino de herradura
brief [briːf] adj breve, corto ♦ n (LAW)
escrito; (task) cometido, encargo ♦ vt
informar; **~s** npl (for men) calzoncillos
mpl; (for women) bragas fpl; **~case** n
cartera (SP), portafolio (AM); **~ing** n
(PRESS) informe m; **~ly** adv (glance)
fugazmente; (say) en pocas palabras
brigadier [brɪgə'dɪə*] n general m de
brigada
bright [braɪt] adj brillante; (room)

luminoso; (*day*) de sol; (*person: clever*)
listo, inteligente; (: *lively*) alegre; (*colour*)
vivo; (*future*) prometedor(a); **~en**
(*also:* **~en up**) *vt* (*room*) hacer más alegre;
(*event*) alegrar ♦ *vi* (*weather*) despejarse;
(*person*) animarse, alegrarse; (*prospects*)
mejorar

brilliance ['brɪljəns] *n* brillo, brillantez *f*;
(*of talent etc*) brillantez

brilliant ['brɪljənt] *adj* brillante; (*inf*)
fenomenal

brim [brɪm] *n* borde *m*; (*of hat*) ala

brine [braɪn] *n* (*CULIN*) salmuera

bring [brɪŋ] (*pt, pp* **brought**) *vt* (*thing,
person: with you*) traer; (: *to sb*) llevar,
conducir; (*trouble, satisfaction*) causar; **~
about** *vt* ocasionar, producir; **~ back** *vt*
volver a traer; (*return*) devolver; **~ down**
vt (*government, plane*) derribar; (*price*)
rebajar; **~ forward** *vt* adelantar; **~ off** *vt*
(*task, plan*) lograr, conseguir; **~ out** *vt*
sacar; (*book etc*) publicar; (*meaning*)
subrayar; **~ round** *vt* (*unconscious
person*) hacer volver en sí; **~ up** *vt* subir;
(*person*) educar, criar; (*question*) sacar a
colación; (*food: vomit*) devolver, vomitar

brink [brɪŋk] *n* borde *m*

brisk [brɪsk] *adj* (*abrupt: tone*) brusco;
(*person*) enérgico, vigoroso; (*pace*) rápido;
(*trade*) activo

bristle ['brɪsl] *n* cerda ♦ *vi*: **to ~ in anger**
temblar de rabia

Britain ['brɪtən] *n* (*also:* **Great ~**) Gran
Bretaña

British ['brɪtɪʃ] *adj* británico ♦ *npl*: **the ~**
los británicos; **~ Isles** *npl*: **the ~ Isles** las
Islas Británicas; **~ Rail** *n* ≈ RENFE *f* (*SP*)

Briton ['brɪtən] *n* británico/a

brittle ['brɪtl] *adj* quebradizo, frágil

broach [brəutʃ] *vt* (*subject*) abordar

broad [brɔːd] *adj* ancho; (*range*) amplio,
(*smile*) abierto; (*general: outlines etc*)
general; (*accent*) cerrado; **in ~ daylight** en
pleno día; **~cast** (*irreg: like* **cast**) *n*
emisión *f* ♦ *vt* (*RADIO*) emitir; (*TV*)
transmitir ♦ *vi* emitir; transmitir; **~en** *vt*
ampliar ♦ *vi* ensancharse; **to ~en one's**

mind hacer más tolerante a uno; **~ly** *adv*
en general; **~-minded** *adj* tolerante,
liberal

broccoli ['brɔkəlɪ] *n* brécol *m*

brochure ['brəuʃuə*] *n* folleto

broil [brɔɪl] *vt* (*CULIN*) asar a la parrilla

broke [brəuk] *pt of* **break** ♦ *adj* (*inf*)
pelado, sin blanca

broken ['brəukən] *pp of* **break** ♦ *adj* roto;
(*machine: also:* **~ down**) averiado; **~ leg**
pierna rota; **in ~ English** en un inglés
imperfecto; **~-hearted** *adj* con el
corazón partido

broker ['brəukə*] *n* agente *m/f*, bolsista
m/f; (*insurance ~*) agente de seguros

brolly ['brɔlɪ] *n* (*BRIT: inf*) paraguas *m inv*

bronchitis [brɔŋ'kaɪtɪs] *n* bronquitis *f*

bronze [brɔnz] *n* bronce *m*

brooch [brəutʃ] *n* prendedor *m*, broche *m*

brood [bruːd] *n* camada, cría ♦ *vi* (*person*)
dejarse obsesionar

broom [brum] *n* escoba; (*BOT*) retama

Bros. *abbr* (= *Brothers*) Hnos

broth [brɔθ] *n* caldo

brothel ['brɔθl] *n* burdel *m*

brother ['brʌðə*] *n* hermano; **~-in-law** *n*
cuñado

brought [brɔːt] *pt, pp of* **bring**

brow [brau] *n* (*forehead*) frente *m*; (*eye~*)
ceja; (*of hill*) cumbre *f*

brown [braun] *adj* (*colour*) marrón; (*hair*)
castaño; (*tanned*) bronceado, moreno ♦ *n*
(*colour*) color *m* marrón o pardo ♦ *vt*
(*CULIN*) dorar; **~ bread** *n* pan integral

Brownie ['braunɪ] *n* niña exploradora; **b~**
(*US: cake*) *pastel de chocolate con nueces*

brown paper *n* papel *m* de estraza

brown sugar *n* azúcar *m* terciado

browse [brauz] *vi* (*through book*) hojear;
(*in shop*) mirar

bruise [bruːz] *n* cardenal *m* (*SP*), moretón
m (*AM*) ♦ *vt* magullar

brunch [brʌnʃ] *n* desayuno-almuerzo

brunette [bruː'net] *n* morena

brunt [brʌnt] *n*: **to bear the ~ of** llevar el
peso de

brush [brʌʃ] *n* cepillo; (*for painting,*

shaving etc) brocha; (*artist's*) pincel *m*; (*with police etc*) roce *m* ♦ *vt* (*sweep*) barrer; (*groom*) cepillar; (*also:* ~ **against**) rozar al pasar; ~ **aside** *vt* rechazar, no hacer caso a; ~ **up** *vt* (*knowledge*) repasar, refrescar; **~wood** *n* (*sticks*) leña

Brussels ['brʌslz] *n* Bruselas; ~ **sprout** *n* col *f* de Bruselas

brute [bruːt] *n* bruto; (*person*) bestia ♦ *adj*: **by ~ force** a fuerza bruta

B.Sc. *abbr* (= *Bachelor of Science*) *licenciado en Ciencias*

BSE *n abbr* (= *bovine spongiform encephalopathy*) encefalopatía espongiforme bovina

bubble ['bʌbl] *n* burbuja ♦ *vi* burbujear, borbotar; ~ **bath** *n* espuma para el baño; ~ **gum** *n* chicle *m* de globo

buck [bʌk] *n* (*rabbit*) conejo macho; (*deer*) gamo; (*US: inf*) dólar *m* ♦ *vi* corcovear; **to pass the ~ (to sb)** echar (a uno) el muerto; ~ **up** *vi* (*cheer up*) animarse, cobrar ánimo

---
Buckingham Palace

ⓘ **Buckingham Palace** *es la residencia oficial del monarca británico en Londres. El palacio se concluyó en 1703 y fue residencia del Duque de Buckingham hasta que, en 1762, pasó a manos de Jorge III. Fue reconstruido en el siglo XIX y posteriormente reformado a principios de este siglo. Una parte del palacio está actualmente abierta al público.*

---

bucket ['bʌkɪt] *n* cubo, balde *m*

buckle ['bʌkl] *n* hebilla ♦ *vt* abrochar con hebilla ♦ *vi* combarse

bud [bʌd] *n* (*of plant*) brote *m*, yema; (*of flower*) capullo ♦ *vi* brotar, echar brotes

Buddhism ['budɪzm] *n* Budismo

budding ['bʌdɪŋ] *adj* en ciernes, en embrión

buddy ['bʌdɪ] (*US*) *n* compañero, compinche *m*

budge [bʌdʒ] *vt* mover; (*fig*) hacer ceder ♦ *vi* moverse, ceder

budgerigar ['bʌdʒərɪgaː*] *n* periquito

budget ['bʌdʒɪt] *n* presupuesto ♦ *vi*: **to ~ for sth** presupuestar algo

budgie ['bʌdʒɪ] *n* = **budgerigar**

buff [bʌf] *adj* (*colour*) color de ante ♦ *n* (*inf: enthusiast*) entusiasta *m/f*

buffalo ['bʌfələu] (*pl* ~ *or* **~es**) *n* (*BRIT*) búfalo; (*US: bison*) bisonte *m*

buffer ['bʌfə*] *n* (*COMPUT*) memoria intermedia; (*RAIL*) tope *m*

buffet[1] ['bufeɪ] *n* (*BRIT: in station*) bar *m*, cafetería; (*food*) buffet *m*; ~ **car** (*BRIT*) (*RAIL*) coche-comedor *m*

buffet[2] ['bʌfɪt] *vt* golpear

bug [bʌg] *n* (*esp US: insect*) bicho, sabandija; (*COMPUT*) error *m*; (*germ*) microbio, bacilo; (*spy device*) micrófono oculto ♦ *vt* (*inf: annoy*) fastidiar; (*room*) poner micrófono oculto en

buggy ['bʌgɪ] *n* cochecito de niño

bugle ['bjuːgl] *n* corneta, clarín *m*

build [bɪld] (*pt, pp* **built**) *n* (*of person*) tipo ♦ *vt* construir, edificar; ~ **up** *vt* (*morale, forces, production*) acrecentar; (*stocks*) acumular; **~er** *n* (*contractor*) contratista *m/f*; **~ing** *n* construcción *f*; (*structure*) edificio; **~ing society** (*BRIT*) *n* sociedad *f* inmobiliaria, cooperativa de construcciones

built [bɪlt] *pt, pp of* **build** ♦ *adj*: **~-in** (*wardrobe etc*) empotrado; **~-up area** *n* zona urbanizada

bulb [bʌlb] *n* (*BOT*) bulbo; (*ELEC*) bombilla (*SP*), foco (*AM*)

Bulgaria [bʌl'gɛərɪə] *n* Bulgaria; **~n** *adj, n* búlgaro/a *m/f*

bulge [bʌldʒ] *n* bulto, protuberancia ♦ *vi* bombearse, pandearse; (*pocket etc*): **to ~ (with)** rebosar (de)

bulk [bʌlk] *n* masa, mole *f*; **in ~** (*COMM*) a granel; **the ~ of** la mayor parte de; **~y** *adj* voluminoso, abultado

bull [bul] *n* toro; (*male elephant, whale*) macho; **~dog** *n* dogo

bulldozer ['buldəuzə*] *n* bulldozer *m*

bullet ['bulɪt] *n* bala

bulletin ['bulɪtɪn] *n* anuncio, parte *m*;

(*journal*) boletín *m*

bulletproof ['bulɪtpruːf] *adj* a prueba de balas

bullfight ['bulfaɪt] *n* corrida de toros; **~er** *n* torero; **~ing** *n* los toros, el toreo

bullion ['buljən] *n* oro (*or* plata) en barras

bullock ['bulək] *n* novillo

bullring ['bulrɪŋ] *n* plaza de toros

bull's-eye *n* centro del blanco

bully ['bulɪ] *n* valentón *m*, matón *m* ♦ *vt* intimidar, tiranizar

bum [bʌm] *n* (*inf: backside*) culo; (*esp US: tramp*) vagabundo

bumblebee ['bʌmblbiː] *n* abejorro

bump [bʌmp] *n* (*blow*) tope *m*, choque *m*; (*jolt*) sacudida; (*on road etc*) bache *m*; (*on head etc*) chichón *m* ♦ *vt* (*strike*) chocar contra; **~ into** *vt fus* chocar contra, tropezar con; (*person*) topar con; **~er** *n* (AUT) parachoques *m inv* ♦ *adj*: **~er crop/harvest** cosecha abundante; **~er cars** *npl* coches *mpl* de choque; **~y** *adj* (*road*) lleno de baches

bun [bʌn] *n* (BRIT: *cake*) pastel *m*; (US: *bread*) bollo; (*of hair*) moño

bunch [bʌntʃ] *n* (*of flowers*) ramo; (*of keys*) manojo; (*of bananas*) piña; (*of people*) grupo; (*pej*) pandilla; **~es** *npl* (*in hair*) coletas *fpl*

bundle ['bʌndl] *n* bulto, fardo; (*of sticks*) haz *m*; (*of papers*) legajo ♦ *vt* (*also: ~ up*) atar, envolver; **to ~ sth/sb into** meter algo/a alguien precipitadamente en

bungalow ['bʌŋgələu] *n* bungalow *m*, chalé *m*

bungle ['bʌŋgl] *vt* hacer mal

bunion ['bʌnjən] *n* juanete *m*

bunk [bʌŋk] *n* litera; **~ beds** *npl* literas *fpl*

bunker ['bʌŋkə*] *n* (*coal store*) carbonera; (MIL) refugio; (GOLF) bunker *m*

bunny ['bʌnɪ] *n* (*also: ~ rabbit*) conejito

buoy [bɔɪ] *n* boya; **~ant** *adj* (*ship*) capaz de flotar; (*economy*) boyante; (*person*) optimista

burden ['bɜːdn] *n* carga ♦ *vt* cargar

bureau [bjuə'rəu] (*pl* **bureaux**) *n* (BRIT:

writing desk) escritorio, buró *m*; (US: *chest of drawers*) cómoda; (*office*) oficina, agencia

bureaucracy [bjuə'rɔkrəsɪ] *n* burocracia

burglar ['bɜːglə*] *n* ladrón/ona *m/f*; **~ alarm** *n* alarma *f* antirrobo; **~y** *n* robo con allanamiento, robo de una casa

burial ['berɪəl] *n* entierro

burly ['bɜːlɪ] *adj* fornido, membrudo

Burma ['bɜːmə] *n* Birmania

burn [bɜːn] (*pt, pp* **burned** *or* **burnt**) *vt* quemar; (*house*) incendiar ♦ *vi* quemarse, arder; incendiarse; (*sting*) escocer ♦ *n* quemadura; **~ down** *vt* incendiar; **~er** *n* (*on cooker etc*) quemador *m*; **~ing** *adj* (*building etc*) en llamas; (*hot: sand etc*) abrasador(a); (*ambition*) ardiente

burrow ['bʌrəu] *n* madriguera ♦ *vi* hacer una madriguera; (*rummage*) hurgar

bursary ['bɜːsərɪ] (BRIT) *n* beca

burst [bɜːst] (*pt, pp* **burst**) *vt* reventar; (*subj: river: banks etc*) romper ♦ *vi* reventarse; (*tyre*) pincharse ♦ *n* (*of gunfire*) ráfaga; (*also: ~ pipe*) reventón *m*; **a ~ of energy/speed/enthusiasm** una explosión de energía/un ímpetu de velocidad/un arranque de entusiasmo; **to ~ into flames** estallar en llamas; **to ~ into tears** deshacerse en lágrimas; **to ~ out laughing** soltar la carcajada; **to ~ open** abrirse de golpe; **to be ~ing with** (*subj: container*) estar lleno a rebosar de; (*person*) reventar por *or* de; **~ into** *vt fus* irrumpir en

bury ['berɪ] *vt* enterrar; (*body*) enterrar, sepultar

bus [bʌs] (*pl* **~es**) *n* autobús *m*

bush [buʃ] *n* arbusto; (*scrub land*) monte *m*; **to beat about the ~** andar(se) con rodeos

bushy [buʃɪ] *adj* (*thick*) espeso, poblado

busily ['bɪzɪlɪ] *adv* afanosamente

business ['bɪznɪs] *n* (*matter*) asunto; (*trading*) comercio, negocios *mpl*; (*firm*) empresa, casa; (*occupation*) oficio; **to be away on ~** estar en viaje de negocios; **it's my ~ to ...** me toca *or* corresponde ...;

it's none of my ~ yo no tengo nada que ver; **he means** ~ habla en serio; **~like** *adj* eficiente; **~man** *n* hombre *m* de negocios; **~ trip** *n* viaje *m* de negocios; **~woman** *n* mujer *f* de negocios

busker [ˈbʌskəʳ] (*BRIT*) *n* músico/a ambulante

bus: ~ **shelter** *n* parada cubierta; ~ **station** *n* estación *f* de autobuses; **~- stop** *n* parada de autobús

bust [bʌst] *n* (*ANAT*) pecho; (*sculpture*) busto ♦ *adj* (*inf: broken*) roto, estropeado; **to go** ~ quebrar

bustle [ˈbʌsl] *n* bullicio, movimiento ♦ *vi* menearse, apresurarse; **bustling** *adj* (*town*) animado, bullicioso

busy [ˈbɪzɪ] *adj* ocupado, atareado; (*shop, street*) concurrido, animado; (*TEL: line*) comunicando ♦ *vt*: **to ~ o.s. with** ocuparse en; **~body** *n* entrometido/a; ~ **signal** (*US*) *n* (*TEL*) señal *f* de comunicando

but [bʌt] *conj* **1** pero; **he's not very bright,** ~ **he's hard-working** no es muy inteligente, pero es trabajador
2 (*in direct contradiction*) sino; **he's not English** ~ **French** no es inglés sino francés; **he didn't sing** ~ **he shouted** no cantó sino que gritó
3 (*showing disagreement, surprise etc*): ~ **that's far too expensive!** ¡pero eso es carísimo!; ~ **it does work!** ¡(pero) sí que funciona!
♦ *prep* (*apart from, except*) menos, salvo; **we've had nothing** ~ **trouble** no hemos tenido más que problemas; **no-one** ~ **him can do it** nadie más que él puede hacerlo; **who** ~ **a lunatic would do such a thing?** ¿sólo un loco haría una cosa así!; ~ **for you/your help** no fue por ti/tu ayuda; **anything** ~ **that** cualquier cosa menos eso
♦ *adv* (*just, only*): **she's** ~ **a child** no es más que una niña; **had I** ~ **known** si lo hubiera sabido; **I can** ~ **try** al menos lo

puedo intentar; **it's all** ~ **finished** está casi acabado

butcher [ˈbutʃəʳ] *n* carnicero ♦ *vt* hacer una carnicería con; (*cattle etc*) matar; **~'s (shop)** *n* carnicería

butler [ˈbʌtləʳ] *n* mayordomo

butt [bʌt] *n* (*barrel*) tonel *m*; (*of gun*) culata; (*of cigarette*) colilla; (*BRIT: fig: target*) blanco ♦ *vt* dar cabezadas contra, top(et)ar; ~ **in** *vi* (*interrupt*) interrumpir

butter [ˈbʌtəʳ] *n* mantequilla ♦ *vt* untar con mantequilla; **~cup** *n* botón *m* de oro

butterfly [ˈbʌtəflaɪ] *n* mariposa; (*SWIMMING: also:* ~ **stroke**) braza de mariposa

buttocks [ˈbʌtəks] *npl* nalgas *fpl*

button [ˈbʌtn] *n* botón *m*; (*US*) placa, chapa ♦ *vt* (*also:* ~ **up**) abotonar, abrochar ♦ *vi* abrocharse

buttress [ˈbʌtrɪs] *n* contrafuerte *m*

buy [baɪ] (*pt, pp* **bought**) *vt* comprar ♦ *n* compra; **to ~ sb sth/sth from sb** comprarle algo a alguien; **to ~ sb a drink** invitar a alguien a tomar algo; **~er** *n* comprador(a) *m/f*

buzz [bʌz] *n* zumbido; (*inf: phone call*) llamada (por teléfono) ♦ *vi* zumbar; **~er** *n* timbre *m*; ~ **word** *n* palabra que está de moda

by [baɪ] *prep* **1** (*referring to cause, agent*) por; de; **killed** ~ **lightning** muerto por un relámpago; **a painting** ~ **Picasso** un cuadro de Picasso
2 (*referring to method, manner, means*): ~ **bus/car/train** en autobús/coche/tren; **to pay** ~ **cheque** pagar con un cheque; ~ **moonlight/candlelight** a la luz de la luna/una vela; ~ **saving hard, he ...** ahorrando, ...
3 (*via, through*) por; **we came** ~ **Dover** vinimos por Dover
4 (*close to, past*): **the house** ~ **the river** la casa junto al río; **she rushed** ~ **me**

pasó a mi lado como una exhalación; **I
go ~ the post office every day** paso por
delante de Correos todos los días
5 (*time: not later than*) para; (: *during*): **~
daylight** de día; **~ 4 o'clock** para las
cuatro; **~ this time tomorrow** mañana a
estas horas; **~ the time I got here it was
too late** cuando llegué ya era demasiado
tarde
6 (*amount*): **~ the metre/kilo** por metro/
kilo; **paid ~ the hour** pagado por hora
7 (MATH, *measure*): **to divide/multiply ~
3** dividir/multiplicar por 3; **a room 3
metres ~ 4** una habitación de 3 metros
por 4; **it's broader ~ a metre** es un
metro más ancho
8 (*according to*) según, de acuerdo con;
it's 3 o'clock ~ my watch según mi reloj,
son las tres; **it's all right ~ me** por mí,
está bien
9: (*all*) **~ oneself** *etc* todo solo; **he did it
(all) ~ himself** lo hizo él solo; **he was
standing (all) ~ himself in a corner**
estaba de pie solo en un rincón
10: **~ the way** a propósito, por cierto;
this wasn't my idea, ~ the way pues, no
fue idea mía
♦ *adv* **1** *see* **go**; **pass** *etc*
2: **~ and ~** finalmente; **they'll come
back ~ and ~** acabarán volviendo; **~ and
large** en líneas generales, en general

bye(-bye) ['baɪ('baɪ)] *excl* adiós, hasta
luego
by(e)-law *n* ordenanza municipal
by: **~-election** (BRIT) *n* elección *f* parcial;
~gone ['baɪgɔn] *adj* pasado, del pasado
♦ *n*: **let ~gones be ~gones** lo pasado,
pasado está; **~pass** ['baɪpɑːs] *n* carretera
de circunvalación; (MED) (operación *f* de)
by-pass *m* ♦ *vt* evitar; **~-product** *n*
subproducto, derivado; (*of situation*)
consecuencia; **~stander** ['baɪstændə*] *n*
espectador(a) *m/f*
byte [baɪt] *n* (COMPUT) byte *m*, octeto
byword ['baɪwɔːd] *n*: **to be a ~ for** ser
conocidísimo por

C, c

C [siː] *n* (MUS) do *m*
C. *abbr* (= centigrade) C.
C.A. *abbr* = chartered accountant
cab [kæb] *n* taxi *m*; (*of truck*) cabina
cabbage ['kæbɪdʒ] *n* col *f*, berza
cabin ['kæbɪn] *n* cabaña; (*on ship*)
camarote *m*; (*on plane*) cabina; **~ crew** *n*
tripulación *f* de cabina; **~ cruiser** *n* yate
m de motor
cabinet ['kæbɪnɪt] *n* (POL) consejo de
ministros; (*furniture*) armario; (*also*:
display ~) vitrina
cable ['keɪbl] *n* cable *m* ♦ *vt* cablegrafiar;
~-car *n* teleférico; **~ television** *n*
televisión *f* por cable
cache [kæʃ] *n* (*of arms, drugs etc*) alijo
cackle ['kækl] *vi* lanzar risotadas; (*hen*)
cacarear
cactus ['kæktəs] (*pl* **cacti**) cacto
cadge [kædʒ] (*inf*) *vt* gorronear
Caesarean [siːˈzɛərɪən] *adj*: **~ (section)**
cesárea
café ['kæfeɪ] *n* café *m*
cafeteria [kæfɪˈtɪərɪə] *n* cafetería
cage [keɪdʒ] *n* jaula
cagey ['keɪdʒɪ] (*inf*) *adj* cauteloso,
reservado
cagoule [kəˈguːl] *n* chubasquero
cajole [kəˈdʒəul] *vt* engatusar
cake [keɪk] *n* (CULIN: *large*) tarta; (: *small*)
pastel *m*; (*of soap*) pastilla; **~d** *adj*: **~d
with** cubierto de
calculate ['kælkjuleɪt] *vt* calcular;
calculation [-ˈleɪʃən] *n* cálculo, cómputo;
calculator *n* calculadora
calendar ['kæləndə*] *n* calendario; **~
month/year** *n* mes *m*/año civil
calf [kɑːf] (*pl* **calves**) *n* (*of cow*) ternero,
becerro; (*of other animals*) cría; (*also*:
~skin) piel *f* de becerro; (ANAT)
pantorrilla
calibre ['kælɪbə*] (US **caliber**) *n* calibre *m*
call [kɔːl] *vt* llamar; (*meeting*) convocar

♦ *vi* (*shout*) llamar; (*TEL*) llamar (por teléfono), telefonear (*esp AM*); (*visit: also:* ~ **in,** ~ **round**) hacer una visita ♦ *n* llamada; **on** ~ (*nurse, doctor etc*) de guardia; ~ **back** *vi* (*return*) volver; (*TEL*) volver a llamar; ~ **for** *vt fus* (*demand*) pedir, exigir; (*fetch*) venir por (*SP*), pasar por (*AM*); ~ **off** *vt* (*cancel: meeting, race*) cancelar; (: *deal*) anular; (: *strike*) desconvocar; ~ **on** *vt fus* (*visit*) visitar; (*turn to*) acudir a; ~ **out** *vi* gritar, dar voces; ~ **up** *vt* (*MIL*) llamar al servicio militar; (*TEL*) llamar; **~box** (*BRIT*) *n* cabina telefónica; **~er** *n* visita; (*TEL*) usuario/a; ~ **girl** *n* prostituta; **~-in** (*US*) *n* (programa *m*) coloquio (por teléfono); **~ing** *n* vocación *f*; (*occupation*) profesión *f*; **~ing card** (*US*) *n* tarjeta comercial *or* de visita

callous [ˈkæləs] *adj* insensible, cruel

calm [kɑːm] *adj* tranquilo; (*sea*) liso, en calma ♦ *n* calma, tranquilidad *f* ♦ *vt* calmar, tranquilizar; ~ **down** *vi* calmarse, tranquilizarse ♦ *vt* calmar, tranquilizar

Calor gas ® [ˈkælə*-*] *n* butano

calorie [ˈkælərɪ] *n* caloría

calves [kɑːvz] *npl of* **calf**

Cambodia [kæmˈbəʊdjə] *n* Camboya

camcorder [ˈkæmkɔːdə*] *n* videocámara

came [keɪm] *pt of* **come**

camel [ˈkæməl] *n* camello

camera [ˈkæmərə] *n* máquina fotográfica; (*CINEMA, TV*) cámara; **in** ~ (*LAW*) a puerta cerrada; **~man** *n* cámara *m*

camouflage [ˈkæməflɑːʒ] *n* camuflaje *m* ♦ *vt* camuflar

camp [kæmp] *n* campamento, camping *m*; (*MIL*) campamento; (*for prisoners*) campo; (*fig: faction*) bando ♦ *vi* acampar ♦ *adj* afectado, afeminado

campaign [kæmˈpeɪn] *n* (*MIL, POL etc*) campaña ♦ *vi* hacer campaña

camp: **~bed** (*BRIT*) *n* cama de campaña; **~er** *n* campista *m/f*; (*vehicle*) caravana; **~ing** *n* camping *m*; **to go ~ing** hacer camping; **~site** *n* camping *m*

campus [ˈkæmpəs] *n* ciudad *f* universitaria

can[1] [kæn] *n* (*of oil, water*) bidón *m*; (*tin*) lata, bote *m* ♦ *vt* enlatar

---
KEYWORD
---

can[2] [kæn] (*negative* **cannot, can't**; *conditional and pt* **could**) *aux vb* **1** (*be able to*) poder; **you ~ do it if you try** puedes hacerlo si lo intentas; **I ~'t see you** no te veo

2 (*know how to*) saber; **I ~ swim/play tennis/drive** sé nadar/jugar al tenis/conducir; ~ **you speak French?** ¿hablas *or* sabes hablar francés?

3 (*may*) poder; ~ **I use your phone?** ¿me dejas *or* puedo usar tu teléfono?

4 (*expressing disbelief, puzzlement etc*): **it ~'t be true!** ¡no puede ser (verdad)!; **what** *CAN* **he want?** ¿qué querrá?

5 (*expressing possibility, suggestion etc*): **he could be in the library** podría estar en la biblioteca; **she could have been delayed** pudo haberse retrasado

---

Canada [ˈkænədə] *n* (el) Canadá; **Canadian** [kəˈneɪdɪən] *adj, n* canadiense *m/f*

canal [kəˈnæl] *n* canal *m*

canary [kəˈneərɪ] *n* canario; **the C~ Islands** *npl* las (Islas) Canarias

cancel [ˈkænsəl] *vt* cancelar; (*train*) suprimir; (*cross out*) tachar, borrar; **~lation** [-ˈleɪʃən] *n* cancelación *f*; supresión *f*

cancer [ˈkænsə*] *n* cáncer *m*; **C~** (*ASTROLOGY*) Cáncer *m*

candid [ˈkændɪd] *adj* franco, abierto

candidate [ˈkændɪdeɪt] *n* candidato/a

candle [ˈkændl] *n* vela; (*in church*) cirio; **~light** *n*: **by ~light** a la luz de una vela; **~stick** *n* (*single*) candelero; (*low*) palmatoria; (*bigger, ornate*) candelabro

candour [ˈkændə*] (*US* **candor**) *n* franqueza

candy [ˈkændɪ] *n* azúcar *m* cande; (*US*) caramelo; **~floss** (*BRIT*) *n* algodón *m* (azucarado)

cane [keɪn] *n* (*BOT*) caña; (*stick*) vara,

palmeta; (for furniture) mimbre f ♦ (BRIT)
vt (SCOL) castigar (con vara)

canister ['kænɪstə*] n bote m, lata; (of gas) bombona

cannabis ['kænəbɪs] n marijuana

canned [kænd] adj en lata, de lata

cannon ['kænən] (pl ~ or ~s) n cañón m

cannot ['kænɔt] = **can not**

canoe [kə'nu:] n canoa; (SPORT) piragua;
~**ing** n piragüismo

canon ['kænən] n (clergyman) canónigo;
(standard) canon m

can-opener n abrelatas m inv

canopy ['kænəpɪ] n dosel m; toldo

can't [kænt] = **can not**

canteen [kæn'ti:n] n (eating place)
cantina; (BRIT: of cutlery) juego

canter ['kæntə*] vi ir a medio galope

canvas ['kænvəs] n (material) lona;
(painting) lienzo; (NAUT) velas fpl

canvass ['kænvəs] vi (POL): **to ~ for**
solicitar votos por ♦ vt (COMM) sondear

canyon ['kænjən] n cañón m

cap [kæp] n (hat) gorra; (of pen) capuchón
m; (of bottle) tapa, tapón m;
(contraceptive) diafragma m; (for toy gun)
cápsula ♦ vt (outdo) superar; (limit)
recortar

capability [keɪpə'bɪlɪtɪ] n capacidad f

capable ['keɪpəbl] adj capaz

capacity [kə'pæsɪtɪ] n capacidad f;
(position) calidad f

cape [keɪp] n capa; (GEO) cabo

caper ['keɪpə*] n (CULIN: gen: ~s)
alcaparra; (prank) broma

capital ['kæpɪtl] n (also: ~ **city**) capital f;
(money) capital m; (also: ~ **letter**)
mayúscula; ~ **gains tax** n impuesto
sobre las ganancias de capital; ~**ism** n
capitalismo; ~**ist** adj, n capitalista m/f;
~**ize on** vt fus aprovechar; ~
punishment n pena de muerte

Capitol

ⓘ El **Capitolio** (**Capitol**) es el edificio del
Congreso (**Congress**) de los Estados
Unidos, situado en la ciudad de

Washington. Por extensión, también se
suele llamar así al edificio en el que tienen
lugar las sesiones parlamentarias de la
cámara de representantes de muchos de los
estados.

Capricorn ['kæprɪkɔːn] n (ASTROLOGY)
Capricornio

capsize [kæp'saɪz] vt volcar, hacer
zozobrar ♦ vi volcarse, zozobrar

capsule ['kæpsjuːl] n cápsula

captain ['kæptɪn] n capitán m

caption ['kæpʃən] n (heading) título; (to
picture) leyenda

captive ['kæptɪv] adj, n cautivo/a m/f

capture ['kæptʃə*] vt prender, apresar;
(animal, COMPUT) capturar; (place) tomar;
(attention) captar, llamar ♦ n
apresamiento; captura; toma; (data ~)
formulación f de datos

car [kɑː*] n coche m, carro (AM), automóvil
m; (US: RAIL) vagón m

carafe [kə'ræf] n jarra

carat ['kærət] n quilate m

caravan ['kærəvæn] n (BRIT) caravana, ruló
f; (in desert) caravana; ~**ning** n: **to go**
~**ning** ir de vacaciones en caravana, viajar
en caravana; ~ **site** (BRIT) n camping m
para caravanas

carbohydrate [kɑːbəu'haɪdreɪt] n hidrato
de carbono; (food) fécula

carbon ['kɑːbən] n carbono; ~ **paper** n
papel m carbón

car boot sale n mercadillo organizado
en un aparcamiento, en el que se exponen
las mercancías en el maletero del coche

carburettor [kɑːbju'retə*] (US **carburetor**)
n carburador m

card [kɑːd] n (material) cartulina; (index ~
etc) ficha; (playing ~) carta, naipe m;
(visiting ~, greetings ~ etc) tarjeta;
~**board** n cartón m

cardiac ['kɑːdɪæk] adj cardíaco

cardigan ['kɑːdɪgən] n rebeca

cardinal ['kɑːdɪnl] adj cardinal;
(importance, principal) esencial ♦ n
cardenal m

card index n fichero
care [keə*] n cuidado; (worry) inquietud f; (charge) cargo, custodia ♦ vi: **to ~ about** (person, animal) tener cariño a; (thing, idea) preocuparse por; **~ of** en casa de, al cuidado de; **in sb's ~** a cargo de uno; **to take ~** de cuidarse de, tener cuidado de; **to take ~ of** cuidar; (problem etc) ocuparse de; **I don't ~** no me importa; **I couldn't ~ less** eso me trae sin cuidado; **~ for** vt fus cuidar a; (like) querer
career [kə'rɪə*] n profesión f; (in work, school) carrera ♦ vi (also: **~ along**) correr a toda velocidad; **~ woman** n mujer f dedicada a su profesión
care: ~free adj despreocupado; **~ful** adj cuidadoso; (cautious) cauteloso; **(be) ~ful!** ¡tenga cuidado!; **~fully** adv con cuidado, cuidadosamente; con cautela; **~less** adj descuidado; (heedless) poco atento; **~lessness** n descuido; falta de atención; **~r** ['keərə*] n enfermero/a m/f (official); (unpaid) persona que cuida a un pariente o vecino
caress [kə'res] n caricia ♦ vt acariciar
caretaker ['keəteɪkə*] n portero/a, conserje m/f
car-ferry n transbordador m para coches
cargo ['kɑ:gəʊ] (pl **~es**) n cargamento, carga
car hire n alquiler m de automóviles
Caribbean [kærɪ'bi:ən] n: **the ~ (Sea)** el (Mar) Caribe
caring ['keərɪŋ] adj humanitario; (behaviour) afectuoso
carnation [kɑ:'neɪʃən] n clavel m
carnival ['kɑ:nɪvəl] n carnaval m; (US: funfair) parque m de atracciones
carol ['kærəl] n: **(Christmas) ~** villancico
carp [kɑ:p] n (fish) carpa
car park (BRIT) n aparcamiento, parking m
carpenter ['kɑ:pɪntə*] n carpintero/a
carpet ['kɑ:pɪt] n alfombra; (fitted) moqueta ♦ vt alfombrar
car phone n teléfono movil
car rental (US) n alquiler m de coches

carriage ['kærɪdʒ] n (BRIT: RAIL) vagón m; (horse-drawn) coche m; (of goods) transporte m; (: cost) porte m, flete m; **~way** (BRIT) n (part of road) calzada
carrier ['kærɪə*] n (transport company) transportista, empresa de transportes; (MED) portador m; **~ bag** (BRIT) n bolsa de papel or plástico
carrot ['kærət] n zanahoria
carry ['kærɪ] vt (subj: person) llevar; (transport) transportar; (involve: responsibilities etc) entrañar, implicar; (MED) ser portador de ♦ vi (sound) oírse; **to get carried away** (fig) entusiasmarse; **~ on** vi (continue) seguir (adelante), continuar ♦ vt proseguir, continuar; **~ out** vt (orders) cumplir; (investigation) llevar a cabo, realizar; **~ cot** (BRIT) n cuna portátil; **~-on** (inf) n (fuss) lío
cart [kɑ:t] n carro, carreta ♦ vt (inf: transport) acarrear
carton ['kɑ:tən] n (box) caja (de cartón); (of milk etc) bote m; (of yogurt) tarrina
cartoon [kɑ:'tu:n] n (PRESS) caricatura; (comic strip) tira cómica; (film) dibujos mpl animados
cartridge ['kɑ:trɪdʒ] n cartucho; (of pen) recambio; (of record player) cápsula
carve [kɑ:v] vt (meat) trinchar; (wood, stone) cincelar, esculpir; (initials etc) grabar; **~ up** vt dividir, repartir; **carving** n (object) escultura; (design) talla; (art) tallado; **carving knife** n trinchante m
car wash n lavado de coches
case [keɪs] n (container) caja; (MED) caso; (for jewels etc) estuche m; (LAW) causa, proceso; (BRIT: also: **suit~**) maleta; **in ~ of** en caso de; **in any ~** en todo caso; **just in ~** por si acaso
cash [kæʃ] n dinero en efectivo, dinero contante ♦ vt cobrar, hacer efectivo; **to pay (in) ~** pagar al contado; **~ on delivery** cóbrese al entregar; **~book** n libro de caja; **~ card** n tarjeta f dinero; **~ desk** (BRIT) n caja; **~ dispenser** n cajero automático
cashew [kæ'ʃu:] n (also: **~ nut**) anacardo

cash flow n flujo de fondos, cash-flow m

cashier [kæ'ʃɪə*] n cajero/a

cashmere ['kæʃmɪə*] n cachemira

cash register n caja

casing ['keɪsɪŋ] n revestimiento

casino [kə'siːnəʊ] n casino

casket ['kɑːskɪt] n cofre m, estuche m; (US: coffin) ataúd m

casserole ['kæsərəʊl] n (food, pot) cazuela

cassette [kæ'set] n cassette f; ~ player/recorder n tocacassettes m inv, cassette m

cast [kɑːst] (pt, pp cast) vt (throw) echar, arrojar, lanzar; (glance, eyes) dirigir; (THEATRE): to ~ sb as Othello dar a uno el papel de Otelo ♦ vi (FISHING) lanzar ♦ n (THEATRE) reparto; (also: plaster~) vaciado; to ~ one's vote votar; to ~ doubt on suscitar dudas acerca de; ~ off vi (NAUT) desamarrar; (KNITTING) cerrar (los puntos); ~ on vi (KNITTING) poner los puntos

castanets [kæstə'nets] npl castañuelas fpl

castaway ['kɑːstəweɪ] n náufrago/a

caster sugar ['kɑːstə*-] (BRIT) n azúcar m extrafino

Castile [kæs'tiːl] n Castilla; **Castilian** adj, n castellano/a m/f

casting vote ['kɑːstɪŋ-] (BRIT) n voto decisivo

cast iron n hierro fundido

castle ['kɑːsl] n castillo; (CHESS) torre f

castor oil ['kɑːstə*-] n aceite m de ricino

casual ['kæʒjul] adj fortuito; (irregular: work etc) eventual, temporero; (unconcerned) despreocupado; (clothes) de sport; ~ly adv de manera despreocupada; (dress) de sport

casualty ['kæʒjultɪ] n víctima, herido; (dead) muerto; (MED: department) urgencias fpl

cat [kæt] n gato; (big ~) felino

Catalan ['kætəlæn] adj, n catalán/ana m/f

catalogue ['kætəlɒg] (US **catalog**) n catálogo ♦ vt catalogar

Catalonia [kætə'ləʊnɪə] n Cataluña

catalyst ['kætəlɪst] n catalizador m

catalytic convertor [kætə'lɪtɪk kən'vɜːtə*]

n catalizador m

catapult ['kætəpʌlt] n tirachinas m inv

catarrh [kə'tɑː*] n catarro

catastrophe [kə'tæstrəfɪ] n catástrofe f

catch [kætʃ] (pt, pp **caught**) vt coger (SP), agarrar (AM); (arrest) detener; (grasp) asir; (breath) contener; (surprise: person) sorprender; (attract: attention) captar; (hear) oír; (MED) contagiarse de, coger; (also: ~ up) alcanzar ♦ vi (fire) encenderse; (in branches etc) enredarse ♦ n (fish etc) pesca; (act of catching) cogida; (hidden problem) dificultad f; (game) pilla-pilla; (of lock) pestillo, cerradura; to ~ fire encenderse; to ~ sight of divisar; ~ on vi (understand) caer en la cuenta; (grow popular) hacerse popular; ~ up vi (fig) ponerse al día; ~ing ['kætʃɪŋ] adj (MED) contagioso; ~ment area ['kætʃmənt-] (BRIT) n zona de captación; ~phrase ['kætʃfreɪz] n lema m, eslogan m; ~y ['kætʃɪ] adj (tune) pegadizo

category ['kætɪgərɪ] n categoría, clase f

cater ['keɪtə*] vi: to ~ for (BRIT) abastecer a; (needs) atender a; (COMM: parties etc) proveer comida a; ~er n abastecedor(a) m/f, proveedor(a) m/f; ~ing n (trade) hostelería

caterpillar ['kætəpɪlə*] n oruga, gusano

cathedral [kə'θiːdrəl] n catedral f

catholic ['kæθəlɪk] adj (tastes etc) amplio; C~ adj, n (REL) católico/a m/f

CAT scan [kæt-] n TAC f, tomografía

Catseye ® ['kæts'aɪ] (BRIT) n (AUT) catafoto

cattle ['kætl] npl ganado

catty ['kætɪ] adj malicioso, rencoroso

caucus ['kɔːkəs] n (POL) camarilla política; (: US: to elect candidates) comité m electoral

caught [kɔːt] pt, pp of **catch**

cauliflower ['kɒlɪflaʊə*] n coliflor f

cause [kɔːz] n causa, motivo, razón f; (principle: also: POL) causa ♦ vt causar

caution ['kɔːʃən] n cautela, prudencia; (warning) advertencia, amonestación f

♦ vt amonestar; **cautious** adj cauteloso, prudente, precavido

cavalry ['kævəlrı] n caballería

cave [keɪv] n cueva, caverna; ~ **in** vi (roof etc) derrumbarse, hundirse

caviar(e) ['kævɪɑ:ˈ] n caviar m

CB n abbr (= Citizens' Band (Radio)) banda ciudadana

CBI n abbr (= Confederation of British Industry) ≈ C.E.O.E. f (SP)

cc abbr = **cubic centimetres**; = **carbon copy**

CD n abbr (= compact disc) DC m; (player) (reproductor m de) disco compacto; ~ **player** n lector m de compact disc, reproductor m de compact disc; ~-**ROM** [si:di:ˈrɔm] n abbr CD-ROM m

cease [si:s] vt, vi cesar; ~**fire** n alto m el fuego; ~**less** adj incesante

cedar ['si:dəˈ] n cedro

ceiling ['si:lɪŋ] n techo; (fig) límite m

celebrate ['sɛlɪbreɪt] vt celebrar ♦ vi divertirse; ~**d** adj célebre; **celebration** [-'breɪʃən] n fiesta, celebración f

celery ['sɛlərɪ] n apio

cell [sɛl] n celda; (BIOL) célula; (ELEC) elemento

cellar ['sɛləˈ] n sótano; (for wine) bodega

cello ['tʃɛləʊ] n violoncelo

Cellophane ® ['sɛləfeɪn] n celofán m

cellphone ['sɛlfəʊn] n teléfono celular

Celt [kɛlt, sɛlt] adj, n celta m/f; ~**ic** adj celta

cement [sə'mɛnt] n cemento; ~ **mixer** n hormigonera

cemetery ['sɛmɪtrɪ] n cementerio

censor ['sɛnsəˈ] n censor m ♦ vt (cut) censurar; ~**ship** n censura

censure ['sɛnʃəˈ] vt censurar

census ['sɛnsəs] n censo

cent [sɛnt] n (US) (coin) centavo, céntimo; see also **per**

centenary [sɛn'ti:nərɪ] n centenario

center ['sɛntəˈ] n (US) = **centre**

centi... [sɛntɪ] prefix: ~**grade** adj centígrado; ~**litre** (US ~**liter**) n centilitro; ~**metre** (US ~**meter**) n centímetro

centipede ['sɛntɪpi:d] n ciempiés m inv

central ['sɛntrəl] adj central; (of house etc) céntrico; **C~ America** n Centroamérica; ~ **heating** n calefacción f central; ~**ize** vt centralizar

centre ['sɛntəˈ] (US **center**) n centro; (fig) núcleo ♦ vt centrar; ~-**forward** n (SPORT) delantero centro; ~-**half** n (SPORT) medio centro

century ['sɛntjurɪ] n siglo; **20th** ~ siglo veinte

ceramic [sɪ'ræmɪk] adj cerámico; ~**s** n cerámica

cereal ['si:rɪəl] n cereal m

ceremony ['sɛrɪmənɪ] n ceremonia; **to stand on** ~ hacer ceremonias, estar de cumplido

certain ['sɜ:tən] adj seguro; (person): **a** ~ **Mr Smith** un tal Sr Smith; (particular, some) cierto; **for** ~ a ciencia cierta; ~**ly** adv (undoubtedly) ciertamente; (of course) desde luego, por supuesto; ~**ty** n certeza, certidumbre f, seguridad f; (inevitability) certeza

certificate [sə'tɪfɪkɪt] n certificado

certified ['sɜ:tɪfaɪd]: ~ **mail** (US) n correo certificado; ~ **public accountant** (US) n contable m/f diplomado/a

certify ['sɜ:tɪfaɪ] vt certificar; (award diploma to) conceder un diploma a; (declare insane) declarar loco

cervical ['sɜ:vɪkl] adj cervical

cervix ['sɜ:vɪks] n cuello del útero

cf. abbr (= compare) cfr

CFC n abbr (= chlorofluorocarbon) CFC m

ch. abbr (= chapter) cap

chain [tʃeɪn] n cadena; (of mountains) cordillera; (of events) sucesión f ♦ vt (also: ~ **up**) encadenar; ~ **reaction** n reacción f en cadena; ~-**smoke** vi fumar un cigarrillo tras otro; ~ **store** n tienda de una cadena, ≈ gran almacén

chair [tʃɛəˈ] n silla; (armchair) sillón m, butaca; (of university) cátedra; (of meeting etc) presidencia ♦ vt (meeting) presidir; ~**lift** n telesilla; ~**man** n presidente m

chalk [tʃɔ:k] n (GEO) creta; (for writing) tiza

(SP), gis *m* *(AM)*

challenge ['tʃælɪndʒ] *n* desafío, reto ♦ *vt* desafiar, retar; *(statement, right)* poner en duda; **to ~ sb to do sth** retar a uno a que haga algo; **challenging** *adj* exigente; *(tone)* de desafío

chamber ['tʃeɪmbə*] *n* cámara, sala; *(POL)* cámara; *(BRIT: LAW: gen pl)* despacho; **~ of commerce** cámara de comercio; **~maid** *n* camarera; **~ music** *n* música de cámara

chamois ['ʃæmwɑː] *n* gamuza

champagne [ʃæm'peɪn] *n* champaña *m*, champán *m*

champion ['tʃæmpɪən] *n* campeón/ona *m/f*; *(of cause)* defensor(a) *m/f*; **~ship** *n* campeonato

chance [tʃɑːns] *n* *(opportunity)* ocasión *f*, oportunidad *f*; *(likelihood)* posibilidad *f*; *(risk)* riesgo *m* ♦ *vt* arriesgar, probar ♦ *adj* fortuito, casual; **to ~ it** arriesgarse, intentarlo; **to take a ~** arriesgarse; **by ~** por casualidad

chancellor ['tʃɑːnsələ*] *n* canciller *m*; **C~ of the Exchequer** *(BRIT)* *n* Ministro de Hacienda

chandelier [ʃændə'lɪə*] *n* araña (de luces)

change [tʃeɪndʒ] *vt* cambiar; *(replace)* cambiar, reemplazar; *(gear, clothes, job)* cambiar de; *(transform)* transformar ♦ *vi* cambiar(se); *(trains)* hacer transbordo; *(traffic lights)* cambiar de color; *(be transformed)*: **to ~ into** transformarse en ♦ *n* cambio; *(alteration)* modificación *f*, transformación *f*; *(of clothes)* muda *f*; *(coins)* suelto, sencillo; *(money returned)* vuelta; **to ~ gear** *(AUT)* cambiar de marcha; **to ~ one's mind** cambiar de opinión *or* idea; **for a ~** para variar; **~able** *adj* *(weather)* cambiable; **~ machine** *n* máquina de cambio; **changing** *adj* cambiante; **changing room** *(BRIT)* *n* vestuario

channel ['tʃænl] *n* *(TV)* canal *m*; *(of river)* cauce *m*; *(groove)* conducto *m*; *(fig: medium)* medio ♦ *vt* *(river etc)* encauzar; **the**

(English) C~ el Canal (de la Mancha); **the C~ Islands** las Islas Normandas; **the C~ Tunnel** el túnel del Canal de la Mancha, el Eurotúnel; **~-hopping** *n* *(TV)* zapping *m*

chant [tʃɑːnt] *n* *(of crowd)* gritos *mpl*; *(REL)* canto ♦ *vt* *(slogan, word)* repetir a gritos

chaos ['keɪɔs] *n* caos *m*

chap [tʃæp] *(BRIT: inf)* *n* *(man)* tío, tipo

chapel ['tʃæpəl] *n* capilla

chaperone ['ʃæpərəʊn] *n* carabina

chaplain ['tʃæplɪn] *n* capellán *m*

chapped [tʃæpt] *adj* agrietado

chapter ['tʃæptə*] *n* capítulo

char [tʃɑː*] *vt* *(burn)* carbonizar, chamuscar

character ['kærɪktə*] *n* carácter *m*, naturaleza, índole *f*; *(moral strength, personality)* carácter; *(in novel, film)* personaje *m*; **~istic** [-'rɪstɪk] *adj* característico ♦ *n* característica

charcoal ['tʃɑːkəʊl] *n* carbón *m* vegetal; *(ART)* carboncillo

charge [tʃɑːdʒ] *n* *(LAW)* cargo, acusación *f*; *(cost)* precio, coste *m*; *(responsibility)* cargo ♦ *vt* *(LAW)*: **to ~ (with)** acusar (de); *(battery)* cargar; *(price)* pedir; *(customer)* cobrar ♦ *vi* precipitarse; *(MIL)* cargar, atacar; **~s** *npl*: **to reverse the ~s** *(BRIT: TEL)* revertir el cobro; **to take ~ of** hacerse cargo de, encargarse de; **to be in ~ of** estar encargado de; *(business)* mandar; **how much do you ~?** ¿cuánto cobra usted?; **to ~ an expense (up) to sb's account** cargar algo a cuenta de alguien; **~ card** *n* tarjeta de cuenta

charity ['tʃærɪtɪ] *n* caridad *f*; *(organization)* sociedad *f* benéfica; *(money, gifts)* limosnas *fpl*

charm [tʃɑːm] *n* encanto, atractivo; *(talisman)* hechizo; *(on bracelet)* dije *m* ♦ *vt* encantar; **~ing** *adj* encantador(a)

chart [tʃɑːt] *n* *(diagram)* cuadro, gráfica; *(map)* carta de navegación ♦ *vt* *(course)* trazar; *(progress)* seguir; **~s** *npl* *(Top 40)*: **the ~s** ≈ los 40 principales *(SP)*

charter ['tʃɑːtə*] *vt* *(plane)* alquilar; *(ship)* fletar ♦ *n* *(document)* carta; *(of university,*

company) estatutos *mpl*; ~ed
accountant (*BRIT*) *n* contable *m/f*
diplomado/a; ~ **flight** *n* vuelo chárter
chase [tʃeɪs] *vt* (*pursue*) perseguir; (*also:* ~
away) ahuyentar ♦ *n* persecución *f*
chasm ['kæzəm] *n* sima
chassis ['ʃæsɪ] *n* chasis *m*
chat [tʃæt] *vi* (*also:* **have a ~**) charlar ♦ *n*
charla; ~ **show** (*BRIT*) *n* programa *m* de
entrevistas
chatter ['tʃætə⁎] *vi* (*person*) charlar; (*teeth*)
castañetear ♦ *n* (*of birds*) parloteo; (*of
people*) charla, cháchara; ~**box** (*inf*) *n*
parlanchín/ina *m/f*
chatty ['tʃætɪ] *adj* (*style*) informal; (*person*)
hablador(a)
chauffeur ['ʃəʊfə⁎] *n* chófer *m*
chauvinist ['ʃəʊvɪnɪst] *n* (*male* ~) machista
m; (*nationalist*) chovinista *m/f*
cheap [tʃiːp] *adj* barato; (*joke*) de mal
gusto; (*poor quality*) de mala calidad
♦ *adv* barato; ~ **day return** *n* billete *m*
de ida y vuelta el mismo día; ~**er** *adj*
más barato; ~**ly** *adv* barato, a bajo
precio
cheat [tʃiːt] *vi* hacer trampa ♦ *vt*: **to ~ sb
(out of sth)** estafar (algo) a uno ♦ *n*
(*person*) tramposo/a
check [tʃek] *vt* (*examine*) controlar; (*facts*)
comprobar; (*halt*) parar, detener;
(*restrain*) refrenar, restringir ♦ *n*
(*inspection*) control *m*, inspección *f*; (*curb*)
freno; (*US: bill*) nota, cuenta; (*US*)
= **cheque**; (*pattern: gen pl*) cuadro ♦ *adj*
(*also:* ~**ed**: *pattern, cloth*) a cuadros; ~ **in**
vi (*at hotel*) firmar el registro; (*at airport*)
facturar el equipaje ♦ *vt* (*luggage*)
facturar; ~ **out** *vi* (*of hotel*) marcharse; ~
up *vi*: **to ~ up on sth** comprobar algo; **to
~ up on sb** investigar a alguien; ~**ered**
(*US*) *adj* = **check**; **chequered**; ~**ers** (*US*)
n juego de damas; ~**-in** (**desk**) *n*
mostrador *m* de facturación; ~**ing
account** (*US*) *n* cuenta corriente; ~**mate**
n jaque *m* mate; ~**out** *n* caja; ~**point** *n*
(punto de) control *m*; ~**room** (*US*) *n*
consigna; ~**up** *n* (*MED*) reconocimiento

general
cheek [tʃiːk] *n* mejilla; (*impudence*)
descaro; **what a ~!** ¡qué cara!; ~**bone** *n*
pómulo; ~**y** *adj* fresco, descarado
cheep [tʃiːp] *vi* piar
cheer [tʃɪə⁎] *vt* vitorear, aplaudir; (*gladden*)
alegrar, animar ♦ *vi* dar vivas ♦ *n* viva *m*;
~**s** *npl* aplausos *mpl*; ~**s!** ¡salud!; ~ **up**
vi animarse ♦ *vt* alegrar, animar; ~**ful** *adj*
alegre
cheerio [tʃɪərɪˈəʊ] (*BRIT*) *excl* ¡hasta luego!
cheese [tʃiːz] *n* queso; ~**board** *n* tabla
de quesos
cheetah ['tʃiːtə] *n* leopardo cazador
chef [ʃef] *n* jefe/a *m/f* de cocina
chemical ['kemɪkəl] *adj* químico ♦ *n*
producto químico
chemist ['kemɪst] *n* (*BRIT: pharmacist*)
farmacéutico/a; (*scientist*) químico/a; ~**ry**
n química; ~**'s (shop)** (*BRIT*) *n* farmacia
cheque [tʃek] (*US* **check**) *n* cheque *m*;
~**book** *n* talonario de cheques (*SP*),
chequera (*AM*); ~ **card** *n* tarjeta de
cheque
chequered ['tʃekəd] (*US* **checkered**) *adj*
(*fig*) accidentado
cherish ['tʃerɪʃ] *vt* (*love*) querer, apreciar;
(*protect*) cuidar; (*hope etc*) abrigar
cherry ['tʃerɪ] *n* cereza; (*also:* ~ **tree**)
cerezo
chess [tʃes] *n* ajedrez *m*; ~**board** *n*
tablero (de ajedrez)
chest [tʃest] *n* (*ANAT*) pecho; (*box*) cofre
m, cajón *m*; ~ **of drawers** *n* cómoda
chestnut ['tʃesnʌt] *n* castaña; ~ **(tree)** *n*
castaño
chew [tʃuː] *vt* mascar, masticar; ~**ing
gum** *n* chicle *m*
chic [ʃiːk] *adj* elegante
chick [tʃɪk] *n* pollito, polluelo; (*inf: girl*)
chica
chicken ['tʃɪkɪn] *n* gallina, pollo; (*food*)
pollo; (*inf: coward*) gallina *m/f*; ~ **out**
(*inf*) *vi* rajarse; ~**pox** *n* varicela
chicory ['tʃɪkərɪ] *n* (*for coffee*) achicoria;
(*salad*) escarola
chief [tʃiːf] *n* jefe/a *m/f* ♦ *adj* principal; ~

executive *n* director(a) *m/f* general; **~ly** *adv* principalmente

chilblain ['tʃɪlbleɪn] *n* sabañón *m*

child [tʃaɪld] (*pl* **children**) *n* niño/a; (*offspring*) hijo/a; **~birth** *n* parto; **~hood** *n* niñez *f*, infancia; **~ish** *adj* pueril, aniñado; **~like** *adj* de niño; **~ minder** (*BRIT*) *n* madre *f* de día; **~ren** ['tʃɪldrən] *npl of* **child**

Chile ['tʃɪlɪ] *n* Chile *m*; **~an** *adj*, *n* chileno/a *m/f*

chill [tʃɪl] *n* frío; (*MED*) resfriado ♦ *vt* enfriar; (*CULIN*) congelar

chil(l)i ['tʃɪlɪ] (*BRIT*) *n* chile *m* (*SP*), ají *m* (*AM*)

chilly ['tʃɪlɪ] *adj* frío

chime [tʃaɪm] *n* repique *m*; (*of clock*) campanada ♦ *vi* repicar; sonar

chimney ['tʃɪmnɪ] *n* chimenea; **~ sweep** *n* deshollinador *m*

chimpanzee [tʃɪmpæn'ziː] *n* chimpancé *m*

chin [tʃɪn] *n* mentón *m*, barbilla

china ['tʃaɪnə] *n* porcelana; (*crockery*) loza

China ['tʃaɪnə] *n* China; **Chinese** [tʃaɪ'niːz] *adj* chino ♦ *n inv* chino/a; (*LING*) chino

chink [tʃɪŋk] *n* (*opening*) grieta, hendedura; (*noise*) tintineo

chip [tʃɪp] *n* (*gen pl*: *CULIN*: *BRIT*) patata (*SP*) *or* papa (*AM*) frita; (: *US*: *also*: **potato ~**) patata *or* papa frita; (*of wood*) astilla; (*of glass, stone*) lasca; (*at poker*) ficha; (*COMPUT*) chip *m* ♦ *vt* (*cup, plate*) desconchar

---

chip shop

i Se denomina **chip shop** o "*fish-and-chip shop*" a un establecimiento en el que se sirven algunas especialidades de comida rápida, muy populares entre los británicos, sobre todo pescado rebozado y patatas fritas.

---

chiropodist [kɪ'rɔpədɪst] (*BRIT*) *n* pedicuro/a, callista *m/f*

chirp [tʃəːp] *vi* (*bird*) gorjear, piar

chisel ['tʃɪzl] *n* (*for wood*) escoplo; (*for stone*) cincel *m*

chit [tʃɪt] *n* nota

chitchat ['tʃɪttʃæt] *n* chismes *mpl*, habladurías *fpl*

chivalry ['tʃɪvəlrɪ] *n* caballerosidad *f*

chives [tʃaɪvz] *npl* cebollinos *mpl*

chlorine ['klɔːriːn] *n* cloro

chock-a-block ['tʃɔkə'blɔk] *adj* atestado

chock-full ['tʃɔk'ful] *adj* atestado

chocolate ['tʃɔklɪt] *n* chocolate *m*; (*sweet*) bombón *m*

choice [tʃɔɪs] *n* elección *f*, selección *f*; (*option*) opción *f*; (*preference*) preferencia ♦ *adj* escogido

choir ['kwaɪə*] *n* coro; **~boy** *n* niño de coro

choke [tʃəuk] *vi* ahogarse; (*on food*) atragantarse ♦ *vt* estrangular, ahogar; (*block*): **to be ~d with** estar atascado de ♦ *n* (*AUT*) estárter *m*

cholesterol [kə'lestərɔl] *n* colesterol *m*

choose [tʃuːz] (*pt* **chose**, *pp* **chosen**) *vt* escoger, elegir; (*team*) seleccionar; **to ~ to do sth** optar por hacer algo

choosy ['tʃuːzɪ] *adj* delicado

chop [tʃɔp] *vt* (*wood*) cortar, tajar; (*CULIN*: *also*: **~ up**) picar ♦ *n* (*CULIN*) chuleta; **~s** *npl* (*jaws*) boca, labios *mpl*

chopper ['tʃɔpə*] *n* (*helicopter*) helicóptero

choppy ['tʃɔpɪ] *adj* (*sea*) picado, agitado

chopsticks ['tʃɔpstɪks] *npl* palillos *mpl*

chord [kɔːd] *n* (*MUS*) acorde *m*

chore [tʃɔː*] *n* faena, tarea; (*routine task*) trabajo rutinario

chorus ['kɔːrəs] *n* coro; (*repeated part of song*) estribillo

chose [tʃəuz] *pt of* **choose**

chosen ['tʃəuzn] *pp of* **choose**

chowder ['tʃaudə*] *n* (*esp US*) sopa de pescado

Christ [kraɪst] *n* Cristo

christen ['krɪsn] *vt* bautizar

Christian ['krɪstɪən] *adj, n* cristiano/a *m/f*; **~ity** [-'ænɪtɪ] *n* cristianismo; **~ name** *n* nombre *m* de pila

Christmas ['krɪsməs] *n* Navidad *f*; **Merry ~!** ¡Felices Pascuas!; **~ card** *n* crismas *m inv*, tarjeta de Navidad; **~ Day** *n* día *m*

de Navidad; **~ Eve** *n* Nochebuena; **~
tree** *n* árbol *m* de Navidad
chrome [krəum] *n* cromo
chronic ['krɒnɪk] *adj* crónico
chronological [krɒnə'lɒdʒɪkəl] *adj*
cronológico
chubby ['tʃʌbɪ] *adj* regordete
chuck [tʃʌk] (*inf*) *vt* lanzar, arrojar; (*BRIT*:
also: **~ up**) abandonar; **~ out** *vt* (*person*)
echar (fuera); (*rubbish etc*) tirar
chuckle ['tʃʌkl] *vi* reírse entre dientes
chug [tʃʌg] *vi* resoplar; (*car, boat: also*: **~
along**) avanzar traqueteando
chum [tʃʌm] *n* compañero/a
chunk [tʃʌŋk] *n* pedazo, trozo
church [tʃəːtʃ] *n* iglesia; **~yard** *n*
cementerio
churn [tʃəːn] *n* (*for butter*) mantequera;
(*for milk*) lechera; **~ out** *vt* producir en
serie
chute [ʃuːt] *n* (*also*: **rubbish ~**) vertedero;
(*for coal etc*) rampa de caída
chutney ['tʃʌtnɪ] *n* condimento a base de
frutas de la India
CIA (*US*) *n abbr* (= *Central Intelligence
Agency*) CIA *f*
CID (*BRIT*) *n abbr* (= *Criminal Investigation
Department*) ≈ B.I.C. *f* (*SP*)
cider ['saɪdə*] *n* sidra
cigar [sɪ'gɑː*] *n* puro
cigarette [sɪgə'rɛt] *n* cigarrillo (*SP*), cigarro
(*AM*); pitillo; **~ case** *n* pitillera; **~ end** *n*
colilla
Cinderella [sɪndə'rɛlə] *n* Cenicienta
cinders ['sɪndəz] *npl* cenizas *fpl*
cine camera ['sɪnɪ-] (*BRIT*) *n* cámara
cinematográfica
cinema ['sɪnəmə] *n* cine *m*
cinnamon ['sɪnəmən] *n* canela
circle ['səːkl] *n* círculo; (*in theatre*)
anfiteatro ♦ *vi* dar vueltas ♦ *vt* (*surround*)
rodear, cercar; (*move round*) dar la vuelta
a
circuit ['səːkɪt] *n* circuito; (*tour*) gira;
(*track*) pista; (*lap*) vuelta; **~ous**
[səː'kjuːtəs] *adj* indirecto
circular ['səːkjulə*] *adj* circular ♦ *n* circular

f
circulate ['səːkjuleɪt] *vi* circular; (*person: at
party etc*) hablar con los invitados ♦ *vt*
poner en circulación; **circulation**
[-'leɪʃən] *n* circulación *f*; (*of newspaper*)
tirada
circumstances ['səːkəmstənsɪz] *npl*
circunstancias *fpl*; (*financial condition*)
situación *f* económica
circus ['səːkəs] *n* circo
CIS *n abbr* (= *Commonwealth of
Independent States*) CEI *f*
cistern ['sɪstən] *n* tanque *m*, depósito; (*in
toilet*) cisterna
citizen ['sɪtɪzn] *n* (*POL*) ciudadano/a; (*of
city*) vecino/a, habitante *m/f*; **~ship** *n*
ciudadanía
citrus fruits ['sɪtrəs-] *npl* agrios *mpl*
city ['sɪtɪ] *n* ciudad *f*; **the C~** *centro
financiero de Londres*
civic ['sɪvɪk] *adj* cívico; (*authorities*)
municipal; **~ centre** (*BRIT*) *n* centro
público
civil ['sɪvɪl] *adj* civil; (*polite*) atento, cortés;
~ engineer *n* ingeniero de caminos(,
canales y puertos); **~ian** [sɪ'vɪlɪən] *adj* civil
(*no militar*) ♦ *n* civil *m/f*, paisano/a
civilization [sɪvɪlaɪ'zeɪʃən] *n* civilización *f*
civilized ['sɪvɪlaɪzd] *adj* civilizado
civil: ~ law *n* derecho civil; **~ servant** *n*
funcionario/a del Estado; **C~ Service** *n*
administración *f* pública; **~ war** *n* guerra
civil
claim [kleɪm] *vt* exigir, reclamar; (*rights
etc*) reivindicar; (*assert*) pretender ♦ *vi* (*for
insurance*) reclamar ♦ *n* reclamación *f*;
pretensión *f*; **~ant** *n* demandante *m/f*
clairvoyant [kleə'vɔɪənt] *n* clarividente *m/f*
clam [klæm] *n* almeja
clamber ['klæmbə*] *vi* trepar
clammy ['klæmɪ] *adj* frío y húmedo
clamour ['klæmə*] (*US* **clamor**) *vi*: **to ~ for**
clamar por, pedir a voces
clamp [klæmp] *n* abrazadera, grapa ♦ *vt*
(*2 things together*) cerrar fuertemente;
(*one thing on another*) afianzar (con
abrazadera); (*AUT: wheel*) poner el cepo a;

~ **down on** vt fus (subj: government, police) reforzar la lucha contra

clang [klæŋ] vi sonar, hacer estruendo

clap [klæp] vi aplaudir; ~**ping** n aplausos mpl

claret ['klærət] n burdeos m inv

clarify ['klærɪfaɪ] vt aclarar

clarinet [klærɪ'net] n clarinete m

clash [klæʃ] n enfrentamiento; choque m; desacuerdo; estruendo ♦ vi (fight) enfrentarse; (beliefs) chocar; (disagree) estar en desacuerdo; (colours) desentonar; (two events) coincidir

clasp [klɑːsp] n (hold) apretón m; (of necklace, bag) cierre m ♦ vt apretar; abrazar

class [klɑːs] n clase f ♦ vt clasificar

classic ['klæsɪk] adj, n clásico; ~**al** adj clásico

classified ['klæsɪfaɪd] adj (information) reservado; ~ **advertisement** n anuncio por palabras

classmate ['klɑːsmeɪt] n compañero/a de clase

classroom ['klɑːsrum] n aula

clatter ['klætə*] n estrépito ♦ vi hacer ruido or estrépito

clause [klɔːz] n cláusula; (LING) oración f

claw [klɔː] n (of cat) uña; (of bird of prey) garra; (of lobster) pinza

clay [kleɪ] n arcilla

clean [kliːn] adj limpio; (record, reputation) bueno, intachable; (joke) decente ♦ vt limpiar; (hands etc) lavar; ~ **out** vt limpiar; ~ **up** vt limpiar, asear; ~**-cut** adj (person) bien parecido; ~**er** n (person) asistenta; (substance) producto para la limpieza; ~**er's** n tintorería; ~**ing** n limpieza; ~**liness** ['klenlɪnɪs] n limpieza

cleanse [klenz] vt limpiar; ~**r** n (for face) crema limpiadora

clean-shaven adj sin barba, afeitado

cleansing department (BRIT) n departamento de limpieza

clear [klɪə*] adj claro; (road, way) libre; (conscience) limpio, tranquilo; (skin) terso; (sky) despejado ♦ vt (space) despejar,

limpiar; (LAW: suspect) absolver; (obstacle) salvar, saltar por encima de; (cheque) aceptar ♦ vi (fog etc) despejarse ♦ adv: ~ **of** a distancia de; **to ~ the table** recoger or levantar la mesa; ~ **up** vt limpiar; (mystery) aclarar, resolver; ~**ance** n (removal) despeje m; (permission) acreditación f; ~**-cut** adj bien definido, nítido; ~**ing** n (in wood) claro; ~**ing bank** (BRIT) n cámara de compensación; ~**ly** adv claramente; (evidently) sin duda; ~**way** (BRIT) n carretera donde no se puede parar

clef [klef] n (MUS) clave f

cleft [kleft] n (in rock) grieta, hendedura

clench [klentʃ] vt apretar, cerrar

clergy ['klɜːdʒɪ] n clero; ~**man** n clérigo

clerical ['klerɪkəl] adj de oficina; (REL) clerical

clerk [klɑːk, (US) klɜːrk] n (BRIT) oficinista m/f; (US) dependiente/a m/f, vendedor(a) m/f

clever ['klevə*] adj (intelligent) inteligente, listo; (skilful) hábil; (device, arrangement) ingenioso

click [klɪk] vt (tongue) chasquear; (heels) taconear

client ['klaɪənt] n cliente m/f

cliff [klɪf] n acantilado

climate ['klaɪmɪt] n clima m

climax ['klaɪmæks] n (of battle, career) apogeo; (of film, book) punto culminante; (sexual) orgasmo

climb [klaɪm] vi subir; (plant) trepar; (move with effort): **to ~ over a wall/into a car** trepar a una tapia/subir a un coche ♦ vt (stairs) subir; (tree) trepar a; (mountain) escalar ♦ n subida; ~**-down** n vuelta atrás; ~**er** n alpinista m/f, (SP), andinista m/f (AM); ~**ing** n alpinismo (SP), andinismo (AM)

clinch [klɪntʃ] vt (deal) cerrar; (argument) remachar

cling [klɪŋ] (pt, pp **clung**) vi: **to ~ to** agarrarse a; (clothes) pegarse a

clinic ['klɪnɪk] n clínica; ~**al** adj clínico; (fig) frío

clink [klɪŋk] vi tintinar

clip [klɪp] n (for hair) horquilla; (also: **paper ~**) sujetapapeles m inv, clip m; (TV, CINEMA) fragmento ♦ vt (cut) cortar; (also: **~ together**) unir; **~pers** npl (for gardening) tijeras fpl; **~ping** n (newspaper) recorte m

clique [kliːk] n camarilla

cloak [kləuk] n capa, manto ♦ vt (fig) encubrir, disimular; **~room** n guardarropa; (BRIT: WC) lavabo (SP), aseos mpl (SP), baño (AM)

clock [klɔk] n reloj m; **~ in** or **on** vi fichar, picar; **~ off** or **out** vi fichar or picar la salida; **~wise** adv en el sentido de las agujas del reloj; **~work** n aparato de relojería ♦ adj (toy) de cuerda

clog [klɔg] n zueco, chanclo ♦ vt atascar ♦ vi (also: **~ up**) atascarse

cloister [ˈklɔɪstə*] n claustro

close¹ [kləus] adj (near): **~ (to)** cerca (de); (friend) íntimo; (connection) estrecho; (examination) detallado, minucioso; (weather) bochornoso; **to have a ~ shave** (fig) escaparse por un pelo ♦ adv cerca; **~ by, ~ at hand** muy cerca; **~ to** prep cerca de

close² [kləuz] vt (shut) cerrar; (end) concluir, terminar ♦ vi (shop etc) cerrarse; (end) concluirse, terminarse ♦ n (end) fin m, final m, conclusión f; **~ down** vi cerrarse definitivamente; **~d** adj (shop etc) cerrado; **~d shop** n taller m gremial

close-knit [kləusˈnɪt] adj (fig) muy unido

closely [ˈkləuslɪ] adv (study) con detalle; (watch) de cerca; (resemble) estrechamente

closet [ˈklɔzɪt] n armario

close-up [ˈkləusʌp] n primer plano

closure [ˈkləuʒə*] n cierre m

clot [klɔt] n (gen: **blood ~**) coágulo; (inf: idiot) imbécil m/f ♦ vi (blood) coagularse

cloth [klɔθ] n (material) tela, paño; (rag) trapo

clothe [kləuð] vt vestir; **~s** npl ropa; **~s brush** n cepillo (para la ropa); **~s line** n cuerda (para tender la ropa); **~s peg** (US

~s pin) n pinza

clothing [ˈkləuðɪŋ] n = **clothes**

cloud [klaud] n nube f; **~burst** n aguacero; **~y** adj nublado, nuboso; (liquid) turbio

clout [klaut] vt dar un tortazo a

clove [kləuv] n clavo; **~ of garlic** diente m de ajo

clover [ˈkləuvə*] n trébol m

clown [klaun] n payaso ♦ vi (also: **~ about, ~ around**) hacer el payaso

cloying [ˈklɔɪɪŋ] adj empalagoso

club [klʌb] n (society) club m; (weapon) porra, cachiporra; (also: **golf ~**) palo ♦ vt aporrear ♦ vi: **to ~ together** (for gift) comprar entre todos; **~s** npl (CARDS) tréboles mpl; **~ class** n (AVIAT) clase f preferente; **~house** n local social, sobre todo en clubs deportivos

cluck [klʌk] vi cloquear

clue [kluː] n pista; (in crosswords) indicación f; **I haven't a ~** no tengo ni idea

clump [klʌmp] n (of trees) grupo

clumsy [ˈklʌmzɪ] adj (person) torpe, desmañado; (tool) difícil de manejar; (movement) desgarbado

clung [klʌŋ] pt, pp of **cling**

cluster [ˈklʌstə*] n grupo ♦ vi agruparse, apiñarse

clutch [klʌtʃ] n (AUT) embrague m; (grasp): **~es** garras fpl ♦ vt asir; agarrar

clutter [ˈklʌtə*] vt atestar

cm abbr (= centimetre) cm

CND n abbr (= Campaign for Nuclear Disarmament) plataforma pro desarme nuclear

Co. abbr = **county; company**

c/o abbr (= care of) c/a, a/c

coach [kəutʃ] n autocar m (SP), coche m de línea; (horse-drawn) coche m; (of train) vagón m, coche m; (SPORT) entrenador(a) m/f, instructor(a) m/f; (tutor) profesor(a) m/f particular ♦ vt (SPORT) entrenar; (student) preparar, enseñar; **~ trip** n excursión f en autocar

coal [kəul] n carbón m; **~ face** n frente m

de carbón; **~field** n yacimiento de carbón

coalition [kəuə'lɪʃən] n coalición f

coalman ['kəulmən] (irreg) n carbonero

coalmine ['kəulmaɪn] n mina de carbón

coarse [kɔːs] adj basto, burdo; (vulgar) grosero, ordinario

coast [kəust] n costa, litoral m ♦ vi (AUT) ir en punto muerto; **~al** adj costero, costanero; **~guard** n guardacostas m inv; **~line** n litoral m

coat [kəut] n abrigo; (of animal) pelaje m, lana; (of paint) mano f, capa ♦ vt cubrir, revestir; **~ of arms** n escudo de armas; **~ hanger** n percha (SP), gancho (AM); **~ing** n capa, baño

coax [kəuks] vt engatusar

cobbler ['kɔblə] n zapatero (remendón)

cobbles ['kɔblz] npl, **cobblestones** ['kɔblstəunz] npl adoquines mpl

cobweb ['kɔbweb] n telaraña

cocaine [kə'keɪn] n cocaína

cock [kɔk] n (rooster) gallo; (male bird) macho ♦ vt (gun) amartillar; **~erel** n gallito

cockle ['kɔkl] n berberecho

cockney ['kɔknɪ] n habitante de ciertos barrios de Londres

cockpit ['kɔkpɪt] n cabina

cockroach ['kɔkrəutʃ] n cucaracha

cocktail ['kɔkteɪl] n coctel m, cóctel m; **~ cabinet** n mueble-bar m; **~ party** n coctel m, cóctel m

cocoa ['kəukəu] n cacao; (drink) chocolate m

coconut ['kəukənʌt] n coco

cod [kɔd] n bacalao

C.O.D. abbr (= cash on delivery) C.A.E.

code [kəud] n código; (cipher) clave f; (dialling ~) prefijo; (post ~) código postal

cod-liver oil ['kɔdlɪvər-] n aceite m de hígado de bacalao

coercion [kəu'əːʃən] n coacción f

coffee ['kɔfɪ] n café m; **~ bar** n (BRIT) cafetería; **~ bean** n grano de café; **~ break** n descanso (para tomar café); **~pot** n cafetera; **~ table** n mesita (para

servir el café)

coffin ['kɔfɪn] n ataúd m

cog [kɔg] n (wheel) rueda dentada; (tooth) diente m

cogent ['kəudʒənt] adj convincente

cognac ['kɔnjæk] n coñac m

coil [kɔɪl] n rollo; (ELEC) bobina, carrete m; (contraceptive) espiral f ♦ vt enrollar

coin [kɔɪn] n moneda ♦ vt (word) inventar, idear; **~age** n moneda; **~-box** n (BRIT) n cabina telefónica

coincide [kəuɪn'saɪd] vi coincidir; (agree) estar de acuerdo; **coincidence** [kəu'ɪnsɪdəns] n casualidad f

Coke ® [kəuk] n Coca-Cola ®

coke [kəuk] n (coal) coque m

colander ['kɔləndə*] n colador m, escurridor m

cold [kəuld] adj frío ♦ n frío; (MED) resfriado; **it's ~** hace frío; **to be ~** (person) tener frío; **to catch ~** enfriarse; **to catch a ~** resfriarse, acatarrarse; **in ~ blood** a sangre fría; **~-shoulder** vt dar or volver la espalda a; **~ sore** n herpes mpl or fpl

coleslaw ['kəulslɔː] n especie de ensalada de col

colic ['kɔlɪk] n cólico

collapse [kə'læps] vi hundirse, derrumbarse; (MED) sufrir un colapso ♦ n hundimiento, derrumbamiento; (MED) colapso; **collapsible** adj plegable

collar ['kɔlə*] n (of coat, shirt) cuello; (of dog etc) collar; **~bone** n clavícula

collateral [kɔ'lætərəl] n garantía colateral

colleague ['kɔliːg] n colega m/f; (at work) compañero, a

collect [kə'lekt] vt (litter, mail etc) recoger; (as a hobby) coleccionar; (BRIT: call and pick up) recoger; (debts, subscriptions etc) recaudar ♦ vi reunirse; (dust) acumularse; **to call ~** (US: TEL) llamar a cobro revertido; **~ion** [kə'lekʃən] n colección f; (of mail, for charity) recogida; **~or** n coleccionista m/f

college ['kɔlɪdʒ] n colegio mayor; (of agriculture, technology) escuela universitaria

collide [kə'laɪd] *vi* chocar

colliery ['kɒlɪərɪ] (*BRIT*) *n* mina de carbón

collision [kə'lɪʒən] *n* choque *m*

colloquial [kə'ləʊkwɪəl] *adj* familiar, coloquial

Colombia [kə'lɒmbɪə] *n* Colombia; **~n** *adj, n* colombiano/a

colon ['kəʊlən] *n* (*sign*) dos puntos; (*MED*) colon *m*

colonel ['kɜːnl] *n* coronel *m*

colonial [kə'ləʊnɪəl] *adj* colonial

colony ['kɒlənɪ] *n* colonia

colour ['kʌlə*] (*US* **color**) *n* color *m* ♦ *vt* color(e)ar; (*dye*) teñir; (*fig: account*) adornar; (: *judgement*) distorsionar ♦ *vi* (*blush*) sonrojarse; **~s** *npl* (*of party, club*) colores *mpl*; **in ~** en color; **~ in** *vt* colorear; **~ bar** *n* segregación *f* racial; **~-blind** *adj* daltónico; **~ed** *adj* de color; (*photo*) en color; **~ film** *n* película en color; **~ful** *adj* lleno de color; (*story*) fantástico; (*person*) excéntrico; **~ing** *n* (*complexion*) tez *f*; (*in food*) colorante *m*; **~ scheme** *n* combinación *f* de colores; **~ television** *n* televisión *f* en color

colt [kəʊlt] *n* potro

column ['kɒləm] *n* columna; **~ist** ['kɒləmnɪst] *n* columnista *m/f*

coma ['kəʊmə] *n* coma *m*

comb [kəʊm] *n* peine *m*; (*ornamental*) peineta ♦ *vt* (*hair*) peinar; (*area*) registrar a fondo

combat ['kɒmbæt] *n* combate *m* ♦ *vt* combatir

combination [kɒmbɪ'neɪʃən] *n* combinación *f*

combine [*vb* kəm'baɪn, *n* 'kɒmbaɪn] *vt* combinar; (*qualities*) reunir ♦ *vi* combinarse ♦ *n* (*ECON*) cartel *m*; **~ (harvester)** *n* cosechadora

---

KEYWORD

come [kʌm] (*pt* **came**, *pp* **come**) *vi* **1** (*movement towards*) venir; **to ~ running** venir corriendo

2 (*arrive*) llegar; **he's ~ here to work** ha venido aquí para trabajar; **to ~ home**

volver a casa

3 (*reach*): **to ~ to** llegar a; **the bill came to £40** la cuenta ascendía a cuarenta libras

4 (*occur*): **an idea came to me** se me ocurrió una idea

5 (*be, become*): **to ~ loose/undone** *etc* aflojarse/desabrocharse, desatarse *etc*; **I've ~ to like him** por fin ha llegado a gustarme

come about *vi* suceder, ocurrir

come across *vt fus* (*person*) topar con; (*thing*) dar con

come away *vi* (*leave*) marcharse; (*become detached*) desprenderse

come back *vi* (*return*) volver

come by *vt fus* (*acquire*) conseguir

come down *vi* (*price*) bajar; (*tree, building*) ser derribado

come forward *vi* presentarse

come from *vt fus* (*place, source*) ser de

come in *vi* (*visitor*) entrar; (*train, report*) llegar; (*fashion*) ponerse de moda; (*on deal etc*) entrar

come in for *vt fus* (*criticism etc*) recibir

come into *vt fus* (*money*) heredar; (*be involved*) tener que ver con; **to ~ into fashion** ponerse de moda

come off *vi* (*button*) soltarse, desprenderse; (*attempt*) salir bien

come on *vi* (*pupil*) progresar; (*work, project*) desarrollarse; (*lights*) encenderse; (*electricity*) volver; **~ on!** ¡vamos!

come out *vi* (*fact*) salir a la luz; (*book, sun*) salir; (*stain*) quitarse

come round *vi* (*after faint, operation*) volver en sí

come to *vi* (*wake*) volver en sí

come up *vi* (*sun*) salir; (*problem*) surgir; (*event*) aproximarse; (*in conversation*) mencionarse

come up against *vt fus* (*resistance etc*) tropezar con

come up with *vt fus* (*idea*) sugerir; (*money*) conseguir

come upon *vt fus* (*find*) dar con

comeback ['kʌmbæk] *n*: **to make a ~**
(*THEATRE*) volver a las tablas
comedian [kə'miːdiən] *n* cómico;
comedienne [-'ɛn] *n* cómica
comedy ['kɒmɪdɪ] *n* comedia; (*humour*)
comicidad *f*
comet ['kɒmɪt] *n* cometa *m*
comeuppance [kʌm'ʌpəns] *n*: **to get
one's ~** llevar su merecido
comfort ['kʌmfət] *n* bienestar *m*; (*relief*)
alivio ♦ *vt* consolar; **~s** *npl* (*of home etc*)
comodidades *fpl*; **~able** *adj* cómodo;
(*financially*) acomodado; (*easy*) fácil;
~ably *adv* (*sit*) cómodamente; (*live*)
holgadamente; **~ station** (*US*) *n* servicios
mpl
comic ['kɒmɪk] *adj* (*also*: **~al**) cómico ♦ *n*
(*comedian*) cómico; (*BRIT: for children*)
tebeo; (*BRIT: for adults*) comic *m*; **~ strip**
n tira cómica
coming ['kʌmɪŋ] *n* venida, llegada ♦ *adj*
que viene; **~(s) and going(s)** *n(pl)* ir y
venir *m*, ajetreo
comma ['kɒmə] *n* coma
command [kə'mɑːnd] *n* orden *f*,
mandato; (*MIL: authority*) mando;
(*mastery*) dominio ♦ *vt* (*troops*) mandar;
(*give orders to*): **to ~ sb to do** mandar *or*
ordenar a uno hacer; **~eer** [kɒmən'dɪə*] *vt*
requisar; **~er** *n* (*MIL*) comandante *m/f*,
jefe/a *m/f*
commemorate [kə'mɛmərеɪt] *vt*
conmemorar
commence [kə'mɛns] *vt, vi* comenzar,
empezar
commend [kə'mɛnd] *vt* elogiar, alabar;
(*recommend*) recomendar
commensurate [kə'mɛnʃərɪt] *adj*: **~ with**
en proporción a, que corresponde a
comment ['kɒmɛnt] *n* comentario ♦ *vi*: **to
~ on** hacer comentarios sobre; **"no ~"**
(*written*) "sin comentarios"; (*spoken*) "no
tengo nada que decir"; **~ary** ['kɒməntəri]
n comentario; **~ator** ['kɒmənteɪtə*] *n*
comentarista *m/f*
commerce ['kɒmɜːs] *n* comercio
commercial [kə'mɜːʃəl] *adj* comercial ♦ *n*

(*TV, RADIO*) anuncio
commiserate [kə'mɪzərеɪt] *vi*: **to ~ with**
compadecerse de, condolerse de
commission [kə'mɪʃən] *n* (*committee, fee*)
comisión *f* ♦ *vt* (*work of art*) encargar;
out of ~ fuera de servicio; **~aire**
[kəmɪʃə'neə*] (*BRIT*) *n* portero; **~er** *n*
(*POLICE*) comisario de policía
commit [kə'mɪt] *vt* (*act*) cometer;
(*resources*) dedicar; (*to sb's care*) entregar;
to ~ o.s. (to do) comprometerse (a
hacer); **to ~ suicide** suicidarse; **~ment** *n*
compromiso; (*to ideology etc*) entrega
committee [kə'mɪtɪ] *n* comité *m*
commodity [kə'mɒdɪtɪ] *n* mercancía
common ['kɒmən] *adj* común; (*pej*)
ordinario ♦ *n* campo común; **the C~s** *npl*
(*BRIT*) (la Cámara de) los Comunes *mpl*;
in ~ en común; **~er** *n* plebeyo; **~ law** *n*
ley *f* consuetudinaria; **~ly** *adv*
comúnmente; **C~ Market** *n* Mercado
Común; **~place** *adj* de lo más común;
~room *n* sala común; **~ sense** *n*
sentido común; **the C~wealth** *n* la
Commonwealth
commotion [kə'məuʃən] *n* tumulto,
confusión *f*
commune [*n* 'kɒmjuːn, *vb* kə'mjuːn] *n*
(*group*) comuna ♦ *vi*: **to ~ with** comulgar
or conversar con
communicate [kə'mjuːnɪkeɪt] *vt*
comunicar ♦ *vi*: **to ~ (with)** comunicarse
(con); (*in writing*) estar en contacto (con)
communication [kəmjuːnɪ'keɪʃən] *n*
comunicación *f*; **~ cord** (*BRIT*) *n* timbre
m de alarma
communion [kə'mjuːnɪən] *n* (*also*: **Holy
C~**) comunión *f*
communiqué [kə'mjuːnɪkeɪ] *n*
comunicado, parte *f*
communism ['kɒmjunɪzəm] *n*
comunismo; **communist** *adj, n*
comunista *m/f*
community [kə'mjuːnɪtɪ] *n* comunidad *f*;
(*large group*) colectividad *f*; **~ centre** *n*
centro social; **~ chest** (*US*) *n* arca
comunitaria, fondo común

commutation ticket [kɔmjuˈteɪʃən-] (*US*) *n* billete *m* de abono

commute [kəˈmjuːt] *vi* viajar a diario de la casa al trabajo ♦ *vt* conmutar; **~r** *n* persona (que viaja ... *see vi*)

compact [*adj* kəmˈpækt, *n* ˈkɔmpækt] *adj* compacto ♦ *vt* (*also:* **powder ~**) polvera; **~ disc** *n* compact disc *m*; **~ disc player** *n* reproductor *m* de disco compacto, compact disc *m*

companion [kəmˈpænɪən] *n* compañero/a; **~ship** *n* compañerismo

company [ˈkʌmpənɪ] *n* compañía; (*COMM*) sociedad *f*, compañía; **to keep sb ~** acompañar a uno; **~ secretary** (*BRIT*) *n* secretario/a de compañía

comparative [kəmˈpærətɪv] *adj* relativo; (*study*) comparativo; **~ly** *adv* (*relatively*) relativamente

compare [kəmˈpɛə*] *vt*: **to ~ sth/sb with/to** comparar algo/a uno con ♦ *vi*: **to ~ (with)** comparase (con); **comparison** [-ˈpærɪsn] *n* comparación *f*

compartment [kəmˈpɑːtmənt] *n* (*also:* RAIL) compartim(i)ento

compass [ˈkʌmpəs] *n* brújula; **~es** *npl* (*MATH*) compás *m*

compassion [kəmˈpæʃən] *n* compasión *f*; **~ate** *adj* compasivo

compatible [kəmˈpætɪbl] *adj* compatible

compel [kəmˈpɛl] *vt* obligar

compensate [ˈkɔmpənseɪt] *vt* compensar ♦ *vi*: **to ~ for** compensar; **compensation** [-ˈseɪʃən] *n* (*for loss*) indemnización *f*

compère [ˈkɔmpɛə*] *n* presentador *m*

compete [kəmˈpiːt] *vi* (*take part*) tomar parte, concurrir; (*vie with*): **to ~ with** competir con, hacer competencia a

competent [ˈkɔmpɪtənt] *adj* competente, capaz

competition [kɔmpɪˈtɪʃən] *n* (*contest*) concurso; (*rivalry*) competencia

competitive [kəmˈpɛtɪtɪv] *adj* (*ECON*, *SPORT*) competitivo

competitor [kəmˈpɛtɪtə*] *n* (*rival*) competidor(a) *m/f*; (*participant*)

concursante *m/f*

complacency [kəmˈpleɪsnsɪ] *n* autosatisfacción *f*

complacent [kəmˈpleɪsənt] *adj* autocomplaciente

complain [kəmˈpleɪn] *vi* quejarse; (*COMM*) reclamar; **~t** *n* queja; reclamación *f*; (*MED*) enfermedad *f*

complement [*n* ˈkɔmplɪmənt, *vb* ˈkɔmplɪment] *n* complemento; (*esp of ship's crew*) dotación *f* ♦ *vt* (*enhance*) complementar; **~ary** [kɔmplɪˈmentərɪ] *adj* complementario

complete [kəmˈpliːt] *adj* (*full*) completo; (*finished*) acabado ♦ *vt* (*fulfil*) completar; (*finish*) acabar; (*a form*) llenar; **~ly** *adv* completamente; **completion** [-ˈpliːʃən] *n* terminación *f*; (*of contract*) realización *f*

complex [ˈkɔmpleks] *adj*, *n* complejo

complexion [kəmˈplekʃən] *n* (*of face*) tez *f*, cutis *m*

compliance [kəmˈplaɪəns] *n* (*submission*) sumisión *f*; (*agreement*) conformidad *f*; **in ~ with** de acuerdo con

complicate [ˈkɔmplɪkeɪt] *vt* complicar; **~d** *adj* complicado; **complication** [-ˈkeɪʃən] *n* complicación *f*

compliment [ˈkɔmplɪmənt] *n* (*formal*) cumplido ♦ *vt* felicitar; **~s** *npl* (*regards*) saludos *mpl*; **to pay sb a ~** hacer cumplidos a uno; **~ary** [-ˈmentərɪ] *adj* lisonjero; (*free*) de favor

comply [kəmˈplaɪ] *vi*: **to ~ with** cumplir con

component [kəmˈpəunənt] *adj* componente ♦ *n* (*TECH*) pieza

compose [kəmˈpəuz] *vt*: **to be ~d of** componerse de; (*music etc*) componer; **to ~ o.s.** tranquilizarse; **~d** *adj* sosegado; **~r** *n* (*MUS*) compositor(a) *m/f*; **composition** [kɔmpəˈzɪʃən] *n* composición *f*

compost [ˈkɔmpɔst] *n* abono (vegetal)

composure [kəmˈpəuʒə*] *n* serenidad *f*, calma

compound [ˈkɔmpaund] *n* (*CHEM*) compuesto; (*LING*) palabra compuesta;

(*enclosure*) recinto ♦ *adj* compuesto; (*fracture*) complicado

comprehend [kɔmprɪˈhɛnd] *vt* comprender; **comprehension** [-ˈhɛnʃən] *n* comprensión *f*

comprehensive [kɔmprɪˈhɛnsɪv] *adj* exhaustivo; (*INSURANCE*) contra todo riesgo; **~ (school)** *n* centro estatal de enseñanza secundaria; ≈ Instituto Nacional de Bachillerato (*SP*)

compress [*vb* kəmˈprɛs, *n* ˈkɔmprɛs] *vt* comprimir; (*information*) condensar ♦ *n* (*MED*) compresa

comprise [kəmˈpraɪz] *vt* (*also:* **be ~d of**) comprender, constar de; (*constitute*) constituir

compromise [ˈkɔmprəmaɪz] *n* (*agreement*) arreglo ♦ *vt* comprometer ♦ *vi* transigir

compulsion [kəmˈpʌlʃən] *n* compulsión *f*; (*force*) obligación *f*

compulsive [kəmˈpʌlsɪv] *adj* compulsivo; (*viewing, reading*) obligado

compulsory [kəmˈpʌlsərɪ] *adj* obligatorio

computer [kəmˈpjuːtə*] *n* ordenador *m*, computador *m*, computadora; **~ game** *n* juego para ordenador; **~-generated** *adj* realizado por ordenador, creado por ordenador; **~ize** *vt* (*data*) computerizar; (*system*) informatizar; **~ programmer** *n* programador(a) *m/f*; **~ programming** *n* programación *f*; **~ science** *n* informática; **computing** [kəmˈpjuːtɪŋ] *n* (*activity, science*) informática

comrade [ˈkɔmrɪd] *n* (*POL, MIL*) camarada; (*friend*) compañero/a; **~ship** *n* camaradería, compañerismo

con [kɔn] *vt* (*deceive*) engañar; (*cheat*) estafar ♦ *n* estafa

conceal [kənˈsiːl] *vt* ocultar

conceit [kənˈsiːt] *n* presunción *f*; **~ed** *adj* presumido

conceive [kənˈsiːv] *vt, vi* concebir

concentrate [ˈkɔnsəntreɪt] *vi* concentrarse ♦ *vt* concentrar

concentration [kɔnsənˈtreɪʃən] *n* concentración *f*

concept [ˈkɔnsɛpt] *n* concepto

concern [kənˈsəːn] *n* (*matter*) asunto; (*COMM*) empresa; (*anxiety*) preocupación *f* ♦ *vt* (*worry*) preocupar; (*involve*) afectar; (*relate to*) tener que ver con; **to be ~ed (about)** interesarse (por), preocuparse (por); **~ing** *prep* sobre, acerca de

concert [ˈkɔnsət] *n* concierto; **~ed** [kənˈsəːtəd] *adj* (*efforts etc*) concertado; **~ hall** *n* sala de conciertos

concerto [kənˈtʃəːtəu] *n* concierto

concession [kənˈsɛʃən] *n* concesión *f*; **tax ~** privilegio fiscal

conclude [kənˈkluːd] *vt* concluir; (*treaty etc*) firmar; (*agreement*) llegar a; (*decide*) llegar a la conclusión de; **conclusion** [-ˈkluːʒən] *n* conclusión *f*; firma; **conclusive** [-ˈkluːsɪv] *adj* decisivo, concluyente

concoct [kənˈkɔkt] *vt* confeccionar; (*plot*) tramar; **~ion** [-ˈkɔkʃən] *n* mezcla

concourse [ˈkɔŋkɔːs] *n* vestíbulo

concrete [ˈkɔŋkriːt] *n* hormigón *m* ♦ *adj* de hormigón; (*fig*) concreto

concur [kənˈkəː*] *vi* estar de acuerdo, asentir

concurrently [kənˈkʌrntlɪ] *adv* al mismo tiempo

concussion [kənˈkʌʃən] *n* conmoción *f* cerebral

condemn [kənˈdɛm] *vt* condenar; (*building*) declarar en ruina

condense [kənˈdɛns] *vi* condensarse ♦ *vt* condensar, abreviar; **~d milk** *n* leche *f* condensada

condition [kənˈdɪʃən] *n* condición *f*, estado; (*requirement*) condición *f* ♦ *vt* condicionar; **on ~ that** a condición (de) que; **~er** *n* suavizante

condolences [kənˈdəulənsɪz] *npl* pésame *m*

condom [ˈkɔndəm] *n* condón *m*

condone [kənˈdəun] *vt* condonar

conducive [kənˈdjuːsɪv] *adj*: **~ to** conducente a

conduct [*n* ˈkɔndʌkt, *vb* kənˈdʌkt] *n* conducta, comportamiento ♦ *vt* (*lead*) conducir; (*manage*) llevar a cabo, dirigir;

(*MUS*) dirigir; **to ~ o.s.** comportarse; **~ed
tour** (*BRIT*) *n* visita acompañada; **~or** *n*
(*of orchestra*) director *m*; (*US: on train*)
revisor(a) *m/f*; (*on bus*) cobrador *m*; (*ELEC*)
conductor *m*; **~ress** *n* (*on bus*)
cobradora

cone [kəun] *n* cono; (*pine ~*) piña; (*on
road*) pivote *m*; (*for ice-cream*) cucurucho

confectioner [kən'fɛkʃənə*] *n* repostero/a;
~'s (shop) *n* confitería; **~y** *n* dulces *mpl*

confer [kən'fəː*] *vt*: **to ~ sth on** otorgar
algo a ♦ *vi* conferenciar

conference ['kɒnfərns] *n* (*meeting*)
reunión *f*; (*convention*) congreso

confess [kən'fɛs] *vt* confesar ♦ *vi* admitir;
~ion [-'fɛʃən] *n* confesión *f*

confetti [kən'fɛtɪ] *n* confeti *m*

confide [kən'faɪd] *vi*: **to ~ in** confiar en

confidence ['kɒnfɪdns] *n* (*also:* **self-~**)
confianza; (*secret*) confidencia; **in ~**
(*speak, write*) en confianza; **~ trick** *n*
timo; **confident** *adj* seguro de sí mismo;
(*certain*) seguro; **confidential**
[kɒnfɪ'dɛnʃəl] *adj* confidencial

confine [kən'faɪn] *vt* (*limit*) limitar; (*shut
up*) encerrar; **~d** *adj* (*space*) reducido;
~ment (*prison*) prisión *f*; **~s** ['kɒnfaɪnz]
npl confines *mpl*

confirm [kən'fəːm] *vt* confirmar; **~ation**
[kɒnfə'meɪʃən] *n* confirmación *f*; **~ed** *adj*
empedernido

confiscate ['kɒnfɪskeɪt] *vt* confiscar

conflict [*n* 'kɒnflɪkt, *vb* kən'flɪkt] *n* conflicto
♦ *vi* (*opinions*) chocar; **~ing** *adj*
contradictorio

conform [kən'fɔːm] *vi* conformarse; **to ~
to** ajustarse a

confound [kən'faund] *vt* confundir

confront [kən'frʌnt] *vt* (*problems*) hacer
frente a; (*enemy, danger*) enfrentarse con;
~ation [kɒnfrən'teɪʃən] *n* enfrentamiento

confuse [kən'fjuːz] *vt* (*perplex*) aturdir,
desconcertar; (*mix up*) confundir;
(*complicate*) complicar; **~d** *adj* confuso;
(*person*) perplejo; **confusing** *adj*
confuso; **confusion** [-'fjuːʒən] *n*
confusión *f*

congeal [kən'dʒiːl] *vi* (*blood*) coagularse;
(*sauce etc*) cuajarse

congested [kən'dʒɛstɪd] *adj*
congestionado; **congestion** *n*
congestión *f*

congratulate [kən'grætjuleɪt] *vt*: **to ~ sb
(on)** felicitar a uno (por);
congratulations [-'leɪʃənz] *npl*
felicitaciones *fpl*; **congratulations!**
¡enhorabuena!

congregate ['kɒngrɪgeɪt] *vi* congregarse;
congregation [-'geɪʃən] *n* (*of a church*)
feligreses *mpl*

congress ['kɒngrɛs] *n* congreso; (*US*): **C~**
Congreso; **C~man** (*irreg*) (*US*) *n*
miembro del Congreso

conifer ['kɒnɪfə*] *n* conífera

conjunctivitis [kəndʒʌŋktɪ'vaɪtɪs] *n*
conjuntivitis *f*

conjure ['kʌndʒə*] *vi* hacer juegos de
manos; **~ up** *vt* (*ghost, spirit*) hacer
aparecer; (*memories*) evocar; **~r** *n*
ilusionista *m/f*

con man ['kɒn-] *n* estafador *m*

connect [kə'nekt] *vt* juntar, unir; (*ELEC*)
conectar; (*TEL: subscriber*) poner; (*: caller*)
poner al habla; (*fig*) relacionar, asociar
♦ *vi*: **to ~ with** (*train*) enlazar con; **to be
~ed with** (*associated*) estar relacionado
con; **~ion** [-ʃən] *n* juntura, unión *f*; (*ELEC*)
conexión *f*; (*RAIL*) enlace *m*; (*TEL*)
comunicación *f*; (*fig*) relación *f*

connive [kə'naɪv] *vi*: **to ~ at** hacer la vista
gorda a

connoisseur [kɒnɪ'sə*] *n* experto/a,
entendido/a

conquer ['kɒŋkə*] *vt* (*territory*) conquistar;
(*enemy, feelings*) vencer; **~or** *n*
conquistador *m*

conquest ['kɒŋkwest] *n* conquista

cons [kɒnz] *npl see* **convenience; pro**

conscience ['kɒnʃəns] *n* conciencia

conscientious [kɒnʃɪ'enʃəs] *adj*
concienzudo; (*objection*) de conciencia

conscious ['kɒnʃəs] *adj* (*deliberate*)
deliberado; (*awake, aware*) consciente;
~ness *n* conciencia; (*MED*) conocimiento

conscript ['kɒnskrɪpt] *n* recluta *m*; **~ion**
[kən'skrɪpʃən] *n* servicio militar
(obligatorio)

consensus [kən'sensəs] *n* consenso

consent [kən'sent] *n* consentimiento ♦ *vi*:
to ~ (to) consentir (en)

consequence ['kɒnsɪkwəns] *n*
consecuencia; (*significance*) importancia

consequently ['kɒnsɪkwəntlɪ] *adv* por
consiguiente

conservation [kɒnsə'veɪʃən] *n*
conservación *f*

conservative [kən'sə:vətɪv] *adj*
conservador(a); (*estimate etc*) cauteloso;
C~ (*BRIT*), *adj*, *n* (*POL*) conservador(a) *m/f*

conservatory [kən'sə:vətrɪ] *n*
invernadero; (*MUS*) conservatorio

conserve [kən'sə:v] *vt* conservar ♦ *n*
conserva

consider [kən'sɪdə*] *vt* considerar; (*take
into account*) tener en cuenta; (*study*)
estudiar, examinar; **to ~ doing sth** pensar
en (la posibilidad de) hacer algo; **~able**
adj considerable; **~ably** *adv*
notablemente; **~ate** *adj* considerado;
consideration [-'reɪʃən] *n* consideración
f; (*factor*) factor *m*; **to give sth further
consideration** estudiar algo más a fondo;
~ing *prep* teniendo en cuenta

consign [kən'saɪn] *vt*: **to ~ to** (*sth
unwanted*) relegar a; (*person*) destinar a;
~ment *n* envío

consist [kən'sɪst] *vi*: **to ~ of** consistir en

consistency [kən'sɪstənsɪ] *n* (*of argument
etc*) coherencia; consecuencia; (*thickness*)
consistencia

consistent [kən'sɪstənt] *adj* (*person*)
consecuente; (*argument etc*) coherente

consolation [kɒnsə'leɪʃən] *n* consuelo

console[1] [kən'səul] *vt* consolar

console[2] ['kɒnsəul] *n* consola

consonant ['kɒnsənənt] *n* consonante *f*

consortium [kən'sɔ:tɪəm] *n* consorcio

conspicuous [kən'spɪkjuəs] *adj* (*visible*)
visible

conspiracy [kən'spɪrəsɪ] *n* conjura,
complot *m*

constable ['kʌnstəbl] (*BRIT*) *n* policía *m/f*;
chief ~ ≈ jefe *m* de policía

constabulary [kən'stæbjulərɪ] *n* ≈ policía

constant ['kɒnstənt] *adj* constante; **~ly**
adv constantemente

constipated ['kɒnstɪpeɪtəd] *adj* estreñido;
constipation [kɒnstɪ'peɪʃən] *n*
estreñimiento

constituency [kən'stɪtjuənsɪ] *n* (*POL: area*)
distrito electoral; (: *electors*) electorado;
constituent [-ənt] *n* (*POL*) elector(a) *m/f*;
(*part*) componente *m*

constitution [kɒnstɪ'tju:ʃən] *n* constitución
f; **~al** *adj* constitucional

constraint [kən'streɪnt] *n* obligación *f*;
(*limit*) restricción *f*

construct [kən'strʌkt] *vt* construir; **~ion**
[-ʃən] *n* construcción *f*; **~ive** *adj*
constructivo

consul ['kɒnsl] *n* cónsul *m/f*; **~ate**
['kɒnsjulɪt] *n* consulado

consult [kən'sʌlt] *vt* consultar; **~ant** *n*
(*BRIT: MED*) especialista *m/f*; (*other
specialist*) asesor(a) *m/f*; **~ation**
[kɒnsəl'teɪʃən] *n* consulta; **~ing room**
(*BRIT*) *n* consultorio

consume [kən'sju:m] *vt* (*eat*) comerse;
(*drink*) beberse; (*fire etc, COMM*) consumir;
~r *n* consumidor(a) *m/f*; **~r goods** *npl*
bienes *mpl* de consumo

consummate ['kɒnsʌmeɪt] *vt* consumar

consumption [kən'sʌmpʃən] *n* consumo

cont. *abbr* (= *continued*) sigue

contact ['kɒntækt] *n* contacto; (*person*)
contacto; (: *pej*) enchufe *m* ♦ *vt* ponerse
en contacto con; **~ lenses** *npl* lentes *fpl*
de contacto

contagious [kən'teɪdʒəs] *adj* contagioso

contain [kən'teɪn] *vt* contener; **to ~ o.s.**
contenerse; **~er** *n* recipiente *m*; (*for
shipping etc*) contenedor *m*

contaminate [kən'tæmɪneɪt] *vt*
contaminar

cont'd *abbr* (= *continued*) sigue

contemplate ['kɒntəmpleɪt] *vt*
contemplar; (*reflect upon*) considerar

contemporary [kən'tempərərɪ] *adj*, *n*

contemporáneo/a *m/f*

contempt [kən'tempt] *n* desprecio; **~ of court** (*LAW*) desacato (a los tribunales); **~ible** *adj* despreciable; **~uous** *adj* desdeñoso

contend [kən'tend] *vt* (*argue*) afirmar ♦ *vi*: **to ~ with/for** luchar contra/por; **~er** *n* (*SPORT*) contendiente *m/f*

content [*adj, vb* kən'tent, *n* 'kɔntent] *adj* (*happy*) contento; (*satisfied*) satisfecho ♦ *vt* contentar; satisfacer ♦ *n* contenido; **~s** *npl* contenido; (**table of**) **~s** índice *m* de materias; **~ed** *adj* contento; satisfecho

contention [kən'tenʃən] *n* (*assertion*) aseveración *f*; (*disagreement*) discusión *f*

contest [*n* 'kɔntest, *vb* kən'test] *n* lucha; (*competition*) concurso ♦ *vt* (*dispute*) impugnar; (*POL*) presentarse como candidato/a en; **~ant** [kən'testənt] *n* concursante *m/f*; (*in fight*) contendiente *m/f*

context ['kɔntekst] *n* contexto

continent ['kɔntinənt] *n* continente *m*; **the C~** (*BRIT*) el continente europeo; **~al** [-'nentl] *adj* continental; **~al breakfast** *n* desayuno estilo europeo; **~al quilt** (*BRIT*) *n* edredón *m*

contingency [kən'tindʒənsi] *n* contingencia

continual [kən'tinjuəl] *adj* continuo; **~ly** *adv* constantemente

continuation [kəntinju'eiʃən] *n* prolongación *f*; (*after interruption*) reanudación *f*

continue [kən'tinju:] *vi, vt* seguir, continuar

continuous [kən'tinjuəs] *adj* continuo

contort [kən'tɔ:t] *vt* retorcer

contour ['kɔntuə*] *n* contorno; (*also:* **line**) curva de nivel

contraband ['kɔntrəbænd] *n* contrabando

contraceptive [kɔntrə'septiv] *adj, n* anticonceptivo

contract [*n* 'kɔntrækt, *vb* kən'trækt] *n* contrato ♦ *vi* (*COMM*): **to ~ to do sth** comprometerse por contrato a hacer algo; (*become smaller*) contraerse,

encogerse ♦ *vt* contraer; **~ion** [kən'trækʃən] *n* contracción *f*; **~or** *n* contratista *m/f*

contradict [kɔntrə'dikt] *vt* contradecir; **~ion** [-ʃən] *n* contradicción *f*

contraption [kən'træpʃən] (*pej*) *n* artilugio *m*

contrary[1] ['kɔntrəri] *adj* contrario ♦ *n* lo contrario; **on the ~** al contrario; **unless you hear to the ~** a no ser que le digan lo contrario

contrary[2] [kən'treəri] *adj* (*perverse*) terco

contrast [*n* 'kɔntrɑ:st, *vt* kən'trɑ:st] *n* contraste *m* ♦ *vt* comparar; **in ~ to** en contraste con

contravene [kɔntrə'vi:n] *vt* infringir

contribute [kən'tribju:t] *vi* contribuir ♦ *vt*: **to ~ £10/an article to** contribuir con 10 libras/un artículo a; **to ~ to** (*charity*) donar a; (*newspaper*) escribir para; (*discussion*) intervenir en; **contribution** [kɔntri'bju:ʃən] *n* (*donation*) donativo; (*BRIT: for social security*) cotización *f*; (*to debate*) intervención *f*; (*to journal*) colaboración *f*; **contributor** *n* contribuyente *m/f*; (*to newspaper*) colaborador(a) *m/f*

contrive [kən'traiv] *vt* (*invent*) idear ♦ *vi*: **to ~ to do** lograr hacer

control [kən'trəul] *vt* controlar; (*process etc*) dirigir; (*machinery*) manejar; (*temper*) dominar; (*disease*) contener ♦ *n* control *m*; **~s** *npl* (*of vehicle*) instrumentos *mpl* de mando; (*of radio*) controles *mpl*; (*governmental*) medidas *fpl* de control; **under ~** bajo control; **to be in ~ of** tener el mando de; **the car went out of ~** se perdió el control del coche; **~led substance** *n* sustancia controlada; **~ panel** *n* tablero de instrumentos; **~ room** *n* sala de mando; **~ tower** *n* (*AVIAT*) torre *f* de control

controversial [kɔntrə'və:ʃl] *adj* polémico

controversy ['kɔntrəvə:si] *n* polémica

convalesce [kɔnvə'les] *vi* convalecer

convector [kən'vektə*] *n* calentador *m* de aire

convene [kən'viːn] *vt* convocar ♦ *vi* reunirse

convenience [kən'viːnɪəns] *n* (*easiness*) comodidad *f*; (*suitability*) idoneidad *f*; (*advantage*) ventaja; **at your ~** cuando le sea conveniente; **all modern ~s, all mod cons** (*BRIT*) todo confort

convenient [kən'viːnɪənt] *adj* (*useful*) útil; (*place, time*) conveniente

convent ['kɒnvənt] *n* convento

convention [kən'venʃən] *n* convención *f*; (*meeting*) asamblea; (*agreement*) convenio; **~al** *adj* convencional

converge [kən'vəːdʒ] *vi* convergir; (*people*): **to ~ on** dirigirse todos a

conversant [kən'vəːsnt] *adj*: **to be ~ with** estar al tanto de

conversation [kɒnvə'seɪʃən] *n* conversación *f*; **~al** *adj* familiar; **~al skill** facilidad *f* de palabra

converse [*n* 'kɒnvəːs, *vb* kən'vəːs] *n* inversa ♦ *vi* conversar; **~ly** [-'vəːslɪ] *adv* a la inversa

conversion [kən'vəːʃən] *n* conversión *f*

convert [*vb* kən'vəːt, *n* 'kɒnvəːt] *vt* (*REL, COMM*) convertir; (*alter*): **to ~ sth into/to** transformar algo en/convertir algo a ♦ *n* converso/a; **~ible** *adj* convertible ♦ *n* descapotable *m*

convey [kən'veɪ] *vt* llevar; (*thanks*) comunicar; (*idea*) expresar; **~or belt** *n* cinta transportadora

convict [*vb* kən'vɪkt, *n* 'kɒnvɪkt] *vt* (*find guilty*) declarar culpable a ♦ *n* presidiario/a; **~ion** [-ʃən] *n* condena; (*belief, certainty*) convicción *f*

convince [kən'vɪns] *vt* convencer; **~d** *adj*: **~d of/that** convencido de/de que; **convincing** *adj* convincente

convoluted ['kɒnvəluːtɪd] *adj* (*argument etc*) enrevesado

convoy ['kɒnvɔɪ] *n* convoy *m*

convulse [kən'vʌls] *vt*: **to be ~d with laughter** desternillarse de risa; **convulsion** [-'vʌlʃən] *n* convulsión *f*

cook [kuk] *vt* (*stew etc*) guisar; (*meal*) preparar ♦ *vi* cocer; (*person*) cocinar ♦ *n* cocinero/a; **~ book** *n* libro de cocina; **~er** *n* cocina; **~ery** *n* cocina; **~ery book** (*BRIT*) *n* = **~ book**; **~ie** (*US*) *n* galleta; **~ing** *n* cocina

cool [kuːl] *adj* fresco; (*not afraid*) tranquilo; (*unfriendly*) frío ♦ *vt* enfriar ♦ *vi* enfriarse; **~ness** *n* frescura; tranquilidad *f*; (*indifference*) falta de entusiasmo

coop [kuːp] *n* gallinero ♦ *vt*: **to ~ up** (*fig*) encerrar

cooperate [kəu'ɒpəreɪt] *vi* cooperar, colaborar; **cooperation** [-'reɪʃən] *n* cooperación *f*, colaboración *f*; **cooperative** [-rətɪv] *adj* (*business*) cooperativo; (*person*) servicial ♦ *n* cooperativa

coordinate [*vb* kəu'ɔːdɪneɪt, *n* kəu'ɔːdɪnət] *vt* coordinar ♦ *n* (*MATH*) coordenada; **~s** *npl* (*clothes*) coordinados *mpl*; **coordination** [-'neɪʃən] *n* coordinación *f*

co-ownership [kəu'əunəʃɪp] *n* co-propiedad *f*

cop [kɒp] (*inf*) *n* poli *m* (*SP*), tira *m* (*AM*)

cope [kəup] *vi*: **to ~ with** (*problem*) hacer frente a

copper ['kɒpə*] *n* (*metal*) cobre *m*; (*BRIT: inf*) poli *m*; **~s** *npl* (*money*) calderilla (*SP*), centavos *mpl* (*AM*)

copulate ['kɒpjuleɪt] *vi* copularse

copy ['kɒpɪ] *n* copia; (*of book etc*) ejemplar *m* ♦ *vt* copiar; **~right** *n* derechos *mpl* de autor

coral ['kɒrəl] *n* coral *m*

cord [kɔːd] *n* cuerda; (*ELEC*) cable *m*; (*fabric*) pana

cordial ['kɔːdɪəl] *adj* cordial ♦ *n* cordial *m*

cordon ['kɔːdn] *n* cordón *m*; **~ off** *vt* acordonar

corduroy ['kɔːdərɔɪ] *n* pana

core [kɔː*] *n* centro, núcleo; (*of fruit*) corazón *m*; (*of problem*) meollo ♦ *vt* quitar el corazón de

coriander [kɒrɪ'ændə*] *n* culantro

cork [kɔːk] *n* corcho; (*tree*) alcornoque *m*; **~screw** *n* sacacorchos *m inv*

corn [kɔːn] *n* (*BRIT: cereal crop*) trigo; (*US: maize*) maíz *m*; (*on foot*) callo; **~ on the**

cob (*CULIN*) maíz en la mazorca (*SP*), choclo (*AM*)

corned beef [ˈkɔːnd-] *n* carne *f* acecinada (en lata)

corner [ˈkɔːnə*] *n* (*outside*) esquina; (*inside*) rincón *m*; (*in road*) curva; (*FOOTBALL*) córner *m*; (*BOXING*) esquina ♦ *vt* (*trap*) arrinconar; (*COMM*) acaparar ♦ *vi* (*in car*) tomar las curvas; **~stone** *n* (*also fig*) piedra angular

cornet [ˈkɔːnɪt] *n* (*MUS*) corneta; (*BRIT: of ice-cream*) cucurucho

cornflakes [ˈkɔːnfleɪks] *npl* copos *mpl* de maíz, cornflakes *mpl*

cornflour [ˈkɔːnflauə*] (*BRIT*), **cornstarch** [ˈkɔːnstɑːtʃ] (*US*) *n* harina de maíz

Cornwall [ˈkɔːnwəl] *n* Cornualles *m*

corny [ˈkɔːnɪ] (*inf*) *adj* gastado

coronary [ˈkɔrənərɪ] *n* (*also:* ~ **thrombosis**) infarto

coronation [kɔrəˈneɪʃən] *n* coronación *f*

coroner [ˈkɔrənə*] *n* juez *m* (de instrucción)

corporal [ˈkɔːpərl] *n* cabo ♦ *adj:* ~ **punishment** castigo corporal

corporate [ˈkɔːpərɪt] *adj* (*action, ownership*) colectivo; (*finance, image*) corporativo

corporation [kɔːpəˈreɪʃən] *n* (*of town*) ayuntamiento; (*COMM*) corporación *f*

corps [kɔː*, *pl* kɔːz] *n inv* cuerpo; **diplomatic ~** cuerpo diplomático; **press ~** gabinete *m* de prensa

corpse [kɔːps] *n* cadáver *m*

correct [kəˈrekt] *adj* justo, exacto; (*proper*) correcto ♦ *vt* corregir; (*exam*) corregir, calificar; **~ion** [-ʃən] *n* (*act*) corrección *f*; (*instance*) rectificación *f*

correspond [kɔrɪsˈpɔnd] *vi* (*write*): **to ~ (with)** escribirse (con); (*be equivalent to*): **to ~ (to)** corresponder (a); (*be in accordance*): **to ~ (with)** corresponder (con); **~ence** *n* correspondencia; **~ence course** *n* curso por correspondencia; **~ent** *n* corresponsal *m/f*

corridor [ˈkɔrɪdɔː*] *n* pasillo

corrode [kəˈrəud] *vt* corroer ♦ *vi* corroerse

corrugated [ˈkɔrəgeɪtɪd] *adj* ondulado; ~ **iron** *n* chapa ondulada

corrupt [kəˈrʌpt] *adj* (*person*) corrupto; (*COMPUT*) corrompido ♦ *vt* corromper; (*COMPUT*) degradar

Corsica [ˈkɔːsɪkə] *n* Córcega

cosmetic [kɔzˈmetɪk] *adj, n* cosmético

cosmopolitan [kɔzməˈpɔlɪtn] *adj* cosmopolita

cost [kɔst] (*pt, pp* **cost**) *n* (*price*) precio; **~s** *npl* (*COMM*) costes *mpl*; (*LAW*) costas *fpl* ♦ *vt* costar, valer ♦ *vt* preparar el presupuesto de; **how much does it ~?** ¿cuánto cuesta?; **to ~ sb time/effort** costarle a uno tiempo/esfuerzo; **it ~ him his life** le costó la vida; **at all ~s** cueste lo que cueste

co-star [ˈkəustɑː*] *n* coprotagonista *m/f*

Costa Rica [ˈkɔstəˈriːkə] *n* Costa Rica; **~n** *adj, n* costarriqueño/a *m/f*

cost-effective [kɔstɪˈfektɪv] *adj* rentable

costly [ˈkɔstlɪ] *adj* costoso

cost-of-living [kɔstəvˈlɪvɪŋ] *adj:* ~ **allowance** plus *m* de carestía de vida; ~ **index** índice *m* del costo de vida

cost price (*BRIT*) *n* precio de coste

costume [ˈkɔstjuːm] *n* traje *m*; (*BRIT: also:* **swimming ~**) traje de baño; ~ **jewellery** *n* bisutería

cosy [ˈkəuzɪ] (*US* **cozy**) *adj* (*person*) cómodo; (*room*) acogedor(a)

cot [kɔt] *n* (*BRIT: child's*) cuna; (*US: campbed*) cama de campaña

cottage [ˈkɔtɪdʒ] *n* casita de campo; (*rustic*) barraca; ~ **cheese** *n* requesón *m*

cotton [ˈkɔtn] *n* algodón *m*; (*thread*) hilo; ~ **on to** (*inf*) *vt fus* caer en la cuenta de; ~ **candy** (*US*) *n* algodón *m* (azucarado); ~ **wool** (*BRIT*) *n* algodón *m* (hidrófilo)

couch [kautʃ] *n* sofá *m*; (*doctor's etc*) diván *m*

couchette [kuːˈʃet] *n* litera

cough [kɔf] *vi* toser ♦ *n* tos *f*; ~ **drop** *n* pastilla para la tos

could [kud] *pt of* **can²**; **~n't = could not**

council [ˈkaunsl] *n* consejo; **city** *or* **town ~** consejo municipal; ~ **estate** (*BRIT*) *n* *urbanización f de viviendas municipales de alquiler;* **~ house** (*BRIT*) *n vivienda municipal de alquiler;* **~lor** *n concejal(a) m/f*

counsel ['kaunsl] *n* (*advice*) consejo; (*lawyer*) abogado/a ♦ *vt* aconsejar; **~lor** *n* consejero/a; **~or** (*US*) *n* abogado/a

count [kaunt] *vt* contar; (*include*) incluir ♦ *vi* contar ♦ *n* cuenta; (*of votes*) escrutinio; (*level*) nivel *m*; (*nobleman*) conde *m*; **~ on** *vt fus* contar con; **~down** *n* cuenta atrás

countenance ['kauntɪnəns] *n* semblante *m*, rostro ♦ *vt* (*tolerate*) aprobar, tolerar

counter ['kauntə*] *n* (*in shop*) mostrador *m*; (*in games*) ficha ♦ *vt* contrarrestar ♦ *adv*: **to run ~ to** ser contrario a, ir en contra de; **~act** *vt* contrarrestar

counterfeit ['kauntəfɪt] *n* falsificación *f*, simulación *f* ♦ *vt* falsificar ♦ *adj* falso, falsificado

counterfoil ['kauntəfɔɪl] *n* talón *m*

counterpart ['kauntəpɑːt] *n* homólogo/a

counter-productive [kauntəprə'dʌktɪv] *adj* contraproducente

countersign ['kauntəsaɪn] *vt* refrendar

countess ['kauntɪs] *n* condesa

countless ['kauntlɪs] *adj* innumerable

country ['kʌntrɪ] *n* país *m*; (*native land*) patria; (*as opposed to town*) campo; (*region*) región *f*, tierra; **~ dancing** (*BRIT*) *n* baile *m* regional; **~ house** *n* casa de campo; **~man** *n* (*irreg*) (*compatriot*) compatriota *m*; (*rural*) campesino, paisano; **~side** *n* campo

county ['kauntɪ] *n* condado

coup [kuː] (*pl* **~s**) *n* (*also*: **~ d'état**) golpe *m* (de estado); (*achievement*) éxito *m*

couple ['kʌpl] *n* (*of things*) par *m*; (*of people*) pareja; (*married* **~**) matrimonio; **a ~ of** un par de

coupon ['kuːpɔn] *n* cupón *m*; (*voucher*) valé *m*

courage ['kʌrɪdʒ] *n* valor *m*, valentía; **~ous** [kə'reɪdʒəs] *adj* valiente

courgette [kuə'ʒɛt] (*BRIT*) *n* calabacín *m* (*SP*), calabacita (*AM*)

courier ['kurɪə*] *n* mensajero/a; (*for tourists*) guía *m/f* (de turismo)

course [kɔːs] *n* (*direction*) dirección *f*; (*of river, SCOL*) curso; (*process*) transcurso; (*MED*): **~ of treatment** tratamiento; (*of ship*) rumbo; (*part of meal*) plato; (*GOLF*) campo; **of ~** desde luego, naturalmente; **of ~!** ¡claro!

court [kɔːt] *n* (*royal*) corte *f*; (*LAW*) tribunal *m*, juzgado; (*TENNIS etc*) pista, cancha ♦ *vt* (*woman*) cortejar a; **to take to ~** demandar

courteous ['kɜːtɪəs] *adj* cortés

courtesy ['kɜːtəsɪ] *n* cortesía; **(by) ~ of** por cortesía de; **~ bus, ~ coach** *n* autobús *m* gratuito

court-house ['kɔːthaus] (*US*) *n* palacio de justicia

courtier ['kɔːtɪə*] *n* cortesano

court-martial (*pl* **courts-martial**) *n* consejo de guerra

courtroom ['kɔːtrum] *n* sala de justicia

courtyard ['kɔːtjɑːd] *n* patio

cousin ['kʌzn] *n* primo/a; **first ~** primo/a carnal, primo/a hermano/a

cove [kəuv] *n* cala, ensenada

covenant ['kʌvənənt] *n* pacto

cover ['kʌvə*] *vt* cubrir; (*feelings, mistake*) ocultar; (*with lid*) tapar; (*book etc*) forrar; (*distance*) recorrer; (*include*) abarcar; (*protect: also: INSURANCE*) cubrir; (*PRESS*) investigar; (*discuss*) tratar ♦ *n* cubierta; (*lid*) tapa; (*for chair etc*) funda; (*envelope*) sobre *m*; (*for book*) forro; (*of magazine*) portada; (*shelter*) abrigo; (*INSURANCE*) cobertura; (*of spy*) cobertura; **~s** *npl* (*on bed*) sábanas; mantas; **to take ~** (*shelter*) protegerse, resguardarse; **under ~** (*indoors*) bajo techo; **under ~ of darkness** al amparo de la oscuridad; **under separate ~** (*COMM*) por separado; **~ up** *vi*: **to ~ up for sb** encubrir a uno; **~age** *n* (*TV, PRESS*) cobertura; **~alls** (*US*) *npl* mono; **~ charge** *n* precio del cubierto; **~ing** *n* capa; **~ing letter** (*US* **~ letter**) *n* carta de explicación; **~ note** *n* (*INSURANCE*) póliza provisional

covert ['kəuvət] *adj* secreto, encubierto

cover-up *n* encubrimiento

cow [kau] *n* vaca; (*inf: woman*) bruja ♦ *vt* intimidar

coward ['kauəd] *n* cobarde *m/f*; **~ice** [-ɪs] *n* cobardía; **~ly** *adj* cobarde

cowboy ['kaubɔɪ] *n* vaquero

cower ['kauə*] *vi* encogerse (de miedo)

coy [kɔɪ] *adj* tímido

cozy ['kəuzɪ] (*US*) *adj* = **cosy**

CPA (*US*) *n abbr* = **certified public accountant**

crab [kræb] *n* cangrejo; **~ apple** *n* manzana silvestre

crack [kræk] *n* grieta; (*noise*) crujido; (*drug*) crack *m* ♦ *vt* agrietar, romper; (*nut*) cascar; (*solve: problem*) resolver; (*: code*) descifrar; (*whip etc*) chasquear; (*knuckles*) crujir; (*joke*) contar ♦ *adj* (*expert*) de primera; **~ down on** *vt fus* adoptar fuertes medidas contra; **~ up** *vi* (*MED*) sufrir una crisis nerviosa; **~er** *n* (*biscuit*) cráquer *m*; (*Christmas ~er*) petardo sorpresa

crackle ['krækl] *vi* crepitar

cradle ['kreɪdl] *n* cuna

craft [krɑːft] *n* (*skill*) arte *m*; (*trade*) oficio; (*cunning*) astucia; (*boat: pl inv*) barco; (*plane: pl inv*) avión *m*

craftsman ['krɑːftsmən] *n* artesano; **~ship** *n* (*quality*) destreza

crafty ['krɑːftɪ] *adj* astuto

crag [kræg] *n* peñasco

cram [kræm] *vt* (*fill*): **to ~ sth with** llenar algo (a reventar) de; (*put*): **to ~ sth into** meter algo a la fuerza en ♦ *vi* (*for exams*) empollar

cramp [kræmp] *n* (*MED*) calambre *m*; **~ed** *adj* apretado, estrecho

cranberry ['krænbərɪ] *n* arándano agrio

crane [kreɪn] *n* (*TECH*) grúa; (*bird*) grulla

crank [kræŋk] *n* manivela; (*person*) chiflado

cranny ['krænɪ] *n see* **nook**

crash [kræʃ] *n* (*noise*) estrépito; (*of cars etc*) choque *m*; (*of plane*) accidente *m* de aviación; (*COMM*) quiebra ♦ *vt* (*car, plane*) estrellar ♦ *vi* (*car, plane*) estrellarse; (*two*

cars) chocar; (*COMM*) quebrar; **~ course** *n* curso acelerado; **~ helmet** *n* casco (protector); **~ landing** *n* aterrizaje *m* forzado

crass [kræs] *adj* grosero, maleducado

crate [kreɪt] *n* cajón *m* de embalaje; (*for bottles*) caja

cravat(e) [krə'væt] *n* pañuelo

crave [kreɪv] *vt, vi*: **to ~ (for)** ansiar, anhelar

crawl [krɔːl] *vi* (*drag o.s.*) arrastrarse; (*child*) andar a gatas, gatear; (*vehicle*) avanzar (lentamente) ♦ *n* (*SWIMMING*) crol *m*

crayfish ['kreɪfɪʃ] *n inv* (*freshwater*) cangrejo de río; (*saltwater*) cigala

crayon ['kreɪən] *n* lápiz *m* de color

craze [kreɪz] *n* (*fashion*) moda

crazy ['kreɪzɪ] *adj* (*person*) loco; (*idea*) disparatado; (*inf: keen*): **~ about sb/sth** loco por uno/algo

creak [kriːk] *vi* (*floorboard*) crujir; (*hinge etc*) chirriar, rechinar

cream [kriːm] *n* (*of milk*) nata, crema; (*lotion*) crema; (*fig*) flor *f* y nata ♦ *adj* (*colour*) color crema; **~ cake** *n* pastel *m* de nata; **~ cheese** *n* queso blanco; **~y** *adj* cremoso; (*colour*) color crema

crease [kriːs] *n* (*fold*) pliegue *m*; (*in trousers*) raya; (*wrinkle*) arruga ♦ *vt* (*wrinkle*) arrugar ♦ *vi* (*wrinkle up*) arrugarse

create [kriː'eɪt] *vt* crear; **creation** [-ʃən] *n* creación *f*; **creative** *adj* creativo; **creator** *n* creador(a) *m/f*

creature ['kriːtʃə*] *n* (*animal*) animal *m*, bicho; (*person*) criatura

crèche [krɛʃ] *n* guardería (infantil)

credence ['kriːdəns] *n*: **to lend** *or* **give ~ to** creer en, dar crédito a

credentials [krɪ'dɛnʃlz] *npl* (*references*) referencias *fpl*; (*identity papers*) documentos *mpl* de identidad

credible ['krɛdɪbl] *adj* creíble; (*trustworthy*) digno de confianza

credit ['krɛdɪt] *n* crédito; (*merit*) honor *m*, mérito ♦ *vt* (*COMM*) abonar; (*believe: also:*

give ~ to) creer, prestar fe a ♦ *adj* crediticio; **~s** *npl* (CINEMA) fichas *fpl* técnicas; **to be in ~** (*person*) tener saldo a favor; **to ~ sb with** (*fig*) reconocer a uno el mérito de; **~ card** *n* tarjeta de crédito; **~or** *n* acreedor(a) *m/f*

creed [kri:d] *n* credo

creek [kri:k] *n* cala, ensenada; (*US*) riachuelo

creep [kri:p] (*pt, pp* **crept**) *vi* arrastrarse; **~er** *n* enredadera; **~y** *adj* (*frightening*) horripilante

cremate [krɪ'meɪt] *vt* incinerar

crematorium [kremə'tɔːrɪəm] (*pl* **crematoria**) *n* crematorio

crêpe [kreɪp] *n* (*fabric*) crespón *m*; (*also:* ~ **rubber**) crepé *m*; ~ **bandage** (BRIT) *n* venda de crepé

crept [krept] *pt, pp of* **creep**

crescent ['kresnt] *n* media luna; (*street*) calle *f* (*en forma de semicírculo*)

cress [kres] *n* berro

crest [krest] *n* (*of bird*) cresta; (*of hill*) cima, cumbre *f*; (*of coat of arms*) blasón *m*; **~fallen** *adj* alicaído

crevice ['krevɪs] *n* grieta, hendedura

crew [kru:] *n* (*of ship etc*) tripulación *f*; (*TV, CINEMA*) equipo; **~cut** *n* corte *m* al rape; **~neck** *n* cuello a la caja

crib [krɪb] *n* cuna ♦ *vt* (*inf*) plagiar

crick [krɪk] *n* (*in neck*) tortícolis *f*

cricket ['krɪkɪt] *n* (*insect*) grillo; (*game*) críquet *m*

crime [kraɪm] *n* (*no pl: illegal activities*) crimen *m*; (*illegal action*) delito; **criminal** ['krɪmɪnl] *n* criminal *m/f*, delincuente *m/f* ♦ *adj* criminal; (*illegal*) delictivo; (*law*) penal

crimson ['krɪmzn] *adj* carmesí

cringe [krɪndʒ] *vi* agacharse, encogerse

crinkle ['krɪŋkl] *vt* arrugar

cripple ['krɪpl] *n* lisiado/a, cojo/a ♦ *vt* lisiar, mutilar

crisis ['kraɪsɪs] (*pl* **crises**) *n* crisis *f inv*

crisp [krɪsp] *adj* fresco; (*manner*) seco; **~s** (BRIT) *npl* patatas *fpl* (SP) *or* papas *fpl* (AM) fritas

crisscross ['krɪskrɔs] *adj* entrelazado

criterion [kraɪ'tɪərɪən] (*pl* **criteria**) *n* criterio

critic ['krɪtɪk] *n* crítico/a; **~al** *adj* crítico; (*illness*) grave; **~ally** *adv* (*speak etc*) en tono crítico; (*ill*) gravemente; **~ism** ['krɪtɪsɪzm] *n* crítica; **~ize** ['krɪtɪsaɪz] *vt* criticar

croak [krəuk] *vi* (*frog*) croar; (*raven*) graznar; (*person*) gruñir

Croatia [krəu'eɪʃə] *n* Croacia

crochet ['krəuʃeɪ] *n* ganchillo

crockery ['krɔkərɪ] *n* loza, vajilla

crocodile ['krɔkədaɪl] *n* cocodrilo

crocus ['krəukəs] *n* croco, crocus *m*

croft [krɔft] *n* granja pequeña

crony ['krəunɪ] (*inf: pej*) *n* compinche *m/f*

crook [kruk] *n* ladrón/ona *m/f*; (*of shepherd*) cayado; **~ed** ['krukɪd] *adj* torcido; (*dishonest*) nada honrado

crop [krɔp] *n* (*produce*) cultivo; (*amount produced*) cosecha; (*riding ~*) látigo de montar ♦ *vt* cortar, recortar; ~ **up** *vi* surgir, presentarse

cross [krɔs] *n* cruz *f*; (*hybrid*) cruce *m* ♦ *vt* (*street etc*) cruzar, atravesar ♦ *adj* de mal humor, enojado; ~ **out** *vt* tachar; ~ **over** *vi* cruzar; **~bar** *n* travesaño; **~country (race)** *n* carrera a campo traviesa, cross *m*; **~-examine** *vt* interrogar; **~-eyed** *adj* bizco; **~fire** *n* fuego cruzado; **~ing** *n* (*sea passage*) travesía; (*also:* **pedestrian ~ing**) paso para peatones; **~ing guard** (US) *n* persona encargada de ayudar a los niños a cruzar la calle; ~ **purposes** *npl*: **to be at ~ purposes** no comprenderse uno a otro; **~reference** *n* referencia, llamada; **~roads** *n* cruce *m*, encrucijada; ~ **section** *n* corte *m* transversal; (*of population*) muestra (representativa); **~walk** (US) *n* paso de peatones; **~wind** *n* viento de costado; **~word** *n* crucigrama *m*

crotch [krɔtʃ] *n* (ANAT, *of garment*) entrepierna

crotchet ['krɔtʃɪt] *n* (MUS) negra

crouch [krautʃ] *vi* agacharse, acurrucarse

crow [krəu] n (bird) cuervo; (of cock) canto, cacareo ♦ vi (cock) cantar

crowbar ['krəubɑ:*] n palanca

crowd [kraud] n muchedumbre f, multitud f ♦ vt (fill) llenar ♦ vi (gather): **to ~ round** reunirse en torno a; (cram): **to ~ in** entrar en tropel; **~ed** adj (full) atestado; (densely populated) superpoblado

crown [kraun] n corona; (of head) coronilla; (for tooth) funda; (of hill) cumbre f ♦ vt coronar; (fig) completar, rematar; **~ jewels** npl joyas fpl reales; **~ prince** n príncipe m heredero

crow's feet npl patas fpl de gallo

crucial ['kru:ʃl] adj decisivo

crucifix ['kru:sɪfɪks] n crucifijo; **~ion** [-'fɪkʃən] n crucifixión f

crude [kru:d] adj (materials) bruto; (fig: basic) tosco; (: vulgar) ordinario; **~ (oil)** n (petróleo) crudo

cruel ['kruəl] adj cruel; **~ty** n crueldad f

cruise [kru:z] n crucero ♦ vi (ship) hacer un crucero; (car) ir a la velocidad de crucero; **~r** n (motorboat) yate m de motor; (warship) crucero

crumb [krʌm] n miga, migaja

crumble ['krʌmbl] vt desmenuzar ♦ vi (building, also fig) desmoronarse; **crumbly** adj que se desmigaja fácilmente

crumpet ['krʌmpɪt] n ≈ bollo para tostar

crumple ['krʌmpl] vt (paper) estrujar; (material) arrugar

crunch [krʌntʃ] vt (with teeth) mascar; (underfoot) hacer crujir ♦ n (fig) hora or momento de la verdad; **~y** adj crujiente

crusade [kru:'seɪd] n cruzada

crush [krʌʃ] n (crowd) aglomeración f; (infatuation): **to have a ~ on sb** estar loco por uno; (drink): **lemon ~** limonada ♦ vt aplastar; (paper) estrujar; (cloth) arrugar; (fruit) exprimir; (opposition) aplastar; (hopes) destruir

crust [krʌst] n corteza; (of snow, ice) costra

crutch [krʌtʃ] n muleta

crux [krʌks] n: **the ~ of** lo esencial de, el quid de

cry [kraɪ] vi llorar; (shout: also: ~ **out**) gritar ♦ n (shriek) chillido; (shout) grito; **~ off** vi echarse atrás

cryptic ['krɪptɪk] adj enigmático, secreto

crystal ['krɪstl] n cristal m; **~-clear** adj claro como el agua

cub [kʌb] n cachorro; (also: ~ **scout**) niño explorador

Cuba ['kju:bə] n Cuba; **~n** adj, n cubano/a m/f

cube [kju:b] n cubo ♦ vt (MATH) cubicar; **cubic** adj cúbico

cubicle ['kju:bɪkl] n (at pool) caseta; (for bed) cubículo

cuckoo ['kuku:] n cuco; ~ **clock** n reloj m de cucú

cucumber ['kju:kʌmbə*] n pepino

cuddle ['kʌdl] vt abrazar ♦ vi abrazarse

cue [kju:] n (snooker ~) taco; (THEATRE etc) señal f

cuff [kʌf] n (of sleeve) puño; (US: of trousers) vuelta; (blow) bofetada; **off the ~** adv de improviso; **~links** npl gemelos mpl

cuisine [kwɪ'zi:n] n cocina

cul-de-sac ['kʌldəsæk] n callejón m sin salida

cull [kʌl] vt (idea) sacar ♦ n (of animals) matanza selectiva

culminate ['kʌlmɪneɪt] vi: **to ~ in** terminar en; **culmination** [-'neɪʃən] n culminación f, colmo

culottes [ku:'lɔts] npl falda pantalón f

culprit ['kʌlprɪt] n culpable m/f

cult [kʌlt] n culto

cultivate ['kʌltɪveɪt] vt (also fig) cultivar; **~d** adj culto; **cultivation** [-'veɪʃən] n cultivo

cultural ['kʌltʃərəl] adj cultural

culture ['kʌltʃə*] n (also fig) cultura; (BIO) cultivo; **~d** adj culto

cumbersome ['kʌmbəsəm] adj de mucho bulto, voluminoso; (process) enrevesado

cunning ['kʌnɪŋ] n astucia ♦ adj astuto

cup [kʌp] n taza; (as prize) copa

cupboard ['kʌbəd] n armario; (kitchen) alacena

cup tie (*BRIT*) *n* partido de copa
curate ['kjʊərɪt] *n* cura *m*
curator [kjʊə'reɪtə*] *n* director(a) *m/f*
curb [kɜːb] *vt* refrenar; (*person*) reprimir
♦ *n* freno; (*US*) bordillo
curdle ['kɜːdl] *vi* cuajarse
cure [kjʊə*] *vt* curar ♦ *n* cura, curación *f*; (*fig: solution*) remedio
curfew ['kɜːfjuː] *n* toque *m* de queda
curiosity [kjʊərɪ'ɔsɪtɪ] *n* curiosidad *f*
curious ['kjʊərɪəs] *adj* curioso; (*person: interested*): **to be ~** sentir curiosidad
curl [kɜːl] *n* rizo ♦ *vt* (*hair*) rizar ♦ *vi* rizarse; **~ up** *vi* (*person*) hacerse un ovillo; **~er** *n* rulo; **~y** *adj* rizado
currant ['kʌrnt] *n* pasa (de Corinto); (*black~, red~*) grosella
currency ['kʌrnsɪ] *n* moneda; **to gain ~** (*fig*) difundirse
current ['kʌrnt] *n* corriente *f* ♦ *adj* (*accepted*) corriente; (*present*) actual; **~ account** (*BRIT*) *n* cuenta corriente; **~ affairs** *npl* noticias *fpl* de actualidad; **~ly** *adv* actualmente
curriculum [kə'rɪkjʊləm] (*pl* **~s** or **curricula**) *n* plan *m* de estudios; **~ vitae** *n* currículum *m*
curry ['kʌrɪ] *n* curry *m* ♦ *vt*: **to ~ favour with** buscar favores con; **~ powder** *n* curry *m* en polvo
curse [kɜːs] *vi* soltar tacos ♦ *vt* maldecir ♦ *n* maldición *f*; (*swearword*) palabrota, taco
cursor ['kɜːsə*] *n* (*COMPUT*) cursor *m*
cursory ['kɜːsərɪ] *adj* rápido, superficial
curt [kɜːt] *adj* corto, seco
curtail [kɜː'teɪl] *vt* (*visit etc*) acortar; (*freedom*) restringir; (*expenses etc*) reducir
curtain ['kɜːtn] *n* cortina; (*THEATRE*) telón *m*
curts(e)y ['kɜːtsɪ] *vi* hacer una reverencia
curve [kɜːv] *n* curva ♦ *vi* (*road*) hacer una curva; (*line etc*) curvarse
cushion ['kʊʃən] *n* cojín *m*; (*of air*) colchón *m* ♦ *vt* (*shock*) amortiguar
custard ['kʌstəd] *n* natillas *fpl*
custody ['kʌstədɪ] *n* custodia; **to take into**

~ detener
custom ['kʌstəm] *n* costumbre *f*; (*COMM*) clientela; **~ary** *adj* acostumbrado
customer ['kʌstəmə*] *n* cliente *m/f*
customized ['kʌstəmaɪzd] *adj* (*car etc*) hecho a encargo
custom-made *adj* hecho a la medida
customs ['kʌstəmz] *npl* aduana; **~ officer** *n* aduanero/a
cut [kʌt] (*pt, pp* **cut**) *vt* cortar; (*price*) rebajar; (*text, programme*) acortar; (*reduce*) reducir ♦ *vi* cortar ♦ *n* (*of garment*) corte *m*; (*in skin*) cortadura; (*in salary etc*) rebaja; (*in spending*) reducción *f*, recorte *m*; (*slice of meat*) tajada; **to ~ a tooth** echar un diente; **~ down** *vt* (*tree*) derribar; (*reduce*) reducir; **~ off** *vt* cortar; (*person, place*) aislar; (*TEL*) desconectar; **~ out** *vt* (*shape*) recortar; (*stop: activity etc*) dejar; (*remove*) quitar; **~ up** *vt* cortar (en pedazos); **~back** *n* reducción *f*
cute [kjuːt] *adj* mono
cuticle ['kjuːtɪkl] *n* cutícula
cutlery ['kʌtlərɪ] *n* cubiertos *mpl*
cutlet ['kʌtlɪt] *n* chuleta; (*nut etc ~*) plato vegetariano hecho con nueces y verdura en forma de chuleta
cut: **~out** *n* (*switch*) dispositivo de seguridad, disyuntor *m*; (*cardboard ~out*) recortable *m*; **~-price** (*US* **~-rate**) *adj* a precio reducido; **~throat** *n* asesino/a ♦ *adj* feroz
cutting ['kʌtɪŋ] *adj* (*remark*) mordaz ♦ *n* (*BRIT: from newspaper*) recorte *m*; (*from plant*) esqueje *m*
CV *n abbr* = **curriculum vitae**
cwt *abbr* = **hundredweight(s)**
cyanide ['saɪənaɪd] *n* cianuro
cycle ['saɪkl] *n* ciclo; (*bicycle*) bicicleta ♦ *vi* ir en bicicleta; **~ lane** *n* carril-bici *m*; **~ path** *n* carril-bici *m*; **cycling** *n* ciclismo; **cyclist** *n* ciclista *m/f*
cyclone ['saɪkləʊn] *n* ciclón *m*
cygnet ['sɪgnɪt] *n* pollo de cisne
cylinder ['sɪlɪndə*] *n* cilindro; (*of gas*) bombona; **~-head gasket** *n* junta de culata

cymbals ['sɪmblz] *npl* platillos *mpl*
cynic ['sɪnɪk] *n* cínico/a; **~al** *adj* cínico; **~ism** ['sɪnɪsɪzəm] *n* cinismo
Cyprus ['saɪprəs] *n* Chipre *f*
cyst [sɪst] *n* quiste *m*; **~itis** [-'taɪtɪs] *n* cistitis *f*
czar [zɑ:*] *n* zar *m*
Czech [tʃɛk] *adj, n* checo/a *m/f*; **~ Republic** *n* la República Checa

D, d

D [di:] *n* (*MUS*) re *m*
dab [dæb] *vt* (*eyes, wound*) tocar (ligeramente); (*paint, cream*) poner un poco de
dabble ['dæbl] *vi*: **to ~ in** ser algo aficionado a
dad [dæd] *n* = **daddy**
daddy ['dædɪ] *n* papá *m*
daffodil ['dæfədɪl] *n* narciso
daft [dɑ:ft] *adj* tonto
dagger ['dægə*] *n* puñal *m*, daga
daily ['deɪlɪ] *adj* diario, cotidiano ♦ *adv* todos los días, cada día
dainty ['deɪntɪ] *adj* delicado
dairy ['dɛərɪ] *n* (*shop*) lechería; (*on farm*) vaquería; **~ farm** *n* granja; **~ products** *npl* productos *mpl* lácteos; **~ store** (*US*) *n* lechería
daisy ['deɪzɪ] *n* margarita
dale [deɪl] *n* valle *m*
dam [dæm] *n* presa ♦ *vt* construir una presa sobre, represar
damage ['dæmɪdʒ] *n* lesión *f*; daño; (*dents etc*) desperfectos *mpl*; (*fig*) perjuicio ♦ *vt* dañar, perjudicar; (*spoil, break*) estropear; **~s** *npl* (*LAW*) daños *mpl* y perjuicios
damn [dæm] *vt* condenar; (*curse*) maldecir ♦ *n* (*inf*): **I don't give a ~** me importa un pito ♦ *adj* (*inf: also:* **~ed**) maldito; **(it)!** ¡maldito sea!; **~ing** *adj* (*evidence*) irrecusable
damp [dæmp] *adj* húmedo, mojado ♦ *n* humedad *f* ♦ *vt* (*also:* **~en**: *cloth, rag*) mojar; (: *enthusiasm*) enfriar

damson ['dæmzən] *n* ciruela damascena
dance [dɑ:ns] *n* baile *m* ♦ *vi* bailar; **~ hall** *n* salón *m* de baile; **~r** *n* bailador(a) *m/f*; (*professional*) bailarín/ina *m/f*; **dancing** *n* baile *m*
dandelion ['dændɪlaɪən] *n* diente *m* de león
dandruff ['dændrəf] *n* caspa
Dane [deɪn] *n* danés/esa *m/f*
danger ['deɪndʒə*] *n* peligro; (*risk*) riesgo; **~!** (*on sign*) ¡peligro de muerte!; **to be in ~ of** correr riesgo de; **~ous** *adj* peligroso; **~ously** *adv* peligrosamente
dangle ['dæŋgl] *vt* colgar ♦ *vi* pender, colgar
Danish ['deɪnɪʃ] *adj* danés/esa ♦ *n* (*LING*) danés *m*
dare [dɛə*] *vt*: **to ~ sb to do** desafiar a uno a hacer ♦ *vi*: **to ~ (to) do sth** atreverse a hacer algo; **I ~ say** (*I suppose*) puede ser (que); **daring** *adj* atrevido, osado ♦ *n* atrevimiento, osadía
dark [dɑ:k] *adj* oscuro; (*hair, complexion*) moreno ♦ *n*: **in the ~** a oscuras; **to be in the ~ about** (*fig*) no saber nada de; **after ~** después del anochecer; **~en** *vt* (*colour*) hacer más oscuro ♦ *vi* oscurecerse; **~ glasses** *npl* gafas *fpl* negras (*SP*), anteojos *mpl* negros (*AM*); **~ness** *n* oscuridad *f*; **~room** *n* cuarto oscuro
darling ['dɑ:lɪŋ] *adj, n* querido/a *m/f*
darn [dɑ:n] *vt* zurcir
dart [dɑ:t] *n* dardo; (*in sewing*) sisa ♦ *vi* precipitarse; **~ away/along** *vi* salir/marchar disparado; **~board** *n* diana; **~s** *n* dardos *mpl*
dash [dæʃ] *n* (*small quantity: of liquid*) gota, chorrito; (: *of solid*) pizca; (*sign*) raya ♦ *vt* (*throw*) tirar; (*hopes*) defraudar ♦ *vi* precipitarse, ir de prisa; **~ away** *or* **off** *vi* marcharse apresuradamente
dashboard ['dæʃbɔ:d] *n* (*AUT*) salpicadero
dashing ['dæʃɪŋ] *adj* gallardo
data ['deɪtə] *npl* datos *mpl*; **~base** *n* base *f* de datos; **~ processing** *n* proceso de datos
date [deɪt] *n* (*day*) fecha; (*with friend*) cita;

(*fruit*) dátil *m* ♦ *vt* fechar; (*person*) salir con; **~ of birth** fecha de nacimiento; **to ~** *adv* hasta la fecha; **~d** *adj* anticuado; **~ rape** *n* violación ocurrida durante una cita con un conocido

daub [dɔ:b] *vt* embadurnar

daughter ['dɔ:tə*] *n* hija; **~-in-law** *n* nuera, hija política

daunting ['dɔ:ntɪŋ] *adj* desalentador(a)

dawdle ['dɔ:dl] *vi* (*go slowly*) andar muy despacio

dawn [dɔ:n] *n* alba, amanecer *m*; (*fig*) nacimiento ♦ *vi* (*day*) amanecer; (*fig*): **it ~ed on him that ...** cayó en la cuenta de que ...

day [deɪ] *n* día *m*; (*working ~*) jornada; (*hey~*) tiempos *mpl*, días *mpl*; **the ~ before/after** el día anterior/siguiente; **the ~ after tomorrow** pasado mañana; **the ~ before yesterday** anteayer; **the following ~** el día siguiente; **by ~** de día; **~break** *n* amanecer *m*; **~dream** *vi* soñar despierto; **~light** *n* luz *f* (del día); **~ return** *n* billete *m* de ida y vuelta (en un día); **~time** *n* día *m*; **~-to-~** *adj* cotidiano

daze [deɪz] *vt* (*stun*) aturdir ♦ *n*: **in a ~** aturdido

dazzle ['dæzl] *vt* deslumbrar

DC *abbr* (= *direct current*) corriente *f* continua

dead [ded] *adj* muerto; (*limb*) dormido; (*telephone*) cortado; (*battery*) agotado ♦ *adv* (*completely*) totalmente; (*exactly*) exactamente; **to shoot sb ~** matar a uno a tiros; **~ tired** muerto (de cansancio); **to stop ~** parar en seco; **the ~** *npl* los muertos; **to be a ~ loss** (*inf: person*) ser un inútil; **~en** *vt* (*blow, sound*) amortiguar; (*pain etc*) aliviar; **~ end** *n* callejón *m* sin salida; **~ heat** *n* (*SPORT*) empate *m*; **~line** *n* fecha (*or* hora) tope; **~lock** *n*: **to reach ~lock** llegar a un punto muerto; **~ly** *adj* mortal, fatal; **~pan** *adj* sin expresión; **the D~ Sea** *n* el Mar Muerto

deaf [def] *adj* sordo; **~en** *vt* ensordecer; **~ness** *n* sordera

deal [di:l] (*pt, pp* **dealt**) *n* (*agreement*) pacto, convenio; (*business ~*) trato ♦ *vt* dar; (*card*) repartir; **a great ~ (of)** bastante, mucho; **~ in** *vt fus* tratar en, comerciar en; **~ with** *vt fus* (*people*) tratar con; (*problem*) ocuparse de; (*subject*) tratar de; **~ings** *npl* (*COMM*) transacciones *fpl*; (*relations*) relaciones *fpl*

dealt [delt] *pt, pp of* **deal**

dean [di:n] *n* (*REL*) deán *m*; (*SCOL: BRIT*) decano; (: *US*) decano; rector *m*

dear [dɪə*] *adj* querido; (*expensive*) caro ♦ *n*: **my ~** mi querido/a ♦ *excl*: **~ me!** ¡Dios mío!; **D~ Sir/Madam** (*in letter*) Muy Señor Mío, Estimado Señor/Estimada Señora; **D~ Mr/Mrs X** Estimado/a Señor(a) X; **~ly** *adv* (*love*) mucho; (*pay*) caro

death [deθ] *n* muerte *f*; **~ certificate** *n* partida de defunción; **~ly** *adj* (*white*) como un muerto; (*silence*) sepulcral; **~ penalty** *n* pena de muerte; **~ rate** *n* mortalidad *f*; **~ toll** *n* número de víctimas

debacle [deɪ'bɑ:kl] *n* desastre *m*

debase [dɪ'beɪs] *vt* degradar

debatable [dɪ'beɪtəbl] *adj* discutible

debate [dɪ'beɪt] *n* debate *m* ♦ *vt* discutir

debit ['debɪt] *n* debe *m* ♦ *vt*: **to ~ a sum to sb** *or* **to sb's account** cargar una suma en cuenta a alguien

debris ['debri:] *n* escombros *mpl*

debt [det] *n* deuda; **to be in ~** tener deudas; **~or** *n* deudor(a) *m/f*

début ['deɪbju:] *n* presentación *f*

decade ['dekeɪd] *n* decenio, década

decadence ['dekədəns] *n* decadencia

decaff ['di:kæf] (*inf*) *n* descafeinado

decaffeinated [dɪ'kæfɪneɪtɪd] *adj* descafeinado

decanter [dɪ'kæntə*] *n* garrafa

decay [dɪ'keɪ] *n* (*of building*) desmoronamiento; (*of tooth*) caries *f inv* ♦ *vi* (*rot*) pudrirse

deceased [dɪ'si:st] *n*: **the ~** el/la difunto/a

deceit [dɪ'si:t] *n* engaño; **~ful** *adj* engañoso; **deceive** [dɪ'si:v] *vt* engañar

December [dɪ'sembə*] n diciembre m

decent ['di:sənt] adj (proper) decente; (person: kind) amable, bueno

deception [dɪ'sepʃən] n engaño

deceptive [dɪ'septɪv] adj engañoso

decibel ['desɪbel] n decibel(io) m

decide [dɪ'saɪd] vt (person) decidir; (question, argument) resolver ♦ vi decidir; **to ~ to do/that** decidir hacer/que; **to ~ on sth** decidirse por algo; **~d** adj (resolute) decidido; (clear, definite) indudable; **~dly** [-dɪdlɪ] adv decididamente; (emphatically) con resolución

deciduous [dɪ'sɪdjuəs] adj de hoja caduca

decimal ['desɪməl] adj decimal ♦ n decimal m; **~ point** n coma decimal

decipher [dɪ'saɪfə*] vt descifrar

decision [dɪ'sɪʒən] n decisión f

decisive [dɪ'saɪsɪv] adj decisivo; (person) decidido

deck [dek] n (NAUT) cubierta; (of bus) piso; (record ~) platina; (of cards) baraja; **~chair** n tumbona

declaration [deklə'reɪʃən] n declaración f

declare [dɪ'kleə*] vt declarar

decline [dɪ'klaɪn] n disminución f, descenso ♦ vt rehusar ♦ vi (person, business) decaer; (strength) disminuir

decoder [di:'kəudə*] n (TV) decodificador m

décor ['deɪkɔ:*] n decoración f; (THEATRE) decorado

decorate ['dekəreɪt] vt (adorn): **to ~ (with)** adornar (de), decorar (de); (paint) pintar; (paper) empapelar; **decoration** [-'reɪʃən] n adorno; (act) decoración f; (medal) condecoración f; **decorator** n (workman) pintor m (decorador)

decorum [dɪ'kɔ:rəm] n decoro

decoy ['di:kɔɪ] n señuelo

decrease [n 'di:kri:s, vb di:'kri:s] n: **~ (in)** disminución f (de) ♦ vt disminuir, reducir ♦ vi reducirse

decree [dɪ'kri:] n decreto; **~ nisi** n sentencia provisional de divorcio

dedicate ['dedɪkeɪt] vt dedicar;

dedication [-'keɪʃən] n (devotion) dedicación f; (in book) dedicatoria

deduce [dɪ'dju:s] vt deducir

deduct [dɪ'dʌkt] vt restar; descontar; **~ion** [dɪ'dʌkʃən] n (amount deducted) descuento; (conclusion) deducción f, conclusión f

deed [di:d] n hecho, acto; (feat) hazaña; (LAW) escritura

deep [di:p] adj profundo; (expressing measurements) de profundidad; (voice) bajo; (breath) profundo; (colour) intenso ♦ adv: **the spectators stood 20 ~** los espectadores se formaron de 20 en fondo; **to be 4 metres ~** tener 4 metros de profundidad; **~en** vt ahondar, profundizar ♦ vi aumentar, crecer; **~-freeze** n congelador m; **~-fry** vt freír en aceite abundante; **~ly** adv (breathe) a pleno pulmón; (interested, moved, grateful) profundamente, hondamente; **~-sea diving** n buceo de altura; **~-seated** adj (beliefs) (profundamente) arraigado

deer [dɪə*] n inv ciervo

deface [dɪ'feɪs] vt (wall, surface) estropear, pintarrajear

default [dɪ'fɔ:lt] n: **by ~** (win) por incomparecencia ♦ adj (COMPUT) por defecto

defeat [dɪ'fi:t] n derrota ♦ vt derrotar, vencer; **~ist** adj, n derrotista m/f

defect [n 'di:fekt, vb dɪ'fekt] n defecto ♦ vi: **to ~ to the enemy** pasarse al enemigo; **~ive** [dɪ'fektɪv] adj defectuoso

defence [dɪ'fens] (US **defense**) n defensa; **~less** adj indefenso

defend [dɪ'fend] vt defender; **~ant** n acusado/a; (in civil case) demandado/a; **~er** n defensor(a) m/f; (SPORT) defensa m/f

defense [dɪ'fens] (US) n = **defence**

defensive [dɪ'fensɪv] adj defensivo ♦ n: **on the ~** a la defensiva

defer [dɪ'fə:*] vt aplazar

defiance [dɪ'faɪəns] n desafío; **in ~ of** en contra de; **defiant** [dɪ'faɪənt] adj *(challenging)* desafiante, retador(a)

deficiency [dɪˈfɪʃənsɪ] *n (lack)* falta; *(defect)* defecto; **deficient** [dɪˈfɪʃənt] *adj* deficiente

deficit [ˈdefɪsɪt] *n* déficit *m*

define [dɪˈfaɪn] *vt (word etc)* definir; *(limits etc)* determinar

definite [ˈdefɪnɪt] *adj (fixed)* determinado; *(obvious)* claro; *(certain)* indudable; **he was ~ about it** no dejó lugar a dudas (sobre ello); **~ly** *adv* desde luego, por supuesto

definition [defɪˈnɪʃən] *n* definición *f*; *(clearness)* nitidez *f*

deflate [diːˈfleɪt] *vt* desinflar

deflect [dɪˈflekt] *vt* desviar

defraud [dɪˈfrɔːd] *vt*: **to ~ sb of sth** estafar algo a uno

defrost [diːˈfrɒst] *vt* descongelar; **~er** *(US) n (demister)* eliminador *m* de vaho

deft [deft] *adj* diestro, hábil

defunct [dɪˈfʌŋkt] *adj* difunto; *(organization etc)* ya que no existe

defuse [diːˈfjuːz] *vt* desactivar; *(situation)* calmar

defy [dɪˈfaɪ] *vt (resist)* oponerse a; *(challenge)* desafiar; *(fig)*: **it defies description** resulta imposible describirlo

degenerate [*vb* dɪˈdʒenəreɪt, *adj* dɪˈdʒenərɪt] *vi* degenerar ♦ *adj* degenerado

degree [dɪˈɡriː] *n* grado; *(SCOL)* título; **to have a ~ in maths** tener una licenciatura en matemáticas; **by ~s** *(gradually)* poco a poco, por etapas; **to some ~** hasta cierto punto

dehydrated [diːhaɪˈdreɪtɪd] *adj* deshidratado; *(milk)* en polvo

de-ice [diːˈaɪs] *vt* deshelar

deign [deɪn] *vi*: **to ~ to do** dignarse hacer

dejected [dɪˈdʒektɪd] *adj* abatido, desanimado

delay [dɪˈleɪ] *vt* demorar, aplazar; *(person)* entretener; *(train)* retrasar ♦ *vi* tardar ♦ *n* demora, retraso; **to be ~ed** retrasarse; **without ~** en seguida, sin tardar

delectable [dɪˈlektəbl] *adj (person)*

encantador(a); *(food)* delicioso

delegate [*n* ˈdelɪɡɪt, *vb* ˈdelɪɡeɪt] *n* delegado/a ♦ *vt (person)* delegar en; *(task)* delegar

delete [dɪˈliːt] *vt* suprimir, tachar

deliberate [*adj* dɪˈlɪbərɪt, *vb* dɪˈlɪbəreɪt] *adj (intentional)* intencionado; *(slow)* pausado, lento ♦ *vi* deliberar; **~ly** *adv (on purpose)* a propósito

delicacy [ˈdelɪkəsɪ] *n* delicadeza; *(choice food)* manjar *m*

delicate [ˈdelɪkɪt] *adj* delicado; *(fragile)* frágil

delicatessen [delɪkəˈtesn] *n* ultramarinos *mpl* finos

delicious [dɪˈlɪʃəs] *adj* delicioso

delight [dɪˈlaɪt] *n (feeling)* placer *m*, deleite *m*; *(person, experience etc)* encanto, delicia ♦ *vt* encantar, deleitar; **to take ~ in** deleitarse en; **~ed** *adj*: **~ed (at** or **with/ to do)** encantado (con/de hacer); **~ful** *adj* encantador(a), delicioso

delinquent [dɪˈlɪŋkwənt] *adj, n* delincuente *m/f*

delirious [dɪˈlɪrɪəs] *adj*: **to be ~** delirar, desvariar; **to be ~ with** estar loco de

deliver [dɪˈlɪvə*] *vt (distribute)* repartir; *(hand over)* entregar; *(message)* comunicar; *(speech)* pronunciar; *(MED)* asistir al parto de; **~y** *n* reparto; entrega; *(of speaker)* modo de expresarse; *(MED)* parto, alumbramiento; **to take ~y of** recibir

delude [dɪˈluːd] *vt* engañar

deluge [ˈdeljuːdʒ] *n* diluvio

delusion [dɪˈluːʒən] *n* ilusión *f*, engaño

de luxe [dəˈlʌks] *adj* de lujo

demand [dɪˈmɑːnd] *vt (gen)* exigir; *(rights)* reclamar ♦ *n* exigencia; *(claim)* reclamación *f*; *(ECON)* demanda; **to be in ~** ser muy solicitado; **on ~** a solicitud; **~ing** *adj (boss)* exigente; *(work)* absorbente

demean [dɪˈmiːn] *vt*: **to ~ o.s.** rebajarse

demeanour [dɪˈmiːnə*] *(US* **demeanor**) *n* porte *m*, conducta

demented [dɪˈmentɪd] *adj* demente

demise [dɪ'maɪz] n (*death*) fallecimiento

demister [diː'mɪstə*] n (*AUT*) eliminador m de vaho

demo ['dɛməu] (*inf*) n abbr (= *demonstration*) manifestación f

democracy [dɪ'mɔkrəsɪ] n democracia; **democrat** ['dɛməkræt] n demócrata m/f; **democratic** [dɛmə'krætɪk] adj democrático; (*US*) demócrata

demolish [dɪ'mɔlɪʃ] vt derribar, demoler; (*fig: argument*) destruir

demon ['diːmən] n (*evil spirit*) demonio

demonstrate ['dɛmənstreɪt] vt demostrar; (*skill, appliance*) mostrar ♦ vi manifestarse; **demonstration** [-'streɪʃən] n (*POL*) manifestación f; (*proof, exhibition*) demostración f; **demonstrator** n (*POL*) manifestante m/f; (*COMM*) demostrador(a) m/f; vendedor(a) m/f

demote [dɪ'məut] vt degradar

demure [dɪ'mjuə*] adj recatado

den [dɛn] n (*of animal*) guarida; (*room*) habitación f

denial [dɪ'naɪəl] n (*refusal*) negativa; (*of report etc*) negación f

denim ['dɛnɪm] n tela vaquera; **~s** npl vaqueros mpl

Denmark ['dɛnmɑːk] n Dinamarca

denomination [dɪnɔmɪ'neɪʃən] n valor m; (*REL*) confesión f

denounce [dɪ'nauns] vt denunciar

dense [dɛns] adj (*crowd*) denso; (*thick*) espeso; (: *foliage etc*) tupido; (*inf: stupid*) torpe; **~ly** adv: **~ly populated** con una alta densidad de población

density ['dɛnsɪtɪ] n densidad f; **single/double-~ disk** n (*COMPUT*) disco de densidad sencilla/doble densidad

dent [dɛnt] n abolladura ♦ vt (*also*: **make a ~ in**) abollar

dental ['dɛntl] adj dental; **~ surgeon** n odontólogo/a

dentist ['dɛntɪst] n dentista m/f

dentures ['dɛntʃəz] npl dentadura (postiza)

deny [dɪ'naɪ] vt negar; (*charge*) rechazar

deodorant [diː'əudərənt] n desodorante m

depart [dɪ'pɑːt] vi irse, marcharse; (*train*) salir; **to ~ from** (*fig: differ from*) apartarse de

department [dɪ'pɑːtmənt] n (*COMM*) sección f; (*SCOL*) departamento; (*POL*) ministerio; **~ store** n gran almacén m

departure [dɪ'pɑːtʃə*] n partida, ida; (*of train*) salida; (*of employee*) marcha; **a new ~** un nuevo rumbo; **~ lounge** n (*at airport*) sala de embarque

depend [dɪ'pɛnd] vi: **to ~ on** depender de; (*rely on*) contar con; **it ~s** depende, según; **~ing on the result** según el resultado; **~able** adj (*person*) formal, serio; (*watch*) exacto; (*car*) seguro; **~ant** n dependiente m/f; **~ent** adj: **to be ~ent on** depender de ♦ n = **dependant**

depict [dɪ'pɪkt] vt (*in picture*) pintar; (*describe*) representar

depleted [dɪ'pliːtɪd] adj reducido

deploy [dɪ'plɔɪ] vt desplegar

deport [dɪ'pɔːt] vt deportar

deposit [dɪ'pɔzɪt] n depósito; (*CHEM*) sedimento; (*of ore, oil*) yacimiento ♦ vt (*gen*) depositar; **~ account** (*BRIT*) n cuenta de ahorros

depot ['dɛpəu] n (*storehouse*) depósito; (*for vehicles*) parque m; (*US*) estación f

depreciate [dɪ'priːʃɪeɪt] vi depreciarse, perder valor

depress [dɪ'prɛs] vt deprimir; (*wages etc*) hacer bajar; (*press down*) apretar; **~ed** adj deprimido; **~ing** adj deprimente; **~ion** [dɪ'prɛʃən] n depresión f

deprivation [dɛprɪ'veɪʃən] n privación f

deprive [dɪ'praɪv] vt: **to ~ sb of** privar a uno de; **~d** adj necesitado

depth [dɛpθ] n profundidad f; (*of cupboard*) fondo; **to be in the ~s of despair** sentir la mayor desesperación; **to be out of one's ~** (*in water*) no hacer pie; (*fig*) sentirse totalmente perdido

deputize ['dɛpjutaɪz] vi: **to ~ for sb** suplir a uno

deputy ['dɛpjutɪ] adj: **~ head** subdirector(a) m/f ♦ n sustituto/a, suplente m/f; (*US: POL*) diputado/a; (*US:*

also: ~ **sheriff**) agente *m* (del sheriff)

derail [dɪ'reɪl] *vt*: **to be ~ed** descarrilarse

deranged [dɪ'reɪndʒd] *adj* trastornado

derby ['dɑːbɪ] (*US*) *n* (*hat*) hongo

derelict ['derɪlɪkt] *adj* abandonado

derisory [dɪ'raɪzərɪ] *adj* (*sum*) irrisorio

derive [dɪ'raɪv] *vt* (*benefit etc*) obtener
  ♦ *vi*: **to ~ from** derivarse de

derogatory [dɪ'rɔgətərɪ] *adj* despectivo

descend [dɪ'send] *vt*, *vi* descender, bajar;
  to ~ from descender de; **to ~ to** rebajarse
  a; **~ant** *n* descendiente *m/f*

descent [dɪ'sent] *n* descenso; (*origin*)
  descendencia

describe [dɪs'kraɪb] *vt* describir;
  description [-'krɪpʃən] *n* descripción *f*;
  (*sort*) clase *f*, género

desecrate ['desɪkreɪt] *vt* profanar

desert [*n* 'dezət, *vb* dɪ'zəːt] *n* desierto ♦ *vt*
  abandonar ♦ *vi* (*MIL*) desertar; **~er**
  [dɪ'zəːtə*] *n* desertor(a) *m/f*; **~ion**
  [dɪ'zəːʃən] *n* deserción *f*; (*LAW*) abandono;
  ~ island *n* isla desierta; **~s** [dɪ'zəːts] *npl*:
  to get one's just ~s llevar su merecido

deserve [dɪ'zəːv] *vt* merecer, ser digno de;
  deserving *adj* (*person*) digno; (*action,
  cause*) meritorio

design [dɪ'zaɪn] *n* (*sketch*) bosquejo;
  (*layout, shape*) diseño; (*pattern*) dibujo;
  (*intention*) intención *f* ♦ *vt* diseñar

designate [*vb* 'dezɪgneɪt, *adj* 'dezɪgnɪt] *vt*
  (*appoint*) nombrar; (*destine*) designar
  ♦ *adj* designado

designer [dɪ'zaɪnə*] *n* diseñador(a) *m/f*;
  (*fashion ~*) modisto/a, diseñador(a) *m/f*
  de moda

desirable [dɪ'zaɪərəbl] *adj* (*proper*)
  deseable; (*attractive*) atractivo

desire [dɪ'zaɪə*] *n* deseo ♦ *vt* desear

desk [desk] *n* (*in office*) escritorio; (*for
  pupil*) pupitre *m*; (*in hotel, at airport*)
  recepción *f*; (*BRIT: in shop, restaurant*) caja

desk-top publishing ['desktɔp-] *n*
  autoedición *f*

desolate ['desəlɪt] *adj* (*place*) desierto;
  (*person*) afligido

despair [dɪs'peə*] *n* desesperación *f* ♦ *vi*:

to ~ of perder la esperanza de

despatch [dɪs'pætʃ] *n*, *vt* = **dispatch**

desperate ['despərɪt] *adj* desesperado;
  (*fugitive*) peligroso; **to be ~ for sth/to do**
  necesitar urgentemente algo/hacer; **~ly**
  adv desesperadamente; (*very*)
  terriblemente, gravemente

desperation [despə'reɪʃən] *n*
  desesperación *f*; **in (sheer) ~**
  (*absolutamente*) desesperado

despicable [dɪs'pɪkəbl] *adj* vil,
  despreciable

despise [dɪs'paɪz] *vt* despreciar

despite [dɪs'paɪt] *prep* a pesar de, pese a

despondent [dɪs'pɔndənt] *adj* deprimido,
  abatido

dessert [dɪ'zəːt] *n* postre *m*; **~spoon** *n*
  cuchara (de postre)

destination [destɪ'neɪʃən] *n* destino

destiny ['destɪnɪ] *n* destino

destitute ['destɪtjuːt] *adj* desamparado,
  indigente

destroy [dɪs'trɔɪ] *vt* destruir; (*animal*)
  sacrificar; **~er** *n* (*NAUT*) destructor *m*

destruction [dɪs'trʌkʃən] *n* destrucción *f*

detach [dɪ'tætʃ] *vt* separar; (*unstick*)
  despegar; **~ed** *adj* (*attitude*) objetivo,
  imparcial; **~ed house** *n* ≈ chalé *m*,
  ≈ chalet *m*; **~ment** *n* (*aloofness*) frialdad
  f; (*MIL*) destacamento

detail ['diːteɪl] *n* detalle *m*; (*no pl: in
  picture etc*) detalles *mpl*; (*trifle*) pequeñez
  f ♦ *vt* detallar; (*MIL*) destacar; **in ~**
  detalladamente; **~ed** *adj* detallado

detain [dɪ'teɪn] *vt* retener; (*in captivity*)
  detener

detect [dɪ'tekt] *vt* descubrir; (*MED, POLICE*)
  identificar; (*MIL, RADAR, TECH*) detectar;
  ~ion [dɪ'tekʃən] *n* descubrimiento;
  identificación *f*; **~ive** *n* detective *m/f*;
  ~ive story *n* novela policíaca; **~or** *n*
  detector *m*

detention [dɪ'tenʃən] *n* detención *f*,
  arresto; (*SCOL*) castigo

deter [dɪ'təː*] *vt* (*dissuade*) disuadir

detergent [dɪ'təːdʒənt] *n* detergente *m*

deteriorate [dɪ'tɪərɪəreɪt] *vi* deteriorarse;

deterioration [-'reɪʃən] *n* deterioro

determination [dɪtɜ:mɪ'neɪʃən] *n* resolución *f*

determine [dɪ'tɜ:mɪn] *vt* determinar; **~d** *adj* (*person*) resuelto, decidido; **~d to do** resuelto a hacer

deterrent [dɪ'terənt] *n* (*MIL*) fuerza de disuasión

detest [dɪ'test] *vt* aborrecer

detonate ['detəneɪt] *vi* estallar ♦ *vt* hacer detonar

detour ['di:tuə*] *n* (*gen*, *US: AUT*) desviación *f*

detract [dɪ'trækt] *vt*: **to ~ from** quitar mérito a, desvirtuar

detriment ['detrɪmənt] *n*: **to the ~ of** en perjuicio de; **~al** [detrɪ'mentl] *adj*: **~al (to)** perjudicial a

devaluation [dɪvælju:'eɪʃən] *n* devaluación *f*

devalue [di:'vælju:] *vt* (*currency*) devaluar; (*fig*) quitar mérito a

devastate ['devəsteɪt] *vt* devastar; (*fig*): **to be ~d by** quedar destrozado por; **devastating** *adj* devastador(a); (*fig*) arrollador(a)

develop [dɪ'veləp] *vt* desarrollar; (*PHOT*) revelar; (*disease*) coger; (*habit*) adquirir; (*fault*) empezar a tener ♦ *vi* desarrollarse; (*advance*) progresar; (*facts*, *symptoms*) aparecer; **~er** *n* promotor *m*; **~ing country** *n* país *m* en (vías de) desarrollo; **~ment** *n* desarrollo; (*advance*) progreso; (*of affair*, *case*) desenvolvimiento; (*of land*) urbanización *f*

deviation [di:vɪ'eɪʃən] *n* desviación *f*

device [dɪ'vaɪs] *n* (*apparatus*) aparato, mecanismo

devil ['devl] *n* diablo, demonio

devious ['di:vɪəs] *adj* taimado

devise [dɪ'vaɪz] *vt* idear, inventar

devoid [dɪ'vɔɪd] *adj*: **~ of** desprovisto de

devolution [di:və'lu:ʃən] *n* (*POL*) descentralización *f*

devote [dɪ'vaut] *vt*: **to ~ sth to** dedicar algo a; **~d** *adj* (*loyal*) leal, fiel; **to be ~d to sb** querer con devoción a alguien; **the**

book is **~d** to politics el libro trata de la política; **~e** [devəu'ti:] *n* entusiasta *m/f*; (*REL*) devoto/a; **devotion** *n* dedicación *f*; (*REL*) devoción *f*

devour [dɪ'vauə*] *vt* devorar

devout [dɪ'vaut] *adj* devoto

dew [dju:] *n* rocío

diabetes [daɪə'bi:ti:z] *n* diabetes *f*; **diabetic** [-'betɪk] *adj*, *n* diabético/a *m/f*

diabolical [daɪə'bɒlɪkəl] (*inf*) *adj* (*weather*, *behaviour*) pésimo

diagnosis [daɪəg'nəusɪs] (*pl* **-ses**) *n* diagnóstico

diagonal [daɪ'ægənl] *adj*, *n* diagonal *f*

diagram ['daɪəgræm] *n* diagrama *m*, esquema *m*

dial ['daɪəl] *n* esfera, cuadrante *m*, cara (*AM*); (*on radio etc*) selector *m*; (*of phone*) disco ♦ *vt* (*number*) marcar

dialling ['daɪəlɪŋ]: **~ code** *n* prefijo; **~ tone** (*US* **dial tone**) *n* (*BRIT*) señal *f* or tono de marcar

dialogue ['daɪəlɒg] (*US* **dialog**) *n* diálogo

diameter [daɪ'æmɪtə*] *n* diámetro

diamond ['daɪəmənd] *n* diamante *m*; (*shape*) rombo; **~s** *npl* (*CARDS*) diamantes *mpl*

diaper ['daɪəpə*] (*US*) *n* pañal *m*

diaphragm ['daɪəfræm] *n* diafragma *m*

diarrhoea [daɪə'ri:ə] (*US* **diarrhea**) *n* diarrea

diary ['daɪərɪ] *n* (*daily account*) diario; (*book*) agenda

dice [daɪs] *n inv* dados *mpl* ♦ *vt* (*CULIN*) cortar en cuadritos

Dictaphone ® ['dɪktəfaun] *n* dictáfono ®

dictate [dɪk'teɪt] *vt* dictar; (*conditions*) imponer; **dictation** [-'teɪʃən] *n* dictado; (*giving of orders*) órdenes *fpl*

dictator [dɪk'teɪtə*] *n* dictador *m*; **~ship** *n* dictadura

dictionary ['dɪkʃənrɪ] *n* diccionario

did [dɪd] *pt of* **do**

didn't ['dɪdənt] = **did not**

die [daɪ] *vi* morir; (*fig: fade*) desvanecerse, desaparecer; **to be dying for sth/to do sth** morirse por algo/de ganas de hacer

algo; ~ **away** *vi* (*sound, light*) perderse;
~ **down** *vi* apagarse; (*wind*) amainar; ~
out *vi* desaparecer

diesel ['diːzəl] *n* vehículo con motor
Diesel; ~ **engine** *n* motor *m* Diesel; ~
(oil) *n* gasoil *m*

diet ['daɪət] *n* dieta; (*restricted food*)
régimen *m* ♦ *vi* (*also*: **be on a ~**) estar a
dieta, hacer régimen

differ ['dɪfə*] *vi*: **to ~ (from)** (*be different*)
ser distinto (a), diferenciarse (de);
(*disagree*) discrepar (de); **~ence** *n*
diferencia; (*disagreement*) desacuerdo;
~ent *adj* diferente, distinto; **~entiate**
[-'renʃieit] *vi*: **to ~entiate (between)**
distinguir (entre); **~ently** *adv* de otro
modo, en forma distinta

difficult ['dɪfɪkəlt] *adj* difícil; **~y** *n*
dificultad *f*

diffident ['dɪfɪdənt] *adj* tímido

dig [dɪg] (*pt, pp* **dug**) *vt* (*hole, ground*)
cavar ♦ *n* (*prod*) empujón *m*;
(*archaeological*) excavación *f*; (*remark*)
indirecta; **to ~ one's nails into** clavar las
uñas en; **~ into** *vt fus* (*savings*)
consumir; **~ up** *vt* (*information*)
desenterrar; (*plant*) desarraigar

digest [*vb* dai'dʒest, *n* 'daidʒest] *vt* (*food*)
digerir; (*facts*) asimilar ♦ *n* resumen *m*;
~ion [dɪ'dʒestʃən] *n* digestión *f*

digit ['dɪdʒɪt] *n* (*number*) dígito; (*finger*)
dedo; **~al** *adj* digital

dignified ['dɪgnɪfaɪd] *adj* grave, solemne

dignity ['dɪgnɪti] *n* dignidad *f*

digress [dai'gres] *vi*: **to ~ from** apartarse
de

digs [dɪgz] (*BRIT: inf*) *npl* pensión *f*,
alojamiento

dilapidated [dɪ'læpɪdeɪtɪd] *adj*
desmoronado, ruinoso

dilemma [dai'lemə] *n* dilema *m*

diligent ['dɪlɪdʒənt] *adj* diligente

dilute [dai'luːt] *vt* diluir

dim [dɪm] *adj* (*light*) débil; (*outline*)
indistinto; (*room*) oscuro; (*inf: stupid*)
lerdo ♦ *vt* (*light*) bajar

dime [daim] (*US*) *n* moneda de diez

centavos

dimension [dɪ'menʃən] *n* dimensión *f*

diminish [dɪ'mɪnɪʃ] *vt, vi* disminuir

diminutive [dɪ'mɪnjutɪv] *adj* diminuto ♦ *n*
(*LING*) diminutivo

dimmers ['dɪməz] (*US*) *npl* (*AUT: dipped
headlights*) luces *fpl* cortas; (: *parking
lights*) luces *fpl* de posición

dimple ['dɪmpl] *n* hoyuelo

din [dɪn] *n* estruendo, estrépito

dine [dain] *vi* cenar; **~r** *n* (*person*)
comensal *m/f*; (*US*) restaurante *m*
económico

dinghy ['dɪŋgɪ] *n* bote *m*; (*also*: **rubber ~**)
lancha (neumática)

dingy ['dɪndʒɪ] *adj* (*room*) sombrío; (*colour*)
sucio

dining car ['dainiŋ-] (*BRIT*) *n* (*RAIL*) coche-
comedor *m*

dining room *n* comedor *m*

dinner ['dɪnə*] *n* (*evening meal*) cena;
(*lunch*) comida; (*public*) cena, banquete
m; ~ **jacket** *n* smoking *m*; ~ **party** *n*
cena; ~ **time** *n* (*evening*) hora de cenar;
(*midday*) hora de comer

dinosaur ['dainəsɔː*] *n* dinosaurio

diocese ['daiəsis] *n* diócesis *f inv*

dip [dɪp] *n* (*slope*) pendiente *m*; (*in sea*)
baño; (*CULIN*) salsa ♦ *vt* (*in water*) mojar;
(*ladle etc*) meter; (*BRIT: AUT*): **to ~ one's
lights** poner luces de cruce ♦ *vi* (*road etc*)
descender, bajar

diploma [dɪ'pləumə] *n* diploma *m*

diplomacy [dɪ'pləuməsi] *n* diplomacia

diplomat ['dɪpləmæt] *n* diplomático/a; **~ic**
[dɪplə'mætɪk] *adj* diplomático

diprod ['dɪprɔd] (*US*) *n* = **dipstick**

dipstick ['dɪpstɪk] (*BRIT*) *n* (*AUT*) varilla de
nivel (del aceite)

dipswitch ['dɪpswɪtʃ] (*BRIT*) *n* (*AUT*)
interruptor *m*

dire [daiə*] *adj* calamitoso

direct [dai'rekt] *adj* directo; (*challenge*)
claro; (*person*) franco ♦ *vt* dirigir; (*order*):
to ~ sb to do sth mandar a uno hacer
algo ♦ *adv* derecho; **can you ~ me to...?**
¿puede indicarme dónde está...?; ~ **debit**

(*BRIT*) *n* domiciliación *f* bancaria de recibos

direction [dɪˈrɛkʃən] *n* dirección *f*; **sense of ~** sentido de la dirección; **~s** *npl* (*instructions*) instrucciones *fpl*; **~s for use** modo de empleo

directly [dɪˈrɛktlɪ] *adv* (*in straight line*) directamente; (*at once*) en seguida

director [dɪˈrɛktəˀ] *n* director(a) *m/f*

directory [dɪˈrɛktərɪ] *n* (*TEL*) guía (telefónica); (*COMPUT*) directorio; **~ enquiries, ~ assistance** (*US*) *n* (servicio de) información *f*

dirt [dɜːt] *n* suciedad *f*; (*earth*) tierra; **~-cheap** *adj* baratísimo; **~y** *adj* sucio; (*joke*) verde (*SP*), colorado (*AM*) ♦ *vt* ensuciar; (*stain*) manchar; **~y trick** *n* juego sucio

disability [dɪsəˈbɪlɪtɪ] *n* incapacidad *f*

disabled [dɪsˈeɪbld] *adj*: **to be physically ~** ser minusválido/a; **to be mentally ~** ser deficiente mental

disadvantage [dɪsədˈvɑːntɪdʒ] *n* desventaja, inconveniente *m*

disagree [dɪsəˈgriː] *vi* (*differ*) discrepar; **to ~ (with)** no estar de acuerdo (con); **~able** *adj* desagradable; (*person*) antipático; **~ment** *n* desacuerdo

disallow [dɪsəˈlaʊ] *vt* (*goal*) anular; (*claim*) rechazar

disappear [dɪsəˈpɪəˀ] *vi* desaparecer; **~ance** *n* desaparición *f*

disappoint [dɪsəˈpɔɪnt] *vt* decepcionar, defraudar; **~ed** *adj* decepcionado; **~ing** *adj* decepcionante; **~ment** *n* decepción *f*

disapproval [dɪsəˈpruːvəl] *n* desaprobación *f*

disapprove [dɪsəˈpruːv] *vi*: **to ~ of** ver mal

disarmament [dɪsˈɑːməmənt] *n* desarme *m*

disarray [dɪsəˈreɪ] *n*: **in ~** (*army, organization*) desorganizado; (*hair, clothes*) desarreglado

disaster [dɪˈzɑːstəˀ] *n* desastre *m*

disband [dɪsˈbænd] *vt* disolver ♦ *vi* desbandarse

disbelief [dɪsbəˈliːf] *n* incredulidad *f*

disc [dɪsk] *n* disco; (*COMPUT*) = **disk**

discard [dɪsˈkɑːd] *vt* (*old things*) tirar; (*fig*) descartar

discern [dɪˈsɜːn] *vt* percibir, discernir; (*understand*) comprender; **~ing** *adj* perspicaz

discharge [*vb* dɪsˈtʃɑːdʒ, *n* ˈdɪstʃɑːdʒ] *vt* (*task, duty*) cumplir; (*waste*) verter; (*patient*) dar de alta; (*employee*) despedir; (*soldier*) licenciar; (*defendant*) poner en libertad ♦ *n* (*ELEC*) descarga; (*MED*) supuración *f*; (*dismissal*) despedida; (*of duty*) desempeño; (*of debt*) pago, descargo

discipline [ˈdɪsɪplɪn] *n* disciplina ♦ *vt* disciplinar; (*punish*) castigar

disc jockey *n* pinchadiscos *m/f inv*

disclaim [dɪsˈkleɪm] *vt* negar

disclose [dɪsˈkləʊz] *vt* revelar; **disclosure** [-ˈkləʊʒəˀ] *n* revelación *f*

disco [ˈdɪskəʊ] *n abbr* = **discothèque**

discomfort [dɪsˈkʌmfət] *n* incomodidad *f*; (*unease*) inquietud *f*; (*physical*) malestar *m*

disconcert [dɪskənˈsɜːt] *vt* desconcertar

disconnect [dɪskəˈnɛkt] *vt* separar; (*ELEC etc*) desconectar

discontent [dɪskənˈtɛnt] *n* descontento; **~ed** *adj* descontento

discontinue [dɪskənˈtɪnjuː] *vt* interrumpir; (*payments*) suspender; **"~d"** (*COMM*) "ya no se fabrica"

discord [ˈdɪskɔːd] *n* discordia; (*MUS*) disonancia

discothèque [ˈdɪskəʊtɛk] *n* discoteca

discount [*n* ˈdɪskaʊnt, *vb* dɪsˈkaʊnt] *n* descuento ♦ *vt* descontar

discourage [dɪsˈkʌrɪdʒ] *vt* desalentar; (*advise against*): **to ~ sb from doing** disuadir a uno de hacer

discover [dɪsˈkʌvəˀ] *vt* descubrir; (*error*) darse cuenta de; **~y** *n* descubrimiento

discredit [dɪsˈkrɛdɪt] *vt* desacreditar

discreet [dɪsˈkriːt] *adj* (*tactful*) discreto; (*careful*) circunspecto, prudente

discrepancy [dɪsˈkrɛpənsɪ] *n* diferencia

discretion [dɪsˈkrɛʃən] *n* (*tact*) discreción

f; **at the ~ of** a criterio de
discriminate [dɪ'skrɪmɪneɪt] *vi*: **to ~ between** distinguir entre; **to ~ against** discriminar contra; **discriminating** *adj* entendido; **discrimination** [-'neɪʃən] *n* (*discernment*) perspicacia; (*bias*) discriminación *f*
discuss [dɪ'skʌs] *vt* discutir; (*a theme*) tratar; **~ion** [dɪ'skʌʃən] *n* discusión *f*
disdain [dɪs'deɪn] *n* desdén *m*
disease [dɪ'ziːz] *n* enfermedad *f*
disembark [dɪsɪm'baːk] *vt, vi* desembarcar
disentangle [dɪsɪn'tæŋgl] *vt* soltar; (*wire, thread*) desenredar
disfigure [dɪs'fɪgə*] *vt* (*person*) desfigurar; (*object*) afear
disgrace [dɪs'greɪs] *n* ignominia; (*shame*) vergüenza, escándalo ♦ *vt* deshonrar; **~ful** *adj* vergonzoso
disgruntled [dɪs'grʌntld] *adj* disgustado, descontento
disguise [dɪs'gaɪz] *n* disfraz *m* ♦ *vt* disfrazar; **in ~** disfrazado
disgust [dɪs'gʌst] *n* repugnancia ♦ *vt* repugnar, dar asco a; **~ing** *adj* repugnante, asqueroso; (*behaviour etc*) vergonzoso
dish [dɪʃ] *n* (*gen*) plato; **to do** *or* **wash the ~es** fregar los platos; **~ out** *vt* repartir; **~ up** *vt* servir; **~cloth** *n* estropajo
dishearten [dɪs'haːtn] *vt* desalentar
dishevelled [dɪ'ʃevəld] (*US* **disheveled**) *adj* (*hair*) despeinado; (*appearance*) desarreglado
dishonest [dɪs'ɔnɪst] *adj* (*person*) poco honrado, tramposo; (*means*) fraudulento; **~y** *n* falta de honradez
dishonour [dɪs'ɔnə*] (*US* **dishonor**) *n* deshonra; **~able** *adj* deshonroso
dishtowel [ˈdɪʃtauəl] (*US*) *n* estropajo
dishwasher [ˈdɪʃwɔʃə*] *n* lavaplatos *m inv*
disillusion [dɪsɪ'luːʒən] *vt* desilusionar
disinfect [dɪsɪn'fekt] *vt* desinfectar; **~ant** *n* desinfectante *m*
disintegrate [dɪs'ɪntɪgreɪt] *vi* disgregarse, desintegrarse
disinterested [dɪs'ɪntrəstɪd] *adj*

desinteresado
disjointed [dɪs'dʒɔɪntɪd] *adj* inconexo
disk [dɪsk] *n* (*esp US*) = **disc**; (*COMPUT*) disco, disquete *m*; **single-/double-sided ~** disco de una cara/dos caras; **~ drive** *n* disc drive *m*; **~ette** *n* = **disk**
dislike [dɪs'laɪk] *n* antipatía, aversión *f* ♦ *vt* tener antipatía a
dislocate [ˈdɪsləkeɪt] *vt* dislocar
dislodge [dɪs'lɔdʒ] *vt* sacar
disloyal [dɪs'lɔɪəl] *adj* desleal
dismal [ˈdɪzml] *adj* (*gloomy*) deprimente, triste; (*very bad*) malísimo, fatal
dismantle [dɪs'mæntl] *vt* desmontar, desarmar
dismay [dɪs'meɪ] *n* consternación *f* ♦ *vt* consternar
dismiss [dɪs'mɪs] *vt* (*worker*) despedir; (*pupils*) dejar marchar; (*soldiers*) dar permiso para irse; (*idea, LAW*) rechazar; (*possibility*) descartar; **~al** *n* despido
dismount [dɪs'maunt] *vi* apearse
disobedient [dɪsə'biːdɪənt] *adj* desobediente
disobey [dɪsə'beɪ] *vt* desobedecer
disorder [dɪs'ɔːdə*] *n* desorden *m*; (*rioting*) disturbios *mpl*; (*MED*) trastorno; **~ly** *adj* desordenado; (*meeting*) alborotado; (*conduct*) escandaloso
disorientated [dɪs'ɔːrɪenteɪtəd] *adj* desorientado
disown [dɪs'əun] *vt* (*action*) renegar de; (*person*) negar cualquier tipo de relación con
disparaging [dɪs'pærɪdʒɪŋ] *adj* despreciativo
dispassionate [dɪs'pæʃənɪt] *adj* (*unbiased*) imparcial
dispatch [dɪs'pætʃ] *vt* enviar ♦ *n* (*sending*) envío; (*PRESS*) informe *m*; (*MIL*) parte *m*
dispel [dɪs'pel] *vt* disipar
dispense [dɪs'pens] *vt* (*medicines*) preparar; **~ with** *vt fus* prescindir de; **~r** *n* (*container*) distribuidor *m* automático; **dispensing chemist** (*BRIT*) *n* farmacia
disperse [dɪs'pəːs] *vt* dispersar ♦ *vi* dispersarse

dispirited [dɪˈspɪrɪtɪd] *adj* desanimado, desalentado

displace [dɪsˈpleɪs] *vt* desplazar, reemplazar; **~d person** *n* (*POL*) desplazado/a

display [dɪsˈpleɪ] *n* (*in shop window*) escaparate *m*; (*exhibition*) exposición *f*; (*COMPUT*) visualización *f*; (*of feeling*) manifestación *f* ♦ *vt* exponer; manifestar; (*ostentatiously*) lucir

displease [dɪsˈpliːz] *vt* (*offend*) ofender; (*annoy*) fastidiar; **~d** *adj*: **~d with** disgustado con; **displeasure** [-ˈplɛʒə*] *n* disgusto

disposable [dɪsˈpəʊzəbl] *adj* desechable; (*income*) disponible; **~ nappy** *n* pañal *m* desechable

disposal [dɪsˈpəʊzl] *n* (*of rubbish*) destrucción *f*; **at one's ~** a su disposición

dispose [dɪsˈpəʊz] *vi*: **to ~ of** (*unwanted goods*) deshacerse de; (*problem etc*) resolver; **~d** *adj*: **~d to do** dispuesto a hacer; **to be well-~d towards sb** estar bien dispuesto hacia uno; **disposition** [dɪspəˈzɪʃən] *n* (*nature*) temperamento; (*inclination*) propensión *f*

disprove [dɪsˈpruːv] *vt* refutar

dispute [dɪsˈpjuːt] *n* disputa; (*also:* **industrial ~**) conflicto (laboral) ♦ *vt* (*argue*) disputar, discutir; (*question*) cuestionar

disqualify [dɪsˈkwɒlɪfaɪ] *vt* (*SPORT*) desclasificar; **to ~ sb for sth/from doing sth** incapacitar a alguien para algo/hacer algo

disquiet [dɪsˈkwaɪət] *n* preocupación *f*, inquietud *f*

disregard [dɪsrɪˈgɑːd] *vt* (*ignore*) no hacer caso de

disrepair [dɪsrɪˈpɛə*] *n*: **to fall into ~** (*building*) desmoronarse

disreputable [dɪsˈrɛpjʊtəbl] *adj* (*person*) de mala fama; (*behaviour*) vergonzoso

disrespectful [dɪsrɪˈspɛktful] *adj* irrespetuoso

disrupt [dɪsˈrʌpt] *vt* (*plans*) desbaratar, trastornar; (*conversation*) interrumpir

dissatisfaction [dɪssætɪsˈfækʃən] *n* disgusto, descontento

dissect [dɪˈsɛkt] *vt* disecar

dissent [dɪˈsɛnt] *n* disensión *f*

dissertation [dɪsəˈteɪʃən] *n* tesina

disservice [dɪsˈsəːvɪs] *n*: **to do sb a ~** perjudicar a alguien

dissimilar [dɪˈsɪmɪlə*] *adj* distinto

dissipate [ˈdɪsɪpeɪt] *vt* disipar; (*waste*) desperdiciar

dissolve [dɪˈzɒlv] *vt* disolver ♦ *vi* disolverse; **to ~ in(to) tears** deshacerse en lágrimas

dissuade [dɪˈsweɪd] *vt*: **to ~ sb (from)** disuadir a uno (de)

distance [ˈdɪstəns] *n* distancia; **in the ~** a lo lejos

distant [ˈdɪstənt] *adj* lejano; (*manner*) reservado, frío

distaste [dɪsˈteɪst] *n* repugnancia; **~ful** *adj* repugnante, desagradable

distended [dɪˈstɛndɪd] *adj* (*stomach*) hinchado

distil [dɪsˈtɪl] (*US* **distill**) *vt* destilar; **~lery** *n* destilería

distinct [dɪsˈtɪŋkt] *adj* (*different*) distinto; (*clear*) claro; (*unmistakeable*) inequívoco; **as ~ from** a diferencia de; **~ion** [dɪsˈtɪŋkʃən] *n* distinción *f*; (*honour*) honor *m*; (*in exam*) sobresaliente *m*; **~ive** *adj* distintivo

distinguish [dɪsˈtɪŋgwɪʃ] *vt* distinguir; **to ~ o.s.** destacarse; **~ed** *adj* (*eminent*) distinguido; **~ing** *adj* (*feature*) distintivo

distort [dɪsˈtɔːt] *vt* distorsionar; (*shape, image*) deformar; **~ion** [dɪsˈtɔːʃən] *n* distorsión *f*; deformación *f*

distract [dɪsˈtrækt] *vt* distraer; **~ed** *adj* distraído; **~ion** [dɪsˈtrækʃən] *n* distracción *f*; (*confusion*) aturdimiento

distraught [dɪsˈtrɔːt] *adj* loco de inquietud

distress [dɪsˈtrɛs] *n* (*anguish*) angustia, aflicción *f* ♦ *vt* afligir; **~ing** *adj* angustioso; doloroso; **~ signal** *n* señal *f* de socorro

distribute [dɪsˈtrɪbjuːt] *vt* distribuir; (*share out*) repartir; **distribution** [-ˈbjuːʃən] *n* distribución f; reparto; **distributor** n (AUT) distribuidor m; (COMM) distribuidora

district ['dɪstrɪkt] n (of country) zona, región f; (of town) barrio; (ADMIN) distrito; **~ attorney** (US) n fiscal m/f; **~ nurse** (BRIT) n enfermera que atiende a pacientes a domicilio

distrust [dɪs'trʌst] n desconfianza ♦ vt desconfiar de

disturb [dɪs'tɜːb] vt (person: bother, interrupt) molestar; (: upset) perturbar, inquietar; (disorganize) alterar; **~ance** n (upheaval) perturbación f; (political etc: gen pl) disturbio; (of mind) trastorno; **~ed** adj (worried, upset) preocupado, angustiado; **emotionally ~ed** trastornado; (childhood) inseguro; **~ing** adj inquietante, perturbador(a)

disuse [dɪs'juːs] n: **to fall into ~** caer en desuso

disused [dɪs'juːzd] adj abandonado

ditch [dɪtʃ] n zanja; (irrigation ~) acequia ♦ vt (inf: partner) deshacerse de; (: plan, car etc) abandonar

dither ['dɪðə*] (pej) vi vacilar

ditto ['dɪtəu] adv ídem, lo mismo

divan [dɪ'væn] n (also: ~ **bed**) cama turca

dive [daɪv] n (from board) salto; (underwater) buceo; (of submarine) sumersión f ♦ vi (swimmer: into water) saltar; (: under water) zambullirse, bucear; (fish, submarine) sumergirse; (bird) lanzarse en picado; **to ~ into** (bag etc) meter la mano en; (place) meterse de prisa en; **~r** n (underwater) buzo

diverse [daɪ'vɜːs] adj diversos/as, varios/as

diversion [daɪ'vɜːʃən] n (BRIT: AUT) desviación f; (distraction, MIL) diversión f; (of funds) distracción f

divert [daɪ'vɜːt] vt (turn aside) desviar

divide [dɪ'vaɪd] vt dividir; (separate) separar ♦ vi dividirse; (road) bifurcarse; **~d highway** (US) n carretera de doble calzada

dividend ['dɪvɪdend] n dividendo; (fig): **to pay ~s** proporcionar beneficios

divine [dɪ'vaɪn] adj (also fig) divino

diving ['daɪvɪŋ] n (SPORT) salto; (underwater) buceo; **~ board** n trampolín m

divinity [dɪ'vɪnɪtɪ] n divinidad f; (SCOL) teología

division [dɪ'vɪʒən] n división f; (sharing out) reparto; (disagreement) diferencias fpl; (COMM) sección f

divorce [dɪ'vɔːs] n divorcio ♦ vt divorciarse de; **~d** adj divorciado; **~e** [-'siː] n divorciado/a

divulge [daɪ'vʌldʒ] vt divulgar, revelar

D.I.Y. (BRIT) adj, n abbr = **do-it-yourself**

dizzy ['dɪzɪ] adj (spell) de mareo; **to feel ~** marearse

DJ n abbr = **disc jockey**

KEYWORD
---

do [duː] (pt **did**, pp **done**) n (inf: party etc): **we're having a little ~ on Saturday** damos una fiestecita el sábado; **it was rather a grand ~** fue un acontecimiento a lo grande

♦ aux vb **1** (in negative constructions: not translated) **I don't understand** no entiendo

2 (to form questions: not translated) **didn't you know?** ¿no lo sabías?; **what ~ you think?** ¿qué opinas?

3 (for emphasis, in polite expressions): **people ~ make mistakes sometimes** sí que se cometen errores a veces; **she does seem rather late** a mí también me parece que se ha retrasado; **~ sit down/ help yourself** siéntate/sírvete por favor; **~ take care!** ¡ten cuidado(, te pido)!

4 (used to avoid repeating vb): **she sings better than I ~** canta mejor que yo; **~ you agree? – yes, I ~/no, I don't** ¿estás de acuerdo? — sí (lo estoy)/no (lo estoy); **she lives in Glasgow – so ~ I** vive en Glasgow — yo también; **he didn't like it and neither did we** no le gustó y a nosotros tampoco; **who made this mess? – I did** ¿quién hizo esta chapuza? — yo; **he asked me to help him and I did** me pidió que le ayudara y lo hice

5 (*in question tags*): **you like him, don't you?** te gusta, ¿verdad? *or* ¿no?; **I don't know him, ~ I?** creo que no le conozco ♦ *vt* **1** (*gen, carry out, perform etc*): **what are you ~ing tonight?** ¿qué haces esta noche?; **what can I ~ for you?** ¿en qué puedo servirle?; **to ~ the washing-up/ cooking** fregar los platos/cocinar; **to ~ one's teeth/hair/nails** lavarse los dientes/arreglarse el pelo/arreglarse las uñas

2 (*AUT etc*): **the car was ~ing 100** el coche iba a 100; **we've done 200 km already** ya hemos hecho 200 km; **he can ~ 100 in that car** puede ir a 100 en ese coche

♦ *vi* **1** (*act, behave*) hacer; **~ as I ~** haz como yo

2 (*get on, fare*): **he's ~ing well/badly at school** va bien/mal en la escuela; **the firm is ~ing well** la empresa anda *or* va bien; **how ~ you ~?** mucho gusto; (*less formal*) ¿qué tal?

3 (*suit*): **will it ~?** ¿sirve?, ¿está *or* va bien?

4 (*be sufficient*) bastar; **will £10 ~?** ¿será bastante con £10?; **that'll ~** así está bien; **that'll ~!** (*in annoyance*) ¡ya está bien!, ¡basta ya!; **to make ~ (with)** arreglárselas (con)

do away with *vt fus* (*kill, disease*) eliminar; (*abolish: law etc*) abolir; (*withdraw*) retirar

do up *vt* (*laces*) atar; (*zip, dress, shirt*) abrochar; (*renovate: room, house*) renovar

do with *vt fus* (*need*): **I could ~ with a drink/some help** no me vendría mal un trago/un poco de ayuda; (*be connected*) tener que ver con; **what has it got to ~ with you?** ¿qué tiene que ver contigo?

do without *vi* ~ pasar sin; **if you're late for tea then you'll ~ without** si llegas tarde tendrás que quedarte sin cenar ♦ *vt fus* pasar sin; **I can ~ without a car** puedo pasar sin coche

dock [dɔk] *n* (*NAUT*) muelle *m*; (*LAW*)

banquillo (de los acusados); **~s** *npl* (*NAUT*) muelles *mpl*, puerto *sg* ♦ *vi* (*enter ~*) atracar (la) muelle; (*SPACE*) acoplarse; **~er** *n* trabajador *m* portuario, estibador *m*; **~yard** *n* astillero

doctor [ˈdɔktə*] *n* médico/a; (*Ph.D. etc*) doctor(a) *m/f* ♦ *vt* (*drink etc*) adulterar; **D~ of Philosophy** *n* Doctor en Filosofía y Letras

document [ˈdɔkjumənt] *n* documento; **~ary** [-ˈmentəri] *adj* documental ♦ *n* documental *m*

dodge [dɔdʒ] *n* (*fig*) truco ♦ *vt* evadir; (*blow*) esquivar

dodgems [ˈdɔdʒəmz] (*BRIT*) *npl* coches *mpl* de choque

doe [dəu] *n* (*deer*) cierva, gama; (*rabbit*) coneja

does [dʌz] *vb see* **do**; **~n't = does not**

dog [dɔg] *n* perro ♦ *vt* seguir los pasos de; (*subj: bad luck*) perseguir; **~ collar** *n* collar *m* de perro; (*of clergyman*) alzacuellos *m inv*; **~-eared** *adj* sobado

dogged [ˈdɔgɪd] *adj* tenaz, obstinado

dogsbody [ˈdɔgzbɔdɪ] (*BRIT: inf*) *n* burro de carga

doings [ˈduɪŋz] *npl* (*activities*) actividades *fpl*

do-it-yourself *n* bricolaje *m*

doldrums [ˈdɔldrəmz] *npl*: **to be in the ~** (*person*) estar abatido; (*business*) estar estancado

dole [dəul] (*BRIT*) *n* (*payment*) subsidio de paro; **on the ~** parado; **~ out** *vt* repartir

doll [dɔl] *n* muñeca; (*US: inf: woman*) muñeca, gachí *f*

dollar [ˈdɔlə*] *n* dólar *m*

dolled up (*inf*) *adj* arreglado

dolphin [ˈdɔlfɪn] *n* delfín *m*

domain [dəˈmeɪn] *n* (*fig*) campo, competencia; (*land*) dominios *mpl*

dome [dəum] *n* (*ARCH*) cúpula

domestic [dəˈmestɪk] *adj* (*animal, duty*) doméstico; (*flight, policy*) nacional; **~ated** *adj* domesticado; (*home-loving*) casero, hogareño

dominate [ˈdɔmɪneɪt] *vt* dominar

domineering [dɔmɪˈnɪərɪŋ] *adj* dominante
dominion [dəˈmɪnɪən] *n* dominio
domino [ˈdɔmɪnəʊ] (*pl* **~es**) *n* ficha de dominó; **~es** *n* (*game*) dominó
don [dɔn] (*BRIT*) *n* profesor(a) *m/f* universitario/a
donate [dəˈneɪt] *vt* donar; **donation** [dəˈneɪʃən] *n* donativo
done [dʌn] *pp of* **do**
donkey [ˈdɔŋkɪ] *n* burro
donor [ˈdəʊnə*] *n* donante *m/f*; **~ card** *n* carnet *m* de donante de órganos
don't [dəʊnt] = **do not**
donut [ˈdəʊnʌt] (*US*) *n* = **doughnut**
doodle [ˈduːdl] *vi* hacer dibujitos *or* garabatos
doom [duːm] *n* (*fate*) suerte *f* ♦ *vt*: **to be ~ed to failure** estar condenado al fracaso
door [dɔː*] *n* puerta; **~bell** *n* timbre *m*; **~handle** *n* tirador *m*; (*of car*) manija; **~man** (*irreg*) *n* (*in hotel*) portero; **~mat** *n* felpudo, estera; **~step** *n* peldaño; **~to-~** *adj* de puerta en puerta; **~way** *n* entrada, puerta
dope [dəʊp] *n* (*inf: illegal drug*) droga; (: *person*) imbécil *m/f* ♦ *vt* (*horse etc*) drogar
dormant [ˈdɔːmənt] *adj* inactivo
dormitory [ˈdɔːmɪtrɪ] *n* (*BRIT*) dormitorio; (*US*) colegio mayor
dormouse [ˈdɔːmaʊs] (*pl* **-mice**) *n* lirón *m*
DOS *n abbr* (= *disk operating system*) DOS *m*
dosage [ˈdəʊsɪdʒ] *n* dosis *f inv*
dose [dəʊs] *n* dósis *f inv*
doss house [ˈdɔss-] (*BRIT*) *n* pensión *f* de mala muerte
dossier [ˈdɔsɪeɪ] *n* expediente *m*, dosier *m*
dot [dɔt] *n* punto ♦ *vi*: **~ted with** salpicado de; **on the ~** *n* en punto
double [ˈdʌbl] *adj* doble ♦ *adv* (*twice*): **to cost ~** costar el doble ♦ *n* doble *m* ♦ *vt* doblar ♦ *vi* doblarse; **on the ~, at the ~** (*BRIT*) corriendo; **~ bass** *n* contrabajo; **~ bed** *n* cama de matrimonio; **~ bend** (*BRIT*) *n* doble curva; **~-breasted** *adj* cruzado; **~cross** *vt* (*trick*) engañar;

(*betray*) traicionar; **~decker** *n* autobús *m* de dos pisos; **~ glazing** (*BRIT*) *n* doble acristalamiento; **~ room** *n* habitación *f* doble; **~s** *n* (*TENNIS*) juego de dobles; **doubly** *adv* doblemente
doubt [daʊt] *n* duda ♦ *vt* dudar; (*suspect*) dudar de; **to ~ that** dudar que; **~ful** *adj* dudoso; (*person*): **to be ~ful about sth** tener dudas sobre algo; **~less** *adv* sin duda
dough [dəʊ] *n* masa, pasta; **~nut** (*US* **donut**) *n* ≈ rosquilla
dove [dʌv] *n* paloma
dovetail [ˈdʌvteɪl] *vi* (*fig*) encajar
dowdy [ˈdaʊdɪ] *adj* (*person*) mal vestido; (*clothes*) pasado de moda
down [daʊn] *n* (*feathers*) plumón *m*, flojel *m* ♦ *adv* (*~wards*) abajo, hacia abajo; (*on the ground*) por *or* en tierra ♦ *prep* abajo ♦ *vt* (*inf: drink*) beberse; **~ with X!** ¡abajo X!; **~-and-out** *n* vagabundo/a; **~-at-heel** *adj* venido a menos; (*appearance*) desaliñado; **~cast** *adj* abatido; **~fall** *n* caída, ruina; **~hearted** *adj* desanimado; **~hill** *adv*: **to go ~hill** (*also fig*) ir cuesta abajo; **~ payment** *n* entrada, pago al contado; **~pour** *n* aguacero; **~right** *adj* (*nonsense, lie*) manifiesto; (*refusal*) terminante; **~size** *vi* (*ECON: company*) reducir la plantilla de

---

Downing Street

i **Downing Street** *es la calle de Londres en la que están las residencias oficiales del Presidente del Gobierno (Prime Minister), tradicionalmente en el No. 10, y del Ministro de Economía (Chancellor of the Exchequer). La calle está situada en el céntrico barrio londinense de Westminster y está cerrada al tráfico de peatones y vehículos. En lenguaje periodístico, se usa también* **Downing Street** *para referirse al primer ministro o al Gobierno.*

Down's syndrome [ˈdaʊnz-] *n* síndrome *m* de Down
down: ~stairs *adv* (*below*) (en la casa de)

abajo; (~wards) escaleras abajo; ~stream adv aguas or río abajo; ~-to-earth adj práctico; ~town adv en el centro de la ciudad; ~ under adv en Australia (or Nueva Zelanda); ~ward [-wəd] adj, adv hacia abajo; ~wards [-wədz] adv hacia abajo

dowry ['dauri] n dote f

doz. abbr = dozen

doze [dəuz] vi dormitar; ~ off vi quedarse medio dormido

dozen ['dʌzn] n docena; a ~ books una docena de libros; ~s of cantidad de

Dr. abbr = doctor; drive

drab [dræb] adj gris, monótono

draft [drɑːft] n (first copy) borrador m; (POL: of bill) anteproyecto; (US: call-up) quinta ♦ vt (plan) preparar; (write roughly) hacer un borrador de; see also draught

draftsman ['drɑːftsmən] (US) n = draughtsman

drag [dræg] vt arrastrar; (river) dragar, rastrear ♦ vi (time) pasar despacio; (play, film etc) hacerse pesado ♦ n (inf) lata; (women's clothing): in ~ vestido de travestí; ~ on vi ser interminable; ~ and drop vt (COMPUT) arrastrar y soltar

dragon ['drægən] n dragón m

dragonfly ['drægənflaɪ] n libélula

drain [dreɪn] n desaguadero; (in street) sumidero; (source of loss): to be a ~ on consumir, agotar ♦ vt (land, marshes) desaguar; (reservoir) desecar; (vegetables) escurrir ♦ vi escurrirse; ~age n (act) desagüe m; (MED, AGR) drenaje m; (sewage) alcantarillado; ~ing board (US ~board) n escurridera, escurridor m; ~pipe n tubo de desagüe

drama ['drɑːmə] n (art) teatro; (play) drama m; (excitement) emoción f; ~tic [drə'mætɪk] adj dramático; ~tist ['dræmətɪst] n dramaturgo/a; ~tize ['dræmətaɪz] vt (events) dramatizar

drank [dræŋk] pt of drink

drape [dreɪp] vt (cloth) colocar; (flag) colgar; ~s (US) npl cortinas fpl

drastic ['dræstɪk] adj (measure) severo; (change) radical, drástico

draught [drɑːft] (US draft) n (of air) corriente f de aire; (NAUT) calado; on ~ (beer) de barril; ~ beer n cerveza de barril; ~board (BRIT) n tablero de damas; ~s (BRIT) n (game) juego de damas

draughtsman ['drɑːftsmən] (US draftsman) (irreg) n delineante m

draw [drɔː] (pt drew, pp drawn) vt (picture) dibujar; (cart) tirar de; (curtain) correr; (take out) sacar; (attract) atraer; (money) retirar; (wages) cobrar ♦ vi (SPORT) empatar ♦ n (SPORT) empate m; (lottery) sorteo; ~ near vi acercarse; ~ out vi (lengthen) alargarse ♦ vt sacar; ~ up vi (stop) pararse ♦ vt (chair) acercar; (document) redactar; ~back n inconveniente m, desventaja; ~bridge n puente m levadizo

drawer [drɔː*] n cajón m

drawing ['drɔːɪŋ] n dibujo; ~ board n tablero de dibujante); ~ pin (BRIT) n chincheta; ~ room n salón m

drawl [drɔːl] n habla lenta y cansina

drawn [drɔːn] pp of draw

dread [dred] n pavor m, terror m ♦ vt temer, tener miedo or pavor a; ~ful adj horroroso

dream [driːm] (pt, pp dreamed or dreamt) n sueño ♦ vt, vi soñar; ~y adj (distracted) soñador(a), distraído; (music) suave

dreary ['drɪərɪ] adj monótono

dredge [dredʒ] vt dragar

dregs [dregz] npl posos mpl; (of humanity) hez f

drench [drentʃ] vt empapar

dress [dres] n vestido; (clothing) ropa ♦ vt vestir; (wound) vendar ♦ vi vestirse; to get ~ed vestirse; ~ up vi vestirse de etiqueta; (in fancy dress) disfrazarse; ~ circle (BRIT) n principal m; ~er n (furniture) aparador m; (: US) cómoda (con espejo); ~ing n (MED) vendaje m; (CULIN) aliño; ~ing gown (BRIT) n bata; ~ing room n (THEATRE) camarín m;

(*SPORT*) vestuario; **~ing table** n tocador m; **~maker** n modista, costurera; **~ rehearsal** n ensayo general

drew [dru:] pt of **draw**

dribble ['drɪbl] vi (baby) babear ♦ vt (ball) regatear

dried [draɪd] adj (fruit) seco; (milk) en polvo

drier ['draɪə*] n = **dryer**

drift [drɪft] n (of current etc) flujo; (of snow) ventisquero; (meaning) significado ♦ vi (boat) ir a la deriva; (sand, snow) amontonarse; **~wood** n madera de deriva

drill [drɪl] n (~ bit) broca; (tool for DIY etc) taladro; (of dentist) fresa; (for mining etc) perforadora, barrena; (MIL) instrucción f ♦ vt perforar, taladrar; (troops) enseñar la instrucción a ♦ vi (for oil) perforar

drink [drɪŋk] (pt **drank**, pp **drunk**) n bebida; (sip) trago ♦ vt, vi beber; **to have a ~** tomar algo; tomar una copa or un trago; **a ~ of water** un trago de agua; **~er** n bebedor(a) m/f; **~ing water** n agua potable

drip [drɪp] n (act) goteo; (one ~) gota; (MED) gota a gota m ♦ vi gotear; **~-dry** adj (shirt) inarrugable; **~ping** n (animal fat) pringue m

drive [draɪv] (pt **drove**, pp **driven**) n (journey) viaje m (en coche); (also: **~way**) entrada; (energy) energía, vigor m; (COMPUT: also: **disk ~**) drive m ♦ vt (car) conducir (SP), manejar (AM); (nail) clavar; (push) empujar; (TECH: motor) impulsar ♦ vi (AUT: at controls) conducir; (: travel) pasearse en coche; **left-/right-hand ~** conducción f a la izquierda/derecha; **to ~ sb mad** volverle loco a uno

drivel ['drɪvl] (inf) n tonterías fpl

driven ['drɪvn] pp of **drive**

driver ['draɪvə*] n conductor(a) m/f (SP), chofer m (AM); (of taxi, bus) chofer; **~'s license** (US) n carnet m de conducir

driveway ['draɪvweɪ] n entrada

driving ['draɪvɪŋ] n el conducir (SP), el manejar (AM); **~ instructor** n

instructor(a) m/f de conducción or manejo; **~ lesson** n clase f de conducción or manejo; **~ licence** (BRIT) n permiso de conducir; **~ school** n autoescuela; **~ test** n examen m de conducción or manejo

drizzle ['drɪzl] n llovizna

drool [dru:l] vi babear

droop [dru:p] vi (flower) marchitarse; (shoulders) encorvarse; (head) inclinarse

drop [drɒp] n (of water) gota; (lessening) baja; (fall) caída ♦ vt dejar caer; (voice, eyes, price) bajar; (passenger) dejar; (omit) omitir ♦ vi (object) caer; (wind) amainar; **~s** npl (MED) gotas fpl; **~ off** vi (sleep) dormirse ♦ vt (passenger) dejar; **~ out** vi (withdraw) retirarse; **~-out** n marginado/a; (SCOL) estudiante que abandona los estudios; **~per** n cuentagotas m inv; **~pings** npl excrementos

drought [draut] n sequía

drove [drəuv] pt of **drive**

drown [draun] vt ahogar ♦ vi ahogarse

drowsy ['drauzɪ] adj soñoliento; **to be ~** tener sueño

drug [drʌg] n medicamento; (narcotic) droga ♦ vt drogar; **to be on ~s** drogarse; **~ addict** n drogadicto/a; **~gist** (US) n farmacéutico; **~store** (US) n farmacia

drum [drʌm] n tambor m; (for oil, petrol) bidón m; **~s** npl batería; **~mer** n tambor m

drunk [drʌŋk] pp of **drink** ♦ adj borracho ♦ n (also: **~ard**) borracho/a; **~en** adj borracho; (laughter, party) de borrachos

dry [draɪ] adj seco; (day) sin lluvia; (climate) árido, seco ♦ vt secar; (tears) enjugarse ♦ vi secarse; **~ up** vi (river) secarse; **~-cleaner's** n tintorería; **~-cleaning** n lavado en seco; **~er** n (for hair) secador m; (US: for clothes) secadora; **~ rot** n putrefacción f fungoide

DSS n abbr = **Department of Social Security**

DTP n abbr (= desk-top publishing) autoedición f

dual ['djuəl] adj doble; **~ carriageway**

(*BRIT*) *n* carretera de doble calzada; **~-purpose** *adj* de doble uso

dubbed [dʌbd] *adj* (*CINEMA*) doblado

dubious ['dju:bɪəs] *adj* indeciso; (*reputation, company*) sospechoso

duchess ['dʌtʃɪs] *n* duquesa

duck [dʌk] *n* pato ♦ *vi* agacharse; **~ling** *n* patito

duct [dʌkt] *n* conducto, canal *m*

dud [dʌd] *n* (*object, tool*) engaño, engañifa ♦ *adj*: **~ cheque** (*BRIT*) cheque *m* sin fondos

due [dju:] *adj* (*owed*): **he is ~ £10** se le deben 10 libras; (*expected: event*): **the meeting is ~ on Wednesday** la reunión tendrá lugar el miércoles; (: *arrival*) **the train is ~ at 8am** el tren tiene su llegada para las 8; (*proper*) debido ♦ *n*: **to give sb his** (*or* **her**) **~** ser justo con alguien ♦ *adv*: **~ north** derecho al norte; **~s** *npl* (*for club, union*) cuota; (*in harbour*) derechos *mpl*; **in ~ course** a su debido tiempo; **~ to** debido a; **to be ~ to** deberse a

duet [dju:'et] *n* dúo

duffel bag ['dʌfəl] *n* bolsa de lona

duffel coat *n* trenca, abrigo de tres cuartos

dug [dʌg] *pt, pp of* **dig**

duke [dju:k] *n* duque *m*

dull [dʌl] *adj* (*light*) débil; (*stupid*) torpe; (*boring*) pesado; (*sound, pain*) sordo; (*weather, day*) gris ♦ *vt* (*pain, grief*) aliviar; (*mind, senses*) entorpecer

duly ['dju:lɪ] *adv* debidamente; (*on time*) a su debido tiempo

dumb [dʌm] *adj* mudo; (*pej: stupid*) estúpido; **~founded** [dʌm'faundɪd] *adj* pasmado

dummy ['dʌmɪ] *n* (*tailor's ~*) maniquí *m*; (*mock-up*) maqueta; (*BRIT: for baby*) chupete *m* ♦ *adj* falso, postizo

dump [dʌmp] *n* (*also*: **rubbish ~**) basurero, vertedero; (*inf: place*) cuchitril *m* ♦ *vt* (*put down*) dejar; (*get rid of*) deshacerse de; (*COMPUT: data*) transferir

dumpling ['dʌmplɪŋ] *n* bola de masa hervida

dumpy ['dʌmpɪ] *adj* regordete/a

dunce [dʌns] *n* zopenco

dung [dʌŋ] *n* estiércol *m*

dungarees [dʌŋgə'ri:z] *npl* mono

dungeon ['dʌndʒən] *n* calabozo

duplex ['dju:pleks] *n* dúplex *m*

duplicate [*n* 'dju:plɪkət, *vb* 'dju:plɪkeɪt] *n* duplicado ♦ *vt* duplicar; (*photocopy*) fotocopiar; (*repeat*) repetir; **in ~** por duplicado

durable ['djuərəbl] *adj* duradero

duration [djuə'reɪʃən] *n* duración *f*

during ['djuərɪŋ] *prep* durante

dusk [dʌsk] *n* crepúsculo, anochecer *m*

dust [dʌst] *n* polvo ♦ *vt* quitar el polvo a, desempolvar; (*cake etc*): **to ~ with** espolvorear de; **~bin** (*BRIT*) *n* cubo de la basura (*SP*), balde *m* (*AM*); **~er** *n* paño, trapo; **~man** (*BRIT irreg*) *n* basurero; **~y** *adj* polvoriento

Dutch [dʌtʃ] *adj* holandés/esa ♦ *n* (*LING*) holandés *m*; **the ~** *npl* los holandeses; **to go ~** (*inf*) pagar cada uno lo suyo; **~man/woman** (*irreg*) *n* holandés/esa *m/f*

duty ['dju:tɪ] *n* deber *m*; (*tax*) derechos *mpl* de aduana; **on ~** de servicio; (*at night etc*) de guardia; **off ~** libre (de servicio); **~-free** *adj* libre de impuestos

duvet ['du:veɪ] (*BRIT*) *n* edredón *m*

dwarf [dwɔ:f] (*pl* **dwarves**) *n* enano/a ♦ *vt* empequeñecer

dwell [dwel] (*pt, pp* **dwelt**) *vi* morar; **~ on** *vt fus* explayarse en

dwindle ['dwɪndl] *vi* menguar, disminuir

dye [daɪ] *n* tinte *m* ♦ *vt* teñir

dying ['daɪɪŋ] *adj* moribundo, agonizante

dyke [daɪk] (*BRIT*) *n* dique *m*

dynamic [daɪ'næmɪk] *adj* dinámico

dynamite ['daɪnəmaɪt] *n* dinamita

dynamo ['daɪnəməu] *n* dinamo *f*

dynasty ['dɪnəstɪ] *n* dinastía

E, e

E [i:] n (MUS) mi m

each [i:tʃ] adj cada inv ♦ pron cada uno;
~ **other** el uno al otro; **they hate ~ other**
se odian (entre ellos o mutuamente);
they have 2 books ~ tienen 2 libros por
persona

eager ['i:gə*] adj (keen) entusiasmado; **to
be ~ to do sth** tener muchas ganas de
hacer algo, impacientarse por hacer algo;
to be ~ for tener muchas ganas de

eagle ['i:gl] n águila

ear [iə*] n oreja; oído; (of corn) espiga;
~**ache** n dolor m de oídos; ~**drum** n
tímpano

earl [ə:l] n conde m

earlier ['ə:liə*] adj anterior ♦ adv antes

early ['ə:li] adv temprano; (before time)
con tiempo, con anticipación ♦ adj
temprano; (settlers etc) primitivo; (death,
departure) prematuro; (reply) pronto; **to
have an ~ night** acostarse temprano; **in
the ~ or ~ in the spring/19th century** a
principios de primavera/del siglo
diecinueve; ~ **retirement** n jubilación f
anticipada

earmark ['iəma:k] vt: **to ~ (for)** reservar
(para), destinar (a)

earn [ə:n] vt (salary) percibir; (interest)
devengar; (praise) merecerse

earnest ['ə:nist] adj (wish) fervoroso;
(person) serio, formal; **in ~** en serio

earnings ['ə:niŋz] npl (personal) sueldo,
ingresos mpl; (company) ganancias fpl

ear: ~**phones** npl auriculares mpl; ~**ring**
n pendiente m, arete m; ~**shot** n: **within
~shot** al alcance del oído

earth [ə:θ] n tierra; (BRIT: ELEC) cable m de
toma de tierra ♦ vt (BRIT: ELEC) conectar a
tierra; ~**enware** n loza (de barro);
~**quake** n terremoto; ~**y** adj (fig: vulgar)
grosero

ease [i:z] n facilidad f; (comfort)
comodidad f ♦ vt (lessen: problem)
mitigar; (: pain) aliviar; (: tension) reducir;
to ~ sth in/out meter/sacar algo con
cuidado; **at ~!** (MIL) ¡descansen!; ~ **off** or
up vi (wind, rain) amainar; (slow down)
aflojar la marcha

easel ['i:zl] n caballete m

easily ['i:zili] adv fácilmente

east [i:st] n este m ♦ adj del este, oriental;
(wind) este ♦ adv al este, hacia el este;
the E~ el Oriente; (POL) los países del Este

Easter ['i:stə*] n Pascua (de Resurrección);
~ **egg** n huevo de Pascua

east: ~**erly** ['i:stəli] adj (to the east) al
este; (from the east) del este; ~**ern**
['i:stən] adj del este, oriental; (oriental)
oriental; (communist) del este; ~**ward(s)**
['i:stwəd(z)] adv hacia el este

easy ['i:zi] adj fácil; (simple) sencillo;
(comfortable) holgado, cómodo; (relaxed)
tranquilo ♦ adv: **to take it** or **things ~**
(not worry) tomarlo con calma; (rest)
descansar; ~ **chair** n sillón m; ~**-going**
adj acomodadizo

eat [i:t] (pt **ate**, pp **eaten**) vt comer; ~
away at vt fus corroer; mermar; ~ **into**
vt fus corroer; (savings) mermar

eaves [i:vz] npl alero m

eavesdrop ['i:vzdrɔp] vi: **to ~ (on)**
escuchar a escondidas

ebb [eb] n reflujo ♦ vi bajar; (fig: also: ~
away) decaer

ebony ['ebəni] n ébano

EC n abbr (= European Community) CE f

eccentric [ik'sentrik] adj, n excéntrico/a
m/f

echo ['ekəu] (pl ~**es**) n eco m ♦ vt (sound)
repetir ♦ vi resonar, hacer eco

éclair [i'kleə*] n pastelillo relleno de crema
y con chocolate por encima

eclipse [i'klips] n eclipse m

ecology [i'kɔlədʒi] n ecología

economic [i:kə'nɔmik] adj económico;
(business etc) rentable; ~**al** adj
económico; ~**s** n (SCOL) economía ♦ npl
(of project etc) rentabilidad f

economize [i'kɔnəmaiz] vi economizar,
ahorrar

economy [ɪ'kɔnəmɪ] *n* economía; **~ class** *n* (*AVIAT*) clase *f* económica; **~ size** *n* tamaño económico

ecstasy ['ɛkstəsɪ] *n* éxtasis *m inv*; (*drug*) éxtasis *m inv*; **ecstatic** [ɛks'tætɪk] *adj* extático

ECU ['eɪkjuː] *n* (= *European Currency Unit*) ECU *m*

Ecuador ['ɛkwədɔːr] *n* Ecuador *m*; **~ian** *adj*, *n* ecuatoriano/a *m/f*

eczema ['ɛksɪmə] *n* eczema *m*

edge [ɛdʒ] *n* (*of knife etc*) filo; (*of object*) borde *m*; (*of lake etc*) orilla ♦ *vt* (*SEWING*) ribetear; **on ~** (*fig*) = **edgy**; **to ~ away from** alejarse poco a poco de; **~ways** *adv*: **he couldn't get a word in ~ways** no pudo meter ni baza

edgy ['ɛdʒɪ] *adj* nervioso, inquieto

edible ['ɛdɪbl] *adj* comestible

Edinburgh ['ɛdɪnbərə] *n* Edimburgo

edit ['ɛdɪt] *vt* (*be editor of*) dirigir; (*text, report*) corregir, preparar; **~ion** [ɪ'dɪʃən] *n* edición *f*; **~or** *n* (*of newspaper*) director(a) *m/f*; (*of column*): **foreign / political ~or** encargado de la sección de extranjero/política; (*of book*) redactor(a) *m/f*; **~orial** [-'tɔːrɪəl] *adj* editorial ♦ *n* editorial *m*

educate ['ɛdjukeɪt] *vt* (*gen*) educar; (*instruct*) instruir

education [ɛdju'keɪʃən] *n* educación *f*; (*schooling*) enseñanza; (*SCOL*) pedagogía; **~al** *adj* (*policy etc*) educacional; (*experience*) docente; (*toy*) educativo

EEC *n abbr* (= *European Economic Community*) CEE *f*

eel [iːl] *n* anguila

eerie ['ɪərɪ] *adj* misterioso

effect [ɪ'fɛkt] *n* efecto ♦ *vt* efectuar, llevar a cabo; **to take ~** (*law*) entrar en vigor *or* vigencia; (*drug*) surtir efecto; **in ~** en realidad; **~ive** *adj* eficaz; (*actual*) verdadero; **~ively** *adv* eficazmente; (*in reality*) efectivamente; **~iveness** *n* eficacia

effeminate [ɪ'fɛmɪnɪt] *adj* afeminado

efficiency [ɪ'fɪʃənsɪ] *n* eficiencia;

rendimiento

efficient [ɪ'fɪʃənt] *adj* eficiente; (*machine*) de buen rendimiento

effort ['ɛfət] *n* esfuerzo; **~less** *adj* sin ningún esfuerzo; (*style*) natural

effusive [ɪ'fjuːsɪv] *adj* efusivo

e.g. *adv abbr* (= *exempli gratia*) p. ej.

egg [ɛg] *n* huevo; **hard-boiled / soft-boiled ~** huevo duro/pasado por agua; **~ on** *vt* incitar; **~cup** *n* huevera; **~ plant** (*esp US*) *n* berenjena; **~shell** *n* cáscara de huevo

ego ['iːgəu] *n* ego; **~tism** *n* egoísmo; **~tist** *n* egoísta *m/f*

Egypt ['iːdʒɪpt] *n* Egipto; **~ian** [ɪ'dʒɪpʃən] *adj*, *n* egipcio/a *m/f*

eiderdown ['aɪdədaun] *n* edredón *m*

eight [eɪt] *num* ocho; **~een** *num* diez y ocho, dieciocho; **eighth** [eɪtθ] *num* octavo; **~y** *num* ochenta

Eire ['ɛərə] *n* Eire *m*

either ['aɪðə*] *adj* cualquiera de los dos; (*both, each*) cada ♦ *pron*: **~ (of them)** cualquiera (de los dos) ♦ *adv* tampoco; **on ~ side** en ambos lados; **I don't like ~** no me gusta ninguno/a de los/las dos; **no, I don't ~** no, yo tampoco ♦ *conj*: **~ yes or no** o sí o no

eject [ɪ'dʒɛkt] *vt* echar, expulsar; (*tenant*) desahuciar; **~or seat** *n* asiento proyectable

elaborate [*adj* ɪ'læbərɪt, *vb* ɪ'læbəreɪt] *adj* (*complex*) complejo ♦ *vt* (*expand*) ampliar; (*refine*) refinar ♦ *vi* explicar con más detalles

elastic [ɪ'læstɪk] *n* elástico ♦ *adj* elástico; (*fig*) flexible; **~ band** (*BRIT*) *n* gomita

elated [ɪ'leɪtɪd] *adj*: **to be ~** regocijarse

elbow ['ɛlbəu] *n* codo

elder ['ɛldə*] *adj* mayor ♦ *n* (*tree*) saúco; (*person*) mayor; **~ly** *adj* de edad, mayor ♦ *npl*: **the ~ly** los mayores

eldest ['ɛldɪst] *adj*, *n* el/la mayor

elect [ɪ'lɛkt] *vt* elegir ♦ *adj*: **the president ~** el presidente electo; **to ~ to do** optar por hacer; **~ion** [ɪ'lɛkʃən] *n* elección *f*; **~ioneering** [ɪlɛkʃə'nɪərɪŋ] *n* campaña

electoral; **~or** *n* elector(a) *m/f*; **~oral** *adj*
electoral; **~orate** *n* electorado

electric [ɪ'lektrɪk] *adj* eléctrico; **~al** *adj*
eléctrico; **~ blanket** *n* manta eléctrica; **~
fire** *n* estufa eléctrica; **~ian** [ɪlek'trɪʃən] *n*
electricista *m/f*; **~ity** [ɪlek'trɪsɪtɪ] *n*
electricidad *f*; **electrify** [ɪ'lektrɪfaɪ] *vt*
(*RAIL*) electrificar; (*fig: audience*) electrizar

electronic [ɪlek'trɒnɪk] *adj* electrónico; **~
mail** *n* correo electrónico; **~s** *n*
electrónica

elegant ['ɛlɪɡənt] *adj* elegante

element ['ɛlɪmənt] *n* elemento; (*of kettle
etc*) resistencia; **~ary** [-'mɛntərɪ] *adj*
elemental; (*primitive*) rudimentario;
(*school*) primario

elephant ['ɛlɪfənt] *n* elefante *m*

elevation [ɛlɪ'veɪʃən] *n* elevación *f*;
(*height*) altura

elevator ['ɛlɪveɪtə*] *n* (*US*) ascensor *m*; (*in
warehouse etc*) montacargas *m inv*

eleven [ɪ'lɛvn] *num* once; **~ses** (*BRIT*) *npl*
café *m* de las once; **~th** *num* undécimo

elicit [ɪ'lɪsɪt] *vt*: **to ~ (from)** sacar (de)

eligible ['ɛlɪdʒəbl] *adj*: **an ~ young man/
woman** un buen partido; **to be ~ for sth**
llenar los requisitos para algo

elm [ɛlm] *n* olmo

elongated ['iːlɒŋɡeɪtɪd] *adj* alargado

elope [ɪ'ləʊp] *vi* fugarse (para casarse)

eloquent ['ɛləkwənt] *adj* elocuente

else [ɛls] *adv*: **something ~** otra cosa;
somewhere ~ en otra parte; **everywhere
~** en todas partes menos aquí; **where ~?**
¿dónde más?, ¿en qué otra parte?; **there
was little ~ to do** apenas quedaba otra
cosa que hacer; **nobody ~ spoke** no
habló nadie más; **~where** *adv* (*be*) en
otra parte; (*go*) a otra parte

elude [ɪ'luːd] *vt* (*subj: idea etc*) escaparse a;
(*capture*) esquivar

elusive [ɪ'luːsɪv] *adj* esquivo; (*quality*)
difícil de encontrar

emaciated [ɪ'meɪsɪeɪtɪd] *adj* demacrado

E-mail, e-mail ['iːmeɪl] *n abbr*
(= *electronic mail*) correo electrónico, e-
mail *m*

emancipate [ɪ'mænsɪpeɪt] *vt* emancipar

embankment [ɪm'bæŋkmənt] *n* terraplén
m

embark [ɪm'bɑːk] *vi* embarcarse ♦ *vt*
embarcar; **to ~ on** (*journey*) emprender;
(*course of action*) lanzarse a; **~ation**
[embɑː'keɪʃən] *n* (*people*) embarco; (*goods*)
embarque *m*

embarrass [ɪm'bærəs] *vt* avergonzar;
(*government etc*) dejar en mal lugar; **~ed**
adj (*laugh, silence*) embarazoso; **~ing** *adj*
(*situation*) violento; (*question*)
embarazoso; **~ment** *n* (*shame*)
vergüenza; (*problem*): **to be an ~ment for
sb** poner en un aprieto a uno

embassy ['ɛmbəsɪ] *n* embajada

embedded [ɪm'bedɪd] *adj* (*object*)
empotrado; (*thorn etc*) clavado

embellish [ɪm'belɪʃ] *vt* embellecer; (*story*)
adornar

embers ['ɛmbəz] *npl* rescoldo, ascua

embezzle [ɪm'bezl] *vt* desfalcar, malversar

embitter [ɪm'bɪtə*] *vt* (*fig: sour*) amargar

embody [ɪm'bɒdɪ] *vt* (*spirit*) encarnar;
(*include*) incorporar

embossed [ɪm'bɒst] *adj* realzado

embrace [ɪm'breɪs] *vt* abrazar, dar un
abrazo a; (*include*) abarcar ♦ *vi* abrazarse
♦ *n* abrazo

embroider [ɪm'brɔɪdə*] *vt* bordar; **~y** *n*
bordado

embryo ['ɛmbrɪəʊ] *n* embrión *m*

emerald ['ɛmərəld] *n* esmeralda

emerge [ɪ'mɜːdʒ] *vi* salir; (*arise*) surgir

emergency [ɪ'mɜːdʒənsɪ] *n* crisis *f inv*; **in
an ~** en caso de urgencia; **state of ~** *n*
estado de emergencia; **~ cord** (*US*) *n*
timbre *m* de alarma; **~ exit** *n* salida de
emergencia; **~ landing** *n* aterrizaje *m*
forzoso; **~ services** *npl* (*fire, police,
ambulance*) servicios *mpl* de urgencia *or*
emergencia

emery board ['ɛmərɪ-] *n* lima de uñas

emigrate ['ɛmɪɡreɪt] *vi* emigrar

emissions [ɪ'mɪʃənz] *npl* emisión *f*

emit [ɪ'mɪt] *vt* emitir; (*smoke*) arrojar;
(*smell*) despedir; (*sound*) producir

emotion [ɪ'məʊʃən] *n* emoción *f*; **~al** *adj* (*needs*) emocional; (*person*) sentimental; (*scene*) conmovedor(a), emocionante; (*speech*) emocionado

emperor ['empərə*] *n* emperador *m*

emphasis ['emfəsɪs] (*pl* **-ses**) *n* énfasis *m inv*

emphasize ['emfəsaɪz] *vt* (*word, point*) subrayar, recalcar; (*feature*) hacer resaltar

emphatic [em'fætɪk] *adj* (*reply*) categórico; (*person*) insistente

empire ['empaɪə*] *n* (*also fig*) imperio

employ [ɪm'plɔɪ] *vt* emplear; **~ee** [-'iː] *n* empleado/a; **~er** *n* patrón/ona *m/f*; empresario; **~ment** *n* (*work*) trabajo; **~ment agency** *n* agencia de colocaciones

empower [ɪm'paʊə*] *vt*: **to ~ sb to do sth** autorizar a uno para hacer algo

empress ['emprɪs] *n* emperatriz *f*

emptiness ['emptɪnɪs] *n* vacío; (*of life etc*) vaciedad *f*

empty ['empti] *adj* vacío; (*place*) desierto; (*house*) desocupado; (*threat*) vano ♦ *vt* vaciar; (*place*) dejar vacío ♦ *vi* vaciarse; (*house etc*) quedar desocupado; **~-handed** *adj* con las manos vacías

EMU *n abbr* (= *European Monetary Union*) UME *f*

emulate ['emjuleɪt] *vt* emular

emulsion [ɪ'mʌlʃən] *n* emulsión *f*; (*also*: **~ paint**) pintura emulsión

enable [ɪ'neɪbl] *vt*: **to ~ sb to do sth** permitir a uno hacer algo

enamel [ɪ'næməl] *n* esmalte *m*; (*also*: **~ paint**) pintura esmaltada

enchant [ɪn'tʃɑːnt] *vt* encantar; **~ing** *adj* encantador(a)

encl. *abbr* (= *enclosed*) adj

enclose [ɪn'kləʊz] *vt* (*land*) cercar; (*letter etc*) adjuntar; **please find ~d** le mandamos adjunto

enclosure [ɪn'kləʊʒə*] *n* cercado, recinto

encompass [ɪn'kʌmpəs] *vt* abarcar

encore [ɒŋ'kɔː*] *excl* ¡otra!, ¡bis! ♦ *n* bis *m*

encounter [ɪn'kaʊntə*] *n* encuentro ♦ *vt* encontrar, encontrarse con; (*difficulty*) tropezar con

encourage [ɪn'kʌrɪdʒ] *vt* alentar, animar; (*activity*) fomentar; (*growth*) estimular; **~ment** *n* estímulo; (*of industry*) fomento

encroach [ɪn'krəʊtʃ] *vi*: **to ~ (up)on** invadir; (*rights*) usurpar; (*time*) adueñarse de

encyclop(a)edia [ensaɪkləʊ'piːdɪə] *n* enciclopedia

end [end] *n* (*gen, also aim*) fin *m*; (*of table*) extremo; (*of street*) final *m*; (*SPORT*) lado ♦ *vt* terminar, acabar; (*also*: **bring to an ~, put an ~ to**) acabar con ♦ *vi* terminar, acabar; **in the ~** al fin; **on ~** (*object*) de punta, de cabeza; **to stand on ~** (*hair*) erizarse; **for hours on ~** hora tras hora; **~ up** *vi*: **to ~ up in** terminar en; (*place*) ir a parar en

endanger [ɪn'deɪndʒə*] *vt* poner en peligro; **an ~ed species** una especie en peligro de extinción

endearing [ɪn'dɪərɪŋ] *adj* simpático, atractivo

endeavour [ɪn'devə*] (*US* **endeavor**) *n* esfuerzo; (*attempt*) tentativa ♦ *vi*: **to ~ to do** esforzarse por hacer; (*try*) procurar hacer

ending ['endɪŋ] *n* (*of book*) desenlace *m*; (*LING*) terminación *f*

endive ['endaɪv] *n* (*chicory*) endibia; (*curly*) escarola

endless ['endlɪs] *adj* interminable, inacabable

endorse [ɪn'dɔːs] *vt* (*cheque*) endosar; (*approve*) aprobar; **~ment** *n* (*on driving licence*) nota de inhabilitación

endure [ɪn'djuə*] *vt* (*bear*) aguantar, soportar ♦ *vi* (*last*) durar

enemy ['enəmɪ] *adj, n* enemigo/a *m/f*

energetic [enə'dʒetɪk] *adj* enérgico

energy ['enədʒɪ] *n* energía

enforce [ɪn'fɔːs] *vt* (*LAW*) hacer cumplir

engage [ɪn'geɪdʒ] *vt* (*attention*) llamar; (*interest*) ocupar; (*in conversation*) abordar; (*worker*) contratar; (*AUT*): **to ~ the clutch** embragar ♦ *vi* (*TECH*) engranar; **to ~ in** dedicarse a, ocuparse en; **~d** *adj* (*BRIT: busy, in use*) ocupado; (*betrothed*) prometido; **to get ~d** prometerse; **~d tone** (*BRIT*) *n* (*TEL*) señal *f* de comunicando; **~ment** *n* (*appointment*) compromiso, cita; (*booking*) contratación *f*; (*to marry*) compromiso; (*period*) noviazgo; **~ment ring** *n* anillo de prometida

engaging [ɪnˈgeɪdʒɪŋ] *adj* atractivo

engine [ˈɛndʒɪn] *n* (*AUT*) motor *m*; (*RAIL*) locomotora; **~ driver** *n* maquinista *m/f*

engineer [ɛndʒɪˈnɪə*] *n* ingeniero; (*BRIT: for repairs*) mecánico; (*on ship, US: RAIL*) maquinista *m*; **~ing** *n* ingeniería

England [ˈɪŋglənd] *n* Inglaterra

English [ˈɪŋglɪʃ] *adj* inglés/esa ♦ *n* (*LING*) inglés *m*; **the ~** *npl* los ingleses *mpl*; **the ~ Channel** *n* (el Canal de) la Mancha; **~man/woman** (*irreg*) *n* inglés/esa *m/f*

engraving [ɪnˈgreɪvɪŋ] *n* grabado

engrossed [ɪnˈgrəʊst] *adj*: **~ in** absorto en

engulf [ɪnˈgʌlf] *vt* (*subj: water*) sumergir, hundir; (*: fire*) prender; (*: fear*) apoderarse de

enhance [ɪnˈhɑːns] *vt* (*gen*) aumentar; (*beauty*) realzar

enjoy [ɪnˈdʒɔɪ] *vt* (*health, fortune*) disfrutar de, gozar de; (*like*) gustarle a uno; **to ~ o.s.** divertirse; **~able** *adj* agradable; (*amusing*) divertido; **~ment** *n* (*joy*) placer *m*; (*activity*) diversión *f*

enlarge [ɪnˈlɑːdʒ] *vt* aumentar; (*broaden*) extender; (*PHOT*) ampliar ♦ *vi*: **to ~ on** (*subject*) tratar con más detalles; **~ment** *n* (*PHOT*) ampliación *f*

enlighten [ɪnˈlaɪtn] *vt* (*inform*) informar; **~ed** *adj* comprensivo; **the E~ment** *n* (*HISTORY*) ≈ la Ilustración, ≈ el Siglo de las Luces

enlist [ɪnˈlɪst] *vt* alistar; (*support*) conseguir ♦ *vi* alistarse

enmity [ˈɛnmɪtɪ] *n* enemistad *f*

enormous [ɪˈnɔːməs] *adj* enorme

enough [ɪˈnʌf] *adj*: **~ time/books** bastante tiempo/bastantes libros ♦ *pron* bastante(s) ♦ *adv*: **big ~** bastante grande; **he has not worked ~** no ha trabajado

bastante; **have you got ~?** ¿tiene usted bastante(s)?; **~ to eat** (lo) suficiente *or* (lo) bastante para comer; **~!** ¡basta ya!; **that's ~, thanks** con eso basta, gracias; **I've had ~ of him** estoy harto de él; **... which, funnily** *or* **oddly ~ ...** ... lo que, por extraño que parezca ...

enquire [ɪnˈkwaɪə*] *vt, vi* = **inquire**

enrage [ɪnˈreɪdʒ] *vt* enfurecer

enrol [ɪnˈrəʊl] (*US* **enroll**) *vt* (*members*) inscribir; (*SCOL*) matricular ♦ *vi* inscribirse; matricularse; **~ment** (*US* **enrollment**) *n* inscripción *f*; matriculación *f*

en route [ɔnˈruːt] *adv* durante el viaje

en suite [ɔnˈswiːt] *adj*: **with ~ bathroom** con baño

ensure [ɪnˈʃuə*] *vt* asegurar

entail [ɪnˈteɪl] *vt* suponer

entangled [ɪnˈtæŋgld] *adj*: **to become ~ (in)** quedarse enredado (en) *or* enmarañado (en)

enter [ˈɛntə*] *vt* (*room*) entrar en; (*club*) hacerse socio de; (*army*) alistarse en; (*sb for a competition*) inscribir; (*write down*) anotar, apuntar; (*COMPUT*) meter ♦ *vi* entrar; **~ for** *vt fus* presentarse para; **~ into** *vt fus* (*discussion etc*) entablar; (*agreement*) llegar a, firmar

enterprise [ˈɛntəpraɪz] *n* empresa; (*spirit*) iniciativa; **free ~** la libre empresa; **private ~** la iniciativa privada; **enterprising** *adj* emprendedor(a)

entertain [ɛntəˈteɪn] *vt* (*amuse*) divertir; (*invite: guest*) invitar (a casa); (*idea*) abrigar; **~er** *n* artista *m/f*; **~ing** *adj* divertido, entretenido; **~ment** *n* (*amusement*) diversión *f*; (*show*) espectáculo

enthralled [ɪnˈθrɔːld] *adj* encantado

enthusiasm [ɪnˈθuːzɪæzəm] *n* entusiasmo

enthusiast [ɪnˈθuːzɪæst] *n* entusiasta *m/f*; **~ic** [-ˈæstɪk] *adj* entusiasta; **to be ~ic about** entusiasmarse por

entire [ɪnˈtaɪə*] *adj* entero; **~ly** *adv* totalmente, en su totalidad; **~ty** [ɪnˈtaɪərətɪ] *n*: **in its ~ty** en su totalidad

entitle [ɪnˈtaɪtl] *vt*: **to ~ sb to sth** dar a

uno derecho a algo; **~d** *adj* (*book*) titulado; **to be ~d to do** tener derecho a hacer

entrance [*n* 'entrəns, *vb* ɪn'trɑːns] *n* entrada ♦ *vt* encantar, hechizar; **to gain ~ to** (*university etc*) ingresar en; **~ examination** *n* examen *m* de ingreso; **~ fee** *n* cuota; **~ ramp** (*US*) *n* (*AUT*) rampa de acceso

entrant ['entrant] *n* (*in race, competition*) participante *m/f*; (*in examination*) candidato/a

entrenched [en'trentʃd] *adj* inamovible

entrepreneur [ɔntrəprə'nəː*] *n* empresario

entrust [ɪn'trʌst] *vt*: **to ~ sth to sb** confiar algo a uno

entry ['entrɪ] *n* entrada; (*in competition*) participación *f*; (*in register*) apunte *m*; (*in account*) partida; (*in reference book*) artículo; **"no ~"** "prohibido el paso"; (*AUT*) "dirección prohibida"; **~ form** *n* hoja de inscripción; **~ phone** *n* portero automático

envelop [ɪn'veləp] *vt* envolver

envelope ['envələup] *n* sobre *m*

envious ['envɪəs] *adj* envidioso; (*look*) de envidia

environment [ɪn'vaɪərnmənt] *n* (*surroundings*) entorno; (*natural world*): **the ~** el medio ambiente; **~al** [-'mentl] *adj* ambiental; medioambiental; **~-friendly** *adj* no perjudicial para el medio ambiente

envisage [ɪn'vɪzɪdʒ] *vt* prever

envoy ['envɔɪ] *n* enviado

envy ['envɪ] *n* envidia ♦ *vt* tener envidia a; **to ~ sb sth** envidiar algo a uno

epic ['epɪk] *n* épica ♦ *adj* épico

epidemic [epɪ'demɪk] *n* epidemia

epilepsy ['epɪlepsɪ] *n* epilepsia

episode ['epɪsəud] *n* episodio

epitomize [ɪ'pɪtəmaɪz] *vt* epitomar, resumir

equal ['iːkwl] *adj* igual; (*treatment*) equitativo ♦ *n* igual *m/f* ♦ *vt* ser igual a; (*fig*) igualar; **to be ~ to** (*task*) estar a la altura de; **~ity** [iː'kwɔlɪtɪ] *n* igualdad *f*;

~ize *vi* (*SPORT*) empatar; **~ly** *adv* igualmente; (*share etc*) a partes iguales

equate [ɪ'kweɪt] *vt*: **to ~ sth with** equiparar algo con; **equation** [ɪ'kweɪʒən] *n* (*MATH*) ecuación *f*

equator [ɪ'kweɪtə*] *n* ecuador *m*

equilibrium [iːkwɪ'lɪbrɪəm] *n* equilibrio

equip [ɪ'kwɪp] *vt* equipar; (*person*) proveer; **to be well ~ped** estar bien equipado; **~ment** *n* equipo; (*tools*) avíos *mpl*

equities ['ekwɪtɪz] (*BRIT*) *npl* (*COMM*) derechos *mpl* sobre *or* en el activo

equivalent [ɪ'kwɪvələnt] *adj*: **~ (to)** equivalente (a) ♦ *n* equivalente *m*

era ['ɪərə] *n* era, época

eradicate [ɪ'rædɪkeɪt] *vt* erradicar

erase [ɪ'reɪz] *vt* borrar; **~r** *n* goma de borrar

erect [ɪ'rekt] *adj* erguido ♦ *vt* erigir, levantar; (*assemble*) montar; **~ion** [-ʃən] *n* construcción *f*; (*assembly*) montaje *m*; (*PHYSIOL*) erección *f*

ERM *n abbr* (= *Exchange Rate Mechanism*) *tipo de cambio europeo*

erode [ɪ'rəud] *vt* (*GEO*) erosionar; (*metal*) corroer, desgastar; (*fig*) desgastar

erotic [ɪ'rɔtɪk] *adj* erótico

errand ['ernd] *n* recado (*SP*), mandado (*AM*)

erratic [ɪ'rætɪk] *adj* desigual, poco uniforme

error ['erə*] *n* error *m*, equivocación *f*

erupt [ɪ'rʌpt] *vi* entrar en erupción; (*fig*) estallar; **~ion** [ɪ'rʌpʃən] *n* erupción *f*; (*of war*) estallido

escalate ['eskəleɪt] *vi* extenderse, intensificarse

escalator ['eskəleɪtə*] *n* escalera móvil

escapade [eskə'peɪd] *n* travesura

escape [ɪ'skeɪp] *n* fuga ♦ *vi* escaparse; (*flee*) huir, evadirse; (*leak*) fugarse ♦ *vt* (*responsibility etc*) evitar, eludir; (*consequences*) escapar a; (*elude*): **his name ~s me** no me sale su nombre; **to ~ from** (*place*) escaparse de; (*person*) escaparse a

escort [*n* 'eskɔːt, *vb* ɪ'skɔːt] *n* acompañante

m/f; (*MIL*) escolta ♦ *vt* acompañar

Eskimo [ˈɛskɪməu] *n* esquimal *m/f*

especially [ɪˈspɛʃlɪ] *adv* (*above all*) sobre todo; (*particularly*) en particular, especialmente

espionage [ɛspɪənɑːʒ] *n* espionaje *m*

esplanade [ɛspləˈneɪd] *n* (*by sea*) paseo marítimo

Esquire [ɪˈskwaɪə] (*abbr* **Esq.**) *n*: **J. Brown, ~** Sr. D. J. Brown

essay [ˈɛseɪ] *n* (*LITERATURE*) ensayo; (*SCOL*: *short*) redacción *f*; (: *long*) trabajo

essence [ˈɛsns] *n* esencia

essential [ɪˈsɛnʃl] *adj* (*necessary*) imprescindible; (*basic*) esencial; **~s** *npl* lo imprescindible, lo esencial; **~ly** *adv* esencialmente

establish [ɪˈstæblɪʃ] *vt* establecer; (*prove*) demostrar; (*relations*) entablar; (*reputation*) ganarse; **~ed** *adj* (*business*) conocido; (*practice*) arraigado; **~ment** *n* establecimiento; **the E~ment** la clase dirigente

estate [ɪˈsteɪt] *n* (*land*) finca, hacienda; (*inheritance*) herencia; (*BRIT*: *also*: **housing ~**) urbanización *f*; **~ agent** (*BRIT*) *n* agente *m/f* inmobiliario/a; **~ car** (*BRIT*) *n* furgoneta

esteem [ɪˈstiːm] *n*: **to hold sb in high ~** estimar en mucho a uno

esthetic [ɪsˈθɛtɪk] (*US*) *adj* = **aesthetic**

estimate [*n* ˈɛstɪmət, *vb* ˈɛstɪmeɪt] *n* estimación *f*, apreciación *f*; (*assessment*) tasa, cálculo; (*COMM*) presupuesto ♦ *vt* estimar, tasar; calcular; **estimation** [-ˈmeɪʃən] *n* opinión *f*, juicio; cálculo

estranged [ɪˈstreɪndʒd] *adj* separado

estuary [ˈɛstjuərɪ] *n* estuario, ría

etc *abbr* (= *et cetera*) etc

eternal [ɪˈtəːnl] *adj* eterno

eternity [ɪˈtəːnɪtɪ] *n* eternidad *f*

ethical [ˈɛθɪkl] *adj* ético; **ethics** [ˈɛθɪks] *n* ética ♦ *npl* moralidad *f*

Ethiopia [iːθɪˈəupɪə] *n* Etiopía

ethnic [ˈɛθnɪk] *adj* étnico; **~ minority** *n* minoría étnica

ethos [ˈiːθɔs] *n* genio, carácter *m*

etiquette [ˈɛtɪkɛt] *n* etiqueta

EU *n abbr* (= *European Union*) UE *f*

euro [ˈjuərəu] *n* euro

Eurocheque [ˈjuərəutʃɛk] *n* Eurocheque *m*

Europe [ˈjuərəp] *n* Europa; **~an** [-ˈpiːən] *adj*, *n* europeo/a *m/f*; **~an Community** *n* Comunidad *f* Europea; **~an Union** *n* Unión *f* Europea

evacuate [ɪˈvækjueɪt] *vt* (*people*) evacuar; (*place*) desocupar

evade [ɪˈveɪd] *vt* evadir, eludir

evaporate [ɪˈvæpəreɪt] *vi* evaporarse; (*fig*) desvanecerse; **~d milk** *n* leche *f* evaporada

evasion [ɪˈveɪʒən] *n* evasión *f*

eve [iːv] *n*: **on the ~ of** en vísperas de

even [ˈiːvn] *adj* (*level*) llano; (*smooth*) liso; (*speed, temperature*) uniforme; (*number*) par ♦ *adv* hasta, incluso; (*introducing a comparison*) aún, todavía; **~ if**, **~ though** aunque +*sub*; **~ more** aun más; **~ so** aun así; **not ~** ni siquiera; **~ he was there** hasta él estuvo allí; **~ on Sundays** incluso los domingos; **to get ~ with sb** ajustar cuentas con uno

evening [ˈiːvnɪŋ] *n* tarde *f*; (*late*) noche *f*; **in the ~** por la tarde; **~ class** *n* clase *f* nocturna; **~ dress** *n* (*no pl*: *formal clothes*) traje *m* de etiqueta; (*woman's*) traje *m* de noche

event [ɪˈvɛnt] *n* suceso, acontecimiento; (*SPORT*) prueba; **in the ~ of** en caso de; **~ful** *adj* (*life*) activo; (*day*) ajetreado

eventual [ɪˈvɛntʃuəl] *adj* final; **~ity** [-ˈælɪtɪ] *n* eventualidad *f*; **~ly** *adv* (*finally*) finalmente; (*in time*) con el tiempo

ever [ˈɛvə*] *adv* (*at any time*) nunca, jamás; (*at all times*) siempre; (*in question*): **why ~ not?** ¿y por qué no?; **the best ~** lo nunca visto; **have you ~ seen it?** ¿lo ha visto usted alguna vez?; **better than ~** mejor que nunca; **~ since** *adv* desde entonces ♦ *conj* después de que; **~green** *n* árbol *m* de hoja perenne; **~lasting** *adj* eterno, perpetuo

---

KEYWORD

every ['ɛvrɪ] adj 1 (each) cada; ~ **one of them** (persons) todos ellos/as; (objects) cada uno de ellos/as; ~ **shop in the town was closed** todas las tiendas de la ciudad estaban cerradas

2 (all possible) todo/a; **I gave you ~ assistance** ... te di toda la ayuda posible; **I have ~ confidence in him** tiene toda mi confianza; **we wish you ~ success** te deseamos toda suerte de éxitos

3 (showing recurrence) todo/a; ~ **day/ week** todos los días/todas las semanas; ~ **other car had been broken into** habían forzado uno de cada dos coches; **she visits me ~ other/third day** me visita cada dos/tres días; ~ **now and then** de vez en cuando

---

every: ~**body** pron = **everyone**; ~**day** adj (daily) cotidiano, de todos los días; (usual) acostumbrado; ~**one** pron todos/ as, todo el mundo; ~**thing** pron todo; **this shop sells ~thing** esta tienda vende de todo; ~**where** adv: **I've been looking for you ~where** te he estado buscando por todas partes; ~**where you go you meet ...** en todas partes encuentras ...

evict [ɪ'vɪkt] vt desahuciar; ~**ion** [ɪ'vɪkʃən] n desahucio

evidence ['ɛvɪdəns] n (proof) prueba; (of witness) testimonio; (sign) indicios mpl; **to give ~** prestar declaración, dar testimonio

evident ['ɛvɪdənt] adj evidente, manifiesto; ~**ly** adv por lo visto

evil ['iːvl] adj malo; (influence) funesto ♦ n mal m

evoke [ɪ'vəuk] vt evocar

evolution [iːvə'luːʃən] n evolución f

evolve [ɪ'vɒlv] vt desarrollar ♦ vi evolucionar, desarrollarse

ewe [juː] n oveja

ex- [ɛks] prefix ex

exact [ɪg'zækt] adj exacto; (person) meticuloso ♦ vt: **to ~ sth (from)** exigir

algo (de); ~**ing** adj exigente; (conditions) arduo; ~**ly** adv exactamente; (indicating agreement) exacto

exaggerate [ɪg'zædʒəreɪt] vt, vi exagerar; **exaggeration** [-'reɪʃən] n exageración f

exalted [ɪg'zɔːltɪd] adj eminente

exam [ɪg'zæm] n abbr (SCOL) = **examination**

examination [ɪgzæmɪ'neɪʃən] n examen m; (MED) reconocimiento

examine [ɪg'zæmɪn] vt examinar; (inspect) inspeccionar, escudriñar; (MED) reconocer; ~**r** n examinador(a) m/f

example [ɪg'zɑːmpl] n ejemplo; **for ~** por ejemplo

exasperate [ɪg'zɑːspəreɪt] vt exasperar, irritar; **exasperation** [-'ʃən] n exasperación f, irritación f

excavate ['ɛkskəveɪt] vt excavar

exceed [ɪk'siːd] vt (amount) exceder; (number) pasar de; (speed limit) sobrepasar; (powers) excederse en; (hopes) superar; ~**ingly** adv sumamente, sobremanera

excellent ['ɛksələnt] adj excelente

except [ɪk'sɛpt] prep (also: ~ **for**, ~**ing**) excepto, salvo ♦ vt exceptuar, excluir; ~ **if/when** excepto si/cuando; ~ **that** salvo que; ~**ion** [ɪk'sɛpʃən] n excepción f; **to take ~ion to** ofenderse por; ~**ional** [ɪk'sɛpʃənl] adj excepcional

excerpt ['ɛksəːpt] n extracto

excess [ɪk'sɛs] n exceso; ~**es** npl (of cruelty etc) atrocidades fpl; ~ **baggage** n exceso de equipaje; ~ **fare** n suplemento; ~**ive** adj excesivo

exchange [ɪks'tʃeɪndʒ] n intercambio; (conversation) diálogo; (also: **telephone ~**) central f (telefónica) ♦ vt: **to ~ (for)** cambiar (por); ~ **rate** n tipo de cambio

exchequer [ɪks'tʃɛkə*] (BRIT) n: **the E~** la Hacienda del Fisco

excise ['ɛksaɪz] n impuestos mpl sobre el alcohol y el tabaco

excite [ɪk'saɪt] vt (stimulate) estimular; (arouse) excitar; ~**d** adj: **to get ~d** emocionarse; ~**ment** n (agitation)

excitación f; (*exhilaration*) emoción f;
exciting *adj* emocionante

exclaim [ɪkˈskleɪm] *vi* exclamar;
exclamation [ɛksklə'meɪʃən] *n*
exclamación f; **exclamation mark** *n*
punto de admiración

exclude [ɪkˈskluːd] *vt* excluir; exceptuar

exclusive [ɪkˈskluːsɪv] *adj* exclusivo; (*club,
district*) selecto; **~ of tax** excluyendo
impuestos; **~ly** *adv* únicamente

excruciating [ɪkˈskruːʃieɪtɪŋ] *adj* (*pain*)
agudísimo, atroz; (*noise, embarrassment*)
horrible

excursion [ɪkˈskəːʃən] *n* (*tourist ~*)
excursión f

excuse [*n* ɪkˈskjuːs, *vb* ɪkˈskjuːz] *n* disculpa,
excusa; (*pretext*) pretexto ♦ *vt* (*justify*)
justificar; (*forgive*) disculpar, perdonar; **to
~ sb from doing sth** dispensar a uno de
hacer algo; **~ me!** (*attracting attention*)
¡por favor!; (*apologizing*) ¡perdón!; **if you
will ~ me** con su permiso

ex-directory [ˈɛksdɪˈrɛktərɪ] (*BRIT*) *adj* que
no consta en la guía

execute [ˈɛksɪkjuːt] *vt* (*plan*) realizar;
(*order*) cumplir; (*person*) ajusticiar,
ejecutar; **execution** [-ˈkjuːʃən] *n*
realización f; cumplimiento; ejecución f

executive [ɪgˈzɛkjutɪv] *n* (*person,
committee*) ejecutivo; (*POL: committee*)
poder *m* ejecutivo ♦ *adj* ejecutivo

exemplify [ɪgˈzɛmplɪfaɪ] *vt* ejemplificar;
(*illustrate*) ilustrar

exempt [ɪgˈzɛmpt] *adj*: **~ from** exento de
♦ *vt*: **to ~ sb from** eximir a uno de; **~ion**
[-ʃən] *n* exención f

exercise [ˈɛksəsaɪz] *n* ejercicio ♦ *vt*
(*patience*) usar de; (*right*) valerse de; (*dog*)
llevar de paseo; (*mind*) preocupar ♦ *vi*
(*also: to take ~*) hacer ejercicio(s); **~ bike**
n ciclostático ® *m*, bicicleta estática; **~
book** *n* cuaderno

exert [ɪgˈzəːt] *vt* ejercer; **to ~ o.s.**
esforzarse; **~ion** [-ʃən] *n* esfuerzo

exhale [ɛksˈheɪl] *vt* despedir ♦ *vi* exhalar

exhaust [ɪgˈzɔːst] *n* (*AUT: also*: **~ pipe**)
escape *m*; (: *fumes*) gases *mpl* de escape

♦ *vt* agotar; **~ed** *adj* agotado; **~ion**
[ɪgˈzɔːstʃən] *n* agotamiento; **nervous ~ion**
postración f nerviosa; **~ive** *adj*
exhaustivo

exhibit [ɪgˈzɪbɪt] *n* (*ART*) obra expuesta;
(*LAW*) objeto expuesto ♦ *vt* (*show:
emotions*) manifestar; (: *courage, skill*)
demostrar; (*paintings*) exponer; **~ion**
[ɛksɪˈbɪʃən] *n* exposición f; (*of talent etc*)
demostración f

exhilarating [ɪgˈzɪləreɪtɪŋ] *adj* estimulante,
tónico

exile [ˈɛksaɪl] *n* exilio; (*person*) exiliado/a
♦ *vt* desterrar, exiliar

exist [ɪgˈzɪst] *vi* existir; (*live*) vivir; **~ence** *n*
existencia; **~ing** *adj* existente, actual

exit [ˈɛksɪt] *n* salida ♦ *vi* (*THEATRE*) hacer
mutis; (*COMPUT*) salir (al sistema); **~ poll**
n encuesta a la salida de los colegios
electorales; **~ ramp** (*US*) *n* (*AUT*) vía de
acceso

exodus [ˈɛksədəs] *n* éxodo

exonerate [ɪgˈzɔnəreɪt] *vt*: **to ~ from**
exculpar de

exotic [ɪgˈzɔtɪk] *adj* exótico

expand [ɪkˈspænd] *vt* ampliar; (*number*)
aumentar ♦ *vi* (*population*) aumentar;
(*trade etc*) expandirse; (*gas, metal*)
dilatarse

expanse [ɪkˈspæns] *n* extensión f

expansion [ɪkˈspænʃən] *n* (*of population*)
aumento; (*of trade*) expansión f

expect [ɪkˈspɛkt] *vt* esperar; (*require*)
contar con; (*suppose*) suponer ♦ *vi*: **to be
~ing** (*pregnant woman*) estar embarazada;
~ancy *n* (*anticipation*) esperanza; **life
~ancy** *n* esperanza de vida; **~ant mother**
n futura madre f; **~ation** [ɛkspɛkˈteɪʃən] *n*
(*hope*) esperanza; (*belief*) expectativa

expedient [ɪkˈspiːdɪənt] *adj* conveniente,
oportuno ♦ *n* recurso, expediente *m*

expedition [ɛkspəˈdɪʃən] *n* expedición f

expel [ɪkˈspɛl] *vt* arrojar; (*from place*)
expulsar

expend [ɪkˈspɛnd] *vt* (*money*) gastar; (*time,
energy*) consumir; **~iture** *n* gastos *mpl*,
desembolso; consumo

expense [ɪkˈspɛns] n gasto, gastos mpl; (high cost) costa; **~s** npl (COMM) gastos mpl; **at the ~ of** a costa de; **~ account** n cuenta de gastos

expensive [ɪkˈspɛnsɪv] adj caro, costoso

experience [ɪkˈspɪərɪəns] n experiencia ♦ vt experimentar; (suffer) sufrir; **~d** adj experimentado

experiment [ɪkˈspɛrɪmənt] n experimento ♦ vi hacer experimentos

expert [ˈɛkspɜːt] adj experto, perito ♦ n experto/a, perito/a; (specialist) especialista m/f; **~ise** [-ˈtiːz] n pericia

expire [ɪkˈspaɪə*] vi caducar, vencer; **expiry** n vencimiento

explain [ɪkˈspleɪn] vt explicar; **explanation** [ɛkspləˈneɪʃən] n explicación f; **explanatory** [ɪkˈsplænətrɪ] adj explicativo; aclaratorio

explicit [ɪkˈsplɪsɪt] adj explícito

explode [ɪkˈspləʊd] vi estallar, explotar; (population) crecer rápidamente; (with anger) reventar

exploit [n ˈɛksplɔɪt, vb ɪkˈsplɔɪt] n hazaña ♦ vt explotar; **~ation** [-ˈteɪʃən] n explotación f

exploratory [ɪkˈsplɔrətrɪ] adj de exploración; (fig: talks) exploratorio, preliminar

explore [ɪkˈsplɔː*] vt explorar; (fig) examinar; investigar; **~r** n explorador(a) m/f

explosion [ɪkˈspləʊʒən] n (also fig) explosión f; **explosive** [ɪksˈpləʊsɪv] adj, n explosivo

exponent [ɪkˈspəʊnənt] n (of theory etc) partidario/a; (of skill etc) exponente m/f

export [vb ɛkˈspɔːt, n ˈɛkspɔːt] vt exportar ♦ n (process) exportación f; (product) producto de exportación ♦ cpd de exportación; **~er** n exportador m

expose [ɪkˈspəʊz] vt exponer; (unmask) desenmascarar; **~d** adj expuesto

exposure [ɪkˈspəʊʒə*] n exposición f; (publicity) publicidad f; (PHOT: speed) velocidad f de obturación; (: shot) fotografía; **to die from ~** (MED) morir de frío; **~ meter** n fotómetro

express [ɪkˈsprɛs] adj (definite) expreso, explícito; (BRIT: letter etc) urgente ♦ n (train) rápido ♦ vt expresar; **~ion** [ɪkˈsprɛʃən] n expresión f; (of actor etc) sentimiento; **~ly** adv expresamente; **~way** n (US) (urban motorway) autopista

exquisite [ɛkˈskwɪzɪt] adj exquisito

extend [ɪkˈstɛnd] vt (visit, street) prolongar; (building) ampliar; (invitation) ofrecer ♦ vi (land) extenderse; (period of time) prolongarse

extension [ɪkˈstɛnʃən] n extensión f; (building) ampliación f; (of time) prolongación f; (TEL: in private house) línea derivada; (: in office) extensión f

extensive [ɪkˈstɛnsɪv] adj extenso; (damage) importante; (knowledge) amplio; **~ly** adv: **he's travelled ~ly** ha viajado por muchos países

extent [ɪkˈstɛnt] n (breadth) extensión f; (scope) alcance m; **to some ~** hasta cierto punto; **to the ~ of...** hasta el punto de...; **to such an ~ that...** hasta tal punto que...; **to what ~?** ¿hasta qué punto?

extenuating [ɪkˈstɛnjueɪtɪŋ] adj: **~ circumstances** circunstancias fpl atenuantes

exterior [ɛkˈstɪərɪə*] adj exterior, externo ♦ n exterior m

external [ɛkˈstɜːnl] adj externo

extinct [ɪkˈstɪŋkt] adj (volcano) extinguido; (race) extinto

extinguish [ɪkˈstɪŋgwɪʃ] vt extinguir, apagar; **~er** n extintor m

extort [ɪkˈstɔːt] vt obtener por fuerza; **~ionate** adj excesivo, exorbitante

extra [ˈɛkstrə] adj adicional ♦ adv (in addition) de más ♦ n (luxury, addition) extra m; (CINEMA, THEATRE) extra m/f, comparsa m/f

extra... [ˈɛkstrə] prefix extra...

extract [vb ɪkˈstrækt, n ˈɛkstrækt] vt sacar; (tooth) extraer; (money, promise) obtener ♦ n extracto

extracurricular [ɛkstrəkəˈrɪkjulə*] adj extraescolar, extra-académico

extradite ['ɛkstrədaɪt] *vt* extraditar
extra: **~marital** *adj* extramatrimonial;
~mural ['ɛkstrə'mjuərl] *adj* extraescolar;
~ordinary [ɪk'strɔːdnrɪ] *adj*
extraordinario; (*odd*) raro
extravagance [ɪk'strævəgəns] *n* derroche
m, despilfarro; (*thing bought*)
extravagancia
extravagant [ɪk'strævəgənt] *adj* (*lavish:
person*) pródigo; (: *gift*) (demasiado) caro;
(*wasteful*) despilfarrador(a)
extreme [ɪk'striːm] *adj* extremo,
extremado ♦ *n* extremo; **~ly** *adv*
sumamente, extremadamente
extricate ['ɛkstrɪkeɪt] *vt:* **to ~ sth/sb from**
librar algo/a uno de
extrovert ['ɛkstrəvəːt] *n* extrovertido/a
eye [aɪ] *n* ojo ♦ *vt* mirar de soslayo, ojear;
to keep an ~ on vigilar; **~bath** *n* ojera;
~brow *n* ceja; **~drops** *npl* gotas *fpl*
para los ojos, colino; **~lash** *n* pestaña;
~lid *n* párpado; **~liner** *n* lápiz *m* de
ojos; **~-opener** *n* revelación *f*, gran
sorpresa; **~shadow** *n* sombreador *m* de
ojos; **~sight** *n* vista; **~sore** *n*
monstruosidad *f*; **~ witness** *n* testigo
m/f presencial

F, f

F [ɛf] *n* (*MUS*) fa *m*
F. *abbr* = **Fahrenheit**
fable ['feɪbl] *n* fábula
fabric ['fæbrɪk] *n* tejido, tela
fabulous ['fæbjuləs] *adj* fabuloso
façade [fə'sɑːd] *n* fachada
face [feɪs] *n* (*ANAT*) cara, rostro; (*of clock*)
esfera (*SP*), cara (*AM*); (*of mountain*) cara,
ladera; (*of building*) fachada ♦ *vt*
(*direction*) estar de cara a; (*situation*) hacer
frente a; (*facts*) aceptar; **~ down** (*person,
card*) boca abajo; **to lose ~**
desprestigiarse; **to make** *or* **pull a ~** hacer
muecas; **in the ~ of** (*difficulties etc*) ante;
on the ~ of it a primera vista; **~ to ~** cara
a cara; **~ up to** *vt fus* hacer frente a,

arrostrar; **~ cloth** (*BRIT*) *n* manopla; **~
cream** *n* crema (de belleza); **~ lift** *n*
estirado facial; (*of building*) renovación *f*;
~ powder *n* polvos *mpl*; **~-saving** *adj*
para salvar las apariencias; **~ value** *n* (*of
stamp*) valor *m* nominal; **to take sth at ~
value** (*fig*) tomar algo en sentido literal
facilities [fə'sɪlɪtɪz] *npl* (*buildings*)
instalaciones *fpl*; (*equipment*) servicios
mpl; **credit ~** facilidades *fpl* de crédito
facing ['feɪsɪŋ] *prep* frente a
facsimile [fæk'sɪmɪlɪ] *n* (*replica*) facsímil(e)
m; (*machine*) telefax *m*; (*fax*) fax *m*
fact [fækt] *n* hecho; **in ~** en realidad
factor ['fæktə*] *n* factor *m*
factory ['fæktərɪ] *n* fábrica
factual ['fæktjuəl] *adj* basado en los
hechos
faculty ['fækltɪ] *n* facultad *f*; (*US: teaching
staff*) personal *m* docente
fad [fæd] *n* novedad *f*, moda
fade [feɪd] *vi* desteñirse; (*sound, smile*)
desvanecerse; (*light*) apagarse; (*flower*)
marchitarse; (*hope, memory*) perderse
fag [fæg] (*BRIT: inf*) *n* (*cigarette*) pitillo (*SP*),
cigarro
fail [feɪl] *vt* (*candidate*) suspender; (*exam*)
no aprobar (*SP*), reprobar (*AM*); (*subj:
memory etc*) fallar a ♦ *vi* suspender; (*be
unsuccessful*) fracasar; (*strength, brakes*)
fallar; (*light*) acabarse; **to ~ to do sth**
(*neglect*) dejar de hacer algo; (*be unable*)
no poder hacer algo; **without ~** sin falta;
~ing *n* falta, defecto ♦ *prep* a falta de;
~ure ['feɪljə*] *n* fracaso; (*person*)
fracasado/a; (*mechanical etc*) fallo
faint [feɪnt] *adj* débil; (*recollection*) vago;
(*mark*) apenas visible ♦ *n* desmayo ♦ *vi*
desmayarse; **to feel ~** estar mareado,
marearse
fair [feə*] *adj* justo; (*hair, person*) rubio; *
(weather*) bueno; (*good enough*) regular;
(*considerable*) considerable ♦ *adv* (*play*)
limpio ♦ *n* feria; (*BRIT: funfair*) parque *m*
de atracciones; **~ly** *adv* (*justly*) con
justicia; (*quite*) bastante; **~ness** *n* justicia,
imparcialidad *f*; **~ play** *n* juego limpio

fairy ['fɛərɪ] *n* hada; **~ tale** *n* cuento de hadas

faith [feɪθ] *n* fe *f*; (*trust*) confianza; (*sect*) religión *f*; **~ful** *adj* (*loyal: troops etc*) leal; (*spouse*) fiel; (*account*) exacto; **~fully** *adv* fielmente; **yours ~fully** (*BRIT: in letters*) le saluda atentamente

fake [feɪk] *n* (*painting etc*) falsificación *f*; (*person*) impostor(a) *m/f* ♦ *adj* falso ♦ *vt* fingir; (*painting etc*) falsificar

falcon ['fɔːlkən] *n* halcón *m*

fall [fɔːl] (*pt* fell, *pp* fallen) *n* caída; (*in price etc*) descenso; (*US*) otoño ♦ *vi* caer(se); (*price*) bajar, descender; **~s** *npl* (*water~*) cascada, salto de agua; **to ~ flat** (*on one's face*) caerse (boca abajo); (*plan*) fracasar; (*joke, story*) no hacer gracia; **~ back** *vi* retroceder; **~ back on** *vt fus* (*remedy etc*) recurrir a; **~ behind** *vi* quedarse atrás; **~ down** *vi* (*person*) caerse; (*building, hopes*) derrumbarse; **~ for** *vt fus* (*trick*) dejarse engañar por; (*person*) enamorarse de; **~ in** *vi* (*roof*) hundirse; (*MIL*) alinearse; **~ off** *vi* caerse; (*diminish*) disminuir; **~ out** *vi* (*friends etc*) reñir; (*hair, teeth*) caerse; **~ through** *vi* (*plan, project*) fracasar

fallacy ['fæləsɪ] *n* error *m*

fallen ['fɔːlən] *pp of* fall

fallout ['fɔːlaut] *n* lluvia radioactiva

fallow ['fæləu] *adj* en barbecho

false [fɔːls] *adj* falso; **under ~ pretences** con engaños; **~ alarm** *n* falsa alarma; **~ teeth** (*BRIT*) *npl* dentadura postiza

falter ['fɔːltə*] *vi* vacilar; (*engine*) fallar

fame [feɪm] *n* fama

familiar [fə'mɪlɪə*] *adj* conocido, familiar; (*tone*) de confianza; **to be ~ with** (*subject*) conocer (bien)

family ['fæmɪlɪ] *n* familia; **~ business** *n* negocio familiar; **~ doctor** *n* médico/a de cabecera

famine ['fæmɪn] *n* hambre *f*, hambruna

famished ['fæmɪʃt] *adj* hambriento

famous ['feɪməs] *adj* famoso, célebre; **~ly** *adv* (*get on*) estupendamente

fan [fæn] *n* abanico; (*ELEC*) ventilador *m*; (*of*
pop star) fan *m/f*; (*SPORT*) hincha *m/f* ♦ *vt* abanicar; (*fire, quarrel*) atizar

fanatic [fə'nætɪk] *n* fanático/a

fan belt *n* correa del ventilador

fanciful ['fænsɪful] *adj* (*design, name*) fantástico

fancy ['fænsɪ] *n* (*whim*) capricho, antojo; (*imagination*) imaginación *f* ♦ *adj* (*luxury*) lujoso, de lujo ♦ *vt* (*feel like, want*) tener ganas de; (*imagine*) imaginarse; (*think*) creer; **to take a ~ to sb** tomar cariño a uno; **he fancies her** (*inf*) le gusta (ella) mucho; **~ dress** *n* disfraz *m*; **~-dress ball** *n* baile *m* de disfraces

fanfare ['fænfɛə*] *n* fanfarria (de trompeta)

fang [fæŋ] *n* colmillo

fantastic [fæn'tæstɪk] *adj* (*enormous*) enorme; (*strange, wonderful*) fantástico

fantasy ['fæntəzɪ] *n* (*dream*) sueño; (*unreality*) fantasía

far [fɑː*] *adj* (*distant*) lejano ♦ *adv* lejos; (*much, greatly*) mucho; **~ away, ~ off** (a lo) lejos; **~ better** mucho mejor; **~ from** lejos de; **by ~** con mucho; **go as ~ as the farm** vaya hasta la granja; **as ~ as I know** que yo sepa; **how ~?** ¿hasta dónde?; (*fig*) ¿hasta qué punto?; **~away** *adj* remoto; (*look*) distraído

farce [fɑːs] *n* farsa

fare [fɛə*] *n* (*on trains, buses*) precio (del billete); (*in taxi: cost*) tarifa; (*food*) comida; **half ~** medio pasaje *m*; **full ~** pasaje completo

Far East *n*: **the ~** el Extremo Oriente

farewell [fɛə'wɛl] *excl*, *n* adiós *m*

farm [fɑːm] *n* granja (*SP*), finca (*AM*), estancia (*AM*) ♦ *vt* cultivar; **~er** *n* granjero (*SP*), estanciero (*AM*); **~hand** *n* peón *m*; **~house** *n* granja, casa de hacienda (*AM*); **~ing** *n* agricultura; (*of crops*) cultivo; (*of animals*) cría; **~land** *n* tierra de cultivo; **~ worker** *n* = **~hand**; **~yard** *n* corral *m*

far-reaching [fɑː'riːtʃɪŋ] *adj* (*reform, effect*) de gran alcance

fart [fɑːt] (*inf!*) *vi* tirarse un pedo (*!*)

farther ['fɑːðə*] *adv* más lejos, más allá

♦ *adj* más lejano
farthest ['fɑ:ðɪst] *superlative of* **far**
fascinate ['fæsɪneɪt] *vt* fascinar;
~**tion** [-'neɪʃən] *n* fascinación *f*
fascism ['fæʃɪzəm] *n* fascismo
fashion ['fæʃən] *n* moda; (~ *industry*)
industria de la moda; (*manner*) manera
♦ *vt* formar; **in** ~ a la moda; **out of** ~
pasado de moda; ~**able** *adj* de moda; ~
show *n* desfile *m* de modelos
fast [fɑ:st] *adj* rápido, veloz; (*clock*):
to be ~ estar
adelantado ♦ *adv* rápidamente, de prisa;
(*stuck, held*) firmemente ♦ *n* ayuno ♦ *vi*
ayunar; ~ **asleep** profundamente
dormido
fasten ['fɑ:sn] *vt* atar, sujetar; (*coat, belt*)
abrochar ♦ *vi* atarse; abrocharse; ~**er**,
~**ing** *n* cierre *m*; (*of door etc*) cerrojo
fast food *n* comida rápida, platos *mpl*
preparados
fastidious [fæs'tɪdɪəs] *adj* (*fussy*)
quisquilloso
fat [fæt] *adj* gordo; (*book*) grueso; (*profit*)
grande, pingüe ♦ *n* grasa; (*on person*)
carnes *fpl*; (*lard*) manteca
fatal ['feɪtl] *adj* (*mistake*) fatal; (*injury*)
mortal; ~**ity** [fə'tælɪtɪ] *n* (*road death etc*)
víctima; ~**ly** *adv* fatalmente; mortalmente
fate [feɪt] *n* destino; (*of person*) suerte *f*;
~**ful** *adj* fatídico
father ['fɑ:ðə*] *n* padre *m*; ~**-in-law** *n*
suegro; ~**ly** *adj* paternal
fathom ['fæðəm] *n* braza ♦ *vt* (*mystery*)
desentrañar; (*understand*) lograr
comprender
fatigue [fə'ti:g] *n* fatiga, cansancio
fatten ['fætn] *vt, vi* engordar
fatty ['fætɪ] *adj* (*food*) graso ♦ *n* (*inf*)
gordito/a, gordinflón/ona *m/f*
fatuous ['fætjuəs] *adj* fatuo, necio
faucet ['fɔ:sɪt] (*US*) *n* grifo (*SP*), llave *f* (*AM*)
fault [fɔ:lt] *n* (*blame*) culpa; (*defect: in
person, machine*) defecto; (*GEO*) falla ♦ *vt*
criticar; **it's my** ~ es culpa mía; **to find** ~
with criticar, poner peros a; **at** ~ culpable;
~**y** *adj* defectuoso

fauna ['fɔ:nə] *n* fauna
favour ['feɪvə*] (*US* **favor**) *n* favor *m*;
(*approval*) aprobación *f* ♦ *vt* (*proposition*)
estar a favor de, aprobar; (*assist*) ser
propicio a; **to do sb a** ~ hacer un favor a
uno; **to find** ~ **with sb** caer en gracia a
uno; **in** ~ **of** a favor de; ~**able** *adj*
favorable; ~**ite** ['feɪvrɪt] *adj, n* favorito,
preferido
fawn [fɔ:n] *n* cervato ♦ *adj* (*also:* ~**-
coloured**) color de cervato, leonado ♦ *vi*:
to ~ **(up)on** adular
fax [fæks] *n* (*document*) fax *m*; (*machine*)
telefax *m* ♦ *vt* mandar por telefax
FBI (*US*) *n abbr* (= *Federal Bureau of
Investigation*) ≈ BIC *f* (*SP*)
fear [fɪə*] *n* miedo, temor *m* ♦ *vt* tener
miedo de, temer; **for** ~ **of** por si; ~**ful** *adj*
temeroso, miedoso; (*awful*) terrible;
~**less** *adj* audaz
feasible ['fi:zəbl] *adj* factible
feast [fi:st] *n* banquete *m*; (*REL: also:* ~
day) fiesta ♦ *vi* festejar
feat [fi:t] *n* hazaña
feather ['feðə*] *n* pluma
feature ['fi:tʃə*] *n* característica; (*article*)
artículo de fondo ♦ *vt* (*subj: film*)
presentar ♦ *vi*: **to** ~ **in** tener un papel
destacado en; ~**s** *npl* (*of face*) facciones
fpl; ~ **film** *n* largometraje *m*
February ['februərɪ] *n* febrero
fed [fed] *pt, pp of* **feed**
federal ['fedərəl] *adj* federal
fed up [fed'ʌp] *adj*: **to be** ~ **(with)** estar
harto (de)
fee [fi:] *n* pago; (*professional*) derechos
mpl, honorarios *mpl*; (*of club*) cuota;
school ~**s** matrícula
feeble ['fi:bl] *adj* débil; (*joke*) flojo
feed [fi:d] (*pt, pp* **fed**) *n* comida; (*of
animal*) pienso; (*on printer*) dispositivo de
alimentación ♦ *vt* alimentar; (*BRIT: baby:
breast~*) dar el pecho a; (*animal*) dar de
comer a; (*data, information*) meter en; **to** ~ **into**
meter en; ~ **on** *vt fus* alimentarse de;
~**back** *n* reacción *f*, feedback *m*
feel [fi:l] (*pt, pp* **felt**) *n* (*sensation*)

sensación f; (*sense of touch*) tacto; (*impression*): **to have the ~ of** parecerse a ♦ *vt* tocar; (*pain etc*) sentir; (*think, believe*) creer; **to ~ hungry/cold** tener hambre/frío; **to ~ lonely/better** sentirse solo/mejor; **I don't ~ well** no me siento bien; **it ~s soft** es suave al tacto; **to ~ like** (*want*) tener ganas de; **~ about** *or* **around** *vi* tantear; **~er** *n* (*of insect*) antena; **~ing** *n* (*physical*) sensación f; (*foreboding*) presentimiento; (*emotion*) sentimiento

feet [fiːt] *npl of* **foot**

feign [feɪn] *vt* fingir

fell [fel] *pt of* **fall** ♦ *vt* (*tree*) talar

fellow ['feləʊ] *n* tipo, tío (*SP*); (*comrade*) compañero; (*of learned society*) socio/a ♦ *cpd*: **~ citizen** *n* conciudadano/a; **~ countryman** (*irreg*) *n* compatriota *m*; **~ men** *npl* semejantes *mpl*; **~ship** *n* compañerismo; (*grant*) beca

felony ['felənɪ] *n* crimen *m*

felt [felt] *pt, pp of* **feel** ♦ *n* fieltro; **~-tip pen** *n* rotulador *m*

female ['fiːmeɪl] *n* (*pej: woman*) mujer f, tía; (*ZOOL*) hembra ♦ *adj* femenino; hembra

feminine ['femɪnɪn] *adj* femenino

feminist ['femɪnɪst] *n* feminista

fence [fens] *n* valla, cerca ♦ *vt* (*also:* **~ in**) cercar ♦ *vi* (*SPORT*) hacer esgrima; **fencing** *n* esgrima

fend [fend] *vi*: **to ~ for o.s.** valerse por sí mismo; **~ off** *vt* (*attack*) rechazar; (*questions*) evadir

fender ['fendə*] *n* guardafuego; (*US: AUT*) parachoques *m inv*

ferment [*vb* fə'ment, *n* 'fɜːment] *vi* fermentar ♦ *n* (*fig*) agitación f

fern [fɜːn] *n* helecho

ferocious [fə'rəʊʃəs] *adj* feroz

ferret ['ferɪt] *n* hurón *m*

ferry ['ferɪ] *n* (*small*) barca (de pasaje), balsa; (*large: also:* **~boat**) transbordador *m* (*SP*), embarcadero (*AM*) ♦ *vt* transportar

fertile ['fɜːtaɪl] *adj* fértil; (*BIOL*) fecundo;

fertilize ['fɜːtɪlaɪz] *vt* (*BIOL*) fecundar; (*AGR*) abonar; **fertilizer** *n* abono

fester ['festə*] *vi* ulcerarse

festival ['festɪvəl] *n* (*REL*) fiesta; (*ART, MUS*) festival *m*

festive ['festɪv] *adj* festivo; **the ~ season** (*BRIT: Christmas*) las Navidades

festivities [fes'tɪvɪtɪz] *npl* fiestas *fpl*

festoon [fes'tuːn] *vt*: **to ~ with** engalanar de

fetch [fetʃ] *vt* ir a buscar; (*sell for*) venderse por

fête [feɪt] *n* fiesta

fetus ['fiːtəs] (*US*) *n* = **foetus**

feud [fjuːd] *n* (*hostility*) enemistad f; (*quarrel*) disputa

fever ['fiːvə*] *n* fiebre f; **~ish** *adj* febril

few [fjuː] *adj* (*not many*) pocos ♦ *pron* pocos; algunos; **a ~** *adj* unos pocos, algunos; **~er** *adj* menos; **~est** *adj* los/las menos

fiancé [fɪ'ɑːnseɪ] *n* novio, prometido; **~e** *n* novia, prometida

fib [fɪb] *n* mentirilla

fibre ['faɪbə*] (*US* **fiber**) *n* fibra; **~glass** (**Fiberglass** ® *US*) *n* fibra de vidrio

fickle ['fɪkl] *adj* inconstante

fiction ['fɪkʃən] *n* ficción f; **~al** *adj* novelesco; **fictitious** [fɪk'tɪʃəs] *adj* ficticio

fiddle ['fɪdl] *n* (*MUS*) violín *m*; (*cheating*) trampa ♦ *vt* (*BRIT: accounts*) falsificar; **~ with** *vt fus* juguetear con

fidget ['fɪdʒɪt] *vi* enredar; **stop ~ing!** ¡estáte quieto!

field [fiːld] *n* campo; (*fig*) campo, esfera; (*SPORT*) campo, cancha (*AM*); **~ marshal** *n* mariscal *m*; **~work** *n* trabajo de campo

fiend [fiːnd] *n* demonio

fierce [fɪəs] *adj* feroz; (*wind, heat*) fuerte; (*fighting, enemy*) encarnizado

fiery ['faɪərɪ] *adj* (*burning*) ardiente; (*temperament*) apasionado

fifteen [fɪf'tiːn] *num* quince

fifth [fɪfθ] *num* quinto

fifty ['fɪftɪ] *num* cincuenta; **~-~** *adj* (*deal, split*) a medias ♦ *adv* a medias, mitad por mitad

fig [fɪg] *n* higo

fight [faɪt] (*pt, pp* **fought**) *n* (*gen*) pelea; (*MIL*) combate *m*; (*struggle*) lucha ♦ *vt* luchar contra; (*cancer, alcoholism*) combatir; (*election*) intentar ganar; (*emotion*) resistir ♦ *vi* pelear, luchar; **~er** *n* combatiente *m/f*; (*plane*) caza *m*; **~ing** *n* combate *m*, pelea

figment ['fɪgmənt] *n*: **a ~ of the imagination** una quimera

figurative ['fɪgjʊrətɪv] *adj* (*meaning*) figurado; (*style*) figurativo

figure ['fɪgə*] *n* (*DRAWING, GEOM*) figura, dibujo; (*number, cipher*) cifra; (*body, outline*) tipo; (*personality*) figura ♦ *vt* (*esp US*) imaginar ♦ *vi* (*appear*) figurar; **~ out** *vt* (*work out*) resolver; **~head** *n* (*NAUT*) mascarón *m* de proa; (*pej: leader*) figura decorativa; **~ of speech** *n* figura retórica

file [faɪl] *n* (*tool*) lima; (*dossier*) expediente *m*; (*folder*) carpeta; (*COMPUT*) fichero; (*row*) fila ♦ *vt* limar; (*LAW: claim*) presentar; (*store*) archivar; **~ in/out** *vi* entrar/salir en fila; **filing cabinet** *n* fichero, archivador *m*

fill [fɪl] *vt* (*space*): **to ~ (with)** llenar (de); (*vacancy, need*) cubrir ♦ *n*: **to eat one's ~** llenarse; **~ in** *vt* rellenar; **~ up** *vt* llenar (hasta el borde) ♦ *vi* (*AUT*) poner gasolina

fillet ['fɪlɪt] *n* filete *m*; **~ steak** *n* filete *m* de ternera

filling ['fɪlɪŋ] *n* (*CULIN*) relleno; (*for tooth*) empaste *m*; **~ station** *n* estación *f* de servicio

film [fɪlm] *n* película ♦ *vt* (*scene*) filmar ♦ *vi* rodar (una película); **~ star** *n* astro, estrella de cine

filter ['fɪltə*] *n* filtro ♦ *vt* filtrar; **~ lane** (*BRIT*) *n* carril *m* de selección; **~-tipped** *adj* con filtro

filth [fɪlθ] *n* suciedad *f*; **~y** *adj* sucio; (*language*) obsceno

fin [fɪn] *n* (*gen*) aleta

final ['faɪnl] *adj* (*last*) final, último; (*definitive*) definitivo, terminante ♦ *n* (*BRIT: SPORT*) final *f*; **~s** *npl* (*SCOL*) examen *m*

final; (*US: SPORT*) final *f*

finale [fɪ'nɑːlɪ] *n* final *m*

final: ~ist *n* (*SPORT*) finalista *m/f*; **~ize** *vt* concluir, completar; **~ly** *adv* (*lastly*) por último, finalmente; (*eventually*) por fin

finance [faɪ'næns] *n* (*money*) fondos *mpl*; **~s** *npl* finanzas *fpl*; (*personal ~s*) situación *f* económica ♦ *vt* financiar; **financial** [-'nænʃəl] *adj* financiero

find [faɪnd] (*pt, pp* **found**) *vt* encontrar, hallar; (*come upon*) descubrir ♦ *n* hallazgo; descubrimiento; **to ~ sb guilty** (*LAW*) declarar culpable a uno; **~ out** *vt* averiguar; (*truth, secret*) descubrir; **to ~ out about** (*subject*) informarse sobre; (*by chance*) enterarse de; **~ings** *npl* (*LAW*) veredicto, fallo; (*of report*) recomendaciones *fpl*

fine [faɪn] *adj* excelente; (*thin*) fino ♦ *adv* (*well*) bien ♦ *n* (*LAW*) multa ♦ *vt* (*LAW*) multar; **to be ~** (*person*) estar bien; (*weather*) hacer buen tiempo; **~ arts** *npl* bellas artes *fpl*

finery ['faɪnərɪ] *n* adornos *mpl*

finger ['fɪŋgə*] *n* dedo ♦ *vt* (*touch*) manosear; **little/index ~** (*dedo*) meñique *m*/índice *m*; **~nail** *n* uña; **~print** *n* huella dactilar; **~tip** *n* yema del dedo

finish ['fɪnɪʃ] *n* (*end*) fin *m*; (*SPORT*) meta; (*polish etc*) acabado ♦ *vt, vi* terminar; **to ~ doing sth** acabar de hacer algo; **to ~ third** llegar el tercero; **~ off** *vt* acabar, terminar; (*kill*) acabar con; **~ up** *vt* acabar, terminar ♦ *vi* ir a parar, terminar; **~ing line** *n* línea de llegada *or* meta

finite ['faɪnaɪt] *adj* finito; (*verb*) conjugado

Finland ['fɪnlənd] *n* Finlandia

Finn [fɪn] *n* finlandés/esa *m/f*; **~ish** *adj* finlandés/esa ♦ *n* (*LING*) finlandés *m*

fir [fə:*] *n* abeto

fire ['faɪə*] *n* fuego; (*in hearth*) lumbre *f*; (*accidental*) incendio; (*heater*) estufa ♦ *vt* (*gun*) disparar; (*interest*) despertar; (*inf: dismiss*) despedir ♦ *vi* (*shoot*) disparar; **on ~** ardiendo, en llamas; **~ alarm** *n* alarma de incendios; **~arm** *n* arma de fuego; **~ brigade** (*US* **~ department**) *n* (*cuerpo*

de) bomberos *mpl*; ~ **engine** *n* coche *m*
de bomberos; ~ **escape** *n* escalera de
incendios; ~ **extinguisher** *n* extintor *m*
(de incendios); ~**guard** *n* rejilla de
protección; ~**man** (*irreg*) *n* bombero;
~**place** *n* chimenea; ~**side** *n*: **by the
~side** al lado de la chimenea; ~ **station**
n parque *m* de bomberos; ~**wood** *n*
leña; ~**works** *npl* fuegos *mpl* artificiales

firing squad ['faɪrɪŋ-] *n* pelotón *m* de
ejecución

firm [fəːm] *adj* firme; (*look, voice*) resuelto
♦ *n* firma, empresa; ~**ly** *adv* firmemente;
resueltamente

first [fəːst] *adj* primero ♦ *adv* (*before
others*) primero; (*when listing reasons etc*)
en primer lugar, primeramente ♦ *n*
(*person: in race*) primero/a; (*AUT*) primera;
(*BRIT: SCOL*) título de licenciado con
calificación de sobresaliente; **at ~** al
principio; ~ **of all** ante todo; ~ **aid** *n*
primera ayuda, primeros auxilios *mpl*; ~-
aid kit *n* botiquín *m*; ~-**class** *adj*
(*excellent*) de primera (categoría); (*ticket
etc*) de primera clase; ~-**hand** *adj* de
primera mano; **F~ Lady** (*esp US*) *n*
primera dama; ~**ly** *adv* en primer lugar;
~ **name** *n* nombre *m* (de pila); ~-**rate**
adj estupendo

fish [fɪʃ] *n inv* pez *m*; (*food*) pescado ♦ *vt,
vi* pescar; **to go ~ing** ir de pesca;
~**erman** (*irreg*) *n* pescador *m*; ~ **farm** *n*
criadero de peces; ~ **fingers** (*BRIT*) *npl*
croquetas *fpl* de pescado; ~**ing boat** *n*
barca de pesca; ~**ing line** *n* sedal *m*;
~**ing rod** *n* caña (de pescar);
~**monger's (shop)** (*BRIT*) *n* pescadería;
~ **sticks** (*US*) *npl* = ~ **fingers**; ~**y** (*inf*)
adj sospechoso

fist [fɪst] *n* puño

fit [fɪt] *adj* (*healthy*) en (buena) forma;
(*proper*) adecuado, apropiado ♦ *vt* (*subj:
clothes*) estar *or* sentar bien a; (*instal*)
poner; (*equip*) proveer, dotar; (*facts*)
cuadrar *or* corresponder con ♦ *vi* (*clothes*)
sentar bien; (*in space, gap*) caber; (*facts*)
coincidir ♦ *n* (*MED*) ataque *m*; ~ **to** (*ready*)

a punto de; ~ **for** apropiado para; **a ~ of
anger/pride** un arranque de cólera/
orgullo; **this dress is a good ~** este
vestido me sienta bien; **by ~s and starts**
a rachas; ~ **in** *vi* (*fig: person*) llevarse bien
(con todos); ~**ful** *adj* espasmódico,
intermitente; ~**ment** *n* módulo adosable;
~**ness** *n* (*MED*) salud *f*; ~**ted carpet** *n*
moqueta; ~**ted kitchen** *n* cocina
amueblada; ~**ter** *n* ajustador *m*; ~**ting**
adj apropiado ♦ *n* (*of dress*) prueba; (*of
piece of equipment*) instalación *f*; ~**ting
room** *n* probador *m*; ~**tings** *npl*
instalaciones *fpl*

five [faɪv] *num* cinco; ~**r** (*inf*) *n* (*BRIT*)
billete *m* de cinco libras; (*US*) billete *m* de
cinco dólares

fix [fɪks] *vt* (*secure*) fijar, asegurar; (*mend*)
arreglar; (*prepare*) preparar ♦ *n*: **to be in
a ~** estar en un aprieto; ~ **up** *vt*
(*meeting*) arreglar; **to ~ sb up with sth**
proveer a uno de algo; ~**ation** [fɪkˈseɪʃən]
n obsesión *f*; ~**ed** *adj* (*prices etc*) fijo;
~**ture** *n* (*SPORT*) encuentro; ~**tures** *npl*
(*cupboards etc*) instalaciones *fpl* fijas

fizzy ['fɪzɪ] *adj* (*drink*) gaseoso

fjord [fjɔːd] *n* fiordo

flabbergasted ['flæbəgɑːstɪd] *adj*
pasmado, alucinado

flabby ['flæbɪ] *adj* gordo

flag [flæg] *n* bandera; (*stone*) losa ♦ *vi*
decaer; **to ~ sb down** hacer señas a uno
para que se pare; ~**pole** *n* asta de
bandera; ~**ship** *n* buque *m* insignia; (*fig*)
bandera

flair [flɛə*] *n* aptitud *f* especial

flak [flæk] *n* (*MIL*) fuego antiaéreo; (*inf:
criticism*) lluvia de críticas

flake [fleɪk] *n* (*of rust, paint*) escama; (*of
snow, soap powder*) copo ♦ *vi* (*also: ~ off*)
desconcharse

flamboyant [flæmˈbɔɪənt] *adj* (*dress*)
vistoso; (*person*) extravagante

flame [fleɪm] *n* llama

flamingo [fləˈmɪŋɡəʊ] *n* flamenco

flammable ['flæməbl] *adj* inflamable

flan [flæn] (*BRIT*) *n* tarta

flank [flæŋk] *n* (*of animal*) ijar *m*; (*of army*) flanco ♦ *vt* flanquear

flannel ['flænl] *n* (*BRIT: also:* **face ~**) manopla; (*fabric*) franela

flap [flæp] *n* (*of pocket, envelope*) solapa ♦ *vt* (*wings, arms*) agitar ♦ *vi* (*sail, flag*) ondear

flare [fleə*] *n* llamarada; (*MIL*) bengala; (*in skirt etc*) vuelo; **~ up** *vi* encenderse; (*fig: person*) encolerizarse; (: *revolt*) estallar

flash [flæʃ] *n* relámpago; (*also:* **news ~**) noticias *fpl* de última hora; (*PHOT*) flash *m* ♦ *vt* (*light, headlights*) lanzar un destello con; (*news, message*) transmitir; (*smile*) lanzar ♦ *vi* brillar; (*hazard light etc*) lanzar destellos; **in a ~** en un instante; **he ~ed by** *or* **past** pasó como un rayo; **~back** *n* (*CINEMA*) flashback *m*; **~bulb** *n* bombilla fusible; **~ cube** *n* cubo de flash; **~light** *n* linterna

flashy ['flæʃi] (*pej*) *adj* ostentoso

flask [flɑːsk] *n* frasco; (*also:* **vacuum ~**) termo

flat [flæt] *adj* llano; (*smooth*) liso; (*tyre*) desinflado; (*battery*) descargado; (*beer*) muerto; (*refusal etc*) rotundo; (*MUS*) desafinado; (*rate*) fijo ♦ *n* (*BRIT: apartment*) piso (*SP*), departamento (*AM*), apartamento; (*AUT*) pinchazo; (*MUS*) bemol *m*; **to work ~ out** trabajar a toda mecha; **~ly** *adv* terminantemente, de plano; **~ten** *vt* (*also:* **~ten out**) allanar; (*smooth out*) alisar; (*building, plants*) arrasar

flatter ['flætə*] *vt* adular, halagar; **~ing** *adj* halagüeño; (*dress*) que favorece; **~y** *n* adulación *f*

flaunt [flɔːnt] *vt* ostentar, lucir

flavour ['fleɪvə*] (*US* **flavor**) *n* sabor *m*, gusto ♦ *vt* sazonar, condimentar; **strawberry-~ed** con sabor a fresa; **~ing** *n* (*in product*) aromatizante *m*

flaw [flɔː] *n* defecto; **~less** *adj* impecable

flax [flæks] *n* lino

flea [fliː] *n* pulga

fleck [flɛk] *n* (*mark*) mota

flee [fliː] (*pt, pp* **fled**) *vt* huir de ♦ *vi* huir,

fugarse

fleece [fliːs] *n* vellón *m*; (*wool*) lana ♦ *vt* (*inf*) desplumar

fleet [fliːt] *n* flota; (*of lorries etc*) escuadra

fleeting ['fliːtɪŋ] *adj* fugaz

Flemish ['flɛmɪʃ] *adj* flamenco

flesh [flɛʃ] *n* carne *f*; (*skin*) piel *f*; (*of fruit*) pulpa; **~ wound** *n* herida superficial

flew [fluː] *pt of* **fly**

flex [flɛks] *n* cordón *m* ♦ *vt* (*muscles*) tensar; **~ible** *adj* flexible

flick [flɪk] *n* capirotazo; chasquido ♦ *vt* (*with hand*) dar un capirotazo a; (*whip etc*) chasquear; (*switch*) accionar; **~ through** *vt fus* hojear

flicker ['flɪkə*] *vi* (*light*) parpadear; (*flame*) vacilar

flier ['flaɪə*] *n* aviador(a) *m/f*

flight [flaɪt] *n* vuelo; (*escape*) huida, fuga; (*also:* **~ of steps**) tramo (de escaleras); **~ attendant** (*US*) *n* camarero/azafata; **~ deck** *n* (*AVIAT*) cabina de mandos; (*NAUT*) cubierta de aterrizaje

flimsy ['flɪmzɪ] *adj* (*thin*) muy ligero; (*building*) endeble; (*excuse*) flojo

flinch [flɪntʃ] *vi* encogerse; **to ~ from** retroceder ante

fling [flɪŋ] (*pt, pp* **flung**) *vt* arrojar

flint [flɪnt] *n* pedernal *m*; (*in lighter*) piedra

flip [flɪp] *vt* dar la vuelta a; (*switch: turn on*) encender; (: *turn off*) apagar; (*coin*) echar a cara o cruz

flippant ['flɪpənt] *adj* poco serio

flipper ['flɪpə*] *n* aleta

flirt [flɜːt] *vi* coquetear, flirtear ♦ *n* coqueta

float [fləut] *n* flotador *m*; (*in procession*) carroza; (*money*) reserva ♦ *vi* flotar; (*swimmer*) hacer la plancha

flock [flɔk] *n* (*of sheep*) rebaño; (*of birds*) bandada ♦ *vi*: **to ~ to** acudir en tropel a

flog [flɔg] *vt* azotar

flood [flʌd] *n* inundación *f*; (*of letters, imports etc*) avalancha ♦ *vt* inundar ♦ *vi* (*place*) inundarse; (*people*): **to ~ into** inundar; **~ing** *n* inundaciones *fpl*; **~light** *n* foco

floor [flɔː*] *n* suelo; (*storey*) piso; (*of sea*)

fondo ♦ vt (*subj: question*) dejar sin respuesta; (: *blow*) derribar; **ground ~, first ~** (*US*) planta baja; **first ~, second ~** (*US*) primer piso; **~board** n tabla; **~ show** n cabaret m

flop [flɔp] n fracaso ♦ vi (*fail*) fracasar; (*fall*) derrumbarse; **~py** adj flojo ♦ n (COMPUT: *also:* **~py disk**) floppy m

flora ['flɔːrə] n flora

floral ['flɔːrl] adj (*pattern*) floreado

florid ['flɔrɪd] adj florido; (*complexion*) rubicundo

florist ['flɒrɪst] n florista m/f; **~'s (shop)** n florería

flounder ['flaundə*] vi (*swimmer*) patalear; (*fig: economy*) estar en dificultades ♦ n (ZOOL) platija

flour [flauə*] n harina

flourish ['flʌrɪʃ] vi florecer ♦ n ademán m, movimiento (ostentoso)

flout [flaut] vt burlarse de

flow [fləu] n (*movement*) flujo; (*of traffic*) circulación f; (*tide*) corriente f ♦ vi (*river, blood*) fluir; (*traffic*) circular; **~ chart** n organigrama m

flower ['flauə*] n flor f ♦ vi florecer; **~ bed** n macizo; **~pot** n tiesto; **~y** adj (*fragrance*) floral; (*pattern*) floreado; (*speech*) florido

flown [fləun] pp of **fly**

flu [fluː] n: **to have ~** tener la gripe

fluctuate ['flʌktjueɪt] vi fluctuar

fluent ['fluːənt] adj (*linguist*) que habla perfectamente; (*speech*) elocuente; **he speaks ~ French, he's ~ in French** domina el francés; **~ly** adv con fluidez

fluff [flʌf] n pelusa; **~y** adj de pelo suave

fluid ['fluːɪd] adj (*movement*) fluido, líquido; (*situation*) inestable ♦ n fluido, líquido

fluke [fluːk] (*inf*) n chiripa

flung [flʌŋ] pt, pp of **fling**

fluoride ['fluəraɪd] n fluoruro

flurry ['flʌrɪ] n (*of snow*) temporal m; **~ of activity** frenesí m de actividad

flush [flʌʃ] n rubor m; (*fig: of youth etc*) resplandor m ♦ vt limpiar con agua ♦ vi

ruborizarse ♦ adj: **~ with** a ras de; **to ~ the toilet** hacer funcionar la cisterna; **~ed** adj ruborizado

flustered ['flʌstəd] adj aturdido

flute [fluːt] n flauta

flutter ['flʌtə*] n (*of wings*) revoloteo, aleteo; **a ~ of panic/excitement** una oleada de pánico/excitación ♦ vi revolotear

flux [flʌks] n: **to be in a state of ~** estar continuamente cambiando

fly [flaɪ] (*pt* **flew**, *pp* **flown**) n mosca; (*on trousers: also:* **flies**) bragueta ♦ vt (*plane*) pilot(e)ar; (*cargo*) transportar (en avión); (*distances*) recorrer (en avión) ♦ vi volar; (*passengers*) ir en avión; (*escape*) evadirse; (*flag*) ondear; **~ away** or **off** vi emprender el vuelo; **~-drive** n: **~-drive holiday** vacaciones que incluyen vuelo y alquiler de coche; **~ing** n (*activity*) (el) volar; (*action*) vuelo ♦ adj: **~ing visit** visita relámpago; **with ~ing colours** con lucimiento; **~ing saucer** n platillo volante; **~ing start** n: **to get off to a ~ing start** empezar con buen pie; **~over** (BRIT) n paso a desnivel or superior; **~sheet** n (*for tent*) doble techo

foal [fəul] n potro

foam [fəum] n espuma ♦ vi hacer espuma; **~ rubber** n goma espuma

fob [fɔb] vt: **to ~ sb off with sth** despachar a uno con algo

focal point ['fəukl-] n (*fig*) centro de atención

focus ['fəukəs] (*pl* **~es**) n foco; (*centre*) centro ♦ vt (*field glasses etc*) enfocar ♦ vi: **to ~ (on)** enfocar (a); (*issue etc*) centrarse en; **in/out of ~** enfocado/desenfocado

fodder ['fɔdə*] n pienso

foetus ['fiːtəs] (*US* **fetus**) n feto

fog [fɔg] n niebla; **~gy** adj: **it's ~gy** hay niebla, está brumoso; **~ lamp** (*US* **~ light**) n (AUT) faro de niebla

foil [fɔɪl] vt frustrar ♦ n hoja; (*kitchen ~*) papel m (de) aluminio; (*complement*) complemento; (FENCING) florete m

fold [fəuld] n (*bend, crease*) pliegue m;

(*AGR*) redil *m* ♦ *vt* doblar; (*arms*) cruzar; ~ **up** *vi* plegarse, doblarse; (*business*) quebrar ♦ *vt* (*map etc*) plegar; ~**er** *n* (*for papers*) carpeta; ~**ing** *adj* (*chair, bed*) plegable

foliage ['fəulɪɪdʒ] *n* follaje *m*

folk [fəuk] *npl* gente *f* ♦ *adj* popular, folklórico; ~**s** *npl* (*family*) familia *sg*, parientes *mpl*; ~**lore** ['fəuklɔ:*] *n* folklore *m*; ~ **song** *n* canción *f* popular *or* folklórica

follow ['fɒləu] *vt* seguir ♦ *vi* seguir; (*result*) resultar; **to ~ suit** hacer lo mismo; ~ **up** *vt* (*letter, offer*) responder a; (*case*) investigar; ~**er** *n* (*of person, belief*) partidario/a; ~**ing** *adj* siguiente ♦ *n* afición *f*, partidarios *mpl*

folly ['fɒlɪ] *n* locura

fond [fɒnd] *adj* (*memory, smile etc*) cariñoso; (*hopes*) ilusorio; **to be ~ of** tener cariño a; (*pastime, food*) ser aficionado a

fondle ['fɒndl] *vt* acariciar

font [fɒnt] *n* pila bautismal; (*TYP*) fundición *f*

food [fu:d] *n* comida; ~ **mixer** *n* batidora; ~ **poisoning** *n* intoxicación *f* alimenticia; ~ **processor** *n* robot *m* de cocina; ~**stuffs** *npl* comestibles *mpl*

fool [fu:l] *n* tonto/a; (*CULIN*) puré *m* de frutas con nata ♦ *vt* engañar ♦ *vi* (*gen*: ~ **around**) bromear; ~**hardy** *adj* temerario; ~**ish** *adj* tonto; (*careless*) imprudente; ~**proof** *adj* (*plan etc*) infalible

foot [fut] (*pl* **feet**) *n* pie *m*; (*measure*) pie *m* (= 304 *mm*); (*of animal*) pata ♦ *vt* (*bill*) pagar; **on ~** a pie; ~**age** *n* (*CINEMA*) imágenes *fpl*; ~**ball** *n* balón *m*; (*game*: *BRIT*) fútbol *m*; (*: US*) fútbol *m* americano; ~**ball player** *n* (*BRIT*: *also*: ~**baller**) futbolista *m*; (*US*) jugador *m* de fútbol americano; ~**brake** *n* freno de pie; ~**bridge** *n* puente *m* para peatones; ~**hills** *npl* estribaciones *fpl*; ~**hold** *n* pie *m* firme; ~**ing** *n* (*fig*) posición *f*; **to lose one's ~ing** perder el pie; ~**lights** *npl* candilejas *fpl*; ~**note** *n* nota (al pie de la página); ~**path** *n* sendero; ~**print** *n*

huella, pisada; ~**step** *n* paso; ~**wear** *n* calzado

┌─────────────┐
│ *KEYWORD* │
└─────────────┘

for [fɔ:] *prep* **1** (*indicating destination, intention*) para; **the train ~ London** el tren con destino a *or* de Londres; **he left ~ Rome** marchó para Roma; **he went ~ the paper** fue por el periódico; **is this ~ me?** ¿es esto para mí?; **it's time ~ lunch** es la hora de comer

2 (*indicating purpose*) para; **what('s it) ~?** ¿para qué (es)?; **to pray ~ peace** rezar por la paz

3 (*on behalf of, representing*): **the MP ~ Hove** el diputado por Hove; **he works ~ the government/a local firm** trabaja para el gobierno/en una empresa local; **I'll ask him ~ you** se lo pediré por ti; **G ~ George** G de Gerona

4 (*because of*) por esta razón; ~ **fear of being criticized** por temor a ser criticado

5 (*with regard to*) para; **it's cold ~ July** hace frío para julio; **he has a gift ~ languages** tiene don de lenguas

6 (*in exchange for*) por; **I sold it ~ £5** lo vendí por £5; **to pay 50 pence ~ a ticket** pagar 50 peniques por un billete

7 (*in favour of*): **are you ~ or against us?** ¿estás con nosotros o contra nosotros?; **I'm all ~ it** estoy totalmente a favor; **vote ~ X** vote (a) X

8 (*referring to distance*): **there are roadworks ~ 5 km** hay obras en 5 km; **we walked ~ miles** caminamos kilómetros y kilómetros

9 (*referring to time*): **he was away ~ 2 years** estuvo fuera (durante) dos años; **it hasn't rained ~ 3 weeks** no ha llovido durante *or* en 3 semanas; **I have known her ~ years** la conozco desde hace años; **can you do it ~ tomorrow?** ¿lo podrás hacer para mañana?

10 (*with infinitive clauses*): **it is not ~ me to decide** la decisión no es cosa mía; **it would be best ~ you to leave** sería mejor que te fueras; **there is still time ~**

you to do it todavía te queda tiempo para hacerlo; **~ this to be possible ...** para que esto sea posible ...
11 (*in spite of*) a pesar de; **~ all his complaints** a pesar de sus quejas
♦ *conj* (*since, as: rather formal*) puesto que

forage ['fɒrɪdʒ] *vi* (*animal*) forrajear; (*person*): **to ~ for** hurgar en busca de
foray ['fɒreɪ] *n* incursión *f*
forbid [fə'bɪd] (*pt* **forbad(e)**, *pp* **forbidden**) *vt* prohibir; **to ~ sb to do sth** prohibir a uno hacer algo; **~ding** *adj* amenazador(a)
force [fɔːs] *n* fuerza ♦ *vt* forzar; (*push*) meter a la fuerza; **to ~ o.s. to do** hacer un esfuerzo por hacer; **the F~s** *npl* (*BRIT*) las Fuerzas Armadas; **in ~** en vigor; **~d** [fɔːst] *adj* forzado; **~-feed** *vt* alimentar a la fuerza; **~ful** *adj* enérgico
forcibly [fə'səblɪ] *adv* a la fuerza; (*speak*) enérgicamente
ford [fɔːd] *n* vado
fore [fɔː*] *n*: **to come to the ~** empezar a destacar
fore: **~arm** *n* antebrazo; **~boding** *n* presentimiento; **~cast** *n* pronóstico ♦ *vt* (*irreg: like* **cast**) pronosticar; **~court** *n* patio; **~finger** *n* (dedo) índice *m*; **~front** *n*: **in the ~front of** en la vanguardia de
forego *vt* **= forgo**
foregone ['fɔːgɒn] *pp of* **forego** ♦ *adj*: **it's a ~ conclusion** es una conclusión evidente
foreground ['fɔːgraʊnd] *n* primer plano
forehead ['fɒrɪd] *n* frente *f*
foreign ['fɒrɪn] *adj* extranjero; (*trade*) exterior; (*object*) extraño; **~er** *n* extranjero/a; **~ exchange** *n* divisas *fpl*; **F~ Office** (*BRIT*) *n* Ministerio de Asuntos Exteriores; **F~ Secretary** (*BRIT*) *n* Ministro de Asuntos Exteriores
fore: **~leg** *n* pata delantera; **~man** (*irreg*) *n* capataz *m*; (*in construction*) maestro de obras; **~most** *adj* principal ♦ *adv*: **first**

and ~most ante todo
forensic [fə'rɛnsɪk] *adj* forense
fore: **~runner** *n* precursor(a) *m/f*; **~see** (*pt* **foresaw**, *pp* **foreseen**) *vt* prever; **~seeable** *adj* previsible; **~shadow** *vt* prefigurar, anunciar; **~sight** *n* previsión *f*
forest ['fɒrɪst] *n* bosque *m*
forestry ['fɒrɪstrɪ] *n* silvicultura
foretaste ['fɔːteɪst] *n* muestra
foretell [fɔː'tɛl] (*pt, pp* **foretold**) *vt* predecir, pronosticar
forever [fə'rɛvə*] *adv* para siempre; (*endlessly*) constantemente
foreword ['fɔːwəːd] *n* prefacio
forfeit ['fɔːfɪt] *vt* perder
forgave [fə'geɪv] *pt of* **forgive**
forge [fɔːdʒ] *n* herrería ♦ *vt* (*signature, money*) falsificar; (*metal*) forjar; **~ ahead** *vi* avanzar mucho; **~ry** *n* falsificación *f*
forget [fə'gɛt] (*pt* **forgot**, *pp* **forgotten**) *vt* olvidar ♦ *vi* olvidarse; **~ful** *adj* despistado; **~-me-not** *n* nomeolvides *f inv*
forgive [fə'gɪv] (*pt* **forgave**, *pp* **forgiven**) *vt* perdonar; **to ~ sb for sth** perdonar algo a uno; **~ness** *n* perdón *m*
forgo [fɔː'gəʊ] (*pt* **forwent**, *pp* **forgone**) *vt* (*give up*) renunciar a; (*go without*) privarse de
forgot [fə'gɒt] *pt of* **forget**
forgotten [fə'gɒtn] *pp of* **forget**
fork [fɔːk] *n* (*for eating*) tenedor *m*; (*for gardening*) horca; (*of roads*) bifurcación *f* ♦ *vi* (*road*) bifurcarse; **~ out** (*inf*) *vt* (*pay*) desembolsar; **~-lift truck** *n* máquina elevadora
forlorn [fə'lɔːn] *adj* (*person*) triste, melancólico; (*place*) abandonado; (*attempt, hope*) desesperado
form [fɔːm] *n* forma; (*BRIT: SCOL*) clase *f*; (*document*) formulario ♦ *vt* formar; (*idea*) concebir; (*habit*) adquirir; **in top ~** en plena forma; **to ~ a queue** hacer cola
formal ['fɔːmal] *adj* (*offer, receipt*) por escrito; (*person etc*) correcto; (*occasion, dinner*) de etiqueta; (*dress*) correcto; (*garden*) (de estilo) clásico; **~ity** [-'mælɪtɪ]

n (*procedure*) trámite *m*; corrección *f*; etiqueta; **~ly** *adv* oficialmente

format ['fɔːmæt] *n* formato ♦ *vt* (*COMPUT*) formatear

formative ['fɔːmətɪv] *adj* (*years*) de formación; (*influence*) formativo

former ['fɔːmə*] *adj* anterior; (*earlier*) antiguo; (*ex*) ex; **the ~ ... the latter ...** aquél ... éste ...; **~ly** *adv* antes

formula ['fɔːmjulə] *n* fórmula

forsake [fə'seɪk] (*pt* **forsook**, *pp* **forsaken**) *vt* (*gen*) abandonar; (*plan*) renunciar a

fort [fɔːt] *n* fuerte *m*

forte ['fɔːtɪ] *n* fuerte *m*

forth [fɔːθ] *adv*: **back and ~** de acá para allá; **and so ~** y así sucesivamente; **~coming** *adj* próximo, venidero; (*help, information*) disponible; (*character*) comunicativo; **~right** *adj* franco; **~with** *adv* en el acto

fortify ['fɔːtɪfaɪ] *vt* (*city*) fortificar; (*person*) fortalecer

fortitude ['fɔːtɪtjuːd] *n* fortaleza

fortnight ['fɔːtnaɪt] (*BRIT*) *n* quince días *mpl*; quincena; **~ly** *adj* de cada quince días, quincenal ♦ *adv* cada quince días, quincenalmente

fortress ['fɔːtrɪs] *n* fortaleza

fortunate ['fɔːtʃənɪt] *adj* afortunado; **it is ~ that ...** (es una) suerte que ...; **~ly** *adv* afortunadamente

fortune ['fɔːtʃən] *n* suerte *f*; (*wealth*) fortuna; **~-teller** *n* adivino/a

forty ['fɔːtɪ] *num* cuarenta

forum ['fɔːrəm] *n* foro

forward ['fɔːwəd] *adj* (*movement, position*) avanzado; (*front*) delantero; (*in time*) adelantado; (*not shy*) atrevido ♦ *n* (*SPORT*) delantero ♦ *vt* (*letter*) remitir; (*career*) promocionar; **to move ~** avanzar; **~(s)** *adv* (hacia) adelante

fossil ['fɔsl] *n* fósil *m*

foster ['fɔstə*] *vt* (*child*) acoger en una familia; fomentar; **~ child** *n* hijo/a adoptivo/a

fought [fɔːt] *pt, pp of* **fight**

foul [faul] *adj* sucio, puerco; (*weather, smell etc*) asqueroso; (*language*) grosero; (*temper*) malísimo ♦ *n* (*SPORT*) falta ♦ *vt* (*dirty*) ensuciar; **~ play** *n* (*LAW*) muerte *f* violenta

found [faund] *pt, pp of* **find** ♦ *vt* fundar; **~ation** [-'deɪʃən] *n* (*act*) fundación *f*; (*basis*) base *f*; (*also*: **~ation cream**) crema base; **~ations** *npl* (*of building*) cimientos *mpl*

founder ['faundə*] *n* fundador(a) *m/f* ♦ *vi* hundirse

foundry ['faundrɪ] *n* fundición *f*

fountain ['fauntɪn] *n* fuente *f*; **~ pen** *n* pluma (estilográfica) (*SP*), pluma-fuente *f* (*AM*)

four [fɔː*] *num* cuatro; **on all ~s** a gatas; **~-poster (bed)** *n* cama de dosel; **~teen** *num* catorce; **~th** *num* cuarto

fowl [faul] *n* ave *f* (de corral)

fox [fɔks] *n* zorro ♦ *vt* confundir

foyer ['fɔɪeɪ] *n* vestíbulo

fraction ['frækʃən] *n* fracción *f*

fracture ['fræktʃə*] *n* fractura

fragile ['frædʒaɪl] *adj* frágil

fragment ['frægmənt] *n* fragmento

fragrant ['freɪgrənt] *adj* fragante, oloroso

frail [freɪl] *adj* frágil; (*person*) débil

frame [freɪm] *n* (*TECH*) armazón *m*; (*of person*) cuerpo; (*of picture, door etc*) marco; (*of spectacles: also*: **~s**) montura ♦ *vt* enmarcar; **~ of mind** *n* estado de ánimo; **~work** *n* marco

France [frɑːns] *n* Francia

franchise ['fræntʃaɪz] *n* (*POL*) derecho de votar, sufragio; (*COMM*) licencia, concesión *f*

frank [fræŋk] *adj* franco ♦ *vt* (*letter*) franquear; **~ly** *adv* francamente

frantic ['fræntɪk] *adj* (*distraught*) desesperado; (*hectic*) frenético

fraternity [frə'təːnɪtɪ] *n* (*feeling*) fraternidad *f*; (*group of people*) círculos *mpl*

fraud [frɔːd] *n* fraude *m*; (*person*) impostor/a *m/f*

fraught [frɔːt] *adj*: **~ with** lleno de

fray [freɪ] *vi* deshilacharse

freak [friːk] *n* (*person*) fenómeno; (*event*)

suceso anormal

freckle ['frɛkl] n peca

free [friː] adj libre; (gratis) gratuito ♦ vt (prisoner etc) poner en libertad; (jammed object) soltar; ~ **(of charge), for** ~ gratis; ~**dom** ['friːdəm] n libertad f; **F~fone** ® ['friːfəun] n número gratuito; ~**-for-all** n riña general; ~ **gift** n prima; ~**hold** n propiedad f vitalicia; ~ **kick** n tiro libre; ~**lance** adj independiente ♦ adv por cuenta propia; ~**ly** adv libremente, (liberally) generosamente; **F~mason** n francmasón m; **F~post** ® n porte m pagado; ~**-range** adj (hen, eggs) de granja; ~ **trade** n libre comercio; ~**way** (US) n autopista; ~ **will** n libre albedrío; **of one's own** ~ **will** por su propia voluntad

freeze [friːz] (pt **froze**, pp **frozen**) vi (weather) helar; (liquid, pipe, person) helarse, congelarse ♦ vt helar; (food, prices, salaries) congelar ♦ n helada; (on arms, wages) congelación f; ~**-dried** adj liofilizado; ~**r** n congelador m (SP), congeladora (AM)

freezing ['friːzɪŋ] adj helado; **3 degrees below** ~ tres grados bajo cero; ~ **point** n punto de congelación

freight [freɪt] n (goods) carga; (money charged) flete m; ~ **train** (US) n tren m de mercancías

French [frɛntʃ] adj francés/esa ♦ n (LING) francés m; **the** ~ npl los franceses; ~ **bean** n judía verde; ~ **fried potatoes** npl patatas fpl (SP) or papas fpl (AM) fritas; ~ **fries** (US) npl = ~ **fried potatoes**; ~**man/woman** (irreg) n francés/esa m/f; ~ **window** n puerta de cristal

frenzy ['frɛnzɪ] n frenesí m

frequent [adj 'friːkwənt, vb frɪ'kwɛnt] adj frecuente ♦ vt frecuentar; ~**ly** [-əntlɪ] adv frecuentemente, a menudo

fresh [frɛʃ] adj fresco; (bread) tierno; (new) nuevo; ~**en** vi (wind, air) soplar más recio; ~**en up** vi (person) arreglarse, lavarse; ~**er** (BRIT: inf) n (UNIV) estudiante

m/f de primer año; ~**ly** adv (made, painted etc) recién; ~**man** (US irreg) n = ~**er**; ~**ness** n frescura; ~**water** adj (fish) de agua dulce

fret [frɛt] vi inquietarse

friar ['fraɪə*] n fraile m; (before name) fray m

friction ['frɪkʃən] n fricción f

Friday ['fraɪdɪ] n viernes m inv

fridge [frɪdʒ] (BRIT) n nevera (SP), refrigeradora (AM)

fried [fraɪd] adj frito

friend [frɛnd] n amigo/a; ~**ly** adj simpático; (government) amigo; (place) acogedor(a); (match) amistoso; ~**ly fire** fuego amigo, disparos mpl del propio bando; ~**ship** n amistad f

frieze [friːz] n friso

fright [fraɪt] n (terror) terror m; (scare) susto; **to take** ~ asustarse; ~**en** vt asustar; ~**ened** adj asustado; ~**ening** adj espantoso; ~**ful** adj espantoso, horrible

frill [frɪl] n volante m

fringe [frɪndʒ] n (BRIT: of hair) flequillo; (on lampshade etc) flecos mpl; (of forest etc) borde m, margen m; ~ **benefits** npl beneficios mpl marginales

frisk [frɪsk] vt cachear, registrar

frisky ['frɪskɪ] adj juguetón/ona

fritter ['frɪtə*] n buñuelo; ~ **away** vt desperdiciar

frivolous ['frɪvələs] adj frívolo

frizzy ['frɪzɪ] adj rizado

fro [frəu] see **to**

frock [frɔk] n vestido

frog [frɔg] n rana; ~**man** n hombre-rana m

frolic ['frɔlɪk] vi juguetear

| KEYWORD |

from [frɔm] prep **1** (indicating starting place) de, desde; **where do you come ~?** ¿de dónde eres?; ~ **London to Glasgow** de Londres a Glasgow; **to escape** ~ **sth/ sb** escaparse de algo/alguien

2 (indicating origin etc) de; **a letter/ telephone call** ~ **my sister** una carta/

llamada de mi hermana; **tell him ~ me that ...** dígale de mi parte que ...
3 (*indicating time*): **~ one o'clock to** *or* **until** *or* **till two** (de(sde) la una a *or* hasta las dos; **~ January (on)** a partir de enero
4 (*indicating distance*) de; **the hotel is 1 km ~ the beach** el hotel está a 1 km de la playa
5 (*indicating price, number etc*) de; **prices range ~ £10 to £50** los precios van desde £10 a *or* hasta £50; **the interest rate was increased ~ 9% to 10%** el tipo de interés fue incrementado de un 9% a un 10%
6 (*indicating difference*) de; **he can't tell red ~ green** no sabe distinguir el rojo del verde; **to be different ~ sb/sth** ser diferente a algo/alguien
7 (*because of, on the basis of*): **~ what he says** por lo que dice; **weak ~ hunger** debilitado por el hambre

front [frʌnt] *n* (*foremost part*) parte *f* delantera; (*of house*) fachada; (*of dress*) delantero; (*promenade: also*: **sea ~**) paseo marítimo; (*MIL, POL, METEOROLOGY*) frente *m*; (*fig: appearances*) apariencias *fpl* ♦ *adj* (*wheel, leg*) delantero; (*row, line*) primero; **in ~ (of)** delante (de); **~ door** *n* puerta principal; **~ier** ['frʌntɪə*] *n* frontera; **~ page** *n* primera plana; **~ room** (*BRIT*) *n* salón *m*, sala; **~-wheel drive** *n* tracción *f* delantera
frost [frɔst] *n* helada; (*also*: **hoar~**) escarcha; **~bite** *n* congelación *f*; **~ed** *adj* (*glass*) deslustrado; **~y** *adj* (*weather*) de helada; (*welcome etc*) glacial
froth [frɔθ] *n* espuma
frown [fraun] *vi* fruncir el ceño
froze [frəuz] *pt of* **freeze**
frozen ['frəuzn] *pp of* **freeze**
fruit [fru:t] *n inv* fruta; fruto; (*fig*) fruto; resultados *mpl*; **~erer** *n* frutero/a; **~erer's (shop)** *n* frutería; **~ful** *adj* provechoso; **~ion** [fru:'ɪʃən] *n*: **to come to ~ion** realizarse; **~ juice** *n* zumo (*SP*) *or* jugo (*AM*) de fruta; **~ machine** (*BRIT*) *n*

máquina *f* tragaperras; **~ salad** *n* macedonia (*SP*) *or* ensalada (*AM*) de frutas
frustrate [frʌs'treɪt] *vt* frustrar
fry [fraɪ] (*pt, pp* **fried**) *vt* freír; **small ~** gente *f* menuda; **~ing pan** *n* sartén *f*
ft. *abbr* = **foot**; **feet**
fudge [fʌdʒ] *n* (*CULIN*) caramelo blando
fuel [fjuəl] *n* (*for heating*) combustible *m*; (*coal*) carbón *m*; (*wood*) leña; (*for engine*) carburante *m*; **~ oil** *n* fuel oil *m*; **~ tank** *n* depósito (de combustible)
fugitive ['fju:dʒɪtɪv] *n* fugitivo/a
fulfil [ful'fɪl] *vt* (*function*) cumplir con; (*condition*) satisfacer; (*wish, desire*) realizar; **~ment** (*US* **fulfillment**) *n* satisfacción *f*; (*of promise, desire*) realización *f*
full [ful] *adj* lleno; (*fig*) pleno; (*complete*) completo; (*maximum*) máximo; (*information*) detallado; (*price*) íntegro; (*skirt*) amplio ♦ *adv*: **to know ~ well that** saber perfectamente que; **I'm ~ (up)** no puedo más; **~ employment** pleno empleo; **a ~ two hours** dos horas completas; **at ~ speed** a máxima velocidad; **in ~** (*reproduce, quote*) íntegramente; **~-length** *adj* (*novel etc*) entero; (*coat*) largo; (*portrait*) de cuerpo entero; **~ moon** *n* luna llena; **~-scale** *adj* (*attack, war*) en gran escala; (*model*) de tamaño natural; **~ stop** *n* punto; **~-time** *adj* (*work*) de tiempo completo ♦ *adv*: **to work ~-time** trabajar a tiempo completo; **~y** *adv* completamente; (*at least*) por lo menos; **~y-fledged** *adj* (*teacher, barrister*) diplomado
fumble ['fʌmbl] *vi*: **to ~ with** manejar torpemente
fume [fju:m] *vi* (*rage*) estar furioso; **~s** *npl* humo, gases *mpl*
fun [fʌn] *n* (*amusement*) diversión *f*; **to have ~** divertirse; **for ~** en broma; **to make ~ of** burlarse de
function ['fʌŋkʃən] *n* función *f* ♦ *vi* funcionar; **~al** *adj* (*operational*) en buen estado; (*practical*) funcional
fund [fʌnd] *n* fondo; (*reserve*) reserva; **~s** *npl* (*money*) fondos *mpl*

fundamental [fʌndəˈmɛntl] *adj* fundamental

funeral [ˈfjuːnərəl] *n* (*burial*) entierro; (*ceremony*) funerales *mpl*; **~ parlour** (*BRIT*) *n* funeraria; **~ service** *n* misa de difuntos, funeral *m*

funfair [ˈfʌnfɛə*] (*BRIT*) *n* parque *m* de atracciones

fungus [ˈfʌŋgəs] (*pl* **fungi**) *n* hongo; (*mould*) moho

funnel [ˈfʌnl] *n* embudo; (*of ship*) chimenea

funny [ˈfʌnɪ] *adj* gracioso, divertido; (*strange*) curioso, raro

fur [fəː*] *n* piel *f*; (*BRIT: in kettle etc*) sarro; **~ coat** *n* abrigo de pieles

furious [ˈfjuərɪəs] *adj* furioso; (*effort*) violento

furlong [ˈfəːlɔŋ] *n* octava parte de una milla, = 201.17 m

furnace [ˈfəːnɪs] *n* horno

furnish [ˈfəːnɪʃ] *vt* amueblar; (*supply*) suministrar; (*information*) facilitar; **~ings** *npl* muebles *mpl*

furniture [ˈfəːnɪtʃə*] *n* muebles *mpl*; **piece of ~** mueble *m*

furrow [ˈfʌrəu] *n* surco

furry [ˈfəːrɪ] *adj* peludo

further [ˈfəːðə*] *adj* (*new*) nuevo, adicional ♦ *adv* más lejos; (*more*) más; (*moreover*) además ♦ *vt* promover, adelantar; **~ education** *n* educación *f* superior; **~more** [fəːðəˈmɔː*] *adv* además

furthest [ˈfəːðɪst] *superlative of* **far**

fury [ˈfjuərɪ] *n* furia

fuse [fjuːz] (*US* **fuze**) *n* fusible *m*; (*for bomb etc*) mecha ♦ *vt* (*metal*) fundir; (*fig*) fusionar ♦ *vi* fundirse; fusionarse; (*BRIT: ELEC*): **to ~ the lights** fundir los plomos; **~ box** *n* caja de fusibles

fuss [fʌs] *n* (*excitement*) conmoción *f*; (*trouble*) alboroto; **to make a ~** armar un lío *or* jaleo; **to make a ~ of sb** mimar a uno; **~y** *adj* (*person*) exigente; (*too ornate*) recargado

futile [ˈfjuːtaɪl] *adj* vano

future [ˈfjuːtʃə*] *adj* futuro; (*coming*) venidero ♦ *n* futuro; (*prospects*) porvenir; **in ~** de ahora en adelante

fuze [fjuːz] (*US*) = **fuse**

fuzzy [ˈfʌzɪ] *adj* (*PHOT*) borroso; (*hair*) muy rizado

G, g

G [dʒiː] *n* (*MUS*) sol *m*

g. *abbr* (= *gram(s)*) gr.

G7 *abbr* (= *Group of Seven*) el grupo de los 7

gabble [ˈgæbl] *vi* hablar atropelladamente

gable [ˈgeɪbl] *n* aguilón *m*

gadget [ˈgædʒɪt] *n* aparato

Gaelic [ˈgeɪlɪk] *adj, n* (*LING*) gaélico

gag [gæg] *n* (*on mouth*) mordaza; (*joke*) chiste *m* ♦ *vt* amordazar

gaiety [ˈgeɪtɪ] *n* alegría

gaily [ˈgeɪlɪ] *adv* alegremente

gain [geɪn] *n*: **~ (in)** aumento (de); (*profit*) ganancia ♦ *vt* ganar ♦ *vi* (*watch*) adelantarse; **to ~ from/by sth** sacar provecho de algo; **to ~ on sb** ganar terreno a uno; **to ~ 3 lbs (in weight)** engordar 3 libras

gal. *abbr* = **gallon**

gala [ˈgaːlə] *n* fiesta

gale [geɪl] *n* (*wind*) vendaval *m*

gallant [ˈgælənt] *adj* valiente; (*towards ladies*) atento

gall bladder [ˈgɔːl-] *n* vesícula biliar

gallery [ˈgælərɪ] *n* (*also*: **art ~**: *public*) pinacoteca; (: *private*) galería de arte; (*for spectators*) tribuna

gallon [ˈgælən] *n* galón *m* (*BRIT* = 4,546 *litros, US* = 3,785 *litros*)

gallop [ˈgæləp] *n* galope *m* ♦ *vi* galopar

gallows [ˈgæləuz] *n* horca

gallstone [ˈgɔːlstəun] *n* cálculo biliario

galore [gəˈlɔː*] *adv* en cantidad, en abundancia

gambit [ˈgæmbɪt] *n* (*fig*): (**opening**) **~** estrategia (inicial)

gamble [ˈgæmbl] *n* (*risk*) riesgo ♦ *vt* jugar, apostar ♦ *vi* (*take a risk*) jugárselas; (*bet*) apostar; **to ~ on** apostar a; (*success etc*) contar con; **~r** n jugador(a) *m/f*; **gambling** n juego

game [geɪm] n juego; (*match*) partido; (*of cards*) partida; (*HUNTING*) caza ♦ *adj* (*willing*): **to be ~ for anything** atreverse a todo; **big ~** caza mayor; **~keeper** n guardabosques *m inv*

gammon ['gæmən] n (*bacon*) tocino ahumado; (*ham*) jamón *m* ahumado

gamut ['gæmət] n gama

gang [gæŋ] n (*of criminals*) pandilla; (*of friends etc*) grupo; (*of workmen*) brigada; **~ up** vi: **to ~ up on sb** aliarse contra uno

gangster ['gæŋstə*] n gángster *m*

gangway ['gæŋweɪ] n (*on ship*) pasarela; (*BRIT: in theatre, bus etc*) pasillo

gaol [dʒeɪl] (*BRIT*) n, vt = **jail**

gap [gæp] n vacío, hueco (*AM*); (*in trees, traffic*) claro; (*in time*) intervalo; (*difference*): **~ (between)** diferencia (entre)

gape [geɪp] vi mirar boquiabierto; (*shirt etc*) abrirse (completamente); **gaping** *adj* (completamente) abierto

garage ['gærɑːʒ] n garaje *m*; (*for repairs*) taller *m*

garbage ['gɑːbɪdʒ] (*US*) n basura; (*inf: nonsense*) tonterías *fpl*; **~ can** n cubo (*SP*) *or* bote *m* (*AM*) de la basura

garbled ['gɑːbld] *adj* (*distorted*) falsificado, amañado

garden ['gɑːdn] n jardín *m*; **~s** *npl* (*park*) parque *m*; **~er** n jardinero/a; **~ing** n jardinería

gargle ['gɑːgl] vi hacer gárgaras, gargarear (*AM*)

garish ['gɛərɪʃ] *adj* chillón/ona

garland ['gɑːlənd] n guirnalda

garlic ['gɑːlɪk] n ajo

garment ['gɑːmənt] n prenda (de vestir)

garnish ['gɑːnɪʃ] vt (*CULIN*) aderezar

garrison ['gærɪsn] n guarnición *f*

garter ['gɑːtə*] n (*for sock*) liga; (*US*) liguero

gas [gæs] n gas *m*; (*fuel*) combustible *m*; (*US: gasoline*) gasolina ♦ vt asfixiar con gas; **~ cooker** (*BRIT*) n cocina de gas; **~**

cylinder n bombona de gas; **~ fire** n estufa de gas

gash [gæʃ] n raja; (*wound*) cuchillada ♦ vt rajar; acuchillar

gasket ['gæskɪt] n (*AUT*) junta de culata

gas mask n careta antigás

gas meter n contador *m* de gas

gasoline ['gæsəliːn] (*US*) n gasolina

gasp [gɑːsp] n boqueada; (*of shock etc*) grito sofocado ♦ vi (*pant*) jadear

gas station (*US*) n gasolinera

gastric ['gæstrɪk] *adj* gástrico

gate [geɪt] n puerta; (*iron ~*) verja; **~crash** (*BRIT*) vt colarse en; **~way** n (*also fig*) puerta

gather ['gæðə*] vt (*flowers, fruit*) coger (*SP*), recoger; (*assemble*) reunir; (*pick up*) recoger; (*SEWING*) fruncir; (*understand*) entender ♦ vi (*assemble*) reunirse; **to ~ speed** ganar velocidad; **~ing** n reunión *f*, asamblea

gaudy ['gɔːdɪ] *adj* chillón/ona

gauge [geɪdʒ] n (*instrument*) indicador *m* ♦ vt medir; (*fig*) juzgar

gaunt [gɔːnt] *adj* (*haggard*) demacrado; (*stark*) desolado

gauntlet ['gɔːntlɪt] n (*fig*): **to run the ~ of** exponerse a; **to throw down the ~** arrojar el guante

gauze [gɔːz] n gasa

gave [geɪv] pt of **give**

gay [geɪ] *adj* (*homosexual*) gay; (*joyful*) alegre; (*colour*) vivo

gaze [geɪz] n mirada fija ♦ vi: **to ~ at sth** mirar algo fijamente

gazelle [gəˈzɛl] n gacela

gazumping [gəˈzʌmpɪŋ] (*BRIT*) n la subida del precio de una casa una vez que ya ha sido apalabrado

GB *abbr* = **Great Britain**

GCE n *abbr* (*BRIT*) = *General Certificate of Education*

GCSE (*BRIT*) n *abbr* (= *General Certificate of Secondary Education*) examen de reválida que se hace a los 16 años

gear [gɪə*] n equipo, herramientas *fpl*; (*TECH*) engranaje *m*; (*AUT*) velocidad *f*,

marcha ♦ vt (fig: adapt): **to ~ sth to**
adaptar or ajustar algo a; **top** or **high**
(US)/**low ~** cuarta/primera velocidad; **in ~**
en marcha; **~ box** n caja de cambios; **~**
lever n palanca de cambio; **~ shift** (US)
n = **~ lever**

geese [giːs] npl of **goose**

gel [dʒel] n gel m

gem [dʒem] n piedra preciosa

Gemini ['dʒemɪnaɪ] n Géminis m, Gemelos
mpl

gender ['dʒendə*] n género

gene [dʒiːn] n gen(e) m

general ['dʒenərl] n general m ♦ adj
general; **in ~** en general; **~ delivery** (US)
n lista de correos; **~ election** n
elecciones fpl generales; **~ly** adv
generalmente, en general; **~**
practitioner n médico general

generate ['dʒenəreɪt] vt (ELEC) generar;
(jobs, profits) producir

generation [dʒenə'reɪʃən] n generación f

generator ['dʒenəreɪtə*] n generador m

generosity [dʒenə'rɒsɪtɪ] n generosidad f

generous ['dʒenərəs] adj generoso

genetic [dʒɪ'netɪk] adj: **~ engineering**
ingeniería genética; **~ fingerprinting**
identificación f genética

Geneva [dʒɪ'niːvə] n Ginebra

genial ['dʒiːnɪəl] adj afable, simpático

genitals ['dʒenɪtlz] npl (órganos mpl)
genitales mpl

genius ['dʒiːnɪəs] n genio

genteel [dʒen'tiːl] adj fino, elegante

gentle ['dʒentl] adj apacible, dulce;
(animal) manso; (breeze, curve etc) suave

gentleman ['dʒentlmən] (irreg) n señor m;
(well-bred man) caballero

gently ['dʒentlɪ] adv dulcemente;
suavemente

gentry ['dʒentrɪ] n alta burguesía

gents [dʒents] n aseos mpl (de caballeros)

genuine ['dʒenjuɪn] adj auténtico; (person)
sincero

geography [dʒɪ'ɒgrəfɪ] n geografía

geology [dʒɪ'ɒlədʒɪ] n geología

geometric(al) [dʒɪə'metrɪk(l)] adj

geométrico

geranium [dʒɪ'reɪnjəm] n geranio

geriatric [dʒerɪ'ætrɪk] adj, n geriátrico/a
m/f

germ [dʒɜːm] n (microbe) microbio,
bacteria; (seed, fig) germen m

German ['dʒɜːmən] adj alemán/ana ♦ n
alemán/ana m/f; (LING) alemán m; **~**
measles n rubéola

Germany ['dʒɜːmənɪ] n Alemania

gesture ['dʒestjə*] n gesto; (symbol)
muestra

┌─────────────┐
│ KEYWORD │
└─────────────┘

get [get] (pt, pp **got**, pp **gotten** (US)) vi 1
(become, be) ponerse, volverse; **to ~ old/**
tired envejecer/cansarse; **to ~ drunk**
emborracharse; **to ~ dirty** ensuciarse; **to ~**
married casarse; **when do I ~ paid?**
¿cuándo me pagan or se me paga?; **it's**
~ting late se está haciendo tarde
2 (go): **to ~ to/from** llegar a/de; **to ~**
home llegar a casa
3 (begin) empezar a; **to ~ to know sb**
(llegar a) conocer a uno; **I'm ~ting to like**
him me está empezando a gustar; **let's go**
going or **started** ¡vamos (a empezar)!
4 (modal aux vb): **you've got to do it**
tienes que hacerlo
♦ vt 1: **to ~ sth done** (finish) terminar
algo; (have done) mandar hacer algo; **to ~**
one's hair cut cortarse el pelo; **to ~ the**
car going or **to go** arrancar el coche; **to**
~ sb to do sth conseguir or hacer que
alguien haga algo; **to ~ sth/sb ready**
preparar algo/a alguien
2 (obtain: money, permission, results)
conseguir; (find: job, flat) encontrar;
(fetch: person, doctor) buscar; (object) ir a
buscar, traer; **to ~ sth for sb** conseguir
algo para alguien; **~ me Mr Jones,**
please (TEL) póngame or comuníqueme
(AM) con el Sr. Jones, por favor; **can I ~**
you a drink? ¿quieres algo de beber?
3 (receive: present, letter) recibir; (acquire:
reputation) alcanzar; (: prize) ganar; **what**
did you ~ for your birthday? ¿qué te

regalaron por tu cumpleaños?; **how much did you ~ for the painting?** ¿cuánto sacaste por el cuadro?

4 (*catch*) coger (*SP*), agarrar (*AM*); (*hit: target etc*) dar en; **to ~ sb by the arm/throat** coger *or* agarrar a uno por el brazo/cuello; **~ him!** ¡cógelo! (*SP*), ¡atrápalo! (*AM*); **the bullet got him in the leg** la bala le dio en la pierna

5 (*take, move*) llevar; **to ~ sth to sb** hacer llegar algo a alguien; **do you think we'll ~ it through the door?** ¿crees que lo podremos meter por la puerta?

6 (*catch, take: plane, bus etc*) coger (*SP*), tomar (*AM*); **where do I ~ the train for Birmingham?** ¿dónde se coge *or* se toma el tren para Birmingham?

7 (*understand*) entender; (*hear*) oír; **I've got it!** ¡ya lo tengo!, ¡eureka!; **I don't ~ your meaning** no te entiendo; **I'm sorry, I didn't ~ your name** lo siento, no cogí tu nombre

8 (*have, possess*): **to have got** tener
get about *vi* salir mucho; (*news*) divulgarse
get along *vi* (*agree*) llevarse bien; (*depart*) marcharse; (*manage*) = **get by**
get at *vt fus* (*attack*) atacar; (*reach*) alcanzar
get away *vi* marcharse; (*escape*) escaparse
get away with *vt fus* hacer impunemente
get back *vi* (*return*) volver ♦ *vt* recobrar
get by *vi* (*pass*) lograr pasar; (*manage*) arreglárselas
get down *vi* bajarse ♦ *vt fus* bajar ♦ *vt* bajar; (*depress*) deprimir
get down to *vt fus* (*work*) ponerse a
get in *vi* entrar; (*train*) llegar; (*arrive home*) volver a casa, regresar
get into *vt fus* entrar en; (*vehicle*) subir a; **to ~ into a rage** enfadarse
get off *vi* (*from train etc*) bajar; (*depart: person, car*) marcharse ♦ *vt* (*remove*) quitar ♦ *vt fus* (*train, bus*) bajar de
get on *vi* (*at exam etc*): **how are you**

~ting on? ¿cómo te va?; (*agree*): **to ~ on (with)** llevarse bien (con) ♦ *vt fus* subir a
get out *vi* salir; (*of vehicle*) bajar ♦ *vt* sacar
get out of *vt fus* salir de; (*duty etc*) escaparse de
get over *vt fus* (*illness*) recobrarse de
get round *vt fus* rodear; (*fig: person*) engatusar a
get through *vi* (*TEL*) lograr comunicarse
get through to *vt fus* (*TEL*) comunicar con
get together *vi* reunirse ♦ *vt* reunir, juntar
get up *vi* (*rise*) levantarse ♦ *vt fus* subir
get up to *vt fus* (*reach*) llegar a; (*prank*) hacer

geyser ['giːzə*] *n* (*water heater*) calentador *m* de agua; (*GEO*) géiser *m*
ghastly ['gɑːstlɪ] *adj* horrible
gherkin ['gɜːkɪn] *n* pepinillo *m*
ghetto blaster ['gɛtəʊblɑːstə*] *n* cassette *m* portátil de gran tamaño
ghost [gəʊst] *n* fantasma *m*
giant ['dʒaɪənt] *n* gigante *m/f* ♦ *adj* gigantesco, gigante
gibberish ['dʒɪbərɪʃ] *n* galimatías *m*
giblets ['dʒɪblɪts] *npl* menudillos *mpl*
Gibraltar [dʒɪ'brɔːltə*] *n* Gibraltar *m*
giddy ['gɪdɪ] *adj* mareado
gift [gɪft] *n* regalo; (*ability*) talento; **~ed** *adj* dotado; **~ token** *or* **voucher** *n* vale *m* canjeable por un regalo
gigantic [dʒaɪ'gæntɪk] *adj* gigantesco
giggle ['gɪgl] *vi* reírse tontamente
gill [dʒɪl] *n* (*measure*) = 0.25 pints (*BRIT* = 0.148l, *US* = 0.118l)
gills [gɪlz] *npl* (*of fish*) branquias *fpl*, agallas *fpl*
gilt [gɪlt] *adj*, *n* dorado; **~-edged** *adj* (*COMM*) de máxima garantía
gimmick ['gɪmɪk] *n* truco
gin [dʒɪn] *n* ginebra
ginger ['dʒɪndʒə*] *n* jengibre *m*; **~ ale** = **~ beer**; **~ beer** (*BRIT*) *n* gaseosa de

jengibre; **~bread** *n* pan *m* (*or* galleta) de jengibre

gingerly ['dʒɪndʒəlɪ] *adv* con cautela

gipsy ['dʒɪpsɪ] *n* = **gypsy**

giraffe [dʒɪ'rɑːf] *n* jirafa

girder ['ɡəːdə*] *n* viga

girl [ɡəːl] *n* (*small*) niña; (*young woman*) chica, joven *f*, muchacha; (*daughter*) hija; **an English ~** una (chica) inglesa; **~friend** *n* (*of girl*) amiga; (*of boy*) novia; **~ish** *adj* de niña

giro ['dʒaɪrəʊ] *n* (BRIT: bank ~) giro bancario; (*post office ~*) giro postal; (*state benefit*) cheque quincenal del subsidio de desempleo

gist [dʒɪst] *n* lo esencial

give [ɡɪv] (*pt* **gave**, *pp* **given**) *vt* dar; (*deliver*) entregar; (*as gift*) regalar ♦ *vi* (*break*) romperse; (*stretch: fabric*) dar de sí; **to ~ sb sth, ~ sth to sb** dar algo a uno; **~ away** *vt* (*give free*) regalar; (*betray*) traicionar; (*disclose*) revelar; **~ back** *vt* devolver; **~ in** *vi* ceder ♦ *vt* entregar; **~ off** *vt* despedir; **~ out** *vt* distribuir; **~ up** *vi* rendirse, darse por vencido ♦ *vt* renunciar a; **to ~ up smoking** dejar de fumar; **to ~ o.s. up** entregarse; **~ way** *vi* ceder; (BRIT: AUT) ceder el paso

glacier ['ɡlæsɪə*] *n* glaciar *m*

glad [ɡlæd] *adj* contento

gladly ['ɡlædlɪ] *adv* con mucho gusto

glamorous ['ɡlæmərəs] *adj* encantador(a), atractivo; **glamour** ['ɡlæmə*] *n* encanto, atractivo

glance [ɡlɑːns] *n* ojeada, mirada ♦ *vi*: **to ~ at** echar una ojeada a; **glancing** *adj* (*blow*) oblicuo

gland [ɡlænd] *n* glándula

glare [ɡlɛə*] *n* (*of anger*) mirada feroz; (*of light*) deslumbramiento, brillo; **to be in the ~ of publicity** ser el foco de la atención pública ♦ *vi* deslumbrar; **to ~ at** mirar con odio a; **glaring** *adj* (*mistake*) manifiesto

glass [ɡlɑːs] *n* vidrio, cristal *m*; (*for drinking*) vaso; (: *with stem*) copa; **~es** *npl*

(*spectacles*) gafas *fpl*; **~house** *n* invernadero; **~ware** *n* cristalería

glaze [ɡleɪz] *vt* (*window*) poner cristales a; (*pottery*) vidriar ♦ *n* vidriado; **glazier** ['ɡleɪzɪə*] *n* vidriero/a

gleam [ɡliːm] *vi* brillar

glean [ɡliːn] *vt* (*information*) recoger

glee [ɡliː] *n* alegría, regocijo

glen [ɡlɛn] *n* cañada

glib [ɡlɪb] *adj* de mucha labia; (*promise, response*) poco sincero

glide [ɡlaɪd] *vi* deslizarse; (AVIAT, *birds*) planear; **~r** *n* (AVIAT) planeador *m*; **gliding** *n* (AVIAT) vuelo sin motor

glimmer ['ɡlɪmə*] *n* luz *f* tenue; (*of interest*) muestra; (*of hope*) rayo

glimpse [ɡlɪmps] *n* vislumbre *m* ♦ *vt* vislumbrar, entrever

glint [ɡlɪnt] *vi* centellear

glisten ['ɡlɪsn] *vi* relucir, brillar

glitter ['ɡlɪtə*] *vi* relucir, brillar

gloat [ɡləʊt] *vi*: **to ~ over** recrearse en

global ['ɡləʊbl] *adj* mundial; **~ warming** (re)calentamiento global *or* de la tierra

globe [ɡləʊb] *n* globo; (*model*) globo terráqueo

gloom [ɡluːm] *n* tinieblas *fpl*, oscuridad *f*; (*sadness*) tristeza, melancolía; **~y** *adj* (*dark*) oscuro; (*sad*) triste; (*pessimistic*) pesimista

glorious ['ɡlɔːrɪəs] *adj* glorioso; (*weather etc*) magnífico

glory ['ɡlɔːrɪ] *n* gloria

gloss [ɡlɔs] *n* (*shine*) brillo; (*paint*) pintura de aceite; **~ over** *vt fus* disimular

glossary ['ɡlɔsərɪ] *n* glosario

glossy ['ɡlɔsɪ] *adj* lustroso; (*magazine*) de lujo

glove [ɡlʌv] *n* guante *m*; **~ compartment** *n* (AUT) guantera

glow [ɡləʊ] *vi* brillar

glower ['ɡlaʊə*] *vi*: **to ~ at** mirar con ceño

glue [ɡluː] *n* goma (de pegar), cemento ♦ *vt* pegar

glum [ɡlʌm] *adj* (*person, tone*) melancólico

glut [ɡlʌt] *n* superabundancia

glutton ['ɡlʌtn] *n* glotón/ona *m/f*; **a ~ for**

work un(a) trabajador(a) incansable

gnat [næt] *n* mosquito

gnaw [nɔ:] *vt* roer

gnome [nəum] *n* gnomo

go [gəu] (*pt* **went**, *pp* **gone**; *pl* **~es**) *vi* ir; (*travel*) viajar; (*depart*) irse, marcharse; (*work*) funcionar, marchar; (*be sold*) venderse; (*time*) pasar; (*fit, suit*): **to ~ with** hacer juego con; (*become*) ponerse; (*break etc*) estropearse, romperse ♦ *n*: **to have a ~ (at)** probar suerte (con); **to be on the ~** no parar; **whose ~ is it?** ¿a quién le toca?; **he's going to do it** va a hacerlo; **to ~ for a walk** ir de paseo; **to ~ dancing** ir a bailar; **how did it ~?** ¿qué tal salió *or* resultó?, ¿cómo ha ido?; **to ~ round the back** pasar por detrás; **~ about** *vi* (*rumour*) propagarse ♦ *vt fus*: **how do I ~ about this?** ¿cómo me las arreglo para hacer esto?; **~ ahead** *vi* seguir adelante; **~ along** *vi* ir ♦ *vt fus* bordear; **to ~ along with** (*agree*) estar de acuerdo con; **~ away** *vi* irse, marcharse; **~ back** *vi* volver; **~ back on** *vt fus* (*promise*) faltar a; **~ by** *vi* (*time*) pasar ♦ *vt fus* guiarse por; **~ down** *vi* bajar; (*ship*) hundirse; (*sun*) ponerse ♦ *vt fus* bajar; **~ for** *vt fus* (*fetch*) ir por; (*like*) gustar; (*attack*) atacar; **~ in** *vi* entrar; **~ in for** *vt fus* (*competition*) presentarse a; **~ into** *vt fus* entrar en; (*investigate*) investigar; (*embark on*) dedicarse a; **~ off** *vi* irse, marcharse; (*food*) pasarse; (*explode*) estallar; (*event*) realizarse ♦ *vt fus* dejar de gustar; **I'm going off him/the idea** ya no me gusta tanto él/la idea; **~ on** *vi* (*continue*) seguir, continuar; (*happen*) pasar, ocurrir; **to ~ on doing sth** seguir haciendo algo; **~ out** *vi* salir; (*fire, light*) apagarse; **~ over** *vi* (*ship*) zozobrar ♦ *vt fus* (*check*) revisar; **~ through** *vt fus* (*town etc*) atravesar; **~ up** *vi, vt fus* subir; **~ without** *vt fus* pasarse sin

goad [gəud] *vt* aguijonear

go-ahead *adj* (*person*) dinámico; (*firm*) innovador(a) ♦ *n* luz *f* verde

goal [gəul] *n* meta; (*score*) gol *m*;

~keeper *n* portero; **~-post** *n* poste *m* (de la portería)

goat [gəut] *n* cabra

gobble ['gɔbl] *vt* (*also*: **~ down**, **~ up**) tragarse, engullir

go-between *n* intermediario/a

god [gɔd] *n* dios *m*; **G~** *n* Dios *m*; **~child** *n* ahijado/a; **~daughter** *n* ahijada; **~dess** *n* diosa; **~father** *n* padrino; **~-forsaken** *adj* dejado de la mano de Dios; **~mother** *n* madrina; **~send** *n* don *m* del cielo; **~son** *n* ahijado

goggles ['gɔglz] *npl* gafas *fpl*

going ['gəuɪŋ] *n* (*conditions*) estado del terreno ♦ *adj*: **the ~ rate** la tarifa corriente *or* en vigor

gold [gəuld] *n* oro ♦ *adj* de oro; **~en** *adj* (*made of ~*) de oro; (*~ in colour*) dorado; **~fish** *n* pez *m* de colores; **~mine** *n* (*also fig*) mina de oro; **~-plated** *adj* chapado en oro; **~smith** *n* orfebre *m/f*

golf [gɔlf] *n* golf *m*; **~ ball** *n* (*for game*) pelota de golf; (*on typewriter*) esfera; **~ club** *n* club *m* de golf; (*stick*) palo (de golf); **~ course** *n* campo de golf; **~er** *n* golfista *m/f*

gone [gɔn] *pp* de **go**

good [gud] *adj* bueno; (*pleasant*) agradable; (*kind*) bueno, amable; (*well-behaved*) educado ♦ *n* bien *m*, provecho; **~s** *npl* (*COMM*) mercancías *fpl*; **~!** ¡qué bien!; **to be ~ at** tener aptitud para; **to be ~ for** servir para; **it's ~ for you** te hace bien; **would you be ~ enough to ...?** ¿podría hacerme el favor de ...?, ¿sería tan amable de ...?; **a ~ deal (of)** mucho; **a ~ many** muchos; **to make ~** reparar; **it's no ~ complaining** no vale la pena (de) quejarse; **for ~** para siempre, definitivamente; **~ morning/afternoon** ¡buenos días/buenas tardes!; **~ evening!** ¡buenas noches!; **~ night!** ¡buenas noches!; **~bye!** ¡adiós!; **to say ~bye** despedirse; **G~ Friday** *n* Viernes *m* Santo; **~-looking** *adj* guapo; **~-natured** *adj* amable, simpático; **~ness** *n* (*of person*) bondad *f*; **for ~ness sake!** ¡por

Dios!; **~ness gracious!** ¡Dios mío!; **~s train** (BRIT) n tren m de mercancías; **~will** n buena voluntad f

goose [guːs] (pl **geese**) n ganso, oca

gooseberry ['guzbəri] n grosella espinosa; **to play ~** hacer de carabina

gooseflesh ['guːsfleʃ] n = **goose pimples**

goose pimples npl carne f de gallina

gore [gɔː*] vt cornear ♦ n sangre f

gorge [gɔːdʒ] n barranco ♦ vr: **to ~ o.s. (on)** atracarse (de)

gorgeous ['gɔːdʒəs] adj (thing) precioso; (weather) espléndido; (person) guapísimo

gorilla [gə'rɪlə] n gorila m

gorse [gɔːs] n tojo

gory ['gɔːrɪ] adj sangriento

go-slow (BRIT) n huelga de manos caídas

gospel ['gɔspəl] n evangelio

gossip ['gɔsɪp] n (scandal) cotilleo, chismes mpl; (chat) charla; (scandalmonger) cotilla m/f, chismoso/a ♦ vi cotillear

got [gɔt] pt, pp of **get**; **~ten** (US) pp of **get**

gout [gaut] n gota

govern ['gʌvən] vt gobernar; (influence) dominar; **~ess** n institutriz f; **~ment** n gobierno; **~or** n gobernador(a) m/f; (of school etc) miembro del consejo; (of jail) director(a) m/f

gown [gaun] n traje m; (of teacher, BRIT: of judge) toga

G.P. n abbr = **general practitioner**

grab [græb] vt coger (SP) or agarrar (AM), arrebatar ♦ vi: **to ~ at** intentar agarrar

grace [greɪs] n gracia ♦ vt honrar; (adorn) adornar; **5 days'** ~ un plazo de 5 días; **~ful** adj grácil, ágil; (style, shape) elegante, gracioso; **gracious** ['greɪʃəs] adj amable

grade [greɪd] n (quality) clase f, calidad f; (in hierarchy) grado; (SCOL: mark) nota; (US: school class) curso ♦ vt clasificar; **~ crossing** (US) n paso a nivel; **~ school** (US) n escuela primaria

gradient ['greɪdɪənt] n pendiente f

gradual ['grædjuəl] adj paulatino; **~ly** adv

paulatinamente

graduate [n 'grædjuɪt, vb 'grædjueɪt] n (US: of high school) graduado/a; (of university) licenciado/a ♦ vi graduarse; licenciarse; **graduation** [-'eɪʃən] n (ceremony) entrega del título

graffiti [grə'fiːtɪ] n pintadas fpl

graft [grɑːft] n (AGR, MED) injerto; (BRIT: inf) trabajo duro; (bribery) corrupción f ♦ vt injertar

grain [greɪn] n (single particle) grano; (corn) granos mpl, cereales mpl; (of wood) fibra

gram [græm] n gramo

grammar ['græmə*] n gramática; **~ school** (BRIT) n ≈ instituto de segunda enseñanza, liceo (SP)

grammatical [grə'mætɪkl] adj gramatical

gramme [græm] n = **gram**

gramophone ['græməfəun] (BRIT) n tocadiscos m inv

grand [grænd] adj magnífico, imponente; (wonderful) estupendo; (gesture etc) grandioso; **~children** npl nietos mpl; **~dad** (inf) n yayo, abuelito; **~daughter** n nieta; **~eur** ['grændjə*] n magnificencia, lo grandioso; **~father** n abuelo; **~ma** (inf) n yaya, abuelita; **~mother** n abuela; **~pa** (inf) n = **~dad**; **~parents** npl abuelos mpl; **~ piano** n piano de cola; **~son** n nieto; **~stand** n (SPORT) tribuna

granite ['grænɪt] n granito

granny ['grænɪ] (inf) n abuelita, yaya

grant [grɑːnt] vt (concede) conceder; (admit) reconocer ♦ n (SCOL) beca; (ADMIN) subvención f; **to take sth/sb for ~ed** dar algo por sentado/no hacer ningún caso a uno

granulated sugar ['grænjuːleɪtɪd-] (BRIT) n azúcar m blanquilla

grape [greɪp] n uva

grapefruit ['greɪpfruːt] n pomelo (SP), toronja (AM)

graph [grɑːf] n gráfica; **~ic** ['græfɪk] adj gráfico; **~ics** n artes fpl gráficas ♦ npl (drawings) dibujos mpl

grapple ['græpl] vi: **to ~ with sth/sb**

agarrar a algo/uno

grasp [grɑːsp] vt agarrar, asir; (understand) comprender ♦ n (grip) asimiento; (understanding) comprensión f; **~ing** adj (mean) avaro

grass [grɑːs] n hierba; (lawn) césped m; **~hopper** n saltamontes m inv; **~-roots** adj (fig) popular

grate [greɪt] n parrilla de chimenea ♦ vi: **to ~ (on)** chirriar (sobre) ♦ vt (CULIN) rallar

grateful ['greɪtful] adj agradecido

grater ['greɪtə*] n rallador m

gratifying ['grætɪfaɪɪŋ] adj grato

grating ['greɪtɪŋ] n (iron bars) reja ♦ adj (noise) áspero

gratitude ['grætɪtjuːd] n agradecimiento

gratuity [grə'tjuːɪtɪ] n gratificación f

grave [greɪv] n tumba ♦ adj serio, grave

gravel ['grævl] n grava

gravestone ['greɪvstəun] n lápida

graveyard ['greɪvjɑːd] n cementerio

gravity ['grævɪtɪ] n gravedad f

gravy ['greɪvɪ] n salsa de carne

gray [greɪ] adj = **grey**

graze [greɪz] vi pacer ♦ vt (touch lightly) rozar; (scrape) raspar ♦ n (MED) abrasión f

grease [griːs] n (fat) grasa; (lubricant) lubricante m ♦ vt engrasar; lubrificar; **~proof paper** (BRIT) n papel m apergaminado; **greasy** adj grasiento

great [greɪt] adj grande; (inf) magnífico, estupendo; **G~ Britain** n Gran Bretaña; **~-grandfather** n bisabuelo; **~-grandmother** n bisabuela; **~ly** adv muy; (with verb) mucho; **~ness** n grandeza

Greece [griːs] n Grecia

greed [griːd] n (also: **~iness**) codicia, avaricia; (for food) gula; (for power etc) avidez f; **~y** adj avaro; (for food) glotón/ona

Greek [griːk] adj griego ♦ n griego/a; (LING) griego

green [griːn] adj (also POL) verde; (inexperienced) novato ♦ n verde m; (stretch of grass) césped m; (GOLF) green

m; **~s** npl (vegetables) verduras fpl; **~ belt** n zona verde; **~ card** n (AUT) carta verde; (US: work permit) permiso de trabajo para los extranjeros en EE. UU.; **~ery** n verdura; **~grocer** (BRIT) n verdulero/a; **~house** n invernadero; **~house effect** n efecto invernadero; **~house gas** n gases mpl de invernadero; **~ish** adj verdoso

Greenland ['griːnlənd] n Groenlandia

greet [griːt] vt (welcome) dar la bienvenida a; (receive: news) recibir; **~ing** n (welcome) bienvenida; **~ing(s) card** n tarjeta de felicitación

grenade [grə'neɪd] n granada

grew [gruː] pt of **grow**

grey [greɪ] adj gris; (weather) sombrío; **~-haired** adj canoso; **~hound** n galgo

grid [grɪd] n reja; (ELEC) red f; **~lock** n (traffic jam) retención f

grief [griːf] n dolor m, pena

grievance ['griːvəns] n motivo de queja, agravio

grieve [griːv] vi afligirse, acongojarse ♦ vt dar pena a; **to ~ for** llorar por

grievous ['griːvəs] adj: **~ bodily harm** (LAW) daños mpl corporales graves

grill [grɪl] n (on cooker) parrilla; (also: **mixed ~**) parrillada ♦ vt (BRIT) asar a la parrilla; (inf: question) interrogar

grille [grɪl] n reja; (AUT) rejilla

grim [grɪm] adj (place) sombrío; (situation) triste; (person) ceñudo

grimace [grɪ'meɪs] n mueca ♦ vi hacer muecas

grime [graɪm] n mugre f, suciedad f

grin [grɪn] n sonrisa abierta ♦ vi sonreír abiertamente

grind [graɪnd] (pt, pp **ground**) vt (coffee, pepper etc) moler; (US: meat) picar; (make sharp) afilar ♦ n (work) rutina

grip [grɪp] n (hold) asimiento; (control) control m, dominio; (of tyre etc): **to have a good/bad ~** agarrarse bien/mal; (handle) asidero; (holdall) maletín m ♦ vt agarrar; (viewer, reader) fascinar; **to get to ~s with** enfrentarse con; **~ping** adj absorbente

grisly ['grızlı] *adj* horripilante, horrible

gristle ['grısl] *n* ternilla

grit [grıt] *n* gravilla; (*courage*) valor *m* ♦ *vt* (*road*) poner gravilla en; **to ~ one's teeth** apretar los dientes

groan [grəun] *n* gemido; quejido ♦ *vi* gemir; quejarse

grocer ['grəusə*] *n* tendero (de ultramarinos (*SP*)); **~ies** *npl* comestibles *mpl*; **~'s (shop)** *n* tienda de ultramarinos *or* de abarrotes (*AM*)

groin [grɔın] *n* ingle *f*

groom [gru:m] *n* mozo/a de cuadra; (*also:* **bride~**) novio ♦ *vt* (*horse*) almohazar; (*fig*): **to ~ sb for** preparar a uno para; **well-~ed** de buena presencia

groove [gru:v] *n* ranura, surco

grope [grəup]: **to ~ for** *vt fus* buscar a tientas

gross [grəus] *adj* (*neglect, injustice*) grave; (*vulgar: behaviour*) grosero; (*: appearance*) de mal gusto; (*COMM*) bruto; **~ly** *adv* (*greatly*) enormemente

grotto ['grɔtəu] *n* gruta

grotty ['grɔtı] (*inf*) *adj* horrible

ground [graund] *pt, pp of* **grind** ♦ *n* suelo, tierra; (*SPORT*) campo, terreno; (*reason: gen pl*) causa, razón *f*; (*US: also:* **~ wire**) tierra ♦ *vt* (*plane*) mantener en tierra; (*US: ELEC*) conectar con tierra; **~s** *npl* (*of coffee etc*) poso; (*gardens etc*) jardines *mpl*, parque *m*; **on the ~** en el suelo; **to the ~** al suelo; **to gain/lose ~** ganar/perder terreno; **~ cloth** (*US*) *n* = **~sheet**; **~ing** *n* (*in education*) conocimientos *mpl* básicos; **~less** *adj* infundado; **~sheet** (*BRIT*) *n* tela impermeable; suelo; **~ staff** *n* personal *m* de tierra; **~work** *n* preparación *f*

group [gru:p] *n* grupo; (*musical*) conjunto ♦ *vt* (*also:* **~ together**) agrupar ♦ *vi* (*also:* **~ together**) agruparse

grouse [graus] *n inv* (*bird*) urogallo ♦ *vi* (*complain*) quejarse

grove [grəuv] *n* arboleda

grovel ['grɔvl] *vi* (*fig*): **to ~ before**

humillarse ante

grow [grəu] (*pt* **grew**, *pp* **grown**) *vi* crecer; (*increase*) aumentar; (*expand*) desarrollarse; (*become*) volverse; **to ~ rich/weak** enriquecerse/debilitarse ♦ *vt* cultivar; (*hair, beard*) dejar crecer; **~ up** *vi* crecer, hacerse hombre/mujer; **~er** *n* cultivador(a) *m/f*, productor(a) *m/f*; **~ing** *adj* creciente

growl [graul] *vi* gruñir

grown [grəun] *pp of* **grow**; **~-up** *n* adulto, mayor *m/f*

growth [grəuθ] *n* crecimiento, desarrollo; (*what has grown*) brote *m*; (*MED*) tumor *m*

grub [grʌb] *n* larva, gusano; (*inf: food*) comida

grubby ['grʌbı] *adj* sucio, mugriento

grudge [grʌdʒ] *n* (motivo de) rencor *m* ♦ *vt*: **to ~ sb sth** dar algo a uno de mala gana; **to bear sb a ~** guardar rencor a uno

gruelling ['gruəlıŋ] (*US* **grueling**) *adj* penoso, duro

gruesome ['gru:səm] *adj* horrible

gruff [grʌf] *adj* (*voice*) ronco; (*manner*) brusco

grumble ['grʌmbl] *vi* refunfuñar, quejarse

grumpy ['grʌmpı] *adj* gruñón/ona

grunt [grʌnt] *vi* gruñir

G-string ['dʒi:strıŋ] *n* taparrabo

guarantee [gærən'ti:] *n* garantía ♦ *vt* garantizar

guard [gɑ:d] *n* (*squad*) guardia; (*one man*) guardia *m*; (*BRIT: RAIL*) jefe *m* de tren; (*on machine*) dispositivo de seguridad; (*also:* **fire~**) rejilla de protección ♦ *vt* guardar; (*prisoner*) vigilar; **to be on one's ~** estar alerta; **~ against** *vt fus* (*prevent*) protegerse de; **~ed** *adj* (*fig*) cauteloso; **~ian** *n* guardián/ana *m/f*; (*of minor*) tutor(a) *m/f*; **~'s van** *n* (*BRIT: RAIL*) furgón *m*

Guatemala [gwætı'mɑ:lə] *n* Guatemala; **~n** *adj, n* guatemalteco/a *m/f*

guerrilla [gə'rılə] *n* guerrillero/a

guess [ges] *vi* adivinar; (*US*) suponer ♦ *vt*

adivinar; suponer ♦ *n* suposición *f*, conjetura; **to take** *or* **have a ~** tratar de adivinar; **~work** *n* conjeturas *fpl*

guest [gest] *n* invitado/a; (*in hotel*) huésped(a) *m/f*; **~ house** *n* casa de huéspedes, pensión *f*; **~ room** *n* cuarto de huéspedes

guffaw [gʌˈfɔ:] *vi* reírse a carcajadas

guidance [ˈgaɪdəns] *n* (*advice*) consejos *mpl*

guide [gaɪd] *n* (*person*) guía *m/f*; (*book, fig*) guía ♦ *vt* (*round museum etc*) guiar; (*lead*) conducir; (*direct*) orientar; **(girl) ~** *n* exploradora; **~book** *n* guía; **~ dog** *n* perro *m* guía; **~lines** *npl* (*advice*) directrices *fpl*

guild [gɪld] *n* gremio

guilt [gɪlt] *n* culpabilidad *f*; **~y** *adj* culpable

guinea pig [ˈgɪnɪ-] *n* cobaya; (*fig*) conejillo de Indias

guise [gaɪz] *n*: **in** *or* **under the ~ of** bajo apariencia de

guitar [gɪˈtɑ:ˀ] *n* guitarra

gulf [gʌlf] *n* golfo; (*abyss*) abismo

gull [gʌl] *n* gaviota

gullible [ˈgʌlɪbl] *adj* crédulo

gully [ˈgʌlɪ] *n* barranco

gulp [gʌlp] *vi* tragar saliva ♦ *vt* (*also: ~ down*) tragarse

gum [gʌm] *n* (*ANAT*) encía; (*glue*) goma, cemento; (*sweet*) caramelo de goma; (*also:* **chewing-~**) chicle *m* ♦ *vt* pegar con goma; **~boots** (*BRIT*) *npl* botas *fpl* de goma

gun [gʌn] *n* (*small*) pistola, revólver *m*; (*shotgun*) escopeta; (*rifle*) fusil *m*; (*cannon*) cañón *m*; **~boat** *n* cañonero; **~fire** *n* disparos *mpl*; **~man** *n* pistolero; **~point** *n*: **at ~point** a mano armada; **~powder** *n* pólvora; **~shot** *n* escopetazo

gurgle [ˈgɜ:gl] *vi* (*baby*) gorgotear; (*water*) borbotear

gush [gʌʃ] *vi* salir a raudales; (*person*) deshacerse en efusiones

gust [gʌst] *n* (*of wind*) ráfaga

gusto [ˈgʌstəu] *n* entusiasmo

gut [gʌt] *n* intestino; **~s** *npl* (*ANAT*) tripas *fpl*; (*courage*) valor *m*

gutter [ˈgʌtəˀ] *n* (*of roof*) canalón *m*; (*in street*) cuneta

guy [gaɪ] *n* (*also:* **~rope**) cuerda; (*inf: man*) tío (*SP*), tipo; (*figure*) monigote *m*

<table>
<tr><td>Guy Fawkes' Night</td></tr>
</table>

i La noche del cinco de noviembre, **Guy Fawkes' Night**, *se celebra en el Reino Unido el fracaso de la conspiración de la pólvora ("Gunpowder Plot"), un intento fallido de volar el parlamento de Jaime I en 1605. Esa noche se lanzan fuegos artificiales y se hacen hogueras en las que se queman unos muñecos de trapo que representan a* **Guy Fawkes**, *uno de los cabecillas de la revuelta. Días antes, los niños tienen por costumbre pedir a los transeúntes "a penny for the guy", dinero que emplean en comprar cohetes y petardos.*

guzzle [ˈgʌzl] *vi* tragar ♦ *vt* engullir

gym [dʒɪm] *n* (*also:* **gymnasium**) gimnasio; (*also:* **gymnastics**) gimnasia; **~nast** *n* gimnasta *m/f*; **~ shoes** *npl* zapatillas *fpl* (de deporte); **~ slip** (*BRIT*) *n* túnica de colegiala

gynaecologist [gaɪnɪˈkɒlədʒɪst] (*US* **gynecologist**) *n* ginecólogo/a

gypsy [ˈdʒɪpsɪ] *n* gitano/a

H, h

haberdashery [hæbəˈdæʃərɪ] (*BRIT*) *n* mercería

habit [ˈhæbɪt] *n* hábito, costumbre *f*; (*drug ~*) adicción *f*; (*costume*) hábito

habitual [həˈbɪtjuəl] *adj* acostumbrado, habitual; (*drinker, liar*) empedernido

hack [hæk] *vt* (*cut*) cortar; (*slice*) tajar ♦ *n* (*pej: writer*) escritor(a) *m/f* a sueldo; **~er** *n* (*COMPUT*) pirata *m/f* informático/a

hackneyed [ˈhæknɪd] *adj* trillado

had [hæd] *pt, pp of* **have**

haddock ['hædək] (*pl* ~ *or* ~**s**) *n especie de merluza*

hadn't ['hædnt] = **had not**

haemorrhage ['heməridʒ] (*US* **hemorrhage**) *n* hemorragia

haemorrhoids ['heməridz] (*US* **hemorrhoids**) *npl* hemorroides *fpl*

haggle ['hægl] *vi* regatear

Hague [heig] *n*: **The ~** La Haya

hail [heil] *n* granizo; (*fig*) lluvia ♦ *vt* saludar; (*taxi*) llamar a; (*acclaim*) aclamar ♦ *vi* granizar; ~**stone** *n* (piedra de) granizo

hair [heə*] *n* pelo, cabellos *mpl*; (*one* ~) pelo, cabello; (*on legs etc*) vello; **to do one's ~** arreglarse el pelo; **to have grey ~** tener canas *fpl*; ~**brush** *n* cepillo (para el pelo); ~**cut** *n* corte *m* (de pelo); ~**do** *n* peinado; ~**dresser** *n* peluquero/a; ~**dresser's** *n* peluquería; ~ **dryer** *n* secador *m* de pelo; ~**grip** *n* horquilla; ~**net** *n* redecilla; ~**piece** *n* postizo; ~**pin** *n* horquilla; ~**pin bend** (*US* ~**pin curve**) *n* curva de horquilla; ~**raising** *adj* espeluznante; ~ **removing cream** *n* crema depilatoria; ~ **spray** *n* laca; ~**style** *n* peinado; ~**y** *adj* peludo; velludo; (*inf: frightening*) espeluznante

hake [heik] (*pl inv or* ~**s**) *n* merluza

half [hɑːf] (*pl* **halves**) *n* mitad *f*; (*of beer*) ≈ caña (*SP*), media pinta; (*RAIL, BUS*) billete *m* de niño ♦ *adj* medio ♦ *adv* medio, a medias; **two and a ~** dos y media; ~ **a dozen** media docena; ~ **a pound** media libra; **to cut sth in ~** cortar algo por la mitad; ~**-caste** ['hɑːfkɑːst] *n* mestizo/a; ~**-hearted** *adj* indiferente, poco entusiasta; ~**-hour** *n* media hora; ~**-mast** *n*: **at ~-mast** (*flag*) a media asta; ~**-price** *adj, adv* a mitad de precio; ~ **term** (*BRIT*) *n* (*SCOL*) *vacaciones de mediados del trimestre*; ~**-time** *n* descanso; ~**way** *adv* a medio camino; (*in period of time*) a mitad de

hall [hɔːl] *n* (*for concerts*) sala; (*entrance way*) hall *m*; vestíbulo; ~ **of residence** (*BRIT*) *n* residencia

hallmark ['hɔːlmɑːk] *n* sello

hallo [hə'ləu] *excl* = **hello**

Hallowe'en [hæləu'iːn] *n* víspera de Todos los Santos

Hallowe'en

ⓘ *La tradición anglosajona dice que en la noche del 31 de octubre,* **Hallowe'en**, *víspera de Todos los Santos, es posible ver a brujas y fantasmas. En este día los niños se disfrazan y van de puerta en puerta llevando un farol hecho con una calabaza en forma de cabeza humana. Cuando se les abre la puerta gritan "trick or treat", amenazando con gastar una broma a quien no les dé golosinas o algo de calderilla.*

---

hallucination [həluːsɪ'neɪʃən] *n* alucinación *f*

hallway ['hɔːlweɪ] *n* vestíbulo

halo ['heiləu] *n* (*of saint*) halo, aureola

halt [hɔːlt] *n* (*stop*) alto, parada ♦ *vt* parar; interrumpir ♦ *vi* pararse

halve [hɑːv] *vt* partir por la mitad

halves [hɑːvz] *npl of* **half**

ham [hæm] *n* jamón *m* (cocido)

hamburger ['hæmbəːgə*] *n* hamburguesa

hamlet ['hæmlɪt] *n* aldea

hammer ['hæmə*] *n* martillo ♦ *vt* (*nail*) clavar; (*force*): **to ~ an idea into sb/a message across** meter una idea en la cabeza a uno/machacar una idea ♦ *vi* dar golpes

hammock ['hæmək] *n* hamaca

hamper ['hæmpə*] *vt* estorbar ♦ *n* cesto

hand [hænd] *n* mano *f*; (*of clock*) aguja; (*writing*) letra; (*worker*) obrero ♦ *vt* dar, pasar; **to give** *or* **lend sb a ~** echar una mano a uno, ayudar a uno; **at ~** a mano; **in ~** (*time*) libre; (*job etc*) entre manos; **on ~** (*person, services*) a mano, al alcance; **to ~** (*information etc*) a mano; **on the one ~ ..., on the other ~ ...** por una parte ..., por otra (parte) ...; ~ **in** *vt* entregar; ~ **out** *vt* distribuir; ~ **over** *vt* (*deliver*)

entregar; ~**bag** n bolso (*SP*),
cartera (*AM*); ~**book** n manual m; ~**brake** n freno de
mano; ~**cuffs** npl esposas fpl; ~**ful** n
puñado

handicap ['hændɪkæp] n minusvalía;
(*disadvantage*) desventaja; (*SPORT*)
handicap m ♦ vt estorbar; **mentally /
physically ~ped** deficiente m/f (mental)/
minusválido/a (físico/a)

handicraft ['hændɪkrɑːft] n artesanía;
(*object*) objeto de artesanía

handiwork ['hændɪwəːk] n obra

handkerchief ['hæŋkətʃɪf] n pañuelo

handle ['hændl] n (of door etc) tirador m;
(of cup etc) asa; (of knife etc) mango; (for
winding) manivela ♦ vt (touch) tocar; (deal
with) encargarse de; (treat: people)
manejar; "~ **with care**" "(manéjese) con
cuidado"; **to fly off the ~** perder los
estribos; ~**bar(s)** n(pl) manillar m

hand: ~ **luggage** n equipaje m de mano;
~**made** adj hecho a mano; ~**out** n
(money etc) limosna; (leaflet) folleto; ~**rail**
n pasamanos m inv; ~**shake** n apretón
m de manos

handsome ['hænsəm] adj guapo;
(building) bello; (fig: profit) considerable

handwriting ['hændraɪtɪŋ] n letra

handy ['hændɪ] adj (close at hand) a la
mano; (tool etc) práctico; (skilful) hábil,
diestro

hang [hæŋ] (pt, pp hung) vt colgar;
(criminal: pt, pp hanged) ahorcar ♦ vi
(painting, coat etc) colgar; (hair, drapery)
caer; **to get the ~ of sth** (inf) lograr
dominar algo; ~ **about** or **around** vi
haraganear; ~ **on** vi (wait) esperar; ~ **up**
vi (TEL) colgar ♦ vt colgar

hanger ['hæŋə*] n percha; ~-**on** n
parásito

hang: ~-**gliding** ['-glaɪdɪŋ] n vuelo libre;
~**over** n (after drinking) resaca; ~-**up** n
complejo

hanker ['hæŋkə*] vi: **to ~ after** añorar

hankie ['hæŋkɪ], **hanky** ['hæŋkɪ] n abbr =
handkerchief

haphazard [hæp'hæzəd] adj fortuito

happen ['hæpən] vi suceder, ocurrir;
(chance): **he ~ed to hear/see** dió la
casualidad de que oyó/vió; **as it ~s** da la
casualidad de que; ~**ing** n suceso,
acontecimiento

happily ['hæpɪlɪ] adv (luckily)
afortunadamente; (cheerfully) alegremente

happiness ['hæpɪnɪs] n felicidad f;
(cheerfulness) alegría

happy ['hæpɪ] adj feliz; (cheerful) alegre; **to
be ~ (with)** estar contento (con); **to be ~
to do** estar encantado de hacer; ~
birthday! ¡feliz cumpleaños!; ~**-go-lucky**
adj despreocupado; ~ **hour** n horas en
las que la bebida es más barata, happy
hour f

harass ['hærəs] vt acosar, hostigar;
~**ment** n persecución f

harbour ['hɑːbə*] (US **harbor**) n puerto
♦ vt (fugitive) dar abrigo a; (hope etc)
abrigar

hard [hɑːd] adj duro; (difficult) difícil;
(work) arduo; (person) severo; (fact)
innegable ♦ adv (work) mucho, duro;
(think) profundamente; **to look ~ at**
clavar los ojos en; **to try ~** esforzarse; **no
~ feelings!** ¡sin rencor(es)!; **to be ~ of
hearing** ser duro de oído; **to be ~ done
by** ser tratado injustamente; ~**back** n
libro en cartoné; ~ **cash** n dinero
contante; ~ **disk** n (COMPUT) disco duro
or rígido; ~**en** vt endurecer; (fig) curtir
♦ vi endurecerse; curtirse; ~-**headed** adj
realista; ~ **labour** n trabajos mpl
forzados

hardly ['hɑːdlɪ] adv apenas; ~ **ever** casi
nunca

hard: ~**ship** n privación f; ~ **shoulder**
(BRIT) n (AUT) arcén m; ~-**up** (inf) adj sin
un duro (SP), sin plata (AM); ~**ware** n
ferretería; (COMPUT) hardware m; (MIL)
armamento; ~**ware shop** n ferretería;
~-**wearing** adj resistente, duradero; ~-
working adj trabajador(a)

hardy ['hɑːdɪ] adj fuerte; (plant) resistente

hare [hɛə*] n liebre f; ~-**brained** adj
descabellado

harm [hɑːm] n daño, mal m ♦ vt (person) hacer daño a; (health, interests) perjudicar; (thing) dañar; **out of ~'s way** a salvo; **~ful** adj dañino; **~less** adj (person) inofensivo; (joke etc) inocente

harmony ['hɑːmənɪ] n armonía

harness ['hɑːnɪs] n arreos mpl; (for child) arnés m; (safety ~) arneses mpl ♦ vt (horse) enjaezar; (resources) aprovechar

harp [hɑːp] n arpa ♦ vi: **to ~ on (about)** machacar (con)

harrowing ['hærəʊɪŋ] adj angustioso

harsh [hɑːʃ] adj (cruel) duro, cruel; (severe) severo; (sound) áspero; (light) deslumbrador(a)

harvest ['hɑːvɪst] n (~ time) siega; (of cereals etc) cosecha; (of grapes) vendimia ♦ vt cosechar

has [hæz] vb see **have**

hash [hæʃ] n (CULIN) picadillo; (fig: mess) lío

hashish ['hæʃɪʃ] n hachís m

hasn't ['hæznt] = **has not**

hassle ['hæsl] (inf) n lata

haste [heɪst] n prisa; **~n** ['heɪsn] vt acelerar ♦ vi darse prisa; **hastily** adv de prisa; precipitadamente; **hasty** adj apresurado; (rash) precipitado

hat [hæt] n sombrero

hatch [hætʃ] n (NAUT: also: **~way**) escotilla; (also: **service ~**) ventanilla ♦ vi (bird) salir del cascarón ♦ vt incubar; (plot) tramar; **5 eggs have ~ed** han salido 5 pollos

hatchback ['hætʃbæk] n (AUT) tres or cinco puertas m

hatchet ['hætʃɪt] n hacha

hate [heɪt] vt odiar, aborrecer ♦ n odio; **~ful** adj odioso; **hatred** ['heɪtrɪd] n odio

haughty ['hɔːtɪ] adj altanero

haul [hɔːl] vt tirar ♦ n (of fish) redada; (of stolen goods etc) botín m; **~age** (BRIT) n transporte m; (costs) gastos mpl de transporte; **~ier** (US **~er**) n transportista m/f

haunch [hɔːntʃ] n anca; (of meat) pierna

haunt [hɔːnt] vt (subj: ghost) aparecerse en; (obsess) obsesionar ♦ n guarida

have [hæv] (pt, pp **had**) aux vb **1** (gen) haber; **to ~ arrived/eaten** haber llegado/comido; **having finished** or **when he had finished, he left** cuando hubo acabado, se fue

2 (in tag questions): **you've done it, ~n't you?** lo has hecho, ¿verdad? or ¿no?

3 (in short answers and questions): **I ~n't** no; **so I ~** pues, es verdad; **we ~n't paid – yes we ~!** no hemos pagado — ¡sí que hemos pagado!; **I've been there before, ~ you?** he estado allí antes, ¿y tú?

♦ modal aux vb (be obliged): **to ~ (got) to do sth** tener que hacer algo; **you ~n't to tell her** no hay que or no debes decírselo

♦ vt **1** (possess): **he has (got) blue eyes/dark hair** tiene los ojos azules/el pelo negro

2 (referring to meals etc): **to ~ breakfast/lunch/dinner** desayunar/comer/cenar; **to ~ a drink/a cigarette** tomar algo/fumar un cigarrillo

3 (receive) recibir; (obtain) obtener; **may I ~ your address?** ¿puedes darme tu dirección?; **you can ~ it for £5** te lo puedes quedar por £5; **I must ~ it by tomorrow** lo necesito para mañana; **to ~ a baby** tener un niño or bebé

4 (maintain, allow): **I won't ~ it/this nonsense!** ¡no lo permitiré!/¡no permitiré estas tonterías!; **we can't ~ that** no podemos permitir eso

5: **to ~ sth done** hacer or mandar hacer algo; **to ~ one's hair cut** cortarse el pelo; **to ~ sb do sth** hacer que alguien haga algo

6 (experience, suffer): **to ~ a cold/flu** tener un resfriado/la gripe; **she had her bag stolen/her arm broken** le robaron el bolso/se rompió un brazo; **to ~ an operation** operarse

7 (+noun): **to ~ a swim/walk/bath/rest** nadar/dar un paseo/darse un baño/descansar; **let's ~ a look** vamos a ver; **to**

~ **a meeting/party** celebrar una reunión/una fiesta; **let me** ~ **a try** déjame intentarlo
have out *vt*: **to** ~ **it out with sb** (*settle a problem etc*) dejar las cosas en claro con alguien

haven ['heɪvn] *n* puerto; (*fig*) refugio
haven't ['hævnt] = **have not**
havoc ['hævək] *n* estragos *mpl*
hawk [hɔːk] *n* halcón *m*
hay [heɪ] *n* heno; ~ **fever** *n* fiebre *f* del heno; ~**stack** *n* almiar *m*
haywire ['heɪwaɪə*] (*inf*) *adj*: **to go** ~ (*plan*) embrollarse
hazard ['hæzəd] *n* peligro ♦ *vt* aventurar; ~**ous** *adj* peligroso; ~ **warning lights** *npl* (*AUT*) señales *fpl* de emergencia
haze [heɪz] *n* neblina
hazelnut ['heɪzlnʌt] *n* avellana
hazy ['heɪzɪ] *adj* brumoso; (*idea*) vago
he [hiː] *pron* él; ~ **who ...** él que ..., quien ...
head [hɛd] *n* cabeza; (*leader*) jefe/a *m/f*; (*of school*) director(a) *m/f* ♦ *vt* (*list*) encabezar; (*group*) capitanear; (*company*) dirigir; ~**s** (**or tails**) cara (o cruz); ~ **first** de cabeza; ~ **over heels** (*in love*) perdidamente; **to** ~ **the ball** cabecear (la pelota); ~ **for** *vt fus* dirigirse a; (*disaster*) ir camino de; ~**ache** *n* dolor *m* de cabeza; ~**dress** *n* tocado; ~**ing** *n* título; ~**lamp** (*BRIT*) *n* = ~**light**; ~**light** *n* faro; ~**line** *n* titular *m*; ~**long** *adv* (*fall*) de cabeza; (*rush*) precipitadamente; ~**master/mistress** *n* director(a) *m/f* (de escuela); ~ **office** *n* oficina central, central *f*; ~-**on** *adj* (*collision*) de frente; ~**phones** *npl* auriculares *mpl*; ~**quarters** *npl* sede *f* central; (*MIL*) cuartel *m* general; ~**rest** *n* reposa-cabezas *m inv*; ~**room** *n* (*in car*) altura interior; (*under bridge*) (límite *m* de) altura; ~**scarf** *n* pañuelo; ~**strong** *adj* testarudo; ~ **waiter** *n* maître *m*; ~**way** *n*: **to make** ~**way** (*fig*) hacer progresos; ~**wind** *n* viento contrario; ~**y** *adj*

(*experience, period*) apasionante; (*wine*) cabezón; (*atmosphere*) embriagador(a)
heal [hiːl] *vt* curar ♦ *vi* cicatrizarse
health [hɛlθ] *n* salud *f*; ~ **food** *n* alimentos *mpl* orgánicos; **the H~ Service** (*BRIT*) *n* el servicio de salud pública; ≈ el Insalud (*SP*); ~**y** *adj* sano, saludable
heap [hiːp] *n* montón *m* ♦ *vt*: **to** ~ (**up**) amontonar; **to** ~ **sth with** llenar algo hasta arriba de; ~**s of** un montón de
hear [hɪə*] (*pt, pp* **heard**) *vt* (*also LAW*) oír; (*news*) saber ♦ *vi* oír; **to** ~ **about** oír hablar de; **to** ~ **from sb** tener noticias de uno; ~**ing** *n* (*sense*) oído; (*LAW*) vista; ~**ing aid** *n* audífono; ~**say** *n* rumores *mpl*, hablillas *fpl*
hearse [həːs] *n* coche *m* fúnebre
heart [hɑːt] *n* corazón *m*; (*fig*) valor *m*; (*of lettuce*) cogollo; ~**s** *npl* (*CARDS*) corazones *mpl*; **to lose/take** ~ descorazonarse/cobrar ánimo; **at** ~ en el fondo; **by** ~ (*learn, know*) de memoria; ~ **attack** *n* infarto (de miocardio); ~**beat** *n* latido (del corazón); ~**breaking** *adj* desgarrador(a); ~**broken** *adj*: **she was** ~**broken about it** esto le partió el corazón; ~**burn** *n* acedía; ~ **failure** *n* fallo cardíaco; ~**felt** *adj* (*deeply felt*) más sentido
hearth [hɑːθ] *n* (*fireplace*) chimenea
hearty ['hɑːtɪ] *adj* (*person*) campechano; (*laugh*) sano; (*dislike, support*) absoluto
heat [hiːt] *n* calor *m*; (*SPORT: also*: **qualifying** ~) prueba eliminatoria ♦ *vt* calentar; ~ **up** *vi* calentarse ♦ *vt* calentar; ~**ed** *adj* caliente; (*fig*) acalorado; ~**er** *n* estufa; (*in car*) calefacción *f*
heath [hiːθ] (*BRIT*) *n* brezal *m*
heather ['hɛðə*] *n* brezo
heating ['hiːtɪŋ] *n* calefacción *f*
heatstroke ['hiːtstrəuk] *n* insolación *f*
heatwave ['hiːtweɪv] *n* ola de calor
heave [hiːv] *vt* (*pull*) tirar; (*push*) empujar con esfuerzo; (*lift*) levantar (con esfuerzo) ♦ *vi* (*chest*) palpitar; (*retch*) tener náuseas ♦ *n* tirón *m*; empujón *m*; **to** ~ **a sigh**

suspirar

heaven ['hɛvn] *n* cielo; (*fig*) una maravilla; **~ly** *adj* celestial; (*fig*) maravilloso

heavily ['hɛvɪlɪ] *adv* pesadamente; (*drink, smoke*) con exceso; (*sleep, sigh*) profundamente; (*depend*) mucho

heavy ['hɛvɪ] *adj* pesado; (*work, blow*) duro; (*sea, rain, meal*) fuerte; (*drinker, smoker*) grande; (*responsibility*) grave; (*schedule*) ocupado; (*weather*) bochornoso; **~ goods vehicle** *n* vehículo pesado; **~weight** *n* (*SPORT*) peso pesado

Hebrew ['hi:bru:] *adj, n* (*LING*) hebreo

heckle ['hɛkl] *vt* interrumpir

hectic ['hɛktɪk] *adj* agitado

he'd [hi:d] = **he would**; **he had**

hedge [hɛdʒ] *n* seto ♦ *vi* contestar con evasivas; **to ~ one's bets** (*fig*) cubrirse

hedgehog ['hɛdʒhɔg] *n* erizo

heed [hi:d] *vt* (*also:* **take ~ of**) (*pay attention to*) hacer caso de; **~less** *adj:* **to be ~less (of)** no hacer caso (de)

heel [hi:l] *n* talón *m*; (*of shoe*) tacón *m* ♦ *vt* (*shoe*) poner tacón a

hefty ['hɛftɪ] *adj* (*person*) fornido; (*parcel, profit*) gordo

heifer ['hɛfə*] *n* novilla, ternera

height [haɪt] *n* (*of person*) estatura; (*of building*) altura; (*high ground*) cerro; (*altitude*) altitud *f*; (*fig: of season*): **at the ~ of summer** en los días más calurosos del verano; (*: of power etc*) cúspide *f*; (*: of stupidity etc*) colmo; **~en** *vt* elevar; (*fig*) aumentar

heir [ɛə*] *n* heredero; **~ess** *n* heredera; **~loom** *n* reliquia de familia

held [hɛld] *pt, pp of* **hold**

helicopter ['hɛlɪkɔptə*] *n* helicóptero

hell [hɛl] *n* infierno; **~!** (*inf*) ¡demonios!

he'll [hi:l] = **he will**; **he shall**

hello [hə'ləu] *excl* ¡hola!; (*to attract attention*) ¡oiga!; (*surprise*) ¡caramba!

helm [hɛlm] *n* (*NAUT*) timón *m*

helmet ['hɛlmɪt] *n* casco

help [hɛlp] *n* ayuda; (*cleaner etc*) criada, asistenta ♦ *vt* ayudar; **~!** ¡socorro!; **~**

yourself sírvete; **he can't ~ it** no es culpa suya; **~er** *n* ayudante *m/f*; **~ful** *adj* útil; (*person*) servicial; (*advice*) útil; **~ing** *n* ración *f*; **~less** *adj* (*incapable*) incapaz; (*defenceless*) indefenso

hem [hɛm] *n* dobladillo ♦ *vt* poner *or* coser el dobladillo; **~ in** *vt* cercar

hemorrhage ['hɛmərɪdʒ] (*US*) *n* = **haemorrhage**

hemorrhoids ['hɛmərɔɪdz] (*US*) *npl* = **haemorrhoids**

hen [hɛn] *n* gallina; (*female bird*) hembra

hence [hɛns] *adv* (*therefore*) por lo tanto; **2 years ~** de aquí a 2 años; **~forth** *adv* de hoy en adelante

hepatitis [hepə'taɪtɪs] *n* hepatitis *f*

her [hə:*] *pron* (*direct*) la; (*indirect*) le; (*stressed, after prep*) ella ♦ *adj* su; *see also* **me**; **my**

herald ['hɛrəld] *n* heraldo ♦ *vt* anunciar; **~ry** *n* heráldica

herb [hə:b] *n* hierba

herd [hə:d] *n* rebaño

here [hɪə*] *adv* aquí; (*at this point*) en este punto; **~!** (*present*) ¡presente!; **~ is/are** aquí está/están; **~ she is** aquí está; **~after** *adv* en el futuro; **~by** *adv* (*in letter*) por la presente

heritage ['hɛrɪtɪdʒ] *n* patrimonio

hermit ['hə:mɪt] *n* ermitaño/a

hernia ['hə:nɪə] *n* hernia

hero ['hɪərəu] (*pl* **~es**) *n* héroe *m*; (*in book, film*) protagonista *m*

heroin ['hɛrəuɪn] *n* heroína

heroine ['hɛrəuɪn] *n* heroína; (*in book, film*) protagonista

heron ['hɛrən] *n* garza

herring ['hɛrɪŋ] *n* arenque *m*

hers [hə:z] *pron* (el) suyo/(la) suya *etc*; *see also* **mine**[1]

herself [hə:'sɛlf] *pron* (*reflexive*) se; (*emphatic*) ella misma; (*after prep*) sí (misma); *see also* **oneself**

he's [hi:z] = **he is**; **he has**

hesitant ['hɛzɪtənt] *adj* vacilante

hesitate ['hɛzɪteɪt] *vi* vacilar; (*in speech*) titubear; (*be unwilling*) resistirse a;

hesitation [ˈheɪʃən] *n* indecisión *f*; titubeo; dudas *fpl*

heterosexual [hetərəʊˈseksjuəl] *adj* heterosexual

heyday [ˈheɪdeɪ] *n*: **the ~ of** el apogeo de

HGV *n abbr* = **heavy goods vehicle**

hi [haɪ] *excl* ¡hola!; (*to attract attention*) ¡oiga!

hiatus [haɪˈeɪtəs] *n* vacío

hibernate [ˈhaɪbəneɪt] *vi* invernar

hiccough [ˈhɪkʌp] = **hiccup**

hiccup [ˈhɪkʌp] *vi* hipar; **~s** *npl* hipo

hide [haɪd] (*pt* **hid**, *pp* **hidden**) *n* (*skin*) piel *f* ♦ *vt* esconder, ocultar ♦ *vi*: **to ~ (from sb)** esconderse *or* ocultarse (de uno); **~-and-seek** *n* escondite *m*

hideous [ˈhɪdɪəs] *adj* horrible

hiding [ˈhaɪdɪŋ] *n* (*beating*) paliza; **to be in ~** (*concealed*) estar escondido

hierarchy [ˈhaɪərɑːkɪ] *n* jerarquía

hi-fi [ˈhaɪfaɪ] *n* estéreo, hifi *m* ♦ *adj* de alta fidelidad

high [haɪ] *adj* alto; (*speed, number*) grande; (*price*) elevado; (*wind*) fuerte; (*voice*) agudo ♦ *adv* alto, a gran altura; **it is 20 m ~** tiene 20 m de alta *or* altura; **~ in the air** en las alturas; **~brow** *adj* intelectual; **~chair** *n* silla alta; **~er education** *n* educación *f or* enseñanza superior; **~-handed** *adj* despótico; **~-heeled** *adj* de tacón alto; **~ jump** *n* (*SPORT*) salto de altura; **the H~lands** *npl* las tierras altas de Escocia; **~light** *n* (*fig*: *of event*) punto culminante; (*in hair*) reflejo ♦ *vt* subrayar; **~ly** *adv* (*paid*) muy bien; (*critical, confidential*) sumamente; (*a lot*): **to speak/think ~ly of** hablar muy bien de/ tener en mucho a; **~ly strung** *adj* hipertenso; **~ness** *n* altura; **Her** *or* **His H~ness** Su Alteza; **~-pitched** *adj* agudo; **~-rise block** *n* torre *f* de pisos; **~ school** *n* ≈ Instituto Nacional de Bachillerato (*SP*); **~ season** *n* (*BRIT*) temporada alta; **~ street** *n* (*BRIT*) calle *f* mayor; **~way** *n* carretera, (*US*) carretera nacional; autopista; **H~way Code** (*BRIT*) *n* código de la circulación

hijack [ˈhaɪdʒæk] *vt* secuestrar; **~er** *n* secuestrador(a) *m/f*

hike [haɪk] *vi* (*go walking*) ir de excursión (a pie) ♦ *n* caminata; **~r** *n* excursionista *m/f*; **hiking** *n* senderismo

hilarious [hɪˈlɛərɪəs] *adj* divertidísimo

hill [hɪl] *n* colina; (*high*) montaña; (*slope*) cuesta; **~side** *n* ladera; **~ walking** *n* senderismo (de montaña); **~y** *adj* montañoso

hilt [hɪlt] *n* (*of sword*) empuñadura; **to the ~** (*fig*: *support*) incondicionalmente

him [hɪm] *pron* (*direct*) le, lo; (*indirect*) le; (*stressed, after prep*) él; *see also* **me**; **~self** *pron* (*reflexive*) se; (*emphatic*) él mismo; (*after prep*) sí (mismo); *see also* **oneself**

hinder [ˈhɪndə*] *vt* estorbar, impedir; **hindrance** [ˈhɪndrəns] *n* estorbo

hindsight [ˈhaɪndsaɪt] *n*: **with ~** en retrospectiva

Hindu [ˈhɪnduː] *n* hindú *m/f*

hinge [hɪndʒ] *n* bisagra, gozne *m* ♦ *vi* (*fig*): **to ~ on** depender de

hint [hɪnt] *n* indirecta; (*advice*) consejo; (*sign*) dejo ♦ *vt*: **to ~ that** insinuar que ♦ *vi*: **to ~ at** hacer alusión a

hip [hɪp] *n* cadera

hippopotamus [hɪpəˈpɒtəməs] (*pl* **~es** *or* **hippopotami**) *n* hipopótamo

hire [ˈhaɪə*] *vt* (*BRIT*: *car, equipment*) alquilar; (*worker*) contratar ♦ *n* alquiler *m*; **for ~** se alquila; (*taxi*) libre; **~(d) car** (*BRIT*) *n* coche *m* de alquiler; **~ purchase** (*BRIT*) *n* compra a plazos

his [hɪz] *pron* (el) suyo/(la) suya *etc* ♦ *adj* su; *see also* **mine**[1]; **my**

Hispanic [hɪsˈpænɪk] *adj* hispánico

hiss [hɪs] *vi* silbar

historian [hɪsˈtɔːrɪən] *n* historiador(a) *m/f*

historic(al) [hɪsˈtɒrɪk(l)] *adj* histórico

history [ˈhɪstərɪ] *n* historia

hit [hɪt] (*pt, pp* **hit**) *vt* (*strike*) golpear, pegar; (*reach*: *target*) alcanzar; (*collide with*: *car*) chocar contra; (*fig*: *affect*) afectar ♦ *n* golpe *m*; (*success*) éxito; **to ~ it off with sb** llevarse bien con uno; **~-**

and-run driver n conductor(a) que atropella y huye

hitch [hɪtʃ] vt (fasten) atar, amarrar; (also: ~ **up**) remangar ♦ n (difficulty) dificultad f; **to ~ a lift** hacer autostop

hitch-hike vi hacer autostop; **~hiking** n autostop m

hi-tech [haɪˈtɛk] adj de alta tecnología

hitherto [ˈhɪðəˈtuː] adv hasta ahora

HIV n abbr (= human immunodeficiency virus) VIH m; **~-negative/positive** adj VIH negativo/positivo

hive [haɪv] n colmena

HMS abbr = **His (Her) Majesty's Ship**

hoard [hɔːd] n (treasure) tesoro; (stockpile) provisión f ♦ vt acumular; (goods in short supply) acaparar; **~ing** n (for posters) cartelera

hoarse [hɔːs] adj ronco

hoax [həʊks] n trampa

hob [hɔb] n quemador m

hobble [ˈhɔbl] vi cojear

hobby [ˈhɔbɪ] n pasatiempo, afición f

hobo [ˈhəʊbəʊ] (US) n vagabundo

hockey [ˈhɔkɪ] n hockey m

hog [hɔg] n cerdo, puerco ♦ vt (fig) acaparar; **to go the whole ~** poner toda la carne en el asador

hoist [hɔɪst] n (crane) grúa ♦ vt levantar, alzar; (flag, sail) izar

hold [həʊld] (pt, pp **held**) vt sostener; (contain) contener; (have: power, qualification) tener; (keep back) retener; (believe) sostener; (consider) considerar; (keep in position) **to ~ one's head up** mantener la cabeza alta; (meeting) celebrar ♦ vi (withstand pressure) resistir ♦ n (grasp) asimiento; (fig) dominio; **~ the line!** (TEL) ¡no cuelgue!; **to ~ one's own** (fig) defenderse; **to catch or get (a) ~ of** agarrarse or asirse de; **~ back** vt retener; (secret) ocultar; **~ down** vt (person) sujetar; (job) mantener; **~ off** vt (enemy) rechazar; **~ on** vi agarrarse bien; (wait) esperar; **~ on!** (TEL) ¡(espere) un momento!; **~ on to** vt fus agarrarse a; (keep) guardar; **~ out** vt

ofrecer ♦ vi (resist) resistir; **~ up** vt (raise) levantar; (support) apoyar; (delay) retrasar; (rob) asaltar; **~all** (BRIT) n bolsa; **~er** n (container) receptáculo; (of ticket, record) poseedor(a) m/f; (of office, title etc) titular m/f; **~ing** n (share) interés m; (farmland) parcela; **~up** n (robbery) atraco; (delay) retraso; (BRIT: in traffic) embotellamiento

hole [həʊl] n agujero

holiday [ˈhɔlɪdɪ] n vacaciones fpl; (public ~) (día m de) fiesta, día m feriado; **on ~** de vacaciones; **~ camp** (BRIT: also: **~ centre**) centro de vacaciones; **~-maker** (BRIT) n turista m/f; **~ resort** n centro turístico

holiness [ˈhəʊlɪnɪs] n santidad f

Holland [ˈhɔlənd] n Holanda

hollow [ˈhɔləʊ] adj hueco; (claim) vacío; (eyes) hundido; (sound) sordo ♦ n hueco; (in ground) hoyo ♦ vt: **to ~ out** excavar

holly [ˈhɔlɪ] n acebo

holocaust [ˈhɔləkɔːst] n holocausto

holy [ˈhəʊlɪ] adj santo, sagrado; (water) bendito

homage [ˈhɔmɪdʒ] n homenaje m

home [həʊm] n casa; (country) patria; (institution) asilo ♦ cpd (domestic) casero, de casa; (ECON, POL) nacional ♦ adv (direction) a casa; (right in: nail etc) a fondo; **at ~** en casa; (in country) en su país; (fig) como pez en el agua; **to go/ come ~** ir/volver a casa; **make yourself at ~** ¡estás en tu casa!; **~ address** n domicilio; **~land** n tierra natal; **~less** adj sin hogar, sin casa; **~ly** adj (simple) sencillo; **~-made** adj casero; **H~ Office** (BRIT) n Ministerio del Interior; **~ rule** n autonomía; **H~ Secretary** (BRIT) n Ministro del Interior; **~sick** adj: **to be ~sick** tener morriña, sentir nostalgia; **~ town** n ciudad f natal; **~ward** [ˈhəʊmwəd] adj (journey) hacia casa; **~work** n deberes mpl

homoeopathic [həʊmɪəˈpæθɪk] (US **homeopathic**) adj homeopático

homosexual [hɔməʊˈsɛksjuəl] adj, n homosexual m/f

Honduran [hɔnˈdjuərən] *adj*, *n* hondureño/a *m/f*

Honduras [hɔnˈdjuərəs] *n* Honduras *f*

honest [ˈɔnɪst] *adj* honrado; (*sincere*) franco, sincero; **~ly** *adv* honradamente; francamente; **~y** *n* honradez *f*

honey [ˈhʌnɪ] *n* miel *f*; **~comb** *n* panal *m*; **~moon** *n* luna de miel; **~suckle** *n* madreselva

honk [hɔŋk] *vi* (*AUT*) tocar el pito, pitar

honorary [ˈɔnərəri] *adj* (*member, president*) de honor; (*title*) honorífico; **~ degree** doctorado honoris causa

honour [ˈɔnə*] (*US* **honor**) *vt* honrar; (*commitment, promise*) cumplir con ♦ *n* honor *m*, honra; **~able** *adj* honorable; **~s degree** *n* (*SCOL*) título de licenciado con calificación alta

hood [hud] *n* capucha; (*BRIT*: *AUT*) capota; (*US*: *AUT*) capó *m*; (*of cooker*) campana de humos

hoof [huːf] (*pl* **hooves**) *n* pezuña

hook [huk] *n* gancho; (*on dress*) corchete *m*, broche *m*; (*for fishing*) anzuelo ♦ *vt* enganchar; (*fish*) pescar

hooligan [ˈhuːlɪgən] *n* gamberro

hoop [huːp] *n* aro

hooray [huːˈreɪ] *excl* = **hurray**

hoot [huːt] (*BRIT*) *vi* (*AUT*) tocar el pito, pitar; (*siren*) sonar la sirena; (*owl*) ulular; **~er** (*BRIT*) *n* (*AUT*) pito, claxon *m* (*NAUT*) sirena

Hoover ® [ˈhuːvə*] (*BRIT*) *n* aspiradora ♦ *vt*: **h~** pasar la aspiradora por

hooves [huːvz] *npl of* **hoof**

hop [hɔp] *vi* saltar, brincar; (*on one foot*) saltar con un pie

hope [həup] *vt*, *vi* esperar ♦ *n* esperanza; **I ~ so/not** espero que sí/no; **~ful** *adj* (*person*) optimista; (*situation*) prometedor(a); **~fully** *adv* con esperanza; (*one hopes*): **~fully he will recover** esperamos que se recupere; **~less** *adj* desesperado; (*person*): **to be ~less** ser un desastre

hops [hɔps] *npl* lúpulo

horizon [həˈraɪzn] *n* horizonte *m*; **~tal** [hɔrɪˈzɔntl] *adj* horizontal

hormone [ˈhɔːməun] *n* hormona

horn [hɔːn] *n* cuerno; (*MUS*: *also*: **French ~**) trompa; (*AUT*) pito, claxon *m*

hornet [ˈhɔːnɪt] *n* avispón *m*

horoscope [ˈhɔrəskəup] *n* horóscopo

horrible [ˈhɔrɪbl] *adj* horrible

horrid [ˈhɔrɪd] *adj* horrible, horroroso

horrify [ˈhɔrɪfaɪ] *vt* horrorizar

horror [ˈhɔrə*] *n* horror *m*; **~ film** *n* película de horror

hors d'œuvre [ɔːˈdəːvrə] *n* entremeses *mpl*

horse [hɔːs] *n* caballo; **~back** *n*: **on ~back** a caballo; **~ chestnut** (*tree*) castaño de Indias; (*nut*) castaña de Indias; **~man/woman** (*irreg*) *n* jinete/a *m/f*; **~power** *n* caballo (de fuerza); **~-racing** *n* carreras *fpl* de caballos; **~radish** *n* rábano picante; **~shoe** *n* herradura

hose [həuz] *n* (*also*: **~pipe**) manguera

hospitable [hɔsˈpɪtəbl] *adj* hospitalario

hospital [ˈhɔspɪtl] *n* hospital *m*

hospitality [hɔspɪˈtælɪtɪ] *n* hospitalidad *f*

host [həust] *n* anfitrión *m*; (*TV, RADIO*) presentador *m*; (*REL*) hostia; (*large number*): **a ~ of** multitud de

hostage [ˈhɔstɪdʒ] *n* rehén *m*

hostel [ˈhɔstl] *n* hostal *m*; **(youth) ~** albergue *m* juvenil

hostess [ˈhəustɪs] *n* anfitriona; (*BRIT*: **air ~**) azafata; (*TV, RADIO*) presentadora

hostile [ˈhɔstaɪl] *adj* hostil

hot [hɔt] *adj* caliente; (*weather*) caluroso, de calor; (*as opposed to warm*) muy caliente; (*spicy*) picante; **to be ~** (*person*) tener calor; (*object*) estar caliente; (*weather*) hacer calor; **~bed** *n* (*fig*) semillero; **~ dog** *n* perro caliente

hotel [həuˈtel] *n* hotel *m*

hot: **~house** *n* invernadero; **~ line** *n* (*POL*) teléfono rojo; **~ly** *adv* con pasión, apasionadamente; **~-water bottle** *n* bolsa de agua caliente

hound [haund] *vt* acosar ♦ *n* perro (de caza)

hour [ˈauə*] *n* hora; **~ly** *adj* (de) cada hora

house [*n* haus, *pl* 'hauzɪz, *vb* hauz] *n* (*gen*, *firm*) casa; (*POL*) cámara; (*THEATRE*) sala ♦ *vt* (*person*) alojar; (*collection*) albergar; **on the ~** (*fig*) la casa invita; **~ arrest** *n* arresto domiciliario; **~boat** *n* casa flotante; **~bound** *adj* confinado en casa; **~breaking** *n* allanamiento de morada; **~hold** *n* familia; (*home*) casa; **~keeper** *n* ama de llaves; **~keeping** *n* (*work*) trabajos *mpl* domésticos; **~keeping (money)** *n* dinero para gastos domésticos; **~-warming party** *n* fiesta de estreno de una casa; **~wife** (*irreg*) *n* ama de casa; **~work** *n* faenas *fpl* (de la casa)

housing ['hauzɪŋ] *n* (*act*) alojamiento; (*houses*) viviendas *fpl*; **~ development** *n* urbanización *f*; **~ estate** (*BRIT*) *n* = **~ development**

hovel ['hɔvl] *n* casucha

hover ['hɔvə*] *vi* flotar (en el aire); **~craft** *n* aerodeslizador *m*

how [hau] *adv* (*in what way*) cómo; **~ are you?** ¿cómo estás?; **~ much milk/many people?** ¿cuánta leche/gente?; **~ much does it cost?** ¿cuánto cuesta?; **~ long have you been here?** ¿cuánto hace que estás aquí?; **~ old are you?** ¿cuántos años tienes?; **~ tall is he?** ¿cómo es de alto?; **~ is school?** ¿cómo (te) va (en) la escuela?; **~ was the film?** ¿qué tal la película?; **~ lovely/awful!** ¡qué bonito/horror!

however [hau'ɛvə*] *adv*: **~ I do it** lo haga como lo haga; **~ cold it is** por mucho frío que haga; **~ fast he runs** por muy rápido que corra; **~ did you do it?** ¿cómo lo hiciste? ♦ *conj* sin embargo, no obstante

howl [haul] *n* aullido ♦ *vi* aullar; (*person*) dar alaridos; (*wind*) ulular

H.P. *n abbr* = **hire purchase**

h.p. *abbr* = **horse power**

HQ *n abbr* = **headquarters**

hub [hʌb] *n* (*of wheel*) cubo; (*fig*) centro

hubcap ['hʌbkæp] *n* tapacubos *m inv*

huddle ['hʌdl] *vi*: **to ~ together** acurrucarse

hue [hju:] *n* color *m*, matiz *m*

huff [hʌf] *n*: **in a ~** enojado

hug [hʌg] *vt* abrazar; (*thing*) apretar con los brazos

huge [hju:dʒ] *adj* enorme

hull [hʌl] *n* (*of ship*) casco

hullo [hə'ləu] *excl* = **hello**

hum [hʌm] *vt* tararear, canturrear ♦ *vi* tararear, canturrear; (*insect*) zumbar

human ['hju:mən] *adj*, *n* humano; **~e** [hju:'meɪn] *adj* humano, humanitario; **~itarian** [hju:mænɪ'tɛərɪən] *adj* humanitario; **~ity** [hju:'mænɪtɪ] *n* humanidad *f*

humble ['hʌmbl] *adj* humilde

humdrum ['hʌmdrʌm] *adj* (*boring*) monótono, aburrido

humid ['hju:mɪd] *adj* húmedo

humiliate [hju:'mɪlɪeɪt] *vt* humillar

humorous ['hju:mərəs] *adj* gracioso, divertido

humour ['hju:mə*] (*US* **humor**) *n* humorismo, sentido del humor; (*mood*) humor *m* ♦ *vt* (*person*) complacer

hump [hʌmp] *n* (*in ground*) montículo; (*camel's*) giba

hunch [hʌntʃ] *n* (*premonition*) presentimiento; **~back** *n* joroba *m/f*; **~ed** *adj* jorobado

hundred ['hʌndrəd] *num* ciento; (*before n*) cien; **~s of** centenares de; **~weight** *n* (*BRIT*) = 50.8 kg; 112 lb; (*US*) = 45.3 kg; 100 lb

hung [hʌŋ] *pt*, *pp of* **hang**

Hungarian [hʌŋ'gɛərɪən] *adj*, *n* húngaro/a *m/f*

Hungary ['hʌŋgərɪ] *n* Hungría

hunger ['hʌŋgə*] *n* hambre *f* ♦ *vi*: **to ~ for** (*fig*) tener hambre de, anhelar; **~ strike** *n* huelga de hambre

hungry ['hʌŋgrɪ] *adj*: **~ (for)** hambriento (de); **to be ~** tener hambre

hunk [hʌŋk] *n* (*of bread etc*) trozo, pedazo

hunt [hʌnt] *vt* (*seek*) buscar; (*SPORT*) cazar ♦ *vi* (*search*): **to ~ (for)** buscar; (*SPORT*) cazar ♦ *n* búsqueda; caza, cacería; **~er** *n* cazador(a) *m/f*; **~ing** *n* caza

hurdle ['hɜːdl] *n* (*SPORT*) valla; (*fig*) obstáculo

hurl [hɜːl] *vt* lanzar, arrojar

hurrah [huˈrɑː] *excl* = **hurray**

hurray [huˈreɪ] *excl* ¡viva!

hurricane ['hʌrɪkən] *n* huracán *m*

hurried ['hʌrɪd] *adj* (*rushed*) hecho de prisa; **~ly** *adv* con prisa, apresuradamente

hurry ['hʌrɪ] *n* prisa ♦ *vi* (*also*: **~ up**) apresurarse, darse prisa ♦ *vt* (*also*: **~ up**: *person*) dar prisa a; (: *work*) apresurar, hacer de prisa; **to be in a ~** tener prisa

hurt [hɜːt] (*pt, pp* **hurt**) *vt* hacer daño a ♦ *vi* doler ♦ *adj* lastimado; **~ful** *adj* (*remark etc*) hiriente

hurtle ['hɜːtl] *vi*: **to ~ past** pasar como un rayo; **to ~ down** ir a toda velocidad

husband ['hʌzbənd] *n* marido

hush [hʌʃ] *n* silencio ♦ *vt* hacer callar; **~!** ¡chitón!, ¡cállate!; **~ up** *vt* encubrir

husk [hʌsk] *n* (*of wheat*) cáscara

husky ['hʌskɪ] *adj* ronco ♦ *n* perro esquimal

hustle ['hʌsl] *vt* (*hurry*) dar prisa a ♦ *n*: **~ and bustle** ajetreo

hut [hʌt] *n* cabaña; (*shed*) cobertizo

hutch [hʌtʃ] *n* conejera

hyacinth ['haɪəsɪnθ] *n* jacinto

hydrant ['haɪdrənt] *n* (*also*: **fire ~**) boca de incendios

hydraulic [haɪˈdrɔːlɪk] *adj* hidráulico

hydroelectric [haɪdrəʊˈlektrɪk] *adj* hidroeléctrico

hydrofoil ['haɪdrəfɔɪl] *n* aerodeslizador *m*

hydrogen ['haɪdrədʒən] *n* hidrógeno

hygiene ['haɪdʒiːn] *n* higiene *f*; **hygienic** [-ˈdʒiːnɪk] *adj* higiénico

hymn [hɪm] *n* himno

hype [haɪp] (*inf*) *n* bombardeo publicitario

hypermarket ['haɪpəmɑːkɪt] *n* hipermercado

hyphen ['haɪfn] *n* guión *m*

hypnotize ['hɪpnətaɪz] *vt* hipnotizar

hypocrisy [hɪˈpɒkrɪsɪ] *n* hipocresía; **hypocrite** ['hɪpəkrɪt] *n* hipócrita *m/f*; **hypocritical** [hɪpəˈkrɪtɪkl] *adj* hipócrita

hypothesis [haɪˈpɒθɪsɪs] (*pl* **hypotheses**) *n* hipótesis *f inv*

hysteria [hɪˈstɪərɪə] *n* histeria; **hysterical** [-ˈsterɪkl] *adj* histérico; (*funny*) para morirse de risa; **hysterics** [-ˈsterɪks] *npl* histeria; **to be in hysterics** (*fig*) morirse de risa

I, i

I [aɪ] *pron* yo

ice [aɪs] *n* hielo; (*~ cream*) helado ♦ *vt* (*cake*) alcorzar ♦ *vi* (*also*: **~ over, ~ up**) helarse; **~berg** *n* iceberg *m*; **~box** *n* (*BRIT*) congelador *m*; (*US*) nevera (*SP*), refrigeradora (*AM*); **~ cream** *n* helado; **~ cube** *n* cubito de hielo; **~d** *adj* (*cake*) escarchado; (*drink*) helado; **~ hockey** *n* hockey *m* sobre hielo

Iceland ['aɪslənd] *n* Islandia

ice: **~ lolly** (*BRIT*) *n* polo; **~ rink** *n* pista de hielo; **~ skating** *n* patinaje *m* sobre hielo

icicle ['aɪsɪkl] *n* carámbano

icing ['aɪsɪŋ] *n* (*CULIN*) alcorza; **~ sugar** (*BRIT*) *n* azúcar *m* glas(eado)

icy ['aɪsɪ] *adj* helado

I'd [aɪd] = **I would**; **I had**

idea [aɪˈdɪə] *n* idea

ideal [aɪˈdɪəl] *n* ideal *m* ♦ *adj* ideal

identical [aɪˈdentɪkl] *adj* idéntico

identification [aɪdentɪfɪˈkeɪʃən] *n* identificación *f*; **(means of) ~** documentos *mpl* personales

identify [aɪˈdentɪfaɪ] *vt* identificar

Identikit ® [aɪˈdentɪkɪt] *n*: **~ (picture)** retrato-robot *m*

identity [aɪˈdentɪtɪ] *n* identidad *f*; **~ card** *n* carnet *m* de identidad

ideology [aɪdɪˈɒlədʒɪ] *n* ideología

idiom ['ɪdɪəm] *n* modismo; (*style of speaking*) lenguaje *m*

idiosyncrasy [ɪdɪəʊˈsɪŋkrəsɪ] *n* idiosincrasia

idiot ['ɪdɪət] *n* idiota *m/f*; **~ic** [-ˈɒtɪk] *adj* tonto

idle ['aɪdl] *adj* (*inactive*) ocioso; (*lazy*) holgazán/ana; (*unemployed*) parado, desocupado; (*machinery etc*) parado; (*talk etc*) frívolo ♦ *vi* (*machine*) marchar en vacío

idol ['aɪdl] *n* ídolo; **~ize** *vt* idolatrar

i.e. *abbr* (= *that is*) esto es

if [ɪf] *conj* si; **~ necessary** si fuera necesario, si hiciese falta; **~ I were you** yo en tu lugar; **~ so/not** de ser así/si no; **~ only I could!** ¡ojalá pudiera!; *see also* **as**; **even**

igloo ['ɪgluː] *n* iglú *m*

ignite [ɪg'naɪt] *vt* (*set fire to*) encender ♦ *vi* encenderse

ignition [ɪg'nɪʃən] *n* (AUT: *process*) ignición *f*; (: *mechanism*) encendido; **to switch on/off the ~** arrancar/apagar el motor; **~ key** *n* (AUT) llave *f* de contacto

ignorant ['ɪgnərənt] *adj* ignorante; **to be ~ of** ignorar

ignore [ɪg'nɔː*] *vt* (*person, advice*) no hacer caso de; (*fact*) pasar por alto

I'll [aɪl] = **I will; I shall**

ill [ɪl] *adj* enfermo, malo ♦ *n* mal *m* ♦ *adv* mal; **to be taken ~** ponerse enfermo; **~-advised** *adj* (*decision*) imprudente; **~-at-ease** *adj* incómodo

illegal [ɪ'liːgl] *adj* ilegal

illegible [ɪ'ledʒɪbl] *adj* ilegible

illegitimate [ɪlɪ'dʒɪtɪmət] *adj* ilegítimo

ill-fated *adj* malogrado

ill feeling *n* rencor *m*

illicit [ɪ'lɪsɪt] *adj* ilícito

illiterate [ɪ'lɪtərət] *adj* analfabeto

ill: ~-mannered *adj* mal educado; **~ness** *n* enfermedad *f*; **~-treat** *vt* maltratar

illuminate [ɪ'luːmɪneɪt] *vt* (*room, street*) iluminar, alumbrar; **illumination** [-'neɪʃən] *n* alumbrado; **illuminations** *npl* (*decorative lights*) iluminaciones *fpl*, luces *fpl*

illusion [ɪ'luːʒən] *n* ilusión *f*; (*trick*) truco

illustrate ['ɪləstreɪt] *vt* ilustrar

illustration [ɪlə'streɪʃən] *n* (*act of illustrating*) ilustración *f*; (*example*) ejemplo, ilustración *f*; (*in book*) lámina

illustrious [ɪ'lʌstrɪəs] *adj* ilustre

I'm [aɪm] = **I am**

image ['ɪmɪdʒ] *n* imagen *f*; **~ry** [-ərɪ] *n* imágenes *fpl*

imaginary [ɪ'mædʒɪnərɪ] *adj* imaginario

imagination [ɪmædʒɪ'neɪʃən] *n* imaginación *f*; (*inventiveness*) inventiva

imaginative [ɪ'mædʒɪnətɪv] *adj* imaginativo

imagine [ɪ'mædʒɪn] *vt* imaginarse

imbalance [ɪm'bæləns] *n* desequilibrio

imitate ['ɪmɪteɪt] *vt* imitar; **imitation** [ɪmɪ'teɪʃən] *n* imitación *f*; (*copy*) copia

immaculate [ɪ'mækjulət] *adj* inmaculado

immaterial [ɪmə'tɪərɪəl] *adj* (*unimportant*) sin importancia

immature [ɪmə'tjuə*] *adj* (*person*) inmaduro

immediate [ɪ'miːdɪət] *adj* inmediato; (*pressing*) urgente, apremiante; (*nearest: family*) próximo; (: *neighbourhood*) inmediato; **~ly** *adv* (*at once*) en seguida; (*directly*) inmediatamente; **~ly next to** muy junto a

immense [ɪ'mɛns] *adj* inmenso, enorme; (*importance*) enorme

immerse [ɪ'məːs] *vt* (*submerge*) sumergir; **to be ~d in** (*fig*) estar absorto en

immersion heater [ɪ'məːʃən-] (BRIT) *n* calentador *m* de inmersión

immigrant ['ɪmɪgrənt] *n* inmigrante *m/f*; **immigration** [ɪmɪ'greɪʃən] *n* inmigración *f*

imminent ['ɪmɪnənt] *adj* inminente

immobile [ɪ'məubaɪl] *adj* inmóvil

immoral [ɪ'mɔrl] *adj* inmoral

immortal [ɪ'mɔːtl] *adj* inmortal

immune [ɪ'mjuːn] *adj*: **~ (to)** inmune (a); **immunity** *n* (MED, *of diplomat*) inmunidad *f*

immunize ['ɪmjunaɪz] *vt* inmunizar

impact ['ɪmpækt] *n* impacto

impair [ɪm'pɛə*] *vt* perjudicar

impart [ɪm'pɑːt] *vt* comunicar; (*flavour*) proporcionar

impartial [ɪm'pɑːʃl] *adj* imparcial

impassable [ɪm'pɑːsəbl] *adj* (*barrier*) infranqueable; (*river, road*) intransitable

impassive [ɪmˈpæsɪv] *adj* impasible

impatience [ɪmˈpeɪʃəns] *n* impaciencia

impatient [ɪmˈpeɪʃənt] *adj* impaciente; **to get** *or* **grow ~** impacientarse

impeccable [ɪmˈpekəbl] *adj* impecable

impede [ɪmˈpiːd] *vt* estorbar

impediment [ɪmˈpedɪmənt] *n* obstáculo, estorbo; (*also*: **speech ~**) defecto (del habla)

impending [ɪmˈpendɪŋ] *adj* inminente

imperative [ɪmˈperətɪv] *adj* (*tone*) imperioso; (*need*) imprescindible

imperfect [ɪmˈpɜːfɪkt] *adj* (*goods etc*) defectuoso ♦ *n* (*LING*: *also*: **~ tense**) imperfecto

imperial [ɪmˈpɪərɪəl] *adj* imperial

impersonal [ɪmˈpɜːsənl] *adj* impersonal

impersonate [ɪmˈpɜːsəneɪt] *vt* hacerse pasar por; (*THEATRE*) imitar

impertinent [ɪmˈpɜːtɪnənt] *adj* impertinente, insolente

impervious [ɪmˈpɜːvɪəs] *adj* impermeable; (*fig*): **~ to** insensible a

impetuous [ɪmˈpetjuəs] *adj* impetuoso

impetus [ˈɪmpətəs] *n* ímpetu *m*; (*fig*) impulso

impinge [ɪmˈpɪndʒ]: **to ~ on** *vt fus* (*affect*) afectar a

implement [*n* ˈɪmplɪmənt, *vb* ˈɪmplɪment] *n* herramienta; (*for cooking*) utensilio ♦ *vt* (*regulation*) hacer efectivo; (*plan*) realizar

implicit [ɪmˈplɪsɪt] *adj* implícito; (*belief, trust*) absoluto

imply [ɪmˈplaɪ] *vt* (*involve*) suponer; (*hint*) dar a entender que

impolite [ɪmpəˈlaɪt] *adj* mal educado

import [*vb* ɪmˈpɔːt, *n* ˈɪmpɔːt] *vt* importar ♦ *n* (*COMM*) importación *f*; (: *article*) producto importado; (*meaning*) significado, sentido

importance [ɪmˈpɔːtəns] *n* importancia

important [ɪmˈpɔːtənt] *adj* importante; **it's not ~** no importa, no tiene importancia

importer [ɪmˈpɔːtə*] *n* importador(a) *m/f*

impose [ɪmˈpəʊz] *vt* imponer ♦ *vi*: **to ~ on sb** abusar de uno; **imposing** *adj* imponente, impresionante

imposition [ɪmpəˈzɪʃn] *n* (*of tax etc*) imposición *f*; **to be an ~ on** (*person*) molestar a

impossible [ɪmˈpɒsɪbl] *adj* imposible; (*person*) insoportable

impotent [ˈɪmpətənt] *adj* impotente

impound [ɪmˈpaund] *vt* embargar

impoverished [ɪmˈpɒvərɪʃt] *adj* necesitado

impractical [ɪmˈpræktɪkl] *adj* (*person, plan*) poco práctico

imprecise [ɪmprɪˈsaɪs] *adj* impreciso

impregnable [ɪmˈpregnəbl] *adj* (*castle*) inexpugnable

impress [ɪmˈpres] *vt* impresionar; (*mark*) estampar; **to ~ sth on sb** hacer entender algo a uno

impression [ɪmˈpreʃən] *n* impresión *f*; (*imitation*) imitación *f*; **to be under the ~ that** tener la impresión de que; **~ist** *n* impresionista *m/f*

impressive [ɪmˈpresɪv] *adj* impresionante

imprint [ˈɪmprɪnt] *n* (*outline*) huella; (*PUBLISHING*) pie *m* de imprenta

imprison [ɪmˈprɪzn] *vt* encarcelar; **~ment** *n* encarcelamiento; (*term of ~ment*) cárcel *f*

improbable [ɪmˈprɒbəbl] *adj* improbable, inverosímil

improper [ɪmˈprɒpə*] *adj* (*unsuitable*: *conduct etc*) incorrecto; (: *activities*) deshonesto

improve [ɪmˈpruːv] *vt* mejorar; (*foreign language*) perfeccionar ♦ *vi* mejorarse; **~ment** *n* mejoramiento; perfección *f*; progreso

improvise [ˈɪmprəvaɪz] *vt, vi* improvisar

impulse [ˈɪmpʌls] *n* impulso; **to act on ~** obrar sin reflexión; **impulsive** [-ˈpʌlsɪv] *adj* irreflexivo

impure [ɪmˈpjuə*] *adj* (*adulterated*) adulterado; (*morally*) impuro; **impurity** *n* impureza

KEYWORD

in [ɪn] *prep* **1** (*indicating place, position, with place names*) en; **~ the house/garden** en (la) casa/el jardín; **~ here/there** aquí/ahí or allí dentro; **~ London/England** en Londres/Inglaterra

2 (*indicating time*) en; **~ spring** en (la) primavera; **~ the afternoon** por la tarde; **at 4 o'clock ~ the afternoon** a las 4 de la tarde; **I did it ~ 3 hours/days** lo hice en 3 horas/días; **I'll see you ~ 2 weeks** *or* **~ 2 weeks' time** te veré dentro de 2 semanas

3 (*indicating manner etc*) en; **~ a loud/soft voice** en voz alta/baja; **~ pencil/ink** a lápiz/bolígrafo; **the boy ~ the blue shirt** el chico de la camisa azul

4 (*indicating circumstances*): **~ the sun/shade/rain** al sol/a la sombra/bajo la lluvia; **a change ~ policy** un cambio de política

5 (*indicating mood, state*): **~ tears** en lágrimas, llorando; **~ anger/despair** enfadado/desesperado; **to live ~ luxury** vivir lujosamente

6 (*with ratios, numbers*): **1 ~ 10 households, 1 household ~ 10** una de cada 10 familias; **20 pence ~ the pound** 20 peniques por libra; **they lined up ~ twos** se alinearon de dos en dos

7 (*referring to people, works*) en; entre; **the disease is common ~ children** la enfermedad es común entre los niños; **~ (the works of) Dickens** en (las obras de) Dickens

8 (*indicating profession etc*): **to be ~ teaching** estar en la enseñanza

9 (*after superlative*) de; **the best pupil ~ the class** el/la mejor alumno/a de la clase

10 (*with present participle*): **~ saying this** al decir esto

♦ *adv*: **to be ~** (*person: at home*) estar en casa; (*work*) estar; (*train, ship, plane*) haber llegado; (*in fashion*) estar de moda; **she'll be ~ later today** llegará más tarde hoy; **to ask sb ~** hacer pasar a uno; **to run/limp** *etc* **~** entrar corriendo/cojeando *etc*

♦ *n*: **the ~s and outs** (*of proposal,*

situation etc) los detalles

---

in. *abbr* = **inch**
inability [ɪnə'bɪlɪtɪ] *n*: **~ (to do)** incapacidad *f* (de hacer)
inaccurate [ɪn'ækjurət] *adj* inexacto, incorrecto
inadequate [ɪn'ædɪkwət] *adj* (*income, reply etc*) insuficiente; (*person*) incapaz
inadvertently [ɪnəd'vɜːtntlɪ] *adv* por descuido
inadvisable [ɪnəd'vaɪzəbl] *adj* poco aconsejable
inane [ɪ'neɪn] *adj* necio, fatuo
inanimate [ɪn'ænɪmət] *adj* inanimado
inappropriate [ɪnə'prəuprɪət] *adj* inadecuado; (*improper*) poco oportuno
inarticulate [ɪnɑː'tɪkjulət] *adj* (*person*) incapaz de expresarse; (*speech*) mal pronunciado
inasmuch as [ɪnəz'mʌtʃ-] *conj* puesto que, ya que
inauguration [ɪnɔːgju'reɪʃən] *n* ceremonia de apertura
inborn [ɪn'bɔːn] *adj* (*quality*) innato
inbred [ɪn'bred] *adj* innato; (*family*) engendrado por endogamia
Inc. *abbr* (*US:* = *incorporated*) S.A.
incapable [ɪn'keɪpəbl] *adj* incapaz
incapacitate [ɪnkə'pæsɪteɪt] *vt*: **to ~ sb** incapacitar a uno
incense [*n* 'ɪnsɛns, *vb* ɪn'sɛns] *n* incienso
♦ *vt* (*anger*) indignar, encolerizar
incentive [ɪn'sɛntɪv] *n* incentivo, estímulo
incessant [ɪn'sɛsnt] *adj* incesante, continuo; **~ly** *adv* constantemente
incest ['ɪnsɛst] *n* incesto
inch [ɪntʃ] *n* pulgada; **to be within an ~ of** estar a dos dedos de; **he didn't give an ~** no dio concesión alguna
incident ['ɪnsɪdnt] *n* incidente *m*
incidental [ɪnsɪ'dɛntl] *adj* accesorio; **~ to** relacionado con; **~ly** [-'dɛntəlɪ] *adv* (*by the way*) a propósito
incite [ɪn'saɪt] *vt* provocar
inclination [ɪnklɪ'neɪʃən] *n* (*tendency*) tendencia, inclinación *f*; (*desire*) deseo;

(*disposition*) propensión *f*

incline [*n* 'ınklaın, *vb* ın'klaın] *n* pendiente *m*, cuesta ♦ *vt* (*head*) poner de lado ♦ *vi* inclinarse; **to be ~d to** (*tend*) ser propenso a

include [ın'kluːd] *vt* (*incorporate*) incluir; (*in letter*) adjuntar; **including** *prep* incluso, inclusive

inclusion [ın'kluːʒən] *n* inclusión *f*

inclusive [ın'kluːsıv] *adj* inclusivo; **~ of tax** incluidos los impuestos

income ['ınkʌm] *n* (*earned*) ingresos *mpl*; (*from property etc*) renta; (*from investment etc*) rédito; **~ tax** *n* impuesto sobre la renta

incoming ['ınkʌmıŋ] *adj* (*flight, government etc*) entrante

incomparable [ın'kɔmpərəbl] *adj* incomparable, sin par

incompatible [ınkəm'pætıbl] *adj* incompatible

incompetent [ın'kɔmpıtənt] *adj* incompetente

incomplete [ınkəm'pliːt] *adj* (*partial: achievement etc*) incompleto; (*unfinished: painting etc*) inacabado

incongruous [ın'kɔŋgruəs] *adj* (*strange*) discordante; (*inappropriate*) incongruente

inconsiderate [ınkən'sıdərət] *adj* desconsiderado

inconsistent [ınkən'sıstənt] *adj* inconsecuente; (*contradictory*) incongruente; **~ with** (que) no concuerda con

inconspicuous [ınkən'spıkjuəs] *adj* (*colour, building etc*) discreto; (*person*) que llama poco la atención

inconvenience [ınkən'viːnjəns] *n* inconvenientes *mpl*; (*trouble*) molestia, incomodidad *f* ♦ *vt* incomodar

inconvenient [ınkən'viːnjənt] *adj* incómodo, poco práctico; (*time, place, visitor*) inoportuno

incorporate [ın'kɔːpəreıt] *vt* incorporar; (*contain*) comprender; (*add*) agregar; **~d** *adj*: **~d company** (*US*) ≈ sociedad *f* anónima

incorrect [ınkə'rɛkt] *adj* incorrecto

increase [*n* 'ınkriːs, *vb* ın'kriːs] *n* aumento ♦ *vi* aumentar; (*grow*) crecer; (*price*) subir ♦ *vt* aumentar; (*price*) subir; **increasing** *adj* creciente; **increasingly** *adv* cada vez más, más y más

incredible [ın'krɛdıbl] *adj* increíble

incubator ['ınkjubeıtə*] *n* incubadora

incumbent [ın'kʌmbənt] *adj*: **it is ~ on him to ...** le incumbe ...

incur [ın'kəː*] *vt* (*expenditure*) incurrir; (*loss*) sufrir; (*anger, disapproval*) provocar

indebted [ın'dɛtıd] *adj*: **to be ~ to sb** estar agradecido a uno

indecent [ın'diːsnt] *adj* indecente; **~ assault** (*BRIT*) *n* atentado contra el pudor; **~ exposure** *n* exhibicionismo

indecisive [ındı'saısıv] *adj* indeciso

indeed [ın'diːd] *adv* efectivamente, en realidad; (*in fact*) en efecto; (*furthermore*) es más; **yes ~!** ¡claro que sí!

indefinitely [ın'dɛfınıtlı] *adv* (*wait*) indefinidamente

indemnity [ın'dɛmnıtı] *n* (*insurance*) indemnidad *f*; (*compensation*) indemnización *f*

independence [ındı'pɛndns] *n* independencia

Independence Day
---

*ⓘ El cuatro de julio es **Independence Day**, la fiesta nacional de Estados Unidos, que se celebra en conmemoración de la Declaración de Independencia, escrita por Thomas Jefferson y aprobada en 1776. En ella se proclamaba la independencia total de Gran Bretaña de las trece colonias americanas que serían el origen de los Estados Unidos de América.*

---

independent [ındı'pɛndənt] *adj* independiente

index ['ındɛks] (*pl* **~es**) *n* (*in book*) índice *m*; (: *in library etc*) catálogo; (*pl* **indices**: *ratio, sign*) exponente *m*; **~ card** *n* ficha; **~ed** (*US*) *adj* = **~-linked**; **~ finger** *n* índice *m*; **~-linked** (*BRIT*) *adj* vinculado al índice del coste de la vida

India ['ɪndɪə] *n* la India; **~n** *adj, n* indio/a *m/f*; **Red ~n** piel roja *m/f*; **~n Ocean** *n*: **the ~n Ocean** el Océano Índico

indicate ['ɪndɪkeɪt] *vt* indicar; **indication** [-'keɪʃən] *n* indicio, señal *f*; **indicative** [ɪn'dɪkətɪv] *adj*: **to be indicative of** indicar; **indicator** *n* indicador *m*; (*AUT*) intermitente *m*

indices ['ɪndɪsiːz] *npl of* **index**

indictment [ɪn'daɪtmənt] *n* acusación *f*

indifferent [ɪn'dɪfrənt] *adj* indiferente; (*mediocre*) regular

indigenous [ɪn'dɪdʒɪnəs] *adj* indígena

indigestion [ɪndɪ'dʒestʃən] *n* indigestión *f*

indignant [ɪn'dɪgnənt] *adj*: **to be ~ at sth/with sb** indignarse por algo/con uno

indigo ['ɪndɪgəʊ] *adj* de color añil ♦ *n* añil *m*

indirect [ɪndɪ'rɛkt] *adj* indirecto

indiscreet [ɪndɪ'skriːt] *adj* indiscreto, imprudente

indiscriminate [ɪndɪ'skrɪmɪnət] *adj* indiscriminado

indisputable [ɪndɪ'spjuːtəbl] *adj* incontestable

indistinct [ɪndɪ'stɪŋkt] *adj* (*noise, memory etc*) confuso

individual [ɪndɪ'vɪdjuəl] *n* individuo ♦ *adj* individual; (*personal*) personal; (*particular*) particular; **~ly** *adv* (*singly*) individualmente

indoctrinate [ɪn'dɒktrɪneɪt] *vt* adoctrinar

indoor ['ɪndɔː*] *adj* (*swimming pool*) cubierto; (*plant*) de interior; (*sport*) bajo cubierta; **~s** [ɪn'dɔːz] *adv* dentro

induce [ɪn'djuːs] *vt* inducir, persuadir; (*bring about*) producir; (*birth*) provocar; **~ment** *n* (*incentive*) incentivo; (*pej: bribe*) soborno

indulge [ɪn'dʌldʒ] *vt* (*whim*) satisfacer; (*person*) complacer; (*child*) mimar ♦ *vi*: **to ~ in** darse el gusto de; **~nce** *n* vicio; (*leniency*) indulgencia; **~nt** *adj* indulgente

industrial [ɪn'dʌstrɪəl] *adj* industrial; **~ action** *n* huelga; **~ estate** (*BRIT*) *n* polígono (*SP*) *or* zona (*AM*) industrial; **~ist**

n industrial *m/f*; **~ize** *vt* industrializar; **~ park** (*US*) *n* = **~ estate**

industrious [ɪn'dʌstrɪəs] *adj* trabajador(a); (*student*) aplicado

industry ['ɪndəstrɪ] *n* industria; (*diligence*) aplicación *f*

inebriated [ɪ'niːbrɪeɪtɪd] *adj* borracho

inedible [ɪn'ɛdɪbl] *adj* incomible; (*poisonous*) no comestible

ineffective [ɪnɪ'fɛktɪv] *adj* ineficaz, inútil

ineffectual [ɪnɪ'fɛktjuəl] *adj* = **ineffective**

inefficient [ɪnɪ'fɪʃənt] *adj* ineficaz, ineficiente

inept [ɪ'nɛpt] *adj* incompetente

inequality [ɪnɪ'kwɒlɪtɪ] *n* desigualdad *f*

inert [ɪ'nɜːt] *adj* inerte, inactivo; (*immobile*) inmóvil

inescapable [ɪnɪ'skeɪpəbl] *adj* ineludible

inevitable [ɪn'ɛvɪtəbl] *adj* inevitable; **inevitably** *adv* inevitablemente

inexcusable [ɪnɪks'kjuːzəbl] *adj* imperdonable

inexpensive [ɪnɪk'spɛnsɪv] *adj* económico

inexperienced [ɪnɪk'spɪərɪənst] *adj* inexperto

infallible [ɪn'fælɪbl] *adj* infalible

infamous ['ɪnfəməs] *adj* infame

infancy ['ɪnfənsɪ] *n* infancia

infant ['ɪnfənt] *n* niño/a; (*baby*) niño pequeño, bebé *m*; (*pej*) aniñado

infantry ['ɪnfəntrɪ] *n* infantería

infant school (*BRIT*) *n* parvulario

infatuated [ɪn'fætjueɪtɪd] *adj*: **~ with** (*in love*) loco por

infatuation [ɪnfætju'eɪʃən] *n* enamoramiento, pasión *f*

infect [ɪn'fɛkt] *vt* (*wound*) infectar; (*food*) contaminar; (*person, animal*) contagiar; **~ion** [ɪn'fɛkʃən] *n* infección *f*; (*fig*) contagio; **~ious** [ɪn'fɛkʃəs] *adj* (*also fig*) contagioso

infer [ɪn'fɜː*] *vt* deducir, inferir

inferior [ɪn'fɪərɪə*] *adj, n* inferior *m/f*; **~ity** [-rɪ'ɔrətɪ] *n* inferioridad *f*

infertile [ɪn'fɜːtaɪl] *adj* estéril; (*person*) infecundo

infested [ɪn'fɛstɪd] *adj*: **~ with** plagado de

in-fighting *n* (fig) lucha(s) *f(pl)* interna(s)

infinite ['ɪnfɪnɪt] *adj* infinito

infinitive [ɪn'fɪnɪtɪv] *n* infinitivo

infinity [ɪn'fɪnɪtɪ] *n* infinito; (*an ~*) infinidad *f*

infirmary [ɪn'fə:mərɪ] *n* hospital *m*

inflamed [ɪn'fleɪmd] *adj*: **to become ~** inflamarse

inflammable [ɪn'flæməbl] *adj* inflamable

inflammation [ɪnflə'meɪʃən] *n* inflamación *f*

inflatable [ɪn'fleɪtəbl] *adj* (*ball, boat*) inflable

inflate [ɪn'fleɪt] *vt* (*tyre, price etc*) inflar; (*fig*) hinchar; **inflation** [ɪn'fleɪʃən] *n* (*ECON*) inflación *f*

inflexible [ɪn'fleksəbl] *adj* (*rule*) rígido; (*person*) inflexible

inflict [ɪn'flɪkt] *vt*: **to ~ sth on sb** infligir algo en uno

influence ['ɪnfluəns] *n* influencia ♦ *vt* influir en, influenciar; **under the ~ of alcohol** en estado de embriaguez; **influential** [-'enfl] *adj* influyente

influenza [ɪnflu'enzə] *n* gripe *f*

influx ['ɪnflʌks] *n* afluencia

inform [ɪn'fɔ:m] *vt*: **to ~ sb of sth** informar a uno sobre *or* de algo ♦ *vi*: **to ~ on sb** delatar a uno

informal [ɪn'fɔ:məl] *adj* (*manner, tone*) familiar; (*dress, interview, occasion*) informal; (*visit, meeting*) extraoficial; **~ity** [-'mælɪtɪ] *n* informalidad *f*; sencillez *f*

informant [ɪn'fɔ:mənt] *n* informante *m/f*

information [ɪnfə'meɪʃən] *n* información *f*; (*knowledge*) conocimientos *mpl*; **a piece of ~** un dato; **~ desk** *n* (mostrador *m* de) información *f*; **~ office** *n* información *f*

informative [ɪn'fɔ:mətɪv] *adj* informativo

informer [ɪn'fɔ:mə*] *n* (*also*: **police ~**) soplón/ona *m/f*

infra-red [ɪnfrə'red] *adj* infrarrojo

infrastructure ['ɪnfrəstrʌktʃə*] *n* (*of system etc*) infraestructura

infringe [ɪn'frɪndʒ] *vt* infringir, violar ♦ *vi*: **to ~ on** abusar de; **~ment** *n* infracción *f*; (*of rights*) usurpación *f*

infuriating [ɪn'fjuərɪeɪtɪŋ] *adj* (*habit, noise*) enloquecedor(a)

ingenious [ɪn'dʒi:njəs] *adj* ingenioso; **ingenuity** [-dʒɪ'nju:ɪtɪ] *n* ingeniosidad *f*

ingenuous [ɪn'dʒenjuəs] *adj* ingenuo

ingot ['ɪŋgət] *n* lingote *m*, barra

ingrained [ɪn'greɪnd] *adj* arraigado

ingratiate [ɪn'greɪʃɪeɪt] *vt*: **to ~ o.s. with** congraciarse con

ingredient [ɪn'gri:dɪənt] *n* ingrediente *m*

inhabit [ɪn'hæbɪt] *vt* vivir en; **~ant** *n* habitante *m/f*

inhale [ɪn'heɪl] *vt* inhalar ♦ *vi* (*breathe in*) aspirar; (*in smoking*) tragar

inherent [ɪn'hɪərənt] *adj*: **~ in** *or* **to** inherente a

inherit [ɪn'herɪt] *vt* heredar; **~ance** *n* herencia; (*fig*) patrimonio

inhibit [ɪn'hɪbɪt] *vt* inhibir, impedir; **~ed** *adj* (*PSYCH*) cohibido; **~ion** [-'bɪʃən] *n* cohibición *f*

inhospitable [ɪnhɔs'pɪtəbl] *adj* (*person*) inhospitalario; (*place*) inhóspito

inhuman [ɪn'hju:mən] *adj* inhumano

initial [ɪ'nɪʃl] *adj* primero ♦ *n* inicial *f* ♦ *vt* firmar con las iniciales; **~s** *npl* (*as signature*) iniciales *fpl*; (*abbreviation*) siglas *fpl*; **~ly** *adv* al principio

initiate [ɪ'nɪʃɪeɪt] *vt* iniciar; **to ~ proceedings against sb** (*LAW*) entablar proceso contra uno

initiative [ɪ'nɪʃətɪv] *n* iniciativa

inject [ɪn'dʒekt] *vt* inyectar; **to ~ sb with sth** inyectar algo a uno; **~ion** [ɪn'dʒekʃən] *n* inyección *f*

injunction [ɪn'dʒʌŋkʃən] *n* interdicto

injure ['ɪndʒə*] *vt* (*hurt*) herir, lastimar; (*fig: reputation etc*) perjudicar; **~d** *adj* (*person, arm*) herido, lastimado; **injury** *n* herida, lesión *f*; (*wrong*) perjuicio, daño; **injury time** *n* (*SPORT*) (tiempo de) descuento

injustice [ɪn'dʒʌstɪs] *n* injusticia

ink [ɪŋk] *n* tinta

inkling ['ɪŋklɪŋ] *n* sospecha; (*idea*) idea

inlaid ['ɪnleɪd] *adj* (*with wood, gems etc*) incrustado

inland [adj 'ɪnlənd, adv ɪn'lænd] adj (waterway, port etc) interior ♦ adv tierra adentro; **I~ Revenue** (BRIT) n departamento de impuestos; ≈ Hacienda (SP)

in-laws npl suegros mpl

inlet ['ɪnlet] n (GEO) ensenada, cala; (TECH) admisión f, entrada

inmate ['ɪnmeɪt] n (in prison) preso/a; presidiario/a; (in asylum) internado/a

inn [ɪn] n posada, mesón m

innate [ɪ'neɪt] adj innato

inner ['ɪnə*] adj (courtyard, calm) interior; (feelings) íntimo; **~ city** n barrios deprimidos del centro de una ciudad; **~ tube** n (of tyre) cámara (SP), llanta (AM)

innings ['ɪnɪŋz] n (CRICKET) entrada, turno

innocent ['ɪnəsnt] adj inocente

innocuous [ɪ'nɔkjuəs] adj inocuo

innovation [ɪnəu'veɪʃən] n novedad f

innuendo [ɪnju'ɛndəu] (pl ~es) n indirecta

inoculation [ɪnɔkju'leɪʃən] n inoculación f

in-patient n paciente m/f interno/a

input ['ɪnput] n entrada; (of resources) inversión f; (COMPUT) entrada de datos

inquest ['ɪnkwest] n (coroner's) encuesta judicial

inquire [ɪn'kwaɪə*] vi preguntar ♦ vt: **to ~ whether** preguntar si; **to ~ about** (person) preguntar por; (fact) informarse de; **~ into** vt fus investigar, indagar; **inquiry** n pregunta; (investigation) investigación f, pesquisa; **"Inquiries"** "Información"; **inquiry office** (BRIT) n oficina de información

inquisitive [ɪn'kwɪzɪtɪv] adj (curious) curioso

ins. abbr = **inches**

insane [ɪn'seɪn] adj loco; (MED) demente

insanity [ɪn'sænɪtɪ] n demencia, locura

inscription [ɪn'skrɪpʃən] n inscripción f; (in book) dedicatoria

inscrutable [ɪn'skru:təbl] adj inescrutable, insondable

insect ['ɪnsekt] n insecto; **~icide** [ɪn'sektɪsaɪd] n insecticida m; **~ repellent** n loción f contra insectos

insecure [ɪnsɪ'kjuə*] adj inseguro

insemination [ɪnsemɪ'neɪʃən] n: **artificial ~** inseminación f artificial

insensitive [ɪn'sensɪtɪv] adj insensible

insert [vb ɪn'sə:t, n 'ɪnsə:t] vt (into sth) introducir ♦ n encarte m; **~ion** [ɪn'sə:ʃən] n inserción f

in-service ['ɪnsə:vɪs] adj (training, course) a cargo de la empresa

inshore [ɪn'ʃɔ:*] adj de bajura ♦ adv (be) cerca de la orilla; (move) hacia la orilla

inside ['ɪn'saɪd] n interior m ♦ adj interior, interno ♦ adv (be) (por) dentro; (go) hacia dentro ♦ prep dentro de; (of time): **~ 10 minutes** en menos de 10 minutos; **~s** npl (inf: stomach) tripas fpl; **~ information** n información f confidencial; **~ lane** n (AUT: in Britain) carril m izquierdo; (: in US, Europe etc) carril m derecho; **~ out** adv (turn) al revés; (know) a fondo

insider dealing, insider trading n (STOCK EXCHANGE) abuso de información privilegiada

insight ['ɪnsaɪt] n perspicacia

insignificant [ɪnsɪg'nɪfɪknt] adj insignificante

insincere [ɪnsɪn'sɪə*] adj poco sincero

insinuate [ɪn'sɪnjueɪt] vt insinuar

insipid [ɪn'sɪpɪd] adj soso, insulso

insist [ɪn'sɪst] vi insistir; **to ~ on** insistir en; **to ~ that** insistir en que; (claim) exigir que; **~ent** adj insistente; (noise, action) persistente

insole ['ɪnsəul] n plantilla

insolent ['ɪnsələnt] adj insolente, descarado

insomnia [ɪn'sɔmnɪə] n insomnio

inspect [ɪn'spekt] vt inspeccionar, examinar; (troops) pasar revista a; **~ion** [ɪn'spekʃən] n inspección f, examen m; (of troops) revista; **~or** n inspector(a) m/f; (BRIT: on buses, trains) revisor(a) m/f

inspiration [ɪnspə'reɪʃən] n inspiración f; **inspire** [ɪn'spaɪə*] vt inspirar

instability [ɪnstə'bɪlɪtɪ] n inestabilidad f

install [ɪn'stɔ:l] vt instalar; (official)

nombrar; **~ation** [ɪnstəˈleɪʃən] *n*
instalación *f*

instalment [ɪnˈstɔːlmənt] (*US* **installment**)
n plazo; (*of story*) entrega; (*of TV serial
etc*) capítulo; **in ~s** (*pay, receive*) a plazos

instance [ˈɪnstəns] *n* ejemplo, caso; **for ~**
por ejemplo; **in the first ~** en primer
lugar

instant [ˈɪnstənt] *n* instante *m*, momento
♦ *adj* inmediato; (*coffee etc*) instantáneo;
~ly *adv* en seguida

instead [ɪnˈsted] *adv* en cambio; **~ of** en
lugar de, en vez de

instep [ˈɪnstep] *n* empeine *m*

instil [ɪnˈstɪl] *vt*: **to ~ sth into** inculcar algo
a

instinct [ˈɪnstɪŋkt] *n* instinto

institute [ˈɪnstɪtjuːt] *n* instituto;
(*professional body*) colegio ♦ *vt* (*begin*)
iniciar, empezar; (*proceedings*) entablar;
(*system, rule*) establecer

institution [ɪnstɪˈtjuːʃən] *n* institución *f*;
(*MED: home*) asilo; (: *asylum*) manicomio;
(*of system etc*) establecimiento; (*of
custom*) iniciación *f*

instruct [ɪnˈstrʌkt] *vt*: **to ~ sb in sth**
instruir a uno en *or* sobre algo; **to ~ sb to
do sth** dar instrucciones a uno de hacer
algo; **~ion** [ɪnˈstrʌkʃən] *n* (*teaching*)
instrucción *f*; **~ions** *npl* (*orders*) órdenes
fpl; **~ions (for use)** modo de empleo;
~or *n* instructor(a) *m/f*

instrument [ˈɪnstrəmənt] *n* instrumento;
~al [-ˈmentl] *adj* (*MUS*) instrumental; **to
be ~al in** ser (el) artífice de; **~ panel** *n*
tablero (de instrumentos)

insufficient [ɪnsəˈfɪʃənt] *adj* insuficiente

insular [ˈɪnsjʊlə*] *adj* insular; (*person*)
estrecho de miras

insulate [ˈɪnsjʊleɪt] *vt* aislar; **insulation**
[-ˈleɪʃən] *n* aislamiento

insulin [ˈɪnsjʊlɪn] *n* insulina

insult [*n* ˈɪnsʌlt, *vb* ɪnˈsʌlt] *n* insulto ♦ *vt*
insultar; **~ing** *adj* insultante

insurance [ɪnˈʃʊərəns] *n* seguro; **fire/life
~** seguro contra incendios/sobre la vida; **~
agent** *n* agente *m/f* de seguros; **~**

policy *n* póliza (de seguros)

insure [ɪnˈʃʊə*] *vt* asegurar

intact [ɪnˈtækt] *adj* íntegro; (*unharmed*)
intacto

intake [ˈɪnteɪk] *n* (*of food*) ingestión *f*; (*of
air*) consumo; (*BRIT: SCOL*): **an ~ of 200 a
year** 200 matriculados al año

integral [ˈɪntɪgrəl] *adj* (*whole*) íntegro;
(*part*) integrante

integrate [ˈɪntɪgreɪt] *vt* integrar ♦ *vi*
integrarse

integrity [ɪnˈtegrɪtɪ] *n* honradez *f*, rectitud
f

intellect [ˈɪntəlekt] *n* intelecto; **~ual**
[-ˈlektjuəl] *adj*, *n* intelectual *m/f*

intelligence [ɪnˈtelɪdʒəns] *n* inteligencia

intelligent [ɪnˈtelɪdʒənt] *adj* inteligente

intelligible [ɪnˈtelɪdʒɪbl] *adj* inteligible,
comprensible

intend [ɪnˈtend] *vt* (*gift etc*): **to ~ sth for**
destinar algo a; **to ~ to do sth** tener
intención de *or* pensar hacer algo

intense [ɪnˈtens] *adj* intenso; **~ly** *adv*
(*extremely*) sumamente

intensify [ɪnˈtensɪfaɪ] *vt* intensificar;
(*increase*) aumentar

intensive [ɪnˈtensɪv] *adj* intensivo; **~ care
unit** *n* unidad *f* de vigilancia intensiva

intent [ɪnˈtent] *n* propósito; (*LAW*)
premeditación *f* ♦ *adj* (*absorbed*) absorto;
(*attentive*) atento; **to all ~s and purposes**
prácticamente; **to be ~ on doing sth**
estar resuelto a hacer algo

intention [ɪnˈtenʃən] *n* intención *f*,
propósito; **~al** *adj* deliberado; **~ally** *adv*
a propósito

intently [ɪnˈtentlɪ] *adv* atentamente,
fijamente

interact [ɪntərˈækt] *vi* influirse
mutuamente; **~ive** *adj* (*COMPUT*)
interactivo

interchange [ˈɪntətʃeɪndʒ] *n* intercambio;
(*on motorway*) intersección *f*; **~able** *adj*
intercambiable

intercom [ˈɪntəkɔm] *n* interfono

intercourse [ˈɪntəkɔːs] *n* (*sexual*)
relaciones *fpl* sexuales

interest ['ɪntrɪst] *n* (*also* COMM) interés *m*
♦ *vt* interesar; **to be ~ed in** interesarse
por; **~ing** *adj* interesante; **~ rate** *n* tipo
or tasa de interés

interface ['ɪntəfeɪs] *n* (COMPUT) junción *f*

interfere [ɪntə'fɪə*] *vi*: **to ~ in** (*quarrel,
other people's business*) entrometerse en;
to ~ with (*hinder*) estorbar; (*damage*)
estropear

interference [ɪntə'fɪərəns] *n* intromisión *f*;
(RADIO, TV) interferencia

interim ['ɪntərɪm] *n*: **in the ~** en el ínterin
♦ *adj* provisional

interior [ɪn'tɪərɪə*] *n* interior *m* ♦ *adj*
interior; **~ designer** *n* interiorista *m/f*

interjection [ɪntə'dʒekʃən] *n* interposición
f; (LING) interjección *f*

interlock [ɪntə'lɔk] *vi* entrelazarse

interlude ['ɪntəluːd] *n* intervalo; (THEATRE)
intermedio

intermediate [ɪntə'miːdɪət] *adj*
intermedio

intermission [ɪntə'mɪʃən] *n* intermisión *f*;
(THEATRE) descanso

intern [*vb* ɪn'tɜːn, *n* 'ɪntɜːn] *vt* internar ♦ *n*
(US) interno/a

internal [ɪn'tɜːnl] *adj* (*layout, pipes,
security*) interior; (*injury, structure, memo*)
internal; **~ly** *adv* "**not to be taken ~ly**"
"uso externo"; **I~ Revenue Service**
(US) *n* departamento de impuestos;
≈ Hacienda (SP)

international [ɪntə'næʃənl] *adj*
internacional ♦ *n* (BRIT: *match*) partido
internacional

Internet ['ɪntənet] *n*: **the ~** Internet *m or f*

interplay ['ɪntəpleɪ] *n* interacción *f*

interpret [ɪn'tɜːprɪt] *vt* interpretar;
(*translate*) traducir; (*understand*) entender
♦ *vi* hacer de intérprete; **~er** *n* intérprete
m/f

interrelated [ɪntərɪ'leɪtɪd] *adj*
interrelacionado

interrogate [ɪn'terəʊgeɪt] *vt* interrogar;
interrogation [-'geɪʃən] *n* interrogatorio

interrupt [ɪntə'rʌpt] *vt*, *vi* interrumpir;
~ion [-'rʌpʃən] *n* interrupción *f*

intersect [ɪntə'sekt] *vi* (*roads*) cruzarse;
~ion [-'sekʃən] *n* (*of roads*) cruce *m*

intersperse [ɪntə'spɜːs] *vt*: **to ~ with**
salpicar de

intertwine [ɪntə'twaɪn] *vt* entrelazarse

interval ['ɪntəvl] *n* intervalo; (BRIT: THEATRE,
SPORT) descanso; (: SCOL) recreo; **at ~s** a
ratos, de vez en cuando

intervene [ɪntə'viːn] *vi* intervenir; (*event*)
interponerse; (*time*) transcurrir;
intervention *n* intervención *f*

interview ['ɪntəvjuː] *n* entrevista ♦ *vt*
entrevistarse con; **~er** *n* entrevistador(a)
m/f

intestine [ɪn'testɪn] *n* intestino

intimacy ['ɪntɪməsɪ] *n* intimidad *f*

intimate [*adj* 'ɪntɪmət, *vb* 'ɪntɪmeɪt] *adj*
íntimo; (*friendship*) estrecho; (*knowledge*)
profundo ♦ *vt* dar a entender

into ['ɪntuː] *prep* en; (*towards*) a; (*inside*)
hacia el interior de; **~ 3 pieces/French**
en 3 pedazos/al francés

intolerable [ɪn'tɔlərəbl] *adj* intolerable,
insoportable

intolerant [ɪn'tɔlərənt] *adj*: **~ (of)**
intolerante (con *or* para)

intoxicated [ɪn'tɔksɪkeɪtɪd] *adj*
embriagado

intractable [ɪn'træktəbl] *adj* (*person*)
intratable; (*problem*) espinoso

intransitive [ɪn'trænsɪtɪv] *adj* intransitivo

intravenous [ɪntrə'viːnəs] *adj* intravenoso

in-tray *n* bandeja de entrada

intricate ['ɪntrɪkət] *adj* (*design, pattern*)
intrincado

intrigue [ɪn'triːg] *n* intriga ♦ *vt* fascinar;
intriguing *adj* fascinante

intrinsic [ɪn'trɪnsɪk] *adj* intrínseco

introduce [ɪntrə'djuːs] *vt* introducir,
meter; (*speaker, TV show etc*) presentar;
to ~ sb (to sb) presentar uno (a otro); **to
~ sb to** (*pastime, technique*) introducir a
uno a; **introduction** [-'dʌkʃən] *n*
introducción *f*; (*of person*) presentación *f*;
introductory [-'dʌktərɪ] *adj*
introductorio; (*lesson, offer*) de
introducción

introvert ['ɪntrəvəːt] *n* introvertido/a ♦ *adj* (*also:* **~ed**) introvertido

intrude [ɪn'truːd] *vi* (*person*) entrometerse; **to ~ on** estorbar; **~r** *n* intruso/a; **intrusion** [-ʒən] *n* invasión *f*

intuition [ɪntjuː'ɪʃən] *n* intuición *f*

inundate ['ɪnʌndeɪt] *vt*: **to ~ with** inundar de

invade [ɪn'veɪd] *vt* invadir

invalid [*n* 'ɪnvəlɪd, *adj* ɪn'vælɪd] *n* (*MED*) minusválido/a ♦ *adj* (*not valid*) inválido, nulo

invaluable [ɪn'væljuəbl] *adj* inestimable

invariable [ɪn'vɛərɪəbl] *adj* invariable

invent [ɪn'vɛnt] *vt* inventar; **~ion** [ɪn'vɛnʃən] *n* invento, (*lie*) ficción *f*, mentira; **~ive** *adj* inventivo; **~or** *n* inventor(a) *m/f*

inventory ['ɪnvəntrɪ] *n* inventario

invert [ɪn'vəːt] *vt* invertir

inverted commas (*BRIT*) *npl* comillas *fpl*

invest [ɪn'vɛst] *vt* invertir ♦ *vi*: **to ~ in** (*company etc*) invertir dinero en; (*fig: sth useful*) comprar

investigate [ɪn'vɛstɪɡeɪt] *vt* investigar; **investigation** [-'ɡeɪʃən] *n* investigación *f*, pesquisa

investment [ɪn'vɛstmənt] *n* inversión *f*

investor [ɪn'vɛstə*] *n* inversionista *m/f*

invigilator [ɪn'vɪdʒɪleɪtə*] *n* persona que vigila en un examen

invigorating [ɪn'vɪɡəreɪtɪŋ] *adj* vigorizante

invisible [ɪn'vɪzɪbl] *adj* invisible

invitation [ɪnvɪ'teɪʃən] *n* invitación *f*

invite [ɪn'vaɪt] *vt* invitar; (*opinions etc*) solicitar, pedir; **inviting** *adj* atractivo; (*food*) apetitoso

invoice ['ɪnvɔɪs] *n* factura ♦ *vt* facturar

involuntary [ɪn'vɔləntrɪ] *adj* involuntario

involve [ɪn'vɔlv] *vt* suponer, implicar; (*concern, affect*) tener que ver con; corresponder; **to ~ sb (in sth)** comprometer a uno (con algo); **~d** *adj* complicado; **to be ~d in** (*take part*) tomar parte en; (*be engrossed*) estar muy metido en; **~ment** *n* participación *f*; dedicación *f*

inward ['ɪnwəd] *adj* (*movement*) interior, interno; (*thought, feeling*) íntimo; **~(s)** *adv* hacia dentro

I/O *abbr* (*COMPUT = input/output*) entrada/salida

iodine ['aɪəudiːn] *n* yodo

ion ['aɪən] *n* ion *m*; **ioniser** ['aɪənaɪzə*] *n* ionizador *m*

iota [aɪ'əutə] *n* jota, ápice *m*

IOU *n abbr* (= *I owe you*) pagaré *m*

IQ *n abbr* (= *intelligence quotient*) cociente *m* intelectual

IRA *n abbr* (= *Irish Republican Army*) IRA *m*

Iran [ɪ'rɑːn] *n* Irán *m*; **~ian** [ɪ'reɪnɪən] *adj*, *n* iraní *m/f*

Iraq [ɪ'rɑːk] *n* Iraq *m*; **~i** *adj*, *n* iraquí *m/f*

irate [aɪ'reɪt] *adj* enojado, airado

Ireland ['aɪələnd] *n* Irlanda

iris ['aɪrɪs] (*pl* **~es**) *n* (*ANAT*) iris *m*; (*BOT*) lirio

Irish ['aɪrɪʃ] *adj* irlandés/esa ♦ *npl*: **the ~** los irlandeses; **~man/woman** (*irreg*) *n* irlandés/esa *m/f*; **~ Sea** *n*: **the ~ Sea** el mar de Irlanda

iron ['aɪən] *n* hierro; (*for clothes*) plancha ♦ *cpd* de hierro ♦ *vt* (*clothes*) planchar; **~ out** *vt* (*fig*) allanar

ironic(al) [aɪ'rɔnɪk(l)] *adj* irónico

ironing ['aɪənɪŋ] *n* (*activity*) planchado; (*clothes: ironed*) ropa planchada; (: *to be ironed*) ropa por planchar; **~ board** *n* tabla de planchar

ironmonger's (shop) ['aɪənmʌŋɡəz] (*BRIT*) *n* ferretería, quincallería

irony ['aɪrənɪ] *n* ironía

irrational [ɪ'ræʃənl] *adj* irracional

irreconcilable [ɪrekən'saɪləbl] *adj* (*ideas*) incompatible; (*enemies*) irreconciliable

irregular [ɪ'reɡjulə*] *adj* irregular; (*surface*) desigual; (*action, event*) anómalo; (*behaviour*) poco ortodoxo

irrelevant [ɪ'reləvənt] *adj* fuera de lugar, inoportuno

irresolute [ɪ'rezəluːt] *adj* indeciso

irrespective [ɪrɪ'spektɪv]: **~ of** *prep* sin tener en cuenta, no importa

irresponsible [ɪrɪˈspɔnsɪbl] *adj* (*act*) irresponsable; (*person*) poco serio

irrigate [ˈɪrɪgeɪt] *vt* regar; **irrigation** [-ˈgeɪʃən] *n* riego

irritable [ˈɪrɪtəbl] *adj* (*person*) de mal humor

irritate [ˈɪrɪteɪt] *vt* fastidiar; (*MED*) picar; **irritating** *adj* fastidioso; **irritation** [-ˈteɪʃən] *n* fastidio; irritación; picazón *f*, picor *m*

IRS (*US*) *n abbr* = **Internal Revenue Service**

is [ɪz] *vb see* **be**

Islam [ˈɪzlɑːm] *n* Islam *m*; **~ic** [ɪzˈlæmɪk] *adj* islámico

island [ˈaɪlənd] *n* isla; **~er** *n* isleño/a

isle [aɪl] *n* isla

isn't [ˈɪznt] = **is not**

isolate [ˈaɪsəleɪt] *vt* aislar; **~d** *adj* aislado; **isolation** [-ˈleɪʃən] *n* aislamiento

Israel [ˈɪzreɪl] *n* Israel *m*; **~i** [ɪzˈreɪlɪ] *adj, n* israelí *m/f*

issue [ˈɪsjuː] *n* (*problem, subject, most important part*) cuestión *f*; (*outcome*) resultado; (*of banknotes etc*) emisión *f*; (*of newspaper etc*) edición *f* ♦ *vt* (*rations, equipment*) distribuir, repartir; (*orders*) dar; (*certificate, passport*) expedir; (*decree*) promulgar; (*magazine*) publicar; (*cheques*) extender; (*banknotes, stamps*) emitir; **at ~** en cuestión; **to take ~ with sb (over)** estar en desacuerdo con uno (sobre); **to make an ~ of sth** hacer una cuestión de algo

Istanbul [ɪstænˈbuːl] *n* Estambul *m*

⎡*KEYWORD*⎤

it [ɪt] *pron* **1** (*specific: subject: not generally translated*) él/ella; (: *direct object*) lo, la; (: *indirect object*) le; (*after prep*) él/ella; (*abstract concept*) ello; **~'s on the table** está en la mesa; **I can't find ~** no lo (*or* la) encuentro; **give ~ to me** dámelo (*or* dámela); **I spoke to him about ~** le hablé del asunto; **what did you learn from ~?** ¿qué aprendiste de él (*or* ella)?; **did you go to ~?** (*party, concert etc*) ¿fuiste?

2 (*impersonal*): **~'s raining** llueve, está lloviendo; **~'s 6 o'clock/the 10th of August** son las 6/es el 10 de agosto; **how far is ~? – ~'s 10 miles/2 hours on the train** ¿a qué distancia está? — a 10 millas/2 horas en tren; **who is ~? – ~'s me** ¿quién es? — soy yo

Italian [ɪˈtæljən] *adj* italiano ♦ *n* italiano/a; (*LING*) italiano

italics [ɪˈtælɪks] *npl* cursiva

Italy [ˈɪtəlɪ] *n* Italia

itch [ɪtʃ] *n* picazón *f* ♦ *vi* (*part of body*) picar; **to ~ to do sth** rabiar por hacer algo; **~y** *adj*: **my hand is ~y** me pica la mano

it'd [ˈɪtd] = **it would; it had**

item [ˈaɪtəm] *n* artículo; (*on agenda*) asunto (a tratar); (*also*: **news ~**) noticia; **~ize** *vt* detallar

itinerary [aɪˈtɪnərərɪ] *n* itinerario

it'll [ˈɪtl] = **it will; it shall**

its [ɪts] *adj* su; sus *pl*

it's [ɪts] = **it is; it has**

itself [ɪtˈsɛlf] *pron* (*reflexive*) sí mismo/a; (*emphatic*) él mismo/ella misma

ITV *n abbr* (*BRIT*: = *Independent Television*) *cadena de televisión comercial independiente del Estado*

I.U.D. *n abbr* (= *intra-uterine device*) DIU *m*

I've [aɪv] = **I have**

ivory [ˈaɪvərɪ] *n* marfil *m*

ivy [ˈaɪvɪ] *n* (*BOT*) hiedra

J, j

jab [dʒæb] *vt*: **to ~ sth into sth** clavar algo en algo ♦ *n* (*inf*) (*MED*) pinchazo

jack [dʒæk] *n* (*AUT*) gato; (*CARDS*) sota; **~ up** *vt* (*AUT*) levantar con gato

jackal [ˈdʒækɔːl] *n* (*ZOOL*) chacal *m*

jacket [ˈdʒækɪt] *n* chaqueta, americana, saco (*AM*); (*of book*) sobrecubierta

jack: **~-knife** *vi* colear; **~ plug** *n* (*ELEC*) enchufe *m* de clavija; **~pot** *n* premio gordo

jaded ['dʒeɪdɪd] *adj* (*tired*) cansado; (*fed-up*) hastiado

jagged ['dʒægɪd] *adj* dentado

jail [dʒeɪl] *n* cárcel *f* ♦ *vt* encarcelar

jam [dʒæm] *n* mermelada; (*also:* **traffic ~**) embotellamiento; (*inf: difficulty*) apuro ♦ *vt* (*passage etc*) obstruir; (*mechanism, drawer etc*) atascar; (*RADIO*) interferir ♦ *vi* atascarse, trabarse; **to ~ sth into sth** meter algo a la fuerza en algo

Jamaica [dʒə'meɪkə] *n* Jamaica

jangle ['dʒæŋgl] *vi* entrechocar (ruidosamente)

janitor ['dʒænɪtə*] *n* (*caretaker*) portero, conserje *m*

January ['dʒænjuərɪ] *n* enero

Japan [dʒə'pæn] *n* (el) Japón; **~ese** [dʒæpə'niːz] *adj* japonés/esa ♦ *n inv* japonés/esa *m/f*; (*LING*) japonés *m*

jar [dʒɑː*] *n* tarro, bote *m* ♦ *vi* (*sound*) chirriar; (*colours*) desentonar

jargon ['dʒɑːgən] *n* jerga

jasmine ['dʒæzmɪn] *n* jazmín *m*

jaundice ['dʒɔːndɪs] *n* ictericia

jaunt [dʒɔːnt] *n* excursión *f*

javelin ['dʒævlɪn] *n* jabalina

jaw [dʒɔː] *n* mandíbula

jay [dʒeɪ] *n* (*ZOOL*) arrendajo

jaywalker ['dʒeɪwɔːkə*] *n* peatón/ona *m/f* imprudente

jazz [dʒæz] *n* jazz *m*; **~ up** *vt* (*liven up*) animar, avivar

jealous ['dʒeləs] *adj* celoso; (*envious*) envidioso; **~y** *n* celos *mpl*; envidia

jeans [dʒiːnz] *npl* vaqueros *mpl*, tejanos *mpl*

Jeep ® [dʒiːp] *n* jeep *m*

jeer [dʒɪə*] *vi*: **to ~ (at)** (*mock*) mofarse (de)

jelly ['dʒelɪ] *n* (*jam*) jalea; (*dessert etc*) gelatina; **~fish** *n inv* medusa (*SP*), aguaviva (*AM*)

jeopardy ['dʒepədɪ] *n*: **to be in ~** estar en peligro

jerk [dʒɑːk] *n* (*jolt*) sacudida; (*wrench*) tirón *m*; (*inf*) imbécil *m/f* ♦ *vt* tirar

bruscamente de ♦ *vi* (*vehicle*) traquetear

jersey ['dʒɑːzɪ] *n* jersey *m*; (*fabric*) (tejido de) punto

Jesus ['dʒiːzəs] *n* Jesús *m*

jet [dʒet] *n* (*of gas, liquid*) chorro; (*AVIAT*) avión *m* a reacción; **~-black** *adj* negro como el azabache; **~ engine** *n* motor *m* a reacción; **~ lag** *n* desorientación *f* después de un largo vuelo

jettison ['dʒetɪsn] *vt* desechar

jetty ['dʒetɪ] *n* muelle *m*, embarcadero

Jew [dʒuː] *n* judío

jewel ['dʒuːəl] *n* joya; (*in watch*) rubí *m*; **~ler** (*US* **~er**) *n* joyero/a; **~ler's (shop)** (*US* **~ry store**) *n* joyería; **~lery** (*US* **~ry**) *n* joyas *fpl*, alhajas *fpl*

Jewess ['dʒuːɪs] *n* judía

Jewish ['dʒuːɪʃ] *adj* judío

jibe [dʒaɪb] *n* mofa

jiffy ['dʒɪfɪ] (*inf*) *n*: **in a ~** en un santiamén

jigsaw ['dʒɪgsɔː] *n* (*also:* **~ puzzle**) rompecabezas *m inv*, puzle *m*

jilt [dʒɪlt] *vt* dejar plantado a

jingle ['dʒɪŋgl] *n* musiquilla ♦ *vi* tintinear

jinx [dʒɪŋks] *n*: **there's a ~ on it** está gafado

jitters ['dʒɪtəz] (*inf*) *npl*: **to get the ~** ponerse nervioso

job [dʒɔb] *n* (*task*) tarea; (*post*) empleo; **it's not my ~** no me incumbe a mí; **it's a good ~ that ...** menos mal que ...; **just the ~!** ¡estupendo!; **~ centre** (*BRIT*) *n* oficina estatal de colocaciones; **~less** *adj* sin trabajo

jockey ['dʒɔkɪ] *n* jockey *m/f* ♦ *vi*: **to ~ for position** maniobrar para conseguir una posición

jog [dʒɔg] *vt* empujar (ligeramente) ♦ *vi* (*run*) hacer footing; **to ~ sb's memory** refrescar la memoria a uno; **~ along** *vi* (*fig*) ir tirando; **~ging** *n* footing *m*

join [dʒɔɪn] *vt* (*things*) juntar, unir; (*club*) hacerse socio de; (*POL: party*) afiliarse a; (*queue*) ponerse en; (*meet: people*) reunirse con ♦ *n* juntura; (*rivers*) confluir ♦ *n* juntura; **~ in** *vi* tomar parte, participar ♦ *vt fus* tomar parte or participar en; ~ **up** vi reunirse; (MIL) alistarse

joiner ['dʒɔɪnə*] (BRIT) n carpintero/a; **~y** n carpintería

joint [dʒɔɪnt] n (TECH) junta, unión f; (ANAT) articulación f; (BRIT: CULIN) pieza de carne (para asar); (inf: place) tugurio; (: of cannabis) porro ♦ adj (common) común; (combined) combinado; ~ **account** (with bank etc) cuenta común

joke [dʒəuk] n chiste m; (also: **practical ~**) broma ♦ vi bromear; **to play a ~ on** gastar una broma a; **~r** n (CARDS) comodín m

jolly ['dʒɔlɪ] adj (merry) alegre; (enjoyable) divertido ♦ adv (BRIT: inf) muy, terriblemente

jolt [dʒəult] n (jerk) sacudida; (shock) susto ♦ vt (physically) sacudir; (emotionally) asustar

jostle ['dʒɔsl] vt dar empellones a, codear

jot [dʒɔt] n: **not one ~** ni jota, ni pizca; **~ down** vt apuntar; **~ter** (BRIT) n bloc m

journal ['dʒɜːnl] n (magazine) revista; (diary) periódico, diario; **~ism** n periodismo; **~ist** n periodista m/f, reportero/a

journey ['dʒɜːnɪ] n viaje m; (distance covered) trayecto

jovial ['dʒəuvɪəl] adj risueño, jovial

joy [dʒɔɪ] n alegría; **~ful** adj alegre; **~ous** adj alegre; **~ ride** n (illegal) paseo en coche robado; **~rider** n gamberro que roba un coche para dar una vuelta y luego abandonarlo; **~ stick** n (AVIAT) palanca de mando; (COMPUT) palanca de control

JP n abbr = **Justice of the Peace**

Jr abbr = **junior**

jubilant ['dʒuːbɪlnt] adj jubiloso

judge [dʒʌdʒ] n juez m/f; (fig: expert) perito ♦ vt juzgar; (consider) considerar; **judg(e)ment** n juicio

judiciary [dʒuːˈdɪʃɪərɪ] n poder m judicial

judicious [dʒuːˈdɪʃəs] adj juicioso

judo ['dʒuːdəu] n judo

jug [dʒʌg] n jarra

juggernaut ['dʒʌgənɔːt] (BRIT) n (huge truck) trailer m

juggle ['dʒʌgl] vi hacer juegos malabares; **~r** n malabarista m/f

juice [dʒuːs] n zumo, jugo (esp AM); **juicy** adj jugoso

jukebox ['dʒuːkbɔks] n máquina de discos

July [dʒuːˈlaɪ] n julio

jumble ['dʒʌmbl] n revoltijo ♦ vt (also: ~ **up**) revolver; **~ sale** (BRIT) n venta de objetos usados con fines benéficos

---
jumble sale

ℹ️ Los **jumble sales** son unos
mercadillos que se organizan con fines
benéficos en los locales de un colegio,
iglesia u otro centro público. En ellos
puede comprarse todo tipo de artículos
baratos de segunda mano, sobre todo ropa,
juguetes, libros, vajillas o muebles.

---

jumbo (jet) ['dʒʌmbəu-] n jumbo

jump [dʒʌmp] vi saltar, dar saltos; (with fear etc) pegar un bote; (increase) aumentar ♦ vt saltar ♦ n salto; aumento; **to ~ the queue** colarse

jumper ['dʒʌmpə*] n (BRIT: pullover) suéter m, jersey m; (US: dress) mandil m; **~ cables** (US) npl = **jump leads**

jump leads (BRIT) npl cables mpl puente de batería

jumpy ['dʒʌmpɪ] (inf) adj nervioso

Jun. abbr = **junior**

junction ['dʒʌŋkʃən] n (BRIT: of roads) cruce m; (RAIL) empalme m

juncture ['dʒʌŋktʃə*] n: **at this ~** en este momento, en esta coyuntura

June [dʒuːn] n junio

jungle ['dʒʌŋgl] n selva, jungla

junior ['dʒuːnɪə*] adj (in age) menor, más joven; (brother/sister etc): **7 years her ~** siete años menor que ella; (position) subalterno ♦ n menor m/f, joven m/f; **~ school** (BRIT) n escuela primaria

junk [dʒʌŋk] n (cheap goods) baratijas fpl; (rubbish) basura; **~ food** n alimentos preparados y envasados de escaso valor nutritivo

junkie ['dʒʌŋkı] (*inf*) *n* drogadicto/a, yonqui *m/f*

junk mail *n* propaganda de buzón

junk shop *n* tienda de objetos usados

Junr *abbr* = **junior**

juror ['dʒuərə*] *n* jurado

jury ['dʒuərı] *n* jurado

just [dʒʌst] *adj* justo ♦ *adv* (*exactly*) exactamente; (*only*) sólo, solamente; **he's ~ done it/left** acaba de hacerlo/irse; **~ right** perfecto; **~ two o'clock** las dos en punto; **she's ~ as clever as you** (ella) es tan lista como tú; **~ as well that ...** menos mal que ...; **~ as he was leaving** en el momento en que se marchaba; **~ before/enough** justo antes/lo suficiente; **~ here** aquí mismo; **he ~ missed** ha fallado por poco; **~ listen to this** escucha esto un momento

justice ['dʒʌstıs] *n* justicia; (*US: judge*) juez *m*; **to do ~ to** (*fig*) hacer justicia a; **J~ of the Peace** *n* juez *m* de paz

justify ['dʒʌstıfaı] *vt* justificar; (*text*) alinear

jut [dʒʌt] *vi* (*also*: **~ out**) sobresalir

juvenile ['dʒuːvənaıl] *adj* (*court*) de menores; (*humour, mentality*) infantil ♦ *n* menor *m* de edad

K, k

K *abbr* (= *one thousand*) mil; (= *kilobyte*) kilobyte *m*, kiloccteto

kangaroo [kæŋgə'ruː] *n* canguro

karate [kə'rɑːtı] *n* karate *m*

kebab [kə'bæb] *n* pincho moruno

keel [kiːl] *n* quilla; **on an even ~** (*fig*) en equilibrio

keen [kiːn] *adj* (*interest, desire*) grande, vivo; (*eye, intelligence*) agudo; (*competition*) reñido; (*edge*) afilado; (*eager*) entusiasta; **to be ~ to do** *or* **on doing sth** tener muchas ganas de hacer algo; **to be ~ on sth/sb** interesarse por algo/uno

keep [kiːp] (*pt, pp* **kept**) *vt* (*preserve, store*)

guardar; (*hold back*) quedarse con; (*maintain*) mantener; (*detain*) detener; (*shop*) ser propietario de; (*feed: family etc*) mantener; (*promise*) cumplir; (*chickens, bees etc*) criar; (*accounts*) llevar; (*diary*) escribir; (*prevent*): **to ~ sb from doing sth** impedir a uno hacer algo ♦ *vi* (*food*) conservarse; (*remain*) seguir, continuar ♦ *n* (*of castle*) torreón *m*; (*food etc*) comida, subsistencia; (*inf*): **for ~s** para siempre; **to ~ doing sth** seguir haciendo algo; **to ~ sb happy** tener a uno contento; **to ~ a place tidy** mantener un lugar limpio; **to ~ sth to o.s.** guardar algo para sí mismo; **to ~ sth (back) from sb** ocultar algo a uno; **to ~ time** (*clock*) mantener la hora exacta; **~ on** *vi*: **to ~ on doing** seguir *or* continuar haciendo; **to ~ on (about sth)** no parar de hablar (de algo); **~ out** *vi* (*stay out*) permanecer fuera; **"~ out"** "prohibida la entrada"; **~ up** *vt* mantener, conservar ♦ *vi* no retrasarse; **to ~ up with** (*pace*) ir al paso de; (*level*) mantenerse a la altura de; **~er** *n* guardián/ana *m/f*; **~-fit** *n* gimnasia (para mantenerse en forma); **~ing** *n* (*care*) cuidado; **in ~ing with** de acuerdo con; **~sake** *n* recuerdo

kennel ['kenl] *n* perrera; **~s** *npl* residencia canina

Kenya ['kenjə] *n* Kenia

kept [kept] *pt, pp of* **keep**

kerb [kəːb] (*BRIT*) *n* bordillo

kernel ['kəːnl] *n* (*nut*) almendra; (*fig*) meollo

ketchup ['ketʃəp] *n* salsa de tomate, catsup *m*

kettle ['ketl] *n* hervidor *m* de agua; **~ drum** *n* (*MUS*) timbal *m*

key [kiː] *n* llave *f*; (*MUS*) tono; (*of piano, typewriter*) tecla ♦ *adj* (*issue etc*) clave *inv* ♦ *vt* (*also*: **~ in**) teclear; **~board** *n* teclado; **~ed up** *adj* (*person*) nervioso; **~hole** *n* ojo (de la cerradura); **~hole surgery** *n* cirugía cerrada, cirugía no invasiva; **~note** *n* (*MUS*) tónica; (*of speech*) punto principal *or* clave; **~ring** *n*

llavero
khaki [ˈkɑːkɪ] n caqui
kick [kɪk] vt dar una patada or un puntapié
a; (inf: habit) quitarse de ♦ vi (horse) dar
coces ♦ n patada; puntapié m; (of animal)
coz f; (thrill): **he does it for ~s** lo hace
por pura diversión; **~ off** vi (SPORT) hacer
el saque inicial
kid [kɪd] n (inf: child) chiquillo/a; (animal)
cabrito; (leather) cabritilla ♦ vi (inf)
bromear
kidnap [ˈkɪdnæp] vt secuestrar; **~per** n
secuestrador(a) m/f; **~ping** n secuestro
kidney [ˈkɪdnɪ] n riñón m
kill [kɪl] vt matar; (murder) asesinar ♦ n
matanza; **to ~ time** matar el tiempo; **~er**
n asesino/a; **~ing** n (one) asesinato;
(several) matanza; **to make a ~ing** (fig)
hacer su agosto; **~joy** n (BRIT) aguafiestas
m/f inv
kiln [kɪln] n horno
kilo [ˈkiːləu] n kilo; **~byte** n (COMPUT)
kilobyte m, kiloccteto; **~gram(me)**
[ˈkɪləugræm] n kilo, kilogramo; **~metre**
[ˈkɪləmiːtə*] (US **~meter**) n kilómetro;
~watt [ˈkɪləuwɔt] n kilovatio
kilt [kɪlt] n falda escocesa
kin [kɪn] n see **next**
kind [kaɪnd] adj amable, atento ♦ n clase
f, especie f; (species) género; **in ~** (COMM)
en especie; **a ~ of** una especie de; **to be
two of a ~** ser tal para cual
kindergarten [ˈkɪndəgɑːtn] n jardín m de
la infancia
kind-hearted adj bondadoso, de buen
corazón
kindle [ˈkɪndl] vt encender; (arouse)
despertar
kindly [ˈkaɪndlɪ] adj bondadoso; cariñoso
♦ adv bondadosamente, amablemente;
will you ~ ... sea usted tan amable de ...
kindness [ˈkaɪndnɪs] n (quality) bondad f,
amabilidad f; (act) favor m
king [kɪŋ] n rey m; **~dom** n reino;
~fisher n martín m pescador; **~-size**
adj de tamaño extra
kiosk [ˈkiːɔsk] n quiosco; (BRIT: TEL) cabina

kipper [ˈkɪpə*] n arenque m ahumado
kiss [kɪs] n beso ♦ vt besar; **to ~ (each
other)** besarse; **~ of life** n respiración f
boca a boca
kit [kɪt] n (equipment) equipo; (tools etc)
(caja de) herramientas fpl; (assembly ~)
juego de armar
kitchen [ˈkɪtʃɪn] n cocina; **~ sink** n
fregadero
kite [kaɪt] n (toy) cometa
kitten [ˈkɪtn] n gatito/a
kitty [ˈkɪtɪ] n (pool of money) fondo común
km abbr (= kilometre) km
knack [næk] n: **to have the ~ of doing
sth** tener el don de hacer algo
knapsack [ˈnæpsæk] n mochila
knead [niːd] vt amasar
knee [niː] n rodilla; **~cap** n rótula
kneel [niːl] (pt, pp knelt) vi (also: ~ **down**)
arrodillarse
knew [njuː] pt of **know**
knickers [ˈnɪkəz] (BRIT) npl bragas fpl
knife [naɪf] (pl knives) n cuchillo ♦ vt
acuchillar
knight [naɪt] n caballero; (CHESS) caballo;
~hood (BRIT) n (title): **to receive a
~hood** recibir el título de Sir
knit [nɪt] vt tejer, tricotar ♦ vi hacer punto,
tricotar; (bones) soldarse; **to ~ one's
brows** fruncir el ceño; **~ting** n labor f de
punto; **~ting machine** n máquina de
tricotar; **~ting needle** n aguja de hacer
punto; **~wear** n prendas fpl de punto
knives [naɪvz] npl of **knife**
knob [nɔb] n (of door) tirador m; (of stick)
puño; (on radio, TV) botón m
knock [nɔk] vt (strike) golpear; (bump into)
chocar contra; (inf) criticar ♦ vi (at door
etc): **to ~ at/on** llamar a ♦ n golpe m;
(on door) llamada; **~ down** vt atropellar;
~ off (inf) vi (finish) salir del trabajo ♦ vt
(from price) descontar; (inf: steal) birlar; **~
out** vt dejar sin sentido; (BOXING) poner
fuera de combate, dejar K.O.; (in
competition) eliminar; **~ over** vt (object)
tirar; (person) atropellar; **~er** n (on door)
aldabón m; **~out** n (BOXING) K.O. m,

knockout *m* ♦ *cpd* (*competition etc*) eliminatorio

knot [nɔt] *n* nudo ♦ *vt* anudar

know [nəu] (*pt* **knew**, *pp* **known**) *vt* (*facts*) saber; (*be acquainted with*) conocer; (*recognize*) reconocer, conocer; **to ~ how to swim** saber nadar; **to ~ about** *or* **of sb/sth** saber de uno/algo; **~-all** *n* sabelotodo *m/f*; **~-how** *n* conocimientos *mpl*; **~ing** *adj* (*look*) de complicidad; **~ingly** *adv* (*purposely*) adrede; (*smile, look*) con complicidad

knowledge ['nɔlɪdʒ] *n* conocimiento; (*learning*) saber *m*, conocimientos *mpl*; **~able** *adj* entendido

knuckle ['nʌkl] *n* nudillo

Koran [kɔ'rɑːn] *n* Corán *m*

Korea [kɔ'rɪə] *n* Corea

kosher ['kəuʃə*] *adj* autorizado por la ley judía

L, l

L (*BRIT*) *abbr* = **learner driver**

l. *abbr* (= *litre*) l

lab [læb] *n abbr* = **laboratory**

label ['leɪbl] *n* etiqueta ♦ *vt* poner etiqueta a

labor *etc* ['leɪbə*] (*US*) = **labour**

laboratory [lə'bɔrətərɪ] *n* laboratorio

laborious [lə'bɔːrɪəs] *adj* penoso

labour ['leɪbə*] (*US* **labor**) *n* (*hard work*) trabajo; (~ *force*) mano *f* de obra; (*MED*): **to be in ~** estar de parto ♦ *vi*: **to ~ (at sth)** trabajar (en algo) ♦ *vt*: **to ~ a point** insistir en un punto; **L~**, **the L~ party** (*BRIT*) el partido laborista, los laboristas *mpl*; **~ed** *adj* (*breathing*) fatigoso; **~er** *n* peón *m*; **farm ~er** peón *m*; (*day ~er*) jornalero

lace [leɪs] *n* encaje *m*; (*of shoe etc*) cordón *m* ♦ *vt* (*shoes: also*: ~ **up**) atarse (los zapatos)

lack [læk] *n* (*absence*) falta ♦ *vt* faltarle a uno, carecer de; **through** *or* **for ~ of** por falta de; **to be ~ing** faltar, no haber; **to**

be ~ing in sth faltarle a uno algo

lacquer ['lækə*] *n* laca

lad [læd] *n* muchacho, chico

ladder ['lædə*] *n* escalera (de mano); (*BRIT*: *in tights*) carrera

laden ['leɪdn] *adj*: ~ **(with)** cargado (de)

ladle ['leɪdl] *n* cucharón *m*

lady ['leɪdɪ] *n* señora; (*dignified, graceful*) dama; **"ladies and gentlemen ..."** "señoras y caballeros ..."; **young ~** señorita; **the ladies' (room)** los servicios de señoras; **~bird** (*US* **~bug**) *n* mariquita; **~like** *adj* fino; **L~ship** *n*: **your L~ship** su Señoría

lag [læg] *n* retraso ♦ *vi* (*also*: ~ **behind**) retrasarse, quedarse atrás ♦ *vt* (*pipes*) revestir

lager ['lɑːgə*] *n* cerveza (rubia)

lagoon [lə'guːn] *n* laguna

laid [leɪd] *pt, pp of* **lay**; ~ **back** (*inf*) *adj* relajado; ~ **up** *adj*: **to be ~ up (with)** tener que guardar cama (a causa de)

lain [leɪn] *pp of* **lie**

lake [leɪk] *n* lago

lamb [læm] *n* cordero; (*meat*) (carne *f* de) cordero; ~ **chop** *n* chuleta de cordero; **lambswool** *n* lana de cordero

lame [leɪm] *adj* cojo; (*excuse*) poco convincente

lament [lə'ment] *n* quejo ♦ *vt* lamentarse de

laminated ['læmɪneɪtɪd] *adj* (*metal*) laminado; (*wood*) contrachapado; (*surface*) plastificado

lamp [læmp] *n* lámpara; **~post** (*BRIT*) *n* (poste *m* de) farol *m*; **~shade** *n* pantalla

lance [lɑːns] *vt* (*MED*) abrir con lanceta

land [lænd] *n* tierra; (*country*) país *m*; (*piece of* ~) terreno; (*estate*) tierras *fpl*, finca ♦ *vi* (*from ship*) desembarcar; (*AVIAT*) aterrizar; (*fig: fall*) caer, terminar ♦ *vt* (*passengers, goods*) desembarcar; **to ~ sb with sth** (*inf*) hacer cargar a uno con algo; ~ **up** *vi*: **to ~ up in/at** ir a parar a/ en; **~fill site** ['lændfɪl-] *n* vertedero; **~ing** *n* aterrizaje *m*; (*of staircase*) rellano; **~ing gear** *n* (*AVIAT*) tren *m* de aterrizaje;

~lady n (of rented house, pub etc) dueña; **~lord** n propietario; (of pub etc) patrón m; **~mark** n lugar m conocido; **to be a ~mark** (fig) marcar un hito histórico; **~owner** n terrateniente m/f; **~scape** n paisaje m; **~scape gardener** n arquitecto de jardines; **~slide** n (GEO) corrimiento de tierras; (fig: POL) victoria arrolladora

lane [leɪn] n (in country) camino; (AUT) carril m; (in race) calle f

language ['læŋgwɪdʒ] n lenguaje m; (national tongue) idioma m, lengua; **bad ~** palabrotas fpl; **~ laboratory** n laboratorio de idiomas

lank [læŋk] adj (hair) lacio

lanky ['læŋkɪ] adj larguirucho

lantern ['læntn] n linterna, farol m

lap [læp] n (of track) vuelta; (of body) regazo; **to sit on sb's ~** sentarse en las rodillas de uno ♦ vt (also: **~ up**) beber a lengüetadas ♦ vi (waves) chapotear; **~ up** vt tragarse

lapel [lə'pɛl] n solapa

Lapland ['læplænd] n Laponia

lapse [læps] n fallo; (moral) desliz m; (of time) intervalo ♦ vi (expire) caducar; (time) pasar, transcurrir; **to ~ into bad habits** caer en malos hábitos

laptop (computer) ['læptɔp-] n (ordenador m) portátil m

larch [lɑːtʃ] n alerce m

lard [lɑːd] n manteca (de cerdo)

larder ['lɑːdə*] n despensa

large [lɑːdʒ] adj grande; **at ~** (free) en libertad; (generally) en general; **~ly** adv (mostly) en su mayor parte; (introducing reason) en gran parte; **~-scale** adj (map) en gran escala; (fig) importante

lark [lɑːk] n (bird) alondra; (joke) broma

laryngitis [lærɪn'dʒaɪtɪs] n laringitis f

laser ['leɪzə*] n láser m; **~ printer** n impresora (por) láser

lash [læʃ] n latigazo; (also: **eye~**) pestaña ♦ vt azotar; (tie) atar a/atar; **~ out** vi: **to ~ out (at sb)** (hit) arremeter (contra uno); **to ~ out against**

sb lanzar invectivas contra uno

lass [læs] (BRIT) n chica

lasso [læ'suː] n lazo

last [lɑːst] adj último; (end: of series etc) final ♦ adv (most recently) la última vez; (finally) por último ♦ vi durar; (continue) continuar, seguir; **~ night** anoche; **~ week** la semana pasada; **at ~** por fin; **~ but one** penúltimo; **~-ditch** adj (attempt) último, desesperado; **~ing** adj duradero; **~ly** adv por último, finalmente; **~-minute** adj de última hora

latch [lætʃ] n pestillo

late [leɪt] adj (far on: in time, process etc) al final de; (not on time) tarde, atrasado; (dead) fallecido ♦ adv tarde; (behind time, schedule) con retraso; **of ~** últimamente; **~ at night** a última hora de la noche; **in ~ May** hacia fines de mayo; **the ~ Mr X** el difunto Sr X; **~comer** n recién llegado/a; **~ly** adv últimamente; **~r** adj (date etc) posterior; (version etc) más reciente ♦ adv más tarde, después; **~st** ['leɪtɪst] adj último; **at the ~st** a más tardar

lathe [leɪð] n torno

lather ['lɑːðə*] n espuma (de jabón) ♦ vt enjabonar

Latin ['lætɪn] n latín m ♦ adj latino; **~ America** n América latina; **~-American** adj, n latinoamericano/a

latitude ['lætɪtjuːd] n latitud f; (fig) libertad f

latter ['lætə*] adj último; (of two) segundo ♦ n: **the ~** el último, éste; **~ly** adv últimamente

laudable ['lɔːdəbl] adj loable

laugh [lɑːf] n risa ♦ vi reír(se); (to do sth) **for a ~** (hacer algo) en broma; **~ at** vt fus reírse de; **~ off** vt tomar algo a risa; **~able** adj ridículo; **~ing stock** n: **the ~ing stock of** el hazmerreír de; **~ter** n risa

launch [lɔːntʃ] n lanzamiento; (boat) lancha ♦ vt (ship) botar; (rocket etc) lanzar; (fig) comenzar; **~ into** vt fus lanzarse a; **~(ing) pad** n plataforma de lanzamiento

launder ['lɔːndə*] *vt* lavar
Launderette ® [lɔːn'drɛt] (*BRIT*) *n*
lavandería (automática)
Laundromat ® ['lɔːndrəmæt] (*US*) *n*
= **Launderette**
laundry ['lɔːndrɪ] *n* (*dirty*) ropa sucia;
(*clean*) colada; (*room*) lavadero
lavatory ['lævətərɪ] *n* wáter *m*
lavender ['lævəndə*] *n* lavanda
lavish ['lævɪʃ] *adj* (*amount*) abundante;
(*person*): ~ **with** pródigo en ♦ *vt*: **to** ~ **sth**
on sb colmar a uno de algo
law [lɔː] *n* ley *f*; (*SCOL*) derecho; (*a rule*)
regla; (*professions connected with* ~)
jurisprudencia; **~-abiding** *adj* respetuoso
de la ley; ~ **and order** *n* orden *m*
público; ~ **court** *n* tribunal *m* (de
justicia); **~ful** *adj* legítimo, lícito; **~less**
adj (*action*) criminal
lawn [lɔːn] *n* césped *m*; **~mower** *n*
cortacésped *m*; ~ **tennis** *n* tenis *m* sobre
hierba
law school (*US*) *n* (*SCOL*) facultad *f* de
derecho
lawsuit ['lɔːsuːt] *n* pleito
lawyer ['lɔːjə*] *n* abogado/a; (*for sales,
wills etc*) notario/a
lax [læks] *adj* laxo
laxative ['læksətɪv] *n* laxante *m*
lay [leɪ] (*pt*, *pp* **laid**) *pt of* **lie** ♦ *adj*
(*not expert*) lego ♦ *vt* (*place*) colocar;
(*eggs, table*) poner; (*cable*) tender;
(*carpet*) extender; ~ **aside** *or* **by** *vt* dejar
a un lado; ~ **down** *vt* (*pen etc*) dejar;
(*rules etc*) establecer; **to** ~ **down the law**
(*pej*) imponer las normas; ~ **off** *vt*
(*workers*) despedir; ~ **on** *vt* (*meal,
facilities*) proveer; ~ **out** *vt* (*spread out*)
disponer, exponer; **~about** (*inf*) *n* vago/
a; **~-by** *n* (*BRIT: AUT*) área de
aparcamiento
layer ['leɪə*] *n* capa
layman ['leɪmən] (*irreg*) *n* lego
layout ['leɪaut] *n* (*design*) plan *m*, trazado;
(*PRESS*) composición *f*
laze [leɪz] *vi* (*also*: ~ **about**) holgazanear
lazy ['leɪzɪ] *adj* perezoso, vago; (*movement*)

lento
lb. *abbr* = **pound** (*weight*)
lead[1] [liːd] (*pt*, *pp* **led**) *n* (*front position*)
delantera; (*clue*) pista; (*ELEC*) cable *m*; (*for
dog*) correa; (*THEATRE*) papel *m* principal
♦ *vt* (*walk etc in front of*) ir a la cabeza
de; (*guide*): **to** ~ **sb somewhere** conducir
a uno a algún sitio; (*be leader of*) dirigir;
(*start, guide: activity*) protagonizar ♦ *vi*
(*road, pipe etc*) conducir a; (*SPORT*) ir
primero; **to be in the** ~ (*SPORT*) llevar la
delantera; (*fig*) ir a la cabeza; **to** ~ **the
way** (*also fig*) llevar la delantera; ~ **away**
vt llevar; ~ **back** *vt* (*person, route*) llevar
de vuelta; ~ **on** *vt* (*tease*) engañar; ~ **to**
vt fus producir, provocar; ~ **up to** *vt fus*
(*events*) conducir a; (*in conversation*)
preparar el terreno para
lead[2] [lɛd] *n* (*metal*) plomo; (*in pencil*)
mina; **~ed petrol** *n* gasolina con plomo
leader ['liːdə*] *n* jefe/a *m/f*, líder *m*;
(*SPORT*) líder *m*; **~ship** *n* dirección *f*;
(*position*) mando; (*quality*) iniciativa
leading ['liːdɪŋ] *adj* (*main*) principal; (*first*)
primero; (*front*) delantero; ~ **lady** *n*
(*THEATRE*) primera actriz *f*; ~ **light** *n*
(*person*) figura principal; ~ **man** (*irreg*) *n*
(*THEATRE*) primer galán *m*
lead singer [liːd-] *n* cantante *m/f*
leaf [liːf] (*pl* **leaves**) *n* hoja ♦ *vi*: **to** ~
through hojear; **to turn over a new** ~
reformarse
leaflet ['liːflɪt] *n* folleto
league [liːg] *n* sociedad *f*; (*FOOTBALL*) liga;
to be in ~ **with** haberse confabulado con
leak [liːk] *n* (*of liquid, gas*) escape *m*, fuga;
(*in pipe*) agujero; (*in roof*) gotera; (*in
security*) filtración *f* ♦ *vi* (*shoes, ship*)
hacer agua; (*pipe*) tener (un) escape;
(*roof*) gotear; (*liquid, gas*) escaparse,
fugarse; (*fig*) divulgarse ♦ *vt* (*fig*) filtrar
lean [liːn] (*pt*, *pp* **leaned** *or* **leant**) *adj*
(*thin*) flaco; (*meat*) magro ♦ *vt*: **to** ~ **sth
on sth** apoyar algo en algo ♦ *vi* (*slope*)
inclinarse; **to** ~ **against** apoyarse contra;
to ~ **on** apoyarse en; ~ **back/forward**
vi inclinarse hacia atrás/adelante; ~ **out**

vi asomarse; ~ **over** *vi* inclinarse; **~ing**
n: **~ing (towards)** inclinación *f* (hacia);
leant [lɛnt] *pt, pp of* **lean**

leap [liːp] (*pt, pp* **leaped** *or* **leapt**) *n* salto
♦ *vi* saltar; **~frog** *n* pídola; **~ year** *n*
año bisiesto

learn [ləːn] (*pt, pp* **learned** *or* **learnt**) *vt*
aprender ♦ *vi* aprender; **to ~ about sth**
enterarse de algo; **to ~ to do sth**
aprender a hacer algo; **~ed** [ˈləːnɪd] *adj*
erudito; **~er** *n* (*BRIT: also:* **~er driver**)
principiante *m/f*; **~ing** *n* el saber *m*,
conocimientos *mpl*

lease [liːs] *n* arriendo ♦ *vt* arrendar

leash [liːʃ] *n* correa

least [liːst] *adj*: **the ~** (*slightest*) el menor,
el más pequeño; (*smallest amount of*)
mínimo ♦ *adv* (*+vb*) menos; (*+adj*): **the ~**
expensive el/la menos costoso/a; **the ~**
possible effort el menor esfuerzo posible;
at ~ por lo menos, al menos; **you could**
at ~ have written por lo menos podías
haber escrito; **not in the ~** en absoluto

leather [ˈlɛðə*] *n* cuero

leave [liːv] (*pt, pp* **left**) *vt* dejar; (*go away*
from) abandonar; (*place etc: permanently*)
salir de ♦ *vi* irse; (*train etc*) salir ♦ *n*
permiso; **to ~ sth to sb** (*money etc*) legar
algo a uno; (*responsibility etc*) encargar a
uno de algo; **to be left** quedar, sobrar;
there's some milk left over sobra *or*
queda algo de leche; **on ~** de permiso; **~**
behind *vt* (*on purpose*) dejar;
(*accidentally*) dejarse; **~ out** *vt* omitir; **~**
of absence *n* permiso de ausentarse

leaves [liːvz] *npl of* **leaf**

Lebanon [ˈlɛbənən] *n*: **the ~** el Líbano

lecherous [ˈlɛtʃərəs] (*pej*) *adj* lascivo

lecture [ˈlɛktʃə*] *n* conferencia; (*SCOL*)
clase *f* ♦ *vi* dar una clase ♦ *vt* (*scold*): **to**
~ sb on *or* **about sth** echar una
reprimenda a uno por algo; **to give a ~**
on dar una conferencia sobre; **~r** *n*
conferenciante *m/f*; (*BRIT: at university*)
profesor(a) *m/f*

led [lɛd] *pt, pp of* **lead**

ledge [lɛdʒ] *n* repisa; (*of window*) alféizar

m; (*of mountain*) saliente *m*

ledger [ˈlɛdʒə*] *n* libro mayor

leech [liːtʃ] *n* sanguijuela

leek [liːk] *n* puerro

leer [lɪə*] *vi*: **to ~ at sb** mirar de manera
lasciva a uno

leeway [ˈliːweɪ] *n* (*fig*): **to have some ~**
tener cierta libertad de acción

left [lɛft] *pt, pp of* **leave** ♦ *adj* izquierdo;
(*remaining*): **there are 2 ~** quedan dos
♦ *n* izquierda ♦ *adv* a la izquierda; **on** *or*
to the ~ a la izquierda; **the L~** (*POL*) la
izquierda; **~-handed** *adj* zurdo; **the ~-**
hand side *n* la izquierda; **~-luggage**
(office) (*BRIT*) *n* consigna; **~-overs** *npl*
sobras *fpl*; **~-wing** *adj* (*POL*) de
izquierdas, izquierdista

leg [lɛg] *n* pierna; (*of animal, chair*) pata;
(*trouser ~*) pernera; (*CULIN: of lamb*)
pierna; (*of chicken*) pata; (*of journey*)
etapa

legacy [ˈlɛgəsɪ] *n* herencia

legal [ˈliːgl] *adj* (*permitted by law*) lícito; (*of*
law) legal; **~ holiday** (*US*) *n* fiesta oficial;
~ize *vt* legalizar; **~ly** *adv* legalmente; **~**
tender *n* moneda de curso legal

legend [ˈlɛdʒənd] *n* (*also fig: person*)
leyenda

legislation [lɛdʒɪsˈleɪʃən] *n* legislación *f*

legislature [ˈlɛdʒɪslətʃə*] *n* cuerpo
legislativo

legitimate [lɪˈdʒɪtɪmət] *adj* legítimo

leg-room *n* espacio para las piernas

leisure [ˈlɛʒə*] *n* ocio, tiempo libre; **at ~**
con tranquilidad; **~ centre** *n* centro de
recreo; **~ly** *adj* sin prisa, lento

lemon [ˈlɛmən] *n* limón *m*; **~ade** *n* (*fizzy*)
gaseosa; **~ tea** *n* té *m* con limón

lend [lɛnd] (*pt, pp* **lent**) *vt*: **to ~ sth to sb**
prestar algo a alguien; **~ing library** *n*
biblioteca de préstamo

length [lɛŋθ] *n* (*size*) largo, longitud *f*;
(*distance*): **the ~ of** todo lo largo de; (*of*
swimming pool, cloth) largo; (*of wood,*
string) trozo; (*amount of time*) duración *f*;
at ~ (*at last*) por fin, finalmente;
(*lengthily*) largamente; **~en** *vt* alargar

♦ *vi* alargarse; **~ways** *adv* a lo largo; **~y** *adj* largo, extenso

lenient ['li:niənt] *adj* indulgente

lens [lenz] *n* (*of spectacles*) lente *f*; (*of camera*) objetivo

Lent [lent] *n* Cuaresma

lent [lent] *pt, pp of* **lend**

lentil ['lentl] *n* lenteja

Leo ['li:əu] *n* Leo

leotard ['li:ətɑ:d] *n* mallas *fpl*

leprosy ['leprəsɪ] *n* lepra

lesbian ['lezbɪən] *n* lesbiana

less [les] *adj* (*in size, degree etc*) menor; (*in quality*) menos ♦ *pron, adv* menos ♦ *prep*: **~ tax/10% discount** menos impuestos/el 10 por ciento de descuento; **~ than half** menos de la mitad; **~ than ever** menos que nunca; **~ and ~** cada vez menos; **the ~ he works ...** cuanto menos trabaja ...; **~en** *vi* disminuir, reducirse ♦ *vt* disminuir, reducir; **~er** ['lesə*] *adj* menor; **to a ~er extent** en menor grado

lesson ['lesn] *n* clase *f*; (*warning*) lección *f*

let [let] (*pt, pp* **let**) *vt* (*allow*) dejar, permitir; (*BRIT: lease*) alquilar; **to ~ sb do sth** dejar que uno haga algo; **to ~ sb know sth** comunicar algo a uno; **~'s go** ¡vamos!; **~ him come** que venga; **"to ~"** "se alquila"; **~ down** *vt* (*tyre*) desinflar; (*disappoint*) defraudar; **~ go** *vi, vt* soltar; **~ in** *vt* dejar entrar; (*visitor etc*) hacer pasar; **~ off** *vt* (*culprit*) dejar escapar; (*gun*) disparar; (*bomb*) accionar; (*firework*) hacer estallar; **~ on** (*inf*) *vi* divulgar; **~ out** *vt* dejar salir; (*sound*) soltar; **~ up** *vi* amainar, disminuir

lethal ['li:θl] *adj* (*weapon*) mortífero; (*poison, wound*) mortal

letter ['letə*] *n* (*of alphabet*) letra; (*correspondence*) carta; **~ bomb** *n* carta-bomba; **~box** (*BRIT*) *n* buzón *m*; **~ing** *n* letras *fpl*

lettuce ['letɪs] *n* lechuga

let-up *n* disminución *f*

leukaemia [lu:'ki:mɪə] (*US* **leukemia**) *n* leucemia

level ['levl] *adj* (*flat*) llano ♦ *adv*: **to draw**

~ with llegar a la altura de ♦ *n* nivel *m*; (*height*) altura ♦ *vt* nivelar; allanar; (*destroy: building*) derribar; (: *forest*) arrasar; **to be ~ with** estar a nivel de; **"A" ~s** (*BRIT*) *npl* ≈ exámenes *mpl* de bachillerato superior, B.U.P.; **"O" ~s** (*BRIT*) *npl* ≈ exámenes *mpl* de octavo de básica; **on the ~** (*fig: honest*) serio; **~ off** *or* **out** *vi* (*prices etc*) estabilizarse; **~ crossing** (*BRIT*) *n* paso a nivel; **~-headed** *adj* sensato

lever ['li:və*] *n* (*also fig*) palanca ♦ *vt*: **to ~ up** levantar con palanca; **~age** *n* (*using bar etc*) apalancamiento; (*fig: influence*) influencia

levy ['levɪ] *n* impuesto ♦ *vt* exigir, recaudar

lewd [lu:d] *adj* lascivo; (*joke*) obsceno, colorado (*AM*)

liability [laɪə'bɪlətɪ] *n* (*pej: person, thing*) estorbo, lastre *m*; (*JUR: responsibility*) responsabilidad *f*; **liabilities** *npl* (*COMM*) pasivo

liable ['laɪəbl] *adj* (*subject*): **~ to** sujeto a; (*responsible*): **~ for** responsable de; (*likely*): **~ to do** propenso a hacer

liaise [lɪ'eɪz] *vi*: **to ~ with** enlazar con; **liaison** [li:'eɪzɒn] *n* (*coordination*) enlace *m*; (*affair*) relaciones *fpl* amorosas

liar ['laɪə*] *n* mentiroso/a

libel ['laɪbl] *n* calumnia ♦ *vt* calumniar

liberal ['lɪbərəl] *adj* liberal; (*offer, amount etc*) generoso

liberate ['lɪbəreɪt] *vt* (*people: from poverty etc*) librar; (*prisoner*) libertar; (*country*) liberar

liberty ['lɪbətɪ] *n* libertad *f*; (*criminal*): **to be at ~** estar en libertad; **to be at ~ to do** estar libre para hacer; **to take the ~ of doing sth** tomarse la libertad de hacer algo

Libra ['li:brə] *n* Libra

librarian [laɪ'brɛərɪən] *n* bibliotecario/a

library ['laɪbrərɪ] *n* biblioteca

libretto [lɪ'brɛtəu] *n* libreto

Libya ['lɪbɪə] *n* Libia; **~n** *adj, n* libio/a *m/f*

lice [laɪs] *npl of* **louse**

licence ['laɪsəns] (*US* **license**) *n* licencia;

(*permit*) permiso; (*also:* **driving ~**, (*US*) **driver's ~**) carnet *m* de conducir (*SP*), permiso (*AM*)

license ['laɪsəns] *n* (*US*) = **licence** ♦ *vt* autorizar, dar permiso a; **~d** *adj* (*for alcohol*) autorizado para vender bebidas alcohólicas; (*car*) matriculado; **~ plate** (*US*) *n* placa (de matrícula)

lick [lɪk] *vt* lamer; (*inf: defeat*) dar una paliza a; **to ~ one's lips** relamerse

licorice ['lɪkərɪs] (*US*) *n* = **liquorice**

lid [lɪd] *n* (*of box, case*) tapa; (*of pan*) tapadera

lido ['laɪdəu] *n* (*BRIT*) piscina

lie [laɪ] (*pt* **lay,** *pp* **lain**) *vi* (*rest*) estar echado, estar acostado; (*of object: be situated*) estar, encontrarse; (*tell lies: pt, pp* **lied**) mentir ♦ *n* mentira; **to ~ low** (*fig*) mantenerse a escondidas; **~ about** *or* **around** *vi* (*things*) estar tirado, (*BRIT: people*) estar tumbado; **~-down** (*BRIT*) *n*: **to have a ~-down** echarse (una siesta); **~-in** (*BRIT*) *n*: **to have a ~-in** quedarse en la cama

lieu [lu:]: **in ~ of** *prep* en lugar de

lieutenant [lef'tenənt, (*US*) lu:'tenənt] *n* (*MIL*) teniente *m*

life [laɪf] (*pl* **lives**) *n* vida; **to come to ~** animarse; **~ assurance** (*BRIT*) *n* seguro de vida; **~belt** (*BRIT*) *n* salvavidas *m inv*; **~boat** *n* lancha de socorro; **~guard** *n* vigilante *m/f*, socorrista *m/f*; **~ insurance** *n* = **~ assurance; ~ jacket** *n* chaleco salvavidas; **~less** *adj* sin vida; (*dull*) soso; **~like** *adj* (*model etc*) que parece vivo; (*realistic*) realista; **~long** *adj* de toda la vida; **~ preserver** (*US*) *n* cinturón *m*/chaleco salvavidas; **~ sentence** *n* cadena perpetua; **~-size** *adj* de tamaño natural; **~ span** *n* vida; **~style** *n* estilo de vida; **~ support system** *n* (*MED*) sistema *m* de respiración asistida; **~time** *n* (*of person*) vida; (*of thing*) período de vida

lift [lɪft] *vt* levantar, suprimir; (*end: ban, rule*) levantar ♦ *vi* (*fog*) disiparse ♦ *n* (*BRIT: machine*) ascensor *m*; **to give sb a**

~ (*BRIT*) llevar a uno en el coche; **~-off** *n* despegue *m*

light [laɪt] (*pt, pp* **lighted** *or* **lit**) *n* luz *f*; (*lamp*) luz *f*, lámpara; (*AUT*) faro; (*for cigarette etc*): **have you got a ~?** ¿tienes fuego? ♦ *vt* (*candle, cigarette, fire*) encender (*SP*), prender (*AM*); (*room*) alumbrar ♦ *adj* (*colour*) claro; (*not heavy, also fig*) ligero; (*room*) con mucha luz; (*gentle, graceful*) ágil; **~s** *npl* (*traffic ~s*) semáforos *mpl*; **to come to ~** salir a luz; **in the ~ of** (*new evidence etc*) a la luz de; **~ up** *vi* (*smoke*) encender un cigarrillo; (*face*) iluminarse ♦ *vt* (*illuminate*) iluminar, alumbrar; (*set fire to*) encender; **~ bulb** *n* bombilla (*SP*), foco (*AM*); **~en** *vt* (*make less heavy*) aligerar; **~er** *n* (*also:* **cigarette ~er**) encendedor *m*, mechero; **~-headed** *adj* (*dizzy*) mareado; (*excited*) exaltado; **~-hearted** *adj* (*person*) alegre; (*remark etc*) divertido; **~house** *n* faro; **~ing** *n* (*system*) alumbrado; **~ly** *adv* ligeramente; (*not seriously*) con poca seriedad; **to get off ~ly** ser castigado con poca severidad; **~ness** *n* (*in weight*) ligereza

lightning ['laɪtnɪŋ] *n* relámpago, rayo; **~ conductor** (*US* **~ rod**) *n* pararrayos *m inv*

light: **~ pen** *n* lápiz *m* óptico; **~weight** *adj* (*suit*) ligero ♦ *n* (*BOXING*) peso ligero; **~ year** *n* año luz

like [laɪk] *vt* gustarle a uno ♦ *prep* como ♦ *adj* parecido, semejante ♦ *n*: **and the ~** y otros por el estilo; **his ~s and dislikes** sus gustos y aversiones; **I would ~, I'd ~** me gustaría; (*for purchase*) quisiera; **would you ~ a coffee?** ¿te apetece un café?; **I ~ swimming** me gusta nadar; **she ~s apples** le gustan las manzanas; **to be** *or* **look ~ sb/sth** parecerse a alguien/algo; **what does it look/taste/sound ~?** ¿cómo es/a qué sabe/cómo suena?; **that's just ~ him** es muy de él, es característico de él; **do it ~ this** hazlo así; **it is nothing ~ ...** no tiene parecido alguno con ...; **~able** *adj* simpático, agradable

likelihood ['laɪklɪhud] n probabilidad f
likely ['laɪklɪ] adj probable; **he's ~ to
leave** es probable que se vaya; **not ~!** ¡ni
hablar!
likeness ['laɪknɪs] n semejanza, parecido;
that's a good ~ se parece mucho
likewise ['laɪkwaɪz] adv igualmente; **to do
~** hacer lo mismo
liking ['laɪkɪŋ] n: **~ (for)** (person) cariño (a);
(thing) afición (a); **to be to sb's ~** ser del
gusto de uno
lilac ['laɪlək] n (tree) lilo; (flower) lila
lily ['lɪlɪ] n lirio, azucena; **~ of the valley** n
lirio de los valles
limb [lɪm] n miembro
limber ['lɪmbə*]: **to ~ up** vi (SPORT) hacer
ejercicios de calentamiento
limbo ['lɪmbəu] n: **to be in ~** (fig) quedar a
la expectativa
lime [laɪm] n (tree) limero; (fruit) lima;
(GEO) cal f
limelight ['laɪmlaɪt] n: **to be in the ~** (fig)
ser el centro de atención
limerick ['lɪmərɪk] n especie de poema
humorístico
limestone ['laɪmstəun] n piedra caliza
limit ['lɪmɪt] n límite m ♦ vt limitar; **~ed**
adj limitado; **to be ~ed to** limitarse a;
~ed (liability) company (BRIT) n
sociedad f anónima
limousine ['lɪməzi:n] n limusina
limp [lɪmp] n: **to have a ~** tener cojera
♦ vi cojear ♦ adj flojo; (material) fláccido
limpet ['lɪmpɪt] n lapa
line [laɪn] n línea; (rope) cuerda; (for
fishing) sedal m; (wire) hilo; (row, series)
fila, hilera; (of writing) renglón m, línea;
(of song) verso; (on hand) arruga; (RAIL) vía
♦ vt (road etc) llenar; (SEWING) forrar; **to ~
the streets** llenar las aceras; **in ~ with**
alineado con; (according to) de acuerdo
con; **~ up** vi hacer cola ♦ vt alinear;
(prepare) preparar; organizar
lined [laɪnd] adj (face) arrugado; (paper)
rayado
linen ['lɪnɪn] n ropa blanca; (cloth) lino
liner ['laɪnə*] n vapor m de línea,

transatlántico; (for bin) bolsa (de basura)
linesman ['laɪnzmən] n (SPORT) juez m de
línea
line-up n (US: queue) cola; (SPORT)
alineación f
linger ['lɪŋgə*] vi retrasarse, tardar en
marcharse; (smell, tradition) persistir
lingerie ['lænʒəri:] n lencería
linguist ['lɪŋgwɪst] n lingüista m/f; **~ics** n
lingüística
lining ['laɪnɪŋ] n forro; (ANAT) (membrana)
mucosa
link [lɪŋk] n (of a chain) eslabón m;
(relationship) relación f, vínculo ♦ vt
vincular, unir; (associate): **to ~ with** or **to**
relacionar con; **~s** npl (GOLF) campo de
golf; **~ up** vt acoplar ♦ vi unirse
lino ['laɪnəu] n = **linoleum**
linoleum [lɪ'nəuliəm] n linóleo
lion ['laɪən] n león m; **~ess** n leona
lip [lɪp] n labio
liposuction ['lɪpəusʌkʃən] n liposucción f
lip: **~read** vi leer los labios; **~ salve** n
crema protectora para labios; **~ service**
n: **to pay ~ service to sth** (pej) prometer
algo de boquilla; **~stick** n lápiz m de
labios, carmín m
liqueur [lɪ'kjuə*] n licor m
liquid ['lɪkwɪd] adj, n líquido; **~ize** [-aɪz] vt
(CULIN) licuar; **~izer** [-aɪzə*] n licuadora
liquor ['lɪkə*] n licor m, bebidas fpl
alcohólicas
liquorice ['lɪkərɪs] (BRIT) n regaliz m
liquor store (US) n bodega, tienda de
vinos y bebidas alcohólicas
Lisbon ['lɪzbən] n Lisboa
lisp [lɪsp] n ceceo ♦ vi cecear
list [lɪst] n lista ♦ vt (mention) enumerar;
(put on a list) poner en una lista; **~ed
building** (BRIT) n monumento declarado
de interés histórico-artístico
listen ['lɪsn] vi escuchar, oír; **to ~ to sb/
sth** escuchar a uno/algo; **~er** n oyente
m/f; (RADIO) radioyente m/f
listless ['lɪstlɪs] adj apático, indiferente
lit [lɪt] pt, pp of **light**
liter ['li:tə*] (US) n = **litre**

literacy ['lɪtərəsɪ] *n* capacidad *f* de leer y escribir
literal ['lɪtərl] *adj* literal
literary ['lɪtərərɪ] *adj* literario
literate ['lɪtərət] *adj* que sabe leer y escribir; (*educated*) culto
literature ['lɪtərɪtʃə*] *n* literatura *f*; (*brochures etc*) folletos *mpl*
lithe [laɪð] *adj* ágil
litigation [lɪtɪ'ɡeɪʃən] *n* litigio
litre ['liːtə*] (*US* **liter**) *n* litro
litter ['lɪtə*] *n* (*rubbish*) basura; (*young animals*) camada, cría; **~ bin** (*BRIT*) *n* papelera; **~ed** *adj*: **~ed with** (*scattered*) lleno de
little ['lɪtl] *adj* (*small*) pequeño; (*not much*) poco ♦ *adv* poco; **a ~** un poco (de); **~ house/bird** casita/pajarito; **a ~ bit** un poquito; **~ by ~** poco a poco; **~ finger** *n* dedo meñique
live¹ [laɪv] *adj* (*animal*) vivo; (*wire*) conectado; (*broadcast*) en directo; (*shell*) cargado
live² [lɪv] *vi* vivir; **~ down** *vt* hacer olvidar; **~ on** *vt fus* (*food, salary*) vivir de; **~ together** *vi* vivir juntos; **~ up to** *vt fus* (*fulfil*) cumplir con
livelihood ['laɪvlɪhud] *n* sustento
lively ['laɪvlɪ] *adj* vivo; (*interesting: place, book etc*) animado
liven up ['laɪvn-] *vt* animar ♦ *vi* animarse
liver ['lɪvə*] *n* hígado
lives [laɪvz] *npl of* **life**
livestock ['laɪvstɔk] *n* ganado
livid ['lɪvɪd] *adj* lívido; (*furious*) furioso
living ['lɪvɪŋ] *adj* (*alive*) vivo ♦ *n*: **to earn** *or* **make a ~** ganarse la vida; **~ conditions** *npl* condiciones *fpl* de vida; **~ room** *n* sala (de estar); **~ standards** *npl* nivel *m* de vida; **~ wage** *n* jornal *m* suficiente para vivir
lizard ['lɪzəd] *n* lagarto; (*small*) lagartija
load [ləud] *n* carga; (*weight*) peso ♦ *vt* (*COMPUT*) cargar; (*also:* **~ up**): **to ~ (with)** cargar (con *or* de); **a ~ of rubbish** (*inf*) tonterías *fpl*; **a ~ of, ~s of** (*fig*) (gran) cantidad de, montones de; **~ed** *adj*

(*vehicle*): **to be ~ed with** estar cargado de; (*question*) intencionado; (*inf: rich*) forrado (de dinero)
loaf [ləuf] (*pl* **loaves**) *n* (barra de) pan *m*
loan [ləun] *n* préstamo ♦ *vt* prestar; **on ~** prestado
loath [ləuθ] *adj*: **to be ~ to do sth** estar poco dispuesto a hacer algo
loathe [ləuð] *vt* aborrecer; (*person*) odiar; **loathing** *n* aversión *f*; odio
loaves [ləuvz] *npl of* **loaf**
lobby ['lɔbɪ] *n* vestíbulo, sala de espera; (*POL: pressure group*) grupo de presión ♦ *vt* presionar
lobster ['lɔbstə*] *n* langosta
local ['ləukl] *adj* local ♦ *n* (*pub*) bar *m*; **the ~s** los vecinos, los del lugar; **~ anaesthetic** *n* (*MED*) anestesia local; **~ authority** *n* municipio, ayuntamiento (*SP*); **~ call** *n* (*TEL*) llamada local; **~ government** *n* gobierno municipal; **~ity** [-'kælɪtɪ] *n* localidad *f*; **~ly** [-kəlɪ] *adv* en la vecindad; por aquí
locate [ləu'keɪt] *vt* (*find*) localizar; (*situate*): **to be ~d in** estar situado en
location [ləu'keɪʃən] *n* situación *f*; **on ~** (*CINEMA*) en exteriores
loch [lɔx] *n* lago
lock [lɔk] *n* (*of door, box*) cerradura; (*of canal*) esclusa; (*of hair*) mechón *m* ♦ *vt* (*with key*) cerrar (con llave) ♦ *vi* (*door etc*) cerrarse (con llave); (*wheels*) trabarse; **~ in** *vt* encerrar; **~ out** *vt* (*person*) cerrar la puerta a; **~ up** *vt* (*criminal*) meter en la cárcel; (*mental patient*) encerrar; (*house*) cerrar (con llave) ♦ *vi* echar la llave
locker ['lɔkə*] *n* casillero
locket ['lɔkɪt] *n* medallón *m*
locksmith ['lɔksmɪθ] *n* cerrajero/a
lockup ['lɔkʌp] *n* (*jail, cell*) cárcel *f*
locum ['ləukəm] *n* (*MED*) (médico/a) interino/a
locust ['ləukəst] *n* langosta
lodge [lɔdʒ] *n* casita (del guarda) ♦ *vi* (*person*): **to ~ (with)** alojarse (en casa de); (*bullet, bone*) incrustarse ♦ *vt* (*complaint*) presentar; **~r** *n* huésped(a) *m/f*

lodgings ['lɔdʒɪŋz] *npl* alojamiento
loft [lɔft] *n* desván *m*
lofty ['lɔftɪ] *adj* (*noble*) sublime; (*haughty*) altanero
log [lɔg] *n* (*of wood*) leño, tronco; (*written account*) diario ♦ *vt* anotar
logbook ['lɔgbuk] *n* (*NAUT*) diario de a bordo; (*AVIAT*) libro de vuelo; (*of car*) documentación *f* (del coche *SP*) *or* carro (*AM*)
loggerheads ['lɔgəhedz] *npl*: **to be at ~ (with)** estar en desacuerdo (con)
logic ['lɔdʒɪk] *n* lógica; **~al** *adj* lógico
logo ['ləugəu] *n* logotipo
loin [lɔɪn] *n* (*CULIN*) lomo, solomillo
loiter ['lɔɪtə*] *vi* (*linger*) entretenerse
loll [lɔl] *vi* (*also*: **~ about**) repantigarse
lollipop ['lɔlɪpɔp] *n* chupa-chups ® *m inv*, pirulí *m*; **~ man/lady** (*BRIT irreg*) *n persona encargada de ayudar a los niños a cruzar la calle*

---
lollipop man/lollipop lady

i *En el Reino Unido, se llama **lollipop man** o **lollipop lady** a la persona que se ocupa de parar el tráfico en los alrededores de los colegios para que los niños crucen sin peligro. Suelen ser personas ya jubiladas, vestidas con una gabardina de color llamativo y llevan una señal de stop portátil, la cual recuerda por su forma a una piruleta, y de ahí su nombre.*

London ['lʌndən] *n* Londres; **~er** *n* londinense *m/f*
lone [ləun] *adj* solitario
loneliness ['ləunlɪnɪs] *n* soledad *f*; aislamiento
lonely ['ləunlɪ] *adj* (*situation*) solitario; (*person*) solo; (*place*) aislado
long [lɔŋ] *adj* largo ♦ *adv* mucho tiempo, largamente ♦ *vi*: **to ~ for sth** anhelar algo; **so** *or* **as ~ as** mientras, con tal que; **don't be ~!** ¡no tardéis!, ¡vuelve pronto!; **how ~ is the street?** ¿cuánto tiene la calle de largo?; **how ~ is the lesson?**

¿cuánto dura la clase?; **6 metres ~** que mide 6 metros, de 6 metros de largo; **6 months ~** que dura 6 meses, de 6 meses de duración; **all night ~** toda la noche; **he no ~er comes** ya no viene; **~ before** mucho antes; **before ~** (*+future*) dentro de poco; (*+past*) poco tiempo después; **at ~ last** al fin, por fin; **~-distance** *adj* (*race*) de larga distancia; (*call*) interurbano; **~-haired** *adj* de pelo largo; **~hand** *n* escritura sin abreviaturas; **~ing** *n* anhelo, ansia; (*nostalgia*) nostalgia ♦ *adj* anhelante
longitude ['lɔŋgɪtjuːd] *n* longitud *f*
long: **~ jump** *n* salto de longitud; **~-life** *adj* (*batteries*) de larga duración; (*milk*) uperizado; **~-lost** *adj* desaparecido hace mucho tiempo; **~-range** *adj* (*plan*) de gran alcance; (*missile*) de largo alcance; **~-sighted** (*BRIT*) *adj* présbita; **~-standing** *adj* de mucho tiempo; **~-suffering** *adj* sufrido; **~-term** *adj* a largo plazo; **~ wave** *n* onda larga; **~-winded** *adj* prolijo
loo [luː] (*BRIT*: *inf*) *n* wáter *m*
look [luk] *vi* mirar; (*seem*) parecer; (*building etc*): **to ~ south/on to the sea** dar al sur/al mar ♦ *n* (*gen*): **to have a ~** mirar; (*glance*) mirada; (*appearance*) aire *m*, aspecto; **~s** *npl* (*good ~s*) belleza; **(here)!** (*expressing annoyance etc*) ¡oye!; **~!** (*expressing surprise*) ¡mira!; **~ after** *vt fus* (*care for*) cuidar a; (*deal with*) encargarse de; **~ at** *vt fus* mirar; (*read quickly*) echar un vistazo a; **~ back** *vi* mirar hacia atrás; **~ down on** *vt fus* (*fig*) despreciar, mirar con desprecio; **~ for** *vt fus* buscar; **~ forward to** *vt fus* esperar con ilusión; (*in letters*): **we ~ forward to hearing from you** quedamos a la espera de sus gratas noticias; **~ into** *vt* investigar; **~ on** *vi* mirar (como espectador); **~ out** *vi* (*beware*): **to ~ out (for)** tener cuidado (de); **~ out for** *vt fus* (*seek*) buscar; (*await*) esperar; **~ round** *vi* volver la cabeza; **~ through** *vt fus* (*examine*) examinar; **~ to** *vt fus* (*rely on*)

contar con; **~ up** *vi* mirar hacia arriba; (*improve*) mejorar ♦ *vt* (*word*) buscar; **~ up to** *vt fus* admirar; **~-out** *n* (*tower etc*) puesto de observación; (*person*) vigía *m/f*; **to be on the ~-out for sth** estar al acecho de algo

loom [luːm] *vi*: **~ (up)** (*threaten*) surgir, amenazar; (*event: approach*) aproximarse

loony ['luːnɪ] (*inf*) *n, adj* loco/a *m/f*

loop [luːp] *n* lazo ♦ *vt*: **to ~ sth round sth** pasar algo alrededor de algo; **~hole** *n* escapatoria

loose [luːs] *adj* suelto; (*clothes*) ancho; (*morals, discipline*) relajado; **to be on the ~** estar en libertad; **to be at a ~ end** *or* **at ~ ends** (*US*) no saber qué hacer; **~ change** *n* cambio; **~ chippings** *npl* (*on road*) gravilla suelta; **~ly** *adv* libremente, aproximadamente; **~n** *vt* aflojar

loot [luːt] *n* botín *m* ♦ *vt* saquear

lop off [lɔp-] *vt* (*branches*) podar

lop-sided *adj* torcido

lord [lɔːd] *n* señor *m*; **L~ Smith** Lord Smith; **the L~** el Señor; **my ~** (*to bishop*) Ilustrísima; (*to noble etc*) Señor; **good L~!** ¡Dios mío!; **the (House of) L~s** (*BRIT*) la Cámara de los Lores; **~ship** *n*: **your L~ship** su Señoría

lore [lɔː*] *n* tradiciones *fpl*

lorry ['lɔrɪ] (*BRIT*) *n* camión *m*; **~ driver** *n* camionero/a

lose [luːz] (*pt, pp* lost) *vt* perder ♦ *vi* perder, ser vencido; **to ~ (time)** (*clock*) atrasarse; **~r** *n* perdedor(a) *m/f*

loss [lɔs] *n* pérdida; **heavy ~es** (*MIL*) grandes pérdidas; **to be at a ~** no saber qué hacer; **to make a ~** sufrir pérdidas

lost [lɔst] *pt, pp of* lose ♦ *adj* perdido; **~ property** (*US ~ and found*) *n* objetos *mpl* perdidos

lot [lɔt] *n* (*group: of things*) grupo; (*at auctions*) lote *m*; **the ~** el todo, todos; **a ~** (*large number: of books etc*) muchos; (*a great deal*) mucho, bastante; **a ~ of, ~s of** mucho(s) (*pl*); **I read a ~** leo bastante; **to draw ~s (for sth)** echar suertes (para

decidir algo)

lotion ['ləuʃən] *n* loción *f*

lottery ['lɔtərɪ] *n* lotería

loud [laud] *adj* (*voice, sound*) fuerte; (*laugh, shout*) estrepitoso; (*condemnation etc*) enérgico; (*gaudy*) chillón/ona ♦ *adv* (*speak etc*) fuerte; **out ~** en voz alta; **~hailer** (*BRIT*) *n* megáfono; **~ly** *adv* (*noisily*) fuerte; (*aloud*) en voz alta; **~speaker** *n* altavoz *m*

lounge [laundʒ] *n* salón *m*, sala (de estar); (*at airport etc*) sala; (*BRIT: also*: **~-bar**) salón-bar *m* ♦ *vi* (*also*: **~ about** *or* **around**) reposar, holgazanear

louse [laus] (*pl* lice) *n* piojo

lousy ['lauzɪ] (*inf*) *adj* (*bad quality*) malísimo, asqueroso; (*ill*) fatal

lout [laut] *n* gamberro/a

lovable ['lʌvəbl] *adj* amable, simpático

love [lʌv] *n* (*romantic, sexual*) amor *m*; (*kind, caring*) cariño ♦ *vt* amar, querer; (*thing, activity*) encantarle a uno; **"~ from Anne"** (*on letter*) "un abrazo (de) Anne"; **to ~ to do** encantarle a uno hacer; **to be/fall in ~ with** estar enamorado/ enamorarse de; **to make ~** hacer el amor; **for the ~ of** por amor de; **"15 ~"** (*TENNIS*) "15 a cero"; **I ~ paella** me encanta la paella; **~ affair** *n* aventura sentimental; **~ letter** *n* carta de amor; **~ life** *n* vida sentimental

lovely ['lʌvlɪ] *adj* (*delightful*) encantador(a); (*beautiful*) precioso

lover ['lʌvə*] *n* amante *m/f*; (*person in love*) enamorado; (*amateur*): **a ~ of** un(a) aficionado/a *or* un(a) amante de

loving ['lʌvɪŋ] *adj* amoroso, cariñoso; (*action*) tierno

low [ləu] *adj, ad* bajo ♦ *n* (*METEOROLOGY*) área de baja presión; **to be ~ on** (*supplies etc*) andar mal de; **to feel ~** sentirse deprimido; **to turn (down) ~** bajar; **~- alcohol** *adj* de bajo contenido en alcohol; **~-calorie** *adj* bajo en calorías; **~-cut** *adj* (*dress*) escotado

lower ['ləuə*] *adj* más bajo; (*less important*) menos importante ♦ *vt* bajar;

(reduce) reducir ♦ *vr*: **to ~ o.s. to** *(fig)* rebajarse a

low: ~-fat *adj (milk, yoghurt)* desnatado; *(diet)* bajo en calorías; **~lands** *npl (GEO)* tierras *fpl* bajas; **~ly** *adj* humilde, inferior; **~ season** *n* la temporada baja

loyal ['lɔɪəl] *adj* leal; **~ty** *n* lealtad *f*

lozenge ['lɔzɪndʒ] *n (MED)* pastilla

L.P. *n abbr* (= *long-playing record*) elepé *m*

L-plates ['ɛl-] *(BRIT)* *npl* placas *fpl* de aprendiz de conductor

⬛ **L-plates**

ⓘ *En el Reino Unido las personas que están aprendiendo a conducir deben llevar en la parte delantera y trasera de su vehículo unas placas blancas con una L en rojo conocidas como L-plates (de learner). No es necesario que asistan a clases teóricas sino que, desde el principio, se les entrega un carnet de conducir provisional ("provisional driving licence") para que realicen sus prácticas, aunque no pueden circular por las autopistas y deben ir siempre acompañadas por un conductor con carnet definitivo ("full driving licence").*

Ltd *abbr* (= *limited company*) S.A.

lubricate ['lu:brɪkeɪt] *vt* lubricar, engrasar

luck [lʌk] *n* suerte *f*; **bad ~** mala suerte; **good ~!** ¡que tengas suerte!, ¡suerte!; **bad or hard or tough ~!** ¡qué pena!; **~ily** *adv* afortunadamente; **~y** *adj* afortunado; *(at cards etc)* con suerte; *(object)* que trae suerte

ludicrous ['lu:dɪkrəs] *adj* absurdo

lug [lʌg] *vt (drag)* arrastrar

luggage ['lʌgɪdʒ] *n* equipaje *m*; **~ rack** *n (on car)* baca, portaequipajes *m inv*

lukewarm ['lu:kwɔ:m] *adj* tibio

lull [lʌl] *n* tregua ♦ *vt*: **to ~ sb to sleep** arrullar a uno; **to ~ sb into a false sense of security** dar a alguien una falsa sensación de seguridad

lullaby ['lʌləbaɪ] *n* nana

lumbago [lʌm'beɪgəu] *n* lumbago

lumber ['lʌmbə*] *n (junk)* trastos *mpl* viejos; *(wood)* maderos *mpl*; **~ with** *vt*: **to be ~ed with** tener que cargar con algo; **~jack** *n* maderero

luminous ['lu:mɪnəs] *adj* luminoso

lump [lʌmp] *n* terrón *m*; *(fragment)* trozo; *(swelling)* bulto ♦ *vt (also:* **~ together**) juntar; **~ sum** *n* suma global; **~y** *adj (sauce)* lleno de grumos; *(mattress)* lleno de bultos

lunatic ['lu:nətɪk] *adj* loco

lunch [lʌntʃ] *n* almuerzo, comida ♦ *vi* almorzar

luncheon ['lʌntʃən] *n* almuerzo; **~ voucher** *(BRIT) n* vale *m* de comida

lunch time *n* hora de comer

lung [lʌŋ] *n* pulmón *m*

lunge [lʌndʒ] *vi (also:* **~ forward**) abalanzarse; **to ~ at** arremeter contra

lurch [lɜ:tʃ] *vi* dar sacudidas ♦ *n* sacudida; **to leave sb in the ~** dejar a uno plantado

lure [luə*] *n (attraction)* atracción *f* ♦ *vt* tentar

lurid ['luərɪd] *adj (colour)* chillón/ona; *(account)* espeluznante

lurk [lɜ:k] *vi (person, animal)* estar al acecho; *(fig)* acechar

luscious ['lʌʃəs] *adj (attractive: person, thing)* precioso; *(food)* delicioso

lush [lʌʃ] *adj* exuberante

lust [lʌst] *n* lujuria; *(greed)* codicia

lustre ['lʌstə*] *(US luster) n* lustre *m*, brillo

lusty ['lʌstɪ] *adj* robusto, fuerte

Luxembourg ['lʌksəmbə:g] *n* Luxemburgo

luxuriant [lʌg'zjuərɪənt] *adj* exuberante

luxurious [lʌg'zjuərɪəs] *adj* lujoso

luxury ['lʌkʃərɪ] *n* lujo ♦ *cpd* de lujo

lying ['laɪɪŋ] *n* mentiras *fpl* ♦ *adj* mentiroso

lyrical ['lɪrɪkl] *adj* lírico

lyrics ['lɪrɪks] *npl (of song)* letra

M, m

m. *abbr* = **metre; mile; million**
M.A. *abbr* = **Master of Arts**
mac [mæk] (*BRIT*) *n* impermeable *m*
macaroni [mækə'rəʊnɪ] *n* macarrones *mpl*
machine [mə'ʃiːn] *n* máquina ♦ *vt* (*dress etc*) coser a máquina; (*TECH*) hacer a máquina; **~ gun** *n* ametralladora; **~ language** *n* (*COMPUT*) lenguaje *m* máquina; **~ry** *n* maquinaria; (*fig*) mecanismo
macho ['mætʃəʊ] *adj* machista
mackerel ['mækrəl] *n inv* caballa
mackintosh ['mækɪntɔʃ] (*BRIT*) *n* impermeable *m*
mad [mæd] *adj* loco; (*idea*) disparatado; (*angry*) furioso; (*keen*): **to be ~ about sth** volverle loco a uno algo
madam ['mædəm] *n* señora
madden ['mædn] *vt* volver loco
made [meɪd] *pt, pp of* **make**
Madeira [mə'dɪərə] *n* (*GEO*) Madera; (*wine*) vino de Madera
made-to-measure (*BRIT*) *adj* hecho a la medida
madly ['mædlɪ] *adv* locamente
madman ['mædmən] (*irreg*) *n* loco
madness ['mædnɪs] *n* locura
Madrid [mə'drɪd] *n* Madrid
magazine [mægə'ziːn] *n* revista; (*RADIO, TV*) programa *m* magazina
maggot ['mægət] *n* gusano
magic ['mædʒɪk] *n* magia ♦ *adj* mágico; **~ian** [mə'dʒɪʃən] *n* mago/a; (*conjurer*) prestidigitador(a) *m/f*
magistrate ['mædʒɪstreɪt] *n* juez *m/f* (*municipal*)
magnet ['mægnɪt] *n* imán *m*; **~ic** [-'netɪk] *adj* magnético; (*personality*) atrayente
magnificent [mæg'nɪfɪsənt] *adj* magnífico
magnify ['mægnɪfaɪ] *vt* (*object*) ampliar; (*sound*) aumentar; **~ing glass** *n* lupa
magpie ['mægpaɪ] *n* urraca
mahogany [mə'hɔgənɪ] *n* caoba

maid [meɪd] *n* criada; **old ~** (*pej*) solterona
maiden ['meɪdn] *n* doncella ♦ *adj* (*aunt etc*) solterona; (*speech, voyage*) inaugural; **~ name** *n* nombre *m* de soltera
mail [meɪl] *n* correo; (*letters*) cartas *fpl* ♦ *vt* echar al correo; **~box** (*US*) *n* buzón *m*; **~ing list** *n* lista de direcciones; **~-order** *n* pedido postal
maim [meɪm] *vt* mutilar, lisiar
main [meɪn] *adj* principal, mayor ♦ *n* (*pipe*) cañería maestra; (*US*) red *f* eléctrica; **the ~s** *npl* (*BRIT: ELEC*) la red eléctrica; **in the ~** en general; **~frame** *n* (*COMPUT*) ordenador *m* central; **~land** *n* tierra firme; **~ly** *adv* principalmente; **~ road** *n* carretera; **~stay** *n* (*fig*) pilar *m*; **~stream** *n* corriente *f* principal
maintain [meɪn'teɪn] *vt* mantener; **maintenance** ['meɪntənəns] *n* mantenimiento; (*LAW*) manutención *f*
maize [meɪz] (*BRIT*) *n* maíz *m* (*SP*), choclo (*AM*)
majestic [mə'dʒestɪk] *adj* majestuoso
majesty ['mædʒɪstɪ] *n* majestad *f*; (*title*): **Your M~** Su Majestad
major ['meɪdʒə*] *n* (*MIL*) comandante *m* ♦ *adj* principal; (*MUS*) mayor
Majorca [mə'jɔːkə] *n* Mallorca
majority [mə'dʒɔrɪtɪ] *n* mayoría
make [meɪk] (*pt, pp* **made**) *vt* hacer; (*manufacture*) fabricar; (*mistake*) cometer; (*speech*) pronunciar; (*cause to be*): **to ~ sb sad** poner triste a alguien; (*force*): **to ~ sb do sth** obligar a alguien a hacer algo; (*earn*) ganar; (*equal*): **2 and 2 ~ 4** 2 y 2 son 4 ♦ *n* marca; **to ~ the bed** hacer la cama; **to ~ a fool of sb** poner a alguien en ridículo; **to ~ a profit/loss** obtener ganancias/sufrir pérdidas; **to ~ it** (*arrive*) llegar; (*achieve sth*) tener éxito; **what time do you ~ it?** ¿qué hora tienes?; **to ~ do with** contentarse con; **~ for** *vt fus* (*place*) dirigirse a; **~ out** *vt* (*decipher*) descifrar; (*understand*) entender; (*see*) distinguir; (*cheque*) extender; **~ up** *vt* (*invent*) inventar; (*prepare*) hacer; (*constitute*) constituir ♦ *vi* reconciliarse;

(with cosmetics) maquillarse; **~ up for** *vt fus* compensar; **~-believe** *n* ficción *f*, invención *f*; **~r** *n* fabricante *m/f*; *(of film, programme)* autor(a) *m/f*; **~shift** *adj* improvisado; **~-up** *n* maquillaje *m*; **~-up remover** *n* desmaquillador *m*

making ['meɪkɪŋ] *n* (*fig*): **in the ~** en vías de formación; **to have the ~s of** *(person)* tener madera de

Malaysia [mə'leɪzɪə] *n* Malasia, Malaysia

male [meɪl] *n* (*BIOL*) macho ♦ *adj* (*sex, attitude*) masculino; *(child etc)* varón

malfunction [mæl'fʌŋkʃən] *n* mal funcionamiento

malice ['mælɪs] *n* malicia; **malicious** [mə'lɪʃəs] *adj* malicioso; rencoroso

malignant [mə'lɪgnənt] *adj* (*MED*) maligno

mall [mɔːl] (*US*) *n* (*also:* **shopping ~**) centro comercial

mallet ['mælɪt] *n* mazo

malnutrition [mælnjuː'trɪʃən] *n* desnutrición *f*

malpractice [mæl'præktɪs] *n* negligencia profesional

malt [mɔːlt] *n* malta; *(whisky)* whisky *m* de malta

Malta ['mɔːltə] *n* Malta; **Maltese** [-'tiːz] *adj, n inv* maltés/esa *m/f*

mammal ['mæml] *n* mamífero

mammoth ['mæməθ] *n* mamut *m* ♦ *adj* gigantesco

man [mæn] (*pl* **men**) *n* hombre *m*; *(~kind)* el hombre ♦ *vt* (*NAUT*) tripular; (*MIL*) guarnecer; *(operate: machine)* manejar; **an old ~** un viejo; **~ and wife** marido y mujer

manage ['mænɪdʒ] *vi* arreglárselas, ir tirando ♦ *vt* (*be in charge of*) dirigir; (*control: person*) manejar; (: *ship*) gobernar; **~able** *adj* manejable; **~ment** *n* dirección *f*; **~r** *n* director(a) *m/f*; (*of pop star*) mánayer *m/f*; (*SPORT*) entrenador(a) *m/f*; **~ress** *n* directora; entrenadora; **~rial** [-ə'dʒɪərɪəl] *adj* directivo; **managing director** *n* director(a) *m/f* general

mandarin ['mændərɪn] *n* (*also:* **~ orange**)

mandarina; *(person)* mandarín *m*

mandatory ['mændətərɪ] *adj* obligatorio

mane [meɪn] *n* (*of horse*) crin *f*; *(of lion)* melena

maneuver [mə'nuːvə*] (*US*) = **manoeuvre**

manfully ['mænfəlɪ] *adv* valientemente

mangle ['mæŋgl] *vt* mutilar, destrozar

man: **~handle** *vt* maltratar; **~hole** *n* agujero de acceso; **~hood** *n* edad *f* viril; *(state)* virilidad *f*; **~-hour** *n* hora-hombre *f*; **~hunt** *n* (*POLICE*) búsqueda y captura

mania ['meɪnɪə] *n* manía; **~c** ['meɪnɪæk] *n* maníaco/a; *(fig)* maniático

manic ['mænɪk] *adj* frenético; **~-depressive** *n* maníaco/a depresivo/a

manicure ['mænɪkjuə*] *n* manicura

manifest ['mænɪfest] *vt* manifestar, mostrar ♦ *adj* manifiesto

manifesto [mænɪ'festəu] *n* manifiesto

manipulate [mə'nɪpjuleɪt] *vt* manipular

man: **~kind** [mæn'kaɪnd] *n* humanidad *f*, género humano; **~ly** *adj* varonil; **~-made** *adj* artificial

manner ['mænə*] *n* manera, modo; *(behaviour)* conducta, manera de ser; *(type)*: **all ~ of things** toda clase de cosas; **~s** *npl* (*behaviour*) modales *mpl*; **bad ~s** mala educación; **~ism** *n* peculiaridad *f* de lenguaje (*or* de comportamiento)

manoeuvre [mə'nuːvə*] (*US* **maneuver**) *vt, vi* maniobrar ♦ *n* maniobra

manor ['mænə*] *n* (*also:* **~ house**) casa solariega

manpower ['mænpauə*] *n* mano *f* de obra

mansion ['mænʃən] *n* palacio, casa grande

manslaughter ['mænslɔːtə*] *n* homicidio no premeditado

mantelpiece ['mæntlpiːs] *n* repisa, chimenea

manual ['mænjuəl] *adj* manual ♦ *n* manual *m*

manufacture [mænju'fæktʃə*] *vt* fabricar ♦ *n* fabricación *f*; **~r** *n* fabricante *m/f*

manure [mə'njuə*] *n* estiércol *m*

manuscript ['mænjuskrɪpt] *n* manuscrito

many ['menɪ] *adj, pron* muchos/as; **a**

great ~ muchísimos, un buen número de;
~ a time muchas veces

map [mæp] n mapa m; **to ~ out** vt
proyectar

maple ['meɪpl] n arce m (SP), maple m
(AM)

mar [mɑ:*] vt estropear

marathon ['mærəθən] n maratón m

marble ['mɑ:bl] n mármol m; (toy) canica

March [mɑ:tʃ] n marzo

march [mɑ:tʃ] vi (MIL) marchar;
(demonstrators) manifestarse ♦ n marcha;
(demonstration) manifestación f

mare [meə*] n yegua

margarine [mɑ:dʒə'ri:n] n margarina

margin ['mɑ:dʒɪn] n margen m; (COMM:
profit ~) margen m de beneficios; **~al** adj
marginal; **~al seat** n (POL) escaño
electoral difícil de asegurar

marigold ['mærɪgəʊld] n caléndula

marijuana [mærɪ'wɑ:nə] n marijuana

marina [mə'ri:nə] n puerto deportivo

marinate ['mærɪneɪt] vt marinar

marine [mə'ri:n] adj marino ♦ n soldado
de marina

marital ['mærɪtl] adj matrimonial; **~ status**
estado civil

marjoram ['mɑ:dʒərəm] n mejorana

mark [mɑ:k] n marca, señal f; (in snow,
mud etc) huella; (stain) mancha; (BRIT:
SCOL) nota; (currency) marco ♦ vt marcar;
manchar; (damage: furniture) rayar;
(indicate: place etc) señalar; (BRIT: SCOL)
calificar, corregir; **to ~ time** marcar el
paso; (fig) marcar(se) un ritmo; **~ed** adj
(obvious) marcado, acusado; **~er** n (sign)
marcador m; (bookmark) señal f (de libro)

market ['mɑ:kɪt] n mercado ♦ vt (COMM)
comercializar; **~ garden** (BRIT) n huerto;
~ing n márketing m; **~place** n
mercado; **~ research** n análisis m inv
de mercados

marksman ['mɑ:ksmən] n tirador m

marmalade ['mɑ:məleɪd] n mermelada de
naranja

maroon [mə'ru:n] vt: **to be ~ed** quedar
aislado; (fig) quedar abandonado

marquee [mɑ:'ki:] n entoldado

marriage ['mærɪdʒ] n (relationship,
institution) matrimonio; (wedding) boda;
(act) casamiento; **~ certificate** n partida
de casamiento

married ['mærɪd] adj casado; (life, love)
conyugal

marrow ['mærəʊ] n médula; (vegetable)
calabacín m

marry ['mærɪ] vt casarse con; (subj: father,
priest etc) casar ♦ vi (also: **get married**)
casarse

Mars [mɑ:z] n Marte m

marsh [mɑ:ʃ] n pantano; (salt ~) marisma

marshal ['mɑ:ʃl] n (MIL) mariscal m; (at
sports meeting etc) oficial m; (US: of police,
fire department) jefe/a m/f ♦ vt (thoughts
etc) ordenar; (soldiers) formar

marshy ['mɑ:ʃɪ] adj pantanoso

martial law ['mɑ:ʃl-] n ley f marcial

martyr ['mɑ:tə*] n mártir m/f; **~dom** n
martirio

marvel ['mɑ:vl] n maravilla, prodigio ♦ vi:
to ~ (at) maravillarse (de); **~lous** (US
~ous) adj maravilloso

Marxist ['mɑ:ksɪst] adj, n marxista m/f

marzipan ['mɑ:zɪpæn] n mazapán m

mascara [mæs'kɑ:rə] n rímel m

masculine ['mæskjʊlɪn] adj masculino

mash [mæʃ] vt machacar; **~ed potatoes**
npl puré m de patatas (SP) or papas (AM)

mask [mɑ:sk] n máscara ♦ vt (cover): **to ~
one's face** ocultarse la cara; (hide:
feelings) esconder

mason ['meɪsn] n (also: **stone~**) albañil m;
(also: **free~**) masón m; **~ry** n (in building)
mampostería

masquerade [mæskə'reɪd] vi: **to ~ as**
disfrazarse de, hacerse pasar por

mass [mæs] n (people) muchedumbre f;
(of air, liquid etc) masa; (of mass, hair etc)
gran cantidad f; (REL) misa ♦ cpd masivo
♦ vi reunirse; concentrarse; **the ~es** npl
las masas; **~es of** (inf) montones de

massacre ['mæsəkə*] n masacre f

massage ['mæsɑ:ʒ] n masaje m ♦ vt dar
masaje en

masseur [mæˈsəː*] *n* masajista *m*

masseuse [mæˈsəːz] *n* masajista *f*

massive [ˈmæsɪv] *adj* enorme; *(support, changes)* masivo

mass media *npl* medios *mpl* de comunicación

mass production *n* fabricación *f* en serie

mast [mɑːst] *n* (*NAUT*) mástil *m*; (*RADIO etc*) torre *f*

master [ˈmɑːstə*] *n* (*of servant*) amo; (*of situation*) dueño, maestro; (*in primary school*) maestro; (*in secondary school*) profesor *m*; (*title for boys*): **M~ X** Señorito X ♦ *vt* dominar; **M~ of Arts/Science** *n* licenciatura superior en Letras/Ciencias; **~ly** *adj* magistral; **~mind** *n* inteligencia superior ♦ *vt* dirigir, planear; **~piece** *n* obra maestra; **~y** *n* maestría

mat [mæt] *n* estera; (*also*: **door~**) felpudo; (*also*: **table ~**) salvamanteles *m inv*, posavasos *m inv* ♦ *adj* = **matt**

match [mætʃ] *n* cerilla, fósforo; (*game*) partido; (*equal*) igual *m/f* ♦ *vt* (*go well with*) hacer juego con; (*equal*) igualar; (*correspond to*) corresponderse con; (*pair*: *also*: **~ up**) casar con ♦ *vi* hacer juego; **to be a good ~** hacer juego; **~box** *n* caja de cerillas; **~ing** *adj* que hace juego

mate [meɪt] *n* (*work~*) colega *m/f*; (*inf*: *friend*) amigo/a; (*animal*) macho *m/* hembra *f*; (*in merchant navy*) segundo de a bordo ♦ *vi* acoplarse, aparearse ♦ *vt* aparear

material [məˈtɪərɪəl] *n* (*substance*) materia; (*information*) material *m*; (*cloth*) tela, tejido ♦ *adj* material; (*important*) esencial; **~s** *npl* materiales *mpl*

maternal [məˈtəːnl] *adj* maternal

maternity [məˈtəːnɪtɪ] *n* maternidad *f*; **~ dress** *n* vestido premamá

math [mæθ] (*US*) *n* = **mathematics**

mathematical [mæθəˈmætɪkl] *adj* matemático

mathematician [mæθəməˈtɪʃən] *n* matemático/a

mathematics [mæθəˈmætɪks] *n*

matemáticas *fpl*

maths [mæθs] (*BRIT*) *n* = **mathematics**

matinée [ˈmætɪneɪ] *n* sesión *f* de tarde

matrices [ˈmeɪtrɪsiːz] *npl* of **matrix**

matriculation [mətrɪkjuˈleɪʃən] *n* (formalización *f* de) matrícula

matrimony [ˈmætrɪmənɪ] *n* matrimonio

matrix [ˈmeɪtrɪks] (*pl* **matrices**) *n* matriz *f*

matron [ˈmeɪtrən] *n* enfermera *f* jefe; (*in school*) ama de llaves

mat(t) [mæt] *adj* mate

matted [ˈmætɪd] *adj* enmarañado

matter [ˈmætə*] *n* cuestión *f*, asunto; (*PHYSICS*) sustancia, materia; (*reading ~*) material *m*; (*MED*: *pus*) pus *m* ♦ *vi* importar; **~s** *npl* (*affairs*) asuntos *mpl*, temas *mpl*; **it doesn't ~** no importa; **what's the ~?** ¿qué pasa?; **no ~ what** pase lo que pase; **as a ~ of course** por rutina; **as a ~ of fact** de hecho; **~-of-fact** *adj* prosaico, práctico

mattress [ˈmætrɪs] *n* colchón *m*

mature [məˈtjuə*] *adj* maduro ♦ *vi* madurar; **maturity** *n* madurez *f*

maul [mɔːl] *vt* magullar

mauve [məuv] *adj* de color malva (*SP*) *or* guinda (*AM*)

maximum [ˈmæksɪməm] (*pl* **maxima**) *adj* máximo ♦ *n* máximo

May [meɪ] *n* mayo

may [meɪ] (*conditional*: **might**) *vi* (*indicating possibility*): **he ~ come** puede que venga; (*be allowed to*): **~ I smoke?** ¿puedo fumar?; (*wishes*): **~ God bless you!** ¡que Dios le bendiga!; **you ~ as well go** bien puedes irte

maybe [ˈmeɪbiː] *adv* quizá(s)

May Day *n* el primero de Mayo

mayhem [ˈmeɪhem] *n* caos *m* total

mayonnaise [meɪəˈneɪz] *n* mayonesa

mayor [meə*] *n* alcalde *m*; **~ess** *n* alcaldesa

maze [meɪz] *n* laberinto

M.D. *abbr* = **Doctor of Medicine**

me [miː] *pron* (*direct*) me; (*stressed, after pron*) mí; **can you hear ~?** ¿me oyes?; **he heard ME!** me oyó a mí; **it's ~** soy yo;

give them to ~ dámelos/las; **with /
without ~** conmigo/sin mí

meadow ['mɛdəu] *n* prado, pradera

meagre ['mi:gə*] (*US* **meager**) *adj* escaso,
pobre

meal [mi:l] *n* comida; (*flour*) harina;
~time *n* hora de comer

mean [mi:n] (*pt, pp* **meant**) *adj* (*with
money*) tacaño; (*unkind*) mezquino, malo;
(*shabby*) humilde; (*average*) medio ♦ *vt*
(*signify*) querer decir, significar; (*refer to*)
referirse a; (*intend*): **to ~ to do sth** pensar
or pretender hacer algo ♦ *n* medio,
término medio; **~s** *npl* (*way*) medio,
manera; (*money*) recursos *mpl*, medios
mpl; **by ~s of** mediante, por medio de;
by all ~s! ¡naturalmente!, ¡claro que sí!;
do you ~ it? ¿lo dices en serio?; **what do
you ~?** ¿qué quiere decir?; **to be meant
for sb/sth** ser para uno/algo

meander [mɪ'ændə*] *vi* (*river*) serpentear

meaning ['mi:nɪŋ] *n* significado, sentido;
(*purpose*) sentido, propósito; **~ful** *adj*
significativo; **~less** *adj* sin sentido

meanness ['mi:nnɪs] *n* (*with money*)
tacañería; (*unkindness*) maldad *f*,
mezquindad *f*; (*shabbiness*) humildad *f*

meant [mɛnt] *pt, pp of* **mean**

meantime ['mi:ntaɪm] *adv* (*also*: **in the ~**)
mientras tanto

meanwhile ['mi:nwaɪl] *adv* = **meantime**

measles ['mi:zlz] *n* sarampión *m*

measure ['mɛʒə*] *vt, vi* medir ♦ *n*
medida; (*ruler*) regla; **~ments** *npl*
medidas *fpl*

meat [mi:t] *n* carne *f*; **cold ~** fiambre *m*;
~ball *n* albóndiga; **~ pie** *n* pastel *m* de
carne

Mecca ['mɛkə] *n* La Meca

mechanic [mɪ'kænɪk] *n* mecánico/a; **~s** *n*
mecánica ♦ *npl* mecanismo; **~al** *adj*
mecánico

mechanism ['mɛkənɪzəm] *n* mecanismo

medal ['mɛdl] *n* medalla; **~lion** [mɪ'dælɪən]
n medallón *m*; **~list** (*US* **~ist**) *n* (*SPORT*)
medallista *m/f*

meddle ['mɛdl] *vi*: **to ~ in** entrometerse

en; **to ~ with sth** manosear algo

media ['mi:dɪə] *npl* medios *mpl* de
comunicación ♦ *npl of* **medium**

mediaeval [mɛdɪ'i:vl] *adj* = **medieval**

mediate ['mi:dɪeɪt] *vi* mediar; **mediator**
n intermediario/a, mediador(a) *m/f*

Medicaid ® ['mɛdɪkeɪd] (*US*) *n programa
de ayuda médica para los pobres*

medical ['mɛdɪkl] *adj* médico ♦ *n*
reconocimiento médico

Medicare ® ['mɛdɪkeə*] (*US*) *n programa
de ayuda médica para los ancianos*

medication [mɛdɪ'keɪʃən] *n* medicación *f*

medicine ['mɛdsɪn] *n* medicina; (*drug*)
medicamento

medieval [mɛdɪ'i:vl] *adj* medieval

mediocre [mi:dɪ'əukə*] *adj* mediocre

meditate ['mɛdɪteɪt] *vi* meditar

Mediterranean [mɛdɪtə'reɪnɪən] *adj*
mediterráneo; **the ~ (Sea)** el (Mar)
Mediterráneo

medium ['mi:dɪəm] (*pl* **media**) *adj*
mediano, regular ♦ *n* (*means*) medio; (*pl
mediums: person*) médium *m/f*; **~ wave** *n*
onda media

meek [mi:k] *adj* manso, sumiso

meet [mi:t] (*pt, pp* **met**) *vt* encontrar;
(*accidentally*) encontrarse con, tropezar
con; (*by arrangement*) reunirse con; (*for
the first time*) conocer; (*go and fetch*) ir a
buscar; (*opponent*) enfrentarse con;
(*obligations*) cumplir; (*encounter: problem*)
hacer frente a; (*need*) satisfacer ♦ *vi*
encontrarse; (*in session*) reunirse; (*join:
objects*) unirse; (*for the first time*)
conocerse; **~ with** *vt fus* (*difficulty*)
tropezar con; **to ~ with success** tener
éxito; **~ing** *n* encuentro; (*arranged*) cita,
compromiso; (*business ~ing*) reunión *f*;
(*POL*) mítin *m*

megabyte ['mɛgəbaɪt] *n* (*COMPUT*)
megabyte *m*, megaocteto

megaphone ['mɛgəfəun] *n* megáfono

melancholy ['mɛlənkəlɪ] *n* melancolía
♦ *adj* melancólico

mellow ['mɛləu] *adj* (*wine*) añejo; (*sound,
colour*) suave ♦ *vi* (*person*) ablandar

melody ['mɛlədɪ] *n* melodía

melon ['mɛlən] *n* melón *m*

melt [mɛlt] *vi* (*metal*) fundirse; (*snow*) derretirse ♦ *vt* fundir; **~down** *n* (*in nuclear reactor*) fusión *f* de un reactor (nuclear); **~ing pot** *n* (*fig*) crisol *m*

member ['mɛmbə*] *n* (*gen*, *ANAT*) miembro; (*of club*) socio/a; **M~ of Parliament** (*BRIT*) diputado/a; **M~ of the European Parliament** (*BRIT*) eurodiputado/a; **~ship** *n* (*members*) número de miembros; (*state*) filiación *f*; **~ship card** *n* carnet *m* de socio

memento [mə'mɛntəu] *n* recuerdo

memo ['mɛməu] *n* apunte *m*, nota

memoirs ['mɛmwɑ:z] *npl* memorias *fpl*

memorandum [mɛmə'rændəm] (*pl* **memoranda**) *n* apunte *m*, nota; (*official note*) acta

memorial [mɪ'mɔ:rɪəl] *n* monumento conmemorativo ♦ *adj* conmemorativo

memorize ['mɛməraɪz] *vt* aprender de memoria

memory ['mɛmərɪ] *n* (*also*: *COMPUT*) memoria; (*instance*) recuerdo; (*of dead person*): **in ~ of** a la memoria de

men [mɛn] *npl of* **man**

menace ['mɛnəs] *n* amenaza ♦ *vt* amenazar; **menacing** *adj* amenazador(a)

mend [mɛnd] *vt* reparar, arreglar; (*darn*) zurcir ♦ *vi* reponerse ♦ *n*: **to be on the ~** ir mejorando; **to ~ one's ways** enmendarse; **~ing** *n* reparación *f*; (*clothes*) ropa por remendar

meningitis [mɛnɪn'dʒaɪtɪs] *n* meningitis *f*

menopause ['mɛnəupɔ:z] *n* menopausia

menstruation [mɛnstru'eɪʃən] *n* menstruación *f*

mental ['mɛntl] *adj* mental; **~ity** [-'tælɪtɪ] *n* mentalidad *f*

mention ['mɛnʃən] *n* mención *f* ♦ *vt* mencionar; (*speak of*) hablar de; **don't ~ it!** ¡de nada!

menu ['mɛnju:] *n* (*set* ~) menú *m*; (*printed*) carta; (*COMPUT*) menú *m*

MEP *n abbr* = **Member of the European Parliament**

merchandise ['mə:tʃəndaɪz] *n* mercancías *fpl*

merchant ['mə:tʃənt] *n* comerciante *m/f*; **~ bank** (*BRIT*) *n* banco comercial; **~ navy** (*US* **~ marine**) *n* marina mercante

merciful ['mə:sɪful] *adj* compasivo; (*fortunate*) afortunado

merciless ['mə:sɪlɪs] *adj* despiadado

mercury ['mə:kjurɪ] *n* mercurio

mercy ['mə:sɪ] *n* compasión *f*; (*REL*) misericordia; **at the ~ of** a la merced de

merely ['mɪəlɪ] *adv* simplemente, sólo

merge [mə:dʒ] *vt* (*join*) unir ♦ *vi* unirse; (*COMM*) fusionarse; (*colours etc*) fundirse; **~r** *n* (*COMM*) fusión *f*

meringue [mə'ræŋ] *n* merengue *m*

merit ['mɛrɪt] *n* mérito ♦ *vt* merecer

mermaid ['mə:meɪd] *n* sirena

merry ['mɛrɪ] *adj* alegre; **M~ Christmas!** ¡Felices Pascuas!; **~-go-round** *n* tiovivo

mesh [mɛʃ] *n* malla

mesmerize ['mɛzməraɪz] *vt* hipnotizar

mess [mɛs] *n* (*muddle*: *of situation*) confusión *f*; (: *of room*) revoltijo; (*dirt*) porquería; (*MIL*) comedor *m*; **~ about** *or* **around** (*inf*) *vi* perder el tiempo; (*pass the time*) entretenerse; **~ about** *or* **around with** (*inf*) *vt fus* divertirse con; **~ up** *vt* (*spoil*) estropear; (*dirty*) ensuciar

message ['mɛsɪdʒ] *n* recado, mensaje *m*

messenger ['mɛsɪndʒə*] *n* mensajero/a

Messrs *abbr* (*on letters*: = *Messieurs*) Sres

messy ['mɛsɪ] *adj* (*dirty*) sucio; (*untidy*) desordenado

met [mɛt] *pt*, *pp of* **meet**

metal ['mɛtl] *n* metal *m*; **~lic** [-'tælɪk] *adj* metálico

metaphor ['mɛtəfə*] *n* metáfora

meteor ['mi:tɪə*] *n* meteoro; **~ite** [-aɪt] *n* meteorito

meteorology [mi:tɪə'rɔlədʒɪ] *n* meteorología

meter ['mi:tə*] *n* (*instrument*) contador *m*; (*US: unit*) = **metre** ♦ *vt* (*US: POST*) franquear

method ['mɛθəd] *n* método

meths [mɛθs] (BRIT) n, **methylated spirit** ['mɛθɪleɪtɪd-] (BRIT) n alcohol m metilado or desnaturalizado

metre ['miːtə*] (US **meter**) n metro

metric ['mɛtrɪk] adj métrico

metropolitan [mɛtrə'pɔlɪtən] adj metropolitano; **the M~ Police** (BRIT) la policía londinense

mettle ['mɛtl] n: **to be on one's ~** estar dispuesto a mostrar todo lo que uno vale

mew [mjuː] vi (cat) maullar

mews [mjuːz] n: ~ **flat** (BRIT) piso *acondicionado en antiguos establos o cocheras*

Mexican ['mɛksɪkən] adj, n mejicano/a m/f, mexicano/a m/f

Mexico ['mɛksɪkəu] n Méjico (SP), México (AM); ~ **City** n Ciudad f de Méjico or México

miaow [miː'au] vi maullar

mice [maɪs] npl of **mouse**

micro... [maɪkrəu] prefix micro...; **~chip** n microplaqueta; **~(computer)** n microordenador m; **~phone** n micrófono; **~processor** n microprocesador m; **~scope** n microscopio; **~wave** n (also: **~wave oven**) horno microondas

mid [mɪd] adj: **in ~ May** a mediados de mayo; **in ~ afternoon** a media tarde; **in ~ air** en el aire; **~day** n mediodía m

middle ['mɪdl] n centro; (half-way point) medio; (waist) cintura ♦ adj de en medio; (course, way) intermedio; **in the ~ of the night** en plena noche; **~-aged** adj de mediana edad; **the M~ Ages** npl la Edad Media; **~-class** adj de clase media; **the ~ class(es)** n(pl) la clase media; **M~ East** n Oriente m Medio; **~man** n intermediario; ~ **name** n segundo nombre; **~-of-the-road** adj moderado; **~weight** n (BOXING) peso medio

middling ['mɪdlɪŋ] adj mediano

midge [mɪdʒ] n mosquito

midget ['mɪdʒɪt] n enano/a

Midlands ['mɪdləndz] npl: **the ~** *la región central de Inglaterra*

midnight ['mɪdnaɪt] n medianoche f

midst [mɪdst] n: **in the ~ of** (crowd) en medio de; (situation, action) en mitad de

midsummer [mɪd'sʌmə*] n: **in ~** en pleno verano

midway [mɪd'weɪ] adj, adv: ~ **(between)** a medio camino (entre); ~ **through** a la mitad (de)

midweek [mɪd'wiːk] adv entre semana

midwife ['mɪdwaɪf] (pl **midwives**) n comadrona, partera

might [maɪt] vb see **may** ♦ n fuerza, poder m; **~y** adj fuerte, poderoso

migraine ['miːgreɪn] n jaqueca

migrant ['maɪɡrənt] n adj (bird) migratorio; (worker) emigrante

migrate [maɪ'ɡreɪt] vi emigrar

mike [maɪk] n abbr (= microphone) micro

mild [maɪld] adj (person) apacible; (climate) templado; (slight) ligero; (taste) suave; (illness) leve; **~ly** adv ligeramente; suavemente; **to put it ~ly** para no decir más

mile [maɪl] n milla; **~age** n número de millas, ≈ kilometraje m; **~ometer** [maɪ'lɔmɪtə*] n ≈ cuentakilómetros m inv; **~stone** n mojón m

militant ['mɪlɪtnt] adj, n militante m/f

military ['mɪlɪtərɪ] adj militar

militia [mɪ'lɪʃə] n milicia

milk [mɪlk] n leche f ♦ vt (cow) ordeñar; (fig) chupar; ~ **chocolate** n chocolate m con leche; **~man** (irreg) n lechero; **~ shake** n batido, malteada (AM); **~y** adj lechoso; **M~y Way** n Vía Láctea

mill [mɪl] n (windmill etc) molino; (coffee ~) molinillo; (factory) fábrica ♦ vt moler ♦ vi (also: ~ **about**) arremolinarse

millennium [mɪ'lɛnɪəm] (pl **~s** or **millennia**) n milenio, milenario

miller ['mɪlə*] n molinero

milli... ['mɪlɪ] prefix: **~gram(me)** n miligramo; **~metre** (US **~meter**) n milímetro

million ['mɪljən] n millón m; **a ~ times** un millón de veces; **~aire** [-jə'nɛə*] n millonario/a

milometer [mar'lɒmɪtə*] (*BRIT*) *n*
= **mileometer**

mime [maɪm] *n* mímica; (*actor*) mimo/a
♦ *vt* remedar ♦ *vi* actuar de mimo

mimic ['mɪmɪk] *n* imitador(a) *m/f* ♦ *adj*
mímico ♦ *vt* remedar, imitar

min. *abbr* = **minimum; minute(s)**

mince [mɪns] *vt* picar ♦ *n* (*BRIT: CULIN*)
carne *f* picada; **~meat** *n* conserva de
fruta picada; (*US: meat*) carne *f* picada; ~
pie *n* empanadilla rellena de fruta
picada; **~r** *n* picadora de carne

mind [maɪnd] *n* mente *f*; (*intellect*)
intelecto; (*contrasted with matter*) espíritu
m ♦ *vt* (*attend to, look after*) ocuparse de,
cuidar; (*be careful of*) tener cuidado con;
(*object to*): **I don't ~ the noise** no me
molesta el ruido; **it is on my ~** me
preocupa; **to bear sth in ~** tomar *or*
tener algo en cuenta; **to make up one's
~** decidirse; **I don't ~** me es igual; **~ you,
...** te advierto que ...; **never ~!** ¡es igual!,
¡no importa!; (*don't worry*) ¡no te
preocupes!; **"~ the step"** "cuidado con
el escalón"; **~er** *n* guardaespaldas *m inv*;
(*child ~er*) ≈ niñera; **~ful** *adj*: **~ful of**
consciente de; **~less** *adj* (*crime*) sin
motivo; (*work*) de autómata

mine¹ [maɪn] *pron* el mío/la mía *etc*; **a
friend of ~** un(a) amigo/a mío/mía ♦ *adj*:
this book is ~ este libro es mío

mine² [maɪn] *n* mina ♦ *vt* (*coal*) extraer;
(*bomb: beach etc*) minar; **~field** *n* campo
de minas; **~r** *n* minero/a

mineral ['mɪnərəl] *adj* mineral ♦ *n* mineral
m; **~s** *npl* (*BRIT: soft drinks*) refrescos *mpl*;
~ water *n* agua mineral

mingle ['mɪŋgl] *vi*: **to ~ with** mezclarse
con

miniature ['mɪnətʃə*] *adj* (en) miniatura
♦ *n* miniatura

minibus ['mɪnɪbʌs] *n* microbús *m*

minimal ['mɪnɪml] *adj* mínimo

minimize ['mɪnɪmaɪz] *vt* minimizar; (*play
down*) empequeñecer

minimum ['mɪnɪməm] (*pl* **minima**) *n*, *adj*
mínimo

mining ['maɪnɪŋ] *n* explotación *f* minera

miniskirt ['mɪnɪskɜːt] *n* minifalda

minister ['mɪnɪstə*] *n* (*BRIT: POL*) ministro/a
(*SP*), secretario/a (*AM*); (*REL*) pastor *m*
♦ *vi*: **to ~ to** atender a

ministry ['mɪnɪstrɪ] *n* (*BRIT: POL*) ministerio
(*SP*), secretaría (*AM*); (*REL*) sacerdocio

mink [mɪŋk] *n* visón *m*

minnow ['mɪnəu] *n* pececillo (*de agua
dulce*)

minor ['maɪnə*] *adj* (*repairs, injuries*) leve;
(*poet, planet*) menor; (*MUS*) menor ♦ *n*
(*LAW*) menor *m* de edad

Minorca [mɪ'nɔːkə] *n* Menorca

minority [maɪ'nɔrɪtɪ] *n* minoría

mint [mɪnt] *n* (*plant*) menta, hierbabuena;
(*sweet*) caramelo de menta ♦ *vt* (*coins*)
acuñar; **the (Royal) M~, the (US) M~** la
Casa de la Moneda; **in ~ condition** en
perfecto estado

minus ['maɪnəs] *n* (*also*: **~ sign**) signo de
menos ♦ *prep* menos; **12 ~ 6 equals 6**
12 menos 6 son 6; **~ 24°C** menos 24
grados

minute¹ ['mɪnɪt] *n* minuto; (*fig*)
momento; **~s** *npl* (*of meeting*) actas *fpl*;
at the last ~ a última hora

minute² [maɪ'njuːt] *adj* diminuto; (*search*)
minucioso

miracle ['mɪrəkl] *n* milagro

mirage ['mɪrɑːʒ] *n* espejismo

mirror ['mɪrə*] *n* espejo; (*in car*) retrovisor
m

mirth [mɜːθ] *n* alegría

misadventure [mɪsəd'ventʃə*] *n* desgracia

misapprehension [mɪsæprɪ'henʃən] *n*
equivocación *f*

misappropriate [mɪsə'prəuprɪeɪt] *vt*
malversar

misbehave [mɪsbɪ'heɪv] *vi* portarse mal

miscalculate [mɪs'kælkjuleɪt] *vt* calcular
mal

miscarriage ['mɪskærɪdʒ] *n* (*MED*) aborto;
~ of justice error *m* judicial

miscellaneous [mɪsɪ'leɪnɪəs] *adj* varios/
as, diversos/as

mischief ['mɪstʃɪf] *n* travesuras *fpl*,

diabluras *fpl*; (*maliciousness*) malicia;
mischievous [-ʃɪvəs] *adj* travieso

misconception [mɪskən'sepʃən] *n* idea
equivocada; equivocación *f*

misconduct [mɪs'kɔndʌkt] *n* mala
conducta; **professional ~** falta profesional

misdemeanour [mɪsdɪ'miːnə*] (*US*
misdemeanor) *n* delito, ofensa

miser ['maɪzə*] *n* avaro/a

miserable ['mɪzərəbl] *adj* (*unhappy*) triste,
desgraciado; (*unpleasant, contemptible*)
miserable

miserly ['maɪzəlɪ] *adj* avariento, tacaño

misery ['mɪzərɪ] *n* tristeza; (*wretchedness*)
miseria, desdicha

misfire [mɪs'faɪə*] *vi* fallar

misfit ['mɪsfɪt] *n* inadaptado/a

misfortune [mɪs'fɔːtʃən] *n* desgracia

misgiving [mɪs'gɪvɪŋ] *n* (*apprehension*)
presentimiento; **to have ~s about sth**
tener dudas acerca de algo

misguided [mɪs'gaɪdɪd] *adj* equivocado

mishandle [mɪs'hændl] *vt* (*mismanage*)
manejar mal

mishap ['mɪshæp] *n* desgracia,
contratiempo

misinform [mɪsɪn'fɔːm] *vt* informar mal

misinterpret [mɪsɪn'təːprɪt] *vt* interpretar
mal

misjudge [mɪs'dʒʌdʒ] *vt* juzgar mal

mislay [mɪs'leɪ] (*irreg*) *vt* extraviar, perder

mislead [mɪs'liːd] (*irreg*) *vt* llevar a
conclusiones erróneas; **~ing** *adj*
engañoso

mismanage [mɪs'mænɪdʒ] *vt* administrar
mal

misplace [mɪs'pleɪs] *vt* extraviar

misprint ['mɪsprɪnt] *n* errata, error *m* de
imprenta

Miss [mɪs] *n* Señorita

miss [mɪs] *vt* (*train etc*) perder; (*fail to hit:
target*) errar; (*regret the absence of*): **I ~
him** (yo) le echo de menos *or* a faltar;
(*fail to see*): **you can't ~ it** no tiene
pérdida ♦ *vi* fallar ♦ *n* (*shot*) tiro fallido *or*
perdido; **~ out** (*BRIT*) *vt* omitir

misshapen [mɪs'ʃeɪpən] *adj* deforme

missile ['mɪsaɪl] *n* (*AVIAT*) mísil *m*; (*object
thrown*) proyectil *m*

missing ['mɪsɪŋ] *adj* (*pupil*) ausente;
(*thing*) perdido; (*MIL*): **~ in action**
desaparecido en combate

mission ['mɪʃən] *n* misión *f*; (*official
representation*) delegación *f*; **~ary** *n*
misionero/a

mist [mɪst] *n* (*light*) neblina; (*heavy*) niebla;
(*at sea*) bruma ♦ *vi* (*eyes: also:* **~ over,** **~
up**) llenarse de lágrimas; (*BRIT: windows:
also:* **~ over, ~ up**) empañarse

mistake [mɪs'teɪk] (*vt: irreg*) *n* error *m*
♦ *vt* entender mal; **by ~** por
equivocación; **to make a ~** equivocarse;
to ~ A for B confundir A con B;
mistaken *pp of* **mistake** ♦ *adj*
equivocado; **to be mistaken** equivocarse,
engañarse

mister ['mɪstə*] (*inf*) *n* señor *m*; *see* **Mr**

mistletoe ['mɪsltəu] *n* muérdago

mistook [mɪs'tuk] *pt of* **mistake**

mistress ['mɪstrɪs] *n* (*lover*) amante *f*; (*of
house*) señora (de la casa); (*BRIT: in
primary school*) maestra; (*in secondary
school*) profesora; (*of situation*) dueña

mistrust [mɪs'trʌst] *vt* desconfiar de

misty ['mɪstɪ] *adj* (*day*) de niebla; (*glasses
etc*) empañado

misunderstand [mɪsʌndə'stænd] (*irreg*)
vt, vi entender mal; **~ing** *n*
malentendido

misuse [*n* mɪs'juːs, *vb* mɪs'juːz] *n* mal uso *m*;
(*of power*) abuso; (*of funds*) malversación *f*
♦ *vt* abusar de; malversar

mitt(en) ['mɪt(n)] *n* manopla

mix [mɪks] *vt* mezclar; (*combine*) unir ♦ *vi*
mezclarse; (*people*) llevarse bien ♦ *n*
mezcla; **~ up** *vt* mezclar; (*confuse*)
confundir; **~ed** *adj* mixto; (*feelings etc*)
encontrado; **~ed-up** *adj* (*confused*)
confuso, revuelto; **~er** *n* (*for food*)
licuadora; (*for drinks*) coctelera; (*person*):
he's a good ~er tiene don de gentes;
~ture *n* mezcla; (*also:* **cough ~ture**)
jarabe *m*; **~up** *n* confusión *f*

mm *abbr* (= *millimetre*) mm

moan [məun] *n* gemido ♦ *vi* gemir; (*inf: complain*): **to ~ (about)** quejarse (de)

moat [məut] *n* foso

mob [mɔb] *n* multitud *f* ♦ *vt* acosar

mobile ['məubaɪl] *adj* móvil ♦ *n* móvil *m*; **~ home** *n* caravana; **~ phone** *n* teléfono portátil

mock [mɔk] *vt* (*ridicule*) ridiculizar; (*laugh at*) burlarse de ♦ *adj* fingido; **~ exam** *examen preparatorio antes de los exámenes oficiales*; **~ery** *n* burla; **~-up** *n* maqueta

mod [mɔd] *adj see* **convenience**

mode [məud] *n* modo

model ['mɔdl] *n* modelo; (*fashion ~, artist's ~*) modelo *m/f* ♦ *adj* modelo ♦ *vt* (*with clay etc*) modelar (*copy*): **to ~ o.s. on** tomar como modelo a ♦ *vi* ser modelo; **to ~ clothes** pasar modelos, ser modelo; **~ railway** *n* ferrocarril *m* de juguete

modem ['məudəm] *n* modem *m*

moderate [*adj* 'mɔdərət, *vb* 'mɔdəreɪt] *adj* moderado/a ♦ *vi* moderarse, calmarse ♦ *vt* moderar

modern ['mɔdən] *adj* moderno; **~ize** *vt* modernizar

modest ['mɔdɪst] *adj* modesto; (*small*) módico; **~y** *n* modestia

modify ['mɔdɪfaɪ] *vt* modificar

mogul ['məugəl] *n* (*fig*) magnate *m*

mohair ['məuhɛə*] *n* mohair *m*

moist [mɔɪst] *adj* húmedo; **~en** ['mɔɪsn] *vt* humedecer; **~ure** ['mɔɪstʃə*] *n* humedad *f*; **~urizer** ['mɔɪstʃəraɪzə*] *n* crema hidratante

molar ['məulə*] *n* muela

mold [məuld] (*US*) *n, vt* = **mould**

mole [məul] *n* (*animal, spy*) topo; (*spot*) lunar *m*

molest [məu'lest] *vt* importunar; (*assault sexually*) abusar sexualmente de

mollycoddle ['mɔlɪkɔdl] *vt* mimar

molt [məult] (*US*) *vi* = **moult**

molten ['məultən] *adj* fundido; (*lava*) líquido

mom [mɔm] (*US*) *n* = **mum**

moment ['məumənt] *n* momento; **at the ~** de momento, por ahora; **~ary** *adj* momentáneo; **~ous** [-'mentəs] *adj* trascendental, importante

momentum [məu'mentəm] *n* momento; (*fig*) ímpetu *m*; **to gather ~** cobrar velocidad; (*fig*) ganar fuerza

mommy ['mɔmɪ] (*US*) *n* = **mummy**

Monaco ['mɔnəkəu] *n* Mónaco

monarch ['mɔnək] *n* monarca *m/f*; **~y** *n* monarquía

monastery ['mɔnəstərɪ] *n* monasterio

Monday ['mʌndɪ] *n* lunes *m inv*

monetary ['mʌnɪtərɪ] *adj* monetario

money ['mʌnɪ] *n* dinero; (*currency*) moneda; **to make ~** ganar dinero; **~ order** *n* giro; **~-spinner** (*inf*) *n*: **to be a ~-spinner** dar mucho dinero

mongrel ['mʌŋgrəl] *n* (*dog*) perro mestizo

monitor ['mɔnɪtə*] *n* (*SCOL*) monitor *m*; (*also:* **television ~**) receptor *m* de control; (*of computer*) monitor *m* ♦ *vt* controlar

monk [mʌŋk] *n* monje *m*

monkey ['mʌŋkɪ] *n* mono; **~ nut** (*BRIT*) *n* cacahuete *m* (*SP*), maní *m* (*AM*); **~ wrench** *n* llave *f* inglesa

monopoly [mə'nɔpəlɪ] *n* monopolio

monotone ['mɔnətəun] *n* voz *f* (*or* tono) monocorde

monotonous [mə'nɔtənəs] *adj* monótono

monsoon [mɔn'suːn] *n* monzón *m*

monster ['mɔnstə*] *n* monstruo

monstrous ['mɔnstrəs] *adj* (*huge*) enorme; (*atrocious, ugly*) monstruoso

month [mʌnθ] *n* mes *m*; **~ly** *adj* mensual ♦ *adv* mensualmente

monument ['mɔnjumənt] *n* monumento

moo [muː] *vi* mugir

mood [muːd] *n* humor *m*; (*of crowd, group*) clima *m*; **to be in a good/bad ~** estar de buen/mal humor; **~y** *adj* (*changeable*) de humor variable; (*sullen*) malhumorado

moon [muːn] *n* luna; **~light** *n* luz *f* de la luna; **~lighting** *n* pluriempleo; **~lit** *adj*: **a ~lit night** una noche de luna

Moor [muə*] *n* moro/a

moor [muə*] n páramo ♦ vt (ship) amarrar
♦ vi echar las amarras
Moorish ['muərɪʃ] adj moro; (architecture)
árabe, morisco
moorland ['muələnd] n páramo, brezal m
moose [muːs] n inv alce m
mop [mɔp] n fregona; (of hair) greña,
melena ♦ vt fregar; **~ up** vt limpiar
mope [məup] vi estar or andar deprimido
moped ['məupɛd] n ciclomotor m
moral ['mɔrl] adj moral ♦ n moraleja; **~s**
npl moralidad f, moral f
morale [mɔ'rɑːl] n moral f
morality [mə'rælɪtɪ] n moralidad f
morass ['mɔræs] n pantano

<u>KEYWORD</u>

more [mɔː*] adj 1 (greater in number etc)
más; **~ people/work than before** más
gente/trabajo que antes
2 (additional) más; **do you want (some)
~ tea?** ¿quieres más té?; **is there any ~
wine?** ¿queda vino?; **it'll take a few ~
weeks** tardará unas semanas más; **it's 2
kms ~ to the house** faltan 2 kms para la
casa; **~ time/letters than we expected**
más tiempo del que/más cartas de las
que esperábamos
♦ pron (greater amount, additional
amount) más; **~ than 10** más de 10; **it
cost ~ than the other one/than we
expected** costó más que el otro/más de
lo que esperábamos; **is there any ~?**
¿hay más?; **many/much ~** muchos(as)/
mucho(a) más
♦ adv más; **~ dangerous/easily (than)**
más peligroso/fácilmente (que); **~ and ~
expensive** cada vez más caro; **~ or less**
más o menos; **~ than ever** más que
nunca

moreover [mɔː'rəuvə*] adv además, por
otra parte
morning ['mɔːnɪŋ] n mañana; (early ~)
madrugada ♦ cpd matutino, de la
mañana; **in the ~** por la mañana; **7
o'clock in the ~** las 7 de la mañana; **~**

sickness n náuseas fpl matutinas
Morocco [mə'rɔkəu] n Marruecos m
moron ['mɔːrɔn] (inf) n imbécil m/f
morphine ['mɔːfiːn] n morfina
Morse [mɔːs] n (also: **~ code**) (código)
Morse
morsel ['mɔːsl] n (of food) bocado
mortar ['mɔːtə*] n argamasa
mortgage ['mɔːɡɪdʒ] n hipoteca ♦ vt
hipotecar; **~ company** (US) n ≈ banco
hipotecario
mortuary ['mɔːtjuərɪ] n depósito de
cadáveres
Moscow ['mɔskəu] n Moscú
Moslem ['mɔzləm] adj, n = **Muslim**
mosque [mɔsk] n mezquita
mosquito [mɔs'kiːtəu] (pl **~es**) n
mosquito (SP), zancudo (AM)
moss [mɔs] n musgo
most [məust] adj la mayor parte de, la
mayoría de ♦ pron la mayor parte, la
mayoría ♦ adv el más; (very) muy; **the ~**
(also: +adj) el más; **~ of them** la mayor
parte de ellos; **I saw the ~** yo vi el que
más; **at the (very) ~** a lo sumo, todo lo
más; **to make the ~ of** aprovechar (al
máximo); **a ~ interesting book** un libro
interesantísimo; **~ly** adv en su mayor
parte, principalmente
MOT (BRIT) n abbr (= Ministry of
Transport): **the ~ (test)** inspección (anual)
obligatoria de coches y camiones
motel [məu'tɛl] n motel m
moth [mɔθ] n mariposa nocturna; (clothes
~) polilla
mother ['mʌðə*] n madre f ♦ adj materno
♦ vt (care for) cuidar (como una madre);
~hood n maternidad f; **~-in-law** n
suegra; **~ly** adj maternal; **~-of-pearl** n
nácar m; **~-to-be** n futura madre f; **~
tongue** n lengua materna
motion ['məuʃən] n movimiento; (gesture)
ademán m, señal f; (at meeting) moción f
♦ vt, vi: **to ~ to (to) sb to do sth** hacer
señas a uno para que haga algo; **~less**
adj inmóvil; **~ picture** n película
motivated ['məutɪveɪtɪd] adj motivado

motive ['məʊtɪv] *n* motivo
motley ['mɒtlɪ] *adj* variado
motor ['məʊtə*] *n* motor *m*; (*BRIT*: *inf*: *vehicle*) coche *m* (*SP*), carro (*AM*), automóvil *m* ♦ *adj* motor (*f*: *motora or motriz*); **~bike** *n* moto *f*; **~boat** *n* lancha motora; **~car** (*BRIT*) *n* coche *m*, carro, automóvil *m*; **~cycle** *n* motocicleta; **~cycle racing** *n* motociclismo; **~cyclist** *n* motociclista *m/f*; **~ing** (*BRIT*) *n* automovilismo; **~ist** *n* conductor(a) *m/f*, automovilista *m/f*; **~ racing** (*BRIT*) *n* carreras *fpl* de coches, automovilismo; **~ vehicle** *n* automóvil *m*; **~way** (*BRIT*) *n* autopista
mottled ['mɒtld] *adj* abigarrado, multicolor
motto ['mɒtəʊ] (*pl* **~es**) *n* lema *m*; (*watchword*) consigna
mould [məʊld] (*US* **mold**) *n* molde *m*; (*mildew*) moho ♦ *vt* moldear; (*fig*) formar; **~y** *adj* enmohecido
moult [məʊlt] (*US* **molt**) *vi* mudar la piel (*or* las plumas)
mound [maʊnd] *n* montón *m*, montículo
mount [maʊnt] *n* monte *m* ♦ *vt* montar, subir a; (*jewel*) engarzar; (*picture*) enmarcar; (*exhibition etc*) organizar ♦ *vi* (*increase*) aumentar; **~ up** *vi* aumentar
mountain ['maʊntɪn] *n* montaña ♦ *cpd* de montaña; **~ bike** *n* bicicleta de montaña; **~eer** [-'nɪə*] *n* montañero/a (*SP*), andinista *m/f* (*AM*); **~eering** [-'nɪərɪŋ] *n* montañismo, andinismo; **~ous** *adj* montañoso; **~ rescue team** *n* equipo de rescate de montaña; **~side** *n* ladera de la montaña
mourn [mɔːn] *vt* llorar, lamentar ♦ *vi*: **to ~ for** llorar la muerte de; **~er** *n* doliente *m/f*; dolorido/a; **~ing** *n* luto; **in ~ing** de luto
mouse [maʊs] (*pl* **mice**) *n* (*ZOOL, COMPUT*) ratón *m*; **~trap** *n* ratonera
mousse [muːs] *n* (*CULIN*) crema batida; (*for hair*) espuma (moldeadora)
moustache [məs'tɑːʃ] (*US* **mustache**) *n* bigote *m*

mousy ['maʊsɪ] *adj* (*hair*) pardusco
mouth [maʊθ, *pl* maʊðz] *n* boca; (*of river*) desembocadura; **~ful** *n* bocado; **~ organ** *n* armónica; **~piece** *n* (*of musical instrument*) boquilla; (*spokesman*) portavoz *m/f*; **~wash** *n* enjuague *m*; **~watering** *adj* apetitoso
movable ['muːvəbl] *adj* movible
move [muːv] *n* (*movement*) movimiento; (*in game*) jugada; (: *turn to play*) turno; (*change: of house*) mudanza; (: *of job*) cambio de trabajo ♦ *vt* mover; (*emotionally*) conmover; (*POL: resolution etc*) proponer ♦ *vi* moverse; (*traffic*) circular; (*also*: **~ house**) trasladarse, mudarse; **to ~ sb to do sth** mover a uno a hacer algo; **to get a ~ on** darse prisa; **~ about** *or* **around** *vi* moverse; (*travel*) viajar; **~ along** *vi* avanzar, adelantarse; **~ away** *vi* alejarse; **~ back** *vi* retroceder; **~ forward** *vi* avanzar; **~ in** *vi* (*to a house*) instalarse; (*police, soldiers*) intervenir; **~ on** *vi* ponerse en camino; **~ out** *vi* (*of house*) mudarse; **~ over** *vi* apartarse, hacer sitio; **~ up** *vi* (*employee*) ser ascendido
moveable ['muːvəbl] *adj* = **movable**
movement ['muːvmənt] *n* movimiento
movie ['muːvɪ] *n* película; **to go to the ~s** ir al cine
moving ['muːvɪŋ] *adj* (*emotional*) conmovedor(a); (*that moves*) móvil
mow [məʊ] (*pt* **mowed**, *pp* **mowed** *or* **mown**) *vt* (*grass, corn*) cortar, segar; **~ down** *vt* (*shoot*) acribillar; **~er** *n* (*also*: **lawn~er**) cortacéspedes *m inv*, segadora
MP *n abbr* = **Member of Parliament**
m.p.h. *abbr* = **miles per hour** (*60 m.p.h.* = *96 k.p.h.*)
Mr ['mɪstə*] (*US* **Mr.**) *n*: **~ Smith** (el) Sr. Smith
Mrs ['mɪsɪz] (*US* **Mrs.**) *n*: **~ Smith** (la) Sra. Smith
Ms [mɪz] (*US* **Ms.**) *n* (= *Miss or Mrs*): **~ Smith** (la) Sr(t)a. Smith
M.Sc. *abbr* = **Master of Science**
much [mʌtʃ] *adj* mucho ♦ *adv* mucho;

(*before pp*) muy ♦ *n or pron* mucho; **how ~ is it?** ¿cuánto es?, ¿cuánto cuesta?; **too ~** demasiado; **it's not ~** no es mucho; **as ~ as** tanto como; **however ~ he tries** por mucho que se esfuerce

muck [mʌk] *n* suciedad *f*; **~ about** or **around** (*inf*) *vi* perder el tiempo; (*enjoy o.s.*) entretenerse; **~ up** (*inf*) *vt* arruinar, estropear

mud [mʌd] *n* barro, lodo

muddle ['mʌdl] *n* desorden *m*, confusión *f*; (*mix-up*) embrollo, lío ♦ *vt* (*also:* **~ up**) embrollar, confundir; **~ through** *vi* salir del paso

muddy ['mʌdɪ] *adj* fangoso, cubierto de lodo

mudguard ['mʌdgɑːd] *n* guardabarros *m inv*

muffin ['mʌfin] *n* panecillo dulce

muffle ['mʌfl] *vt* (*sound*) amortiguar; (*against cold*) embozar; **~d** *adj* (*noise etc*) amortiguado, apagado; **~r** (*US*) *n* (*AUT*) silenciador *m*

mug [mʌg] *n* taza grande (*sin platillo*); (*for beer*) jarra; (*inf: face*) jeta; (: *fool*) bobo ♦ *vt* (*assault*) asaltar; **~ging** *n* asalto

muggy ['mʌgɪ] *adj* bochornoso

mule [mjuːl] *n* mula

multi... [mʌltɪ] *prefix* multi...

multi-level [mʌltɪ'levl] (*US*) *adj* = **multistorey**

multiple ['mʌltɪpl] *adj* múltiple ♦ *n* múltiplo; **~ sclerosis** *n* esclerosis *f* múltiple

multiplex cinema ['mʌltɪpleks-] *n* multicines *mpl*

multiplication [mʌltɪplɪ'keɪʃən] *n* multiplicación *f*

multiply ['mʌltɪplaɪ] *vt* multiplicar ♦ *vi* multiplicarse

multistorey [mʌltɪ'stɔːrɪ] (*BRIT*) *adj* de muchos pisos

multitude ['mʌltɪtjuːd] *n* multitud *f*

mum [mʌm] (*BRIT: inf*) *n* mamá ♦ *adj*: **to keep ~** mantener la boca cerrada

mumble ['mʌmbl] *vt, vi* hablar entre dientes, refunfuñar

mummy ['mʌmɪ] *n* (*BRIT: mother*) mamá; (*embalmed*) momia

mumps [mʌmps] *n* paperas *fpl*

munch [mʌntʃ] *vt, vi* mascar

mundane [mʌn'deɪn] *adj* trivial

municipal [mjuː'nɪsɪpl] *adj* municipal

murder ['mɜːdə*] *n* asesinato; (*in law*) homicidio ♦ *vt* asesinar, matar; **~er/ess** *n* asesino/a; **~ous** *adj* homicida

murky ['mɜːkɪ] *adj* (*water*) turbio; (*street, night*) lóbrego

murmur ['mɜːmə*] *n* murmullo ♦ *vt, vi* murmurar

muscle ['mʌsl] *n* músculo; (*fig: strength*) garra, fuerza; **~ in** *vi* entrometerse; **muscular** ['mʌskjulə*] *adj* muscular; (*person*) musculoso

muse [mjuːz] *vi* meditar ♦ *n* musa

museum [mjuː'zɪəm] *n* museo

mushroom ['mʌʃrum] *n* seta, hongo; (*CULIN*) champiñón *m* ♦ *vi* crecer de la noche a la mañana

music ['mjuːzɪk] *n* música; **~al** *adj* musical; (*sound*) melodioso; (*person*) con talento musical ♦ *n* (*show*) comedia musical; **~al instrument** *n* instrumento musical; **~ hall** *n* teatro de variedades; **~ian** [-'zɪʃən] *n* músico/a

Muslim ['mʌzlɪm] *adj, n* musulmán/ana *m/f*

muslin ['mʌzlɪn] *n* muselina

mussel ['mʌsl] *n* mejillón *m*

must [mʌst] *aux vb* (*obligation*): **I ~ do it** debo hacerlo, tengo que hacerlo; (*probability*): **he ~ be there by now** ya debe (de) estar allí ♦ *n*: **it's a ~** es imprescindible

mustache ['mʌstæʃ] (*US*) *n* = **moustache**

mustard ['mʌstəd] *n* mostaza

muster ['mʌstə*] *vt* juntar, reunir

mustn't ['mʌsnt] = **must not**

mute [mjuːt] *adj, n* mudo/a *m/f*

muted ['mjuːtɪd] *adj* callado; (*colour*) apagado

mutiny ['mjuːtɪnɪ] *n* motín *m* ♦ *vi* amotinarse

mutter ['mʌtə*] *vt, vi* murmurar

mutton ['mʌtn] *n* carne *f* de cordero

mutual ['mjuːtʃʊəl] *adj* mutuo; (*interest*) común; **~ly** *adv* mutuamente

muzzle ['mʌzl] *n* hocico; (*for dog*) bozal *m*; (*of gun*) boca ♦ *vt* (*dog*) poner un bozal a

my [maɪ] *adj* mi(s); **~ house/brother/ sisters** mi casa/mi hermano/mis hermanas; **I've washed ~ hair/cut ~ finger** me he lavado el pelo/cortado un dedo; **is this ~ pen or yours?** ¿es este bolígrafo mío o tuyo?

myself [maɪˈsɛlf] *pron* (*reflexive*) me; (*emphatic*) yo mismo; (*after prep*) mí (mismo); *see also* **oneself**

mysterious [mɪsˈtɪərɪəs] *adj* misterioso

mystery ['mɪstərɪ] *n* misterio

mystify ['mɪstɪfaɪ] *vt* (*perplex*) dejar perplejo

myth [mɪθ] *n* mito

N, n

n/a *abbr* (= *not applicable*) no interesa

nag [næg] *vt* (*scold*) regañar; **~ging** *adj* (*doubt*) persistente; (*pain*) continuo

nail [neɪl] *n* (*human*) uña; (*metal*) clavo ♦ *vt* clavar; **to ~ sth to sth** clavar algo en algo; **to ~ sb down to doing sth** comprometer a uno a que haga algo; **~brush** *n* cepillo para las uñas; **~file** *n* lima para las uñas; **~ polish** *n* esmalte *m or* laca para las uñas; **~ polish remover** *n* quitaesmalte *m*; **~ scissors** *npl* tijeras *fpl* para las uñas; **~ varnish** (*BRIT*) *n* = **~ polish**

naïve [naɪˈiːv] *adj* ingenuo

naked ['neɪkɪd] *adj* (*nude*) desnudo; (*flame*) expuesto al aire

name [neɪm] *n* nombre *m*; (*surname*) apellido; (*reputation*) fama, renombre *m* ♦ *vt* (*child*) poner nombre a; (*criminal*) identificar; (*price, date etc*) fijar; **what's your ~?** ¿cómo se llama?; **by ~** de nombre; **in the ~ of** en nombre de; **to give one's ~ and address** dar sus señas;

~ly *adv* a saber; **~sake** *n* tocayo/a

nanny ['nænɪ] *n* niñera

nap [næp] *n* (*sleep*) sueñecito, siesta

nape [neɪp] *n*: **~ of the neck** nuca, cogote *m*

napkin ['næpkɪn] *n* (*also*: **table ~**) servilleta

nappy ['næpɪ] (*BRIT*) *n* pañal *m*; **~ rash** *n* prurito

narcotic [nɑːˈkɔtɪk] *adj, n* narcótico

narrow ['nærəʊ] *adj* estrecho, angosto; (*fig: majority etc*) corto; (: *ideas etc*) estrecho ♦ *vi* (*road*) estrecharse; (*diminish*) reducirse; **to have a ~ escape** escaparse por los pelos; **to ~ sth down** reducir algo; **~ly** *adv* (*miss*) por poco; **~-minded** *adj* de miras estrechas

nasty ['nɑːstɪ] *adj* (*remark*) feo; (*person*) antipático; (*revolting: taste, smell*) asqueroso; (*wound, disease etc*) peligroso, grave

nation ['neɪʃən] *n* nación *f*

national ['næʃənl] *adj, n* nacional *m/f*; **~ dress** *n* vestido nacional; **N~ Health Service** (*BRIT*) *n* servicio nacional de salud pública; ≈ Insalud *m* (*SP*); **N~ Insurance** (*BRIT*) *n* seguro social nacional; **~ism** *n* nacionalismo; **~ist** *adj, n* nacionalista *m/f*; **~ity** [-ˈnælɪtɪ] *n* nacionalidad *f*; **~ize** *vt* nacionalizar; **~ly** *adv* (*nationwide*) en escala nacional; (*as a nation*) nacionalmente, como nación; **~ park** (*BRIT*) *n* parque *m* nacional

nationwide ['neɪʃənwaɪd] *adj* en escala *or* a nivel nacional

native ['neɪtɪv] *n* (*local inhabitant*) natural *m/f*, nacional *m/f* ♦ *adj* (*indigenous*) indígena; (*country*) natal; (*innate*) natural, innato; **a ~ of Russia** un(a) natural *m/f* de Rusia; **a ~ speaker of French** un hablante nativo de francés; **N~ American** *adj, n* americano/a indígena, amerindio/a; **~ language** *n* lengua materna

Nativity [nəˈtɪvɪtɪ] *n*: **the ~** Navidad *f*

NATO ['neɪtəʊ] *n abbr* (= *North Atlantic Treaty Organization*) OTAN *f*

natural ['nætʃrəl] *adj* natural; **~ly** *adv*

(*speak etc*) naturalmente; (*of course*) desde luego, por supuesto

nature ['neɪtʃə*] *n* (*also:* **N~**) naturaleza; (*group, sort*) género, clase *f*; (*character*) carácter *m*, genio; **by ~** por *or* de naturaleza

naught [nɔ:t] = **nought**

naughty ['nɔ:tɪ] *adj* (*child*) travieso

nausea ['nɔ:sɪə] *n* náuseas *fpl*

nautical ['nɔ:tɪkl] *adj* náutico, marítimo; (*mile*) marino

naval ['neɪvl] *adj* naval, de marina; **~ officer** *n* oficial *m/f* de marina

nave [neɪv] *n* nave *f*

navel ['neɪvl] *n* ombligo

navigate ['nævɪgeɪt] *vt* gobernar ♦ *vi* navegar; (*AUT*) ir de copiloto; **navigation** [-'geɪʃən] *n* (*action*) navegación *f*; (*science*) náutica; **navigator** *n* navegador(a) *m/f*, navegante *m/f*; (*AUT*) copiloto *m/f*

navvy ['nævɪ] (*BRIT*) *n* peón *m* caminero

navy ['neɪvɪ] *n* marina de guerra; (*ships*) armada, flota; **~(-blue)** *adj* azul marino

Nazi ['nɑ:tsɪ] *n* nazi *m/f*

NB *abbr* (= *nota bene*) nótese

near [nɪə*] *adj* (*place, relation*) cercano; (*time*) próximo ♦ *adv* cerca ♦ *prep* (*also:* **~ to**: *space*) cerca de, junto a; (: *time*) cerca de ♦ *vt* acercarse a, aproximarse a; **~by** [nɪə'baɪ] *adj* cercano, próximo ♦ *adv* cerca; **~ly** *adv* casi, por poco; **I ~ly fell** por poco me caigo; **~ miss** *n* tiro cercano; **~side** *n* (*AUT: in Britain*) lado izquierdo; (: *in US, Europe etc*) lado derecho; **~-sighted** *adj* miope, corto de vista

neat [ni:t] *adj* (*place*) ordenado, bien cuidado; (*person*) pulcro; (*plan*) ingenioso; (*spirits*) solo; **~ly** *adv* (*tidily*) con esmero; (*skilfully*) ingeniosamente

necessarily ['nesɪsrɪlɪ] *adv* necesariamente

necessary ['nesɪsrɪ] *adj* necesario, preciso

necessitate [nɪ'sesɪteɪt] *vt* hacer necesario

necessity [nɪ'sesɪtɪ] *n* necesidad *f*; **necessities** *npl* artículos *mpl* de primera necesidad

neck [nek] *n* (*of person, garment, bottle*) cuello; (*of animal*) pescuezo ♦ *vi* (*inf*) besuquearse; **~ and ~** parejos; **~lace** ['neklɪs] *n* collar *m*; **~line** *n* escote *m*; **~tie** ['nektaɪ] *n* corbata

née [neɪ] *adj*: **~ Scott** de soltera Scott

need [ni:d] *n* (*lack*) escasez *f*, falta; (*necessity*) necesidad *f* ♦ *vt* (*require*) necesitar; **I ~ to do it** tengo que *or* debo hacerlo; **you don't ~ to go** no hace falta que (te) vayas

needle ['ni:dl] *n* aguja ♦ *vt* (*fig: inf*) picar, fastidiar

needless ['ni:dlɪs] *adj* innecesario; **~ to say** huelga decir que

needlework ['ni:dlwə:k] *n* (*activity*) costura, labor *f* de aguja

needn't ['ni:dnt] = **need not**

needy ['ni:dɪ] *adj* necesitado

negative ['negətɪv] *n* (*PHOT*) negativo; (*LING*) negación *f* ♦ *adj* negativo; **~ equity** *n* situación que se da cuando el valor de la vivienda es menor que el de la hipoteca que pesa sobre ella

neglect [nɪ'glekt] *vt* (*one's duty*) faltar a, no cumplir con; (*child*) descuidar, desatender ♦ *n* (*of house, garden etc*) abandono; (*of child*) desatención *f*; (*of duty*) incumplimiento

negligee ['neglɪʒeɪ] *n* (*nightgown*) salto de cama

negotiate [nɪ'gəʊʃɪeɪt] *vt* (*treaty, loan*) negociar; (*obstacle*) franquear; (*bend in road*) tomar ♦ *vi*: **to ~ (with)** negociar (con); **negotiation** [-'eɪʃən] *n* negociación *f*, gestión *f*

neigh [neɪ] *vi* relinchar

neighbour ['neɪbə*] (*US* **neighbor**) *n* vecino/a; **~hood** *n* (*place*) vecindad *f*, barrio; (*people*) vecindario; **~ing** *adj* vecino; **~ly** *adj* (*person*) amable; (*attitude*) de buen vecino

neither ['naɪðə*] *adj* ni ♦ *conj*: **I didn't move and ~ did John** no me he movido, ni Juan tampoco ♦ *pron* ninguno ♦ *adv*: **~ good nor bad** ni bueno ni malo; **~ is true** ninguno/a de los/las dos es cierto/a

neon ['niːɔn] *n* neón *m*; ~ **light** *n* lámpara de neón

nephew ['nɛvjuː] *n* sobrino

nerve [nɜːv] *n* (*ANAT*) nervio; (*courage*) valor *m*; (*impudence*) descaro, frescura; **a fit of ~s** un ataque de nervios; **~-racking** *adj* desquiciante

nervous ['nɜːvəs] *adj* (*anxious, ANAT*) nervioso; (*timid*) tímido, miedoso; ~ **breakdown** *n* crisis *f* nerviosa

nest [nɛst] *n* (*of bird*) nido; (*wasps' ~*) avispero ♦ *vi* anidar; ~ **egg** *n* (*fig*) ahorros *mpl*

nestle ['nɛsl] *vi*: **to ~ down** acurrucarse

net [nɛt] *n* (*gen*) red *f*; (*fabric*) tul *m* ♦ *adj* (*COMM*) neto, líquido ♦ *vt* coger (*SP*) or agarrar (*AM*) con red; (*SPORT*) marcar; **~ball** *n* básquet *m*

Netherlands ['nɛðələndz] *npl*: **the ~** los Países Bajos

nett [nɛt] *adj* = **net**

netting ['nɛtɪŋ] *n* red *f*, redes *fpl*

nettle ['nɛtl] *n* ortiga

network ['nɛtwɜːk] *n* red *f*

neurotic [njuə'rɔtɪk] *adj, n* neurótico/a *m/f*

neuter ['njuːtə*] *adj* (*LING*) neutro ♦ *vt* castrar, capar

neutral ['njuːtrəl] *adj* (*person*) neutral; (*colour etc, ELEC*) neutro ♦ *n* (*AUT*) punto muerto; **~ize** *vt* neutralizar

never ['nɛvə*] *adv* nunca, jamás; **I ~ went** no fui nunca; ~ **in my life** jamás en la vida; *see also* **mind**; **~-ending** *adj* interminable, sin fin; **~theless** [nɛvəðə'lɛs] *adv* sin embargo, no obstante

new [njuː] *adj* nuevo; (*brand new*) a estrenar; (*recent*) reciente; **N~ Age** *n* Nueva Era; **~born** *adj* recién nacido; **~comer** ['njuːkʌmə*] *n* recién venido/a *or* llegado/a; **~fangled** (*pej*) *adj* modernísimo; **~found** *adj* (*friend*) nuevo; (*enthusiasm*) recién adquirido; **~ly** *adv* nuevamente, recién; **~ly-weds** *npl* recién casados *mpl*

news [njuːz] *n* noticias *fpl*; **a piece of ~** una noticia; **the ~** (*RADIO, TV*) las noticias *fpl*; ~ **agency** *n* agencia de noticias; **~agent** (*BRIT*) *n* vendedor(a) *m/f* de periódicos; **~caster** *n* presentador(a) *m/f*, locutor(a) *m/f*; ~ **flash** *n* noticia de última hora; **~letter** *n* hoja informativa, boletín *m*; **~paper** *n* periódico, diario; **~print** *n* papel *m* de periódico; **~reader** *n* = **~caster**; **~reel** *n* noticiario; **~ stand** *n* quiosco *or* puesto de periódicos

newt [njuːt] *n* tritón *m*

New Year *n* Año Nuevo; **~'s Day** *n* Día *m* de Año Nuevo; **~'s Eve** *n* Nochevieja

New York ['njuː'jɔːk] *n* Nueva York

New Zealand [njuː'ziːlənd] *n* Nueva Zelanda; **~er** *n* neozelandés/esa *m/f*

next [nɛkst] *adj* (*house, room*) vecino; (*bus stop, meeting*) próximo; (*following: page etc*) siguiente ♦ *adv* después; **the ~ day** el día siguiente; ~ **time** la próxima vez; ~ **year** el año próximo *or* que viene; ~ **to** junto a, al lado de; ~ **to nothing** casi nada; ~ **please!** ¡el siguiente! ~ **door** *adv* en la casa de al lado ♦ *adj* vecino, de al lado; **~-of-kin** *n* pariente *m* más cercano

NHS *n abbr* = **National Health Service**

nib [nɪb] *n* plumilla

nibble ['nɪbl] *vt* mordisquear, mordiscar

Nicaragua [nɪkə'ræɡjuə] *n* Nicaragua; **~n** *adj, n* nicaragüense *m/f*

nice [naɪs] *adj* (*likeable*) simpático; (*kind*) amable; (*pleasant*) agradable; (*attractive*) bonito, mono, lindo (*AM*); **~ly** *adv* amablemente; bien

nick [nɪk] *n* (*wound*) rasguño; (*cut, indentation*) mella, muesca ♦ *vt* (*inf*) birlar, robar; **in the ~ of time** justo a tiempo

nickel ['nɪkl] *n* níquel *m*; (*US*) moneda de 5 centavos

nickname ['nɪkneɪm] *n* apodo, mote *m* ♦ *vt* apodar

nicotine ['nɪkətiːn] *n* nicotina

niece [niːs] *n* sobrina

Nigeria [naɪ'dʒɪərɪə] *n* Nigeria; **~n** *adj, n* nigeriano/a *m/f*

niggling ['nɪɡlɪŋ] *adj* (*trifling*) nimio,

insignificante; (*annoying*) molesto
night [naɪt] *n* noche *f*; (*evening*) tarde *f*;
the ~ before last anteanoche; **at ~, by ~**
de noche, por la noche; **~cap** *n* (*drink*)
bebida que se toma antes de acostarse; **~
club** *n* cabaret *m*; **~dress** (*BRIT*) *n*
camisón *m*; **~fall** *n* anochecer *m*;
~gown *n* = **~dress**; **~ie** ['naɪti] *n*
= **~dress**
nightingale ['naɪtɪŋgeɪl] *n* ruiseñor *m*
night: **~life** *n* vida nocturna; **~ly** *adj* de
todas las noches ♦ *adv* todas las noches,
cada noche; **~mare** *n* pesadilla; **~
porter** *n* portero de noche; **~ school** *n*
clase(s) *f(pl)* nocturna(s); **~ shift** *n* turno
nocturno *or* de noche; **~-time** *n* noche *f*;
~ watchman *n* vigilante *m* nocturno
nil [nɪl] (*BRIT*) *n* (*SPORT*) cero, nada
Nile [naɪl] *n*: **the ~** el Nilo
nimble ['nɪmbl] *adj* (*agile*) ágil, ligero;
(*skilful*) diestro
nine [naɪn] *num* nueve; **~teen** *num*
diecinueve, diez y nueve; **~ty** *num*
noventa
ninth [naɪnθ] *adj* noveno
nip [nɪp] *vt* (*pinch*) pellizcar; (*bite*) morder
nipple ['nɪpl] *n* (*ANAT*) pezón *m*
nitrogen ['naɪtrədʒən] *n* nitrógeno

|KEYWORD|

no [nəu] (*pl* **~es**) *adv* (*opposite of "yes"*)
no; **are you coming? – ~ (I'm not)**
¿vienes? — no; **would you like some
more? – ~ thank you** ¿quieres más? —
no gracias
♦ *adj* (*not any*): **I have ~ money/time/
books** no tengo dinero/tiempo/libros; **~
other man would have done it** ningún
otro lo hubiera hecho; **"~ entry"**
"prohibido el paso"; **"~ smoking"**
"prohibido fumar"
♦ *n* no *m*

---

nobility [nəu'bɪlɪtɪ] *n* nobleza
noble ['nəubl] *adj* noble
nobody ['nəubədɪ] *pron* nadie
nod [nɔd] *vi* saludar con la cabeza; (*in*

agreement) decir que sí con la cabeza;
(*doze*) dar cabezadas ♦ *vt*: **to ~ one's
head** inclinar la cabeza ♦ *n* inclinación *f*
de cabeza; **~ off** *vi* dar cabezadas
noise [nɔɪz] *n* ruido; (*din*) escándalo,
estrépito; **noisy** *adj* ruidoso; (*child*)
escandaloso
nominate ['nɔmɪneɪt] *vt* (*propose*)
proponer; (*appoint*) nombrar; **nominee**
[-'niː] *n* candidato/a
non... [nɔn] *prefix* no, des..., in...; **~-
alcoholic** *adj* no alcohólico; **~chalant**
adj indiferente; **~-committal** *adj*
evasivo; **~descript** *adj* soso
none [nʌn] *pron* ninguno/a ♦ *adv* de
ninguna manera; **~ of you** ninguno de
vosotros; **I've ~ left** no me queda
ninguno/a; **he's ~ the worse for it** no le
ha hecho ningún mal
nonentity [nɔ'nentɪtɪ] *n* cero a la
izquierda, nulidad *f*
nonetheless [nʌnðə'les] *adv* sin
embargo, no obstante
non-existent *adj* inexistente
non-fiction *n* literatura no novelesca
nonplussed [nɔn'plʌst] *adj* perplejo
nonsense ['nɔnsəns] *n* tonterías *fpl*,
disparates *fpl*; **~!** ¡qué tonterías!
non: **~-smoker** *n* no fumador(a) *m/f*; **~-
smoking** *adj* (de) no fumador; **~-stick**
adj (*pan, surface*) antiadherente; **~-stop**
adj continuo; (*RAIL*) directo ♦ *adv* sin
parar
noodles ['nuːdlz] *npl* tallarines *mpl*
nook [nuk] *n*: **~s and crannies** escondrijos
mpl
noon [nuːn] *n* mediodía *m*
no-one *pron* = **nobody**
noose [nuːs] *n* (*hangman's*) dogal *m*
nor [nɔː*] *conj* = **neither** ♦ *adv see* **neither**
norm [nɔːm] *n* norma
normal ['nɔːml] *adj* normal; **~ly** *adv*
normalmente
north [nɔːθ] *n* norte *m* ♦ *adj* del norte,
norteño ♦ *adv* al *or* hacia el norte; **N~
Africa** *n* África del Norte; **N~ America**
n América del Norte; **~-east** *n* nor(d)este

m; **~erly** ['nɔ:ðəlɪ] *adj (point, direction)*
norteño; **~ern** ['nɔ:ðən] *adj* norteño, del
norte; **N~ern Ireland** *n* Irlanda del
Norte; **N~ Pole** *n* Polo Norte; **N~ Sea**
n Mar *m* del Norte; **~ward(s)**
['nɔ:θwəd(z)] *adv* hacia el norte; **~-west** *n*
nor(d)oeste *m*

Norway ['nɔ:weɪ] *n* Noruega; **Norwegian**
[-'wi:dʒən] *adj* noruego/a ♦ *n* noruego/a;
(LING) noruego

nose [nəuz] *n (ANAT)* nariz *f*; *(ZOOL)*
hocico; *(sense of smell)* olfato ♦ *vi*: **to ~
about** curiosear; **~bleed** *n* hemorragia
nasal; **~-dive** *n (of plane: deliberate)*
picado vertical; *(: involuntary)* caída en
picado; **~y** *(inf) adj* curioso, fisgón/ona

nostalgia [nɔs'tældʒɪə] *n* nostalgia

nostril ['nɔstrɪl] *n* ventana de la nariz

nosy ['nəuzɪ] *(inf) adj* = **nosey**

not [nɔt] *adv* no; **~ that ...** no es que ...;
it's too late, isn't it? es demasiado
tarde, ¿verdad *or* no?; **~ yet/now**
todavía/ahora no; **why ~?** ¿por qué no?;
see also **all**; **only**

notably ['nəutəblɪ] *adv* especialmente

notary ['nəutərɪ] *n* notario/a

notch [nɔtʃ] *n* muesca, corte *m*

note [nəut] *n (MUS, record, letter)* nota;
(banknote) billete *m*; *(tone)* tono ♦ *vt*
(observe) notar, observar; *(write down)*
apuntar, anotar; **~book** *n* libreta,
cuaderno; **~d** ['nəutɪd] *adj* célebre,
conocido; **~pad** *n* bloc *m*; **~paper** *n*
papel *m* para cartas

nothing ['nʌθɪŋ] *n* nada; *(zero)* cero; **he
does ~** no hace nada; **~ new** nada
nuevo; **~ much** no mucho; **for ~** *(free)*
gratis, sin pago; *(in vain)* en balde

notice ['nəutɪs] *n (announcement)* anuncio;
(warning) aviso; *(dismissal)* despido;
(resignation) dimisión *f*; *(period of time)*
plazo ♦ *vt (observe)* notar, observar; **to
bring sth to sb's ~** *(attention)* llamar la
atención de uno sobre algo; **to take ~ of**
tomar nota de, prestar atención a; **at
short ~** con poca anticipación; **until
further ~** hasta nuevo aviso; **to hand in**

one's ~ dimitir; **~able** *adj* evidente,
obvio; **~ board** *(BRIT) n* tablón *m* de
anuncios

notify ['nəutɪfaɪ] *vt*: **to ~ sb (of sth)**
comunicar (algo) a uno

notion ['nəuʃən] *n* idea; *(opinion)* opinión *f*

notorious [nəu'tɔ:rɪəs] *adj* notorio

nougat ['nu:gɑ:] *n* turrón *m*

nought [nɔ:t] *n* cero

noun [naun] *n* nombre *m*, sustantivo

nourish ['nʌrɪʃ] *vt* nutrir; *(fig)* alimentar;
~ing *adj* nutritivo; **~ment** *n* alimento,
sustento

novel ['nɔvl] *n* novela ♦ *adj (new)* nuevo,
original; *(unexpected)* insólito; **~ist** *n*
novelista *m/f*; **~ty** *n* novedad *f*

November [nəu'vɛmbə*] *n* noviembre *m*

novice ['nɔvɪs] *n (REL)* novicio/a

now [nau] *adv (at the present time)* ahora;
(these days) actualmente, hoy día ♦ *conj*:
~ (that) ya que, ahora que; **right ~** ahora
mismo; **by ~** ya; **just ~** ahora mismo; **~
and then, ~ and again** de vez en
cuando; **from ~ on** de ahora en adelante;
~adays ['nauədeɪz] *adv* hoy (en) día,
actualmente

nowhere ['nəuwɛə*] *adv (direction)* a
ninguna parte; *(location)* en ninguna
parte

nozzle ['nɔzl] *n* boquilla

nuance ['nju:ɑ:ns] *n* matiz *m*

nuclear ['nju:klɪə*] *adj* nuclear

nucleus ['nju:klɪəs] *(pl* **nuclei)** *n* núcleo

nude [nju:d] *adj*, *n* desnudo/a *m/f*; **in the
~** desnudo

nudge [nʌdʒ] *vt* dar un codazo a

nudist ['nju:dɪst] *n* nudista *m/f*

nuisance ['nju:sns] *n* molestia, fastidio;
(person) pesado, latoso; **what a ~!** ¡qué
lata!

null [nʌl] *adj*: **~ and void** nulo y sin efecto

numb [nʌm] *adj*: **~ with cold/fear**
entumecido por el frío/paralizado de
miedo

number ['nʌmbə*] *n* número; *(quantity)*
cantidad *f* ♦ *vt (pages etc)* numerar,
poner número a; *(amount to)* sumar,

ascender a; **to be ~ed among** figurar
entre; **a ~ of** varios, algunos; **they were
ten in ~** eran diez; **~ plate** (BRIT) n
matrícula, placa
numeral ['nju:mərəl] n número, cifra
numerate ['nju:mərit] adj competente en
la aritmética
numerous ['nju:mərəs] adj numeroso
nun [nʌn] n monja, religiosa
nurse [nə:s] n enfermero/a; (also: **~maid**)
niñera ♦ vt (patient) cuidar, atender
nursery ['nə:sərɪ] n (institution) guardería
infantil; (room) cuarto de los niños; (for
plants) criadero, semillero; **~ rhyme** n
canción f infantil; **~ school** n parvulario,
escuela de párvulos; **~ slope** (BRIT) n
(SKI) cuesta para principiantes
nursing ['nə:sɪŋ] n (profession) profesión f
de enfermera; (care) asistencia, cuidado;
~ home n clínica de reposo
nut [nʌt] n (TECH) tuerca; (BOT) nuez f;
~crackers npl cascanueces m inv
nutmeg ['nʌtmeg] n nuez f moscada
nutritious [nju:'trɪʃəs] adj nutritivo,
alimenticio
nuts [nʌts] (inf) adj loco
nutshell ['nʌtʃel] n: **in a ~** en resumidas
cuentas
nylon ['naɪlɔn] n nilón m ♦ adj de nilón

O, o

oak [əuk] n roble m ♦ adj de roble
O.A.P. (BRIT) n abbr = **old-age
pensioner**
oar [ɔ:*] n remo
oasis [əu'eɪsɪs] (pl **oases**) n oasis m inv
oath [əuθ] n juramento; (swear word)
palabrota; **on** (BRIT) or **under ~** bajo
juramento
oatmeal ['əutmi:l] n harina de avena
oats [əuts] n avena
obedience [ə'bi:dɪəns] n obediencia
obedient [ə'bi:dɪənt] adj obediente
obey [ə'beɪ] vt obedecer; (instructions,
regulations) cumplir

obituary [ə'bɪtjuərɪ] n necrología
object [n 'ɔbdʒɪkt, vb əb'dʒɛkt] n objeto;
(purpose) objeto, propósito; (LING)
complemento ♦ vi: **to ~ to** estar en
contra de; (proposal) oponerse a; **to ~
that** objetar que; **expense is no ~** no
importa cuánto cuesta; **I ~!** ¡yo protesto!;
~ion [əb'dʒɛkʃən] n protesta; **I have no
~ion to ...** no tengo inconveniente en
que ...; **~ionable** [əb'dʒɛkʃənəbl] adj
desagradable; (conduct) censurable; **~ive**
adj, n objetivo
obligation [ɔblɪ'geɪʃən] n obligación f;
(debt) deber m; **without ~** sin
compromiso
oblige [ə'blaɪdʒ] vt (do a favour for)
complacer, hacer un favor a; **to ~ sb to
do sth** forzar or obligar a uno a hacer
algo; **to be ~d to sb for sth** estarle
agradecido a uno por algo; **obliging** adj
servicial, atento
oblique [ə'bli:k] adj oblicuo; (allusion)
indirecto
obliterate [ə'blɪtəreɪt] vt borrar
oblivion [ə'blɪvɪən] n olvido; **oblivious**
[-ɪəs] adj: **oblivious of** inconsciente de
oblong ['ɔblɔŋ] adj rectangular ♦ n
rectángulo
obnoxious [əb'nɔkʃəs] adj odioso,
detestable; (smell) nauseabundo
oboe ['əubəu] n oboe m
obscene [əb'si:n] adj obsceno
obscure [əb'skjuə*] adj oscuro ♦ vt
oscurecer; (hide: sun) esconder
observant [əb'zə:vnt] adj observador(a)
observation [ɔbzə'veɪʃən] n observación f;
(MED) examen m
observe [əb'zə:v] vt observar; (rule)
cumplir; **~r** n observador(a) m/f
obsess [əb'sɛs] vt obsesionar; **~ive** adj
obsesivo; obsesionante
obsolete ['ɔbsəli:t] adj: **to be ~** estar en
desuso
obstacle ['ɔbstəkl] n obstáculo; (nuisance)
estorbo; **~ race** n carrera de obstáculos
obstinate ['ɔbstɪnɪt] adj terco, porfiado;
(determined) obstinado

obstruct [əbˈstrʌkt] *vt* obstruir; (*hinder*) estorbar, obstaculizar; **~ion** [əbˈstrʌkʃən] *n* (*action*) obstrucción *f*; (*object*) estorbo, obstáculo

obtain [əbˈteɪn] *vt* obtener; (*achieve*) conseguir

obvious [ˈɔbvɪəs] *adj* obvio, evidente; **~ly** *adv* evidentemente, naturalmente; **~ly not** por supuesto que no

occasion [əˈkeɪʒən] *n* oportunidad *f*, ocasión *f*; (*event*) acontecimiento; **~al** *adj* poco frecuente, ocasional; **~ally** *adv* de vez en cuando

occupant [ˈɔkjupənt] *n* (*of house*) inquilino/a; (*of car*) ocupante *m/f*

occupation [ɔkjuˈpeɪʃən] *n* ocupación *f*; (*job*) trabajo; (*pastime*) ocupaciones *fpl*; **~al hazard** *n* riesgo profesional

occupier [ˈɔkjupaɪə*] *n* inquilino/a

occupy [ˈɔkjupaɪ] *vt* (*seat, post, time*) ocupar; (*house*) habitar; **to ~ o.s. in doing** pasar el tiempo haciendo

occur [əˈkɜ:*] *vi* pasar, suceder; **to ~ to sb** ocurrírsele a uno; **~rence** [əˈkʌrəns] *n* acontecimiento; (*existence*) existencia

ocean [ˈəuʃən] *n* océano

o'clock [əˈklɔk] *adv*: **it is 5 ~** son las 5

OCR *n abbr* = **optical character recognition / reader**

October [ɔkˈtəubə*] *n* octubre *m*

octopus [ˈɔktəpəs] *n* pulpo

odd [ɔd] *adj* extraño, raro; (*number*) impar; (*sock, shoe etc*) suelto; **60-~** 60 y pico; **at ~ times** de vez en cuando; **to be the ~ one out** estar de más; **~ity** *n* rareza; (*person*) excéntrico; **~-job man** *n* chico para todo; **~ jobs** *npl* bricolaje *m*; **~ly** *adv* curiosamente, extrañamente; *see also* **enough**; **~ments** *npl* (*COMM*) retales *mpl*; **~s** *npl* (*in betting*) puntos *mpl* de ventaja; **it makes no ~s** da lo mismo; **at ~s** reñidos/as; **~s and ends** minucias *fpl*

odometer [ɔˈdɔmɪtə*] (*US*) *n* cuentakilómetros *m inv*

odour [ˈəudə*] (*US* **odor**) *n* olor *m*; (*unpleasant*) hedor *m*

KEYWORD

of [ɔv, əv] *prep* **1** (*gen*) de; **a friend ~ ours** un amigo nuestro; **a boy ~ 10** un chico de 10 años; **that was kind ~ you** eso fue muy amable por *or* de tu parte

2 (*expressing quantity, amount, dates etc*) de; **a kilo ~ flour** un kilo de harina; **there were 3 ~ them** había tres; **3 ~ us went** tres de nosotros fuimos; **the 5th ~ July** el 5 de julio

3 (*from, out of*) de; **made ~ wood** (hecho) de madera

---

off [ɔf] *adj, adv* (*engine*) desconectado; (*light*) apagado; (*tap*) cerrado; (*BRIT: food: bad*) pasado, malo; (*: milk*) cortado; (*cancelled*) cancelado ♦ *prep* de; **to be ~** (*to leave*) irse, marcharse; **to be ~ sick** estar enfermo *or* de baja; **a day ~** un día libre *or* sin trabajar; **to have an ~ day** tener un día malo; **he had his coat ~** se había quitado el abrigo; **10% ~** (*COMM*) (con el) 10% de descuento; **5 km ~ (the road)** a 5 km (de la carretera); **~ the coast** frente a la costa; **I'm ~ meat** (*no longer eat/like it*) paso de la carne; **on the ~ chance** por si acaso; **~ and on** de vez en cuando

offal [ˈɔfl] (*BRIT*) *n* (*CULIN*) menudencias *fpl*

off-colour [ɔfˈkʌlə*] (*BRIT*) *adj* (*ill*) indispuesto

offence [əˈfɛns] (*US* **offense**) *n* (*crime*) delito; **to take ~ at** ofenderse por

offend [əˈfɛnd] *vt* (*person*) ofender; **~er** *n* delincuente *m/f*

offensive [əˈfɛnsɪv] *adj* ofensivo; (*smell etc*) repugnante ♦ *n* (*MIL*) ofensiva

offer [ˈɔfə*] *n* oferta, ofrecimiento; (*proposal*) propuesta ♦ *vt* ofrecer; (*opportunity*) facilitar; **"on ~"** (*COMM*) "en oferta"; **~ing** *n* ofrenda

offhand [ɔfˈhænd] *adj* informal ♦ *adv* de improviso

office [ˈɔfɪs] *n* (*place*) oficina; (*room*) despacho; (*position*) carga, oficio; **doctor's ~** (*US*) consultorio; **to take ~**

entrar en funciones; ~ **automation** n
ofimática, buromática; ~ **block** (US ~
building) n bloque m de oficinas; ~
hours npl horas fpl de oficina; (US: MED)
horas fpl de consulta
officer ['ɔfisə*] n (MIL etc) oficial m/f; (also:
police ~) agente m/f de policía; (of
organization) director(a) m/f
office worker n oficinista m/f
official [ə'fɪʃl] adj oficial, autorizado ♦ n
funcionario, oficial m
offing ['ɔfɪŋ] n: **in the ~** (fig) en
perspectiva
off: **~-licence** (BRIT) n (shop) bodega,
tienda de vinos y bebidas alcohólicas; **~-
line** adj, adv (COMPUT) fuera de línea; **~-
peak** adj (electricity) de banda
económica; (ticket) billete de precio
reducido por viajar fuera de las horas
punta; **~-putting** (BRIT) adj (person)
asqueroso; (remark) desalentador(a); **~-
season** adj, adv fuera de temporada

offset ['ɔfset] (irreg) vt contrarrestar,
compensar
offshoot ['ɔfʃuːt] n (fig) ramificación f
offshore [ɔf'ʃɔː*] adj (breeze, island)
costera; (fishing) de bajura
offside ['ɔf'saɪd] adj (SPORT) fuera de
juego; (AUT: in UK) del lado derecho; (: in
US, Europe etc) del lado izquierdo
offspring ['ɔfsprɪŋ] n inv descendencia f
off: **~stage** adv entre bastidores; **~-the-**

peg (US **~-the-rack**) adv confeccionado;
~-white adj color crudo
often ['ɔfn] adv a menudo, con frecuencia;
how ~ do you go? ¿cada cuánto vas?
oh [əu] excl ¡ah!
oil [ɔɪl] n aceite m; (petroleum) petróleo;
(for heating) aceite m combustible ♦ vt
engrasar; **~can** n lata de aceite; **~field** n
campo petrolífero; **~ filter** n (AUT) filtro
de aceite; **~ painting** n pintura al óleo;
~ rig n torre f de perforación; **~ tanker**
n petrolero; (truck) camión m cisterna; **~
well** n pozo de petróleo); **~y** adj
aceitoso; (food) grasiento
ointment ['ɔɪntmənt] n ungüento
O.K., okay ['əu'keɪ] excl O.K., ¡está bien!,
¡vale! (SP) ♦ adj bien ♦ vt dar el visto
bueno a
old [əuld] adj viejo; (former) antiguo; **how
~ are you?** ¿cuántos años tienes?, ¿qué
edad tienes?; **he's 10 years ~** tiene 10
años; **~er brother** hermano mayor; **~
age** n vejez f; **~-age pensioner** (BRIT)
n jubilado/a; **~-fashioned** adj
anticuado, pasado de moda
olive ['ɔlɪv] n (fruit) aceituna; (tree) olivo
♦ adj (also: **~-green**) verde oliva; **~ oil** n
aceite m de oliva
Olympic [əu'lɪmpɪk] adj olímpico; **the ~
Games, the ~s** las Olimpíadas
omelet(te) ['ɔmlɪt] n tortilla (SP), tortilla
de huevo (AM)
omen ['əumən] n presagio
ominous ['ɔmɪnəs] adj de mal agüero,
amenazador(a)
omit [əu'mɪt] vt omitir

┌─────────────┐
│ KEYWORD   │
└─────────────┘

on [ɔn] prep **1** (indicating position) en;
sobre; **~ the wall** en la pared; **it's ~ the
table** está sobre or en la mesa; **~ the left**
a la izquierda
2 (indicating means, method, condition
etc): **~ foot** a pie; **~ the train/plane** (go)
en tren/avión; (be) en el tren/el avión; **~
the radio/television/telephone** por or
en la radio/televisión/al teléfono; **to be ~**

drugs drogarse; (*MED*) estar a tratamiento; **to be ~ holiday/business** estar de vacaciones/en viaje de negocios **3** (*referring to time*): **~ Friday** el viernes; **~ Fridays** los viernes; **~ June 20th** el 20 de junio; **a week ~ Friday** del viernes en una semana; **~ arrival** al llegar; **~ seeing this** al ver esto **4** (*about, concerning*) sobre, acerca de; **a book ~ physics** un libro de *or* sobre física ♦ *adv* **1** (*referring to dress*): **to have one's coat ~** tener *or* llevar el abrigo puesto; **she put her gloves ~** se puso los guantes **2** (*referring to covering*): **"screw the lid ~ tightly"** "cerrar bien la tapa" **3** (*further, continuously*): **to walk** *etc* **~** seguir caminando *etc* ♦ *adj* **1** (*functioning, in operation*: *machine, radio, TV, light*) encendido/a (*SP*), prendido/a (*AM*); (: *tap*) abierto/a; (: *brakes*) echado/a, puesto/a; **is the meeting still ~?** (*in progress*) ¿todavía continúa la reunión?; (*not cancelled*) ¿va a haber reunión al fin?; **there's a good film ~ at the cinema** ponen una buena película en el cine **2**: **that's not ~!** (*inf: not possible*) ¡eso ni hablar!; (: *not acceptable*) ¡eso no se hace!

once [wʌns] *adv* una vez; (*formerly*) antiguamente ♦ *conj* una vez que; **~ he had left/it was done** una vez que se había marchado/se hizo; **at ~** en seguida, inmediatamente; (*simultaneously*) a la vez; **~ a week** una vez por semana; **~ more** otra vez; **~ and for all** de una vez por todas; **~ upon a time** érase una vez

oncoming [ˈɒnkʌmɪŋ] *adj* (*traffic*) que viene de frente

KEYWORD

one [wʌn] *num* un(o)/una; **~ hundred and fifty** ciento cincuenta; **~ by ~** uno a uno ♦ *adj* **1** (*sole*) único; **the ~ book which** el único libro que; **the ~ man who** el único que

2 (*same*) mismo/a; **they came in the ~ car** vinieron en un solo coche ♦ *pron* **1**: **this ~** éste/ésta; **that ~** ése/ésa; (*more remote*) aquél/aquella; **I've already got (a red) ~** ya tengo uno/a (rojo/a); **~ by ~** uno/a por uno/a **2**: **~ another** os (*SP*), se (+*el uno al otro, unos a otros etc*); **do you two ever see ~ another?** ¿vosotros dos os veis alguna vez? (*SP*), ¿se ven ustedes dos alguna vez?; **the boys didn't dare look at ~ another** los chicos no se atrevieron a mirarse (el uno al otro); **they all kissed ~ another** se besaron unos a otros **3** (*impers*): **~ never knows** nunca se sabe; **to cut ~'s finger** cortarse el dedo; **~ needs to eat** hay que comer

one: **~-day excursion** (*US*) *n* billete *m* de ida y vuelta en un día; **~-man** *adj* (*business*) individual; **~-man band** *n* hombre-orquesta *m*; **~-off** (*BRIT: inf*) *n* (*event*) acontecimiento único

oneself [wʌnˈself] *pron* (*reflexive*) se; (*after prep*) sí; (*emphatic*) uno/a mismo/a; **to hurt ~** hacerse daño; **to keep sth for ~** guardarse algo; **to talk to ~** hablar solo

one: **~-sided** *adj* (*argument*) parcial; **~-to-~** *adj* (*relationship*) de dos; **~-way** *adj* (*street*) de sentido único

ongoing [ˈɒngəʊɪŋ] *adj* continuo

onion [ˈʌnjən] *n* cebolla

on-line *adj, adv* (*COMPUT*) en línea

onlooker [ˈɒnlʊkəʳ] *n* espectador(a) *m/f*

only [ˈəʊnlɪ] *adv* solamente, sólo ♦ *adj* único, solo ♦ *conj* solamente que, pero; **an ~ child** un hijo único; **not ~ ... but also ...** no sólo ... sino también ...

onset [ˈɒnset] *n* comienzo

onshore [ˈɒnʃɔːʳ] *adj* (*wind*) que sopla del mar hacia la tierra

onslaught [ˈɒnslɔːt] *n* ataque *m*, embestida

onto [ˈɒntʊ] *prep* = **on to**

onward(s) [ˈɒnwəd(z)] *adv* (*move*) (hacia) adelante; **from that time ~** desde entonces en adelante

onyx ['ɒnɪks] n ónice m

ooze [u:z] vi rezumar

opaque [əʊ'peɪk] adj opaco

OPEC ['əʊpɛk] n abbr (= Organization of Petroleum-Exporting Countries) OPEP f

open ['əʊpn] adj abierto; (car) descubierto; (road, view) despejado; (meeting) público; (admiration) manifiesto ♦ vt abrir ♦ vi abrirse; (book etc: commence) comenzar; **in the ~ (air)** al aire libre; **~ on to** vt fus (subj: room, door) dar a; **~ up** vt abrir; (blocked road) despejar ♦ vi abrirse, empezar; **~ing** n abertura; (start) comienzo; (opportunity) oportunidad f; **~ing hours** npl horario de apertura; **~ learning** n enseñanza flexible a tiempo parcial; **~ly** adv abiertamente; **~-minded** adj imparcial; **~-necked** adj (shirt) desabrochado; sin corbata; **~-plan** adj: **~-plan office** gran oficina sin particiones

---

Open University

i La **Open University**, *fundada en 1969, está especializada en impartir cursos a distancia que no exigen una dedicación exclusiva. Cuenta con sus propios materiales de apoyo, entre ellos programas de radio y televisión emitidos por la BBC y para conseguir los créditos de la licenciatura es necesaria la presentación de unos trabajos y la asistencia a los cursos de verano.*

---

opera ['ɒpərə] n ópera f; **~ house** n teatro de la ópera

operate ['ɒpəreɪt] vt (machine) hacer funcionar; (company) dirigir ♦ vi funcionar; **to ~ on sb** (MED) operar a uno

operatic [ɒpə'rætɪk] adj de ópera

operating table ['ɒpəreɪtɪŋ-] n mesa de operaciones

operating theatre n sala de operaciones

operation [ɒpə'reɪʃən] n operación f; (of machine) funcionamiento; **to be in ~** estar funcionando or en funcionamiento; **to**

have an ~ (MED) ser operado; **~al** adj operacional, en buen estado

operative ['ɒpərətɪv] adj en vigor

operator ['ɒpəreɪtə*] n (of machine) maquinista m/f, operario/a; (TEL) operador(a) m/f, telefonista m/f

opinion [ə'pɪnɪən] n opinión f; **in my ~** en mi opinión, a mi juicio; **~ated** adj testarudo; **~ poll** n encuesta, sondeo

opponent [ə'pəʊnənt] n adversario/a, contrincante m/f

opportunity [ɒpə'tju:nɪtɪ] n oportunidad f; **to take the ~ of doing** aprovechar la ocasión para hacer

oppose [ə'pəʊz] vt oponerse a; **to be ~d to sth** oponerse a algo; **as ~d to** a diferencia de; **opposing** adj opuesto, contrario

opposite ['ɒpəzɪt] adj opuesto, contrario a; (house etc) de enfrente ♦ adv en frente ♦ prep en frente de, frente a ♦ n lo contrario

opposition [ɒpə'zɪʃən] n oposición f

oppressive [ə'prɛsɪv] adj opresivo; (weather) agobiante

opt [ɒpt] vi: **to ~ for** optar por; **to ~ to do** optar por hacer; **~ out** vi: **to ~ out of** optar por no hacer

optical ['ɒptɪkl] adj óptico

optician [ɒp'tɪʃən] n óptico m/f

optimist ['ɒptɪmɪst] n optimista m/f; **~ic** [-'mɪstɪk] adj optimista

option ['ɒpʃən] n opción f; **~al** adj facultativo, discrecional

or [ɔ:*] conj o; (before o, ho) u; (with negative): **he hasn't seen ~ heard anything** no ha visto ni oído nada; **~ else** si no

oral ['ɔ:rəl] adj oral ♦ n examen m oral

orange ['ɒrɪndʒ] n (fruit) naranja ♦ adj color naranja

orbit ['ɔ:bɪt] n órbita ♦ vt, vi orbitar

orchard ['ɔ:tʃəd] n huerto

orchestra ['ɔ:kɪstrə] n orquesta; (US: seating) platea

orchid ['ɔ:kɪd] n orquídea

ordain [ɔ:'deɪn] vt (REL) ordenar, decretar

ordeal [ɔː'diːl] *n* experiencia horrorosa
order ['ɔːdə*] *n* orden *m*; (*command*) orden *f*; (*good ~*) buen estado; (*COMM*) pedido ♦ *vt* (*also:* **put in ~**) arreglar, poner en orden; (*COMM*) pedir; (*command*) mandar, ordenar; **in ~** en orden; (*of document*) en regla; **in (working) ~** en funcionamiento; **in ~ to do/that** para hacer/que; **on ~** (*COMM*) pedido; **to be out of ~** estar desordenado; (*not working*) no funcionar; **to ~ sb to do sth** mandar a uno hacer algo; **~ form** *n* hoja de pedido; **~ly** *n* (*MIL*) ordenanza *m*; (*MED*) enfermero/a (auxiliar) ♦ *adj* ordenado
ordinary ['ɔːdnrɪ] *adj* corriente, normal; (*pej*) común y corriente; **out of the ~** fuera de lo común
Ordnance Survey ['ɔːdnəns-] (*BRIT*) *n* servicio oficial de topografía
ore [ɔː*] *n* mineral *m*
organ ['ɔːgən] *n* órgano; **~ic** [ɔː'gænɪk] *adj* orgánico; **~ism** *n* organismo
organization [ɔːgənaɪ'zeɪʃən] *n* organización *f*
organize ['ɔːgənaɪz] *vt* organizar; **~r** *n* organizador(a) *m/f*
orgasm ['ɔːgæzəm] *n* orgasmo
orgy ['ɔːdʒɪ] *n* orgía
Orient ['ɔːrɪənt] *n* Oriente *m*; **oriental** [-'entl] *adj* oriental
orientate ['ɔːrɪənteɪt] *vt*: **to ~ o.s.** orientarse
origin ['ɔrɪdʒɪn] *n* origen *m*
original [ə'rɪdʒɪnl] *adj* original; (*first*) primero; (*earlier*) primitivo ♦ *n* original *m*; **~ly** *adv* al principio
originate [ə'rɪdʒɪneɪt] *vi*: **to ~ from, to ~ in** surgir de, tener su origen en
Orkney ['ɔːknɪ] *n* (*also:* **the Orkney Islands**) las Orcadas
ornament ['ɔːnəmənt] *n* adorno; (*trinket*) chuchería; **~al** [-'mentl] *adj* decorativo, de adorno
ornate [ɔː'neɪt] *adj* muy ornado, vistoso
orphan ['ɔːfn] *n* huérfano/a
orthopaedic [ɔːθə'piːdɪk] (*US* **orthopedic**)

adj ortopédico
ostensibly [ɔs'tensɪblɪ] *adv* aparentemente
ostentatious [ɔsten'teɪʃəs] *adj* ostentoso
osteopath ['ɔstɪəpæθ] *n* osteópata *m/f*
ostracize ['ɔstrəsaɪz] *vt* hacer el vacío a
ostrich ['ɔstrɪtʃ] *n* avestruz *m*
other ['ʌðə*] *adj* otro ♦ *pron*: **the ~ (one)** el/la otro/a ♦ *adv*: **~ than** aparte de; **~s** (*~ people*) otros; **the ~ day** el otro día; **~wise** *adv* de otra manera ♦ *conj* (*if not*) si no
otter ['ɔtə*] *n* nutria
ouch [autʃ] *excl* ¡ay!
ought [ɔːt] (*pt* **ought**) *aux vb*: **I ~ to do it** debería hacerlo; **this ~ to have been corrected** esto debiera haberse corregido; **he ~ to win** (*probability*) debe *or* debiera ganar
ounce [auns] *n* onza (*28.35g*)
our ['auə*] *adj* nuestro; *see also* **my**; **~s** *pron* (el) nuestro/(la) nuestra *etc*; *see also* **mine**[1]; **~selves** *pron pl* (*reflexive, after prep*) nosotros; (*emphatic*) nosotros mismos; *see also* **oneself**
oust [aust] *vt* desalojar
out [aut] *adv* fuera, afuera; (*not at home*) fuera (de casa); (*light, fire*) apagado; **~ there** allí (fuera); **he's ~** (*absent*) no está, ha salido; **to be ~ in one's calculations** equivocarse (en sus cálculos); **to run ~** salir corriendo; **~ loud** en alta voz; **~ of** (*outside*) fuera de; (*because of: anger etc*) por; **~ of petrol** sin gasolina; **"~ of order"** "no funciona"; **~-and-~** *adj* (*liar, thief etc*) redomado, empedernido; **~back** *n* interior *m*; **~board** *adj*: **~board motor** (*motor m*) fuera borda *m*; **~break** *n* (*of war*) comienzo; (*of disease*) epidemia; (*of violence etc*) ola; **~burst** *n* explosión *f*, arranque *m*; **~cast** *n* paria *m/f*; **~come** *n* resultado; **~crop** *n* (*of rock*) afloramiento; **~cry** *n* protestas *fpl*; **~dated** *adj* anticuado, fuera de moda; **~do** (*irreg*) *vt* superar; **~door** *adj* exterior, de aire libre; (*clothes*) de calle; **~doors** *adv* al aire libre
outer ['autə*] *adj* exterior, externo; **~**

space n espacio exterior
outfit ['autfɪt] n (clothes) conjunto
out: ~**going** adj (character) extrovertido;
(retiring: president etc) saliente; ~**goings**
(BRIT) npl gastos mpl; ~**grow** (irreg) vt:
he has ~grown his clothes su ropa le
queda pequeña ya; ~**house** n
dependencia; ~**ing** ['autɪŋ] n excursión f,
paseo
out: ~**law** n proscrito ♦ vt proscribir; ~**lay**
n inversión f; ~**let** n salida f; (of pipe)
desagüe m; (US: ELEC) toma de corriente;
(also: retail ~**let**) punto de venta; ~**line**
n (shape) contorno, perfil m; (sketch,
plan) esbozo ♦ vt (plan etc) esbozar; **in**
~**line** (fig) a grandes rasgos; ~**live** vt
sobrevivir a; ~**look** n (fig: prospects)
perspectivas fpl; (: for weather)
pronóstico; ~**lying** adj remoto, aislado;
~**moded** adj anticuado, pasado de
moda; ~**number** vt superar en número;
~**-of-date** adj (passport) caducado;
(clothes) pasado de moda; ~**-of-the-way**
adj apartado; ~**patient** n paciente m/f
externo/a; ~**post** n puesto avanzado;
~**put** n (volumen m de) producción f,
rendimiento; (COMPUT) salida
outrage ['autreɪdʒ] n escándalo; (atrocity)
atrocidad f ♦ vt ultrajar; ~**ous** [-'reɪdʒəs]
adj monstruoso
outright [adv aut'raɪt, adj 'autraɪt] adv (ask,
deny) francamente; (refuse)
rotundamente; (win) de manera absoluta;
(be killed) en el acto ♦ adj franco,
rotundo
outset ['autset] n principio
outside [aut'saɪd] n exterior m ♦ adj
exterior, externo ♦ adv fuera ♦ prep fuera
de; (beyond) más allá de; **at the ~** (fig) a
lo sumo; ~ **lane** n (AUT: in Britain) carril
m de la derecha; (: in US, Europe etc)
carril m de la izquierda; ~ **line** n (TEL)
línea (exterior); ~**r** n (stranger) extraño,
forastero
out: ~**size** adj (clothes) de talla grande;
~**skirts** npl alrededores mpl, afueras fpl;
~**spoken** adj muy franco; ~**standing**

adj excepcional, destacado; (remaining)
pendiente; ~**stay** vt: **to ~stay one's
welcome** quedarse más de la cuenta;
~**stretched** adj (hand) extendido;
~**strip** vt (competitors, demand) dejar
atrás, aventajar; ~**-tray** n bandeja de
salida
outward ['autwəd] adj externo; (journey)
de ida
outweigh [aut'weɪ] vt pesar más que
outwit [aut'wɪt] vt ser más listo que
oval ['əuvl] adj ovalado ♦ n óvalo
ovary ['əuvərɪ] n ovario
oven ['ʌvn] n horno; ~**proof** adj
resistente al horno
over ['əuvə*] adv encima, por encima
♦ adj (or adv) (finished) terminado;
(surplus) de sobra ♦ prep (por) encima de;
(above) sobre; (on the other side of) al
otro lado de; (more than) más de;
(during) durante; ~ **here** (por) aquí; ~
there (por) allí or allá; **all ~** (everywhere)
por todas partes; ~ **and ~ (again)** una y
otra vez; ~ **and above** además de; **to ask
sb ~** invitar a uno a casa; **to bend ~**
inclinarse
overall [adj, n 'əuvərɔːl, adv əuvər'ɔːl] adj
(length etc) total; (study) de conjunto
♦ adv en conjunto ♦ n (BRIT)
guardapolvo; ~**s** npl mono (SP), overol m
(AM)
over: ~**awe** vt: **to be ~awed (by)** quedar
impresionado (con); ~**balance** vi perder
el equilibrio; ~**board** adv (NAUT) por la
borda; ~**book** [əuvə'buk] vt sobrereservar
overcast ['əuvəkɑːst] adj encapotado
overcharge [əuvə'tʃɑːdʒ] vt: **to ~ sb**
cobrar un precio excesivo a uno
overcoat ['əuvəkəut] n abrigo, sobretodo
overcome [əuvə'kʌm] (irreg) vt vencer;
(difficulty) superar
over: ~**crowded** adj atestado de gente;
(city, country) superpoblado; ~**do** (irreg)
vt exagerar; (overcook) cocer demasiado;
to ~do it (work etc) pasarse; ~**dose** n
sobredosis f inv; ~**draft** n saldo deudor;
~**drawn** adj (account) en descubierto;

~**due** *adj* retrasado; ~**estimate**
[əuvər'estimeit] *vt* sobreestimar
overflow [*vb* əuvə'fləu, *n* 'əuvəfləu] *vi*
desbordarse ♦ *n* (*also*: ~ **pipe**) (cañería
de) desagüe *m*
overgrown [əuvə'grəun] *adj* (*garden*)
invadido por la vegetación
overhaul [*vb* əuvə'hɔːl, *n* 'əuvəhɔːl] *vt*
revisar, repasar ♦ *n* revisión *f*
overhead [*adv* əuvə'hed, *adj*, *n* 'əuvəhed]
adv por arriba *or* encima ♦ *adj* (*cable*)
aéreo ♦ *n* (*US*) = ~**s**; ~**s** *npl* (*expenses*)
gastos *mpl* generales
over: ~**hear** (*irreg*) *vt* oír por casualidad;
~**heat** *vi* (*engine*) recalentarse; ~**joyed**
adj encantado, lleno de alegría
overland ['əuvəlænd] *adj*, *adv* por tierra
overlap [əuvə'læp] *vi* traslaparse
over: ~**leaf** *adv* al dorso; ~**load** *vt*
sobrecargar; ~**look** *vt* (*have view of*) dar
a, tener vistas a; (*miss: by mistake*) pasar
por alto; (*excuse*) perdonar
overnight [əuvə'nait] *adv* durante la
noche; (*fig*) de la noche a la mañana
♦ *adj* de noche; **to stay** ~ pasar la noche
overpass ['əuvəpɑːs] (*US*) *n* paso superior
overpower [əuvə'pauə*] *vt* dominar; (*fig*)
embargar; ~**ing** *adj* (*heat*) agobiante;
(*smell*) penetrante
over: ~**rate** *vt* sobreestimar; ~**ride** (*irreg*)
vt no hacer caso de; ~**riding** *adj*
predominante; ~**rule** *vt* (*decision*) anular;
(*claim*) denegar; ~**run** (*irreg*) *vt* (*country*)
invadir; (*time limit*) rebasar, exceder
overseas [əuvə'siːz] *adv* (*abroad: live*) en
el extranjero; (: *travel*) al extranjero ♦ *adj*
(*trade*) exterior; (*visitor*) extranjero
overshadow [əuvə'ʃædəu] *vt*: **to be** ~**ed**
by estar a la sombra de
overshoot [əuvə'ʃuːt] (*irreg*) *vt* excederse
oversight ['əuvəsait] *n* descuido
oversleep [əuvə'sliːp] (*irreg*) *vi* quedarse
dormido
overstep [əuvə'step] *vt*: **to** ~ **the mark**
pasarse de la raya
overt [əu'vɜːt] *adj* abierto
overtake [əuvə'teik] (*irreg*) *vt* sobrepasar;

(*BRIT: AUT*) adelantar
over: ~**throw** (*irreg*) *vt* (*government*)
derrocar; ~**time** *n* horas *fpl*
extraordinarias; ~**tone** *n* (*fig*) tono
overture ['əuvətʃuə*] *n* (*MUS*) obertura;
(*fig*) preludio
over: ~**turn** *vt* volcar; (*fig: plan*)
desbaratar; (: *government*) derrocar ♦ *vi*
volcar; ~**weight** *adj* demasiado gordo *or*
pesado; ~**whelm** *vt* aplastar; (*subj:
emotion*) sobrecoger; ~**whelming** *adj*
(*victory, defeat*) arrollador(a); (*feeling*)
irresistible; ~**work** *vi* trabajar demasiado;
~**wrought** [əuvə'rɔːt] *adj* sobreexcitado
owe [əu] *vt*: **to** ~ **sb sth, to** ~ **sth to sb**
deber algo a uno; **owing to** *prep* debido
a, por causa de
owl [aul] *n* búho, lechuza
own [əun] *vt* tener, poseer ♦ *adj* propio; **a**
room of my ~ una habitación propia; **to**
get one's ~ **back** tomar revancha; **on**
one's ~ solo, a solas; ~ **up** *vi* confesar;
~**er** *n* dueño/a; ~**ership** *n* posesión *f*
ox [ɔks] (*pl* ~**en**) *n* buey *m*; ~**tail** *n*: ~**tail**
soup sopa de rabo de buey
oxygen ['ɔksidʒən] *n* oxígeno
oyster ['ɔistə*] *n* ostra
oz. *abbr* = **ounce(s)**
ozone ['əuzəun]: ~ **friendly** *adj* que no
daña la capa de ozono; ~ **hole** *n* agujero
m de/en la capa de ozono; ~ **layer** *n*
capa *f* de ozono

P, p

p [piː] *abbr* = **penny; pence**
P.A. *n abbr* = **personal assistant; public**
address system
p.a. *abbr* = **per annum**
pa [pɑː] (*inf*) *n* papá *m*
pace [peis] *n* paso ♦ *vi*: **to** ~ **up and down**
pasearse de un lado a otro; **to keep** ~
with llevar al mismo paso que; ~**maker**
n (*MED*) regulador *m* cardíaco,
marcapasos *m inv*; (*SPORT: also*: ~**setter**)
liebre *f*

Pacific [pə'sɪfɪk] *n*: **the ~ (Ocean)** el (Océano) Pacífico

pack [pæk] *n* (*packet*) paquete *m*; (*of hounds*) jauría; (*of people*) manada, bando; (*of cards*) baraja; (*bundle*) fardo; (*US: of cigarettes*) paquete *m*; (*back ~*) mochila ♦ *vt* (*fill*) llenar; (*in suitcase etc*) meter, poner; (*cram*) llenar, atestar; **to ~ (one's bags)** hacerse la maleta; **to ~ sb off** despachar a uno; **~ it in!** (*inf*) ¡déjalo!

package ['pækɪdʒ] *n* paquete *m*; (*bulky*) bulto; (*also*: **~ deal**) acuerdo global; **~ holiday** *n* vacaciones *fpl* organizadas; **~ tour** *n* viaje *m* organizado

packed lunch *n* almuerzo frío

packet ['pækɪt] *n* paquete *m*

packing ['pækɪŋ] *n* embalaje *m*; **~ case** *n* cajón *m* de embalaje

pact [pækt] *n* pacto

pad [pæd] *n* (*of paper*) bloc *m*; (*cushion*) cojinete *m*; (*inf: home*) casa ♦ *vt* rellenar; **~ding** *n* (*material*) relleno

paddle ['pædl] *n* (*oar*) canalete *m*; (*US: for table tennis*) paleta ♦ *vt* impulsar con canalete ♦ *vi* (*with feet*) chapotear; **paddling pool** (*BRIT*) *n* estanque *m* de juegos

paddock ['pædək] *n* corral *m*

padlock ['pædlɒk] *n* candado

paediatrics [piːdɪ'ætrɪks] (*US* **pediatrics**) *n* pediatría

pagan ['peɪɡən] *adj*, *n* pagano/a *m/f*

page [peɪdʒ] *n* (*of book*) página; (*of newspaper*) plana; (*also*: **~ boy**) paje *m* ♦ *vt* (*in hotel etc*) llamar por altavoz a

pageant ['pædʒənt] *n* (*procession*) desfile *m*; (*show*) espectáculo; **~ry** *n* pompa

pager ['peɪdʒə*] *n* (*TEL*) busca *m*

paging device ['peɪdʒɪŋ-] *n* = **pager**

paid [peɪd] *pt*, *pp of* **pay** ♦ *adj* (*work*) remunerado; (*holiday*) pagado; (*official etc*) a sueldo; **to put ~ to** (*BRIT*) acabar con

pail [peɪl] *n* cubo, balde *m*

pain [peɪn] *n* dolor *m*; **to be in ~** sufrir; **to take ~s to do sth** tomarse grandes molestias en hacer algo; **~ed** *adj* (*expression*) afligido; **~ful** *adj* doloroso; (*difficult*) penoso; (*disagreeable*) desagradable; **~fully** *adv* (*fig: very*) terriblemente; **~killer** *n* analgésico; **~less** *adj* que no causa dolor; **~staking** ['peɪnzteɪkɪŋ] *adj* (*person*) concienzudo, esmerado

paint [peɪnt] *n* pintura ♦ *vt* pintar; **to ~ the door blue** pintar la puerta de azul; **~brush** *n* (*artist's*) pincel *m*; (*decorator's*) brocha; **~er** *n* pintor(a) *m/f*; **~ing** *n* pintura; **~work** *n* pintura

pair [peə*] *n* (*of shoes, gloves etc*) par *m*; (*of people*) pareja; **a ~ of scissors** unas tijeras; **a ~ of trousers** unos pantalones, un pantalón

pajamas [pə'dʒɑːməz] (*US*) *npl* pijama *m*

Pakistan [pɑːkɪ'stɑːn] *n* Paquistán *m*; **~i** *adj*, *n* paquistaní *m/f*

pal [pæl] (*inf*) *n* compinche *m/f*, compañero/a

palace ['pæləs] *n* palacio

palatable ['pælɪtəbl] *adj* sabroso

palate ['pælɪt] *n* paladar *m*

pale [peɪl] *adj* (*gen*) pálido; (*colour*) claro ♦ *n*: **to be beyond the ~** pasarse de la raya

Palestine ['pælɪstaɪn] *n* Palestina; **Palestinian** [-'tɪnɪən] *adj*, *n* palestino/a *m/f*

palette ['pælɪt] *n* paleta

pall [pɔːl] *vi* perder el sabor

pallet ['pælɪt] *n* (*for goods*) pallet *m*

pallid ['pælɪd] *adj* pálido

palm [pɑːm] *n* (*ANAT*) palma; (*also*: **~ tree**) palmera, palma ♦ *vt*: **to ~ sth off on sb** (*inf*) encajar algo a uno; **P~ Sunday** *n* Domingo de Ramos

paltry ['pɔːltrɪ] *adj* irrisorio

pamper ['pæmpə*] *vt* mimar

pamphlet ['pæmflət] *n* folleto

pan [pæn] *n* (*also*: **sauce~**) cacerola, cazuela, olla; (*also*: **frying ~**) sartén *f*

Panama ['pænəmɑː] *n* Panamá *m*; **the ~ Canal** el Canal de Panamá

pancake ['pænkeɪk] *n* crepe *f*

panda ['pændə] *n* panda *m*; **~ car** (*BRIT*) *n*

coche *m* Z (*SP*)

pandemonium [pændɪˈməʊnɪəm] *n* jaleo

pander [ˈpændə*] *vi*: **to ~ to** complacer a

pane [peɪn] *n* cristal *m*

panel [ˈpænl] *n* (*of wood etc*) panel *m*; (*RADIO, TV*) panel *m* de invitados; **~ling** (*US* **~ing**) *n* paneles *mpl*

pang [pæŋ] *n*: **a ~ of regret** (una punzada de) remordimiento; **hunger ~s** dolores *mpl* del hambre

panic [ˈpænɪk] *n* (terror *m*) pánico ♦ *vi* dejarse llevar por el pánico; **~ky** *adj* (*person*) asustadizo; **~-stricken** *adj* preso de pánico

pansy [ˈpænzɪ] *n* (*BOT*) pensamiento; (*inf*: *pej*) maricón *m*

pant [pænt] *vi* jadear

panther [ˈpænθə*] *n* pantera

panties [ˈpæntɪz] *npl* bragas *fpl*, pantis *mpl*

pantihose [ˈpæntɪhəʊz] (*US*) *n* pantimedias *fpl*

pantomime [ˈpæntəmaɪm] (*BRIT*) *n* revista musical representada en Navidad, basada en cuentos de hadas

---

pantomime

ⓘ *En época navideña se ponen en escena en los teatros británicos las llamadas* **pantomimes**, *que son versiones libres de cuentos tradicionales como Aladino o El gato con botas. En ella nunca faltan personajes como la dama ("dame"), papel que siempre interpreta un actor, el protagonista joven ("principal boy"), normalmente interpretado por una actriz, y el malvado ("villain"). Es un espectáculo familiar en el que se anima al público a participar y aunque va dirigido principalmente a los niños, cuenta con grandes dosis de humor para adultos.*

---

pantry [ˈpæntrɪ] *n* despensa

pants [pænts] *n* (*BRIT: underwear: woman's*) bragas *fpl*; (: *man's*) calzoncillos *mpl*; (*US: trousers*) pantalones *mpl*

paper [ˈpeɪpə*] *n* papel *m*; (*also:* **news~**)

periódico, diario; (*academic essay*) ensayo; (*exam*) examen *m* ♦ *adj* de papel ♦ *vt* empapelar (*SP*), tapizar (*AM*); **~s** *npl* (*also:* **identity ~s**) papeles *mpl*, documentos *mpl*; **~back** *n* libro en rústica; **~ bag** *n* bolsa de papel; **~ clip** *n* clip *m*; **~ hankie** *n* pañuelo de papel; **~weight** *n* pisapapeles *m inv*; **~work** *n* trabajo administrativo

paprika [ˈpæprɪkə] *n* pimentón *m*

par [pɑ:*] *n* par *f*; (*GOLF*) par *m*; **to be on a ~ with** estar a la par con

parachute [ˈpærəʃu:t] *n* paracaídas *m inv*

parade [pəˈreɪd] *n* desfile *m* ♦ *vt* (*show off*) hacer alarde de ♦ *vi* desfilar; (*MIL*) pasar revista

paradise [ˈpærədaɪs] *n* paraíso

paradox [ˈpærədɔks] *n* paradoja; **~ically** [-ˈdɔksɪklɪ] *adv* paradójicamente

paraffin [ˈpærəfɪn] (*BRIT*) *n* (*also:* **~ oil**) parafina

paragon [ˈpærəgən] *n* modelo

paragraph [ˈpærəgrɑ:f] *n* párrafo

parallel [ˈpærəlel] *adj* en paralelo; (*fig*) semejante ♦ *n* (*line*) paralela; (*fig, GEO*) paralelo

paralyse [ˈpærəlaɪz] *vt* paralizar

paralysis [pəˈrælɪsɪs] *n* parálisis *f inv*

paralyze [ˈpærəlaɪz] (*US*) *vt* = **paralyse**

paramount [ˈpærəmaʊnt] *adj*: **of ~ importance** de suma importancia

paranoid [ˈpærənɔɪd] *adj* (*person, feeling*) paranoico

paraphernalia [pærəfəˈneɪlɪə] *n* (*gear*) avíos *mpl*

parasite [ˈpærəsaɪt] *n* parásito/a

parasol [ˈpærəsɔl] *n* sombrilla, quitasol *m*

paratrooper [ˈpærətru:pə*] *n* paracaidista *m/f*

parcel [ˈpɑ:sl] *n* paquete *m* ♦ *vt* (*also:* **~ up**) empaquetar, embalar

parched [pɑ:tʃt] *adj* (*person*) muerto de sed

parchment [ˈpɑ:tʃmənt] *n* pergamino

pardon [ˈpɑ:dn] *n* (*LAW*) indulto ♦ *vt* perdonar; **~ me!, I beg your ~!** (*I'm sorry!*) ¡perdone usted!; **(I beg your) ~?, ~**

me? (US) (what did you say?) ¿cómo?
parent ['pɛərənt] n (mother) madre f;
(father) padre m; **~s** npl padres mpl; **~al**
[pə'rɛntl] adj paternal/maternal
parenthesis [pə'rɛnθɪsɪs] (pl
parentheses) n paréntesis m inv
Paris ['pærɪs] n París
parish ['pærɪʃ] n parroquia
Parisian [pə'rɪzɪən] adj, n parisiense m/f
park [pɑːk] n parque m ♦ vt aparcar,
estacionar ♦ vi aparcar, estacionarse
parking ['pɑːkɪŋ] n aparcamiento,
estacionamiento; **"no ~"** "prohibido
estacionarse"; **~ lot** (US) n parking m; **~
meter** n parquímetro; **~ ticket** n multa
de aparcamiento
parliament ['pɑːləmənt] n parlamento;
(Spanish) Cortes fpl; **~ary** [-'mɛntərɪ] adj
parlamentario

ℹ️ El Parlamento británico (**Parliament**)
tiene como sede el palacio de
Westminster, también llamado "Houses of
Parliament" y consta de dos cámaras. La
Cámara de los Comunes ("House of
Commons"), compuesta por 650 diputados
(**Members of Parliament**) elegidos por
sufragio universal en su respectiva
circunscripción electoral (**constituency**),
se reúne 175 días al año y sus sesiones
son moderadas por el Presidente de la
Cámara (**Speaker**). La cámara alta es la
Cámara de los Lores ("House of
Lords") y
está formada por miembros que han sido
nombrados por el monarca o que han
heredado su escaño. Su poder es limitado,
aunque actúa como tribunal supremo de
apelación, excepto en Escocia.

parlour ['pɑːlə*] (US **parlor**) n sala de
recibo, salón m, living m (AM)
parochial [pə'rəʊkɪəl] (pej) adj de miras
estrechas
parole [pə'rəʊl] n: **on ~** libre bajo palabra
parquet ['pɑːkeɪ] n: **~ floor(ing)** parquet
m

parrot ['pærət] n loro, papagayo
parry ['pærɪ] vt parar
parsley ['pɑːslɪ] n perejil m
parsnip ['pɑːsnɪp] n chirivía
parson ['pɑːsn] n cura m
part [pɑːt] n (gen, MUS) parte f; (bit) trozo;
(of machine) pieza; (THEATRE etc) papel m;
(of serial) entrega; (US: in hair) raya ♦ adv
= **partly** ♦ vt separar ♦ vi (people)
separarse; (crowd) apartarse; **to take ~ in**
tomar parte or participar en; **to take sth
in good ~** tomar algo en buena parte; **to
take sb's ~** defender a uno; **for my ~** por
mi parte; **for the most ~** en su mayor
parte; **to ~ one's hair** hacerse la raya; **~
with** vt fus ceder, entregar; (money)
pagar; **~ exchange** (BRIT) n: **in ~
exchange** como parte del pago
partial ['pɑːʃl] adj parcial; **to be ~ to** ser
aficionado a
participant [pɑː'tɪsɪpənt] n (in competition)
concursante m/f; (in campaign etc)
participante m/f
participate [pɑː'tɪsɪpeɪt] vi: **to ~ in**
participar en; **participation** [-'peɪʃən] n
participación f
participle ['pɑːtɪsɪpl] n participio
particle ['pɑːtɪkl] n partícula; (of dust)
grano
particular [pə'tɪkjulə*] adj (special)
particular; (concrete) concreto; (given)
determinado; (fussy) quisquilloso;
(demanding) exigente; **~s** npl
(information) datos mpl; (details)
pormenores mpl; **in ~** en particular; **~ly**
adv (in particular) sobre todo; (difficult,
good etc) especialmente
parting ['pɑːtɪŋ] n (act of) separación f;
(farewell) despedida; (BRIT: in hair) raya
♦ adj de despedida
partisan [pɑːtɪ'zæn] adj partidista ♦ n
partidario/a
partition [pɑː'tɪʃən] n (POL) división f;
(wall) tabique m
partly ['pɑːtlɪ] adv en parte
partner ['pɑːtnə*] n (COMM) socio/a;
(SPORT, at dance) pareja; (spouse) cónyuge

m/f; (*lover*) compañero/a; **~ship** *n*
asociación *f*; (*COMM*) sociedad *f*
partridge ['pɑːtrɪdʒ] *n* perdiz *f*
part-time *adj, adv* a tiempo parcial
party ['pɑːtɪ] *n* (*POL*) partido; (*celebration*)
fiesta; (*group*) grupo; (*LAW*) parte *f*
interesada ♦ *cpd* (*POL*) de partido; **~
dress** *n* vestido de fiesta
pass [pɑːs] *vt* (*time, object*) pasar; (*place*)
pasar por; (*overtake*) rebasar; (*exam*)
aprobar; (*approve*) aprobar ♦ *vi* pasar;
(*SCOL*) aprobar, ser aprobado ♦ *n* (*permit*)
permiso; (*membership card*) carnet *m*; (*in
mountains*) puerto, desfiladero; (*SPORT*)
pase *m*; (*SCOL: also:* **~ mark**): **to get a ~
in** aprobar en; **to ~ sth through sth** pasar
algo por algo; **to make a ~ at sb** (*inf*)
hacer proposiciones a uno; **~ away** *vi*
fallecer; **~ by** *vi* pasar ♦ *vt* (*ignore*) pasar
por alto; **~ for** *vt fus* pasar por; **~ on** *vt*
transmitir; **~ out** *vi* desmayarse; **~ up** *vt*
(*opportunity*) renunciar a; **~able** *adj*
(*road*) transitable; (*tolerable*) pasable
passage ['pæsɪdʒ] *n* (*also:* **~way**) pasillo;
(*act of passing*) tránsito; (*fare, in book*)
pasaje *m*; (*by boat*) travesía; (*ANAT*) tubo
passbook ['pɑːsbuk] *n* libreta de banco
passenger ['pæsɪndʒə*] *n* pasajero/a,
viajero/a
passer-by [pɑːsə'baɪ] *n* transeúnte *m/f*
passing ['pɑːsɪŋ] *adj* pasajero; **in ~** de
paso; **~ place** *n* (*AUT*) apartadero
passion ['pæʃən] *n* pasión *f*; **~ate** *adj*
apasionado
passive ['pæsɪv] *adj* (*gen, also LING*)
pasivo; **~ smoking** *n* efectos del tabaco
en fumadores pasivos
Passover ['pɑːsəuvə*] *n* Pascua (de los
judíos)
passport ['pɑːspɔːt] *n* pasaporte *m*; **~
control** *n* control *m* de pasaporte; **~
office** *n* oficina de pasaportes
password ['pɑːswɜːd] *n* contraseña
past [pɑːst] *prep* (*in front of*) por delante
de; (*further than*) más allá de; (*later than*)
después de ♦ *adj* pasado; (*president etc*)
antiguo ♦ *n* (*time*) pasado; (*of person*)

antecedentes *mpl*; **he's ~ forty** tiene más
de cuarenta años; **ten/quarter ~ eight** las
ocho y diez/cuarto; **for the ~ few/3 days**
durante los últimos días/últimos 3 días; **to
run ~ sb** pasar a uno corriendo
pasta ['pæstə] *n* pasta
paste [peɪst] *n* pasta; (*glue*) engrudo ♦ *vt*
pegar
pasteurized ['pæstəraɪzd] *adj* pasteurizado
pastille ['pæstl] *n* pastilla
pastime ['pɑːstaɪm] *n* pasatiempo
pastry ['peɪstrɪ] *n* (*dough*) pasta; (*cake*)
pastel *m*
pasture ['pɑːstʃə*] *n* pasto
pasty¹ ['pæstɪ] *n* empanada
pasty² ['peɪstɪ] *adj* (*complexion*) pálido
pat [pæt] *vt* dar una palmadita a; (*dog etc*)
acariciar
patch [pætʃ] *n* (*of material, eye ~*) parche
m; (*mended part*) remiendo; (*of land*)
terreno ♦ *vt* remendar; **(to go through) a
bad ~** (pasar por) una mala racha; **~ up**
vt reparar; (*quarrel*) hacer las paces en;
~work *n* labor *m* de retazos; **~y** *adj*
desigual
pâté ['pæteɪ] *n* paté *m*
patent ['peɪtnt] *n* patente *f* ♦ *vt* patentar
♦ *adj* patente, evidente; **~ leather** *n*
charol *m*
paternal [pə'tɜːnl] *adj* paternal; (*relation*)
paterno
path [pɑːθ] *n* camino, sendero; (*trail, track*)
pista; (*of missile*) trayectoria
pathetic [pə'θetɪk] *adj* patético, lastimoso;
(*very bad*) malísimo
pathological [pæθə'lɔdʒɪkəl] *adj*
patológico
pathway ['pɑːθweɪ] *n* sendero, vereda
patience ['peɪʃns] *n* paciencia; (*BRIT:
CARDS*) solitario
patient ['peɪʃnt] *n* paciente *m/f* ♦ *adj*
paciente, sufrido
patio ['pætɪəu] *n* patio
patriot ['peɪtrɪət] *n* patriota *m/f*; **~ic**
[pætrɪ'ɔtɪk] *adj* patriótico
patrol [pə'trəul] *n* patrulla ♦ *vt* patrullar
por; **~ car** *n* coche *m* patrulla; **~man**

(US irreg) n policía m
patron ['peɪtrən] n (in shop) cliente m/f;
(of charity) patrocinador(a) m/f; **~ of the
arts** mecenas m; **~ize** ['pætrənaɪz] vt
(shop) ser cliente de; (artist etc) proteger;
(look down on) condescender con; **~
saint** n santo/a patrón/ona m/f
patter ['pætə*] n golpeteo; (sales talk) labia
♦ vi (rain) tamborilear
pattern ['pætən] n (SEWING) patrón m;
(design) dibujo
pauper ['pɔːpə*] n pobre m/f
pause [pɔːz] n pausa ♦ vi hacer una pausa
pave [peɪv] vt pavimentar; **to ~ the way
for** preparar el terreno para
pavement ['peɪvmənt] (BRIT) n acera (SP),
vereda (AM)
pavilion [pə'vɪlɪən] n (SPORT) caseta
paving ['peɪvɪŋ] n pavimento, enlosado; **~
stone** n losa
paw [pɔː] n pata
pawn [pɔːn] n (CHESS) peón m; (fig)
instrumento ♦ vt empeñar; **~ broker** n
prestamista m/f; **~shop** n monte m de
piedad
pay [peɪ] (pt, pp **paid**) n (wage etc) sueldo,
salario ♦ vt pagar ♦ vi (be profitable)
rendir; **to ~ attention (to)** prestar
atención (a); **to ~ sb a visit** hacer una
visita a uno; **to ~ one's respects to sb**
presentar sus respetos a uno; **~ back** vt
(money) reembolsar; (person) pagar; **~ for**
vt fus pagar; **~ in** vt ingresar; **~ off** vt
saldar ♦ vi (scheme, decision) dar
resultado; **~ up** vt pagar (de mala gana);
~able adj: **~able to** pagadero a; **~ day**
n día m de paga; **~ee** n portador(a) m/f;
~ envelope (US) n = **~ packet**; **~ment**
n pago; **monthly ~ment** mensualidad f; **~
packet** (BRIT) n sobre m (de paga); **~
phone** n teléfono público; **~roll** n
nómina; **~ slip** n recibo de sueldo; **~
television** n televisión f de pago
PC n abbr = **personal computer**; (BRIT)
= **police constable** ♦ adj abbr
= **politically correct**
p.c. abbr = **per cent**

pea [piː] n guisante m (SP), chícharo (AM),
arveja (AM)
peace [piːs] n paz f; (calm) paz f,
tranquilidad f; (calm) tranquilo, sosegado
~ful adj (gentle) pacífico;
peach [piːtʃ] n melocotón m (SP), durazno
(AM)
peacock ['piːkɔk] n pavo real
peak [piːk] n (of mountain) cumbre f,
cima; (of cap) visera; (fig) cumbre f; **~
hours** npl, **~ period** n horas fpl punta
peal [piːl] n (of bells) repique m; **~ of
laughter** carcajada
peanut ['piːnʌt] n cacahuete m (SP), maní
m (AM); **~ butter** manteca de cacahuete
or maní
pear [pεə*] n pera
pearl [pəːl] n perla
peasant ['pεznt] n campesino/a
peat [piːt] n turba
pebble ['pεbl] n guijarro
peck [pεk] vt (also: **~ at**) picotear ♦ n
picotazo; (kiss) besito; **~ing order** n
orden m de jerarquía; **~ish** (BRIT: inf) adj:
I feel ~ish tengo ganas de picar algo
peculiar [pɪ'kjuːlɪə*] adj (odd) extraño,
raro; (typical) propio, característico; **~ to**
propio de
pedal ['pεdl] n pedal m ♦ vi pedalear
pedantic [pɪ'dæntɪk] adj pedante
peddler ['pεdlə*] n: **drug ~** traficante m/f;
camello
pedestrian [pɪ'dεstrɪən] n peatón/ona m/f
♦ adj pedestre; **~ crossing** (BRIT) n paso
de peatones; **~ precinct** (BRIT), **~ zone**
(US) n zona peatonal
pediatrics [piːdɪ'ætrɪks] (US) n
= **paediatrics**
pedigree ['pεdɪgriː] n genealogía; (of
animal) raza, pedigrí m ♦ cpd (animal) de
raza, de casta
pee [piː] (inf) vi mear
peek [piːk] vi mirar a hurtadillas
peel [piːl] n piel f; (of orange, lemon)
cáscara; (: removed) peladuras fpl ♦ vt
pelar ♦ vi (paint etc) desconcharse;
(wallpaper) despegarse, desprenderse;

(skin) pelar

peep [piːp] *n* (*BRIT: look*) mirada furtiva; (*sound*) pío ♦ *vi* (*BRIT: look*) mirar furtivamente; **~ out** *vi* salir (un poco); **~hole** *n* mirilla

peer [pɪə*] *vi*: **to ~ at** esudriñar ♦ *n* (*noble*) par *m*; (*equal*) igual *m*; (*contemporary*) contemporáneo/a; **~age** *n* nobleza

peeved [piːvd] *adj* enojado

peg [pɛg] *n* (*for coat etc*) gancho, colgadero; (*BRIT: also*: **clothes ~**) pinza

Pekingese [piːkɪˈniːz] *n* (*dog*) pequinés/esa *m/f*

pelican [ˈpɛlɪkən] *n* pelícano; **~ crossing** (*BRIT*) *n* (*AUT*) paso de peatones señalizado

pellet [ˈpɛlɪt] *n* bolita; (*bullet*) perdigón *m*

pelt [pɛlt] *vt*: **to ~ sb with sth** arrojarle algo a uno ♦ *vi* (*rain*) llover a cántaros: (*inf: run*) correr ♦ *n* pellejo

pen [pɛn] *n* (*fountain ~*) pluma; (*ballpoint ~*) bolígrafo; (*for sheep*) redil *m*

penal [ˈpiːnl] *adj* penal; **~ize** *vt* castigar

penalty [ˈpɛnltɪ] *n* (*gen*) pena; (*fine*) multa; **~ (kick)** *n* (*FOOTBALL*) penalty *m*; (*RUGBY*) golpe *m* de castigo

penance [ˈpɛnəns] *n* penitencia

pence [pɛns] *npl of* **penny**

pencil [ˈpɛnsl] *n* lápiz *m*, lapicero (*AM*); **~ case** *n* estuche *m*; **~ sharpener** *n* sacapuntas *m inv*

pendant [ˈpɛndnt] *n* pendiente *m*

pending [ˈpɛndɪŋ] *prep* antes de ♦ *adj* pendiente

pendulum [ˈpɛndjuləm] *n* péndulo

penetrate [ˈpɛnɪtreɪt] *vt* penetrar

penfriend [ˈpɛnfrɛnd] (*BRIT*) *n* amigo/a por carta

penguin [ˈpɛŋgwɪn] *n* pingüino

penicillin [pɛnɪˈsɪlɪn] *n* penicilina

peninsula [pəˈnɪnsjulə] *n* península

penis [ˈpiːnɪs] *n* pene *m*

penitentiary [pɛnɪˈtɛnʃərɪ] (*US*) *n* cárcel *f*, presidio

penknife [ˈpɛnnaɪf] *n* navaja

pen name *n* seudónimo

penniless [ˈpɛnɪlɪs] *adj* sin dinero

penny [ˈpɛnɪ] (*pl* **pennies** *or* (*BRIT*) **pence**) *n* penique *m*; (*US*) centavo

penpal [ˈpɛnpæl] *n* amigo/a por carta

pension [ˈpɛnʃən] *n* (*state benefit*) jubilación *f*; **~er** (*BRIT*) *n* jubilado/a; **~ fund** *n* caja *or* fondo de pensiones

pentagon [ˈpɛntəgən] *n*: **the P~** (*US: POL*) el Pentágono

Pentagon

i *Se conoce como* **Pentagon** *al edificio de planta pentagonal que acoge las dependencias del Ministerio de Defensa estadounidense ("Department of Defense") en Arlington, Virginia. En lenguaje periodístico se aplica también a la dirección militar del país.*

Pentecost [ˈpɛntɪkɔst] *n* Pentecostés *m*

penthouse [ˈpɛnthaus] *n* ático de lujo

pent-up [ˈpɛntʌp] *adj* reprimido

people [ˈpiːpl] *npl* gente *f*; (*citizens*) pueblo, ciudadanos *mpl*; (*POL*): **the ~** el pueblo ♦ *n* (*nation, race*) pueblo, nación *f*; **several ~ came** vinieron varias personas; **~ say that ...** dice la gente que ...

pep [pɛp] (*inf*): **~ up** *vt* animar

pepper [ˈpɛpə*] *n* (*spice*) pimienta; (*vegetable*) pimiento ♦ *vt*: **to ~ with** (*fig*) salpicar de; **~mint** *n* (*sweet*) pastilla de menta

peptalk [ˈpɛptɔːk] *n*: **to give sb a ~** darle a uno una inyección de ánimo

per [pəː*] *prep* por; **~ day/person** por día/persona; **~ annum** al año; **~ capita** *adj*, *adv* per cápita

perceive [pəˈsiːv] *vt* percibir; (*realize*) darse cuenta de

per cent *n* por ciento

percentage [pəˈsɛntɪdʒ] *n* porcentaje *m*

perception [pəˈsɛpʃən] *n* percepción *f*; (*insight*) perspicacia; (*opinion etc*) opinión *f*; **perceptive** [-ˈsɛptɪv] *adj* perspicaz

perch [pəːtʃ] *n* (*fish*) perca; (*for bird*) percha ♦ *vi*: **to ~ (on)** (*bird*) posarse (en); (*person*) encaramarse (en)

percolator ['pəːkəleɪtə*] n (also: **coffee ~**) cafetera de filtro

perennial [pə'rɛnɪəl] adj perenne

perfect [adj, n 'pəːfɪkt, vb pə'fɛkt] adj perfecto ♦ n (also: **~ tense**) perfecto ♦ vt perfeccionar; **~ly** ['pəːfɪktlɪ] adv perfectamente

perforate ['pəːfəreɪt] vt perforar

perform [pə'fɔːm] vt (carry out) realizar, llevar a cabo; (THEATRE) representar; (piece of music) interpretar ♦ vi (well, badly) funcionar; **~ance** n (of a play) representación f; (of actor, athlete etc) actuación f; (of car, engine, company) rendimiento f; (of economy) resultados mpl; **~er** n (actor) actor m, actriz f

perfume ['pəːfjuːm] n perfume m

perhaps [pə'hæps] adv quizá(s), tal vez

peril ['pɛrɪl] n peligro, riesgo

perimeter [pə'rɪmɪtə*] n perímetro

period ['pɪərɪəd] n período; (SCOL) clase f; (full stop) punto; (MED) regla ♦ adj (costume, furniture) de época; **~ic(al)** [-'ɔdɪk(l)] adj periódico; **~ical** [-'ɔdɪkl] n periódico; **~ically** [-'ɔdɪklɪ] adv de vez en cuando, cada cierto tiempo

peripheral [pə'rɪfərəl] adj periférico ♦ n (COMPUT) periférico, unidad f periférica

perish ['pɛrɪʃ] vi perecer; (decay) echarse a perder; **~able** adj perecedero

perjury ['pəːdʒərɪ] n (LAW) perjurio

perk [pəːk] n extra m; **~ up** vi (cheer up) animarse

perm [pəːm] n permanente f

permanent ['pəːmənənt] adj permanente

permeate ['pəːmɪeɪt] vi penetrar, trascender ♦ vt penetrar, trascender a

permissible [pə'mɪsɪbl] adj permisible, lícito

permission [pə'mɪʃən] n permiso

permissive [pə'mɪsɪv] adj permisivo

permit [n 'pəːmɪt, vb pə'mɪt] n permiso, licencia ♦ vt permitir

perplex [pə'plɛks] vt dejar perplejo

persecute ['pəːsɪkjuːt] vt perseguir

persevere [pəːsɪ'vɪə*] vi persistir

Persian ['pəːʃən] adj, n persa m/f; **the ~ Gulf** el Golfo Pérsico

persist [pə'sɪst] vi: **to ~ (in doing sth)** persistir (en hacer algo); **~ence** n empeño; **~ent** adj persistente; (determined) porfiado

person ['pəːsn] n persona; **in ~** en persona; **~al** adj personal; individual; (visit) en persona; **~al assistant** n ayudante m/f personal; **~al column** n anuncios mpl personales; **~al computer** n ordenador m personal; **~ality** [-'nælɪtɪ] n personalidad f; **~ally** adv personalmente; (in person) en persona; **to take sth ~ally** tomarse algo a mal; **~al organizer** n agenda; **~al stereo** n Walkman ® m; **~ify** [-'sɔnɪfaɪ] vt encarnar

personnel [pəːsə'nɛl] n personal m

perspective [pə'spɛktɪv] n perspectiva

Perspex ® ['pəːspɛks] n plexiglás ® m

perspiration [pəːspɪ'reɪʃən] n transpiración f

persuade [pə'sweɪd] vt: **to ~ sb to do sth** persuadir a uno para que haga algo

Peru [pə'ruː] n el Perú; **Peruvian** adj, n peruano/a m/f

perverse [pə'vəːs] adj perverso; (wayward) travieso

pervert [n 'pəːvəːt, vb pə'vəːt] n pervertido/a ♦ vt pervertir; (truth, sb's words) tergiversar

pessimist ['pɛsɪmɪst] n pesimista m/f; **~ic** [-'mɪstɪk] adj pesimista

pest [pɛst] n (insect) insecto nocivo; (fig) lata, molestia

pester ['pɛstə*] vt molestar, acosar

pesticide ['pɛstɪsaɪd] n pesticida m

pet [pɛt] n animal m doméstico ♦ cpd favorito ♦ vt acariciar; **teacher's ~** favorito/a (del profesor); **~ hate** manía

petal ['pɛtl] n pétalo

peter ['piːtə*]: **to ~ out** vi agotarse, acabarse

petite [pə'tiːt] adj chiquita

petition [pə'tɪʃən] n petición f

petrified ['pɛtrɪfaɪd] adj horrorizado

petrol ['pɛtrəl] (BRIT) n gasolina; **two/four-star ~** gasolina normal/súper; **~ can**

n bidón *m* de gasolina
petroleum [pə'trəʊlɪəm] *n* petróleo
petrol: ~ **pump** (*BRIT*) *n* (*in garage*)
surtidor *m* de gasolina; ~ **station** (*BRIT*)
n gasolinera; ~ **tank** (*BRIT*) *n* depósito
(de gasolina)
petticoat ['pɛtɪkəʊt] *n* enaguas *fpl*
petty ['pɛtɪ] *adj* (*mean*) mezquino;
(*unimportant*) insignificante; ~ **cash** *n*
dinero para gastos menores; ~ **officer** *n*
contramaestre *m*
petulant ['pɛtjʊlənt] *adj* malhumorado
pew [pju:] *n* banco
pewter ['pju:tə*] *n* peltre *m*
phantom ['fæntəm] *n* fantasma *m*
pharmacist ['fɑːməsɪst] *n* farmacéutico/a
pharmacy ['fɑːməsɪ] *n* farmacia
phase [feɪz] *n* fase *f* ♦ *vt*: **to ~ sth in/out**
introducir/retirar algo por etapas
Ph.D. *abbr* = **Doctor of Philosophy**
pheasant ['fɛznt] *n* faisán *m*
phenomenon [fə'nɒmɪnən] (*pl*
phenomena) *n* fenómeno
philanthropist [fɪ'lænθrəpɪst] *n*
filántropo/a
Philippines ['fɪlɪpiːnz] *npl*: **the ~** las
Filipinas
philosopher [fɪ'lɒsəfə*] *n* filósofo/a
philosophy [fɪ'lɒsəfɪ] *n* filosofía
phobia ['fəʊbjə] *n* fobia
phone [fəʊn] *n* teléfono ♦ *vt* telefonear,
llamar por teléfono; **to be on the ~** tener
teléfono; (*be calling*) estar hablando por
teléfono; ~ **back** *vt*, *vi* volver a llamar; ~
up *vt*, *vi* llamar por teléfono; ~ **book** *n*
guía telefónica; ~ **booth** *n* cabina
telefónica; ~ **box** (*BRIT*) *n* = ~ **booth**; ~
call *n* llamada (telefónica); ~**card** *n*
teletarjeta; ~**-in** (*BRIT*) *n* (*RADIO*, *TV*)
programa *m* de participación (telefónica)
phonetics [fə'nɛtɪks] *n* fonética
phoney ['fəʊnɪ] *adj* falso
photo ['fəʊtəʊ] *n* foto *f*; ~**copier** *n*
fotocopiadora; ~**copy** *n* fotocopia ♦ *vt*
fotocopiar
photograph ['fəʊtəgrɑːf] *n* fotografía ♦ *vt*
fotografiar; ~**er** [fə'tɒgrəfə*] *n* fotógrafo;

~**y** [fə'tɒgrəfɪ] *n* fotografía
phrase [freɪz] *n* frase *f* ♦ *vt* expresar; ~
book *n* libro de frases
physical ['fɪzɪkl] *adj* físico; ~ **education**
n educación *f* física; ~**ly** *adv* físicamente
physician [fɪ'zɪʃən] *n* médico/a
physicist ['fɪzɪsɪst] *n* físico/a
physics ['fɪzɪks] *n* física
physiotherapy [fɪzɪəʊ'θɛrəpɪ] *n*
fisioterapia
physique [fɪ'ziːk] *n* físico
pianist ['piːənɪst] *n* pianista *m/f*
piano [pɪ'ænəʊ] *n* piano
pick [pɪk] *n* (*tool: also*: ~**-axe**) pico,
piqueta ♦ *vt* (*select*) elegir, escoger;
(*gather*) coger (*SP*), recoger; (*remove, take
out*) sacar, quitar; (*lock*) abrir con ganzúa;
take your ~ escoja lo que quiera; **the ~
of** lo mejor de; **to ~ one's nose/teeth**
hurgarse las narices/limpiarse los dientes;
to ~ a quarrel with sb meterse con
alguien; ~ **at** *vt fus*: **to ~ at one's food**
comer con poco apetito; ~ **on** *vt fus*
(*person*) meterse con; ~ **out** *vt* escoger;
(*distinguish*) identificar; ~ **up** *vi* (*improve:
sales*) ir mejor; (: *patient*) reponerse;
(: *FINANCE*) recobrarse ♦ *vt* recoger;
(*learn*) aprender; (*POLICE: arrest*) detener;
(*person: for sex*) ligar; (*RADIO*) captar; **to ~
up speed** acelerarse; **to ~ o.s. up**
levantarse
picket ['pɪkɪt] *n* piquete *m* ♦ *vt* piquetear
pickle ['pɪkl] *n* (*also*: ~**s**: *as condiment*)
escabeche *m*; (*fig: mess*) apuro ♦ *vt*
encurtir
pickpocket ['pɪkpɒkɪt] *n* carterista *m/f*
pickup ['pɪkʌp] *n* (*small truck*) furgoneta
picnic ['pɪknɪk] *n* merienda ♦ *vi* ir de
merienda; ~ **area** *n* zona de picnic;
(*AUT*) área de descanso
picture ['pɪktʃə*] *n* cuadro; (*painting*)
pintura; (*photograph*) fotografía; (*TV*)
imagen *f*; (*film*) película; (*fig: description*)
descripción *f*; (: *situation*) situación *f* ♦ *vt*
(*imagine*) imaginar; **the ~s** *npl*: **the ~s** (*BRIT*)
el cine; ~ **book** *n* libro de dibujos
picturesque [pɪktʃə'rɛsk] *adj* pintoresco

pie [paɪ] n pastel m; (open) tarta; (small: of meat) empanada

piece [piːs] n pedazo, trozo; (of cake) trozo; (item): **a ~ of clothing/furniture/advice** una prenda (de vestir)/un mueble/un consejo ♦ vt: **to ~ together** juntar; (TECH) armar; **to take to ~s** desmontar; **~meal** adv poco a poco; **~work** n trabajo a destajo

pie chart n gráfico de sectores or tarta

pier [pɪə*] n muelle m, embarcadero

pierce [pɪəs] vt perforar

piercing [ˈpɪəsɪŋ] adj penetrante

pig [pɪg] n cerdo (SP), puerco (SP), chancho (AM); (pej: unkind person) asqueroso; (: greedy person) glotón/ona m/f

pigeon [ˈpɪdʒən] n paloma; (as food) pichón m; **~hole** n casilla

piggy bank [ˈpɪgɪ-] n hucha (en forma de cerdito)

pig: ~headed [ˈpɪgˈhɛdɪd] adj terco, testarudo; **~let** [ˈpɪglɪt] n cochinillo; **~skin** n piel f de cerdo; **~sty** [ˈpɪgstaɪ] n pocilga; **~tail** n (girl's) trenza; (Chinese, TAUR) coleta

pike [paɪk] n (fish) lucio

pilchard [ˈpɪltʃəd] n sardina

pile [paɪl] n montón m; (of carpet, cloth) pelo ♦ vt (also: **~ up**) amontonar; (fig) acumular ♦ vi (also: **~ up**) amontonarse; acumularse; **~ into** vt fus (car) meterse en; **~s** [paɪlz] npl (MED) almorranas fpl, hemorroides mpl; **~-up** n (AUT) accidente m múltiple

pilfering [ˈpɪlfərɪŋ] n ratería

pilgrim [ˈpɪlgrɪm] n peregrino/a; **~age** n peregrinación f, romería

pill [pɪl] n píldora; **the ~** la píldora

pillage [ˈpɪlɪdʒ] vt pillar, saquear

pillar [ˈpɪlə*] n pilar m; **~ box** (BRIT) n buzón m

pillion [ˈpɪljən] n (of motorcycle) asiento trasero

pillow [ˈpɪləu] n almohada; **~case** n funda

pilot [ˈpaɪlət] n piloto ♦ cpd (scheme etc) piloto ♦ vt pilotar; **~ light** n piloto

pimp [pɪmp] n chulo (SP), cafiche m (AM)

pimple [ˈpɪmpl] n grano

PIN n abbr (= personal identification number) número personal

pin [pɪn] n alfiler m ♦ vt prender (con alfiler); **~s and needles** hormigueo; **to ~ sb down** (fig) hacer que uno concrete; **to ~ sth on sb** (fig) colgarle a uno el sambenito de algo

pinafore [ˈpɪnəfɔː*] n delantal m; **~ dress** (BRIT) n mandil m

pinball [ˈpɪnbɔːl] n mesa americana

pincers [ˈpɪnsəz] npl pinzas fpl, tenazas fpl

pinch [pɪntʃ] n (of salt etc) pizca ♦ vt pellizcar; (inf: steal) birlar; **at a ~** en caso de apuro

pincushion [ˈpɪnkuʃən] n acerico

pine [paɪn] n (also: **~ tree, wood**) pino ♦ vi: **to ~ for** suspirar por; **~ away** vi morirse de pena

pineapple [ˈpaɪnæpl] n piña, ananás m

ping [pɪŋ] n (noise) sonido agudo; **~-pong** ® n pingpong ® m

pink [pɪŋk] adj rosado, (color de) rosa ♦ n (colour) rosa; (BOT) clavel m, clavellina

pinpoint [ˈpɪnpɔɪnt] vt precisar

pint [paɪnt] n pinta (BRIT = 568cc; US = 473cc); (BRIT: inf: of beer) pinta de cerveza, ≈ jarra (SP)

pin-up n fotografía erótica

pioneer [paɪəˈnɪə*] n pionero/a

pious [ˈpaɪəs] adj piadoso, devoto

pip [pɪp] n (seed) pepita; **the ~s** (BRIT) la señal

pipe [paɪp] n tubo, caño; (for smoking) pipa ♦ vt conducir en cañerías; **~s** npl (gen) cañería; (also: **bag~s**) gaita; **~ cleaner** n limpiapipas m inv; **~ dream** n sueño imposible; **~line** n (for oil) oleoducto; (for gas) gasoducto; **~r** n gaitero/a

piping [ˈpaɪpɪŋ] adv: **to be ~ hot** estar que quema

piquant [ˈpiːkənt] adj picante; (fig) agudo

pique [piːk] n pique m, resentimiento

pirate [ˈpaɪərət] n pirata m/f ♦ vt (cassette,

book) piratear; **~ radio** (*BRIT*) *n* emisora pirata

Pisces ['paɪsi:z] *n* Piscis *m*

piss [pɪs] (*inf!*) *vi* mear; **~ed** (*inf!*) *adj* (*drunk*) borracho

pistol ['pɪstl] *n* pistola

piston ['pɪstən] *n* pistón *m*, émbolo

pit [pɪt] *n* hoyo; (*also*: **coal ~**) mina; (*in garage*) foso de inspección; (*also*: **orchestra ~**) platea ♦ *vt*: **to ~ one's wits against sb** medir fuerzas con uno; **~s** *npl* (*AUT*) box *m*

pitch [pɪtʃ] *n* (*MUS*) tono; (*BRIT*: *SPORT*) campo, terreno; (*fig*) punto; (*tar*) brea ♦ *vt* (*throw*) arrojar, lanzar ♦ *vi* (*fall*) caer(se); **to ~ a tent** montar una tienda (de campaña); **~-black** *adj* negro como boca de lobo; **~ed battle** *n* batalla campal

pitfall ['pɪtfɔ:l] *n* riesgo

pith [pɪθ] *n* (*of orange*) médula

pithy ['pɪθɪ] *adj* (*fig*) jugoso

pitiful ['pɪtɪful] *adj* (*touching*) lastimoso, conmovedor(a)

pitiless ['pɪtɪlɪs] *adj* despiadado

pittance ['pɪtns] *n* miseria

pity ['pɪtɪ] *n* compasión *f*, piedad *f* ♦ *vt* compadecer(se de); **what a ~!** ¡qué pena!

pizza ['pi:tsə] *n* pizza

placard ['plækɑ:d] *n* letrero; (*in march etc*) pancarta

placate [plə'keɪt] *vt* apaciguar

place [pleɪs] *n* lugar *m*, sitio; (*seat*) plaza, asiento; (*post*) puesto; (*home*): **at/to his ~** en/a su casa; (*role: in society etc*) papel *m* ♦ *vt* (*object*) poner, colocar; (*identify*) reconocer; **to take ~** tener lugar; **to be ~d** (*in race, exam*) colocarse; **out of ~** (*not suitable*) fuera de lugar; **in the first ~** en primer lugar; **to change ~s with sb** cambiarse de sitio con uno; **~ of birth** lugar *m* de nacimiento

placid ['plæsɪd] *adj* apacible

plague [pleɪg] *n* plaga; (*MED*) peste *f* ♦ *vt* (*fig*) acosar, atormentar

plaice [pleɪs] *n inv* platija

plaid [plæd] *n* (*material*) tartán *m*

plain [pleɪn] *adj* (*unpatterned*) liso; (*clear*) claro, evidente; (*simple*) sencillo; (*not handsome*) poco atractivo ♦ *adv* claramente ♦ *n* llano, llanura; **~ chocolate** *n* chocolate *m* amargo; **~-clothes** *adj* (*police*) vestido de paisano; **~ly** *adv* claramente

plaintiff ['pleɪntɪf] *n* demandante *m/f*

plait [plæt] *n* trenza

plan [plæn] *n* (*drawing*) plano; (*scheme*) plan *m*, proyecto ♦ *vt* proyectar, planificar ♦ *vi* hacer proyectos; **to ~ to do** pensar hacer

plane [pleɪn] *n* (*AVIAT*) avión *m*; (*MATH, fig*) plano; (*also*: **~ tree**) plátano; (*tool*) cepillo

planet ['plænɪt] *n* planeta *m*

plank [plæŋk] *n* tabla

planner ['plænə*] *n* planificador(a) *m/f*

planning ['plænɪŋ] *n* planificación *f*; **family ~** planificación familiar; **~ permission** *n* permiso para realizar obras

plant [plɑ:nt] *n* planta; (*machinery*) maquinaria; (*factory*) fábrica ♦ *vt* plantar; (*field*) sembrar; (*bomb*) colocar

plaster ['plɑ:stə*] *n* (*for walls*) yeso; (*also*: **~ of Paris**) yeso mate; (*BRIT: also*: **sticking ~**) tirita (*SP*), esparadrapo, curita (*AM*) ♦ *vt* enyesar; (*cover*): **to ~ with** llenar *or* cubrir de; **~ed** (*inf*) *adj* borracho; **~er** *n* yesero

plastic ['plæstɪk] *n* plástico ♦ *adj* de plástico; **~ bag** *n* bolsa de plástico

Plasticine ® ['plæstɪsi:n] (*BRIT*) *n* plastilina ®

plastic surgery *n* cirujía plástica

plate [pleɪt] *n* (*dish*) plato; (*metal, in book*) lámina; (*dental ~*) placa de dentadura postiza

plateau ['plætəu] (*pl* **~s** *or* **~x**) *n* meseta, altiplanicie *f*

plateaux ['plætəuz] *npl of* **plateau**

plate glass *n* vidrio cilindrado

platform ['plætfɔ:m] *n* (*RAIL*) andén *m*; (*stage, BRIT: on bus*) plataforma; (*at meeting*) tribuna; (*POL*) programa *m* (electoral)

platinum ['plætɪnəm] *adj, n* platino

platoon [plə'tu:n] n pelotón m

platter ['plætə*] n fuente f

plausible ['plɔ:zɪbl] adj verosímil; (*person*) convincente

play [pleɪ] n (THEATRE) obra, comedia ♦ vt (*game*) jugar; (*compete against*) jugar contra; (*instrument*) tocar; (*part: in play etc*) hacer el papel de; (*tape, record*) poner ♦ vi jugar; (*band*) tocar; (*tape, record*) sonar; **to ~ safe** ir a lo seguro; **~ down** vt quitar importancia a; **~ up** vi (*cause trouble to*) dar guerra; **~boy** n playboy m; **~er** n jugador(a) m/f; (THEATRE) actor/actriz m/f; (MUS) músico/a; **~ful** adj juguetón/ona; **~ground** n (*in school*) patio de recreo; (*in park*) parque m infantil; **~group** n jardín m de niños; **~ing card** n naipe m, carta; **~ing field** n campo de deportes; **~mate** n compañero/a de juego; **~-off** n (SPORT) (partido de) desempate m; **~pen** n corral m; **~thing** n juguete m; **~time** n (SCOL) recreo; **~wright** n dramaturgo m

plc abbr (= *public limited company*) ≈ S.A.

plea [pli:] n súplica, petición f; (LAW) alegato, defensa, **~ bargaining** n (LAW) acuerdo entre fiscal y defensor para agilizar los trámites judiciales

plead [pli:d] vt (LAW): **to ~ sb's case** defender a uno; (*give as excuse*) poner como pretexto ♦ vi (LAW) declararse; (*beg*): **to ~ with sb** suplicar or rogar a uno

pleasant ['plɛznt] adj agradable; **~ries** npl cortesías fpl

please [pli:z] excl ¡por favor! ♦ vt (*give pleasure to*) dar gusto a, agradar ♦ vi (*think fit*): **do as you ~** haz lo que quieras; **~ yourself!** (*inf*) ¡haz lo que quieras!, ¡como quieras!; **~d** adj (*happy*) alegre, contento; **~d (with)** satisfecho (de); **~d to meet you** ¡encantado!, ¡tanto gusto!; **pleasing** adj agradable, grato

pleasure ['plɛʒə*] n placer m, gusto; **"it's a ~!"** "el gusto es mío"

pleat [pli:t] n pliegue m

pledge [plɛdʒ] n (*promise*) promesa, voto

♦ vt prometer

plentiful ['plɛntɪful] adj copioso, abundante

plenty ['plɛntɪ] n: **~ of** mucho(s)/a(s)

pliable ['plaɪəbl] adj flexible

pliers ['plaɪəz] npl alicates mpl, tenazas fpl

plight [plaɪt] n situación f difícil

plimsolls ['plɪmsəlz] (BRIT) npl zapatos mpl de tenis

plinth [plɪnθ] n plinto

plod [plɔd] vi caminar con paso pesado; (*fig*) trabajar laboriosamente

plonk [plɔŋk] (*inf*) n (BRIT: *wine*) vino peleón ♦ vt: **to ~ sth down** dejar caer algo

plot [plɔt] n (*scheme*) complot m, conjura; (*of story, play*) argumento; (*of land*) terreno, lote m (AM) ♦ vt (*mark out*) trazar; (*conspire*) tramar, urdir ♦ vi conspirar

plough [plau] (US **plow**) n arado ♦ vt (*earth*) arar; **to ~ money into** invertir dinero en; **~ through** vt fus (*crowd*) abrirse paso por la fuerza por; **~man's lunch** (BRIT) n almuerzo de pub a base de pan, queso y encurtidos

pluck [plʌk] vt (*fruit*) coger (SP), recoger (AM); (*musical instrument*) puntear; (*bird*) desplumar; (*eyebrows*) depilar; **to ~ up courage** hacer de tripas corazón

plug [plʌg] n tapón m; (ELEC) enchufe m, clavija; (AUT: *also:* **spark(ing) ~**) bujía ♦ vt (*hole*) tapar; (*inf: advertise*) dar publicidad a; **~ in** vt (ELEC) enchufar

plum [plʌm] n (*fruit*) ciruela

plumb [plʌm] vt: **to ~ the depths of** alcanzar los mayores extremos de

plumber ['plʌmə*] n fontanero/a (SP), plomero/a (AM)

plumbing ['plʌmɪŋ] n (*trade*) fontanería, plomería; (*piping*) cañería

plummet ['plʌmɪt] vi: **to ~ (down)** caer a plomo

plump [plʌmp] adj rechoncho, rollizo ♦ vi: **to ~ for** (*inf: choose*) optar por; **~ up** vt mullir

plunder ['plʌndə*] vt pillar, saquear

plunge [plʌndʒ] *n* zambullida ♦ *vt*
sumergir, hundir ♦ *vi* (*fall*) caer; (*dive*)
saltar; (*person*) arrojarse; **to take the ~**
lanzarse; **plunging** *adj*: **plunging
neckline** escote *m* pronunciado

pluperfect [pluː'pɜːfɪkt] *n*
pluscuamperfecto

plural ['pluərl] *adj* plural ♦ *n* plural *m*

plus [plʌs] *n* (*also*: **~ sign**) signo más
♦ *prep* más, y, además de; **ten/twenty ~**
más de diez/veinte

plush [plʌʃ] *adj* lujoso

plutonium [pluː'təunɪəm] *n* plutonio

ply [plaɪ] *vt* (*a trade*) ejercer ♦ *vi* (*ship*) ir y
venir ♦ *n* (*of wool, rope*) cabo; **to ~ sb
with drink** insistir en ofrecer a uno
muchas copas; **~wood** *n* madera
contrachapada

P.M. *n abbr* = **Prime Minister**

p.m. *adv abbr* (= *post meridiem*) de la
tarde *or* noche

pneumatic [njuː'mætɪk] *adj* neumático; **~
drill** *n* martillo neumático

pneumonia [njuː'məunɪə] *n* pulmonía

poach [pəutʃ] *vt* (*cook*) escalfar; (*steal*)
cazar (*or* pescar) en vedado ♦ *vi* cazar (*or*
pescar) en vedado; **~ed** *adj* escalfado;
~er *n* cazador(a) *m/f* furtivo/a

P.O. Box *n abbr* = **Post Office Box**

pocket ['pɔkɪt] *n* bolsillo; (*fig: small area*)
bolsa ♦ *vt* meter en el bolsillo; (*steal*)
embolsar; **to be out of ~** (*BRIT*) salir
perdiendo; **~book** (*US*) *n* cartera; **~
calculator** *n* calculadora de bolsillo; **~
knife** *n* navaja; **~ money** *n* asignación *f*

pod [pɔd] *n* vaina

podgy ['pɔdʒɪ] *adj* gordinflón/ona

podiatrist [pɔ'diːətrɪst] (*US*) *n* pedicuro/a

poem ['pəuɪm] *n* poema *m*

poet ['pəuɪt] *n* poeta *m/f*; **~ic** [-'etɪk] *adj*
poético; **~ry** *n* poesía

poignant ['pɔɪnjənt] *adj* conmovedor(a)

point [pɔɪnt] *n* punto; (*tip*) punta;
(*purpose*) fin *m*, propósito; (*use*) utilidad *f*;
(*significant part*) lo significativo; (*moment*)
momento; (*ELEC*) toma (de corriente);
(*also*: **decimal ~**): **2 ~ 3 (2.3)** dos coma

tres (2,3) ♦ *vt* señalar; (*gun etc*): **to ~ sth
at sb** apuntar algo a uno ♦ *vi*: **to ~ at**
señalar; **~s** *npl* (*AUT*) contactos *mpl*; (*RAIL*)
agujas *fpl*; **to be on the ~ of doing sth**
estar a punto de hacer algo; **to make a ~
of** poner empeño en; **to get/miss the ~**
comprender/no comprender; **to come to
the ~** ir al meollo; **there's no ~ (in
doing)** no tiene sentido (hacer); **~ out** *vt*
señalar; **~ to** *vt fus* (*fig*) indicar, señalar;
~-blank *adv* (*say, refuse*) sin más hablar;
(*also*: **at ~-blank range**) a quemarropa;
~ed *adj* (*shape*) puntiagudo, afilado;
(*remark*) intencionado; **~edly** *adv*
intencionadamente; **~er** *n* (*needle*) aguja,
indicador *m*; **~less** *adj* sin sentido; **~ of
view** *n* punto de vista

poise [pɔɪz] *n* aplomo, elegancia

poison ['pɔɪzn] *n* veneno ♦ *vt* envenenar;
~ing *n* envenenamiento; **~ous** *adj*
venenoso; (*fumes etc*) tóxico

poke [pəuk] *vt* (*jab with finger, stick etc*)
empujar; (*put*): **to ~ sth in(to)** introducir
algo en; **~ about** *vi* fisgonear

poker ['pəukə*] *n* atizador *m*; (*CARDS*)
póker *m*

poky ['pəukɪ] *adj* estrecho

Poland ['pəulənd] *n* Polonia

polar ['pəulə*] *adj* polar; **~ bear** *n* oso
polar

Pole [pəul] *n* polaco/a

pole [pəul] *n* palo; (*fixed*) poste *m*; (*GEO*)
polo; **~ bean** (*US*) *n* ≈ judía verde; **~
vault** *n* salto con pértiga

police [pə'liːs] *n* policía ♦ *vt* vigilar; **~ car**
n coche-patrulla *m*; **~man** (*irreg*) *n*
policía *m*, guardia *m*; **~ state** *n* estado
policial; **~ station** *n* comisaría *f*;
~woman (*irreg*) *n* mujer *f* policía

policy ['pɔlɪsɪ] *n* política; (*also*: **insurance
~**) póliza

polio ['pəulɪəu] *n* polio *f*

Polish ['pəulɪʃ] *adj* polaco ♦ *n* (*LING*)
polaco

polish ['pɔlɪʃ] *n* (*for shoes*) betún *m*; (*for
floor*) cera (de lustrar); (*shine*) brillo, lustre
m; (*fig: refinement*) educación *f* ♦ *vt*

(shoes) limpiar; *(make shiny)* pulir, sacar brillo a; **~ off** *vt (food)* despachar; **~ed** *adj (fig: person)* elegante

polite [pə'laɪt] *adj* cortés, atento; **~ness** *n* cortesía

political [pə'lɪtɪkl] *adj* político; **~ly** *adv* políticamente; **~ly correct** políticamente correcto

politician [pɔlɪ'tɪʃən] *n* político/a

politics ['pɔlɪtɪks] *n* política

poll [pəul] *n (election)* votación *f*; *(also:* **opinion ~**) sondeo, encuesta ♦ *vt (votes)* obtener

pollen ['pɔlən] *n* polen *m*

polling day ['pəulɪŋ-] *n* día *m* de elecciones

polling station *n* centro electoral

pollute [pə'luːt] *vt* contaminar

pollution [pə'luːʃən] *n* polución *f*, contaminación *f* del medio ambiente

polo ['pəuləu] *n (sport)* polo; **~-necked** *adj* de cuello vuelto; **~ shirt** *n* polo, niqui *m*

polyester [pɔlɪ'estə*] *n* poliéster *m*

polystyrene [pɔlɪ'staɪriːn] *n* poliestireno

polythene ['pɔlɪθiːn] *(BRIT) n* politeno

pomegranate ['pɔmɪɡrænɪt] *n* granada

pomp [pɔmp] *n* pompa

pompous ['pɔmpəs] *adj* pomposo

pond [pɔnd] *n (natural)* charca; *(artificial)* estanque *m*

ponder ['pɔndə*] *vt* meditar

ponderous ['pɔndərəs] *adj* pesado

pong [pɔŋ] *(BRIT: inf) n* hedor *m*

pony ['pəuni] *n* poney *m*, jaca, potro *(AM)*; **~tail** *n* cola de caballo; **~ trekking** *(BRIT)* excursión *f* a caballo

poodle ['puːdl] *n* caniche *m*

pool [puːl] *n (natural)* charca; *(also:* **swimming ~**) piscina *(SP)*, alberca *(AM)*; *(fig: of light etc)* charco; *(SPORT)* chapolín *m* ♦ *vt* juntar; **~s** *npl (football ~s)* quinielas *fpl*; **typing ~** servicio de mecanografía

poor [puə*] *adj* pobre; *(bad)* de mala calidad ♦ *npl*: **the ~** los pobres; **~ly** *adj* mal, enfermo ♦ *adv* mal

pop [pɔp] *n (sound)* ruido seco; *(MUS)* *(música)* pop *m*; *(inf: father)* papá *m*; *(drink)* gaseosa ♦ *vt (put quickly)* meter *(de prisa)* ♦ *vi* reventar; *(cork)* saltar; **~ in/out** *vi* entrar/salir un momento; **~ up** *vi* aparecer inesperadamente; **~corn** *n* palomitas *fpl*

pope [pəup] *n* papa *m*

poplar ['pɔplə*] *n* álamo

popper ['pɔpə*] *(BRIT) n* automático

poppy ['pɔpɪ] *n* amapola

Popsicle ® ['pɔpsɪkl] *(US) n* polo

pop star *n* estrella del pop

populace ['pɔpjuləs] *n* pueblo, plebe *f*

popular ['pɔpjulə*] *adj* popular

population [pɔpju'leɪʃən] *n* población *f*

porcelain ['pɔːslɪn] *n* porcelana

porch [pɔːtʃ] *n* pórtico, entrada; *(US)* veranda

porcupine ['pɔːkjupaɪn] *n* puerco *m* espín

pore [pɔː*] *n* poro ♦ *vi*: **to ~ over** engolfarse en

pork [pɔːk] *n* carne *f* de cerdo *(SP)* or chancho *(AM)*

pornography [pɔː'nɔɡrəfɪ] *n* pornografía

porpoise ['pɔːpəs] *n* marsopa

porridge ['pɔrɪdʒ] *n* gachas *fpl* de avena

port [pɔːt] *n* puerto; *(NAUT: left side)* babor *m*; *(wine)* vino de Oporto; **~ of call** puerto de escala

portable ['pɔːtəbl] *adj* portátil

porter ['pɔːtə*] *n (for luggage)* maletero; *(doorkeeper)* portero/a, conserje *m/f*

portfolio [pɔːt'fəuləu] *n* cartera

porthole ['pɔːthəul] *n* portilla

portion ['pɔːʃən] *n* porción *f*; *(of food)* ración *f*

portrait ['pɔːtreɪt] *n* retrato

portray [pɔː'treɪ] *vt* retratar; *(subj: actor)* representar

Portugal ['pɔːtjuɡl] *n* Portugal *m*

Portuguese [pɔːtju'ɡiːz] *adj* portugués/esa ♦ *n inv* portugués/esa *m/f*; *(LING)* portugués *m*

pose [pəuz] *n* postura, actitud *f* ♦ *vi* *(pretend)*: **to ~ as** hacerse pasar por ♦ *vt* *(question)* plantear; **to ~ for** posar para

posh [pɒʃ] (*inf*) *adj* elegante, de lujo

position [pə'zɪʃən] *n* posición *f*; (*job*) puesto; (*situation*) situación *f* ♦ *vt* colocar

positive ['pɒzɪtɪv] *adj* positivo; (*certain*) seguro; (*definite*) definitivo

possess [pə'zɛs] *vt* poseer; **~ion** [pə'zɛʃən] *n* posesión *f*; **~ions** *npl* (*belongings*) pertenencias *fpl*

possibility [pɒsɪ'bɪlɪtɪ] *n* posibilidad *f*

possible ['pɒsɪbl] *adj* posible; **as big as ~** lo más grande posible; **possibly** *adv* posiblemente; **I cannot possibly come** me es imposible venir

post [pəust] *n* (*BRIT: system*) correos *mpl*; (*BRIT: letters, delivery*) correo; (*job, situation*) puesto; (*pole*) poste *m* ♦ *vt* (*BRIT: send by post*) echar al correo; (*BRIT: appoint*): **to ~ to** enviar a; **~age** *n* porte *m*, franqueo; **~age stamp** *n* sello de correos; **~al** *adj* postal, de correos; **~al order** *n* giro postal; **~box** (*BRIT*) *n* buzón *m*; **~card** *n* tarjeta postal; **~code** (*BRIT*) *n* código postal

postdate [pəust'deɪt] *vt* (*cheque*) poner fecha adelantada a

poster ['pəustə*] *n* cartel *m*

poste restante [pəust'rɛstɔ̃nt] (*BRIT*) *n* lista de correos

postgraduate ['pəust'grædjuət] *n* posgraduado/a

posthumous ['pɒstjuməs] *adj* póstumo

postman ['pəustmən] (*irreg*) *n* cartero

postmark ['pəustmɑːk] *n* matasellos *m inv*

post-mortem [-'mɔːtəm] *n* autopsia

post office *n* (*building*) (oficina de) correos *m*; (*organization*): **the Post Office** Administración *f* General de Correos; **Post Office Box** *n* apartado postal (*SP*), casilla de correos (*AM*)

postpone [pəs'pəun] *vt* aplazar

postscript ['pəustskrɪpt] *n* posdata

posture ['pɒstʃə*] *n* postura, actitud *f*

postwar [pəust'wɔː*] *adj* de la posguerra

posy ['pəuzɪ] *n* ramillete *m* (de flores)

pot [pɒt] *n* (*for cooking*) olla *f*; (*tea~*) tetera; (*coffee~*) cafetera; (*for flowers*) maceta; (*for jam*) tarro, pote *m*; (*inf: marijuana*)

chocolate *m* ♦ *vt* (*plant*) poner en tiesto; **to go to ~** (*inf*) irse al traste

potato [pə'teɪtəu] (*pl* **~es**) *n* patata (*SP*), papa (*AM*); **~ peeler** *n* pelapatatas *m inv*

potent ['pəutnt] *adj* potente, poderoso; (*drink*) fuerte

potential [pə'tɛnʃl] *adj* potencial, posible ♦ *n* potencial *m*; **~ly** *adv* en potencia

pothole ['pɒthəul] *n* (*in road*) bache *m*; (*BRIT: underground*) gruta; **potholing** (*BRIT*) *n*: **to go potholing** dedicarse a la espeleología

potluck [pɒt'lʌk] *n*: **to take ~** tomar lo que haya

potted ['pɒtɪd] *adj* (*food*) en conserva; (*plant*) en tiesto *or* maceta; (*shortened*) resumido

potter ['pɒtə*] *n* alfarero/a ♦ *vi*: **to ~ around, ~ about** (*BRIT*) hacer trabajitos; **~y** *n* cerámica; (*factory*) alfarería

potty ['pɒtɪ] *n* orinal *m* de niño

pouch [pautʃ] *n* (*ZOOL*) bolsa; (*for tobacco*) petaca

poultry ['pəultrɪ] *n* aves *fpl* de corral; (*meat*) pollo

pounce [pauns] *vi*: **to ~ on** precipitarse sobre

pound [paund] *n* libra (*weight = 453g or 16oz; money = 100 pence*) ♦ *vt* (*beat*) golpear; (*crush*) machacar ♦ *vi* (*heart*) latir; **~ sterling** *n* libra esterlina

pour [pɔː*] *vt* echar; (*tea etc*) servir ♦ *vi* correr, fluir; **to ~ sb a drink** servirle a uno una copa; **~ away or off** *vt* vaciar, verter; **~ in** *vi* (*people*) entrar en tropel; **~ out** *vi* salir en tropel ♦ *vt* (*drink*) echar, servir; (*fig*) **to ~ out one's feelings** desahogarse; **~ing** *adj*: **~ing rain** lluvia torrencial

pout [paut] *vi* hacer pucheros

poverty ['pɒvətɪ] *n* pobreza, miseria; **~-stricken** *adj* necesitado

powder ['paudə*] *n* polvo; (*face ~*) polvos *mpl* ♦ *vt* polvorear; **to ~ one's face** empolvarse la cara; **~ compact** *n* polvera; **~ed milk** *n* leche *f* en polvo; **~ room** *n* aseos *mpl*

power ['pauə*] n poder m; (strength) fuerza; (nation, TECH) potencia; (drive) empuje m; (ELEC) fuerza, energía ♦ vt impulsar; **to be in ~** (POL) estar en el poder; **~ cut** (BRIT) n apagón m; **~ed** adj: **~ed by** impulsado por; **~ failure** n = **~ cut**; **~ful** adj poderoso; (engine) potente; (speech etc) convincente; **~less** adj: **~less (to do)** incapaz (de hacer); **~ point** (BRIT) n enchufe m; **~ station** n central f eléctrica

p.p. abbr (= per procurationem): **~ J. Smith** p.p. (por poder de) J. Smith; (= pages) págs

PR n abbr = **public relations**

practical ['præktɪkl] adj práctico; **~ity** [-'kælɪtɪ] n factibilidad f; **~ joke** n broma pesada; **~ly** adv (almost) casi

practice ['præktɪs] n (habit) costumbre f; (exercise) práctica, ejercicio; (training) adiestramiento; (MED: of profession) práctica, ejercicio; (MED, LAW: business) consulta ♦ vt, vi (US) = **practise**; **in ~** (in reality) en la práctica; **out of ~** desentrenado

practise ['præktɪs] (US **practice**) vt (carry out) practicar; (profession) ejercer; (train at) practicar ♦ vi ejercer; (train) practicar; **practising** adj (Christian etc) practicante; (lawyer) en ejercicio

practitioner [præk'tɪʃənə*] n (MED) médico/a

prairie ['prɛərɪ] n pampa

praise [preɪz] n alabanza(s) f(pl), elogio(s) m(pl) ♦ vt alabar, elogiar; **~worthy** adj loable

pram [præm] (BRIT) n cochecito de niño

prank [præŋk] n travesura

prawn [prɔ:n] n gamba; **~ cocktail** n cóctel m de gambas

pray [preɪ] vi rezar

prayer [prɛə*] n oración f, rezo; (entreaty) ruego, súplica

preach [pri:tʃ] vi (also fig) predicar; **~er** n predicador(a) m/f

precaution [prɪ'kɔ:ʃən] n precaución f

precede [prɪ'si:d] vt, vi preceder

precedent ['prɛsɪdənt] n precedente m

preceding [prɪ'si:dɪŋ] adj anterior

precinct ['pri:sɪŋkt] n recinto; **~s** npl contornos mpl; **pedestrian ~** (BRIT) zona peatonal; **shopping ~** (BRIT) centro comercial

precious ['prɛʃəs] adj precioso

precipitate [prɪ'sɪpɪteɪt] vt precipitar

precise [prɪ'saɪs] adj preciso, exacto; **~ly** adv precisamente, exactamente

precocious [prɪ'kəʊʃəs] adj precoz

precondition [pri:kən'dɪʃən] n condición f previa

predecessor ['pri:dɪsɛsə*] n antecesor(a) m/f

predicament [prɪ'dɪkəmənt] n apuro

predict [prɪ'dɪkt] vt pronosticar; **~able** adj previsible; **~ion** [-'dɪkʃən] n predicción f

predominantly [prɪ'dɒmɪnəntlɪ] adv en su mayoría

pre-empt [pri:'ɛmt] vt adelantarse a

preen [pri:n] vt: **to ~ itself** (bird) limpiarse (las plumas); **to ~ o.s.** pavonearse

preface ['prɛfəs] n prefacio

prefect ['pri:fɛkt] (BRIT) n (in school) monitor(a) m/f

prefer [prɪ'fə:*] vt preferir; **to ~ doing** or **to do** preferir hacer; **~able** ['prɛfrəbl] adj preferible; **~ably** ['prɛfrəblɪ] adv de preferencia; **~ence** ['prɛfrəns] n preferencia; (priority) prioridad f; **~ential** [prɛfə'rɛnʃəl] adj preferente

prefix ['pri:fɪks] n prefijo

pregnancy ['prɛgnənsɪ] n (of woman) embarazo; (of animal) preñez f

pregnant ['prɛgnənt] adj (woman) embarazada; (animal) preñada

prehistoric ['pri:hɪs'tɔrɪk] adj prehistórico

prejudice ['prɛdʒudɪs] n prejuicio; **~d** (person) predispuesto

premarital ['pri:'mærɪtl] adj premarital

premature ['prɛmətʃuə*] adj prematuro

premier ['prɛmɪə*] adj primero, principal ♦ n (POL) primer(a) ministro/a

première ['prɛmɪɛə*] n estreno

premise ['prɛmɪs] n premisa; **~s** npl (of business etc) local m; **on the ~s** en el lugar mismo

premium ['pri:mɪəm] *n* premio; (*insurance*) prima; ~ **bond** (*BRIT*) *n* bono del estado que participa en una lotería nacional

premonition [premə'nɪʃən] *n* presentimiento

preoccupied [pri:'ɔkjupaɪd] *adj* ensimismado

prep [prep] *n* (*SCOL: study*) deberes *mpl*

prepaid [pri:'peɪd] *adj* porte pagado

preparation [prepə'reɪʃən] *n* preparación *f*; ~**s** *npl* preparativos *mpl*

preparatory [prɪ'pærətərɪ] *adj* preparatorio, preliminar; ~ **school** *n* escuela preparatoria

prepare [prɪ'pɛə*] *vt* preparar, disponer; (*CULIN*) preparar ♦ *vi*: **to ~ for** (*action*) prepararse *or* disponerse para; (*event*) hacer preparativos para; ~**d to** dispuesto a; ~**d for** listo para

preposition [prepə'zɪʃən] *n* preposición *f*

preposterous [prɪ'pɔstərəs] *adj* absurdo, ridículo

prep school *n* = **preparatory school**

prerequisite [pri:'rekwɪzɪt] *n* requisito

Presbyterian [prezbɪ'tɪərɪən] *adj*, *n* presbiteriano/a *m/f*

preschool ['pri:sku:l] *adj* preescolar

prescribe [prɪ'skraɪb] *vt* (*MED*) recetar

prescription [prɪ'skrɪpʃən] *n* (*MED*) receta

presence ['prezns] *n* presencia; **in sb's ~** en presencia de uno; ~ **of mind** aplomo

present [*adj, n* 'preznt, *vb* prɪ'zent] *adj* (*in attendance*) presente; (*current*) actual ♦ *n* (*gift*) regalo; (*actuality*): **the ~** la actualidad, el presente ♦ *vt* (*introduce, describe*) presentar; (*expound*) exponer; (*give*) presentar, dar, ofrecer; (*THEATRE*) representar; **to give sb a ~** regalar algo a uno; **at ~** actualmente; ~**able** [prɪ'zentəbl] *adj*: **to make o.s. ~able** arreglarse; ~**ation** [-'teɪʃən] *n* presentación *f*; (*of report etc*) exposición *f*; (*formal ceremony*) entrega de un regalo; ~**-day** *adj* actual; ~**er** [prɪ'zentə*] *n* (*RADIO, TV*) locutor(a) *m/f*; ~**ly** *adv* (*soon*) dentro de poco;

(*now*) ahora

preservative [prɪ'zə:vətɪv] *n* conservante *m*

preserve [prɪ'zə:v] *vt* (*keep safe*) preservar, proteger; (*maintain*) mantener; (*food*) conservar ♦ *n* (*for game*) coto, vedado; (*often pl: jam*) conserva, confitura

president ['prezɪdənt] *n* presidente *m/f*; ~**ial** [-'denʃl] *adj* presidencial

press [pres] *n* (*newspapers*): **the P~** la prensa; (*printer's*) imprenta; (*of button*) pulsación *f* ♦ *vt* empujar; (*button etc*) apretar; (*clothes: iron*) planchar; (*put pressure on: person*) presionar; (*insist*): **to ~ sth on sb** insistir en que uno acepte algo ♦ *vi* (*squeeze*) apretar; (*pressurize*): **to ~ for** presionar por; **we are ~ed for time/money** estamos apurados de tiempo/dinero; ~ **on** *vi* avanzar; (*hurry*) apretar el paso; ~ **agency** *n* agencia de prensa; ~ **conference** *n* rueda de prensa; ~**ing** *adj* apremiante; ~ **stud** (*BRIT*) *n* botón *m* de presión; ~**-up** (*BRIT*) *n* plancha

pressure ['preʃə*] *n* presión *f*; **to put ~ on sb** presionar a uno; ~ **cooker** *n* olla a presión; ~ **gauge** *n* manómetro; ~ **group** *n* grupo de presión; **pressurized** *adj* (*container*) a presión

prestige [pres'ti:ʒ] *n* prestigio

presumably [prɪ'zju:məblɪ] *adv* es de suponer que, cabe presumir que

presume [prɪ'zju:m] *vt*: **to ~ (that)** presumir (que), suponer (que)

pretence [prɪ'tens] (*US* **pretense**) *n* fingimiento; **under false ~s** con engaños

pretend [prɪ'tend] *vt*, *vi* (*feign*) fingir

pretentious [prɪ'tenʃəs] *adj* presumido; (*ostentatious*) ostentoso, aparatoso

pretext ['pri:tekst] *n* pretexto

pretty ['prɪtɪ] *adj* bonito (*SP*), lindo (*AM*) ♦ *adv* bastante

prevail [prɪ'veɪl] *vi* (*gain mastery*) prevalecer; (*be current*) predominar; ~**ing** *adj* (*dominant*) predominante

prevalent ['prevələnt] *adj* (*widespread*) extendido

prevent [prɪ'vɛnt] *vt*: to ~ sb from doing sth impedir a uno hacer algo; to ~ sth from happening evitar que ocurra algo; ~ative *adj* = **preventive**; ~ive *adj* preventivo

preview ['pri:vju:] *n* (*of film*) preestreno

previous ['pri:vɪəs] *adj* previo, anterior; ~ly *adv* antes

prewar [pri:'wɔ:*] *adj* de antes de la guerra

prey [preɪ] *n* presa ♦ *vi*: to ~ on (*feed on*) alimentarse de; it was ~ing on his mind le preocupaba, le obsesionaba

price [praɪs] *n* precio ♦ *vt* (*goods*) fijar el precio de; ~less *adj* que no tiene precio; ~ list tarifa

prick [prɪk] *n* (*sting*) picadura ♦ *vt* pinchar; (*hurt*) picar; to ~ up one's ears aguzar el oído

prickle ['prɪkl] *n* (*sensation*) picor *m*; (*BOT*) espina; **prickly** *adj* espinoso; (*fig: person*) enojadizo; **prickly heat** *n* sarpullido causado por exceso de calor

pride [praɪd] *n* orgullo; (*pej*) soberbia ♦ *vt*: to ~ o.s. on enorgullecerse de

priest [pri:st] *n* sacerdote *m*; ~hood *n* sacerdocio

prim [prɪm] *adj* (*demure*) remilgado; (*prudish*) gazmoño

primarily ['praɪmərɪlɪ] *adv* ante todo

primary ['praɪmərɪ] *adj* (*first in importance*) principal ♦ *n* (*US: POL*) (elección *f*) primaria; ~ **school** (*BRIT*) escuela primaria

prime [praɪm] *adj* primero, principal; (*excellent*) selecto, de primera clase ♦ *n*: in the ~ of life en la flor de la vida ♦ *vt* (*wood, fig*) preparar; ~ **example** ejemplo típico; **P~ Minister** *n* primer(a) ministro/a

primeval [praɪ'mi:vəl] *adj* primitivo

primitive ['prɪmɪtɪv] *adj* primitivo; (*crude*) rudimentario

primrose ['prɪmrəuz] *n* primavera, prímula

Primus (stove) ® ['praɪməs-] (*BRIT*) *n* hornillo de camping

prince [prɪns] *n* príncipe *m*

princess [prɪn'sɛs] *n* princesa

principal ['prɪnsɪpl] *adj* principal, mayor ♦ *n* director(a) *m/f*; ~ity [-'pælɪtɪ] *n* principado

principle ['prɪnsɪpl] *n* principio; **in ~** en principio; **on ~** por principio

print [prɪnt] *n* (*foot~*) huella; (*finger~*) huella dactilar; (*letters*) letra de molde; (*fabric*) estampado; (*ART*) grabado; (*PHOT*) impresión *f* ♦ *vt* imprimir; (*cloth*) estampar; (*write in capitals*) escribir en letras de molde; **out of ~** agotado; **~ed matter** *n* impresos *mpl*; **~er** *n* (*person*) impresor(a) *m/f*; (*machine*) impresora; **~ing** *n* (*art*) imprenta; (*act*) impresión *f*; **~out** *n* (*COMPUT*) impresión *f*

prior ['praɪə*] *adj* anterior, previo; (*more important*) más importante; **~ to** antes de

priority [praɪ'ɔrɪtɪ] *n* prioridad *f*; **to have ~ (over)** tener prioridad (sobre)

prison ['prɪzn] *n* cárcel *f*, prisión *f* ♦ *cpd* carcelario; **~er** *n* (*in prison*) preso/a; (*captured person*) prisionero/a; **~er-of-war** *n* prisionero de guerra

privacy ['prɪvəsɪ] *n* intimidad *f*

private ['praɪvɪt] *adj* (*personal*) particular; (*property, industry, discussion etc*) privado; (*person*) reservado; (*place*) tranquilo ♦ *n* soldado raso; **"~"** (*on envelope*) "confidencial"; (*on door*) "prohibido el paso"; **in ~** en privado; **~ enterprise** *n* empresa privada; **~ eye** *n* detective *m/f* privado/a; **~ property** *n* propiedad *f* privada; **~ school** *n* colegio particular

privet ['prɪvɪt] *n* alheña

privilege ['prɪvɪlɪdʒ] *n* privilegio; (*prerogative*) prerrogativa

privy ['prɪvɪ] *adj*: **to be ~ to** estar enterado de

prize [praɪz] *n* premio ♦ *adj* de primera clase ♦ *vt* apreciar, estimar; **~-giving** *n* distribución *f* de premios; **~winner** *n* premiado/a

pro [prəu] *n* (*SPORT*) profesional *m/f* ♦ *prep* a favor de; **the ~s and cons** los pros y los contras

probability [prɔbə'bɪlɪtɪ] *n* probabilidad *f*;

in all ~ con toda probabilidad

probable ['prɔbəbl] *adj* probable

probably ['prɔbəblɪ] *adv* probablemente

probation [prə'beɪʃən] *n*: **on ~** (*employee*) a prueba; (*LAW*) en libertad condicional

probe [prəub] *n* (*MED, SPACE*) sonda; (*enquiry*) encuesta, investigación *f* ♦ *vt* sondar; (*investigate*) investigar

problem ['prɔbləm] *n* problema *m*

procedure [prə'siːdʒə*] *n* procedimiento; (*bureaucratic*) trámites *mpl*

proceed [prə'siːd] *vi* (*do afterwards*): **to ~ to do sth** proceder a hacer algo; (*continue*): **to ~ (with)** continuar *or* seguir (con); **~ings** *npl* acto(s) (*pl*); (*LAW*) proceso; **~s** ['prəusiːdz] *npl* (*money*) ganancias *fpl*, ingresos *mpl*

process ['prəuses] *n* proceso ♦ *vt* tratar, elaborar; **~ing** *n* tratamiento, elaboración *f*; (*PHOT*) revelado

procession [prə'seʃən] *n* desfile *m*; **funeral ~** cortejo fúnebre

pro-choice [prəu'tʃɔɪs] *adj* en favor del derecho a elegir de la madre

proclaim [prə'kleɪm] *vt* anunciar

procrastinate [prəu'kræstɪneɪt] *vi* demorarse

procure [prə'kjuə*] *vt* conseguir

prod [prɔd] *vt* empujar ♦ *n* empujón *m*

prodigy ['prɔdɪdʒɪ] *n* prodigio

produce [*n* 'prɔdjuːs, *vt* prə'djuːs] *n* (*AGR*) productos *mpl* agrícolas ♦ *vt* producir; (*play, film, programme*) presentar; **~r** *n* productor(a) *m/f*; (*of film, programme*) director(a) *m/f*; (*of record*) productor(a) *m/f*

product ['prɔdʌkt] *n* producto

production [prə'dʌkʃən] *n* producción *f*; (*THEATRE*) presentación *f*; **~ line** *n* línea de producción

productivity [prɔdʌk'tɪvɪtɪ] *n* productividad *f*

profession [prə'feʃən] *n* profesión *f*; **~al** *adj* profesional ♦ *n* profesional *m/f*; (*skilled person*) perito

professor [prə'fesə*] *n* (*BRIT*) catedrático/a; (*US, Canada*) profesor(a) *m/f*

proficient [prə'fɪʃənt] *adj* experto, hábil

profile ['prəufaɪl] *n* perfil *m*

profit ['prɔfɪt] *n* (*COMM*) ganancia ♦ *vi*: **to ~ by** *or* **from** aprovechar *or* sacar provecho de; **~ability** [-ə'bɪlɪtɪ] *n* rentabilidad *f*; **~able** *adj* (*ECON*) rentable

profound [prə'faund] *adj* profundo

profusely [prə'fjuːslɪ] *adv* profusamente

programme ['prəugræm] (*US* **program**) *n* programa *m* ♦ *vt* programar; **~r** (*US* **programer**) *n* programador(a) *m/f*; **programming** (*US* **programing**) *n* programación *f*

progress [*n* 'prəugres, *vi* prə'gres] *n* progreso; (*development*) desarrollo ♦ *vi* progresar, avanzar; **in ~** en curso; **~ive** [-'gresɪv] *adj* progresivo; (*person*) progresista

prohibit [prə'hɪbɪt] *vt* prohibir; **to ~ sb from doing sth** prohibir a uno hacer algo; **~ion** [-'bɪʃn] *n* prohibición *f*; (*US*): **P~ion** Ley *f* Seca

project [*n* 'prɔdʒekt, *vb* prə'dʒekt] *n* proyecto ♦ *vt* proyectar ♦ *vi* (*stick out*) salir, sobresalir; **~ion** [prə'dʒekʃən] *n* proyección *f*; (*overhang*) saliente *m*; **~or** [prə'dʒektə*] *n* proyector *m*

pro-life [prəu'laɪf] *adj* pro-vida

prolong [prə'lɔŋ] *vt* prolongar, extender

prom [prɔm] *n abbr* = **promenade**; (*US: ball*) baile *m* de gala

---

Prom

i *El ciclo de conciertos de música clásica más conocido de Londres es el llamado* **the Proms** *(promenade concerts), que se celebra anualmente en el Royal Albert Hall. Su nombre se debe a que originalmente el público paseaba durante las actuaciones, costumbre que en la actualidad se mantiene de forma simbólica, permitiendo que parte de los asistentes permanezcan de pie. En Estados Unidos se llama* **prom** *a un baile de gala en un centro de educación secundaria o universitaria.*

promenade [prɒmə'nɑːd] n (by sea) paseo marítimo; **~ concert** (BRIT) n concierto (en que parte del público permanece de pie)

prominence ['prɒmɪnəns] n importancia

prominent ['prɒmɪnənt] adj (standing out) saliente; (important) eminente, importante

promiscuous [prə'mɪskjuəs] adj (sexually) promiscuo

promise ['prɒmɪs] n promesa ♦ vt, vi prometer; **promising** adj prometedor(a)

promote [prə'məut] vt (employee) ascender; (product, pop star) hacer propaganda por; (ideas) fomentar; **~r** n (of event) promotor(a) m/f; (of cause etc) impulsor(a) m/f; **promotion** [-'məuʃən] n (advertising campaign) campaña de promoción f; (in rank) ascenso

prompt [prɒmpt] adj rápido ♦ adv: **at 6 o'clock ~** a las seis en punto ♦ n (COMPUT) aviso ♦ vt (urge) mover, incitar; (when talking) instar; (THEATRE) apuntar; **to ~ sb to do sth** instar a uno a hacer algo; **~ly** adv rápidamente; (exactly) puntualmente

prone [prəun] adj (lying) postrado; **~ to** propenso a

prong [prɒŋ] n diente m, punta f

pronoun ['prəunaun] n pronombre m

pronounce [prə'nauns] vt pronunciar; **~d** adj (marked) marcado

pronunciation [prənʌnsɪ'eɪʃən] n pronunciación f

proof [pruːf] n prueba ♦ adj: **~ against** a prueba de

prop [prɒp] n apoyo; (fig) sostén m ♦ vt (also: **~ up**) apoyar; (lean): **to ~ sth against** apoyar algo contra

propaganda [prɒpə'gændə] n propaganda

propel [prə'pel] vt impulsar, propulsar; **~ler** n hélice f

propensity [prə'pensɪtɪ] n propensión f

proper ['prɒpə*] adj (suited, right) propio; (exact) justo; (seemly) correcto, decente; (authentic) verdadero; (referring to place): **the village ~** el pueblo mismo; **~ly** adv (adequately) correctamente; (decently) decentemente; **~ noun** n nombre m propio

property ['prɒpətɪ] n propiedad f; (personal) bienes mpl muebles; **~ owner** n dueño/a de propiedades

prophecy ['prɒfɪsɪ] n profecía

prophesy ['prɒfɪsaɪ] vt (fig) predecir

prophet ['prɒfɪt] n profeta m

proportion [prə'pɔːʃən] n proporción f; (share) parte f; **~al** adj: **~al (to)** en proporción (con); **~al representation** n representación f proporcional; **~ate** adj: **~ate (to)** en proporción (con)

proposal [prə'pəuzl] n (offer of marriage) oferta de matrimonio; (plan) proyecto

propose [prə'pəuz] vt proponer ♦ vi declararse; **to ~ to do** tener intención de hacer

proposition [prɒpə'zɪʃən] n propuesta

proprietor [prə'praɪətə*] n propietario/a, dueño/a

propriety [prə'praɪətɪ] n decoro

pro rata [-'rɑːtə] adv a prorrateo

prose [prəuz] n prosa

prosecute ['prɒsɪkjuːt] vt (LAW) procesar; **prosecution** [-'kjuːʃən] n proceso, causa; (accusing side) acusación f; **prosecutor** n acusador(a) m/f; (also: **public prosecutor**) fiscal m

prospect [n 'prɒspekt, vb prə'spekt] n (possibility) posibilidad f; (outlook) perspectiva ♦ vi: **to ~ for** buscar; **~s** npl (for work etc) perspectivas fpl; **~ing** n prospección f; **~ive** [prə'spektɪv] adj futuro

prospectus [prə'spektəs] n prospecto

prosper ['prɒspə*] vi prosperar; **~ity** [-'spentɪ] n prosperidad f; **~ous** adj próspero

prostitute ['prɒstɪtjuːt] n prostituta; (male) hombre que se dedica a la prostitución

protect [prə'tekt] vt proteger; **~ion** [-'tekʃən] n protección f; **~ive** adj protector(a)

protein ['prəutiːn] n proteína

protest [n 'prəutest, vb prə'test] n protesta

♦ *vi*: **to ~ about** *or* **at/against** protestar de/contra ♦ *vt* (*insist*): **to ~ (that)** insistir en (que)

Protestant ['prɒtɪstənt] *adj, n* protestante *m/f*

protester [prə'tɛstə*] *n* manifestante *m/f*

protracted [prə'træktɪd] *adj* prolongado

protrude [prə'truːd] *vi* salir, sobresalir

proud [praud] *adj* orgulloso; (*pej*) soberbio, altanero

prove [pruːv] *vt* probar; (*show*) demostrar ♦ *vi*: **to ~ (to be) correct** resultar correcto; **to ~ o.s.** probar su valía

proverb ['prɒvəːb] *n* refrán *m*

provide [prə'vaɪd] *vt* proporcionar, dar; **to ~ sb with sth** proveer a uno de algo; **~d (that)** *conj* con tal de que, a condición de que; **~ for** *vt fus* (*person*) mantener a; (*problem etc*) tener en cuenta; **providing** [prə'vaɪdɪŋ] *conj*: **providing (that)** a condición de que, con tal de que

province ['prɒvɪns] *n* provincia; (*fig*) esfera; **provincial** [prə'vɪnʃəl] *adj* provincial; (*pej*) provinciano

provision [prə'vɪʒən] *n* (*supplying*) suministro, abastecimiento; (*of contract etc*) disposición *f*; **~s** *npl* (*food*) comestibles *mpl*; **~al** *adj* provisional

proviso [prə'vaɪzəu] *n* condición *f*, estipulación *f*

provocative [prə'vɒkətɪv] *adj* provocativo

provoke [prə'vəuk] *vt* (*cause*) provocar, incitar; (*anger*) enojar

prowess ['praus] *n* destreza

prowl [praul] *vi* (*also*: **~ about, ~ around**) merodear ♦ *n*: **on the ~** de merodeo; **~er** *n* merodeador(a) *m/f*

proxy ['prɒksɪ] *n*: **by ~** por poderes

prudent ['pruːdənt] *adj* prudente

prune [pruːn] *n* ciruela pasa ♦ *vt* podar

pry [praɪ] *vi*: **to ~ (into)** entrometerse (en)

PS *n abbr* (= *postscript*) P.D.

psalm [sɑːm] *n* salmo

pseudonym ['sjuːdəunɪm] *n* seudónimo

psyche ['saɪkɪ] *n* psique *f*

psychiatric [saɪkɪ'ætrɪk] *adj* psiquiátrico

psychiatrist [saɪ'kaɪətrɪst] *n* psiquiatra *m/f*

psychic ['saɪkɪk] *adj* (*also*: **~al**) psíquico

psychoanalyse [saɪkəu'ænəlaɪz] *vt* psicoanalizar; **psychoanalysis** [-ə'nælɪsɪs] *n* psicoanálisis *m inv*

psychological [saɪkə'lɔdʒɪkl] *adj* psicológico

psychologist [saɪ'kɔlədʒɪst] *n* psicólogo/a

psychology [saɪ'kɔlədʒɪ] *n* psicología

PTO *abbr* (= *please turn over*) sigue

pub [pʌb] *n abbr* (= *public house*) pub *m*, bar *m*

---

pub

i Un **pub** es un local público donde se pueden consumir bebidas alcohólicas. La estricta regulación sobre la venta de alcohol prohíbe que se sirva a menores de 18 años y controla las horas de apertura, aunque éstas son más flexibles desde hace unos años. El **pub** es, además, un lugar de encuentro donde se sirven comidas ligeras o se juega a los dardos o al billar, entre otras actividades.

---

puberty ['pjuːbətɪ] *n* pubertad *f*

public ['pʌblɪk] *adj* público ♦ *n*: **the ~** el público; **in ~** en público; **to make ~** hacer público; **~ address system** *n* megafonía

publican ['pʌblɪkən] *n* tabernero/a

publication [pʌblɪ'keɪʃən] *n* publicación *f*

public: ~ company *n* sociedad *f* anónima; **~ convenience** (*BRIT*) *n* aseos *mpl* públicos (*SP*), sanitarios *mpl* (*AM*); **~ holiday** *n* día de fiesta (*SP*), (día) feriado (*AM*); **~ house** (*BRIT*) *n* bar *m*, pub *m*

publicity [pʌb'lɪsɪtɪ] *n* publicidad *f*

publicize ['pʌblɪsaɪz] *vt* publicitar

publicly ['pʌblɪklɪ] *adv* públicamente, en público

public: ~ opinion *n* opinión *f* pública; **~ relations** *n* relaciones *fpl* públicas; **~ school** *n* (*BRIT*) escuela privada; (*US*) instituto; **~-spirited** *adj* que tiene sentido del deber ciudadano; **~ transport** *n* transporte *m* público

publish ['pʌblɪʃ] *vt* publicar; **~er** *n*

(*person*) editor(a) *m/f*; (*firm*) editorial *f*;
~ing *n* (*industry*) industria del libro
pub lunch *n almuerzo que se sirve en un pub*; **to go for a ~** almorzar *o* comer en un pub
pucker ['pʌkə*] *vt* (*pleat*) arrugar; (*brow etc*) fruncir
pudding ['pudɪŋ] *n* pudín *m*; (*BRIT: dessert*) postre *m*; **black ~** morcilla
puddle ['pʌdl] *n* charco
puff [pʌf] *n* soplo; (*of smoke, air*) bocanada; (*of breathing*) resoplido ♦ *vt*: **to ~ one's pipe** chupar la pipa ♦ *vi* (*pant*) jadear; **to ~** *vt* hinchar; **~ pastry** *n* hojaldre *m*; **~y** *adj* hinchado
pull [pul] *n* (*tug*): **to give sth a ~** dar un tirón a algo ♦ *vt* tirar de; (*press: trigger*) apretar; (*haul*) tirar, arrastrar; (*close: curtain*) echar ♦ *vi* tirar; **to ~ to pieces** hacer pedazos; **to not ~ one's punches** no andarse con bromas; **to ~ one's weight** hacer su parte; **to ~ o.s. together** sobreponerse; **to ~ sb's leg** tomar el pelo a uno; **~ apart** *vt* (*break*) romper; **~ down** *vt* (*building*) derribar; **~ in** *vi* (*car etc*) parar (junto a la acera); (*train*) llegar a la estación; **~ off** *vt* (*deal etc*) cerrar; **~ out** *vi* (*car, train etc*) salir ♦ *vt* sacar, arrancar; **~ over** *vi* (*AUT*) hacerse a un lado; **~ through** *vi* (*MED*) reponerse; **~ up** *vi* (*stop*) parar ♦ *vt* (*raise*) levantar; (*uproot*) arrancar, desarraigar
pulley ['pulɪ] *n* polea
pullover ['puləuvə*] *n* jersey *m*, suéter *m*
pulp [pʌlp] *n* (*of fruit*) pulpa
pulpit ['pulpɪt] *n* púlpito
pulsate [pʌl'seɪt] *vi* pulsar, latir
pulse [pʌls] *n* (*ANAT*) pulso; (*rhythm*) pulsación *f*; (*BOT*) legumbre *f*
pump [pʌmp] *n* bomba; (*shoe*) zapatilla ♦ *vt* sacar con una bomba; **~ up** *vt* inflar
pumpkin ['pʌmpkɪn] *n* calabaza
pun [pʌn] *n* juego de palabras
punch [pʌntʃ] *n* (*blow*) golpe *m*, puñetazo; (*tool*) punzón *m*; (*drink*) ponche *m* ♦ *vt* (*hit*): **to ~ sb/sth** dar un puñetazo *or* golpear a uno/algo; **~line** *n* palabras que

rematan un chiste; **~-up** (*BRIT: inf*) *n* riña
punctual ['pʌŋktjuəl] *adj* puntual
punctuation [pʌŋktju'eɪʃən] *n* puntuación *f*
puncture ['pʌŋktʃə*] (*BRIT*) *n* pinchazo ♦ *vt* pinchar
pungent ['pʌndʒənt] *adj* acre
punish ['pʌnɪʃ] *vt* castigar; **~ment** *n* castigo
punk [pʌŋk] *n* (*also*: **~ rocker**) punki *m/f*; (*also*: **~ rock**) música punk; (*US: inf: hoodlum*) rufián *m*
punt [pʌnt] *n* (*boat*) batea
punter ['pʌntə*] (*BRIT*) *n* (*gambler*) jugador(a) *m/f*; (*inf*) cliente *m/f*
puny ['pju:nɪ] *adj* débil
pup [pʌp] *n* cachorro
pupil ['pju:pl] *n* alumno/a; (*of eye*) pupila
puppet ['pʌpɪt] *n* títere *m*
puppy ['pʌpɪ] *n* cachorro, perrito
purchase ['pə:tʃɪs] *n* compra ♦ *vt* comprar; **~r** *n* comprador(a) *m/f*
pure [pjuə*] *adj* puro
purée ['pjuəreɪ] *n* puré *m*
purely ['pjuəlɪ] *adv* puramente
purge [pə:dʒ] *n* (*MED, POL*) purga ♦ *vt* purgar
purify ['pjuərɪfaɪ] *vt* purificar, depurar
purple ['pə:pl] *adj* purpúreo; morado
purpose ['pə:pəs] *n* propósito; **on ~** a propósito, adrede; **~ful** *adj* resuelto, determinado
purr [pə:*] *vi* ronronear
purse [pə:s] *n* monedero; (*US*) bolsa (*SP*), cartera (*AM*) ♦ *vt* fruncir
pursue [pə'sju:] *vt* seguir; **~r** *n* perseguidor(a) *m/f*
pursuit [pə'sju:t] *n* (*chase*) caza; (*occupation*) actividad *f*
push [puʃ] *n* empuje *m*, empujón *m*; (*of button*) presión *f*; (*drive*) empuje *m* ♦ *vt* empujar; (*button*) apretar; (*promote*) promover ♦ *vi* empujar; (*demand*): **to ~ for** luchar por; **~ aside** *vt* apartar con la mano; **~ off** (*inf*) *vi* largarse; **~ on** *vi* seguir adelante; **~ through** *vi* (*crowd*) abrirse paso a empujones ♦ *vt* (*measure*)

despachar; **~ up** vt (total, prices) hacer subir; **~chair** (BRIT) n sillita de ruedas; **~er** n (drug ~er) traficante m/f de drogas; **~over** (inf) n: **it's a ~over** está tirado; **~-up** (US) n plancha; **~y** (pej) adj agresivo

puss [pus] (inf) n minino

pussy(-cat) ['pusɪ-] (inf) n = **puss**

put [put] (pt, pp **put**) vt (place) poner, colocar; (~ into) meter; (say) expresar; (a question) hacer; (estimate) estimar; **~ about** or **around** vt (rumour) diseminar; **~ across** vt (ideas etc) comunicar; **~ away** vt (store) guardar; **~ back** vt (replace) devolver a su lugar; (postpone) aplazar; **~ by** vt (money) guardar; **~ down** vt (on ground) poner en el suelo; (animal) sacrificar; (in writing) apuntar; (revolt etc) sofocar; (attribute): **to ~ sth down to** atribuir algo a; **~ forward** vt (ideas) presentar, proponer; **~ in** vt (complaint) presentar; (time) dedicar; **~ off** vt (postpone) aplazar; (discourage) desanimar; **~ on** vt ponerse; (light etc) encender; (play etc) presentar; (gain): **to ~ on weight** engordar; (brake) echar; (record, kettle etc) poner; (assume) adoptar; **~ out** vt (fire, light) apagar; (rubbish etc) sacar; (cat etc) echar; (one's hand) alargar; (inf: person): **to be ~ out** alterarse; **~ through** vt (TEL) poner; (plan etc) hacer aprobar; **~ up** vt (raise) levantar, alzar; (hang) colgar; (build) construir; (increase) aumentar; (accommodate) alojar; **~ up with** vt fus aguantar

putt [pʌt] n putt m, golpe m corto; **~ing green** n green m; minigolf m

putty ['pʌtɪ] n masilla

put-up ['putʌp] adj: **~ job** (BRIT) amaño

puzzle ['pʌzl] n rompecabezas m inv; (also: **crossword ~**) crucigrama m; (mystery) misterio ♦ vt dejar perplejo, confundir ♦ vi: **to ~ over sth** devanarse los sesos con algo; **puzzling** adj misterioso, extraño

pyjamas [pɪ'dʒɑːməz] (BRIT) npl pijama m

pylon ['paɪlən] n torre f de conducción eléctrica

pyramid ['pɪrəmɪd] n pirámide f

Pyrenees [pɪrə'niːz] npl: **the ~** los Pirineos

python ['paɪθən] n pitón m

Q, q

quack [kwæk] n graznido; (pej: doctor) curandero/a

quad [kwɒd] n abbr = **quadrangle**; **quadruplet**

quadrangle ['kwɒdræŋgl] n patio

quadruple [kwɒ'drupl] vt, vi cuadruplicar

quadruplets [kwɔː'druːplɪts] npl cuatrillizos/as

quail [kweɪl] n codorniz f ♦ vi: **to ~ at** or **before** amedrentarse ante

quaint [kweɪnt] adj extraño; (picturesque) pintoresco

quake [kweɪk] vi temblar ♦ n abbr = **earthquake**

Quaker ['kweɪkə*] n cuáquero/a

qualification [kwɒlɪfɪ'keɪʃən] n (ability) capacidad f; (often pl: diploma etc) título; (reservation) salvedad f

qualified ['kwɒlɪfaɪd] adj capacitado; (professionally) titulado; (limited) limitado

qualify ['kwɒlɪfaɪ] vt (make competent) capacitar; (modify) modificar ♦ vi (in competition): **to ~ (for)** calificarse (para); (pass examination(s)): **to ~ (as)** calificarse (de), graduarse (en); (be eligible): **to ~ (for)** reunir los requisitos (para)

quality ['kwɒlɪtɪ] n calidad f; (of person) cualidad f; **~ time** n tiempo dedicado a la familia y a los amigos

---
quality press

ⓘ *La expresión* **quality press** *se refiere a los periódicos que dan un tratamiento serio de las noticias, ofreciendo información detallada sobre un amplio espectro de temas y un análisis en profundidad de la actualidad. Por su tamaño, considerablemente mayor que el* *de los periódicos sensacionalistas, se les conoce también como "broadsheets".*

qualm [kwɑ:m] *n* escrúpulo

quandary ['kwɔndrɪ] *n*: **to be in a ~** tener dudas

quantity ['kwɔntɪtɪ] *n* cantidad *f*; **in ~** en grandes cantidades; **~ surveyor** *n* aparejador(a) *m/f*

quarantine ['kwɔrntiːn] *n* cuarentena

quarrel ['kwɔrl] *n* riña, pelea ♦ *vi* reñir, pelearse

quarry ['kwɔrɪ] *n* cantera

quart [kwɔːt] *n* ≈ litro

quarter ['kwɔːtə*] *n* cuarto, cuarta parte *f*; (*US: coin*) moneda de 25 centavos; (*of year*) trimestre *m*; (*district*) barrio ♦ *vt* dividir en cuartos; (*MIL: lodge*) alojar; **~s** *npl* (*barracks*) cuartel *m*; (*living ~s*) alojamiento; **a ~ of an hour** un cuarto de hora; **~ final** *n* cuarto de final; **~ly** *adj* trimestral ♦ *adv* cada 3 meses, trimestralmente

quartet(te) [kwɔː'tet] *n* cuarteto

quartz [kwɔːts] *n* cuarzo

quash [kwɔʃ] *vt* (*verdict*) anular

quaver ['kweɪvə*] (*BRIT*) *n* (*MUS*) corchea ♦ *vi* temblar

quay [kiː] *n* (*also*: **~side**) muelle *m*

queasy ['kwiːzɪ] *adj*: **to feel ~** tener náuseas

queen [kwiːn] *n* reina; (*CARDS etc*) dama; **~ mother** *n* reina madre

queer [kwɪə*] *adj* raro, extraño ♦ *n* (*inf: highly offensive*) maricón *m*

quell [kwel] *vt* (*feeling*) calmar; (*rebellion etc*) sofocar

quench [kwentʃ] *vt*: **to ~ one's thirst** apagar la sed

query ['kwɪərɪ] *n* (*question*) pregunta ♦ *vt* dudar de

quest [kwest] *n* busca, búsqueda

question ['kwestʃən] *n* pregunta; (*doubt*) duda; (*matter*) asunto, cuestión *f* ♦ *vt* (*doubt*) dudar de; (*interrogate*) interrogar, hacer preguntas a; **beyond ~** fuera de toda duda; **out of the ~** imposible; ni

hablar; **~able** *adj* dudoso; **~ mark** *n* punto de interrogación; **~naire** [-'neə*] *n* cuestionario

queue [kjuː] (*BRIT*) *n* cola ♦ *vi* (*also*: **~ up**) hacer cola

quibble ['kwɪbl] *vi* sutilizar

quick [kwɪk] *adj* rápido; (*agile*) ágil; (*mind*) listo ♦ *n*: **cut to the ~** (*fig*) herido en lo vivo; **be ~!** ¡date prisa!; **~en** *vt* apresurar ♦ *vi* apresurarse, darse prisa; **~ly** *adv* rápidamente, de prisa; **~sand** *n* arenas *fpl* movedizas; **~-witted** *adj* perspicaz

quid [kwɪd] (*BRIT: inf*) *n inv* libra

quiet ['kwaɪət] *adj* (*voice, music etc*) bajo; (*person, place*) tranquilo; (*ceremony*) íntimo ♦ *n* silencio; (*calm*) tranquilidad *f* ♦ *vt, vi* (*US*) = **~en**; **~en** (*also*: **~en down**) *vi* calmarse; (*grow silent*) callarse ♦ *vt* calmar; hacer callar; **~ly** *adv* tranquilamente; (*silently*) silenciosamente; **~ness** *n* silencio; tranquilidad *f*

quilt [kwɪlt] *n* edredón *m*

quin [kwɪn] *n abbr* = **quintuplet**

quintet(te) [kwɪn'tet] *n* quinteto

quintuplets [kwɪn'tjuːplɪts] *npl* quintillizos/as

quip [kwɪp] *n* pulla

quirk [kwɜːk] *n* peculiaridad *f*; (*accident*) capricho

quit [kwɪt] (*pt, pp* **quit** *or* **quitted**) *vt* dejar, abandonar; (*premises*) desocupar ♦ *vi* (*give up*) renunciar; (*resign*) dimitir

quite [kwaɪt] *adv* (*rather*) bastante; (*entirely*) completamente; **that's not ~ big enough** no acaba de ser lo bastante grande; **~ a few of them** un buen número de ellos; **~ (so)!** ¡así es!, ¡exactamente!

quits [kwɪts] *adj*: **~ (with)** en paz (con); **let's call it ~** dejémoslo en tablas

quiver ['kwɪvə*] *vi* estremecerse

quiz [kwɪz] *n* concurso ♦ *vt* interrogar; **~zical** *adj* burlón(ona)

quota ['kwəʊtə] *n* cuota

quotation [kwəʊ'teɪʃən] *n* cita; (*estimate*) presupuesto; **~ marks** *npl* comillas *fpl*

quote [kwəʊt] *n* cita; (*estimate*)

presupuesto ♦ *vt* citar; (*price*) cotizar ♦ *vi*:
to ~ from citar de; **~s** *npl* (*inverted commas*) comillas *fpl*

R, r

rabbi ['ræbaɪ] *n* rabino
rabbit ['ræbɪt] *n* conejo; **~ hutch** *n*
conejera
rabble ['ræbl] (*pej*) *n* chusma, populacho
rabies ['reɪbiːz] *n* rabia
RAC (*BRIT*) *n abbr* = **Royal Automobile Club**
rac(c)oon [rə'kuːn] *n* mapache *m*
race [reɪs] *n* carrera; (*species*) raza ♦ *vt*
(*horse*) hacer correr; (*engine*) acelerar ♦ *vi*
(*compete*) competir; (*run*) correr; (*pulse*)
latir a ritmo acelerado; **~ car** (*US*) *n*
= **racing car**; **~ car driver** (*US*) *n*
= **racing driver**; **~course** *n* hipódromo;
~horse *n* caballo de carreras; **~track** *n*
pista; (*for cars*) autódromo
racial ['reɪʃl] *adj* racial
racing ['reɪsɪŋ] *n* carreras *fpl*; **~ car** (*BRIT*)
n coche de carreras; **~ driver** (*BRIT*) *n*
corredor(a) *m/f* de coches
racism ['reɪsɪzəm] *n* racismo; **racist** [-sɪst]
adj, n racista *m/f*
rack [ræk] *n* (*also*: **luggage ~**) rejilla; (*shelf*)
estante *m*; (*also*: **roof ~**) baca,
portaequipajes *m inv*; (*dish ~*)
escurreplatos *m inv*; (*clothes ~*) percha
♦ *vt* atormentar; **to ~ one's brains**
devanarse los sesos
racket ['rækɪt] *n* (*for tennis*) raqueta;
(*noise*) ruido, estrépito; (*swindle*) estafa,
timo
racquet ['rækɪt] *n* raqueta
racy ['reɪsɪ] *adj* picante, salado
radar ['reɪdɑː*] *n* radar *m*
radiant ['reɪdɪənt] *adj* radiante (de
felicidad)
radiate ['reɪdɪeɪt] *vt* (*heat*) radiar; (*emotion*)
irradiar ♦ *vi* (*lines*) extenderse
radiation [reɪdɪ'eɪʃən] *n* radiación *f*
radiator ['reɪdɪeɪtə*] *n* radiador *m*

radical ['rædɪkl] *adj* radical
radii ['reɪdɪaɪ] *npl of* **radius**
radio ['reɪdɪəu] *n* radio *f*; **on the ~** por
radio
radio... [reɪdɪəu] *prefix*: **~active** *adj*
radioactivo; **~graphy** [reɪdɪ'ɔgrəfɪ] *n*
radiografía; **~logy** [reɪdɪ'ɔlədʒɪ] *n*
radiología
radio station *n* emisora
radiotherapy [-'θerəpɪ] *n* radioterapia
radish ['rædɪʃ] *n* rábano
radius ['reɪdɪəs] (*pl* **radii**) *n* radio
RAF *n abbr* = **Royal Air Force**
raffle ['ræfl] *n* rifa, sorteo
raft [rɑːft] *n* balsa; (*also*: **life ~**) balsa
salvavidas
rafter ['rɑːftə*] *n* viga
rag [ræg] *n* (*piece of cloth*) trapo; (*torn
cloth*) harapo; (*pej: newspaper*)
periodicucho; (*for charity*) *actividades
estudiantiles benéficas*; **~s** *npl* (*torn
clothes*) harapos *mpl*; **~ doll** *n* muñeca
de trapo
rage [reɪdʒ] *n* rabia, furor *m* ♦ *vi* (*person*)
rabiar, estar furioso; (*storm*) bramar; **it's
all the ~** (*very fashionable*) está muy de
moda
ragged ['rægɪd] *adj* (*edge*) desigual,
mellado; (*appearance*) andrajoso,
harapiento
raid [reɪd] *n* (*MIL*) incursión *f*; (*criminal*)
asalto; (*by police*) redada ♦ *vt* invadir,
atacar; asaltar
rail [reɪl] *n* (*on stair*) barandilla, pasamanos
m inv; (*on bridge, balcony*) pretil *m*; (*of
ship*) barandilla; (*also*: **towel ~**) toallero;
~s *npl* (*RAIL*) vía; **by ~** por ferrocarril;
~ing(s) *n(pl)* vallado; **~road** (*US*) *n*
= **~way**; **~way** (*BRIT*) *n* ferrocarril *m*, vía
férrea; **~way line** (*BRIT*) *n* línea (de
ferrocarril); **~wayman** (*BRIT irreg*) *n*
ferroviario; **~way station** (*BRIT*) *n*
estación *f* de ferrocarril
rain [reɪn] *n* lluvia ♦ *vi* llover; **in the ~** bajo
la lluvia; **it's ~ing** llueve, está lloviendo;
~bow *n* arco iris; **~coat** *n* impermeable
m; **~drop** *n* gota de lluvia; **~fall** *n* lluvia;

~forest *n* selvas *fpl* tropicales; **~y** *adj* lluvioso

raise [reɪz] *n* aumento ♦ *vt* levantar; (*increase*) aumentar; (*improve: morale*) subir; (*: standards*) mejorar; (*doubts*) suscitar; (*a question*) plantear; (*cattle, family*) criar; (*crop*) cultivar; (*army*) reclutar; (*loan*) obtener; **to ~ one's voice** alzar la voz

raisin ['reɪzn] *n* pasa de Corinto

rake [reɪk] *n* (*tool*) rastrillo; (*person*) libertino ♦ *vt* (*garden*) rastrillar

rally ['rælɪ] *n* (*POL etc*) reunión *f*, mitin *m*; (*AUT*) rallye *m*; (*TENNIS*) peloteo ♦ *vt* reunir ♦ *vi* recuperarse; **~ round** *vt fus* (*fig*) dar apoyo a

RAM [ræm] *n abbr* (= *random access memory*) RAM *f*

ram [ræm] *n* carnero; (*also:* **battering ~**) ariete *m* ♦ *vt* (*crash into*) dar contra, chocar con; (*push: fist etc*) empujar con fuerza

ramble ['ræmbl] *n* caminata, excursión *f* en el campo ♦ *vi* (*pej: also:* **~ on**) divagar; **~r** *n* excursionista *m/f*; (*BOT*) trepadora; **rambling** *adj* (*speech*) inconexo; (*house*) laberíntico; (*BOT*) trepador(a)

ramp [ræmp] *n* rampa; **on/off ~** (*US: AUT*) vía de acceso/salida

rampage [ræm'peɪdʒ] *n*: **to be on the ~** desmandarse ♦ *vi*: **they went rampaging through the town** recorrieron la ciudad armando alboroto

rampant ['ræmpənt] *adj* (*disease etc*): **to be ~** estar extendiéndose mucho

ram raid *vt* atracar (*rompiendo el escaparate con un coche*)

ramshackle ['ræmʃækl] *adj* destartalado

ran [ræn] *pt of* **run**

ranch [rɑːntʃ] *n* hacienda, estancia; **~er** *n* ganadero

rancid ['rænsɪd] *adj* rancio

rancour ['ræŋkə*] (*US* **rancor**) *n* rencor *m*

random ['rændəm] *adj* fortuito, sin orden; (*COMPUT, MATH*) aleatorio ♦ *n*: **at ~** al azar

randy ['rændɪ] (*BRIT: inf*) *adj* cachondo

rang [ræŋ] *pt of* **ring**

range [reɪndʒ] *n* (*of mountains*) cadena de montañas, cordillera; (*of missile*) alcance *m*; (*of voice*) registro; (*series*) serie *f*; (*of products*) surtido; (*BRIT: also:* **kitchen ~**) fogón *m* ♦ *vt* (*place*) colocar; (*arrange*) arreglar ♦ *vi*: **to ~ over** (*extend*) extenderse por; **to ~ from ... to ...** oscilar entre ... y ...

ranger [reɪndʒə*] *n* guardabosques *m inv*

rank [ræŋk] *n* (*row*) fila; (*MIL*) rango; (*status*) categoría; (*BRIT: also:* **taxi ~**) parada de taxis ♦ *vi*: **to ~ among** figurar entre ♦ *adj* fétido, rancio; **the ~ and file** (*fig*) la base

ransack ['rænsæk] *vt* (*search*) registrar; (*plunder*) saquear

ransom ['rænsəm] *n* rescate *m*; **to hold to ~** (*fig*) hacer chantaje a

rant [rænt] *vi* divagar, desvariar

rap [ræp] *vt* golpear, dar un golpecito en ♦ *n* (*music*) rap *m*

rape [reɪp] *n* violación *f*; (*BOT*) colza ♦ *vt* violar; **~ (seed) oil** *n* aceite *m* de colza

rapid ['ræpɪd] *adj* rápido; **~ity** [rə'pɪdɪtɪ] *n* rapidez *f*; **~s** *npl* (*GEO*) rápidos *mpl*

rapist ['reɪpɪst] *n* violador *m*

rapport [ræ'pɔː*] *n* simpatía

rapturous ['ræptʃərəs] *adj* extático

rare [reə*] *adj* raro, poco común; (*CULIN: steak*) poco hecho

rarely ['reəlɪ] *adv* pocas veces

raring ['reərɪŋ] *adj*: **to be ~ to go** (*inf*) tener muchas ganas de empezar

rascal ['rɑːskl] *n* pillo, pícaro

rash [ræʃ] *adj* imprudente, precipitado ♦ *n* (*MED*) sarpullido, erupción *f* (*cutánea*); (*of events*) serie *f*

rasher ['ræʃə*] *n* lonja

raspberry ['rɑːzbərɪ] *n* frambuesa

rasping ['rɑːspɪŋ] *adj*: **a ~ noise** un ruido áspero

rat [ræt] *n* rata

rate [reɪt] *n* (*ratio*) razón *f*; (*price*) precio; (*: of hotel etc*) tarifa; (*of interest*) tipo; (*speed*) velocidad *f* ♦ *vt* tasar; (*estimate*) estimar; **~s** *npl* (*BRIT: property tax*) impuesto municipal; (*fees*) tarifa; **to ~**

sth/sb as considerar algo/a uno como; **~able value** (*BRIT*) *n* valor *m* impuesto; **~payer** (*BRIT*) *n* contribuyente *m/f*

rather ['rɑːðəʳ] *adv*: **it's ~ expensive** es algo caro; (*too much*) es demasiado caro; (*to some extent*) más bien; **there's ~ a lot** hay bastante; **I would** *or* **I'd ~ go** preferiría ir; **or ~** mejor dicho

rating ['reɪtɪŋ] *n* tasación *f*; (*score*) índice *m*; (*of ship*) clase *f*; **~s** *npl* (*RADIO, TV*) niveles *mpl* de audiencia

ratio ['reɪʃɪəu] *n* razón *f*; **in the ~ of 100 to 1** a razón de 100 a 1

ration ['ræʃən] *n* ración *f* ♦ *vt* racionar; **~s** *npl* víveres *mpl*

rational ['ræʃənl] *adj* (*solution, reasoning*) lógico, razonable; (*person*) cuerdo, sensato; **~e** [-'nɑːl] *n* razón *f* fundamental; **~ize** *vt* justificar

rat race *n* lucha incesante por la supervivencia

rattle ['rætl] *n* golpeteo; (*of train etc*) traqueteo; (*for baby*) sonaja, sonajero ♦ *vi* castañetear; (*car, bus*): **to ~ along** traquetear ♦ *vt* hacer sonar agitando; **~snake** *n* serpiente *f* de cascabel

raucous ['rɔːkəs] *adj* estridente, ronco

ravage ['rævɪdʒ] *vt* hacer estragos en, destrozar; **~s** *npl* estragos *mpl*

rave [reɪv] *vi* (*in anger*) encolerizarse; (*with enthusiasm*) entusiasmarse; (*MED*) delirar, desvariar ♦ *n* (*inf*: *party*) rave *m*

raven ['reɪvən] *n* cuervo

ravenous ['rævənəs] *adj* hambriento

ravine [rə'viːn] *n* barranco

raving ['reɪvɪŋ] *adj*: **~ lunatic** loco/a de atar

ravishing ['rævɪʃɪŋ] *adj* encantador(a)

raw [rɔː] *adj* crudo; (*not processed*) bruto; (*sore*) vivo; (*inexperienced*) novato, inexperto; **~ deal** (*inf*) *n* injusticia; **~ material** *n* materia prima

ray [reɪ] *n* rayo; **~ of hope** (rayo de) esperanza

raze [reɪz] *vt* arrasar

razor ['reɪzəʳ] *n* (*open*) navaja; (*safety ~*) máquina de afeitar; (*electric ~*) máquina

(eléctrica) de afeitar; **~ blade** *n* hoja de afeitar

Rd *abbr* = **road**

re [riː] *prep* con referencia a

reach [riːtʃ] *n* alcance *m*; (*of river etc*) extensión *f* entre dos recodos ♦ *vt* alcanzar, llegar a; (*achieve*) lograr ♦ *vi* extenderse; **within ~** al alcance (de la mano); **out of ~** fuera del alcance; **~ out** *vt* (*hand*) tender ♦ *vi*: **to ~ out for sth** alargar *or* tender la mano para tomar algo

react [riː'ækt] *vi* reaccionar; **~ion** [-'ækʃən] *n* reacción *f*

reactor [riː'æktəʳ] *n* (*also*: **nuclear ~**) reactor *m* (nuclear)

read [riːd, *pt, pp* rɛd] (*pt, pp* **read**) *vi* leer ♦ *vt* leer; (*understand*) entender; (*study*) estudiar; **~ out** *vt* leer en alta voz; **~able** *adj* (*writing*) legible; (*book*) leíble; **~er** *n* lector(a) *m/f*; (*BRIT*: *at university*) profesor(a) *m/f* adjunto/a; **~ership** *n* (*of paper etc*) (número de) lectores *mpl*

readily ['rɛdɪlɪ] *adv* (*willingly*) de buena gana; (*easily*) fácilmente; (*quickly*) en seguida

readiness ['rɛdɪnɪs] *n* buena voluntad *f*; (*preparedness*) preparación *f*; **in ~** (*prepared*) listo, preparado

reading ['riːdɪŋ] *n* lectura; (*on instrument*) indicación *f*

ready ['rɛdɪ] *adj* listo, preparado; (*willing*) dispuesto; (*available*) disponible ♦ *adv*: **~-cooked** listo para comer ♦ *n*: **at the ~** (*MIL*) listo para tirar; **to get ~** *vi* prepararse ♦ *vt* preparar; **~-made** *adj* confeccionado; **~-to-wear** *adj* confeccionado

real [rɪəl] *adj* verdadero, auténtico; **in ~ terms** en términos reales; **~ estate** *n* bienes *mpl* raíces; **~istic** [-'lɪstɪk] *adj* realista

reality [riː'ælɪtɪ] *n* realidad *f*

realization [rɪəlaɪ'zeɪʃən] *n* comprensión *f*; (*fulfilment, COMM*) realización *f*

realize ['rɪəlaɪz] *vt* (*understand*) darse cuenta de

really ['rɪəlɪ] *adv* realmente; (*for emphasis*) verdaderamente; (*actually*): **what ~ happened** lo que pasó en realidad; **~?** ¿de veras?; **~!** (*annoyance*) ¡vamos!, ¡por favor!

realm [relm] *n* reino; (*fig*) esfera

realtor ® ['rɪəltɔː*] (*US*) *n* corredor(a) *m/f* de bienes raíces

reap [riːp] *vt* segar; (*fig*) cosechar, recoger

reappear [riːə'pɪə*] *vi* reaparecer

rear [rɪə*] *adj* trasero ♦ *n* parte *f* trasera ♦ *vt* (*cattle, family*) criar ♦ *vi* (*also: ~ up*) (*animal*) encabritarse; **~guard** *n* retaguardia

rearmament [riːˈɑːməmənt] *n* rearme *m*

rearrange [riːəˈreɪndʒ] *vt* ordenar *or* arreglar de nuevo

rear-view mirror *n* (*AUT*) (espejo) retrovisor *m*

reason ['riːzn] *n* razón *f* ♦ *vi*: **to ~ with sb** tratar de que uno entre en razón; **it stands to ~ that** es lógico que; **~able** *adj* razonable; (*sensible*) sensato; **~ably** *adv* razonablemente; **~ing** *n* razonamiento, argumentos *mpl*

reassurance [riːəˈʃuərəns] *n* consuelo

reassure [riːəˈʃuə*] *vt* tranquilizar, alentar; **to ~ sb that** tranquilizar a uno asegurando que

rebate ['riːbeɪt] *n* (*on tax etc*) desgravación *f*

rebel [*n* 'rɛbl, *vi* rɪˈbɛl] *n* rebelde *m/f* ♦ *vi* rebelarse, sublevarse; **~lious** [rɪˈbɛljəs] *adj* rebelde; (*child*) revoltoso

rebirth ['riːbɜːθ] *n* renacimiento

rebound [*vi* rɪˈbaʊnd, *n* 'riːbaʊnd] *vi* (*ball*) rebotar ♦ *n* rebote *m*; **on the ~** (*also fig*) de rebote

rebuff [rɪˈbʌf] *n* desaire *m*, rechazo

rebuild [riːˈbɪld] (*irreg*) *vt* reconstruir

rebuke [rɪˈbjuːk] *n* reprimenda ♦ *vt* reprender

rebut [rɪˈbʌt] *vt* rebatir

recall [*vb* rɪˈkɔːl, *n* 'riːkɔːl] *vt* (*remember*) recordar; (*ambassador etc*) retirar ♦ *n* recuerdo; retirada

recap ['riːkæp], **recapitulate** [riːkəˈpɪtjuleɪt] *vt, vi* recapitular

rec'd *abbr* (= *received*) rbdo

recede [rɪˈsiːd] *vi* (*memory*) ir borrándose; (*hair*) retroceder; **receding** *adj* (*forehead, chin*) huidizo; **to have a receding hairline** tener entradas

receipt [rɪˈsiːt] *n* (*document*) recibo; (*for parcel etc*) acuse *m* de recibo; (*act of receiving*) recepción *f*; **~s** *npl* (*COMM*) ingresos *mpl*

receive [rɪˈsiːv] *vt* recibir; (*guest*) acoger; (*wound*) sufrir; **~r** *n* (*TEL*) auricular *m*; (*RADIO*) receptor *m*; (*of stolen goods*) perista *m/f*; (*COMM*) administrador *m* jurídico

recent ['riːsnt] *adj* reciente; **~ly** *adv* recientemente; **~ly arrived** recién llegado

receptacle [rɪˈsɛptɪkl] *n* receptáculo

reception [rɪˈsɛpʃən] *n* recepción *f*; (*welcome*) acogida; **~ desk** *n* recepción *f*; **~ist** *n* recepcionista *m/f*

recess [rɪˈsɛs] *n* (*in room*) hueco; (*for bed*) nicho; (*secret place*) escondrijo; (*POL etc*: *holiday*) clausura

recession [rɪˈsɛʃən] *n* recesión *f*

recipe ['rɛsɪpɪ] *n* receta; (*for disaster, success*) fórmula

recipient [rɪˈsɪpɪənt] *n* recibidor(a) *m/f*; (*of letter*) destinatario/a

recital [rɪˈsaɪtl] *n* recital *m*

recite [rɪˈsaɪt] *vt* (*poem*) recitar

reckless ['rɛkləs] *adj* temerario, imprudente; (*driving, driver*) peligroso; **~ly** *adv* imprudentemente; de modo peligroso

reckon ['rɛkən] *vt* calcular; (*consider*) considerar; (*think*): **I ~ that ...** me parece que ...; **~ on** *vt fus* contar con; **~ing** *n* cálculo

reclaim [rɪˈkleɪm] *vt* (*land, waste*) recuperar; (*land: from sea*) rescatar; (*demand back*) reclamar

reclamation [rɛkləˈmeɪʃən] *n* (*of land*) acondicionamiento de tierras

recline [rɪˈklaɪn] *vi* reclinarse; **reclining** *adj* (*seat*) reclinable

recluse [rɪˈkluːs] *n* recluso/a

recognition [rekəg'nɪʃən] n reconocimiento; **transformed beyond ~** irreconocible

recognizable ['rekəgnaɪzəbl] adj: **~ (by)** reconocible (por)

recognize ['rekəgnaɪz] vt: **to ~ (by/as)** reconocer (por/como)

recoil [vi rɪ'kɔɪl, n 'riːkɔɪl] vi (person): **to ~ from doing sth** retraerse de hacer algo ♦ n (of gun) retroceso

recollect [rekə'lekt] vt recordar, acordarse de; **~ion** [-'lekʃən] n recuerdo

recommend [rekə'mend] vt recomendar

reconcile ['rekənsaɪl] vt (two people) reconciliar; (two facts) compaginar; **to ~ o.s. to sth** conformarse a algo

recondition [riːkən'dɪʃən] vt (machine) reacondicionar

reconnoitre [rekə'nɔɪtə*] (US **reconnoiter**) vt, vi (MIL) reconocer

reconsider [riːkən'sɪdə*] vt repensar

reconstruct [riːkən'strʌkt] vt reconstruir

record [n 'rekɔːd, vt rɪ'kɔːd] n (MUS) disco; (of meeting etc) acta; (register) registro, partida; (file) archivo; (also: **criminal ~**) antecedentes mpl; (written) expediente m; (SPORT, COMPUT) récord m ♦ vt registrar; (MUS: song etc) grabar; **in ~ time** en un tiempo récord; **off the ~** adj no oficial ♦ adv confidencialmente; **~ card** n (in file) ficha; **~ed delivery** (BRIT) n (POST) entrega con acuse de recibo; **~er** n (MUS) flauta de pico; **~ holder** n (SPORT) actual poseedor(a) m/f del récord; **~ing** n (MUS) grabación f; **~ player** n tocadiscos m inv

recount [rɪ'kaunt] vt contar

re-count ['riːkaunt] n (POL: of votes) segundo escrutinio

recoup [rɪ'kuːp] vt: **to ~ one's losses** recuperar las pérdidas

recourse [rɪ'kɔːs] n: **to have ~ to** recurrir a

recover [rɪ'kʌvə*] vt recuperar ♦ vi (from illness, shock) recuperarse; **~y** n recuperación f

recreation [rekrɪ'eɪʃən] n recreo; **~al** adj de recreo; **~al drug** droga recreativa

recruit [rɪ'kruːt] n recluta m/f ♦ vt reclutar; (staff) contratar

rectangle ['rektæŋgl] n rectángulo; **rectangular** [-'tæŋgjulə*] adj rectangular

rectify ['rektɪfaɪ] vt rectificar

rector ['rektə*] n (REL) párroco; **~y** n casa del párroco

recuperate [rɪ'kuːpəreɪt] vi reponerse, restablecerse

recur [rɪ'kəː*] vi repetirse; (pain, illness) producirse de nuevo; **~rence** [rɪ'kʌrens] n repetición f; **~rent** [rɪ'kʌrent] adj repetido

recycle [riː'saɪkl] vt reciclar

red [red] n rojo ♦ adj rojo; (hair) pelirrojo; (wine) tinto; **to be in the ~** (account) estar en números rojos; (business) tener un saldo negativo; **to give sb the ~ carpet treatment** recibir a uno con todos los honores; **R~ Cross** n Cruz f Roja; **~currant** n grosella roja; **~den** vt enrojecer ♦ vi enrojecerse

redeem [rɪ'diːm] vt redimir; (promises) cumplir; (sth in pawn) desempeñar; (fig, also REL) rescatar; **~ing** adj: **~ing feature** rasgo bueno or favorable

redeploy [riːdɪ'plɔɪ] vt (resources) reorganizar

red: **~-haired** adj pelirrojo; **~-handed** adj: **to be caught ~-handed** cogerse (SP) or pillarse (AM) con las manos en la masa; **~head** n pelirrojo/a; **~ herring** n (fig) pista falsa; **~-hot** adj candente

redirect [riːdaɪ'rekt] vt (mail) reexpedir

red light n: **to go through a ~** (AUT) pasar la luz roja; **red-light district** n barrio rojo

redo [riː'duː] (irreg) vt rehacer

redress [rɪ'dres] vt reparar

Red Sea n: **the ~** el mar Rojo

redskin ['redskɪn] n piel roja m/f

red tape n (fig) trámites mpl

reduce [rɪ'djuːs] vt reducir; **to ~ sb to tears** hacer llorar a uno; **to be ~d to begging** no quedarle a uno otro remedio que pedir limosna; **"~ speed now"** (AUT) "reduzca la velocidad"; **at a ~d price** (of goods) (a precio) rebajado; **reduction** [rɪ'dʌkʃən] n reducción f; (of price) rebaja; (discount) descuento; (smaller-scale copy) copia reducida

redundancy [rɪ'dʌndənsɪ] n (dismissal) despido; (unemployment) desempleo

redundant [rɪ'dʌndnt] adj (BRIT: worker) parado, sin trabajo; (detail, object) superfluo; **to be made ~** quedar(se) sin trabajo

reed [riːd] n (BOT) junco, caña; (MUS) lengüeta

reef [riːf] n (at sea) arrecife m

reek [riːk] vi: **to ~ (of)** apestar (a)

reel [riːl] n carrete m, bobina; (of film) rollo; (dance) baile m escocés ♦ vt (also: ~ **up**) devanar; (also: ~ **in**) sacar ♦ vi (sway) tambalear(se)

ref [ref] (inf) n abbr = **referee**

refectory [rɪ'fektərɪ] n comedor m

refer [rɪ'fɜː*] vt (send: patient) referir; (: matter) remitir ♦ vi: **to ~ to** (allude to) referirse a, aludir a; (apply to) relacionarse con; (consult) consultar

referee [refə'riː] n árbitro; (BRIT: for job application): **to be a ~ for sb** proporcionar referencias a uno ♦ vt (match) arbitrar en

reference ['refrəns] n referencia; (for job application: letter) carta de recomendación; **with ~ to** (COMM: in letter) me remito a; **~ book** n libro de consulta; **~ number** n número de referencia

refill [vt riː'fɪl, n 'riːfɪl] vt rellenar ♦ n repuesto, recambio

refine [rɪ'faɪn] vt refinar; **~d** adj (person) fino; **~ment** n cultura, educación f; (of system) refinamiento

reflect [rɪ'flekt] vt reflejar ♦ vi (think) reflexionar, pensar; **it ~s badly/well on him** le perjudica/le hace honor; **~ion** [-'flekʃən] n (act) reflexión f; (image) reflejo; (criticism) crítica; **on ~ion** pensándolo bien; **~or** n (AUT) captafaros m inv; (of light, heat) reflector m

reflex ['riːfleks] adj, n reflejo; **~ive**

[rɪ'fleksɪv] adj (LING) reflexivo

reform [rɪ'fɔːm] n reforma ♦ vt reformar; **~atory** (US) n reformatorio

refrain [rɪ'freɪn] vi: **to ~ from doing** abstenerse de hacer ♦ n estribillo

refresh [rɪ'freʃ] vt refrescar; **~er course** (BRIT) n curso de repaso; **~ing** adj refrescante; **~ments** npl refrescos mpl

refrigerator [rɪ'frɪdʒəreɪtə*] n nevera (SP), refrigeradora (AM)

refuel [riː'fjuəl] vi repostar (combustible)

refuge ['refjuːdʒ] n refugio, asilo; **to take ~ in** refugiarse en

refugee [refju'dʒiː] n refugiado/a

refund [n 'riːfʌnd, vb rɪ'fʌnd] n reembolso ♦ vt devolver, reembolsar

refurbish [riː'fɜːbɪʃ] vt restaurar, renovar

refusal [rɪ'fjuːzəl] n negativa; **to have first ~ on** tener la primera opción a

refuse[1] ['refjuːs] n basura; **~ collection** n recolección f de basuras

refuse[2] [rɪ'fjuːz] vt rechazar; (invitation) declinar; (permission) denegar ♦ vi: **to ~ to do sth** negarse a hacer algo; (horse) rehusar

regain [rɪ'geɪn] vt recobrar, recuperar

regal ['riːgl] adj regio, real

regard [rɪ'gɑːd] n mirada; (esteem) respeto; (attention) consideración f ♦ vt (consider) considerar; **to give one's ~s to** saludar de su parte a; **"with kindest ~s"** "con muchos recuerdos"; **~ing, as ~s, with ~ to** con respecto a, en cuanto a; **~less** adv a pesar de todo; **~less of** sin reparar en

régime [reɪ'ʒiːm] n régimen m

regiment ['redʒɪmənt] n regimiento; **~al** [-'mentl] adj militar

region ['riːdʒən] n región f; **in the ~ of** (fig) alrededor de; **~al** adj regional

register ['redʒɪstə*] n registro ♦ vt registrar; (birth) declarar; (car) matricular; (letter) certificar; (subj: instrument) marcar, indicar ♦ vi (at hotel) registrarse; (as student) matricularse; (make impression) producir impresión; **~ed** adj (letter, parcel) certificado; **~ed**

trademark *n* marca registrada
registrar [ˈredʒistrɑː*] *n* secretario/a (del registro civil)
registration [redʒisˈtreiʃən] *n* (*act*) declaración *f*; (AUT: *also:* ~ **number**) matrícula
registry [ˈredʒistri] *n* registro; ~ **office** (BRIT) *n* registro civil; **to get married in a** ~ **office** casarse por lo civil
regret [riˈgret] *n* sentimiento, pesar *m* ♦ *vt* sentir, lamentar; ~**fully** *adv* con pesar; ~**table** *adj* lamentable
regular [ˈregjulə*] *adj* regular; (*soldier*) profesional; (*usual*) habitual; (: *doctor*) de cabecera ♦ *n* (*client etc*) cliente/a *m/f* habitual; ~**ly** *adv* con regularidad; (*often*) repetidas veces
regulate [ˈregjuleit] *vt* controlar; **regulation** [-ˈleiʃən] *n* (*rule*) regla, reglamento
rehearsal [riˈhəːsəl] *n* ensayo
rehearse [riˈhəːs] *vt* ensayar
reign [rein] *n* reinado; (*fig*) predominio ♦ *vi* reinar; (*fig*) imperar
reimburse [riːimˈbəːs] *vt* reembolsar
rein [rein] *n* (*for horse*) rienda
reindeer [ˈreindiə*] *n inv* reno
reinforce [riːinˈfɔːs] *vt* reforzar; ~**d concrete** *n* hormigón *m* armado; ~**ments** *npl* (MIL) refuerzos *mpl*
reinstate [riːinˈsteit] *vt* reintegrar; (*tax, law*) reinstaurar
reiterate [riːˈitəreit] *vt* reiterar, repetir
reject [*n* ˈriːdʒekt, *vb* riˈdʒekt] *n* (*thing*) desecho ♦ *vt* rechazar; (*suggestion*) descartar; (*coin*) expulsar; ~**ion** [riˈdʒekʃən] *n* rechazo
rejoice [riˈdʒɔis] *vi*: **to** ~ **at** *or* **over** regocijarse *or* alegrarse de
rejuvenate [riˈdʒuːvəneit] *vt* rejuvenecer
relapse [riˈlæps] *n* recaída
relate [riˈleit] *vt* (*tell*) contar, relatar; (*connect*) relacionar ♦ *vi* relacionarse; ~**d** *adj* afín; (*person*) emparentado; ~**d to** (*subject*) relacionado con; **relating to** *prep* referente a
relation [riˈleiʃən] *n* (*person*) familiar *m/f*,

pariente/a *m/f*; (*link*) relación *f*; ~**s** *npl* (*relatives*) familiares *mpl*; ~**ship** *n* relación *f*; (*personal*) relaciones *fpl*; (*also:* **family** ~**ship**) parentesco
relative [ˈrelətiv] *n* pariente/a *m/f*, familiar *m/f* ♦ *adj* relativo; ~**ly** *adv* (*comparatively*) relativamente
relax [riˈlæks] *vi* descansar; (*unwind*) relajarse ♦ *vt* (*one's grip*) soltar, aflojar; (*control*) relajar; (*mind, person*) descansar; ~**ation** [riːlækˈseiʃən] *n* descanso; (*of rule, control*) relajamiento; (*entertainment*) diversión *f*; ~**ed** *adj* relajado; (*tranquil*) tranquilo; ~**ing** *adj* relajante
relay [ˈriːlei] *n* (*race*) carrera de relevos ♦ *vt* (RADIO, TV) retransmitir
release [riˈliːs] *n* (*liberation*) liberación *f*; (*from prison*) puesta en libertad; (*of gas etc*) escape *m*; (*of film etc*) estreno; (*of record*) lanzamiento ♦ *vt* (*prisoner*) poner en libertad; (*gas*) despedir, arrojar; (*from wreckage*) soltar; (*catch, spring etc*) desenganchar; (*film*) estrenar; (*book*) publicar; (*news*) difundir
relegate [ˈrelegeit] *vt* relegar; (BRIT: SPORT): **to be** ~**d to** bajar a
relent [riˈlent] *vi* ablandarse; ~**less** *adj* implacable
relevant [ˈreləvənt] *adj* (*fact*) pertinente; ~ **to** relacionado con
reliable [riˈlaiəbl] *adj* (*person, firm*) de confianza, de fiar; (*method, machine*) seguro; (*source*) fidedigno; **reliably** *adv*: **to be reliably informed that ...** saber de fuente fidedigna que ...
reliance [riˈlaiəns] *n*: ~ (**on**) dependencia (de)
relic [ˈrelik] *n* (REL) reliquia; (*of the past*) vestigio
relief [riˈliːf] *n* (*from pain, anxiety*) alivio; (*help, supplies*) socorro, ayuda; (ART, GEO) relieve *m*
relieve [riˈliːv] *vt* (*pain*) aliviar; (*bring help to*) ayudar, socorrer; (*take over from*) sustituir; (: *guard*) relevar; **to** ~ **sb of sth** quitar algo a uno; **to** ~ **o.s.** hacer sus necesidades

religion [rɪˈlɪdʒən] n religión f; **religious** adj religioso

relinquish [rɪˈlɪŋkwɪʃ] vt abandonar; (plan, habit) renunciar a

relish [ˈrɛlɪʃ] n (CULIN) salsa; (enjoyment) entusiasmo ♦ vt (food etc) saborear; (enjoy): **to ~ sth** hacerle mucha ilusión a uno algo

relocate [riːləʊˈkeɪt] vt cambiar de lugar, mudar ♦ vi mudarse

reluctance [rɪˈlʌktəns] n renuencia

reluctant [rɪˈlʌktənt] adj renuente; **~ly** adv de mala gana

rely on [rɪˈlaɪ-] vt fus depender de; (trust) contar con

remain [rɪˈmeɪn] vi (survive) quedar; (be left) sobrar; (continue) quedar(se), permanecer; **~der** n resto; **~ing** adj que queda(n); (surviving) restante(s); **~s** npl restos mpl

remand [rɪˈmɑːnd] n: **on ~** detenido (bajo custodia) ♦ vt: **to be ~ed in custody** quedar detenido bajo custodia; **~ home** (BRIT) n reformatorio

remark [rɪˈmɑːk] n comentario ♦ vt comentar; **~able** adj (outstanding) extraordinario

remarry [riːˈmærɪ] vi volver a casarse

remedial [rɪˈmiːdɪəl] adj de recuperación

remedy [ˈrɛmədɪ] n remedio ♦ vt remediar, curar

remember [rɪˈmɛmbəʳ] vt recordar, acordarse de; (bear in mind) tener presente; (send greetings to): **~ me to him** dale recuerdos de mi parte; **remembrance** n recuerdo; **R~ Day** n ≈ día en el que se recuerda a los caídos en las dos guerras mundiales

---

Remembrance Day

ℹ️ *En el Reino Unido el domingo más próximo al 11 de noviembre se conoce como* Remembrance Sunday *o* Remembrance Day, *aniversario de la firma del armisticio de 1918 que puso fin a la Primera Guerra Mundial. Ese día, a las once de la mañana (hora en que se*

---

firmó el armisticio), se recuerda a los que murieron en las dos guerras mundiales con dos minutos de silencio ante los monumentos a los caídos. Allí se colocan coronas de amapolas, flor que también se suele llevar prendida en el pecho tras pagar un donativo destinado a los inválidos de guerra.

---

remind [rɪˈmaɪnd] vt: **to ~ sb to do sth** recordar a uno que haga algo; **to ~ sb of sth** (of fact) recordar algo a uno; **she ~s me of her mother** me recuerda a su madre; **~er** n notificación f; (memento) recuerdo

reminisce [rɛmɪˈnɪs] vi recordar (viejas historias); **reminiscent** adj: **to be reminiscent of sth** recordar algo

remiss [rɪˈmɪs] adj descuidado; **it was ~ of him** fue un descuido de su parte

remission [rɪˈmɪʃən] n remisión f; (of prison sentence) disminución f de pena; (REL) perdón m

remit [rɪˈmɪt] vt (send: money) remitir, enviar; **~tance** n remesa, envío

remnant [ˈrɛmnənt] n resto; (of cloth) retal m; **~s** npl (COMM) restos mpl de serie

remorse [rɪˈmɔːs] n remordimientos mpl; **~ful** adj arrepentido; **~less** adj (fig) implacable, inexorable

remote [rɪˈməʊt] adj (distant) lejano; (person) distante; **~ control** n telecontrol m; **~ly** adv remotamente; (slightly) levemente

remould [ˈriːməʊld] (BRIT) n (tyre) neumático or llanta (AM) recauchutado/a

removable [rɪˈmuːvəbl] adj (detachable) separable

removal [rɪˈmuːvəl] n (taking away) el quitar; (BRIT: from house) mudanza; (from office: dismissal) destitución f; (MED) extirpación f; **~ van** (BRIT) n camión m de mudanzas

remove [rɪˈmuːv] vt quitar; (employee) destituir; (name: from list) tachar, borrar; (doubt) disipar; (abuse) suprimir, acabar con; (MED) extirpar

Renaissance [rɪˈneɪsɑ̃ns] *n*: **the ~** el Renacimiento

render [ˈrɛndəʳ] *vt* (*thanks*) dar; (*aid*) proporcionar, prestar; (*make*): **to ~ sth useless** hacer algo inútil; **~ing** *n* (*MUS etc*) interpretación *f*

rendezvous [ˈrɔndɪvuː] *n* cita

renew [rɪˈnjuː] *vt* renovar; (*resume*) reanudar; (*loan etc*) prorrogar; **~able** *adj* renovable; **~al** *n* reanudación *f*; prórroga

renounce [rɪˈnauns] *vt* renunciar a; (*right, inheritance*) renunciar

renovate [ˈrɛnəveɪt] *vt* renovar

renown [rɪˈnaun] *n* renombre *m*; **~ed** *adj* renombrado

rent [rɛnt] *n* (*for house*) arriendo, renta ♦ *vt* alquilar; **~al** *n* (*for television, car*) alquiler *m*

rep [rɛp] *n abbr* = **representative**; **repertory**

repair [rɪˈpɛəʳ] *n* reparación *f*, compostura ♦ *vt* reparar, componer; (*shoes*) remendar; **in good/bad ~** en buen/mal estado; **~ kit** *n* caja de herramientas

repatriate [riːˈpætrɪeɪt] *vt* repatriar

repay [riːˈpeɪ] (*irreg*) *vt* (*money*) devolver, reembolsar; (*person*) pagar; (*debt*) liquidar; (*sb's efforts*) devolver, corresponder a; **~ment** *n* reembolso, devolución *f*; (*sum of money*) recompensa

repeal [rɪˈpiːl] *n* revocación *f* ♦ *vt* revocar

repeat [rɪˈpiːt] *n* (*RADIO, TV*) reposición *f* ♦ *vt* repetir ♦ *vi* repetirse; **~edly** *adv* repetidas veces

repel [rɪˈpɛl] *vt* (*drive away*) rechazar; (*disgust*) repugnar; **~lent** *adj* repugnante ♦ *n*: **insect ~lent** crema (*or* loción *f*) anti-insectos

repent [rɪˈpɛnt] *vi*: **to ~ (of)** arrepentirse (de); **~ance** *n* arrepentimiento

repercussions [riːpəˈkʌʃənz] *npl* consecuencias *fpl*

repertory [ˈrɛpətərɪ] *n* (*also*: **~ theatre**) teatro de repertorio

repetition [rɛpɪˈtɪʃən] *n* repetición *f*

repetitive [rɪˈpɛtɪtɪv] *adj* repetitivo

replace [rɪˈpleɪs] *vt* (*put back*) devolver a su sitio; (*take the place of*) reemplazar, sustituir; **~ment** *n* (*act*) reposición *f*; (*thing*) recambio; (*person*) suplente *m/f*

replay [ˈriːpleɪ] *n* (*SPORT*) desempate *m*; (*of tape, film*) repetición *f*

replenish [rɪˈplɛnɪʃ] *vt* rellenar; (*stock etc*) reponer

replica [ˈrɛplɪkə] *n* copia, reproducción *f* (exacta)

reply [rɪˈplaɪ] *n* respuesta, contestación *f* ♦ *vi* contestar, responder

report [rɪˈpɔːt] *n* informe *m*; (*PRESS etc*) reportaje *m*; (*BRIT: also*: **school ~**) boletín *m* escolar; (*of gun*) estallido ♦ *vt* informar de; (*PRESS etc*) hacer un reportaje sobre; (*notify: accident, culprit*) denunciar ♦ *vi* (*make a report*) presentar un informe; (*present o.s.*): **to ~ (to sb)** presentarse (ante uno); **~ card** *n* (*US, Scottish*) cartilla escolar; **~edly** *adv* según se dice; **~er** *n* periodista *m/f*

repose [rɪˈpəuz] *n*: **in ~** (*face, mouth*) en reposo

reprehensible [rɛprɪˈhɛnsɪbl] *adj* reprensible, censurable

represent [rɛprɪˈzɛnt] *vt* representar; (*COMM*) ser agente de; (*describe*): **to ~ sth as** describir algo como; **~ation** [-ˈteɪʃən] *n* representación *f*; **~ations** *npl* (*protest*) quejas *fpl*; **~ative** *n* representante *m/f*; (*US: POL*) diputado/a *m/f* ♦ *adj* representativo

repress [rɪˈprɛs] *vt* reprimir; **~ion** [-ˈprɛʃən] *n* represión *f*

reprieve [rɪˈpriːv] *n* (*LAW*) indulto; (*fig*) alivio

reprisals [rɪˈpraɪzlz] *npl* represalias *fpl*

reproach [rɪˈprəutʃ] *n* reproche *m* ♦ *vt*: **to ~ sb for sth** reprochar algo a uno; **~ful** *adj* de reproche, de acusación

reproduce [riːprəˈdjuːs] *vt* reproducir ♦ *vi* reproducirse; **reproduction** [-ˈdʌkʃən] *n* reproducción *f*

reprove [rɪˈpruːv] *vt*: **to ~ sb for sth** reprochar algo a uno

reptile [ˈrɛptaɪl] *n* reptil *m*

republic [rɪˈpʌblɪk] *n* república; **~an** *adj*,

n republicano/a *m/f*
repudiate [rɪ'pjuːdɪeɪt] *vt* rechazar;
(*violence etc*) repudiar
repulsive [rɪ'pʌlsɪv] *adj* repulsivo
reputable ['repjutəbl] *adj* (*make etc*) de
renombre
reputation [repju'teɪʃən] *n* reputación *f*
reputed [rɪ'pjuːtɪd] *adj* supuesto; **~ly** *adv*
según dicen *or* se dice
request [rɪ'kwest] *n* petición *f*; (*formal*)
solicitud *f* ♦ *vt*: **to ~ sth of** *or* **from sb**
solicitar algo a uno; **~ stop** (*BRIT*) *n*
parada discrecional
require [rɪ'kwaɪə*] *vt* (*need: subj: person*)
necesitar, tener necesidad de; (:: *thing*,
situation) exigir; (*want*) pedir; **to ~ sb to
do sth** pedir a uno que haga algo;
~ment *n* requisito; (*need*) necesidad *f*
requisition [rekwɪ'zɪʃən] *n*: **~ (for)**
solicitud *f* (de) ♦ *vt* (*MIL*) requisar
rescue ['reskjuː] *n* rescate *m* ♦ *vt* rescatar;
~ party *n* expedición *f* de salvamento;
~r *n* salvador(a) *m/f*
research [rɪ'səːtʃ] *n* investigaciones *fpl*
♦ *vt* investigar; **~er** *n* investigador(a) *m/f*
resemblance [rɪ'zembləns] *n* parecido
resemble [rɪ'zembl] *vt* parecerse a
resent [rɪ'zent] *vt* tomar a mal; **~ful** *adj*
resentido; **~ment** *n* resentimiento
reservation [rezə'veɪʃən] *n* reserva
reserve [rɪ'zəːv] *n* reserva; (*SPORT*)
suplente *m/f* ♦ *vt* (*seats etc*) reservar; **~s**
npl (*MIL*) reserva; **in ~** de reserva; **~d** *adj*
reservado
reshuffle [riː'ʃʌfl] *n*: **Cabinet ~** (*POL*)
remodelación *f* del gabinete
residence ['rezɪdəns] *n* (*formal: home*)
domicilio; (*length of stay*) permanencia; **~
permit** (*BRIT*) *n* permiso de permanencia
resident ['rezɪdənt] *n* (*of area*) vecino/a;
(*in hotel*) huésped(a) *m/f* ♦ *adj*
(*population*) permanente; (*doctor*)
residente; **~ial** [-'denʃəl] *adj* residencial
residue ['rezɪdjuː] *n* resto
resign [rɪ'zaɪn] *vt* renunciar a ♦ *vi* dimitir;
to ~ o.s. *to* (*situation*) resignarse a;
~ation [rezɪg'neɪʃən] *n* dimisión *f*; (*state of*

mind) resignación *f*; **~ed** *adj* resignado
resilient [rɪ'zɪlɪənt] *adj* (*material*) elástico;
(*person*) resistente
resist [rɪ'zɪst] *vt* resistir, oponerse a;
~ance *n* resistencia
resolute ['rezəluːt] *adj* resuelto; (*refusal*)
tajante
resolution [rezə'luːʃən] *n* (*gen*) resolución
f
resolve [rɪ'zɔlv] *n* resolución *f* ♦ *vt*
resolver ♦ *vi*: **to ~ to do** resolver hacer;
~d *adj* resuelto
resort [rɪ'zɔːt] *n* (*town*) centro turístico;
(*recourse*) recurso ♦ *vi*: **to ~ to** recurrir a;
in the last ~ como último recurso
resounding [rɪ'zaundɪŋ] *adj* sonoro; (*fig*)
clamoroso
resource [rɪ'sɔːs] *n* recurso; **~s** *npl*
recursos *mpl*; **~ful** *adj* despabilado,
ingenioso
respect [rɪs'pekt] *n* respeto ♦ *vt* respetar;
~s *npl* recuerdos *mpl*, saludos *mpl*; **with
~ to** con respecto a; **in this ~** en cuanto a
eso; **~able** *adj* respetable; (*large:
amount*) apreciable; (*passable*) tolerable;
~ful *adj* respetuoso
respective [rɪs'pektɪv] *adj* respectivo; **~ly**
adv respectivamente
respite ['respaɪt] *n* respiro
respond [rɪs'pɔnd] *vi* responder; (*react*)
reaccionar; **response** [-'pɔns] *n*
respuesta; reacción *f*
responsibility [rɪspɔnsɪ'bɪlɪtɪ] *n*
responsabilidad *f*
responsible [rɪs'pɔnsɪbl] *adj* (*character*)
serio, formal; (*job*) de confianza; (*liable*): **~
(for)** responsable (de)
responsive [rɪs'pɔnsɪv] *adj* sensible
rest [rest] *n* descanso, reposo; (*MUS, pause*)
pausa, silencio; (*support*) apoyo;
(*remainder*) resto ♦ *vi* descansar; (*be
supported*): **to ~ on** descansar sobre ♦ *vt*
(*lean*): **to ~ sth on/against** apoyar algo
en *or* sobre/contra; **the ~ of them**
(*people, objects*) los demás; **it ~s with him
to ...** depende de él el que ...
restaurant ['restərən] *n* restaurante *m*; **~**

car (*BRIT*) *n* (*RAIL*) coche-comedor *m*

restful ['restful] *adj* descansado, tranquilo

rest home *n* residencia para jubilados

restive ['restɪv] *adj* inquieto; (*horse*) rebelón(ona)

restless ['restlɪs] *adj* inquieto

restoration [restə'reɪʃən] *n* restauración *f*; devolución *f*

restore [rɪ'stɔː*] *vt* (*building*) restaurar; (*sth stolen*) devolver; (*health*) restablecer; (*to power*) volver a poner a

restrain [rɪs'treɪn] *vt* (*feeling*) contener, refrenar; (*person*): **to ~ (from doing)** disuadir (de hacer); **~ed** *adj* reservado; **~t** *n* (*restriction*) restricción *f*; (*moderation*) moderación *f*; (*of manner*) reserva

restrict [rɪs'trɪkt] *vt* restringir, limitar; **~ion** [-kʃən] *n* restricción *f*, limitación *f*; **~ive** *adj* restrictivo

rest room (*US*) *n* aseos *mpl*

result [rɪ'zʌlt] *n* resultado ♦ *vi*: **to ~ in** terminar en, tener por resultado; **as a ~ of** a consecuencia de

resume [rɪ'zjuːm] *vt* reanudar ♦ *vi* comenzar de nuevo

résumé ['reɪzjuːmeɪ] *n* resumen *m*; (*US*) currículum *m*

resumption [rɪ'zʌmpʃən] *n* reanudación *f*

resurgence [rɪ'səːdʒəns] *n* resurgimiento *m*

resurrection [rezə'rekʃən] *n* resurrección *f*

resuscitate [rɪ'sʌsɪteɪt] *vt* (*MED*) resucitar

retail ['riːteɪl] *adj, adv* al por menor; **~er** *n* detallista *m/f*; **~ price** *n* precio de venta al público

retain [rɪ'teɪn] *vt* (*keep*) retener, conservar; **~er** *n* (*fee*) anticipo

retaliate [rɪ'tælɪeɪt] *vi*: **to ~ (against)** tomar represalias (contra); **retaliation** [-'eɪʃən] *n* represalias *fpl*

retarded [rɪ'tɑːdɪd] *adj* retrasado

retch [retʃ] *vi* dársele a uno arcadas

retentive [rɪ'tentɪv] *adj* (*memory*) retentivo

retire [rɪ'taɪə*] *vi* (*give up work*) jubilarse; (*withdraw*) retirarse; (*go to bed*) acostarse; **~d** *adj* (*person*) jubilado; **~ment** *n* (*giving up work: state*) retiro; (*: act*) jubilación *f*; **retiring** *adj* (*leaving*)

saliente; (*shy*) retraído

retort [rɪ'tɔːt] *vi* contestar

retrace [riː'treɪs] *vt*: **to ~ one's steps** volver sobre sus pasos, desandar lo andado

retract [rɪ'trækt] *vt* (*statement*) retirar; (*claws*) retraer; (*undercarriage, aerial*) replegar

retrain [riː'treɪn] *vt* reciclar; **~ing** *n* readaptación *f* profesional

retread ['riːtred] *n* neumático (*SP*) or llanta (*AM*) recauchutado/a

retreat [rɪ'triːt] *n* (*place*) retiro; (*MIL*) retirada ♦ *vi* retirarse

retribution [retrɪ'bjuːʃən] *n* desquite *m*

retrieval [rɪ'triːvəl] *n* recuperación *f*

retrieve [rɪ'triːv] *vt* recobrar; (*situation, honour*) salvar; (*COMPUT*) recuperar; (*error*) reparar; **~r** *n* perro cobrador

retrospect ['retrəspekt] *n*: **in ~** retrospectivamente; **~ive** [-'spektɪv] *adj* retrospectivo; (*law*) retroactivo

return [rɪ'təːn] *n* (*going or coming back*) vuelta, regreso; (*of sth stolen etc*) devolución *f*; (*FINANCE: from land, shares*) ganancia, ingresos *mpl* ♦ *cpd* (*journey*) de regreso; (*BRIT: ticket*) de ida y vuelta; (*match*) de vuelta ♦ *vi* (*person etc: come or go back*) volver, regresar; (*symptoms etc*) reaparecer; (*regain*): **to ~ to** recuperar ♦ *vt* devolver; (*favour, love etc*) corresponder a; (*verdict*) pronunciar; (*POL: candidate*) elegir; **~s** *npl* (*COMM*) ingresos *mpl*; **in ~ (for)** a cambio (de); **by ~ of post** a vuelta de correo; **many happy ~s (of the day)!** ¡feliz cumpleaños!

reunion [riː'juːnɪən] *n* (*of family*) reunión *f*; (*of two people, school*) reencuentro

reunite [riːjuː'naɪt] *vt* reunir; (*reconcile*) reconciliar

rev [rev] (*AUT*) *n abbr* (= *revolution*) revolución *f* ♦ *vt* (*also*: **~ up**) acelerar

reveal [rɪ'viːl] *vt* revelar; **~ing** *adj* revelador(a)

revel ['revl] *vi*: **to ~ in sth/in doing sth** gozar de algo/con hacer algo

revenge [rɪ'vendʒ] *n* venganza; **to take ~**

on vengarse de

revenue [ˈrevənjuː] n ingresos mpl, rentas fpl

reverberate [rɪˈvəːbəreɪt] vi (sound) resonar, retumbar; (fig: shock) repercutir

reverence [ˈrevərəns] n reverencia

Reverend [ˈrevərənd] adj (in titles): **the ~ John Smith** (Anglican) el Reverendo John Smith; (Catholic) el Padre John Smith; (Protestant) el Pastor John Smith

reversal [rɪˈvəːsl] n (of order) inversión f; (of direction, policy) cambio; (of decision) revocación f

reverse [rɪˈvəːs] n (opposite) contrario; (back: of cloth) revés m; (: of coin) reverso; (: of paper) dorso; (AUT: also: ~ gear) marcha atrás; (setback) revés m ♦ adj (order) inverso; (direction) contrario; (process) opuesto ♦ vt (decision, AUT) dar marcha atrás a; (position, function) invertir ♦ vi (BRIT: AUT) dar marcha atrás; **~-charge call** (BRIT) n llamada a cobro revertido; **reversing lights** (BRIT) npl (AUT) luces fpl de retroceso

revert [rɪˈvəːt] vi: **to ~ to** volver a

review [rɪˈvjuː] n (magazine, MIL) revista; (of book, film) reseña; (US: examination) repaso, examen m ♦ vt repasar, examinar; (MIL) pasar revista a; (book, film) reseñar; **~er** n crítico/a

revise [rɪˈvaɪz] vt (manuscript) corregir; (opinion) modificar; (price, procedure) revisar ♦ vi (study) repasar; **revision** [rɪˈvɪʒən] n corrección f; modificación f; (for exam) repaso

revival [rɪˈvaɪvəl] n (recovery) reanimación f; (of interest) renacimiento; (THEATRE) reestreno; (of faith) despertar m

revive [rɪˈvaɪv] vt resucitar; (custom) restablecer; (hope) despertar; (play) reestrenar ♦ vi (person) volver en sí; (business) reactivarse

revolt [rɪˈvəult] n rebelión f ♦ vi rebelarse, sublevarse ♦ vt dar asco a, repugnar; **~ing** adj asqueroso, repugnante

revolution [revəˈluːʃən] n revolución f; **~ary** adj, n revolucionario/a m/f; **~ize** vt

revolucionar

revolve [rɪˈvɔlv] vi dar vueltas, girar; (life, discussion): **to ~ (a)round** girar en torno a

revolver [rɪˈvɔlvəʳ] n revólver m

revolving [rɪˈvɔlvɪŋ] adj (chair, door etc) giratorio

revue [rɪˈvjuː] n (THEATRE) revista

revulsion [rɪˈvʌlʃən] n asco, repugnancia

reward [rɪˈwɔːd] n premio, recompensa ♦ vt: **to ~ (for)** recompensar or premiar (por); **~ing** adj (fig) valioso

rewind [riːˈwaɪnd] (irreg) vt rebobinar

rewire [riːˈwaɪəʳ] vt (house) renovar la instalación eléctrica de

rheumatism [ˈruːmətɪzəm] n reumatismo, reúma m

Rhine [raɪn] n: **the ~** el (río) Rin

rhinoceros [raɪˈnɔsərəs] n rinoceronte m

rhododendron [rəudəˈdendrn] n rododendro

Rhone [rəun] n: **the ~** el (río) Ródano

rhubarb [ˈruːbɑːb] n ruibarbo

rhyme [raɪm] n rima; (verse) poesía

rhythm [ˈrɪðm] n ritmo

rib [rɪb] n (ANAT) costilla ♦ vt (mock) tomar el pelo a

ribbon [ˈrɪbən] n cinta; **in ~s** (torn) hecho trizas

rice [raɪs] n arroz m; **~ pudding** n arroz m con leche

rich [rɪtʃ] adj rico; (soil) fértil; (food) pesado; (: sweet) empalagoso; (abundant): **~ in** (minerals etc) rico en; **the ~** npl los ricos; **~es** npl riqueza; **~ly** adv ricamente; (deserved, earned) bien

rickets [ˈrɪkɪts] n raquitismo

rid [rɪd] (pt, pp rid) vt: **to ~ sb of sth** librar a uno de algo; **to get ~ of** deshacerse or desembarazarse de

ridden [ˈrɪdn] pp of **ride**

riddle [ˈrɪdl] n (puzzle) acertijo; (mystery) enigma m, misterio ♦ vt: **to be ~d with** ser lleno or plagado de

ride [raɪd] (pt rode, pp ridden) n paseo; (distance covered) viaje m, recorrido ♦ vi (as sport) montar; (go somewhere: on horse, bicycle) dar un paseo, pasearse;

(*travel: on bicycle, motorcycle, bus*) viajar
♦ *vt* (*a horse*) montar a; (*a bicycle,
motorcycle*) andar en; (*distance*) recorrer;
to take sb for a ~ (*fig*) engañar a uno; **~r**
n (*on horse*) jinete/a *m/f*; (*on bicycle*)
ciclista *m/f*; (*on motorcycle*) motociclista
m/f

ridge [rɪdʒ] *n* (*of hill*) cresta; (*of roof*)
caballete *m*; (*wrinkle*) arruga

ridicule ['rɪdɪkjuːl] *n* irrisión *f*, burla ♦ *vt*
poner en ridículo, burlarse de;
ridiculous [-'dɪkjʊləs] *adj* ridículo

riding ['raɪdɪŋ] *n* equitación *f*; **I like ~** me
gusta montar a caballo; **~ school** *n*
escuela de equitación

rife [raɪf] *adj*: **to be ~** ser muy común; **to
be ~ with** abundar en

riffraff ['rɪfræf] *n* gentuza

rifle ['raɪfl] *n* rifle *m*, fusil *m* ♦ *vt* saquear;
~ through *vt* (*papers*) registrar; **~
range** *n* campo de tiro; (*at fair*) tiro al
blanco

rift [rɪft] *n* (*in clouds*) claro; (*fig:
disagreement*) desavenencia

rig [rɪg] *n* (*also: oil ~: at sea*) plataforma
petrolera ♦ *vt* (*election etc*) amañar; **~
out** (*BRIT*) *vt* disfrazar; **~ up** *vt*
improvisar; **~ging** *n* (*NAUT*) aparejo

right [raɪt] *adj* (*correct*) correcto, exacto;
(*suitable*) indicado, debido; (*proper*)
apropiado; (*just*) justo; (*morally good*)
bueno; (*not left*) derecho ♦ *n* bueno;
(*title, claim*) derecho; (*not left*) derecha
♦ *adv* bien, correctamente; (*not left*) a la
derecha; (*exactly*): **~ now** ahora mismo
♦ *vt* enderezar; (*correct*) corregir ♦ *excl*
¡bueno!, ¡está bien!; **to be ~** (*person*)
tener razón; (*answer*) ser correcto; **is that
the ~ time?** (*of clock*) ¿es esa la hora
buena?; **by ~s** en justicia; **on the ~** a la
derecha; **to be in the ~** tener razón; **~
away** en seguida; **~ in the middle**
exactamente en el centro; **~ angle** *n*
ángulo recto; **~eous** ['raɪtʃəs] *adj* justado,
honrado; (*anger*) justificado; **~ful** *adj*
legítimo; **~-handed** *adj* diestro; **~-hand
man** *n* brazo derecho; **~-hand side** *n*

derecha; **~ly** *adv* correctamente,
debidamente; (*with reason*) con razón; **~
of way** *n* (*on path etc*) derecho de paso; **~**
(*AUT*) prioridad *f*; **~-wing** *adj* (*POL*)
derechista

rigid ['rɪdʒɪd] *adj* rígido; (*person, ideas*)
inflexible

rigmarole ['rɪgmərəul] *n* galimatías *m inv*

rigorous ['rɪgərəs] *adj* riguroso

rile [raɪl] *vt* irritar

rim [rɪm] *n* borde *m*; (*of spectacles*) aro; (*of
wheel*) llanta

rind [raɪnd] *n* (*of bacon*) corteza; (*of lemon
etc*) cáscara; (*of cheese*) costra

ring [rɪŋ] (*pt* **rang**, *pp* **rung**) *n* (*of metal*)
aro; (*on finger*) anillo; (*of people*) corro;
(*of objects*) círculo; (*gang*) banda; (*for
boxing*) cuadrilátero; (*of circus*) pista; (*bull
~*) ruedo, plaza; (*sound of bell*) toque *m*
♦ *vi* (*on telephone*) llamar por teléfono;
(*bell*) repicar; (*doorbell, phone*) sonar;
(*also:* **~ out**) sonar ♦ *vt* (*BRIT: TEL*)
llamar, telefonear; (*bell etc*)
hacer sonar; (*doorbell*) tocar; **to give sb a
~** (*BRIT: TEL*) llamar o telefonear a alguien;
~ back (*BRIT*) *vt, vi* (*TEL*) devolver la
llamada; **~ off** (*BRIT*) *vi* (*TEL*) colgar,
cortar la comunicación; **~ up** (*BRIT*) *vt*
(*TEL*) llamar, telefonear; **~ing** *n* (*of bell*)
repique *m*; (*of phone*) el sonar; (*in ears*)
zumbido; **~ing tone** *n* (*TEL*) tono de
llamada; **~leader** *n* (*of gang*) cabecilla
m; **~lets** ['rɪŋlɪts] *npl* rizos *mpl*, bucles
mpl; **~ road** (*BRIT*) *n* carretera periférica
or de circunvalación

rink [rɪŋk] *n* (*also:* **ice ~**) pista de hielo

rinse [rɪns] *n* aclarado; (*dye*) tinte *m* ♦ *vt*
aclarar; (*mouth*) enjuagar

riot ['raɪət] *n* motín *m*, disturbio ♦ *vi*
amotinarse; **to run ~** desmandarse; **~ous**
adj alborotado; (*party*) bullicioso

rip [rɪp] *n* rasgón *m*, rasgadura ♦ *vt* rasgar,
desgarrar ♦ *vi* rasgarse, desgarrarse;
~cord *n* cabo de desgarre

ripe [raɪp] *adj* maduro; **~n** *vt* madurar;
(*cheese*) curar ♦ *vi* madurar

ripple ['rɪpl] *n* onda, rizo; (*sound*)

murmullo ♦ vi rizarse

rise [raɪz] (pt **rose**, pp **risen**) n (slope) cuesta, pendiente f; (hill) altura; (BRIT: in wages) aumento; (in prices, temperature) subida; (fig: to power etc) ascenso ♦ vi subir; (waters) crecer; (sun, moon) salir; (person: from bed etc) levantarse; (also: ~ **up**: rebel) sublevarse; (in rank) ascender; **to give ~ to** dar lugar or origen a; **to ~ to the occasion** ponerse a la altura de las circunstancias; **risen** ['rɪzn] pp of **rise**; **rising** adj (increasing: number) creciente; (: prices) en aumento or alza; (tide) creciente; (sun, moon) naciente

risk [rɪsk] n riesgo, peligro ♦ vt arriesgar; (run the ~ of) exponerse a; **to take** or **run the ~ of doing** correr el riesgo de hacer; **at ~** en peligro; **at one's own ~** bajo su propia responsabilidad; **~y** adj arriesgado, peligroso

rissole ['rɪsəʊl] n croqueta

rite [raɪt] n rito; **last ~s** exequias fpl

ritual ['rɪtjʊəl] adj ritual ♦ n ritual m, rito

rival ['raɪvl] n rival m/f; (in business) competidor(a) m/f ♦ adj rival, opuesto ♦ vt competir con; **~ry** n competencia

river ['rɪvə*] n río ♦ cpd (port) de río; (traffic) fluvial; **up/down ~** río arriba/abajo; **~bank** n orilla (del río); **~bed** n lecho, cauce m

rivet ['rɪvɪt] n roblón m, remache m ♦ vt (fig) captar

Riviera [rɪvɪ'eərə] n: **the (French) ~** la Costa Azul (francesa)

road [rəʊd] n camino; (motorway etc) carretera; (in town) calle f ♦ cpd (accident) de tráfico; **major/minor ~** carretera principal/secundaria; **~ accident** n accidente m de tráfico; **~block** n barricada; **~hog** n loco/a del volante; **~ map** n mapa m de carreteras; **~ rage** n agresividad en la carretera; **~ safety** n seguridad f vial; **~side** n borde m (del camino); **~sign** n señal f de tráfico; **~ user** n usuario/a de la vía pública; **~way** n calzada; **~works** npl obras fpl; **~worthy** adj (car) en buen estado para

circular

roam [rəʊm] vi vagar

roar [rɔː*] n rugido; (of vehicle, storm) estruendo; (of laughter) carcajada ♦ vi rugir; hacer estruendo; **to ~ with laughter** reírse a carcajadas; **to do a ~ing trade** hacer buen negocio

roast [rəʊst] n carne f asada, asado ♦ vt asar; (coffee) tostar; **~ beef** n rosbif m

rob [rɒb] vt robar; **to ~ sb of sth** robar algo a uno; (fig: deprive) quitar algo a uno; **~ber** n ladrón/ona m/f; **~bery** n robo

robe [rəʊb] n (for ceremony etc) toga; (also: **bath~**, US) albornoz m

robin ['rɒbɪn] n petirrojo

robot ['rəʊbɒt] n robot m

robust [rəʊ'bʌst] adj robusto, fuerte

rock [rɒk] n roca; (boulder) peña, peñasco; (US: small stone) piedrecita; (BRIT: sweet) ≈ piruli ♦ vt (swing gently: cradle) balancear, mecer; (: child) arrullar; (shake) sacudir ♦ vi mecerse, balancearse; sacudirse; **on the ~s** (drink) con hielo; (marriage etc) en ruinas; **~ and roll** n rocanrol m; **~-bottom** n (fig) punto más bajo; **~ery** n cuadro alpino

rocket ['rɒkɪt] n cohete m

rocking ['rɒkɪŋ]: **~ chair** n mecedora; **~ horse** n caballo de balancín

rocky ['rɒkɪ] adj rocoso

rod [rɒd] n vara, varilla; (also: **fishing ~**) caña

rode [rəʊd] pt of **ride**

rodent ['rəʊdnt] n roedor m

roe [rəʊ] n (species: also: **~ deer**) corzo; (of fish): **hard/soft ~** hueva/lecha

rogue [rəʊg] n pícaro, pillo

role [rəʊl] n papel m

roll [rəʊl] n rollo; (of bank notes) fajo; (also: **bread ~**) panecillo; (register, list) lista, nómina; (sound: of drums etc) redoble m ♦ vt hacer rodar; (also: **~ up**: string) enrollar; (: sleeves) arremangar; (cigarette) liar; (also: **~ out**: pastry) aplanar; (flatten: road, lawn) apisonar ♦ vi rodar; (drum) redoblar; (ship) balancearse; **~ about** or

around *vi* (*person*) revolcarse; (*object*) rodar (por); **~ by** *vi* (*time*) pasar; **~ over** *vi* dar una vuelta; **~ up** *vi* (*inf: arrive*) aparecer ♦ *vt* (*carpet*) arrollar; **~ call** *n*: **to take a ~ call** pasar lista; **~er** *n* rodillo; (*wheel*) rueda; (*for road*) apisonadora; (*for hair*) rulo; **~erblade** *n* patín *m* (en línea); **~er coaster** *n* montaña rusa; **~er skates** *npl* patines *mpl* de rueda

rolling ['rəulɪŋ] *adj* (*landscape*) ondulado; **~ pin** *n* rodillo (de cocina); **~ stock** *n* (*RAIL*) material *m* rodante

ROM [rɔm] *n abbr* (*COMPUT*: = *read only memory*) ROM *f*

Roman ['rəumən] *adj* romano/a; **~ Catholic** *adj*, *n* católico/a *m/f* (romano/a)

romance [rə'mæns] *n* (*love affair*) amor *m*; (*charm*) lo romántico; (*novel*) novela de amor

Romania [ru:'meɪnɪə] *n* = **Rumania**

Roman numeral *n* número romano

romantic [rə'mæntɪk] *adj* romántico

Rome [rəum] *n* Roma

romp [rɔmp] *n* retozo, juego ♦ *vi* (*also*: **~ about**) jugar, brincar

rompers ['rɔmpəz] *npl* pelele *m*

roof [ru:f] (*pl* **~s**) *n* (*gen*) techo; (*of house*) techo, tejado ♦ *vt* techar, poner techo a; **the ~ of the mouth** el paladar; **~ing** *n* techumbre *f*; **~ rack** *n* (*AUT*) baca, portaequipajes *m inv*

rook [ruk] *n* (*bird*) graja; (*CHESS*) torre *f*

room [ru:m] *n* cuarto, habitación *f*, pieza (*esp AM*); (*also*: **bed~**) dormitorio; (*in school etc*) sala; (*space, scope*) sitio, cabida; **~s** *npl* (*lodging*) alojamiento; **"~s to let"**, **"~s for rent"** (*US*) "se alquilan cuartos"; **single/double ~** habitación individual/doble *or* para dos personas; **~ing house** (*US*) *n* pensión *f*; **~mate** *n* compañero/a de cuarto; **~ service** *n* servicio de habitaciones; **~y** *adj* espacioso; (*garment*) amplio

roost [ru:st] *vi* pasar la noche

rooster ['ru:stə*] *n* gallo

root [ru:t] *n* raíz *f* ♦ *vi* arraigarse; **~ about**

vi (*fig*) buscar y rebuscar; **~ for** *vt fus* (*support*) apoyar a; **~ out** *vt* desarraigar

rope [rəup] *n* cuerda; (*NAUT*) cable *m* ♦ *vt* (*tie*) atar *or* amarrar con (una) cuerda; (*climbers*: *also*: **~ together**) encordarse; (*an area*: *also*: **~ off**) acordonar; **to know the ~s** (*fig*) conocer los trucos (del oficio); **~ in** *vt* (*fig*): **to ~ sb in** persuadir a uno a tomar parte

rosary ['rəuzərɪ] *n* rosario

rose [rəuz] *pt of* **rise** ♦ *n* rosa; (*shrub*) rosal *m*; (*on watering can*) roseta

rosé ['rəuzeɪ] *n* vino rosado

rosebud ['rəuzbʌd] *n* capullo de rosa

rosebush ['rəuzbuʃ] *n* rosal *m*

rosemary ['rəuzmərɪ] *n* romero

roster ['rɔstə*] *n*: **duty ~** lista de deberes

rostrum ['rɔstrəm] *n* tribuna

rosy ['rəuzɪ] *adj* rosado, sonrosado; **a ~ future** un futuro prometedor

rot [rɔt] *n* podredumbre *f*; (*fig: pej*) tonterías *fpl* ♦ *vt* pudrir ♦ *vi* pudrirse

rota ['rəutə] *n* (*sistema m de*) turnos *mpl*

rotary ['rəutərɪ] *adj* rotativo

rotate [rəu'teɪt] *vt* (*revolve*) hacer girar, dar vueltas a; (*jobs*) alternar ♦ *vi* girar, dar vueltas; **rotating** *adj* rotativo; **rotation** [-'teɪʃən] *n* rotación *f*

rotten ['rɔtn] *adj* podrido; (*dishonest*) corrompido; (*inf: bad*) pocho; **to feel ~** (*ill*) sentirse fatal

rotund [rəu'tʌnd] *adj* regordete

rouble ['ru:bl] (*US* **ruble**) *n* rublo

rough [rʌf] *adj* (*skin, surface*) áspero; (*terrain*) quebrado; (*road*) desigual; (*voice*) bronco; (*person, manner*) tosco, grosero; (*weather*) borrascoso; (*treatment*) brutal; (*sea*) picado; (*town, area*) peligroso; (*cloth*) basto; (*plan*) preliminar; (*guess*) aproximado ♦ *n* (*GOLF*): **in the ~** en las hierbas altas; **to ~ it** vivir sin comodidades; **to sleep ~** (*BRIT*) pasar la noche al raso; **~age** *n* fibra(*s*) *f*(*pl*); **~-and-ready** *adj* improvisado; **~ copy** *n* borrador *m*; **~ draft** *n* = **~ copy**; **~ly** *adv* (*handle*) torpemente; (*make*) toscamente; (*speak*) groseramente;

(*approximately*) aproximadamente; **~ness** *n* (*of surface*) aspereza; (*of person*) rudeza

roulette [ruːˈlɛt] *n* ruleta

Roumania [ruːˈmeɪnɪə] *n* = **Rumania**

round [raund] *adj* redondo ♦ *n* círculo; (*BRIT: of toast*) rebanada; (*of policeman*) ronda; (*of milkman*) recorrido; (*of doctor*) visitas *fpl*; (*game: of cards, in competition*) partida; (*of ammunition*) cartucho; (*BOXING*) asalto; (*of talks*) ronda ♦ *vt* (*corner*) doblar ♦ *prep* alrededor de; (*surrounding*): **~ his neck/the table** en su cuello/alrededor de la mesa; (*in a circular movement*): **to move ~ the room/sail ~ the world** dar una vuelta a la habitación/circunnavegar el mundo; (*in various directions*): **to move ~ a room/house** moverse por toda la habitación/casa; (*approximately*) alrededor de ♦ *adv*: **all ~** por todos lados; **the long way ~** por el camino menos directo; **all the year ~** durante todo el año; **it's just ~ the corner** (*fig*) está a la vuelta de la esquina; **~ the clock** *adv* las 24 horas; **to go ~ to sb's (house)** ir a casa de uno; **to go ~ the back** pasar por atrás; **enough to go ~** bastante (para todos); **a ~ of applause** una salva de aplausos; **a ~ of drinks/sandwiches** una ronda de bebidas/bocadillos; **~ off** *vt* (*speech etc*) acabar, poner término a; **~ up** *vt* (*cattle*) acorralar; (*people*) reunir; (*price*) redondear; **~about** *n* (*BRIT*) (*AUT*) isleta; (*at fair*) tiovivo ♦ *adj* (*route, means*) indirecto; **~ers** *n* (*game*) juego similar al *béisbol*; **~ly** *adv* (*fig*) rotundamente; **~ trip** *n* viaje *m* de ida y vuelta; **~up** *n* rodeo; (*of criminals*) redada; (*of news*) resumen *m*

rouse [rauz] *vt* (*wake up*) despertar; (*stir up*) suscitar; **rousing** *adj* (*cheer, welcome*) caluroso

route [ruːt] *n* ruta, camino; (*of bus*) recorrido; (*of shipping*) derrota

routine [ruːˈtiːn] *adj* rutinario ♦ *n* rutina; (*THEATRE*) número

rove [rəuv] *vt* vagar *or* errar por

row¹ [rəu] *n* (*line*) fila, hilera; (*KNITTING*) pasada ♦ *vi* (*in boat*) remar ♦ *vt* conducir remando; **4 days in a ~** 4 días seguidos

row² [rau] *n* (*racket*) escándalo; (*dispute*) bronca, pelea; (*scolding*) regaño ♦ *vi* pelear(se)

rowboat [ˈrəubəut] (*US*) *n* bote *m* de remos

rowdy [ˈraudɪ] *adj* (*person: noisy*) ruidoso; (*occasion*) alborotado

rowing [ˈrəuɪŋ] *n* remo; **~ boat** (*BRIT*) *n* bote *m* de remos

royal [ˈrɔɪəl] *adj* real; **R~ Air Force** *n* Fuerzas *fpl* Aéreas Británicas; **~ty** *n* (*~ persons*) familia real; (*payment to author*) derechos *mpl* de autor

rpm *abbr* (= *revs per minute*) r.p.m.

R.S.V.P. *abbr* (= *répondez s'il vous plaît*) SRC

Rt. Hon. *abbr* (*BRIT*: = *Right Honourable*) *título honorífico de diputado*

rub [rʌb] *vt* frotar; (*scrub*) restregar ♦ *n*: **to give sth a ~** frotar algo; **to ~ sb up** *or* **~ sb** (*US*) **the wrong way** entrarle uno por mal ojo; **~ off** *vi* borrarse; **~ off on** *vt fus* influir en; **~ out** *vt* borrar

rubber [ˈrʌbə*] *n* caucho, goma; (*BRIT: eraser*) goma de borrar; **~ band** *n* goma, gomita; **~ plant** *n* ficus *m*

rubbish [ˈrʌbɪʃ] *n* basura; (*waste*) desperdicios *mpl*; (*fig: pej*) tonterías *fpl*; (*junk*) pacotilla; **~ bin** (*BRIT*) *n* cubo (*SP*) *or* bote *m* (*AM*) de la basura; **~ dump** *n* vertedero, basurero

rubble [ˈrʌbl] *n* escombros *mpl*

ruble [ˈruːbl] (*US*) *n* = **rouble**

ruby [ˈruːbɪ] *n* rubí *m*

rucksack [ˈrʌksæk] *n* mochila

rudder [ˈrʌdə*] *n* timón *m*

ruddy [ˈrʌdɪ] *adj* (*face*) rubicundo; (*inf: damned*) condenado

rude [ruːd] *adj* (*impolite: person*) mal educado; (: *word, manners*) grosero; (*crude*) crudo; (*indecent*) indecente; **~ness** *n* descortesía

ruffle [ˈrʌfl] *vt* (*hair*) despeinar; (*clothes*) arrugar; **to get ~d** (*fig: person*) alterarse

rug [rʌg] *n* alfombra; (*BRIT: blanket*) manta

rugby ['rʌgbɪ] *n* (*also:* ~ **football**) rugby *m*

rugged ['rʌgɪd] *adj* (*landscape*) accidentado; (*features*) robusto

ruin ['ru:ɪn] *n* ruina ♦ *vt* arruinar; (*spoil*) estropear; ~**s** *npl* ruinas *fpl*, restos *mpl*

rule [ru:l] *n* (*norm*) norma, costumbre *f*; (*regulation, ruler*) regla; (*government*) dominio ♦ *vt* (*country, person*) gobernar ♦ *vi* gobernar; (*LAW*) fallar; **as a** ~ por regla general; ~ **out** *vt* excluir; ~**d** *adj* (*paper*) rayado; ~**r** *n* (*sovereign*) soberano; (*for measuring*) regla; **ruling** *adj* (*party*) gobernante; (*class*) dirigente ♦ *n* (*LAW*) fallo, decisión *f*

rum [rʌm] *n* ron *m*

Rumania [ru:'meɪnɪə] *n* Rumanía; ~**n** *adj* rumano/a ♦ *n* rumano/a *m/f*; (*LING*) rumano

rumble ['rʌmbl] *n* (*noise*) ruido sordo ♦ *vi* retumbar, hacer un ruido sordo; (*stomach, pipe*) sonar

rummage ['rʌmɪdʒ] *vi* (*search*) hurgar

rumour ['ru:mə*] (*US* **rumor**) *n* rumor *m* ♦ *vt*: **it is ~ed that ...** se rumorea que ...

rump [rʌmp] *n* (*of animal*) ancas *fpl*, grupa; ~ **steak** *n* filete *m* de lomo

rumpus ['rʌmpəs] *n* lío, jaleo

run [rʌn] (*pt* **ran**, *pp* **run**) *n* (*fast pace*): **at a** ~ corriendo; (*SPORT, in tights*) carrera; (*outing*) paseo, excursión *f*; (*distance travelled*) trayecto; (*series*) serie *f*; (*THEATRE*) temporada; (*SKI*) pista ♦ *vt* correr; (*operate: business*) dirigir; (: *competition, course*) organizar; (: *hotel, house*) administrar, llevar; (*COMPUT*) ejecutar; (*pass: hand*) pasar; (*PRESS: feature*) publicar ♦ *vi* correr; (*work: machine*) funcionar, marchar; (*bus, train: operate*) circular, ir; (: *travel*) ir; (*continue: play*) seguir; (: *contract*) ser válido; (*flow: river*) fluir; (*colours, washing*) desteñirse; (*in election*) ser candidato; **there was a ~ on** (*meat, tickets*) hubo mucha demanda de; **in the long ~** a la larga; **on the ~** en fuga; **I'll ~ you to the station** te llevaré a la estación (en coche); **to ~ a risk** correr

un riesgo; **to ~ a bath** llenar la bañera; ~ **about** *or* **around** *vi* (*children*) correr por todos lados; ~ **across** *vt fus* (*find*) dar *or* topar con; ~ **away** *vi* huir; ~ **down** *vt* (*production*) ir reduciendo; (*factory*) ir restringiendo la producción en; (*subj: car*) atropellar; (*criticize*) criticar; **to be ~ down** (*person: tired*) estar debilitado; ~ **in** (*BRIT*) *vt* (*car*) rodar; ~ **into** *vt fus* (*meet: person, trouble*) tropezar con; (*collide with*) chocar con; ~ **off** *vt* (*water*) dejar correr; (*copies*) sacar ♦ *vi* huir corriendo; ~ **out** *vi* (*person*) salir corriendo; (*liquid*) irse; (*lease*) caducar, vencer; (*money etc*) acabarse; ~ **out of** *vt fus* quedar sin; ~ **over** *vt* (*AUT*) atropellar ♦ *vt fus* (*revise*) repasar; ~ **through** *vt fus* (*instructions*) repasar; ~ **up** *vt* (*debt*) contraer; **to ~ up against** (*difficulties*) tropezar con; ~**away** *adj* (*horse*) desbocado; (*truck*) sin frenos; (*child*) escapado de casa

rung [rʌŋ] *pp of* **ring** ♦ *n* (*of ladder*) escalón *m*, peldaño

runner ['rʌnə*] *n* (*in race: person*) corredor(a) *m/f*; (: *horse*) caballo; (*on sledge*) patín *m*; ~ **bean** (*BRIT*) *n* ≈ judía verde; ~**-up** *n* subcampeón/ona *m/f*

running ['rʌnɪŋ] *n* (*sport*) atletismo; (*business*) administración *f* ♦ *adj* (*water, costs*) corriente; (*commentary*) continuo; **to be in/out of the ~ for sth** tener/no tener posibilidades de ganar algo; **6 days** ~ 6 días seguidos; ~ **commentary** *n* (*TV, RADIO*) comentario en directo; (*on guided tour etc*) comentario detallado; ~ **costs** *npl* gastos *mpl* corrientes

runny ['rʌnɪ] *adj* fluido; (*nose, eyes*) gastante

run-of-the-mill *adj* común y corriente

runt [rʌnt] *n* (*also pej*) redrojo, enano

run-up *n*: ~ **to** (*election etc*) período previo a

runway ['rʌnweɪ] *n* (*AVIAT*) pista de aterrizaje

rural ['ruərl] *adj* rural

rush [rʌʃ] *n* ímpetu *m*; (*hurry*) prisa; (*COMM*) demanda repentina; (*current*) corriente *f* fuerte; (*of feeling*) torrente; (*BOT*) junco ♦ *vt* apresurar; (*work*) hacer de prisa ♦ *vi* correr, precipitarse; **~ hour** *n* horas *fpl* punta

rusk [rʌsk] *n* bizcocho tostado

Russia ['rʌʃə] *n* Rusia; **~n** *adj* ruso/a ♦ *n* ruso/a *m/f*; (*LING*) ruso

rust [rʌst] *n* herrumbre *f*, moho ♦ *vi* oxidarse

rustic ['rʌstɪk] *adj* rústico

rustle ['rʌsl] *vi* susurrar ♦ *vt* (*paper*) hacer crujir

rustproof ['rʌstpruːf] *adj* inoxidable

rusty ['rʌstɪ] *adj* oxidado

rut [rʌt] *n* surco; (*ZOOL*) celo; **to be in a ~** ser esclavo de la rutina

ruthless ['ruːθlɪs] *adj* despiadado

rye [raɪ] *n* centeno

S, s

Sabbath ['sæbəθ] *n* domingo; (*Jewish*) sábado

sabotage ['sæbətɑːʒ] *n* sabotaje *m* ♦ *vt* sabotear

saccharin(e) ['sækərɪn] *n* sacarina

sachet ['sæʃeɪ] *n* sobrecito

sack [sæk] *n* (*bag*) saco, costal *m* ♦ *vt* (*dismiss*) despedir; (*plunder*) saquear; **to get the ~** ser despedido; **~ing** *n* despido; (*material*) arpillera

sacred ['seɪkrɪd] *adj* sagrado, santo

sacrifice ['sækrɪfaɪs] *n* sacrificio ♦ *vt* sacrificar

sad [sæd] *adj* (*unhappy*) triste; (*deplorable*) lamentable

saddle ['sædl] *n* silla (de montar); (*of cycle*) sillín *m* ♦ *vt* (*horse*) ensillar; **to be ~d with sth** (*inf*) quedar cargado con algo; **~bag** *n* alforja

sadistic [sə'dɪstɪk] *adj* sádico

sadly ['sædlɪ] *adv* lamentablemente; **to be ~ lacking in** estar por desgracia carente de

sadness ['sædnɪs] *n* tristeza

s.a.e. *abbr* (= *stamped addressed*

envelope) sobre con las propias señas de uno y con sello

safari [sə'fɑːrɪ] *n* safari *m*

safe [seɪf] *adj* (*out of danger*) fuera de peligro; (*not dangerous, sure*) seguro; (*unharmed*) ileso ♦ *n* caja de caudales, caja fuerte; **~ and sound** sano y salvo; **(just) to be on the ~ side** para mayor seguridad; **~-conduct** *n* salvoconducto; **~-deposit** *n* (*vault*) cámara acorazada; (*box*) caja de seguridad; **~guard** *n* protección *f*, garantía ♦ *vt* proteger, defender; **~keeping** *n* custodia; **~ly** *adv* seguramente, con seguridad; **to arrive ~ly** llegar bien; **~ sex** *n* sexo seguro or sin riesgo

safety ['seɪftɪ] *n* seguridad *f*; **~ belt** *n* cinturón *m* (de seguridad); **~ pin** *n* imperdible *m* (*SP*), seguro (*AM*); **~ valve** *n* válvula de seguridad

saffron ['sæfrən] *n* azafrán *m*

sag [sæg] *vi* aflojarse

sage [seɪdʒ] *n* (*herb*) salvia; (*man*) sabio

Sagittarius [sædʒɪ'teərɪəs] *n* Sagitario

Sahara [sə'hɑːrə] *n*: **the ~ (Desert)** el (desierto del) Sáhara

said [sed] *pt, pp of* **say**

sail [seɪl] *n* (*on boat*) vela; (*trip*): **to go for a ~** dar un paseo en barco ♦ *vt* (*boat*) gobernar ♦ *vi* (*travel: ship*) navegar; (*SPORT*) hacer vela; (*begin voyage*) salir; **they ~ed into Copenhagen** arribaron a Copenhague; **~ through** *vt fus* (*exam*) aprobar sin ningún problema; **~boat** (*US*) *n* velero, barco de vela; **~ing** *n* (*SPORT*) vela; **to go ~ing** hacer vela; **~ing boat** *n* barco de vela; **~ing ship** *n* velero; **~or** *n* marinero, marino

saint [seɪnt] *n* santo; **~ly** *adj* santo

sake [seɪk] *n*: **for the ~ of** por

salad ['sæləd] *n* ensalada; **~ bowl** *n* ensaladera; **~ cream** (*BRIT*) *n* (especie *f* de) mayonesa; **~ dressing** *n* aliño

salary ['sælərɪ] *n* sueldo

sale [seɪl] *n* venta; (*at reduced prices*) liquidación *f*, saldo; (*auction*) subasta; **~s** *npl* (*total amount sold*) ventas *fpl*, facturación f; "**for ~**" "se vende"; **on ~** en venta; **on ~ or return** (*goods*) venta por reposición; **~room** n sala de subastas; **~s assistant** (*US* **~s clerk**) n dependiente/a *m/f*; **salesman/woman** (*irreg*) n (*in shop*) dependiente/a *m/f*; (*representative*) viajante *m/f*

salmon ['sæmən] n *inv* salmón m

salon ['sælɒn] n (*hairdressing ~*) peluquería; (*beauty ~*) salón m de belleza

saloon [sə'lu:n] n (*US*) bar m, taberna; (*BRIT: AUT*) (*coche de*) turismo; (*ship's lounge*) cámara, salón m

salt [sɔlt] n sal f ♦ vt salar; (*put ~ on*) poner sal en; **~ cellar** n salero; **~water** *adj* de agua salada; **~y** *adj* salado

salute [sə'lu:t] n saludo; (*of guns*) salva ♦ vt saludar

salvage ['sælvɪdʒ] n (*saving*) salvamento, recuperación f; (*things saved*) objetos *mpl* salvados ♦ vt salvar

salvation [sæl'veɪʃən] n salvación f; **S~ Army** n Ejército de Salvación

same [seɪm] *adj* mismo ♦ *pron*: **the ~** el/la mismo/a, los/las mismos/as; **the ~ book as** el mismo libro que; **at the ~ time** (*at the ~ moment*) al mismo tiempo; (*yet*) sin embargo; **all** *or* **just the ~** sin embargo, aun así; **to do the ~ (as sb)** hacer lo mismo (que uno); **the ~ to you!** ¡igualmente!

sample ['sɑ:mpl] n muestra ♦ vt (*food*) probar; (*wine*) catar

sanction ['sæŋkʃən] n aprobación f ♦ vt sancionar; aprobar; **~s** *npl* (*POL*) sanciones *fpl*

sanctity ['sæŋktɪtɪ] n santidad f; (*inviolability*) inviolabilidad f

sanctuary ['sæŋktjuərɪ] n santuario; (*refuge*) asilo, refugio; (*for wildlife*) reserva

sand [sænd] n arena; (*beach*) playa ♦ vt (*also*: **~ down**) lijar

sandal ['sændl] n sandalia

sand: **~box** (*US*) n = **~pit**; **~castle** n castillo de arena; **~ dune** n duna; **~paper** n papel m de lija; **~pit** n (*for children*) cajón m de arena; **~stone** n

piedra arenisca

sandwich ['sændwɪtʃ] n bocadillo (*SP*), sandwich m, emparedado (*AM*) ♦ vt intercalar; **~ed between** apretujado entre; **cheese/ham ~** sandwich de queso/jamón; **~ course** (*BRIT*) n curso de medio tiempo

sandy ['sændɪ] *adj* arenoso; (*colour*) rojizo

sane [seɪn] *adj* cuerdo; (*sensible*) sensato

sang [sæŋ] *pt of* **sing**

sanitary ['sænɪtərɪ] *adj* sanitario; (*clean*) higiénico; **~ towel** (*US* **~ napkin**) n paño higiénico, compresa

sanitation [sænɪ'teɪʃən] n (*in house*) servicios *mpl* higiénicos; (*in town*) servicio de desinfección; **~ department** (*US*) n departamento de limpieza y recogida de basuras

sanity ['sænɪtɪ] n cordura; (*of judgment*) sensatez f

sank [sæŋk] *pt of* **sink**

Santa Claus [sæntə'klɔ:z] n San Nicolás, Papá Noel

sap [sæp] n (*of plants*) savia ♦ vt (*strength*) minar, agotar

sapling ['sæplɪŋ] n árbol nuevo *or* joven

sapphire ['sæfaɪə*] n zafiro

sarcasm ['sɑ:kæzm] n sarcasmo

sardine [sɑ:'di:n] n sardina

Sardinia [sɑ:'dɪnɪə] n Cerdeña

sash [sæʃ] n faja

sat [sæt] *pt, pp of* **sit**

Satan ['seɪtn] n Satanás m

satchel ['sætʃl] n (*child's*) cartera (*SP*), mochila (*AM*)

satellite ['sætəlaɪt] n satélite m; **~ dish** n antena de televisión para satélite; **~ television** n televisión f vía satélite

satin ['sætɪn] n raso ♦ *adj* de raso

satire ['sætaɪə*] n sátira

satisfaction [sætɪs'fækʃən] n satisfacción f

satisfactory [sætɪs'fæktərɪ] *adj* satisfactorio

satisfy ['sætɪsfaɪ] vt satisfacer; (*convince*) convencer; **~ing** *adj* satisfactorio

Saturday ['sætədɪ] n sábado

sauce [sɔ:s] n salsa; (*sweet*) crema; jarabe m; **~pan** n cacerola, olla

saucer ['sɔ:sə*] *n* platillo
Saudi ['saudi]: ~ **Arabia** *n* Arabia Saudí
  or Saudita; ~ **(Arabian)** *adj*, *n* saudí *m/*
  f, saudita *m/f*
sauna ['sɔ:nə] *n* sauna
saunter ['sɔ:ntə*] *vi*: **to ~ in/out** entrar/
  salir sin prisa
sausage ['sɔsɪdʒ] *n* salchicha; ~ **roll** *n*
  empanadita de salchicha
sauté ['səuteɪ] *adj* salteado
savage ['sævɪdʒ] *adj* (*cruel, fierce*) feroz,
  furioso; (*primitive*) salvaje ♦ *n* salvaje *m/f*
  ♦ *vt* (*attack*) embestir
save [seɪv] *vt* (*rescue*) salvar, rescatar;
  (*money, time*) ahorrar; (*put by, keep: seat*)
  guardar; (*COMPUT*) salvar (y guardar);
  (*avoid: trouble*) evitar; (*SPORT*) parar ♦ *vi*
  (*also:* ~ **up**) ahorrar ♦ *n* (*SPORT*) parada
  ♦ *prep* salvo, excepto
saving ['seɪvɪŋ] *n* (*on price etc*) economía
  ♦ *adj*: **the ~ grace of** el único mérito de;
  ~**s** *npl* ahorros *mpl*; ~**s account** *n*
  cuenta de ahorros; ~**s bank** *n* caja de
  ahorros
saviour ['seɪvjə*] (*US* **savior**) *n* salvador(a)
  m/f
savour ['seɪvə*] (*US* **savor**) *vt* saborear; ~**y**
  adj sabroso; (*dish: not sweet*) salado
saw [sɔ:] (*pt* **sawed**, *pp* **sawed** *or* **sawn**)
  pt of **see** ♦ *n* (*tool*) sierra ♦ *vt* serrar;
  ~**dust** *n* (a)serrín *m*; ~**mill** *n* aserradero;
  ~**n-off shotgun** *n* escopeta de cañones
  recortados
saxophone ['sæksəfəun] *n* saxófono
say [seɪ] (*pt, pp* **said**) *n*: **to have one's ~**
  expresar su opinión ♦ *vt* decir; **to have a some**
  or **some ~ in sth** tener voz *or* tener que
  ver en algo; **to ~ yes/no** decir que sí/no;
  could you ~ that again? ¿podría repetir
  eso?; **that is to ~** es decir; **that goes
  without ~ing** ni que decir tiene; ~**ing** *n*
  dicho, refrán *m*
scab [skæb] *n* costra; (*pej*) esquirol *m*
scaffold ['skæfəuld] *n* cadalso; ~**ing** *n*
  andamio, andamiaje *m*
scald [skɔ:ld] *n* escaldadura ♦ *vt* escaldar
scale [skeɪl] *n* (*gen, MUS*) escala; (*of fish*)
  escama; (*of salaries, fees etc*) escalafón *m*
  ♦ *vt* (*mountain*) escalar; (*tree*) trepar; ~**s**
  npl (*for weighing: small*) balanza; (*: large*)
  báscula; **on a large ~** en gran escala; ~ **of
  charges** tarifa, lista de precios; ~ **down**
  vt reducir a escala
scallop ['skɔləp] *n* (*ZOOL*) venera; (*SEWING*)
  festón *m*
scalp [skælp] *n* cabellera ♦ *vt* escalpar
scampi ['skæmpɪ] *npl* gambas *fpl*
scan [skæn] *vt* (*examine*) escudriñar;
  (*glance at quickly*) dar un vistazo a; (*TV,
  RADAR*) explorar, registrar ♦ *n* (*MED*): **to
  have a ~** pasar por el escáner
scandal ['skændl] *n* escándalo; (*gossip*)
  chismes *mpl*
Scandinavia [skændɪ'neɪvɪə] *n*
  Escandinavia; ~**n** *adj*, *n* escandinavo/a
  m/f
scant [skænt] *adj* escaso; ~**y** *adj* (*meal*)
  insuficiente; (*clothes*) ligero
scapegoat ['skeɪpgəut] *n* cabeza de turco,
  chivo expiatorio
scar [skɑ:] *n* cicatriz *f*; (*fig*) señal *f* ♦ *vt*
  dejar señales en
scarce [skeəs] *adj* escaso; **to make o.s. ~**
  (*inf*) esfumarse; ~**ly** *adv* apenas; **scarcity**
  n escasez *f*
scare [skeə*] *n* susto, sobresalto; (*panic*)
  pánico ♦ *vt* asustar, espantar; **to ~ sb
  stiff** dar a uno un susto de muerte; **bomb
  ~** amenaza de bomba; ~ **off** *or* **away** *vt*
  ahuyentar; ~**crow** *n* espantapájaros *m*
  inv; ~**d** *adj*: **to be ~d** estar asustado
scarf [skɑ:f] (*pl* ~**s** *or* **scarves**) *n* (*long*)
  bufanda; (*square*) pañuelo
scarlet ['skɑ:lɪt] *adj* escarlata; ~ **fever** *n*
  escarlatina
scarves [skɑ:vz] *npl of* **scarf**
scary ['skeərɪ] (*inf*) *adj* espeluznante
scathing ['skeɪðɪŋ] *adj* mordaz
scatter ['skætə*] *vt* (*spread*) esparcir,
  desparramar; (*put to flight*) dispersar ♦ *vi*
  desparramarse; dispersarse; ~**brained**
  adj ligero de cascos
scavenger ['skævəndʒə*] *n* (*person*)
  basurero/a

scenario [sɪ'nɑːrɪəu] *n* (*THEATRE*) argumento; (*CINEMA*) guión *m*; (*fig*) escenario

scene [siːn] *n* (*THEATRE, fig etc*) escena; (*of crime etc*) escenario; (*view*) panorama *m*; (*fuss*) escándalo; **~ry** *n* (*THEATRE*) decorado; (*landscape*) paisaje *m*; **scenic** *adj* pintoresco

scent [sɛnt] *n* perfume *m*, olor *m*; (*fig: track*) rastro, pista

sceptic ['skɛptɪk] (*US* **skeptic**) *n* escéptico/a; **~al** *adj* escéptico

sceptre ['sɛptə*] (*US* **scepter**) *n* cetro

schedule ['ʃɛdjuːl, (*US*) 'skɛdjuːl] *n* (*timetable*) horario; (*of events*) programa *m*; (*list*) lista ♦ *vt* (*visit*) fijar la hora de; **to arrive on ~** llegar a la hora debida; **to be ahead of/behind ~** estar adelantado/en retraso; **~d flight** *n* vuelo regular

scheme [skiːm] *n* (*plan*) plan *m*, proyecto; (*plot*) intriga; (*arrangement*) disposición *f*; (*pension ~ etc*) sistema *m* ♦ *vi* (*intrigue*) intrigar; **scheming** *adj* intrigante ♦ *n* intrigas *fpl*

schizophrenic [skɪtzə'frɛnɪk] *adj* esquizofrénico

scholar ['skɔlə*] *n* (*pupil*) alumno/a; (*learned person*) sabio/a, erudito/a; **~ship** *n* erudición *f*; (*grant*) beca

school [skuːl] *n* escuela, colegio; (*in university*) facultad *f* ♦ *cpd* escolar; **~ age** *n* edad *f* escolar; **~book** *n* libro de texto; **~boy** *n* alumno; **~ children** *npl* alumnos *mpl*; **~girl** *n* alumna; **~ing** *n* enseñanza; **~master/mistress** *n* (*primary*) maestro/a; (*secondary*) profesor/a *m/f*; **~teacher** *n* (*primary*) maestro/a; (*secondary*) profesor(a) *m/f*

schooner ['skuːnə*] *n* (*ship*) goleta

sciatica [saɪ'ætɪkə] *n* ciática

science ['saɪəns] *n* ciencia; **~ fiction** *n* ciencia-ficción *f*; **scientific** [-'tɪfɪk] *adj* científico; **scientist** *n* científico/a

scissors ['sɪzəz] *npl* tijeras *fpl*; **a pair of ~** unas tijeras

scoff [skɔf] *vt* (*BRIT: inf: eat*) engullir ♦ *vi*: **to ~ (at)** (*mock*) mofarse (de)

scold [skəuld] *vt* regañar

scone [skɔn] *n* pastel de pan

scoop [skuːp] *n* (*for flour etc*) pala; (*PRESS*) exclusiva; **~ out** *vt* excavar; **~ up** *vt* recoger

scooter ['skuːtə*] *n* moto *f*; (*toy*) patinete *m*

scope [skəup] *n* (*of plan*) ámbito; (*of person*) competencia; (*opportunity*) libertad *f* (de acción)

scorch [skɔːtʃ] *vt* (*clothes*) chamuscar; (*earth, grass*) quemar, secar

score [skɔː*] *n* (*points etc*) puntuación *f*; (*MUS*) partitura; (*twenty*) veintena ♦ *vt* (*goal, point*) ganar; (*mark*) rayar; (*achieve: success*) conseguir ♦ *vi* marcar un tanto; (*FOOTBALL*) marcar (un) gol; (*keep score*) llevar el tanteo; **~s of** (*very many*) decenas de; **on that ~** en lo que se refiere a eso; **to ~ 6 out of 10** obtener una puntuación de 6 sobre 10; **~ out** *vt* tachar; **~ over** *vt fus* obtener una victoria sobre; **~board** *n* marcador *m*

scorn [skɔːn] *n* desprecio; **~ful** *adj* desdeñoso, despreciativo

Scorpio ['skɔːpɪəu] *n* Escorpión *m*

scorpion ['skɔːpɪən] *n* alacrán *m*

Scot [skɔt] *n* escocés/esa *m/f*

Scotch [skɔtʃ] *n* whisky *m* escocés

Scotland ['skɔtlənd] *n* Escocia

Scots [skɔts] *adj* escocés/esa; **~man/woman** (*irreg*) *n* escocés/esa *m/f*; **Scottish** ['skɔtɪʃ] *adj* escocés/esa

scoundrel ['skaundrl] *n* canalla *m/f*, sinvergüenza *m/f*

scout [skaut] *n* (*MIL, also:* **boy ~**) explorador *m*; (*also: US*) niña exploradora; **~ around** *vi* reconocer el terreno

scowl [skaul] *vi* fruncir el ceño; **to ~ at sb** mirar con ceño a uno

scrabble ['skræbl] *vi* (*claw*): **to ~ (at)** arañar; (*also: ~ around: search*) revolver todo buscando ♦ *n*: **S~** ® Scrabble ® *m*

scraggy ['skrægɪ] *adj* descarnado

scram [skræm] (*inf*) *vi* largarse

scramble ['skræmbl] *n* (*climb*) subida

(difícil); (*struggle*) pelea ♦ *vi*: **to ~ through/out** abrirse paso/salir con dificultad; **to ~ for** pelear por; **~d eggs** *npl* huevos *mpl* revueltos

scrap [skræp] *n* (*bit*) pedacito; (*fig*) pizca; (*fight*) riña, bronca; (*also*: **~ iron**) chatarra, hierro viejo ♦ *vt* (*discard*) desechar, descartar ♦ *vi* reñir, armar (una) bronca; **~s** *npl* (*waste*) sobras *fpl*, desperdicios *mpl*; **~book** *n* álbum *m* de recortes; **~ dealer** *n* chatarrero/a

scrape [skreɪp] *n*: **to get into a ~** meterse en un lío ♦ *vt* raspar; (*skin etc*) rasguñar; (*~ against*) rozar ♦ *vi*: **to ~ through** (*exam*) aprobar por los pelos; **~ together** *vt* (*money*) arañar, juntar

scrap: **~ heap** *n* (*fig*): **to be on the ~ heap** estar acabado; **~ merchant** (*BRIT*) *n* chatarrero/a; **~ paper** *n* pedazos *mpl* de papel

scratch [skrætʃ] *n* rasguño; (*from claw*) arañazo ♦ *cpd*: **~ team** equipo improvisado ♦ *vt* (*paint, car*) rayar; (*with claw, nail*) rasguñar, arañar; (*rub: nose etc*) rascarse ♦ *vi* rascarse; **to start from ~** partir de cero; **to be up to ~** cumplir con los requisitos

scrawl [skrɔːl] *n* garabatos *mpl* ♦ *vi* hacer garabatos

scrawny [ˈskrɔːnɪ] *adj* flaco

scream [skriːm] *n* chillido ♦ *vi* chillar

screech [skriːtʃ] *vi* chirriar

screen [skriːn] *n* (*CINEMA, TV*) pantalla; (*movable barrier*) biombo ♦ *vt* (*conceal*) tapar; (*from the wind etc*) proteger; (*film*) proyectar; (*candidates etc*) investigar a; **~ing** *n* (*MED*) investigación *f* médica; **~play** *n* guión *m*

screw [skruː] *n* tornillo ♦ *vt* (*also*: **~ in**) atornillar; **~ up** *vt* (*paper etc*) arrugar; **to ~ up one's eyes** arrugar el entrecejo; **~driver** *n* destornillador *m*

scribble [ˈskrɪbl] *n* garabatos *mpl* ♦ *vt, vi* garabatear

script [skrɪpt] *n* (*CINEMA etc*) guión *m*; (*writing*) escritura, letra

Scripture(s) [ˈskrɪptʃə*(z)] *n(pl)* Sagrada Escritura

scroll [skrəʊl] *n* rollo

scrounge [skraʊndʒ] (*inf*) *vt*: **to ~ sth off** *or* **from sb** obtener algo de uno de gorra ♦ *n*: **on the ~** de gorra; **~r** *n* gorrón/ona *m/f*

scrub [skrʌb] *n* (*land*) maleza ♦ *vt* fregar, restregar; (*inf: reject*) cancelar, anular

scruff [skrʌf] *n*: **by the ~ of the neck** por el pescuezo

scruffy [ˈskrʌfɪ] *adj* desaliñado, piojoso

scrum(mage) [ˈskrʌm(mɪdʒ)] *n* (*RUGBY*) melée *f*

scruple [ˈskruːpl] *n* (*gen pl*) escrúpulo

scrutinize [ˈskruːtɪnaɪz] *vt* escudriñar; (*votes*) escrutar; **scrutiny** [ˈskruːtɪnɪ] *n* escrutinio, examen *m*

scuff [skʌf] *vt* (*shoes, floor*) rayar

scuffle [ˈskʌfl] *n* refriega

sculptor [ˈskʌlptə*] *n* escultor(a) *m/f*

sculpture [ˈskʌlptʃə*] *n* escultura

scum [skʌm] *n* (*on liquid*) espuma; (*pej: people*) escoria

scurry [ˈskʌrɪ] *vi* correr; **to ~ off** escabullirse

scuttle [ˈskʌtl] *n* (*also*: **coal ~**) cubo, carbonera ♦ *vt* (*ship*) barrenar ♦ *vi* (*scamper*): **to ~ away, ~ off** escabullirse

scythe [saɪð] *n* guadaña

SDP (*BRIT*) *n abbr* = **Social Democratic Party**

sea [siː] *n* mar *m* ♦ *cpd* de mar, marítimo; **by ~** (*travel*) en barco; **on the ~** (*boat*) en el mar; (*town*) junto al mar; **to be all at ~** (*fig*) estar despistado; **out to ~, at ~** en alta mar; **~board** *n* litoral *m*; **~food** *n* mariscos *mpl*; **~ front** *n* paseo marítimo; **~-going** *adj* de altura; **~gull** *n* gaviota

seal [siːl] *n* (*animal*) foca; (*stamp*) sello ♦ *vt* (*close*) cerrar; **~ off** *vt* (*area*) acordonar

sea level *n* nivel *m* del mar

sea lion *n* león *m* marino

seam [siːm] *n* costura; (*of metal*) juntura; (*of coal*) veta, filón *m*

seaman [ˈsiːmən] (*irreg*) *n* marinero

seance [ˈseɪɔns] *n* sesión *f* de espiritismo

seaplane ['si:pleɪn] n hidroavión m
seaport ['si:pɔ:t] n puerto de mar
search [sə:tʃ] n (for person, thing) busca, búsqueda; (COMPUT) búsqueda; (inspection: of sb's home) registro ♦ vt (look in) buscar en; (examine) examinar; (person, place) registrar ♦ vi: **to ~ for** buscar; **in ~ of** en busca de; **~ through** vt fus registrar; **~ing** adj penetrante; **~light** n reflector m; **~ party** n pelotón m de salvamento; **~ warrant** n mandamiento (judicial)
sea: **~shore** n playa, orilla del mar; **~sick** adj mareado; **~side** n playa, orilla del mar; **~side resort** n centro turístico costero
season ['si:zn] n (of year) estación f; (sporting etc) temporada; (of films etc) ciclo ♦ vt (food) sazonar; **in/out of ~** en sazón/fuera de temporada; **~al** adj estacional; **~ed** adj (fig) experimentado; **~ing** n condimento, aderezo; **~ ticket** n abono
seat [si:t] n (in bus, train) asiento; (chair) silla; (PARLIAMENT) escaño; (buttocks) culo, trasero; (of trousers) culera ♦ vt sentar; **to be ~ed** sentarse; **~ belt** n cinturón m de seguridad
sea: **~ water** n agua del mar; **~weed** n alga marina; **~worthy** adj en condiciones de navegar
sec. abbr = **second(s)**
secluded [sɪ'klu:dɪd] adj retirado
seclusion [sɪ'klu:ʒən] n reclusión f
second ['sekənd] adj segundo ♦ adv en segundo lugar ♦ n segundo; (AUT: also: **~ gear**) segunda; (COMM) artículo con algún desperfecto; (BRIT: SCOL: degree) título de licenciado con calificación de notable ♦ vt (motion) apoyar; **~ary** adj secundario; **~ary school** n escuela secundaria; **~-class** adj de segunda clase ♦ adv (RAIL) en segunda; **~hand** adj de segunda mano, usado; **~ hand** n (on clock) segundero; **~ly** adv en segundo lugar; **~ment** [sɪ'kɔndmənt] (BRIT) n

traslado temporal; **~-rate** adj de segunda categoría; **~ thoughts** npl: **to have ~ thoughts** cambiar de opinión; **on ~ thoughts** or **thought** (US) pensándolo bien
secrecy ['si:krəsɪ] n secreto
secret ['si:krɪt] adj, n secreto; **in ~** en secreto
secretarial [sekrɪ'tɛərɪəl] adj de secretario; (course, staff) de secretariado
secretary ['sekrətərɪ] n secretario/a; **S~ of State (for)** (BRIT: POL) Ministro (de)
secretive ['si:krətɪv] adj reservado, sigiloso
secretly ['si:krɪtlɪ] adv en secreto
sect [sekt] n secta; **~arian** [-'tɛərɪən] adj sectario
section ['sekʃən] n sección f; (part) parte f; (of document) artículo; (of opinion) sector m; (cross-~) corte m transversal
sector ['sektə*] n sector m
secular ['sekjulə*] adj secular, seglar
secure [sɪ'kjuə*] adj seguro; (firmly fixed) firme, fijo ♦ vt (fix) asegurar, afianzar; (get) conseguir
security [sɪ'kjuərɪtɪ] n seguridad f; (for loan) fianza; (: object) prenda
sedate [sɪ'deɪt] adj tranquilo ♦ vt tratar con sedantes
sedation [sɪ'deɪʃən] n (MED) sedación f
sedative ['sedɪtɪv] n sedante m, sedativo
seduce [sɪ'dju:s] vt seducir; **seduction** [-'dʌkʃən] n seducción f; **seductive** [-'dʌktɪv] adj seductor(a)
see [si:] (pt **saw**, pp **seen**) vt ver; (accompany): **to ~ sb to the door** acompañar a uno a la puerta; (understand) ver, comprender ♦ vi ver ♦ n (arz)obispado; **to ~ that** (ensure) asegurar que; **~ you soon!** ¡hasta pronto!; **~ about** vt fus atender a, encargarse de; **~ off** vt despedir; **~ through** vt fus (fig) calar ♦ vt (plan) llevar a cabo; **~ to** vt fus atender a, encargarse de
seed [si:d] n semilla; (in fruit) pepita; (fig: gen pl) germen m; (TENNIS etc) preseleccionado/a; **to go to ~** (plant) granar; (fig) descuidarse; **~ling** n planta

de semillero; **~y** *adj* (*shabby*) desaseado, raído

seeing ['si:ɪŋ] *conj*: **~ (that)** visto que, en vista de que

seek [si:k] (*pt, pp* **sought**) *vt* buscar; (*post*) solicitar

seem [si:m] *vi* parecer; **there ~s to be ...** parece que hay ...; **~ingly** *adv* aparentemente, según parece

seen [si:n] *pp of* **see**

seep [si:p] *vi* filtrarse

seesaw ['si:sɔ:] *n* subibaja

seethe [si:ð] *vi* hervir; **to ~ with anger** estar furioso

see-through *adj* transparente

segment ['segmənt] *n* (*part*) sección *f*; (*of orange*) gajo

segregate ['segrɪgeɪt] *vt* segregar

seize [si:z] *vt* (*grasp*) agarrar, asir; (*take possession of*) secuestrar; (: *territory*) apoderarse de; (*opportunity*) aprovecharse de; **~ (up)on** *vt fus* aprovechar; **~ up** *vi* (*TECH*) agarrotarse

seizure ['si:ʒə*] *n* (*MED*) ataque *m*; (*LAW, of power*) incautación *f*

seldom ['seldəm] *adv* rara vez

select [sɪ'lekt] *adj* selecto, escogido ♦ *vt* escoger, elegir; (*SPORT*) seleccionar; **~ion** [-'lekʃən] *n* selección *f*, elección *f*; (*COMM*) surtido

self [self] (*pl* **selves**) *n* uno mismo; **the ~** el yo ♦ *prefix* auto...; **~-assured** *adj* seguro de sí mismo; **~-catering** (*BRIT*) *adj* (*flat etc*) con cocina; **~-centred** (*US* **~-centered**) *adj* egocéntrico; **~-confidence** *n* confianza en sí mismo; **~-conscious** *adj* cohibido; **~-contained** (*BRIT*) *adj* (*flat*) con entrada particular; **~-control** *n* autodominio; **~-defence** (*US* **~-defense**) *n* defensa propia; **~-discipline** *n* autodisciplina; **~-employed** *adj* que trabaja por cuenta propia; **~-evident** *adj* patente; **~-governing** *adj* autónomo; **~-indulgent** *adj* autocomplaciente; **~-interest** *n* egoísmo; **~ish** *adj* egoísta; **~ishness** *n* egoísmo; **~less** *adj* desinteresado; **~-**

made *adj*: **~-made man** hombre *m* que se ha hecho a sí mismo; **~-pity** *n* lástima de sí mismo; **~-portrait** *n* autorretrato; **~-possessed** *adj* sereno, dueño de sí mismo; **~-preservation** *n* propia conservación *f*; **~-respect** *n* amor *m* propio; **~-righteous** *adj* santurrón/ona; **~-sacrifice** *n* abnegación *f*; **~-satisfied** *adj* satisfecho de sí mismo; **~-service** *adj* de autoservicio; **~-sufficient** *adj* autosuficiente; **~-taught** *adj* autodidacta

sell [sel] (*pt, pp* **sold**) *vt* vender ♦ *vi* venderse; **to ~ at** *or* **for £10** venderse a 10 libras; **~ off** *vt* liquidar; **~ out** *vi*: **to ~ out of tickets/milk** vender todas las entradas/toda la leche; **~-by date** *n* fecha de caducidad; **~er** *n* vendedor(a) *m/f*; **~ing price** *n* precio de venta

Sellotape ® ['seləuteɪp] (*BRIT*) *n* cinta adhesiva, celo (*SP*), scotch *m* (*AM*)

selves [selvz] *npl of* **self**

semblance ['sembləns] *n* apariencia

semen ['si:mən] *n* semen *m*

semester [sɪ'mestə*] (*US*) *n* semestre *m*

semi... ['semɪ] *prefix* semi..., medio...; **~circle** *n* semicírculo; **~colon** *n* punto y coma; **~conductor** *n* semiconductor *m*; **~detached (house)** *n* (*casa*) semiseparada; **~final** *n* semi-final *m*

seminar ['semɪnɑ:*] *n* seminario

seminary ['semɪnərɪ] *n* (*REL*) seminario

semiskilled ['semɪskɪld] *adj* (*work, worker*) semi-cualificada

semi-skimmed (milk) *n* leche semidesnatada

senate ['senɪt] *n* senado; **senator** *n* senador(a) *m/f*

send [send] (*pt, pp* **sent**) *vt* mandar, enviar; (*signal*) transmitir; **~ away** *vt* despachar; **~ away for** *vt fus* pedir; **~ back** *vt* devolver; **~ for** *vt fus* mandar traer; **~ off** *vt* (*goods*) despachar; (*BRIT: SPORT: player*) expulsar; **~ out** *vt* (*invitation*) mandar; (*signal*) emitir; **~ up** *vt* (*person, price*) hacer subir; (*BRIT: parody*) parodiar; **~er** *n* remitente *m/f*;

~-off *n*: **a good ~-off** una buena despedida

senior ['si:nɪə*] *adj* (*older*) mayor, más viejo; (: *on staff*) de más antigüedad; (*of higher rank*) superior; **~ citizen** *n* persona de la tercera edad; **~ity** [-'ɔrɪti] *n* antigüedad *f*

sensation [sen'seɪʃən] *n* sensación *f*; **~al** *adj* sensacional

sense [sens] *n* (*faculty, meaning*) sentido; (*feeling*) sensación *f*; (*good ~*) sentido común, juicio ♦ *vt* sentir, percibir; **it makes ~** tiene sentido; **~less** *adj* estúpido, insensato; (*unconscious*) sin conocimiento; **~ of humour** *n* sentido del humor

sensible ['sensɪbl] *adj* sensato; (*reasonable*) razonable, lógico

sensitive ['sensɪtɪv] *adj* sensible; (*touchy*) susceptible

sensual ['sensjuəl] *adj* sensual

sensuous ['sensjuəs] *adj* sensual

sent [sent] *pt, pp of* **send**

sentence ['sentns] *n* (*LING*) oración *f*; (*LAW*) sentencia, fallo ♦ *vt*: **to ~ sb to death/to 5 years (in prison)** condenar a uno a muerte/a 5 años de cárcel

sentiment ['sentɪmənt] *n* sentimiento; (*opinion*) opinión *f*; **~al** [-'mentl] *adj* sentimental

sentry ['sentrɪ] *n* centinela *m*

separate [*adj* 'seprɪt, *vb* 'sepəreɪt] *adj* separado; (*distinct*) distinto ♦ *vt* separar; (*part*) dividir ♦ *vi* separarse; **~s** *npl* (*clothes*) coordinados *mpl*; **~ly** *adv* por separado; **separation** [-'reɪʃən] *n* separación *f*

September [sep'tembə*] *n* se(p)tiembre *m*

septic ['septɪk] *adj* séptico; **~ tank** *n* fosa séptica

sequel ['si:kwl] *n* consecuencia, resultado; (*of story*) continuación *f*

sequence ['si:kwəns] *n* sucesión *f*, serie *f*; (*CINEMA*) secuencia

sequin ['si:kwɪn] *n* lentejuela

serene [sɪ'ri:n] *adj* sereno, tranquilo

sergeant ['sɑ:dʒənt] *n* sargento

serial ['sɪərɪəl] *n* (*TV*) telenovela, serie *f* televisiva; (*BOOK*) serie *f*; **~ize** *vt* emitir como serial; **~ killer** *n* asesino/a múltiple; **~ number** *n* número de serie

series ['sɪərɪːs] *n inv* serie *f*

serious ['sɪərɪəs] *adj* serio; (*grave*) grave; **~ly** *adv* en serio; (*ill, wounded etc*) gravemente

sermon ['sə:mən] *n* sermón *m*

serrated [sɪ'reɪtɪd] *adj* serrado, dentellado

serum ['sɪərəm] *n* suero

servant ['sə:vənt] *n* servidor(a) *m/f*; (*house ~*) criado/a

serve [sə:v] *vt* servir; (*customer*) atender; (*subj: train*) pasar por; (*apprenticeship*) hacer; (*prison term*) cumplir ♦ *vi* (*at table*) servir; (*TENNIS*) sacar; **to ~ as/for/to do** servir de/para/para hacer ♦ *n* (*TENNIS*) saque *m*; **it ~s him right** se lo tiene merecido; **~ out** *vt* (*food*) servir; **~ up** *vt* = **~ out**

service ['sə:vɪs] *n* servicio; (*REL*) misa; (*AUT*) mantenimiento; (*dishes etc*) juego ♦ *vt* (*car etc*) revisar; (: *repair*) reparar; **the S~s** *npl* las fuerzas armadas; **to be of ~ to sb** ser útil a uno; **~ included/not included** servicio incluído/no incluído; **~able** *adj* servible, utilizable; **~ area** *n* (*on motorway*) area de servicio; **~ charge** (*BRIT*) *n* servicio; **~man** *n* militar *m*; **~ station** *n* estación *f* de servicio

serviette [sə:vɪ'et] (*BRIT*) *n* servilleta

session ['seʃən] *n* sesión *f*; **to be in ~** estar en sesión

set [set] (*pt, pp* **set**) *n* juego; (*RADIO*) aparato; (*TV*) televisor *m*; (*of utensils*) batería; (*of cutlery*) cubierto; (*of books*) colección *f*; (*TENNIS*) set *m*; (*group of people*) grupo; (*CINEMA*) plató *m*; (*THEATRE*) decorado; (*HAIRDRESSING*) marcado ♦ *adj* (*fixed*) fijo, fijado; (*ready*) listo ♦ *vt* (*place*) poner, colocar; (*fix*) fijar; (*adjust*) ajustar, arreglar; (*decide: rules etc*) establecer, decidir ♦ *vi* (*sun*) ponerse; (*jam, jelly*) cuajarse; (*concrete*) fraguar; (*bone*) componerse; **to be ~ on doing sth** estar empeñado en hacer algo; **to ~ to**

music poner música a; **to ~ on fire** incendiar, poner fuego a; **to ~ free** poner en libertad; **to ~ sth going** poner algo en marcha; **to ~ sail** zarpar, hacerse a la vela; ~ **about** *vt fus* ponerse a; ~ **aside** *vt* poner aparte, dejar de lado; (*money, time*) reservar; ~ **back** *vt* (*cost*): **to ~ sb back £5** costar a uno cinco libras; (: *in time*): **to ~ back (by)** retrasar (por); ~ **off** *vi* partir ♦ *vt* (*bomb*) hacer estallar; (*events*) poner en marcha; (*show up well*) hacer resaltar; ~ **out** *vi* partir ♦ *vt* (*arrange*) disponer; (*state*) exponer; **to ~ out to do sth** proponerse hacer algo; ~ **up** *vt* establecer; **~back** *n* revés *m*, contratiempo; ~ **menu** *n* menú *m*

settee [se'ti:] *n* sofá *m*

setting ['setɪŋ] *n* (*scenery*) marco; (*position*) disposición *f*; (*of sun*) puesta; (*of jewel*) engaste *m*, montadura

settle ['setl] *vt* (*argument*) resolver; (*accounts*) ajustar, liquidar; (*MED: calm*) calmar, sosegar ♦ *vi* (*dust etc*) depositarse; (*weather*) serenarse; (*also*: ~ **down**) instalarse; tranquilizarse; **to ~ for sth** convenir en aceptar algo; **to ~ on sth** decidirse por algo; ~ **in** *vi* instalarse; ~ **up** *vi*: **to ~ up with sb** ajustar cuentas con uno; **~ment** *n* (*payment*) liquidación *f*; (*agreement*) acuerdo, convenio; (*village etc*) pueblo; **~r** *n* colono/a, colonizador(a) *m/f*

setup ['setʌp] *n* sistema *m*; (*situation*) situación *f*

seven ['sevn] *num* siete; **~teen** *num* diez y siete, diecisiete; **~th** *num* séptimo; **~ty** *num* setenta

sever ['sevə*] *vt* cortar; (*relations*) romper

several ['sevərl] *adj, pron* varios/as *m/fpl*, algunos/as *m/fpl*; ~ **of us** varios de nosotros

severance ['sevərəns] *n* (*of relations*) ruptura; ~ **pay** *n* indemnización *f* por despido

severe [sɪ'vɪə*] *adj* severo; (*serious*) grave; (*hard*) duro; (*pain*) intenso; **severity** [sɪ'verɪtɪ] *n* severidad *f*; gravedad *f*;

intensidad *f*

sew [səu] (*pt* **sewed**, *pp* **sewn**) *vt, vi* coser; ~ **up** *vt* coser, zurcir

sewage ['su:ɪdʒ] *n* aguas *fpl* residuales

sewer ['su:ə*] *n* alcantarilla, cloaca

sewing ['səuɪŋ] *n* costura; ~ **machine** *n* máquina de coser

sewn [səun] *pp of* **sew**

sex [seks] *n* sexo; (*lovemaking*): **to have ~** hacer el amor; **~ist** *adj, n* sexista *m/f*; **~ual** ['seksjuəl] *adj* sexual; **~y** *adj* sexy

shabby ['ʃæbɪ] *adj* (*person*) desharrapado; (*clothes*) raído, gastado; (*behaviour*) ruin *inv*

shack [ʃæk] *n* choza, chabola

shackles ['ʃæklz] *npl* grillos *mpl*, grilletes *mpl*

shade [ʃeɪd] *n* sombra; (*for lamp*) pantalla; (*for eyes*) visera; (*of colour*) matiz *m*, tonalidad *f*; (*small quantity*): **a ~ (too big/more)** un poquitín (grande/más) ♦ *vt* dar sombra a; (*eyes*) proteger del sol; **in the ~** en la sombra

shadow ['ʃædəu] *n* sombra ♦ *vt* (*follow*) seguir y vigilar; ~ **cabinet** (*BRIT*) *n* (*POL*) *gabinete paralelo formado por el partido de oposición*; **~y** *adj* oscuro; (*dim*) indistinto

shady ['ʃeɪdɪ] *adj* sombreado; (*fig: dishonest*) sospechoso; (: *deal*) turbio

shaft [ʃɑ:ft] *n* (*of arrow, spear*) astil *m*; (*AUT, TECH*) eje *m*, árbol *m*; (*of mine*) pozo; (*of lift*) hueco, caja; (*of light*) rayo

shaggy ['ʃægɪ] *adj* peludo

shake [ʃeɪk] (*pt* **shook**, *pp* **shaken**) *vt* sacudir; (*building*) hacer temblar; (*bottle, cocktail*) agitar ♦ *vi* (*tremble*) temblar; **to ~ one's head** (*in refusal*) negar con la cabeza; (*in dismay*) mover *or* menear la cabeza, incrédulo; **to ~ hands with sb** estrechar la mano a uno; ~ **off** *vt* sacudirse; (*fig*) deshacerse de; ~ **up** *vt* agitar; (*fig*) reorganizar; **shaky** *adj* (*hand, voice*) trémulo; (*building*) inestable

shall [ʃæl] *aux vb*: ~ **I help you?** ¿quieres que te ayude?; **I'll buy three, ~ I?** compro tres, ¿no te parece?

shallow ['ʃæləu] *adj* poco profundo; (*fig*) superficial

sham [ʃæm] *n* fraude *m*, engaño ♦ *vt* fingir, simular

shambles ['ʃæmblz] *n* confusión *f*

shame [ʃeɪm] *n* vergüenza ♦ *vt* avergonzar; **it is a ~ that/to do** es una lástima que/hacer; **what a ~!** ¡qué lástima!; **~ful** *adj* vergonzoso; **~less** *adj* desvergonzado

shampoo [ʃæm'puː] *n* champú *m* ♦ *vt* lavar con champú; **~ and set** *n* lavado y marcado

shamrock ['ʃæmrɔk] *n* trébol *m* (*emblema nacional irlandés*)

shandy ['ʃændɪ] *n* mezcla de cerveza con gaseosa

shan't [ʃɑːnt] = **shall not**

shantytown ['ʃæntɪtaun] *n* barrio de chabolas

shape [ʃeɪp] *n* forma ♦ *vt* formar, dar forma a; (*sb's ideas*) formar; (*sb's life*) determinar; **to take ~** tomar forma; **~ up** *vi* (*events*) desarrollarse; (*person*) formarse; **~d** *suffix*: **heart-~d** en forma de corazón; **~less** *adj* informe, sin forma definida; **~ly** *adj* (*body etc*) esbelto

share [ʃɛə*] *n* (*part*) parte *f*, porción *f*; (*contribution*) cuota; (*COMM*) acción *f* ♦ *vt* dividir; (*have in common*) compartir; **to ~ out (among** *or* **between)** repartir (entre); **~holder** (*BRIT*) *n* accionista *m/f*

shark [ʃɑːk] *n* tiburón *m*

sharp [ʃɑːp] *adj* (*blade, nose*) afilado; (*point*) puntiagudo; (*outline*) definido; (*pain*) intenso; (*MUS*) desafinado; (*contrast*) marcado; (*voice*) agudo; (*person: quick-witted*) astuto; (: *dishonest*) poco escrupuloso ♦ *n* (*MUS*) sostenido ♦ *adv*: **at 2 o'clock ~** a las 2 en punto; **~en** *vt* afilar; (*pencil*) sacar punta a; (*fig*) agudizar; **~ener** *n* (*also*: **pencil ~ener**) sacapuntas *m inv*; **~-eyed** *adj* de vista aguda; **~ly** *adv* (*turn, stop*) bruscamente; (*stand out, contrast*) claramente; (*criticize, retort*) severamente

shatter ['ʃætə*] *vt* hacer añicos *or* pedazos; (*fig: ruin*) destruir, acabar con ♦ *vi* hacerse añicos

shave [ʃeɪv] *vt* afeitar, rasurar ♦ *vi* afeitarse, rasurarse ♦ *n*: **to have a ~** afeitarse; **~r** *n* (*also*: **electric ~r**) máquina de afeitar (eléctrica)

shaving ['ʃeɪvɪŋ] *n* (*action*) el afeitarse, rasurado; **~s** *npl* (*of wood etc*) virutas *fpl*; **~ brush** *n* brocha (de afeitar); **~ cream** *n* crema de afeitar; **~ foam** *n* espuma de afeitar

shawl [ʃɔːl] *n* chal *m*

she [ʃiː] *pron* ella; **~-cat** *n* gata

sheaf [ʃiːf] (*pl* **sheaves**) *n* (*of corn*) gavilla; (*of papers*) fajo

shear [ʃɪə*] (*pt* **sheared**, *pp* **sheared** *or* **shorn**) *vt* esquilar, trasquilar; **~s** *npl* (*for hedge*) tijeras *fpl* de jardín

sheath [ʃiːθ] *n* vaina; (*contraceptive*) preservativo

sheaves [ʃiːvz] *npl of* **sheaf**

shed [ʃɛd] (*pt, pp* **shed**) *n* cobertizo ♦ *vt* (*skin*) mudar; (*tears, blood*) derramar; (*load*) derramar; (*workers*) despedir

she'd [ʃiːd] = **she had; she would**

sheen [ʃiːn] *n* brillo, lustre *m*

sheep [ʃiːp] *n inv* oveja; **~dog** *n* perro pastor; **~skin** *n* piel *f* de carnero

sheer [ʃɪə*] *adj* (*utter*) puro, completo; (*steep*) escarpado; (*material*) diáfano ♦ *adv* verticalmente

sheet [ʃiːt] *n* (*on bed*) sábana; (*of paper*) hoja; (*of glass, metal*) lámina; (*of ice*) capa

sheik(h) [ʃeɪk] *n* jeque *m*

shelf [ʃɛlf] (*pl* **shelves**) *n* estante *m*

shell [ʃɛl] *n* (*on beach*) concha; (*of egg, nut etc*) cáscara; (*explosive*) proyectil *m*, obús *m*; (*of building*) armazón *f* ♦ *vt* (*peas*) desenvainar; (*MIL*) bombardear

she'll [ʃiːl] = **she will; she shall**

shellfish ['ʃɛlfɪʃ] *n inv* crustáceo; (*as food*) mariscos *mpl*

shell suit *n* chándal *m* de calle

shelter ['ʃɛltə*] *n* abrigo, refugio ♦ *vt* (*aid*) amparar, proteger; (*give lodging to*) abrigar ♦ *vi* abrigarse, refugiarse; **~ed** *adj* (*life*) protegido; (*spot*) abrigado; **~ed**

housing n viviendas vigiladas para ancianos y minusválidos

shelve [ʃɛlv] vt (fig) aplazar; **~s** npl of **shelf**

shepherd [ˈʃɛpəd] n pastor m ♦ vt (guide) guiar, conducir; **~'s pie** (BRIT) n pastel de carne y patatas

sherry [ˈʃɛrɪ] n jerez m

she's [ʃiːz] = **she is**; **she has**

Shetland [ˈʃɛtlənd] n (also: **the ~ Isles**) las Islas de Zetlandia

shield [ʃiːld] n escudo; (protection) blindaje m ♦ vt: **to ~ (from)** proteger (de)

shift [ʃɪft] n (change) cambio; (at work) turno ♦ vt trasladar; (remove) quitar ♦ vi moverse; **~ work** n trabajo a turnos; **~y** adj tramposo; (eyes) furtivo

shimmer [ˈʃɪmə*] n reflejo trémulo

shin [ʃɪn] n espinilla

shine [ʃaɪn] (pt, pp **shone**) n brillo, lustre m ♦ vi brillar, relucir ♦ vt (shoes) lustrar, sacar brillo a; **to ~ a torch on sth** dirigir una linterna hacia algo

shingle [ˈʃɪŋɡl] n (on beach) guijarros mpl; **~s** n (MED) herpes mpl or fpl

shiny [ˈʃaɪnɪ] adj brillante, lustroso

ship [ʃɪp] n buque m, barco ♦ vt (goods) embarcar; (send) transportar or enviar por vía marítima; **~building** n construcción f de buques; **~ment** n (goods) envío; **~ping** n (act) embarque m; (traffic) buques mpl; **~wreck** n naufragio ♦ vt: **to be ~wrecked** naufragar; **~yard** n astillero

shire [ˈʃaɪə*] (BRIT) n condado

shirt [ʃəːt] n camisa; **in (one's) ~ sleeves** en mangas de camisa

shit [ʃɪt] (inf!) excl ¡mierda! (!)

shiver [ˈʃɪvə*] n escalofrío ♦ vi temblar, estremecerse; (with cold) tiritar

shoal [ʃəʊl] n (of fish) banco; (fig: also: **~s**) tropel m

shock [ʃɔk] n (impact) choque m; (ELEC) descarga (eléctrica); (emotional) conmoción f; (start) sobresalto, susto; (MED) postración f nerviosa ♦ vt dar un susto a; (offend) escandalizar; **~**

absorber n amortiguador m; **~ing** adj (awful) espantoso; (outrageous) escandaloso

shoddy [ˈʃɔdɪ] adj de pacotilla

shoe [ʃuː] (pt, pp **shod**) n zapato; (for horse) herradura ♦ vt (horse) herrar; **~brush** n cepillo para zapatos; **~lace** n cordón m; **~ polish** n betún m; **~shop** n zapatería; **~string** n (fig): **on a ~string** con muy poco dinero

shone [ʃɔn] pt, pp of **shine**

shook [ʃʊk] pt of **shake**

shoot [ʃuːt] (pt, pp **shot**) n (on branch, seedling) retoño, vástago ♦ vt disparar; (kill) matar a tiros; (wound) pegar un tiro; (execute) fusilar; (film) rodar, filmar ♦ vi (FOOTBALL) chutar; **~ down** vt (plane) derribar; **~ in/out** vi entrar corriendo/ salir disparado; **~ up** vi (prices) dispararse; **~ing** n (shots) tiros mpl; (HUNTING) caza con escopeta; **~ing star** n estrella fugaz

shop [ʃɔp] n tienda; (workshop) taller m ♦ vi (also: **go ~ping**) ir de compras; **~ assistant** (BRIT) n dependiente/a m/f; **~ floor** (BRIT) n (fig) taller m, fábrica; **~keeper** n tendero/a; **~lifting** n mechería; **~per** n comprador(a) m/f; **~ping** n (goods) compras fpl; **~ping bag** n bolsa (de compras); **~ping centre** (US **~ping center**) n centro comercial; **~-soiled** adj deteriorado; **~ steward** (BRIT) n (INDUSTRY) enlace m sindical; **~ window** n escaparate m (SP), vidriera (AM)

shore [ʃɔː*] n orilla ♦ vt: **to ~ (up)** reforzar; **on ~** en tierra

shorn [ʃɔːn] pp of **shear**

short [ʃɔːt] adj corto; (in time) breve, de corta duración; (person) bajo; (curt) brusco, seco; (insufficient) insuficiente; **(a pair of) ~s** (unos) pantalones mpl cortos; **to be ~ of sth** estar falto de algo; **in ~** en pocas palabras; **~ of doing ...** fuera de hacer ...; **it is ~ for** es la forma abreviada de; **to cut ~** (speech, visit) interrumpir, terminar inesperadamente; **everything ~**

of ... todo menos ...; **to fall ~ of** no alcanzar; **to run ~ of** quedarle a uno poco; **to stop ~** parar en seco; **to stop ~ of** detenerse antes de; **~age** n: a **~age of** una falta de; **~bread** n *especie de mantecada*; **~change** vt no dar el cambio completo a; **~circuit** n cortocircuito; **~coming** n defecto, deficiencia; **~(crust) pastry** (BRIT) n pasta quebradiza; **~cut** n atajo; **~en** vt acortar; (visit) interrumpir; **~fall** n déficit m; **~hand** (BRIT) n taquigrafía; **~hand typist** (BRIT) n taquimecanógrafo/a; **~ list** (BRIT) n (for job) lista de candidatos escogidos; **~lived** adj efímero; **~ly** adv en breve, dentro de poco; **~sighted** (BRIT) adj miope; (fig) imprudente; **~staffed** adj: **to be ~staffed** estar falto de personal; **~ story** n cuento; **~tempered** adj enojadizo; **~term** adj (effect) a corto plazo; **~wave** n (RADIO) onda corta

shot [ʃɔt] pt, pp of **shoot** ♦ n (sound) tiro, disparo; (try) tentativa; (injection) inyección f; (PHOT) toma, fotografía; **to be a good/poor ~** (person) tener buena/mala puntería; **like a ~** (without any delay) como un rayo; **~gun** n escopeta

should [ʃud] aux vb: **I ~ go now** debo irme ahora; **he ~ be there now** debe de haber llegado (ya); **I ~ go if I were you** yo en tu lugar me iría; **I ~ like to** me gustaría

shoulder [ˈʃəʊldə*] n hombro ♦ vt (fig) cargar con; **~ bag** n cartera de bandolera; **~ blade** n omóplato

shouldn't [ˈʃudnt] = **should not**

shout [ʃaut] n grito ♦ vt gritar ♦ vi gritar, dar voces; **~ down** vt acallar a gritos; **~ing** n griterío

shove [ʃʌv] n empujón m ♦ vt empujar; (inf: put): **to ~ sth in** meter algo a empellones; **~ off** (inf) vi largarse

shovel [ˈʃʌvl] n pala; (mechanical) excavadora ♦ vt mover con pala

show [ʃəʊ] (pt **showed**, pp **shown**) n (of emotion) demostración f; (semblance)

apariencia; (exhibition) exposición f; (THEATRE) función f, espectáculo; (TV) show m ♦ vt mostrar, enseñar; (courage etc) mostrar, manifestar; (exhibit) exponer; (film) proyectar ♦ vi mostrarse; (appear) aparecer; **for ~** para impresionar; **on ~** (exhibits etc) expuesto; **~ in** vt (person) hacer pasar; **~ off** (pej) vi presumir ♦ vt (display) lucir; **~ out** vt: **to ~ sb out** acompañar a uno a la puerta; **~ up** vi (stand out) destacar; (inf: turn up) aparecer ♦ vt (unmask) desenmascarar; **~ business** n mundo del espectáculo; **~down** n enfrentamiento (final)

shower [ˈʃauə*] n (rain) chaparrón m, chubasco; (of stones etc) lluvia; (for bathing) ducha (SP), regadera (AM) ♦ vi llover ♦ vt (fig): **to ~ sb with sth** colmar a uno de algo; **to have a ~** ducharse; **~proof** adj impermeable

showing [ˈʃəʊɪŋ] n (of film) proyección f

show jumping n hípica

shown [ʃəʊn] pp of **show**

show: ~-off (inf) n (person) presumido/a; **~piece** n (of exhibition etc) objeto cumbre; **~room** n sala de muestras

shrank [ʃræŋk] pt of **shrink**

shrapnel [ˈʃræpnl] n metralla

shred [ʃred] n (gen pl) triza, jirón m ♦ vt hacer trizas; (CULIN) desmenuzar; **~der** n (vegetable ~der) picadora; (document ~der) trituradora (de papel)

shrewd [ʃruːd] adj astuto

shriek [ʃriːk] n chillido ♦ vi chillar

shrill [ʃrɪl] adj agudo, estridente

shrimp [ʃrɪmp] n camarón m

shrine [ʃraɪn] n santuario, sepulcro

shrink [ʃrɪŋk] (pt **shrank**, pp **shrunk**) vi encogerse; (be reduced) reducirse; (also: **~ away**) retroceder ♦ vt encoger ♦ n (inf: pej) loquero/a; **to ~ from (doing) sth** no atreverse a hacer algo; **~wrap** vt embalar con película de plástico

shrivel [ˈʃrɪvl] (also: **~ up**) vt (dry) secar ♦ vi secarse

shroud [ʃraud] n sudario ♦ vt: **~ed in mystery** envuelto en el misterio

Shrove Tuesday [ˈʃrəuv-] *n* martes *m* de carnaval

shrub [ʃrʌb] *n* arbusto; **~bery** *n* arbustos *mpl*

shrug [ʃrʌg] *n* encogimiento de hombros ♦ *vt, vi*: **to ~ (one's shoulders)** encogerse de hombros; **~ off** *vt* negar importancia a

shrunk [ʃrʌŋk] *pp of* **shrink**

shudder [ˈʃʌdə*] *n* estremecimiento, escalofrío ♦ *vi* estremecerse

shuffle [ˈʃʌfl] *vt* (*cards*) barajar ♦ *vi*: **to ~ (one's feet)** arrastrar los pies

shun [ʃʌn] *vt* rehuir, esquivar

shunt [ʃʌnt] *vt* (*train*) maniobrar; (*object*) empujar

shut [ʃʌt] (*pt, pp* **shut**) *vt* cerrar ♦ *vi* cerrarse; **~ down** *vt, vi* cerrar; **~ off** *vt* (*supply etc*) cortar; **~ up** *vi* (*inf: keep quiet*) callarse ♦ *vt* (*close*) cerrar; (*silence*) hacer callar; **~ter** *n* contraventana; (*PHOT*) obturador *m*

shuttle [ˈʃʌtl] *n* lanzadera; (*also: ~ service*) servicio rápido y continuo entre dos puntos: (: *AVIAT*) puente *m* aéreo; **~cock** *n* volante *m*; **~ diplomacy** *n* viajes *mpl* diplomáticos

shy [ʃaɪ] *adj* tímido; **~ness** *n* timidez *f*

Sicily [ˈsɪsɪlɪ] *n* Sicilia

sick [sɪk] *adj* (*ill*) enfermo; (*nauseated*) mareado; (*humour*) negro; (*vomiting*): **to be ~** (*BRIT*) vomitar; **to feel ~** tener náuseas; **to be ~ of** (*fig*) estar harto de; **~ bay** *n* enfermería; **~en** *vt* dar asco a; **~ening** *adj* (*fig*) asqueroso

sickle [ˈsɪkl] *n* hoz *f*

sick: **~ leave** *n* baja por enfermedad; **~ly** *adj* enfermizo; (*smell*) nauseabundo; **~ness** *n* enfermedad *f*, mal *m*; (*vomiting*) náuseas *fpl*; **~ pay** *n* subsidio de enfermedad

side [saɪd] *n* (*gen*) lado; (*of body*) costado; (*of lake*) orilla; (*of hill*) ladera; (*team*) equipo, ♦ *adj* (*door, entrance*) lateral ♦ *vi*: **to ~ with sb** tomar el partido de uno; **by the ~ of** al lado de; **~ by ~** juntos/as; **from ~ to ~** de un lado para otro; **from**

all ~s de todos lados; **to take ~s (with)** tomar partido (con); **~board** *n* aparador *m*; **~boards** (*BRIT*) *npl* = **~burns**; **~burns** *npl* patillas *fpl*; **~ drum** *n* tambor *m*; **~ effect** *n* efecto secundario; **~light** *n* (*AUT*) luz *f* lateral; **~line** *n* (*SPORT*) línea de banda; (*fig*) empleo suplementario; **~long** *adj* de soslayo; **~ order** *n* plato de acompañamiento; **~ show** *n* (*stall*) caseta; **~step** *vt* (*fig*) esquivar; **~ street** *n* calle *f* lateral; **~track** *vt* (*fig*) desviar (de su propósito); **~walk** (*US*) *n* acera; **~ways** *adv* de lado

siding [ˈsaɪdɪŋ] *n* (*RAIL*) apartadero, vía muerta

siege [siːdʒ] *n* cerco, sitio

sieve [sɪv] *n* colador *m* ♦ *vt* cribar

sift [sɪft] *vt* cribar; (*fig: information*) escudriñar

sigh [saɪ] *n* suspiro ♦ *vi* suspirar

sight [saɪt] *n* (*faculty*) vista; (*spectacle*) espectáculo; (*on gun*) mira, alza ♦ *vt* divisar; **in ~** a la vista; **out of ~** fuera de (la) vista; **on ~** (*shoot*) sin previo aviso; **~seeing** *n* excursionismo, turismo; **to go ~seeing** hacer turismo

sign [saɪn] *n* (*with hand*) señal *f*, seña; (*trace*) huella, rastro; (*notice*) letrero; (*written*) signo ♦ *vt* firmar; (*SPORT*) fichar; **to ~ sth over to sb** firmar el traspaso de algo a uno; **~ on** *vi* (*BRIT: as unemployed*) registrarse como desempleado; (*for course*) inscribirse ♦ *vt* (*MIL*) alistar; (*employee*) contratar; **~ up** *vi* (*MIL*) alistarse; (*for course*) inscribirse ♦ *vt* (*player*) fichar

signal [ˈsɪgnl] *n* señal *f* ♦ *vi* señalizar ♦ *vt* (*person*) hacer señas a; (*message*) comunicar por señales; **~man** (*irreg*) *n* (*RAIL*) guardavía *m*

signature [ˈsɪgnətʃə*] *n* firma; **~ tune** *n* sintonía de apertura de un programa

signet ring [ˈsɪgnət-] *n* anillo de sello

significance [sɪgˈnɪfɪkəns] *n* (*importance*) trascendencia

significant [sɪgˈnɪfɪkənt] *adj* significativo; (*important*) trascendente

signify ['sɪgnɪfaɪ] *vt* significar
sign language *n* lenguaje *m* para
sordomudos
signpost ['saɪnpəust] *n* indicador *m*
silence ['saɪlns] *n* silencio ♦ *vt* acallar;
(*guns*) reducir al silencio; **~r** *n* (*on gun*,
BRIT: AUT) silenciador *m*
silent ['saɪlnt] *adj* silencioso; (*not speaking*)
callado; (*film*) mudo; **to remain ~** guardar
silencio; **~ partner** *n* (COMM) socio/a
comanditario/a
silhouette [sɪluː'et] *n* silueta
silicon chip ['sɪlɪkən-] *n* plaqueta de
silicio
silk [sɪlk] *n* seda ♦ *adj* de seda; **~y** *adj*
sedoso
silly ['sɪlɪ] *adj* (*person*) tonto; (*idea*)
absurdo
silt [sɪlt] *n* sedimento
silver ['sɪlvə*] *n* plata; (*money*) moneda
suelta ♦ *adj* de plata; (*colour*) plateado; **~
paper** (BRIT) *n* papel *m* de plata; **~-
plated** *adj* plateado; **~smith** *n* platero/
a; **~ware** *n* plata; **~y** *adj* argentino
similar ['sɪmɪlə*] *adj:* **~ (to)** parecido or
semejante (a); **~ity** [-'lærɪtɪ] *n* semejanza;
~ly *adv* del mismo modo
simmer ['sɪmə*] *vi* hervir a fuego lento
simple ['sɪmpl] *adj* (*easy*) sencillo; (*foolish,
COMM: interest*) simple; **simplicity**
[-'plɪsɪtɪ] *n* sencillez *f*; **simplify** ['sɪmplɪfaɪ]
vt simplificar
simply ['sɪmplɪ] *adv* (*live, talk*)
sencillamente; (*just, merely*) sólo
simulate ['sɪmjuːleɪt] *vt* fingir, simular; **~d**
adj simulado; (*fur*) de imitación
simultaneous [sɪməl'teɪnɪəs] *adj*
simultáneo; **~ly** *adv* simultáneamente
sin [sɪn] *n* pecado ♦ *vi* pecar
since [sɪns] *adv* desde entonces, después
♦ *prep* desde ♦ *conj* (*time*) desde que;
(*because*) ya que, puesto que; **~ then,
ever ~** desde entonces
sincere [sɪn'sɪə*] *adj* sincero; **~ly** *adv:*
yours ~ly (*in letters*) le saluda
atentamente; **sincerity** [-'serɪtɪ] *n*
sinceridad *f*

sinew ['sɪnjuː] *n* tendón *m*
sing [sɪŋ] (*pt* **sang**, *pp* **sung**) *vt, vi* cantar
Singapore [sɪŋə'pɔː*] *n* Singapur *m*
singe [sɪndʒ] *vt* chamuscar
singer ['sɪŋə*] *n* cantante *m/f*
singing ['sɪŋɪŋ] *n* canto
single ['sɪŋgl] *adj* único, solo; (*unmarried*)
soltero; (*not double*) simple, sencillo ♦ *n*
(BRIT: *also:* **~ ticket**) billete *m* sencillo;
(*record*) sencillo, single *m*; **~s** *npl* (TENNIS)
individual *m*; **~ out** *vt* (*choose*) escoger;
~ bed cama individual; **~-breasted** *adj*
recto; **~ file** *n:* **in ~ file** en fila de uno;
~-handed *adv* sin ayuda; **~-minded**
adj resuelto, firme; **~ parent** *n* padre *m*
soltero, madre *f* soltera (*o* divorciado *etc*);
~ parent family familia monoparental; **~
room** *n* cuarto individual
singly ['sɪŋglɪ] *adv* uno por uno
singular ['sɪŋgjulə*] *adj* (*odd*) raro,
extraño; (*outstanding*) excepcional ♦ *n*
(LING) singular *m*
sinister ['sɪnɪstə*] *adj* siniestro
sink [sɪŋk] (*pt* **sank**, *pp* **sunk**) *n* fregadero
♦ *vt* (*ship*) hundir, echar a pique;
(*foundations*) excavar ♦ *vi* (*gen*) hundirse;
to ~ sth into hundir algo en; **~ in** *vi* (*fig*)
penetrar, calar
sinner ['sɪnə*] *n* pecador(a) *m/f*
sinus ['saɪnəs] *n* (ANAT) seno
sip [sɪp] *n* sorbo ♦ *vt* sorber, beber a
sorbitos
siphon ['saɪfən] *n* sifón *m*; **~ off** *vt* desviar
sir [sə*] *n* señor *m*; **S~ John Smith** Sir John
Smith; **yes ~** sí, señor
siren ['saɪərn] *n* sirena
sirloin ['səːlɔɪn] *n* (*also:* **~ steak**) solomillo
sister ['sɪstə*] *n* hermana; (BRIT: *nurse*)
enfermera jefe; **~-in-law** *n* cuñada
sit [sɪt] (*pt, pp* **sat**) *vi* sentarse; (*be sitting*)
estar sentado; (*assembly*) reunirse; (*for
painter*) posar ♦ *vt* (*exam*) presentarse a;
~ down *vi* sentarse; **~ in on** *vt fus*
asistir a; **~ up** *vi* incorporarse; (*not go to
bed*) velar
sitcom ['sɪtkɔm] *n abbr* (= *situation
comedy*) comedia de situación

site [saɪt] n sitio m; (also: **building ~**) solar m
♦ vt situar

sit-in n (demonstration) sentada

sitting ['sɪtɪŋ] n (of assembly etc) sesión f;
(in canteen) turno; **~ room** n sala de
estar

situated ['sɪtjʊeɪtɪd] adj situado

situation [sɪtjʊ'eɪʃən] n situación f; **"~s
vacant"** (BRIT) "ofrecen trabajo"

six [sɪks] num seis; **~teen** num diez y seis,
dieciséis; **~th** num sexto; **~ty** num
sesenta

size [saɪz] n tamaño; (extent) extensión f;
(of clothing) talla; (of shoes) número; **~
up** vt formarse una idea de; **~able** adj
importante, considerable

sizzle ['sɪzl] vi crepitar

skate [skeɪt] n patín m; (fish: pl inv) raya
♦ vi patinar; **~board** n monopatín m;
~boarding n monopatín m; **~r** n
patinador(a) m/f; **skating** n patinaje m;
skating rink n pista de patinaje

skeleton ['skelɪtn] n esqueleto m; (TECH)
armazón f; (outline) esquema m; **~ staff**
n personal m reducido

skeptic etc (US) = **sceptic**

sketch [sketʃ] n (drawing) dibujo m; (outline)
esbozo, bosquejo; (THEATRE) sketch m ♦ vt
dibujar; (plan etc: also: **~ out**) esbozar; **~
book** n libro m de dibujos; **~y** adj
incompleto

skewer ['skjuːə*] n broqueta

ski [skiː] n esquí m ♦ vi esquiar; **~ boot** n
bota de esquí

skid [skɪd] n patinazo ♦ vi patinar

ski: **~er** n esquiador(a) m/f; **~ing** n esquí
m; **~ jump** n salto con esquís

skilful ['skɪlful] (BRIT) adj diestro, experto

ski lift n telesilla m, telesquí m

skill [skɪl] n destreza, pericia; técnica; **~ed**
adj hábil, diestro; (worker) cualificado;
~full (US) adj = **skilful**

skim [skɪm] vt (milk) desnatar; (glide over)
rozar, rasar ♦ vi: **to ~ through** (book)
hojear; **~med milk** n leche f desnatada

skimp [skɪmp] vt (also: **~ on**: work)
chapucear; (cloth etc) escatimar; **~y** adj

escaso; (skirt) muy corto

skin [skɪn] n piel f; (complexion) cutis m
♦ vt (fruit etc) pelar; (animal) despellejar;
~ cancer n cáncer m de piel; **~-deep**
adj superficial; **~ diving** n buceo; **~ny**
adj flaco; **~tight** adj (dress etc) muy
ajustado

skip [skɪp] n brinco, salto; (BRIT: container)
contenedor m ♦ vi brincar; (with rope)
saltar a la comba ♦ vt saltarse

ski: **~ pass** n forfait m (de esquí); **~
pole** n bastón m de esquiar

skipper ['skɪpə*] n (NAUT, SPORT) capitán
m

skipping rope ['skɪpɪŋ-] (BRIT) n comba

skirmish ['skə:mɪʃ] n escaramuza

skirt [skə:t] n falda (SP), pollera (AM) ♦ vt
(go round) ladear; **~ing board** (BRIT) n
rodapié m

ski slope n pista de esquí

ski suit n traje m de esquiar

ski tow n remonte m

skittle ['skɪtl] n bolo; **~s** n (game) boliche
m

skive [skaɪv] (BRIT: inf) vi gandulear

skull [skʌl] n calavera; (ANAT) cráneo

skunk [skʌŋk] n mofeta

sky [skaɪ] n cielo; **~light** n tragaluz m,
claraboya; **~scraper** n rascacielos m inv

slab [slæb] n (stone) bloque m; (flat) losa;
(of cake) trozo

slack [slæk] adj (loose) flojo; (slow) de
poca actividad; (careless) descuidado; **~s**
npl pantalones mpl; **~en** (also: **~en off**)
vi aflojarse ♦ vt aflojar; (speed) disminuir

slag heap ['slæg-] n escorial m,
escombrera

slag off (BRIT: inf) vt poner como un
trapo

slam [slæm] vt (throw) arrojar
(violentamente); (criticize) criticar
duramente ♦ vi (door) cerrarse de golpe;
to ~ the door dar un portazo

slander ['slɑːndə*] n calumnia, difamación
f

slang [slæŋ] n argot m; (jargon) jerga

slant [slɑːnt] n sesgo, inclinación f; (fig)

interpretación *f*; **~ed** *adj* (*fig*) parcial;
~ing *adj* inclinado; (*eyes*) rasgado
slap [slæp] *n* palmada; (*in face*) bofetada
♦ *vt* dar una palmada *or* bofetada a;
(*paint etc*): **to ~ sth on sth** embadurnar
algo con algo ♦ *adv* (*directly*)
exactamente, directamente; **~dash** *adj*
descuidado; **~stick** *n* comedia de golpe
y porrazo; **~-up** *adj*: **a ~-up meal** (*BRIT*)
un banquetazo, una comilona
slash [slæʃ] *vt* acuchillar; (*fig: prices*)
fulminar
slat [slæt] *n* tablilla, listón *m*
slate [sleɪt] *n* pizarra ♦ *vt* (*fig: criticize*)
criticar duramente
slaughter ['slɔ:tə*] *n* (*of animals*) matanza;
(*of people*) carnicería ♦ *vt* matar; **~house**
n matadero
Slav [slɑ:v] *adj* eslavo
slave [sleɪv] *n* esclavo/a ♦ *vi* (*also: ~*
away) sudar tinta; **~ry** *n* esclavitud *f*
slay [sleɪ] (*pt* slew, *pp* slain) *vt* matar
sleazy ['sli:zɪ] *adj* de mala fama
sledge [sledʒ] *n* trineo; **~hammer** *n*
mazo
sleek [sli:k] *adj* (*shiny*) lustroso; (*car etc*)
elegante
sleep [sli:p] (*pt, pp* slept) *n* sueño ♦ *vi*
dormir; **to go to ~** quedarse dormido;
~ around *vi* acostarse con cualquiera; **~ in**
vi (*oversleep*) quedarse dormido; **~er** *n*
(*person*) durmiente *m/f*; (*BRIT: RAIL: on*
track) traviesa; (: *train*) coche-cama *m*;
~ing bag *n* saco de dormir; **~ing car** *n*
coche-cama *m*; **~ing partner** (*BRIT*) *n*
(*COMM*) socio comanditario; **~ing pill** *n*
somnífero; **~less** *adj*: **a ~less night** una
noche en blanco; **~walker** *n*
sonámbulo/a; **~y** *adj* soñoliento; (*place*)
soporífero
sleet [sli:t] *n* aguanieve *f*
sleeve [sli:v] *n* manga; (*TECH*) manguito;
(*of record*) portada; **~less** *adj* sin mangas
sleigh [sleɪ] *n* trineo
sleight [slaɪt] *n*: **~ of hand** escamoteo
slender ['slendə*] *adj* delgado; (*means*)
escaso

slept [slept] *pt, pp of* sleep
slew [slu:] *pt of* slay ♦ *vi* (*BRIT*: *veer*)
torcerse
slice [slaɪs] *n* (*of meat*) tajada; (*of bread*)
rebanada; (*of lemon*) rodaja; (*utensil*) pala
♦ *vt* cortar (en tajos); rebanar
slick [slɪk] *adj* (*skilful*) hábil, diestro; (*clever*)
astuto ♦ *n* (*also*: **oil ~**) marea negra
slide [slaɪd] (*pt, pp* slid) *n* (*movement*)
descenso, desprendimiento; (*in*
playground) tobogán *m*; (*PHOT*)
diapositiva; (*BRIT: also*: **hair ~**) pasador *m*
♦ *vt* correr, deslizar ♦ *vi* (*slip*) resbalarse;
(*glide*) deslizarse; **sliding** *adj* (*door*)
corredizo; **sliding scale** *n* escala móvil
slight [slaɪt] *adj* (*slim*) delgado; (*frail*)
delicado; (*pain etc*) leve; (*trivial*)
insignificante; (*small*) pequeño ♦ *n* desaire
m ♦ *vt* (*insult*) ofender, desairar; **not in**
the ~est en absoluto; **~ly** *adv*
ligeramente, un poco
slim [slɪm] *adj* delgado, esbelto; (*fig:*
chance) remoto ♦ *vi* adelgazar
slime [slaɪm] *n* limo, cieno
slimming ['slɪmɪŋ] *n* adelgazamiento
slimy ['slaɪmɪ] *adj* cenagoso
sling [slɪŋ] (*pt, pp* slung) *n* (*MED*)
cabestrillo; (*weapon*) honda ♦ *vt* tirar,
arrojar
slip [slɪp] *n* (*slide*) resbalón *m*; (*mistake*)
descuido; (*underskirt*) combinación *f*; (*of*
paper) papelito ♦ *vt* (*slide*) deslizar ♦ *vi*
deslizarse; (*stumble*) resbalar(se); (*decline*)
decaer; (*move smoothly*): **to ~ into/out of**
(*room etc*) introducirse en/salirse de; **to**
give sb the ~ eludir a uno; **a ~ of the**
tongue un lapsus; **to ~ sth on/off**
ponerse/quitarse algo; **~ away** *vi*
escabullirse; **~ in** *vt* meter ♦ *vi* meterse;
~ out *vi* (*go out*) salir (un momento); **~**
up *vi* (*make mistake*) equivocarse; meter
la pata; **~ped disc** *n* vértebra dislocada
slipper ['slɪpə*] *n* zapatilla, pantufla
slippery ['slɪpərɪ] *adj* resbaladizo
slip: ~ road (*BRIT*) *n* carretera de acceso;
~-up *n* (*error*) desliz *m*; **~way** *n* grada,
gradas *fpl*

slit [slɪt] *n* (*pt, pp* **slit**) *n* raja; (*cut*) corte *m*
♦ *vt* rajar; cortar

slither ['slɪðə*] *vi* deslizarse

sliver ['slɪvə*] *n* (*of glass, wood*) astilla; (*of cheese etc*) raja

slob [slɔb] (*inf*) *n* abandonado/a

slog [slɔg] (*BRIT*) *vi* sudar tinta; **it was a ~** costó trabajo (hacerlo)

slogan ['sləugən] *n* eslogan *m*, lema *m*

slope [sləup] *n* (*up*) cuesta, pendiente *f*; (*down*) declive *m*; (*side of mountain*) falda, vertiente *m* ♦ *vi*: **to ~ down** estar en declive; **to ~ up** inclinarse; **sloping** *adj* en pendiente; en declive; (*writing*) inclinado

sloppy ['slɔpɪ] *adj* (*work*) descuidado; (*appearance*) desaliñado

slot [slɔt] *n* ranura ♦ *vt*: **to ~ into** encajar en

slot machine *n* (*BRIT: vending machine*) distribuidor *m* automático; (*for gambling*) tragaperras *m inv*

slouch [slautʃ] *vi* andar *etc* con los hombros caídos

Slovenia [sləu'vi:nɪə] *n* Eslovenia

slovenly ['slʌvənlɪ] *adj* desaliñado, desaseado; (*careless*) descuidado

slow [sləu] *adj* lento; (*not clever*) lerdo; (*watch*): **to be ~** atrasar ♦ *adv* lentamente, despacio ♦ *vt, vi* (*also: ~ down, ~ up*) retardar; **"~"** (*road sign*) "disminuir velocidad"; **~down** (*US*) *n* huelga de manos caídas; **~ly** *adv* lentamente, despacio; **~ motion** *n*: **in ~ motion** a cámara lenta

sludge [slʌdʒ] *n* lodo, fango

slug [slʌg] *n* babosa; (*bullet*) posta; **~gish** *adj* lento; (*person*) perezoso

sluice [slu:s] *n* (*gate*) esclusa; (*channel*) canal *m*

slum [slʌm] *n* casucha

slump [slʌmp] *n* (*economic*) depresión *f* ♦ *vi* hundirse; (*prices*) caer en picado

slung [slʌŋ] *pt, pp of* **sling**

slur [slɜ:*] *n*: **to cast a ~ on** insultar ♦ *vt* (*speech*) pronunciar mal

slush [slʌʃ] *n* nieve *f* a medio derretir

slut [slʌt] *n* putona

sly [slaɪ] *adj* astuto; (*smile*) taimado

smack [smæk] *n* bofetada ♦ *vt* dar con la mano a; (*child, on face*) abofetear ♦ *vi*: **to ~ of** saber a, oler a

small [smɔ:l] *adj* pequeño; **~ ads** (*BRIT*) *npl* anuncios *mpl* por palabras; **~ change** *n* suelto, cambio; **~holder** (*BRIT*) *n* granjero/a, parcelero/a; **~ hours** *npl*: **in the ~ hours** a las altas horas (de la noche); **~pox** *n* viruela; **~ talk** *n* cháchara

smart [smɑ:t] *adj* elegante; (*clever*) listo, inteligente; (*quick*) rápido, vivo ♦ *vi* escocer, picar; **~en up** *vi* arreglarse ♦ *vt* arreglar

smash [smæʃ] *n* (*also: ~-up*) choque *m*; (*MUS*) exitazo ♦ *vt* (*break*) hacer pedazos; (*car etc*) estrellar; (*SPORT: record*) batir ♦ *vi* hacerse pedazos; (*against wall etc*) estrellarse; **~ing** (*inf*) *adj* estupendo

smattering ['smætərɪŋ] *n*: **a ~ of** algo de

smear [smɪə*] *n* mancha; (*MED*) frotis *m inv* ♦ *vt* untar; **~ campaign** *n* campaña de desprestigio

smell [smɛl] *n* (*pt, pp* **smelt** *or* **smelled**) *n* olor *m*; (*sense*) olfato ♦ *vt, vi* oler; **~y** *adj* maloliente

smile [smaɪl] *n* sonrisa ♦ *vi* sonreír

smirk [smɜ:k] *n* sonrisa falsa *or* afectada

smith [smɪθ] *n* herrero; **~y** ['smɪðɪ] *n* herrería

smog [smɔg] *n* esmog *m*

smoke [sməuk] *n* humo ♦ *vi* fumar; (*chimney*) echar humo ♦ *vt* (*cigarettes*) fumar; **~d** *adj* (*bacon, glass*) ahumado; **~r** *n* (*person*) fumador(a) *m/f*; (*RAIL*) coche *m* fumador; **~ screen** *n* cortina de humo; **~ shop** (*US*) *n* estanco (*SP*), tabaquería (*AM*); **smoking** *n*: **"no smoking"** "prohibido fumar"; **smoky** *adj* (*room*) lleno de humo; (*taste*) ahumado

smolder ['sməuldə*] (*US*) *vi* = **smoulder**

smooth [smu:ð] *adj* liso; (*sea*) tranquilo; (*flavour, movement*) suave; (*sauce*) fino; (*person: pej*) meloso ♦ *vt* (*also: ~ out*) alisar; (*creases, difficulties*) allanar

smother ['smʌðə*] *vt* sofocar; (*repress*) contener

smoulder ['sməuldə*] (*US* **smolder**) *vi* arder sin llama

smudge [smʌdʒ] *n* mancha ♦ *vt* manchar

smug [smʌg] *adj* presumido; orondo

smuggle ['smʌgl] *vt* pasar de contrabando; **~r** *n* contrabandista *m/f*; **smuggling** *n* contrabando

smutty ['smʌtɪ] *adj* (*fig*) verde, obsceno

snack [snæk] *n* bocado; **~ bar** *n* cafetería

snag [snæg] *n* problema *m*

snail [sneɪl] *n* caracol *m*

snake [sneɪk] *n* serpiente *f*

snap [snæp] *n* (*sound*) chasquido; (*photograph*) foto *f* ♦ *adj* (*decision*) instantáneo ♦ *vt* (*break*) quebrar; (*fingers*) castañetear ♦ *vi* quebrarse; (*fig: speak sharply*) contestar bruscamente; **to ~ shut** cerrarse de golpe; **~ at** *vt fus* (*subj: dog*) intentar morder; **~ off** *vi* partirse; **~ up** *vt* agarrar; **~ fastener** (*US*) *n* botón *m* de presión; **~py** (*inf*) *adj* (*answer*) instantáneo; (*slogan*) conciso; **make it ~py!** (*hurry up*) ¡date prisa!; **~shot** *n* foto *f* (instantánea)

snare [snɛə*] *n* trampa

snarl [snɑːl] *vi* gruñir

snatch [snætʃ] *n* (*small piece*) fragmento ♦ *vt* (**~ away**) arrebatar; (*fig*) agarrar; **to ~ some sleep** encontrar tiempo para dormir

sneak [sniːk] (*pt* (*US*) **snuck**) *vi*: **to ~ in/ out** entrar/salir a hurtadillas ♦ *n* (*inf*) soplón/ona *m/f*; **to ~ up on sb** aparecérsele de improviso a uno; **~ers** *npl* zapatos *mpl* de lona; **~y** *adj* furtivo

sneer [snɪə*] *vi* reír con sarcasmo; (*mock*): **to ~ at** burlarse de

sneeze [sniːz] *vi* estornudar

sniff [snɪf] *vi* sollozar ♦ *vt* husmear, oler; (*drugs*) esnifar

snigger ['snɪgə*] *vi* reírse con disimulo

snip [snɪp] *n* tijeretazo; (*BRIT: inf: bargain*) ganga ♦ *vt* tijeretear

sniper ['snaɪpə*] *n* francotirador(a) *m/f*

snippet ['snɪpɪt] *n* retazo

snob [snɔb] *n* (e)snob *m/f*; **~bery** *n* (e)snobismo; **~bish** *adj* (e)snob

snooker ['snuːkə*] *n* especie de billar

snoop [snuːp] *vi*: **to ~ about** fisgonear

snooze [snuːz] *n* siesta ♦ *vi* echar una siesta

snore [snɔː*] *n* ronquido ♦ *vi* roncar

snorkel ['snɔːkl] *n* (tubo) respirador *m*

snort [snɔːt] *n* bufido ♦ *vi* bufar

snout [snaut] *n* hocico, morro

snow [snəu] *n* nieve *f* ♦ *vi* nevar; **~ball** *n* bola de nieve ♦ *vi* (*fig*) agrandirse, ampliarse; **~bound** *adj* bloqueado por la nieve; **~drift** *n* ventisquero; **~drop** *n* campanilla; **~fall** *n* nevada; **~flake** *n* copo de nieve; **~man** (*irreg*) *n* figura de nieve; **~plough** (*US* **~plow**) *n* quitanieves *m inv*; **~shoe** *n* raqueta (de nieve); **~storm** *n* nevada, nevasca

snub [snʌb] *vt* (*person*) desairar ♦ *n* desaire *m*, repulsa; **~-nosed** *adj* chato

snuff [snʌf] *n* rapé *m*

snug [snʌg] *adj* (*cosy*) cómodo; (*fitted*) ajustado

snuggle ['snʌgl] *vi*: **to ~ up to sb** arrimarse a uno

KEYWORD

---

so [səu] *adv* **1** (*thus, likewise*) así, de este modo; **if ~** de ser así; **I like swimming – ~ do I** a mí me gusta nadar — a mí también; **I've got work to do – ~ has Paul** tengo trabajo que hacer — Paul también; **it's 5 o'clock – ~ it is!** son las cinco — ¡pues es verdad!; **I hope/think ~** espero/creo que sí; **~ far** hasta ahora; (*in past*) hasta este momento

2 (*in comparisons etc: to such a degree*) tan; **~ quickly (that)** tan rápido (que); **~ big (that)** tan grande (que); **she's not ~ clever as her brother** no es tan lista como su hermano; **we were ~ worried** estábamos preocupadísimos

3: **~ much** *adj, adv* tanto; **~ many** tantos/as

4 (*phrases*): **10 or ~** unos 10, 10 o así; **~ long!** (*inf: goodbye*) ¡hasta luego!

♦ *conj* **1** (*expressing purpose*): **~ as to do** para hacer; **~ (that)** para que +*sub*
2 (*expressing result*) así que; **~ you see, I could have gone** así que ya ves, (yo) podría haber ido

soak [səuk] *vt* (*drench*) empapar; (*steep in water*) remojar ♦ *vi* remojarse, estar a remojo; **~ in** *vi* penetrar; **~ up** *vt* absorber

soap [səup] *n* jabón *m*; **~flakes** *npl* escamas *fpl* de jabón; **~ opera** *n* telenovela; **~ powder** *n* jabón *m* en polvo; **~y** *adj* jabonoso

soar [sɔ:*] *vi* (*on wings*) remontarse; (*rocket, prices*) dispararse; (*building etc*) elevarse

sob [sɔb] *n* sollozo ♦ *vi* sollozar

sober ['səubə*] *adj* (*serious*) serio; (*not drunk*) sobrio; (*colour, style*) discreto; **~ up** *vt* quitar la borrachera

so-called *adj* así llamado

soccer ['sɔkə*] *n* fútbol *m*

social ['səuʃl] *adj* social ♦ *n* velada, fiesta; **~ club** *n* club *m*; **~ism** *n* socialismo; **~ist** *adj*, *n* socialista *m/f*; **~ize** *vi*: **to ~ize (with)** alternar (con); **~ly** *adv* socialmente; **~ security** *n* seguridad *f* social; **~ work** *n* asistencia social; **~ worker** *n* asistente/a *m/f* social

society [sə'saɪətɪ] *n* sociedad *f*; (*club*) asociación *f*; (*also*: **high ~**) alta sociedad

sociology [səusɪ'ɔlədʒɪ] *n* sociología

sock [sɔk] *n* calcetín *m*, media (*SP*)

socket ['sɔkɪt] *n* cavidad *f*; (*BRIT: ELEC*) enchufe *m*

sod [sɔd] *n* (*of earth*) césped *m*; (*BRIT: inf!*) cabrón/ona *m/f* (!)

soda ['səudə] *n* (*CHEM*) sosa; (*also*: **~ water**) soda; (*US: also*: **~ pop**) gaseosa

sofa ['səufə] *n* sofá *m*

soft [sɔft] *adj* (*lenient, not hard*) blando; (*gentle, not bright*) suave; **~ drink** *n* bebida no alcohólica; **~en** ['sɔfn] *vt* ablandar; suavizar; (*effect*) amortiguar ♦ *vi* ablandarse; suavizarse; **~ly** *adv* suavemente; (*gently*) delicadamente, con

delicadeza; **~ness** *n* blandura; suavidad *f*; **~ware** *n* (*COMPUT*) software *m*

soggy ['sɔgɪ] *adj* empapado

soil [sɔɪl] *n* (*earth*) tierra, suelo ♦ *vt* ensuciar; **~ed** *adj* sucio

solar ['səulə*] *adj*: **~ energy** *n* energía solar; **~ panel** *n* panel *m* solar

sold [səuld] *pt*, *pp of* **sell**; **~ out** *adj* (*COMM*) agotado

solder ['səuldə*] *vt* soldar ♦ *n* soldadura

soldier ['səuldʒə*] *n* soldado; (*army man*) militar *m*

sole [səul] *n* (*of foot*) planta; (*of shoe*) suela; (*fish: pl inv*) lenguado ♦ *adj* único

solemn ['sɔləm] *adj* solemne

sole trader *n* (*COMM*) comerciante *m* exclusivo

solicit [sə'lɪsɪt] *vt* (*request*) solicitar ♦ *vi* (*prostitute*) importunar

solicitor [sə'lɪsɪtə*] (*BRIT*) *n* (*for wills etc*) ≈ notario/a; (*in court*) ≈ abogado/a

solid ['sɔlɪd] *adj* sólido; (*gold etc*) macizo ♦ *n* sólido; **~s** *npl* (*food*) alimentos *mpl* sólidos

solidarity [sɔlɪ'dærɪtɪ] *n* solidaridad *f*

solitary ['sɔlɪtərɪ] *adj* solitario, solo; **~ confinement** *n* incomunicación *f*

solo ['səuləu] *n* solo ♦ *adv* (*fly*) en solitario; **~ist** *n* solista *m/f*

soluble ['sɔlju:bl] *adj* soluble

solution [sə'lu:ʃən] *n* solución *f*

solve [sɔlv] *vt* resolver, solucionar

solvent ['sɔlvənt] *adj* (*COMM*) solvente ♦ *n* (*CHEM*) solvente *m*

KEYWORD

some [sʌm] *adj* **1** (*a certain amount or number of*): **~ tea/water/biscuits** té/agua/(unas) galletas; **there's ~ milk in the fridge** hay leche en el frigo; **there were ~ people outside** había algunas personas fuera; **I've got ~ money, but not much** tengo algo de dinero, pero no mucho
2 (*certain: in contrasts*) algunos/as; **~ people say that ...** hay quien dice que ...; **~ films were excellent, but most**

were **mediocre** hubo películas
excelentes, pero la mayoría fueron
mediocres
3 (*unspecified*): **~ woman was asking for
you** una mujer estuvo preguntando por
ti; **he was asking for ~ book** (or other)
pedía un libro; **~ day** algún día; **~ day
next week** un día de la semana que
viene
♦ *pron* **1** (*a certain number*): **I've got ~**
(*books etc*) tengo algunos/as
2 (*a certain amount*) algo; **I've got ~**
(*money, milk*) tengo algo; **could I have ~
of that cheese?** ¿me puede dar un poco
de ese queso?; **I've read ~ of the book**
he leído parte del libro
♦ *adv*: **~ 10 people** unas 10 personas,
una decena de personas

some: ~body ['sʌmbədɪ] *pron* =
someone; **~how** *adv* de alguna manera;
(*for some reason*) por una u otra razón;
~one *pron* alguien; **~place** (*US*) *adv*
= **somewhere**
somersault ['sʌməsɔ:lt] *n* (*deliberate*) salto
mortal; (*accidental*) vuelco ♦ *vi* dar un
salto mortal; dar vuelcos
some: ~thing *pron* algo; **would you like
~thing to eat/drink?** ¿te gustaría cenar/
tomar algo?; **~time** *adv* (*in future*) algún
día, en algún momento; (*in past*): **~time
last month** durante el mes pasado;
~times *adv* a veces; **~what** *adv* algo;
~where *adv* (*be*) en alguna parte; (*go*) a
alguna parte; **~where else** (*be*) en otra
parte; (*go*) a otra parte
son [sʌn] *n* hijo
song [sɔŋ] *n* canción *f*
son-in-law *n* yerno
soon [su:n] *adv* pronto, dentro de poco; **~
afterwards** poco después; *see also* **as**;
~er *adv* (*time*) antes, más temprano;
(*preference*): **I would ~er do that** preferiría
hacer eso; **~er or later** tarde o temprano
soot [sut] *n* hollín *m*
soothe [su:ð] *vt* tranquilizar; (*pain*) aliviar
sophisticated [sə'fɪstɪkeɪtɪd] *adj*

sofisticado
sophomore ['sɔfəmɔ:*] (*US*) *n* estudiante
m/f de segundo año
sopping ['sɔpɪŋ] *adj*: **~ (wet)** empapado
soppy ['sɔpɪ] (*pej*) *adj* tonto
soprano [sə'prɑ:nəu] *n* soprano *f*
sorcerer ['sɔ:sərə*] *n* hechicero
sore [sɔ:*] *adj* (*painful*) doloroso, que duele
♦ *n* llaga; **~ly** *adv*: **I am ~ly tempted to**
estoy muy tentado a
sorrow ['sɔrəu] *n* pena, dolor *m*; **~s** *npl*
pesares *mpl*; **~ful** *adj* triste
sorry ['sɔrɪ] *adj* (*regretful*) arrepentido;
(*condition, excuse*) lastimoso; **~!** ¡perdón!,
¡perdone!; **~?** ¿cómo?; **to feel ~ for sb**
tener lástima a uno; **I feel ~ for him** me
da lástima
sort [sɔ:t] *n* clase *f*, género, tipo ♦ *vt* (*also:
~ out: papers*) clasificar; (: *problems*)
arreglar, solucionar; **~ing office** *n* sala
de batalla
SOS *n* SOS *m*
so-so *adv* regular, así así
soufflé ['su:fleɪ] *n* suflé *m*
sought [sɔ:t] *pt, pp of* **seek**
soul [səul] *n* alma; **~ful** *adj* lleno de
sentimiento
sound [saund] *n* (*noise*) sonido, ruido;
(*volume: on TV etc*) volumen *m*; (*GEO*)
estrecho ♦ *adj* (*healthy*) sano; (*safe, not
damaged*) en buen estado; (*reliable:
person*) digno de confianza; (*sensible*)
sensato, razonable; (*secure: investment*)
seguro ♦ *adv*: **~ asleep** profundamente
dormido ♦ *vt* (*alarm*) sonar ♦ *vi* sonar,
resonar; (*fig: seem*) parecer; **to ~ like**
sonar a; **~ out** *vt* sondear; **~ barrier** *n*
barrera del sonido; **~bite** *n* cita jugosa; **~
effects** *npl* efectos *mpl* sonoros; **~ly** *adv*
(*sleep*) profundamente; (*defeated*)
completamente; **~proof** *adj*
insonorizado; **~track** *n* (*of film*) banda
sonora
soup [su:p] *n* (*thick*) sopa; (*thin*) caldo; **~
plate** *n* plato sopero; **~spoon** *n*
cuchara sopera
sour ['sauə*] *adj* agrio; (*milk*) cortado; **it's**

~ **grapes** (*fig*) están verdes
source [sɔːs] *n* fuente *f*
south [sauθ] *n* sur *m* ♦ *adj* del sur, sureño
♦ *adv* al sur, hacia el sur; **S~ Africa** *n*
África del Sur; **S~ African** *adj, n*
sudafricano/a *m/f*; **S~ America** *n*
América del Sur, Sudamérica; **S~**
American *adj, n* sudamericano/a *m/f*;
~-east *n* sudeste *m*; **~erly** ['sʌðəlɪ] *adj*
sur; (*from the* ~) del sur; **~ern** ['sʌðən] *adj*
del sur, meridional; **S~ Pole** Polo Sur;
~ward(s) *adv* hacia el sur; **~-west** *n*
suroeste *m*
souvenir [suːvə'nɪə*] *n* recuerdo
sovereign ['sɒvrɪn] *adj, n* soberano/a *m/f*;
~ty *n* soberanía
soviet ['səuvɪət] *adj* soviético; **the S~**
Union la Unión Soviética
sow¹ [səu] (*pt* **sowed**, *pp* **sown**) *vt*
sembrar
sow² [sau] *n* cerda (*SP*), puerca (*SP*),
chancha (*AM*)
soy [sɔɪ] (*US*) *n* = **soya**
soya ['sɔɪə] (*BRIT*) *n* soja; ~ **bean** *n* haba
de soja; ~ **sauce** *n* salsa de soja
spa [spaː] *n* balneario
space [speɪs] *n* espacio; (*room*) sitio ♦ *cpd*
espacial ♦ *vt* (*also*: ~ **out**) espaciar; **~craft**
n nave *f* espacial; **~man/woman** (*irreg*)
n astronauta *m/f*, cosmonauta *m/f*;
~ship *n* = **~craft**; **spacing** *n* espaciado
spacious ['speɪʃəs] *adj* amplio
spade [speɪd] *n* (*tool*) pala, laya; **~s** *npl*
(*CARDS*: *British*) picas *fpl*; (: *Spanish*)
espadas *fpl*
spaghetti [spə'getɪ] *n* espaguetis *mpl*,
fideos *mpl*
Spain [speɪn] *n* España
span [spæn] *n* (*of bird, plane*) envergadura;
(*of arch*) luz *f*; (*in time*) lapso ♦ *vt*
extenderse sobre, cruzar; (*fig*) abarcar
Spaniard ['spænjəd] *n* español(a) *m/f*
spaniel ['spænjəl] *n* perro de aguas
Spanish ['spænɪʃ] *adj* español(a) ♦ *n*
(*LING*) español *m*, castellano; **the ~** *npl* los
españoles
spank [spæŋk] *vt* zurrar

spanner ['spænə*] (*BRIT*) *n* llave *f* (inglesa)
spare [speə*] *adj* de reserva; (*surplus*)
sobrante, de más ♦ *n* = ~ **part** ♦ *vt* (*do
without*) pasarse sin; (*refrain from hurting*)
perdonar; **to** ~ (*surplus*) sobrante, de
sobra; ~ **part** *n* pieza de repuesto; ~
time *n* tiempo libre; ~ **wheel** *n* (*AUT*)
rueda de recambio
sparingly ['speərɪŋlɪ] *adv* con moderación
spark [spaːk] *n* chispa; (*fig*) chispazo;
~(ing) plug *n* bujía
sparkle ['spaːkl] *n* centelleo, destello ♦ *vi*
(*shine*) relucir, brillar; **sparkling** *adj*
(*eyes, conversation*) brillante; (*wine*)
espumoso; (*mineral water*) con gas
sparrow ['spærəu] *n* gorrión *m*
sparse [spaːs] *adj* esparcido, escaso
spartan ['spaːtən] *adj* (*fig*) espartano
spasm ['spæzəm] *n* (*MED*) espasmo
spastic ['spæstɪk] *n* espástico/a
spat [spæt] *pt, pp of* **spit**
spate [speɪt] *n* (*fig*): **a** ~ **of** un torrente de
spawn [spɔːn] *vi* desovar, frezar ♦ *n*
huevas *fpl*
speak [spiːk] (*pt* **spoke**, *pp* **spoken**) *vt*
(*language*) hablar; (*truth*) decir ♦ *vi*
hablar; (*make a speech*) intervenir; **to** ~ **to**
sb/of *or* **about sth** hablar con uno/de *or*
sobre algo; ~ **up!** ¡habla fuerte!; **~er** *n* (*in
public*) orador(a) *m/f*; (*also*: **loud~er**)
altavoz *m*; (*for stereo etc*) bafle *m*; (*POL*):
the S~er (*BRIT*) el Presidente de la
Cámara de los Comunes; (*US*) el
Presidente del Congreso
spear [spɪə*] *n* lanza ♦ *vt* alancear; **~head**
vt (*attack etc*) encabezar
spec [spek] (*inf*) *n*: **on** ~ como
especulación
special ['speʃl] *adj* especial; (*edition etc*)
extraordinario; (*delivery*) urgente; **~ist** *n*
especialista *m/f*; **~ity** [speʃɪ'ælɪtɪ] *n*
especialidad *f*; **~ize** *vi*: **to ~ize (in)**
especializarse (en); **~ly** *adv* sobre todo,
en particular; **~ty** (*US*) *n* = **~ity**
species ['spiːʃiːz] *n inv* especie *f*
specific [spə'sɪfɪk] *adj* específico; **~ally**
adv específicamente

specify ['spesifai] *vt, vi* especificar, precisar
specimen ['spesiman] *n* ejemplar *m*; (*MED: of urine*) espécimen *m* (: *of blood*) muestra
speck [spɛk] *n* grano, mota
speckled ['spɛkld] *adj* moteado
specs [spɛks] (*inf*) *npl* gafas *fpl* (*SP*), anteojos *mpl*
spectacle ['spɛktəkl] *n* espectáculo; **~s** *npl* (*BRIT: glasses*) gafas *fpl* (*SP*), anteojos *mpl*; **spectacular** [-'tækjulə*] *adj* espectacular; (*success*) impresionante
spectator [spɛk'teitə*] *n* espectador(a) *m/f*
spectrum ['spɛktrəm] (*pl* **spectra**) *n* espectro
speculate ['spɛkjuleit] *vi*: **to ~ (on)** especular (en); **speculation** [spɛkju'leiʃən] *n* especulación *f*
speech [spi:tʃ] *n* (*faculty*) habla; (*formal talk*) discurso; (*spoken language*) lenguaje *m*; **~less** *adj* mudo, estupefacto; **~ therapist** *n* especialista que corrige defectos de pronunciación en los niños
speed [spi:d] *n* velocidad *f*; (*haste*) prisa; (*promptness*) rapidez *f*; **at full** or **top ~** a máxima velocidad; **~ up** *vi* acelerarse ♦ *vt* acelerar; **~boat** *n* lancha motora; **~ily** *adv* rápido, rápidamente; **~ing** *n* (*AUT*) exceso de velocidad; **~ limit** *n* límite *m* de velocidad, velocidad *f* máxima; **~ometer** [spi'dɔmitə*] *n* velocímetro; **~way** *n* (*sport*) pista de carrera; **~y** *adj* (*fast*) veloz, rápido; (*prompt*) pronto
spell [spɛl] (*pt, pp* **spelt** (*BRIT*) or **spelled**) *n* (*also:* **magic ~**) encanto, hechizo; (*period of time*) rato, período ♦ *vt* deletrear; (*fig*) anunciar, presagiar; **to cast a ~ on sb** hechizar a uno; **he can't ~** pone faltas de ortografía; **~bound** *adj* embelesado, hechizado; **~ing** *n* ortografía
spend [spɛnd] (*pt, pp* **spent**) *vt* (*money*) gastar; (*time*) pasar; (*life*) dedicar; **~thrift** *n* derrochador(a) *m/f*, pródigo/a
sperm [spə:m] *n* esperma
sphere [sfiə*] *n* esfera

sphinx [sfiŋks] *n* esfinge *f*
spice [spais] *n* especia ♦ *vt* condimentar
spicy ['spaisi] *adj* picante
spider ['spaidə*] *n* araña
spike [spaik] *n* (*point*) punta; (*BOT*) espiga
spill [spil] (*pt, pp* **spilt** or **spilled**) *vt* derramar, verter ♦ *vi* derramarse; **to ~ over** desbordarse
spin [spin] (*pt, pp* **spun**) *n* (*AVIAT*) barrena; (*trip in car*) paseo (en coche); (*on ball*) efecto ♦ *vt* (*wool etc*) hilar; (*ball etc*) hacer girar ♦ *vi* girar, dar vueltas
spinach ['spinitʃ] *n* espinaca; (*as food*) espinacas *fpl*
spinal ['spainl] *adj* espinal; **~ cord** *n* columna vertebral
spin doctor *n* informador(a) parcial al servicio de un partido político *etc*
spin-dryer (*BRIT*) *n* secador *m* centrífugo
spine [spain] *n* espinazo, columna vertebral; (*thorn*) espina; **~less** *adj* (*fig*) débil, pusilánime
spinning ['spinŋ] *n* hilandería; **~ top** *n* peonza
spin-off *n* derivado, producto secundario
spinster ['spinstə*] *n* soltera
spiral ['spaiərl] *n* espiral *f* ♦ *vi* (*fig: prices*) subir desorbitadamente; **~ staircase** *n* escalera de caracol
spire ['spaiə*] *n* aguja, chapitel *m*
spirit ['spirit] *n* (*soul*) alma *f*; (*ghost*) fantasma *m*; (*attitude, sense*) espíritu *m*; (*courage*) valor *m*, ánimo; **~s** *npl* (*drink*) licor(es) *m(pl)*; **in good ~s** alegre, de buen ánimo; **~ed** *adj* enérgico, vigoroso
spiritual ['spiritjuəl] *adj* espiritual ♦ *n* espiritual *m*
spit [spit] (*pt, pp* **spat**) *n* (*for roasting*) asador *m*, espetón *m*; (*saliva*) saliva ♦ *vi* escupir; (*sound*) chisporrotear; (*rain*) lloviznar
spite [spait] *n* rencor *m*, ojeriza ♦ *vt* causar pena a, mortificar; **in ~ of** a pesar de, pese a; **~ful** *adj* rencoroso, malévolo
spittle ['spitl] *n* saliva, baba
splash [splæʃ] *n* (*sound*) chapoteo; (*of colour*) mancha ♦ *vt* salpicar ♦ *vi* (*also:* **~**

about) chapotear

spleen [spli:n] n (ANAT) bazo

splendid ['splendɪd] adj espléndido

splint [splɪnt] n tablilla

splinter ['splɪntə*] n (of wood etc) astilla; (in finger) espigón m ♦ vi astillarse, hacer astillas

split [splɪt] (pt, pp **split**) n hendedura, raja; (fig) división f; (POL) escisión f ♦ vt partir, rajar; (party) dividir; (share) repartir ♦ vi dividirse, escindirse; ~ **up** vi (couple) separarse; (meeting) acabarse

spoil [spɔɪl] (pt, pp **spoilt** or **spoiled**) vt (damage) dañar; (mar) estropear; (child) mimar, consentir; ~**s** npl despojo, botín m; ~**sport** n aguafiestas m inv

spoke [spəuk] pt of **speak** ♦ n rayo, radio

spoken ['spəukn] pp of **speak**

spokesman ['spəuksmən] (irreg) n portavoz m; **spokeswoman** ['spəukswumən] (irreg) n portavoz f

sponge [spʌndʒ] n esponja; (also: ~ **cake**) bizcocho ♦ vt (wash) lavar con esponja ♦ vi: **to ~ off** or **on sb** vivir a costa de uno; ~ **bag** (BRIT) n esponjera

sponsor ['spɒnsə*] n patrocinador(a) m/f ♦ vt (applicant, proposal etc) proponer; ~**ship** n patrocinio

spontaneous [spɒn'teɪnɪəs] adj espontáneo

spooky ['spu:kɪ] (inf) adj espeluznante, horripilante

spool [spu:l] n carrete m

spoon [spu:n] n cuchara; ~**-feed** vt dar de comer con cuchara a; (fig) tratar como un niño a; ~**ful** n cucharada

sport [spɔ:t] n deporte m; (person): **to be a good ~** ser muy majo ♦ vt (wear) lucir, ostentar; ~**ing** adj deportivo; (generous) caballeroso; **to give sb a ~ing chance** darle a uno una (buena) oportunidad; ~ **jacket** (US) n = ~**s jacket**; ~**s car** n coche m deportivo; ~**s jacket** (BRIT) n chaqueta deportiva; ~**sman** (irreg) n deportista m; ~**smanship** n deportividad f; ~**swear** n trajes mpl de deporte or sport; ~**swoman** (irreg) n

deportista; ~**y** adj deportista

spot [spɒt] n sitio, lugar m; (dot: on pattern) punto, mancha; (pimple) grano; (RADIO) cuña publicitaria; (TV) espacio publicitario; (small amount): **a ~ of** un poquito de ♦ vt (notice) notar, observar; **on the ~** allí mismo; ~ **check** n reconocimiento rápido; ~**less** adj perfectamente limpio; ~**light** n foco, reflector m; (AUT) faro auxiliar; ~**ted** adj (pattern) de puntos; ~**ty** adj (face) con granos

spouse [spauz] n cónyuge m/f

spout [spaut] n (of jug) pico; (of pipe) caño ♦ vi salir en chorro

sprain [spreɪn] n torcedura ♦ vt: **to ~ one's ankle/wrist** torcerse el tobillo/la muñeca

sprang [spræŋ] pt of **spring**

sprawl [sprɔ:l] vi tumbarse

spray [spreɪ] n rociada; (of sea) espuma; (container) atomizador m; (for paint etc) pistola rociadora; (of flowers) ramita ♦ vt rociar; (crops) regar

spread [spred] (pt, pp **spread**) n extensión f; (for bread etc) pasta para untar; (inf: food) comilona ♦ vt extender; (butter) untar; (wings, sails) desplegar; (work, wealth) repartir; (scatter) esparcir ♦ vi (also: ~ **out**: stain) extenderse; (news) diseminarse; ~ **out** vi (move apart) separarse; ~**-eagled** adj a pata tendida; ~**sheet** n hoja electrónica or de cálculo

spree [spri:] n: **to go on a ~** ir de juerga

sprightly ['spraɪtlɪ] adj vivo, enérgico

spring [sprɪŋ] (pt **sprang**, pp **sprung**) n (season) primavera; (leap) salto, brinco; (coiled metal) resorte m; (of water) fuente f, manantial m ♦ vi saltar, brincar; ~ **up** vi (thing: appear) aparecer; (problem) surgir; ~**board** n trampolín m; ~**-clean(ing)** n limpieza general; ~**time** n primavera

sprinkle ['sprɪŋkl] vt (pour: liquid) rociar; (: salt, sugar) espolvorear; **to ~ water on, ~ with water** etc rociar or salpicar de agua etc; ~**r** n (for lawn) rociadera; (to *put out fire)* aparato de rociadura automática

sprint [sprɪnt] *n* esprint *m* ♦ *vi* esprintar

sprout [spraʊt] *vi* brotar, retoñar; **(Brussels) ~s** *npl* coles *fpl* de Bruselas

spruce [spruːs] *n inv* (*BOT*) pícea ♦ *adj* aseado, pulcro

sprung [sprʌŋ] *pp of* **spring**

spun [spʌn] *pt, pp of* **spin**

spur [spəː*] *n* espuela; *(fig)* estímulo, aguijón *m* ♦ *vt (also:* **~ on**) estimular, incitar; **on the ~ of the moment** de improviso

spurious ['spjʊərɪəs] *adj* falso

spurn [spəːn] *vt* desdeñar, rechazar

spurt [spəːt] *n* chorro; *(of energy)* arrebato ♦ *vi* chorrear

spy [spaɪ] *n* espía *m/f* ♦ *vi*: **to ~ on** espiar a ♦ *vt (see)* divisar, lograr ver; **~ing** *n* espionaje *m*

sq. *abbr* = **square**

squabble ['skwɔbl] *vi* reñir, pelear

squad [skwɔd] *n* (*MIL*) pelotón *m*; (*POLICE*) brigada; (*SPORT*) equipo

squadron ['skwɔdrn] *n* (*MIL*) escuadrón *m*; (*AVIAT, NAUT*) escuadra

squalid ['skwɔlɪd] *adj* vil; *(fig: sordid)* sórdido

squall [skwɔːl] *n* (*storm*) chubasco; (*wind*) ráfaga

squalor ['skwɔlə*] *n* miseria

squander ['skwɔndə*] *vt* (*money*) derrochar, despilfarrar; (*chances*) desperdiciar

square [skwɛə*] *n* cuadro; *(in town)* plaza; *(inf: person)* carca *m/f* ♦ *adj* cuadrado; *(inf: ideas, tastes)* trasnochado ♦ *vt* (*arrange*) arreglar; (*MATH*) cuadrar; (*reconcile*) compaginar; **all ~** igual(es); **to have a ~ meal** comer caliente; **2 metres ~** 2 metros en cuadro; **2 ~ metres** 2 metros cuadrados; **~ly** *adv* de lleno

squash [skwɔʃ] *n* (*BRIT: drink*): **lemon/ orange ~** zumo (*SP*) *or* jugo (*AM*) de limón/naranja; (*US: BOT*) calabacín *m*; (*SPORT*) squash *m*, frontenis *m* ♦ *vt* aplastar

squat [skwɔt] *adj* achaparrado ♦ *vi (also:* **~ down**) agacharse, sentarse en cuclillas; **~ter** *n* persona que ocupa ilegalmente una casa

squeak [skwiːk] *vi* (*hinge*) chirriar, rechinar; (*mouse*) chillar

squeal [skwiːl] *vi* chillar, dar gritos agudos

squeamish ['skwiːmɪʃ] *adj* delicado, remilgado

squeeze [skwiːz] *n* presión *f*; (*of hand*) apretón *m*; (*COMM*) restricción *f* ♦ *vt* (*hand, arm*) apretar; **~ out** *vt* exprimir

squelch [skwɛltʃ] *vi* chapotear

squid [skwɪd] *n inv* calamar *m*; (*CULIN*) calamares *mpl*

squiggle ['skwɪgl] *n* garabato

squint [skwɪnt] *vi* bizquear, ser bizco ♦ *n* (*MED*) estrabismo

squirm [skwəːm] *vi* retorcerse, revolverse

squirrel ['skwɪrəl] *n* ardilla

squirt [skwəːt] *vi* salir a chorros ♦ *vt* chiscar

Sr *abbr* = **senior**

St *abbr* = **saint; street**

stab [stæb] *n* (*with knife*) puñalada; (*of pain*) pinchazo; (*inf: try*): **to have a ~ at (doing) sth** intentar (hacer) algo ♦ *vt* apuñalar

stable ['steɪbl] *adj* estable ♦ *n* cuadra, caballeriza

stack [stæk] *n* montón *m*, pila ♦ *vt* amontonar, apilar

stadium ['steɪdɪəm] *n* estadio

staff [stɑːf] *n* (*work force*) personal *m*, plantilla; (*BRIT: SCOL*) cuerpo docente ♦ *vt* proveer de personal

stag [stæg] *n* ciervo, venado

stage [steɪdʒ] *n* escena; (*point*) etapa; (*platform*) plataforma; (*profession*): **the ~** el teatro ♦ *vt* (*play*) poner en escena, representar; (*organize*) montar, organizar; **in ~s** por etapas; **~coach** *n* diligencia; **~ manager** *n* director(a) *m/f* de escena

stagger ['stægə*] *vi* tambalearse ♦ *vt* (*amaze*) asombrar; (*hours, holidays*) escalonar; **~ing** *adj* asombroso

stagnant ['stægnənt] *adj* estancado

stag party n despedida de soltero

staid [steɪd] adj serio, formal

stain [steɪn] n mancha; (colouring) tintura ♦ vt manchar; (wood) teñir; **~ed glass window** n vidriera de colores; **~less steel** n acero inoxidable; **~ remover** n quitamanchas m inv

stair [stɛə*] n (step) peldaño, escalón m; **~s** npl escaleras fpl; **~case** n = **~way**; **~way** n escalera

stake [steɪk] n estaca, poste m; (COMM) interés m; (BETTING) apuesta ♦ vt (money) apostar; (life) arriesgar; (reputation) poner en juego; (claim) presentar una reclamación; **to be at ~** estar en juego

stale [steɪl] adj (bread) duro; (food) pasado; (smell) rancio; (beer) agrio

stalemate ['steɪlmeɪt] n tablas fpl (por ahogado); (fig) estancamiento

stalk [stɔ:k] n tallo, caña ♦ vt acechar, cazar al acecho; **~ off** vi irse airado

stall [stɔ:l] n (in market) puesto; (in stable) casilla (de establo) ♦ vt (AUT) calar; (fig) dar largas a ♦ vi (AUT) calarse; (fig) andarse con rodeos; **~s** npl (BRIT: in cinema, theatre) butacas fpl

stallion ['stælɪən] n semental m

stamina ['stæmɪnə] n resistencia

stammer ['stæmə*] n tartamudeo ♦ vi tartamudear

stamp [stæmp] n sello (SP), estampilla (AM); (mark, also fig) marca, huella; (on document) timbre m ♦ vi (also: **~ one's foot**) patear ♦ vt (mark) marcar; (letter) poner sellos or estampillas en; (with rubber ~) sellar; **~ album** n álbum m para sellos or estampillas; **~ collecting** n filatelia

stampede [stæm'pi:d] n estampida

stance [stæns] n postura

stand [stænd] (pt, pp **stood**) n (position) posición f, postura; (for taxis) parada; (hall ~) perchero; (music ~) atril m; (SPORT) tribuna; (at exhibition) stand m ♦ vi (be) estar, encontrarse; (be on foot) estar de pie; (rise) levantarse; (remain) quedar en pie; (in election) presentar

candidatura ♦ vt (place) poner, colocar; (withstand) aguantar, soportar; (invite to) invitar; **to make a ~** (fig) mantener una postura firme; **to ~ for parliament** (BRIT) presentarse (como candidato) a las elecciones; **~ by** vi (be ready) estar listo ♦ vt fus (opinion) aferrarse a; (person) apoyar; **~ down** vi (withdraw) ceder el puesto; **~ for** vt fus (signify) significar; (tolerate) aguantar, permitir; **~ in for** vt fus suplir a; **~ out** vi destacarse; **~ up** vi levantarse, ponerse de pie; **~ up for** vt fus defender; **~ up to** vt fus hacer frente a

standard ['stændəd] n patrón m, norma; (level) nivel m; (flag) estandarte m ♦ adj (size etc) normal, corriente; (text) básico; **~s** npl (morals) valores mpl morales; **~ lamp** (BRIT) n lámpara de pie; **~ of living** n nivel m de vida

stand-by ['stændbaɪ] n (reserve) recurso seguro; **to be on ~** estar sobre aviso; **~ ticket** n (AVIAT) (billete m) standby m

stand-in ['stændɪn] n suplente m/f

standing ['stændɪŋ] adj (on foot) de pie, en pie; (permanent) permanente ♦ n reputación f; **of many years' ~** que lleva muchos años; **~ joke** n broma permanente; **~ order** (BRIT) n (at bank) orden f de pago permanente; **~ room** n sitio para estar de pie

stand: **~point** n punto de vista; **~still** n: **at a ~still** (industry, traffic) paralizado; (car) parado; **to come to a ~still** quedar paralizado; pararse

stank [stæŋk] pt of **stink**

staple ['steɪpl] n (for papers) grapa ♦ adj (food etc) básico ♦ vt grapar; **~r** n grapadora

star [stɑ:*] n estrella; (celebrity) estrella, astro ♦ vt (THEATRE, CINEMA) ser el/la protagonista de; **the ~s** npl (ASTROLOGY) el horóscopo

starboard ['stɑ:bəd] n estribor m

starch [stɑ:tʃ] n almidón m

stardom ['stɑ:dəm] n estrellato

stare [stɛə*] n mirada fija ♦ vi: **to ~ at**

mirar fijo
starfish [ˈstɑːfɪʃ] *n* estrella de mar
stark [stɑːk] *adj* (*bleak*) severo, escueto
♦ *adv*: ~ **naked** en cueros
starling [ˈstɑːlɪŋ] *n* estornino
starry [ˈstɑːrɪ] *adj* estrellado; ~~**eyed** *adj*
(*innocent*) inocentón/ona, ingenuo
start [stɑːt] *n* principio, comienzo;
(*departure*) salida; (*sudden movement*)
salto, sobresalto; (*advantage*) ventaja ♦ *vt*
empezar, comenzar; (*cause*) causar;
(*found*) fundar; (*engine*) poner en marcha
♦ *vi* comenzar, empezar; (*with fright*)
asustarse, sobresaltarse; (*train etc*) salir; **to**
~ **doing** *or* **to do sth** empezar a hacer
algo; ~ **off** *vi* empezar, comenzar; (*leave*)
salir, ponerse en camino; ~ **up** *vi*
comenzar; (*car*) ponerse en marcha ♦ *vt*
comenzar; poner en marcha; ~**er** *n* (*AUT*)
botón *m* de arranque; (*SPORT: official*) juez
m/f de salida; (*BRIT: CULIN*) entrada; ~**ing**
point *n* punto de partida
startle [ˈstɑːtl] *vt* asustar, sobrecoger;
startling *adj* alarmante
starvation [stɑːˈveɪʃən] *n* hambre *f*
starve [stɑːv] *vi* tener mucha hambre; (*to
death*) morir de hambre ♦ *vt* hacer pasar
hambre
state [steɪt] *n* estado ♦ *vt* (*say, declare*)
afirmar; **the S~s** los Estados Unidos; **to
be in a** ~ estar agitado; ~**ly** *adj*
majestuoso, imponente; ~**ly home** *n*
casa señorial, casa solariega; ~**ment** *n*
afirmación *f*; ~~**sman** (*irreg*) *n* estadista *m*
static [ˈstætɪk] *n* (*RADIO*) parásitos *mpl*
♦ *adj* estático; ~ **electricity** *n* estática
station [ˈsteɪʃən] *n* (*gen*) estación *f*; (*RADIO*)
emisora; (*rank*) posición *f* social ♦ *vt*
colocar, situar; (*MIL*) apostar
stationary [ˈsteɪʃnərɪ] *adj* estacionario, fijo
stationer [ˈsteɪʃənə*] *n* papelero/a; ~'**s
(shop)** (*BRIT*) *n* papelería; ~**y** [-nərɪ] *n*
papel *m* de escribir, artículos *mpl* de
escritorio
station master *n* (*RAIL*) jefe *m* de
estación
station wagon (*US*) *n* ranchera

statistic [stəˈtɪstɪk] *n* estadística; ~**s** *n*
(*science*) estadística
statue [ˈstætjuː] *n* estatua
status [ˈsteɪtəs] *n* estado; (*reputation*)
estatus *m*; ~ **symbol** *n* símbolo de
prestigio
statute [ˈstætjuːt] *n* estatuto, ley *f*;
statutory *adj* estatutario
staunch [stɔːntʃ] *adj* leal, incondicional
stay [steɪ] *n* estancia ♦ *vi* quedar(se); (*as
guest*) hospedarse; **to** ~ **put** seguir en el
mismo sitio; **to** ~ **the night/5 days** pasar
la noche/estar 5 días; ~ **behind** *vi*
quedar atrás; ~ **in** *vi* quedarse en casa; ~
on *vi* quedarse; ~ **out** *vi* (*of house*) no
volver a casa; (*on strike*) permanecer en
huelga; ~ **up** *vi* (*at night*) velar, no
acostarse; ~**ing power** *n* aguante *m*
stead [sted] *n*: **in sb's** ~ en lugar de uno;
to stand sb in good ~ ser muy útil a uno
steadfast [ˈstedfɑːst] *adj* firme, resuelto
steadily [ˈstedɪlɪ] *adv* constantemente;
(*firmly*) firmemente; (*work, walk*) sin parar;
(*gaze*) fijamente
steady [ˈstedɪ] *adj* (*firm*) firme; (*regular*)
regular; (*person, character*) sensato,
juicioso; (*boyfriend*) formal; (*look, voice*)
tranquilo ♦ *vt* (*stabilize*) estabilizar;
(*nerves*) calmar
steak [steɪk] *n* (*gen*) filete *m*; (*beef*) bistec
m
steal [stiːl] (*pt* **stole**, *pp* **stolen**) *vt* robar
♦ *vi* robar; (*move secretly*) andar a
hurtadillas
stealth [stelθ] *n*: **by** ~ a escondidas,
sigilosamente; ~**y** *adj* cauteloso, sigiloso
steam [stiːm] *n* vapor *m*; (*mist*) vaho,
humo ♦ *vt* (*CULIN*) cocer al vapor ♦ *vi*
echar vapor; ~ **engine** *n* máquina de
vapor; ~**er** *n* (*buque m de*) vapor *m*;
~**roller** *n* apisonadora; ~**ship** *n* = ~**er**;
~**y** *adj* (*room*) lleno de vapor; (*window*)
empañado; (*heat, atmosphere*)
bochornoso
steel [stiːl] *n* acero ♦ *adj* de acero;
~**works** *n* acería
steep [stiːp] *adj* escarpado, abrupto; (*stair*)

empinado; (*price*) exorbitante, excesivo ♦ *vt* empapar, remojar

steeple ['sti:pl] *n* aguja; **~chase** *n* carrera de obstáculos

steer [stɪə*] *vt* (*car*) conducir (*SP*), manejar (*AM*); (*person*) dirigir ♦ *vi* conducir, manejar; **~ing** *n* (*AUT*) dirección *f*; **~ing wheel** *n* volante *m*

stem [stem] *n* (*of plant*) tallo; (*of glass*) pie *m* ♦ *vt* detener; (*blood*) restañar; **~ from** *vt fus* ser consecuencia de

stench [stentʃ] *n* hedor *m*

stencil ['stensl] *n* (*pattern*) plantilla ♦ *vt* hacer un cliché de

stenographer [ste'nɔgrəfə*] (*US*) *n* taquígrafo/a

step [step] *n* paso; (*on stair*) peldaño, escalón *m* ♦ *vi*: **to ~ forward/back** dar un paso adelante/hacia atrás; **~s** *npl* (*BRIT*) = **~ladder; in/out of ~ (with)** acorde/en disonancia (con); **~ down** *vi* (*fig*) retirarse; **~ on** *vt fus* pisar; **~ up** *vt* (*increase*) aumentar; **~brother** *n* hermanastro; **~daughter** *n* hijastra; **~father** *n* padrastro; **~ladder** *n* escalera doble *or* de tijera; **~mother** *n* madrastra; **~ping stone** *n* pasadera; **~sister** *n* hermanastra; **~son** *n* hijastro

stereo ['stɪərɪəu] *n* estéreo ♦ *adj* (*also*: **~phonic**) estéreo, estereofónico

sterile ['sterail] *adj* estéril; **sterilize** ['sterilaɪz] *vt* esterilizar

sterling ['stə:lɪŋ] *adj* (*silver*) de ley ♦ *n* (*ECON*) (libras *pl*) esterlinas *fpl*; **one pound ~** una libra esterlina

stern [stə:n] *adj* severo, austero ♦ *n* (*NAUT*) popa

stew [stju:] *n* cocido (*SP*), estofado (*SP*), guisado (*AM*) ♦ *vt* estofar, guisar; (*fruit*) cocer

steward ['stju:əd] *n* camarero; **~ess** *n* (*esp on plane*) azafata

stick [stɪk] (*pt, pp* **stuck**) *n* palo; (*of dynamite*) barreno; (*as weapon*) porra; (*walking ~*) bastón *m* ♦ *vt* (*glue*) pegar; (*inf: put*) meter; (*: tolerate*) aguantar, soportar; (*thrust*): **to ~ sth into** clavar *or*

hincar algo en ♦ *vi* pegarse; (*be unmoveable*) quedarse parado; (*in mind*) quedarse grabado; (*in throat etc*) atascarse; **~ out** *vi* sobresalir; **~ up** *vi* sobresalir; **~ up for** *vt fus* defender; **~er** *n* (*label*) etiqueta engomada; (*with slogan*) pegatina; **~ing plaster** *n* esparadrapo

stick-up ['stɪkʌp] (*inf*) *n* asalto, atraco

sticky ['stɪkɪ] *adj* pegajoso; (*label*) engomado; (*fig*) difícil

stiff [stɪf] *adj* rígido, tieso; (*hard*) duro; (*manner*) estirado; (*difficult*) difícil; (*person*) inflexible; (*price*) exorbitante ♦ *adv*: **scared/bored ~** muerto de miedo/aburrimiento; **~en** *vi* (*muscles etc*) agarrotarse; **~ neck** *n* tortícolis *m inv*; **~ness** *n* rigidez *f*, tiesura

stifle ['staifl] *vt* ahogar, sofocar; **stifling** *adj* (*heat*) sofocante, bochornoso

stigma ['stɪgmə] *n* (*fig*) estigma *m*

stile [stail] *n* portillo, portilla

stiletto [stɪ'letəu] (*BRIT*) *n* (*also*: **~ heel**) tacón *m* de aguja

still [stɪl] *adj* inmóvil, quieto ♦ *adv* todavía; (*even*) aun; (*nonetheless*) sin embargo, aun así; **~born** *adj* nacido muerto; **~ life** *n* naturaleza muerta

stilt [stɪlt] *n* zanco; (*pile*) pilar *m*, soporte *m*

stilted ['stɪltɪd] *adj* afectado

stimulate ['stɪmjuleɪt] *vt* estimular

stimulus ['stɪmjuləs] (*pl* **stimuli**) *n* estímulo, incentivo

sting [stɪŋ] (*pt, pp* **stung**) *n* picadura; (*pain*) escozor *m*, picazón *f*; (*organ*) aguijón *m* ♦ *vt, vi* picar

stingy ['stɪndʒɪ] *adj* tacaño

stink [stɪŋk] (*pt* **stank**, *pp* **stunk**) *n* hedor *m*, tufo ♦ *vi* heder, apestar; **~ing** *adj* hediondo, fétido; (*fig: inf*) horrible

stint [stɪnt] *n* tarea, trabajo ♦ *vi*: **to ~ on** escatimar

stir [stə:*] *n* (*fig: agitation*) conmoción *f* ♦ *vt* (*tea etc*) remover; (*fig: emotions*) provocar ♦ *vi* moverse; **~ up** *vt* (*trouble*) fomentar

stirrup ['stɪrəp] *n* estribo

stitch [stɪtʃ] *n* (*SEWING*) puntada; (*KNITTING*) punto; (*MED*) punto (de sutura); (*pain*) punzada ♦ *vt* coser; (*MED*) suturar

stoat [stəut] *n* armiño

stock [stɔk] *n* (*COMM: reserves*) existencias *fpl*, stock *m*; (*: selection*) surtido; (*AGR*) ganado, ganadería; (*CULIN*) caldo; (*descent*) raza, estirpe *f*; (*FINANCE*) capital *m* ♦ *adj* (*fig: reply etc*) clásico ♦ *vt* (*have in* ~) tener existencias de; **~s and shares** acciones y valores; **in ~** en existencia *or* almacén; **out of ~** agotado; **to take ~ of** (*fig*) asesorar, examinar; **~ up with** *vt fus* abastecerse de; **~broker** ['stɔkbrəukə*] *n* agente *m/f or* corredor(a) *m/f* de bolsa; **~ cube** (*BRIT*) *n* pastilla de caldo; **~ exchange** *n* bolsa

stocking ['stɔkɪŋ] *n* media

stock: **~ market** *n* bolsa (de valores); **~pile** *n* reserva ♦ *vt* acumular, almacenar; **~taking** (*BRIT*) *n* (*COMM*) inventario

stocky ['stɔkɪ] *adj* (*strong*) robusto; (*short*) achaparrado

stodgy ['stɔdʒɪ] *adj* indigesto, pesado

stoke [stəuk] *vt* atizar

stole [stəul] *pt* of **steal** ♦ *n* estola

stolen ['stəuln] *pp* of **steal**

stomach ['stʌmək] *n* (*ANAT*) estómago; (*belly*) vientre *m* ♦ *vt* tragar, aguantar; **~ache** *n* dolor *m* de estómago

stone [stəun] *n* piedra; (*in fruit*) hueso; = 6.348 kg; 14 libras ♦ *adj* de piedra ♦ *vt* apedrear; (*fruit*) deshuesar; **~-cold** *adj* helado; **~-deaf** *adj* sordo como una tapia; **~work** *n* (*art*) cantería; **stony** *adj* pedregoso; (*fig*) frío

stood [stud] *pt*, *pp* of **stand**

stool [stu:l] *n* taburete *m*

stoop [stu:p] *vi* (*also:* **~ down**) doblarse, agacharse; (*also:* **have a ~**) ser cargado de espaldas

stop [stɔp] *n* parada; (*in punctuation*) punto ♦ *vt* parar, detener; (*break off*) suspender; (*block: pay*) suspender; (*: cheque*) invalidar; (*also:* **put a ~ to**) poner término a ♦ *vi* pararse, detenerse; (*end*) acabarse; **to ~ doing sth** dejar de hacer algo; **~ dead** *vi* pararse en seco; **~ off** *vi* interrumpir el viaje; **~ up** *vt* (*hole*) tapar; **~gap** *n* (*person*) interino/a; (*thing*) recurso provisional; **~over** *n* parada; (*AVIAT*) escala

stoppage ['stɔpɪdʒ] *n* (*strike*) paro; (*blockage*) obstrucción *f*

stopper ['stɔpə*] *n* tapón *m*

stop press *n* noticias *fpl* de última hora

stopwatch ['stɔpwɔtʃ] *n* cronómetro

storage ['stɔːrɪdʒ] *n* almacenaje *m*; **~ heater** *n* acumulador *m*

store [stɔː*] *n* (*stock*) provisión *f*; (*depot: BRIT: large shop*) almacén *m*; (*US*) tienda; (*reserve*) reserva, repuesto ♦ *vt* almacenar; **~s** *npl* víveres *mpl*; **in ~** (*fig*): **to be in ~ for sb** esperarle a uno; **~ up** *vt* acumular; **~room** *n* despensa

storey ['stɔːrɪ] (*US* **story**) *n* piso

stork [stɔːk] *n* cigüeña

storm [stɔːm] *n* tormenta; (*fig: of applause*) salva; (*: of criticism*) nube *f* ♦ *vi* (*fig*) rabiar ♦ *vt* tomar por asalto; **~y** *adj* tempestuoso

story ['stɔːrɪ] *n* historia; (*lie*) mentira; (*US*) = **storey**; **~book** *n* libro de cuentos

stout [staut] *adj* (*strong*) sólido; (*fat*) gordo, corpulento; (*resolute*) resuelto ♦ *n* cerveza negra

stove [stəuv] *n* (*for cooking*) cocina; (*for heating*) estufa

stow [stəu] *vt* (*also:* **~ away**) meter, poner; (*NAUT*) estibar; **~away** *n* polizón/ona *m/f*

straggle ['strægl] *vi* (*houses etc*) extenderse; (*lag behind*) rezagarse

straight [streɪt] *adj* recto, derecho; (*frank*) franco, directo; (*simple*) sencillo ♦ *adv* derecho, directamente; (*drink*) sin mezcla; **to put *or* get sth ~** dejar algo en claro; **~ away, ~ off** en seguida; **~en** *vt* (*also:* **~en out**) enderezar, poner derecho; **~-faced** *adj* serio; **~forward** *adj* (*simple*) sencillo; (*honest*) honrado, franco

strain [streɪn] *n* tensión *f*; (*TECH*) presión *f*; (*MED*) torcedura; (*breed*) tipo, variedad *f*

♦ vt (*back etc*) torcerse; (*resources*) agotar; (*stretch*) estirar; (*food, tea*) colar; **~s** npl (MUS) son m; **~ed** adj (*muscle*) torcido; (*laugh*) forzado; (*relations*) tenso; **~er** n colador m

strait [streɪt] n (GEO) estrecho; **to be in dire ~s** pasar grandes apuros; **~-jacket** n camisa de fuerza; **~-laced** adj mojigato, gazmoño

strand [strænd] n (*of thread*) hebra; (*of hair*) trenza; (*of rope*) ramal m

stranded ['strændɪd] adj (*person: without money*) desamparado; (: *without transport*) colgado

strange [streɪndʒ] adj (*not known*) desconocido; (*odd*) extraño, raro; **~ly** adv de un modo raro; *see also* **enough**; **~r** n desconocido/a; (*from another area*) forastero/a

strangle ['stræŋgl] vt estrangular; **~hold** n (*fig*) dominio completo

strap [stræp] n correa; (*of slip, dress*) tirante m

strategic [strə'tiːdʒɪk] adj estratégico

strategy ['strætɪdʒɪ] n estrategia

straw [strɔː] n paja; (*drinking ~*) caña, pajita; **that's the last ~!** ¡eso es el colmo!

strawberry ['strɔːbərɪ] n fresa (SP), frutilla (AM)

stray [streɪ] adj (*animal*) extraviado; (*bullet*) perdido; (*scattered*) disperso ♦ vi extraviarse, perderse

streak [striːk] n raya; (*in hair*) raya ♦ vt rayar ♦ vi: **to ~ past** pasar como un rayo

stream [striːm] n riachuelo, arroyo; (*of people, vehicles*) riada, caravana; (*of smoke, insults etc*) chorro ♦ vt (SCOL) dividir en grupos por habilidad ♦ vi correr, fluir; **to ~ in/out** (*people*) entrar/salir en tropel

streamer ['striːmə*] n serpentina

streamlined ['striːmlaɪnd] adj aerodinámico

street [striːt] n calle f; **~car** (US) n tranvía m; **~ lamp** n farol m; **~ plan** n plano; **~wise** (*inf*) adj que tiene mucha calle

strength [streŋθ] n fuerza; (*of girder, knot*

etc) resistencia; (*fig: power*) poder m; **~en** vt fortalecer, reforzar

strenuous ['strenjuəs] adj (*energetic, determined*) enérgico

stress [stres] n presión f; (*mental strain*) estrés m; (*accent*) acento ♦ vt subrayar, recalcar; (*syllable*) acentuar

stretch [stretʃ] n (*of sand etc*) trecho ♦ vi estirarse; (*extend*): **to ~ to** or **as far as** extenderse hasta ♦ vt extender, estirar; (*make demands of*) exigir el máximo esfuerzo a; **~ out** vi tenderse ♦ vt (*arm etc*) extender; (*spread*) estirar

stretcher ['stretʃə*] n camilla

strewn [struːn] adj: **~ with** cubierto or sembrado de

stricken ['strɪkən] adj (*person*) herido; (*city, industry etc*) condenado; **~ with** (*disease*) afectado por

strict [strɪkt] adj severo; (*exact*) estricto; **~ly** adv severamente; estrictamente

stride [straɪd] (*pt* **strode**, *pp* **stridden**) n zancada, tranco ♦ vi dar zancadas, andar a trancos

strife [straɪf] n lucha

strike [straɪk] (*pt, pp* **struck**) n huelga; (*of oil etc*) descubrimiento; (*attack*) ataque m ♦ vt golpear, pegar; (*oil etc*) descubrir; (*bargain, deal*) cerrar ♦ vi declarar la huelga; (*attack*) atacar; (*clock*) dar la hora; **on ~** (*workers*) en huelga; **to ~ a match** encender un fósforo; **~ down** vt derribar; **~ up** vt (MUS) empezar a tocar; (*conversation*) entablar; (*friendship*) trabar; **~r** n huelguista m/f; (SPORT) delantero; **striking** adj llamativo

string [strɪŋ] (*pt, pp* **strung**) n (*gen*) cuerda; (*row*) hilera ♦ vt: **to ~ together** ensartar; **to ~ out** extenderse; **the ~s** npl (MUS) los instrumentos de cuerda; **to pull ~s** (*fig*) mover palancas; **~ bean** n judía verde, habichuela; **~(ed) instrument** n (MUS) instrumento de cuerda

stringent ['strɪndʒənt] adj riguroso, severo

strip [strɪp] n tira; (*of land*) franja; (*of metal*) cinta, lámina ♦ vt desnudar; (*paint*) quitar; (*also:* **~ down**: *machine*)

desmontar ♦ *vi* desnudarse; ~ **cartoon** *n*
tira cómica (*SP*), historieta (*AM*)
stripe [straɪp] *n* raya; (*MIL*) galón *m*; ~**d**
adj a rayas, rayado
strip lighting *n* alumbrado fluorescente
stripper ['strɪpə*] *n* artista *m/f* de
striptease
strive [straɪv] (*pt* **strove**, *pp* **striven**) *vi*: **to**
~ **for sth/to do sth** luchar por
conseguir/hacer algo
strode [strəud] *pt of* **stride**
stroke [strəuk] *n* (*blow*) golpe *m*;
(*SWIMMING*) brazada; (*MED*) apoplejía; (*of
paintbrush*) toque *m* ♦ *vt* acariciar; **at a** ~
de un solo golpe
stroll [strəul] *n* paseo, vuelta ♦ *vi* dar un
paseo *or* una vuelta; ~**er** (*US*) *n* (*for child*)
sillita de ruedas
strong [strɔŋ] *adj* fuerte; **they are 50** ~
son 50; ~**hold** *n* fortaleza; (*fig*) baluarte
m; ~**ly** *adv* fuertemente, con fuerza;
(*believe*) firmemente; ~**room** *n* cámara
acorazada
strove [strəuv] *pt of* **strive**
struck [strʌk] *pt, pp of* **strike**
structure ['strʌktʃə*] *n* estructura;
(*building*) construcción *f*
struggle ['strʌgl] *n* lucha ♦ *vi* luchar
strum [strʌm] *vt* (*guitar*) rasguear
strung [strʌŋ] *pt, pp of* **string**
strut [strʌt] *n* puntal *m* ♦ *vi* pavonearse
stub [stʌb] *n* (*of ticket etc*) talón *m*; (*of
cigarette*) colilla; **to** ~ **one's toe on sth**
dar con el dedo (del pie) contra algo; ~
out *vt* apagar
stubble ['stʌbl] *n* rastrojo; (*on chin*) barba
(incipiente)
stubborn ['stʌbən] *adj* terco, testarudo
stuck [stʌk] *pt, pp of* **stick** ♦ *adj* (*jammed*)
atascado; ~-**up** *adj* engreído, presumido
stud [stʌd] *n* (*in shirt* ~) corchete *m*; (*of boot*)
taco; (*earring*) pendiente *m* (de bolita);
(*also*: ~ **farm**) caballeriza; (*also*: ~ **horse**)
caballo semental ♦ *vt* (*fig*): ~**ded with**
salpicado de
student ['stju:dənt] *n* estudiante *m/f* ♦ *adj*
estudiantil; ~ **driver** (*US*) *n* aprendiz(a)

m/f
studio ['stju:dɪəu] *n* estudio; (*artist's*) taller
m; ~ **flat** (*US* ~ **apartment**) *n* estudio
studious ['stju:dɪəs] *adj* estudioso;
(*studied*) calculado; ~**ly** *adv* (*carefully*) con
esmero
study ['stʌdɪ] *n* estudio ♦ *vt* estudiar;
(*examine*) examinar, investigar ♦ *vi*
estudiar
stuff [stʌf] *n* materia; (*substance*) material
m, sustancia; (*things*) cosas *fpl* ♦ *vt* llenar;
(*CULIN*) rellenar; (*animals*) disecar; (*inf:
push*) meter; ~**ing** *n* relleno; ~**y** *adj*
(*room*) mal ventilado; (*person*) de miras
estrechas
stumble ['stʌmbl] *vi* tropezar, dar un
traspié; **to** ~ **across**, ~ **on** (*fig*) tropezar
con; **stumbling block** *n* tropiezo,
obstáculo
stump [stʌmp] *n* (*of tree*) tocón *m*; (*of
limb*) muñón *m* ♦ *vt*: **to be** ~**ed for an
answer** no saber qué contestar
stun [stʌn] *vt* dejar sin sentido
stung [stʌŋ] *pt, pp of* **sting**
stunk [stʌŋk] *pp of* **stink**
stunning ['stʌnɪŋ] *adj* (*fig: news*)
pasmoso; (: *outfit etc*) sensacional
stunt [stʌnt] *n* (*in film*) escena peligrosa;
(*publicity* ~) truco publicitario; ~**man**
(*irreg*) *n* doble *m*
stupid ['stju:pɪd] *adj* estúpido, tonto; ~**ity**
[-'pɪdɪtɪ] *n* estupidez *f*
sturdy ['stə:dɪ] *adj* robusto, fuerte
stutter ['stʌtə*] *n* tartamudeo ♦ *vi*
tartamudear
sty [staɪ] *n* (*for pigs*) pocilga
stye [staɪ] *n* (*MED*) orzuelo
style [staɪl] *n* estilo; **stylish** *adj* elegante,
a la moda
stylus ['staɪləs] *n* aguja
suave [swɑ:v] *adj* cortés
sub... [sʌb] *prefix* sub...; ~**conscious** *adj*
subconsciente; ~**contract** *vt*
subcontratar; ~**divide** *vt* subdividir
subdue [səb'dju:] *vt* sojuzgar; (*passions*)
dominar; ~**d** *adj* (*light*) tenue; (*person*)
sumiso, manso

subject [n 'sʌbdʒɪkt, vb səb'dʒekt] n súbdito; (SCOL) asignatura; (matter) tema m; (GRAMMAR) sujeto ♦ vt: **to ~ sb to sth** someter a uno a algo; **to be ~ to** (law) estar sujeto a; (subj: person) ser propenso a; **~ive** [-'dʒektɪv] adj subjetivo; **~ matter** n (content) contenido

sublet [sʌb'let] vt subarrendar

submarine [sʌbmə'riːn] n submarino

submerge [səb'məːdʒ] vt sumergir ♦ vi sumergirse

submissive [səb'mɪsɪv] adj sumiso

submit [səb'mɪt] vt someter ♦ vi: **to ~ to sth** someterse a algo

subnormal [sʌb'nɔːməl] adj anormal

subordinate [sə'bɔːdɪnət] adj, n subordinado/a m/f

subpoena [səb'piːnə] n (LAW) citación f

subscribe [səb'skraɪb] vi suscribir; **to ~ to** (opinion, fund) suscribir, aprobar; (newspaper) suscribirse a; **~r** n (to periodical) subscriptor(a) m/f; (to telephone) abonado/a

subscription [səb'skrɪpʃən] n abono; (to magazine) subscripción f

subsequent ['sʌbsɪkwənt] adj subsiguiente, posterior; **~ly** adv posteriormente, más tarde

subside [səb'saɪd] vi hundirse; (flood) bajar; (wind) amainar; **subsidence** [-'saɪdns] n hundimiento; (in road) socavón m

subsidiary [səb'sɪdɪərɪ] adj secundario ♦ n sucursal f, filial f

subsidize ['sʌbsɪdaɪz] vt subvencionar

subsidy ['sʌbsɪdɪ] n subvención f

subsistence [səb'sɪstəns] n subsistencia; **~ allowance** n salario mínimo

substance ['sʌbstəns] n sustancia

substantial [səb'stænʃl] adj sustancial, sustancioso; (fig) importante

substantiate [səb'stænʃɪeɪt] vt comprobar

substitute ['sʌbstɪtjuːt] n (person) suplente m/f; (thing) sustituto ♦ vt: **to ~ A for B** sustituir A por B, reemplazar B por A

subtitle ['sʌbtaɪtl] n subtítulo

subtle ['sʌtl] adj sutil; **~ty** n sutileza

subtotal [sʌb'teutl] n total m parcial

subtract [səb'trækt] vt restar, sustraer; **~ion** [-'trækʃən] n resta, sustracción f

suburb ['sʌbəːb] n barrio residencial; **the ~s** las afueras (de la ciudad); **~an** [sə'bəːbən] adj suburbano; (train etc) de cercanías; **~ia** [sə'bəːbɪə] n barrios mpl residenciales

subway ['sʌbweɪ] n (BRIT) paso subterráneo or inferior; (US) metro

succeed [sək'siːd] vi (person) tener éxito; (plan) salir bien ♦ vt suceder a; **to ~ in doing** lograr hacer; **~ing** adj (following) sucesivo

success [sək'ses] n éxito; **~ful** adj exitoso; (business) próspero; **to be ~ful (in doing)** lograr (hacer); **~fully** adv con éxito

succession [sək'seʃən] n sucesión f, serie f

successive [sək'sesɪv] adj sucesivo, consecutivo

succinct [sək'sɪŋkt] adj sucinto

such [sʌtʃ] adj tal, semejante; (of that kind): **~ a book** tal libro; (so much): **~ courage** tanto valor ♦ adv tan; **~ a long trip** un viaje tan largo; **~ a lot of** tanto(s)/a(s); **~ as** (like) tal como; **as ~** como tal; **~-and-~** adj tal o cual

suck [sʌk] vt chupar; (bottle) sorber; (breast) mamar; **~er** n (ZOOL) ventosa; (inf) bobo, primo

suction ['sʌkʃən] n succión f

Sudan [su'dæn] n Sudán m

sudden ['sʌdn] adj (rapid) repentino, súbito; (unexpected) imprevisto; **all of a ~** de repente; **~ly** adv de repente

suds [sʌdz] npl espuma de jabón

sue [suː] vt demandar

suede [sweɪd] n ante m (SP), gamuza (AM)

suet ['suɪt] n sebo

Suez ['suːɪz] n: **the ~ Canal** el Canal de Suez

suffer ['sʌfə*] vt sufrir, padecer; (tolerate) aguantar, soportar ♦ vi sufrir; **to ~ from** (illness etc) padecer; **~er** n víctima; (MED) enfermo/a; **~ing** n sufrimiento

sufficient [sə'fɪʃənt] *adj* suficiente, bastante; **~ly** *ad* suficientemente, bastante

suffocate ['sʌfəkeɪt] *vi* ahogarse, asfixiarse; **suffocation** [-'keɪʃən] *n* asfixia

sugar ['ʃugə*] *n* azúcar *m* ♦ *vt* echar azúcar a, azucarar; **~ beet** *n* remolacha; **~ cane** *n* caña de azúcar

suggest [sə'dʒɛst] *vt* sugerir; **~ion** [-'dʒɛstʃən] *n* sugerencia; **~ive** (*pej*) *adj* indecente

suicide ['suɪsaɪd] *n* suicidio; (*person*) suicida *m/f*; *see also* **commit**

suit [suːt] *n* (*man's*) traje *m*; (*woman's*) conjunto; (*LAW*) pleito; (*CARDS*) palo ♦ *vt* convenir; (*clothes*) sentar a, ir bien a; (*adapt*): **to ~ sth to** adaptar *or* ajustar algo a; **well ~ed** (*well matched*): **couple**) hecho el uno para el otro; **~able** *adj* conveniente; (*apt*) indicado; **~ably** *adv* convenientemente; (*impressed*) apropiadamente

suitcase ['suːtkeɪs] *n* maleta (*SP*), valija (*AM*)

suite [swiːt] *n* (*of rooms, MUS*) suite *f*; (*furniture*): **bedroom/dining room ~** (juego de) dormitorio/comedor

suitor ['suːtə*] *n* pretendiente *m*

sulfur ['sʌlfə*] (*US*) *n* = **sulphur**

sulk [sʌlk] *vi* estar de mal humor; **~y** *adj* malhumorado

sullen ['sʌlən] *adj* hosco, malhumorado

sulphur ['sʌlfə*] (*US* **sulfur**) *n* azufre *m*

sultana [sʌl'tɑːnə] *n* (*fruit*) pasa de Esmirna

sultry ['sʌltrɪ] *adj* (*weather*) bochornoso

sum [sʌm] *n* suma; (*total*) total *m*; **~ up** *vt* resumir ♦ *vi* hacer un resumen

summarize ['sʌməraɪz] *vt* resumir

summary ['sʌmərɪ] *n* resumen *m* ♦ *adj* (*justice*) sumario

summer ['sʌmə*] *n* verano ♦ *cpd* de verano; **in ~** en verano; **~ holidays** *npl* vacaciones *fpl* de verano; **~house** *n* (*in garden*) cenador *m*, glorieta; **~time** *n* (*season*) verano; **~ time** *n* (*by clock*) hora de verano

summit ['sʌmɪt] *n* cima, cumbre *f*; (*also:* **~ conference, ~ meeting**) (conferencia) cumbre *f*

summon ['sʌmən] *vt* (*person*) llamar; (*meeting*) convocar; (*LAW*) citar; **~ up** *vt* (*courage*) armarse de; **~s** *n* llamamiento, llamada ♦ *vt* (*LAW*) citar

sump [sʌmp] (*BRIT*) *n* (*AUT*) cárter *m*

sumptuous ['sʌmptjuəs] *adj* suntuoso

sun [sʌn] *n* sol *m*; **~bathe** *vi* tomar el sol; **~block** *n* filtro solar; **~burn** *n* (*painful*) quemadura; (*tan*) bronceado; **~burnt** *adj* quemado por el sol

Sunday ['sʌndɪ] *n* domingo; **~ school** *n* catequesis *f* dominical

sundial ['sʌndaɪəl] *n* reloj *m* de sol

sundown ['sʌndaun] *n* anochecer *m*

sundry ['sʌndrɪ] *adj* varios/as, diversos/as; **all and ~** todos sin excepción; **sundries** *npl* géneros *mpl* diversos

sunflower ['sʌnflauə*] *n* girasol *m*

sung [sʌŋ] *pp of* **sing**

sunglasses ['sʌnglɑːsɪz] *npl* gafas *fpl* (*SP*) *or* anteojos *mpl* de sol

sunk [sʌŋk] *pp of* **sink**

sun: **~light** *n* luz *f* del sol; **~lit** *adj* iluminado por el sol; **~ny** *adj* soleado; (*day*) de sol; (*fig*) alegre; **~rise** *n* salida del sol; **~ roof** *n* (*AUT*) techo corredizo; **~screen** *n* protector *m* solar; **~set** *n* puesta del sol; **~shade** *n* (*over table*) sombrilla; **~shine** *n* sol *m*; **~stroke** *n* insolación *f*; **~tan** *n* bronceado; **~tan oil** *n* aceite *m* bronceador

super ['suːpə*] (*inf*) *adj* genial

superannuation [suːpərænju'eɪʃən] *n* cuota de jubilación

superb [suː'pəːb] *adj* magnífico, espléndido

supercilious [suːpə'sɪlɪəs] *adj* altanero

superfluous [suː'pəːfluəs] *adj* superfluo, de sobra

superhuman [suːpə'hjuːmən] *adj* sobrehumano

superimpose ['suːpərɪm'pəuz] *vt* sobreponer

superintendent [suːpərɪn'tɛndənt] *n*

director(a) *m/f*; (*POLICE*) subjefe/a *m/f*
superior [su'pɪərɪə*] *adj* superior; (*smug*)
desdeñoso ♦ *n* superior *m*; **~ity** [-'ɔrɪtɪ] *n*
superioridad *f*
superlative [su'pə:lətɪv] *n* superlativo
superman ['su:pəmæn] (*irreg*) *n*
superhombre *m*
supermarket ['su:pəmɑ:kɪt] *n*
supermercado
supernatural [su:pə'nætʃərəl] *adj*
sobrenatural ♦ *n*: **the ~** lo sobrenatural
superpower ['su:pəpauə*] *n* (*POL*)
superpotencia
supersede [su:pə'si:d] *vt* suplantar
superstar ['su:pəstɑ:*] *n* gran estrella
superstitious [su:pə'stɪʃəs] *adj*
supersticioso
supertanker ['su:pətæŋkə*] *n*
superpetrolero
supervise ['su:pəvaɪz] *vt* supervisar;
supervision [-'vɪʒən] *n* supervisión *f*;
supervisor *n* supervisor(a) *m/f*
supper ['sʌpə*] *n* cena
supple ['sʌpl] *adj* flexible
supplement [*n* 'sʌplɪmənt, *vb* sʌplɪ'mənt]
n suplemento ♦ *vt* suplir; **~ary**
[-'mentərɪ] *adj* suplementario; **~ary benefit** (*BRIT*) *n*
subsidio suplementario de la seguridad
social
supplier [sə'plaɪə*] *n* (*COMM*)
distribuidor(a) *m/f*
supply [sə'plaɪ] *vt* (*provide*) suministrar;
(*equip*): **to ~ (with)** proveer (de) ♦ *n*
provisión *f*; (*gas, water etc*) suministro;
supplies *npl* (*food*) víveres *mpl*; (*MIL*)
pertrechos *mpl*; **~ teacher** *n* profesor(a)
m/f suplente
support [sə'pɔ:t] *n* apoyo; (*TECH*) soporte
m ♦ *vt* apoyar; (*financially*) mantener;
(*uphold, TECH*) sostener; **~er** *n* (*POL etc*)
partidario/a; (*SPORT*) aficionado/a
suppose [sə'pəuz] *vt* suponer; (*imagine*)
imaginarse; (*duty*): **to be ~d to do sth**
deber hacer algo; **~dly** [sə'pəuzɪdlɪ] *adv*
según cabe suponer; **supposing** *conj* en
caso de que
suppress [sə'prɛs] *vt* suprimir; (*yawn*)

ahogar
supreme [su'pri:m] *adj* supremo
surcharge ['sə:tʃɑ:dʒ] *n* sobretasa, recargo
sure [ʃuə*] *adj* seguro; (*definite, convinced*)
cierto; **to make ~ of sth/that** asegurarse
de algo/asegurar que; **~!** (*of course*)
¡claro!, ¡por supuesto!; **~ enough**
efectivamente; **~ly** *adv* (*certainly*)
seguramente
surf [sə:f] *n* olas *fpl*
surface ['sə:fɪs] *n* superficie *f* ♦ *vt* (*road*)
revestir ♦ *vi* (*also fig*) salir a la superficie;
by ~ mail por vía terrestre
surfboard ['sə:fbɔ:d] *n* tabla (de surf)
surfeit ['sə:fɪt] *n*: **a ~ of** un exceso de
surfing ['sə:fɪŋ] *n* surf *m*
surge [sə:dʒ] *n* oleada, oleaje *m* ♦ *vi*
(*wave*) romper; (*people*) avanzar en tropel
surgeon ['sə:dʒən] *n* cirujano/a
surgery ['sə:dʒərɪ] *n* cirugía; (*BRIT: room*)
consultorio; **~ hours** (*BRIT*) *npl* horas *fpl*
de consulta
surgical ['sə:dʒɪkl] *adj* quirúrgico; **~ spirit**
(*BRIT*) *n* alcohol *m* de 90°
surname ['sə:neɪm] *n* apellido
surpass [sə:'pɑ:s] *vt* superar, exceder
surplus ['sə:pləs] *n* excedente *m*; (*COMM*)
superávit *m* ♦ *adj* excedente, sobrante
surprise [sə'praɪz] *n* sorpresa ♦ *vt*
sorprender; **surprising** *adj*
sorprendente; **surprisingly** *adv*: **it was**
surprisingly easy me *etc* sorprendió lo
fácil que fue
surrender [sə'rɛndə*] *n* rendición *f*,
entrega ♦ *vi* rendirse, entregarse
surreptitious [sʌrəp'tɪʃəs] *adj* subrepticio
surrogate ['sʌrəgɪt] *n* sucedáneo; **~**
mother *n* madre *f* portadora
surround [sə'raund] *vt* rodear, circundar;
(*MIL etc*) cercar; **~ing** *adj* circundante;
~ings *npl* alrededores *mpl*, cercanías *fpl*
surveillance [sə:'veɪləns] *n* vigilancia
survey [*n* 'sə:veɪ, *vb* sə:'veɪ] *n* inspección *f*,
reconocimiento; (*inquiry*) encuesta ♦ *vt*
examinar, inspeccionar; (*look at*) mirar,
contemplar; **~or** *n* agrimensor(a) *m/f*
survival [sə'vaɪvl] *n* supervivencia

survive [sə'vaɪv] *vi* sobrevivir; (*custom etc*) perdurar ♦ *vt* sobrevivir a; **survivor** *n* superviviente *m/f*

susceptible [sə'sɛptəbl] *adj*: ~ **(to)** (*disease*) susceptible (a); (*flattery*) sensible (a)

suspect [*adj, n* 'sʌspɛkt, *vb* səs'pɛkt] *adj, n* sospechoso/a *m/f* ♦ *vt* (*person*) sospechar de; (*think*) sospechar

suspend [səs'pɛnd] *vt* suspender; **~ed sentence** *n* (*LAW*) libertad *f* condicional; **~er belt** *n* portaligas *m inv*; **~ers** *npl* (*BRIT*) ligas *fpl*; (*US*) tirantes *mpl*

suspense [səs'pɛns] *n* incertidumbre *f*, duda; (*in film etc*) suspense *m*; **to keep sb in ~** mantener a uno en suspense

suspension [səs'pɛnʃən] *n* (*gen, AUT*) suspensión *f*; (*of driving licence*) privación *f*; **~ bridge** *n* puente *m* colgante

suspicion [səs'pɪʃən] *n* sospecha; (*distrust*) recelo; **suspicious** [-ʃəs] *adj* receloso; (*causing suspicion*) sospechoso

sustain [səs'teɪn] *vt* sostener, apoyar; (*suffer*) sufrir, padecer; **~able** *adj* sostenible; **~ed** *adj* (*effort*) sostenido

sustenance ['sʌstɪnəns] *n* sustento

swab [swɔb] *n* (*MED*) algodón *m*

swagger ['swægə*] *vi* pavonearse

swallow ['swɔləu] *n* (*bird*) golondrina ♦ *vt* tragar; (*fig, pride*) tragarse; **~ up** *vt* (*savings etc*) consumir

swam [swæm] *pt of* **swim**

swamp [swɔmp] *n* pantano, ciénaga ♦ *vt* (*with water etc*) inundar; (*fig*) abrumar, agobiar; **~y** *adj* pantanoso

swan [swɔn] *n* cisne *m*

swap [swɔp] *n* canje *m*, intercambio ♦ *vt*: **to ~ (for)** cambiar (por)

swarm [swɔːm] *n* (*of bees*) enjambre *m*; (*fig*) multitud *f* ♦ *vi* (*bees*) formar un enjambre; (*people*) pulular; **to be ~ing with** ser un hervidero de

swastika ['swɔstɪkə] *n* esvástika

swat [swɔt] *vt* aplastar

sway [sweɪ] *vi* mecerse, balancearse ♦ *vt* (*influence*) mover, influir en

swear [swɛə*] (*pt* **swore**, *pp* **sworn**) *vi* (*curse*) maldecir; (*promise*) jurar ♦ *vt* jurar; **~word** *n* taco, palabrota

sweat [swɛt] *n* sudor *m* ♦ *vi* sudar

sweater ['swɛtə*] *n* suéter *m*

sweatshirt ['swɛtʃəːt] *n* suéter *m*

sweaty ['swɛtɪ] *adj* sudoroso

Swede [swiːd] *n* sueco/a

swede [swiːd] (*BRIT*) *n* nabo

Sweden ['swiːdn] *n* Suecia; **Swedish** ['swiːdɪʃ] *adj* sueco ♦ *n* (*LING*) sueco

sweep [swiːp] (*pt, pp* **swept**) *n* (*act*) barrido *m*; (*also*: **chimney ~**) deshollinador(a) *m/f* ♦ *vt* barrer; (*with arm*) empujar; (*subj: current*) arrastrar ♦ *vi* barrer; (*arm etc*) moverse rápidamente; (*wind*) soplar con violencia; **~ away** *vt* barrer; **~ past** *vi* pasar majestuosamente; **~ up** *vi* barrer; **~ing** *adj* (*gesture*) dramático; (*generalized*) *statement*) generalizado

sweet [swiːt] *n* (*candy*) dulce *m*, caramelo; (*BRIT: pudding*) postre *m* ♦ *adj* dulce; (*fig: kind*) dulce, amable; (*: attractive*) mono; **~corn** *n* maíz *m*; **~en** *vt* (*add sugar to*) poner azúcar a; (*person*) endulzar; **~heart** *n* novio/a; **~ness** *n* dulzura; **~pea** *n* guisante *m* de olor

swell [swɛl] (*pt* **swelled**, *pp* **swollen** *or* **swelled**) *n* (*of sea*) marejada, oleaje *m* ♦ *adj* (*US: inf: excellent*) estupendo, fenomenal ♦ *vt* hinchar, inflar ♦ *vi* (*also*: **~ up**) hincharse; (*numbers*) aumentar; (*sound, feeling*) ir aumentando; **~ing** *n* (*MED*) hinchazón *f*

sweltering ['swɛltərɪŋ] *adj* sofocante, de mucho calor

swept [swɛpt] *pt, pp of* **sweep**

swerve [swəːv] *vi* desviarse bruscamente

swift [swɪft] *n* (*bird*) vencejo ♦ *adj* rápido, veloz; **~ly** *adv* rápidamente

swig [swɪg] (*inf*) *n* (*drink*) trago

swill [swɪl] *vt* (*also*: **~ out, ~ down**) lavar, limpiar con agua

swim [swɪm] (*pt* **swam**, *pp* **swum**) *n*: **to go for a ~** ir a nadar *or* a bañarse ♦ *vi* nadar; (*head, room*) dar vueltas ♦ *vt* nadar; (*the Channel etc*) cruzar a nado; **~mer** *n* nadador(a) *m/f*; **~ming** *n*

natación f; **~ming cap** n gorro de baño;
~ming costume (*BRIT*) n bañador m,
traje m de baño; **~ming pool** n piscina
(*SP*), alberca (*AM*); **~ming trunks** n
bañador m (de hombre); **~ming suit** n
= **~ming costume**
swindle ['swɪndl] n estafa ♦ vt estafar
swine [swaɪn] (*inf!*) canalla (*!*)
swing [swɪŋ] (*pt, pp* **swung**) n (*in
playground*) columpio; (*movement*)
balanceo, vaivén m; (*change of direction*)
viraje m; (*rhythm*) ritmo ♦ vt balancear;
(*also:* **~ round**) voltear, girar ♦ vi
balancearse, columpiarse; (*also:* **~ round**)
dar media vuelta; **to be in full ~** estar en
plena marcha; **~ bridge** n puente m
giratorio; **~ door** (*US* **~ing door**) n
puerta giratoria
swingeing ['swɪndʒɪŋ] (*BRIT*) adj (*cuts*)
atroz
swipe [swaɪp] vt (*hit*) golpear fuerte; (*inf:
steal*) guindar
swirl [swə:l] vi arremolinarse
Swiss [swɪs] adj, n inv suizo/a m/f
switch [swɪtʃ] n (*for light etc*) interruptor
m; (*change*) cambio ♦ vt (*change*)
cambiar de; **~ off** vt apagar; (*engine*)
parar; **~ on** vt encender (*SP*), prender
(*AM*); (*engine, machine*) arrancar; **~board**
n (*TEL*) centralita (de teléfonos) (*SP*),
conmutador m (*AM*)
Switzerland ['swɪtsələnd] n Suiza
swivel ['swɪvl] vi (*also:* **~ round**) girar
swollen ['swəulən] pp of **swell**
swoon [swu:n] vi desmayarse
swoop [swu:p] n (*by police etc*) redada
♦ vi (*also:* **~ down**) calarse
swop [swɔp] = **swap**
sword [sɔ:d] n espada; **~fish** n pez m
espada
swore [swɔ:*] pt of **swear**
sworn [swɔ:n] pp of **swear** ♦ adj
(*statement*) bajo juramento; (*enemy*)
implacable
swot [swɔt] (*BRIT*) vt, vi empollar
swum [swʌm] pp of **swim**
swung [swʌŋ] pt, pp of **swing**

sycamore ['sɪkəmɔ:*] n sicomoro
syllable ['sɪləbl] n sílaba
syllabus ['sɪləbəs] n programa m de
estudios
symbol ['sɪmbl] n símbolo
symmetry ['sɪmɪtrɪ] n simetría
sympathetic [sɪmpə'θetɪk] adj
(*understanding*) comprensivo; (*likeable*)
simpático; (*showing support*): **~ to(wards)**
bien dispuesto hacia
sympathize ['sɪmpəθaɪz] vi: **to ~ with**
(*person*) compadecerse de; (*feelings*)
comprender; (*cause*) apoyar; **~r** n (*POL*)
simpatizante m/f
sympathy ['sɪmpəθɪ] n (*pity*) compasión f;
sympathies npl (*tendencies*) tendencias
fpl; **with our deepest ~** nuestro más
sentido pésame; **in ~** en solidaridad
symphony ['sɪmfənɪ] n sinfonía
symptom ['sɪmptəm] n síntoma m, indicio
synagogue ['sɪnəgɔg] n sinagoga
syndicate ['sɪndɪkɪt] n (*gen*) sindicato; (*of
newspapers*) agencia (de noticias)
syndrome ['sɪndrəum] n síndrome m
synopsis [sɪ'nɔpsɪs] (*pl* **synopses**) n
sinopsis f inv
synthesis ['sɪnθəsɪs] (*pl* **syntheses**) n
síntesis f inv
synthetic [sɪn'θetɪk] adj sintético
syphilis ['sɪfɪlɪs] n sífilis f
syphon ['saɪfən] = **siphon**
Syria ['sɪrɪə] n Siria; **~n** adj, n sirio/a
syringe [sɪ'rɪndʒ] n jeringa
syrup ['sɪrəp] n jarabe m; (*also:* **golden ~**)
almíbar m
system ['sɪstəm] n sistema m; (*ANAT*)
organismo; **~atic** [-'mætɪk] adj
sistemático, metódico; **~ disk** n
(*COMPUT*) disco del sistema; **~s analyst**
n analista m/f de sistemas

T, t

ta [tɑ:] (*BRIT: inf*) *excl* ¡gracias!
tab [tæb] *n* lengüeta; (*label*) etiqueta; **to keep ~s on** (*fig*) vigilar
tabby ['tæbɪ] *n* (*also:* **~ cat**) gato atigrado
table ['teɪbl] *n* mesa; (*of statistics etc*) cuadro, tabla ♦ *vt* (*BRIT: motion etc*) presentar; **to lay** *or* **set the ~** poner la mesa; **~cloth** *n* mantel *m*; **~ of contents** *n* índice *m* de materias; **~ d'hôte** [tɑ:bl'dəut] *adj* del menú; **~ lamp** *n* lámpara de mesa; **~mat** *n* (*for plate*) posaplatos *m inv*; (*for hot dish*) salvamantel *m*; **~spoon** *n* cuchara de servir; (*also:* **~spoonful**: *as measurement*) cucharada
tablet ['tæblɪt] *n* (*MED*) pastilla, comprimido; (*of stone*) lápida
table tennis *n* ping-pong *m*, tenis *m* de mesa
table wine *n* vino de mesa
tabloid ['tæblɔɪd] *n* periódico popular sensacionalista

> **tabloid press**
>
> ***i*** El término **tabloid press** *o* **tabloids** se usa para referirse a la prensa popular británica, por el tamaño más pequeño de los periódicos. A diferencia de los de la llamada **quality press**, estas publicaciones se caracterizan por un lenguaje sencillo, una presentación llamativa y un contenido sensacionalista, centrado a veces en los escándalos financieros y sexuales de los famosos, por lo que también reciben el nombre peyorativo de "gutter press".

tack [tæk] *n* (*nail*) tachuela; (*fig*) rumbo ♦ *vt* (*nail*) clavar con tachuelas; (*stitch*) hilvanar ♦ *vi* virar
tackle ['tækl] *n* (*fishing ~*) aparejo (de pescar); (*for lifting*) aparejo ♦ *vt* (*difficulty*) enfrentarse con; (*challenge: person*) hacer

frente a; (*grapple with*) agarrar; (*FOOTBALL*) cargar; (*RUGBY*) placar
tacky ['tækɪ] *adj* pegajoso; (*pej*) cutre
tact [tækt] *n* tacto, discreción *f*; **~ful** *adj* discreto, diplomático
tactics ['tæktɪks] *n, npl* táctica
tactless ['tæktlɪs] *adj* indiscreto
tadpole ['tædpəul] *n* renacuajo
tag [tæg] *n* (*label*) etiqueta; **~ along** *vi* ir (*or* venir) también
tail [teɪl] *n* cola; (*of shirt, coat*) faldón *m* ♦ *vt* (*follow*) vigilar a; **~s** *npl* (*formal suit*) levita; **~ away** *vi* (*in size, quality etc*) ir disminuyendo; **~ off** *vi* = **~ away**; **~back** (*BRIT*) *n* (*AUT*) cola; **~ end** *n* cola, parte *f* final; **~gate** *n* (*AUT*) puerta trasera
tailor ['teɪlə*] *n* sastre *m*; **~ing** *n* (*cut*) corte *m*; (*craft*) sastrería; **~-made** *adj* (*also fig*) hecho a la medida
tailwind ['teɪlwɪnd] *n* viento de cola
tainted ['teɪntɪd] *adj* (*food*) pasado; (*water, air*) contaminado; (*fig*) manchado
take [teɪk] (*pt* **took**, *pp* **taken**) *vt* tomar; (*grab*) coger (*SP*), agarrar (*AM*); (*gain: prize*) ganar; (*require: effort, courage*) exigir; (*tolerate: pain etc*) aguantar; (*hold: passengers etc*) tener cabida para; (*accompany, bring, carry*) llevar; (*exam*) presentarse a; **to ~ sth from** (*drawer etc*) sacar algo de; (*person*) quitar algo a; **I ~ it that ...** supongo que ...; **~ after** *vt fus* parecerse a; **~ apart** *vt* desmontar; **~ away** *vt* (*remove*) quitar; (*carry off*) llevar; (*MATH*) restar; **~ back** *vt* (*return*) devolver; (*one's words*) retractarse de; **~ down** *vt* (*building*) derribar; (*letter etc*) apuntar; (*understand*) entender; (*include*) abarcar; (*lodger*) acoger, recibir; **~ off** *vi* (*AVIAT*) despegar ♦ *vt* (*remove*) quitar; **~ on** *vt* (*work*) aceptar; (*employee*) contratar; (*opponent*) desafiar; **~ out** *vt* sacar; **~ over** *vt* (*business*) tomar posesión de; (*country*) tomar el poder ♦ *vi*: **to ~ over from sb** reemplazar a uno; **~ to** *vt fus* (*person*) coger cariño a, encariñarse con; (*activity*) aficionarse a; **~ up** *vt* (*a dress*)

acortar; (*occupy: time, space*) ocupar; (*engage in: hobby etc*) dedicarse a; (*accept*): **to ~ sb up on** aceptar; **~away** (*BRIT*) *adj* (*food*) para llevar ♦ *n* tienda (*or* restaurante *m*) de comida para llevar; **~off** *n* (*AVIAT*) despegue *m*; **~out** (*US*) *n* = **~away**; **~over** *n* (*COMM*) absorción *f*

takings ['teɪkɪŋz] *npl* (*COMM*) ingresos *mpl*

talc [tælk] *n* (*also:* **~um powder**) (polvos de) talco

tale [teɪl] *n* (*story*) cuento; (*account*) relación *f*; **to tell ~s** (*fig*) chivarse

talent ['tælnt] *n* talento; **~ed** *adj* de talento

talk [tɔːk] *n* charla; (*conversation*) conversación *f*; (*gossip*) habladurías *fpl*, chismes *mpl* ♦ *vi* hablar; **~s** *npl* (*POL etc*) conversaciones *fpl*; **to ~ about** hablar de; **to ~ sb into doing sth** convencer a uno para que haga algo; **to ~ sb out of doing sth** disuadir a uno de que haga algo; **to ~ shop** hablar del trabajo; **~ over** *vt* discutir; **~ative** *adj* hablador(a); **~ show** *n* programa *m* de entrevistas

tall [tɔːl] *adj* alto; (*object*) grande; **to be 6 feet ~** (*person*) medir 1 metro 80

tally ['tælɪ] *n* cuenta ♦ *vi*: **to ~ (with)** corresponder (con)

talon ['tæln] *n* garra

tambourine [tæmbə'riːn] *n* pandereta

tame [teɪm] *adj* domesticado; (*fig*) mediocre

tamper ['tæmpə*] *vi*: **to ~ with** tocar, andar con

tampon ['tæmpən] *n* tampón *m*

tan [tæn] *n* (*also:* **sun~**) bronceado ♦ *vi* ponerse moreno ♦ *adj* (*colour*) marrón

tang [tæŋ] *n* sabor *m* fuerte

tangent ['tændʒənt] *n* (*MATH*) tangente *f*; **to go off at a ~** (*fig*) salirse por la tangente

tangerine [tændʒə'riːn] *n* mandarina

tangle ['tæŋgl] *n* enredo; **to get in(to) a ~** enredarse

tank [tæŋk] *n* (*water ~*) depósito, tanque *m*; (*for fish*) acuario; (*MIL*) tanque *m*

tanker ['tæŋkə*] *n* (*ship*) buque *m* cisterna;

(*truck*) camión *m* cisterna

tanned [tænd] *adj* (*skin*) moreno

tantalizing ['tæntəlaɪzɪŋ] *adj* tentador(a)

tantamount ['tæntəmaunt] *adj*: **~ to** equivalente a

tantrum ['tæntrəm] *n* rabieta

tap [tæp] *n* (*BRIT: on sink etc*) grifo (*SP*), canilla (*AM*); (*gas ~*) llave *f*; (*gentle blow*) golpecito ♦ *vt* (*hit gently*) dar golpecitos en; (*resources*) utilizar, explotar; (*telephone*) intervenir; **on ~** (*fig: resources*) a mano; **~ dancing** *n* claqué *m*

tape [teɪp] *n* (*also:* **magnetic ~**) cinta magnética; (*cassette*) cassette *f*, cinta; (*sticky ~*) cinta adhesiva; (*for tying*) cinta ♦ *vt* (*record*) grabar (en cinta); (*stick with ~*) pegar con cinta adhesiva; **~ deck** *n* grabadora; **~ measure** *n* cinta métrica, metro

taper ['teɪpə*] *n* cirio ♦ *vi* afilarse

tape recorder *n* grabadora

tapestry ['tæpɪstrɪ] *n* (*object*) tapiz *m*; (*art*) tapicería

tar [tɑː] *n* alquitrán *m*, brea

target ['tɑːgɪt] *n* (*gen*) blanco

tariff ['tærɪf] *n* (*on goods*) arancel *m*; (*BRIT: in hotels etc*) tarifa

tarmac ['tɑːmæk] *n* (*BRIT: on road*) asfaltado; (*AVIAT*) pista (de aterrizaje)

tarnish ['tɑːnɪʃ] *vt* deslustrar

tarpaulin [tɑː'pɔːlɪn] *n* lona impermeabilizada

tarragon ['tærəgən] *n* estragón *m*

tart [tɑːt] *n* (*CULIN*) tarta; (*BRIT: inf: prostitute*) puta ♦ *adj* agrio, ácido; **~ up** (*BRIT: inf*) *vt* (*building*) remozar; **to ~ o.s. up** acicalarse

tartan ['tɑːtn] *n* tejido escocés *m*

tartar ['tɑːtə*] *n* (*on teeth*) sarro; **~(e) sauce** *n* salsa tártara

task [tɑːsk] *n* tarea; **to take to ~** reprender; **~ force** *n* (*MIL, POLICE*) grupo de operaciones

taste [teɪst] *n* (*sense*) gusto; (*flavour*) sabor *m*; (*also:* **after~**) sabor *m*, dejo; (*sample*): **have a ~!** ¡prueba un poquito!; (*fig*) muestra, idea ♦ *vt* (*also fig*) probar ♦ *vi*:

to ~ of *or* **like** (*fish, garlic etc*) saber a;
you can ~ the garlic (in it) se nota el
sabor a ajo; **in good/bad ~** de buen/mal
gusto; **~ful** *adj* de buen gusto; **~less**
adj (*food*) soso; (*remark etc*) de mal gusto;
tasty *adj* sabroso, rico

tatters ['tætəz] *npl:* **in ~** hecho jirones

tattoo [tə'tu:] *n* tatuaje *m*; (*spectacle*)
espectáculo militar ♦ *vt* tatuar

tatty ['tætɪ] (*BRIT: inf*) *adj* cochambroso

taught [tɔ:t] *pt, pp of* **teach**

taunt [tɔ:nt] *n* burla ♦ *vt* burlarse de

Taurus ['tɔ:rəs] *n* Tauro

taut [tɔ:t] *adj* tirante, tenso

tax [tæks] *n* impuesto ♦ *vt* gravar (con un
impuesto); (*fig: memory*) poner a prueba
(*: patience*) agotar; **~able** *adj* (*income*)
gravable; **~ation** [-'seɪʃən] *n* impuestos
mpl; **~ avoidance** *n* evasión *f* de
impuestos; **~ disc** (*BRIT*) *n* (*AUT*) pegatina
del impuesto de circulación; **~ evasion**
n evasión *f* fiscal; **~-free** *adj* libre de
impuestos

taxi ['tæksɪ] *n* taxi *m* ♦ *vi* (*AVIAT*) rodar por
la pista; **~ driver** *n* taxista *m/f*; **~ rank**
(*BRIT*) *n* = **~ stand**; **~ stand** *n* parada de
taxis

tax: ~ payer *n* contribuyente *m/f*; **~
relief** *n* desgravación *f* fiscal; **~ return** *n*
declaración *f* de ingresos

TB *n abbr* = **tuberculosis**

tea [ti:] *n* té *m*; (*BRIT: meal*) ≈ merienda
(*SP*); cena; **high ~** (*BRIT*) merienda-cena
(*SP*); **~ bag** *n* bolsita de té; **~ break**
(*BRIT*) *n* descanso para el té

teach [ti:tʃ] (*pt, pp* **taught**) *vt:* **to ~ sb
sth, ~ sth to sb** enseñar algo a uno ♦ *vi*
(*be a teacher*) ser profesor(a), enseñar;
~er *n* (*in secondary school*) profesor(a)
m/f; (*in primary school*) maestro/a,
profesor(a) de EGB; **~ing** *n* enseñanza

tea cosy *n* cubretetera *m*

teacup ['ti:kʌp] *n* taza para el té

teak [ti:k] *n* (madera de) teca

team [ti:m] *n* equipo *m*; (*of horses*) tiro;
~work *n* trabajo en equipo

teapot ['ti:pɔt] *n* tetera

tear¹ [tɪə*] *n* lágrima; **in ~s** llorando

tear² [tɛə*] (*pt* **tore**, *pp* **torn**) *n* rasgón *m*,
desgarrón *m* ♦ *vt* romper, rasgar ♦ *vi*
rasgarse; **~ along** *vi* (*rush*) precipitarse;
~ up *vt* (*sheet of paper etc*) romper

tearful ['tɪəfəl] *adj* lloroso

tear gas ['tɪə-] *n* gas *m* lacrimógeno

tearoom ['ti:ru:m] *n* salón *m* de té

tease [ti:z] *vt* tomar el pelo a

tea set *n* servicio de té

teaspoon *n* cucharita; (*also:* **~ful:** *as
measurement*) cucharadita

teat [ti:t] *n* (*of bottle*) tetina

teatime ['ti:taɪm] *n* hora del té

tea towel (*BRIT*) *n* paño de cocina

technical ['tɛknɪkl] *adj* técnico; **~
college** (*BRIT*) *n* ≈ escuela de artes y
oficios (*SP*); **~ity** [-'kælɪtɪ] *n* (*point of law*)
formalismo; (*detail*) detalle *m* técnico; **~ly**
adv en teoría; (*regarding technique*)
técnicamente

technician [tɛk'nɪʃn] *n* técnico/a

technique [tɛk'ni:k] *n* técnica

technological [tɛknə'lɔdʒɪkl] *adj*
tecnológico

technology [tɛk'nɔlədʒɪ] *n* tecnología

teddy (bear) ['tɛdɪ-] *n* osito de felpa

tedious ['ti:dɪəs] *adj* pesado, aburrido

teem [ti:m] *vi:* **to ~ with** rebosar de; **it is
~ing (with rain)** llueve a cántaros

teenage ['ti:neɪdʒ] *adj* (*fashions etc*)
juvenil; (*children*) quinceañero; **~r** *n*
quinceañero/a

teens [ti:nz] *npl:* **to be in one's ~** ser
adolescente

tee-shirt ['ti:ʃə:t] *n* = **T-shirt**

teeter ['ti:tə*] *vi* balancearse; (*fig*): **to ~ on
the edge of ...** estar al borde de ...

teeth [ti:θ] *npl of* **tooth**

teethe [ti:ð] *vi* echar los dientes

teething ['ti:ðɪŋ]: **~ ring** *n* mordedor *m*;
~ troubles *npl* (*fig*) dificultades *fpl*
iniciales

teetotal ['ti:'təutl] *adj* abstemio

telegram ['tɛlɪgræm] *n* telegrama *m*

telegraph ['tɛlɪgrɑ:f] *n* telégrafo; **~ pole**
n poste *m* telegráfico

telepathy [təˈlepəθɪ] *n* telepatía

telephone [ˈtelɪfəun] *n* teléfono ♦ *vt* llamar por teléfono, telefonear; (*message*) dar por teléfono; **to be on the ~** (*talking*) hablar por teléfono; (*possessing ~*) tener teléfono; **~ booth** *n* cabina telefónica; **~ box** (*BRIT*) *n* = **~ booth**; **~ call** *n* llamada (telefónica); **~ directory** *n* guía (telefónica); **~ number** *n* número de teléfono; **telephonist** [təˈlefənɪst] (*BRIT*) *n* telefonista *m/f*

telescope [ˈtelɪskəup] *n* telescopio

television [ˈtelɪvɪʒən] *n* televisión *f*; **on ~** en la televisión; **~ set** *n* televisor *m*

tell [tel] (*pt*, *pp* **told**) *vt* decir; (*relate: story*) contar; (*distinguish*): **to ~ sth from** distinguir algo de ♦ *vi* (*talk*): **to ~ (of)** contar; (*have effect*) tener efecto; **to ~ sb to do sth** mandar a uno hacer algo; **~ off** *vt*: **to ~ sb off** regañar a uno; **~er** *n* (*in bank*) cajero/a; **~ing** *adj* (*remark, detail*) revelador(a); **~tale** *adj* (*sign*) indicador(a)

telly [ˈtelɪ] (*BRIT: inf*) *n abbr* (= *television*) tele *f*

temp [temp] *n abbr* (*BRIT*: = *temporary*) temporero/a

temper [ˈtempə*] *n* (*nature*) carácter *m*; (*mood*) humor *m*; (*bad*~) (mal) genio; (*fit of anger*) acceso de ira ♦ *vt* (*moderate*) moderar; **to be in a ~** estar furioso; **to lose one's ~** enfadarse, enojarse

temperament [ˈtempərəmənt] *n* (*nature*) temperamento

temperate [ˈtempərət] *adj* (*climate etc*) templado

temperature [ˈtemprətʃə*] *n* temperatura; **to have** *or* **run a ~** tener fiebre

temple [ˈtempl] *n* (*building*) templo; (*ANAT*) sien *f*

tempo [ˈtempəu] (*pl* **tempos** *or* **tempi**) *n* (*MUS*) tempo, tiempo; (*fig*) ritmo

temporarily [ˈtempərərɪlɪ] *adv* temporalmente

temporary [ˈtempərərɪ] *adj* provisional; (*passing*) transitorio; (*worker*) temporero; (*job*) temporal

tempt [tempt] *vt* tentar; **to ~ sb into doing sth** tentar *or* inducir a uno a hacer algo; **~ation** [-ˈteɪʃən] *n* tentación *f*; **~ing** *adj* tentador(a); (*food*) apetitoso/a

ten [ten] *num* diez

tenacity [təˈnæsɪtɪ] *n* tenacidad *f*

tenancy [ˈtenənsɪ] *n* arrendamiento, alquiler *m*

tenant [ˈtenənt] *n* inquilino/a

tend [tend] *vt* cuidar ♦ *vi*: **to ~ to do sth** tener tendencia a hacer algo

tendency [ˈtendənsɪ] *n* tendencia

tender [ˈtendə*] *adj* (*person, care*) tierno, cariñoso; (*meat*) tierno; (*sore*) sensible ♦ *n* (*COMM: offer*) oferta; (*money*): **legal ~** moneda de curso legal ♦ *vt* ofrecer; **~ness** *n* ternura; (*of meat*) blandura

tenement [ˈtenəmənt] *n* casa de pisos (*SP*)

tennis [ˈtenɪs] *n* tenis *m*; **~ ball** *n* pelota de tenis; **~ court** *n* cancha de tenis; **~ player** *n* tenista *m/f*; **~ racket** *n* raqueta de tenis

tenor [ˈtenə*] *n* (*MUS*) tenor *m*

tenpin bowling [ˈtenpɪn-] *n* (juego de los) bolos

tense [tens] *adj* (*person*) nervioso; (*moment, atmosphere*) tenso; (*muscle*) tenso, en tensión ♦ *n* (*LING*) tiempo

tension [ˈtenʃən] *n* tensión *f*

tent [tent] *n* tienda (de campaña) (*SP*), carpa (*AM*)

tentative [ˈtentətɪv] *adj* (*person, smile*) indeciso; (*conclusion, plans*) provisional

tenterhooks [ˈtentəhuks] *npl*: **on ~** sobre ascuas

tenth [tenθ] *num* décimo

tent peg *n* clavija, estaca

tent pole *n* mástil *m*

tenuous [ˈtenjuəs] *adj* tenue

tenure [ˈtenjuə*] *n* (*of land etc*) tenencia; (*of office*) ejercicio

tepid [ˈtepɪd] *adj* tibio

term [tə:m] *n* (*word*) término; (*period*) período; (*SCOL*) trimestre *m* ♦ *vt* llamar; **~s** *npl* (*conditions, COMM*) condiciones *fpl*; **in the short/long ~** a corto/largo plazo; **to be on good ~s with sb** llevarse bien con uno; **to come to ~s with** (*problem*) aceptar

terminal ['tə:mɪnl] *adj* (*disease*) mortal; (*patient*) terminal ♦ *n* (*ELEC*) borne *m*; (*COMPUT*) terminal *m*; (*also:* **air ~**) terminal *f*; (*BRIT: also:* **coach ~**) (estación *f*) terminal *f*

terminate ['tə:mɪneɪt] *vt* terminar

terminus ['tə:mɪnəs] (*pl* **termini**) *n* término, (estación *f*) terminal *f*

terrace ['terəs] *n* terraza; (*BRIT: row of houses*) hilera de casas adosadas; **the ~s** (*BRIT: SPORT*) las gradas *fpl*; **~d** *adj* (*garden*) en terrazas; (*house*) adosado

terrain [tɛ'reɪn] *n* terreno

terrible ['terɪbl] *adj* terrible, horrible; (*inf*) atroz; **terribly** *adv* terriblemente; (*very badly*) malísimamente

terrier ['terɪə*] *n* terrier *m*

terrific [tə'rɪfɪk] *adj* (*very great*) tremendo; (*wonderful*) fantástico, fenomenal

terrify ['terɪfaɪ] *vt* aterrorizar

territory ['terɪtəri] *n* (*also fig*) territorio

terror ['terə*] *n* terror *m*; **~ism** *n* terrorismo; **~ist** *n* terrorista *m/f*

test [test] *n* (*gen, CHEM*) prueba; (*MED*) examen *m*; (*SCOL*) examen *m*, test *m*; (*also:* **driving ~**) examen *m* de conducir ♦ *vt* probar, poner a prueba; (*MED, SCOL*) examinar

testament ['testəmənt] *n* testamento; **the Old/New T~** el Antiguo/Nuevo Testamento

testicle ['testɪkl] *n* testículo

testify ['testɪfaɪ] *vi* (*LAW*) prestar declaración; **to ~ to sth** atestiguar algo

testimony ['testɪməni] *n* (*LAW*) testimonio

test: ~ match *n* (*CRICKET, RUGBY*) partido internacional; **~ tube** *n* probeta

tetanus ['tetənəs] *n* tétano

tether ['teðə*] *vt* atar (con una cuerda) ♦ *n*: **to be at the end of one's ~** no aguantar más

text [tekst] *n* texto; **~book** *n* libro de texto

textiles ['tekstaɪlz] *npl* textiles *mpl*; (*textile industry*) industria textil

texture ['tekstʃə*] *n* textura

Thailand ['taɪlænd] *n* Tailandia

Thames [temz] *n*: **the ~** el (río) Támesis

than [ðæn] *conj* (*in comparisons*): **more ~ 10/once** más de 10/una vez; **I have more/less ~ you/Paul** tengo más/menos que tú/Paul; **she is older ~ you think** es mayor de lo que piensas

thank [θæŋk] *vt* dar las gracias a, agradecer; **~ you (very much)** muchas gracias; **~ God!** ¡gracias a Dios!; **~s** *npl* gracias *fpl* ♦ *excl* (*also:* **many ~s**, **~s a lot**) ¡gracias!; **~s to** *prep* gracias a; **~ful** *adj*: **~ful (for)** agradecido (por); **~less** *adj* ingrato; **T~sgiving (Day)** *n* día *m* de Acción de Gracias

---

Thanksgiving (Day)

ⓘ En Estados Unidos el cuarto jueves de noviembre es **Thanksgiving Day**, *fiesta oficial en la que se recuerda la celebración que hicieron los primeros colonos norteamericanos ("Pilgrims" o "Pilgrim Fathers") tras la estupenda cosecha de 1621, por la que se dan gracias a Dios. En Canadá se celebra una fiesta semejante el segundo lunes de octubre, aunque no está relacionada con dicha fecha histórica.*

KEYWORD

that [ðæt] (*pl* **those**) *adj* (*demonstrative*) ese/a, *pl* esos/as; (*more remote*) aquel/ aquella, *pl* aquellos/as; **leave those books on the table** deja esos libros sobre la mesa; **~ one** ése/ésa; (*more remote*) aquél/aquélla; **~ one over there** ése/ésa de ahí; aquél/aquélla de allí

♦ *pron* **1** (*demonstrative*) ése/a, *pl* ésos/as; (*neuter*) eso; (*more remote*) aquél/aquélla, *pl* aquellos/as; (*neuter*) aquello; **what's ~?** ¿qué es eso (*or* aquello)?; **who's ~?** ¿quién es ése/a (*or* aquél/aquélla)?; **is ~ you?** ¿eres tú?; **will you eat all ~?** ¿vas a comer todo eso?; **~'s my house** ésa es mi casa; **~'s what he said** eso es lo que

dijo; **~ is (to say)** es decir
2 (*relative: subject, object*) que; (*with preposition*) (el/la) que *etc*, el/la cual *etc*; **the book (~) I read** el libro que leí; **the books ~ are in the library** los libros que están en la biblioteca; **all (~) I have** todo lo que tengo; **the box (~) I put it in** la caja en la que *or* donde lo puse; **the people (~) I spoke to** la gente con la que hablé
3 (*relative: of time*) que; **the day (~) he came** el día (en) que vino
♦ *conj* que; **he thought ~ I was ill** creyó que yo estaba enfermo
♦ *adv* (*demonstrative*): **I can't work ~ much** no puedo trabajar tanto; **I didn't realise it was ~ bad** no creí que fuera tan malo; **~ high** así de alto

thatched [θætʃt] *adj* (*roof*) de paja; (*cottage*) con tejado de paja
thaw [θɔː] *n* deshielo ♦ *vi* (*ice*) derretirse; (*food*) descongelarse ♦ *vt* (*food*) descongelar

KEYWORD

the [ðiː, ðə] *def art* **1** (*gen*) el, *f* la, *pl* los, *fpl* las (*NB* = el *immediately before f n beginning with stressed (h)a*; a+el = al; de+el = del); **~ boy/girl** el chico/la chica; **~ books/flowers** los libros/las flores; **to ~ postman/from ~ drawer** al cartero/del cajón; **I haven't ~ time/money** no tengo tiempo/dinero
2 (+*adj to form n*) los; lo; **~ rich and ~ poor** los ricos y los pobres; **to attempt ~ impossible** intentar lo imposible
3 (*in titles*): **Elizabeth ~ First** Isabel primera; **Peter ~ Great** Pedro el Grande
4 (*in comparisons*): **~ more he works ~ more he earns** cuanto más trabaja más gana

theatre ['θɪətə*] (*US* **theater**) *n* teatro; (*also*: **lecture ~**) aula; (*MED*: *also*: **operating ~**) quirófano; **~-goer** *n* aficionado/a al teatro

theatrical [θɪ'ætrɪkl] *adj* teatral
theft [θeft] *n* robo
their [ðeə*] *adj* su; **~s** *pron* (el) suyo/(la) suya *etc*; *see also* **my**; **mine**[1]
them [ðem, ðəm] *pron* (*direct*) los/las; (*indirect*) les; (*stressed, after prep*) ellos/ellas; *see also* **me**
theme [θiːm] *n* tema *m*; **~ park** *n* parque de atracciones (*en torno a un tema central*); **~ song** *n* tema *m* (*musical*)
themselves [ðəm'selvz] *pl pron* (*subject*) ellos mismos/ellas mismas; (*complement*) se; (*after prep*) sí (mismos/as); *see also* **oneself**
then [ðen] *adv* (*at that time*) entonces; (*next*) después; (*later*) luego, después; (*and also*) además ♦ *conj* (*therefore*) en ese caso, entonces ♦ *adj*: **the ~ president** el entonces presidente; **by ~** para entonces; **from ~ on** desde entonces
theology [θɪ'ɒlədʒɪ] *n* teología
theory ['θɪərɪ] *n* teoría
therapist ['θerəpɪst] *n* terapeuta *m/f*
therapy ['θerəpɪ] *n* terapia

KEYWORD

there ['ðeə*] *adv* **1**: **~ is, ~ are** hay; **~ is no-one here/no bread left** no hay nadie aquí/no queda pan; **~ has been an accident** ha habido un accidente
2 (*referring to place*) ahí; (*distant*) allí; **it's ~** está ahí; **put it in/on/up/down ~** ponlo ahí dentro/encima/arriba/abajo; **I want that book ~** quiero ese libro de ahí; **~ he is!** ¡ahí está!
3: **~, ~** (*esp to child*) ea, ea

there: **~abouts** *adv* por ahí; **~after** *adv* después; **~by** *adv* así, de ese modo; **~fore** *adv* por lo tanto; **~'s = there is**; **there has**
thermal ['θɜːml] *adj* termal; (*paper*) térmico
thermometer [θə'mɒmɪtə*] *n* termómetro
Thermos ® ['θɜːməs] *n* (*also*: **~ flask**) termo
thermostat ['θɜːməustæt] *n* termostato

thesaurus [θɪˈsɔːrəs] *n* tesoro

these [ðiːz] *pl adj* estos/as ♦ *pl pron* éstos/as

thesis [ˈθiːsɪs] (*pl* **theses**) *n* tesis *f inv*

they [ðeɪ] *pl pron* ellos/ellas; (*stressed*) ellos (mismos)/ellas (mismas); **~ say that ...** (*it is said that*) se dice que ...; **~'d = they had; they would; ~'ll = they shall; they will; ~'re = they are; ~'ve = they have**

thick [θɪk] *adj* (*in consistency*) espeso; (*in size*) grueso; (*stupid*) torpe ♦ *n*: **in the ~ of the battle** en lo más reñido de la batalla; **it's 20 cm ~** tiene 20 cm de espesor; **~en** *vi* espesarse ♦ *vt* (*sauce etc*) espesar; **~ness** *n* espesor *m*; grueso; **~set** *adj* fornido

thief [θiːf] (*pl* **thieves**) *n* ladrón/ona *m/f*

thigh [θaɪ] *n* muslo

thimble [ˈθɪmbl] *n* dedal *m*

thin [θɪn] *adj* (*person, animal*) flaco; (*in size*) delgado; (*in consistency*) poco espeso; (*hair, crowd*) escaso ♦ *vt*: **to ~ (down)** diluir

thing [θɪŋ] *n* cosa; (*object*) objeto, artículo; (*matter*) asunto; (*mania*): **to have a ~ about sb/sth** estar obsesionado con uno/algo; **~s** *npl* (*belongings*) efectos *mpl* (personales); **the best ~ would be to ...** lo mejor sería ...; **how are ~s?** ¿qué tal?

think [θɪŋk] (*pt, pp* **thought**) *vi* pensar ♦ *vt* pensar, creer; **what did you ~ of them?** ¿qué te parecieron?; **to ~ about sth/sb** pensar en algo/uno; **I'll ~ about it** lo pensaré; **to ~ of doing sth** pensar en hacer algo; **I ~ so/not** creo que sí/no; **to ~ well of sb** tener buen concepto de uno; **~ over** *vt* reflexionar sobre, meditar; **~ up** *vt* (*plan etc*) idear; **~ tank** *n* gabinete *m* de estrategia

thinly [ˈθɪnlɪ] *adv* (*cut*) fino; (*spread*) ligeramente

third [θɜːd] *adj* (*before n*) tercer(a); (*following n*) tercero/a ♦ *n* tercero/a; (*fraction*) tercio; (*BRIT: SCOL: degree*) título de licenciado con calificación de aprobado; **~ly** *adv* en tercer lugar; **~ party insurance** (*BRIT*) *n* seguro contra

terceros; **~-rate** *adj* (de calidad) mediocre; **T~ World** *n* Tercer Mundo

thirst [θɜːst] *n* sed *f*; **~y** *adj* (*person, animal*) sediento; (*work*) que da sed; **to be ~y** tener sed

thirteen [ˈθɜːˈtiːn] *num* trece

thirty [ˈθɜːtɪ] *num* treinta

KEYWORD

this [ðɪs] (*pl* **these**) *adj* (*demonstrative*) este/a; *pl* estos/as; (*neuter*) esto; **~ man/ woman** este hombre/esta mujer; **these children/flowers** estos chicos/estas flores; **~ one (here)** éste/a, esto (de aquí) ♦ *pron* (*demonstrative*) éste/a; *pl* éstos/as; (*neuter*) esto; **who is ~?** ¿quién es éste/ ésta?; **what is ~?** ¿qué es esto?; **~ is where I live** aquí vivo; **~ is what he said** esto es lo que dijo; **~ is Mr Brown** (*in introductions*) le presento al Sr. Brown; (*photo*) éste es el Sr. Brown; (*on telephone*) habla el Sr. Brown ♦ *adv* (*demonstrative*): **~ high/long** *etc* así de alto/largo *etc*; **~ far** hasta aquí

---

thistle [ˈθɪsl] *n* cardo

thorn [θɔːn] *n* espina

thorough [ˈθʌrə] *adj* (*search*) minucioso; (*wash*) a fondo; (*knowledge, research*) profundo; (*person*) meticuloso; **~bred** *adj* (*horse*) de pura sangre; **~fare** *n* calle *f*; **"no ~fare"** "prohibido el paso"; **~ly** *adv* (*search*) minuciosamente; (*study*) profundamente; (*wash*) a fondo; (*utterly: bad, wet etc*) completamente, totalmente

those [ðəuz] *pl adj* esos/esas; (*more remote*) aquellos/as

though [ðəu] *conj* aunque ♦ *adv* sin embargo

thought [θɔːt] *pt, pp of* **think** ♦ *n* pensamiento; (*opinion*) opinión *f*; **~ful** *adj* pensativo; (*serious*) serio; (*considerate*) atento; **~less** *adj* desconsiderado

thousand [ˈθauzənd] *num* mil; **two ~** dos mil; **~s of** miles de; **~th** *num* milésimo

thrash [θræʃ] *vt* azotar; (*defeat*) derrotar; **~ about** *or* **around** *vi* debatirse; **~ out** *vt* discutir a fondo

thread [θred] *n* hilo; (*of screw*) rosca ♦ *vt* (*needle*) enhebrar; **~bare** *adj* raído

threat [θret] *n* amenaza; **~en** *vi* amenazar ♦ *vt*: **to ~en sb with/to do** amenazar a uno con/con hacer

three [θri:] *num* tres; **~-dimensional** *adj* tridimensional; **~-piece suit** *n* traje *m* de tres piezas; **~-piece suite** *n* tresillo; **~-ply** *adj* (*wool*) de tres cabos

threshold ['θreʃhəuld] *n* umbral *m*

threw [θru:] *pt of* **throw**

thrifty ['θrɪftɪ] *adj* económico

thrill [θrɪl] *n* (*excitement*) emoción *f*; (*shudder*) estremecimiento ♦ *vt* emocionar; **to be ~ed** (*with gift etc*) estar encantado; **~er** *n* novela (or obra or película) de suspense; **~ing** *adj* emocionante

thrive [θraɪv] (*pt, pp* **thrived**) *vi* (*grow*) crecer; (*do well*): **to ~ on sth** sentarle muy bien a uno algo; **thriving** *adj* próspero

throat [θrəut] *n* garganta; **to have a sore ~** tener dolor de garganta

throb [θrɔb] *vi* latir; dar punzadas; vibrar

throes [θrəuz] *npl*: **in the ~ of** en medio de

throne [θrəun] *n* trono

throng [θrɔŋ] *n* multitud *f*, muchedumbre *f* ♦ *vt* agolparse en

throttle ['θrɔtl] *n* (*AUT*) acelerador *m* ♦ *vt* estrangular

through [θru:] *prep* por, a través de; (*time*) durante; (*by means of*) por medio de, mediante; (*owing to*) gracias a ♦ *adj* (*ticket, train*) directo ♦ *adv* completamente, de parte a parte; de principio a fin; **to put sb ~ to sb** (*TEL*) poner or pasar a uno con uno; **to be ~** (*TEL*) tener comunicación; (*have finished*) haber terminado; **"no ~ road"** (*BRIT*) "calle sin salida"; **~out** *prep* (*place*) por todas partes de, por todo; (*time*) durante todo ♦ *adv* por or en todas partes

throw [θrəu] (*pt* **threw**, *pp* **thrown**) *n* tiro; (*SPORT*) lanzamiento ♦ *vt* tirar, echar; (*SPORT*) lanzar; (*rider*) derribar; (*fig*)

desconcertar; **to ~ a party** dar una fiesta; **~ away** *vt* tirar; (*money*) derrochar; **~ off** *vt* deshacerse de; **~ out** *vt* tirar; (*person*) echar; expulsar; **~ up** *vi* vomitar; **~away** *adj* para tirar, desechable; (*remark*) hecho de paso; **~-in** *n* (*SPORT*) saque *m*

thru [θru:] (*US*) = **through**

thrush [θrʌʃ] *n* zorzal *m*, tordo

thrust [θrʌst] (*pt, pp* **thrust**) *vt* empujar (con fuerza)

thud [θʌd] *n* golpe *m* sordo

thug [θʌg] *n* gamberro/a

thumb [θʌm] *n* (*ANAT*) pulgar *m*; **to ~ a lift** hacer autostop; **~ through** *vt fus* (*book*) hojear; **~tack** (*US*) *n* chincheta (*SP*)

thump [θʌmp] *n* golpe *m*; (*sound*) ruido seco or sordo ♦ *vt* golpear ♦ *vi* (*heart etc*) palpitar

thunder ['θʌndə*] *n* trueno ♦ *vi* tronar; (*train etc*): **to ~ past** pasar como un trueno; **~bolt** *n* rayo; **~clap** *n* trueno; **~storm** *n* tormenta; **~y** *adj* tormentoso

Thursday ['θə:zdɪ] *n* jueves *m inv*

thus [ðʌs] *adv* así, de este modo

thyme [taɪm] *n* tomillo

thyroid ['θaɪrɔɪd] *n* (*also*: **~ gland**) tiroides *m inv*

tic [tɪk] *n* tic *m*

tick [tɪk] *n* (*sound: of clock*) tictac *m*; (*mark*) palomita; (*ZOOL*) garrapata; (*BRIT: inf*): **in a ~** en un instante ♦ *vi* hacer tictac ♦ *vt* marcar; **~ off** *vt* marcar; (*person*) reñir; **~ over** *vi* (*engine*) girar en marcha lenta; (*fig*) ir tirando

ticket ['tɪkɪt] *n* billete *m* (*SP*), tíquet *m*, boleto (*AM*); (*for cinema etc*) entrada (*SP*), boleto (*AM*); (*in shop: on goods*) etiqueta (*for raffle*) papeleta; (*for library*) tarjeta; (*parking ~*) multa por estacionamiento ilegal; **~ collector** *n* revisor(a) *m/f*; **~ office** *n* (*THEATRE*) taquilla (*SP*), boletería (*AM*); (*RAIL*) despacho de billetes (*SP*) or boletos (*AM*)

tickle ['tɪkl] *vt* hacer cosquillas a ♦ *vi* hacer cosquillas; **ticklish** *adj* (*person*) cosquilloso; (*problem*) delicado

tidal ['taɪdl] *adj* de marea; **~ wave** *n* maremoto

tidbit ['tɪdbɪt] (*US*) *n* = **titbit**

tiddlywinks ['tɪdlɪwɪŋks] *n juego infantil con fichas de plástico*

tide [taɪd] *n* marea; (*fig: of events etc*) curso, marcha; **~ over** *vt* (*help out*) ayudar a salir del apuro

tidy ['taɪdɪ] *adj* (*room etc*) ordenado; (*dress, work*) limpio; (*person*) (bien) arreglado ♦ *vt* (*also:* **~ up**) poner en orden

tie [taɪ] *n* (*string etc*) atadura; (*BRIT: also:* **neck~**) corbata; (*fig: link*) vínculo, lazo; (*SPORT etc: draw*) empate *m* ♦ *vt* atar ♦ *vi* (*SPORT etc*) empatar; **to ~ in a bow** atar con un lazo; **to ~ a knot in sth** hacer un nudo en algo; **~ down** *vt* (*fig: person: restrict*) atar; (: *to price, date etc*) obligar a; **~ up** *vt* (*parcel*) envolver; (*dog, person*) atar; (*arrangements*) concluir; **to be ~d up** (*busy*) estar ocupado

tier [tɪə*] *n* grada; (*of cake*) piso

tiger ['taɪgə*] *n* tigre *m*

tight [taɪt] *adj* (*rope*) tirante; (*money*) escaso; (*clothes*) ajustado; (*bend*) cerrado; (*shoes, schedule*) apretado; (*budget*) ajustado; (*security*) estricto; (*inf: drunk*) borracho ♦ *adv* (*squeeze*) muy fuerte; (*shut*) bien; **~en** *vt* (*rope*) estirar; (*screw, grip*) apretar; (*security*) reforzar ♦ *vi* estirarse; apretarse; **~-fisted** *adj* tacaño; **~ly** *adv* (*grasp*) muy fuerte; **~rope** *n* cuerda floja; **~s** (*BRIT*) *npl* panti *mpl*

tile [taɪl] *n* (*on roof*) teja; (*on floor*) baldosa; (*on wall*) azulejo; **~d** *adj* de tejas; embaldosado; (*wall*) alicatado

till [tɪl] *n* caja (registradora) ♦ *vt* (*land*) cultivar ♦ *prep, conj* = **until**

tilt [tɪlt] *vt* inclinar ♦ *vi* inclinarse

timber ['tɪmbə*] *n* (*material*) madera

time [taɪm] *n* tiempo; (*epoch: often pl*) época; (*by clock*) hora; (*moment*) momento; (*occasion*) vez *f*; (*MUS*) compás *m* ♦ *vt* calcular o medir el tiempo de; (*race*) cronometrar; (*remark, visit etc*) elegir el momento para; **a long ~** mucho

tiempo; **4 at a ~** de 4 en 4; **4 a la vez;** **for the ~ being** de momento, por ahora; **from ~ to ~** de vez en cuando; **at ~s** a veces; **in ~** (*soon enough*) a tiempo; (*after some time*) con el tiempo; (*MUS*) al compás; **in a week's ~** dentro de una semana; **in no ~** en un abrir y cerrar de ojos; **any ~** cuando sea; **on ~** a la hora; **5 ~s 5** 5 por 5; **what ~ is it?** ¿qué hora es?; **to have a good ~** pasarlo bien, divertirse; **~ bomb** *n* bomba de efecto retardado; **~less** *adj* eterno; **~ limit** *n* plazo; **~ly** *adj* oportuno; **~ off** *n* tiempo libre; **~r** *n* (*in kitchen etc*) programador *m* horario; **~ scale** (*BRIT*) *n* escala de tiempo; **~-share** *n* apartamento (*or* casa) a tiempo compartido; **~ switch** (*BRIT*) *n* interruptor *m* (horario); **~table** *n* horario; **~ zone** *n* huso horario

timid ['tɪmɪd] *adj* tímido

timing ['taɪmɪŋ] *n* (*SPORT*) cronometraje *m*; **the ~ of his resignation** el momento que eligió para dimitir

tin [tɪn] *n* estaño; (*also:* **~ plate**) hojalata; (*BRIT: can*) lata; **~foil** *n* papel *m* de estaño

tinge [tɪndʒ] *n* matiz *m* ♦ *vt*: **~d with** teñido de

tingle ['tɪŋgl] *vi* (*person*): **to ~ (with)** estremecerse (de); (*hands etc*) hormiguear

tinker ['tɪŋkə*]: **~ with** *vt fus* jugar con, tocar

tinned [tɪnd] (*BRIT*) *adj* (*food*) en lata, en conserva

tin opener [-əʊpnə*] (*BRIT*) *n* abrelatas *m inv*

tinsel ['tɪnsl] *n* (guirnalda de) espumillón *m*

tint [tɪnt] *n* matiz *m*; (*for hair*) tinte *m*; **~ed** *adj* (*hair*) teñido; (*glass, spectacles*) ahumado

tiny ['taɪnɪ] *adj* minúsculo, pequeñito

tip [tɪp] *n* (*end*) punta; (*gratuity*) propina; (*BRIT: for rubbish*) vertedero; (*advice*) consejo ♦ *vt* (*waiter*) dar una propina a; (*tilt*) inclinar; (*empty: also:* **~ out**) vaciar, echar; (*overturn: also:* **~ over**) volcar; **~-**

off n (hint) advertencia; **~ped** (BRIT) adj (cigarette) con filtro
Tipp-Ex ® ['tɪpeks] n Tipp-Ex ® m
tipsy ['tɪpsɪ] (inf) adj alegre, mareado
tiptoe ['tɪptəu] n: **on ~** de puntillas
tire ['taɪə*] n (US) = **tyre** ♦ vt cansar ♦ vi (gen) cansarse; (become bored) aburrirse; **~d** adj cansado; **to be ~d of sth** estar harto de algo; **~less** adj incansable; **~some** adj aburrido; **tiring** adj cansado
tissue ['tɪʃuː] n tejido; (paper handkerchief) pañuelo de papel, kleenex ® m; **~ paper** n papel m de seda
tit [tɪt] n (bird) herrerillo común; **to give ~ for tat** dar ojo por ojo
titbit ['tɪtbɪt] (US **tidbit**) n (food) golosina; (news) noticia sabrosa
title ['taɪtl] n título; **~ deed** n (LAW) título de propiedad; **~ role** n papel m principal
TM abbr = **trademark**

to [tuː, tə] prep 1 (direction) a; **to go ~ France/London/school/the station** ir a Francia/Londres/al colegio/a la estación; **to go ~ Claude's/the doctor's** ir a casa de Claude/al médico; **the road ~ Edinburgh** la carretera de Edimburgo
2 (as far as) hasta, a; **from here ~ London** de aquí a or hasta Londres; **to count ~ 10** contar hasta 10; **from 40 ~ 50 people** entre 40 y 50 personas
3 (with expressions of time): **a quarter/twenty ~ 5** las 5 menos cuarto/veinte
4 (for, of): **the key ~ the front door** la llave de la puerta principal; **she is secretary ~ the director** es la secretaria del director; **a letter ~ his wife** una carta a or para su mujer
5 (expressing indirect object) a; **to give sth ~ sb** darle algo a alguien; **to talk ~ sb** hablar con alguien; **to be a danger ~ sb** ser un peligro para alguien; **to carry out repairs ~ sth** hacer reparaciones en algo
6 (in relation to): **3 goals ~ 2** 3 goles a 2; **30 miles ~ the gallon** ≈ 9,4 litros a los cien (kms)

7 (purpose, result): **to come ~ sb's aid** venir en auxilio or ayuda de alguien; **to sentence sb ~ death** condenar a uno a muerte; **~ my great surprise** con gran sorpresa mía
♦ with vb 1 (simple infin): **~ go/eat** ir/comer
2 (following another vb): **to want/try/start ~ do** querer/intentar/empezar a hacer; see also relevant vb
3 (with vb omitted): **I don't want ~** no quiero
4 (purpose, result) para; **I did it ~ help you** lo hice para ayudarte; **he came ~ see you** vino a verte
5 (equivalent to relative clause): **I have things ~ do** tengo cosas que hacer; **the main thing is ~ try** lo principal es intentarlo
6 (after adj etc): **ready ~ go** listo para irse; **too old ~ ...** demasiado viejo (como) para ...
♦ adv: **pull/push the door ~** tirar de/empujar la puerta

toad [təud] n sapo; **~stool** n hongo venenoso
toast [təust] n (CULIN) tostada; (drink, speech) brindis m ♦ vt (CULIN) tostar; (drink to) brindar por; **~er** n tostador m
tobacco [tə'bækəu] n tabaco; **~nist** n estanquero/a (SP), tabaquero/a (AM); **~nist's (shop)** (BRIT) n estanco (SP), tabaquería (AM)
toboggan [tə'bɔgən] n tobogán m
today [tə'deɪ] adv, n (also fig) hoy m
toddler ['tɔdlə*] n niño/a (que empieza a andar)
toe [təu] n dedo (del pie); (of shoe) punta; **to ~ the line** (fig) conformarse; **~nail** n uña del pie
toffee ['tɔfi] n toffee m; **~ apple** (BRIT) n manzana acaramelada
together [tə'geðə*] adv juntos; (at same time) al mismo tiempo, a la vez; **~ with** junto con
toil [tɔɪl] n trabajo duro, labor f ♦ vi

trabajar duramente

toilet ['tɔɪlət] *n* retrete *m*; (*BRIT: room*) servicios *mpl* (*SP*), wáter *m* (*SP*), sanitario (*AM*) ♦ *cpd* (*soap etc*) de aseo; **~ paper** *n* papel *m* higiénico; **~ries** *npl* artículos *mpl* de tocador; **~ roll** *n* rollo de papel higiénico

token ['təukən] *n* (*sign*) señal *f*, muestra; (*souvenir*) recuerdo; (*disc*) ficha ♦ *adj* (*strike, payment etc*) simbólico; **book/record ~** (*BRIT*) vale *m* para comprar libros/discos; **gift ~** (*BRIT*) vale-regalo

Tokyo ['təukjəu] *n* Tokio, Tokio

told [təuld] *pt, pp of* **tell**

tolerable ['tɔlərəbl] *adj* (*bearable*) soportable; (*fairly good*) pasable

tolerant ['tɔlərnt] *adj*: **~ of** tolerante con

tolerate ['tɔləreɪt] *vt* tolerar

toll [təul] *n* (*of casualties*) número de víctimas; (*tax, charge*) peaje *m* ♦ *vi* (*bell*) doblar

tomato [tə'mɑːtəu] (*pl* **~es**) *n* tomate *m*

tomb [tuːm] *n* tumba

tomboy ['tɔmbɔɪ] *n* marimacho

tombstone ['tuːmstəun] *n* lápida

tomcat ['tɔmkæt] *n* gato (macho)

tomorrow [tə'mɔrəu] *adv, n* (*also: fig*) mañana; **the day after ~** pasado mañana; **~ morning** mañana por la mañana

ton [tʌn] *n* tonelada (*BRIT* = 1016 kg; *US* = 907 kg); (*metric ~*) tonelada métrica; **~s of** (*inf*) montones de

tone [təun] *n* tono ♦ *vi* (*also: ~ in*) armonizar; **~ down** *vt* (*criticism*) suavizar; (*colour*) atenuar; **~ up** *vt* (*muscles*) tonificar; **~-deaf** *adj* con mal oído

tongs [tɔŋz] *npl* (*for coal*) tenazas *fpl*; (*curling ~*) tenacillas *fpl*

tongue [tʌŋ] *n* lengua; **~ in cheek** irónicamente; **~-tied** *adj* (*fig*) mudo; **~-twister** *n* trabalenguas *m inv*

tonic ['tɔnɪk] *n* (*MED, also fig*) tónico; (*also: ~ water*) (agua) tónica

tonight [tə'naɪt] *adv, n* esta noche; esta tarde

tonsil ['tɔnsl] *n* amígdala; **~litis** [-'laɪtɪs] *n* amigdalitis *f*

too [tuː] *adv* (*excessively*) demasiado; (*also*) también; **~ much** demasiado; **~ many** demasiados/as

took [tuk] *pt of* **take**

tool [tuːl] *n* herramienta; **~ box** *n* caja de herramientas

toot [tuːt] *n* pitido ♦ *vi* tocar el pito

tooth [tuːθ] (*pl* **teeth**) *n* (*ANAT, TECH*) diente *m*; (*molar*) muela; **~ache** *n* dolor *m* de muelas; **~brush** *n* cepillo de dientes; **~paste** *n* pasta de dientes; **~pick** *n* palillo

top [tɔp] *n* (*of mountain*) cumbre *f*, cima; (*of tree*) copa; (*of head*) coronilla; (*of ladder, page*) lo alto; (*of table*) superficie *f*; (*of cupboard*) parte *f* de arriba; (*lid: of box*) tapa; (*: of bottle, jar*) tapón *m*; (*of list etc*) cabeza; (*toy*) peonza; (*garment*) blusa; camiseta ♦ *adj* de arriba; (*in rank*) principal, primero; (*best*) mejor ♦ *vt* (*exceed*) exceder; (*be first in*) encabezar; **on ~ of** (*above*) sobre, encima de; (*in addition to*) además de; **from ~ to bottom** de pies a cabeza; **~ off** (*US*) *vt* = **~ up**; **~ up** *vt* llenar; **~ floor** *n* último piso; **~ hat** *n* sombrero de copa; **~-heavy** *adj* (*object*) mal equilibrado

topic ['tɔpɪk] *n* tema *m*; **~al** *adj* actual

top: ~less *adj* (*bather, bikini*) topless *inv*; **~-level** *adj* (*talks*) al más alto nivel; **~most** *adj* más alto

topple ['tɔpl] *vt* derribar ♦ *vi* caerse

top-secret *adj* de alto secreto

topsy-turvy ['tɔpsɪ'təːvɪ] *adj* al revés ♦ *adv* patas arriba

torch [tɔːtʃ] *n* antorcha; (*BRIT: electric*) linterna

tore [tɔː*] *pt of* **tear2**

torment [*n* 'tɔːmɛnt, *vt* tɔː'mɛnt] *n* tormento ♦ *vt* atormentar; (*fig: annoy*) fastidiar

torn [tɔːn] *pp of* **tear2**

torrent ['tɔrnt] *n* torrente *m*

tortoise ['tɔːtəs] *n* tortuga; **~shell** ['tɔːtəʃel] *adj* de carey

torture ['tɔːtʃə*] *n* tortura ♦ *vt* torturar; (*fig*) atormentar

Tory ['tɔːrɪ] (*BRIT*) *adj*, *n* (*POL*) conservador(a) *m/f*

toss [tɒs] *vt* tirar, echar; (*one's head*) sacudir; **to ~ a coin** echar a cara o cruz; **to ~ up for sth** jugar a cara o cruz algo; **to ~ and turn** (*in bed*) dar vueltas

tot [tɒt] *n* (*BRIT: drink*) copita; (*child*) nene/a *m/f*

total ['təutl] *adj* total, entero; (*emphatic: failure etc*) completo, total ♦ *n* total *m*, suma ♦ *vt* (*add up*) sumar; (*amount to*) ascender a; **~ly** *adv* totalmente

totter ['tɔtə*] *vi* tambalearse

touch [tʌtʃ] *n* tacto; (*contact*) contacto ♦ *vt* tocar; (*emotionally*) conmover; **a ~ of** (*fig*) un poquito de; **to get in ~ with sb** ponerse en contacto con uno; **to lose ~** (*friends*) perder contacto; **~ on** *vt fus* (*topic*) aludir (*brevemente*) a; **~ up** *vt* (*paint*) retocar; **~-and-go** *adj* arriesgado; **~down** *n* aterrizaje *m*; (*on sea*) amerizaje *m*; (*US: FOOTBALL*) ensayo; **~ed** *adj* (*moved*) conmovido; **~ing** *adj* (*moving*) conmovedor(a); **~line** *n* (*SPORT*) línea de banda; **~y** *adj* (*person*) quisquilloso

tough [tʌf] *adj* (*material*) resistente; (*meat*) duro; (*problem etc*) difícil; (*policy, stance*) inflexible; (*person*) fuerte; **~en** *vt* endurecer

toupée ['tuːpeɪ] *n* peluca

tour ['tuə*] *n* viaje *m*, vuelta; (*also: package ~*) viaje *m* todo comprendido; (*of town, museum*) visita; (*by band etc*) gira ♦ *vt* recorrer, visitar; **~ guide** *n* guía *m* turístico, guía *f* turística

tourism ['tuərɪzm] *n* turismo

tourist ['tuərɪst] *n* turista *m/f* ♦ *cpd* turístico; **~ office** *n* oficina de turismo

tousled ['tauzld] *adj* (*hair*) despeinado

tout [taut] *vi*: **to ~ for business** solicitar clientes ♦ *n* (*also: ticket ~*) revendedor(a) *m/f*

tow [təu] *vt* remolcar; **"on** *or* **in** (*US*) **~"** (*AUT*) "a remolque"

toward(s) [tə'wɔːd(z)] *prep* hacia; (*attitude*) respecto a, con; (*purpose*) para

towel ['tauəl] *n* toalla; **~ling** *n* (*fabric*) felpa; **~ rail** (*US* **~ rack**) *n* toallero

tower ['tauə*] *n* torre *f*; **~ block** (*BRIT*) *n* torre *f* (de pisos); **~ing** *adj* muy alto, imponente

town [taun] *n* ciudad *f*; **to go to ~** ir a la ciudad; (*fig*) echar la casa por la ventana; **~ centre** *n* centro de la ciudad; **~ council** *n* ayuntamiento, consejo municipal; **~ hall** *n* ayuntamiento; **~ plan** *n* plano de la ciudad; **~ planning** *n* urbanismo

towrope ['təurəup] *n* cable *m* de remolque

tow truck (*US*) *n* camión *m* grúa

toy [tɔɪ] *n* juguete *m*; **~ with** *vt fus* jugar con; (*idea*) acariciar; **~shop** *n* juguetería

trace [treɪs] *n* rastro ♦ *vt* (*draw*) trazar, delinear; (*locate*) encontrar; (*follow*) seguir la pista de; **tracing paper** *n* papel *m* de calco

track [træk] *n* (*mark*) huella, pista; (*path: gen*) camino, senda; (: *of bullet etc*) trayectoria; (: *of suspect, animal*) pista, rastro; (*RAIL*) vía; (*SPORT*) pista; (*on tape, record*) canción *f* ♦ *vt* seguir la pista de; **to keep ~ of** mantenerse al tanto de, seguir; **~ down** *vt* (*prey*) seguir el rastro de; (*sth lost*) encontrar; **~suit** *n* chandal *m*

tract [trækt] *n* (*GEO*) región *f*

traction ['trækʃən] *n* (*power*) tracción *f*; **in ~** (*MED*) en tracción

tractor ['træktə*] *n* tractor *m*

trade [treɪd] *n* comercio; (*skill, job*) oficio ♦ *vi* negociar, comerciar ♦ *vt* (*exchange*): **to ~ sth (for sth)** cambiar algo (por algo); **~ in** *vt* (*old car etc*) ofrecer como parte del pago; **~ fair** *n* feria comercial; **~mark** *n* marca de fábrica; **~ name** *n* marca registrada; **~r** *n* comerciante *m/f*; **~sman** (*irreg*) *n* (*shopkeeper*) tendero; **~ union** *n* sindicato; **~ unionist** *n* sindicalista *m/f*

tradition [trə'dɪʃən] *n* tradición *f*; **~al** *adj* tradicional

traffic ['træfɪk] *n* (*gen, AUT*) tráfico, circulación *f*, tránsito (*AM*) ♦ *vi*: **to ~ in** (*pej: liquor, drugs*) traficar en; **~ circle**

(US) n isleta; **~ jam** n embotellamiento;
~ lights npl semáforo; **~ warden** n
guardia m/f de tráfico
tragedy ['trædʒədɪ] n tragedia
tragic ['trædʒɪk] adj trágico
trail [treɪl] n (tracks) rastro, pista; (path)
camino, sendero; (dust, smoke) estela ♦ vt
(drag) arrastrar; (follow) seguir la pista de
♦ vi arrastrar; (in contest etc) ir perdiendo;
~ behind vi quedar a la zaga; **~er** n
(AUT) remolque m; (caravan) caravana f;
(CINEMA) trailer m, avance m; **~er truck**
(US) n trailer m
train [treɪn] n tren m; (of dress) cola;
(series) serie f ♦ vt (educate, teach skills to)
formar; (sportsman) entrenar; (dog)
adiestrar; (point: gun etc) apuntar
a ♦ vi (SPORT) entrenarse; (learn a skill): **to**
~ as a teacher etc estudiar para profesor
etc; **one's ~ of thought** el razonamiento
de uno; **~ed** adj (worker) cualificado,
(animal) amaestrado; **~ee** [treɪ'niː] n
aprendiz(a) m/f; **~er** n (SPORT: coach)
entrenador(a) m/f; (: shoe): **~ers**
zapatillas fpl (de deporte); (of animals)
domador(a) m/f; **~ing** n formación f;
entrenamiento; **to be in ~ing** (SPORT)
estar entrenando; **~ing college** n (gen)
colegio de formación profesional; (for
teachers) escuela de formación del
profesorado; **~ing shoes** npl zapatillas
fpl (de deporte)
trait [treɪt] n rasgo
traitor ['treɪtə*] n traidor(a) m/f
tram [træm] (BRIT) n (also: **~car**) tranvía m
tramp [træmp] n (person) vagabundo/a;
(inf: pej: woman) puta
trample ['træmpl] vt: **to ~ (underfoot)**
pisotear
trampoline ['træmpəliːn] n trampolín m
tranquil ['træŋkwɪl] adj tranquilo; **~lizer** n
(MED) tranquilizante m
transact [træn'zækt] vt (business)
despachar; **~ion** [-'zækʃən] n transacción
f, operación f
transfer [n 'trænsfə:*, vb træns'fə:*] n (of
employees) traslado; (of money, power)

transferencia; (SPORT) traspaso; (picture,
design) calcomanía ♦ vt trasladar;
transferir; **to ~ the charges** (BRIT: TEL)
llamar a cobro revertido
transform [træns'fɔːm] vt transformar
transfusion [træns'fjuːʒən] n transfusión f
transient ['trænzɪənt] adj transitorio
transistor [træn'zɪstə*] n (ELEC) transistor
m; **~ radio** n transistor m
transit ['trænzɪt] n: **in ~** en tránsito
transitive ['trænzɪtɪv] adj (LING) transitivo
transit lounge n sala de tránsito
translate [trænz'leɪt] vt traducir;
translation [-'leɪʃən] n traducción f;
translator n traductor(a) m/f
transmit [trænz'mɪt] vt transmitir; **~ter** n
transmisor m
transparency [træns'pɛərnsɪ] n
transparencia; (BRIT: PHOT) diapositiva
transparent [træns'pærnt] adj
transparente
transpire [træns'paɪə*] vi (turn out)
resultar; (happen) ocurrir, suceder; **it ~d**
that ... se supo que ...
transplant ['trænsplɑːnt] n (MED)
transplante m
transport [n 'trænspɔːt, vt træns'pɔːt] n
transporte m; (car) coche m (SP), carro
(AM), automóvil m ♦ vt transportar;
~ation [-'teɪʃən] n transporte m; **~ café**
(BRIT) n bar-restaurant m de carretera
transvestite [trænz'vestaɪt] n travestí m/f
trap [træp] n (snare, trick) trampa;
(carriage) cabriolé m ♦ vt coger (SP) or
agarrar (AM) en una trampa; (trick)
engañar; (confine) atrapar; **~ door** n
escotilla
trapeze [trə'piːz] n trapecio
trappings ['træpɪŋz] npl adornos mpl
trash [træʃ] n (rubbish) basura; (pej): **the**
book/film is ~ el libro/la película no vale
nada; (nonsense) tonterías fpl; **~ can** (US)
n cubo (SP) or balde m (AM) de la basura
travel ['trævl] n el viajar ♦ vi viajar ♦ vt
(distance) recorrer; **~s** npl (journeys) viajes
mpl; **~ agent** n agente m/f de viajes;
~ler (US **~er**) n viajero/a; **~ler's**

cheque (US **~er's check**) n cheque m de viajero; **~ling** (US **~ing**) n los viajes, el viajar; **~ sickness** n mareo

trawler ['trɔːlə*] n pesquero de arrastre

tray [treɪ] n bandeja; (on desk) cajón m

treacherous ['tretʃərəs] adj traidor, traicionero; (dangerous) peligroso

treacle ['triːkl] (BRIT) n melaza

tread [tred] (pt **trod**, pp **trodden**) n (step) paso, pisada; (sound) ruido de pasos; (of stair) escalón m; (of tyre) banda de rodadura ♦ vi pisar; **~ on** vt fus pisar

treason ['triːzn] n traición f

treasure ['treʒə*] n (also fig) tesoro ♦ vt (value: object, friendship) apreciar; (: memory) guardar

treasurer ['treʒərə*] n tesorero/a

treasury ['treʒərɪ] n: **the T~** el Ministerio de Hacienda

treat [triːt] n (present) regalo ♦ vt tratar; **to ~ sb to sth** invitar a uno a algo

treatment ['triːtmənt] n tratamiento

treaty ['triːtɪ] n tratado

treble ['trebl] adj triple ♦ vt triplicar ♦ vi triplicarse; **~ clef** n (MUS) clave f de sol

tree [triː] n árbol m; **~ trunk** n tronco (de árbol)

trek [trek] n (long journey) viaje m largo y difícil; (tiring walk) caminata

trellis ['trelɪs] n enrejado

tremble ['trembl] vi temblar

tremendous [trɪ'mendəs] adj tremendo, enorme; (excellent) estupendo

tremor ['tremə*] n temblor m; (also: **earth ~**) temblor m de tierra

trench [trentʃ] n zanja

trend [trend] n (tendency) tendencia; (of events) curso; (fashion) moda; **~y** adj de moda

trespass ['trespəs] vi: **to ~ on** entrar sin permiso en; **"no ~ing"** "prohibido el paso"

trestle ['tresl] n caballete m

trial ['traɪəl] n (LAW) juicio, proceso; (test: of machine etc) prueba; **~s** npl (hardships) dificultades fpl; **by ~ and error** a fuerza de probar

triangle ['traɪæŋgl] n (MATH, MUS) triángulo

tribe [traɪb] n tribu f

tribunal [traɪ'bjuːnl] n tribunal m

tributary ['trɪbjutərɪ] n (river) afluente m

tribute ['trɪbjuːt] n homenaje m, tributo; **to pay ~ to** rendir homenaje a

trick [trɪk] n (skill, knack) tino, truco; (conjuring ~) truco; (joke) broma; (CARDS) baza ♦ vt engañar; **to play a ~ on sb** gastar una broma a uno; **that should do the ~** a ver si funciona así; **~ery** n engaño

trickle ['trɪkl] n (of water etc) goteo ♦ vi gotear

tricky ['trɪkɪ] adj difícil; delicado

tricycle ['traɪsɪkl] n triciclo

trifle ['traɪfl] n bagatela; (CULIN) dulce m de bizcocho borracho, gelatina, fruta y natillas ♦ adv: **a ~ long** un poquito largo; **trifling** adj insignificante

trigger ['trɪgə*] n (of gun) gatillo; **~ off** vt desencadenar

trim [trɪm] adj (house, garden) en buen estado; (person, figure) esbelto ♦ n (haircut etc) recorte m; (on car) guarnición f ♦ vt (neaten) arreglar; (cut) recortar; (decorate) adornar; (NAUT: a sail) orientar; **~mings** npl (CULIN) guarnición f

trip [trɪp] n viaje m; (excursion) excursión f; (stumble) traspié m ♦ vi (stumble) tropezar; (go lightly) andar a paso ligero; **on a ~** de viaje; **~ up** vi tropezar, caerse ♦ vt hacer tropezar or caer

tripe [traɪp] n (CULIN) callos mpl

triple ['trɪpl] adj triple; **triplets** ['trɪplɪts] npl trillizos/as mpl/fpl; **triplicate** ['trɪplɪkət] n: **in triplicate** por triplicado

trite [traɪt] adj trillado

triumph ['traɪʌmf] n triunfo ♦ vi: **to ~ (over)** vencer; **~ant** [traɪ'ʌmfənt] adj (team etc) vencedor(a); (wave, return) triunfal

trivia ['trɪvɪə] npl trivialidades fpl

trivial ['trɪvɪəl] adj insignificante; (commonplace) banal

trod [trɒd] pt of **tread**

trodden ['trɔdn] *pp of* **tread**

trolley ['trɔlɪ] *n* carrito; (*also*: **~ bus**) trolebús *m*

trombone [trɔm'bəun] *n* trombón *m*

troop [tru:p] *n* grupo, banda; **~s** *npl* (MIL) tropas *fpl*; **~ in/out** *vi* entrar/salir en tropel; **~ing the colour** *n* (*ceremony*) presentación *f* de la bandera

trophy ['trəufɪ] *n* trofeo

tropical ['trɔpɪkl] *adj* tropical

trot [trɔt] *n* trote *m* ♦ *vi* trotar; **on the ~** (BRIT: *fig*) seguidos/as

trouble ['trʌbl] *n* problema *m*, dificultad *f*; (*worry*) preocupación *f*; (*bother, effort*) molestia, esfuerzo; (*unrest*) inquietud *f*; (MED): **stomach** *etc* **~** problemas *mpl* gástricos *etc* ♦ *vt* (*disturb*) molestar; (*worry*) preocupar, inquietar ♦ *vi*: **to ~ to do sth** molestarse en hacer algo; **~s** *npl* (POL *etc*) conflictos *mpl*; (*personal*) problemas *mpl*; **to be in ~** estar en un apuro; **it's no ~!** ¡no es molestia (ninguna)!; **what's the ~?** (*with broken TV etc*) ¿cuál es el problema?; (*doctor to patient*) ¿qué pasa?; **~d** *adj* (*person*) preocupado; (*country, epoch, life*) agitado; **~maker** *n* agitador(a) *m/f*; (*child*) alborotador *m*; **~shooter** *n* (*in conflict*) conciliador/a *m/f*; **~some** *adj* molesto

trough [trɔf] *n* (*also*: **drinking ~**) abrevadero; (*also*: **feeding ~**) comedero; (*depression*) depresión *f*

troupe [tru:p] *n* grupo

trousers ['trauzəz] *npl* pantalones *mpl*; **short ~** pantalones *mpl* cortos

trousseau ['tru:səu] (*pl* **~x** *or* **~s**) *n* ajuar *m*

trout [traut] *n inv* trucha

trowel ['trauəl] *n* (*of gardener*) palita; (*of builder*) paleta

truant ['truənt] *n*: **to play ~** (BRIT) hacer novillos

truce [tru:s] *n* tregua

truck [trʌk] *n* (*lorry*) camión *m*; (RAIL) vagón *m*; **~ driver** *n* camionero; **~ farm** (US) *n* huerto

true [tru:] *adj* verdadero; (*accurate*) exacto;

(*genuine*) auténtico; (*faithful*) fiel; **to come ~** realizarse

truffle ['trʌfl] *n* trufa

truly ['tru:lɪ] *adv* (*really*) realmente; (*truthfully*) verdaderamente; (*faithfully*): **yours ~** (*in letter*) le saluda atentamente

trump [trʌmp] *n* triunfo

trumpet ['trʌmpɪt] *n* trompeta

truncheon ['trʌntʃən] *n* porra

trundle ['trʌndl] *vi*: **to ~ along** ir sin prisas

trunk [trʌŋk] *n* (*of tree, person*) tronco; (*of elephant*) trompa; (*case*) baúl *m*; (US: AUT) maletero; **~s** *npl* (*also*: **swimming ~s**) bañador *m* (de hombre)

truss [trʌs] *vt*: **~ (up)** atar

trust [trʌst] *n* confianza; (*responsibility*) responsabilidad *f*; (LAW) fideicomiso ♦ *vt* (*rely on*) tener confianza en; (*hope*) esperar; (*entrust*): **to ~ sth to sb** confiar algo a uno; **to take sth on ~** aceptar algo a ojos cerrados; **~ed** *adj* de confianza; **~ee** [trʌs'ti:] *n* (LAW) fideicomisario; (*of school*) administrador *m*; **~ful** *adj* confiado; **~ing** *adj* confiado; **~worthy** *adj* digno de confianza

truth [tru:θ, *pl* tru:ðz] *n* verdad *f*; **~ful** *adj* veraz

try [traɪ] *n* tentativa, intento; (RUGBY) ensayo ♦ *vt* (*attempt*) intentar; (*test*: *also*: **~ out**) probar, someter a prueba; (LAW) juzgar, procesar; (*strain*: *patience*) hacer perder ♦ *vi* probar; **to have a ~** probar suerte; **to ~ to do sth** intentar hacer algo; **~ again!** ¡vuelve a probar!; **~ harder!** ¡esfuérzate más!; **well, I tried** al menos lo intenté; **~ on** *vt* (*clothes*) probarse; **~ing** *adj* (*experience*) cansado; (*person*) pesado

T-shirt ['ti:ʃə:t] *n* camiseta

T-square *n* regla en T

tub [tʌb] *n* cubo (SP), balde *m* (AM); (*bath*) tina, bañera

tube [tju:b] *n* tubo; (BRIT: *underground*) metro; (*for tyre*) cámara de aire

tuberculosis [tjubə:kju'ləusɪs] *n* tuberculosis *f inv*

tube station (BRIT) *n* estación *f* de metro

tubular ['tju:bjulə*] *adj* tubular

TUC (*BRIT*) *n abbr* (= *Trades Union Congress*) *federación nacional de sindicatos*

tuck [tʌk] *vt* (*put*) poner; **~ away** *vt* (*money*) guardar; (*building*): **to be ~ed away** esconderse, ocultarse; **~ in** *vt* meter dentro; (*child*) arropar ♦ *vi* (*eat*) comer con apetito; **~ up** *vt* (*child*) arropar; **~ shop** *n* (*SCOL*) tienda; ≈ bar *m* (del colegio) (*SP*)

Tuesday ['tju:zdɪ] *n* martes *m inv*

tuft [tʌft] *n* mechón *m*; (*of grass etc*) manojo

tug [tʌg] *n* (*ship*) remolcador *m* ♦ *vt* tirar de; **~-of-war** *n* lucha de tiro de cuerda; (*fig*) tira y afloja *m*

tuition [tju:'ɪʃən] *n* (*BRIT*) enseñanza; (: *private* ~) clases *fpl* particulares; (*US: school fees*) matrícula

tulip ['tju:lɪp] *n* tulipán *m*

tumble ['tʌmbl] *n* (*fall*) caída ♦ *vi* caer; **to ~ to sth** (*inf*) caer en la cuenta de algo; **~down** *adj* destartalado; **~ dryer** (*BRIT*) *n* secadora

tumbler ['tʌmblə*] *n* (*glass*) vaso

tummy ['tʌmɪ] (*inf*) *n* barriga, tripa

tumour ['tju:mə*] (*US* **tumor**) *n* tumor *m*

tuna ['tju:nə] *n inv* (*also:* **~ fish**) atún *m*

tune [tju:n] *n* melodía ♦ *vt* (*MUS*) afinar; (*RADIO, TV, AUT*) sintonizar; **to be in/out of ~** (*instrument*) estar afinado/desafinado; (*singer*) cantar afinadamente/desafinar; **to be in/out of ~ with** (*fig*) estar de acuerdo/en desacuerdo con; **~ in** *vi*: **to ~ in (to)** (*RADIO, TV*) sintonizar (con); **~ up** *vi* (*musician*) afinar (su instrumento); **~ful** *adj* melodioso; **~r** *n*: **piano ~r** afinador(a) *m/f* de pianos

tunic ['tju:nɪk] *n* túnica

Tunisia [tju:'nɪzɪə] *n* Túnez *m*

tunnel ['tʌnl] *n* túnel *m*; (*in mine*) galería ♦ *vi* construir un túnel/una galería

turban ['tə:bən] *n* turbante *m*

turbulent ['tə:bjulənt] *adj* turbulento

tureen [tə'ri:n] *n* sopera

turf [tə:f] *n* césped *m*; (*clod*) tepe *m* ♦ *vt* cubrir con césped; **~ out** (*inf*) *vt* echar a

la calle

Turk [tə:k] *n* turco/a

Turkey ['tə:kɪ] *n* Turquía

turkey ['tə:kɪ] *n* pavo

Turkish ['tə:kɪʃ] *adj, n* turco

turmoil ['tə:mɔɪl] *n*: **in ~** revuelto

turn [tə:n] *n* turno; (*in road*) curva; (*of mind, events*) rumbo; (*THEATRE*) número; (*MED*) ataque *m* ♦ *vt* girar, volver; (*collar, steak*) dar la vuelta a; (*page*) pasar; (*change*): **to ~ sth into** convertir algo en ♦ *vi* volver; (*person: look back*) volverse; (*reverse direction*) dar la vuelta; (*milk*) cortarse; (*become*): **to ~ nasty/forty** ponerse feo/cumplir los cuarenta; **a good ~** un favor; **it gave me quite a ~** me dio un susto; **"no left ~"** (*AUT*) "prohibido girar a la izquierda"; **it's your ~** te toca a ti; **in ~** por turnos; **to take ~s (at)** turnarse (en); **~ away** *vi* apartar la vista ♦ *vi* rechazar; **~ back** *vi* volverse atrás ♦ *vt* hacer retroceder; (*clock*) retrasar; **~ down** *vt* (*refuse*) rechazar; (*reduce*) bajar; (*fold*) doblar; **~ in** *vi* (*inf: go to bed*) acostarse ♦ *vt* (*fold*) doblar hacia dentro; **~ off** *vi* (*from road*) desviarse ♦ *vt* (*light, radio etc*) apagar; (*tap*) cerrar; (*engine*) parar; **~ on** *vt* (*light, radio etc*) encender (*SP*), prender (*AM*); (*tap*) abrir; (*engine*) poner en marcha; **~ out** *vt* (*light, gas*) apagar; (*produce*) producir ♦ *vi* (*voters*) concurrir; **to ~ out to be ...** resultar ser ...; **~ over** *vi* (*person*) volverse ♦ *vt* (*object*) dar la vuelta a; (*page*) volver; **~ round** *vi* volverse; (*rotate*) girar; **~ up** *vi* (*person*) llegar, presentarse; (*lost object*) aparecer ♦ *vt* (*gen*) subir; **~ing** *n* (*in road*) vuelta; **~ing point** *n* (*fig*) momento decisivo

turnip ['tə:nɪp] *n* nabo

turn: **~out** *n* concurrencia; **~over** *n* (*COMM: amount of money*) volumen *m* de ventas; (: *of goods*) movimiento; **~pike** (*US*) *n* autopista de peaje; **~stile** *n* torniquete *m*; **~table** *n* plato; **~-up** (*BRIT*) *n* (*on trousers*) vuelta

turpentine ['tə:pəntaɪn] *n* (*also:* **turps**)

trementina

turquoise ['tə:kwɔɪz] *n* (*stone*) turquesa
♦ *adj* color turquesa

turret ['tʌrɪt] *n* torreón *m*

turtle ['tə:tl] *n* galápago *m*; **~neck
(sweater)** *n* jersey *m* de cuello vuelto

tusk [tʌsk] *n* colmillo

tutor ['tju:tə*] *n* profesor(a) *m/f*; **~ial**
[-'tɔ:rɪəl] *n* (*SCOL*) seminario

tuxedo [tʌk'si:dəu] (*US*) *n* smóking *m*,
esmoquin *m*

TV [ti:'vi:] *n abbr* (= *television*) tele *f*

twang [twæŋ] *n* (*of instrument*) punteado;
(*of voice*) timbre *m* nasal

tweezers ['twi:zəz] *npl* pinzas *fpl* (de
depilar)

twelfth [twɛlfθ] *num* duodécimo

twelve [twɛlv] *num* doce; **at ~ o'clock**
(*midday*) a mediodía; (*midnight*) a
medianoche

twentieth ['twɛntɪɪθ] *adj* vigésimo

twenty ['twɛntɪ] *num* veinte

twice [twaɪs] *adv* dos veces; **~ as much**
dos veces más

twiddle ['twɪdl] *vi*: **to ~ (with) sth** dar
vueltas a algo; **to ~ one's thumbs** (*fig*)
estar mano sobre mano

twig [twɪg] *n* ramita

twilight ['twaɪlaɪt] *n* crepúsculo

twin [twɪn] *adj, n* gemelo/a *m/f* ♦ *vt*
hermanar; **~-bedded room** *n*
habitación *f* doble

twine [twaɪn] *n* bramante *m* ♦ *vi* (*plant*)
enroscarse

twinge [twɪndʒ] *n* (*of pain*) punzada; (*of
conscience*) remordimiento

twinkle ['twɪŋkl] *vi* centellear; (*eyes*) brillar

twirl [twə:l] *vt* dar vueltas a ♦ *vi* dar
vueltas

twist [twɪst] *n* (*action*) torsión *f*; (*in road,
coil*) vuelta; (*in wire, flex*) doblez *f*; (*in
story*) giro ♦ *vt* torcer; (*weave*) trenzar;
(*roll around*) enrollar; (*fig*) deformar ♦ *vi*
serpentear

twit [twɪt] (*inf*) *n* tonto

twitch [twɪtʃ] *n* (*pull*) tirón *m*; (*nervous*) tic
m ♦ *vi* crisparse

two [tu:] *num* dos; **to put ~ and ~
together** (*fig*) atar cabos; **~-door** *adj*
(*AUT*) de dos puertas; **~-faced** *adj* (*pej*:
person) falso; **~fold** *adv*: **to increase
~fold** doblarse; **~-piece (suit)** *n* traje *m*
de dos piezas; **~-piece (swimsuit)** *n*
dos piezas *m inv*, bikini *m*; **~some** *n*
(*people*) pareja; **~-way** *adj*: **~-way traffic**
circulación *f* de dos sentidos

tycoon [taɪ'ku:n] *n*: **(business) ~** magnate
m

type [taɪp] *n* (*category*) tipo, género;
(*model*) tipo; (*TYP*) tipo, letra ♦ *vt* (*letter
etc*) escribir a máquina; **~cast** *adj*
(*actor*) encasillado; **~face** *n* letra;
~script *n* texto mecanografiado;
~writer *n* máquina de escribir; **~written**
adj mecanografiado

typhoid ['taɪfɔɪd] *n* tifoidea

typical ['tɪpɪkl] *adj* típico

typing ['taɪpɪŋ] *n* mecanografía

typist ['taɪpɪst] *n* mecanógrafo/a

tyrant ['taɪərnt] *n* tirano/a

tyre ['taɪə*] (*US* **tire**) *n* neumático (*SP*),
llanta (*AM*); **~ pressure** *n* presión *f* de
los neumáticos

U, u

U-bend ['ju:'bɛnd] *n* (*AUT, in pipe*) recodo

udder ['ʌdə*] *n* ubre *f*

UFO ['ju:fəu] *n abbr* (= *unidentified flying
object*) OVNI *m*

ugh [ə:h] *excl* ¡uf!

ugly ['ʌglɪ] *adj* feo; (*dangerous*) peligroso

UHT *abbr*: **~ milk** leche *f* UHT, leche *f*
uperizada

UK *n abbr* = **United Kingdom**

ulcer ['ʌlsə*] *n* úlcera; (*mouth ~*) llaga

Ulster ['ʌlstə*] *n* Ulster *m*

ulterior [ʌl'tɪərɪə*] *adj*: **~ motive** segundas
intenciones *fpl*

ultimate ['ʌltɪmət] *adj* último, final;
(*greatest*) máximo; **~ly** *adv* (*in the end*)
por último, al final; (*fundamentally*) a or
en fin de cuentas

umbilical cord [ʌmˈbɪlɪkl-] n cordón m umbilical

umbrella [ʌmˈbrelə] n paraguas m inv; (for sun) sombrilla

umpire [ˈʌmpaɪə*] n árbitro

umpteen [ʌmpˈtiːn] adj enésimos/as; ~th adj: for the ~th time por enésima vez

UN n abbr (= United Nations) NN. UU.

unable [ʌnˈeɪbl] adj: to be ~ to do sth no poder hacer algo

unaccompanied [ʌnəˈkʌmpənɪd] adj no acompañado; (song) sin acompañamiento

unaccustomed [ʌnəˈkʌstəmd] adj: to be ~ to no estar acostumbrado a

unanimous [juːˈnænɪməs] adj unánime

unarmed [ʌnˈɑːmd] adj (defenceless) inerme; (without weapon) desarmado

unattached [ʌnəˈtætʃt] adj (person) soltero y sin compromiso; (part etc) suelto

unattended [ʌnəˈtendɪd] adj desatendido

unattractive [ʌnəˈtræktɪv] adj poco atractivo

unauthorized [ʌnˈɔːθəraɪzd] adj no autorizado

unavoidable [ʌnəˈvɔɪdəbl] adj inevitable

unaware [ʌnəˈweə*] adj: to be ~ of ignorar; ~s adv de improviso

unbalanced [ʌnˈbælənst] adj (report) poco objetivo; (mentally) trastornado

unbearable [ʌnˈbeərəbl] adj insoportable

unbeatable [ʌnˈbiːtəbl] adj (team) invencible; (price) inmejorable; (quality) insuperable

unbelievable [ʌnbɪˈliːvəbl] adj increíble

unbend [ʌnˈbend] (irreg) vi (relax) relajarse ♦ vt (wire) enderezar

unbiased [ʌnˈbaɪəst] adj imparcial

unborn [ʌnˈbɔːn] adj que va a nacer

unbroken [ʌnˈbrəʊkən] adj (seal) intacto; (series) continuo; (record) no batido; (spirit) indómito

unbutton [ʌnˈbʌtn] vt desabrochar

uncalled-for [ʌnˈkɔːldfɔː*] adj gratuito, inmerecido

uncanny [ʌnˈkænɪ] adj extraño

unceremonious [ˈʌnserɪˈməʊnɪəs] adj (abrupt, rude) brusco, hosco

uncertain [ʌnˈsəːtn] adj incierto; (indecisive) indeciso

unchanged [ʌnˈtʃeɪndʒd] adj igual, sin cambios

uncivilized [ʌnˈsɪvɪlaɪzd] adj inculto; (fig: behaviour etc) bárbaro; (hour) inoportuno

uncle [ˈʌŋkl] n tío

uncomfortable [ʌnˈkʌmfətəbl] adj incómodo; (uneasy) inquieto

uncommon [ʌnˈkɔmən] adj poco común, raro

uncompromising [ʌnˈkɔmprəmaɪzɪŋ] adj intransigente

unconcerned [ʌnkənˈsəːnd] adj indiferente, despreocupado

unconditional [ʌnkənˈdɪʃənl] adj incondicional

unconscious [ʌnˈkɔnʃəs] adj sin sentido; (unaware): to be ~ of no darse cuenta de ♦ n: the ~ el inconsciente

uncontrollable [ʌnkənˈtrəʊləbl] adj (child etc) incontrolable; (temper) indomable; (laughter) incontenible

unconventional [ʌnkənˈvenʃənl] adj poco convencional

uncouth [ʌnˈkuːθ] adj grosero, inculto

uncover [ʌnˈkʌvə*] vt descubrir; (take lid off) destapar

undecided [ʌndɪˈsaɪdɪd] adj (character) indeciso; (question) no resuelto

under [ˈʌndə*] prep debajo de; (less than) menos de; (according to) según, de acuerdo con; (sb's leadership) bajo ♦ adv debajo, abajo; ~ there allí abajo; ~ repair en reparación

under... [ˈʌndə*] prefix sub; ~age adj menor de edad; (drinking etc) de los menores de edad; ~carriage (BRIT) n (AVIAT) tren m de aterrizaje; ~charge vt cobrar menos de la cuenta; ~clothes npl ropa interior (SP) or íntima (AM); ~coat n (paint) primera mano; ~cover adj clandestino; ~current n (fig) corriente f oculta; ~cut vt irreg vender más barato que; ~developed adj subdesarrollado; ~dog n desvalido/a; ~done adj (CULIN) poco hecho;

~**estimate** *vt* subestimar; ~**exposed** *adj* (PHOT) subexpuesto; ~**fed** *adj* subalimentado; ~**foot** *adv* con los pies; ~**go** *vt irreg* sufrir; (*treatment*) recibir; ~**graduate** *n* estudiante *m/f*; ~**ground** *n* (BRIT: *railway*) metro; (POL) movimiento clandestino ♦ *adj* (*car park*) subterráneo ♦ *adv* (*work*) en la clandestinidad; ~**growth** *n* maleza; ~**hand(ed)** *adj* (*fig*) socarrón; ~**lie** *vt irreg* (*fig*) ser la razón fundamental de; ~**line** *vt* subrayar; ~**mine** *vt* socavar, minar; ~**neath** [ʌndə'niːθ] *adv* debajo ♦ *prep* debajo de, bajo; ~**paid** *adj* mal pagado; ~**pants** *npl* calzoncillos *mpl*; ~**pass** (BRIT) *n* paso subterráneo; ~**privileged** *adj* desposeído; ~**rate** *vt* menospreciar, subestimar; ~**shirt** (US) *n* camiseta; ~**shorts** (US) *npl* calzoncillos *mpl*; ~**side** *n* parte *f* inferior; ~**skirt** (BRIT) *n* enaguas *fpl*

understand [ʌndə'stænd] (*irreg*) *vt*, *vi* entender, comprender; (*assume*) tener entendido; ~**able** *adj* comprensible; ~**ing** *adj* comprensivo ♦ *n* comprensión *f*, entendimiento; (*agreement*) acuerdo

understatement ['ʌndəsteɪtmənt] *n* modestia (excesiva); **that's an ~!** ¡eso es decir poco!

understood [ʌndə'stud] *pt*, *pp* of **understand** ♦ *adj* (*agreed*) acordado; (*implied*): **it is ~ that** se sobreentiende que

understudy ['ʌndəstʌdɪ] *n* suplente *m/f*

undertake [ʌndə'teɪk] (*irreg*) *vt* emprender; **to ~ to do sth** comprometerse a hacer algo

undertaker ['ʌndəteɪkə*] *n* director(a) *m/f* de pompas fúnebres

undertaking ['ʌndəteɪkɪŋ] *n* empresa; (*promise*) promesa

under: ~**tone** *n*: **in an ~tone** en voz baja; ~**water** *adv* bajo el agua ♦ *adj* submarino; ~**wear** *n* ropa interior (SP) or íntima (AM); ~**world** *n* (of *crime*) hampa, inframundo; ~**writer** *n* (INSURANCE) asegurador(a) *m/f*

undesirable [ʌndɪ'zaɪrəbl] *adj* (*person*) indeseable; (*thing*) poco aconsejable

undo [ʌn'duː] (*irreg*) *vt* (*laces*) desatar; (*button etc*) desabrochar; (*spoil*) deshacer; ~**ing** *n* ruina, perdición *f*

undoubted [ʌn'dautɪd] *adj* indudable

undress [ʌn'dres] *vi* desnudarse

undulating ['ʌndjuleɪtɪŋ] *adj* ondulante

unduly [ʌn'djuːlɪ] *adv* excesivamente, demasiado

unearth [ʌn'əːθ] *vt* desenterrar

unearthly [ʌn'əːθlɪ] *adj* (*hour*) inverosímil

uneasy [ʌn'iːzɪ] *adj* intranquilo, preocupado; (*feeling*) desagradable; (*peace*) inseguro

uneducated [ʌn'edjukeɪtɪd] *adj* ignorante, inculto

unemployed [ʌnɪm'plɔɪd] *adj* parado, sin trabajo ♦ *npl*: **the ~** los parados

unemployment [ʌnɪm'plɔɪmənt] *n* paro, desempleo

unending [ʌn'endɪŋ] *adj* interminable

unerring [ʌn'əːrɪŋ] *adj* infalible

uneven [ʌn'iːvn] *adj* desigual; (*road etc*) lleno de baches

unexpected [ʌnɪk'spektɪd] *adj* inesperado; ~**ly** *adv* inesperadamente

unfailing [ʌn'feɪlɪŋ] *adj* (*support*) indefectible; (*energy*) inagotable

unfair [ʌn'feə*] *adj*: ~ **(to sb)** injusto (con uno)

unfaithful [ʌn'feɪθful] *adj* infiel

unfamiliar [ʌnfə'mɪlɪə*] *adj* extraño, desconocido; **to be ~ with** desconocer

unfashionable [ʌn'fæʃnəbl] *adj* pasado or fuera de moda

unfasten [ʌn'fɑːsn] *vt* (*knot*) desatar; (*dress*) desabrochar; (*open*) abrir

unfavourable [ʌn'feɪvərəbl] (US **unfavorable**) *adj* desfavorable

unfeeling [ʌn'fiːlɪŋ] *adj* insensible

unfinished [ʌn'fɪnɪʃt] *adj* inacabado, sin terminar

unfit [ʌn'fɪt] *adj* bajo de forma; (*incompetent*): ~ **(for)** incapaz (de); ~ **for work** no apto para trabajar

unfold [ʌn'fəuld] *vt* desdoblar ♦ *vi* abrirse

unforeseen [ˈʌnfɔːˈsiːn] *adj* imprevisto
unforgettable [ʌnfəˈgetəbl] *adj* inolvidable
unfortunate [ʌnˈfɔːtʃnət] *adj* desgraciado; (*event, remark*) inoportuno; **~ly** *adv* desgraciadamente
unfounded [ʌnˈfaundɪd] *adj* infundado
unfriendly [ʌnˈfrendlɪ] *adj* antipático; (*behaviour, remark*) hostil, poco amigable
ungainly [ʌnˈgeɪnlɪ] *adj* desgarbado
ungodly [ʌnˈgɒdlɪ] *adj*: **at an ~ hour** a una hora inverosímil
ungrateful [ʌnˈgreɪtful] *adj* ingrato
unhappiness [ʌnˈhæpɪnɪs] *n* tristeza, desdicha
unhappy [ʌnˈhæpɪ] *adj* (*sad*) triste; (*unfortunate*) desgraciado; (*childhood*) infeliz; **~ about/with** (*arrangements etc*) poco contento con, descontento de
unharmed [ʌnˈhɑːmd] *adj* ileso
unhealthy [ʌnˈhelθɪ] *adj* (*place*) malsano; (*person*) enfermizo; (*fig: interest*) morboso
unheard-of *adj* inaudito, sin precedente
unhurt [ʌnˈhɜːt] *adj* ileso
unidentified [ʌnaɪˈdentɪfaɪd] *adj* no identificado, sin identificar; *see also* **UFO**
uniform [ˈjuːnɪfɔːm] *n* uniforme *m* ♦ *adj* uniforme
unify [ˈjuːnɪfaɪ] *vt* unificar, unir
uninhabited [ʌnɪnˈhæbɪtɪd] *adj* desierto
unintentional [ʌnɪnˈtenʃənəl] *adj* involuntario
union [ˈjuːnjən] *n* unión *f*; (*also:* **trade ~**) sindicato ♦ *cpd* sindical; **U~ Jack** *n* bandera del Reino Unido
unique [juːˈniːk] *adj* único
unison [ˈjuːnɪsn] *n*: **in ~** (*speak, reply, sing*) al unísono
unit [ˈjuːnɪt] *n* unidad *f*; (*section: of furniture etc*) elemento; (*team*) grupo; **kitchen ~** módulo de cocina
unite [juːˈnaɪt] *vt* unir ♦ *vi* unirse; **~d** *adj* unido; (*effort*) conjunto; **U~d Kingdom** *n* Reino Unido; **U~d Nations (Organization)** *n* Naciones *fpl* Unidas; **U~d States (of America)** *n* Estados *mpl* Unidos

unit trust (*BRIT*) *n* bono fiduciario
unity [ˈjuːnɪtɪ] *n* unidad *f*
universe [ˈjuːnɪvəːs] *n* universo
university [juːnɪˈvəːsɪtɪ] *n* universidad *f*
unjust [ʌnˈdʒʌst] *adj* injusto
unkempt [ʌnˈkempt] *adj* (*appearance*) descuidado; (*hair*) despeinado
unkind [ʌnˈkaɪnd] *adj* poco amable; (*behaviour, comment*) cruel
unknown [ʌnˈnəun] *adj* desconocido
unlawful [ʌnˈlɔːful] *adj* ilegal, ilícito
unleaded [ʌnˈledɪd] *adj* (*petrol, fuel*) sin plombo
unless [ʌnˈles] *conj* a menos que; **~ he comes** a menos que venga; **~ otherwise stated** salvo indicación contraria
unlike [ʌnˈlaɪk] *adj* (*not alike*) distinto de *or* a; (*not like*) poco propio de ♦ *prep* a diferencia de
unlikely [ʌnˈlaɪklɪ] *adj* improbable; (*unexpected*) inverosímil
unlimited [ʌnˈlɪmɪtɪd] *adj* ilimitado
unlisted [ʌnˈlɪstɪd] (*US*) *adj* (*TEL*) que no consta en la guía
unload [ʌnˈləud] *vt* descargar
unlock [ʌnˈlɒk] *vt* abrir (con llave)
unlucky [ʌnˈlʌkɪ] *adj* desgraciado; (*object, number*) que da mala suerte; **to be ~** tener mala suerte
unmarried [ʌnˈmærɪd] *adj* soltero
unmistak(e)able [ʌnmɪsˈteɪkəbl] *adj* inconfundible
unnatural [ʌnˈnætʃrəl] *adj* (*gen*) antinatural; (*manner*) afectado; (*habit*) perverso
unnecessary [ʌnˈnesəsərɪ] *adj* innecesario, inútil
unnoticed [ʌnˈnəutɪst] *adj*: **to go** *or* **pass ~** pasar desapercibido
UNO [ˈjuːnəu] *n abbr* (= *United Nations Organization*) ONU *f*
unobtainable [ʌnəbˈteɪnəbl] *adj* inconseguible; (*TEL*) inexistente
unobtrusive [ʌnəbˈtruːsɪv] *adj* discreto
unofficial [ʌnəˈfɪʃl] *adj* no oficial; (*news*) sin confirmar
unorthodox [ʌnˈɔːθədɔks] *adj* poco

ortodoxo; (*REL*) heterodoxo

unpack [ʌnˈpæk] *vi* deshacer las maletas
♦ *vt* deshacer

unpalatable [ʌnˈpælətəbl] *adj* incomible;
(*truth*) desagradable

unparalleled [ʌnˈpærəleld] *adj*
(*unequalled*) incomparable

unpleasant [ʌnˈpleznt] *adj* (*disagreeable*)
desagradable; (*person, manner*) antipático

unplug [ʌnˈplʌg] *vt* desenchufar,
desconectar

unpopular [ʌnˈpɔpjulə*] *adj* impopular,
poco popular

unprecedented [ʌnˈpresɪdəntɪd] *adj* sin
precedentes

unpredictable [ʌnprɪˈdɪktəbl] *adj*
imprevisible

unprofessional [ʌnprəˈfeʃənl] *adj*
(*attitude, conduct*) poco ético

unqualified [ʌnˈkwɔlɪfaɪd] *adj* sin título,
no cualificado; (*success*) total

unquestionably [ʌnˈkwestʃənəblɪ] *adv*
indiscutiblemente

unreal [ʌnˈrɪəl] *adj* irreal; (*extraordinary*)
increíble

unrealistic [ʌnrɪəˈlɪstɪk] *adj* poco realista

unreasonable [ʌnˈriːznəbl] *adj*
irrazonable; (*demand*) excesivo

unrelated [ʌnrɪˈleɪtɪd] *adj* sin relación;
(*family*) no emparentado

unreliable [ʌnrɪˈlaɪəbl] *adj* (*person*)
informal; (*machine*) poco fiable

unremitting [ʌnrɪˈmɪtɪŋ] *adj* constante

unreservedly [ʌnrɪˈzɜːvɪdlɪ] *adv* sin
reserva

unrest [ʌnˈrest] *n* inquietud *f*, malestar *m*;
(*POL*) disturbios *mpl*

unroll [ʌnˈrəʊl] *vt* desenrollar

unruly [ʌnˈruːlɪ] *adj* indisciplinado

unsafe [ʌnˈseɪf] *adj* peligroso

unsaid [ʌnˈsed] *adj*: **to leave sth ~** dejar
algo sin decir

unsatisfactory [ˈʌnsætɪsˈfæktərɪ] *adj* poco
satisfactorio

unsavoury [ʌnˈseɪvərɪ] (*US* **unsavory**) *adj*
(*fig*) repugnante

unscrew [ʌnˈskruː] *vt* destornillar

unscrupulous [ʌnˈskruːpjuləs] *adj* sin
escrúpulos

unsettled [ʌnˈsetld] *adj* inquieto,
intranquilo; (*weather*) variable

unshaven [ʌnˈʃeɪvn] *adj* sin afeitar

unsightly [ʌnˈsaɪtlɪ] *adj* feo

unskilled [ʌnˈskɪld] *adj* (*work*) no
especializado; (*worker*) no cualificado

unspeakable [ʌnˈspiːkəbl] *adj* indecible;
(*awful*) incalificable

unstable [ʌnˈsteɪbl] *adj* inestable

unsteady [ʌnˈstedɪ] *adj* inestable

unstuck [ʌnˈstʌk] *adj*: **to come ~**
despegarse; (*fig*) fracasar

unsuccessful [ʌnsəkˈsesful] *adj* (*attempt*)
infructuoso; (*writer, proposal*) sin éxito; **to
be ~** (*in attempting sth*) no tener éxito,
fracasar; **~ly** *adv* en vano, sin éxito

unsuitable [ʌnˈsuːtəbl] *adj* inapropiado;
(*time*) inoportuno

unsure [ʌnˈʃuə*] *adj* inseguro, poco
seguro

unsuspecting [ˈʌnsəsˈpektɪŋ] *adj*
desprevenido

unsympathetic [ʌnsɪmpəˈθetɪk] *adj* poco
comprensivo; (*unlikeable*) antipático

unthinkable [ʌnˈθɪŋkəbl] *adj*
inconcebible, impensable

untidy [ʌnˈtaɪdɪ] *adj* (*room*) desordenado;
(*appearance*) desaliñado

untie [ʌnˈtaɪ] *vt* desatar

until [ʌnˈtɪl] *prep* hasta ♦ *conj* hasta que; **~
he comes** hasta que venga; **~ now** hasta
ahora; **~ then** hasta entonces

untimely [ʌnˈtaɪmlɪ] *adj* inoportuno;
(*death*) prematuro

untold [ʌnˈtəʊld] *adj* (*story*) nunca
contado; (*suffering*) indecible; (*wealth*)
incalculable

untoward [ʌntəˈwɔːd] *adj* adverso

unused [ʌnˈjuːzd] *adj* sin usar

unusual [ʌnˈjuːʒʊəl] *adj* insólito, poco
común; (*exceptional*) inusitado

unveil [ʌnˈveɪl] *vt* (*statue*) descubrir

unwanted [ʌnˈwɔntɪd] *adj* (*clothing*) viejo;
(*pregnancy*) no deseado

unwelcome [ʌnˈwelkəm] *adj* inoportuno;

(news) desagradable

unwell [ʌn'wɛl] *adj*: **to be/feel ~** estar indispuesto/sentirse mal

unwieldy [ʌn'wiːldɪ] *adj* difícil de manejar

unwilling [ʌn'wɪlɪŋ] *adj*: **to be ~ to do sth** estar poco dispuesto a hacer algo; **~ly** *adv* de mala gana

unwind [ʌn'waɪnd] *(irreg: like* wind²*) vt* desenvolver ♦ *vi (relax)* relajarse

unwise [ʌn'waɪz] *adj* imprudente

unwitting [ʌn'wɪtɪŋ] *adj* inconsciente

unworthy [ʌn'wəːðɪ] *adj* indigno

unwrap [ʌn'ræp] *vt* desenvolver

unwritten [ʌn'rɪtn] *adj (agreement)* tácito; *(rules, law)* no escrito

---
KEYWORD
---

up [ʌp] *prep*: **to go/be ~ sth** subir/estar subido en algo; **he went ~ the stairs/the hill** subió las escaleras/la colina; **we walked/climbed ~ the hill** subimos la colina; **they live further ~ the street** viven más arriba en la calle; **go ~ that road and turn left** sigue por esa calle y gira a la izquierda

♦ *adv* **1** *(upwards, higher)* más arriba; **~ in the mountains** en lo alto (de la montaña); **put it a bit higher ~** ponlo un poco más arriba *or* alto; **~ there** ahí *or* allí arriba; **~ above** en lo alto, por encima, arriba

2: **to be ~** *(out of bed)* estar levantado; *(prices, level)* haber subido

3: **~ to** *(as far as)* hasta; **~ to now** hasta ahora *or* la fecha

4: **to be ~ to** *(depending on)*: **it's ~ to you** depende de ti; **he's not ~ to it** *(job, task etc)* no es capaz de hacerlo; **his work is not ~ to the required standard** su trabajo no da la talla; *(inf: be doing)*: **what is he ~ to?** ¿que estará tramando?

♦ *n*: **~s and downs** altibajos *mpl*

upbringing ['ʌpbrɪŋɪŋ] *n* educación *f*

update [ʌp'deɪt] *vt* poner al día

upgrade [ʌp'greɪd] *vt (house)* modernizar; *(employee)* ascender

upheaval [ʌp'hiːvl] *n* trastornos *mpl*; *(POL)* agitación *f*

uphill [ʌp'hɪl] *adj* cuesta arriba; *(fig: task)* penoso, difícil ♦ *adv*: **to go ~** ir cuesta arriba

uphold [ʌp'həʊld] *(irreg) vt* defender

upholstery [ʌp'həʊlstərɪ] *n* tapicería

upkeep ['ʌpkiːp] *n* mantenimiento

upon [ə'pɔn] *prep* sobre

upper ['ʌpə*] *adj* superior, de arriba ♦ *n* *(of shoe: also:* **~s)** empeine *m*; **~-class** *adj* de clase alta; **~ hand** *n*: **to have the ~ hand** tener la sartén por el mango; **~most** *adj* el más alto; **what was ~most in my mind** lo que me preocupaba más

upright ['ʌpraɪt] *adj* derecho; *(vertical)* vertical; *(fig)* honrado

uprising ['ʌpraɪzɪŋ] *n* sublevación *f*

uproar ['ʌprɔː*] *n* escándalo

uproot [ʌp'ruːt] *vt (also fig)* desarraigar

upset [*n* 'ʌpsɛt, *vb, adj* ʌp'sɛt] *n (to plan etc)* revés *m*, contratiempo; *(MED)* trastorno ♦ *(irreg) vt (glass etc)* volcar; *(plan)* alterar; *(person)* molestar, disgustar ♦ *adj* molesto, disgustado; *(stomach)* revuelto

upshot ['ʌpʃɔt] *n* resultado

upside-down *adv* al revés; **to turn a place ~** *(fig)* revolverlo todo

upstairs [ʌp'stɛəz] *adv* arriba ♦ *adj (room)* de arriba ♦ *n* el piso superior

upstart ['ʌpstɑːt] *n* advenedizo/a

upstream [ʌp'striːm] *adv* río arriba

uptake ['ʌpteɪk] *n*: **to be quick/slow on the ~** ser muy listo/torpe

uptight [ʌp'taɪt] *adj* tenso, nervioso

up-to-date *adj* al día

upturn ['ʌptəːn] *n (in luck)* mejora; *(COMM: in market)* resurgimiento económico

upward ['ʌpwəd] *adj* ascendente; **~(s)** *adv* hacia arriba; *(more than)*: **~(s) of** más de

urban ['əːbən] *adj* urbano

urchin ['əːtʃɪn] *n* pilluelo, golfillo

urge [əːdʒ] *n (desire)* deseo ♦ *vt*: **to ~ sb to do sth** animar a uno a hacer algo

urgent ['əːdʒənt] *adj* urgente; *(voice)*

perentorio
urinate ['juərɪneɪt] *vi* orinar
urine ['juərɪn] *n* orina, orines *mpl*
urn [ə:n] *n* urna; (*also*: **tea ~**) cacharro
metálico grande para hacer té
Uruguay ['juərəgwaɪ] *n* Uruguay; **~an**
[-'gwaɪən] *adj, n* uruguayo/a *m/f*
US *n abbr* (= *United States*) EE. UU.
us [ʌs] *pron* nos; (*after prep*) nosotros/as;
see also **me**
USA *n abbr* (= *United States* (*of America*))
EE. UU.
usage ['ju:zɪdʒ] *n* (*LING*) uso
use [*n* ju:s, *vb* ju:z] *n* uso, empleo;
(*usefulness*) utilidad *f* ♦ *vt* usar, emplear;
she ~d to do it (ella) solía *or*
acostumbraba hacerlo; **in ~** en uso; **out**
of ~ en desuso; **to be of ~** servir; **it's no**
~ (*pointless*) es inútil; (*not useful*) no sirve;
to be ~d to estar acostumbrado a,
acostumbrar; **~ up** *vt* (*food*) consumir;
(*money*) gastar; **~d** *adj* (*car*) usado; **~ful**
adj útil; **~fulness** *n* utilidad *f*; **~less** *adj*
(*unusable*) inservible; (*pointless*) inútil;
(*person*) inepto; **~r** *n* usuario/a; **~r-**
friendly *adj* (*computer*) amistoso
usher ['ʌʃə*] *n* (*at wedding*) ujier *m*; **~ette**
[-'ret] *n* (*in cinema*) acomodadora
USSR *n* (*HIST*): **the ~** la URSS
usual ['ju:ʒuəl] *adj* normal, corriente; **as ~**
como de costumbre; **~ly** *adv*
normalmente
utensil [ju:'tensl] *n* utensilio; **kitchen ~s**
batería de cocina
uterus ['ju:tərəs] *n* útero
utility [ju:'tɪlɪtɪ] *n* utilidad *f*; (*public ~*)
(*empresa de*) servicio público; **~ room** *n*
ofis *m*
utilize ['ju:tɪlaɪz] *vt* utilizar
utmost ['ʌtməust] *adj* mayor ♦ *n*: **to do**
one's ~ hacer todo lo posible
utter ['ʌtə*] *adj* total, completo ♦ *vt*
pronunciar, proferir; **~ly** *adv*
completamente, totalmente
U-turn ['ju:'tə:n] *n* viraje *m* en redondo

V, v

v. *abbr* = **verse; versus;** (= *volt*) v;
(= *vide*) véase
vacancy ['veɪkənsɪ] *n* (*BRIT*: *job*) vacante *f*;
(*room*) habitación *f* libre; **"no**
vacancies" "completo"
vacant ['veɪkənt] *adj* desocupado, libre;
(*expression*) distraído
vacate [və'keɪt] *vt* (*house, room*)
desocupar; (*job*) dejar (vacante)
vacation [və'keɪʃən] *n* vacaciones *fpl*
vaccinate ['væksɪneɪt] *vt* vacunar
vaccine ['væksi:n] *n* vacuna
vacuum ['vækjum] *n* vacío; **~ cleaner** *n*
aspiradora; **~flask** (*BRIT*) *n* termo; **~-**
packed *adj* empaquetado al vacío
vagina [və'dʒaɪnə] *n* vagina
vagrant ['veɪgrənt] *n* vagabundo/a
vague [veɪg] *adj* vago; (*memory*) borroso;
(*ambiguous*) impreciso; (*person: absent-*
minded) distraído; (: *evasive*): **to be ~** no
decir las cosas claramente; **~ly** *adv*
vagamente; distraídamente; con evasivas
vain [veɪn] *adj* (*conceited*) presumido;
(*useless*) vano, inútil; **in ~** en vano
valentine ['væləntaɪn] *n* (*also*: **~ card**)
tarjeta del Día de los Enamorados
valet ['væleɪ] *n* ayuda *m* de cámara
valid ['vælɪd] *adj* válido; (*ticket*) valedero;
(*law*) vigente
valley ['vælɪ] *n* valle *m*
valuable ['væljuəbl] *adj* (*jewel*) de valor;
(*time*) valioso; **~s** *npl* objetos *mpl* de
valor
valuation [vælju'eɪʃən] *n* tasación *f*,
valuación *f*; (*judgement of quality*)
valoración *f*
value ['vælju:] *n* valor *m*; (*importance*)
importancia ♦ *vt* (*fix price of*) tasar,
valorar; (*esteem*) apreciar; **~s** *npl*
(*principles*) principios *mpl*; **~ added tax**
(*BRIT*) *n* impuesto sobre el valor añadido;
~d *adj* (*appreciated*) apreciado
valve [vælv] *n* válvula

van [væn] *n* (*AUT*) furgoneta (*SP*), camioneta (*AM*)

vandal ['vændl] *n* vándalo/a; **~ism** *n* vandalismo; **~ize** *vt* dañar, destruir

vanilla [və'nɪlə] *n* vainilla

vanish ['vænɪʃ] *vi* desaparecer

vanity ['vænɪtɪ] *n* vanidad *f*

vantage point ['vɑːntɪdʒ-] *n* (*for views*) punto panorámico

vapour ['veɪpə*] (*US* **vapor**) *n* vapor *m*; (*on breath, window*) vaho

variable ['veərɪəbl] *adj* variable

variation [veərɪ'eɪʃən] *n* variación *f*

varicose ['værɪkəus] *adj*: **~ veins** varices *fpl*

varied ['veərɪd] *adj* variado

variety [və'raɪətɪ] *n* (*diversity*) diversidad *f*; (*type*) variedad *f*; **~ show** *n* espectáculo de variedades

various ['veərɪəs] *adj* (*several: people*) varios/as; (*reasons*) diversos/as

varnish ['vɑːnɪʃ] *n* barniz *m*; (*nail ~*) esmalte *m* ♦ *vt* barnizar; (*nails*) pintar (con esmalte)

vary ['veərɪ] *vt* variar; (*change*) cambiar ♦ *vi* variar

vase [vɑːz] *n* florero

Vaseline ® ['væsɪliːn] *n* vaselina ®

vast [vɑːst] *adj* enorme

VAT [væt] (*BRIT*) *n abbr* (= *value added tax*) IVA *m*

vat [væt] *n* tina, tinaja

Vatican ['vætɪkən] *n*: **the ~** el Vaticano

vault [vɔːlt] *n* (*of roof*) bóveda; (*tomb*) panteón *m*; (*in bank*) cámara acorazada ♦ *vt* (*also*: **~ over**) saltar (por encima de)

vaunted ['vɔːntɪd] *adj*: **much ~** cacareado, alardeado

VCR *n abbr* = **video cassette recorder**

VD *n abbr* = **venereal disease**

VDU *n abbr* (= *visual display unit*) UPV *f*

veal [viːl] *n* ternera

veer [vɪə*] *vi* (*vehicle*) virar; (*wind*) girar

vegan ['viːgən] *n* vegetariano/a estricto/a, vegetaliano/a

vegeburger ['vɛdʒɪbəːgə*] *n* hamburguesa vegetal

vegetable ['vɛdʒtəbl] *n* (*BOT*) vegetal *m*; (*edible plant*) legumbre *f*, hortaliza ♦ *adj* vegetal; **~s** *npl* (*cooked*) verduras *fpl*

vegetarian [vɛdʒɪ'teərɪən] *adj, n* vegetariano/a *m/f*

vehement ['viːɪmənt] *adj* vehemente, apasionado

vehicle ['viːɪkl] *n* vehículo; (*fig*) medio

veil [veɪl] *n* velo ♦ *vt* velar; **~ed** *adj* (*fig*) velado

vein [veɪn] *n* vena; (*of ore etc*) veta

velocity [vɪ'lɒsɪtɪ] *n* velocidad *f*

velvet ['vɛlvɪt] *n* terciopelo

vending machine ['vɛndɪŋ-] *n* distribuidor *m* automático

veneer [və'nɪə*] *n* chapa, enchapado; (*fig*) barniz *m*

venereal disease [vɪ'nɪərɪəl-] *n* enfermedad *f* venérea

Venetian blind [vɪ'niːʃən-] *n* persiana

Venezuela [vɛnɪ'zweɪlə] *n* Venezuela; **~n** *adj, n* venezolano/a *m/f*

vengeance ['vɛndʒəns] *n* venganza; **with a ~** (*fig*) con creces

venison ['vɛnɪsn] *n* carne *f* de venado

venom ['vɛnəm] *n* veneno; (*bitterness*) odio; **~ous** *adj* venenoso; lleno de odio

vent [vɛnt] *n* (*in jacket*) respiradero; (*in wall*) rejilla (de ventilación) ♦ *vt* (*fig: feelings*) desahogar

ventilator ['vɛntɪleɪtə*] *n* ventilador *m*

venture ['vɛntʃə*] *n* empresa ♦ *vt* (*opinion*) ofrecer ♦ *vi* arriesgarse, lanzarse; **business ~** empresa comercial

venue ['vɛnjuː] *n* lugar *m*

veranda(h) [və'rændə] *n* terraza

verb [vəːb] *n* verbo; **~al** *adj* verbal

verbatim [vəː'beɪtɪm] *adj, adv* palabra por palabra

verdict ['vəːdɪkt] *n* veredicto, fallo; (*fig*) opinión *f*, juicio

verge [vəːdʒ] (*BRIT*) *n* borde *m*; **"soft ~s"** (*AUT*) "arcén *m* no asfaltado"; **to be on the ~ of doing sth** estar a punto de hacer algo; **~ on** *vt fus* rayar en

verify ['vɛrɪfaɪ] *vt* comprobar, verificar

vermin ['vəːmɪn] *npl* (*animals*) alimañas

fpl; (*insects, fig*) parásitos *mpl*

vermouth ['vəːməθ] *n* vermut *m*

versatile ['vəːsətaɪl] *adj* (*person*) polifacético; (*machine, tool etc*) versátil

verse [vəːs] *n* poesía; (*stanza*) estrofa; (*in bible*) versículo

version ['vəːʃən] *n* versión *f*

versus ['vəːsəs] *prep* contra

vertebra ['vəːtɪbrə] (*pl* **~e**) *n* vértebra

vertical ['vəːtɪkl] *adj* vertical

verve [vəːv] *n* brío

very ['verɪ] *adv* muy ♦ *adj*: **the ~ book which** el mismo libro que; **the ~ last** el último de todos; **at the ~ least** al menos; **~ much** muchísimo

vessel ['vesl] *n* (*ship*) barco; (*container*) vasija; *see* **blood**

vest [vest] *n* (*BRIT*) camiseta; (*US: waistcoat*) chaleco; **~ed interests** *npl* (*COMM*) intereses *mpl* creados

vet [vet] *vt* fastidiar; (*candidate*) investigar ♦ *n abbr* (*BRIT*) = **veterinary surgeon**

veteran ['vetərn] *n* veterano

veterinary surgeon ['vetrɪnərɪ] (*US* **veterinarian**) *n* veterinario/a *m/f*

veto ['viːtəu] (*pl* **~es**) *n* veto ♦ *vt* prohibir, poner el veto a

vex [veks] *vt* fastidiar; **~ed** *adj* (*question*) controvertido

VHF *abbr* (= *very high frequency*) muy alta frecuencia

via ['vaɪə] *prep* por, por medio de

vibrant ['vaɪbrənt] *adj* (*lively*) animado; (*bright*) vivo; (*voice*) vibrante

vibrate [vaɪ'breɪt] *vi* vibrar

vicar ['vɪkə*] *n* párroco (de la Iglesia Anglicana); **~age** *n* parroquia

vice [vaɪs] *n* (*evil*) vicio; (*TECH*) torno de banco

vice- [vaɪs] *prefix* vice-; **~-chairman** *n* vicepresidente *m*

vice squad *n* brigada antivicio

vice versa ['vaɪsɪ'vəːsə] *adv* viceversa

vicinity [vɪ'sɪnɪtɪ] *n*: **in the ~ (of)** cercano (a)

vicious ['vɪʃəs] *adj* (*attack*) violento; (*words*) cruel; (*horse, dog*) resabido; **~**

circle *n* círculo vicioso

victim ['vɪktɪm] *n* víctima

victor ['vɪktə*] *n* vencedor(a) *m/f*

victory ['vɪktərɪ] *n* victoria

video ['vɪdɪəu] *cpd* video ♦ *n* (~ *film*) videofilm *m*; (*also*: ~ **cassette**) videocassette *f*; (*also*: ~ **cassette recorder**) magnetoscopio; ~ **game** *n* videojuego; ~ **tape** *n* cinta de vídeo

vie [vaɪ] *vi*: **to ~ (with sb for sth)** competir (con uno por algo)

Vienna [vɪ'enə] *n* Viena

Vietnam [vjet'næm] *n* Vietnam *m*; **~ese** [-nə'miːz] *n inv, adj* vietnamita *m/f*

view [vjuː] *n* vista; (*outlook*) perspectiva; (*opinion*) opinión *f*, criterio ♦ *vt* (*look at*) mirar; (*fig*) considerar; **on ~** (*in museum etc*) expuesto; **in full ~ (of)** en plena vista (de); **in ~ of the weather/the fact that** en vista del tiempo/del hecho de que; **in my ~** en mi opinión; **~er** *n* espectador(a) *m/f*; (*TV*) telespectador(a) *m/f*; **~finder** *n* visor *m* de imagen; **~point** *n* (*attitude*) punto de vista; (*place*) mirador *m*

vigour ['vɪgə*] (*US* **vigor**) *n* energía, vigor *m*

vile [vaɪl] *adj* vil, infame; (*smell*) asqueroso; (*temper*) endemoniado

villa ['vɪlə] *n* (*country house*) casa de campo; (*suburban house*) chalet *m*

village ['vɪlɪdʒ] *n* aldea; **~r** *n* aldeano/a

villain ['vɪlən] *n* (*scoundrel*) malvado/a; (*in novel*) malo; (*BRIT: criminal*) maleante *m/f*

vindicate ['vɪndɪkeɪt] *vt* vindicar, justificar

vindictive [vɪn'dɪktɪv] *adj* vengativo

vine [vaɪn] *n* vid *f*

vinegar ['vɪnɪgə*] *n* vinagre *m*

vineyard ['vɪnjɑːd] *n* viña, viñedo

vintage ['vɪntɪdʒ] *n* (*year*) vendimia, cosecha ♦ *cpd* de época; **~ wine** *n* vino añejo

vinyl ['vaɪnl] *n* vinilo

viola [vɪ'əulə] *n* (*MUS*) viola

violate ['vaɪəleɪt] *vt* violar

violence ['vaɪələns] *n* violencia

violent ['vaɪələnt] *adj* violento; (*intense*) intenso

violet ['vaɪələt] *adj* violado, violeta ♦ *n* (*plant*) violeta

violin [vaɪə'lɪn] *n* violín *m*; **~ist** *n* violinista *m/f*

VIP *n abbr* (= *very important person*) VIP *m*

virgin ['vɜːdʒɪn] *n* virgen *f*

Virgo ['vɜːgəu] *n* Virgo

virtually ['vɜːtjuəlɪ] *adv* prácticamente

virtual reality ['vɜːtjuəl-] *n* (*COMPUT*) mundo *or* realidad *f* virtual

virtue ['vɜːtjuː] *n* virtud *f*; (*advantage*) ventaja; **by ~ of** en virtud de

virtuous ['vɜːtjuəs] *adj* virtuoso

virus ['vaɪərəs] *n* (*also: COMPUT*) virus *m*

visa ['viːzə] *n* visado (*SP*), visa (*AM*)

visible ['vɪzəbl] *adj* visible

vision ['vɪʒən] *n* (*sight*) vista; (*foresight, in dream*) visión *f*

visit ['vɪzɪt] *n* visita ♦ *vt* (*person: US: also: ~ with*) visitar, hacer una visita a; (*place*) ir a, (ir a) conocer; **~ing hours** *npl* (*in hospital etc*) horas *fpl* de visita; **~or** *n* (*in museum*) visitante *m/f*; (*invited to house*) visita; (*tourist*) turista *m/f*

visor ['vaɪzə*] *n* visera

visual ['vɪzjuəl] *adj* visual; **~ aid** *n* medio visual; **~ display unit** *n* unidad *f* de presentación visual; **~ize** *vt* imaginarse

vital ['vaɪtl] *adj* (*essential*) esencial, imprescindible; (*dynamic*) dinámico; (*organ*) vital; **~ly** *adv*: **~ly important** de primera importancia; **~ statistics** *npl* (*fig*) medidas *fpl* vitales

vitamin ['vɪtəmɪn] *n* vitamina

vivacious [vɪ'veɪʃəs] *adj* vivaz, alegre

vivid ['vɪvɪd] *adj* (*account*) gráfico; (*light*) intenso; (*imagination, memory*) vivo; **~ly** *adv* gráficamente; (*remember*) como si fuera hoy

V-neck ['viːnɛk] *n* cuello de pico

vocabulary [vəu'kæbjulərɪ] *n* vocabulario

vocal ['vəukl] *adj* vocal; (*articulate*) elocuente; **~ cords** *npl* cuerdas *fpl* vocales

vocation [vəu'keɪʃən] *n* vocación *f*; **~al** *adj* profesional

vodka ['vɔdkə] *n* vodka *m*

vogue [vəug] *n*: **in ~** en boga, de moda

voice [vɔɪs] *n* voz *f* ♦ *vt* expresar

void [vɔɪd] *n* vacío; (*hole*) hueco ♦ *adj* (*invalid*) nulo, inválido; (*empty*): **~ of** carente *or* desprovisto de

volatile ['vɔlətaɪl] *adj* (*situation*) inestable; (*person*) voluble; (*liquid*) volátil

volcano [vɔl'keɪnəu] (*pl* **~es**) *n* volcán *m*

volition [və'lɪʃən] *n*: **of one's own ~** de su propia voluntad

volley ['vɔlɪ] *n* (*of gunfire*) descarga; (*of stones etc*) lluvia; (*fig*) torrente *m*; (*TENNIS etc*) volea; **~ball** *n* vol(e)ibol *m*

volt [vəult] *n* voltio; **~age** *n* voltaje *m*

volume ['vɔljuːm] *n* (*gen*) volumen *m*; (*book*) tomo

voluntary ['vɔləntərɪ] *adj* voluntario

volunteer [vɔlən'tɪə*] *n* voluntario/a ♦ *vt* (*information*) ofrecer ♦ *vi* ofrecerse (de voluntario); **to ~ to do** ofrecerse a hacer

vomit ['vɔmɪt] *n* vómito ♦ *vt, vi* vomitar

vote [vəut] *n* voto; (*votes cast*) votación *f*; (*right to ~*) derecho de votar; (*franchise*) sufragio ♦ *vt* (*chairman*) elegir; (*propose*): **to ~ that** proponer que ♦ *vi* votar, ir a votar; **~ of thanks** voto de gracias; **~r** *n* votante *m/f*; **voting** *n* votación *f*

vouch [vautʃ]: **to ~ for** *vt fus* garantizar, responder de

voucher ['vautʃə*] *n* (*for meal, petrol*) vale *m*

vow [vau] *n* voto ♦ *vt*: **to ~ to do/that** jurar hacer/que

vowel ['vauəl] *n* vocal *f*

voyage ['vɔɪdʒ] *n* viaje *m*

vulgar ['vʌlgə*] *adj* (*rude*) ordinario, grosero; (*in bad taste*) de mal gusto; **~ity** [-'gærɪtɪ] *n* grosería; mal gusto

vulnerable ['vʌlnərəbl] *adj* vulnerable

vulture ['vʌltʃə*] *n* buitre *m*

W, w

wad [wɒd] *n* bolita; (*of banknotes etc*) fajo

waddle ['wɒdl] *vi* anadear

wade [weɪd] *vi*: **to ~ through** (*water*) vadear; (*fig: book*) leer con dificultad; **wading pool** (*US*) *n* piscina para niños

wafer ['weɪfə*] *n* galleta, barquillo

waffle ['wɒfl] *n* (*CULIN*) gofre *m* ♦ *vi* dar el rollo

waft [wɒft] *vt* llevar por el aire ♦ *vi* flotar

wag [wæg] *vt* menear, agitar ♦ *vi* moverse, menearse

wage [weɪdʒ] *n* (*also*: **~s**) sueldo, salario ♦ *vt*: **to ~ war** hacer la guerra; **~ earner** *n* asalariado/a; **~ packet** *n* sobre *m* de paga

wager ['weɪdʒə*] *n* apuesta

wag(g)on ['wægən] *n* (*horse-drawn*) carro; (*BRIT: RAIL*) vagón *m*

wail [weɪl] *n* gemido ♦ *vi* gemir

waist [weɪst] *n* cintura, talle *m*; **~coat** (*BRIT*) *n* chaleco; **~line** *n* talle *m*

wait [weɪt] *n* (*interval*) pausa ♦ *vi* esperar; **to lie in ~ for** acechar a; **I can't ~ to** (*fig*) estoy deseando; **to ~ for** esperar (a); **~ behind** *vi* quedarse; **~ on** *vt fus* servir a; **~er** *n* camarero; **~ing** *n*: **"no ~ing"** (*BRIT: AUT*) "prohibido estacionarse"; **~ing list** *n* lista de espera; **~ing room** *n* sala de espera; **~ress** *n* camarera

waive [weɪv] *vt* suspender

wake [weɪk] (*pt* **woke** *or* **waked**, *pp* **woken** *or* **waked**) *vt* (*also*: **~ up**) despertar ♦ *vi* (*also*: **~ up**) despertarse ♦ *n* (*for dead person*) vela, velatorio; (*NAUT*) estela; **waken** *vt*, *vi* = **wake**

Wales [weɪlz] *n* País *m* de Gales; **the Prince of ~** el príncipe de Gales

walk [wɔːk] *n* (*stroll*) paseo; (*hike*) excursión *f* a pie, caminata; (*gait*) paso, andar *m*; (*in park etc*) paseo, alameda ♦ *vi* andar, caminar; (*for pleasure, exercise*) pasear ♦ *vt* (*distance*) recorrer a pie, andar; (*dog*) pasear; **10 minutes' ~**

from here a 10 minutos de aquí andando; **people from all ~s of life** gente de todas las esferas; **~ out** *vi* (*audience*) salir; (*workers*) declararse en huelga; **~ out on** (*inf*) *vt fus* abandonar; **~er** *n* (*person*) paseante *m/f*; **~ie-talkie** ['wɔːkɪ'tɔːkɪ] *n* walkie-talkie *m*; **~ing** *n* el andar; **~ing shoes** *npl* zapatos *mpl* para andar; **~ing stick** *n* bastón *m*; **W~man** ® *n* Walkman ® *m*; **~out** *n* huelga; **~over** (*inf*) *n*: **it was a ~over** fue pan comido; **~way** *n* paseo

wall [wɔːl] *n* pared *f*; (*exterior*) muro; (*city ~ etc*) muralla; **~ed** *adj* amurallado; (*garden*) con tapia

wallet ['wɒlɪt] *n* cartera (*SP*), billetera (*AM*)

wallflower ['wɔːlflaʊə*] *n* alhelí *m*; **to be a ~** (*fig*) comer pavo

wallow ['wɒləʊ] *vi* revolcarse

wallpaper ['wɔːlpeɪpə*] *n* papel *m* pintado ♦ *vt* empapelar

walnut ['wɔːlnʌt] *n* nuez *f*; (*tree*) nogal *m*

walrus ['wɔːlrəs] (*pl* ~ *or* **~es**) *n* morsa

waltz [wɔːlts] *n* vals *m* ♦ *vi* bailar el vals

wand [wɒnd] *n* (*also*: **magic ~**) varita (mágica)

wander ['wɒndə*] *vi* (*person*) vagar; deambular; (*thoughts*) divagar ♦ *vt* recorrer, vagar por

wane [weɪn] *vi* menguar

wangle ['wæŋgl] (*BRIT: inf*) *vt* agenciarse

want [wɒnt] *vt* querer, desear; (*need*) necesitar ♦ *n*: **for ~ of** por falta de; **~s** *npl* (*needs*) necesidades *fpl*; **to ~ to do** querer hacer; **to ~ sb to do sth** querer que uno haga algo; **~ed** *adj* (*criminal*) buscado; **"~ed"** (*in advertisements*) "se busca"; **~ing** *adj*: **to be found ~ing** no estar a la altura de las circunstancias

war [wɔː*] *n* guerra; **to make ~ (on)** (*also fig*) declarar la guerra (a)

ward [wɔːd] *n* (*in hospital*) sala; (*POL*) distrito electoral; (*LAW: child: also*: **~ of court**) pupilo/a; **~ off** *vt* (*blow*) desviar, parar; (*attack*) rechazar

warden ['wɔːdn] *n* (*BRIT: of institution*)

director(a) *m/f*; (*of park, game reserve*) guardián/ana *m/f*; (BRIT: *also*: **traffic ~**) guardia *m/f*

warder ['wɔːdə*] (BRIT) *n* guardián/ana *m/f*, carcelero/a

wardrobe ['wɔːdrəub] *n* armario, guardarropa, ropero (*esp AM*)

warehouse ['wɛəhaus] *n* almacén *m*, depósito

wares [wɛəz] *npl* mercancías *fpl*

warfare ['wɔːfɛə*] *n* guerra

warhead ['wɔːhed] *n* cabeza armada

warily ['wɛərɪlɪ] *adv* con cautela, cautelosamente

warm [wɔːm] *adj* caliente; (*thanks*) efusivo; (*clothes etc*) abrigado; (*welcome, day*) caluroso; **it's ~** hace calor; **I'm ~** tengo calor; **~ up** *vi* (*room*) calentarse; (*person*) entrar en calor; (*athlete*) hacer ejercicios de calentamiento ♦ *vt* calentar; **~-hearted** *adj* afectuoso; **~ly** *adv* afectuosamente; **~th** *n* calor *m*

warn [wɔːn] *vt* avisar, advertir; **~ing** *n* aviso, advertencia; **~ing light** *n* luz *f* de advertencia; **~ing triangle** *n* (AUT) triángulo señalizador

warp [wɔːp] *vi* (*wood*) combarse ♦ *vt* combar; (*mind*) pervertir

warrant ['wɔrnt] *n* autorización *f*; (LAW: *to arrest*) orden *f* de detención; (: *to search*) mandamiento de registro

warranty ['wɔrəntɪ] *n* garantía

warren ['wɔrən] *n* (*of rabbits*) madriguera; (*fig*) laberinto

warrior ['wɔrɪə*] *n* guerrero/a

Warsaw ['wɔːsɔː] *n* Varsovia

warship ['wɔːʃɪp] *n* buque *m* o barco de guerra

wart [wɔːt] *n* verruga

wartime ['wɔːtaɪm] *n*: **in ~** en tiempos de guerra, en la guerra

wary ['wɛərɪ] *adj* cauteloso

was [wɔz] *pt of* **be**

wash [wɔʃ] *vt* lavar ♦ *vi* lavarse; (*sea etc*): **to ~ against/over sth** llegar hasta/cubrir algo ♦ *n* (*clothes etc*) lavado; (*of ship*) estela; **to have a ~** lavarse; **~ away** *vt*

(*stain*) quitar lavando; (*subj: river etc*) llevarse; **~ off** *vi* quitarse (al lavar); **~ up** *vi* (BRIT) fregar los platos; (US) lavarse; **~able** *adj* lavable; **~basin** (US **~bowl**) *n* lavabo; **~ cloth** (US) *n* manopla; **~er** *n* (TECH) arandela; **~ing** *n* (*dirty*) ropa sucia; (*clean*) colada; **~ing machine** *n* lavadora; **~ing powder** (BRIT) *n* detergente *m* (en polvo)

Washington ['wɔʃɪŋtən] *n* Washington *m*

wash: ~ing-up (BRIT) *n* fregado, platos *mpl* (para fregar); **~ing-up liquid** (BRIT) *n* líquido lavavajillas; **~-out** (*inf*) *n* fracaso; **~room** (US) *n* servicios *mpl*

wasn't ['wɔznt] = **was not**

wasp [wɔsp] *n* avispa

wastage ['weɪstɪdʒ] *n* desgaste *m*; (*loss*) pérdida

waste [weɪst] *n* derroche *m*, despilfarro; (*of time*) pérdida; (*food*) sobras *fpl*; (*rubbish*) basura, desperdicios *mpl* ♦ *adj* (*material*) de desecho; (*left over*) sobrante; (*land*) baldío, descampado ♦ *vt* malgastar, derrochar; (*time*) perder; (*opportunity*) desperdiciar; **~s** *npl* (*area of land*) tierras *fpl* baldías; **~ away** *vi* consumirse; **~ disposal unit** (BRIT) *n* triturador *m* de basura; **~ful** *adj* derrochador(a); (*process*) antieconómico; **~ ground** (BRIT) *n* terreno baldío; **~paper basket** *n* papelera; **~ pipe** *n* tubo de desagüe

watch [wɔtʃ] *n* (*also*: **wrist ~**) reloj *m*; (MIL: *group of guards*) centinela *m*; (*act*) vigilancia; (NAUT: *spell of duty*) guardia ♦ *vt* (*look at*) mirar, observar; (: *match, programme*) ver; (*spy on, guard*) vigilar; (*be careful of*) cuidarse de, tener cuidado de ♦ *vi* ver, mirar; (*keep guard*) montar guardia; **~ out** *vi* cuidarse, tener cuidado; **~dog** *n* perro guardián; (*fig*) persona u organismo encargado de asegurarse de que las empresas actúan dentro de la legalidad; **~ful** *adj* vigilante, sobre aviso; **~maker** *n* relojero/a; **~man** (*irreg*) *n* see **night**; **~ strap** *n* pulsera (de reloj)

water ['wɔːtə*] n agua ♦ vt (plant) regar ♦ vi (eyes) llorar; (mouth) hacerse la boca agua; ~ **down** vt (milk etc) aguar; (fig: story) dulcificar, diluir; ~ **closet** n wáter m; ~**colour** n acuarela; ~**cress** n berro; ~**fall** n cascada, salto de agua; ~ **heater** n calentador m de agua; ~**ing can** n regadera; ~ **lily** n nenúfar m; ~**line** n (NAUT) línea de flotación; ~**logged** adj (ground) inundado; ~ **main** n cañería del agua; ~**melon** n sandía; ~**proof** adj impermeable; ~**shed** n (GEO) cuenca; (fig) momento crítico; ~**skiing** n esquí m acuático; ~**tight** adj hermético; ~**way** n vía fluvial or navegable; ~**works** n central f depuradora; ~**y** adj (coffee etc) aguado; (eyes) lloroso

watt [wɔt] n vatio

wave [weɪv] n (of hand) señal f con la mano; (on water) ola; (RADIO, in hair) onda; (fig) oleada ♦ vi agitar la mano; (flag etc) ondear ♦ vt (handkerchief, gun) agitar; ~**length** n longitud f de onda

waver ['weɪvə*] vi (voice, love etc) flaquear; (person) vacilar

wavy ['weɪvɪ] adj ondulado

wax [wæks] n cera ♦ vt encerar ♦ vi (moon) crecer; ~ **paper** (US) n papel m apergaminado; ~**works** n museo de cera ♦ npl figuras fpl de cera

way [weɪ] n camino; (distance) trayecto, recorrido; (direction) dirección f, sentido; (manner) modo, manera; (habit) costumbre f; **which ~? – this ~** ¿por dónde?, ¿en qué dirección? — por aquí; **on the ~** (en route) en (el) camino; **to be on one's ~** estar en camino; **to be in the ~** bloquear el camino; (fig) estorbar; **to go out of one's ~ to do sth** desvivirse por hacer algo; **under ~** en marcha; **to lose one's ~** extraviarse; **in a ~** en cierto modo or sentido; **no ~!** (inf) ¡de eso nada!; **by the ~** ... a propósito ...; **"~ in"** (BRIT) "entrada"; **"~ out"** (BRIT) "salida"; **the ~ back** el camino de vuelta; **"give ~"** (BRIT: AUT) "ceda el paso"

waylay [weɪ'leɪ] (irreg) vt salir al paso a

wayward ['weɪwəd] adj díscolo

W.C. n (BRIT) wáter m

we [wiː] pl pron nosotros/as

weak [wiːk] adj débil, flojo; (tea etc) claro; ~**en** vi debilitarse; (give way) ceder ♦ vt debilitar; ~**ling** n debilucho/a; (morally) persona de poco carácter; ~**ness** n debilidad f; (fault) punto débil; **to have a ~ness for** tener debilidad por

wealth [welθ] n riqueza; (of details) abundancia; ~**y** adj rico

wean [wiːn] vt destetar

weapon ['wepən] n arma

wear [weə*] (pt **wore**, pp **worn**) n (use) uso; (deterioration through use) desgaste m; (clothing): **sports/baby~** ropa de deportes/de niños ♦ vt (clothes) llevar; (shoes) calzar; (damage: through use) gastar, usar ♦ vi (last) durar; (rub through etc) desgastarse; **evening ~** ropa de etiqueta; ~ **away** vt gastar ♦ vi desgastarse; ~ **down** vt gastar; (strength) agotar; ~ **off** vi (pain etc) pasar, desaparecer; ~ **out** vt desgastar; (person, strength) agotar; ~ **and tear** n desgaste m

weary ['wɪərɪ] adj cansado; (dispirited) abatido ♦ vi: **to ~ of** cansarse de

weasel ['wiːzl] n (ZOOL) comadreja

weather ['weðə*] n tiempo ♦ vt (storm, crisis) hacer frente a; **under the ~** (fig: ill) indispuesto, pachucho; ~**-beaten** adj (skin) curtido; (building) deteriorado por la intemperie; ~**cock** n veleta; ~ **forecast** n boletín m meteorológico; ~**man** (irreg: inf) n hombre m del tiempo; ~ **vane** n = ~**cock**

weave [wiːv] (pt **wove**, pp **woven**) vt (cloth) tejer; (fig) entretejer; ~**r** n tejedor(a) m/f; **weaving** n tejeduría

web [web] n (of spider) telaraña; (on duck's foot) membrana; (network) red f

website ['websaɪt] n espacio Web

wed [wed] (pt, pp **wedded**) vt casar ♦ vi casarse

we'd [wiːd] = **we had**; **we would**

wedding ['wedɪŋ] n boda, casamiento;

silver / golden ~ (anniversary) bodas *fpl* de plata/de oro; **~ day** *n* día *m* de la boda; **~ dress** *n* traje *m* de novia; **~ present** *n* regalo de boda; **~ ring** *n* alianza

wedge [wedʒ] *n* (*of wood etc*) cuña; (*of cake*) trozo ♦ *vt* acuñar; (*push*) apretar

Wednesday ['wɛnzdɪ] *n* miércoles *m inv*

wee [wi:] (*Scottish*) *adj* pequeñito

weed [wi:d] *n* mala hierba, maleza ♦ *vt* escardar, desherbar; **~killer** *n* herbicida *m*; **~y** *adj* (*person*) mequetréfico

week [wi:k] *n* semana; **a ~ today/on Friday** de hoy/del viernes en ocho días; **~day** *n* día *m* laborable; **~end** *n* fin *m* de semana; **~ly** *adv* semanalmente, cada semana ♦ *adj* semanal ♦ *n* semanario

weep [wi:p] (*pt, pp* **wept**) *vi, vt* llorar; **~ing willow** *n* sauce *m* llorón

weigh [weɪ] *vt, vi* pesar; **to ~ anchor** levar anclas; **~ down** *vt* sobrecargar; (*fig: with worry*) agobiar; **~ up** *vt* sopesar

weight [weɪt] *n* peso; (*metal ~*) pesa; **to lose / put on ~** adelgazar/engordar; **~ing** *n* (*allowance*): **(London) ~ing** dietas (*por residir en Londres*); **~lifter** *n* levantador *m* de pesas; **~y** *adj* pesado; (*matters*) de relevancia *or* peso

weir [wɪə*] *n* presa

weird [wɪəd] *adj* raro, extraño

welcome ['wɛlkəm] *adj* bienvenido ♦ *n* bienvenida ♦ *vt* dar la bienvenida a; (*be glad of*) alegrarse de; **thank you — you're ~** gracias — de nada

weld [wɛld] *n* soldadura ♦ *vt* soldar

welfare ['wɛlfɛə*] *n* bienestar *m*; (*social aid*) asistencia social; **~ state** *n* estado del bienestar

well [wɛl] *n* fuente *f*, pozo ♦ *adv* bien ♦ *adj*: **to be ~** estar bien (de salud) ♦ *excl* ¡vaya!, ¡bueno!; **as ~** también; **as ~ as** además de; **~ done!** ¡bien hecho!; **get ~ soon!** ¡que te mejores pronto!; **to do ~** (*business*) ir bien; (*person*) tener éxito; **~ up** *vi* (*tears*) saltar

we'll [wi:l] = **we will; we shall**

well: ~-behaved *adj* bueno; **~-being** *n*

bienestar *m*; **~-built** *adj* (*person*) fornido; **~-deserved** *adj* merecido; **~-dressed** *adj* bien vestido; **~-groomed** *adj* de buena presencia; **~-heeled** (*inf*) *adj* (*wealthy*) rico

wellingtons ['wɛlɪŋtənz] *npl* (*also:* **wellington boots**) botas *fpl* de goma

well: ~-known *adj* (*person*) conocido; **~-mannered** *adj* educado; **~-meaning** *adj* bienintencionado; **~-off** *adj* acomodado; **~-read** *adj* leído; **~-to-do** *adj* acomodado; **~-wisher** *n* admirador(a) *m/f*

Welsh [wɛlʃ] *adj* galés/esa ♦ *n* (*LING*) galés *m*; **the ~** *npl* los galeses; **~man** (*irreg*) *n* galés *m*; **~ rarebit** *n* pan *m* con queso tostado; **~woman** (*irreg*) *n* galesa

went [wɛnt] *pt of* **go**

wept [wɛpt] *pt, pp of* **weep**

were [wə:*] *pt of* **be**

we're [wɪə*] = **we are**

weren't [wə:nt] = **were not**

west [wɛst] *n* oeste *m* ♦ *adj* occidental, del oeste ♦ *adv* al *or* hacia el oeste; **the W~** el Oeste, el Occidente; **W~ Country** (*BRIT*) *n*: **the W~ Country** el suroeste de Inglaterra; **~erly** *adj* occidental; (*wind*) del oeste; **~ern** *adj* occidental ♦ *n* (*CINEMA*) película del oeste; **W~ Germany** *n* Alemania Occidental; **W~ Indian** *adj, n* antillano/a *m/f*; **W~ Indies** *npl* Antillas *fpl*; **~ward(s)** *adv* hacia el oeste

wet [wɛt] *adj* (*damp*) húmedo; (*~ through*) mojado; (*rainy*) lluvioso ♦ *n* (*BRIT*) (*POL*) conservador(a) *m/f* moderado/a; **to get ~** mojarse; **"~ paint"** "recién pintado"; **~suit** *n* traje *m* térmico

we've [wi:v] = **we have**

whack [wæk] *vt* dar un buen golpe a

whale [weɪl] *n* (*ZOOL*) ballena

wharf [wɔ:f] (*pl* **wharves**) *n* muelle *m*

KEYWORD

what [wɔt] *adj* **1** (*in direct/indirect questions*) qué; **~ size is he?** ¿qué talla usa?; **~ colour/shape is it?** ¿de qué

color/forma es?
2 (*in exclamations*): ~ **a mess!** ¡qué
desastre!; ~ **a fool I am!** ¡qué tonto soy!
♦ *pron* 1 (*interrogative*) qué; ~ **are you
doing?** ¿qué haces *or* estás haciendo?; ~
is happening? ¿qué pasa *or* está
pasando?; ~ **is it called?** ¿cómo se
llama?; ~ **about me?** ¿y yo qué?; ~ **about
doing ...?** ¿qué tal si hacemos ...?
2 (*relative*) lo que; **I saw ~ you did/was on
the table** vi lo que hiciste/había en la mesa
♦ *excl* (*disbelieving*) ¡cómo!; **~, no coffee!**
¡que no hay café!

whatever [wɔt'ɛvə*] *adj*: ~ **book you
choose** cualquier libro que elijas ♦ *pron*:
do ~ is necessary haga lo que sea
necesario; ~ **happens** pase lo que pase;
no reason ~ ninguna razón sea la que
sea; **nothing ~** nada en absoluto
whatsoever [wɔtsəu'ɛvə*] *adj* = **whatever**
wheat [wiːt] *n* trigo
wheedle ['wiːdl] *vt*: **to ~ sb into doing
sth** engatusar a uno para que haga algo;
to ~ sth out of sb sonsacar algo a uno
wheel [wiːl] *n* rueda; (*AUT: also*: **steering
~**) volante *m*; (*NAUT*) timón *m* ♦ *vt* (*pram
etc*) empujar ♦ *vi* (*also*: ~ **round**) dar la
vuelta, girar; **~barrow** *n* carretilla;
~chair *n* silla de ruedas; ~ **clamp** *n*
(*AUT*) cepo
wheeze [wiːz] *vi* resollar

when [wɛn] *adv* cuando; ~ **did it happen?**
¿cuándo ocurrió?; **I know ~ it happened**
sé cuándo ocurrió
♦ *conj* 1 (*at, during, after the time that*)
cuando; **be careful ~ you cross the road**
ten cuidado al cruzar la calle; **that was ~
I needed you** fue entonces que te
necesité
2 (*on, at which*): **on the day ~ I met him**
el día en qué le conocí
3 (*whereas*) cuando

whenever [wɛn'ɛvə*] *conj* cuando; (*every
time that*) cada vez que ♦ *adv* cuando
sea
where [wɛə*] *adv* dónde ♦ *conj* donde;
this is ~ aquí es donde; **~abouts** *adv*
dónde ♦ *n*: **nobody knows his ~abouts**
nadie conoce su paradero; **~as** *conj* visto
que, mientras; **~by** *pron* por lo cual;
wherever [-'ɛvə*] *conj* dondequiera que;
(*interrogative*) dónde; **~withal** *n* recursos
mpl
whether ['wɛðə*] *conj* si; **I don't know ~
to accept or not** no sé si aceptar o no; ~
you go or not vayas o no vayas

which [wɪtʃ] *adj* 1 (*interrogative: direct,
indirect*) qué; ~ **picture(s) do you want?**
¿qué cuadro(s) quieres?; ~ **one?** ¿cuál?
2: **in ~ case** en cuyo caso; **we got there
at 8 pm, by ~ time the cinema was full**
llegamos allí a las 8, cuando el cine
estaba lleno
♦ *pron* 1 (*interrogative*) cual; **I don't mind
~** el/la que sea
2 (*relative: replacing noun*) que;
(: *replacing clause*) lo que; (: *after
preposition*) (el/la) que *etc*, el/la cual *etc*;
the apple ~ you ate/~ is on the table la
manzana que comiste/que está en la
mesa; **the chair on ~ you are sitting** la
silla en la que estás sentado; **he said he
knew, ~ is true/I feared** dijo que lo
sabía, lo cual *or* lo que es cierto/me temía

whichever [wɪtʃ'ɛvə*] *adj*: **take ~ book
you prefer** coja (SP) el libro que prefiera;
~ **book you take** cualquier libro que coja
while [waɪl] *n* rato, momento ♦ *conj*
mientras; (*although*) aunque; **for a ~**
durante algún tiempo; ~ **away** *vt* pasar
whim [wɪm] *n* capricho
whimper ['wɪmpə*] *n* sollozo ♦ *vi*
lloriquear
whimsical ['wɪmzɪkl] *adj* (*person*)
caprichoso; (*look*) juguetón/ona
whine [waɪn] *n* (*of pain*) gemido; (*of*

engine) zumbido; (*of siren*) aullido ♦ *vi*
gemir; zumbar; (*fig: complain*) gimotear
whip [wɪp] *n* látigo; (*POL: person*)
*encargado de la disciplina partidaria en
el parlamento* ♦ *vt* azotar; (*CULIN*) batir;
(*move quickly*): **to ~ sth out/off** sacar/
quitar algo de un tirón; **~ped cream** *n*
nata *or* crema montada; **~-round** (*BRIT*)
n colecta
whirl [wɜːl] *vt* hacer girar, dar vueltas a
♦ *vi* girar, dar vueltas; (*leaves etc*)
arremolinarse; **~pool** *n* remolino; **~wind**
n torbellino
whirr [wɜː*] *vi* zumbar
whisk [wɪsk] *n* (*CULIN*) batidor *m* ♦ *vt*
(*CULIN*) batir; **to ~ sb away** *or* **off** llevar
volando a uno
whiskers ['wɪskəz] *npl* (*of animal*) bigotes
mpl; (*of man*) patillas *fpl*
whiskey ['wɪskɪ] (*US, Ireland*) *n* = **whisky**
whisky ['wɪskɪ] *n* whisky *m*
whisper ['wɪspə*] *n* susurro ♦ *vi*, *vt*
susurrar
whistle ['wɪsl] *n* (*sound*) silbido; (*object*)
silbato ♦ *vi* silbar
white [waɪt] *adj* blanco; (*pale*) pálido ♦ *n*
blanco; (*of egg*) clara; **~ coffee** (*BRIT*) *n*
café *m* con leche; **~-collar worker** *n*
oficinista *m/f*; **~ elephant** *n* (*fig*) maula;
~ lie *n* mentirilla; **~ paper** *n* (*POL*) libro
rojo; **~wash** *n* (*paint*) jalbegue *m*, cal *f*
♦ *vt* (*also fig*) blanquear
whiting ['waɪtɪŋ] *n inv* (*fish*) pescadilla
Whitsun ['wɪtsn] *n* pentecostés *m*
whizz [wɪz] *vi*: **to ~ past** *or* **by** pasar a
toda velocidad; **~ kid** (*inf*) *n* prodigio

who [huː] *pron* 1 (*interrogative*) quién; **~ is
it?, ~'s there?** ¿quién es?; **~ are you
looking for?** ¿a quién buscas?; **I told her
~ I was** le dije quién era yo
2 (*relative*) que; **the man/woman ~
spoke to me** el hombre/la mujer que
habló conmigo; **those ~ can swim** los
que saben *or* sepan nadar

whodun(n)it [huːˈdʌnɪt] (*inf*) *n* novela
policíaca
whoever [huːˈɛvə*] *pron*: **~ finds it**
cualquiera *or* quienquiera que lo
encuentre; **ask ~ you like** pregunta a
quien quieras; **~ he marries** no importa
con quién se case
whole [həul] *adj* (*entire*) todo, entero; (*not
broken*) intacto ♦ *n* todo; (*all*): **the ~ of
the town** toda la ciudad, la ciudad entera
♦ *n* (*total*) total *m*; (*sum*) conjunto; **on
the ~, as a ~** en general; **~food(s)** *n(pl)*
alimento(s) *m(pl)* integral(es); **~hearted**
adj sincero, cordial; **~meal** *adj* integral;
~sale *n* venta al por mayor ♦ *adj* al por
mayor; (*fig: destruction*) sistemático;
~saler *n* mayorista *m/f*; **~some** *adj*
sano; **~wheat** *adj* = **~meal**; **wholly** *adv*
totalmente, enteramente

whom [huːm] *pron* 1 (*interrogative*): **~ did
you see?** ¿a quién viste?; **to ~ did you
give it?** ¿a quién se lo diste?; **tell me
from ~ you received it** dígame de quién
lo recibió
2 (*relative*) que; **to ~** a quien(es); **of ~** de
quien(es), del/de la que *etc*; **the man ~ I
saw/to ~ I wrote** el hombre que vi/a
quien escribí; **the lady about/with ~ I
was talking** la señora de (la) que/con
quien *or* (la) que hablaba

whooping cough ['huːpɪŋ-] *n* tos *f*
ferina
whore [hɔː*] (*inf: pej*) *n* puta

whose [huːz] *adj* 1 (*possessive:
interrogative*): **~ book is this?, ~ is this
book?** ¿de quién es este libro?; **~ pencil
have you taken?** ¿de quién es el lápiz
que has cogido?; **~ daughter are you?**
¿de quién eres hija?
2 (*possessive: relative*) cuyo/a, *pl* cuyos/as;
the man ~ son you rescued el hombre
cuyo hijo rescataste; **those ~ passports I**

have aquellas personas cuyos pasaportes tengo; **the woman ~ car was stolen** la mujer a quien le robaron el coche ♦ *pron* de quién; **~ is this?** ¿de quién es esto?; **I know ~ it is** sé de quién es

why [waɪ] *adv* por qué; **~ not?** ¿por qué no?; **~ not do it now?** ¿por qué no lo haces (*or* hacemos *etc*) ahora?
♦ *conj*: **I wonder ~ he said that** me pregunto por qué dijo eso; **that's not ~ I'm here** no es por eso (por lo) que estoy aquí; **the reason ~** la razón por la que
♦ *excl* (*expressing surprise, shock, annoyance*) ¡hombre!, ¡vaya! (*explaining*): **~, it's you!** ¡hombre, eres tú!; **~, that's impossible** ¡pero sí eso es imposible!

wicked ['wɪkɪd] *adj* malvado, cruel
wicket ['wɪkɪt] *n* (CRICKET: *stumps*) palos *mpl*; (: *grass area*) terreno de juego
wide [waɪd] *adj* ancho; (*area, knowledge*) vasto, grande; (*choice*) amplio ♦ *adv*: **to open ~** abrir de par en par; **to shoot ~** errar el tiro; **~-angle lens** *n* objetivo de gran angular; **~-awake** *adj* bien despierto; **~ly** *adv* (*travelled*) mucho; (*spaced*) muy; **it is ~ly believed/known that ...** mucha gente piensa/sabe que ...; **~n** *vt* ensanchar; (*experience*) ampliar ♦ *vi* ensancharse; **~ open** *adj* abierto de par en par; **~spread** *adj* extendido, general
widow ['wɪdəu] *n* viuda; **~ed** *adj* viudo; **~er** *n* viudo
width [wɪdθ] *n* anchura; (*of cloth*) ancho
wield [wiːld] *vt* (*sword*) blandir; (*power*) ejercer
wife [waɪf] (*pl* **wives**) *n* mujer *f*, esposa
wig [wɪg] *n* peluca
wiggle ['wɪgl] *vt* menear
wild [waɪld] *adj* (*animal*) salvaje; (*plant*) silvestre; (*person*) furioso, violento; (*idea*) descabellado; (*rough*: *sea*) bravo; (: *land*) agreste; (: *weather*) muy revuelto; **~s** *npl*

regiones *fpl* salvajes, tierras *fpl* vírgenes; **~erness** ['wɪldənɪs] *n* desierto; **~life** *n* fauna; **~ly** *adv* (*behave*) locamente; (*lash out*) a diestro y siniestro; (*guess*) a lo loco; (*happy*) a más no poder
wilful ['wɪlful] (US **willful**) *adj* (*action*) deliberado; (*obstinate*) testarudo

will [wɪl] *aux vb* **1** (*forming future tense*): **I ~ finish it tomorrow** lo terminaré *or* voy a terminar mañana; **I ~ have finished it by tomorrow** lo habré terminado para mañana; **~ you do it? - yes I ~/no I won't** ¿lo harás? — sí/no
2 (*in conjectures, predictions*): **he ~** *or* **he'll be there by now** ya habrá *or* debe (de) haber llegado; **that ~ be the postman** será *or* debe ser el cartero
3 (*in commands, requests, offers*): **~ you be quiet!** ¿quieres callarte?; **~ you help me?** ¿quieres ayudarme?; **~ you have a cup of tea?** ¿te apetece un té?; **I won't put up with it!** ¡no lo soporto!
♦ *vt* (*pt, pp* **willed**): **to ~ sb to do sth** desear que alguien haga algo; **he ~ed himself to go on** con gran fuerza de voluntad, continuó
♦ *n* voluntad *f*; (*testament*) testamento

willing ['wɪlɪŋ] *adj* (*with goodwill*) de buena voluntad; (*enthusiastic*) entusiasta; **he's ~ to do it** está dispuesto a hacerlo; **~ly** *adv* con mucho gusto; **~ness** *n* buena voluntad
willow ['wɪləu] *n* sauce *m*
willpower ['wɪlpauə*] *n* fuerza de voluntad
willy-nilly [wɪlɪ'nɪlɪ] *adv* quiérase o no
wilt [wɪlt] *vi* marchitarse
win [wɪn] (*pt, pp* **won**) *n* victoria, triunfo
♦ *vt* ganar; (*obtain*) conseguir, lograr ♦ *vi* ganar; **~ over** *vt* convencer a; **~ round** (BRIT) *vt* = **~ over**
wince [wɪns] *vi* encogerse
winch [wɪntʃ] *n* torno
wind[1] [wɪnd] *n* viento; (MED) gases *mpl*

♦ *vt* (*take breath away from*) dejar sin aliento a

wind² [waɪnd] (*pt, pp* **wound**) *vt* enrollar; (*wrap*) envolver; (*clock, toy*) dar cuerda a ♦ *vi* (*road, river*) serpentear; ~ **up** *vt* (*clock*) dar cuerda a; (*debate, meeting*) concluir, terminar

windfall ['wɪndfɔːl] *n* golpe *m* de suerte

winding ['waɪndɪŋ] *adj* (*road*) tortuoso; (*staircase*) de caracol

wind instrument [wɪnd-] *n* (*MUS*) instrumento de viento

windmill ['wɪndmɪl] *n* molino de viento

window ['wɪndəu] *n* ventana; (*in car, train*) ventanilla; (*in shop etc*) escaparate *m* (*SP*), vitrina (*AM*); ~ **box** *n* jardinera de ventana; ~ **cleaner** *n* (*person*) limpiador *m* de cristales; ~ **ledge** *n* alféizar *m*, repisa; ~ **pane** *n* cristal *m*; ~~**shopping** *n*: **to go** ~~**shopping**, ir de escaparates; ~**sill** *n* alféizar *m*, repisa

windpipe ['wɪndpaɪp] *n* tráquea

wind power *n* energía eólica

windscreen ['wɪndskriːn] (*US* **windshield**) *n* parabrisas *m inv*; ~ **washer** *n* lavaparabrisas *m inv*; ~ **wiper** *n* limpiaparabrisas *m inv*

windswept ['wɪndswept] *adj* azotado por el viento

windy ['wɪndɪ] *adj* de mucho viento; **it's** ~ hace viento

wine [waɪn] *n* vino; ~ **bar** *n* enoteca; ~ **cellar** *n* bodega; ~ **glass** *n* copa (para vino); ~ **list** *n* lista de vinos; ~ **waiter** *n* escanciador *m*

wing [wɪŋ] *n* ala; (*AUT*) aleta; ~**s** *npl* (*THEATRE*) bastidores *mpl*; ~**er** *n* (*SPORT*) extremo

wink [wɪŋk] *n* guiño, pestañeo ♦ *vi* guiñar, pestañear

winner ['wɪnə*] *n* ganador(a) *m/f*

winning ['wɪnɪŋ] *adj* (*team*) ganador(a); (*goal*) decisivo; (*smile*) encantador(a); ~**s** *npl* ganancias *fpl*

winter ['wɪntə*] *n* invierno ♦ *vi* invernar; **wintry** ['wɪntrɪ] *adj* invernal

wipe [waɪp] *n*: **to give sth a** ~ pasar un

trapo sobre algo ♦ *vt* limpiar; (*tape*) borrar; ~ **off** *vt* limpiar con un trapo; (*remove*) quitar; ~ **out** *vt* (*debt*) liquidar; (*memory*) borrar; (*destroy*) destruir; ~ **up** *vt* limpiar

wire ['waɪə*] *n* alambre *m*; (*ELEC*) cable *m* (eléctrico); (*TEL*) telegrama *m* ♦ *vt* (*house*) poner la instalación eléctrica en; (*also*: ~ **up**) conectar; (*person: telegram*) telegrafiar

wireless ['waɪəlɪs] (*BRIT*) *n* radio *f*

wiring ['waɪərɪŋ] *n* instalación *f* eléctrica

wiry ['waɪərɪ] *adj* (*person*) enjuto y fuerte; (*hair*) crespo

wisdom ['wɪzdəm] *n* sabiduría, saber *m*; (*good sense*) cordura; ~ **tooth** *n* muela del juicio

wise [waɪz] *adj* sabio; (*sensible*) juicioso

...wise [waɪz] *suffix*: **time~** en cuanto a *or* respecto al tiempo

wish [wɪʃ] *n* deseo ♦ *vt* querer; **best ~es** (*on birthday etc*) felicidades *fpl*; **with best ~es** (*in letter*) saludos *mpl*, recuerdos *mpl*; **to ~ sb goodbye** despedirse de uno; **he ~ed me well** me deseó mucha suerte; **to ~ to do/sb to do sth** querer hacer/ que alguien haga algo; **to ~ for** desear; ~**ful** *adj*: **it's ~ful thinking** eso sería soñar

wisp [wɪsp] *n* mechón *m*; (*of smoke*) voluta

wistful ['wɪstful] *adj* pensativo

wit [wɪt] *n* ingenio, gracia; (*also*: ~**s**) inteligencia; (*person*) chistoso/a

witch [wɪtʃ] *n* bruja; ~**craft** *n* brujería; ~~**hunt** *n* (*fig*) caza de brujas

---

KEYWORD

---

with [wɪð, wɪθ] *prep* **1** (*accompanying, in the company of*) con (con+mí, ti, sí = conmigo, contigo, consigo); **I was** ~ **him** estaba con él; **we stayed** ~ **friends** nos quedamos en casa de unos amigos; **I'm (not)** ~ **you** (*understand*) (no) te entiendo; **to be** ~ **it** (*inf: person: up-to-date*) estar al tanto; (*: alert*) ser despabilado

2 (*descriptive, indicating manner etc*) con; de; **a room** ~ **a view** una habitación con vistas; **the man** ~ **the grey hat/blue eyes** el hombre del sombrero gris/de los ojos azules; **red ~ anger** rojo de ira; **to shake ~ fear** temblar de miedo; **to fill sth ~ water** llenar algo de agua

withdraw [wɪθ'drɔ:] (*irreg*) *vt* retirar, sacar ♦ *vi* retirarse; **to ~ money (from the bank)** retirar fondos (del banco); **~al** *n* retirada; (*of money*) reintegro; **~al symptoms** *npl* (*MED*) síndrome *m* de abstinencia; **~n** *adj* (*person*) reservado, introvertido

wither ['wɪðə*] *vi* marchitarse

withhold [wɪθ'həuld] (*irreg*) *vt* (*money*) retener; (*decision*) aplazar; (*permission*) negar; (*information*) ocultar

within [wɪð'ɪn] *prep* dentro de ♦ *adv* dentro; **~ reach (of)** al alcance (de); **~ sight (of)** a la vista (de); **~ the week** antes de acabar la semana; **~ a mile (of)** a menos de una milla (de)

without [wɪð'aut] *prep* sin; **to go ~ sth** pasar sin algo

withstand [wɪθ'stænd] (*irreg*) *vt* resistir a

witness ['wɪtnɪs] *n* testigo *m/f* ♦ *vt* (*event*) presenciar; (*document*) atestiguar la veracidad de; **to bear ~ to** (*fig*) ser testimonio de; **~ box** *n* tribuna de los testigos; **~ stand** (*US*) *n* = **~ box**

witty ['wɪtɪ] *adj* ingenioso

wives [waɪvz] *npl of* **wife**

wk *abbr* = **week**

wobble ['wɔbl] *vi* temblar; (*chair*) cojear

woe [wəu] *n* desgracia

woke [wəuk] *pt of* **wake**

woken ['wəukən] *pp of* **wake**

wolf [wulf] *n* lobo; **wolves** [wulvz] *npl of* **wolf**

woman ['wumən] (*pl* **women**) *n* mujer *f*; **~ doctor** *n* médica; **women's lib** (*inf: pej*) *n* liberación *f* de la mujer; **~ly** *adj* femenino

womb [wu:m] *n* matriz *f*, útero

women ['wɪmɪn] *npl of* **woman**

won [wʌn] *pt, pp of* **win**

wonder ['wʌndə*] *n* maravilla, prodigio; (*feeling*) asombro ♦ *vi*: **to ~ whether/why** preguntarse si/por qué; **to ~ at**

asombrarse de; **to ~ about** pensar sobre *or* en; **it's no ~ (that)** no es de extrañarse (que +*subjun*); **~ful** *adj* maravilloso

won't [wəunt] = **will not**

wood [wud] *n* (*timber*) madera; (*forest*) bosque *m*; **~ carving** *n* (*act*) tallado en madera; (*object*) talla en madera; **~ed** *adj* arbolado; **~en** *adj* de madera; (*fig*) inexpresivo; **~pecker** *n* pájaro carpintero; **~wind** *n* (*MUS*) instrumentos *mpl* de viento de madera; **~work** *n* carpintería; **~worm** *n* carcoma

wool [wul] *n* lana; **to pull the ~ over sb's eyes** (*fig*) engatusar a uno; **~en** (*US*) *adj* = **~len**; **~len** *adj* de lana; **~lens** *npl* géneros *mpl* de lana; **~ly** *adj* lanudo, de lana; (*fig: ideas*) confuso; **~y** (*US*) *adj* = **~ly**

word [wə:d] *n* palabra; (*news*) noticia; (*promise*) palabra (de honor) ♦ *vt* redactar; **in other ~s** en otras palabras; **to break/keep one's ~** faltar a la palabra/cumplir la promesa; **to have ~s with sb** reñir con uno; **~ing** *n* redacción *f*; **~ processing** *n* proceso de textos; **~ processor** *n* procesador *m* de textos

wore [wɔ:*] *pt of* **wear**

work [wə:k] *n* trabajo; (*job*) empleo, trabajo; (*ART, LITERATURE*) obra ♦ *vi* trabajar; (*mechanism*) funcionar, marchar; (*medicine*) ser eficaz, surtir efecto ♦ *vt* (*shape*) trabajar; (*stone etc*) tallar; (*mine etc*) explotar; (*machine*) manejar, hacer funcionar; **~s** *n* (*BRIT: factory*) fábrica ♦ *npl* (*of clock, machine*) mecanismo; **to be out of ~** estar parado, no tener trabajo; **to ~ loose** (*part*) desprenderse; (*knot*) aflojarse; **~ on** *vt fus* trabajar en, dedicarse a; (*principle*) basarse en; **~ out** *vi* (*plans etc*) salir bien, funcionar ♦ *vt* (*problem*) resolver; (*plan*) elaborar; **it ~s out at £100** suma 100 libras; **~ up** *vt*: **to get ~ed up** excitarse; **~able** *adj* (*solution*) práctico, factible; **~aholic** [wə:kə'hɔlɪk] *n* trabajador(a) obsesivo/a *m/f*; **~er** *n* trabajador(a) *m/f*, obrero/a; **~force** *n* mano *f* de obra; **~ing class** *n* clase *f* obrera; **~ing-class** *adj* obrero; **~ing order** *n*: **in ~ing order** en funcionamiento; **~man** (*irreg*) *n* obrero; **~manship** *n* habilidad *f*, trabajo; **~sheet** *n* hoja de trabajo; **~shop** *n* taller *m*; **~ station** *n* puesto *or* estación *f* de trabajo; **~-to-rule** (*BRIT*) *n* huelga de celo

world [wə:ld] *n* mundo ♦ *cpd* (*champion*) del mundo; (*power, war*) mundial; **to think the ~ of sb** (*fig*) tener un concepto muy alto de uno; **~ly** *adj* mundano; **~-wide** *adj* mundial, universal; **W~-Wide Web** *n*: **the W~-Wide Web** el World Wide Web

worm [wə:m] *n* (*also:* **earth~**) lombriz *f*

worn [wɔ:n] *pp of* **wear** ♦ *adj* usado; **~-out** *adj* (*object*) gastado; (*person*) rendido, agotado

worried ['wʌrɪd] *adj* preocupado

worry ['wʌrɪ] *n* preocupación *f* ♦ *vt* preocupar, inquietar ♦ *vi* preocuparse; **~ing** *adj* inquietante

worse [wə:s] *adj, adv* peor ♦ *n* lo peor; **a change for the ~** un empeoramiento; **~n** *vt, vi* empeorar; **~ off** *adj* (*financially*): **to be ~ off** tener menos dinero; (*fig*): **you'll be ~ off this way** de esta forma estarás peor que nunca

worship ['wə:ʃɪp] *n* adoración *f* ♦ *vt* adorar; **Your W~** (*BRIT: to mayor*) señor alcalde; (*: to judge*) señor juez

worst [wə:st] *adj, adv* peor ♦ *n* lo peor; **at ~** en lo peor de los casos

worth [wə:θ] *n* valor *m* ♦ *adj*: **to be ~** valer; (*fig*) ♦ *it's ~ it* vale *or* merece la pena; **to be ~ one's while (to do)** merecer la pena (hacer); **~less** *adj* sin valor; (*useless*) inútil; **~while** *adj* (*activity*) que merece la pena; (*cause*) loable

worthy ['wə:ðɪ] *adj* respetable; (*motive*) honesto; **~ of** digno de

───────────────
| KEYWORD |
───────────────

would [wud] *aux vb* **1** (*conditional tense*): **if you asked him he ~ do it** si se lo pidieras, lo haría; **if you had asked him he ~ have done it** si se lo hubieras pedido, lo habría *or* hubiera hecho
2 (*in offers, invitations, requests*): **~ you like a biscuit?** ¿quieres una galleta?; (*formal*) ¿querría una galleta?; **~ you ask him to come in?** ¿quiere hacerle pasar?; **~ you open the window please?** ¿quiere *or* podría abrir la ventana, por favor?
3 (*in indirect speech*): **I said I ~ do it** dije que lo haría
4 (*emphatic*): **it WOULD have to snow today!** ¡tenía que nevar precisamente hoy!
5 (*insistence*): **she ~n't behave** no quiso comportarse bien
6 (*conjecture*): **it ~ have been midnight** sería medianoche; **it ~ seem so** parece ser que sí
7 (*indicating habit*): **he ~ go there on Mondays** iba allí los lunes

───────────────

would-be (*pej*) *adj* presunto

wouldn't ['wudnt] = **would not**

wound¹ [wu:nd] *n* herida ♦ *vt* herir

wound² [waund] *pt, pp of* **wind**

wove [wəuv] *pt of* **weave**

woven ['wəuvən] *pp of* **weave**

wrap [ræp] *vt* (*also:* **~ up**) envolver; **~per** *n* (*on chocolate*) papel *m*; (*BRIT: of book*) sobrecubierta; **~ping paper** *n* papel *m* de envolver; (*fancy*) papel *m* de regalo

wreak [ri:k] *vt*: **to ~ havoc (on)** hacer estragos (en); **to ~ vengeance (on)** vengarse (de)

wreath [ri:θ, *pl* ri:ðz] *n* (*funeral ~*) corona

wreck [rek] *n* (*ship: destruction*) naufragio; (*: remains*) restos *mpl* del barco; (*pej: person*) ruina ♦ *vt* (*car etc*) destrozar; (*chances*) arruinar; **~age** *n* restos *mpl*; (*of building*) escombros *mpl*

wren [ren] *n* (*ZOOL*) reyezuelo

wrench [rentʃ] *n* (*TECH*) llave *f* inglesa; (*tug*) tirón *m*; (*fig*) dolor *m* ♦ *vt* arrancar; **to ~ sth from sb** arrebatar algo violentamente a uno

wrestle ['resl] *vi*: **to ~ (with sb)** luchar (con *or* contra uno); **~r** *n* luchador(a) *m/f*

(de lucha libre); **wrestling** n lucha libre
wretched ['rɛtʃɪd] *adj* miserable
wriggle ['rɪgl] *vi* (*also:* ~ **about**) menearse, retorcerse
wring [rɪŋ] (*pt, pp* **wrung**) *vt* retorcer; (*wet clothes*) escurrir; (*fig*): **to ~ sth out of sb** sacar algo por la fuerza a uno
wrinkle ['rɪŋkl] *n* arruga ♦ *vt* arrugar ♦ *vi* arrugarse
wrist [rɪst] *n* muñeca; **~watch** *n* reloj *m* de pulsera
writ [rɪt] *n* mandato judicial
write [raɪt] (*pt* **wrote**, *pp* **written**) *vt* escribir; (*cheque*) extender ♦ *vi* escribir; ~ **down** *vt* escribir; (*note*) apuntar; ~ **off** *vt* (*debt*) borrar (como incobrable); (*fig*) desechar por inútil; ~ **out** *vt* escribir; ~ **up** *vt* redactar; **~-off** *n* siniestro total; **~r** *n* escritor(a) *m/f*
writhe [raɪð] *vi* retorcerse
writing ['raɪtɪŋ] *n* escritura; (*hand-~*) letra; (*of author*) obras *fpl*; **in ~** por escrito; ~ **paper** *n* papel *m* de escribir
written ['rɪtn] *pp of* **write**
wrong [rɔŋ] *adj* (*wicked*) malo; (*unfair*) injusto; (*incorrect*) equivocado, incorrecto; (*not suitable*) inoportuno, inconveniente; (*reverse*) del revés ♦ *adv* equivocadamente ♦ *n* injusticia ♦ *vt* ser injusto con; **you are ~ to do it** haces mal en hacerlo; **you are ~ about that, you've got it ~** en eso estás equivocado; **to be in the ~** no tener razón, tener la culpa; **what's ~?** ¿qué pasa?; **to go ~** (*person*) equivocarse; (*plan*) salir mal; (*machine*) estropearse; **~ful** *adj* injusto; **~ly** *adv* mal, incorrectamente; (*by mistake*) por error; ~ **number** *n* (*TEL*): **you've got the ~ number** se ha equivocado de número
wrote [rəut] *pt of* **write**
wrought iron [rɔ:t-] *n* hierro forjado
wrung [rʌŋ] *pt, pp of* **wring**
wt. *abbr* = **weight**
WWW *n abbr* (= *World Wide Web*) WWW *m*

X, x

Xmas ['ɛksməs] *n abbr* = **Christmas**
X-ray ['ɛksreɪ] *n* radiografía ♦ *vt* radiografiar, sacar radiografías de
xylophone ['zaɪləfəun] *n* xilófono

Y, y

yacht [jɔt] *n* yate *m*; **~ing** *n* (*sport*) balandrismo; **~sman/woman** (*irreg*) *n* balandrista *m/f*
Yank [jæŋk] (*pej*) *n* yanqui *m/f*
Yankee ['jæŋkɪ] (*pej*) *n* = **Yank**
yap [jæp] *vi* (*dog*) aullar
yard [jɑ:d] *n* patio; (*measure*) yarda; **~stick** *n* (*fig*) criterio, norma
yarn [jɑ:n] *n* hilo; (*tale*) cuento, historia
yawn [jɔ:n] *n* bostezo ♦ *vi* bostezar; **~ing** *adj* (*gap*) muy abierto
yd(s). *abbr* = **yard(s)**
yeah [jɛə] (*inf*) *adv* sí
year [jɪə*] *n* año; **to be 8 ~s old** tener 8 años; **an eight-~-old child** un niño de ocho años (de edad); **~ly** *adj* anual ♦ *adv* anualmente, cada año
yearn [jə:n] *vi*: **to ~ for sth** añorar algo, suspirar por algo
yeast [ji:st] *n* levadura
yell [jɛl] *n* grito, alarido ♦ *vi* gritar
yellow ['jɛləu] *adj* amarillo
yelp [jɛlp] *n* aullido ♦ *vi* aullar
yes [jɛs] *adv* sí ♦ *n* sí *m*; **to say/answer ~** decir/contestar que sí
yesterday ['jɛstədɪ] *adv* ayer ♦ *n* ayer *m*; ~ **morning/evening** ayer por la mañana/tarde; **all day ~** todo el día de ayer
yet [jɛt] *adv* ya; (*negative*) todavía ♦ *conj* sin embargo, a pesar de todo; **it is not finished ~** todavía no está acabado; **the best ~** el/la mejor hasta ahora; **as ~** hasta ahora, todavía
yew [ju:] *n* tejo
yield [ji:ld] *n* (*AGR*) cosecha; (*COMM*)

rendimiento ♦ *vt* ceder; (*results*) producir, dar; (*profit*) rendir ♦ *vi* rendirse, ceder; (*US: AUT*) ceder el paso

YMCA *n abbr* (= *Young Men's Christian Association*) Asociación *f* de Jóvenes Cristianos

yog(h)ourt ['jəugət] *n* yogur *m*

yog(h)urt ['jəugət] *n* = **yog(h)ourt**

yoke [jəuk] *n* yugo

yolk [jəuk] *n* yema (de huevo)

KEYWORD

you [ju:] *pron* **1** (*subject: familiar*) tú, *pl* vosotros/as (*SP*), ustedes (*AM*); (*polite*) usted, *pl* ustedes; ~ **are very kind** eres/es *etc* muy amable; ~ **Spanish enjoy your food** a vosotros (*or* ustedes) los españoles os (*or* les) gusta la comida; ~ **and I will go** iremos tú y yo

2 (*object: direct: familiar*) te, *pl* os (*SP*), les (*AM*); (*polite*) le, *pl* les, *f* la, *pl* las; **I know** ~ te/le *etc* conozco

3 (*object: indirect: familiar*) te, *pl* os (*SP*), les (*AM*); (*polite*) le, *pl* les; **I gave the letter to** ~ **yesterday** te/os *etc* di la carta ayer

4 (*stressed*): **I told** YOU **to do it** te dije a ti que lo hicieras, es a ti a quien dije que lo hicieras; *see also* **3, 5**

5 (*after prep: NB:* con+ti = **contigo**: *familiar*) ti, *pl* vosotros/as (*SP*), ustedes (*AM*); (*: polite*) usted, *pl* ustedes; **it's for** ~ es para ti/vosotros *etc*

6 (*comparisons: familiar*) tú, *pl* vosotros/as (*SP*), ustedes (*AM*); (*: polite*) usted, *pl* ustedes; **she's younger than** ~ es más joven que tú/vosotros *etc*

7 (*impersonal: one*): **fresh air does** ~ **good** el aire puro (*te*) hace bien; ~ **never know** nunca se sabe; ~ **can't do that!** ¡eso no se hace!

---

you'd [ju:d] = **you had; you would**

you'll [ju:l] = **you will; you shall**

young [jʌŋ] *adj* joven ♦ *npl* (*of animal*) cría; (*people*): **the** ~ los jóvenes, la juventud; ~**er** *adj* (*brother etc*) menor;

~**ster** *n* joven *m/f*

your [jɔː*] *adj* tu; (*pl*) vuestro; (*formal*) su; *see also* **my**

you're [juə*] = **you are**

yours [jɔːz] *pron* tuyo; (*pl*) vuestro; (*formal*) suyo; *see also* **faithfully; mine**[1]; **sincerely**

yourself [jɔː'sɛlf] *pron* tú mismo; (*complement*) te; (*after prep*) ti (*mismo*); (*formal*) usted mismo; (*: complement*) se; (*: after prep*) sí (*mismo*); **yourselves** *pl pron* vosotros mismos; (*after prep*) vosotros (*mismos*); (*formal*) ustedes (*mismos*); (*: complement*) se; (*: after prep*) sí mismos; *see also* **oneself**

youth [ju:θ, *pl* ju:ðz] *n* juventud *f*; (*young man*) joven *m*; ~ **club** *n* club *m* juvenil; ~**ful** *adj* juvenil; ~ **hostel** *n* albergue *m* de juventud

you've [ju:v] = **you have**

Yugoslav ['ju:gəuslɑ:v] *adj, n* yugo(e)slavo/a *m/f*

Yugoslavia [ju:gəu'slɑ:vɪə] *n* Yugoslavia

yuppie ['jʌpɪ] (*inf*) *adj, n* yupi *m/f*, yupy *m/f*

YWCA *n abbr* (= *Young Women's Christian Association*) Asociación *f* de Jóvenes Cristianas

Z, z

zany ['zeɪnɪ] *adj* estrafalario

zap [zæp] *vt* (*COMPUT*) borrar

zeal [zi:l] *n* celo, entusiasmo; ~**ous** ['zɛləs] *adj* celoso, entusiasta

zebra ['zi:brə] *n* cebra; ~ **crossing** (*BRIT*) *n* paso de peatones

zero ['zɪərəu] *n* cero

zest [zest] *n* ánimo, vivacidad *f*; (*of orange*) piel *f*

zigzag ['zɪgzæg] *n* zigzag *m* ♦ *vi* zigzaguear, hacer eses

zinc [zɪŋk] *n* cinc *m*, zinc *m*

zip [zɪp] *n* (*also*: ~ **fastener,** (*US*) ~**per**) cremallera (*SP*), cierre *m* (*AM*) ♦ *vt* (*also*: ~ **up**) cerrar la cremallera de; ~ **code** (*US*)

   n código postal
zodiac ['zəudɪæk] *n* zodíaco
zone [zəun] *n* zona
zoo [zu:] *n* (jardín *m*) zoo *m*
zoology [zu'ɔlədʒɪ] *n* zoología

zoom [zu:m] *vi*: **to ~ past** pasar
   zumbando; **~ lens** *n* zoom *m*
zucchini [zu:'ki:nɪ] (*US*) *n(pl)*
   calabacín(ines) *m(pl)*